T0184700

Lecture Notes in Computer Science 10174

Commenced Publication in 1973
Founding and Former Series Editors:
Gerhard Goos, Juris Hartmanis, and Jan van Leeuwen

Editorial Board

David Hutchison
  Lancaster University, Lancaster, UK
Takeo Kanade
  Carnegie Mellon University, Pittsburgh, PA, USA
Josef Kittler
  University of Surrey, Guildford, UK
Jon M. Kleinberg
  Cornell University, Ithaca, NY, USA
Friedemann Mattern
  ETH Zurich, Zurich, Switzerland
John C. Mitchell
  Stanford University, Stanford, CA, USA
Moni Naor
  Weizmann Institute of Science, Rehovot, Israel
C. Pandu Rangan
  Indian Institute of Technology, Madras, India
Bernhard Steffen
  TU Dortmund University, Dortmund, Germany
Demetri Terzopoulos
  University of California, Los Angeles, CA, USA
Doug Tygar
  University of California, Berkeley, CA, USA
Gerhard Weikum
  Max Planck Institute for Informatics, Saarbrücken, Germany

More information about this series at http://www.springer.com/series/7410

Serge Fehr (Ed.)

Public-Key Cryptography – PKC 2017

20th IACR International Conference
on Practice and Theory in Public-Key Cryptography
Amsterdam, The Netherlands, March 28–31, 2017
Proceedings, Part I

Springer

Editor
Serge Fehr
CWI
Amsterdam
The Netherlands

ISSN 0302-9743   ISSN 1611-3349   (electronic)
Lecture Notes in Computer Science
ISBN 978-3-662-54364-1   ISBN 978-3-662-54365-8   (eBook)
DOI 10.1007/978-3-662-54365-8

Library of Congress Control Number: 2017932641

LNCS Sublibrary: SL4 – Security and Cryptology

© International Association for Cryptologic Research 2017
This work is subject to copyright. All rights are reserved by the Publisher, whether the whole or part of the material is concerned, specifically the rights of translation, reprinting, reuse of illustrations, recitation, broadcasting, reproduction on microfilms or in any other physical way, and transmission or information storage and retrieval, electronic adaptation, computer software, or by similar or dissimilar methodology now known or hereafter developed.
The use of general descriptive names, registered names, trademarks, service marks, etc. in this publication does not imply, even in the absence of a specific statement, that such names are exempt from the relevant protective laws and regulations and therefore free for general use.
The publisher, the authors and the editors are safe to assume that the advice and information in this book are believed to be true and accurate at the date of publication. Neither the publisher nor the authors or the editors give a warranty, express or implied, with respect to the material contained herein or for any errors or omissions that may have been made. The publisher remains neutral with regard to jurisdictional claims in published maps and institutional affiliations.

Printed on acid-free paper

This Springer imprint is published by Springer Nature
The registered company is Springer-Verlag GmbH Germany
The registered company address is: Heidelberger Platz 3, 14197 Berlin, Germany

Preface

The 20th IACR International Conference on Practice and Theory of Public-Key Cryptography (PKC 2017) was held March 28–31, 2017, in Amsterdam, The Netherlands. The conference is sponsored by the International Association for Cryptologic Research (IACR) and has an explicit focus on public-key cryptography.

These proceedings, consisting of two volumes, feature 36 papers; these were selected by the Program Committee from 160 qualified submissions. Each submission was reviewed independently by at least three reviewers, or four in the case of Program Committee member submissions. Following the initial reviewing phase, the submissions and their reviews were discussed over a period of one month, before final decisions were then made. During this discussion phase, the Program Committee made substantial use of a newer feature of the submission/review software, which allows direct yet anonymous communication between the Program Committee and the authors; I think this interaction proved very useful in resolving pending issues and questions.

The reviewing and selection process was an intensive and time-consuming task, and I thank the members of the Program Committee, along with the external reviewers, for all their hard work and their excellent job. I also want to acknowledge Shai Halevi for his awesome submission/review software, which tremendously simplifies the program chair's work, and I thank him for his 24/7 and always-prompt assistance.

The conference program also included two invited talks, one by Vipul Goyal on "Recent Advances in Non-Malleable Cryptography," and the other by Kenny Paterson on "The Evolution of Public Key Cryptography in SSL/TLS." I would like to thank the two invited speakers as well as all the other speakers for their contributions to the program.

I also want to thank all the authors who submitted papers; you made it very challenging for the Program Committee to decide on what should be "the best" submissions — which of course is very much a matter of taste and perspective. I know that having good papers rejected because of a tough competition, and because there is always some amount of randomness involved, is disappointing, but I am optimistic that these "unlucky" papers will find their place and get the deserved recognition.

Last but not least, I would like to thank Marc Stevens, the general chair, for setting up a great conference and ensuring a smooth running of the event, and Ronald Cramer for his advisory support and allowing me to tap into his experience.

January 2017   Serge Fehr

PKC 2017

The 20th International Conference on Practice and Theory of Public-Key Cryptography

Amsterdam, The Netherlands
March 28–31, 2017

Sponsored by the
International Association of Cryptologic Research

General Chair

Marc Stevens   CWI Amsterdam, The Netherlands

Program Chair

Serge Fehr   CWI Amsterdam, The Netherlands

Program Committee

Masayuki Abe	NTT Secure Platform Labs, Japan
Fabrice Benhamouda	IBM Research, USA
Nir Bitansky	MIT, USA
Zvika Brakerski	Weizmann Institute of Science, Israel
Nishanth Chandran	Microsoft Research, India
Dana Dachman-Soled	University of Maryland, USA
Nico Döttling	UC Berkeley, USA
Léo Ducas	CWI Amsterdam, The Netherlands
Sebastian Faust	Ruhr-University Bochum, Germany
Dario Fiore	IMDEA Software Institute, Spain
Pierre-Alain Fouque	Rennes 1 University, France
Georg Fuchsbauer	ENS, France
Sanjam Garg	UC Berkeley, USA
Jens Groth	University College London, UK
Carmit Hazay	Bar-Ilan University, Israel
Dennis Hofheinz	KIT, Germany
Tibor Jager	Paderborn University, Germany
Abhishek Jain	Johns Hopkins University, USA
Marcel Keller	University of Bristol, UK
Markulf Kohlweiss	Microsoft Research, UK
Vadim Lyubashevsky	IBM Research Zurich, Switzerland

Takahiro Matsuda	AIST, Japan
Adam O'Neill	Georgetown University, USA
Arpita Patra	Indian Institute of Science, India
Ludovic Perret	Sorbonnes University, UPMC/Inria/CNRS, France
Christophe Petit	University of Oxford, UK
Vanishree Rao	PARC, USA
Alessandra Scafuro	North Carolina State University, USA
Gil Segev	Hebrew University of Jerusalem, Israel
Fang Song	Portland State University, USA
Daniele Venturi	Sapienza University of Rome, Italy
Ivan Visconti	University of Salerno, Italy
Hoeteck Wee	ENS, France
Vassilis Zikas	Rensselaer Polytechnic Institute, USA

External Reviewers

Hamza Abusalah	Mahdi Cheraghchi	Kristina Hostakova
Shashank Agrawal	Céline Chevalier	Vincenzo Iovino
Tristan Allard	Seung Geol Choi	Malika Izabachène
Miguel Ambrona	Arka Rai Choudhary	Sune Jakobsen
Daniel Apon	Kai-Min Chung	Marc Joye
Diego F. Aranha	Aloni Cohen	Charanjit Jutla
Nuttapong Attrapadung	Sandro Coretti	Ali El Kaafarani
Christian Badertscher	Véronique Cortier	Bhavana Kanukurthi
Saikrishna Badrinarayanan	Anamaria Costache	Koray Karabina
Shi Bai	Geoffroy Couteau	Aniket Kate
Foteini Baldimtsi	Lisa Eckey	Dakshita Khurana
Marshall Ball	Antonio Faonio	Eike Kiltz
Carsten Baum	Luca di Feo	Taechan Kim
David Bernhard	Tore Kasper Frederiksen	Elena Kirshanova
Silvio Biagioni	Tommaso Gagliardoni	Fuyuki Kitagawa
Jean-Francois Biasse	Steven Galbraith	Yutaro Kiyomura
Olivier Blazy	David Galindo	Susumu Kiyoshima
Jonathan Bootle	Pierrick Gaudry	Lisa Kohl
Joppe Bos	Romain Gay	Ilan Komargodski
Cecilia Boschini	Marilyn George	Yashvanth Kondi
Florian Bourse	Essam Ghadafi	Venkata Koppula
Elette Boyle	Junqing Gong	Luke Kowalczyk
Chris Brzuska	Aurore Guillevic	Juliane Krämer
Angelo De Caro	Felix Günther	Mukul Kulkarni
Wouter Castryck	Ryo Hiromasa	Thijs Laarhoven
Dario Catalano	Mohammad Hajiabadi	Sebastian Lauer
Andrea Cerulli	Yoshikazu Hanatani	Moon Sung Lee
Pyrros Chaidos	Ethan Heilman	Tancrède Lepoint
Jie Chen	Justin Holmgren	Qinyi Li

Benoît Libert
Satyanarayana Lokam
Patrick Longa
Steve Lu
Yun Lu
Bernardo Magri
Mary Maller
Alex Malozemoff
Antonio Marcedone
Giorgia Azzurra Marson
Daniel Masny
Nicolas Meloni
Peihan Miao
Giacomo Micheli
Michele Minelli
Ameer Mohammed
Pratyay Mukherjee
Debdeep Mukhopadhyay
Patrick Märtens
Pierrick Méaux
Michael Naehrig
Gregory Neven
Anca Nitulescu
Luca Nizzardo
Ariel Nof
Koji Nuida
Maciej Obremski
Miyako Ohkubo
Cristina Onete
Michele Orrù
Daniel Page
Jiaxin Pan

Dimitris Papadopoulos
Sunoo Park
Anat Paskin-Cherniavsky
Alain Passelègue
Valerio Pastro
Cécile Pierrot
Rafael del Pino
Rachel Player
Oxana Poburinnaya
David Pointcheval
Antigoni Polychroniadou
Manoj Prabhakaran
Benjamin Pring
Srinivasan Raghuraman
Joost Renes
Răzvan Roşie
Dragos Rotaru
Tim Ruffing
Akshayaram Srinivasan
Yusuke Sakai
Kazuo Sakiyama
John M. Schanck
Benedikt Schmidt
Peter Scholl
Jacob Schuldt
Peter Schwabe
Sven Schäge
Ido Shahaf
Igor Shparlinski
Shashank Singh
Luisa Siniscalchi
Ben Smith

Douglas Stebila
Kim Taechan
Atsushi Takayasu
Vanessa Teague
Adrien Thillard
Aishwarya
   Thiruvengadam
Yan Bo Ti
Mehdi Tibouchi
Junichi Tomida
Daniel Tschudi
Dominique Unruh
Alexander Ushakov
Satyanarayana Vusirikala
Xiao Wang
Yohei Watanabe
Avi Weinstock
Mor Weiss
David Wu
Keita Xagawa
Shota Yamada
Takashi Yamakawa
Avishay Yanai
Eylon Yogev
Kazuki Yoneyama
Yang Yu
Mark Zhandry
Jean Karim Zinzindohoué
Michael Zohner

Contents – Part I

Leakage-Resilient and Non-Malleable Codes

Number Theory and Diffie-Hellman

Contents – Part II

Real-World Schemes

Multiparty Computation

Primitives

Cryptanalysis

LP Solutions of Vectorial Integer Subset Sums – Cryptanalysis of Galbraith's Binary Matrix LWE

Gottfried Herold[✉] and Alexander May

Faculty of Mathematics, Horst Görtz Institute for IT-Security,
Ruhr-University Bochum, Bochum, Germany
{gottfried.herold,alex.may}@rub.de

Abstract. We consider Galbraith's space efficient LWE variant, where the $(m \times n)$-matrix A is binary. In this binary case, solving a vectorial subset sum problem over the integers allows for decryption. We show how to solve this problem using (Integer) Linear Programming. Our attack requires only a fraction of a second for all instances in a regime for m that cannot be attacked by current lattice algorithms. E.g. we are able to solve 100 instances of Galbraith's small LWE challenge $(n, m) = (256, 400)$ all in a fraction of a second. We also show under a mild assumption that instances with $m \leq 2n$ can be broken in polynomial time via LP relaxation. Moreover, we develop a method that identifies weak instances for Galbraith's large LWE challenge $(n, m) = (256, 640)$.

Keywords: Binary matrix LWE · Linear programming · Cryptanalysis

1 Introduction

Over the last decade, the Learning with Errors (LWE) problem [16] has proved to be extremely versatile for the construction of various cryptographic primitives. Since LWE is as hard as worst-case lattice problems, it is consider one of the most important post-quantum candidates. Let us recall that an LWE instance consists of a random $(m \times n)$-matrix $\mathbf{A}$ with elements from $\mathbb{Z}_q$ and an m-dimensional vector $\boldsymbol{b} \in \mathbb{Z}_q^m$, where $\boldsymbol{b} = \mathbf{A}\boldsymbol{s} + \boldsymbol{e} \bmod q$ with a secret random $\boldsymbol{s} \in \mathbb{Z}_q^n$ and where the entries of $\boldsymbol{e} \in \mathbb{Z}_q^m$ are from a discretized normal distribution.

The LWE decisional problem is to distinguish $(\mathbf{A}, \boldsymbol{b})$ from $(\mathbf{A}, \boldsymbol{u})$ for random $\boldsymbol{u} \in \mathbb{Z}_q^m$. While LWE has some intriguing hardness properties, it is known that one has to choose quite large n in order to reach a desired security level against lattice reduction attacks. This in turn makes the size of LWE instances $(\mathbf{A}, \boldsymbol{b})$, and thus the size of public keys, undesirably large. For practical reasons, people therefore looked into various variants of LWE, such as ring-LWE [13,14], LWE with short secret [2,15] or LWE with short error [10,15]. Recently, some special instances of ring-LWE were identified to have serious weaknesses [4,6], but these instances were not suggested for cryptographic use. Moreover, it was shown that LWE with binary secrets and errors can be attacked in slightly subexponential time $2^{\mathcal{O}(n/\log\log n)}$

© International Association for Cryptologic Research 2017
S. Fehr (Ed.): PKC 2017, Part I, LNCS 10174, pp. 3–15, 2017.
DOI: 10.1007/978-3-662-54365-8_1

by a BKW-type algorithm [11], where LWE dimension $n = 128$ was practically broken within half a day. Also, LWE with binary secret leads to more efficient lattice attacks [3]. While choosing special variants of LWE seems to slightly decrease the security, the improved attacks do not substantially endanger the security of these variants in general.

In this paper, we look at another LWE variant due to Galbraith [8]. In this variant, $\mathbf{A}$ is replaced by a *binary* matrix. This makes Galbraith's variant very tempting for low-weight devices that are not capable of storing a sufficiently large LWE instance.

In [8], Galbraith instantiates Regev's encryption system [16] with his binary matrix $\mathbf{A}$ and suggests to use the parameters $(n, m, q) = (256, 640, 4093)$ that were originally proposed by Lindner and Peikert [12] for Regev's original scheme. Galbraith also gives a thorough security analysis based on lattices, where in his experiments he fixes n and tries to break encryption for increasing m. Based on this analysis, he concludes that instances with $m \geq 400$ might be hard to break with lattice techniques.

For Regev's original scheme, security follows from hardness of LWE for appropriate parameters; this is not automatically the case for binary matrix $\mathbf{A}$ without changing parameters. For Galbraith's choices, in order to break encryption, one can solve an equation of the form $\boldsymbol{u}\mathbf{A} = \boldsymbol{c}_1$ for a known matrix $\mathbf{A} \in \{0, 1\}^{m \times n}$, some known ciphertext component $\boldsymbol{c}_1 \in \mathbb{Z}^n$ and some unknown vector $\boldsymbol{u} \in \{0, 1\}^m$. In other words, one has to find a subset of all rows of $\mathbf{A}$ that sums to $\boldsymbol{c}_1$. We call this problem therefore a *vectorial integer subset sum*. If the unknown vector $\boldsymbol{u}$ is short, a vectorial integer subset sum can certainly be solved by finding a closest vector in some appropriate lattice. This is the standard analysis that was carried out in [8] against this avenue of attack.

However, a vectorial integer subset sum is by its definition also an Integer Linear Programming (ILP) problem. Namely, we are looking for an integral solution $\boldsymbol{u} \in \mathbb{Z}^m$ of m linear equations over the integers. While it is known that ILP is in general NP-hard, it is also known that in many cases removing the integrality constraint on $\boldsymbol{u}$ provides a lot of useful information about the problem. Removing the integrality constraint is called a *LP relaxation* of the problem. Without integrality constraints, the resulting problem can be solved in polynomial time, using e.g. the ellipsoid method [9].

We show under a mild assumption on $\mathbf{A}$ that the vectorial subset sum problem can for parameters $m \leq 2n$ be solved by its LP relaxation (with success probability $\frac{1}{2}$). More precisely, the LP solution has the property that it is already integral. This in turn means that vectorial integer subset sums with $m \leq 2n$ can be solved in polynomial time. In practice, we are able to solve instances with $n = 256$ and $m \leq 2n$ in a fraction of a second. Notice that this is already a regime for m that seems to be infeasible to reach with current lattice reduction algorithms.

However, $m \leq 2n$ does not quite suffice to break Galbraith's $(n, m) = (256, 640)$-challenge in practice. Namely, when we look at instances with $m > 2n$ the success probability of our MATLAB ILP solver drops quite quickly – when we allow only some fixed, small computation time. Yet, when looking at a large number of instances of our vectorial integer subset sums, we realize experimentally that there is still a significant number of weak instances that are vulnerable to LP relaxation with some additional tricks (such as e.g. the cutting plane method). More concretely, we are able to show that at least 1 out of 2^{15} instances of Regev-type encryptions with $(n, m) = (256, 640)$ can be solved in about 30 min. Interestingly, we are able to compute a simple score for every instance I that accurately predicts whether I is indeed weak – based on an estimation of the volume of the search space that comes from the LP relaxation. We find that such a quick test for identifying weak instances I is a quite remarkable property of Linear Programming. We are not aware of a similar property for other cryptanalytic methods. We hope that our results motivate more cryptanalytic research using (Integer) Linear Programming.

Note that our attack breaks Galbraith's instantiation of LWE encryption with binary matrices, but does not break binary LWE itself. Due to that, our attack allows ciphertext recovery, but not key recovery.

Our paper is organized as follows. In Sect. 2, we recall Galbraith's scheme and its cryptanalysis challenges. In Sect. 3, we model vectorial integer subset sums in form of an Integer Linear Programming. We attack instances with $m \leq 2n$ in Sect. 4 and show that they actually admit a polynomial time attack. In Sect. 5, we show how to identify weak instances for large m and we present our experimental results for Galbraith's large challenge $(n, m) = (256, 640)$.

2 Galbraith's Binary Matrix LWE

Let us briefly recall Regev's LWE encryption scheme. Let q be prime. One chooses a public $\mathbf{A} \in_R \mathbb{Z}_q^{m \times n}$ and a private $s \in_R \mathbb{Z}_q^n$. One then compute $b = \mathbf{A}s + e \bmod q$, where the e_i are sampled from a discrete normal distribution with mean 0 and standard deviation σ. The public key consists of $(\mathbf{A}, b)$.

For encrypting some message $M \in \{0, 1\}$, one chooses a random nonce $u \in_R \{0, 1\}^m$ and computes the ciphertext

$$c = (c_1, c_2) = (u\mathbf{A} \bmod q, \langle u, b \rangle + M \lfloor \tfrac{q}{2} \rfloor \bmod q) \in \mathbb{Z}_q^n \times \mathbb{Z}_q.$$

For decryption to 0 respectively 1, one checks whether $c_1 s - c_2$ is closer to 0 respectively $\frac{q}{2}$.

After analyzing lattice attacks, Lindner and Peikert [12] suggest to use the parameters

$$(n, m, q) = (256, 640, 4093)$$

for medium security level and estimate that these parameters offer roughly 128-bit security. However, for these parameters the public key $(\mathbf{A}, b)$ has already 247 kilobytes, which is way too much for constrained devices.

Therefore, Galbraith [8] suggested to construct the public matrix $\mathbf{A}$ with **binary entries** simply from the seed of a PRNG. All that one has to store in this case is the seed itself, and the vector b. A similar trick is also used in other contexts to shorten the public key size [5].

Moreover, Galbraith gives a thorough security analysis of his LWE variant, based on its lattice complexity. In his security analysis he considers the problem of recovering the nonce u from

$$c_1 = uA. \tag{1}$$

Notice that since now $A \in \{0,1\}^{m \times n}$, every entry of c_1 is an inner product of two random binary length-m vectors. Thus, the entries of c_1 are random variables from a binomial distribution $B(m, \frac{1}{4})$ with expected value $\frac{m}{4}$. Since $\frac{m}{4} \ll q$, the equality $c_1 = uA$ does not only hold modulo q, but also over the integers.

Hence, recovering u from (c_1, A) can be seen as a *vectorial integer subset sum* problem. Once u is recovered, one can easily subtract $\langle u, b \rangle$ from c_2 and thus recover the message m. Hence, solving the vectorial integer subset sum problem gives a *ciphertext only message recovery attack*.

We would like to stress that this attack does not allow for key recovery of s. We also note that in Regev's original scheme, the security proof shows IND-CPA security assuming that the LWE problem is hard. For this reduction, we need that c_1 is essentially independent of A, which is proven using the Leftover Hash Lemma by setting parameters sufficiently large. In particular, u is required to have sufficient entropy and Eq. (1) has many solutions for u in Regev's non-binary scheme, whereas the parameters in Galbraith's binary scheme are set such that u is the unique solution to Eq. (1). Due to that, our attack does not give an attack on binary LWE. In fact, binary LWE was shown to be at least as secure as standard LWE in [1], provided n is increased by a factor $\mathcal{O}(\log q)$. Consequently, it seems unlikely that the attack extends to binary LWE.

2.1   Previous Cryptanalysis and Resulting Parameter Suggestions

In his security analysis, Galbraith attacks the vectorial integer subset sum by lattice methods. Namely, he first finds an arbitrary integer solution $w \in \mathbb{Z}^m$ with $c_1 = wA$. Then he solves CVP with target vector w in the lattice

$$L = \{v \in \mathbb{Z}^m \mid vA \equiv 0 \bmod q\}.$$

Let v be a CVP-solution, then we usually have $u = w - v$.

Galbraith reports that for $n = 256$ and $m \in [260, 340]$, the CVP-method works well. He further conjectures that with additional tricks one should be able to handle values up to $m = 380$ or 390, but that "it would be impressive to solve cases with $m > 400$ without exploiting weeks or months of computing resources".

Based on his analysis, Galbraith raised the two following cryptanalysis challenges:

– C1 with $(n, m) = (256, 400)$: The goal is to compute u from (A, c_1) in less than a day on an ordinary PC.
– C2 with $(n, m) = (256, 640)$: The goal is mount an attack using current computing facilities that would take less than a year.

According to Galbraith, breaking C1 should be interpreted "as causing embarrassment to the author", while C2 should be considered a "total break".

3 Modeling Our Vectorial Integer Subset Sum as an Integer Linear Program

In the canonical form of an Integer Linear Program (ILP), one is given *linear constraints*

$$\mathbf{A}'\boldsymbol{x} \leq \boldsymbol{b}', \boldsymbol{x} \geq 0 \text{ and } \boldsymbol{x} \in \mathbb{Z}^m,$$

for which one has to maximize a *linear objective function* $\langle \boldsymbol{f}, \boldsymbol{x} \rangle$ for some $\boldsymbol{f} \in \mathbb{R}^m$ that can be freely chosen.

Notice that it is straightforward to map our vectorial integer subset sum problem $\boldsymbol{u}A = \boldsymbol{c}_1$ from Eq. (1) into an ILP. Namely, we define the inequalities

$$
\begin{aligned}
\mathbf{A}^{\mathsf{T}}\boldsymbol{u} &\leq \boldsymbol{c}_1 \\
-\mathbf{A}^{\mathsf{T}}\boldsymbol{u} &\leq -\boldsymbol{c}_1 \text{ and} \\
u_i &\leq 1 \text{ for all } i = 1, \ldots, m. \\
u_i &\geq 0 \text{ for all } i = 1, \ldots, m.
\end{aligned}
\tag{2}
$$

We can for simplicity chose $\boldsymbol{f} = \boldsymbol{0}$, since we are interested in *any* feasible solution to Eq. (2), and it is not hard to see that by the choice of our parameters our solution $\boldsymbol{u}$ is a unique feasible solution. Namely, look at the map

$$
\begin{aligned}
\{0,1\}^m &\to \left(B\left(m, \tfrac{1}{4}\right) \right)^n, \\
\boldsymbol{u} &\mapsto \boldsymbol{u}\mathbf{A},
\end{aligned}
$$

where $X \sim B(m, \frac{1}{4})$ is a binomially distribution random variable with m experiments and $\Pr[X = 1] = \frac{1}{4}$ for each experiment. Notice that the jth entry, $1 \leq j \leq n$, of $\boldsymbol{u}\mathbf{A}$ can be written as $u_1 a_{1,j} + \ldots + u_m a_{m,j}$, where we have the event X_i that $u_i a_{i,j} = 1$ iff $u_i = a_{i,j} = 1$, i.e. with probability $\frac{1}{4}$. Hence, we can model the entries of $\boldsymbol{u}\mathbf{A}$ as random variables from $B(m, \frac{1}{4})$.

For the usual parameter choice $q > m$, the solution $\boldsymbol{u}$ of Eq. (2) is unique as long as this map is injective, i.e. as long as the entropy of $\left(B(m, \frac{1}{4}) \right)^n$ is larger than m. The entropy of the binomial distribution $\left(B(m, \frac{1}{4}) \right)^n$ is roughly $\frac{n}{2} \log_2(\frac{3}{8}\pi e m)$. Thus, one can compute for which m we obtain unique solutions $\boldsymbol{u}$. Choosing e.g. $n = 256$, we receive unique $\boldsymbol{u}$ for $m \leq 1500$. Hence, in the remaining paper we can safely assume unique solutions to our vectorial subset sum problem.

4 Attacking $m \leq 2n$: Solving Challenge C1

We ran 100 instances of Eq. (2) on an ordinary 2.8 GHz laptop with $n = 256$ and increasing m. We used the ILP solver from MATLAB 2015, which was stopped whenever it did not find a solution after time $t_{\max} = 10$ s. We found that the success probability of our attack dropped from 100% at $m = 490$ to approximately 1% at $m = 590$, cf. Table 1. The largest drop of success probability takes place slightly after $m = 2n$.

For comparison, we also solved the LP relaxation, i.e. Eq. (2) without integrality constraint on $\boldsymbol{u}$. This is much faster than ILP, so we solved 1000 instances for each m. We checked whether the returned non-integral solution matched our desired integral solution for $\boldsymbol{u}$, in which case we call a run successful. The success rate of LP relaxation is also given in Table 1.

It turns out that Galbraith's small C1 challenge can already solely be solved by its LP relaxation. Since LP relaxation is only the starting point for ILP, it does not come as a surprise that ILP has a slightly larger success rate. However, it is impressive that LP relaxation alone is already powerful enough to solve a significant fraction of all instances.

Table 1. Success probability for solving Eq. (2) for $n = 256$. We used MATLAB 2015 and restricted to $t_{\max} = 10\,\mathrm{s}$ for the ILP.

m	400	450	480	490	500	510	512	520
Success (ILP)	100%	100%	100%	100%	96%	83%	79%	63%
Success (LP)	100%	99.6%	93.3%	82.3%	68.8%	55.6%	48.1%	35.4%
m	530	540	550	560	570	580	590	600
Success (ILP)	60%	32%	25%	12%	3%	1%	1%	0%
Success (LP)	19.8%	11.0%	4.5%	1.9%	0.8%	0.3%	0%	0%

We now give a theoretical justification for the strength of LP relaxation, showing that under some mild heuristic, for $m \leq 2n$, the solution of the LP relaxation is unique. Since, by construction, we know that there is an integral solution $\boldsymbol{u}$ to Eq. (2), uniqueness of the solution directly implies that the LP solver has to find the desired $\boldsymbol{u}$.

In the following lemma, we replace our linear constraints from $\mathbf{A}$ by some random linear constraints from some matrix $\bar{\mathbf{A}}$ over the reals. This will give us already uniqueness of the solution $\boldsymbol{u}$. Afterwards, we will argue why replacing $\bar{\mathbf{A}}$ back by our LWE matrix $\mathbf{A}$ should not affect the lemma's statement.

Lemma 1. *Let $\boldsymbol{u} \in \{0,1\}^{2n}$. Let $\bar{\mathbf{A}} \in \mathbb{R}^{n \times 2n}$ be a random matrix, whose rows are uniformly distributed on the sphere around $\mathbf{0} \in \mathbb{R}^{2n}$. Then*

$$Pr[\nexists \boldsymbol{x} \in (\mathbb{R} \cap [0,1])^{2n} \mid \bar{\mathbf{A}}\boldsymbol{x} = \bar{\mathbf{A}}\boldsymbol{u}, \boldsymbol{x} \neq \boldsymbol{u}] = \frac{1}{2}.$$

Proof. Let us look at the $2n$-dimensional unit cube $U_{2n} = \{\boldsymbol{x} \in (\mathbb{R} \cap [0,1])^{2n}\}$. Obviously $\mathbf{0}, \boldsymbol{u} \in U_{2n}$, both lying at corners of U_{2n}. Now, let us assume wlog. that $\boldsymbol{u} = \mathbf{0}$ (which can be achieved by reflections). Let H be the hyperplane defined by the kernel of $\bar{\mathbf{A}}$.

Since $\bar{\mathbf{A}}$ is randomly chosen from $\mathbb{R}^{n \times 2n}$, it has full rank n with probability 1: since we chose the entries of $\bar{\mathbf{A}}$ from the reals $\mathbb{R}$, we avoid any problems that might arise from co-linearity. Thus, H as well as its orthogonal complement $H^{\perp}$

have dimension n. Notice that $H^{\perp} = \text{Im}(\bar{\mathbf{A}}^{\mathsf{T}})$. By construction, both H and $H^{\perp}$ intersect U_{2n} in the corner $\mathbf{0} = \mathbf{u}$. We are interested whether one of the hyperplanes goes through U_{2n}.

The answer to this question is given by Farkas' Lemma [7], which tells us that *exactly one* of H and $H^{\perp}$ passes through U_{2n}. Notice first that not both can pass through U_{2n}. Now assume that H intersects U_{2n} only in the zero point $\mathbf{0}$. Then Farkas' Lemma tells us that there is a vector in its orthogonal complement $H^{\perp}$ that fully intersects U_{2n}. Notice that again by having vectors over the reals, the intersection $H^{\perp} \cap U_{2n}$ is n-dimensional.

By the randomness of $\bar{\mathbf{A}}$, the orientation of H in $\mathbb{R}^{2n}$ is uniformly random, and hence the same holds for the orientation of $H^{\perp}$. Since H and $H^{\perp}$ share exactly the same distribution, and since by Farkas' Lemma exactly one out of both has a trivial intersection with U_{2n}, we have

$$\Pr[H \cap U_{2n} = \{\mathbf{u}\}] = \Pr[H^{\perp} \cap U_{2n} = \{\mathbf{u}\}] = \frac{1}{2}.$$

Let $\mathbf{b} = \bar{\mathbf{A}}\mathbf{u} = \mathbf{0}$. Since $H = \ker(\bar{\mathbf{A}})$, it follows that $\mathbf{u}$ is a unique solution to the equation $\mathbf{A}\mathbf{x} = \mathbf{b}$ in the case that H has trivial intersection with U_{2n}. $\qquad\square$

Theorem 1. *Under the heuristic assumption that our matrix $\mathbf{A}^{\mathsf{T}}$ behaves like a random $(n \times m)$-matrix, whose rows are uniformly distributed on the sphere around 0^m, LP relaxation solves Eq. (2) in polynomial time for all $m \leq 2n$.*

Proof. Notice that the case $m = 2n$ follows directly from Lemma 1, since LP relaxation has to find the unique solution $\mathbf{u}$, and its running time is polynomial using e.g. the ellipsoid method. For the case $m < 2n$ we can simply append $2n - m$ additional columns to $\mathbf{A}^{\mathsf{T}}$, and add a random subset of these to $\mathbf{c}_1$.

Now let us say a word about the heuristic assumption from Theorem 1. Our assumption requires that the discretized $\mathbf{A}^{\mathsf{T}}$ defines a random orientation of a hyperplane just as $\bar{\mathbf{A}}$. Since $\mathbf{A}^{\mathsf{T}}$ has by definition only positive entries, its columns always have non-negative inner product with the all-one vector 1^n. This minor technical problem can be fixed easily by centering the entries of $\mathbf{A}^{\mathsf{T}}$ around 0 via the following transformation of Eq. (2):

First, guess the Hamming weight $w = \sum_{i=1}^{m} u_i$. Then subtract $(\frac{1}{2}, \ldots, \frac{1}{2})$ from every column vector of $\mathbf{A}^{\mathsf{T}}$ and finally subtract $\frac{w}{2}$ from every entry of $\mathbf{c}_1$. After this transformation $\mathbf{A}^{\mathsf{T}}$ has entries uniform from $\{\pm\frac{1}{2}\}$ and should fulfill the desired heuristic assumption of Theorem 1.

5 Attacking $m = 640$: Solving Challenge C2

In order to tackle the $m = 640$ challenge, we could in principle proceed as in the previous section, identify a weak instance for e.g. $m = 590$, brute-force guess 50 coordinates of $\mathbf{u}$ and run each time an ILP solver for 10 s.

However, we found out experimentally that even in dimension $m = 640$ the density of weak instances is not negligible. Hence, it seems to be much more effective to identify weak instances than to brute-force coordinates. So in the following we try to identify what makes particular instances weak.

We follow the paradigm that an ILP is the easier to solve, the more the LP relaxation "knows about the problem". In particular, we expect that a problem is easy to solve if the solution polytope P of the LP relaxation of Eq. (2) is small. In the extreme case, if $P = \{u\}$, then the problem can be solved by the LP solver alone (cf. Theorem 1). To quantify the size of the solution space in an easy-to-compute way, we compute the length of a random projection of P. It turns out that this length, henceforth called *score* gives a very good prediction on the hardness of an instance.

More concretely, for an instance $I = (\mathbf{A}, c)$, we choose a vector r with random direction. Then we maximize and minimize the linear objective function $\langle r, u \rangle$ under the linear constraints given by the LP relaxation of Eq. (2) and consider their difference D. Clearly, $S_r := \frac{D}{\|r\|}$ is the length of the orthogonal projection of P onto the span of r. Formally, the *score* of an instance I wrt. to some direction r is defined as follows.

Definition 1. *Let $I = (\mathbf{A}, c)$ be an instance. Consider the solution polytope P of the LP relaxation of Eq. (2), i.e. P is defined as $P = [0,1]^m \cap \{x \mid \mathbf{A}^\mathsf{T} x = c\}$. Let $r \in \mathbb{R}^m$. Then the score S_r is defined via*

$$f_{\max} := \max_{x \in P} \langle r, x \rangle$$
$$f_{\min} := \min_{x \in P} \langle r, x \rangle \tag{3}$$
$$S_r := \frac{f_{\max} - f_{\min}}{\|r\|}$$

Note that S_r can be computed by solving two LP problems, hence in polynomial time.

Since S_r quantifies the search space for the ILP, instances with small score should be easier to compute. For $m = 640$, we computed the scores of 2^{19} instances, which took approximately 1 s per instance.

Independence of r and Reliability of Our Score. We experimentally confirm that for a given instance I, the value of S_r is mainly a function of I and does not depend significantly on the particular choice of r. Therefore, we choose the fixed vector $r = (1, \dots, 1, -1, \dots, -1)$ for r with exactly $\frac{m}{2}$ ones and $\frac{m}{2}$ -1's. We use the score $S = S_r$ for this particular choice of r and sort instances according to S.

We confirm that the score S is a very good predictor for the success of ILP solvers and the success probability drops considerably at some cutoff value for S. E.g. for $m = 520$ and within a 10 s time limit, we find that we can solve

- $>99\%$ of instances with $S \leq 1.22$,
- 60% of instances with $1.22 \leq S \leq 1.54$ and
- $<3\%$ of instances with $S > 1.54$.

Distribution of S. Average values for S can be found in Table 2. Figure 1 shows the distribution of S. Note that while the distribution looks suspiciously Gaussian for $m = 640$, there is a considerable negative skewness and the tail distribution towards 0 is much fatter than for a Gaussian (cf. Fig. 2). This fat tail enables us to find a significant fraction of weak instances even for large m.

Notice that a score $S = 0$ basically means that LP relaxation finds the solution.

Table 2. Average values for S for $n = 256$ and varying m. We used 1000 instances for each m.

m	400	450	480	490	500	510	512	520
average of S	0	0.002	0.07	0.22	0.43	0.69	0.83	1.15
m	530	540	550	560	570	580	590	600
average of S	1.76	2.16	2.74	3.16	3.60	4.04	4.34	4.80
m	610	620	630	640				
average of S	5.18	5.52	5.83	6.18				

Results for $m = 640$. We generated a large number $N = 2^{19}$ of instances with $n = 256$, $m = 640$, and tried to solve only those 271 instances with the lowest score S, which in our case meant $S < 3.2$. We were able to solve 16 out of those 271 weakest instances in half an hour each. We found 15 instances with $S < 2.175$, of which we solved 12. The largest value of S, for which we could solve an instance, was $S \approx 2.6$.

Fixing Coordinates. Let us provide some more detailed explanation why an ILP solver works well on instances with small score S. Consider some $r \in \{0, \pm 1\}^m$ of low Hamming weight $|r|_1 = w$, so $\|r\| = \sqrt{w}$. Heuristically, we expect that S_r should be approximately S, as S_r mainly depends on the instance and not on the choice of r. Of course, for a vector $r \in \{0, \pm 1\}^m$ with low Hamming weight we have

$$S_r = \frac{1}{\sqrt{w}} \left(\max_{x \in P} \langle r, x \rangle - \min_{x \in P} \langle r, x \rangle \right) \le \frac{1}{\sqrt{w}} \left(\max_{x \in [0,1]^m} \langle r, x \rangle - \min_{x \in [0,1]^m} \langle r, x \rangle \right) = \sqrt{w},$$

but that only means we should expect S_r to be even smaller. Since we know that for the true integer solution u, we have $\langle r, u \rangle \in \mathbb{Z}$, we can add the *cuts* $\langle r, u \rangle \le \lfloor f_{\max} \rfloor$ and $\langle r, u \rangle \ge \lceil f_{\min} \rceil$ to the set of equations, where $f_{\max}$ resp. $f_{\min}$ are the maximum resp. minimum computed for S_r.

This is a special case of what is called *cut generation* in Integer Linear Programming. If $S_r < \sqrt{w}$, i.e. $f_{\max} - f_{\min} < w$, then adding such a new inequality always makes the solution space of the LP relaxation smaller. In fact, such an inequality restricts the possible set that w out of the m variables u_i can jointly obtain. So if $S_r < \sqrt{w}$ for many different r, we get lots of sparse relations between the u_i. Such inequalities are called *good cuts*.

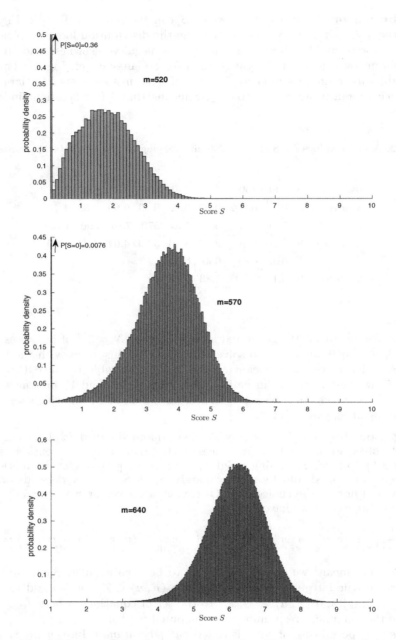

Fig. 1. pdf's of S for $n = 256$ and varying values of m. Note that the y-axis is cropped and does not show the true density at $S = 0$ (where the distribution technically does not even have a finite continuous density). We rather give the probability for $S = 0$. For $m = 640$, we never encountered an instance with $S = 0$.

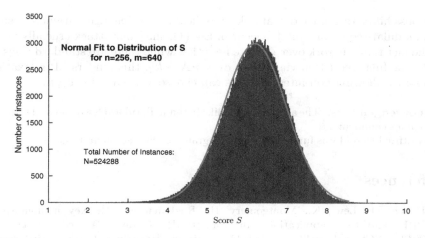

Fig. 2. Comparison of distribution of S for $n = 256$, $m = 640$ with a normal distribution. The distribution of S has negative skewness and a much fatter tail towards 0. Hence, we obtain more weak instances than we would expect from a normal distribution.

In particular, consider the case $w = 1$ and $\boldsymbol{r} = (0, 0, \ldots, 0, 1, 0, \ldots, 0)$, i.e. we maximize/minimize an individual variable u_i over P. If this maximum is <1, we know that $u_i = 0$ holds and if the minimum is >0, we know $u_i = 1$. So if $S_{\boldsymbol{r}} < 1$ holds for some $\boldsymbol{r}$ with $|\boldsymbol{r}|_1 = 1$, we can fix one of the u_i's and reduce the number of unknowns by one – which makes fixing further u_i's even easier. If the score S is small, we expect that the ILP solver can find lots of such good cuts, possibly even cuts with $w = 1$.

Indeed, in all instances that we could solve, some variables could be fixed by such good cuts with $w = 1$. For dimensions $m \leq 550$, most instances that were solved by the ILP could be solved by such cuts alone.

In fact, we preprocessed our 271 weak instances for $m = 640$ by trying to fix each individual coordinate. This alone was sufficient to determine an average of >100 individual coordinates of the solution $\boldsymbol{u}$ for $S < 2.175$, and in one case it was sufficient to completely solve the problem.

6   Conclusion

According to Galbraith's metric for the challenge C2 in Sect. 3, the results of Sect. 5 can be seen as total break for binary matrix LWE. On the other hand, one could easily avoid weak instances I by simply rejecting weak I's during ciphertext generation. This would however violate the idea of lightweight encryption with binary matrix LWE.

Still, during our experiments we got the feeling that the vectorial integer subset sum problem gets indeed hard for large m, even for its weakest instances. So Galbraith's variant might be safely instantiated for large m, but currently we find it hard to determine m's that fulfill a concrete security level of e.g. 128 bit.

One possibility to render our attack inapplicable is to change parameters such that modular reductions mod q occur in Eq. (1), since our attack crucially relies on the fact that we work over $\mathbb{Z}$. Note here that while there are standard ways to model modular reduction via ILP as $c_1 = uA - kq$, this renders LP relaxation useless: by allowing non-integral k, we can choose any value for c_1, u.

Acknowledgements. The authors would like to thank Bernhard Esslinger and Patricia Wienen for comments.

Gottfried Herold was funded by the ERC grant 307952 (acronym FSC).

References

1. Boneh, D., Lewi, K., Montgomery, H., Raghunathan, A.: Key homomorphic PRFs and their applications. In: Canetti, R., Garay, J.A. (eds.) CRYPTO 2013. LNCS, vol. 8042, pp. 410–428. Springer, Heidelberg (2013). doi:10.1007/978-3-642-40041-4_23
2. Brakerski, Z., Langlois, A., Peikert, C., Regev, O., Stehlé, D.: Classical hardness of learning with errors. In: Boneh, D., Roughgarden, T., Feigenbaum, J., (eds.), 45th ACM STOC, Palo Alto, CA, USA, 1–4 June, pp. 575–584. ACM Press (2013)
3. Buchmann, J.A., Göpfert, F., Player, R., Wunderer, T.: On the hardness of LWE with binary error: revisiting the hybrid lattice-reduction and meet-in-the-middle attack. IACR Cryptology ePrint Archive, p. 89 (2016)
4. Castryck, W., Iliashenko, I., Vercauteren, F.: Provably weak instances of ring-LWE revisited. In: Fischlin, M., Coron, J.-S. (eds.) EUROCRYPT 2016. LNCS, vol. 9665, pp. 147–167. Springer, Heidelberg (2016). doi:10.1007/978-3-662-49890-3_6
5. Coron, J.-S., Naccache, D., Tibouchi, M.: Public key compression and modulus switching for fully homomorphic encryption over the integers. In: Pointcheval, D., Johansson, T. (eds.) EUROCRYPT 2012. LNCS, vol. 7237, pp. 446–464. Springer, Heidelberg (2012). doi:10.1007/978-3-642-29011-4_27
6. Elias, Y., Lauter, K.E., Ozman, E., Stange, K.E.: Provably weak instances of ring-LWE. In: Gennaro, R., Robshaw, M. (eds.) CRYPTO 2015. LNCS, vol. 9215, pp. 63–92. Springer, Heidelberg (2015). doi:10.1007/978-3-662-47989-6_4
7. Farkas, J.: Theorie der einfachen Ungleichungen. J. für die reine und angewandte Mathematik (Crelle's Journal) **124**, 1–27 (1902). http://resolver.sub.uni-goettingen.de/purl?GDZPPN002165023
8. Galbraith, S.D.: Space-efficient variants of cryptosystems based on learning with errors (2013). https://www.math.auckland.ac.nz/sgal018/pubs.html
9. Grötschel, M., Lovász, L., Schrijver, A.: Geometric Algorithms and Combinatorial Optimization. Algorithms and Combinatorics. Springer, Heidelberg (2012). doi:10.1007/978-3-642-78240-4. ISBN 978-3-642-78240-4
10. Güneysu, T., Lyubashevsky, V., Pöppelmann, T.: Practical lattice-based cryptography: a signature scheme for embedded systems. In: Prouff, E., Schaumont, P. (eds.) CHES 2012. LNCS, vol. 7428, pp. 530–547. Springer, Heidelberg (2012). doi:10.1007/978-3-642-33027-8_31
11. Kirchner, P., Fouque, P.-A.: An improved BKW algorithm for LWE with applications to cryptography and lattices. In: Gennaro, R., Robshaw, M. (eds.) CRYPTO 2015. LNCS, vol. 9215, pp. 43–62. Springer, Heidelberg (2015). doi:10.1007/978-3-662-47989-6_3

12. Lindner, R., Peikert, C.: Better key sizes (and attacks) for LWE-based encryption. In: Kiayias, A. (ed.) CT-RSA 2011. LNCS, vol. 6558, pp. 319–339. Springer, Heidelberg (2011). doi:10.1007/978-3-642-19074-2_21
13. Lyubashevsky, V., Peikert, C., Regev, O.: On ideal lattices and learning with errors over rings. In: Gilbert, H. (ed.) EUROCRYPT 2010. LNCS, vol. 6110, pp. 1–23. Springer, Heidelberg (2010). doi:10.1007/978-3-642-13190-5_1
14. Lyubashevsky, V., Peikert, C., Regev, O.: A toolkit for ring-LWE cryptography. In: Johansson, T., Nguyen, P.Q. (eds.) EUROCRYPT 2013. LNCS, vol. 7881, pp. 35–54. Springer, Heidelberg (2013). doi:10.1007/978-3-642-38348-9_3
15. Micciancio, D., Peikert, C.: Hardness of SIS and LWE with small parameters. In: Canetti, R., Garay, J.A. (eds.) CRYPTO 2013. LNCS, vol. 8042, pp. 21–39. Springer, Heidelberg (2013). doi:10.1007/978-3-642-40041-4_2
16. Regev, O.: On lattices, learning with errors, random linear codes, and cryptography. In: STOC, pp. 84–93. ACM (2005)

Improved Algorithms for the Approximate k-List Problem in Euclidean Norm

Gottfried Herold[(✉)] and Elena Kirshanova

Faculty of Mathematics, Horst Görtz Institute for IT-Security,
Ruhr University Bochum, Bochum, Germany
{gottfried.herold,elena.kirshanova}@rub.de

Abstract. We present an algorithm for the approximate k-List problem for the Euclidean distance that improves upon the Bai-Laarhoven-Stehlé (BLS) algorithm from ANTS'16. The improvement stems from the observation that almost all the solutions to the approximate k-List problem form a particular configuration in n-dimensional space. Due to special properties of configurations, it is much easier to verify whether a k-tuple forms a configuration rather than checking whether it gives a solution to the k-List problem. Thus, phrasing the k-List problem as a problem of finding such configurations immediately gives a better algorithm. Furthermore, the search for configurations can be sped up using techniques from Locality-Sensitive Hashing (LSH). Stated in terms of configuration-search, our LSH-like algorithm offers a broader picture on previous LSH algorithms.

For the Shortest Vector Problem, our configuration-search algorithm results in an exponential improvement for memory-efficient sieving algorithms. For $k = 3$, it allows us to bring down the complexity of the BLS sieve algorithm on an n-dimensional lattice from $2^{0.4812n+o(n)}$ to $2^{0.3962n+o(n)}$ with the same space requirement $2^{0.1887n+o(n)}$. Note that our algorithm beats the Gauss Sieve algorithm with time resp. space of $2^{0.415n+o(n)}$ resp. $2^{0.208n+o(n)}$, while being easy to implement. Using LSH techniques, we can further reduce the time complexity down to $2^{0.3717n+o(n)}$ while retaining a memory complexity of $2^{0.1887n+o(n)}$.

1 Introduction

The k-List problem is defined as follows: given k lists $L_1, \ldots, L_k$ of elements from a set X, find k-tuples $(x_1, \ldots, x_k) \in L_1 \times \ldots \times L_k$ that satisfy some condition C. For example, Wagner [19] considers $X \subset \{0,1\}^n$, and a tuple $(x_1, \ldots, x_k)$ is a solution if $x_1 \oplus \ldots \oplus x_n = 0^n$. In this form, the problem has found numerous applications in cryptography [14] and learning theory [6].

For ℓ_2-norm conditions with $X \subset \mathbb{R}^n$ and $k = 2$, the task of finding pairs $(\boldsymbol{x}_1, \boldsymbol{x}_2) \in L_1 \times L_2$, s.t. $\|\boldsymbol{x}_1 + \boldsymbol{x}_2\| < \min\{\|\boldsymbol{x}_1\|, \|\boldsymbol{x}_2\|\}$, is at the heart of certain algorithms for the Shortest Vector Problem (SVP). Such algorithms, called *sieving* algorithms [1,17], are asymptotically the fastest SVP solvers known so far.

© International Association for Cryptologic Research 2017
S. Fehr (Ed.): PKC 2017, Part I, LNCS 10174, pp. 16–40, 2017.
DOI: 10.1007/978-3-662-54365-8_2

Sieving algorithms look at pairs of lattice vectors that sum up to a short(er) vector. Once enough such sums are found, repeat the search by combining these shorter vectors into even shorter ones and so on. It is not difficult to see that in order to find even one pair where the sum is shorter than both the summands, we need an exponential number of lattice vectors, so the memory requirement is exponential. In practice, due to the large memory-requirement, sieving algorithms are outperformed by the asymptotically slower Kannan enumeration [10].

Naturally, the question arises whether one can reduce the constant in the exponent of the memory complexity of sieving algorithms at the expense of running time. An affirmative answer is obtained in the recently proposed k-list sieving by Bai, Laarhoven, and Stehlé [4] (BLS, for short). For constant k, they present an algorithm that, given input lists $L_1, \ldots, L_k$ of elements from the n-sphere S^n with radius 1, outputs k-tuples with the property $\|x_1 + \ldots + x_n\| < 1$. They provide the running time and memory-complexities for $k = 3, 4$.

We improve and generalize upon the BLS k-list algorithm. Our results are as follows:

1. We present an algorithm that on input $L_1, \ldots, L_k \subset \mathsf{S}^n$, outputs k-tuples $(x_1, \ldots, x_k), \in L_1 \times \ldots \times L_k$, s.t. all *pairs* (x_i, x_j) in a tuple satisfy certain inner product constraints. We call this problem the Configuration problem (Definition 3).
2. We give a concentration result on the distribution of scalar products of $x_1, \ldots x_k \in \mathsf{S}^n$ (Theorems 1 and 2), which implies that finding vectors that sum to a shorter vector can be reduced to the above Configuration problem.
3. By working out the properties of the aforementioned distribution, we *prove* the conjectured formula (Eq. (3.2) from [4]) on the input list-sizes (Theorem 3), s.t. we can expect a constant success probability for sieving. We provide closed formulas for the running times for both algorithms: BLS and our Algorithm 1 (Theorem 4). Algorithm 1 achieves an exponential speed-up compared the BLS algorithm.
4. To further reduce the running time of our algorithm, we introduce the so-called Configuration Extension Algorithm (Algorithm 2). It has an effect similar to Locality-Sensitive Hashing as it shrinks the lists in a helpful way. This is a natural generalization of LSH to our framework of configurations. We briefly explain how to combine Algorithm 1 and the Configuration Extension in Sect. 7. A complete description can be found in the full version.

Roadmap. Section 2 gives basic notations and states the problem we consider in this work. Section 3 introduces configurations – a novel tool that aids the analysis in succeeding Sects. 4 and 5 where we present our algorithm for the k-List problem and prove its running time. Our generalization of Locality Sensitive Hashing – Configuration Extension – is described in Sect. 6 and its application to the k-list problem in Sect. 7. We conclude with experimental results confirming our analysis in Sect. 8. We defer some of the proofs and details on the Configuration Extension Algorithm to the appendices as these are not necessary to understand the main part.

2   Preliminaries

Notations. We denote by $\mathsf{S}^n \subset \mathbb{R}^{n+1}$ the n-dimensional unit sphere. We use soft-$\mathcal{O}$ notation to denote running times: $T = \widetilde{\mathcal{O}}(2^{cn})$ means that we suppress subexponential factors. We use sub-indices $\mathcal{O}_k(.)$ in the $\mathcal{O}$-notation to stress that the asymptotic result holds for k fixed. For any set $\boldsymbol{x}_1, \ldots, \boldsymbol{x}_k$ of vectors in some $\mathbb{R}^n$, the *Gram matrix* $C \in \mathbb{R}^{k \times k}$ is given by the set of pairwise scalar products. It is a complete invariant of the $\boldsymbol{x}_1, \ldots, \boldsymbol{x}_k$ up to simultaneous rotation and reflection of all $\boldsymbol{x}_i$'s. For such matrices $C \in \mathbb{R}^{k \times k}$ and $I \subset \{1, \ldots, k\}$, we write $C[I]$ for the appropriate $|I| \times |I|$-submatrix with rows and columns from I.

As we consider distances wrt. the ℓ_2-norm, the approximate k-List problem we consider in this work is the following computational problem:

Definition 1 (Approximate k-List problem). *Let $0 < t < \sqrt{k}$. Assume we are given k lists $L_1, \ldots, L_k$ of equal exponential size, whose entries are iid. uniformly chosen vectors from the n-sphere S^n. The task is to output an $1 - o(1)$-fraction of all solutions, where solutions are k-tuples $\boldsymbol{x}_1 \in L_1, \ldots, \boldsymbol{x}_k \in L_k$ satisfying $\|\boldsymbol{x}_1 + \cdots + \boldsymbol{x}_k\|^2 \leq t^2$.*

We consider the case where t, k are constant and the input lists are of size c^n for some constant $\mathsf{c} > 1$. We are interested in the asymptotic complexity for $n \to \infty$. To simplify the exposition, we pretend that we can compute with real numbers; all our algorithms work with sufficiently precise approximations (possibly losing an $o(1)$-fraction of solutions due to rounding). This does not affect the asymptotics. Note that the problem becomes trivial for $t > \sqrt{k}$, since all but an $1 - o(1)$-fraction of k-tuples from $L_1 \times \cdots \times L_k$ satisfy $\|\boldsymbol{x}_1 + \ldots + \boldsymbol{x}_k\|^2 \approx k$ (random $\boldsymbol{x}_i \in \mathsf{S}^n$ are almost orthogonal with high probability, cf. Theorem 1). In the case $t > \sqrt{k}$, we need to ask that $\|\boldsymbol{x}_1 + \ldots + \boldsymbol{x}_k\|^2 \geq t^2$ to get a meaningful problem. Then all our results apply to the case $t > \sqrt{k}$ as well.

In our definition, we allow to drop a $o(1)$-fraction of solutions, which is fine for the sieving applications. In fact, we will propose an algorithm that drops an exponentially small fraction of solutions and our asymptotic improvement compared to BLS crucially relies on dropping more solutions than BLS. For this reason, we are only interested in the case where the expected number of solutions is exponential.

Relation to the Approximate Shortest Vector Problem. The main incentive to look at the approximate k-List problem (as in Definition 1) is its straightforward application to the so-called sieving algorithms for the shortest vector problem (SVP) on an n-dimensional lattice (see Sect. 7.2 for a more comprehensive discussion). The complexity of these sieving algorithms is completely determined by the complexity of an approximate k-List solver called as main subroutine. So one can instantiate a lattice sieving algorithm using an approximate k-List solver (the ability to choose k allows a memory-efficient instantiations of such a solver). This is observed and fully explained in [4]. For $k = 3$, the running time for the SVP algorithm presented in [4] is $2^{0.4812n+o(n)}$ requiring $2^{0.1887n+o(n)}$

memory. Running our Algorithm 1 instead as a k-List solver within the SVP sieving, one obtains a running time of $2^{0.3962n+o(n)}$ with the same memory complexity $2^{0.1887n+o(n)}$. As explained in Sect. 7.2, we can reduce the running time even further down to $2^{0.3717n+o(n)}$ with no asymptotic increase in memory by using a combination of Algorithm 1 and the LSH-like Configuration Extension Algorithm. This combined algorithm is fully described in the full version of the paper.

In the applications to sieving, we have $t = 1$ and actually look for solutions $\| \pm x_1 \pm \cdots \pm x_k \| \leq 1$ with arbitrary signs. This is clearly equivalent by considering the above problem separately for each of the $2^k = \mathcal{O}(1)$ choices of signs. Further, the lists $L_1, \ldots, L_k$ can actually be equal. Our algorithm works for this case as well. In these settings, some obvious optimizations are possible, but they do not affect the asymptotics.

Our methods are also applicable to lists of different sizes, but we stick to the case of equal list sizes to simplify the formulas for the running times.

3   Configurations

Whether a given k-tuple $x_1, \ldots, x_k$ is a solution to the approximate k-List problem is invariant under simultaneous rotations/reflections of all x_i and we want to look at k-tuples up to such symmetry by what we call configurations of points. As we are concerned with the ℓ_2-norm, a complete invariant of k-tuples up to symmetry is given by the set of pairwise scalar products and we define configurations for this norm:

Definition 2 (Configuration). *The* configuration $C = \mathrm{Conf}\,(x_1, \ldots, x_k)$ *of k points $x_1, \ldots, x_k \in \mathsf{S}^n$ is defined as the Gram matrix $C_{i,j} = \langle x_i, x_j \rangle$.*

Clearly, the configuration of the k-tuple $x_1, \ldots, x_k$ determines the length of the sum $\|\sum_i x_i\|$:

$$\Big\|\sum_i x_i\Big\|^2 = \sum_{i,j} \langle x_i, x_j \rangle = k + 2\sum_{i<j} \langle x_i, x_j \rangle. \tag{1}$$

We denote by

$$\mathscr{C} = \{C \in \mathbb{R}^{k \times k} \mid C \text{ symmetric positive semi-definite, } C_{i,i} = 1 \ \forall i\},$$

$$\mathscr{C}_{\leq t} = \{C \in \mathscr{C} \mid \sum_{i,j} C_{i,j} \leq t^2\} \subset \mathscr{C}$$

the spaces of all possible configurations resp. those which give a length of at most t. The spaces $\mathscr{C}$ and $\mathscr{C}_{\leq t}$ are compact and convex. For fixed k, it is helpful from an algorithmic point of view to think of $\mathscr{C}$ as a finite set: for any $\varepsilon > 0$, we can cover $\mathscr{C}$ by finitely many ε-balls, so we can efficiently enumerate $\mathscr{C}$.

In the context of the approximate k-List problem with target length t, a k-tuple $x_1, \ldots, x_k$ is a solution iff $\mathrm{Conf}\,(x_1, \ldots, x_k) \in \mathscr{C}_{\leq t}$. For that reason, we call a configuration in $\mathscr{C}_{\leq t}$ *good*. An obvious way to solve the approximate k-List problem is to enumerate over all good configurations and solve the following k-List configuration problem:

Definition 3 (Configuration problem). *On input k exponentially-sized lists $L_1, \ldots, L_k$ of vectors from S^n, a target configuration $C \in \mathscr{C}$ and some $\varepsilon > 0$, the task is to output all k-tuples $\boldsymbol{x}_1 \in L_1, \ldots, \boldsymbol{x}_k \in L_k$, such that $|\langle \boldsymbol{x}_i, \boldsymbol{x}_j \rangle - C_{ij}| \le \varepsilon$ for all i, j. Such k-tuples are called solutions to the problem.*

Remark 1. Due to $\langle \boldsymbol{x}_i, \boldsymbol{x}_j \rangle$ taking real values, it does not make sense to ask for exact equality to C, but rather we introduce some $\varepsilon > 0$. We shorthand write $C \approx_\varepsilon C'$ for $|C_{i,j} - C'_{i,j}| \le \varepsilon$. Formally, our analysis will show that for fixed $\varepsilon > 0$, we obtain running times and list sizes of the form $\widetilde{\mathcal{O}}_\varepsilon(2^{(c+f(\varepsilon))n})$ for some unspecified continuous f with $\lim_{\varepsilon \to 0} f(\varepsilon) = 0$. Letting $\varepsilon \to 0$ sufficiently slowly, we absorb $f(\varepsilon)$ into the $\widetilde{\mathcal{O}}(.)$-notation and omit it.

As opposed to the approximate k-List problem, being a solution to the k-List configuration problem is a locally checkable property [12]: it is a conjunction of conditions involving only *pairs* $\boldsymbol{x}_i, \boldsymbol{x}_j$. It is this and the following observation that we leverage to improve on the results of [4].

It turns out that the configurations attained by the solutions to the approximate k-List problem are concentrated around a single good configuration, which is the good configuration with the highest amount of symmetry. So in fact, we only need to solve the configuration problem for this particular good configuration. The following theorem describes the distribution of configurations:

Theorem 1. *Let $\boldsymbol{x}_1, \ldots, \boldsymbol{x}_k \in \mathsf{S}^n$ be independent, uniformly distributed on the n-sphere, $n > k$. Then the configuration $C = C(\boldsymbol{x}_1, \ldots, \boldsymbol{x}_k)$ follows a distribution $\mu_\mathscr{C}$ on $\mathscr{C}$ with density given by*

$$\mu_\mathscr{C} = W_{n,k} \cdot \det(C)^{\frac{1}{2}(n-k)} \mathrm{d}\mathscr{C} = \widetilde{\mathcal{O}}_k\Big(\det(C)^{\frac{n}{2}} \Big) \mathrm{d}\mathscr{C},$$

where $W_{n,k} = \pi^{-\frac{k(k-1)}{4}} \prod_{i=0}^{k-1} \frac{\Gamma(\frac{n+1}{2})}{\Gamma(\frac{n+1-i}{2})} = \mathcal{O}_k\big(n^{\frac{k(k-1)}{4}}\big)$ is a normalization constant that only depends on n and k. Here, the reference measure $\mathrm{d}\mathscr{C}$ is given by $\mathrm{d}\mathscr{C} = \mathrm{d}C_{1,2} \cdots \mathrm{d}C_{(k-1),k}$ (i.e. the Lebesgue measure in a natural parametrization).

Proof. We derive this by an approximate normalization of the so-called Wishart distribution [20]. Observe that we can sample $C \leftarrow \mu_\mathscr{C}$ in the following way: We sample $\boldsymbol{x}_1, \ldots, \boldsymbol{x}_k \in \mathbb{R}^{n+1}$ iid from spherical $n + 1$-dimensional Gaussians, such that the direction of each $\boldsymbol{x}_i$ is uniform over S^n. Note that the lengths of the $\boldsymbol{x}_i$ are not normalized to 1. Then we set $A_{i,j} := \langle \boldsymbol{x}_i, \boldsymbol{x}_j \rangle$. Finally, normalize to $C_{i,j} := \frac{A_{i,j}}{\sqrt{A_{i,i} A_{j,j}}}$.

The joint distribution of the $A_{i,j}$ is (by definition) given by the so-called Wishart distribution. [20] Its density for $n + 1 > k - 1$ is known to be

$$\rho_{\text{Wishart}} = \frac{e^{-\frac{1}{2} \operatorname{Tr} A} \cdot \det(A)^{\frac{n+1-k-1}{2}}}{2^{\frac{(n+1)k}{2}} \pi^{\frac{k(k-1)}{4}} \prod_{i=0}^{k-1} \Gamma(\frac{n+1-i}{2})} \mathrm{d}A \tag{2}$$

where the reference density $\mathrm{d}A$ is given by $\mathrm{d}A = \prod_{i \le j} \mathrm{d}A_{i,j}$. We refer to [8] for a relatively simple computation of that density. Consider the change of variables on $\mathbb{R}^{k(k+1)/2}$ given by

$$
\begin{aligned}
&\Phi\big(A_{1,1}, A_{2,2}, \ldots, A_{k,k}, A_{1,2}, \ldots, A_{k-1,k}\big) \\
&= \Big(A_{1,1}, A_{2,2}, \ldots, A_{k,k}, \frac{A_{1,2}}{\sqrt{A_{1,1}A_{2,2}}}, \ldots, \frac{A_{k,k-1}}{\sqrt{A_{k-1,k-1}A_{k,k}}}\Big),
\end{aligned}
$$

i.e. we map the $A_{i,j}$'s to $C_{i,j}$'s while keeping the $A_{i,i}$'s to make the transformation bijective almost everywhere. The Jacobian $D\Phi$ of Φ is a triangular matrix and its determinant is easily seen to be

$$
\big|\det(D\Phi)\big| = \prod_i \frac{1}{\sqrt{A_{i,i}}^{\,k-1}}.
$$

Further, note that $A = TCT$, where T is a diagonal matrix with diagonal $\sqrt{A_{1,1}}, \ldots, \sqrt{A_{k,k}}$. In particular, $\det(A) = \det(C) \cdot \prod_i A_{i,i}$. Consequently, we can transform the Wishart density into $\big(A_{1,1}, \ldots, A_{k,k}, C_{1,2}, \ldots, C_{k-1,k}\big)$-coordinates as

$$
\rho_{\text{Wishart}} = \frac{e^{-\frac{1}{2}\sum_i A_{i,i}} \det(C)^{\frac{n-k}{2}} \prod_i A_{i,i}^{\frac{n-k}{2}}}{2^{\frac{(n+1)k}{2}} \pi^{\frac{k(k-1)}{4}} \prod_{i=0}^{k-1} \Gamma(\frac{n-i+1}{2})} \prod_i \sqrt{A_{i,i}}^{\,k-1} \prod_i \mathrm{d}A_{i,i} \prod_{i<j} \mathrm{d}C_{i,j}.
$$

The desired $\mu_{\mathscr{C}}$ is obtained from ρ_{Wishart} by integrating out $\mathrm{d}A_{1,1}\mathrm{d}A_{2,2}\cdots\mathrm{d}A_{k,k}$. We can immediately see that $\mu_{\mathscr{C}}$ takes the form $\mu_{\mathscr{C}} = W_{n,k} \det(C)^{\frac{n-k}{2}} \mathrm{d}\mathscr{C}$ for some constants $W_{n,k}$. We compute $W_{n,k}$ as

$$
\begin{aligned}
W_{n,k} &= \int_{A_{1,1}} \cdots \int_{A_{k,k}} \frac{e^{-\frac{1}{2}\sum_i A_{i,i}} \prod_i A_{i,i}^{\frac{n-k}{2}}}{2^{\frac{(n+1)k}{2}} \pi^{\frac{k(k-1)}{4}} \prod_{i=0}^{k-1} \Gamma(\frac{n-i+1}{2})} \prod_i \sqrt{A_{i,i}}^{\,k-1} \prod_i \mathrm{d}A_{i,i} \\
&= \frac{1}{2^{\frac{(n+1)k}{2}} \pi^{\frac{k(k-1)}{4}} \prod_{i=0}^{k-1} \Gamma(\frac{n-i+1}{2})} \Big(\int_{A_{1,1}=0}^{+\infty} A_{1,1}^{\frac{n-1}{2}} e^{-\frac{1}{2}A_{1,1}} \, \mathrm{d}A_{1,1}\Big)^k \\
&= \frac{2^{\frac{(n+1)k}{2}}}{2^{\frac{(n+1)k}{2}} \pi^{\frac{k(k-1)}{4}} \prod_{i=0}^{k-1} \Gamma(\frac{n-i+1}{2})} \Big(\int_{A_{1,1}=0}^{+\infty} \big(\tfrac{A_{1,1}}{2}\big)^{\frac{n+1}{2}-1} e^{-\frac{1}{2}A_{1,1}} \tfrac{1}{2}\mathrm{d}A_{1,1}\Big)^k \\
&= \frac{1}{\pi^{\frac{k(k-1)}{4}} \prod_{i=0}^{k-1} \Gamma(\frac{n-i+1}{2})} \Big(\int_{x=0}^{+\infty} x^{\frac{n+1}{2}-1} e^{-x} \, \mathrm{d}x\Big)^k \\
&= \frac{\Gamma(\frac{n+1}{2})^k}{\pi^{\frac{k(k-1)}{4}} \prod_{i=0}^{k-1} \Gamma(\frac{n-i+1}{2})}.
\end{aligned}
$$

Finally, note that as a consequence of Stirling's formula, we have $\frac{\Gamma(n+z)}{\Gamma(n)} = \mathcal{O}_z(n^z)$ for any fixed z and $n \to \infty$. From this, we get

$$
W_{n,k} = \frac{\Gamma(\frac{n+1}{2})^k}{\pi^{\frac{k(k-1)}{4}} \prod_{i=0}^{k-1} \Gamma(\frac{n-i+1}{2})} = \mathcal{O}_k\Big(n^{\sum_{i=0}^{k-1} \frac{i}{2}}\Big) = \mathcal{O}_k\Big(n^{\frac{k(k-1)}{4}}\Big).
$$

The configurations C that we care about the most have the highest amount of symmetry. We call a configuration C balanced if $C_{i,j} = C_{i',j'}$ for all $i \neq j$, $i' \neq j'$. To compute the determinant $\det(C)$ for such balanced configurations, we have the following lemma:

Lemma 1.

$$Let\ C = \begin{pmatrix} 1 & a & a & \dots & a \\ a & 1 & a & \dots & a \\ a & a & 1 & \dots & a \\ \vdots & & & \ddots & \vdots \\ a & a & a & \dots & 1 \end{pmatrix} \in \mathbb{R}^{k \times k}.$$

Then $\det(C) = (1-a)^{k-1}(1 + (k-1)a)$.

Proof. We have $C = (1-a) \cdot \mathbb{1}_k + a \cdot \mathbf{1} \cdot \mathbf{1}^{\mathbf{t}}$, where $\mathbf{1} \in \mathbb{R}^{k \times 1}$ is an all-ones vector. Sylvester's Determinant Theorem [2] gives

$$\det(C) = (1-a)^k \det\big(\mathbb{1}_k + \tfrac{a}{1-a}\mathbf{1} \cdot \mathbf{1}^{\mathbf{t}}\big) = (1-a)^k \det\big(\mathbb{1}_1 + \tfrac{a}{1-a}\mathbf{1}^{\mathbf{t}} \cdot \mathbf{1}\big)$$
$$= (1-a)^k(1 + \tfrac{a}{1-a}k) = (1-a)^{k-1}(1 + (k-1)a).$$

For fixed k and C, the probability density $\widetilde{\mathcal{O}}\big(\det(C)^{\frac{n}{2}}\big)$ of $\mu_{\mathscr{C}}$ is exponential in n. Since $C \in \mathscr{C}$ can only vary in a compact space, taking integrals will asymptotically pick the maximum value: in particular, we have for the probability that a uniformly random k-tuple $\boldsymbol{x}_1, \dots, \boldsymbol{x}_k$ is good:

$$\int_{C \text{ good}} \mu_{\mathscr{C}} = \widetilde{\mathcal{O}}\Big(\max_{C \text{ good}} \det(C)^{\frac{n}{2}}\Big). \tag{3}$$

We now compute this maximum.

Theorem 2. *Let* $0 < t < \sqrt{k}$ *be some target length and consider the subset* $\mathscr{C}_{\leq t} \subset \mathscr{C}$ *of good configurations for target length at most* t. *Then* $\det(C)$ *attains its unique maximum over* $\mathscr{C}_{\leq t}$ *at the balanced configuration* $C_{Bal,t}$, *defined by* $C_{i,j} = \frac{t^2-k}{k^2-k}$ *for all* $i \neq j$ *with maximal value*

$$\det(C)_{\max} = \det(C_{Bal,t}) = \frac{t^2}{k}\Big(\frac{k^2 - t^2}{k^2 - k}\Big)^{k-1}.$$

In particular, for $t = 1$, *this gives* $C_{i,j} = -\frac{1}{k}$ *and* $\det(C)_{\max} = \frac{(k+1)^{k-1}}{k^k}$. *Consequently, for any fixed* k *and any fixed* $\varepsilon > 0$, *the probability that a randomly chosen solution to the approximate* k-*List problem is* ε-*close to* $C_{Bal,t}$ *converges exponentially fast to* 1 *as* $n \to \infty$.

Proof. It suffices to show that C is balanced at the maximum, i.e. that all $C_{i,j}$ with $i \neq j$ are equal. Then computing the actual values is straightforward from (1) and Lemma 1. Assume $k \geq 3$, as there is nothing to show otherwise.

For the proof, it is convenient to replace the conditions $C_{i,i} = 1$ for all i by the (weaker) condition $\text{Tr}\,(C) = k$. Let $\mathscr{C}'_{\leq t}$ denote the set of all symmetric, positive semi-definite $C \in \mathbb{R}^{k \times k}$ with $\text{Tr}\,(C) = k$ and $\sum_{i,j} C_{i,j} \leq t^2$. We maximize $\det(C)$ over $\mathscr{C}'_{\leq t}$ and our proof will show that $C_{i,i} = 1$ is satisfied at the maximum.

Let $C \in \mathscr{C}'_{\leq t}$. Since C is symmetric, positive semi-definite, there exists an orthonormal basis $v_1, \ldots, v_k$ of eigenvectors with eigenvalues $0 \leq \lambda_1 \leq \ldots \leq \lambda_k$.

Clearly, $\sum_i \lambda_i = \text{Tr}\,(C) = k$ and our objective $\det(C)$ is given by $\det(C) = \prod_i \lambda_i$. We can write $\sum_{i,j} C_{i,j}$ as $\mathbf{1}^{\text{t}} C \mathbf{1}$ for an all-ones vector $\mathbf{1}$. We will show that if $\det(C)$ is maximal, then $\mathbf{1}$ is an eigenvector of C. Since

$$t^2 \geq \mathbf{1}^{\text{t}} C \mathbf{1} \geq \lambda_1 \|\mathbf{1}\|^2 = k\lambda_1, \tag{4}$$

for the smallest eigenvalue λ_1 of C, we have $\lambda_1 \leq \frac{t^2}{k} < 1$. For fixed λ_1, maximizing $\det(C) = \lambda_1 \cdot \prod_{i=2}^{k} \lambda_i$ under $\sum_{i=2}^{k} \lambda_i = k - \lambda_1$ gives (via the Arithmetic Mean-Geometric Mean Inequality)

$$\det(C) \leq \lambda_1 \left(\frac{k - \lambda_1}{k - 1} \right)^{k-1}.$$

The derivative of the right-hand side wrt. λ_1 is $\frac{k(1-\lambda_1)}{k-1} \left(\frac{k-\lambda_1}{k-1} \right)^{k-2} > 0$, so we can bound it by plugging in the maximal $\lambda_1 = \frac{t^2}{k}$:

$$\det(C) \leq \lambda_1 \left(\frac{k - \lambda_1}{k - 1} \right)^{k-1} \leq \frac{t^2}{k} \left(\frac{k - \frac{t^2}{k}}{k - 1} \right)^{k-1} = \frac{t^2}{k} \left(\frac{k^2 - t}{k^2 - k} \right)^{k-1} \tag{5}$$

The inequalities (5) are satisfied with equality iff $\lambda_2 = \ldots = \lambda_k$ and $\lambda_1 = \frac{t^2}{k}$. In this case, we can compute the value of λ_2 as $\lambda_2 = \frac{k^2 - t^2}{k(k-1)}$ from $\text{Tr}\,(C) = k$. The condition $\lambda_1 = \frac{t^2}{k}$ means that (4) is satisfied with equality, which implies that $\mathbf{1}$ is an eigenvector with eigenvalue λ_1. So wlog. $v_1 = \frac{1}{\sqrt{k}}\mathbf{1}$. Since the v_i's are orthonormal, we have $\mathbb{1}_k = \sum_i v_i v_i^{\text{t}}$, where $\mathbb{1}_k$ is the $k \times k$ identity matrix. Since we can write C as $C = \sum_i \lambda_i v_i v_i^{\text{t}}$, we obtain

$$C = \sum_i \lambda_i v_i v_i^{\text{t}} = (\lambda_1 - \lambda_2) v_1 v_1^{\text{t}} + \lambda_2 \sum_{i=1}^{k} v_i v_i^{\text{t}} = \frac{\lambda_1 - \lambda_2}{k} \mathbf{1}\mathbf{1}^{\text{t}} + \lambda_2 \cdot \mathbb{1}_k,$$

for $\det(C)$ maximal. From $C = \frac{\lambda_1 - \lambda_2}{k} \mathbf{1}\mathbf{1}^{\text{t}} + \lambda_2 \cdot \mathbb{1}_k$, we see that all diagonal entries of C are equal to $\lambda_2 + \frac{\lambda_1 - \lambda_2}{k}$ and the off-diagonal entries are all equal to $\frac{\lambda_1 - \lambda_2}{k}$. So all $C_{i,i}$ are equal with $C_{i,i} = 1$, because $\text{Tr}\,(C) = k$, and C is balanced.

For the case $t > \sqrt{k}$, and $\mathscr{C}_{\leq t}$ replaced by $\mathscr{C}_{\geq t}$, the statement can be proven analogously. Note that we need to consider the largest eigenvalue rather than the smallest in the proof. We remark that for $t = 1$, the condition $\langle x_i, x_j \rangle = C_{i,j} = -\frac{1}{k}$ for all $i \neq j$ is equivalent to saying that $x_1, \ldots, x_k$ are k points of a regular $k + 1$-simplex whose center is the origin. The missing $k + 1^{\text{th}}$ point of the simplex is $-\sum_i x_i$, i.e. the negative of the sum (see Fig. 1).

A corollary of our concentration result is the following formula for the expected size of the output lists in the approximate k-List problem.

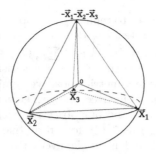

Fig. 1. A regular tetrahedron (3–simplex) represents a balanced configuration for $k = 3$.

Corollary 1. *Let k, t be fixed. Then the expected number of solutions to the approximate k-List problem with input lists of length $|L|$ is*

$$\mathbb{E}[\#solutions] = \widetilde{\mathcal{O}}\left(|L|^k \left(\frac{t^2}{k}\left(\frac{k^2 - t^2}{k^2 - k}\right)^{k-1}\right)^{\frac{n}{2}}\right). \tag{6}$$

Proof. By Theorems 1 and 2, the probability that any k-tuple is a solution is given by $\widetilde{\mathcal{O}}(\det(C_{\mathrm{Bal},t})^{\frac{n}{2}})$. The claim follows immediately.

In particular, this allows us to prove the following conjecture of [4]:

Theorem 3. *Let k be fixed and $t = 1$. If in the approximate k-List problem, the length $|L|$ of each input list is equal to the expected length of the output list, then $|L| = \widetilde{\mathcal{O}}\left(\left(\frac{k^{\frac{k}{k-1}}}{k+1}\right)^{\frac{n}{2}}\right).$*

Proof. This follows from simple algebraic manipulation of (6).

Our concentration result shows that it is enough to solve the configuration problem for $C_{\mathrm{Bal},t}$.

Corollary 2. *Let k, t be fixed. Then the approximate k-List problem with target length t can be solved in essentially the same time as the k-List configuration problem with target configuration $C_{\mathrm{Bal},t}$ for any fixed $\varepsilon > 0$.*

Proof. On input $L_1, \ldots, L_k$, solve the k-List configuration problem with target configuration $C_{\mathrm{Bal},t}$. Restrict to those solutions whose sum has length at most t. By Theorem 2, this will find all but an exponentially small fraction of solutions to the approximate k-List problem. Since we only need to output a $1 - o(1)$-fraction of the solutions, this solves the problem.

4   Algorithm

In this section we present our algorithm for the Configuration problem (Definition 3). On input it receives k lists $L_1, \ldots, L_k$, a target configuration C in the form of a Gram matrix $C_{i,j} = \langle \boldsymbol{x}_i, \boldsymbol{x}_j \rangle \in \mathbb{R}^{k \times k}$ and a small $\varepsilon > 0$. The algorithm proceeds as follows: it picks an $\boldsymbol{x}_1 \in L_1$ and filters all the remaining lists with respect to the values $\langle \boldsymbol{x}_1, \boldsymbol{x}_i \rangle$ for all $2 \leq i \leq k$. More precisely, $\boldsymbol{x}_i \in L_i$ 'survives' the filter if $|\langle \boldsymbol{x}_1, \boldsymbol{x}_i \rangle - C_{1,i}| \leq \varepsilon$. We put such an $\boldsymbol{x}_i$ into $L_i^{(1)}$ (the superscript indicates how many filters were applied to the original list L_i). On this step, all the k-tuples of the form $(\boldsymbol{x}_1, \boldsymbol{x}_2, \ldots, \boldsymbol{x}_k) \in \{\boldsymbol{x}_1\} \times L_2^{(1)} \times \ldots \times L_k^{(1)}$ with a fixed first component $\boldsymbol{x}_1$ partially match the target configuration: all scalar products involving $\boldsymbol{x}_1$ are as desired. In addition, the lists $L_i^{(1)}$ become much shorter than the original ones.

Next, we choose an $\boldsymbol{x}_2 \in L_2^{(1)}$ and create smaller lists $L_i^{(2)}$ from $L_i^{(1)}$ by filtering out all the $\boldsymbol{x}_i \in L_i^{(1)}$ that do not satisfy $|\langle \boldsymbol{x}_2, \boldsymbol{x}_i \rangle - C_{2,i}| \leq \varepsilon$ for all $3 \leq i \leq k$. A tuple of the form $(\boldsymbol{x}_1, \boldsymbol{x}_2, \boldsymbol{x}_3, \ldots, \boldsymbol{x}_k) \in \{\boldsymbol{x}_1\} \times \{\boldsymbol{x}_2\} \times L_3^{(2)} \times \ldots \times L_k^{(2)}$ satisfies the target configuration $C_{i,j}$ for $i = 1, 2$. We proceed with this list-filtering strategy until we have fixed all $\boldsymbol{x}_i$ for $1 \leq i \leq k$. We output all such k-tuples. Note that our algorithm becomes the trivial brute-force algorithm once we are down to 2 lists to be processed. As soon as we have fixed $\boldsymbol{x}_1, \ldots, \boldsymbol{x}_{k-2}$ and created $L_{k-1}^{(k-2)}, L_k^{(k-2)}$, our algorithm iterates over $L_{k-1}^{(k-2)}$ and checks the scalar product with every element from $L_k^{(k-2)}$.

Our algorithm is detailed in Algorithm 1 and illustrated in Fig. 2a.

Algorithm 1. k-List for the Configuration Problem

Input: $L_1, \ldots, L_k$ – lists of vectors from $\mathbf{S}^n$. $C_{i,j} = \langle \boldsymbol{x}_i, \boldsymbol{x}_j \rangle \in \mathbb{R}^{k \times k}$ – Gram matrix. $\varepsilon > 0$.
Output: L_{out} – list of k-tuples $\boldsymbol{x}_1 \in L_1, \ldots, \boldsymbol{x}_k \in L_k$, s.t. $|\langle \boldsymbol{x}_i, \boldsymbol{x}_j \rangle - C_{ij}| \leq \varepsilon$, for all i, j.

1: $L_{\text{out}} \leftarrow \{\}$
2: **for all** $\boldsymbol{x}_1 \in L_1$ **do**
3:      **for all** $j = 2 \ldots k$ **do**
4:          $L_j^{(1)} \leftarrow \text{FILTER}(\boldsymbol{x}_1, L_j, C_{1,j}, \varepsilon)$
5:      **for all** $\boldsymbol{x}_2 \in L_2^{(1)}$ **do**
6:          **for all** $j = 3 \ldots k$ **do**
7:              $L_j^{(2)} \leftarrow \text{FILTER}(\boldsymbol{x}_2, L_j^{(1)}, C_{2,j}, \varepsilon)$
8:          $\ddots$
9:          **for all** $\boldsymbol{x}_k \in L_k^{(k-1)}$ **do**
10:            $L_{\text{out}} \leftarrow L_{\text{out}} \cup \{(\boldsymbol{x}_1, \ldots \boldsymbol{x}_k)\}$
11: **return** L_{out}

1: **function** FILTER$(\boldsymbol{x}, L, c, \varepsilon)$
2:      $L' \leftarrow \{\}$
3:      **for all** $\boldsymbol{x}' \in L$ **do**
4:          **if** $|\langle \boldsymbol{x}, \boldsymbol{x}' \rangle - c| \leq \varepsilon$ **then**
5:              $L' \leftarrow L' \cup \{\boldsymbol{x}'\}$
6:      **return** L'

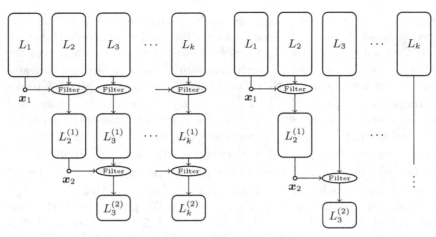

(a) Pictorial representation of Alg. 1. At level i, a filter receives as input $\boldsymbol{x}_i$ and a vector $\boldsymbol{x}_j$ from $L_j^{(i-1)}$ (for the input lists, $L = L^{(0)}$). $\boldsymbol{x}_j$ passes through the filter if $|\langle \boldsymbol{x}_i, \boldsymbol{x}_j \rangle - C_{i,j}| \leq \varepsilon$, in which case it is added to $L_j^{(i)}$. The configuration C is a global parameter.

(b) The k-List algorithm given in [4]. The main difference is that a filter receives as inputs $\boldsymbol{x}_i$ and a vector $\boldsymbol{x}_j \in L_j$, as opposed to $\boldsymbol{x}_j \in L_j^{(i-1)}$. Technically, in [4], $\boldsymbol{x}_i$ survives the filter if $|\langle \boldsymbol{x}_i, \boldsymbol{x}_1 + \ldots + \boldsymbol{x}_{i-1} \rangle| \geq c_i$ for some predefined c_i. Due to our concentration results, this description is equivalent to the one given in [4] in the sense that the returned solutions are (up to a subexponential fraction) the same.

Fig. 2. k-List algorithms for the configuration problem. Left: Our Algorithm 1. Right: k-tuple sieve algorithm of [4].

5 Analysis

In this section we analyze the complexity of Algorithm 1 for the Configuration problem. First, we should mention that the memory complexity is completely determined by the input list-sizes $|L_i|$ (remember that we restrict to constant k) and it does not change the asymptotics when we apply k filters. In practice, all intermediate lists $L_i^{(j)}$ can be implemented by storing pointers to the elements of the original lists.

In the following, we compute the expected sizes of filtered lists $L_i^{(j)}$ and establish the expected running time of Algorithm 1. Since our algorithm has an exponential running time of 2^{cn} for some $c = \Theta(1)$, we are interested in determining c (which depends on k) and we ignore polynomial factors, e.g. we do not take into account time spent for computing inner products.

Theorem 4. *Let k be fixed. Algorithm 1 given as input k lists $L_1, \ldots, L_k \subset \mathsf{S}^n$ of the same size $|L|$, a target balanced configuration $C_{Bal,t} \in \mathbb{R}^{k \times k}$, a target length*

$0 < t < \sqrt{k}$, and $\varepsilon > 0$, outputs the list L_{out} of solutions to the Configuration problem. The expected running time of Algorithm 1 is

$$T = \widetilde{\mathcal{O}}\Big(|L| \cdot \max_{1 \le i \le k-1} |L|^i \cdot \frac{(k^2 - t^2)^i}{(k^2 - k)^{i+1}} \cdot \Big(\frac{(k^2 - k + (i-1)(t^2 - k))^2}{k^2 - k + (i-2)(t^2 - k)}\Big)^{\frac{n}{2}}\Big). \quad (7)$$

In particular, for $t = 1$ and $|L_{out}| = |L|$ it holds that

$$T = \widetilde{\mathcal{O}}\Big(\Big(\frac{k^{\frac{1}{k-1}}}{k+1} \cdot \max_{1 \le i \le k-1} k^{\frac{i}{k-1}} \cdot \frac{(k - i + 1)^2}{k - i + 2}\Big)^{\frac{n}{2}}\Big). \quad (8)$$

Remark 2. In the proof below we also show that the expected running time of the k-List algorithm presented in [4] is (see also Fig. 3 for a comparison) for $t = 1, |L_{out}| = |L|$

$$T_{\mathrm{BLS}} = \widetilde{\mathcal{O}}\Big(\Big(\frac{k^{\frac{k}{k-1}}}{(k+1)^2} \cdot \max_{1 \le i \le k-1} \big(k^{\frac{i}{k-1}} \cdot (k - i + 1)\big)\Big)^{\frac{n}{2}}\Big). \quad (9)$$

Corollary 3. *For $k = 3$, $t = 1$, and $|L| = |L_{out}|$ (the most interesting setting for SVP), Algorithm 1 has running time*

$$T = 2^{0.3962n + o(n)}, \quad (10)$$

requiring $|L| = 2^{0.1887n + o(n)}$ memory.

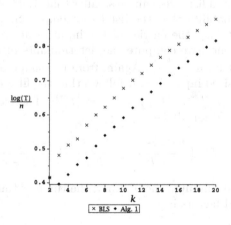

Fig. 3. Running exponents scaled by $1/n$ for the target length $t = 1$. For $k = 2$, both algorithms are the Nguyen-Vidick sieve [18] with $\log(T)/n = 0.415$ (naive brute-force over two lists). For $k = 3$, Algorithm 1 achieves $\log(T)/n = 0.3962$.

Proof (Proof of Theorem 4). The correctness of the algorithm is straightforward: let us associate the lists $L^{(i)}$ with a level i where i indicates the number of filtering steps applied to L (we identify the input lists with the 0th level: $L_i = L_i^{(0)}$). So for executing the filtering for the ith time, we choose an $\boldsymbol{x}_i \in L_i^{(i-1)}$ that satisfies the condition $|\langle \boldsymbol{x}_i, \boldsymbol{x}_{i-1} \rangle - C_{i,i-1}| \leq \varepsilon$ (for a fixed $\boldsymbol{x}_{i-1}$) and append to a previously obtained $(i-1)$-tuple $(\boldsymbol{x}_1, \ldots, \boldsymbol{x}_{i-1})$. Thus on the last level, we put into L_{out} a k-tuple $(\boldsymbol{x}_1, \ldots, \boldsymbol{x}_k)$ that is a solution to the Configuration problem.

Let us first estimate the size of the list $L_i^{(i-1)}$ output by the filtering process applied to the list $L_i^{(i-2)}$ for $i > 1$ (i.e. the left-most lists on Fig. 2a). Recall that all elements $\boldsymbol{x}_i \in L_i^{(i-1)}$ satisfy $|\langle \boldsymbol{x}_i, \boldsymbol{x}_j \rangle - C_{i,j}| \leq \varepsilon$, $1 \leq j \leq i - 1$. Then the *total* number of i-tuples $(\boldsymbol{x}_1, \boldsymbol{x}_2, \ldots, \boldsymbol{x}_i) \in L_1 \times L_2^{(1)} \times \ldots \times L_i^{(i-1)}$ considered by the algorithm is determined by the probability that in a random i-tuple, all pairs $(\boldsymbol{x}_j, \boldsymbol{x}_{j'}), 1 \leq j, j' \leq i$ satisfy the inner product constraints given by $C_{j,j'}$. This probability is given by Theorem 1 and since the input lists are of the same size $|L|$, we have[1]

$$|L_1| \cdot |L_2^{(1)}| \cdot \ldots |L_i^{(i-1)}| = |L|^i \cdot \det(C[1 \ldots i])^{\frac{n}{2}}, \tag{11}$$

where $\det(C[1 \ldots i])$ denotes the i-th principal minor of C. Using (11) for two consecutive values of i and dividing, we obtain

$$|L_{i+1}^{(i)}| = |L| \cdot \left(\frac{\det(C[1 \ldots i + 1])}{\det(C[1 \ldots i])} \right)^{\frac{n}{2}}. \tag{12}$$

Note that these expected list sizes can be smaller than 1. This should be thought of as the inverse probability that the list is not empty. Since we target a balanced configuration $C_{\text{Bal},t}$, the entries of the input Gram matrix are specified by Theorem 2 and, hence, we compute the determinants in the above quotient by applying Lemma 1 for $a = \frac{t^k - k}{k^2 - k}$. Again, from the shape of the Gram matrix $C_{\text{Bal},t}$ and the equal-sized input lists, it follows that the filtered list on each level are of the same size: $|L_{i+1}^{(i)}| = |L_{i+2}^{(i)}| = \ldots = |L_k^{(i)}|$. Therefore, for all filtering levels $0 \leq j \leq k - 1$ and for all $j + 1 \leq i \leq k$,

$$|L_i^{(j)}| = |L| \cdot \left(\frac{k^2 - t^2}{k^2 - k} \cdot \frac{k^2 - k + j(t^2 - k)}{k^2 - k + (j-1)(t^2 - k)} \right)^{\frac{n}{2}}. \tag{13}$$

Now let us discuss the running time. Clearly, the running time of Algorithm 1 is (up to subexponential factors in n)

$$T = |L_1^{(0)}| \cdot (|L_2^{(0)}| + |L_2^{(1)}| \cdot (|L_3^{(1)}| + |L_3^{(2)}| \cdot (\ldots \cdot (|L_k^{(k-2)}| + |L_k^{(k-1)}|)))\ldots).$$

---

[1] Throughout this proof, the equations that involve list-sizes $|L|$ and running time T are assumed to have $\widetilde{\mathcal{O}}(\cdot)$ on the right-hand side. We omit it for clarity.

Multiplying out and observing that $|L_k^{(k-2)}| > |L_k^{(k-1)}|$, so we may ignore the very last term, we deduce that the total running time is (up to subexponential factors) given by

$$T = |L| \cdot \max_{1 \leq i \leq k-1} |L^{(i-1)}| \cdot \prod_{j=1}^{i-1} |L^{(j)}|, \tag{14}$$

where $|L^{(j)}|$ is the size of any filtered list on level j (so we omit the subscripts). Consider the value $i_{\max}$ of i where the maximum is attained in the above formula. The meaning of $i_{\max}$ is that the total cost over all loops to create the lists $L_j^{(i_{\max})}$ is dominating the running time. At this level, the lists $L_j^{(i_{\max})}$ become small enough such that iterating over them (i.e. creation of $L_j^{(i_{\max}+1)}$) does not contribute asymptotically. Plugging in Eqs. (11) and (12) into (14), we obtain

$$T = |L| \cdot \max_{1 \leq i \leq k-1} |L|^i \left(\frac{(\det C[1 \dots i])^2}{\det C[1 \dots (i-1)]} \right)^{\frac{n}{2}}. \tag{15}$$

Using Lemma 1, we obtain the desired expression for the running time.

For the case $t = 1$ and $|L_{\mathrm{out}}| = |L|$, the result of Theorem 3 on the size of the input lists $|L|$ yields a compact formula for the filtered lists:

$$\left| L_i^{(j)} \right| = \left(k^{\frac{1}{k-1}} \cdot \frac{k-j}{k-j+1} \right)^{\frac{n}{2}}. \tag{16}$$

Plugging this into either (14) or (15), the running time stated in (8) easily follows.

It remains to show the complexity of the BLS algorithm [4], claimed in Remark 2. We do not give a complete description of the algorithm but illustrate it in Fig. 2b. We change the presentation of the algorithm to our configuration setting: in the original description, a vector $\boldsymbol{x}_i$ survives the filter if it satisfies $|\langle \boldsymbol{x}_i, \boldsymbol{x}_1 + \dots + \boldsymbol{x}_{i-1} \rangle| \geq c_i$ for a predefined c_i (a sequence $(c_1, \dots, c_{k-1}) \in \mathbb{R}^{k-1}$ is given as input to the BLS algorithm). Our concentration result (Theorem 1) also applies here and the condition $|\langle \boldsymbol{x}_i, \boldsymbol{x}_1 + \dots + \boldsymbol{x}_{i-1} \rangle| \geq c_i$ is equivalent to a pairwise constraint on the $\langle \boldsymbol{x}_i, \boldsymbol{x}_j \rangle$ up to losing an exponentially small fraction of solutions. The optimal sequence of c_i's corresponds to the balanced configuration $C_{\mathrm{Bal},t}$ derived in Theorem 2. Indeed, Table 1 in [4] corresponds exactly to $C_{\mathrm{Bal},t}$ for $t = 1$. So we may rephrase their filtering where instead of shrinking the list L_i by taking inner products with the sum $\boldsymbol{x}_1 + \dots + \boldsymbol{x}_{i-1}$, we filter L_i gradually by considering $\langle \boldsymbol{x}_i, \boldsymbol{x}_j \rangle$ for $1 \leq j \leq i-1$.

It follows that the filtered lists $L^{(i)}$ on level i are of the same size (in leading order) for both our and BLS algorithms. In particular, Eq. (12) holds for the expected list-sizes of the BLS algorithm. The crucial difference lies in the construction of these lists. To construct the list $L_i^{(i-1)}$ in BLS, the filtering procedure is applied not to $L_i^{(i-2)}$, but to a (larger) input-list L_i. Hence, the running time is (cf. (14)), ignoring subexponential factors

$$T_{\mathrm{BLS}} = |L_1| \cdot (|L_2| + |L_2^{(1)}| \cdot (|L_3| + |L_3^{(2)}| \cdot (\ldots \cdot (|L_k| + |L_k^{(k-1)}|)))\ldots)$$
$$= |L|^2 \cdot \max_{1 \leq i \leq k-1} \cdot \prod_{j=1}^{i-1} |L^{(j)}|.$$

The result follows after substituting (16) into the above product.

6   Configuration Extension

For $k = 2$, the asymptotically best algorithm with running time $T = \left(\frac{3}{2}\right)^{\frac{n}{2}}$ for $t = 1$ is due to [5], using techniques from Locally Sensitive Hashing. We generalize this to what we call Configuration Extension. To explain the LSH technique, consider the (equivalent) approximate 2-List problem with $t = 1$, where we want to bound the norm of the difference $\|\boldsymbol{x}_1 - \boldsymbol{x}_2\|^2 \leq 1$ rather than the sum, i.e. we want to find points that are close. The basic idea is to choose a family of hash functions $\mathscr{H}$, such that for $h \in \mathscr{H}$, the probability that $h(\boldsymbol{x}_1) = h(\boldsymbol{x}_2)$ is large if $\boldsymbol{x}_1$ and $\boldsymbol{x}_2$ are close, and small if they are far apart. Using such an $h \in \mathscr{H}$, we can bucket our lists according to h and then only look for pairs $\boldsymbol{x}_1, \boldsymbol{x}_2$ that collide under h. Repeat with several $h \in \mathscr{H}$ as appropriate to find all/most solutions. We may view such an $h \in \mathscr{H}$ as a collection of preimages $D_{h,z} = h^{-1}(z)$ and the algorithm first determines which elements $\boldsymbol{x}_1, \boldsymbol{x}_2$ are in some given $D_{h,z}$ (filtering the list using $D_{h,z}$) and then searches for solutions only among those. Note that, conceptually, we only really need the $D_{h,z}$ and not the functions h. Indeed, there is actually no need for the $D_{h,z}$ to be a partition of S^n for given h, and h need not even exist. Rather, we may have an arbitrary collection of sets $D^{(r)}$, with r belonging to some index set. The existence of functions h would help in efficiency when filtering. However, [5] (and also [16], stated for the ℓ_1-norm) give a technique to efficiently construct and apply filters $D^{(r)}$ without such an h in an amortized way.

The natural choice for $D^{(r)}$ is to choose all points with distance at most d for some $d > 0$ from some reference point $\boldsymbol{v}^{(r)}$ (that is typically not from any L_i). This way, a random pair $\boldsymbol{x}_1, \boldsymbol{x}_2 \in D^{(r)}$ has a higher chance to be close to each other than uniformly random points $\boldsymbol{x}_1, \boldsymbol{x}_2 \in \mathsf{S}^n$. Notationally, let us call (a description of) $D^{(r)}$ together with the filtered lists an *instance*, where $1 \leq r \leq R$ and R is the number of instances.

In our situation, we look for small sums rather than small differences. The above translates to asking that $\boldsymbol{x}_1$ is close to $\boldsymbol{v}^{(r)}$ and that $\boldsymbol{x}_2$ is far apart from $\boldsymbol{v}^{(r)}$ (or, equivalently, that $\boldsymbol{x}_2$ is close to $-\boldsymbol{v}^{(r)}$). In general, one may (for $k > 2$) consider not just a single $\boldsymbol{v}^{(r)}$ but rather several *related* $\boldsymbol{v}_1^{(r)}, \ldots, \boldsymbol{v}_m^{(r)}$. So an instance consists of m points $\boldsymbol{v}_1^{(r)}, \ldots, \boldsymbol{v}_m^{(r)}$ and shrunk lists $L_i^{\prime(r)}$ where $L_i^{\prime(r)} \subset L_i$ is obtained by taking those $x_i \in L_i$ that have some prescribed distances $d_{i,j}$

to $\boldsymbol{v}_j^{(r)}$. Note that the $d_{i,j}$ may depend on i and so need not treat the lists symmetrically. As a consequence, it does no longer make sense to think of this technique in terms of hash collisions in our setting.

We organize all the distances between $\boldsymbol{v}$'s and $\boldsymbol{x}$'s that occur into a single matrix C (i.e. a configuration) that governs the distances between $\boldsymbol{v}$'s and $\boldsymbol{x}$'s: the $\langle \boldsymbol{v}_j, \boldsymbol{v}_{j'} \rangle$-entries of C describe the relation between the $\boldsymbol{v}$'s and the $\langle \boldsymbol{x}_i, \boldsymbol{v}_j \rangle$-entries of C describe the $d_{i,j}$. The $\langle \boldsymbol{x}_i, \boldsymbol{x}_{i'} \rangle$-entries come from the approximate k-List problem we want to solve. While not relevant for constructing actual $\boldsymbol{v}_j^{(r)}$'s and $L_i'^{(r)}$'s, the $\langle \boldsymbol{x}_i, \boldsymbol{x}_{i'} \rangle$-entries are needed to choose the number R of instances.

For our applications to sieving, the elements from the input list L_i may possibly be not uniform from all of S^n due to previous processing of the lists. Rather, the elements $\boldsymbol{x}_i$ from L_i have some prescribed distance $d_{i,j}$ to (known) $\boldsymbol{v}_j$'s: e.g. in Algorithm 1, we fix $\boldsymbol{x}_1 \in L_1$ that we use to filter the remaining $k-1$ lists; we model this by taking $\boldsymbol{x}_1$ as one of the $\boldsymbol{v}_j$'s (and reducing k by 1). Another possibility is that we use configuration extension on lists that are the output of a previous application of configuration extension.

In general, we consider "old" points $\boldsymbol{v}_j$ and wish to create "new" points $\boldsymbol{v}_\ell$, so we have actually three different types of rows/columns in C, corresponding to the list elements, old and new points.

Definition 4 (Configuration Extension). *Consider a configuration matrix C. We consider C as being indexed by disjoint sets $I_{lists}, I_{old}, I_{new}$. Here, $|I_{lists}| = k$ corresponds to the input lists, $|I_{old}| = m_{old}$ corresponds to the "old" points, $|I_{new}| = m_{new}$ corresponds to the "new" points. We denote appropriate square submatrices by $C[I_{lists}]$ etc. By configuration extension, we mean an algorithm* ConfExt *that takes as input k exponentially large lists $L_i \subset \mathsf{S}^n$ for $i \in I_{lists}$, m_{old} "old" points $\boldsymbol{v}_j \in \mathsf{S}^n$, $j \in I_{old}$ and the matrix C. Assume that each input list separately satisfies the given configuration constraints wrt. the old points:* $\mathrm{Conf}\,(\boldsymbol{x}_i, (\boldsymbol{v}_j)_{j \in I_{old}}) \approx C[i, I_{old}]$ *for $i \in I_{lists}$, $\boldsymbol{x}_i \in L_i$.*

It outputs R instances, where each instance consists of m_{new} points $\boldsymbol{v}_\ell$, $\ell \in I_{new}$ and shrunk lists $L_i' \subset L_i$, where $\mathrm{Conf}\,((\boldsymbol{v}_j)_{j \in I_{old}}, (\boldsymbol{v}_\ell)_{\ell \in I_{new}}) \approx C[I_{old}, I_{new}]$ *and each $\boldsymbol{x}_i' \in L_i'$ satisfies*

$$\mathrm{Conf}\,(\boldsymbol{x}_i', (\boldsymbol{v}_j)_{j \in I_{old}}, (\boldsymbol{v}_\ell)_{\ell \in I_{old}}) \approx C[i, I_{old}, I_{new}].$$

The instances are output one-by-one in a streaming fashion. This is important, since the total size of the output usually exceeds the amount of available memory.

The naive way to implement configuration extension is as follows: independently for each instance, sample uniform $\boldsymbol{v}_\ell$'s conditioned on the given constraints and then make a single pass over each input list L_i to construct L_i'. This would require $\widetilde{\mathcal{O}}(\max_i |L_i| \cdot R)$ time. However, using the block coding/stripe techniques of [5,16], one can do much better. The central observation is that if we subdivide the coordinates into blocks, then a configuration constraint on all coordinates is (up to losing a subexponential fraction of solutions) equivalent to independent configuration constraints on each block. The basic idea is then to construct the v_ℓ's in a block-wise fashion such that an exponential number of instances have the same v_ℓ's on a block of coordinates. We can then amortize the construction of the L'_i's among such instances, since we can first construct some intermediate $L''_i \subset L_i$ that is compatible with the v_ℓ's on the shared block of coordinates. To actually construct $L'_i \subset L''_i$, we only need to pass over L''_i rather than L_i. Of course, this foregos independence of the v_ℓ's across different instances, but one can show that they are still independent enough to ensure that we will find most solutions if the number of instances is large enough.

Adapting these techniques of [5,16] to our framework is straightforward, but extremely technical. We work out the details in the full version of the paper.

A rough summary of the properties of our Configuration Extension Algorithm ConfExt (see the full version for a proof) is given by the following:

Theorem 5. *Use notation as in Definition 4. Assume that C, k, m_{old}, m_{new} do not depend on n. Then our algorithm* ConfExt, *given as input C, k, m_{old}, m_{new}, old points v_j and exponentially large lists $L_1, \ldots, L_k$ of points from S^n, outputs*

$$R = \widetilde{\mathcal{O}}\left(\frac{\det(C[I_{old}, I_{new}]) \cdot \det(C[I_{lists}, I_{old}])}{\det(C[I_{lists}, I_{old}, I_{new}]) \cdot \det(C[I_{old}])} \right)^{\frac{n}{2}} \quad (17)$$

instances, where each output instance consists of m_{new} points v_ℓ and sublists $L'_i \subset L_i$. In each such output instance, the new points $(v_\ell)_{\ell \in I_{new}}$ are chosen uniformly conditioned on the constraints (but not independent across instances). Consider solution k-tuples, i.e. $x_i \in L_i$ with $\mathrm{Conf}\,((x_i)_{i \in I_{lists}}) \approx C[I_{lists}]$. With overwhelming probability, for every solution k-tuple $(x_i)_{i \in I_{lists}}$, there exists at least one instance such that all $x_i \in L'_i$ for this instance, so we retain all solutions. Assume further that the elements from the input lists L_i, $i \in I_{lists}$ are iid uniformly distributed conditioned on the configuration $\mathrm{Conf}\,(x_i, (v_j)_{j \in I_{old}})$ for $x_i \in L_i$, which is assumed to be compatible with C. Then the expected size of the output lists per instance is given by

$$\mathbb{E}[|L'_i|] = |L_i| \cdot \widetilde{\mathcal{O}}\left(\left(\frac{\det(C[i, I_{old}, I_{new}]) \cdot \det(C[I_{old}])}{\det(C[I_{old}, I_{new}]) \cdot \det(C[i, I_{old}])} \right)^{n/2} \right).$$

Assume that all these expected output list sizes are exponentially increasing in n (rather than decreasing). Then the running time of the algorithm is given by $\widetilde{\mathcal{O}}(R \cdot \max_i \mathbb{E}[|L'_i|])$ (essentially the size of the output) and the memory complexity is given by $\widetilde{\mathcal{O}}(\max_i |L_i|)$ (essentially the size of the input).

7   Improved k-List Algorithm with Configuration Extension

Now we explain how to use the Configuration Extension Algorithm within the k-List Algorithm 1 to speed-up the search for configurations. In fact, there is a whole family of algorithms obtained by combining Filter from Algorithm 1 and the configuration extension algorithm ConfExt. The combined algorithm is given in Algorithm 2.

Recall that Algorithm 1 takes as inputs k lists $L_1, \ldots, L_k$ of equal size and processes the lists in several levels (cf. Fig. 2a). The lists $L_j^{(i)}$ for $j \geq i$ at the ith level (where the input lists correspond to the 0th level) are obtained by brute-forcing over $x_i \in L_i^{(i-1)}$ and running Filter on $L_j^{(i-1)}$ and x_i.

We can use ConfExt in the following way: before using Filter on $L_j^{(i-1)}$, we run ConfExt to create R instances with smaller sublists $L_j^{\prime(i-1)} \subset L_j^{(i-1)}$. We then apply Filter to each of these $L_j^{\prime(i-1)}$ rather than to $L_j^{(i-1)}$. The advantage is that for a given instance, the $L_j^{\prime(i-1)}$ are dependent (over the choice of j), so we expect a higher chance to find solutions.

In principle, one can use ConfExt on any level, i.e. we alternate between using ConfExt and Filter. Note that the x_i's that we brute-force over in order to apply Filter become "old" v_j's in the context of the following applications of ConfExt.

It turns out that among the variety of potential combinations of Filter and ConfExt, some are more promising than others. From the analysis of Algorithm 1, we know that the running time is dominated by the cost of filtering (appropriately multiplied by the number of times we need to filter) to create lists at some level $i_{\max}$. The value of $i_{\max}$ can be deduced from Eq. (14), where the individual contribution $|L| \cdot |L^{(i-1)}| \cdot \prod_{j=1}^{i-1} |L^{(j)}|$ in that formula exactly corresponds to the total cost of creating all lists at the i-th level.

It makes sense to use ConfExt to reduce the cost of filtering at this critical level. This means that we use ConfExt on the lists $L_j^{(i_{\max}-1)}$, $j \geq i_{\max} - 1$. Let us choose $m_{\text{new}} = 1$ new point v_ℓ. The lists $L_j^{(i_{\max}-1)}$ are already reduced by enforcing configuration constraints with $x_1 \in L_1, \ldots, x_{i_{\max}-1} \in L_{i_{\max}-1}$ from previous applications of Filter. This means that the $x_1, \ldots, x_{i_{\max}-1}$ take the role of "old" v_j's in ConfExt. The configuration $C^{ext} \in \mathbb{R}^{(k+1) \times (k+1)}$ for ConfExt is obtained as follows: The $C^{ext}[I_{\text{lists}}, I_{\text{old}}]$-part is given by the target configuration. The rest (which means the last row/column corresponding to the single "new" point) can be chosen freely and is subject to optimization. Note that the optimization problem does not depend on n.

This approach is taken in Algorithm 2. Note that for levels below $i_{\max}$, it does not matter whether we continue to use our Filter approach or just brute-force: if $i_{\max} = k$, there are no levels below. If $i_{\max} < k$, the lists are small from this level downward and brute-force becomes cheap enough not to affect the asymptotics.

Let us focus on the case where the input list sizes are the same as the output list sizes, which is the relevant case for applications to Shortest Vector sieving. It turns out (numerically) that in this case, the approach taken by Algorithm 2 is optimal for most values of k. The reason is as follows: Let T be the contribution to the running time of Algorithm 1 from level $i_{\max}$, which is asymptotically the same as the total running time. The second-largest contribution, denoted T' comes from level $i_{\max} - 1$. The improvement in running time from using ConfExt to reduce T decreases with k and is typically not enough to push it below T'.

Consequently, using ConfExt between other levels will not help. We also observed that choosing $m_{\mathrm{new}} = 1$ was usually optimal for k up to 10. Exceptions to these observations occur when T and T' are very close (this happens, e.g. for $k = 6$) or when k is small and the benefit from using ConfExt is large (i.e. $k = 3$).

Since the case $k = 3$ is particularly interesting for the Shortest Vector sieving (see Sect. 7.2), we present the 3-List algorithm separately in Sect. 7.1.

Algorithm 2. k-List with Configuration Extension

Input: $L_1, \ldots, L_k$ – input lists. $C \in \mathbb{R}^{k \times k}$ – target configuration. $\varepsilon > 0$ – measure of closeness.
Output: L_{out} – list of k-tuples $x_1 \in L_1, \ldots, x_k \in L_k$, s.t. $|\langle x_i, x_j \rangle - C_{ij}| \leq \varepsilon$, for all i, j.

1: $i_{\max}, C^{ext} = \mathrm{PREPROCESS}(k, C_{i,j} \in \mathbb{R}^{k \times k})$
2: $L_{\mathrm{out}} \leftarrow \{\}$
3: **for all** $x_1 \in L_1$ **do**
4: 　　 $L_j^{(1)} \leftarrow \mathrm{FILTER}(x_1, L_j, C_{1,j}, \varepsilon)$ 　　　　　　　　　　　　　 ▷ $j = 2, \ldots, k$

5: 　　　　 **for all** $x_{i_{\max}-1} \in L_{i_{\max}-1}^{(i_{\max}-2)}$ **do**
6: 　　　　　　 $L_j^{(i_{\max}-1)} \leftarrow \mathrm{FILTER}(x_{i_{\max}-1}, L_j^{i_{\max}-2}, C_{i_{\max}-1,j}, \varepsilon)$ 　 ▷ $j = i_{\max}, \ldots, k$
7: 　　　　　　 $I_{\mathrm{old}} \leftarrow \{1, \ldots, i_{\max} - 1\}$, $I_{\mathrm{lists}} \leftarrow \{i_{\max}, \ldots, k\}$, $I_{\mathrm{new}} \leftarrow \{k+1\}$.
8: 　　　　　　 $m_{\mathrm{old}} \leftarrow i_{\max} - 1$, $k' \leftarrow k + 1 - i_{\max}$, $m_{\mathrm{new}} \leftarrow 1$.
9: 　　　　　　 $v_j \leftarrow x_j$ for $j \in I_{\mathrm{old}}$.
10: 　　　　　　 Call ConfExt$(n, k', m_{\mathrm{old}}, m_{\mathrm{new}}, C^{ext}, L_{i_{\max}}^{(i_{\max}-1)}, \ldots, L_k^{(i_{\max}-1)}, (v_j)_{j \in I_{\mathrm{old}}}, \varepsilon)$
11: 　　　　　　 **for all** output instances $w, L_{i_{\max}}'^{(i_{\max}-1)}, \ldots, L_k'^{(i_{\max}-1)}$ **do** ▷ Output is streamed
12: 　　　　　　　　 **for all** $x_{i_{\max}} \in L_j'^{(i_{\max}-1)}$ **do**
13: 　　　　　　　　　　 $L_j^{(i_{\max})} \leftarrow \mathrm{FILTER}(x_{i_{\max}}, L_j'^{(i_{\max}-1)}, C_{i_{\max},j}, \varepsilon)$ 　　 ▷ $j = i_{\max} + 1 \ldots k$
14: 　　　　　　　　　　 Brute-force over $L_j^{(i_{\max})}$ to obtain $x_{i_{\max}+1}, \ldots, x_k$ compatible with C
15: 　　　　　　　　　　 $L_{\mathrm{out}} \leftarrow L_{\mathrm{out}} \cup \{(x_1, \ldots, x_k)\}$
16: **return** L_{out}

1: **procedure** PREPROCESS$(k, C \in \mathbb{R}^{k \times k})$
2: 　　 Determine $i_{\max}$ using Eq. (14)
3: 　　 Set $C^{ext}[\{1, \ldots, k\}] \leftarrow C$.
4: 　　 Determine optimal $C_{i,k+1}^{ext} = C_{k+1,i}^{ext}$ by numerical optimization.
5: 　　 **return** $i_{\max}, C^{ext} \in \mathbb{R}^{(k+1) \times (k+1)}$

1: **function** FILTER(x, L, c, ε): See Algorithm 1

7.1 Improved 3-List Algorithm

The case $k = 3$ stands out from the above discussion as one can achieve a faster algorithm running the Configuration Extension Algorithm on *two* points v_1, v_2. This case is also interesting in applications to lattice sieving, so we detail on it below.

From Eq. (14) we have $i_{\max} = 2$, or more precisely, the running time of the 3-List algorithm (without Configuration Extension) is $T = |L_1| \cdot |L_2^{(1)}| \cdot |L_3^{(1)}|$. So we start shrinking the lists right from the beginning which corresponds to $m_{\mathrm{old}} = 0$. For the balance configuration as the target, we have $C[I_{\mathrm{lists}}] = -1/3$ on the off-diagonals. With the help of an optimization solver, we obtain the optimal values for $\langle \boldsymbol{x}_i, \boldsymbol{v}_j \rangle$ for $i = \{1,2,3\}$ and $j = \{1,2\}$, and for $\langle \boldsymbol{v}_1, \boldsymbol{v}_2 \rangle$ (there are 7 values to optimize for), so the input to the Configuration Extension Algorithm is determined. The target configuration is of the form

$$C = \begin{pmatrix} 1 & -1/3 & -1/3 & 0.47 & -0.15 \\ -1/3 & 1 & -1/3 & -0.17 & 0.26 \\ -1/3 & -1/3 & 1 & -0.19 & -0.14 \\ 0.47 & -0.17 & -0.19 & 1 & -0.26 \\ -0.15 & 0.26 & -0.14 & -0.26 & 1 \end{pmatrix} \tag{18}$$

and the number of instances is given by $R = \widetilde{\mathcal{O}}(1.4038^n)$ according to (17). The algorithm runs in a streamed fashion: the lists L'_1, L'_2, L'_3 in line 2 of Algorithm 3 are obtained instance by instance and, hence, lines 3 to 9 are repeated R times.

Algorithm 3. 3-List with Configuration Extension

Input: L_1, L_2, L_3 – input lists of vectors from S^n, $|L| = 2^{0.1887n + o(n)}$
$\quad\quad C \in \mathbb{R}^{5 \times 5}$ as in Eq. (18), $\rho = 1.4038$, $\varepsilon > 0$
Output: $L_{\text{out}} \subset L_1 \times L_2 \times L_3$, s.t. $|\langle \boldsymbol{x}_i, \boldsymbol{x}_j \rangle - C_{ij}| \leq \varepsilon$, for all $1 \leq i, j \leq 3$.

1: $L_{\text{out}} \leftarrow \{\}$
2: $L'_1, L'_2, L'_3 \leftarrow \mathsf{ConfExt}(k = 3, m_{\text{old}} = 0, m_{\text{new}} = 2, C \in \mathbb{R}^{5 \times 5}, \varepsilon, L_1, L_2, L_3, (n_1, \dots, n_t))$
3: $\quad$ **for all** $\boldsymbol{x}_1 \in L'_1$ **do**
4: $\quad\quad L_2^{(1)} \leftarrow \text{FILTER}(\boldsymbol{x}_1, L'_2, -1/3, \varepsilon)$
5: $\quad\quad L_3^{(1)} \leftarrow \text{FILTER}(\boldsymbol{x}_1, L'_3, -1/3, \varepsilon)$
6: $\quad\quad$ **for all** $\boldsymbol{x}_2 \in L_2^{(1)}$ **do**
7: $\quad\quad\quad$ **for all** $\boldsymbol{x}_3 \in L_3^{(1)}$ **do**
8: $\quad\quad\quad\quad$ **if** $|\langle \boldsymbol{x}_2, \boldsymbol{x}_3 \rangle + 1/3| \leq \varepsilon$ **then**
9: $\quad\quad\quad\quad\quad L_{\text{out}} \leftarrow (\boldsymbol{x}_1, \boldsymbol{x}_2, \boldsymbol{x}_3)$
10: **return** L_{out}
1: **function** $\text{FILTER}(\boldsymbol{x}, L, c, \varepsilon)$: See Algorithm 1

From Theorem 3, it follows that if the input lists satisfy $|L| = 2^{0.1887n + o(n)}$, then we expect $|L_{\text{out}}| = |L|$. Also from Eq. (8), it follows that the 3-List Algorithm 1 (i.e. without combining with the Configuration Extension Algorithm) has running time of $2^{0.3962n + o(n)}$. The above Algorithm 3 brings it down to $2^{0.3717n + o(n)}$.

7.2 Application to the Shortest Vector Problem

In this section we briefly discuss how certain shortest vector algorithms can benefit from our improvement for the approximate k-List problem. We start by stating the approximate shortest vector problem.

On input, we are given a full-rank lattice $\mathcal{L}(B)$ described by a matrix $B \in \mathbb{R}^{n \times n}$ (with polynomially-sized entries) whose columns correspond to basis vectors, and some constant $c \geq 1$. The task is to output a nonzero lattice vector $x \in \mathcal{L}(B)$, s.t. $\|x\| \leq c\lambda_1(B)$ where $\lambda_1(B)$ denotes the length of the shortest nonzero vector in $\mathcal{L}(B)$. x is a solution to the approximate shortest vector problem.

The AKS sieving algorithm (introduced by Ajtai, Kumar, and Sivakumar in [1]) is currently the best (heuristic) algorithm for the approximate shortest vector problem: for an n-dimensional lattice, the running time and memory are of order 2^n. Sieving algorithms have two flavours: the Nguyen-Vidick sieve [18] and the Gauss sieve [17]. Both make polynomial in n number of calls to the approximate 2-List solver. Without LSH-techniques, the running time both the Nguyen-Vidick and the Gauss sieve is the running time of the approximate 2-List algorithm: $2^{0.415n+o(n)}$ with $2^{0.208n+o(n)}$ memory. Using our 3-List Algorithm 1 instead, the running time can be reduced to $2^{0.3962n+o(n)}$ (with only $2^{0.1887n+o(n)}$ memory) introducing essentially no polynomial overhead. Using Algorithm 3, we achieve even better asymptotics: $2^{0.3717n+o(n)}$, but it might be too involved for practical speed-ups due very large polynomial overhead for too little exponential gain in realistic dimensions.

Now we describe the Nguyen-Vidick sieve that uses a k-List solver as a main subroutine (see [4] for a more formal description). We start by sampling lattice-vectors $x \in \mathcal{L}(B) \cap B_n(2^{O(n)} \cdot \lambda_1(B))$, where $B_n(R)$ denotes an n-dimensional ball of radius R. This can be done using, for example, Klein's nearest plane procedure [11]. In the k-List Nguyen-Vidick for $k > 2$, we sample many such lattice-vectors, put them in a list L, and search for k-tuples $x_1, \ldots, x_k \in L \times \ldots \times L$ s.t. $\|x_1 + \ldots + x_k\| \leq \gamma \cdot \max_{1 \leq i \leq k} x_i$ for some $\gamma < 1$. The sum $x_1 + \ldots + x_k$ is put into L_{out}. The size of L is chosen in a way to guarantee that $|L| \approx |L_{\text{out}}|$. The search for short k-tuples is repeated over the list L_{out}. Note that since with each new iteration we obtain vectors that are shorter by a constant factor γ, starting with $2^{O(n)}$ approximation to the shortest vector (this property is guaranteed by Klein's sampling algorithm applied to an LLL-reduced basis), we need only linear in n iterations to find the desired $x \in \mathcal{L}(B)$.

Naturally, we would like to apply our approximate k-List algorithm to k copies of the list L to implement the search for short sums. Indeed, we can do so by making a commonly used assumption: we assume the lattice-vectors we put into the lists lie uniformly on a spherical shell (on a very thin shell, essentially a sphere). The heuristic here is that it does not affect the behaviour of the algorithm. Intuitively, the discreteness of a lattice should not be "visible" to the algorithm (at least not until we find the approximate shortest vector).

We conclude by noting that our improved k-List Algorithm can as well be used within the Gauss sieve, which is known to perform faster in practice than the Nguyen-Vidick sieve. An iteration of the original 2-Gauss sieve as described in [17], searches for pairs (p, v), s.t. $\|p + v\| < \max\{\|p\|, \|v\|\}$, where $p \in \mathcal{L}(B)$ is *fixed*, $v \in L \subset \mathcal{L}(B)$, and $p \neq v$. Once such a pair is found and $\|p\| > \|v\|$, we set $p' \leftarrow p + v$ and proceed with the search over (p', v), otherwise if $\|p\| < \|v\|$, we delete $v \in L$ and store the sum $p + v$ as p-input point for the next iteration. Once no pair is found, we add p' to L. On the next iteration, the search is repeated with another p which is obtained either by reducing some deleted $v \in L$ before, or by sampling from $\mathcal{L}(B)$. The idea is to keep only those vectors in L that *cannot* form a pair with a shorter sum. Bai, Laarhoven, and Stehlé in [4], generalize it to k-Gauss sieve by keeping only those vectors in L that do not form a shorter k-sum. In the language of configuration search, we look for configurations $(p, v_1, \ldots, v_{k-1}) \in \{p\} \times L \times \ldots \times L$ where the first point is fixed, so we apply our Algorithm 1 on $k - 1$ (identical) lists.

Unfortunately, applying LSH/configuration extension-techniques for the Gauss Sieve is much more involved than for the Nguyen-Vidick Sieve. For $k = 2$, [13] applies LSH techniques, but this requires an exponential increase in memory (which runs counter to our goal). We do not know whether these techniques extend to our setting. At any rate, since the gain from LSH/Configuration Extension techniques decreases with k (with the biggest jump from $k = 2$ to $k = 3$), while the overhead increases, gaining a practical speed-up from LSH/Configuration Extension within the Gauss sieve for $k \geq 3$ seems unrealistic.

Open Questions. We present all our algorithms for a *fixed* k, and in the analysis, we suppress all the prefactors (in running time and list-sizes) for fixed k in the $\mathcal{O}_k(.)$ notation. Taking a closer look at how these factors depend on k, we notice (see, for example, the expression for $W_{n,k}$ in Theorem 1) that exponents of the polynomial prefactors depend on k. It prevents us from discussing the case $k \to \infty$, which is an interesting question especially in light of SVP. Another similar question is the optimal choice of ε and how it affects the pre-factors.

8 Experimental Results

We implement the 3-Gauss sieve algorithm in collaboration with S. Bai [3]. The implementation is based on the program developed by Bai, Laarhoven, and Stehlé in [4], making the approaches comparable.

Lattice bases are generated by the SVP challenge generator [7]. It produces a lattice generated by the columns of the matrix

$$
B = \begin{pmatrix} p & x_1 & \ldots & x_{n-1} \\ 0 & 1 & \ldots & 0 \\ \vdots & \vdots & \ddots & \vdots \\ 0 & 0 & \ldots & 1 \end{pmatrix},
$$

where p is a large prime, and $x_i < p$ for all i. Lattices of this type are random in the sense of Goldstein and Mayer [9].

For all the dimensions except 80, the bases are preprocessed with BKZ reduction of block-size 20. For $n = 80$, the block-size is 30. For our input lattices, we do not know their minimum λ_1. The algorithm terminates when it finds many linearly dependent triples (v_1, v_2, v_3). We set a counter for such an event and terminate the algorithm once this counter goes over a pre-defined threshold.

Table 1. Experimental results for k-tuple Gauss sieve. The running times T are given in seconds, $|L|$ is the maximal size of the list L. ε is the approximation parameter for the subroutine Filter of Algorithm 1. The best running-time per dimension is type-set bold.

n	2-sieve	BLS 3-sieve	Algorithm 1 for $k = 3$			
			$\varepsilon = 0.0$	$\varepsilon = 0.015$	$\varepsilon = 0.3$	$\varepsilon = 0.4$
	$T, |L|$	$T, |L|$	$T, |L|$	$T, |L|$	$T, |L|$	$T, |L|$
60	1.38e3, 13257	1.02e4, 4936	1.32e3, 7763	1.26e3, 7386	1.26e3, 6751	**1.08e3, 6296**
62	2.88e3, 19193	1.62e4, 6239	2.8e3, 10356	3.1e3, 9386	**1.8e3, 8583**	2.2e3, 8436
64	8.64e3, 24178	5.5e4, 8369	5.7e3, 13573	3.6e3, 12369	**3.36e3, 11142**	4.0e4, 10934
66	1.75e4, 31707	9.66e4, 10853	1.5e4, 17810	1.38e4, 16039	**9.1e3, 14822**	1.2e4, 14428
68	3.95e4, 43160	2.3e5, 14270	2.34e4, 24135	2.0e4, 21327	**1.68e4, 19640**	1.86e4, 18355
70	6.4e4, 58083	6.2e5, 19484	6.21e4, 32168	3.48e5, 26954	**3.3e4, 25307**	3.42e4, 24420
72	2.67e5, 77984	1.2e6, 25034	7.6e4, 40671	7.2e4, 37091	**6.16e4, 34063**	6.35e4, 34032
74	3.45e5, 106654	–	2.28e5, 54198	2.08e5, 47951	**2.02e5, 43661**	2.03e5, 40882
76	4.67e5, 142397	–	3.58e5, 71431	2.92e5, 64620	**2.42e5, 56587**	2.53e5, 54848
78	9.3e5, 188905	–	–	–	**4.6e5, 74610**	4.8e5, 70494
80	–	–	–	–	**9.47e5, 98169**	9.9e5, 98094

The intuition behind this idea is straightforward: at some point the list L will contain very short basis-vectors and the remaining list-vectors will be their linear combinations. Trying to reduced the latter will ultimately produce the zero-vector. The same termination condition was already used in [15], where the authors experimentally determine a threshold of such "zero-sum" triples.

Up to $n = 64$, the experiments are repeated 5 times (i.e. on 5 random lattices), for the dimensions less than 80, 3 times. For the running times and the list-sizes presented in the table below, the average is taken. For $n = 80$, the experiment was performed once.

Our tests confirm a noticeable speed-up of the 3-Gauss sieve when our Configuration Search Algorithm 1 is used. Moreover, as the analysis suggests (see Fig. 3), our algorithm outperforms the naive 2-Gauss sieve while using much less memory. The results can be found in Table 1.

Another interesting aspect of the algorithm is the list-sizes when compared with BLS. Despite the fact that, asymptotically, the size of the list $|L|$ is the same for our and for the BLS algorithms, in practice our algorithm requires a longer list (cf. the right numbers in each column). This is due to the fact that we filter out a larger fraction of solutions. Also notice that increasing ε – the approximation to the target configuration, we achieve an additional speed-up. This becomes obvious once we look at the Filter procedure: allowing for a smaller inner-product throws away less vectors, which in turn results in a shorter list L. For the range of dimensions we consider, we experimentally found $\varepsilon = 0.3$ to be a good choice.

Acknowledgments. We would like to thank the authors of [4], Shi Bai, Damien Stehlé, and Thijs Laarhoven for constructive discussions.

Elena Kirshanova was supported by UbiCrypt, the research training group 1817/1 funded by the DFG. Gottfried Herold was funded by ERC grant 307952 (acronym FSC).

References

1. Ajtai, M., Kumar, R., Sivakumar, D.: A sieve algorithm for the shortest lattice vector problem. In: Proceedings of STOC, pp. 601–610 (2001)
2. Akritas, A.G., Akritas, E.K., Malaschonok, G.I.: Symbolic computation, new trends and developments various proofs of Sylvester's (determinant) identity. Math. Comput. Simul. **42**(4), 585–593 (1996)
3. Bai, S.: Personal Communication, August 2016
4. Bai, S., Laarhoven, T., Stehlé, D.: Tuple lattice sieving. LMS J. Comput. Math. **19A**, 146–162 (2016). doi:10.1112/S1461157016000292. Algorithmic Number Theory Symposium (ANTS) XII
5. Becker, A., Ducas, L., Gama, N., Laarhoven, T.: New directions in nearest neighbor searching with applications to lattice sieving. In: Krauthgamer, R. (eds.) Proceedings of the Twenty-Seventh Annual ACM-SIAM Symposium on Discrete Algorithms, SODA 2016, Arlington, VA, USA, pp. 10–24. SIAM, 10–12 January 2016
6. Blum, A., Kalai, A., Wasserman, H.: Noise-tolerant learning, the parity problem, and the statistical query model. J. ACM **50**, 506–519 (2003)
7. SVP Challenge: SVP challenge generator. http://latticechallenge.org/svp-challenge
8. Ghosh, M., Sinha, B.K.: A simple derivation of the Wishart distribution. Am. Stat. **56**(2), 100–101 (2002)
9. Goldstein, D., Mayer, A.: On the equidistribution of Hecke points. Forum Mathematicum **15**(3), 165–189 (2006)
10. Kannan, R.: Improved algorithms for integer programming and related lattice problems. In: Proceedings of STOC, pp. 193–206 (1983)
11. Klein, P.: Finding the closest lattice vector when it's unusually close. In: Proceedings of the Eleventh Annual ACM-SIAM Symposium on Discrete Algorithms, SODA 2000, pp. 937–941 (2000)
12. Kupferman, O., Lustig, Y., Vardi, M.Y.: On locally checkable properties. In: Hermann, M., Voronkov, A. (eds.) LPAR 2006. LNCS (LNAI), vol. 4246, pp. 302–316. Springer, Heidelberg (2006). doi:10.1007/11916277_21
13. Laarhoven, T.: Sieving for shortest vectors in lattices using angular locality-sensitive hashing. In: Gennaro, R., Robshaw, M. (eds.) CRYPTO 2015. LNCS, vol. 9215, pp. 3–22. Springer, Heidelberg (2015)
14. Lyubashevsky, V.: The parity problem in the presence of noise, decoding random linear codes, and the subset sum problem. In: Chekuri, C., Jansen, K., Rolim, J.D.P., Trevisan, L. (eds.) APPROX/RANDOM -2005. LNCS, vol. 3624, pp. 378–389. Springer, Heidelberg (2005). doi:10.1007/11538462_32
15. Mariano, A., Laarhoven, T., Bischof, C.: Parallel (probable) lock-free hash sieve: a practical sieving algorithm for the SVP. In: 44th International Conference on Parallel Processing (ICPP), pp. 590–599, September 2015
16. May, A., Ozerov, I.: On computing nearest neighbors with applications to decoding of binary linear codes. In: Oswald, E., Fischlin, M. (eds.) EUROCRYPT 2015. LNCS, vol. 9056, pp. 203–228. Springer, Heidelberg (2015). doi:10.1007/978-3-662-46800-5_9

17. Micciancio, D., Voulgaris, P.: Faster exponential time algorithms for the shortest vector problem. In: Proceedings of the Twenty-First Annual ACM-SIAM Symposium on Discrete Algorithms, SODA 2010, pp. 1468–1480 (2010)
18. Nguyen, P.Q., Vidick, T.: Sieve algorithms for the shortest vector problem are practical. J. Math. Crypt. **2**, 181–207 (2008)
19. Wagner, D.: A generalized birthday problem. In: Yung, M. (ed.) CRYPTO 2002. LNCS, vol. 2442, pp. 288–304. Springer, Heidelberg (2002). doi:10.1007/3-540-45708-9_19
20. Wishart, J.: The generalized product moment distribution in samples from a normal multivariate population. Biometrika **20A**(1–2), 32–52 (1928)

Zeroizing Attacks on Indistinguishability Obfuscation over CLT13

Jean-Sébastien Coron[1], Moon Sung Lee[1], Tancrède Lepoint[2($\boxtimes$)],
and Mehdi Tibouchi[3]

[1] University of Luxembourg, Luxembourg City, Luxembourg
[2] SRI International, New York City, NY, USA
tancrede.lepoint@sri.com
[3] NTT Secure Platform Laboratories, Tokyo, Japan

Abstract. In this work, we describe a new polynomial-time attack on
the multilinear maps of Coron, Lepoint, and Tibouchi (CLT13), when
used in candidate indistinguishability obfuscation (iO) schemes. More
specifically, we show that given the obfuscation of the simple branching
program that computes the always zero functionality previously considered by Miles, Sahai and Zhandry (Crypto 2016), one can recover the
secret parameters of CLT13 in polynomial time via an extension of the
zeroizing attack of Coron et al. (Crypto 2015). Our attack is generaliz-
able to arbitrary *oblivious* branching programs for arbitrary functionality, and allows (1) to recover the secret parameters of CLT13, and then
(2) to recover the randomized branching program entirely. Our analysis
thus shows that almost all single-input variants of iO over CLT13 are
insecure.

1 Introduction

Since their introduction, all candidates for multilinear maps [GGH13a, CLT13,
GGH15] have been shown to suffer from zeroizing attacks [GGH13a, CHL+15,
GGH15], sometimes even when no low-level encoding of zero was made available
to the adversary [CGH+15]. However, the leading application of multilinear
maps, indistinguishability obfuscation, has until now remained little affected by
this kind of attacks. This resistance seemed to come from the fact that the particular combinations enforced in indistinguishability obfuscation constructions
did not allow enough freedom to obtain a simple system of successful zero-tests
that could be solved using linear algebraic techniques; see the discussion on the
limitations of zeroizing attacks in [CGH+15, Sect. 1.2].

Attacks Against iO (Related Work). Attacks against simplified variants
of certain obfuscation schemes instantiated over the Coron-Lepoint-Tibouchi
(CLT13) multilinear maps [CLT13] have been described in [CGH+15]. Firstly,
the GGHRSW branching-program (BP) obfuscation procedure from [GGH+13b]
has been shown to be broken for branching programs with a special "decomposable" structure where the inputs bits can be partitioned in three sets, and so

© International Association for Cryptologic Research 2017
S. Fehr (Ed.): PKC 2017, Part I, LNCS 10174, pp. 41–58, 2017.
DOI: 10.1007/978-3-662-54365-8_3

that one set only affects the first steps of the BP, a second set the middle steps of the BP, and the last set the final steps of the BP. Secondly, the simple variants of the circuit obfuscation procedures from [Zim15, AB15] has been shown to be broken for simple circuits, such as point functions.

Recently in [MSZ16], Miles, Sahai and Zhandry introduced annihilation attacks against multilinear maps, and applied them to cryptanalyze in polynomial-time several candidate iO schemes [BGK+14, MSW14, AGIS14, PST14, BMSZ16] over the Garg-Gentry-Halevi (GGH13) multilinear maps [GGH13a]. The core idea of the attack against to differentiate whether an obfuscated program $\mathcal{O}$ comes from a branching program $\mathbf{A}$ or a branching program $\mathbf{A}'$ is the following: evaluate specific inputs x_i's that evaluate to 0 on $\mathbf{A}$ and $\mathbf{A}'$, get the zero-tested values $y_i = O(x_i)$, and then evaluate an annihilating polynomial $Q_{\mathbf{A}}$ constructed from $\mathbf{A}$ over the y_i's. When $\mathbf{A}$ was obfuscated, $Q_{\mathbf{A}}(y)$ belongs to an ideal $\mathcal{I}$ independent of y and $\mathbf{A}$; otherwise $Q_{\mathbf{A}}(y) \notin \mathcal{I}$ with high probability. Annihilation polynomials can also be used to attack the order revealing encryption scheme proposed in [BLR+15]. Concurrently to our work, Chen, Gentry and Halevi [CGH16] used annihilation polynomials to attack the initial GGHRSW candidate iO scheme [GGH+13b] and Apon et al. [ADGM16] introduced the notion of *partially inequivalent* branching programs, shown to be sufficient for annihilation attacks.

Our Contributions. In the remaining of the document, we cryptanalyze several constructions of indistinguishability obfuscation [GGH+13b, MSW14, AGIS14, PST14, BGK+14, BMSZ16] when instantiated over CLT13. More specifically, we show the following theorem.

Theorem 1. *Let $\mathcal{O}$ denote the single-input variant of the iO candidates in* [GGH+13b, MSW14, AGIS14, PST14, BGK+14, BMSZ16] *(over CLT13 multilinear maps). There exists a branching program $\mathbf{A}$ such that, given $\mathcal{O}(\mathbf{A})$, one can break the CLT13 multilinear maps in polynomial-time.*

To show this, we use the branching program $\mathbf{A}$ that computes the always-zero function previously considered in [MSZ16], in which every matrix is simply the identity matrix. This branching program does not fit in the framework of the zeroizing attacks proposed in [CGH+15], but we show that one can reconstruct the three-ways structure required by the zeroizing attacks by using tensor products. More precisely, consider a branching program evaluation on input x

$$A(x) = \widehat{\mathbf{A}}_0 \times \prod_{i=1}^{2t} \widehat{\mathbf{A}}_{i,x_{\mathsf{inp}(i)}} \times \widehat{\mathbf{A}}_{2t+1} \times p_{zt} \bmod x_0,$$

where $\mathsf{inp}(i) = \min(i, 2t + 1 - i)$ denotes the input bit used at the i-th step of the computation and $\widehat{\mathbf{A}} = \{\widehat{\mathbf{A}}_0, \widehat{\mathbf{A}}_{2t+1}, \widehat{\mathbf{A}}_{i,b} \mid i \in [2t], b \in \{0,1\}\}$ is the obfuscated branching program. We show that $A(x)$ can be rewritten as a product of consecutive factors

$$A(x) = \mathbf{B}(x) \times \mathbf{C}(x) \times \mathbf{D}(x) \times \mathbf{C}'(x) \times \mathbf{B}'(x) \times p_{zt} \bmod x_0$$
$$= \left(\mathbf{B}'(x)^T \otimes \mathbf{B}(x)\right) \times \left(\mathbf{C}'(x)^T \otimes \mathbf{C}(x)\right) \times \mathrm{vec}\left(\mathbf{D}(x)\right) \times p_{zt} \bmod x_0,$$

where the factors $\boldsymbol{B}'(x)^T \otimes \boldsymbol{B}(x), \boldsymbol{C}'(x)^T \otimes \boldsymbol{C}(x)$ and $\boldsymbol{D}(x)$ that can be made to vary independently, and $\mathsf{vec}(\boldsymbol{D})$ denotes the vector formed by stacking the columns of the matrix $\boldsymbol{D}$ on top of each other. We then show how to extend the zeroizing attack approach described in [CHL+15, CGH+15] to construct a block diagonal matrix, and apply the Cayley-Hamilton theorem to recover all the secrets embedded in the CLT13 public parameters. Once the multilinear map secret parameters have been recovered, one can then *recover the randomized branching program* $\widetilde{\boldsymbol{A}}$ completely. Thus, one can distinguish between the obfuscation of two branching programs whenever they are inequivalent under Kilian's randomization.

Our attack is applicable to the single-input version of the candidate obfuscators from [MSW14, AGIS14, PST14, BGK+14, BMSZ16], to the GGHRSW obfuscator [GGH+13b] (as opposed to annihilations attacks).

Last, but not least, we then show how to *generalize* our attack to branching programs with an essentially arbitrary structure, including oblivious branching programs, and to programs achieving essentially arbitrary functionalities. This shows that the previously mentioned single-input obfuscators should be considered broken when instantiated with CLT13.

2   Preliminaries

Notation. We use $[a]_n$ or $a \bmod n$ to denote a unique integer $x \in (-\frac{n}{2}, \frac{n}{2}]$ which is congruent to a modulo n. A set $\{1, 2, \ldots, n\}$ is denoted by $[n]$. Vectors and matrices will be denoted by bold letters. The transpose of a matrix $\boldsymbol{A}$ is denoted by $\boldsymbol{A}^T$.

2.1   Kronecker Product of Matrices

For any two matrices $\boldsymbol{A} \in R^{m \times n}$ and $\boldsymbol{B} \in R^{p \times q}$, we define the *Kronecker product* (or tensor product) of $\boldsymbol{A}$ and $\boldsymbol{B}$ as the block matrix $\boldsymbol{A} \otimes \boldsymbol{B} \in R^{(mp) \times (nq)}$ given by:

$$\boldsymbol{A} \otimes \boldsymbol{B} = \begin{bmatrix} a_{11}\boldsymbol{B} & \cdots & a_{1n}\boldsymbol{B} \\ \vdots & \ddots & \vdots \\ a_{m1}\boldsymbol{B} & \cdots & a_{mn}\boldsymbol{B} \end{bmatrix}, \quad \text{where } \boldsymbol{A} = (a_{ij}).$$

We will be using the following important property of the Kronecker product. Consider a matrix $\boldsymbol{C} \in R^{n \times m}$ and let $\boldsymbol{c}_i \in R^n$, $i = 1, \ldots, m$ be its column vectors, so that $\boldsymbol{C} = [\boldsymbol{c}_1, \ldots, \boldsymbol{c}_m]$. We denote by $\mathsf{vec}(\boldsymbol{C})$ the column vector of dimension mn formed by stacking the columns $\boldsymbol{c}_i$ of $\boldsymbol{C}$ on top of one another:

$$\mathsf{vec}(\boldsymbol{C}) = \begin{bmatrix} \boldsymbol{c}_1 \\ \vdots \\ \boldsymbol{c}_m \end{bmatrix} \in R^{mn}.$$

Now for any three matrices A, B, and C for which the matrix product $A \cdot B \cdot C$ is defined, the following property holds [Lau04, Chap. 13]:

$$\mathsf{vec}(A \cdot B \cdot C) = (C^T \otimes A) \cdot \mathsf{vec}(B)$$

(this follows from the fact that $\mathsf{vec}(xy^T) = y \otimes x$ for any two column vectors x and y). Note that for any column vector c, $\mathsf{vec}(c) = c$. This property has concurrently and independently been used in the variant of annihilation attacks introduced by Apon et al. [ADGM16].

2.2 CLT13 Multilinear Map

We briefly recall the asymmetric CLT13 scheme; we refer to [CLT13] for a full description. The CLT13 scheme relies on the Chinese Remainder Theorem (CRT) representation. For large secret primes p_k's, let $x_0 = \prod_{k=1}^{n} p_k$. We denote by $\mathsf{CRT}(a_1, a_2, \ldots, a_n)$ or $\mathsf{CRT}(a_k)_k$ the number $a \in \mathbb{Z}_{x_0}$ such that $a \equiv a_k \pmod{p_k}$ for all $k \in [n]$. The plaintext space of CLT13 scheme is $\mathbb{Z}_{g_1} \times \mathbb{Z}_{g_2} \times \cdots \times \mathbb{Z}_{g_n}$ for small secret integers g_k's. An encoding of a vector $\mathbf{a} = (a_1, \ldots, a_n)$ at level set $S = \{i_0\}$ is an integer $\alpha \in \mathbb{Z}_{x_0}$ such that $\alpha = [\mathsf{CRT}(a_1 + g_1 r_1, \ldots, a_n + g_n r_n)/z_{i_0}]_{x_0}$ for small r_k's, and where z_{i_0} is a secret mask in $\mathbb{Z}_{x_0}$ uniformly chosen during the parameters generation procedure of the multilinear map. To support a κ-level multilinearity, κ distinct z_i's are used. We do not consider the straddling set system [BGK+14] since it is not relevant to our attacks.

Additions between encodings in the same level set can be done by modular additions in $\mathbb{Z}_{x_0}$. Multiplication between encodings can be done by modular multiplication in $\mathbb{Z}_{x_0}$, only when those encodings are in disjoint level sets, and the resulting encoding level set is the union of the input level sets. At the top level set $[\kappa]$, an encoding of zero can be tested by multiplying it by the zero-test parameter $p_{zt} = [\prod_{i=1}^{\kappa} z_i \cdot \mathsf{CRT}(p_k^* h_k g_k^{-1})_k]_{x_0}$ in $\mathbb{Z}_{x_0}$ where $p_k^* = x_0/p_k$, and comparing the result to x_0. If the result is small, then the encoding encodes a zero vector.[1]

2.3 Indistinguishability Obfuscation

We borrow the definition of indistinguishability obfuscation from [GGH+13b], where iO for circuits are defined.

Definition 1 (Indistinguishability Obfuscator (iO)). *A uniform PPT machine iO is called an indistinguishability obfuscator for a circuit class $\{C_\lambda\}$ if the following conditions are satisfied:*

– *For all security parameters $\lambda \in \mathbb{N}$, for all $C \in C_\lambda$, for all inputs x, we have that*

$$Pr[C'(x) = C(x) \; : \; C' \leftarrow iO(\lambda, C)] = 1.$$

---

[1] In this paper, for simplicity of notation, we only consider a single zero-testing element instead of a vector thereof [CLT13].

- *For any (not necessarily uniform) PPT distinguisher D, there exists a negligible function α such that the following holds: For all security parameters $\lambda \in \mathbb{N}$, for all pairs of circuits $C_0, C_1 \in \mathcal{C}_\lambda$, we have that if $C_0(x) = C_1(x)$ for all inputs x, then*

$$|Pr[D(iO(\lambda, C_0)) = 1] - Pr[D(iO(\lambda, C_1)) = 1]| \leq \alpha(\lambda).$$

Circuits can be directly obfuscated using circuit obfuscators [Zim15, AB15, DGG+16]. However, most of the iO candidate obfuscators (see [GGH+13b, MSW14, AGIS14, PST14, BMSZ16, GMM+16]) first convert the circuits to matrix branching programs, randomize them, and then obfuscated them using a candidate multilinear maps scheme such as [GGH13a, CLT13, GGH15].

Obviously, for the converted branching program $\boldsymbol{B}$, the iO obfuscator $\mathcal{O}$ should preserve the functionality: $\boldsymbol{B}(x) = \mathcal{O}(\boldsymbol{B})(x)$ for all x. Moreover, for two functionally-equivalent branching programs $\boldsymbol{B}$ and $\boldsymbol{B}'$, $\mathcal{O}(\mathbf{B})$ and $\mathcal{O}(\mathbf{B}')$ should be computationally indistinguishable, unless they have different length or types of matrices. The concrete instance of such branching programs and their obfuscations are described in Sects. 3.1 and 3.2, respectively.

Note that, while the candidate multilinear maps [GGH13a, CLT13, GGH15] have recently been found to fail to securely realize multi-party key exchanges (see [HJ16, CHL+15, CLLT16a]), few weaknesses were found in the iO candidates over CLT13 (and GGH15 [GGH15]), mainly due to the absence of the low-level encodings of zeroes in the public domain. In [CGH+15], Coron et al. described an attack against the circuit obfuscators for simple circuits, and the GGHRSW obfuscator for branching programs with a special decomposable structure (but not on oblivious branching programs). Annihilations attacks [MSZ16] were recently introduced and allowed to break many iO candidates over GGH13; however, they do not carry to obfuscators over CLT13 as far as we know.

3   Zeroizing Attack on Indistinguishability Obfuscation of Simple Branching Programs

For simplicity, we describe our attack on the simple single input branching program introduced in [MSZ16]. We will show how to generalize our attack to oblivious branching programs with arbitrary functionalities in Sect. 4.

3.1   Target Branching Program

We consider the following branching program $\mathbf{A}$ that evaluates to zero for all t-bit inputs. Let us first define the function which describes what input bit is examined at the i-th step:

$$\mathsf{inp}(i) = \min(i, 2t + 1 - i) \text{ for } i \in [2t].$$

Now, the branching program is defined as follows:

$$\mathbf{A} = \{\mathsf{inp}, \boldsymbol{A}_0, \boldsymbol{A}_{2t+1}, \boldsymbol{A}_{i,b} \mid i \in [2t], b \in \{0, 1\}\},$$

where

$$\boldsymbol{A}_0 = [0\ 1],\ \boldsymbol{A}_{2t+1} = [1\ 0]^T,\ \boldsymbol{A}_{i,0} = \boldsymbol{A}_{i,1} = \begin{bmatrix} 1 & 0 \\ 0 & 1 \end{bmatrix}\ \text{for } i \in [2t].$$

It is evaluated in the usual way on $x \in \{0,1\}^t$:

$$\mathbf{A}(x) := \boldsymbol{A}_0 \times \prod_{i=1}^{2t} \boldsymbol{A}_{i,x_{\mathsf{inp}(i)}} \times \boldsymbol{A}_{2t+1}.$$

3.2   Obfuscation of Branching Programs

To obfuscate a branching program, we follow the standard recipe of indistinguishability obfuscation constructions: use Kilian style randomization with extra scalar multiplications by random numbers, and encode the resulting matrices with the candidate multilinear maps.

Let us describe the obfuscation procedure of the branching program $\mathbf{A}$ from Sect. 3.1, over the CLT13 multilinear map. Let $\prod_{k=1}^{n} \mathbb{Z}_{g_k}$ be the plaintext space of the CLT13 map, and denote $g = \prod_{k=1}^{n} g_k$. We first choose random invertible matrices $\{\boldsymbol{R}_i \in \mathbb{Z}_g^{2 \times 2}\}_{i \in [2t+1]}$ and non-zero scalars $\{\alpha_{i,b} \in \mathbb{Z}_g\}_{i \in [2t], b \in \{0,1\}}$. Then the matrices in the branching program $\mathbf{A}$ are randomized using Kilian randomization, and we define $\widetilde{\mathbf{A}}$ the randomized branching program:

$$\widetilde{\mathbf{A}} = \{\mathsf{inp}, \widetilde{\boldsymbol{A}}_0, \widetilde{\boldsymbol{A}}_{2t+1}, \widetilde{\boldsymbol{A}}_{i,b} \mid i \in [2t], b \in \{0,1\}\}$$

where

$$\widetilde{\boldsymbol{A}}_0 = \boldsymbol{A}_0 \cdot \boldsymbol{R}_1^{-1},\ \widetilde{\boldsymbol{A}}_{2t+1} = \boldsymbol{R}_{2t+1} \cdot \boldsymbol{A}_{2t+1},\ \widetilde{\boldsymbol{A}}_{i,b} = \alpha_{i,b} \cdot \boldsymbol{R}_i \cdot \boldsymbol{A}_{i,b} \cdot \boldsymbol{R}_{i+1}^{-1},$$

for $i \in [2t]$, $b \in \{0,1\}$.

Next, the randomized branching program $\widetilde{\mathbf{A}}$ is encoded using the CLT13 scheme. In order to evaluate the randomized branching program, our multilinear map must accommodate $\kappa = 2t + 2$ products, i.e. the multilinearity level is set to $[\kappa]$. Each element $\tilde{a} \in \mathbb{Z}_g$ of the matrices $\widetilde{\boldsymbol{A}}_{i,b}$'s is considered as a vector $([\tilde{a}]_{g_1}, \dots, [\tilde{a}]_{g_n}) \in \mathbb{Z}_{g_1} \times \cdots \times \mathbb{Z}_{g_n}$, and encoded as an integer $\hat{a} \in \mathbb{Z}_{x_0}$ at level $S = \{i\}$. In particular, we have that $\hat{a} = [\mathsf{CRT}([\tilde{a}]_{g_1} + g_1 r_1, \dots, [\tilde{a}]_{g_n} + g_n r_n)/z_i]_{x_0}$ for small random integers r_k's. The matrices $\widetilde{\boldsymbol{A}}_0$ and $\widetilde{\boldsymbol{A}}_{2t+1}$ are encoded analogously.

The resulting obfuscated branching program is

$$\widehat{\mathbf{A}} = \{\mathsf{inp}, \widehat{\boldsymbol{A}}_0, \widehat{\boldsymbol{A}}_{2t+1}, \widehat{\boldsymbol{A}}_{i,b} \mid i \in [2t], b \in \{0,1\}\}$$

where $\widehat{\boldsymbol{A}}_{i,b}$ is an entry-wise encoding of $\widetilde{\boldsymbol{A}}_{i,b}$. The obfuscated branching program $\widehat{\mathbf{A}}$ can be evaluated in the usual way: define $A(x)$ be

$$A(x) := \widehat{\boldsymbol{A}}_0 \times \prod_{i=1}^{2t} \widehat{\boldsymbol{A}}_{i,x_{\mathsf{inp}(i)}} \times \widehat{\boldsymbol{A}}_{2t+1} \times p_{zt} \bmod x_0.$$

Then $\widehat{\mathbf{A}}(x) = 0$ if and only if $A(x)$ is small compared to x_0.

3.3   Attack over CLT13 Encoding

As in the previous zeroizing attacks [CHL+15,CGH+15] against the CLT13 graded encoding scheme, our approach will be to decompose the zero-tested values $A(x)$ into a product of several factors that can be made to vary independently. We then use those varying factors to construct a matrix that will reveal the factorization of the modulus x_0, and hence entirely break the security of the scheme.

To obtain this decomposition, we will rely on the identity $\mathsf{vec}(\boldsymbol{ABC}) = (\boldsymbol{C}^T \otimes \boldsymbol{A})\,\mathsf{vec}(\boldsymbol{B})$ (see Sect. 2.1). First, we define several matrices $\boldsymbol{B}(x)$, $\boldsymbol{B}'(x)$, $\boldsymbol{C}(x)$, $\boldsymbol{C}'(x)$, and $\boldsymbol{D}(x)$ as products of consecutive factors appearing in the product $A(x)$:

$$A(x) := \widehat{\boldsymbol{A}}_0 \times \prod_{i=1}^{2t} \widehat{\boldsymbol{A}}_{i,x_{\mathsf{inp}(i)}} \times \widehat{\boldsymbol{A}}_{2t+1} \times p_{zt} \bmod x_0$$

$$= \underbrace{\widehat{\boldsymbol{A}}_0 \cdot \prod_{i=1}^{s} \widehat{\boldsymbol{A}}_{i,x_{\mathsf{inp}(i)}}}_{\boldsymbol{B}(x)} \times \underbrace{\widehat{\boldsymbol{A}}_{s+1,x_{\mathsf{inp}(s+1)}}}_{\boldsymbol{C}(x)} \times \underbrace{\prod_{i=s+2}^{2t-s-1} \widehat{\boldsymbol{A}}_{i,x_{\mathsf{inp}(i)}}}_{\boldsymbol{D}(x)}$$

$$\times \underbrace{\widehat{\boldsymbol{A}}_{2t-s,x_{\mathsf{inp}(2t-s)}}}_{\boldsymbol{C}'(x)} \times \underbrace{\prod_{i=2t-s+1}^{2t} \widehat{\boldsymbol{A}}_{i,x_{\mathsf{inp}(i)}} \cdot \widehat{\boldsymbol{A}}_{2t+1}}_{\boldsymbol{B}'(x)} \times p_{zt} \bmod x_0 \qquad (1)$$

for a specific $s \in [1, t-2]$. Using the identity above, we can then rewrite $A(x)$ as follows:

$$A(x) = \boldsymbol{B}(x) \times (\boldsymbol{C}(x)\boldsymbol{D}(x)\boldsymbol{C}'(x)) \times \boldsymbol{B}'(x) \times p_{zt} \bmod x_0$$

$$= \mathsf{vec}\Big(\boldsymbol{B}(x) \times (\boldsymbol{C}(x)\boldsymbol{D}(x)\boldsymbol{C}'(x)) \times \boldsymbol{B}'(x)\Big) \times p_{zt} \bmod x_0$$

$$= \left(\boldsymbol{B}'(x)^T \otimes \boldsymbol{B}(x)\right) \times \mathsf{vec}\left(\boldsymbol{C}(x)\boldsymbol{D}(x)\boldsymbol{C}'(x)\right) \times p_{zt} \bmod x_0$$

$$= \left(\boldsymbol{B}'(x)^T \otimes \boldsymbol{B}(x)\right) \times \left(\boldsymbol{C}'(x)^T \otimes \boldsymbol{C}(x)\right) \times \mathsf{vec}\left(\boldsymbol{D}(x)\right) \times p_{zt} \bmod x_0.$$

Note that in the above equation, $\boldsymbol{B}'(x)^T \otimes \boldsymbol{B}(x)$ is a row vector of dimension 4, $\boldsymbol{C}'(x)^T \otimes \boldsymbol{C}(x)$ is a 4×4 matrix, and $\mathsf{vec}\left(\boldsymbol{D}(x)\right)$ is a column vector of dimension 4.

Furthermore, recall that CRT values have the property that $\mathsf{CRT}(p_k^* \cdot u_k)_k = \sum_k p_k^* \cdot u_k \bmod x_0$ for any tuple $(u_k)_k$, and the relation holds over $\mathbb{Z}$ when the u_k's are small compared to the p_k's. Now, for a multilinear encoding α with level set S, denote by $[\alpha]^{(k)}$ its underlying CRT component modulo p_k (and similarly for vectors and matrices of encodings); in other words:

$$\alpha = \mathsf{CRT}\left([\alpha]^{(1)}, \ldots, [\alpha]^{(n)}\right) \cdot \prod_{i \in S} z_i^{-1} \bmod x_0.$$

With that notation and since $p_{zt} = \prod_{i=1}^{\kappa} z_i \cdot \sum_{k=1}^{n} h_k p_k^* g_k^{-1} \bmod x_0$, where n is the number of primes p_k in x_0, the expression of $A(x)$ can be extended further as:

$$A(x) = \left[\ldots \left[\boldsymbol{B'}(x)^T \otimes \boldsymbol{B}(x) \right]^{(k)} \ldots \right]$$

$$\times \begin{bmatrix} \ddots & & \\ & p_k^* h_k g_k^{-1} \cdot \left[\boldsymbol{C'}(x)^T \otimes \boldsymbol{C}(x) \right]^{(k)} & \\ & & \ddots \end{bmatrix} \times \begin{bmatrix} \vdots \\ \left[\mathsf{vec}(\boldsymbol{D}(x)) \right]^{(k)} \\ \vdots \end{bmatrix}, \quad (2)$$

where the three matrices are respectively of dimensions $1 \times 4n$, $4n \times 4n$ and $4n \times 1$. For all x, the fact that the branching program evaluates to zero (and hence $A(x)$ is an encoding of zero) ensures that the relation holds over $\mathbb{Q}$ and not just modulo x_0: indeed, it guarantees that the factor that each p_k^* gets multiplied with is small modulo p_k.

Now the key point of the attack is that the first matrix in the relation above depends only on the first s bits of the input x, the second matrix only on the $(s+1)$-st bit of x, and the third matrix on the remaining $(t-s-1)$ bits of x. Given integers i, j, b with $0 \le i < 2^s$, $0 \le j < 2^{t-s-1}$ and $b \in \{0,1\}$, denote by $W_{ij}^{(b)}$ the value $A(x) \in \mathbb{Z}$ corresponding to the input x whose first s bits are the binary expansion of i, whose last $(t-s-1)$ bits are the binary expansion of j and whose $(s+1)$-st bit is b. By the above, we can write $W_{ij}^{(b)}$ in the form:

$$W_{ij}^{(b)} = \boldsymbol{X}_i \cdot \boldsymbol{U}^{(b)} \cdot \boldsymbol{Y}_j$$

where $\boldsymbol{X}_i$ is the row vector of size $4n$, $\boldsymbol{Y}_j$ the column vector of size $4n$ and $\boldsymbol{U}^{(b)}$ the square matrix of size $4n$ that appear in Eq. (2).

Assuming that $2^{\min(s,t-s-1)} \ge 4n$ (which can be achieved by taking $s = \lfloor t/2 \rfloor$ as long as $2^{t/2} \ge 8n$), we can thus form two matrices $\boldsymbol{W}^{(0)}, \boldsymbol{W}^{(1)}$ with any choice of $4n$ indices i and j, and those matrices satisfy a relation of the form $\boldsymbol{W}^{(b)} = \boldsymbol{X} \cdot \boldsymbol{U}^{(b)} \cdot \boldsymbol{Y}$ with $\boldsymbol{X}, \boldsymbol{Y}$ square matrices of dimension $4n$ independent of b. The attack strategy is then similar to [CGH+15]. With high probability on the sets of indices i and j, these matrices will be invertible over $\mathbb{Q}$, and we will have:

$$\boldsymbol{W}^{(0)} \left(\boldsymbol{W}^{(1)} \right)^{-1} = \left(\boldsymbol{X} \boldsymbol{U}^{(0)} \boldsymbol{Y} \right) \cdot \left(\boldsymbol{X} \boldsymbol{U}^{(1)} \boldsymbol{Y} \right)^{-1} = \boldsymbol{X} \cdot \boldsymbol{U}^{(0)} \left(\boldsymbol{U}^{(1)} \right)^{-1} \cdot \boldsymbol{X}^{-1}.$$

In particular, the characteristic polynomials of the matrices $\boldsymbol{W}^{(0)} \left(\boldsymbol{W}^{(1)} \right)^{-1}$ and $\boldsymbol{U}^{(0)} \left(\boldsymbol{U}^{(1)} \right)^{-1}$ are equal, and since we know the $\boldsymbol{W}^{(b)}$, we can compute that common polynomial P in polynomial time, together with its factorization. Now the latter matrix is block diagonal, and satisfies:

$$\boldsymbol{U}^{(0)} \left(\boldsymbol{U}^{(1)} \right)^{-1} \equiv \begin{bmatrix} \ddots & & \\ & \boldsymbol{\Gamma} \bmod p_k & \\ & & \ddots \end{bmatrix} \pmod{x_0}$$

where $\boldsymbol{\Gamma} = \left(\boldsymbol{C}_0'^T \otimes \boldsymbol{C}_0\right) \cdot \left(\boldsymbol{C}_1'^T \otimes \boldsymbol{C}_1\right)^{-1}$ (with obvious definitions for $\boldsymbol{C}_0$, $\boldsymbol{C}_0'$, $\boldsymbol{C}_1$, $\boldsymbol{C}_1'$). Therefore, P decomposes as a product of factors P_k, $k = 1, \ldots, n$, such that $P_k(\boldsymbol{\Gamma}) \equiv 0 \pmod{p_k}$. Moreover, as characteristic polynomials over $\mathbb{Q}$ are essentially random matrices, the polynomials P_k should heuristically be irreducible with high probability, and hence occur directly in the factorization of P (that assumption, which is well verified in practice, appears as Conjecture 1 in [CGH+15, Sect. 3.3]). This yields to the complete recovery of the p_k's as $p_k = \gcd\left(x_0, P_k(\boldsymbol{\Gamma})\right)$, where the P_k are the irreducible factors of P.

Clearly, once the p_k's are found, it is straightforward to break indistinguishability obfuscation. Indeed, given any two multilinear encodings at level $\{i\}$, applying rational reconstruction to their ratio modulo p_k reveals $z_i \bmod p_k$, and hence the entire z_i. Then, even if the g_k's are kept secret, rational reconstruction again applied to p_{zt} allows to recover them. This makes it possible to completely "decrypt" multilinear encodings, and hence obtain the full original randomized branching program $\widetilde{\mathbf{A}}$.

In particular, we can distinguish between the obfuscation of two branching programs whenever they are inequivalent under Kilian's randomization.

3.4 Implementation of the Attack

Since the attack relies on some heuristic assumptions regarding e.g. the irreducibility of the factors of the characteristic polynomial of $\boldsymbol{U}^{(0)}\left(\boldsymbol{U}^{(1)}\right)^{-1}$ corresponding to its block diagonal submatrices, we have written an implementation to check that these assumptions were indeed satisfied in practice. The source code in Sage [S+16] is provided in the full version [CLLT16b].

Running that implementation, we have verified that we could always recover the full factorization of x_0 efficiently.

4 Generality of Our Attack

In the previous section, we have described a zeroizing attack that breaks CLT13-based indistinguishability obfuscation for a specific branching program (previously considered in [MSZ16]) for which no previous attack was known in the CLT13 setting. In particular, that program does not have the decomposable structure required to apply the attack of [CGH+15, Sect. 3.4]. In that sense, we do extend the scope of zeroizing attacks beyond the setting of [CGH+15].

However, our attack setting may seem quite special at first glance. In particular, the following aspects of our attack may seem to restrict its generality:

- we have described our attack against a somewhat simplified obfuscation construction, that yields 2×2 matrix encodings and does not include all the countermeasures against potential attacks suggested in [GGH+13b] and later papers;
- our attack appears to rely in a crucial way on the specific structure of the branching program $\mathbf{A}$ (and its inp function in particular) in order to achieve the partitioning necessary to apply zeroizing techniques;

- we only target a branching program for a very simple functionality (the identically zero function).

In this section, we show that all of these limitations can be overcome, so that our attack is in fact quite general:

- we can apply it to almost all proposed (single-input) iO candidates instantiated over CLT13 multilinear maps, including the single-input variants of [GGH+13b, MSW14, AGIS14, PST14, BGK+14, BMSZ16];
- we can extend it to branching programs with an essentially arbitrary structure, including oblivious branching programs;
- we can mount it with programs achieving essentially arbitrary functionalities.

4.1 Attacking Other Obfuscators

The attack of Sect. 3 targets a somewhat simplified obfuscator that takes a branching program, randomizes it using Kilian-style random matrices together with multiplicative bundling with random scalars $\alpha_{i,b}$, and outputs multilinear encodings of the resulting randomized matrices directly. Actual candidate constructions of indistinguishability obfuscation in the literature, on the other hand, are usually more complicated, and typically involve extending the matrices in the original branching program using diagonal blocks that get canceled out when carrying out multilinear zero testing. The goal of these changes is usually to protect against classes of attacks that could exploit the particular algebraic structure of branching programs in undesirable ways—see e.g. [GMM+16] and references therein.

However, for the most part, these additional security features have no incidence on the applicability of our attack. This is because we only rely on the zero-testing of top-level multilinear encodings of zero being small—the precise algebraic structure of the matrices involved is essentially irrelevant for our purposes. This is in contrast, in particular, with Miles et al.'s annihilation attacks [MSZ16], which do exploit algebraic properties of the branching program matrices (such as low-degree polynomial relations they satisfy), and hence get thwarted by the submatrices used in [GGH+13b, GMM+16]. Recently, Chen, Gentry and Halevi extended annihilation attacks to [GGH+13b] using the "multiplicative bundling" scalars.

More precisely, the only difference between proposed obfuscators that matters in our attack is the dimension of the matrix encodings involved. If the obfuscated branching program $\widehat{\mathbf{A}}$ consists of $w \times w$ matrices instead of 2×2 matrices as in Sect. 3, $\boldsymbol{C}'(x)^T \otimes \boldsymbol{C}(x)$ is of dimension w^2. As a result, we need to construct matrices $\boldsymbol{W}^{(b)}$ of dimension $w^2 n$, and in particular the number t of input bits should satisfy $2^{t/2} \geq 2w^2 n$.

Note that this condition is never a restriction in non-trivial cases: this is because $2^{t/2} < 2w^2 n$ implies that there is only a logarithmic number of input bits, or in other words a polynomial-size domain. But indistinguishability obfuscation for functions with a polynomial-size domain is trivial: it is equivalent to giving out the graph of the function in full, since it is a canonical (hence indistinguishable) representation, and anyone with access to an obfuscation can recover it in polynomial time.

We finish this paragraph by reviewing several candidate iO constructions and discussing how they fit within the argument above. This will prove Theorem 1, which we now recall.

Theorem 1. *Let $\mathcal{O}$ denote the single-input variant of the iO candidates in* [GGH+13b, MSW14, AGIS14, PST14, BGK+14, BMSZ16] *(over CLT13 multilinear maps). There exists a branching program* **A** *such that, given* $\mathcal{O}(\mathbf{A})$*, one can break the CLT13 multilinear maps in polynomial-time.*

[AGIS14, MSW14, BMSZ16]. The obfuscator described in Sect. 3.2 is essentially identical to the single-input versions of the constructions from [AGIS14, MSW14, BMSZ16]. The only difference is that those papers do not directly encode matrices at singleton multilinear levels $\{i\}$, but use a more complicated level structure involving straddling sets. Since our attack relies on the honest evaluation of the obfuscated branching program, it automatically respects the multilinear level structure of any correct obfuscator. Therefore, it applies to those schemes *without any change*.

[GGH+13b]. The main difference between the obfuscator described in Sect. 3.2 and the one proposed in [GGH+13b] is that the latter extends the original branching program matrices $\boldsymbol{A}_{i,b}$ by random diagonal matrices $\boldsymbol{\Delta}_{i,b}$ of dimension $d = 8t+10$ before applying Kilian's randomization and multilinear encoding (and the matrices $\boldsymbol{A}_{i,b}$ themselves are assumed to be of dimension 5 instead of 2, to accommodate for the original formulation of Barrington's theorem). In other words, the randomized branching program $\widetilde{\mathbf{A}}$ has the form:

$$\widetilde{\boldsymbol{A}}_{i,b} = \alpha_{i,b}\boldsymbol{R}_i \cdot \begin{bmatrix} \boldsymbol{A}_{i,b} & \\ & \boldsymbol{\Delta}_{i,b} \end{bmatrix} \cdot \boldsymbol{R}_{i+1}^{-1},$$

with the bookend matrices $\widetilde{\boldsymbol{A}}_0$, $\widetilde{\boldsymbol{A}}_{2t+1}$ adapted in such a way that the condition:

$$\mathbf{A}(x) = 0 \quad \text{if and only if} \quad \widetilde{\boldsymbol{A}}_0 \cdot \prod_i \widetilde{\boldsymbol{A}}_{i,x_{\mathsf{inp}(i)}} \cdot \widetilde{\boldsymbol{A}}_{2t+1} = 0$$

continues to hold. Because that condition holds, our attack applies in exactly the same way, except again for the fact that the dimension of encoded matrices $\widetilde{\boldsymbol{A}}_{i,b}$ increases from 2 to $w = d + 5 = 8t + 15$. This means that the condition on t becomes $2^{t/2} \geq 2(8t + 15)^2 n$, which is, again, not a meaningful restriction.

[PST14]. The situation for the obfuscator of [PST14] is similar. In that scheme, the randomized branching program $\widetilde{\mathbf{A}}$ takes the form:

$$\widetilde{\boldsymbol{A}}_{i,b} = \alpha_{i,b}\boldsymbol{R}_i \cdot \begin{bmatrix} \boldsymbol{A}_{i,b} & \\ & \boldsymbol{I}_5 \end{bmatrix} \cdot \boldsymbol{R}_{i+1}^{-1},$$

where I_5 is simply the 5×5 identity matrix, and the original branching program matrices are also assumed to be of dimension 5. Again, our attack extends to that setting directly, the only difference being that the dimension of encoded matrices $\widetilde{A}_{i,b}$ increases from 2 to $w = 10$. The fact that the scheme from [PST14] uses straddling sets has, again, no bearing on the applicability of our techniques.

[BGK+14]. In the [BGK+14] obfuscator, the shape of the obfuscated branching program and the zero-testing condition look a bit different. More precisely, in that scheme, the randomized branching program is basically the same as $\widetilde{A}$ from Sect. 3.2 *together with* the values $\alpha_{i,b}$ of the scalar randomizers except that they use random vectors for A_0 and A_{2t+1}. And $\alpha_{i,b}$ and $A_0 \cdot A_{2t+1}$ are also included in the randomized branching program. Moreover, the zero-testing condition is modified: $\widetilde{A}(x) = 0$ if and only if

$$\widetilde{A}_0 \cdot \prod_i \widetilde{A}_{i,x_{\mathsf{inp}(i)}} \cdot \widetilde{A}_{2t+1} = \gamma \cdot \prod_i \alpha_{i,x_{\mathsf{inp}(i)}}, \tag{3}$$

where $\gamma = A_0 \cdot A_{2t+1}$. The output of the obfuscator is then essentially the same obfuscated branching program $\widehat{A}$ from Sect. 3.2 *together with* encodings $\widehat{\alpha}_{i,b}$ of the values $\alpha_{i,b}$ at the same multilinear level as $\widehat{A}_{i,b}$ as well as the encoding $\widehat{\gamma}$ of γ. And the evaluation is carried out by applying zero-testing to Eq. (3), given multilinear encodings $\widehat{A}_0$, $\widehat{A}_{2t+1}$, $\widehat{A}_{i,b}$, $\widehat{\alpha}_{i,b}$, and $\widehat{\gamma}$.

Our attack can be adapted to this construction. Since multiplication between scalars is commutative, the scalar values on the right-hand side of (3) can be *freely* decomposed into several parts. In view of (1), let us decompose the set $[2t]$ into a partition: $S_1 = \{1, \ldots, s, 2t - s + 1, \ldots, 2t\}$, $S_2 = \{s + 1, 2t - s\}$, and $S_3 = \{s + 2, \ldots, 2t - s - 1\}$. Then we can decompose the above mentioned scalar values into three parts:

$$\gamma \prod_i \alpha_{i,x_{\mathsf{inp}(i)}} = \gamma \prod_{i \in S_1} \alpha_{i,x_{\mathsf{inp}(i)}} \times \prod_{i \in S_2} \alpha_{i,x_{\mathsf{inp}(i)}} \times \prod_{i \in S_3} \alpha_{i,x_{\mathsf{inp}(i)}}.$$

Since the left hand side of (3) is the same as in Sect. 3.2, the expression in (2) can be extended to the zero-testing of (3) as follows:

$$A(x) = \left[\ldots \left[B'(x)^T \otimes B(x) \right]^{(k)} \left[\delta_1 \right]^{(k)} \ldots \right]$$

$$\times \begin{bmatrix} \ddots & & \\ & \begin{matrix} p_k^* h_k g_k^{-1} \cdot \left[C'(x)^T \otimes C(x) \right]^{(k)} \\ p_k^* h_k g_k^{-1} \cdot \left[\delta_2 \right]^{(k)} \end{matrix} & \\ & & \ddots \end{bmatrix}$$

$$\times \begin{bmatrix} \vdots \\ \left[\mathsf{vec}(D(x)) \right]^{(k)} \\ -\left[\delta_3 \right]^{(k)} \\ \vdots \end{bmatrix},$$

where $\delta_1 = \widehat{\gamma} \prod_{i \in S_1} \widehat{\alpha}_{i,x_{\mathsf{inp}(i)}}$, $\delta_2 = \prod_{i \in S_2} \widehat{\alpha}_{i,x_{\mathsf{inp}(i)}}$, and $\delta_3 = \prod_{i \in S_3} \widehat{\alpha}_{i,x_{\mathsf{inp}(i)}}$.

Here, the three matrices are respectively of dimensions $1 \times 5n$, $5n \times 5n$ and $5n \times 1$ when $w = 2$. And we can then complete the attack in a manner similar to Sect. 3.3. The condition for this attack to succeed becomes: $2^{t/2} \geq 2(w^2 + 1)n$.

4.2   Attacking Branching Programs with Arbitrary Structure

Another apparent limitation of our attack is related to the particular structure of the branching program $\mathbf{A}$, and in particular its inp function. Indeed, the key point of our attack is our ability to obtain a *partitioning* of the branching program, i.e. express the associated zero-test value $A(x)$ as a product of three successive factors depending on disjoint subsets of input bits. We achieved this by observing that $A(x)$ can be put in the form:

$$A(x) = \mathbf{B}(x) \cdot \mathbf{C}(x) \cdot \mathbf{D}(x) \cdot \mathbf{C}'(x) \cdot \mathbf{B}'(x) \times p_{zt} \bmod x_0$$

where $\mathbf{B}(x), \mathbf{B}'(x)$ depend on one subset of input bits, $\mathbf{C}(x), \mathbf{C}'(x)$ a different, disjoint subset, and $\mathbf{D}(x)$ on a third subset disjoint from the first two. We then used the tensor product identity mentioned in Sect. 2.1 to reorder those matrices so as to get a factor depending only on $\mathbf{B}(x)$ and $\mathbf{B}'(x)$ on the left, another one depending only on $\mathbf{C}(x)$ and $\mathbf{C}'(x)$ in the middle, and a last one depending only on $\mathbf{D}(x)$ on the right:

$$A(x) = \left(\mathbf{B}'(x)^T \otimes \mathbf{B}(x)\right) \times \left(\mathbf{C}'(x)^T \otimes \mathbf{C}(x)\right) \times \mathsf{vec}\left(\mathbf{D}(x)\right) \times p_{zt} \bmod x_0.$$

This technique seems to rely in an essential way on the order in which input bits are assigned to successive branching program layers, and although we did not come up with the branching program $\mathbf{A}$ ourselves (as it was proposed earlier in [MSZ16]), we have to admit that it is rather special.

Indeed, proposed candidate iO constructions are often supposed to operate on *oblivious* branching programs, whose length is a multiple of the number t of input bits and whose inp function is fixed to $\mathsf{inp}(i) = (i \bmod t) + 1$ (i.e. the input bits are associated to successive layers in cyclic order). This is natural, since all branching programs can be trivially converted to that form, and a canonical inp function is needed to ensure indistinguishability. However, the branching program $\mathbf{A}$ above is *not* oblivious, and it is not immediately clear that our partitioning technique based on tensor products extends to that case.

Fortunately, it turns out that our technique does extend to oblivious (and hence to arbitrary) branching programs as well, at the cost of an increase in the dimension of the matrix encodings involved. There is in fact a simple greedy algorithm that will convert any scalar expression consisting of a product of three types of matrices $\mathbf{B}_i$, $\mathbf{C}_i$, $\mathbf{D}_i$ to an equal product of three factors, the first of which involves only the $\mathbf{B}_i$'s, the second only the $\mathbf{C}_i$'s and the third only the $\mathbf{D}_i$'s. Writing down a description of the algorithm would be somewhat tedious, but it is easy to understand on an example.

If we consider for example an oblivious branching program $\mathbf{A}_2$ of length $2t$ (i.e. with two groups of t layers associated with all successive input bits), the corresponding zero-test value can be put in the form:

$$A(x) = \boldsymbol{B} \cdot \boldsymbol{C} \cdot \boldsymbol{D} \cdot \boldsymbol{B}' \cdot \boldsymbol{C}' \cdot \boldsymbol{D}' \cdot p_{zt} \bmod x_0$$

where, again, $\boldsymbol{B}, \boldsymbol{B}'$ depend on one subset of input bits, $\boldsymbol{C}, \boldsymbol{C}'$ a different, disjoint subset, and $\boldsymbol{D}, \boldsymbol{D}'$ on a third subset disjoint from the first two (and we omit the dependence of these matrices on x to simplify notations). The matrices all have dimension $w \times w$, except the first and the last, which are of dimension $1 \times w$ and $w \times 1$ respectively. Denoting by A_{zt} the value such that $A(x) = A_{zt} \cdot p_{zt} \bmod x_0$, we can then put A_{zt} in the desired partitioned form as follows:

$$
\begin{aligned}
A_{zt} &= \boldsymbol{BC} \cdot \mathsf{vec}\left(\boldsymbol{D} \cdot (\boldsymbol{B}'\boldsymbol{C}') \cdot \boldsymbol{D}'\right) \\
&= \boldsymbol{BC}\left(\boldsymbol{D}'^T \otimes \boldsymbol{D}\right) \mathsf{vec}(\boldsymbol{I}_w \boldsymbol{B}'\boldsymbol{C}') \\
&= \boldsymbol{BC}\left(\boldsymbol{D}'^T \otimes \boldsymbol{D}\right)\left(\boldsymbol{C}'^T \otimes \boldsymbol{I}_w\right) \mathsf{vec}(\boldsymbol{B}') \\
&= \left(\mathsf{vec}(\boldsymbol{B}')^T \otimes \boldsymbol{B}\right) \cdot \mathsf{vec}\left(\boldsymbol{C}\left(\boldsymbol{D}'^T \otimes \boldsymbol{D}\right)\left(\boldsymbol{C}'^T \otimes \boldsymbol{I}_w\right)\right) \\
&= \left(\mathsf{vec}(\boldsymbol{B}')^T \otimes \boldsymbol{B}\right) \cdot \left(\boldsymbol{C}' \otimes \boldsymbol{I}_w \otimes \boldsymbol{C}\right) \cdot \mathsf{vec}\left(\boldsymbol{D}'^T \otimes \boldsymbol{D}\right),
\end{aligned}
$$

and clearly a similar procedure works for any number of layer groups, allowing us to adapt the attack to oblivious branching programs in general.

However, for an oblivious branching program of length mt (with m groups of t layers), we can see that the dimension of the resulting square matrix in the middle is given by w^{2m-1}, and therefore, we need to have $2^{t/2} \geq nw^{2m-1}$ to obtain sufficiently many zeros to apply the zeroizing technique. As a result, we can attack oblivious branching programs only when the number m of layer groups is not too large compared to the number t of input bits. In particular, we cannot break the obfuscation of oblivious branching programs with length greater than $\omega(t^2)$ using that technique.

Thus, in principle, using oblivious branching programs whose length is quite large compared to the number of inputs might be an effective countermeasure against our attack. It remains to be seen whether further improvements could yield to a successful attack against oblivious branching programs of length $\Omega(t^c)$ for $c > 2$.

On the flip side, we will see below that by adding "dummy" input bits, we can *pad* essentially any oblivious branching program into another oblivious branching program that computes the same functionality (ignoring the dummy input bits), with the same number of layer groups, and whose obfuscation is broken using our techniques.

4.3   Attacking Arbitrary Functionalities

The attack on Sect. 3 was described against a branching program for the always-zero function. Since we do not use any property of the underlying matrices other than the fact that the program evaluates to zero on many inputs, it is clear that the attack should extend to branching programs for other functionalities as well. Describing the class of functionalities we can capture in that way is not easy, however.

If we take for example a branching program $\mathbf{A}''$ with the same input size, the same length and the same inp function as $\mathbf{A}$ (and with encoding matrices of dimension w, say), then a sufficient condition for the attack to apply to $\mathbf{A}''$ is essentially that we can find sufficiently many "contiguous" inputs on which the program evaluates to zero. More precisely, suppose that we can find a subset R of the set $[t]$ of input bit indices and an assignment $(y_r)_{r \in R} \in \{0,1\}^R$ of these input bits such that $\mathbf{A}''$ evaluates to zero on all inputs $x \in \{0,1\}^t$ that coincide with (y_r) on R. In other words:

$$\left(\forall r \in R, \; x_r = y_r\right) \implies \mathbf{A}''(x) = 0.$$

Then we can break the obfuscation of $\mathbf{A}''$ using the obfuscator of Sect. 3.2 as soon as $2^{(t-r)/2} \geq 2w^2n$. The idea is simply to apply the attack in Sect. 3.3 with s chosen in such a way that $s+1$ is exactly the $(\lfloor (t-r)/2 \rfloor + 1)$-st element of $[t] \setminus R$ (in increasing order). Then, $A(x)$ satisfies Eq. (2) for all values of x with $x_r = y_r$ for $r \in R$. This provides at least $2^{(t-r)/2-1}$ choices for $\boldsymbol{X}_i$, $2^{(t-r)/2-1}$ for $\boldsymbol{Y}_j$ and two choices for $\boldsymbol{U}^{(b)}$, so we have enough zero values to apply the attack.

While the condition above is quite contrived, it should be satisfied by many branching programs (especially as $t-r$ can be chosen to be logarithmic: it follows that almost all functionalities should satisfy the condition), including many natural examples (a branching program whose underlying circuit is the nontrivial conjunction of two sub-circuits, one of which depends only on $t-r$ input bits would be an example). But it gives little insight into the class of functionalities we end up capturing.

A different angle of approach towards this problem is the padding technique already considered in [MSZ16, Sect. 3.3]. Given a branching program $\mathbf{A}_0$ implementing any functionality and for which we can find an input where it evaluates to zero, we can convert it into another branching program $\mathbf{A}_0^*$ with slightly more input bits, that implements the same functionality (it simply ignores the additional dummy input bits and evaluates to the same values as $\mathbf{A}_0$ everywhere), and whose obfuscation is broken using our attack.

This is in fact trivial: take the branching program $\mathbf{A}_0$, and append to it (before the final bookend matrix) additional layers associated with the new input bits consisting entirely of identity matrices, in the same order as the inp function of the branching program $\mathbf{A}$ from Sect. 3.1. Since all the added layers contain only identity matrices, they do not change the functionality at all. Then, if we simply fix the non-dummy input bits to the value on which we know $\mathbf{A}_0$ vanishes, we are exactly reduced to the setting of Sect. 3.3, and our attack applies directly.

This may be a bit *too* trivial, however, since we could just as well append a branching program with a "decomposable" structure in the sense of [CGH+15, Sect. 3.4], and the corresponding attack would apply already.

A less trivial observation is that we can start from any *oblivious* branching program $\mathbf{A}_0$ (for which we know an input evaluating to zero), and convert it to another *oblivious* branching program $\mathbf{A}_0^*$ with more input bits but the same number of layer groups, that implements the same functionality in the sense above, and whose obfuscation is, again, broken using our attack.

The idea this time is to add layers associated with the dummy input bits with all-identity matrices in each layer group. This does not change the functionality, and once we fix the original input bits to the input evaluating to zero, we are reduced to breaking an oblivious branching program for the always-zero function with a fixed number m of layer groups and a number of input bits that we can choose. By the discussion of Sect. 4.2 above, if the matrix encodings are of dimension w, it suffice to add t dummy inputs bits where $2^{t/2} \geq nw^{2m-1}$, which is always achievable.

5   Conclusion

Our attack shows that the single-input candidate iO constructions for branching programs over the CLT13 multilinear map proposed in the literature should be considered insecure. We leave as a challenging open problem how to extend our attack to the dual-input iO schemes.

Acknowledgments. This work has been supported in part by the European Union's H2020 Programme under grant agreement number ICT-644209. We thank the PKC 2017 reviewers for their careful reading of the paper and their diligent comments.

References

[AB15]   Applebaum, B., Brakerski, Z.: Obfuscating circuits via composite-order graded encoding. In: Dodis, Y., Nielsen, J.B. (eds.) TCC 2015. LNCS, vol. 9015, pp. 528–556. Springer, Heidelberg (2015). doi:10.1007/978-3-662-46497-7_21

[ADGM16]   Apon, D., Döttling, N., Garg, S., Mukherjee, P.: Cryptanalysis of indistinguishability obfuscations of circuits over GGH13. Cryptology ePrint Archive, Report 2016/1003 (2016). https://eprint.iacr.org/2016/1003

[AGIS14]   Ananth, P.V., Gupta, D., Ishai, Y., Sahai, A.: Optimizing obfuscation: avoiding barrington's theorem. In: Ahn, G.-J., Yung, M., Li, N. (eds.) ACM CCS, pp. 646–658. ACM (2014)

[BGK+14]   Barak, B., Garg, S., Kalai, Y.T., Paneth, O., Sahai, A.: Protecting obfuscation against algebraic attacks. In: Nguyen, P.Q., Oswald, E. (eds.) EUROCRYPT 2014. LNCS, vol. 8441, pp. 221–238. Springer, Heidelberg (2014). doi:10.1007/978-3-642-55220-5_13

[BLR+15]   Boneh, D., Lewi, K., Raykova, M., Sahai, A., Zhandry, M., Zimmerman, J.: Semantically secure order-revealing encryption: multi-input functional encryption without obfuscation. In: Oswald, E., Fischlin, M. (eds.) EUROCRYPT 2015. LNCS, vol. 9057, pp. 563–594. Springer, Heidelberg (2015). doi:10.1007/978-3-662-46803-6_19

[BMSZ16]   Badrinarayanan, S., Miles, E., Sahai, A., Zhandry, M.: Post-zeroizing obfuscation: new mathematical tools, and the case of evasive circuits. In: Fischlin, M., Coron, J.-S. (eds.) EUROCRYPT 2016. LNCS, vol. 9666, pp. 764–791. Springer, Heidelberg (2016). doi:10.1007/978-3-662-49896-5_27

[CGH+15] Coron, J.-S., et al.: Zeroizing without low-level zeroes: new MMAP attacks and their limitations. In: Gennaro, R., Robshaw, M. (eds.) CRYPTO 2015. LNCS, vol. 9215, pp. 247–266. Springer, Heidelberg (2015). doi:10.1007/978-3-662-47989-6_12

[CGH16] Chen, Y., Gentry, C., Halevi, S.: Cryptanalyses of candidate branching program obfuscators. Cryptology ePrint Archive, Report 2016/998 (2016). https://eprint.iacr.org/2016/998

[CHL+15] Cheon, J.H., Han, K., Lee, C., Ryu, H., Stehlé, D.: Cryptanalysis of the multilinear map over the integers. In: Oswald, E., Fischlin, M. (eds.) EUROCRYPT 2015. LNCS, vol. 9056, pp. 3–12. Springer, Heidelberg (2015). doi:10.1007/978-3-662-46800-5_1

[CLLT16a] Coron, J.-S., Lee, M.S., Lepoint, T., Tibouchi, M.: Cryptanalysis of GGH15 multilinear maps. In: Robshaw, M., Katz, J. (eds.) CRYPTO 2016. LNCS, vol. 9815, pp. 607–628. Springer, Heidelberg (2016). doi:10.1007/978-3-662-53008-5_21

[CLLT16b] Coron, J., Lee, M.S., Lepoint, T., Tibouchi, M.: Zeroizing attacks on indistinguishability obfuscation over CLT13. Cryptology ePrint Archive, Report 2016/1011 (2016). https://eprint.iacr.org/2016/1011

[CLT13] Coron, J.-S., Lepoint, T., Tibouchi, M.: Practical multilinear maps over the integers. In: Canetti, R., Garay, J.A. (eds.) CRYPTO 2013. LNCS, vol. 8042, pp. 476–493. Springer, Heidelberg (2013). doi:10.1007/978-3-642-40041-4_26

[DGG+16] Döttling, N., Garg, S., Gupta, D., Miao, P., Mukherjee, P.: Obfuscation from low noise multilinear maps. Cryptology ePrint Archive, Report 2016/599 (2016). https://eprint.iacr.org/2016/599

[GGH13a] Garg, S., Gentry, C., Halevi, S.: Candidate multilinear maps from ideal lattices. In: Johansson, T., Nguyen, P.Q. (eds.) EUROCRYPT 2013. LNCS, vol. 7881, pp. 1–17. Springer, Heidelberg (2013). doi:10.1007/978-3-642-38348-9_1

[GGH+13b] Garg, S., Gentry, C., Halevi, S., Raykova, M., Sahai, A., Waters, B.: Candidate indistinguishability obfuscation and functional encryption for all circuits. In: Proceedings of the FOCS, pp. 40–49. IEEE Computer Society (2013)

[GGH15] Gentry, C., Gorbunov, S., Halevi, S.: Graph-induced multilinear maps from lattices. In: Dodis, Y., Nielsen, J.B. (eds.) TCC 2015. LNCS, vol. 9015, pp. 498–527. Springer, Heidelberg (2015). doi:10.1007/978-3-662-46497-7_20

[GMM+16] Garg, S., Miles, E., Mukherjee, P., Sahai, A., Srinivasan, A., Zhandry, M.: Secure obfuscation in a weak multilinear map model. In: Hirt, M., Smith, A. (eds.) TCC 2016. LNCS, vol. 9986, pp. 241–268. Springer, Heidelberg (2016). doi:10.1007/978-3-662-53644-5_10

[HJ16] Hu, Y., Jia, H.: Cryptanalysis of GGH map. In: Fischlin, M., Coron, J.-S. (eds.) EUROCRYPT 2016. LNCS, vol. 9665, pp. 537–565. Springer, Heidelberg (2016). doi:10.1007/978-3-662-49890-3_21

[Lau04] Laub, A.J.: Matrix Analysis for Scientists and Engineers. Society for Industrial and Applied Mathematics, Philadelphia (2004)

[MSW14] Miles, E., Sahai, A., Weiss, M.: Protecting obfuscation against arithmetic attacks. Cryptology ePrint Archive, Report 2014/878 (2014). https://eprint.iacr.org/2014/878

[MSZ16] Miles, E., Sahai, A., Zhandry, M.: Annihilation attacks for multilinear maps: cryptanalysis of indistinguishability obfuscation over GGH13. In: Robshaw, M., Katz, J. (eds.) CRYPTO 2016. LNCS, vol. 9815, pp. 629–658. Springer, Heidelberg (2016). doi:10.1007/978-3-662-53008-5_22

[PST14] Pass, R., Seth, K., Telang, S.: Indistinguishability obfuscation from semantically-secure multilinear encodings. In: Garay, J.A., Gennaro, R. (eds.) CRYPTO 2014. LNCS, vol. 8616, pp. 500–517. Springer, Heidelberg (2014). doi:10.1007/978-3-662-44371-2_28

[S+16] Stein, W., et al.: Sage Mathematics Software (Version 7.0) (2016). http://www.sagemath.org

[Zim15] Zimmerman, J.: How to obfuscate programs directly. In: Oswald, E., Fischlin, M. (eds.) EUROCRYPT 2015. LNCS, vol. 9057, pp. 439–467. Springer, Heidelberg (2015). doi:10.1007/978-3-662-46803-6_15

Protocols

Cut Down the Tree to Achieve Constant Complexity in Divisible E-cash

David Pointcheval[1], Olivier Sanders[2]([✉]), and Jacques Traoré[3]

[1] CNRS, ENS, INRIA, PSL Research University, Paris, France
[2] Orange Labs, Applied Crypto Group, Cesson-Sévigné, France
`oliviersanders@live.fr`
[3] Orange Labs, Applied Crypto Group, Caen, France

Abstract. Divisible e-cash, proposed in 1991 by Okamoto and Ohta, addresses a practical concern of electronic money, the problem of paying the exact amount. Users of such systems can indeed withdraw coins of a large value N and then divide it into many pieces of any desired values $V \leq N$. Such a primitive therefore allows to avoid the use of several denominations or change issues. Since its introduction, many constructions have been proposed but all of them make use of the same framework: they associate each coin with a binary tree, which implies, at least, a logarithmic complexity for the spendings.

In this paper, we propose the first divisible e-cash system without such a tree structure, and so without its inherent downsides. Our construction is the first one to achieve constant-time spendings while offering a quite easy management of the coins. It compares favorably with the state-of-the-art, while being provably secure in the standard model.

1 Introduction

Electronic payment systems have a strong impact on individual's privacy, and this is often underestimated by the users. Transaction informations, such as payee's identity, date and location, allow a third party (usually, the financial institution) to learn a lot of things about the users: individuals' whereabouts, religious beliefs, health status, etc., which can eventually be quite sensitive.

However, secure e-payment and strong privacy are not incompatible, as shown by Chaum in 1982 [12]: he introduced the concept of electronic cash (*e-cash*), the digital analogue of regular cash, and in particular with its anonymity property. Typically, e-cash systems consider three kinds of parties, the bank, users and merchants. The bank issues coins, which can be withdrawn by users, and then be spent to merchants. Eventually, the merchants deposit the money on their account at the bank. It is better when the spending process does not involve the bank, in which case the e-cash system is said *offline*. Ideally, users and merchants should form a single set, which means that anyone receiving a coin should be able to spend it again without depositing it to the bank. Unfortunately, such a solution, called *transferable* e-cash implies [13] coins of growing size which quickly becomes cumbersome.

© International Association for Cryptologic Research 2017
S. Fehr (Ed.): PKC 2017, Part I, LNCS 10174, pp. 61–90, 2017.
DOI: 10.1007/978-3-662-54365-8_4

Although most of the features of regular cash, such as anonymity, can be reproduced by e-cash, there is one fundamental difference between these two systems: the latter can easily by duplicated, as any digital information. This property is a major issue for money, since dishonest users could spend several times the same coin to different merchants. To deter this bad behavior, e-cash systems must enable (1) detection of double-spending (*i.e.* the reuse of a spent coin), or alternatively over-spending (*i.e.* spending more money than withdrawn) and (2) identification of defrauders.

Unfortunately, achieving such properties becomes tricky when anonymity of transactions is required. Indeed, the bank can no longer trace the users' payments and check that, for each of them, the global amount spent remains lower than the amount he withdrew. To enable detection of double-spending/over-spending, most of the e-cash systems then make use of serial numbers: every coin is associated with a unique number, only known to its owner until he spends the coin. The serial number is indeed revealed during the transaction and stored by the bank in a database. The bank can thus detect any reuse of serial numbers and so any double-spending.

1.1   Divisible E-cash

In 1991, Okamoto and Ohta [21] showed that e-cash can do more than simply emulate regular cash. They introduced the notion of *divisible* e-cash, where users withdraw coins of value N and have the ability of dividing it into many pieces of any desired values $V_i \leq N$ such that $\sum_i V_i = N$. Such a property enables the user to pay the exact amount whatever the amount of the initially withdrawn coin was, which was a problem for traditional e-cash (and regular cash) systems. The authors proposed a framework representing each coin of value $N = 2^n$ by a binary tree where each leaf is associated with a serial number, and so with a value 1. When a user wants to spend a value $2^\ell \leq N$, he reveals an information related to a node s of depth $n - \ell$, allowing the bank to recover the 2^ℓ serial numbers associated with the leaves descending from s. The benefit of this tree structure is to provide a partial control on the amount of serial numbers the user reveals. The latter can indeed send them by batches of 2^ℓ, for any $0 \leq \ell \leq n$, which is much more efficient than sending them one by one, while ensuring that no information on serial numbers which do not descend from the spent nodes will leak.

Following this seminal work, a large number of constructions (including for example the following papers [2,8–11,20]) have been proposed, all of them making use of this framework, with a binary tree. In 2007, Canard and Gouget [8] proposed the first anonymous construction in the random oracle model, and recently, Canard *et al.* [10] showed that both anonymity and efficiency can be achieved in the standard model.

However, this binary tree structure has a major downside: it is tailored to spend powers of 2. Unfortunately, such an event is unlikely in real life. In practice, to pay a value V, the users must write $V = \sum_i b_i \cdot 2^i$, for $b_i \in \{0,1\}$ and then repeat the **Spend** protocol v times, where $v = \sum_i b_i$. Therefore, the *constant-time*

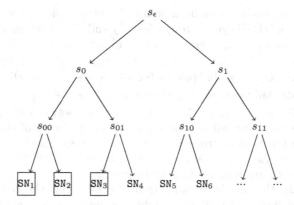

Fig. 1. Tree-based divisible coin

property claimed by several constructions is somewhat misleading: spendings can be performed in constant-time as long as V is a power of 2 but not in the general case, and in the worst case the complexity is logarithmic.

Moreover, this structure makes the coin management slightly more difficult. Indeed, let us consider the case illustrated by the Fig. 1, where a user has already spent a value $V_1 = 3$ and so revealed the first three serial numbers SN_1, SN_2 and SN_3. Now assume that the user wants to spend a value $V_2 = 2$. He cannot use the node s_{01}, since SN_3 has already been revealed and so must use s_{10} or s_{11}. This means that the serial number SN_4 will remain isolated, and the user will have to spend it later as a unit. It is then necessary to maintain a list of unspent serial numbers and try to avoid the presence of several "holes" in the tree, which thereafter restricts a lot the value that can be spent at once.

1.2   Our Contribution

In this work, we aim at a greater simplicity and a better efficiency, and propose the first divisible e-cash system which truly achieves constant-time spendings. The main novelty of our construction it that we get rid of the tree structure and so of its inherent downsides that we have described above. Our scheme enables users to reveal, by sending a constant number of elements, the sequence of V serial numbers $SN_j, \ldots, SN_{j+V-1}$, for any j and V of their choice (provided that $j + V - 1 \leq N$), even if V is not a power of 2. If we reconsider the previous example, this means that the user can now reveal, with a constant complexity, $SN_4, \ldots, SN_{4+V_2-1}$, for any value V_2.

We start from [10], which introduced the idea of a unique coin's structure, but make several changes to achieve constant-time spendings. The most important one is that we generate the public parameters in such a way that a same element can be used for spendings of any possible amount. This stands in sharp contrast with previous constructions where each element was associated with a node of the tree and so with a unique amount. More specifically, we use bilinear groups (*i.e.* a set of three cyclic groups $\mathbb{G}_1$, $\mathbb{G}_2$ and $\mathbb{G}_T$ of prime order p, along with a bilinear map $e : \mathbb{G}_1 \times \mathbb{G}_2 \rightarrow \mathbb{G}_T$) and set the N serial numbers of a coin as $\mathtt{SN}_j = e(s, \widetilde{g})^{x \cdot y^j}$, for $j = 1, \ldots, N$, where x is the coin's secret and $(y, s, \widetilde{g}) \in \mathbb{Z}_p \times \mathbb{G}_1 \times \mathbb{G}_2$ are global parameters of the system (not all public). These parameters additionally contain the elements $s_j = s^{y^j} \in \mathbb{G}_1$, for $j = 1, \ldots, N$ and $\widetilde{g}_j = \widetilde{g}^{y^j} \in \mathbb{G}_2$, for $j = 1, \ldots, N-1$. The relations between all these elements (namely the fact that they all depend on y) are at the heart of the efficiency of our construction but have a strong impact on anonymity. Indeed, (1) they could be used by an adversary to link transactions together and (2) they make the anonymity property much more difficult to prove.

Regarding (2), the problem comes from the fact that the reduction in the anonymity proof must take all these relations into account while being able to reveal the non-critical serial numbers $\{e(s, \widetilde{g})^{x \cdot y^j}\}_{j=1}^{j^*-1} \cup \{e(s, \widetilde{g})^{x \cdot y^j}\}_{j=j^*+V^*}^{N}$ and to insert the challenge serial numbers in $\{e(s, \widetilde{g})^{x \cdot y^j}\}_{j=j^*}^{j^*+V^*-1}$, for any $j^*, V^* \in [1, N]$. Nonetheless, we manage to prove the anonymity of our construction under an assumption which, albeit new and rather complex, does not depend on either j^* and V^*. We stress that the latter point was far from obvious. We also investigate in the full version [22] another way of generating the public parameters which allows to rely on a more classical assumption but at the cost of significant increase of the complexity (which nevertheless remains constant).

Regarding (1), we must pay attention to the way the serial numbers $\mathtt{SN}_i$, for $i = j, \ldots, j+V-1$, are revealed during a spending of value V. For example, we show in Sect. 4.1 that the solution from [10] (namely sending s_j^x) would trivially be insecure in our setting. The user will then rather send s_j^x encrypted in a way that prevents anyone from testing relations between spendings while ensuring that only a specific amount of serial numbers can be recovered from it.

Our **Spend** protocol is then quite efficient: it mostly consists in sending an encryption of s_j^x along with a proof of well-formedness. As illustrated on Fig. 3 of Sect. 5.2, it outperforms the state-of-the-art [11,20], whose complexity logarithmically depends on the spent value V. Since spending is the operation subject to the strongest time constraints (for example, it should be performed in less than 300 ms in a public transport system [19]) we argue that our construction makes all the features of e-cash systems much more accessible.

1.3   Organization

In Sect. 2, we recall some definitions and present the computational assumptions underlying the security of our scheme. Section 3 reviews the syntax of a divisible E-cash system along with security properties definitions. We provide in Sect. 4 a high level description of our construction and a more detailed presentation in Sect. 5. The latter additionally contains a comparison with state-of-the-art. Eventually, the security analysis is performed in Sect. 6.

Due to space limitations, the description of an alternative scheme which is less efficient, but whose anonymity relies on a quite classical assumption, is postponed to the full version [22]. The latter also presents an instantiation of our divisible e-cash system and contains a proof of hardness of our new assumption in the generic bilinear group model.

2 Preliminaries

2.1 Bilinear Groups

Bilinear groups are a set of three cyclic groups $\mathbb{G}_1$, $\mathbb{G}_2$, and $\mathbb{G}_T$ of prime order p, along with a bilinear map $e : \mathbb{G}_1 \times \mathbb{G}_2 \to \mathbb{G}_T$ with the following properties:

1. for all $g \in \mathbb{G}_1, \widetilde{g} \in \mathbb{G}_2$ and $a, b \in \mathbb{Z}_p$, $e(g^a, \widetilde{g}^b) = e(g, \widetilde{g})^{a \cdot b}$;
2. for $g \neq 1_{\mathbb{G}_1}$ and $\widetilde{g} \neq 1_{\mathbb{G}_2}$, $e(g, \widetilde{g}) \neq 1_{\mathbb{G}_T}$;
3. the map e is efficiently computable.

Galbraith et al. [16] defined three types of pairings: in Type-1, $\mathbb{G}_1 = \mathbb{G}_2$; in Type-2, $\mathbb{G}_1 \neq \mathbb{G}_2$ but there exists an efficient homomorphism $\phi : \mathbb{G}_2 \to \mathbb{G}_1$, while no efficient one exists in the other direction; in Type-3, $\mathbb{G}_1 \neq \mathbb{G}_2$ and no efficiently computable homomorphism exists between $\mathbb{G}_1$ and $\mathbb{G}_2$, in either direction.

Although Type-1 pairings were mostly used in the early-age of pairing-based cryptography, they have been gradually discarded in favour of Type-3 pairings. Indeed, the latter offer a better efficiency and are compatible with several computational assumptions, such as the SXDH and the $N - \mathsf{MXDH}'$ ones we present below, which do not hold in the former.

2.2 Computational Assumptions

Our security analysis makes use of the SXDH, $q - \mathsf{SDH}$ [6] and $N - \mathsf{BDHI}$ [5] assumptions which have been considered reasonable for Type-3 pairings.

Definition 1 (SXDH assumption). *For $k \in \{1, 2\}$, the DDH assumption is hard in $\mathbb{G}_k$ if, given $(g, g^x, g^y, g^z) \in \mathbb{G}_k^4$, it is hard to distinguish whether $z = x \cdot y$ or z is random. The SXDH assumption holds if DDH is hard in both $\mathbb{G}_1$ and $\mathbb{G}_2$*

Definition 2 ($q-\mathsf{SDH}$ assumption). *Given $(g, g^x, g^{x^2}, ..., g^{x^q}) \in \mathbb{G}_1$, it is hard to output a pair $(m, g^{\frac{1}{x+m}}) \in \mathbb{Z}_p \times \mathbb{G}_1$.*

Definition 3 ($N - \mathsf{BDHI}$ assumption). *Given $(\{g^{y^i}\}_{i=0}^N, \{\widetilde{g}^{y^i}\}_{i=0}^N) \in \mathbb{G}_1^{N+1} \times \mathbb{G}_2^{N+1}$, it is hard to compute $G = e(g, \widetilde{g})^{1/y} \in \mathbb{G}_T$.*

However, the anonymity of our construction relies on a new assumption, that we call $N - \mathsf{MXDH}'$. To provide more confidence in the latter, we first introduced a weaker variant, called $N - \mathsf{MXDH}$, that holds (as we prove it in the full version [22]) in the generic bilinear group model for Type-3 pairings and next prove that both variants are actually related as stated in Theorem 6.

Definition 4. $\forall N \in \mathbb{N}^*$, we define $C = N^3 - N^2$, $S = C + 1$, $E = N^2 - N$, $D = S + E$ and $P = D + C$, along with the following assumptions.

- **(N – MXDH assumption).** Given $\{(g^{\gamma^k})_{k=0}^P, (g^{\alpha \cdot \delta \cdot \gamma^{-k}})_{k=0}^E, (g^{\chi \cdot \gamma^k})_{k=D+1}^P,$
  $(g^{\alpha \cdot \gamma^{-k}}, g^{\chi \cdot \gamma^k/\alpha})_{k=0}^C\} \in \mathbb{G}_1^{P+E+3S+1}$, as well as $(\widetilde{g}^{\gamma^k}, \widetilde{g}^{\alpha \cdot \gamma^{-k}})_{k=0}^C \in \mathbb{G}_2^{2S}$ and
  an element $g^z \in \mathbb{G}_1$, it is hard to decide whether $z = \delta + \chi \gamma^D/\alpha$ or z is
  random.
- **(N – MXDH$'$ assumption).** Given $\{(g^{\gamma^k}, h^{\gamma^k})_{k=0}^P, (g^{\alpha \cdot \delta \cdot \gamma^{-k}}, h^{\alpha \cdot \delta \cdot \gamma^{-k}})_{k=0}^E,$
  $(g^{\chi \cdot \gamma^k}, h^{\chi \cdot \gamma^k})_{k=D+1}^P, (g^{\alpha \cdot \gamma^{-k}}, g^{\chi \cdot \gamma^k/\alpha}, h^{\chi \cdot \gamma^k/\alpha})_{k=0}^C\} \in \mathbb{G}_1^{2P+5S+2E+2}$, as well as
  $(\widetilde{g}^{\gamma^k}, \widetilde{g}^{\alpha \cdot \gamma^{-k}})_{k=0}^C \in \mathbb{G}_2^{2S}$ and a pair $(g^{z_1}, h^{z_2}) \in \mathbb{G}_1^2$, it is hard to decide whether
  $z_1 = z_2 = \delta + \chi \gamma^D/\alpha$ or (z_1, z_2) is random.

In the full version [22], we present another divisible e-cash protocol whose proof relies on a more classical assumption, but at the cost of larger public parameters and more complex (but still constant-size) protocols.

Regarding the N – MXDH assumption, the core idea is that the elements provided in an instance allow to compute the sets $\mathcal{S}_1 = \{e(g, \widetilde{g})^{\chi \cdot \gamma^k}\}_{k=0}^{S-1}$ and $\mathcal{S}_2 = \{e(g, \widetilde{g})^{\chi \cdot \gamma^k}\}_{k=D+1}^{P+C}$ but no element of $\mathcal{S}_3 = \{e(g, \widetilde{g})^{\chi \cdot \gamma^k}\}_{k=S}^D$. In the security proof, we will manage to force the V^* "challenge" serial numbers $\text{SN}_{j^*}, \ldots,$ $\text{SN}_{j^*+V^*-1}$ (where V^* is the amount of the challenge transaction, *i.e* the one where the adversary tries to identify the spender) to belong to $\mathcal{S}_3$ while ensuring that the other ones belong to $\mathcal{S}_1 \cup \mathcal{S}_2$ and so can be simulated. This requires a great flexibility from the assumption, since the number V^* and the index j^* are adaptively chosen by the adversary. If N is the amount of the divisible coin, this means that it must be possible, for any $(j^*, V^*) \in [1, N]^2$, to insert $j^* - 1$ serial numbers in $\mathcal{S}_1$, V^* in $\mathcal{S}_3$ and $N + 1 - (j^* + V^*)$ in $\mathcal{S}_2$, all of these sets being constant. We show in Sect. 6.3 that this is the case when the integers C, S, E, D and P are chosen as in the above definition.

Theorem 5. *The N – MXDH assumption holds in the generic bilinear group model: after q_G group and pairing oracle queries, no adversary can solve the N – MXDH problem with probability greater than $2N^3 \cdot (7N^3 + q_G)^2/p$.*

The proof, that is quite classical, can be found in the full version [22]. It is worthy to note that the integer N will represent the amount of a divisible coin and so will remain negligible compared to p. For example, a typical value for N is 1000 which allows users to withdraw coins of value 10\$, if the basic unit is the cent.

Theorem 6. *The N – MXDH$'$ assumption holds if both the DDH assumption in $\mathbb{G}_1$ and the N – MXDH assumption hold.*

Proof. Let $\mathcal{A}$ be an adversary against the N – MXDH$'$ assumption with a non-negligible advantage

$$\text{Adv}(\mathcal{A}) = |\Pr[\mathcal{A}(\mathcal{S}, g^z, h^z)|z = \delta + \chi \cdot \gamma^D/\alpha] - \Pr[\mathcal{A}(\mathcal{S}, g^{z_1}, h^{z_2})|z_1, z_2 \xleftarrow{\$} \mathbb{Z}_p]|,$$

where $\mathcal{S}$ refers to the set of all elements, except g^{z_1} and h^{z_2}, provided in an $N - \mathsf{MXDH}'$ challenge. We define hybrid distributions:

$$\mathsf{Adv}_1(\mathcal{A}) = |\Pr[\mathcal{A}(\mathcal{S}, g^z, h^z)|z = \delta + \chi \cdot \gamma^D/\alpha] - \Pr[\mathcal{A}(\mathcal{S}, g^z, h^z)|z \xleftarrow{\$} \mathbb{Z}_p]|$$

$$\mathsf{Adv}_2(\mathcal{A}) = |\Pr[\mathcal{A}(\mathcal{S}, g^z, h^z)|z \xleftarrow{\$} \mathbb{Z}_p] - \Pr[\mathcal{A}(\mathcal{S}, g^{z_1}, h^{z_2})|z_1, z_2 \xleftarrow{\$} \mathbb{Z}_p]|,$$

we then have: $\mathsf{Adv}(\mathcal{A}) \leq \mathsf{Adv}_1(\mathcal{A}) + \mathsf{Adv}_2(\mathcal{A})$.

Since $\mathsf{Adv}(\mathcal{A})$ is non-negligible, at least $\mathsf{Adv}_1(\mathcal{A})$ or $\mathsf{Adv}_2(\mathcal{A})$ is non-negligible.

In the former case, $\mathcal{A}$ can be used to break the $N - \mathsf{MXDH}$ assumption: from an $N - \mathsf{MXDH}$ instance, one can generate an $N - \mathsf{MXDH}'$ instance with a random scalar c and setting $h = g^c$. By running $\mathcal{A}$ on this instance, it gives a valid guess for it if and only if this would be a valid guess for the $N - \mathsf{MXDH}$ instance. The advantage is thus the same.

In the latter case, $\mathcal{A}$ can be used to break the DDH assumption in $\mathbb{G}_1$. Indeed, let (g, g^{z_1}, h, h^{z_2}) be a DDH challenge. One can compute a valid set $\mathcal{S}$ from g and h by using random (known) scalars α, γ and δ, and then run $\mathcal{A}$ on $(\mathcal{S}, g^{z_1}, h^{z_2})$. $\square$

One can note that the $N - \mathsf{MXDH}$ and $N - \mathsf{MXDH}'$ assumptions would actually be equivalent if the former implied the DDH assumption in $\mathbb{G}_1$ (which does not seem to be true). Nevertheless, this theorem shows that the $N - \mathsf{MXDH}'$ assumption is not much stronger than the $N - \mathsf{MXDH}$ one, since the DDH assumption can be considered reasonable.

2.3 Digital Signature Scheme

A digital signature scheme Σ is defined by three algorithms:

- the key generation algorithm $\Sigma.\mathsf{Keygen}$ which outputs a pair of signing and verification keys $(\mathsf{sk}, \mathsf{pk})$ – we assume that sk always contains pk;
- the signing algorithm $\Sigma.\mathsf{Sign}$ which, on input the signing key sk and a message m, outputs a signature σ;
- and the verification algorithm $\Sigma.\mathsf{Verify}$ which, on input m, σ and pk, outputs 1 if σ is a valid signature on m under pk, and 0 otherwise.

The standard security notion for a signature scheme is *existential unforgeability under chosen-message attacks* (EUF-CMA) [17] which means that it is hard, even given access to a signing oracle, to output a valid pair (m, σ) for a message m never asked to the oracle. In this paper we will also use variants, first with *selective chosen-message attacks* (SCMA) which restricts means for the adversary by limiting the oracle queries to be asked before having seen the key pk; or with *one-time signature* (OTS), which limits the adversary to ask one query only to the signing oracle; and with *strong unforgeability* (SUF) which relaxes the goal of the adversary which must now output a valid pair (m, σ) that was not returned by the signing oracle (a new signature for an already signed message is a valid forgery).

2.4   Groth-Sahai Proof Systems

In [18], Groth and Sahai proposed a non-interactive proof system, in the common reference string (CRS) model, which captures most of the relations for bilinear groups. There are two types of setup for the CRS that yield either perfect soundness or perfect witness indistinguishability, while being computationally indistinguishable (under the SXDH assumption, in our setting).

To prove that some variables satisfy a set of relations, the prover first commits to them (by using the elements from the CRS) and then computes one proof element per relation. Efficient non-interactive witness undistinguishable proofs are available for

- pairing-product equations, for variables $\{X_i\}_{i=1}^n \in \mathbb{G}_1$, $\{\widetilde{X}_i\}_{i=1}^n \in \mathbb{G}_2$ and constant $t_T \in \mathbb{G}_T$, $\{A_i\}_{i=1}^n \in \mathbb{G}_1$, $\{\widetilde{B}_i\}_{i=1}^n \in \mathbb{G}_2$, $\{a_{i,j}\}_{i,j=1}^n \in \mathbb{Z}_p$:

$$\prod_{i=1}^n e(A_i, \widetilde{X}_i) \prod_{i=1}^n e(X_i, \widetilde{B}_i) \prod_{i=1}^n \prod_{j=1}^n e(X_i, \widetilde{X}_j)^{a_{i,j}} = t_T;$$

- or multi-exponentiation equations, for variables $\{X_i\}_{i=1}^n \in \mathbb{G}_k$, $\{y_i\}_{i=1}^n \in \mathbb{Z}_p$ and constant $T \in \mathbb{G}_k$, $\{A_i\}_{i=1}^n \in \mathbb{G}_k$, $\{b_i\}_{i=1}^n \in \mathbb{Z}_p$, $\{a_{i,j}\}_{i,j=1}^n \in \mathbb{Z}_p$ for $k \in \{1, 2\}$:

$$\prod_{i=1}^n A_i^{y_i} \prod_{j=1}^n X_j^{b_j} \prod_{i=1}^n \prod_{j=1}^n X_j^{y_i \cdot a_{i,j}} = T.$$

Multi-exponentiation equations and pairing-product equations such that $t_T = 1_{\mathbb{G}_T}$ also admit non-interactive zero-knowledge (NIZK) proofs at no additional cost.

3   Divisible E-cash System

We recall in this section the syntax and the security model of a divisible e-cash system, as described in [10].

3.1   Syntax

A divisible e-cash system is defined by the following algorithms, that involve three types of entities, the bank $\mathcal{B}$, a user $\mathcal{U}$ and a merchant $\mathcal{M}$.

- Setup($1^k, N$): On input a security parameter k and an integer N, this probabilistic algorithm outputs the public parameters pp for divisible coins of global value N. We assume that pp are implicit to the other algorithms, and that they include k and N. They are also an implicit input to the adversary, we will then omit them.
- BKeygen(): This probabilistic algorithm executed by the bank $\mathcal{B}$ outputs a key pair (bsk, bpk). It also sets L as an empty list, that will store all deposited coins. We assume that bsk contains bpk.

- Keygen(): This probabilistic algorithm executed by a user $\mathcal{U}$ (resp. a merchant $\mathcal{M}$) outputs a key pair (usk, upk) (resp. (msk, mpk)). We assume that usk (resp. msk) contains upk (resp. mpk).
- Withdraw($\mathcal{B}$(bsk, upk), $\mathcal{U}$(usk, bpk)): This is an interactive protocol between the bank $\mathcal{B}$ and a user $\mathcal{U}$. At the end of this protocol, the user gets a divisible coin C of value N or outputs $\perp$ (in case of failure) while the bank stores the transcript Tr of the protocol execution or outputs $\perp$.
- Spend($\mathcal{U}$(usk, C, bpk, mpk, V), $\mathcal{M}$(msk, bpk, V)): This is an interactive protocol between a user $\mathcal{U}$ and a merchant $\mathcal{M}$. At the end of the protocol the merchant gets a master serial number Z of value V (the amount of the transaction they previously agreed on) along with a proof of validity Π or outputs $\perp$. $\mathcal{U}$ either updates C or outputs $\perp$.
- Deposit($\mathcal{M}$(msk, bpk, (V, Z, Π)), $\mathcal{B}$(bsk, L, mpk)): This is an interactive protocol between a merchant $\mathcal{M}$ and the bank $\mathcal{B}$. $\mathcal{B}$ first checks the validity of the transcript (V, Z, Π) and that it has not already been deposited. If one of these conditions is not fulfilled, then $\mathcal{B}$ aborts and outputs $\perp$. At the end of the protocol $\mathcal{B}$ stores the V serial numbers $\mathrm{SN}_1, \ldots, \mathrm{SN}_V$ derived from Z in L or returns a transcript (V', Z', Π') such that SN_i is also a serial number derived from Z', for some $i \in [1, V]$.
- Identify($(v_1, Z_1, \Pi_1), (v_2, Z_2, \Pi_2)$, bpk): On inputs two different valid transcripts (v_1, Z_1, Π_1) and (v_2, Z_2, Π_2), this deterministic algorithm outputs a user's public key upk if there is a collision between the serial numbers derived from Z_1 and from Z_2, and $\perp$ otherwise.

3.2 Security Model

Informally, to reconcile the interests of all parties, a divisible e-cash system should (1) ensure detection of double-spending/over-spending and identification of the defrauders, (2) preserve privacy of its users, (3) ensure that none of them can be falsely accused of fraud. Regarding the first point, we recall that reuse of money cannot be prevented (since digital coin can always be duplicated) but the guarantee of being identified should constitute a strong incentive not to cheat. The third point implicitly ensures that a coin can only be spent by its owner.

These security properties were formally defined as *traceability*, *anonymity* and *exculpability* by the authors of [10]. For consistency, we recall the associated security games, in Fig. 2, which make use of the following oracles:

- $\mathcal{O}$Add() is an oracle used by the adversary $\mathcal{A}$ to register a new honest user (resp. merchant). The oracle runs the Keygen algorithm, stores usk (resp. msk) and returns upk (resp. mpk) to $\mathcal{A}$. In this case, upk (resp. mpk) is said *honest*.
- $\mathcal{O}$Corrupt(upk/mpk) is an oracle used by $\mathcal{A}$ to corrupt an honest user (resp. merchant) whose public key is upk (resp. mpk). The oracle then returns the corresponding secret key usk (resp. msk) to $\mathcal{A}$ along with the secret values of every coin withdrawn by this user. From now on, upk (resp. mpk) is said *corrupted*.

$\text{Exp}_{\mathcal{A}}^{tra}(1^k, N)$ – Traceability Security Game

1. $pp \leftarrow \text{Setup}(1^k, N)$
2. $(\text{bsk}, \text{bpk}) \leftarrow \text{BKeygen}()$
3. $[(V_1, Z_1, \Pi_1), \ldots, (V_u, Z_u, \Pi_u)] \xleftarrow{\$} \mathcal{A}^{\mathcal{O}\text{Add}, \mathcal{O}\text{Corrupt}, \mathcal{O}\text{AddCorrupt}, \mathcal{O}\text{Withdraw}_{\mathcal{B}}, \mathcal{O}\text{Spend}}(\text{bpk})$
4. If $\sum_{i=1}^{u} V_i > m \cdot N$ and $\forall i \neq j, \text{Identify}((V_i, Z_i, \Pi_i), (V_j, Z_j, \Pi_j)) = \perp$,
   then return 1
5. Return 0

$\text{Exp}_{\mathcal{A}}^{excu}(1^k, N)$ – Exculpability Security Game

1. $pp \leftarrow \text{Setup}(1^k, N)$
2. $\text{bpk} \leftarrow \mathcal{A}()$
3. $[(V_1, Z_1, \Pi_1), (V_2, Z_2, \Pi_2)] \leftarrow \mathcal{A}^{\mathcal{O}\text{Add}, \mathcal{O}\text{Corrupt}, \mathcal{O}\text{AddCorrupt}, \mathcal{O}\text{Withdraw}_{\mathcal{U}}, \mathcal{O}\text{Spend}}()$
4. If $\text{Identify}((V_1, Z_1, \Pi_1), (V_2, Z_2, \Pi_2), \text{bpk}) = \text{upk}$ and upk not corrupted,
   then return 1
5. Return 0

$\text{Exp}_{\mathcal{A}}^{anon-b}(1^k, N)$ – Anonymity Security Game

1. $pp \leftarrow \text{Setup}(1^k, N)$
2. $\text{bpk} \leftarrow \mathcal{A}()$
3. $(V, \text{upk}_0, \text{upk}_1, \text{mpk}) \leftarrow \mathcal{A}^{\mathcal{O}\text{Add}, \mathcal{O}\text{Corrupt}, \mathcal{O}\text{AddCorrupt}, \mathcal{O}\text{Withdraw}_{\mathcal{U}}, \mathcal{O}\text{Spend}}()$
4. If upk_i is not registered for $i \in \{0, 1\}$, then return 0
5. If $c_{\text{upk}_i} > m_{\text{upk}_i} \cdot N - V$ for $i \in \{0, 1\}$, then return 0
6. $(V, Z, \Pi) \leftarrow \text{Spend}(C(\text{usk}_b, C, \text{mpk}, V), \mathcal{A}())$
7. $c_{\text{upk}_{1-b}} \leftarrow c_{\text{upk}_{1-b}} + V$
8. $b^* \leftarrow \mathcal{A}^{\mathcal{O}\text{Add}, \mathcal{O}\text{Corrupt}, \mathcal{O}\text{AddCorrupt}, \mathcal{O}\text{Withdraw}_{\mathcal{U}}, \mathcal{O}\text{Spend}}()$
9. If upk_i has been corrupted for $i \in \{0, 1\}$, then return 0
10. Return $(b = b^*)$

Fig. 2. Security games for anonymous divisible E-cash

- $\mathcal{O}\text{AddCorrupt}(\text{upk}/\text{mpk})$ is an oracle used by $\mathcal{A}$ to register a new corrupted user (resp. merchant) whose public key is upk (resp. mpk). In this case, upk (resp. mpk) is said *corrupted*. The adversary could use this oracle on a public key already registered (during a previous $\mathcal{O}\text{Add}$ query) but for simplicity, we do not consider such case as it will gain nothing more than using the $\mathcal{O}\text{Corrupt}$ oracle on the same public key.
- $\mathcal{O}\text{Withdraw}_{\mathcal{U}}(\text{upk})$ is an oracle that executes the user's side of the Withdraw protocol. This oracle will be used by $\mathcal{A}$ playing the role of the bank against the user with public key upk.
- $\mathcal{O}\text{Withdraw}_{\mathcal{B}}(\text{upk})$ is an oracle that executes the bank's side of the Withdraw protocol. This oracle will be used by $\mathcal{A}$ playing the role of a user whose public key is upk against the bank.
- $\mathcal{O}\text{Spend}(\text{upk}, V)$ is an oracle that executes the user's side of the Spend protocol for a value V. This oracle will be used by $\mathcal{A}$ playing the role of the merchant $\mathcal{M}$.

In the experiments, users are denoted by their public keys upk, c_{upk} denotes the amount already spent by user upk during $\mathcal{O}$Spend queries and m_{upk} the number of divisible coins that he has withdrawn. This means that the total amount available by a user upk is $m_{\mathsf{upk}} \cdot N$. The number of coins withdrawn by all users during an experiment is denoted by m.

In the anonymity security game, we differ a little bit from [10]: while c_{upk_b} is increased by V at step 6 during the Spend protocol, $c_{\mathsf{upk}_{1-b}}$ is also increased by V at step 7 to avoid $\mathcal{A}$ trivially wins by trying to make one of the two players to overspend money.

Let $\mathcal{A}$ be a probabilistic polynomial adversary. A divisible E-cash system is:

- *traceable* if $\mathsf{Succ}^{tra}(\mathcal{A}) = \Pr[\mathsf{Exp}_{\mathcal{A}}^{tra}(1^k, V) = 1]$ is negligible for any $\mathcal{A}$;
- *exculpable* if $\mathsf{Succ}^{excu}(\mathcal{A}) = \Pr[\mathsf{Exp}_{\mathcal{A}}^{excu}(1^k, V) = 1]$ is negligible for any $\mathcal{A}$;
- *anonymous* if $\mathsf{Adv}^{anon}(\mathcal{A}) = |\Pr[\mathsf{Exp}_{\mathcal{A}}^{anon-1}(1^k, V)] - \Pr[\mathsf{Exp}_{\mathcal{A}}^{anon-0}(1^k, V)]|$ is negligible for any $\mathcal{A}$.

4 Our Construction

4.1 High Level Description

Our Approach. We start from [10,11], in order to keep the quite easy and efficient withdrawal procedure (which mostly consists in certifying secret scalars). But we would like to improve on the spending procedure, and namely to get everything really constant (both in time and in size). Indeed, the user should be able to send only one information revealing the serial numbers, corresponding to the amount to be spent. But he should also be able to choose the sequence he discloses. For example, if he wants to pay a value V with a coin whose $(j-1)$ first serial numbers have already been used, then he should be able to send an element $\phi_{V,j}$ revealing the V serial numbers $\mathsf{SN}_j, \ldots, \mathsf{SN}_{j+V-1}$.

Description. All the serial numbers have the same structure, and are just customized by a random secret scalar x which constitutes the secret of the coin (our withdrawals are thus similar to the ones of [10,11]). More specifically, the public parameters contain the N values $s_j = s^{y^j}$ (for $j = 1, \ldots, N$), with a public group element $s \in \mathbb{G}_1$, and some secret scalar $y \xleftarrow{\$} \mathbb{Z}_p$: for any coin's secret x, this defines the serial numbers $\mathsf{SN}_j = e(s, \widetilde{g})^{x \cdot y^j}$.

The critical point is to find a way to construct the unique $\phi_{V,j}$ and to decide which elements should be provided in the public parameters pp to enable the bank to compute the serial numbers (all the expected ones, but not more).

First Attempt. One could define $\phi_{V,j}$ as s_j^x, in which case pp should contain the set $\mathcal{S} = \{\widetilde{g}_k = \widetilde{g}^{y^k}\}_{k=0}^{N-1}$. Indeed, a user with a fresh coin (*i.e.* never involved in a spending) must be able to spend a value N by revealing s_1^x and so the bank needs to know $\mathcal{S}$ to recover $\mathsf{SN}_i \leftarrow e(s_1^x, \widetilde{g}_{i-1})$, for $i = 1, \ldots, N$. One can note that $\mathcal{S}$ is actually enough for any spending, since, for any $j \in [1, N]$, recovering $\mathrm{SN}_j, \ldots, \mathrm{SN}_{j+V-1}$ from $\phi_{V,j}$ still requires elements from $\{\widetilde{g}_k\}_{k=0}^{V-1}$.

However, there is an obvious problem with this solution. Once $\mathcal{S}$ is published, nothing prevents the bank from computing more serial numbers than the amount V of the transaction. For example, if a user with a fresh coin spends a value 1, then the bank is still able to recover all the serial numbers from $\phi_{1,1} = s_1^x$.

Our Solution. It is therefore necessary to provide a way, for the user, to control the amount of serial numbers which can be recovered from the element s_j^x. To this end, we define N (one for each possible value $V \in [1, N]$) ElGamal [14] public keys $h_V = g^{a_V}$ and add the sets $\mathcal{S}_V = \{\widetilde{g}_k^{-a_V}\}_{k=0}^{V-1}$, for $V = 1, \ldots, N$, to pp. To reveal V serial numbers from s_j^x, the user now encrypts it under h_V, which defines $\phi_{V,j}$ as $(c_0 = g^r, c_1 = s_j^x \cdot h_V^r)$, for some $r \in \mathbb{Z}_p$. By using the elements from $\mathcal{S}_V$, the bank is still able to compute the V serial numbers since:

$$
\begin{aligned}
e(c_1, \widetilde{g}_k) \cdot e(c_0, \widetilde{g}_k^{-a_V}) &= e(s_j^x \cdot h_V^r, \widetilde{g}_k) \cdot e(g^r, \widetilde{g}_k^{-a_V}) \\
&= e(s_j^x, \widetilde{g}_k) \cdot e(h_V^r, \widetilde{g}_k) \cdot e(g^r, \widetilde{g}_k^{-a_V}) \\
&= e(s^{y^j \cdot x}, \widetilde{g}^{y^k}) \cdot e(g^{a_V \cdot r}, \widetilde{g}_k) \cdot e(g^{-a_V \cdot r}, \widetilde{g}_k) \\
&= e(s, \widetilde{g})^{x \cdot y^{j+k}} = \mathrm{SN}_{j+k},
\end{aligned}
$$

for $k = 0, \ldots, V - 1$. But now, it can no longer derive additional serial numbers because $\mathcal{S}_V$ only contains V elements. Moreover, the elements of the other sets $\mathcal{S}_{V'}$, for $V' \neq V$, are useless since they correspond to other public keys.

One can note that ElGamal encryption was also used in [11] but to prevent an adversary from testing relations across the different levels of the tree. We here use it to enable a total control on the amount of revealed serial numbers. A same element s_j^x can thus be involved in spendings of different values, which is the basis of the efficiency and the flexibility of our scheme.

Security Analysis. An interesting feature of our solution is that the bank does not need to know the index j to compute the serial numbers. This is due to the fact that $\mathrm{SN}_{j+1} = \mathrm{SN}_j^y$, for all $j \in [1, N-1]$ and so that the computation of a serial number is independent from j. Therefore, a spending does not reveal any additional information about the coin (such as the spent part) and so achieves the strongest notion of anonymity.

However, this has implications on the security analysis, since one must take into account the relations between the different serial numbers. Anonymity will then rely on a new assumption, called $N - \mathrm{MXDH}'$, which seems reasonable for Type-3 pairings, as we explain in Sect. 2.2.

Validity of a Transaction. Serial numbers are central to the detection of double-spending and so to ensure the traceability of the scheme. It is therefore necessary, during a spending of value V, to force the user to send a valid element $\phi_{V,j}$, by requesting a proof that the latter is well-formed. The user must then prove that (1) $\phi_{V,j}$ is an ElGamal encryption of some s_j^x under h_V (which is known since it corresponds to the spent amount), where (2) x has been certified, and (3) s_j is a valid parameter for a transaction of value V. The first two statements can easily be handled using the Groth-Sahai [18] methodology, but this is not the case for the third one. Indeed, as we explained, s_j (and so the index j) cannot be revealed unless breaking the anonymity of the scheme which would only achieve a weaker unlinkability property (as defined in [10]).

We could use the solution from [10] which consists in certifying each s_j under the public keys $\mathsf{pk}^1, \ldots, \mathsf{pk}^{N-j+1}$ and to prove that the s_j to be used is certified under the public key pk^V. However, such a solution is quite efficient for tree-based schemes where each s_j is associated with a unique node and so with a single amount, but not for our scheme where s_j can be involved in any transaction of value V such that $V \in [1, N - j + 1]$. This would dramatically increase the bank's public key since it would contain about $N^2/2$ certificates.

While our public parameters will be of quadratic size, because of the sets $\mathcal{S}_V$, we hope the part necessary to the user to be at most linear in N. We will then use another solution which exploits the relation $e(s_j, \widetilde{g}_{V-1}) = e(s_{j+V-1}, \widetilde{g})$. To prove that $j \leq N - V + 1$, the user will thus simply prove that there is some s_k, for $k \in [1, N]$, such that $e(s_j, \widetilde{g}_{V-1}) = e(s_k, \widetilde{g})$. This can be done efficiently if a certificate on each s_k is provided by the bank. One may note that this proof only ensures that $j \leq N - V + 1$ and not that $j \geq 1$. However, we will show, in the security analysis, that a user is unlikely to produce a proof for an element $s_j \notin \{s_1, \ldots, s_N\}$.

Security Tags. Detection of double-spending may not be sufficient to deter users from cheating. To prevent frauds it is also necessary to provide a way to identify dishonest users. Since we aim at achieving the anonymity property, such an identification cannot rely on some trusted entity with the power of tracing any user of the system. We will then use the standard technique of security tags which allows to recover the spender's identity from any pair of transactions detected as a double-spending. Similarly to the constructions of [10,11], we will add to the public parameters the elements t_j such that, $\forall j \in [1, N]$, $t_j = s_j^c$ for some $c \in \mathbb{Z}_p$ and define, for a transaction involving $\phi_{V,j}$, the security tag as $\psi_{V,j} = (g^{r'}, \mathsf{upk}^R \cdot t_j^x \cdot h_V^{r'})$ where upk is the user's public key and R is some public information related to the transaction. As we prove below, such a tag hides the identity of a spender as long as he does not double-spend its coin.

Remark 7. Divisible e-cash systems do not usually specify the way the coin should be spent. As explained above, our construction is the first one to allow sequential spendings, contrarily to tree-based construction where the coins may contain several holes (see Sect. 1.1). Therefore, for sake of simplicity, we assume in the following that the user sequentially reveals the serial numbers and so we associate each coin to an index j. The latter means that $\mathsf{SN}_1, \ldots, \mathsf{SN}_{j-1}$ have already been revealed and that the next spending of value V will reveal $\mathsf{SN}_j, \ldots, \mathsf{SN}_{j+V-1}$.

However, we stress that the user is free to spend the coin as he wants. The only constraint is that two spendings must not reveal the same serial numbers, otherwise the user will be accused of double-spending.

4.2 Setup

Public Parameters. Let $(p, \mathbb{G}_1, \mathbb{G}_2, \mathbb{G}_T, e)$ be the description of bilinear groups of prime order p, elements g, h, u_1, u_2, w be generators of $\mathbb{G}_1$, $\widetilde{g}$ be a generator of $\mathbb{G}_2$, and H be collision-resistant hash function onto $\mathbb{Z}_p$. A trusted authority generates $(z, y) \xleftarrow{\$} \mathbb{Z}_p^2$ and, for $i = 1, \ldots, N$ (where N is the value of the coin), $a_i \xleftarrow{\$} \mathbb{Z}_p$. It then computes the public parameters as follows:

- $(s, t) \leftarrow (g^z, h^z)$;
- $(s_j, t_j) \leftarrow (s^{y^j}, t^{y^j})$, for $j = 1, \ldots, N$;
- $\widetilde{g}_k \leftarrow \widetilde{g}^{y^k}$, for $k = 0, \ldots, N - 1$;
- $h_i \leftarrow g^{a_i}$, for $i = 1, \ldots, N$;
- $\widetilde{h}_{i,k} \leftarrow \widetilde{g}^{-a_i \cdot y^k}$, for $i = 1, \ldots, N$ and $k = 0, \ldots, i - 1$.

These parameters can also be cooperatively generated by a set of users and the bank, in a way similar to the one described in [10]. The point is that none of these entities should know the scalars $(a_i)_i$, y or z.

We divide the public parameters pp into two parts, $pp_{\mathcal{U}} \leftarrow \{g, h, u_1, u_2, w, H, \{h_i\}_{i=1}^N, \{(s_j, t_j)\}_{j=1}^N\}$ and $pp_{\mathcal{B}} \leftarrow \{\{\widetilde{g}_k\}_{k=0}^{N-1}, \{(\widetilde{h}_{i,k})_{k=0}^{i-1}\}_{i=1}^N\}$. The former contains the elements necessary to all the entities of the system whereas the latter contains the elements only useful to the bank during the Deposit protocol. We therefore assume that the users and the merchants only store $pp_{\mathcal{U}}$ and discard $pp_{\mathcal{B}}$. Note that the former is linear in N, while the latter is quadratic.

Our protocols make use of NIZK and NIWI proofs for multi-exponentiations and pairing-product equations which are covered by the Groth-Sahai proof system [18]. We then add to $pp_{\mathcal{U}}$ the description of a CRS for the perfect soundness setting and of a one-time signature scheme Σ_{ots} (e.g. the one from [6]).

5   Our Divisible E-cash System

In this section, we provide an extended description of our new protocol and then discuss its efficiency. We describe a concrete instantiation in the full version [22].

5.1   The Protocol

- Keygen(): Each user (resp. merchant) selects a random usk $\leftarrow \mathbb{Z}_p$ (resp. msk) and gets upk $\leftarrow g^{\mathsf{usk}}$ (resp. mpk $\leftarrow g^{\mathsf{msk}}$). In the following, we assume that upk (resp. mpk) is public, meaning that anyone can get an authentic copy of it.

- BKeygen(): The bank has two important roles to play. It must (1) deliver new coins to users during withdrawals and (2) control the transactions to detect double-spendings and identify the defrauders.

  The first point will require a signature scheme Σ_1 whose message space is $\mathbb{G}_1^2$ to certify the secret values associated with the withdrawn coins. We can therefore use the construction from [1] which is optimal in type-3 bilinear groups.

  The second point relies on the proof of validity of the elements $\phi_{V,j}$ sent during a transaction. As explained above, such a proof requires that the elements s_k are certified, for $k = 1, \ldots, N$. For the same reasons, their dual elements t_k must be certified too. It is therefore necessary to select a structure-preserving signature scheme Σ_0 whose message space is $\mathbb{G}_1^2$. We can then still choose the one from [1] but our security analysis shows that a scheme achieving a weaker security notion would be enough.

  Once the schemes Σ_0 and Σ_1 are selected, the bank generates $(\mathsf{sk}_0, \mathsf{pk}_0) \leftarrow \Sigma_0.\mathsf{Keygen}(pp)$ and $(\mathsf{sk}_1, \mathsf{pk}_1) \leftarrow \Sigma_1.\mathsf{Keygen}(pp)$. It then computes $\tau_j \leftarrow \Sigma_0.\mathsf{Sign}(\mathsf{sk}_0, (s_j, t_j))$ for all $j \in 1, \ldots, N$ and sets $\mathsf{bsk} \leftarrow \mathsf{sk}_1$ and $\mathsf{bpk} \leftarrow \{\mathsf{pk}_0, \mathsf{pk}_1, \tau_1, \ldots, \tau_N\}$.
- Withdraw($\mathcal{B}(\mathsf{bsk}, \mathsf{upk}), \mathcal{U}(\mathsf{usk}, \mathsf{bpk})$): As explained in the previous section, each coin is associated with a random scalar x, which implicitly defines its serial numbers as $\mathsf{SN}_k = e(s_j^x, \tilde{g}) = e(s, \tilde{g})^{x \cdot y^k}$, for $k = 1, \ldots, N$. Delivering a new coin thus essentially consists in certifying this scalar x. However, for security reasons, it is necessary to bind the latter with the identity of its owner. Indeed, if this coin is double-spent, it must be possible to identify the user who has withdrawn it. This could be done by certifying the pair $(x, \mathsf{usk}) \in \mathbb{Z}_p^2$ (without revealing them), using for example the scheme from [7], but, in the standard model, the bank will rather certify the pair $(u_1^{\mathsf{usk}}, u_2^x) \in \mathbb{G}_1^2$. This is due to the fact that scalars cannot be efficiently extracted from Groth-Sahai proofs, contrarily to group elements in $\mathbb{G}_1$.

  In practice, the user computes u_1^{usk} and $u_2^{x_1}$ for some random $x_1 \xleftarrow{\$} \mathbb{Z}_p$ and sends them to the bank along with upk. He then proves knowledge of x_1 and usk in a zero-knowledge way (using, for example, the Schnorr's interactive protocol [23]). If the bank accepts the proof, it generates a random $x_2 \xleftarrow{\$} \mathbb{Z}_p$, computes $u \xleftarrow{\$} u_2^{x_1} \cdot u_2^{x_2}$ and $\sigma \leftarrow \Sigma_1.\mathsf{Sign}(\mathsf{sk}_1, (u_1^{\mathsf{usk}}, u))$ (unless u was used in a previous withdrawal) and returns σ and x_2 to the user. The latter then sets the coin's secret $x \leftarrow x_1 + x_2$ and coin state $C \leftarrow (x, \sigma, 1)$: the last element of C is the index of the next serial number to be used. Hence the remaining amount on the coin is $N + 1$ minus this index.

  Informally, the cooperative generation of the scalar x allows us to exclude (with overwhelming probability) false positives, *i.e.* a collision in the list L of serial numbers maintained by the bank which would not be due to an actual double-spending. We refer to Remark 8 for more details.
- Spend($\mathcal{U}(\mathsf{usk}, C, \mathsf{bpk}, \mathsf{mpk}, V), \mathcal{M}(\mathsf{msk}, \mathsf{bpk}, V)$): Let $C = (x, \sigma, j)$ be the coin the user wishes to spend. The latter selects two random scalars $(r_1, r_2) \xleftarrow{\$} \mathbb{Z}_p^2$ and computes $R \leftarrow H(info)$, $\phi_{V,j} \leftarrow (g^{r_1}, s_j^x \cdot h_V^{r_1})$ and $\psi_{V,j} \leftarrow (g^{r_2}, \mathsf{upk}^R \cdot t_j^x \cdot h_V^{r_2})$,

where *info* is some information related to the transaction (such as the date, the amount, the merchant's public key,...).

Now, he must prove that (1) his coin C is valid and (2) that the elements $\phi_{V,j}$ and $\psi_{V,j}$ are well-formed. The first point consists in proving knowledge of a valid signature σ on $(u_1^{\mathsf{usk}}, u_2^x)$, whereas the second point requires to prove knowledge of τ_{j+V-1} on (s_{j+V-1}, t_{j+V-1}). This can be efficiently done in the standard model by using the Groth-Sahai methodology [18].

Unfortunately, the resulting proofs can be re-randomized which enables a dishonest merchant to deposit several versions of the same transcript. To prevent such a randomization, the user generates a one-time signature key pair $(\mathsf{sk}_{ots}, \mathsf{pk}_{ots})$ which will be used to sign the whole transcript. To ensure that only the spender can produce this signature, the public key pk_{ots} will be certified into $\mu \leftarrow w^{\frac{1}{\mathsf{usk}+H(\mathsf{pk}_{ots})}}$. One may note that these problems do not arise in the ROM since the proofs would be simply converted into a (non-randomizable) signature of knowledge by using the Fiat-Shamir heuristic [15].

More formally, once the user has computed $\phi_{V,j}$, $\psi_{V,j}$ and μ, he computes Groth-Sahai commitments to $\mathsf{usk}, x, r_1, r_2, s_j, t_j, s_{j+V-1}, t_{j+V-1}, \tau_{j+V-1}, \sigma, \mu$, $U_1 = u_1^{\mathsf{usk}}$ and $U_2 = u_2^x$. He next provides:

1. a NIZK proof π that the committed values satisfy:

$$\phi_{V,j} = (g^{r_1}, s_j^x \cdot h_V^{r_1}) \qquad \wedge \qquad \psi_{V,j} = (g^{r_2}, (g^R)^{\mathsf{usk}} \cdot t_j^x \cdot h_V^{r_2})$$
$$\wedge \quad U_2 = u_2^x \quad \wedge \quad U_1 = u_1^{\mathsf{usk}} \quad \wedge \quad \mu^{(\mathsf{usk}+H(\mathsf{pk}_{ots}))} = w$$
$$\wedge \quad e(s_j, \widetilde{g}_{V-1}) = e(s_{j+V-1}, \widetilde{g}) \qquad \wedge \qquad e(t_j, \widetilde{g}_{V-1}) = e(t_{j+V-1}, \widetilde{g})$$

2. a NIWI proof π' that the committed values satisfy:

$$1 = \Sigma_0.\mathtt{Verify}(\mathsf{pk}_0, (s_{j+V-1}, t_{j+V-1}), \tau_{j+V-1})$$
$$\wedge \quad 1 = \Sigma_1.\mathtt{Verify}(\mathsf{pk}_1, (U_1, U_2), \sigma).$$

Finally, he computes $\eta \leftarrow \Sigma_{ots}.\mathtt{Sign}(\mathsf{sk}_{ots}, H(R||\phi_{V,j}||\psi_{V,j}||\pi||\pi'))$ and sends it to $\mathcal{M}$ along with $\mathsf{pk}_{ots}, \phi_{V,j}, \psi_{V,j}, \pi$ and π'.

The merchant accepts if the proofs and the signatures are correct in which case he stores $(V, Z, \Pi) \leftarrow (V, (\phi_{V,j}, \psi_{V,j}), (\pi, \pi', \mathsf{pk}_{ots}, \eta))$ while the user updates its coin $C \leftarrow (x, \sigma, j + V)$.

– $\mathtt{Deposit}(\mathcal{M}(\mathsf{msk}, \mathsf{bpk}, (V, Z, \Pi)), \mathcal{B}(\mathsf{bsk}, L, \mathsf{mpk}))$: When a transcript is deposited by a merchant, the bank parses it as $(V, (\phi_{V,j}, \psi_{V,j}), (\pi, \pi', \mathsf{pk}_{ots}, \eta))$ and checks its validity (in the same way as the merchant did during the $\mathtt{Spend}$ protocol). $\mathcal{B}$ also verifies that it does not already exist in its database. If everything is correct, $\mathcal{B}$ derives the serial numbers from $\phi_{V,j} = (\phi_{V,j}[1], \phi_{V,j}[2])$ by computing $\mathtt{SN}_k \leftarrow e(\phi_{V,j}[2], \widetilde{g}_k) \cdot e(\phi_{V,j}[1], \widetilde{h}_{V,k})$, for $k = 0, \dots, V - 1$. If none of these serial numbers is in L, the bank adds them to this list and stores the associated transcript. Else, there is at least one $\mathtt{SN}' \in L$ (associated with a transcript (V', Z', Π')) and one $k^* \in [0, V - 1]$ such that $\mathtt{SN}' = \mathtt{SN}_{k^*}$. The bank then outputs the two transcripts (V, Z, Π) and (V', Z', Π') as a proof of a double-spending.

– $\mathtt{Identify}((V_1, Z_1, \Pi_1), (V_2, Z_2, \Pi_2), \mathsf{bpk})$: The first step before identifying a double-spender is to check the validity of both transcripts and that there is a collision between their serial numbers, $i.e.$ there are $k_1 \in [0, V_1 - 1]$ and $k_2 \in [0, V_2 - 1]$ such that:

$$\mathsf{SN}_{k_1} = e(\phi_{V_1, j_1}[2], \tilde{g}_{k_1}) \cdot e(\phi_{V_1, j_1}[1], \tilde{h}_{V_1, k_1})$$
$$= e(\phi_{V_2, j_2}[2], \tilde{g}_{k_2}) \cdot e(\phi_{V_2, j_2}[1], \tilde{h}_{V_2, k_2}) = \mathsf{SN}_{k_2}$$

Let T_b be $e(\psi_{V_b, j_b}[2], \tilde{g}_{k_b}) \cdot e(\psi_{V_b, j_b}[1], \tilde{h}_{V_b, k_b})$, for $b \in \{1, 2\}$. The algorithm checks, for each registered public key upk_i, whether $T_1 \cdot T_2^{-1} = e(\mathsf{upk}_i, \tilde{g}_{k_1}^{R_1} \cdot \tilde{g}_{k_2}^{-R_2})$ until it gets a match. It then returns the corresponding key upk^* (or $\perp$ if the previous equality does not hold for any upk_i), allowing anyone to verify, without the linear cost in the number of users, that the identification is correct.

Remark 8. A collision in the list L means that two transcripts $(V_1, Z_1, \Pi_1) \neq (V_2, Z_2, \Pi_2)$ lead to a same serial number SN. Let $Z_b = (\phi_{V_b, j_b}, \psi_{V_b, j_b})$, for $b \in \{1, 2\}$, the soundness of the NIZK proofs produced by the users during the spendings implies that:

$$e(\phi_{V_1, j_1}[2], \tilde{g}_{k_1}) \cdot e(\phi_{V_1, j_1}[1], \tilde{h}_{V_1, k_1}) = e(\mathsf{s}_1, \tilde{g}_{k_1})^{x_1} = \mathsf{SN}$$
$$= e(\mathsf{s}_2, \tilde{g}_{k_2})^{x_2} = e(\phi_{V_2, j_2}[2], \tilde{g}_{k_2}) \cdot e(\phi_{V_2, j_2}[1], \tilde{h}_{V_2, k_2})$$

for some $k_1 \in [0, V_1 - 1]$, $k_2 \in [0, V_2 - 1]$ and certified scalars x_1 and x_2, where the elements s_1 and s_2 verify, with $\ell_1, \ell_2 \in [1, N]$:

$$e(\mathsf{s}_1, \tilde{g}_{V_1 - 1}) = e(\mathsf{s}_{\ell_1}, \tilde{g}) \text{ and } e(\mathsf{s}_2, \tilde{g}_{V_2 - 1}) = e(\mathsf{s}_{\ell_2}, \tilde{g}).$$

Therefore, we have, for $b \in \{1, 2\}$, $e(\mathsf{s}_b, \tilde{g}) = e(\mathsf{s}, \tilde{g})^{y^{\ell_b - V_b + 1}}$, and so

$$\mathsf{SN} = e(\mathsf{s}, \tilde{g})^{x_1 \cdot y^{\ell_1 - V_1 + 1 + k_1}} = e(\mathsf{s}, \tilde{g})^{x_2 \cdot y^{\ell_2 - V_2 + 1 + k_2}}$$

A collision thus implies that $x_1 \cdot x_2^{-1} = y^{\ell_2 - \ell_1 + V_1 - V_2 + k_2 - k_1}$. Since x_1 and x_2 are randomly (and cooperatively) chosen, without knowledge of y, a collision for $x_1 \neq x_2$ will only occur with negligible probability. We can then assume that these scalars are equal and so that the collision in L is due to a double-spending.

Remark 9. The soundness of the proofs implies that the $\mathtt{Identify}$ algorithm will output, with overwhelming probability, an identity upk each time a collision is found in L. Indeed, let $(V_1, Z_1, \Pi_1), (V_2, Z_2, \Pi_2)$ be the two involved transcripts, and k_1, k_2 such that:

$$\mathsf{SN}_{k_1} = e(\phi_{V_1, j_1}[2], \tilde{g}_{k_1}) \cdot e(\phi_{V_1, j_1}[1], \tilde{h}_{V_1, k_1})$$
$$= e(\phi_{V_2, j_2}[2], \tilde{g}_{k_2}) \cdot e(\phi_{V_2, j_2}[1], \tilde{h}_{V_2, k_2}) = \mathsf{SN}_{k_2}$$

For $b \in \{1, 2\}$, if Π_b is sound, then $(\phi_{V_b, j_b}[1], \phi_{V_b, j_b}[2]) = (g^{r_b}, s_{j_b}^{x_b} \cdot h_{V_b}^{r_b})$ for some $r_b \in \mathbb{Z}_p$ and so:

$$\mathsf{SN}_{k_1} = e(s_{j_1}^{x_1}, \widetilde{g}_{k_1}) = e(s_{j_2}^{x_2}, \widetilde{g}_{k_2}) = \mathsf{SN}_{k_2} \tag{1}$$

For the same reasons, $T_b = e(\psi_{V_b, j_b}[2], \widetilde{g}_{k_b}) \cdot e(\psi_{V_b, j_b}[1], \widetilde{h}_{V_b, k_b}) = e(\mathsf{upk}_b^{R_b} \cdot t_{j_b}^{x_b}, \widetilde{g}_{k_b})$, for $b \in \{1, 2\}$.

As explained in the previous remark, the equality (1) is unlikely to hold for different scalars x_1 and x_2. We may then assume that $x_1 = x_2 = x$ and so that $\mathsf{upk}_1 = \mathsf{upk}_2 = \mathsf{upk}$ since the bank verifies, during a withdrawal, that the same scalar x (or equivalently the same public value $u = u_2^x$) is not used by two different users.

The relation (1) also implies that $e(t_{j_1}^x, \widetilde{g}_{k_1}) = e(t_{j_2}^x, \widetilde{g}_{k_2})$ and so that:

$$T_1 \cdot T_2^{-1} = e(\mathsf{upk}^{R_1}, \widetilde{g}_{k_1}) \cdot e(\mathsf{upk}^{R_2}, \widetilde{g}_{k_2})^{-1} = e(\mathsf{upk}, \widetilde{g}_{k_1}^{R_1} \cdot \widetilde{g}_{k_2}^{-R_2}).$$

The defrauder's identity upk will then be returned by the algorithm $\mathtt{Identify}$, unless $\widetilde{g}_{k_1}^{R_1} \cdot \widetilde{g}_{k_2}^{-R_2} = 1_{\mathbb{G}_2}$. However, such an equality is very unlikely for distinct k_1 and k_2 (for the same reasons as the ones given in Remark 8) but also for $k_1 = k_2$ since it would imply that $R_1 = R_2$ and so a collision on the hash function H.

The security of our divisible E-Cash system is stated by the following theorems, whose proofs can be found in the next section.

Theorem 10. *In the standard model, our divisible E-Cash system is **traceable** under the $N - \mathsf{BDHI}$ assumption if Σ_0 is an EUF-SCMA signature scheme, Σ_1 is an EUF-CMA signature scheme, and H is a collision-resistant hash function.*

Theorem 11. *Let q be a bound on the number of $\mathcal{OSpend}$ queries made by the adversary. In the standard model, our divisible E-Cash system achieves the **exculpability property** under the $q - \mathsf{SDH}$ assumption if Σ_{ots} is a SUF-OTS signature scheme, and H is a collision-resistant hash function.*

Theorem 12. *In the standard model, our divisible E-Cash system is **anonymous** under the SXDH and the $N - \mathsf{MXDH}'$ assumptions.*

Remark 13. A downside of our construction is that its anonymity relies on a quite complex assumption. This is due to the fact that most elements of the public parameters are related, which must be taken into account by the assumption. As we explain in the full version [22], we can rely on a more conventional assumption (while keeping the constant size property) by generating these parameters independently. Unfortunately, this has a strong impact on the efficiency of the protocol. Such a solution must then be considered as a tradeoff between efficiency and security assumption.

5.2   Efficiency

We compare in Fig. 3, the efficiency of our construction with the state-of-the-art, and namely Martens [20] (which improves the construction of [9]) and

Schemes	Martens [20]	Canard *et al* [11]	Our work
Parameters			
$pp_{\mathcal{U}} \cup$ bpk	$(N+2)\ \mathbb{G}_1 + N\ \mathbb{G}_2$ + pk	$(4N+n+4)\ \mathbb{G}_1$ + 2 pk + N |Sign|	$(3N+5)\ \mathbb{G}_1$ + 2 pk + N |Sign|
$pp_{\mathcal{B}}$	-	$(4N-1)\ \mathbb{G}_2$	$(N^2+3N+2)/2\ \mathbb{G}_2$
Withdraw Protocol			
Computations	$\mathsf{ME}_{\mathbb{G}_1}(N)$ + Sign	$2\ \mathsf{E}_{\mathbb{G}_1}$ + Sign	$2\ \mathsf{E}_{\mathbb{G}_1}$ + Sign
Coin Size	$2N\ \mathbb{Z}_p + \mathbb{G}_1 + $|Sign|	$2\ \mathbb{Z}_p + $|Sign|	$2\ \mathbb{Z}_p + $|Sign|
Spend Protocol			
Computations	$(1+2v)\ \mathsf{E}_{\mathbb{G}_1}$ $+ v\ \mathsf{ME}_{\mathbb{G}_1}(N-V)$ $+ v\ \mathsf{ME}_{\mathbb{G}_2}(V)$ + Sign $+ $ NIZK$\{(2v+2)\ \mathsf{E}_{\mathbb{G}_1}$ $+ v\ \mathsf{P}$ + Sign$\}$	$(1+7v)\ \mathsf{E}_{\mathbb{G}_1}$ + Sign $+ $ NIZK$\{(3+4v)\ \mathsf{E}_{\mathbb{G}_1}$ $+ 2v\ \mathsf{P}$ $+ (1+v)$ Sign$\}$	$8\ \mathsf{E}_{\mathbb{G}_1}$ + Sign $+ $ NIZK$\{7\ \mathsf{E}_{\mathbb{G}_1} + 2\ \mathsf{P}$ $+ 2$ Sign$\}$
Communications	$2v\ \mathbb{G}_1 + $|Sign| $+ $|NIZK|	$4v\ \mathbb{G}_1 + $|Sign| $+ $|NIZK|	$4\ \mathbb{G}_1 + $|Sign| $+ $|NIZK|
Deposit Protocol			
Computations	$2V\ \mathsf{E}_{\mathbb{G}_1}$	$2V\ \mathsf{P}$	$2V\ \mathsf{P}$
Communications	$V\ SN + $|Spend|	$V\ SN + $|Spend|	$V\ SN + $|Spend|

Fig. 3. Efficiency comparison between related works and our construction for coins of value N and Spend and Deposit of value V ($V \leq N$). The computation and communication complexities are given from the user's point of view. (n denotes the smallest integer such that $N \leq 2^n$ and v the Hamming weight of V. $\mathsf{E}_{\mathbb{G}}$ refers to an exponentiation in $\mathbb{G}$, $\mathsf{ME}_{\mathbb{G}}(m)$ to a multi-exponentiation with m different bases in $\mathbb{G}$, P to a pairing computation, and Sign to the cost of the signing protocol whose public key is pk. NIZK$\{\mathsf{E}_{\mathbb{G}}\}$ denotes the cost of a NIZK proof of a multi-exponentiation equation in $\mathbb{G}$, NIZK$\{\mathsf{P}\}$ the one of a pairing-product equation, and NIZK$\{$Sign$\}$ the one of a valid signature. Finally, SN refers to the size of a serial number and \|Spend\| to the size of the transcript of the Spend protocol.)

Canard *et al.* [11]. One can note that our table differs from those provided in these papers. This is mostly due to the fact that they only describe the most favorable case, where the spent value V is a power of 2. However, in real life, such an event is quite unlikely. Most of the time, the users of such systems will then have to write $V = \sum b_i \cdot 2^i$, for $b_i \in \{0,1\}$ and repeat the Spend protocol for each $b_i = 1$. Our description therefore considers the Hamming weight v of V (*i.e.* the number of b_i such that $b_i = 1$) but, for a proper comparison, also takes into account the possible optimisations of batch spendings (for example proving that the user's secret is certified can be done only once).

Another difference with [20] comes from the fact that the author considered that "a multi-base exponentiation takes a similar time as a single-base exponentiation". Although some works (*e.g.* [4]) have shown that an N-base exponentiation can be done more efficiently that N single-base exponentiations, considering that the cost of the former is equivalent to the one of a single exponentiation is a strong assumption, in particular when N can be greater than 1000 (if the coin's value is greater than 10\$). Our table therefore distinguishes multi-base exponentiations from single ones.

An important feature for an electronic payment system is the efficiency of its Spend protocol. This is indeed the one subject to the strongest time constraints. For example, public transport services require that payments should be performed in less than 300ms [19], to avoid congestion in front of turnstiles. From this perspective, our scheme is the most effective one and, above all, is the first one to achieve constant time (and size) spendings, no matter which value is spent. Moreover, our divisible E-Cash system offers the same efficiency as the withdrawals of [11], while keeping a reasonable size for the parameters $pp_{\mathcal{U}}$. Indeed, in our protocol, $pp_{\mathcal{U}}$ just requires 230 KBytes of storage space for $N = 1024$ (defining the coin's value as 10.24\$) if Barreto-Naehrig curves [3] are used to instantiate the bilinear groups. For the same settings, pp_U amounts to 263 KBytes for [11] and 98 KBytes for [20].

From the bank's point of view, the downside of our scheme is the additional parameters pp_B that the bank must store, and they amount to 33 MBytes, but it should not be a problem for this entity. As for the other schemes, each deposit of a value V requires to store V serial numbers whose size can be adjusted by using an appropriate hash function (see Remark 14 below).

Remark 14. As explained in [10], the bank does not need to store the serial numbers but only their smaller hash values, as fingerprints. Therefore, the size of the V elements SN computed during a deposit of value V is the same for all the schemes. The Deposit size then mostly depends on the size of the Spend transcripts. By achieving smaller, constant-size spendings, we thus alleviate the storage burden of the bank and so improve the scalability of our divisible E-Cash system.

Remark 15. Public identification of defrauders has an impact on the complexity of the system. This roughly doubles the size of the parameters and requires several additional computations during a spending. Such a property also has consequences on the security analysis which must rely on a stronger assumption (namely the $N - \mathsf{MXDH'}$ one instead of its weaker variant) involving more challenge elements.

However, in some situations, it can be possible to consider an authority which would be trusted to revoke user's anonymity only in case of fraud. The resulting e-cash system, called *fair*, obviously weakens anonymity but may be a reasonable tradeoff between user's privacy and legal constraints.

Our scheme can be modified to add such an entity. One way would be to entrust it with the extraction key of the Groth-Sahai proof system. It could then extract the element $U_1 = u_1^{\mathsf{usk}}$ from any transaction and so identify the spender. The elements t_j would then become unnecessary and could be discarded from the public parameters. Moreover, the elements $\psi_{V,j}$, along with the associated proofs, would also become useless during the Spend protocol. The complexity of the scheme would then be significantly improved. The consequences of these changes on the security analysis are discussed in Remark 21 of the next section.

6   Security Analysis

6.1   Proof of Theorem 10: Traceability

Let us consider a successful adversary $\mathcal{A}$ which manages to spend more than he has withdrawn without being traced. This formally means that it is able to produce, after q_w withdrawals, u valid transcripts $\{(V_i, Z_i, \Pi_i)\}_{i=1}^u$ representing an amount of $\sum_{i=1}^u V_i > N \cdot q_w$, but such that $\texttt{Identify}((V_i, Z_i, \Pi_i), (V_j, Z_j, \Pi_j)) = \bot$, for all $i \neq j$. We can have the three following cases:

- Type-1 Forgeries: $\exists i$ such that Π_i contains commitments to a pair (s_{ℓ_i}, t_{ℓ_i}) which was not signed in a τ_ℓ by the bank, during the key generation phase;
- Type-2 Forgeries: $\exists i$ such that Π_i contains commitments to a pair $(u_1^{\mathsf{usk}}, u_2^x)$ which was never signed by the bank, during a $\mathcal{O}\texttt{Withdraw}_{\mathcal{U}}$ query;
- Type-3 Forgeries: $\forall 1 \leq i \leq u$, $\exists \tau_{\ell_i}$ in bpk which is a valid signature on the pair (s_{ℓ_i}, t_{ℓ_i}) committed in Π_i and the pairs $(u_1^{\mathsf{usk}}, u_2^x)$ involved in this transcript were signed by the bank during a $\mathcal{O}\texttt{Withdraw}_{\mathcal{U}}$ query, but identification fails.

Intuitively, the first two cases imply an attack against the signatures schemes Σ_0 or Σ_1, respectively. This is formally stated by the two following lemmas:

Lemma 16. *Any Type-1 forger $\mathcal{A}$ with success probability ε can be converted into an adversary against the EUF-SCMA security of Σ_0 with the same success probability.*

Proof. The reduction $\mathcal{R}$ generates the public parameters (the group elements), and sends $\{(s_j, t_j)\}_{j=1}^N$ to the signing oracle of the EUF-SCMA security experiment which returns the signatures $\{\tau_j\}_{j=1}^N$ along with the challenge public key pk. It can run $\Sigma_1.\mathsf{Keygen}$ to get the key pair $(\mathsf{sk}_1, \mathsf{pk}_1)$ and set bpk as $(\mathsf{pk}_0 = \mathsf{pk}, \mathsf{pk}_1, \tau_1, \ldots, \tau_N)$. One may note that $\mathcal{R}$ is able to answer any query from $\mathcal{A}$ since it knows $\mathsf{bsk} = \mathsf{sk}_1$.

At the end of the game, $\mathcal{R}$ extracts (it has generated the CRS of the Groth-Sahai proofs system and so knows the related extraction keys) from Π_i, for $i \in [1, u]$, a valid signature τ_{ℓ_i} on some pair (s_{ℓ_i}, t_{ℓ_i}) under the public key pk. Since $\mathcal{A}$ is a Type-1 forger with success probability ε, at least one of these pairs does not belong to the set $\{(s_j, t_j)\}_{j=1}^N$ and so is valid forgery which can be used to break the EUF-SCMA security of Σ_0, with probability ε. $\square$

Lemma 17. *Any Type-2 forger $\mathcal{A}$ with success probability ε can be converted into an adversary against the EUF-CMA security of Σ_1 with the same success probability.*

Proof. The reduction $\mathcal{R}$ generates the public parameters (the group elements) and its public key as usual except that it sets pk_1 as pk, the challenge public key in the EUF-CMA security experiment. $\mathcal{R}$ can then directly answer all the queries except the $\mathcal{O}\mathtt{Withdraw}_\mathcal{B}$ ones for which it will forward the pairs $(u_1^{\mathsf{usk}}, u_2^x)$ to the signing oracle and forward the resulting signature σ to $\mathcal{A}$.

The game ends when $\mathcal{A}$ outputs u transcripts such that one of them, $(2^\ell, Z, \Pi)$, contains a commitment to a pair $(u_1^{\mathsf{usk}}, u_2^x)$ which was never signed by the bank during a $\mathcal{O}\mathtt{Withdraw}_\mathcal{B}$ query. The soundness of the proof implies that it also contains a commitment to an element σ such that $\Sigma_1.\mathtt{Verify}((u_1^{\mathsf{usk}}, u_2^x), \sigma, \mathsf{pk}) = 1$. Such a forgery can then be used to break the EUF-CMA security of Σ_1. □

Now, it remains to evaluate the success probability of a Type-3 forger. The following lemma shows that it is negligible under $N - \mathsf{BDHI}$ assumption.

Lemma 18. *Any Type-3 forger $\mathcal{A}$ with success probability ε can be converted into an adversary against the $N - \mathsf{BDHI}$ assumption with the same success probability.*

Proof. Let $(\{g^{y^i}\}_{i=0}^N, \{\widetilde{g}^{y^i}\}_{i=0}^N) \in \mathbb{G}_1^{N+1} \times \mathbb{G}_2^{N+1}$ be a $N - \mathsf{BDHI}$ challenge. The reduction $\mathcal{R}$ generates random scalars $c, z' \leftarrow \mathbb{Z}_p$ and $a_i \leftarrow \mathbb{Z}_p$, for $i = 1, \ldots, N$, and sets the public parameters as follows:

- $(s_j, t_j) \leftarrow ((g^{y^{j-1}})^{z'}, (g^{y^{j-1}})^{c \cdot z'})$, for $j = 1, \ldots, N$;
- $\widetilde{g}_k \leftarrow \widetilde{g}^{y^k}$, for $k = 0, \ldots, N - 1$;
- $h_i \leftarrow g^{a_i}$, for $i = 1, \ldots, N$;
- $\widetilde{h}_{i,k} \leftarrow (\widetilde{g}^{y^k})^{-a_i}$, for $i = 1, \ldots, N$ and $k = 0, \ldots, i - 1$.

By setting $(s, t) = (g^{z' \cdot y^{-1}}, g^{c \cdot z' \cdot y^{-1}})$—recall that this pair is not published in pp—, one can easily check that the simulation is correct: $s_j = s^{y^j}$ and $t_j = t^{y^j}$. $\mathcal{R}$ then generates the CRS for the perfect soundness setting and stores the extraction keys. Finally, it computes the bank's key pair $(\mathsf{bsk}, \mathsf{bpk})$ as usual and so is able to answer every oracle queries.

At the end of the game, $\mathcal{R}$ extracts the elements $s^{(i)}$ committed in Π_i, for $i = 1, \ldots, u$. Each of these proofs also contains a commitment to signature τ_{ℓ_i} on the pair (s_{ℓ_i}, t_{ℓ_i}) such that: $e(s^{(i)}, \widetilde{g}_{V_i-1}) = e(s_{\ell_i}, \widetilde{g})$. Since we here consider Type-3 forgeries, $\ell_i \in [1, N]$ (otherwise $\tau_{\ell_i} \notin \mathsf{bpk}$) and so $s_{\ell_i} = s^{y^{\ell_i}}$. Therefore, we have $s^{(i)} = s^{y^{\ell_i - V_i + 1}}$, where $\ell_i - V_i + 1 \leq N - V_i + 1$. We then distinguish the two following cases.

- Case 1: $\forall i \in [1, u], \ell_i - V_i + 1 \geq 1$;
- Case 2: $\exists i \in [1, u]$ such that $\ell_i - V_i + 1 < 1$.

The first case means that $\mathcal{A}$ only used valid elements $s^{(i)}$ (*i.e.* $s^{(i)} = s_{j_i}$ such that $j_i \in [1, N - V_i + 1]$) to construct the proofs Π_i. So all the $(\sum_{i=1}^u V_i)$ serial numbers derived from the u transcripts returned by $\mathcal{A}$ belong to the set $\mathcal{S} = \{\cup_{k=1}^{q_w} \{e(s, \widetilde{g})^{x_k \cdot y^\ell}\}_{\ell=1}^N\}$, where $\{x_k\}_{k=1}^{q_w}$ is the list of the scalars certified by the bank during the $\mathcal{O}\texttt{Withdraw}_{\mathcal{U}}$ queries. An over-spending means that $\sum_{i=1}^{u} V_i > N \cdot q_w = |\mathcal{S}|$, so there is at least one collision in the list of the serial numbers. However, a collision without identification of a defrauder is unlikely, as we explained in Remark 9. Hence, case 1 can only occur with negligible probability.

Now, let us consider the second case: when such a case occurs, $\mathcal{R}$ is able to extract the element $s^{y^{\ell_i - V_i + 1}}$ such that $\ell_i - V_i + 1 \leq 0$, and compute $\mathbf{g} \leftarrow (s^{y^{\ell_i - V_i + 1}})^{1/z'} = g^{y^{\ell_i - V_i}}$ with $1 - N \leq \ell_i - V_i \leq -1$. Let k_i be the integer such that $\ell_i - V_i + k_i = -1$. The previous inequalities imply that $k_i \in [0, N-2]$ and so $\mathcal{R}$ can break the $N - \mathsf{BDHI}$ assumption by returning $e(g, \widetilde{g})^{y^{-1}} = e(\mathbf{g}, \widetilde{g}_{k_i})$. $\square$

6.2   Proof of Theorem 11: Exculpability

The goal of the adversary $\mathcal{A}$ is to make the identify procedure to claim an honest user upk guilty of double-spending: it publishes two valid transcripts (V_1, Z_1, Π_1) and (V_2, Z_2, Π_2) such that $\mathsf{upk} = \texttt{Identify}((V_1, Z_1, \Pi_1), (V_2, Z_2, \Pi_2))$, while this user did not perform the two transactions (maybe one). We can obviously assume that one of these transcripts has been forged by $\mathcal{A}$.

Let us consider a successful adversary. We distinguish the two following cases:

- Type-1 forgeries: the public key pk_{ots} of the one-time signature scheme used in this forged transcript is one of those used by the honest user to answer $\mathcal{O}\texttt{Spend}$ queries.
- Type-2 forgeries: pk_{ots} was never used by this honest user.

Lemma 19. *Let q_s be a bound on the number of $\mathcal{O}\texttt{Spend}$ queries. Any Type-1 forger $\mathcal{A}$ with success probability ε can be converted into an adversary against the SUF-OTS security of the one-time signature scheme Σ_{ots} with success probability greater than ε/q_s.*

Proof. The reduction $\mathcal{R}$ generates the public parameters along with the bank's key pair and selects an integer $i^* \in [1, q_s]$. Upon receiving the ith $\mathcal{O}\texttt{Spend}$ query, it acts normally if $i \neq i^*$, but uses the public key pk_{ots}^* and the signing oracle of the SUF-OTS security experiment if $i = i^*$.

Let pk_{ots} be the public key involved in the forged transcript. $\mathcal{R}$ aborts if $\mathsf{pk}_{ots} \neq \mathsf{pk}_{ots}^*$, which occurs with probability $1 - 1/q_s$. Else, the forged transcript contains a new one-time signature η under pk_{ots}^* which can be used against the security of Σ_{ots}. $\square$

Lemma 20. *Let q_s (resp. q_a) be a bound on the number of $\mathcal{O}\texttt{Spend}$ queries (resp. $\mathcal{O}\texttt{Add}$ queries). Any Type-2 forger $\mathcal{A}$ with success probability ε can be converted into an adversary against the $q_s - \mathsf{SDH}$ assumption with success probability ε/q_a.*

Proof. Let $(g, g^\alpha, \ldots, g^{\alpha^{q_s}})$ be a $q_s - \mathsf{SDH}$ challenge, the reduction $\mathcal{R}$ will make a guess on the user upk^* framed by $\mathcal{A}$ and will act as if its secret key was α. Therefore, it selects $1 \leq i^* \leq q_a$ and generates the public parameters as in the $\texttt{Setup}$ algorithm except that it sets u_1 as g^z for some random $z \in \mathbb{Z}_p$.

Next, it computes q_s key pairs $(\mathsf{sk}_{ots}^{(i)}, \mathsf{pk}_{ots}^{(i)}) \leftarrow \Sigma_{ots}.\mathsf{Keygen}(1^k)$ and sets w as $g^{\prod_{i=1}^{q_s}(\alpha+H(\mathsf{pk}_{ots}^{(i)}))}$ (which is possible using the $q_s - \mathsf{SDH}$ challenge [6], since the exponent is a polynomial in α of degree q_s). The reduction will answer the oracle queries as follows.

- $\mathcal{O}\mathsf{Add}()$ queries: When the adversary makes the ith $\mathcal{O}\mathsf{Add}$ query to register a user, $\mathcal{R}$ runs the Keygen algorithm if $i \neq i^*$ and sets $\mathsf{upk}^* \leftarrow g^\alpha$ otherwise.
- $\mathcal{O}\mathsf{Corrupt}(\mathsf{upk}/\mathsf{mpk})$ queries: $\mathcal{R}$ returns the secret key if $\mathsf{upk} \neq \mathsf{upk}^*$ and aborts otherwise.
- $\mathcal{O}\mathsf{AddCorrupt}(\mathsf{upk}/\mathsf{mpk})$ queries: $\mathcal{R}$ stores the public key which is now considered as registered.
- $\mathcal{O}\mathsf{Withdraw}_{\mathcal{U}}(\mathsf{bsk}, \mathsf{upk})$ queries: $\mathcal{R}$ acts normally if $\mathsf{upk} \neq \mathsf{upk}^*$ and simulates the interactive proof of knowledge of α otherwise.
- $\mathcal{O}\mathsf{Spend}(\mathsf{upk}, V)$ queries: $\mathcal{R}$ acts normally if $\mathsf{upk} \neq \mathsf{upk}^*$. Else, to answer the jth query on upk^*, it computes $\mu \leftarrow g^{\prod_{i=1, i\neq j}^{q_s}(\alpha+H(\mathsf{pk}_{ots}^{(i)}))}$ which satisfies $\mu = w^{1/(\alpha+H(\mathsf{pk}_{ots}^{(j)}))}$, and uses $\mathsf{sk}_{ots}^{(j)}$ as in the Spend protocol.

The adversary then outputs two valid transcripts (V_1, Z_1, Π_1) and (V_2, Z_2, Π_2) which accuse upk of double-spending. If $\mathsf{upk} \neq \mathsf{upk}^*$ then $\mathcal{R}$ aborts which will occur with probability $1 - 1/q_a$. Else, the soundness of the proof implies that the forged transcript was signed under pk_{ots} and so that the proof involves an element $\mu = w^{\frac{1}{\alpha+H(\mathsf{pk}_{ots})}}$. Since here we consider Type-2 attacks, $\mathsf{pk}_{ots} \notin \{\mathsf{pk}_{ots}^{(i)}\}_i$. Therefore, $H(\mathsf{pk}_{ots}) \notin \{H(\mathsf{pk}_{ots}^{(i)})\}_i$ with overwhelming probability, due to the collision-resistance of the hash function H. The element μ can then be used to break the $q_s - \mathsf{SDH}$ assumption in $\mathbb{G}_1$ (as in [6]). $\square$

6.3   Proof of Theorem 12: Anonymity

In this proof, we assume that the coins are spent in a sequential way: the index j in $C = (x, \sigma, j)$ is increased by V after each spending of an amount V, and the new j is used in the next spending. A next coin is used when the previous coin is finished. But the proof would also apply if the user could adaptively choose the coin (x, σ), as well as (j, V) for every spending.

We can make the proof with a sequence of games, starting from the initial game for anonymity, with a random bit b (see Fig. 2), where the simulator emulates the challenger but correctly generating all the secret values. The advantage is ε, and we want to show it is negligible.

In a next game, the simulator makes a guess on the amount $V^* \in [1, N]$ chosen by the adversary during the step 3 of the anonymity experiment (see Fig. 2) and also makes a guess $j^* \in [1, N - V^* + 1]$ for the actual index of the coin of the user upk_b at the challenge time (but this challenge value could be chosen by the adversary, as said above). In addition, we denote q_w the bound on the number of $\mathcal{O}\mathsf{Withdraw}_{\mathcal{U}}$ queries, and the simulator selects a random integer $\ell^* \in [1, q_w]$, for the expected index of the $\mathcal{O}\mathsf{Withdraw}_{\mathcal{U}}$ query that generates the coin that will be used in the challenge. If during the simulation it appears they are not correct, one stops the simulation. This guess does not affect the success probability of the adversary, when the guess is correct, but just reduces the advantage from ε to $2\varepsilon/(q_w N^2)$.

Next, the simulator generates the CRS for the Groth-Sahai proofs in the perfect witness indistinguishability setting, so that it can later simulate the proofs. This is indistinguishable from the previous game under the SXDH assumption.

Now, the simulator will simulate the public parameters from an $N - \mathsf{MXDH}'$ challenge:

- $(g^{\gamma^k}, h^{\gamma^k})_{k=0}^P \in \mathbb{G}_1^{2P+2}$,
- $(g^{\alpha \cdot \delta \cdot \gamma^{-k}}, h^{\alpha \cdot \delta \cdot \gamma^{-k}})_{k=0}^E \in \mathbb{G}_1^{2E+2}$,
- $(g^{\chi \cdot \gamma^k}, h^{\chi \cdot \gamma^k})_{k=D+1}^P \in \mathbb{G}_1^{2C}$,
- and $((g^{\alpha \cdot \gamma^{-k}})_{k=0}^C, (g^{\chi \cdot \gamma^k/\alpha}, h^{\chi \cdot \gamma^k/\alpha})_{k=0}^C,) \in \mathbb{G}_1^{3S}$,
- as well as $(\widetilde{g}^{\gamma^k}, \widetilde{g}^{\alpha \cdot \gamma^{-k}})_{k=0}^C \in \mathbb{G}_2^{2S}$,
- and a pair $(g^{z_1}, h^{z_2}) \in \mathbb{G}_1^2$ be an $N - \mathsf{MXDH}'$ challenge.

We recall that $C = N^3 - N^2$, $S = C + 1$, $E = N^2 - N$, $D = S + E = N^3 - N + 1$ and $P = D + C = 2N^3 - N^2 - N + 1$. Let d be the quotient of the division of N^2 by V^* (i.e. $N^2 = d \cdot V^* + r_d$ with $0 \leq r_d < V^*$), then the simulator constructs the public parameters as follows.

- g and h are defined from g^{γ^k} and h^{γ^k} respectively, with $k = 0$;
- $u_1 \xleftarrow{\$} \mathbb{G}_1$ and $u_2 \leftarrow g^{w \cdot \gamma^P}$, for a random $w \in \mathbb{Z}_p$;
- $\widetilde{g}$ is defined from $\widetilde{g}^{\gamma^k}$, with $k = 0$;
- $(s_j, t_j) \leftarrow (g^{\gamma^{D+d(1-V^*+j-j^*)}}, h^{\gamma^{D+d(1-V^*+j-j^*)}})$, for $j = 1, \ldots, N$;
- $\widetilde{g}_k \leftarrow \widetilde{g}^{\gamma^{d \cdot k}}$, for $k = 0, \ldots, N-1$;
- $h_i \leftarrow g^{w_i \cdot \alpha \cdot \gamma^{d(-i+1)}}$, for $i \in [1, \ldots, N]$, with w_i a random scalar;
- $\widetilde{h}_{i,k} \leftarrow \widetilde{g}^{-w_i \cdot \alpha \cdot \gamma^{d(k-i+1)}}$, for $i \in [1, \ldots, N]$ and $k = 0, \ldots, i-1$.

We must check that

(1) the simulation of the parameters is correct: let us define $y = \gamma^d$, $(s, t) = (g^{\gamma^{D+d(1-V^*-j^*)}}, h^{\gamma^{D+d(1-V^*-j^*)}})$, and $a_i = \alpha \cdot w_i \cdot \gamma^{d(-i+1)}$ for $i \in [1, \ldots, N]$. We then have:
  - $(s_j, t_j) = ((g^{\gamma^{D+d(1-V^*-j^*)}})^{\gamma^{d \cdot j}}, (h^{\gamma^{D+d(1-V^*-j^*)}})^{\gamma^{d \cdot j}}) = (s^{y^j}, t^{y^j})$;
  - $\widetilde{g}_k = \widetilde{g}^{y^k}$, for $k = 0, \ldots, N-1$;
  - $h_i = g^{a_i}$, for $i = 1, \ldots, N$;
  - $\widetilde{h}_{i,k} = \widetilde{g}^{-a_i \cdot y^k}$, for $i = 1, \ldots, N$ and $k = 0, \ldots, i-1$.
  The simulation is therefore correct;

(2) all of these elements can be provided from the $N - \mathsf{MXDH}'$ challenge: First, recall that $N^2 = d \cdot V^* + r_d$ with $0 \leq r_d < V^* \leq N$. Then $2 \leq V^* + j^* \leq N+1$ and $N \leq d \leq N^2$.

  Let us consider the pairs $(s_j, t_j) = (g^{\gamma^{D+d(1-V^*+j-j^*)}}, h^{\gamma^{D+d(1-V^*+j-j^*)}})$, for $j = 1, \ldots, N$: $1 + j - (V^* + j^*) \geq 2 - (N+1) \geq -N+1$, therefore,

$d(1-V^*+j-j^*) \geq -d(N-1) \geq -N^2(N-1) \geq -C$. Moreover, $d(1-V^*+j-j^*) \leq d(N-1) \leq N^2(N-1) \leq C$. Hence $D-C \leq D+d(1-V^*+j-j^*) \leq D+C = P$. Since $D = S+E = C+1+E$, $D-C = E+1 = N^2-N+1 \geq 0$. Hence, the pairs (s_j, t_j) can be defined from the tuple $(g^{\gamma^k}, h^{\gamma^k})_{k=0}^P$ of the $N - \mathsf{MXDH}'$ instance.

About the elements $\widetilde{g}_k = \widetilde{g}^{\gamma^{d \cdot k}}$, since we have $0 \leq d \cdot k \leq N^2(N-1) = C$, for $k = 0, \ldots, N-1$, they all are in the tuple $(\widetilde{g}^{\gamma^k})_{k=0}^C$.

Eventually, let us consider the elements $h_i = g^{w_i \cdot \alpha \cdot \gamma^{d(-i+1)}}$ and $\widetilde{h}_{i,k} = \widetilde{g}^{-w_i \cdot \alpha \cdot \gamma^{d(k-i+1)}}$, for $i \in [1, N]$ and $k \in [0, i-1]$. Since $-C \leq -d(N-1) \leq d(-i+1) \leq 0$ and $-C \leq d(k-i+1) \leq 0$, they all can be computed from the tuples $(g^{\alpha \cdot \gamma^{-k}})_{k=0}^C$ and $(\widetilde{g}^{\alpha \cdot \gamma^{-k}})_{k=0}^C$, just using the additional random scalar w_i.

The reduction $\mathcal{R}$ is thus able to generate the public parameters from the $N - \mathsf{MXDH}'$ instance.

The simulator now has to answer all the oracle queries, with all the secret keys.

- $\mathcal{O}\mathtt{Add}()$ queries: run the $\mathtt{Keygen}$ algorithm and return upk (or mpk);
- $\mathcal{O}\mathtt{Withdraw}_{\mathcal{U}}(\mathsf{bsk}, \mathsf{upk})$ queries: for the ℓth $\mathcal{O}\mathtt{Withdraw}_{\mathcal{U}}$ query, the simulator plays normally if $\ell \neq \ell^*$, but sending the pair $(u_1^{\mathsf{usk}}, (g^{\chi \cdot \gamma^P})^w = u_2^\chi)$ otherwise (using the $N - \mathsf{MXDH}'$ instance). It can then simulate the proof of knowledge and receives a scalar x' along with a signature σ on $(u_1^{\mathsf{usk}}, u_2^{x^*})$, where $x^* = \chi + x'$. The coin is then implicitly defined as $C^* = (x^*, \sigma, 1)$ and we will now denote its owner by upk^*;
- $\mathcal{O}\mathtt{Corrupt}(\mathsf{upk}/\mathsf{mpk})$ queries: the simulator plays normally (if the guesses are correct, upk^* cannot be asked to be corrupted);
- $\mathcal{O}\mathtt{AddCorrupt}(\mathsf{upk}/\mathsf{mpk})$: the simulator stores the public key which is now considered as registered;
- $\mathcal{O}\mathtt{Spend}(\mathsf{upk}, V)$ queries: if the coin to be used for the spending has not been withdrawn during the $\ell^* - \mathcal{O}\mathtt{Withdraw}_{\mathcal{U}}$-query, then the simulator knows all the secret keys, and so it can play normally. Else, it proceeds as follows. One can first remark that if the guesses are correct, $j \notin [j^* - V + 1, j^* + V^* - 1]$. Otherwise this spending and the challenge spending would lead to a double-spending.
  - If $j \geq j^* + V^*$, then $D + d(1 - V^* + j - j^*) \geq D + d \geq D + 1$, so $s_j^{x^*}$ and $t_j^{x^*}$ can be computed from the tuple $(g^{\chi \cdot \gamma^k}, h^{\chi \cdot \gamma^k})_{k=D+1}^P$. Indeed,

$$s_j^{x^*} = (g^{\gamma^{D+d(1-V^*+j-j^*)}})^{x^*} = g^{\chi \cdot \gamma^{D+d(1-V^*+j-j^*)}} \cdot (g^{\gamma^{D+d(1-V^*+j-j^*)}})^{x'}$$
$$t_j^{x^*} = (h^{\gamma^{D+d(1-V^*+j-j^*)}})^{x^*} = h^{\chi \cdot \gamma^{D+d(1-V^*+j-j^*)}} \cdot (h^{\gamma^{D+d(1-V^*+j-j^*)}})^{x'}.$$

The simulator can then send ElGamal encryptions of $s_j^{x^*}$ and $t_j^{x^*} \cdot g^{R \cdot \mathsf{usk}^*}$ under h_V (which yields valid ϕ_{V^*, j^*} and ψ_{V^*, j^*}) along with simulated proofs.

- If $j \leq j^* - V$, then we proceed as follows.

  Let $r \leftarrow -\chi \cdot \gamma^{D+d(-V^*+1+j-j^*)+d(V-1)}/\alpha$ and $(r_1', r_2') \xleftarrow{\$} \mathbb{Z}_p^2$. Then, $(g^{r/w_V+r_1'}, s_j^{x'} \cdot h_V^{r_1'})$ and $(h^{r/w_V} \cdot g^{r_2'}, t_j^{x'} \cdot g^{R \cdot \text{usk}^*} \cdot h_V^{r_2'})$ are valid pairs $\phi_{V,j}$ and $\psi_{V,j}$ which can be computed from the tuple $(g^{\chi \cdot \gamma^k/\alpha}, h^{\chi \cdot \gamma^k/\alpha})_{k=0}^C$ of the $N - \text{MXDH}'$ instance: Since $d \cdot V^* = N^2 - r_d > N^2 - N$,

$$D + d(-V^* + 1 + j - j^*) + d(V-1) = D + d(V - V^* + j - j^*)$$
$$\leq D - d \cdot V^* < D - N^2 + N < D - E = S = C + 1$$

This is thus less or equal to C, as the indices of the tuple.

It then remains to prove that $(g^{r/w_V+r_1'}, s_j^{x'} \cdot h_V^{r_1'})$ and $(h^{r/w_V} \cdot g^{r_2'}, t_j^{x'} \cdot g^{R \cdot \text{usk}^*} \cdot h_V^{r_2'})$ are valid ElGamal encryptions of $s_j^{x^*}$ and $t_j^{x^*} \cdot g^{R \cdot \text{usk}^*}$ under h_V. Let c be the secret scalar such that $h = g^c$, $r_1 = r/w_V + r_1'$ and $r_2 = c \cdot r/w_V + r_2'$, we then have: $g^{r_1} = g^{r/w_V+r_1'}$ and

$$s_j^{x^*} \cdot h_V^{r_1} = s_j^\chi \cdot s_j^{x'} \cdot h_V^{r/w_V+r_1'}$$
$$= g^{\chi \cdot \gamma^{D+d(1-V^*+j-j^*)}} \cdot (g^{w_V \cdot \alpha \cdot \gamma^{d(-V+1)}})^{r/w_V} \cdot s_j^{x'} \cdot h_V^{r_1'}$$
$$= g^{\chi \cdot \gamma^{D+d(1-V^*+j-j^*)}} \cdot g^{-\chi \cdot \gamma^{D+d(1-V^*+j-j^*)}} \cdot s_j^{x'} \cdot h_V^{r_1'})$$
$$= s_j^{x'} \cdot h_V^{r_1'}$$

Similarly, $g^{r_2} = h^{r/w_W} \cdot g^{r_2'}$ and as just above

$$t_j^{x^*} \cdot g^{R \cdot \text{usk}^*} \cdot h_V^{r_2} = t_j^{x'} \cdot t_j^\chi \cdot g^{R \cdot \text{usk}^*} \cdot h_V^{c \cdot r/w_V} \cdot h_V^{r_2'}$$
$$= t_j^{x'} \cdot h^{\chi \cdot \gamma^{D+d(1-V^*+j-j^*)}} \cdot g^{R \cdot \text{usk}^*} \cdot h^{-\chi \cdot \gamma^{D+d(1-V^*+j-j^*)}} \cdot h_V^{r_2'}$$
$$= t_j^{x'} \cdot g^{R \cdot \text{usk}^*} \cdot h_V^{r_2'}$$

The spending is thus correctly simulated since r_1' and r_2' are random scalars.

During the challenge phase (*i.e.* the step 3 of the anonymity experiment), $\mathcal{A}$ outputs two public keys upk_0 and upk_1 along a value V. If the guesses were correct, $V = V^*$, $\text{upk}^* = \text{upk}_b$ and the coin involving x^* is spent, at index $j = j^*$. The simulator selects random r_1' and r_2', computes $R \leftarrow H(info)$, and returns, along with the simulated proofs, the pairs

$$\phi_{V^*, j^*} = ((g^{z_1})^{-1/w_{V^*}} \cdot g^{r_1'}, s_j^{x'} \cdot g^{-\delta \cdot \alpha \cdot \gamma^{-d(V^*-1)}} \cdot h_{V^*}^{r_1'})$$
$$\psi_{V^*, j^*} = ((h^{z_2})^{-1/w_{V^*}} \cdot g^{r_2'}, t_j^{x'} \cdot g^{R \cdot \text{usk}^*} \cdot h^{-\delta \cdot \alpha \cdot \gamma^{-d(V^*-1)}} \cdot h_{V^*}^{r_2'}).$$

One can note that $-d(V^* - 1) \geq -N^2 + N = -E$ and so that the pair $(g^{\delta \cdot \alpha \cdot \gamma^{-d(V^*-1)}}, h^{\delta \cdot \alpha \cdot \gamma^{-d(V^*-1)}})$ belongs to the tuple $(g^{\alpha \cdot \delta \cdot \gamma^{-k}}, h^{\alpha \cdot \delta \cdot \gamma^{-k}})_{k=0}^E$.

Let $r_1 = -z_1/w_{V^*} + r_1'$ and $r_2 = -(c \cdot z_2)/w_{V^*} + r_2'$. If $z_1 = z_2 = \delta + \chi \cdot \gamma^D/\alpha$, then

$$
\begin{aligned}
(g^{r_1}, s_{j^*}^{x^*} \cdot h_{V^*}^{r_1}) &= (g^{r_1}, s_{j^*}^{\chi} \cdot s_{j^*}^{x'} \cdot h_{V^*}^{-z_1/w_{V^*}} \cdot h_{V^*}^{r_1'}) \\
&= (g^{r_1}, s_{j^*}^{\chi} \cdot s_{j^*}^{x'} \cdot g^{-\chi \cdot \gamma^{D+d(1-V^*)}} \cdot g^{-\delta \cdot \alpha \gamma^{d(1-V^*)}} \cdot h_{V^*}^{r_1'}) \\
&= (g^{-z_1/w_{V^*}+r_1'}, s_{j^*}^{x'} \cdot g^{-\delta \cdot \alpha \gamma^{d(1-V^*)}} \cdot h_{V^*}^{r_1'}) = \phi_{V^*,j^*}
\end{aligned}
$$

and

$$
\begin{aligned}
(g^{r_2}, t_{j^*}^{x^*} \cdot g^{R \cdot \mathsf{usk}^*} \cdot h_{V^*}^{r_2}) &= (g^{r_2}, t_{j^*}^{\chi} \cdot t_{j^*}^{x'} \cdot h_{V^*}^{-(c \cdot z_2)/w_{V^*}} \cdot g^{R \cdot \mathsf{usk}^*} \cdot h_{V^*}^{r_2'}) \\
&= (g^{r_2}, t_{j^*}^{\chi} \cdot t_{j^*}^{x'} \cdot h^{-\chi \cdot \gamma^{D+d(1-V^*)}} \cdot h^{-\delta \cdot \alpha \gamma^{d(1-V^*)}} \cdot g^{R \cdot \mathsf{usk}^*} \cdot h_{V^*}^{r_2'}) \\
&= (h^{-z_2/w_{V^*}} \cdot g^{r_2}, t_{j^*}^{x'} \cdot h^{-\delta \cdot \alpha \gamma^{d(1-V^*)}} \cdot g^{R \cdot \mathsf{usk}^*} \cdot h_{V^*}^{r_2'}) = \psi_{V^*,j^*}
\end{aligned}
$$

The challenge spending is thus correctly simulated too.

In the next game, we replace the $N - \mathsf{MXDH}'$ instance by a random instance, with random z_1 and z_2. From the simulation of ϕ_{V^*,j^*} and ψ_{V^*,j^*}, we see that they perfectly hide upk^*. Hence, the advantage of the adversary in this last game is exactly zero.

Remark 21. One can note that the h-based elements $h^{z_2}, \{h^{\gamma^k}\}_{k=0}^P$, $\{h^{\alpha \cdot \delta \cdot \gamma^{-k}}\}_{k=0}^E, \{h^{\chi \cdot \gamma^k}\}_{k=D+1}^P$ and $\{h^{\chi \cdot \gamma^k/\alpha}\}_{k=0}^C$ provided in the $N - \mathsf{MXDH}'$ challenge are only useful to simulate the security tags $\psi_{V,j}$ and ψ_{V^*,j^*}. In the case of fair divisible E-Cash system, they would no longer be necessary (see Remark 15) and so the security of the resulting scheme could simply rely on the weaker $N - \mathsf{MXDH}$ assumption.

7 Conclusion

We have proposed the first divisible e-cash system which achieves constant-time spendings, regardless of the spent value. Moreover, our solution keeps the best features of state-of-the-art, such as the efficiency of the withdrawals from [10] and the scalability of [11]. We argue that this is a major step towards the practical use of an e-cash system.

This also shows that the binary-tree structure, used by previous constructions, can be avoided. It may therefore open up new possibilities and incite new work in this area. We provide another construction in the full version [22] whose security proof relies on a more classical assumption, still avoiding the tree structure, but with larger public parameters.

Acknowledgments. We thank the anonymous reviewers for their useful remarks. This work was supported in part by the European Research Council under the European Community's Seventh Framework Programme (FP7/2007-2013 Grant Agreement no. 339563 – CryptoCloud).

References

1. Abe, M., Groth, J., Haralambiev, K., Ohkubo, M.: Optimal structure-preserving signatures in asymmetric bilinear groups. In: Rogaway, P. (ed.) CRYPTO 2011. LNCS, vol. 6841, pp. 649–666. Springer, Heidelberg (2011). doi:10.1007/978-3-642-22792-9_37

2. Au, M.H., Susilo, W., Mu, Y.: Practical anonymous divisible E-cash from bounded accumulators. In: Tsudik, G. (ed.) FC 2008. LNCS, vol. 5143, pp. 287–301. Springer, Heidelberg (2008). doi:10.1007/978-3-540-85230-8_26

3. Barreto, P.S.L.M., Naehrig, M.: Pairing-friendly elliptic curves of prime order. In: Preneel, B., Tavares, S. (eds.) SAC 2005. LNCS, vol. 3897, pp. 319–331. Springer, Heidelberg (2006). doi:10.1007/11693383_22

4. Bellare, M., Garay, J.A., Rabin, T.: Fast batch verification for modular exponentiation and digital signatures. In: Nyberg, K. (ed.) EUROCRYPT 1998. LNCS, vol. 1403, pp. 236–250. Springer, Heidelberg (1998). doi:10.1007/BFb0054130

5. Boneh, D., Boyen, X.: Efficient selective-ID secure identity-based encryption without random oracles. In: Cachin, C., Camenisch, J.L. (eds.) EUROCRYPT 2004. LNCS, vol. 3027, pp. 223–238. Springer, Heidelberg (2004). doi:10.1007/978-3-540-24676-3_14

6. Boneh, D., Boyen, X.: Short signatures without random oracles and the SDH assumption in bilinear groups. J. Cryptol. **21**(2), 149–177 (2008)

7. Camenisch, J., Lysyanskaya, A.: Signature schemes and anonymous credentials from bilinear maps. In: Franklin, M. (ed.) CRYPTO 2004. LNCS, vol. 3152, pp. 56–72. Springer, Heidelberg (2004). doi:10.1007/978-3-540-28628-8_4

8. Canard, S., Gouget, A.: Divisible E-cash systems can be truly anonymous. In: Naor, M. (ed.) EUROCRYPT 2007. LNCS, vol. 4515, pp. 482–497. Springer, Heidelberg (2007). doi:10.1007/978-3-540-72540-4_28

9. Canard, S., Gouget, A.: Multiple denominations in E-cash with compact transaction data. In: Sion, R. (ed.) FC 2010. LNCS, vol. 6052, pp. 82–97. Springer, Heidelberg (2010). doi:10.1007/978-3-642-14577-3_9

10. Canard, S., Pointcheval, D., Sanders, O., Traoré, J.: Divisible E-cash made practical. In: Katz, J. (ed.) PKC 2015. LNCS, vol. 9020, pp. 77–100. Springer, Heidelberg (2015). doi:10.1007/978-3-662-46447-2_4

11. Canard, S., Pointcheval, D., Sanders, O., Traoré, J.: scalable divisible E-cash. In: Malkin, T., Kolesnikov, V., Lewko, A.B., Polychronakis, M. (eds.) ACNS 2015. LNCS, vol. 9092, pp. 287–306. Springer, Cham (2015). doi:10.1007/978-3-319-28166-7_14

12. Chaum, D.: Blind signatures for untraceable payments. In: Chaum, D., Rivest, R.L., Sherman, A.T. (eds.) CRYPTO 1982, pp. 199–203. Plenum Press, New York (1982)

13. Chaum, D., Pedersen, T.P.: Transferred cash grows in size. In: Rueppel, R.A. (ed.) EUROCRYPT 1992. LNCS, vol. 658, pp. 390–407. Springer, Heidelberg (1993). doi:10.1007/3-540-47555-9_32

14. ElGamal, T.: A public key cryptosystem and a signature scheme based on discrete logarithms. In: Blakley, G.R., Chaum, D. (eds.) CRYPTO 1984. LNCS, vol. 196, pp. 10–18. Springer, Heidelberg (1985). doi:10.1007/3-540-39568-7_2

15. Fiat, A., Shamir, A.: How to prove yourself: practical solutions to identification and signature problems. In: Odlyzko, A.M. (ed.) CRYPTO 1986. LNCS, vol. 263, pp. 186–194. Springer, Heidelberg (1987). doi:10.1007/3-540-47721-7_12

16. Galbraith, S.D., Paterson, K.G., Smart, N.P.: Pairings for cryptographers. Discrete Appl. Math. **156**(16), 3113–3121 (2008)
17. Goldwasser, S., Micali, S., Rivest, R.L.: A digital signature scheme secure against adaptive chosen-message attacks. SIAM J. Comput. **17**(2), 281–308 (1988)
18. Groth, J., Sahai, A.: Efficient non-interactive proof systems for bilinear groups. In: Smart, N. (ed.) EUROCRYPT 2008. LNCS, vol. 4965, pp. 415–432. Springer, Heidelberg (2008). doi:10.1007/978-3-540-78967-3_24
19. GSMA: White paper: mobile NFC in transport (2012). http://www.gsma.com/digitalcommerce/wp-content/uploads/2012/10/Transport_White_Paper_April13_amended.pdf
20. Märtens, P.: Practical divisible E-cash. Cryptology ePrint Archive, Report 2015/318 (2015). http://eprint.iacr.org/2015/318
21. Okamoto, T., Ohta, K.: Universal electronic cash. In: Feigenbaum, J. (ed.) CRYPTO 1991. LNCS, vol. 576, pp. 324–337. Springer, Heidelberg (1992). doi:10.1007/3-540-46766-1_27
22. Pointcheval, D., Sanders, O., Traoré, J.: Cut down the tree to achieve constant complexity in divisible E-cash. Cryptology ePrint Archive, Report 2015/972 (2015). http://eprint.iacr.org/2015/972
23. Schnorr, C.P.: Efficient identification and signatures for smart cards. In: Brassard, G. (ed.) CRYPTO 1989. LNCS, vol. 435, pp. 239–252. Springer, New York (1990). doi:10.1007/0-387-34805-0_22

Asymptotically Tight Bounds for Composing ORAM with PIR

Ittai Abraham[1], Christopher W. Fletcher[2], Kartik Nayak[3(✉)], Benny Pinkas[4], and Ling Ren[5]

[1] VMware Research, Herzliya, Israel
iabraham@vmware.com
[2] University of Illinois, Urbana-Champaign, IL, USA
cwfletch@illinois.edu
[3] University of Maryland, College Park, MD, USA
kartik@cs.umd.edu
[4] Bar Ilan University, Ramat Gan, Israel
benny@pinkas.net
[5] MIT, Cambridge, MA, USA
renling@mit.edu

Abstract. Oblivious RAM (ORAM) is a cryptographic primitive that allows a trusted client to outsource storage to an untrusted server while hiding the client's memory access patterns to the server. The last three decades of research on ORAMs have reduced the bandwidth blowup of ORAM schemes from $O(\sqrt{N})$ to $O(1)$. However, all schemes that achieve a bandwidth blowup smaller than $O(\log N)$ use expensive computations such as homomorphic encryptions. In this paper, we achieve a sub-logarithmic bandwidth blowup of $O(\log_d N)$ (where d is a free parameter) without using expensive computation. We do so by using a d-ary tree and a two server private information retrieval (PIR) protocol based on inexpensive XOR operations at the servers. We also show a $\Omega(\log_{cD} N)$ lower bound on bandwidth blowup in the modified model involving PIR operations. Here, c is the number of blocks stored by the client and D is the number blocks on which PIR operations are performed. Our construction matches this lower bound implying that the lower bound is tight for certain parameter ranges. Finally, we show that C-ORAM (CCS 15) and CHf-ORAM violate the lower bound. Combined with concrete attacks on C-ORAM/CHf-ORAM, we claim that there exist security flaws in these constructions.

1 Introduction

Oblivious RAM is a cryptographic primitive that allows a client to privately outsource storage to an untrusted server without revealing any information about its data accesses, i.e., the server learns nothing about the data or the sequence of addresses accessed. It was first proposed by Goldreich and Ostrovsky [22,23]. Since the initial theoretical work three decades ago, there has been a lot of effort to improve ORAMs either as a stand-alone primitive [2,9,12,19,24,25,27,37,39,

© International Association for Cryptologic Research 2017
S. Fehr (Ed.): PKC 2017, Part I, LNCS 10174, pp. 91–120, 2017.
DOI: 10.1007/978-3-662-54365-8_5

40, 42, 44, 48, 51, 53, 58] or for applications including secure outsourced storage [3, 33, 41, 49, 50, 59], secure processors [15–17, 36, 43, 45, 46] and secure multi-party computation [20, 34, 35, 54, 55, 60].

The standard ORAM model assumes the server to be a simple storage device that only supports *read* and *write* operations. In this model, numerous works have improved the bandwidth blowup (or bandwidth overhead) — the amount of communication between the client and the server relative to an insecure scenario that does not protect access patterns — from $O(\log^3 N)$ to $O(\log N)$ where N is the number of logical data blocks. But none could achieve sub-logarithmic bandwidth blowup so far. In this sense, though not provably insurmountable [5], the $\Omega(\log N)$ bandwidth blowup barrier does seem hard to surpass.

To this end, a line of work deviates from the standard model and assumes the existence of two non-colluding servers [34, 41, 49] with inexpensive server computation (e.g., XOR) or no server computation. But these constructions have been unable to surpass the $\Omega(\log N)$ bandwidth blowup barrier.

Another line of work allows the server to perform some computation. The most recent works involving server computation achieved $O(1)$ width blowup [2, 12, 39, 40]. But this improvement in bandwidth comes with a huge cost in the amount of server computation. In both Apon et al. [2] and Devadas et al. [12], the server runs the ORAM algorithm using homomorphic encryption (fully homomorphic and additively homomorphic, respectively) with little client intervention. In practice, in both schemes, the time for server computation will far exceed the time for server-client communication and become the new bottleneck.

Thus, the state of the art leaves the following natural question:

Can we construct a sub−logarithmic ORAM without expensive computation?

A recent construction called CHf-ORAM [39] claims to have solved the above challenge by combining ORAM with private information retrieval (PIR). Using four non-colluding servers, CHf-ORAM claims to achieve $O(1)$ bandwidth blowup using simple XOR-based PIR protocols. However, we realized that there exist security flaws in CHf-ORAM and its predecessor C-ORAM [40]. We give two concrete attacks on a slight variant of C-ORAM, highlighting some subtleties that the current C-ORAM proof does not capture.

Private information retrieval (PIR) and Oblivious RAM (ORAM) are two closely related concepts, and they both hide access patterns. In fact, PIR is frequently applied to ORAM constructions to improve bandwidth blowup [37, 39–41, 61]. This led us to ask the following question:

What is the asymptotically optimal bandwidth blowup one can achieve by using PIR in an ORAM construction?

In order to answer this question, we build on the seminal work of Goldreich and Ostrovsky [23] and derive a $\Omega(\log_{cD} N)$ bandwidth lower bound for ORAMs that leverage only PIR and PIR-write on top of the traditional model. Here, c is the number of blocks stored by the client and D is the number of blocks on which PIR/PIR-write operations are performed. C-ORAM and CHf-ORAM violate this lower bound, and thus cannot be secure.

Given the insecurity of C-ORAM and CHf-ORAM, the former question remains open. We then positively answer the former question with a concrete and provably secure construction. Our construction relies on a d-ary ORAM tree and a private information retrieval (PIR) protocol involving two non-colluding servers, where the servers perform simple XOR computations. Our construction achieves $O(\log_d N)$ bandwidth blowup with $c = O(1)$ blocks of client storage and PIR operations on $D = d \cdot \mathsf{polylog}(N)$ blocks. Therefore, it matches the $\Omega(\log_{cD} N)$ lower bound when $d = \Omega(\log N)$, implying that under certain parameter ranges our construction is asymptotically optimal and the lower bound is asymptotically tight.

We remark that there is a concurrent and independent work, MSKT-ORAM, that achieves comparable bandwidth blowup using similar techniques [62].[1] Our construction has several advantages over the concurrent work and we make a more detailed comparison in Sect. 2.

1.1 Our Contributions

Our contributions in this paper can be summarized as follows:

1. **ORAM with sub-logarithmic bandwidth blowup.** We show a provably secure ORAM construction that achieves a bandwidth blowup of $O(\log_d N)$ (where d is a parameter) using $O(1)$ blocks of client storage. Our construction uses a d-ary tree and a PIR protocol (Sect. 4).
2. **Extending the Goldreich-Ostrovsky lower bound to allow PIR operation.** For a client storing c blocks of data and performing a PIR on D blocks at a time, we show that the ORAM bandwidth blowup is lower bounded by $\Omega(\log_{cD} N)$ (Sect. 5). Our construction matches this lower bound implying that the lower bound is tight and that our construction is asymptotically optimal for certain parameter ranges.
3. **Security flaws in prior works.** Using our lower bound and other concrete attacks, we show that the bandwidth blowup claimed by C-ORAM and CHf-ORAM [39, 40] is not achievable (Sect. 6).

1.2 Overview of Our Construction

On a high level, an ORAM access has two phases. The first phase, called *retrieval*, fetches and possibly updates the data block requested by the client. The second phase, called *eviction*, reshuffles some data blocks on the server. Many recent

---

[1] The title of that paper claims "constant bandwidth", which would have been immediately ruled out by our lower bound. On a closer look, the bandwidth blowup is actually $O(\log_d N)$. This calls for our lower bound to clear the confusion in this direction.

Table 1. Comparison with existing Oblivious RAM schemes. N denotes the number of logical blocks stored by the ORAM. In [44,53], a stash of $\Omega(\lambda)$ blocks ensures a failure probability of $e^{\Omega(-\lambda)}$. For a negligible (in N) failure probability, these works set $\lambda = \omega(\log N)$.

Construction	Bandwidth blowup	Client storage	Block size	Server computation	#Servers
Path ORAM [53]	$8 \log N$	$O(\lambda)$	$\Omega(\log^2 N)$	-	1
Ring ORAM [44]	$2.5 \log N$	$O(\lambda)$	$\Omega(\log^2 N)$	XOR	1
Onion ORAM [12]	$O(1)$	$O(1)$	$\tilde{\Omega}(\log^5 N)$	Homomorphic enc.	1
This work	$4 \log_d N$	$O(1)$	$\Omega(d\lambda \log N)$	XOR	2
(with $d = \log N$)	$4 \log N / \log \log N$		$\Omega(\lambda \log^2 N)$		

ORAM constructions [12,44,53,54] are based on binary trees, in which the bandwidth overhead on retrieval and eviction are both $\Theta(\log N)$ due to the tree height.

Our construction uses a tree with larger fan-out $d = \omega(1)$, which decreases the tree height to $O(\log_d N) = O(\frac{\log N}{\log d})$. Based on a d-ary tree, we design a new eviction algorithm whose bandwidth overhead is $O(\log_d N)$. However, it increases the bandwidth overhead by more than a factor of d on retrieval in the standard model. We then use two-server private information retrieval (Sect. 3.3) to reduce the retrieval bandwidth to $O(1)$ (assuming moderately large block size). Our basic eviction algorithm also requires $\Omega(d \log N)$ blocks of client storage. We again rely on two-server PIR to reduce the client storage to $O(1)$. Overall, we obtain a two-server ORAM with $O(1)$ client storage and $O(\log_d N)$, i.e., sub-logarithmic bandwidth overhead (Table 1).

Although our bandwidth blowup decreases with the tree fan-out d, we cannot keep increasing d for free due to block metadata. We discuss the trade-off regarding d in Sect. 4.4.

2   Related Work

Oblivious RAM was first introduced by Goldreich and Ostrovsky around three decades ago [22,23]. They proposed two constructions. The latter of the two used a hierarchy of buffers of exponentially increasing size, which was later known as the hierarchical ORAM framework.

They achieved $O(\log^3 N)$ amortized bandwidth blowup under constant client storage, $\Omega(\log N)$ block size and computational security. Their model assumes the server to be a simple storage device that is capable of only "read" and "write" operations. In this model, they show an $\Omega(\log_c N)$ lower bound on the bandwidth blowup, where c is the number of blocks stored by the client.

Follow-up works [24,25,27,57,58] in the hierarchical ORAM framework reduced the bandwidth blowup from $O(\log^3 N)$ to $O(\log^2 N / \log \log N)$. Most of these works also used constant client storage and computational security, and bandwidth blowups are amortized and holds for $\Omega(\log N)$ block size. Ajtai [1] and Damgård et al. [10] showed ORAM constructions that are statistically secure. This was followed by the statistically secure ORAM construction by Shi et al. [48], who introduced the tree-based paradigm. ORAM constructions in the tree-based paradigm have improved the bandwidth blowup from $O(\log^3 N)$ to $O(\log N)$ [9,19,44,48,53,54]. Circuit ORAM [54] gets very close to the Goldreich-Ostrovsky lower bound, achieving $O(\log N)\omega(1)$ bandwidth blowup with constant client storage for moderately large blocks of size $\Omega(\log^2 N)$. Most tree-based ORAMs achieved statistical access pattern security, and obtained the desired bandwidth blowup in the worst-case instead of an amortized blowup. But the reported bandwidth results only hold for moderately large blocks of size $\Omega(\log^2 N)$ due to the use of the ORAM recursion technique [48].

It is worth noting that our d-ary tree idea is similar to the techniques in the following papers. Kushilevitz et al. [27] achieves $O(\log^2 N/\log\log N)$ bandwidth blowup using $\Theta(\log N)$ buffers for every large level. Gentry et al. [19] uses a $\Theta(\log N)$-ary tree and a push-to-leaf procedure along a deterministic path to achieve $O(\log^2 N/\log\log N)$ blowup. An concurrent work [62] uses a $\Theta(\log N)$-ary tree, which we compare to in detail later. In all cases, the idea is to balance the (sometimes implicit) bandwidth mismatch between the retrieval phase and the eviction phase.

Many works deviated from the traditional ORAM model defined by Goldreich and Ostrovsky by introducing multiple non-colluding servers and/or server-side computation. Some of these papers refer to their work as oblivious outsourced storage, but we still refer to them as ORAMs. We review these works below.

ORAMs using multiple non-colluding servers. Constructions in this category so far have not been able to surpass the $\Omega(\log N)$ bandwidth barrier (except CHf-ORAM [39] which we discuss later in this section) [34,41,49]. Lu and Ostrovsky [34] achieved a bandwidth blowup of $O(\log N)$. In their scheme, each non-colluding server performs permutations that are hidden to the other server due to which the Goldreich-Ostrovsky lower bound does not apply. Stefanov and Shi [49] implemented a practical system using two servers and $O(\sqrt{N})$ client storage. Their client storage can be reduced to $O(1)$ using the standard recursion technique [48]. Their construction required $O(1)$ client-to-server bandwidth blowup and $O(\log N)$ server-to-server bandwidth blowup.

ORAMs with server computation. There exist many ORAM schemes that allow the server to do computation on data blocks [2,11,12,20,37,40,44,50, 51,57,59,61]. Most of these works still require $\Omega(\log N)$ bandwidth blowup, except the following ones. Apon et al. [2] use fully homomorphic encryption to achieve an $O(1)$ bandwidth blowup. However, the large overhead of FHE makes the scheme impractical. Onion ORAM [12] improves upon Apon et al. to achieve an $O(1)$ bandwidth blowup by using only additively homomorphic encryption or somewhat homomorphic encryption. The amount of server computation is significantly reduced (compared to FHE) but is still quite large. In addition, the $O(1)$ bandwidth blowup of Onion ORAM can only be achieved for very large block sizes $(B = \Omega(\log^5 N))$. Both these schemes circumvent the

Goldreich-Ostrovsky lower bound by using homomorphic operations on the server side that require little client intervention.

Independent and concurrent work. MSKT-ORAM [62] is an independent and concurrent work that achieves comparable bandwidth blowup using similar techniques, i.e., a d-ary tree and two-server PIR applied to a poly-logarithmic number of blocks. Our construction has several advantages stemming from the following major differences: While we extended the most recent tree-based ORAM, Onion ORAM [12], to a d-ary tree, MSKT-ORAM builds on top of the very first tree-based ORAM by Shi et al. [48] and extends it to a d-ary tree. Thus, MSKT-ORAM does not take advantage of the new techniques invented afterwards, such as small block recursion [52], reverse lexicographical order [19], higher bucket load [44], reduced eviction frequency [44], and an empty bucket invariant [12]. As a result, MSKT-ORAM requires a block size as large as $\Omega(N^\epsilon)$ for some constant ϵ, while we only require blocks of size polylog(N) bits; MSKT-ORAM has a $\omega(\log N)$ server storage blowup, while our construction has a constant size server storage blowup (Sect. 4.1); MSKT-ORAM needs a PIR, a physical read and a physical write operation to evict each block, while we can eliminate the need for the physical read due to the empty bucket/slice invariant (cf. Lemma 2 and Sect. 4.3); MSKT-ORAM also spends at least 2× more bandwidth for both blocks and metadata during eviction, since Shi et al. [48] requires two evictions after every access.

Oblivious RAM lower bound. As mentioned earlier, Goldreich and Ostrovsky presented a lower bound of $\Omega(\log_c N)$ where c is the amount of client storage in blocks. Their lower bound modeled the server as a simple storage device capable of reading and writing blocks. Boyle and Naor revisit the ORAM lower bound to relate it to the size of circuits for sorting [5]. In our work, we extend the lower bound suggested by Goldreich and Ostrovsky to encompass private information retrieval (PIR) as a possible operation performed by the client and obtain a lower bound of $\Omega(\log_{cD}(N))$ in Sect. 5. Here, c is the number of blocks stored by the client and D is the number of blocks that a PIR is performed on. C-ORAM [40] and CHf-ORAM [39] violate the lower bound and must have security flaws. Boyle and Naor showed that an ORAM lower bound is difficult to obtain in a general model, i.e., if the client is not restricted to a small set of operations.

Other related work. There has also been work to optimize ORAM for the number of rounds of communication [14,18,57], response time [11], parallelism [4,7] and various other parameters [3,47]. Liu et al. developed compiler techniques to achieve obliviousness with fewer ORAM accesses [30–32]. Some data structures can be made oblivious without using a full ORAM [26,38,56].

Private information retrieval. A Private information retrieval (PIR) protocol allows a user to retrieve some data block from a server without revealing the block that was retrieved. It was first introduced by Chor et al. [8]. In our work, we use a simple two server $O(N)$ scheme from [8] to reduce the bandwidth cost of accessing a block.

3   Preliminaries

3.1   Problem Definition

Consider a scenario where a trusted client wishes to store data to a remote untrusted server while preserving privacy. First, the client can protect confidentiality of the data using standard encryption schemes. However, the access pattern of the client, i.e., the order in which the client accesses the data, can also reveal information. Oblivious RAM algorithms address this problem by *hiding* the data access pattern, i.e., hiding which blocks were read/written from the server. Intuitively, a server observing the resulting *physical* access pattern should not be able to learn anything about the *logical* access pattern of the client.

The ORAM model traditionally treats the server as a simple storage device [22,23]. But recent works have extended the ORAM model to allow for server computation [2,12]. Informally, an ORAM that allows server computation can be defined as follows:

Definition 1 (Informal). *Let $\boldsymbol{y} = ((a_1, op_1, data_1), \ldots, (a_t, op_t, data_t))$ be the client's logical data request sequence of length t. For each tuple $\boldsymbol{y}_i = (a_i, op_i, data_i)$, a_i represents the logical address of the data block accessed by the client, $op_i \in \{\mathsf{Read}, \mathsf{Write}\}$ and $data_i$ is the data being written ($data_i = \perp$ if $op_i = \mathsf{Read}$).*

Let $ORAM(\boldsymbol{y})$ represent the ORAM client's sequence of interactions with the server. We say an ORAM algorithm is correct if for each access $i \in [t]$, $ORAM(\boldsymbol{y}_i)$ returns data that is consistent with $\boldsymbol{y}_i$ except with $negl(|\boldsymbol{y}|)$ probability. We say an ORAM algorithm is secure if for two access patterns $\boldsymbol{y}$ and $\boldsymbol{z}$ with $|\boldsymbol{y}| = |\boldsymbol{z}|$, their access patterns $ORAM(\boldsymbol{y})$ and $ORAM(\boldsymbol{z})$ are computationally or statistically indistinguishable. Respectively, the ORAM algorithms are called computationally or statistically secure.

The sequence of interaction $ORAM(\boldsymbol{y})$ may include simple physical read/write requests, PIR requests, or any other complex protocols between the client and the server.

Bandwidth blowup. In order to hide data access patterns, $ORAM(\boldsymbol{y})$ involves more communication between the server and the client than $\boldsymbol{y}$. We define *bandwidth blowup* as the ratio between the amount of communication (measured in bits) in $ORAM(\boldsymbol{y})$ to the amount of communication in $\boldsymbol{y}$. Each unit of logic data accessed by a client is referred to as a *block*. We denote N to be the total number of logic data blocks in the ORAM.

3.2   Tree-Based ORAMs

In a tree-based ORAM, server storage is organized as a binary tree [48]. As mentioned in the introduction, instead of a binary tree, in this work we use a d-ary tree. Hence this brief introduction presents the general case and considers d as an independent parameter.

```
 1: function Access(a, op, data)
 2:    l ← PosMap[a]
 3:    data ← ReadBlock(l, a)
 4:    l' ← UniformRandom(0, d^L − 1)
 5:    PosMap[a] ← l'
 6:    if op = read then
 7:        return data to client
 8:    else
 9:        data ← data'
10:    Write data to the root bucket
11:    evict()
```

Fig. 1. Tree-based ORAM data access algorithm. Here, PosMap is a map from an address a to a leaf l of the tree. ReadBlock(l, a) retrieves a block of data with address a from a path of buckets along leaf l.

Server storage. We consider d-ary tree with $L + 1$ levels, from level 0 to level L. Thus, level i has d^i nodes. Recall that N is the total number of logical blocks stored by the client. Then L is roughly $\log_d N$. Each node in the tree is called a *bucket* and each bucket contains Z slots for logical blocks. A slot can also be empty — in this case, we say it contains a *dummy* block; otherwise, we say it contains a *real* block. Each block stores B bits of information. Dummy blocks and real blocks are both encrypted using randomized symmetric encryption.

Metadata. Aside from the B bits of block data, tree-based ORAMs also store some metadata for each block. The metadata stores the block identifier and whether the block is real or dummy. The client also maintains a position map PosMap that maps each real block to a random leaf in the tree.

In this work, we first assume that the client stores all the metadata locally. We then describe how this metadata can be offloaded to the server (Sect. 4.3) to achieve $O(1)$ client storage.

Invariant. Tree-based ORAM maintains the invariant that if a block is mapped to a leaf l of the tree, the block must be in some bucket on the path from the root to the leaf l. Since a leaf uniquely determines a path and vice versa, we use the two terms interchangeably.

Access. The pseudo-code for an access algorithm in a tree-based ORAM is described in Fig. 1. To access a block with logical address a, the client performs the following operations:

1. Look up the local PosMap to figure out the path l it is mapped to (line 2).
2. Download and decrypt every block on path p, discarding every block that does not have address a. Due to the invariant, the client is guaranteed to find block a on path l. This is done by ReadBlock(l, a) in Fig. 1 line 3.
3. Remap block a to a new random path l' (i.e., update PosMap), i.e. logically remove block a from its old position (lines 4 and 5).

4. Re-encrypt block a and append it to the root bucket (line 10, encryption is not shown in the figure).
5. Invoke an eviction procedure to percolate blocks towards leaves (line 11).

The first four steps correspond to the retrieval phase, and are similar for many tree-based ORAMs [12,48,53]. Tree-based ORAMs differ in their eviction procedures (which also affect the bucket size Z). Existing tree-based ORAM schemes when extended to use a d-ary tree do not achieve sub-logarithmic bandwidth blowup due to inefficient eviction. Hence, a main contribution of this paper is to construct such an eviction scheme (Sect. 4).

3.3 Private Information Retrieval

Private information retrieval (PIR) allows a user to download one item from an unprocessed database known to a server, without revealing to the server which item is downloaded [8]. More formally, the setting has a server which is holding a list of records $Y = (y_1, y_2, \cdots, y_m)$, and a user who wants to download record y_i without revealing i to the server. A PIR scheme must enable this operation while requiring communication that is strictly smaller than the size of the database (otherwise, a trivial solution could have the user hide i by simply downloading the entire database.) The database records are usually public data records, or records which are owned by the server, and therefore the user cannot encrypt or otherwise preprocess them.

Two categories of PIR techniques exist – one operates in a setting with a single server and the other requires the existence of two or more non-colluding servers. Single-server PIR protocols, such as [6,21,28], have been adopted by Path-PIR [37] and Onion ORAM [12] to improve bandwidth. A downside, however, is that they require the server to perform operations on homomorphically encrypted ciphertexts [29], making server computation the new bottleneck. PIR in the presence of two or more non-colluding servers is conceptually simpler and involves much less computation — typically only simple XOR operations. It can also guarantee information-theoretic security (whereas it is known that single-server PIR cannot be unconditionally secure).

The original investigation of two-server PIR assumed that each database record is a single bit. The initial PIR paper described a two-server PIR protocol with $O(m^{1/3})$ communication [8] (and more efficient protocols with more than two servers). This result was only recently improved to obtain a communication of $m^{O(\sqrt{\log\log m/\log m})}$ [13].

In the setting of ORAM, we are interested in a PIR of long records, where the number of bits in each record $|y_j|$ is in the same order as the total number of records m. In this case there is a simple PIR protocol that was adopted in [41]: The database of records is replicated across the two servers, $\mathcal{S}_1$ and $\mathcal{S}_2$. Suppose that the user is interested in retrieving record i. For the request, the user generates a random bit string of length m, $X = (x_1, x_2, \cdots, x_m)$. He then generates $X' = (x'_1, x'_2, \cdots, x'_m)$ by flipping the i-th bit in X, i.e., $x'_i = \bar{x}_i$ and $x'_j = x_j$ for $j \neq i$. The user then sends X to $\mathcal{S}_1$, and X' to $\mathcal{S}_2$. $\mathcal{S}_1$ computes and responds with $\sum_j x_j \cdot y_j$ while $\mathcal{S}_2$ computes and responds with $\sum_j x_j' \cdot y_j$. Here, the sums represent a bit-wise XOR, and $\cdot$ represents a bit-wise AND. The user then sums up (XORs) the two responses to obtain $\sum_j (x_j + x_j') \cdot y_j = y_i$. The above protocol is denoted as $\mathsf{TwoServerPIR}(\mathcal{S}_1, \mathcal{S}_2, Y, i)$. The communication overhead is $O(|y_j| + m) = O(|y_j|)$.

PIR-writes. Analogous to PIR, we can define PIR-write operations. Our construction in this paper does not use PIR-writes, but we briefly mention it below since our lower bound in Sect. 5 allows PIR-writes.

A PIR-write operation lets a user update one record among a list of records on a server without revealing to the server which record is updated. Notice that now the records can no longer be public data; they have to be encrypted. Otherwise, the server can trivially figure out which record is updated by comparing their values before and after the update.

4   The Construction

Our construction follows the tree-based ORAM paradigm in the previous section (Sect. 3.2). In this section, we present the changes in server storage and the retrieval and eviction strategies to obtain a sub-logarithmic bandwidth overhead. Figure 2 shows the pseudocode of our construction. Figure 3 shows how servers store blocks and an example eviction for our construction.

Server storage. Our construction uses two servers $\mathcal{S}_1$ and $\mathcal{S}_2$, both storing identical information (hence, Fig. 3 shows only one tree). Our d-ary tree has $L + 1$ levels, numbered from 0 (the root) to L (the leaves). Each node in the tree is called a *bucket*. Each bucket consists of Z slots that can each store one block. Slots from the non-root buckets are equally divided into d *slices*, each of size Z/d. Each leaf bucket has an bucket aux that can store Z blocks.

Metadata. Our construction requires metadata similar to the description in Sect. 3.2, i.e., the position map PosMap and a block identifier for each slot. As mentioned, we assume the client stores all metadata locally for the cloud storage application, but can easily outsource them to the server without asymptotically increasing bandwidth blowup (Sect. 4.3).

Initialization. Initially, the ORAM tree at both servers contain all dummy blocks. The position map is initialized to contain independent and uniformly random numbers for each block. The client initializes each block using a logical write operation. If the client issues a logical read operation to a block that has never been initialized, the behavior of the ORAM is undefined.

Access. Each client request is represented as a tuple $(a, \mathsf{op}, \mathsf{data}')$ where a is the address of the block, $\mathsf{op} \in \{\mathsf{Read}, \mathsf{Write}\}$ and data' is the data to be written ($\mathsf{data}' = \perp$ if $\mathsf{op} = \mathsf{Read}$). The client maintains a counter cnt for the total number of accesses made so far. For each access $(a, \mathsf{op}, \mathsf{data}')$, the client does the following (refer Fig. 2):

1: Persistent variables cnt, G initialized to 0
2: cnt is the number of accesses performed so far since the previous eviction
3: G is the number of evictions performed so far, represented in base d
4: Let $\mathcal{P}(l)$ be the path from root to leaf l, and $\mathcal{P}(l, k)$ be the k-th bucket on $\mathcal{P}(l)$.

5: **function** Access(a, op, data$'$)
6:   $l \leftarrow$ PosMap[a]
7:   data $\leftarrow$ ReadBlock(l, a)
8:   **if** op = read **then**
9:     return data to client
10: **else**
11:    data $\leftarrow$ data$'$
12:    $l' \leftarrow$ UniformRandom($0, d^L - 1$)
13:    PosMap[a] $\leftarrow l'$
14:    Write data to the cnt-th slot of the root bucket
15:    cnt := cnt $+ 1$ mod $Z/2$
16:    **if** cnt = 0 **then**
17:      $l_e \leftarrow$ reverse(G)
18:      EvictAlongPath(l_e)
19:      $G \leftarrow G + 1$ mod d^L

20: **function** ReadBlock(l, a)
21:    $(\mathsf{id}_1, \mathsf{id}_2, \dots, \mathsf{id}_{ZL}) \leftarrow$ Retrieve block identifiers on $\mathcal{P}(l)$
22:    Suppose $\mathsf{id}_i = a$
23:    **return** TwoServerPIR($\mathcal{S}_1, \mathcal{S}_2, \mathcal{P}(l), i$)

24: **function** EvictAlongPath(l_e)
25:    **for** $k \leftarrow 0$ to $L - 1$ **do**
26:      Let s be the $(k + 1)$-th digit of G *// For each bucket, $(k + 1)$-th digit accesses slices in a round-robin manner.*
27:      EvictToSlices(l_e, k, s)
28:      *// Additional processing for the leaf bucket $\mathcal{P}(l_e, L)$ to make it empty*
29:      Read all blocks in $\mathcal{P}(l_e, L)$ and its auxiliary bucket $\mathcal{P}(l_e, \mathsf{aux})$
30:      Move all real blocks from $\mathcal{P}(l_e, L)$ to $\mathcal{P}(l_e, \mathsf{aux})$

31: **function** EvictToSlices(l_e, k, s)
32:    *// Evict from bucket $\mathcal{P}(l_e, k)$ to the s-th slice of each of its d children*
33:    Download all blocks in $\mathcal{P}(l_e, k)$
34:    **for** $t \leftarrow 1$ to d **do**
35:      Let S be the s-th slice of the t-th child of $\mathcal{P}(l_e, k)$
36:      Let T be the set of real blocks in $\mathcal{P}(l_e, k)$ that can be evicted to S
37:      Upload T to S and pad remaining slots in S with dummy blocks

Fig. 2. Access and eviction algorithm for our oblivious RAM construction.

1. The client looks up position map PosMap[a] to obtain the leaf l associated with block a (line 6).
2. Let $\mathcal{P}(l)$ represent the path from root to leaf l, and $\mathcal{P}(l, k)$ represent the k-th bucket on $\mathcal{P}(l)$. The client retrieves the block identifiers on the path $(\mathsf{id}_1, \mathsf{id}_2 \dots, \mathsf{id}_{ZL})$ from its local storage. Due to the tree-based ORAM

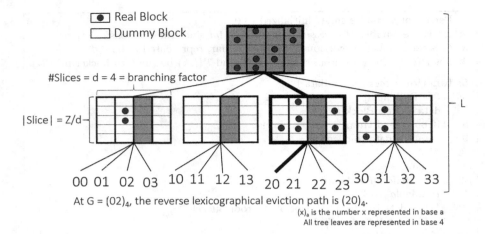

At $G = (02)_4$, the reverse lexicographical eviction path is $(20)_4$.

$(x)_a$ is the number x represented in base a
All tree leaves are represented in base 4

Fig. 3. Example eviction path for a three-level 4-ary tree at $G = 2$ i.e. $G = (02)_4$. For evicting the root bucket into its children buckets, the client downloads blue colored root bucket and writes to the blue colored slices of its children. The figure shows load of the buckets just before eviction from the root bucket. (Color figure online)

invariant, one of the identifiers on the path will be a. Without loss of generality, assume $\mathsf{id}_i = a$ (lines 21 and 22).

3. The client invokes a two-server PIR protocol $\mathsf{TwoServerPIR}(\mathcal{S}_1, \mathcal{S}_2, \mathcal{P}(l), i)$ to retrieve the block with address a (line 23).

4. The client updates the data field of the block a to data$'$ if op = Write. It sets a new leaf l' for the block and updates PosMap. It updates the metadata to remove the block from the tree. It appends the block a to the cnt-th slot of the root bucket (lines 8–14).

5. The client increments cnt. If cnt $= Z/2$, the client resets cnt and performs the eviction procedure described below (lines 15–19).

Eviction. The eviction procedure of our construction is a generalization of the eviction procedure of Onion ORAM [12]. It differs from Onion ORAM in the following two ways. First, we apply the eviction scheme on a reverse lexicographical ordering [19] over a d-ary tree instead of a binary tree. Second, when evicting from each bucket along a path, we write to only one slice of each child bucket (instead of writing to the entire child buckets). This is essential for our construction to achieve sub-logarithmic bandwidth blowup.

As shown in Fig. 2, we evict every $Z/2$ accesses along reverse lexicographical ordering of paths. Given that we have a d-ary tree instead of a binary tree, we represent the paths as numbers with base d. We use a counter G to maintain the next path l_e that should be evicted. Eviction is performed for each non-leaf bucket on path $\mathcal{P}(l_e)$. For the k-th bucket from the root, denoted $\mathcal{P}(l_e, k)$, the client first downloads the bucket $\mathcal{P}(l_e, k)$. It then uploads all real blocks to the s-th slice (which will be empty before this operation) of each of its children

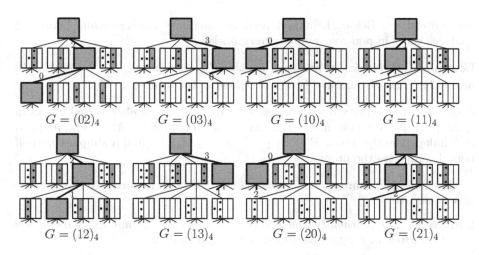

$G = (02)_4$ $G = (03)_4$ $G = (10)_4$ $G = (11)_4$

$G = (12)_4$ $G = (13)_4$ $G = (20)_4$ $G = (21)_4$

Fig. 4. Buckets and slices accessed for $2d$ **consecutive evictions.** Here, $d = 4$ and $G = \#$ evictions mod d^L. $(x)_a$ denotes the number x represented in base a. The dots in the slices represent real blocks at the end of the eviction operation. Note that for each bucket, slices are accessed (written into) in a round-robin manner. If an eviction path passes through a bucket at level i at t-th eviction then it passes through it again at $t + d^i$ evictions.

where s is the $(k + 1)$-th digit of G. (We show in Sect. 4.2 that there will be sufficient room in these slices.) After this operation, the bucket $\mathcal{P}(l_e, k)$ will be empty. Due to the reverse lexicographical order of eviction paths, $\mathcal{P}(l_e, k)$ will be a child bucket for the next $d - 1$ evictions involving it (refer Fig. 4 for an example), during each of which the slice being written to will be empty. For the last level (level L), the client downloads all blocks in the leaf bucket $\mathcal{P}(l_e, L)$ and its auxiliary bucket $\mathcal{P}(l_e, \mathsf{aux})$. It moves all real blocks to the auxiliary bucket $\mathcal{P}(l_e, \mathsf{aux})$ and uploads both buckets to the server.

Example. An example showing $2d$ consecutive evictions is in Fig. 4 for $d = 4$. In the example, we start with eviction number $G = (02)_4$. Observe that the third child of the root bucket is emptied at $G = (02)_4$ as the reverse lexicographic eviction path $(20)_4$ passes through it. In the next $d - 1$ evictions, one slice of the bucket is written to in a round-robin manner. Finally, at eviction number $G = (12)_4$, when the path $(21)_4$ passes through it again, the last slice is written into after which the entire bucket is emptied again. Similarly, it can be easily seen that for each bucket at level i, a slice is written into every d^{i-1} evictions and the bucket is emptied every d^i evictions.

4.1 Parameterization and Overflow Analysis

We show that the buckets (and slices) in the tree overflow with negligible probability. In our construction, the root bucket and the auxiliary buckets are not partitioned into slices. Eviction is performed every $Z/2$ accesses, so the root bucket never overflows. Below, Lemma 1 analyzes auxiliary buckets while Lemma 2 analyzes slices in non-root non-auxiliary buckets.

Lemma 1. *If the size of auxiliary buckets Z_{aux} satisfies $N \leq d^L \cdot Z_{\text{aux}}/2$, the probability that an auxiliary bucket overflows is bounded by $e^{-\frac{Z_{\text{aux}}}{6}}$.*

Proof. For an auxiliary bucket b, define $Y(b)$ to be the number of real blocks in b. Each of the N blocks in the ORAM has a probability of d^{-L} to be mapped to b independently. Thus, $E[Y(b)] \leq N \cdot d^{-L} \leq Z_{\text{aux}}/2$, and a simple Chernoff bound completes the proof. □

The following lemma generalizes Onion ORAM [12] Lemma 1 to the scenario of a d-ary tree.

Lemma 2. *The probability that a slice of a non-root and non-auxiliary bucket overflows after an eviction operation is bounded by $e^{-\frac{Z}{6d}}$.*

Proof. Consider a bucket b, and its i-th slice b_i. Define $Y(b)$ to be the number of real blocks in b, and $Y(b_i)$ to be the number of blocks in b_i after an eviction operation.

We will first assume that all slices have infinite capacity and show that $E[Y(b_i)] \leq Z/2d$, i.e., the expected number of blocks in a non-root slice after an eviction operation is no more than $Z/2d$ at any time. Then, we bound the overflow probability given a finite capacity.

For a non-root and non-auxiliary bucket b, we define variables $\overline{m}$ and $m_i, 1 \leq i \leq d$: the last EvictAlongPath operation where b is on the eviction path is the $\overline{m}$-th EvictAlongPath operation, and the EvictAlongPath operation where b is a sibling bucket with eviction happening to slice i is the m_i-th EvictAlongPath operation. Clearly, during eviction to one of the d slices, the bucket b is on the eviction path. Thus, one of m_i is equal to $\overline{m}$. We also time-stamp the blocks as follows. When a block is accessed and remapped, it gets a time stamp m^*, if the next EvictAlongPath would be the m^*-th EvictAlongPath operation.

Now consider b_i and $Y(b_i)$. There exist the following cases:

1. If $\overline{m} \geq m_i$, then $Y(b_i) = 0$, because the entire bucket b becomes empty when it is a parent bucket during the $\overline{m}$-th EvictAlongPath operation, and the next eviction that evicts blocks to slice b_i has not occurred.
2. If $\overline{m} < m_i$, we must have $m_{i-1} < m_i$. Otherwise, m_i is the smallest among $m_1, \ldots, m_d$ and it must be that $\overline{m} \geq m_i$. We consider blocks with what time stamp range can end up in b_i.
   - Blocks with time stamp $m^* \leq \overline{m}$ will not be in b_i as these blocks would have been evicted out of b in the $\overline{m}$-th EvictAlongPath operation.
   - Blocks with time stamp $\overline{m} < m^* \leq m_{i-1}$ or $m^* > m_i$ will not be in b_i as these blocks are evicted to either slices $\leq i - 1$ or slices $> i$ respectively.
   - Blocks with time stamp $m_{i-1} < m^* \leq m_i$ can be evicted to b_i.

There are at most $(m_i - m_{i-1})Z/2$ blocks with time stamp $m_{i-1} < m^* \leq m_i$. Each of these blocks go to bucket b independently with probability d^{-j}, where j is the level of b. Due to the deterministic reverse lexicographic ordering of eviction paths, it is easy to see that $m_i - m_{i-1} = d^{j-1}$. Therefore, $E[Y(b_i)] \leq d^{j-1} \cdot Z/2 \cdot d^{-j} = Z/2d$.

In either case, we have $\mu = E[Y(b_i)] \leq Z/2d$. Now that we have independence and the expected number of blocks in a bucket, using a Chernoff bound with $\delta = 1$, a slice b_i overflows with probability

$$\Pr[Y(b_i) > (1+\delta)u] \leq e^{-\frac{\delta^2 \mu}{3}} = e^{-\frac{Z}{6d}}. \qquad \square$$

Combining the two lemmas, we can set $Z = \Omega(d\lambda)$ and $Z_{\mathsf{aux}} = \Omega(\lambda)$. The probability that any slice or any bucket overflows is $e^{-\Omega(\lambda)}$. Following prior work [12,44,53], it suffices to set $\lambda = \omega(\log N)$ for $N^{-\omega(1)}$ failure probability, i.e., negligible in N.

Server Storage. The amount of server storage in our construction is

$$Z_{\mathsf{aux}} \cdot d^L + Z \cdot \Sigma_{i=0}^L d^i = \Theta(N).$$

4.2   Security Analysis

Similar to all tree based ORAMs, for each access, the client performs the retrieval phase on a random path. The use of PIR hides the location of the requested block on that random path. Eviction is performed on a publicly known reverse lexicographical ordering of paths. Along the eviction path, each bucket and a predetermined slice in each child buckets are downloaded/uploaded. Thus, all client operations observed by the servers are independent of the logical client access patterns.

4.3   Reducing Client Storage

In the construction described so far, the client stores the $\Theta(N \log N)$-bit position map, $\Theta(N \log N)$-bit metadata for all block and uses $\Theta(d\lambda)$ blocks of temporary storage during the eviction operation. In this section, we optimize our scheme to reduce the client storage to $O(1)$ blocks.

A. Position map. The position map for the main ORAM has a $\Theta(\log N)$-bit entry for each of the N blocks, amounting to $\Theta(N \log N)$ bits of storage.

Position map can be stored recursively in smaller ORAMs as discussed by Shi et al. [48]. As discussed in [52], when the data block size is $\Omega(\log^2 N)$ (which is the case for our scheme), using a small block size for recursive position map ORAMs, the asymptotic cost of recursion would be insignificant compared to the main ORAM tree. Hence, recursion does not increase to the bandwidth blowup asymptotically.

```
1: function EvictToSlices(l_e, k, s)
2:     // Evict from bucket P(l_e, k) to the s-th slice of each of its d children
3:     Download metadata for bucket P(l_e, k) from S_1
4:     for t ← 1 to d
5:         Let S be the s-th slice of the t-th child of P(l_e, k) and S_i be its i-th slot //
           S is empty
6:         for each S_i ∈ S
7:             if ∃j such that the j-th block in P(l_e, k) can be evicted to S then
8:                 block = TwoServerPIR(S_1, S_2, P(l_e, k), j)
9:                 Locally update the metadata for the j-th block in P(l_e, k) to be dummy
10:                Upload block along with its metadata to S_i on both servers
11:            else // no such j exists, do a dummy PIR and a dummy upload
12:                Run TwoServerPIR(S_1, S_2, P(l_e, k), 1) and discard its output
13:                Upload a dummy block with a dummy identifier to S_i on both servers
14:        Upload the updated metadata of P(l_e, k) to S_1
```

Fig. 5. Evicting to children slices using $O(1)$ blocks of client storage.

B. Metadata for each block in the tree. For each block of the tree, we store whether the block is real or dummy. If it is real, the identifying address is stored. This amounts to another $\Theta(N \log N)$ bits of storage.

We can store the metadata of each block along with the block data on the server. However, this would require downloading metadata from the server during retrieval before performing each PIR operation. For $Z = O(d\lambda)$, $L < \log_d N$ and a size of $O(\log N)$ bits for storing the identifier and whether the block is dummy, the total amount of metadata downloaded for an access is $O(d\lambda \log N \log_d N)$. Thus, for a block size of $\Omega(d\lambda \log N \log_d N)$ bits, the asymptotic bandwidth for downloading this metadata is absorbed.

C. Temporary storage for an eviction operation. During an eviction operation, the client downloads a bucket and a slice from each of its d children. This is equivalent to downloading two buckets. Thus, for each step of the eviction operation the client needs to store $Z = O(d\lambda)$ blocks.

We now show how this client storage can be reduced to $O(1)$. At a high level, the client needs to perform the eviction from a bucket to its children buckets without downloading the entire buckets. If the client can only store one block, it needs to download one block at a time from the parent bucket and upload it to one of its children buckets. And the client needs to do so obliviously. We achieve this by hiding which block from the parent bucket is downloaded, again using PIR, and letting the client upload to the children buckets in a deterministic order. The new EvictToSlices algorithm for evicting a parent bucket to its children slices is shown in Fig. 5.

To perform the eviction from a bucket $P(l_e, k)$ to a slice S of its t-th child, the client first downloads the metadata corresponding to $P(l_e, k)$ (line 3). The client uploads to each slot i in S (denoted S_i) sequentially, one slot at a time (line 3).

Before this eviction, each slot S_i will be empty due to Lemma 2. There are two cases:

1. If there exists a real block in $\mathcal{P}(l_e, k)$ that can be evicted to S, the client downloads that block from $\mathcal{P}(l_e, k)$ using PIR (thus hiding its location in $\mathcal{P}(l_e, k)$), and uploads it (re-encrypted) to S_i (lines 7–10).
2. If no real block in $\mathcal{P}(l_e, k)$ can be evicted to S, the client performs a dummy PIR to download an arbitrary block from $\mathcal{P}(l_e, k)$, discards the PIR output, and uploads an encrypted dummy block to S_i (lines 11–13).

Thus, for each $S_i \in S$ in order, the client downloads a block from the parent bucket using PIR (without revealing its position or whether its a dummy PIR) and uploads a block to S_i. This eviction process requires $O(1)$ blocks of storage.

4.4   Bandwidth Analysis

Bandwidth blowup. We analyze the bandwidth blowup of our construction while temporarily ignoring metadata for simplicity. The bandwidth blowup for retrieving a block using PIR is $O(1)$. On evictions, for each bucket on the path, the client downloads the parent bucket and uploads to one slice from each of the d child buckets, which is equivalent to two buckets of bandwidth. Thus, an eviction costs $2ZL$ blocks of bandwidth and it is performed every $Z/2$ accesses, giving an amortized bandwidth blowup of $4L < 4\log_d N$. Overall, the bandwidth blowup of our scheme is $O(\log_d N)$.

Trade-off regarding d. Although our bandwidth blowup decreases with d, we cannot keep increasing d for free. The reason is that the client needs to download a $\Theta(\log N)$-bit metadata for all $d\lambda \log_d N$ blocks on a path, on each access and eviction. Recursion contributes another $O(\log^3 N)$ bits, but that is no greater than the metadata overhead. So the raw bandwidth (in bits) per access is $O(B \log_d N + d\lambda \log_d N \log N)$. While we usually focus on the multiplicative blowup term, when d becomes too large, the additive term will dominate. Thus, the aforementioned bandwidth blowup only holds if the block size is $B = \Omega(d\lambda \log N)$. (If the client has large local storage and stores metadata locally, the block size B can be a $\log N$ factor smaller.)

In other words, the optimal d should be determined as a function of the block size B and the number of blocks N. For instance, for an application using moderately large block size $B = \Omega(\lambda \log^2 N)$, we can set $d = \Theta(\log N)$ and the bandwidth blowup is $O(\log N / \log \log N)$. If some application uses very large blocks such as $B = \Omega(\sqrt{N}\lambda \log N)$, then we can set $d = \Theta(\sqrt{N})$ and achieve a bandwidth blowup of $O(1)$.

5   Extending the Goldreich-Ostrovsky Lower Bound

Goldreich and Ostrovsky [23] gave an $\Omega(\log_c N)$ lower bound on the bandwidth overhead assuming perfect correctness, perfect security and assuming the client to be restricted to the following operations: reading from a memory location and writing to a memory location. Here, N represents the number of logical blocks stored on the server and c is the number of logical blocks stored by the client.

In this section, we first review (a slight variant of) the original Goldreich-Ostrovsky lower bound and its proof from [23]. We then extend the model to include PIR and PIR-write as possible client operations, and analyze how this changes the bound.

Following Goldreich-Ostrovsky and Boyle-Naor [5,23] (both papers considered the client as a CPU) we will use client and CPU interchangeably, and refer to client storage as c registers.

5.1   Original Lower Bound

We present a slight variant of the CPU used in the original lower bound work [23]:

Definition 2. *A CPU is modeled as a probabilistic random-access-machine* (RAM) *which has c registers and is restricted to the following operations:*

- READ$_i$ *reads a block from memory into a CPU register: For an* addr $\in [N]$, *set* Reg$[i] \leftarrow$ val, *where* val *is the content of the memory at location* addr.
- WRITE$_i$ *moves a block from a CPU register to memory: For some $i \in [c]$ and* addr $\in [N]$, *write the data in* Reg$[i]$ *to location* addr *in the memory.*

Our RAM model has slightly different operations than the original analysis in [23] to simplify the exposition. This will cause only constant factor differences in the bound. Given this model, the original lower bound can be stated as:

Theorem 1. *Every statistically oblivious simulation of a probabilistic RAM (Definition 2), which can access N blocks of data and hold c blocks in the CPU, on input y makes at least $max\{|y|, \Omega(t \cdot \log_c N)\}$ accesses to simulate $t = \mathsf{poly}(N)$ steps.*

Proof. As described by Goldreich and Ostrovsky [23], the task of simulating an ORAM can be modeled as a game in between three players

1. The CPU, which can hold at most c blocks and has access to a random function f
2. the program request sequence of length t
3. the observer

The CPU knows the program request sequence ahead of time. Suppose the request access sequence is represented as $r_1, \ldots, r_t$. The game takes place on a memory consisting of N cells, each capable of storing a single block.

The game proceeds for t rounds. In each round i, the CPU loads r_i in one of its registers in such a way that the observer does not learn r_i. The CPU does so by making a sequence of operations as described in Definition 2. At any time during the game, the CPU can store at most c blocks in memory. Round i ends when the CPU holds block r_i.

For a t sized request sequence, the CPU's response can be represented by two q sized sequences. The first sequence consists of an externally visible access pattern. Each entry in this sequence is a single address (each of which is sufficient to implement either READ$_i$ or WRITE$_i$). The second sequence consists of hidden operations performed by the CPU. Let us consider the possible number of *hidden actions* that can be taken by the CPU, *for a fixed visible access pattern*. For each visible read address, the block that is read can be stored in one of the c registers in the CPU. Likewise, for each visible write address, the block written back could have been removed from any one of the c registers in the CPU. Thus, hidden from the observer, the system can evolve in c ways on a READ and c ways on a WRITE.

Given that the CPU stores c blocks, a q length sequence can satisfy at most c^q program access sequences. Therefore, each visible access sequence can satisfy at most $(2c)^q c^q$ program request sequences. For perfect security, the visible access sequence should be able to satisfy all N^t possible request sequences, i.e.,

$$N^t \leq (2c)^q c^q$$

or $q \geq \frac{t \log N}{\log c + \log(2c)} = \Omega\left(t \log_c N\right)$. $\qquad\qquad\qquad\qquad$ □

The above is a bound on the number of operations. Since each operation incurs at least 1 block of bandwidth, we also obtain an amortized bandwidth blowup lower bound of $\Omega(\log_c N)$.[2]

5.2   Augmented Lower Bound (After Adding PIR)

We now extend the above result to allow the CPU to perform PIR and PIR-write.

Definition 3. *A PIR-augmented CPU is modeled as a probabilistic random-access-machine* PIR-RAM *which has c registers and is restricted to the following operations:*

– READ$_i$ *as described in Definition 2.*
– WRITE$_i$ *as described in Definition 2.*
– PIR-READ$_i$ *reads a block from memory into a CPU register using PIR: For a set of at most D addresses, set* Reg$[i] \leftarrow$ val, *where* val *can be the content of the memory at any of the locations in the set.*
– PIR-WRITE$_i$ *moves a block from a CPU register into memory privately using a PIR-WRITE operation: For a set of at most D addresses, write the data in* Reg$[i]$ *to a location among one of the D addresses.*

Theorem 2. *Every statistically oblivious simulation of a probabilistic* PIR-RAM *(Definition 3), which can access N blocks of data and hold c blocks in the CPU and perform PIR on a maximum of D blocks, on input y makes at least* $max\{|y|, \Omega(t \cdot \log_{cD} N)\}$ *accesses to simulate $t = $ poly(N) steps.*

---

[2] If we assume that the memory is initially permuted by the CPU unknown to the server, then the total number of program request sequences is at most $M^M (2c)^q c^q$ where $M = $ poly(N) is the physical memory size. Hence, we have $q = \Omega((t - M) \log_c N)$.

Proof. The proof follows the same framework as the original lower bound. The number of operations in the visible and hidden sequences due to READ$_i$ or WRITE$_i$ operations is unchanged. Now, the visible sequence additionally reveals the set of D addresses accessed on a PIR request for PIR-READ$_i$/PIR-WRITE$_i$. In each of these operations, the client can select one out of D possible memory blocks to read/write in the visible memory. Furthermore, for each of the above D outcomes, the client can add the read block to (or remove the written block from) any one of the c local registers. Thus, the system can evolve in cD possible ways for each of the PIR-READ and PIR-WRITE operations.

Extending the original argument, each visible access sequence can satisfy $(2c + 2cD)^q c^q$ program request sequences. For perfect security, the visible access sequence should be able to satisfy all N^t possible request sequences, i.e.,

$$N^t \leq (2c + 2cD)^q c^q$$

or $q \geq \frac{t \log N}{\log c + \log(2c + 2cD)} = \Omega\left(\frac{t \log N}{\log(cD)}\right)$.   □

Again, the bound is on the number of operations. Since each of the four operations incurs at least 1 block of bandwidth, a bound on the number of operations translates to a bound on amortized bandwidth blowup.

5.3   Discussion

Accounting for failure probability. The above lower bound assumes perfect security, i.e., each visible physical access sequence should be able to satisfy all possible program request sequences. However, using an argument similar to Wang et al. [54], the same lower bound can be extended to work for up to $O(1)$ failure probability (and hence, negligible failure probability).

PIR as a black box. Our lower bound is independent of the implementation details of the PIR and PIR-write operations. The bound is applicable to any statistically secure PIR construction that meets the interface in Definition 3, regardless of the number of servers it uses. We also note that although the lower bound considers PIR-WRITE as a possible operation, our construction does not use this primitive.

Our construction and the lower bound. Our construction matches this lower bound for certain parameter ranges. We use $c = 1$ register and perform a PIR operation on $D = O(d \cdot poly(\log N))$ blocks. Thus, our lower bound is asymptotically tight for $d = \Omega(\log N)$ when the data block size $B = \Omega(d \log^2 N)$.

C-ORAM, CHf-ORAM and the lower bound. We discuss how the lower bound is applicable to C-ORAM [40] and CHf-ORAM [39] in Sect. 6.2.

Circumventing the lower bound. The lower bound on bandwidth only applies to black-box usage of PIR. Onion ORAM [12] circumvents the lower bound and achieves $O(1)$ bandwidth blowup. The reason is that the homomorphic select operation in Onion ORAM (a non-black-box usage of PIR) does not consume one unit of bandwidth. Therefore, while the number of operations in Onion ORAM is still subject to the bound, the bound does not translate to a bound on bandwidth blowup. It is also possible to circumvent the lower bound by adding other operations (e.g., FHE [2]).

6 Security Analysis of C-ORAM

C-ORAM [40] is a CCS'15 paper that achieves constant bandwidth blowup over smaller block sizes and performs less server computation (compared to Onion ORAM [12]). C-ORAM introduces an eviction procedure that publicly and homomorphically merges bucket contents. CHf-ORAM [39] extends C-ORAM with four non-colluding servers to avoid homomorphic encryption. In this section, we first give a short review of C-ORAM and CHf-ORAM. We then use the lower bound described in the previous section to show that the results obtained by C-ORAM and CHf-ORAM are impossible. Lastly, we give two concrete attacks that apply to both C-ORAM and CHf-ORAM.

6.1 A Review of C-ORAM

C-ORAM follows the tree-based ORAM framework in Sect. 3.2. It has a large bucket size $Z = \omega(\log N)$ and performs one eviction every $\chi = O(Z)$ accesses. On accesses, it relies on single-server PIR (or 2-server PIR in the case of CHf-ORAM) to achieve constant bandwidth. Each eviction goes down a path in the reverse lexicographical order. For each bucket on the path, C-ORAM moves all blocks in it into the two child buckets. To perform this eviction procedure using constant bandwidth, C-ORAM proposes the following "oblivious merge" operation.

Each bucket may contain three types of blocks: real, noisy and zero. Essentially, C-ORAM has two types of dummy blocks. A zero block is a dummy block whose plaintext value is 0; a noisy block is a dummy block whose plaintext value is arbitrary. Metadata in each bucket or maintained by the client tracks the type of each block. C-ORAM then encrypts each block using an additive homomorphic encryption. Notice that if the server homomorphically merges an encrypted real block with an encrypted zero block, the result would be an encryption of the real block, i.e., $E(r) + E(0) = E(r)$ for a plaintext real block r. However, if a real block is merged with a noisy block or another real block, then the content cannot be recovered. If a zero block is merged with a noisy block, it is "contaminated" and becomes a noisy block. Therefore, in order to merge two buckets, C-ORAM needs to permute and align the two buckets in a very specific way, i.e., a real block in one bucket must always be aligned with a zero block in the other bucket. Crucially, C-ORAM also prioritizes aligning two noisy blocks such that it contaminates as few zero blocks as possible.

To make the presentation clear, we distinguish "permute" and "shuffle" operations. Whenever we say a set of blocks are "shuffled", we mean the client downloads all the blocks, shuffles them secretly and uploads them back to the server;

the server has no idea how the blocks are shuffled. Whenever we say a set of blocks are "permuted", we mean the client instructs the server to permute them, and the server sees the permutation. Therefore, permuting a set of blocks does not provide any obfuscation effect. Its only purpose is to enforce the merging rules in C-ORAM, i.e., a real block should be merged with a zero block, and a noisy block should be merged with another noisy block if possible.

Each eviction goes down a path, and merges each bucket on the path into its two children. Note that shuffling all buckets involved an eviction would take more than constant bandwidth. Therefore, when two buckets need to be merged in C-ORAM, they are permuted and not shuffled, and the server sees the permutations. It is unnecessary to permute both buckets. It is equivalent to permuting only the parent bucket and merging it into the child bucket. Now we try to analyze whether these permutations leak information about the access pattern. C-ORAM argues that if the client secretly and randomly shuffles the root bucket before each eviction, then all permutations look random and leak no information to the server. Unfortunately, this belief is incorrect.

6.2   C-ORAM, CHf-ORAM and the Lower Bound

C-ORAM and CHf-ORAM introduced three new operations on top of the standard ORAM model: download a block from a path of poly-logarithmic blocks using PIR-READ, upload a block to one hidden location in a bucket using PIR-WRITE, and an oblivious merge operation. In an oblivious merge operation, the server applies plaintext permutations (chosen by the client) to buckets before merging them. This operation creates only one possible outcome to the system state, since no action is hidden from the server. Thus oblivious merge does not affect the lower bound in Sect. 5.

CHf-ORAM achieves statistical security with negligible failure probability and is thus subject to the lower bound in Theorem 2. The number of operations required for t logical accesses is $\Omega(\frac{t \log N}{\log(cD)})$ where $c = O(1)$ and $D = \mathsf{polylog}(N)$. Thus, its bandwidth blowup is lower bounded by $\Omega(\frac{\log N}{\log \log N})$. Instead, CHf-ORAM claims to have achieved $O(1)$ bandwidth, implying a flaw in its construction.

C-ORAM achieves computational security due to the use of single-server PIR-READ/PIR-WRITE, and thus does not directly violate the lower bound. However, unless carefully shown otherwise, it is extremely unlikely that any security flaw of CHf-ORAM can be fixed by merely replacing information theoretically secure PIR with computationally secure PIR.

6.3   An Attack on the Optimized Construction of C-ORAM

This subsection and the next one give two concrete attacks to C-ORAM to give some insights on why it is insecure. Before we start, the following analogy may aid understanding. Imagine a trivially broken ORAM as follows. The client randomly shuffles all N blocks only *once* initially and keeps track of the mapping locally. Then for each request, the client simply retrieves the requested block. Each access is clearly to a random location due to the initial shuffle. But if the same block is requested multiple times, these accesses will go to the same location and this correlation reveals information.

C-ORAM essentially used a flawed argument like the above. While each permutation looks random in isolation, there is correlation among permutations, and the correlation leaks information. Both of our attacks exploit this fact.

Our first attack is on the optimized construction of C-ORAM, i.e., the "Second Construction" in Sect. 3.3. The goal of the second construction is to decrease D, i.e., the number of blocks to perform PIR on. The idea is to, on every access, "clone" the requested path to temporary memory, and perform a C-ORAM eviction operation (which we call a "shadow eviction") along the cloned path. By the ORAM invariant, the block of interest now lives in the leaf bucket and PIR to only the leaf bucket (not the entire path) is sufficient to retrieve the block. The cloned path is thrown out after the PIR operation.

This scheme suffers from correlations among permutation operations when a pair of buckets (a parent and its child) are part of multiple shadow evictions in between being involved in two regular evictions. Note that due to randomness (even if one eviction happens after every access, as suggested in C-ORAM), there is non-negligible probability that a pair of buckets deep in the tree are involved in more than 1 shadow evictions between two regular evictions. In each shadow eviction, the normal C-ORAM eviction rules apply: a real block can only be merged with a zero block, and a noisy block is prioritized to be merged with another noisy block. Since the contents of the two buckets remain the same across these shadow evictions, it is easy to see that certain slots in one bucket (e.g., the real blocks) will repeatedly "prefer" certain slots in the other bucket (e.g., zero blocks). This bias can reveal the number of real blocks in the bucket. It is well known that revealing bucket load in tree ORAMs is sufficient to leak the access pattern [48]: more recently accessed blocks will be in buckets higher in the tree than less recently used blocks.

6.4   An Attack on the Basic Construction of C-ORAM

Our second attack applies to both the basic version and the optimized version of C-ORAM. For this attack, we need the first three evictions. Recall that the basic C-ORAM performs one eviction every χ accesses, so we need client access sequences of length 3χ. Concretely, consider the following two client access patterns:

1. Access the same block 3χ times, i.e., $X = \{a_1, \ldots, a_{3\chi}\}$ where $a_i = a, \forall i$
2. Access 3χ distinct blocks, i.e., $X' = \{a_1, \ldots, a_{3\chi}\}$ where $a_i \neq a_j, \forall i \neq j$.

In this attack, we assume that initially all blocks in the C-ORAM tree are zero blocks. Our attack also works if initially the server stores all real blocks in leaf buckets, and all non-leaf buckets only contain zero blocks. We believe these

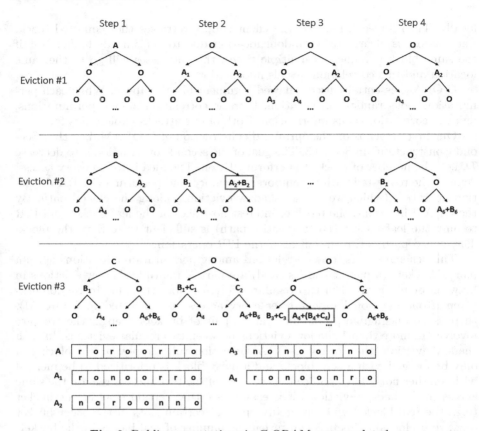

Fig. 6. Public permutations in C-ORAM are correlated.

are the two most natural initial states for tree-based ORAMs.[3] With access pattern X, the root will contain 1 real block, $\chi - 1$ noisy blocks and $Z - \chi$ zero blocks before each eviction. With access pattern X', the root will contain χ real blocks, 0 noisy block and $Z - \chi$ zero blocks before each eviction.

Figure 6 walks through the first three evictions in C-ORAM, and highlights a pair of correlated permutations during the 2nd and 3rd eviction. The figure shows the first three levels of the tree. O represents a bucket full of zero blocks. Initially, all blocks are zero. A, B and C are the three buckets of blocks injected into the root before the 1st, 2nd and 3rd eviction, respectively. A, B and C are all randomly shuffled by the client.

On the first eviction (first row), A is injected to the root. The bottom of the figure depicts an example of A assuming a small bucket size $Z = 8$ and $\chi = 4$. It

---

[3] Through personal communication with the C-ORAM authors, we learnt that C-ORAM does not start in these two initial states. Instead, they assume each bucket contains an equal number of noisy and zero blocks that are shuffled randomly. However, the C-ORAM paper did not specify what the initial state is.

contains $\chi = 4$ real blocks, denoted r, and 4 zero blocks, denoted o. This would be the case when the original access pattern is X' and four distinct blocks are accessed. A is then evicted to the next level, producing A_1 and A_2. They are then merged with the two children (both are all-zero buckets O), leaving the root empty. A_1 contains the set of blocks mapped to the left half of the tree, and A_2 contains the set of blocks mapped to the right half of the tree. In the example at the bottom, we assume 3 blocks are mapped to the left half and 1 block is mapped to the right half. Notice that A_1 and A_2 are correlated. All the real blocks in A_1 are noisy blocks (denoted n) in A_2 and vice versa. On the other hand, all the zero blocks in A_1 are zero blocks in A_2 as well. We remark that A_1 and A_2 will be independently permuted (not shown in the figure). The two permutations will be truly random because merging with empty buckets imposes no restrictions on how the two buckets are aligned. But as we noted earlier the permutations do not provide any security benefits since the attacker sees the permutation in clear. The attacker can easily apply the inverse permutation to get the same view as our example in which the correlation exists.

The first eviction continues down the leftmost path and evicts A_1 into A_3 and A_4, and further evicts A_3 down the tree (not shown). Again, a public random permutation is applied for every merge, and similar correlations exist among all the derivative of A once the attacker applies the inverse permutation.

The second eviction (second row) injects another shuffled bucket B. B produces B_1 and B_2. B_1 is randomly permuted and merged with a zero bucket. B_2, however, needs to be permuted according to the C-ORAM rules (described in Sect. 6.1) to align with A_2. After that, the eviction goes on to evict the merged bucket $A_2 + B_2$ and its children (not shown).

On the third eviction (third row), we focus on the left half of the tree. C similarly produces C_1 and C_2. C_1 is permuted and merged with B_1. The merged bucket is then permuted again to be merged with A_4. This latter permutation (to align $B_4 + C_4$ with A_4) will have a strong correlation with the one that aligns A_2 and B_2 in the second row. More crucially, the type of correlation is very different depending on whether the client access pattern is X or X', thereby revealing the access pattern.

First consider access pattern X. In this case, A_2, B_2, A_4 and B_4 mostly contain noisy and zero blocks (there are at most 3 real blocks in the system). Furthermore, the noisy blocks occupy the same set of locations in A_2 and A_4, and also in B_2 and B_4. If two noisy blocks are aligned during $A_2 + B_2$, those two slots are also likely to be aligned in $A_4 + B_4$ because C-ORAM prioritizes noisy-noisy merge. Define the number of repetitions between two permutations π and π' to be the size of the set $\{i \mid \pi(i) = \pi'(i)\}$. If we simply count the number of repetitions between the above two permutations, it will be significantly higher than 1, which is the expected value for two random permutations.

Now consider access pattern X'. In this case, A_2, B_2, A_4 and B_4 will all contain a moderate number of real blocks. Recall that all real blocks in A_2 (B_2) are noisy blocks in A_4 (B_4) and vice versa, while all zero blocks in A_2 (B_2) are zero blocks in A_4 (B_4). Now once a real block in A_2 is aligned with a zero block in B_2, that same slot in A_4—a noisy block—tends to avoid that previous slot in B_4—a zero block—again because C-ORAM prioritizes noisy-noisy merge. If we again count the number of repetitions between these two permutations, it will be much lower than the expected value 1 for two random permutations.

Utilizing these two different types of correlation, the attacker can easily distinguish X and X' by counting the repeated entries between the two highlighted permutations above. We implement the above attack and run the experiment 10000 times with $Z = 60$ and $\chi = 20$. For access pattern (i), the average number of repetition we get is 1.96. For access pattern (ii), the average number of repetition is merely 0.81. We repeat the same experiment with $Z = 120$ and $\chi = 40$, and reproduce the results: 1.94 and 0.86. This shows our attack easily distinguishes the two access patterns.

7   Conclusion and Open Problems

In this work, we design an Oblivious RAM with sub-logarithmic overhead where the servers only perform XOR operations. We achieve this by using a novel eviction scheme over a d-ary tree to obtain an eviction overhead of $O(\log_d N)$ and using two-server PIR to reduce the cost to retrieve a block. We show a lower bound of $\Omega(\log_{cD} N)$ for bandwidth blowup for a client storing c blocks of data and performing a PIR on D blocks of data at a time. Our construction matches our lower bound under certain parameter ranges. C-ORAM [40] and CHf-ORAM [39] violate the lower bound and have security flaws.

While we do achieve a sub-logarithmic bandwidth blowup, we do so by using a two server PIR and server computation. It is still an open question whether a sub-logarithmic bandwidth blowup can be obtained in the original model defined by Goldreich and Ostrovsky (the GO bound does not rule it out if the client uses $c = \omega(1)$ storage). Also, all known ORAM schemes that achieve $O(\log N)$ bandwidth blowup require a block size of $\Omega(\log^2 N)$. Whether this bound (or a sub-logarithmic bound) can be obtained for smaller block sizes remains open.

Acknowledgements. We would like to thank authors of C-ORAM (Tarik Moataz, Travis Mayberry and Erik-Oliver Blass) for discussions and inputs on algorithmic details of C-ORAM. We would like to thank Dahlia Malkhi, Jonathan Katz, Elaine Shi, Hubert Chan and Xiao Wang for helpful discussions on this work. This work is funded in part by NSF awards #1111599, #1563722 and a Google Ph.D. Fellowship award.

References

1. Ajtai, M.: Oblivious RAMs without cryptogrpahic assumptions. In: Proceedings of the forty-second ACM symposium on Theory of computing, pp. 181–190. ACM (2010)

2. Apon, D., Katz, J., Shi, E., Thiruvengadam, A.: Verifiable oblivious storage. In: Krawczyk, H. (ed.) PKC 2014. LNCS, vol. 8383, pp. 131–148. Springer, Heidelberg (2014). doi:10.1007/978-3-642-54631-0_8

3. Bindschaedler, V., Naveed, M., Pan, X., Wang, X., Huang, Y.: Practicing oblivious access on cloud storage: the gap, the fallacy, and the new way forward. In Proceedings of the 22nd ACM SIGSAC Conference on Computer and Communications Security, pp. 837–849. ACM (2015)
4. Boyle, E., Chung, K.-M., Pass, R.: Oblivious parallel RAM and applications. In: Kushilevitz, E., Malkin, T. (eds.) TCC 2016. LNCS, vol. 9563, pp. 175–204. Springer, Heidelberg (2016)
5. Boyle, E., Naor, M.: Is there an oblivious RAM lower bound? In: Proceedings of the ACM Conference on Innovations in Theoretical Computer Science, pp. 357–368. ACM (2016)
6. Cachin, C., Micali, S., Stadler, M.: Computationally private information retrieval with polylogarithmic communication. In: Stern, J. (ed.) EUROCRYPT 1999. LNCS, vol. 1592, pp. 402–414. Springer, Heidelberg (1999). doi:10.1007/3-540-48910-X_28
7. Chen, B., Lin, H., Tessaro, S.: Oblivious parallel RAM: improved efficiency and generic constructions. In: Kushilevitz, E., Malkin, T. (eds.) TCC 2016. LNCS, vol. 9563, pp. 205–234. Springer, Heidelberg (2016). doi:10.1007/978-3-662-49099-0_8
8. Chor, B., Kushilevitz, E., Goldreich, O., Sudan, M.: Private information retrieval. J. ACM (JACM) 45(6), 965–981 (1998)
9. Chung, K.-M., Liu, Z., Pass, R.: Statistically-secure ORAM with $\tilde{O}(\log^2 n)$ overhead. In: Sarkar, P., Iwata, T. (eds.) ASIACRYPT 2014. LNCS, vol. 8874, pp. 62–81. Springer, Heidelberg (2014). doi:10.1007/978-3-662-45608-8_4
10. Damgård, I., Meldgaard, S., Nielsen, J.B.: Perfectly secure oblivious RAM without random oracles. In: Ishai, Y. (ed.) TCC 2011. LNCS, vol. 6597, pp. 144–163. Springer, Heidelberg (2011)
11. Dautrich, J., Stefanov, E., Shi, E.: Burst ORAM: Minimizing ORAM response times for bursty access patterns. In: 23rd USENIX Security Symposium (USENIX Security 14), pp. 749–764 (2014)
12. Devadas, S., Dijk, M., Fletcher, C.W., Ren, L., Shi, E., Wichs, D.: Onion ORAM: a constant bandwidth blowup oblivious RAM. In: Kushilevitz, E., Malkin, T. (eds.) TCC 2016. LNCS, vol. 9563, pp. 145–174. Springer, Heidelberg (2016). doi:10.1007/978-3-662-49099-0_6
13. Dvir., Z., Gopi, S.: 2-server PIR with sub-polynomial communication. In: Servedio, R.A., Rubinfeld, R. (eds.) Proceedings of the Forty-Seventh Annual ACM on Symposium on Theory of Computing, STOC, Portland, OR, USA, 14–17 June, pp. 577–584. ACM (2015)
14. Fletcher, C., Naveed, M., Ren, L., Shi, E., Stefanov, E.: Bucket ORAM: single online roundtrip, constant bandwidth oblivious RAM. Technical report (2015)
15. Fletcher, C.W., Dijk, M.V., Devadas, S.: A secure processor architecture for encrypted computation on untrusted programs. In: Proceedings of the Seventh ACM Workshop on Scalable Trusted Computing, pp. 3–8. ACM (2012)
16. Fletcher, C.W., Ren, L., Kwon, A., van Dijk, M., Devadas, S.: Freecursive ORAM: [nearly] free recursion and integrity verification for position-based oblivious RAM. In: ACM SIGPLAN Notices, vol. 50, pp. 103–116. ACM (2015)
17. Fletcher, C.W., Ren, L., Kwon, A., van Dijk, M., Stefanov, E., Serpanos, D., Devadas, S.: A low-latency, low-area hardware oblivious RAM controller. In: IEEE 23rd Annual International Symposium on Field-Programmable Custom Computing Machines (FCCM), pp. 215–222. IEEE (2015)
18. Garg, S., Mohassel, P., Papamanthou, C., Tworam: Round-optimal oblivious RAM with applications to searchable encryption. Cryptology ePrint Archive, Report 2015/1010 (2015)

19. Gentry, C., Goldman, K.A., Halevi, S., Julta, C., Raykova, M., Wichs, D.: Optimizing ORAM and using it efficiently for secure computation. In: Cristofaro, E., Wright, M. (eds.) PETS 2013. LNCS, vol. 7981, pp. 1–18. Springer, Heidelberg (2013). doi:10.1007/978-3-642-39077-7_1

20. Gentry, C., Halevi, S., Jutla, C., Raykova, M.: Private database access with HE-over-ORAM architecture. In: Malkin, T., Kolesnikov, V., Lewko, A.B., Polychronakis, M. (eds.) ACNS 2015. LNCS, vol. 9092, pp. 172–191. Springer, Cham (2015). doi:10.1007/978-3-319-28166-7_9

21. Gentry, C., Ramzan, Z.: Single-database private information retrieval with constant communication rate. In: Caires, L., Italiano, G.F., Monteiro, L., Palamidessi, C., Yung, M. (eds.) ICALP 2005. LNCS, vol. 3580, pp. 803–815. Springer, Heidelberg (2005)

22. Goldreich, O.: Towards a theory of software protection and simulation by oblivious RAMs. In: Proceedings of the nineteenth annual ACM symposium on Theory of computing, pp. 182–194. ACM (1987)

23. Goldreich, O., Ostrovsky, R.: Software protection and simulation on oblivious RAMs. J. ACM (JACM) 43(3), 431–473 (1996)

24. Goodrich, M.T., Mitzenmacher, M.: Privacy-preserving access of outsourced data via oblivious RAM simulation. In: Aceto, L., Henzinger, M., Sgall, J. (eds.) ICALP 2011. LNCS, vol. 6756, pp. 576–587. Springer, Heidelberg (2011). doi:10.1007/978-3-642-22012-8_46

25. Goodrich, M.T., Mitzenmacher, M., Ohrimenko, O., Tamassia, R.: Privacy-preserving group data access via stateless oblivious RAM simulation. In: Proceedings of the Twenty-Third Annual ACM-SIAM Symposium on Discrete Algorithms, pp. 157–167. SIAM (2012)

26. Keller, M., Scholl, P.: Efficient, oblivious data structures for MPC. In: Sarkar, P., Iwata, T. (eds.) ASIACRYPT 2014. LNCS, vol. 8874, pp. 506–525. Springer, Heidelberg (2014). doi:10.1007/978-3-662-45608-8_27

27. Kushilevitz, E., Lu, S., Ostrovsky, R.: On the (in)security of hash-based oblivious RAM and a new balancing scheme. In: Proceedings of the Twenty-Third Annual ACM-SIAM Symposium on Discrete Algorithms, pp. 143–156. SIAM (2012)

28. Kushilevitz, E., Ostrovsky, R.: Replication is not needed: single database, computationally-private information retrieval. In: 38th Annual Symposium on Foundations of Computer Science, FOCS 1997, Miami Beach, Florida, USA, 19–22 October, pp. 364–373. IEEE Computer Society (1997)

29. Lipmaa, H.: An oblivious transfer protocol with log-squared communication. In: Zhou, J., Lopez, J., Deng, R.H., Bao, F. (eds.) ISC 2005. LNCS, vol. 3650, pp. 314–328. Springer, Heidelberg (2005). doi:10.1007/11556992_23

30. Liu, C., Harris, A., Maas, M., Hicks, M., Tiwari, M., Shi, E.: GhostRider: a hardware-software system for memory trace oblivious computation. In: ACM SIGARCH Computer Architecture News, vol. 43, pp. 87–101. ACM (2015)

31. Liu, C., Huang, Y., Shi, E., Katz, J., Hicks, M.: Automating efficient RAM-model secure computation. In: 2014 IEEE Symposium on Security and Privacy, pp. 623–638. IEEE (2014)

32. Liu, C., Wang, X.S., Nayak, K., Huang, Y., Shi, E.: ObliVM: a programming framework for secure computation. In: 2015 IEEE Symposium on Security and Privacy, pp. 359–376. IEEE (2015)

33. Lorch, J.R., Parno, B., Mickens, J., Raykova, M., Schiffman, J.: Shroud: ensuring private access to large-scale data in the data center. In: Presented as part of the 11th USENIX Conference on File and Storage Technologies (FAST 2013), pp. 199–213 (2013)

34. Lu, S., Ostrovsky, R.: Distributed oblivious RAM for secure two-party computation. In: Sahai, A. (ed.) TCC 2013. LNCS, vol. 7785, pp. 377–396. Springer, Heidelberg (2013)
35. Lu, S., Ostrovsky, R.: How to garble RAM programs? In: Johansson, T., Nguyen, P.Q. (eds.) EUROCRYPT 2013. LNCS, vol. 7881, pp. 719–734. Springer, Heidelberg (2013). doi:10.1007/978-3-642-38348-9_42
36. Maas, M., Love, E., Stefanov, E., Tiwari, M., Shi, E., Asanovic, K., Kubiatowicz, J., Song, D.: PHANTOM: practical oblivious computation in a secure processor. In Proceedings of the ACM SIGSAC Conference on Computer and Communications Security, pp. 311–324. ACM (2013)
37. Mayberry, T., Blass, E.-O., Chan, A.H.: Efficient private file retrieval by combining ORAM and PIR. In: NDSS, Citeseer (2014)
38. Mitchell, J.C., Zimmerman, J.: Data-oblivious data structures. In: Theoretical Aspects of Computer Science (STACS) (2014)
39. Moataz, T., Blass, E.-O., Mayberry, T.: CHf-ORAM: a constant communication ORAM without homomorphic encryption. Cryptology ePrint Archive, Report 2015/1116 (2015)
40. Moataz, T., Mayberry, T., Blass, E.-O.: Constant communication ORAM with small blocksize. In: Proceedings of the 22nd ACM SIGSAC Conference on Computer and Communications Security, pp. 862–873. ACM (2015)
41. Ostrovsky, R., Shoup, V.: Private information storage. In: Proceedings of the Twenty-Ninth Annual ACM Symposium on Theory of Computing, pp. 294–303. ACM (1997)
42. Pinkas, B., Reinman, T.: Oblivious RAM revisited. In: Rabin, T. (ed.) CRYPTO 2010. LNCS, vol. 6223, pp. 502–519. Springer, Heidelberg (2010). doi:10.1007/978-3-642-14623-7_27
43. Rane, A., Lin, C., Tiwari, M.: Raccoon: closing digital side-channels through obfuscated execution. In: 24th USENIX Security Symposium (USENIX Security 15), pp. 431–446 (2015)
44. Ren, L., Fletcher, C., Kwon, A., Stefanov, E., Shi, E., Van Dijk, M., Devadas, S., Constants count: practical improvements to oblivious RAM. In 24th USENIX Security Symposium (USENIX Security 15), pp. 415–430 (2015)
45. Ren, L., Fletcher, C.W., Yu, X., Van Dijk, M., Devadas, S.: Integrity verification for path oblivious-ram. In: High Performance Extreme Computing Conference (HPEC). Institute of Electrical and Electronics Engineers (IEEE) (2013)
46. Ren, L., Yu, X., Fletcher, C.W., Van Dijk, M., Devadas, S.: Design space exploration and optimization of path oblivious RAM in secure processors. In: ACM SIGARCH Computer Architecture News, vol. 41, pp. 571–582. ACM (2013)
47. Sahin, C., Zakhary, V., El Abbadi, A., Lin, H.R., Tessaro, S.: TaoStore: overcoming asynchronicity in oblivious data storage. In: IEEE Symposium on Security and Privacy (SP) (2016)
48. Shi, E., Chan, T.-H.H., Stefanov, E., Li, M.: Oblivious RAM with $O((\log N)^3)$ worst-case cost. In: Lee, D.H., Wang, X. (eds.) ASIACRYPT 2011. LNCS, vol. 7073, pp. 197–214. Springer, Heidelberg (2011). doi:10.1007/978-3-642-25385-0_11
49. Stefanov, E., Shi, E.: Multi-cloud oblivious storage. In Proceedings of the 2013 ACM SIGSAC Conference on Computer and Communications Security, pp. 247–258. ACM (2013)
50. Stefanov, E., Shi, E.: ObliviStore: high performance oblivious cloud storage. In: IEEE Symposium on Security and Privacy (SP), pp. 253–267. IEEE (2013)
51. Stefanov, E., Shi, E., Song, D.X.: Towards practical oblivious RAM. In: NDSS, The Internet Society (2012)

52. Stefanov, E., van Dijk, M., Shi, E., Chan, T.-H.H., Fletcher, C., Ren, L., Yu, X., Devadas, S.: Path ORAM: an extremely simple oblivious RAM protocol. Cryptology ePrint Archive, Report 2013/280 v. 3 (2013). http://eprint.iacr.org/2013/280

53. Stefanov, E., Van Dijk, M., Shi, E., Fletcher, C., Ren, L., Yu, X., Devadas, S.: Path ORAM: an extremely simple oblivious RAM protocol. In: Proceedings of the ACM SIGSAC Conference on Computer and Communications Security, pp. 299–310. ACM (2013)

54. Wang, X., Chan, H., Shi, E.: Circuit ORAM: on tightness of the Goldreich-Ostrovsky lower bound. In: Proceedings of the 22nd ACM SIGSAC Conference on Computer and Communications Security, pp. 850–861. ACM (2015)

55. Wang, X.S., Huang, Y., Chan, T.-H.H., Shelat, A., Shi, E.: SCORAM: oblivious RAM for secure computation. In: Proceedings of the ACM SIGSAC Conference on Computer and Communications Security, CCS 2014, pp. 191–202, New York, NY, USA. ACM (2014)

56. Wang, X.S., Nayak, K., Liu, C., Chan, T., Shi, E., Stefanov, E., Huang, Y.: Oblivious data structures. In: Proceedings of the ACM SIGSAC Conference on Computer and Communications Security, pp. 215–226. ACM (2014)

57. Williams, P., Sion, R.: SR-ORAM: single round-trip oblivious RAM. ACNS, industrial track, pp. 19–33 (2012)

58. Williams, P., Sion, R., Carbunar, B.: Building castles out of mud: practical access pattern privacy and correctness on untrusted storage. In: Proceedings of the 15th ACM Conference on Computer and Communications Security, pp. 139–148. ACM (2008)

59. Williams, P., Sion, R., Tomescu, A.: PrivateFS: a parallel oblivious file system. In: Proceedings of the 2012 ACM Conference on Computer and Communications Security, pp. 977–988. ACM (2012)

60. Zahur, S., Wang, X.S., Raykova, M., Gascón, A., Doerner, J., Evans, D., Katz, J.: Revisiting square-root ORAM: efficient random access in multi-party computation. In: IEEE Symposium on Security and Privacy, SP, San Jose, CA, USA, 22–26 May, pp. 218–234 (2016)

61. Zhang, J., Ma, Q., Zhang, W., Qiao, D.: KT-ORAM: a bandwidth-efficient ORAM built on K-ary tree of PIR nodes (2014)

62. Zhang, J., Ma, Q., Zhang, W., Qiao, D.: MSKT-ORAM: a constant bandwidth ORAM without homomorphic encryption. IACR Cryptology ePrint Archive, Report 2016/882 (2016)

Predictable Arguments of Knowledge

Antonio Faonio[1]([✉]), Jesper Buus Nielsen[1], and Daniele Venturi[2]

[1] Department of Computer Science, Aarhus University, Aarhus, Denmark
afaonio@gmail.com
[2] Sapienza, University of Rome, Rome, Italy

Abstract. We initiate a formal investigation on the power of *predictability* for argument of knowledge systems for *NP*. Specifically, we consider private-coin argument systems where the answer of the prover can be predicted, given the private randomness of the verifier; we call such protocols Predictable Arguments of Knowledge (PAoK).

Our study encompasses a full characterization of PAoK, showing that such arguments can be made extremely laconic, with the prover sending a single bit, and assumed to have only one round (i.e., two messages) of communication without loss of generality.

We additionally explore PAoK satisfying additional properties (including zero-knowledge and the possibility of re-using the same challenge across multiple executions with the prover), present several constructions of PAoK relying on different cryptographic tools, and discuss applications to cryptography.

1 Introduction

Consider the classical proof system for Graphs Non-Isomorphism where, on common input two graphs (G_0, G_1), the verifier chooses a random bit b, and sends a uniformly random permutation of the graph G_b to the prover. If the two graphs are not isomorphic the prover replies correctly sending back the value b.

A peculiar property of the above proof system is that the verifier knows in advance the answer of the prover, i.e., the answer given by the prover is *predictable*. Another property is that it uses only one round of communication and that the prover sends a single bit. Following the work of Goldreich *et al.* [30] we call a proof system with these properties *extremely laconic*.

In this paper, we study the notion of predictability in interactive proof systems for *NP*. More specifically, we focus on the cryptographic setting where the prover's strategy is efficiently computable and, moreover, we aim for the notion of knowledge soundness, where any convincing polynomial-time prover must "know" the witness relative to the instance being proven.

We formalize this notion of Predictable Arguments of Knowledge (PAoK), explore their properties and applications, and provide several constructions based on various cryptographic tools and assumptions.

Our Contributions and Techniques. We proceed to describe our results and techniques in more details.

© International Association for Cryptologic Research 2017
S. Fehr (Ed.): PKC 2017, Part I, LNCS 10174, pp. 121–150, 2017.
DOI: 10.1007/978-3-662-54365-8_6

Characterizing PAoK. Syntactically a PAoK is a multi-round protocol $(\mathcal{P}, \mathcal{V})$ where in each round: (i) The verifier $\mathcal{V}$, given the instance x and private coins r, generates a challenge c (that is sent to $\mathcal{P}$) together with a predicted answer b; (ii) The prover $\mathcal{P}$, given (x, w, c), generates an answer a. The prover is said to convince the verifier if and only if $a = b$ in all rounds.

Apart from being complete—meaning that an honest prover convinces the verifier with overwhelming probability—PAoK satisfy the standard property of *knowledge soundness*. Informally, this means that given any successful prover convincing the verifier on instance x with probability ϵ, there exists an efficient extractor recovering a witness for x with probability polynomially related to ϵ. Looking ahead, our definition of knowledge soundness is parametrized by a so-called instance sampler. Intuitively this means that only instances sampled through the sampler are extractable, and allows to consider more fine-grained flavours of extractability.[1]

Our first result is that PAoK can always be made extremely laconic, both in term of round complexity and of message complexity (i.e., the number of bits sent by the prover). Such a characterization is obtained as follows:

- First, we show that one can collapse any multi-round PAoK into a one-round PAoK with higher message complexity. Let $(\mathcal{P}, \mathcal{V})$ be a ρ-round PAoK, where $\mathcal{V}$ generates several challenges $(c_1, \ldots, c_\rho)$ with c_i used during round i.[2] We turn $(\mathcal{P}, \mathcal{V})$ into a one-round predictable argument $(\tilde{\mathcal{P}}, \tilde{\mathcal{V}})$ where the multi-round PAoK is "cut" at a random index $i^* \in [\rho]$; this essentially means that $\tilde{\mathcal{V}}$ runs $\mathcal{V}$ and forwards $(c_1, \ldots, c_{i^*})$, whereas $\tilde{\mathcal{P}}$ runs $\mathcal{P}$ and replies with $(a_1, \ldots, a_{i^*})$. One can show that, if the initial PAoK has knowledge error ϵ, the transformed PAoK has knowledge error ϵ/ρ. The latter can finally be made negligible via parallel repetition. It is important to notice that parallel repetition, in general, does not amplify soundness for argument systems [5, 39]. However, it is well known that for secret-coin one-round arguments (such as PAoK), parallel repetition amplifies (knowledge) soundness at an exponential rate [5].
- Second, we show how to reduce the prover's answer length to a single bit[3] as follows. Let $(\mathcal{P}, \mathcal{V})$ be a PAoK with ℓ-bit answers. We define a new PAoK $(\mathcal{P}', \mathcal{V}')$ where the verifier $\mathcal{V}'$ runs $\mathcal{V}$ in order to obtain a pair (c, b), samples randomness r, and defines the new predicted answer to be the inner product between b and r. Given challenge (c, r) the prover $\mathcal{P}'$ simply runs $\mathcal{P}$ in order to obtain a and defines the answer to be the inner product between a and r. Knowledge soundness follows by the Goldreich-Levin hard-core bit theorem [28].

---

[1] Similar fine-grained definitions have already been considered in the literature, e.g., for differing-inputs obfuscation [6].

[2] It is easy to see that generating all the challenges at the same time, independently of the prover's answers, is without loss of generality.

[3] This further justifies our interest to arguments (as opposed to *proofs*) for *NP* as Goldreich *et al.* [30] showed that unless the polynomial-time hierarchy collapses there does not exist a laconic proof system for all *NP*.

Interestingly, we can wrap up the two results together showing that any PAoK, no matter of the round or message complexity, can be made extremely laconic.

Constructions. Next, we turn to constructing PAoK. Our starting point is the observation that full-fledged PAoK for a relation R imply (and in fact are equivalent to) extractable witness encryption [31] (Ext-WE) for the same relation R. Briefly, a witness encryption scheme allows to encrypt an arbitrary message using a statement x belonging to an *NP*-language L; decryption can be performed by anyone knowing a valid witness w for x. Extractable security means that from any adversary breaking semantic security of the encryption scheme, we can obtain an extractor computing a valid witness for x.

The equivalence between PAoK and Ext-WE can be seen as follows:

- From Ext-WE to PAoK we encrypt a random bit a using the encryption scheme and then ask the prover to return a.
- From PAoK to Ext-WE, we first make the PAoK extremely laconic, then we generate a challenge/answer pair (c, a) for the PAoK, and encrypt a single bit β as $(c, a \oplus \beta)$.[4]

In light of the recent work by Garg *et al.* [23], the above result can be seen as a negative result. In particular, [23] shows that, under the conjecture that a certain special-purpose obfuscator exists, it is impossible to have an Ext-WE scheme for a specific *NP* relation. The reason for this depends on the auxiliary information that an adversary might have on the input: The assumed special-purpose obfuscator could be used to obfuscate the auxiliary input in a way that allows to decrypt ciphertexts, without revealing any information about the witness. As stated in [23], such a negative result can be interpreted as an "implausibility result" on the existence of Ext-WE with arbitrary auxiliary input for all of *NP*. Given the equivalence between PAoK and Ext-WE such an implausibility result carries over to PAoK as well.[5]

Motivated by the above discussion, we propose two constructions of PAoK that circumvent the implausibility result of [23] by either restricting to specific *NP* relations, or by focusing on PAoK where knowledge soundness is only required to hold for a specific class of instance samplers (and thus for restricted auxiliary inputs). More in details:

- We show a simple connection between PAoK and so-called Extractable Hash-Proof Systems[6] [42] (Ext-HPS): Given an Ext-HPS for a relation R it is possible to construct a PAoK for a related relation R' in a natural way.

---

[4] Domain extension for Ext-WE can be obtained by encrypting each bit of a message individually.

[5] Very recently, Bellare *et al.* [7] show that assuming sub-exponential one-way functions and sub-exponential indistinguishability obfuscation, differing-input obfuscation for Turing Machines [2] is impossible. While this result adds another negative evidence, it does not apply directly to Ext-WE.

[6] The connection between Hash Proof Systems and Witness Encryption was already noted by [23].

– We can construct a PAoK for a specific instance sampler by assuming a weak[7] form of differing-inputs obfuscation. The challenge c corresponds to an obfuscation of the circuit that hard-wires the instance x and a random value b, and upon input w returns b if and only if (x, w) is in the relation.

Interestingly, we can show that, for the special case of so-called random self-reducible relations,[8] a PAoK with knowledge soundness w.r.t. the instance sampler that corresponds to the algorithm for re-randomizing an instance in the language, can be generically leveraged to obtain a full-fledged PAoK (with arbitrary auxiliary input) for any NP-relation that is random-self reducible.

Zero-Knowledge PAoK. Notice that, as opposed to standard arguments, predictable arguments are non-trivial to construct even without requiring them to be zero-knowledge (or even witness indistinguishable).[9] Nevertheless, it is possible (and interesting) to consider PAoK that additionally satisfy the zero-knowledge property. It is well known that argument systems with a deterministic prover, such as PAoK, cannot be zero-knowledge in the plain model [29]. Motivated by this, given any PAoK (for some fixed relation), we propose two different transformations to obtain a zero-knowledge PAoK (for the same relation):

– The first transformation is in the non-programmable random oracle model. Here we exploit the fact that PAoK are honest-verifier zero-knowledge. Our strategy is to force the malicious verifier to act honestly; we achieve this by having the prover check that the challenge was honestly generated using randomness provided by the random oracle. In case the check fails the prover will not reveal the answer, but instead it will output a special symbol $\bot$. To ensure knowledge soundness we define the check to be dependent on the prover's message, in such a way that a malicious prover cannot obtain the (private) randomness of the verifier in case it does not already know the correct answer.
– The second transformation is in the common random string (CRS) model, and works as follows. The verifier sends the challenge c together with a non-interactive zero-knowledge proof π that c is "well formed" (i.e., there exists random coins r such that the verifier of the underlying PAoK with coins r returns a pair (c, b)).

We leave it as an interesting open problem to construct a witness indistinguishable PAoK in the plain model.

Predictable ZAP. In the basic definition of PAoK, the verifier generates the challenge c (together with the predicted answer b) depending on the instance x

---

[7] Namely, following the terminology in [6], extractability only holds for a specific class of circuit samplers, related to the underlying instance sampler.
[8] Roughly speaking, a random self-reducible relation is a relation for which average-case hardness implies worst-case hardness.
[9] This is because the trivial protocol where the prover forwards a witness is not predictable.

being proven. We also look at the special case where the challenge is generated in an instance-independent manner, together with a trapdoor that later allows to predict the prover's answer a. The goal here is to have the *same* challenge being used across multiple executions of a PAoK with the prover.

Protocols of this type have been already considered in the literature under the name of ZAP [17]. There are however a few crucial differences: (i) ZAP are public-coin, whereas predictable arguments are secret-coin; (ii) ZAP are witness indistinguishable, whereas predictable arguments are interesting even without requiring such a property. Hence, we formalize the notion of Predictable ZAP (PZAP) which is a kind of secret-coin ZAP in which the prover's answer can be predicted (given the secret coins of the verifier and some trapdoor), and the same challenge can be re-used across multiple executions. We insist on PZAP satisfying knowledge soundness, but we do not require them to be witness indistinguishable; the definition of knowledge soundness features a malicious prover that can adaptively choose the target instance while keeping oracle access to the verifier algorithm. We also consider a weaker flavour, where the prover has no access to the verifier. We give a construction of PZAP relying on the recently introduced tool of Extractable Witness PRF [43]. We also show that weak PZAP can be generically leveraged to PZAP using standard cryptographic tools. This result shows that, under some standard cryptographic assumptions, for any construction of weak PZAP there exists *another* construction satisfying the definition of PZAP. It is interesting to understand if given a construction of weak PZAP the construction itself already satisfies the definition of PZAP. We give a negative evidence for this question. Namely, we show a black-box separation between weak PZAP and PZAP, ruling out a large class of black-box reductions from the former to the latter.

Applications. Although we find the concept of PAoK to be interesting in its own right, we also discuss applications of PAoK to proving lower bounds in two different cryptographic settings:

– Leakage-tolerant interactive protocols (as introduced by Bitanski *et al.* [9]) are interactive protocols whose security degrades gracefully in the presence of arbitrary leakage on the state of the players.

   Previous work [36] showed that any leakage-tolerant interactive protocol for secure message transmission, tolerating leakage of poly-logarithmic size on the state of the receiver, needs to have secret keys which are as long as the total number of bits transmitted using that key. Using PAoK, we can strengthen this negative result to hold already for leakage of a constant number of bits. Details are deferred in the full version of the paper [21].
– Non-malleable codes (as introduced by Dziembowski *et al.* [18]) allow to encode a message in such a way that the decoding of a tampered codeword either yields the original message or a completely unrelated value.

   Previous work [22] showed an interesting application of non-malleable codes to protecting arbitrary computation (carried out by a von Neumann architecture) against tampering attacks. This result requires to assume a leakage- and tamper-free CPU which is used to carry out "simple" operations on a constant number of encodings.

A natural idea to weaken the assumption of a leakage-proof CPU, would be to design a code which remains non-malleable even given a small amount of leakage on the encoded message. Subsequent to our work [19], the concept of PAoK has been exploited to show that such non-malleable codes tolerating leakage from the encoding process cannot exist (under the assumption that collision-resistant hash functions exist).

Giving up on Knowledge Extraction. As already discussed above, the implausibility result of Garg *et al.* [23] has negative implications on some of our results. We were able to circumvent these implications by either constructing PAoK for restricted relations, or by considering weaker flavours of extractability. Yet another way to circumvent the implausibility result of [23] is to give up on knowledge soundness and to consider instead standard computational soundness (i.e., a computationally bounded malicious prover cannot convince the verifier into accepting a false statement).

Let us call a multi-round, predictable, computationally sound interactive protocol a *predictable argument*. It is easy to see that all our results for PAoK continue to hold for predictable arguments. In particular: (i) Predictable arguments can be assumed w.l.o.g. to be extremely laconic; (ii) There exists a predictable argument for a relation R if and only if there exists a (non-extractable) witness encryption scheme for R; (iii) We can construct a predictable argument for a relation R given any hash-proof system for R;[10] (iv) Computationally sound PZAP can be obtained based on any (non-extractable) Witness PRF.

Additional Related Work. A study of interactive proofs with laconic provers was already in [27,30]. They did not investigate proofs of *knowledge*, though. As explained above our notion of PAoK is intimately related to extractable witness encryption, as first proposed by Goldwasser *et al.* [31]— where it is argued that the construction of Garg *et al.* [24] is extractable. See [1,16] for more recent work on witness encryption.

In [25], Garg *et al.* introduce the concept of Efficiently Extractable Non-Interactive Istance-Dependent Commitment Scheme (Ext-NI-ID Commitment for short). The primitive resembles the concept of PAoK, however there is a crucial difference. Ext-NI-ID Commitments are statistical hiding, this implies that an Ext-NI-ID can be used to construct a Predictable Argument with "statistical soundness" for the same language, however, the reverse implication does not hold.

---

[10] We note that, in the other direction, predictable arguments seem to imply some kind of hash-proof system where "statistical smoothness" is replaced by "computational smoothness." We leave it as an interesting direction for future research to explore potential applications of such "computationally smooth" hash-proof systems and their connection to trapdoor hash-proof system (see Benhamouda *et al.* [8]).

The problem we faced to amplify knowledge soundness of PAoK shares similarities with the problem of amplifying computational soundness for argument systems. Although it is well known that parallel repetition does not work in general [5,39], there are some exceptions such as 3-message arguments [5,13], public-coin arguments [15,38], and simulatable arguments [14,33] (a generalization of both 3-message and public-coin). Relevant to ours is the work of Haitner on random-terminating arguments [32].

Roadmap. We start by setting some basic notation, in Sect. 2. The definition of PAoK, together with their characterization in terms of round-complexity and amount of prover communication, can be found in Sect. 3. In Sect. 4 we explore constructions of PAoK for random self-reducible relations. The two compilers yielding zero-knowledge PAoK in the CRS model and in the non-programmable random oracle model are presented in Sect. 5. In Sect. 6 we investigate the concept of predictable ZAP. Finally, in Sect. 7, we discuss a few interesting open problems related to our work.

2   Preliminaries

For $a, b \in \mathbb{R}$, we let $[a, b] = \{x \in \mathbb{R} : a \leq x \leq b\}$; for $a \in \mathbb{N}$ we let $[a] = \{1, 2, \ldots, a\}$. If x is a string, we denote its length by $|x|$; if $\mathcal{X}$ is a set, $|\mathcal{X}|$ represents the number of elements in $\mathcal{X}$. When x is chosen randomly in $\mathcal{X}$, we write $x \leftarrow_\$ \mathcal{X}$. When $\mathcal{A}$ is an algorithm, we write $y \leftarrow_\$ \mathcal{A}(x)$ to denote a run of $\mathcal{A}$ on input x and output y; if $\mathcal{A}$ is randomized, then y is a random variable and $\mathcal{A}(x; r)$ denotes a run of $\mathcal{A}$ on input x and randomness r. An algorithm $\mathcal{A}$ is *probabilistic polynomial-time* (PPT) if $\mathcal{A}$ is randomized and for any input $x, r \in \{0, 1\}^*$ the computation of $\mathcal{A}(x; r)$ terminates in at most $poly(|x|)$ steps. Vectors and matrices are typeset in boldface. For a vector $\mathbf{v} = (v_1, \ldots, v_n)$ we sometimes write $\mathbf{v}[i]$ for the i-th element of $\mathbf{v}$. We use Maj to denote the majority function.

Throughout the paper we let $\kappa \in \mathbb{N}$ denote the security parameter. We say that a function $\nu : \mathbb{N} \to [0, 1]$ is negligible in the security parameter, if $\nu(\kappa) = \kappa^{-\omega(1)}$. A function $\mu : \mathbb{N} \to [0, 1]$ is noticeable in the security parameter, if there exists a positive polynomial $p(\cdot)$ such that $\nu(\kappa) \geq 1/p(\kappa)$ for infinitely many $\kappa \geq \kappa_0$.

Let X and Y be a pair of random variables. The statistical distance between X and Y is defined as $\Delta(X, Y) := \max_{\mathcal{D}} |\Pr[\mathcal{D}(X) = 1] - \Pr[\mathcal{D}(Y) = 1]|$, where the maximum is taken over all (possibly unbounded) distinguishers. In case the maximum is taken over all PPT distinghuishers, we sometimes speak of computational distance. For two ensembles $\mathcal{X} = \{X_\kappa\}_{\kappa \in \mathbb{N}}$ and $\mathcal{Y} = \{Y_\kappa\}_{\kappa \in \mathbb{N}}$, we write $\mathcal{X} \equiv \mathcal{Y}$ to denote that $\mathcal{X}$ and $\mathcal{Y}$ are identically distributed, $\mathcal{X} \overset{s}{\approx} \mathcal{Y}$ to denote that $\mathcal{X}$ and $\mathcal{Y}$ are statistically close (i.e., their statistical distance is bounded by a negligible function of the security parameter), and $\mathcal{X} \overset{c}{\approx} \mathcal{Y}$ to denote that $\mathcal{X}$ and $\mathcal{Y}$ are computationally indistinguishable.

Interactive Protocols. Let $R \subseteq \{0,1\}^* \times \{0,1\}^*$ be an *NP*-relation, naturally defining a language $L_R := \{x : \exists w \text{ s.t. } (x,w) \in R\}$. We are typically interested in efficiently samplable relations, for which there exists a PPT algorithm SamR taking as input the security parameter (and random coins r) and outputting a pair $(x,w) \in R$. An interactive protocol $\Pi = (\mathcal{P}, \mathcal{V})$ for R features a prover $\mathcal{P}$ (holding a value $x \in L_R$ together with a corresponding witness w) and a verifier $\mathcal{V}$ (holding x), where the goal of the prover is to convince the verifier that $x \in L_R$. At the end of the protocol execution, the verifier outputs either acc or rej. We write $\langle \mathcal{P}(1^\kappa, x, w), \mathcal{V}(1^\kappa, x) \rangle$ for the random variable corresponding to the verifier's verdict, and $\mathcal{P}(1^\kappa, x, w) \leftrightarows \mathcal{V}(1^\kappa, x)$ for the random variable corresponding to a transcript of protocol Π on input (x, w).

Unless stated otherwise, all interactive protocols considered in this paper are *secret-coin*, meaning that the verifier's strategy depends on a secretly kept random tape. We also call Π a ρ-round protocol if the protocol consists of ρ rounds, where each round features a message from the verifier to the prover and viceversa

3   Predictable Arguments of Knowledge

We start by defining Predictable Arguments of Knowledge (PAoK) as multi-round interactive protocols in which the verifier generates a challenge (to be sent to the prover) and can at the same time predict the prover's answer to that challenge; we insist on (computational) extractable security, meaning that from any prover convincing a verifier with some probability we can extract a witness with probability related to the prover's success probability.

The main result of this section is that PAoK can be assumed without loss of generality to be extremely laconic (i.e., the prover sends a single bit and the protocol consists of a single round of communication). More in detail, in Sect. 3.1, we show that any multi-round PAoK can be squeezed into a one-round PAoK. In Sect. 3.2 we show that, for any $\ell \in \mathbb{N}$, the existence of a PAoK where the prover answer is of length ℓ bits implies the existence of a laconic PAoK.

The Definition. In a multi-round protocol the verifier produces many challenges $\mathbf{c} = (c_1, \ldots, c_\rho)$. W.l.o.g. in a predictable argument, we can assume that all the challenges are generated together and then forwarded one-by-one to the prover; this is because the answers are known *in advance*. Specifically, a ρ-round predictable argument is fully specified by a tuple of algorithms $\Pi = (\mathsf{Chall}, \mathsf{Resp})$, as described below:

1. $\mathcal{V}$ samples $(\mathbf{c}, \mathbf{b}) \leftarrow_\$ \mathsf{Chall}(1^\kappa, x)$, where $\mathbf{c} := (c_1, \ldots, c_\rho)$ and $\mathbf{b} := (b_1, \ldots, b_\rho)$.
2. For all $i \in [\rho]$ in increasing sequence:
    - $\mathcal{V}$ forwards c_i to $\mathcal{P}$;
    - $\mathcal{P}$ computes $(a_1, \ldots, a_i) := \mathsf{Resp}(1^\kappa, x, w, c_1, \ldots, c_i)$ and forwards a_i to $\mathcal{V}$;
    - $\mathcal{V}$ checks that $a_i = b_i$, and returns rej if this is not the case.
3. If all challenges are answered correctly, $\mathcal{V}$ returns acc.

Notice that the algorithm Resp takes as input all challenges up-to round i in order to generate the i-th answer.[11]

We say that prover $\mathcal{P}$ and verifier $\mathcal{V}$, running the protocol above, *execute a PAoK Π* upon input security parameter 1^κ, common input x, and prover's private input w; we denote with $\langle \mathcal{P}(1^\kappa, x, w), \mathcal{V}(1^\kappa, x) \rangle_\Pi$ (or, when Π is clear from the context, simply $\langle \mathcal{P}(1^\kappa, x, w), \mathcal{V}(1^\kappa, x) \rangle$) the output of such interaction. We say that a prover $\mathcal{P}$ *succeeds* on the instance x and auxiliary input w if $\langle \mathcal{P}(1^\kappa, x, w), \mathcal{V}(1^\kappa, x) \rangle = \mathtt{acc}$. We give a granular definition of extractability that is parametrized by an efficient instance sampler $\mathcal{S}$, and that roughly says that the protocol is sound and moreover sampled instances are extractable. Here, the sampler is simply an algorithm taking as input the security parameter and auxiliary input $z_S \in \{0,1\}^*$, and outputting an instance x together with auxiliary information $aux \in \{0,1\}^*$.

Definition 1 (Predictable Arguments of Knowledge). *Let $\Pi = (\mathsf{Chall}, \mathsf{Resp})$ be a ρ-round predictable argument for an NP relation R, with ℓ-bit prover's answer. Consider the properties below.*

Completeness: *There exists a negligible function $\nu : \mathbb{N} \to [0,1]$ such that for all sequences $\{(x_\kappa, w_\kappa)\}_{\kappa \geqslant 0}$ where $(x_\kappa, w_\kappa) \in R$, we have that:*

$$\Pr_{\mathcal{P}, \mathcal{V}} [\langle \mathcal{P}(1^\kappa, x_\kappa, w_\kappa), \mathcal{V}(1^\kappa, x_\kappa) \rangle = \mathtt{rej}] \leqslant \nu(\kappa).$$

$(\mathcal{S}, f, \epsilon)$-Knowledge soundness: *For all PPT provers $\mathcal{P}^*$ there exists a PPT extractor $\mathcal{K}$ such that for all auxiliary inputs $z_P, z_S \in \{0,1\}^*$ the following holds. Whenever*

$$p(\kappa) := \Pr_{\mathcal{P}^*, \mathcal{V}, r_S} [\langle \mathcal{P}^*(1^\kappa, aux, x, z_P), \mathcal{V}(x) \rangle = \mathtt{acc} : (x, aux) := \mathcal{S}(1^\kappa, z_S; r_S)] > \epsilon(\kappa)$$

then

$$\Pr_{\mathcal{K}, r_S} \left[\begin{array}{l} \exists w \ s.t. \ f(w) = y \\ (x, w) \in R \end{array} : \begin{array}{l} (x, aux) := \mathcal{S}(1^\kappa, z_S; r_S), \\ y \leftarrow_\$ \mathcal{K}(1^\kappa, x, z_P, z_S, aux) \end{array} \right] \geqslant p(\kappa) - \epsilon(\kappa).$$

We call Π a ρ-round $\mathcal{S}$-PAoK for R, if Π satisfies completeness and $(\mathcal{S}, f, \epsilon)$-knowledge soundness for any efficient computable function f, and moreover $\epsilon - 2^{-\rho\ell}$ is negligible. We call Π an $\mathcal{S}$-PAoK for R, if Π is a 1-round $\mathcal{S}$-PAoK and we call it a laconic $\mathcal{S}$-PAoK if Π is an $\mathcal{S}$-PAoK and $\ell = 1$. Sometimes we also say that Π is a ρ-round $(f, \mathcal{S})$-PAoK if knowledge soundness holds for a specific function f.

Consider the dummy sampler $\mathcal{S}_{\mathsf{dummy}}$ that parses its input z_S as (x, aux) and then outputs the pair (x, aux). We call Π a ρ-round (f, ϵ)-PAoK for R, if Π satisfies completeness and $(\mathcal{S}_{\mathsf{dummy}}, f, \epsilon)$-knowledge soundness. We say that Π is a ρ-round PAoK for R, if Π is a ρ-round $\mathcal{S}_{\mathsf{dummy}}$-PAoK for R.

---

[11] In the description above we let Resp output also all previous answers $a_1, \ldots, a_{i-1}$; while this is not necessary it can be assumed w.l.o.g. and will simplify the proof of Theorem 1.

The reason why the above definition is parametrized by the function f instead of considering the relation $R' = \{(x, y) : \exists w \text{ s.t. } (x, w) \in R \wedge y = f(w)\}$ is that such a relation might not be an NP-relation (as it might be hard to check whether $\exists w$ s.t. $(x, w) \in R \wedge y = f(w)$. Our definition, instead, ensures that the honest prover knows w but we can only extract $f(w)$. Also note that, in the above definition, the prover $\mathcal{P}^*$ takes as input the auxiliary information returned by the sampler.

3.1   On Multi-round PAoK

In this section we show that multi-round PAoK can be squeezed into a one-round PAoK (maintaining knowledge soundness).

Let $\Pi = (\mathsf{Chall}, \mathsf{Resp})$ be a ρ-round PAoK. Consider the following protocol between prover $\tilde{\mathcal{P}}_n$ and verifier $\tilde{\mathcal{V}}_n$—let us call it the *collapsed protocol* for future reference—for a parameter $n \in \mathbb{N}$ to be determined later:

- Repeat the following sub-protocol $\tilde{\Pi} = (\tilde{\mathcal{P}}, \tilde{\mathcal{V}})$ in parallel for all $j \in [n]$:
  - $\tilde{\mathcal{V}}$ runs $(\mathbf{c}^j, \mathbf{b}^j) \leftarrow_\$ \mathsf{Chall}(1^\kappa, x)$; let $\mathbf{c}^j = (c_1^j, \ldots, c_\rho^j)$ and similarly $\mathbf{b}^j = (b_1^j, \ldots, b_\rho^j)$. Then, $\tilde{\mathcal{V}}$ samples a random index $i_j^* \leftarrow_\$ [\rho]$, and forwards $(c_1^j, \ldots, c_{i_j^*}^j)$ to $\tilde{\mathcal{P}}$.
  - $\tilde{\mathcal{P}}$, given a pair (x, w) and challenges $(c_1^j, \ldots, c_{i_j^*}^j)$, computes $(a_1^j, \ldots, a_{i_j^*}^j) \leftarrow_\$ \mathsf{Resp}(1^\kappa, x, w, c_1^j, \ldots, c_{i_j^*}^j)$ and forwards $(a_1^j, \ldots, a_{i_j^*}^j)$ to $\tilde{\mathcal{V}}$.
  - $\tilde{\mathcal{V}}$ is said to accept the j-th parallel execution if and only if $a_i^j = b_i^j$ for all $i \in [i_j^*]$
- Return acc if and only if all parallel executions are accepting.

We write $\tilde{\Pi}_n := (\tilde{\mathcal{P}}_n, \tilde{\mathcal{V}}_n)$ for the n-fold repetition of the sub-protocol $\tilde{\Pi} = (\tilde{\mathcal{P}}, \tilde{\mathcal{V}})$. Note that the sub-protocol $\tilde{\Pi}$ is the one-round protocol (described above) that simply cuts the multi-round protocol Π to a random round. We show the following theorem:

Theorem 1. *For any polynomial $\rho(\cdot)$ and any function f if Π is a $\rho(\kappa)$-round f-PAoK, then the above defined collapsed protocol $\tilde{\Pi}_n = (\tilde{\mathcal{P}}_n, \tilde{\mathcal{V}}_n)$ with parameter $n = \omega(\rho \log \kappa)$ is an f-PAoK.*

We give an intuition for the proof. For simplicity, assume that Π is a $\frac{1}{3}$-PAoK for the relation R. We claim that the knowledge error of the collapsed protocol is not bigger than $1 - \frac{2}{3\rho}$. To see this, consider a prover $\mathcal{P}^*$ for the original protocol Π which at the i-th iteration (where $i \in [\rho]$) forwards the challenge $c_1, \ldots, c_i$ to a malicious prover $\tilde{\mathcal{P}}^*$ for the collapsed protocol. Notice that conditioned on $i^* = i$ the challenge has exactly the same distribution as a challenge for the collapsed protocol. The prover $\mathcal{P}^*$ fails if the malicious prover $\tilde{\mathcal{P}}^*$ of the collapsed protocol answered wrongly at least one of the queries that he received. So if we suppose that $\tilde{\mathcal{P}}^*$ succeeds with probability strictly bigger than $1 - \frac{2}{3\rho}$, then, by the union bound, the failing probability of $\mathcal{P}^*$ is strictly bounded by $\frac{2}{3\rho} \cdot \rho$, therefore $\mathcal{P}^*$ succeeds with probability strictly bigger than $\frac{1}{3}$.

Finally, we can make the knowledge soundness error of the collapsed protocol negligible via parallel repetition. It is important to notice that parallel repetition, in general, does not amplify soundness for argument systems [5,39]. Luckily, it does so (at an exponential rate) in the special case of secret-coin one-round arguments (such as PAoK) [5]. The proof of the above theorem relies on the well-known fact that parallel repetition decreases the (knowledge) soundness error of one-round arguments at an exponential rate.

Lemma 1 (Theorem 4.1 of [5], adapted to one-round protocols). *Let* $\Pi = (\mathcal{P}, \mathcal{V})$ *be a one-round argument of knowledge and denote by* $\Pi_n = (\mathcal{P}_n, \mathcal{V}_n)$ *the one-round protocol that consists of the n-fold repetition of the initial protocol* Π. *Suppose* $0 < \alpha, \beta < 1$ *and* $n \geqslant 2$ *is an integer. Suppose* $\alpha > (16/\beta) \cdot e^{-\beta \cdot n/128}$. *Then there is an oracle algorithm* $\mathcal{R}$ *such that for any prover* $\mathcal{P}^*$, *verifier* $\mathcal{V}$ *and input string* x, *the following is true: If* $\Pr[\langle \mathcal{P}^*(1^\kappa, x, aux), \mathcal{V}_n(x)\rangle = \mathsf{acc}] \geqslant 2\alpha$ *then* $\Pr[\langle \mathcal{R}^{\mathcal{P}^*}(1^\kappa, x, aux), \mathcal{V}(x)\rangle = \mathsf{acc}] \geqslant 1 - \beta$. *Furthermore,* $\mathcal{R}^{\mathcal{P}^*}$ *runs in time* $poly(n, |x|, \alpha^{-1})$.

Proof (of Theorem 1). Let $\tilde{\mathcal{P}}_n^*$ be a prover for the collapsed protocol such that for some x and z succeeds with probability at least κ^{-c} for some constant c. Let $\alpha = \frac{1}{2}\kappa^{-c}$ and $\beta = \frac{1}{2\rho}$, notice that setting $n = \omega(\rho \log \kappa)$ the following equation holds for κ big enough:

$$\frac{1}{2}\kappa^{-c} = \alpha > (16/\beta) \cdot e^{-\beta \cdot n/128} = 32\rho \cdot e^{-\omega(\log \kappa)/256}.$$

We can apply Lemma 1 with the parameters α and β set as above. Therefore, consider a single instance of the sub-protocol $\tilde{\Pi}$, the prover $\mathcal{R}^{\tilde{\mathcal{P}}_n}$ succeeds with probability $1 - \beta = 1 - \frac{1}{2\rho}$.

We build a prover $\mathcal{P}^*$ for Π that succeeds with probability $\frac{1}{2}$. Specifically, Let $\tilde{\mathcal{P}}^* := \mathcal{R}^{\tilde{\mathcal{P}}_n^*}$ and let $\mathcal{P}^*$ interact with the verifier $\mathcal{V}$ of the multi-round protocol as follow:

1. $\mathcal{V}$ samples $(\mathbf{c}, \mathbf{b}) \leftarrow_\$ \mathsf{Chall}(1^\kappa, x)$, where $\mathbf{c} := (c_1, \dots, c_\rho)$ and $\mathbf{b} := (b_1, \dots, b_\rho)$.
2. For all $i \in [\rho]$ in increasing sequence:
   - Upon input challenge c_i from the verifier $\mathcal{V}$, prover $\mathcal{P}^*$ runs internally $\tilde{\mathcal{P}}^*$ on input $(1^\kappa, x)$ and challenge $(c_1, \dots, c_i)$. If $\tilde{\mathcal{P}}^*$ outputs $(a_1, \dots, a_i)$, then $\mathcal{P}^*$ forwards a_i to $\mathcal{V}$; otherwise it aborts.

Rewriting explicitly the acceptance probability of $\tilde{\mathcal{P}}^*$ in the collapsed protocol on (x, z):

$$\Pr\left[\tilde{\mathcal{P}}^*(1^\kappa, x, z, c_1, \dots, c_i) = (b_1, \dots, b_i) : (\mathbf{c}, \mathbf{b}) \leftarrow_\$ \mathsf{Chall}(1^\kappa, x), i \leftarrow_\$ [\rho]\right] \geqslant 1 - \frac{1}{2\rho}.$$

Let W_i be the event that $a_i = b_i$ in the interaction between $\mathcal{P}^*$ and $\mathcal{V}$ described above. We can write:

$$\Pr[\langle \mathcal{P}^*(1^\kappa, x, z), \mathcal{V}(1^\kappa, x)\rangle = \mathsf{acc}]$$

$$= \Pr[\forall i \in [\rho] : W_i] = 1 - \Pr[\exists i \in [\rho] : \neg W_i] \geqslant 1 - \sum_{i \in [\rho]} \Pr[\neg W_i]$$

$$= 1 - \rho \cdot \mathbb{E}_{i \leftarrow\$ [\rho]} \big[\Pr[\mathcal{P}^*(1^\kappa, x, c_1, \ldots, c_i) \neq a_i : (\mathbf{c}, \mathbf{b}) \leftarrow\$ \mathsf{Chall}(1^\kappa, x)] \big]$$

$$\geqslant 1 - \left(\tfrac{1}{2\rho}\right) \cdot \rho = \tfrac{1}{2}. \tag{1}$$

where the equations above follow by the definition of average and by our assumption on the success probability of $\tilde{\mathcal{P}}^*$ on (x, z). Notice that for any successful $\tilde{\mathcal{P}}_n^*$ we can define an extractor that is the same extractor for the machine $\mathcal{P}^*$ executing $\tilde{\mathcal{P}}^* = \mathcal{R}^{\tilde{\mathcal{P}}_n^*}$ as a subroutine. Moreover, since $\tilde{\mathcal{P}}_n^*$ succeeds with probability κ^{-c} then $\mathcal{P}^*$ runs in polynomial time.

3.2   Laconic PAoK

We show that laconic PAoK (where the size of the prover's answer is $\ell = 1$ bit) are in fact equivalent to PAoK.

Theorem 2. *Let R be an NP relation. If there exists a PAoK for R then there exists a* laconic *PAoK for R.*

The proof of the theorem, which appears in the full version of the paper [21], relies on the Goldreich-Levin Theorem [26, Theorem 2.5.2]. Here is the intuition. Let $(\mathcal{P}, \mathcal{V})$ be a PAoK with ℓ-bit answers. We define a new PAoK $(\mathcal{P}', \mathcal{V}')$ where the verifier $\mathcal{V}'$ runs $\mathcal{V}$ in order to obtain a pair (c, b), samples randomness r, and defines the new predicted answer to be the inner product between b and r. Given challenge (c, r) the prover $\mathcal{P}'$ simply runs $\mathcal{P}$ in order to obtain a and defines the answer to be the inner product between a and r. Knowledge soundness follows by the Goldreich-Levin theorem.

4   Constructing PAoK

We explore constructions of PAoK. For space reasons we defer to the full version of the paper [21] the constructions based on Extractable Witness Encryption [24, 31] and on Extractable Hash-Proof Systems [42].

In Sect. 4.1, we focus on constructing PAoK for so-called random self-reducible relations. In particular, we show that, for such relations, a fully-extractable PAoK can be obtained by generically leveraging a PAoK for a (much weaker) specific sampler (which depends on the random self-reducible relation).

In Sect. 4.2, we show that a PAoK for a specific sampler can be obtained generically by using a differing-input obfuscator [6] for a related (specific) circuit sampler.

4.1 PAoK for Random Self-reducible Languages

We construct a PAoK for languages that are random self-reducible. Roughly speaking, a random self-reducible language is a language for which average-case hardness implies worst-case hardness. Random self-reducibility is a very natural property, with many applications in cryptography (see, e.g., [3,37,40]). Informally a function is random self-reducible if, given an algorithm that computes the function on random inputs, one can compute the function on any input. When considering *NP* relations, one has to take a little more care while defining random self-reducibility. We say that $\mathcal{O}_R(\cdot)$ is an *oracle* for the relation R, if on any input $x \in L_R$ we have that $(x, \mathcal{O}_R(x)) \in R$.

Definition 2 (Self-reducible relation). *An NP-relation R for a language L is random self-reducible if there exists a tuple of PPT algorithms $\mathcal{W} :=$ $(\mathcal{W}_{\mathsf{smp}}, \mathcal{W}_{\mathsf{cmp}}, \mathcal{W}_{\mathsf{inv}})$ such that, for any oracle $\mathcal{O}_R$ for the relation $R \subseteq X \times W$, the following holds*

Correctness. *For any $x \in L_R$ and for any $r \in \{0,1\}^{p(|x|)}$, let $x' := \mathcal{W}_{\mathsf{smp}}(x; r)$ and $w := \mathcal{W}_{\mathsf{cmp}}(x, w'; r)$ where $w' \leftarrow \mathcal{O}_R(x')$. Then $(x, w) \in R$.*
Witness re-constructability. *For any $x \in L_R$ and for any $r \in \{0,1\}^{p(|x|)}$, let $x' := \mathcal{W}_{\mathsf{smp}}(x; r)$ and $w := \mathcal{W}_{\mathsf{cmp}}(x, w'; r)$ where $w' \leftarrow \mathcal{O}_R(x')$, and define $w'' := \mathcal{W}_{\mathsf{inv}}(x, w; r)$. Then $(x', w'') \in R$.*
Uniformity. *For any x the output of $\mathcal{W}_{\mathsf{smp}}(x)$ is uniformly distributed over X.*

We call the tuple of algorithms $\mathcal{W}$ an average-to-worst-case (AWC) reduction with witness re-constructibility.

Notice that the reduction $\mathcal{W}$ has access to a "powerful" oracle that produces a witness for a randomized instance, and uses such witness to compute a witness for the original instance. Moreover, for any fixed instance the function can be easily inverted. The witness re-constructibility property is not standard in the context of random self reducibility, however we note that it holds for many interesting random self-reducible relationships (e.g., for the case of discrete logarithm).

Theorem 3. *Let R be an NP-relation which has AWC reduction $\mathcal{W} = (\mathcal{W}_{\mathsf{smp}}, \mathcal{W}_{\mathsf{cmp}}, \mathcal{W}_{\mathsf{inv}})$ with witness re-constructability. If there exists a $(\mathcal{W}_{\mathsf{smp}}, \epsilon)$-PAoK for the relation R, then there exists an ϵ-PAoK for R.*

The proof of the above theorem is deferred to the full version of the paper [21]. Here we discuss some intuition. Let $\Pi' := (\mathsf{Chall}', \mathsf{Resp}')$ be a PAoK (w.r.t. the sampler $\mathcal{W}_{\mathsf{smp}}$) for R, the idea of the construction is to map the input instance x into a random instance x' using $\mathcal{W}_{\mathsf{smp}}(x; r)$ for a random r, then sample a challenge using the algorithm Chall' on input instance x' and additionally send the prover the auxiliary information r needed to compute a valid witness w' for x'. The response algorithm first computes the valid witness w' for the instance x' using $\mathcal{W}_{\mathsf{inv}}$ and then answers the challenge. Let Π be the PAoK described above, given a prover $\mathcal{P}^*$ for Π we need to define a knowledge extractor $\mathcal{K}$. The point is that $\mathcal{P}^*$ can equivalently be seen as a prover for Π' where instances are sampled using $\mathcal{W}_{\mathsf{smp}}(x;\cdot)$. For this scenario the knowledge soundness of Π provides a knowledge extractor $\mathcal{K}'$, and such an extractor can output a valid witness for a uniformly sampled instance. This is where we use the random self-reducibility property. The extractor $\mathcal{K}'$, in fact, can be seen as an oracle for the relation R that with noticeable probability produces a valid witness for a uniformly chosen instance. Therefore, using the AWC reduction $\mathcal{W}$ with oracle access to $\mathcal{K}'$ we can reconstruct a valid witness for the instance x.

4.2   PAoK for a Specific Sampler

We use the framework for obfuscation proposed by Bellare *et al.* in [6]. A circuit sampling algorithm is a PPT algorithm $\mathcal{S} = \{\mathcal{S}_\kappa\}_{\kappa \in \mathbb{N}}$ whose output is distributed over $\mathcal{C}_\kappa \times \mathcal{C}_\kappa \times \{0,1\}^{p(\kappa)}$, for a class of circuit $\mathcal{C} = \{\mathcal{C}_\kappa\}_{\kappa \in \mathbb{N}}$ and a polynomial p. We assume that for every $C_0, C_1 \in \mathcal{C}_\kappa$ it holds that $|C_0| = |C_1|$. Given any class of samplers $\mathbf{S}$ for a class of circuits $\mathcal{C}$ consider the following definition:

Definition 3 (S-Obfuscator). *A PPT algorithm Obf is an $\mathbf{S}$-obfuscator for the parametrized collection of circuits $\mathcal{C} = \{\mathcal{C}_\kappa\}_{\kappa \in \mathbb{N}}$ if the following requirements are met.*

- **Correctness:** $\forall \kappa, \forall C \in \mathcal{C}_\kappa, \forall x : \Pr[C'(x) = C(x) : C' \leftarrow_\$ \textsf{Obf}(1^\kappa, C)] = 1.$
- **Security:** *For every sampler $\mathcal{S} \in \mathbf{S}$, for every PPT (distinguishing) algorithm $\mathcal{D}$, and every auxiliary inputs $z_D, z_S \in \{0,1\}^*$, there exists a negligible function $\nu : \mathbb{N} \to [0,1]$ such that for all $\kappa \in \mathbb{N}$:*

$$\left| \Pr\left[\mathcal{D}(C', aux, z_D, z_S) = 1 : \begin{array}{c} (C_0, C_1, aux) \leftarrow_\$ \mathcal{S}(1^\kappa, z_S), \\ C' \leftarrow_\$ \textsf{Obf}(1^\kappa, C_0) \end{array} \right] \right.$$
$$\left. - \Pr\left[\mathcal{D}(C', aux, z_D, z_S) = 1 : \begin{array}{c} (C_0, C_1, aux) \leftarrow_\$ \mathcal{S}(1^\kappa, z_S), \\ C' \leftarrow_\$ \textsf{Obf}(1^\kappa, C_1) \end{array} \right] \right| \leqslant \nu(\kappa),$$

where the probability is over the coins of $\mathcal{S}$ and Obf.

Abusing the notation, given a circuit sampler $\mathcal{S}$, we say that Obf is an $\mathcal{S}$-obfuscator if it is an $\{\mathcal{S}\}$-obfuscator. It is easy to see that the above definition allows to consider various flavours of obfuscation as a special case (including indistinguishability and differing-input obfuscation [4]). In particular, we say that a circuit sampler is differing-input if for any PPT adversary $\mathcal{A}$ and any auxiliary input $z_S \in \{0,1\}^*$ there exists a negligible function $\nu : \mathbb{N} \to [0,1]$ such that the following holds:

$$\Pr\left[C_0(x) \neq C_1(x) : \begin{array}{c} (C_0, C_1, aux) \leftarrow_\$ \mathcal{S}(1^\kappa, z_S) \\ x \leftarrow \mathcal{A}(C_0, C_1, aux, z_S) \end{array} \right] \leqslant \nu(\kappa).$$

Let $\mathbf{S}^{\mathrm{diff}}$ be the class of all differing-input samplers; it is clear that an $\mathbf{S}^{\mathrm{diff}}$-obfuscator is equivalent to a differing-input obfuscator.

Consider the following construction of a PAoK $\Pi = (\mathsf{Chall}, \mathsf{Resp})$ for a relation R.

- Upon input $(1^\kappa, x)$ algorithm $\mathsf{Chall}(1^\kappa, x)$ outputs $c := \mathsf{Obf}(C_{x,b})$ where $b \leftarrow_\$ \{0,1\}^\kappa$ and $C_{x,b}$ is the circuit that hard-wires x and b and, upon input a value w, it returns b if and only if $(x, w) \in R$ (and $\perp$ otherwise).
- Upon input $(1^\kappa, x, w, c)$, algorithm $\mathsf{Resp}(1^\kappa, x, w, c)$ executes $a := c(w)$ and outputs a.

Given an arbitrary instance sampler $\mathcal{S}$, let $\mathsf{CS}[\mathcal{S}]$ be the circuit samplers that sample randomness $r' := r\|b$, execute $(x, aux) := \mathcal{S}(1^\kappa, z_\mathcal{S}; r)$, and output the tuple $(C_{x,b}, C_{x,\perp}, aux\|b)$. We prove the following result, whose proof appears in the full version of the paper [21].

Theorem 4. *Let $\mathcal{S}$ be an arbitrary instance sampler and $\mathcal{S}^{\mathrm{diff}}$ and $\mathsf{CS}[\mathcal{S}]$ be as above. If $\mathsf{CS}[\mathcal{S}] \in \mathcal{S}^{\mathrm{diff}}$ and Obf is a $\mathsf{CS}[\mathcal{S}]$-obfuscator, then the protocol Π described above is an $\mathcal{S}$-PAoK for the relation R.*

By combining Theorem 4 together with Theorem 3 we get the following corollary.

Corollary 1. *Let R be a random self-reducible NP-relation which is witness reconstructible and has AWC reduction $\mathcal{W} = (\mathcal{W}_{\mathsf{smp}}, \mathcal{W}_{\mathsf{cmp}}, \mathcal{W}_{\mathsf{inv}})$. If there exists a $\mathsf{CS}[\mathcal{W}_{\mathsf{smp}}]$-obfuscator and $\mathsf{CS}[\mathcal{W}_{\mathsf{smp}}] \in \mathcal{S}^{\mathrm{diff}}$ then there exists a PAoK for R.*

5   On Zero Knowledge

One can easily verify that PAoK are always honest-verifier zero-knowledge, since the answer to a (honest) challenge from the verifier can be predicted without knowing a valid witness.

It is also not too hard to see that in general PAoK may not be witness indistinguishable (more details in the full version of the paper [21]).

Furthermore, we note that PAoK in the plain model can be zero-knowledge only for trivial languages. The reason is that predictable arguments have inherently deterministic provers and, as shown by Goldreich and Oren [29, Theorem 4.5], the zero-knowledge property for such protocols is achievable only for languages in *BPP*.

In this section we show how to circumvent this impossibility using setup assumptions. In particular, we show how to transform any PAoK into another PAoK additionally satisfying the zero-knowledge property (without giving up on predictability). We provide two solutions. The first one in the common random string (CRS) model,[12] while the second one is in the non-programmable random oracle (NPRO) model.

---

[12] This model is sometimes also known as the Uniform Random String (URS) model.

5.1   Compiler in the CRS Model

We start by recalling the standard notion of zero-knowledge interactive protocols in the CRS model. Interactive protocols in the CRS model are defined analogously to interactive protocols in the plain model (cf. Sect. 2), with the only difference that at setup a uniformly random string $\omega \leftarrow_\$ \{0,1\}^\ell$ is sampled and both the prover and the verifier additionally take ω as input. For space reasons, the definition of zero-knowledge protocols in the CRS model is given in the full version of the paper [21].

The Compiler. Our first compiler is based on a NIZK-PoK system (see full version for the formal definition). Let $\Pi = (\mathsf{Chall}, \mathsf{Resp})$ be a PAoK for a relation R, and assume that Chall uses at most $\rho(|x|, \kappa)$ random bits for a polynomial ρ. Let $\mathcal{NIZK} = (\ell, \mathsf{Prove}, \mathsf{Ver})$ be a NIZK for the relation

$$R_{\mathsf{chal}} = \{((c,x),r) : \exists b \text{ s.t. } (c,b) := \mathsf{Chall}(1^\kappa, x; r)\}.$$

Consider the following one-round PAoK $\Pi' = (\mathsf{Chall}', \mathsf{Resp}')$ in the CRS model.

- At setup a uniform CRS $\omega \leftarrow_\$ \{0,1\}^\ell$ is sampled.
- Algorithm Chall' takes as input $(1^\kappa, \omega, x)$ and proceeds as follows:
    1. Sample random tape $r \leftarrow_\$ \{0,1\}^\rho$.
    2. Generate a proof $\pi \leftarrow_\$ \mathsf{Prove}(\omega, (c,x), r)$ for $((c,x),r) \in R_{\mathsf{chal}}$.
    3. Output $c' := (c, \pi)$.
- Algorithm Resp' takes as input $(1^\kappa, \omega, x, w, c')$ and proceeds as follows:
    1. Parse $c' := (c, \pi)$; in case $\mathsf{Ver}(\omega, (c,x), \pi) = 0$ return $\perp$.
    2. Output $b' := \mathsf{Resp}(1^\kappa, x, w, c)$.

Roughly speaking, in the above construction the verifier sends the challenge c together with a NIZK-PoK π that c is "well formed" (i.e., there exist random coins r such that the verifier of the underlying PAoK with coins r returns a pair (c, b)); the prover answers only in case the proof π is correct. We show the following result, whose proof appears in the full version of the paper [21].

Theorem 5. *Let Π be a PAoK for the relation $R \in NP$ and let $\mathcal{NIZK}$ be a NIZK-PoK for the relation R_{chal}. Then the protocol Π' is a ZK-PAoK in the CRS model.*

The knowledge soundness of Π' follows almost directly from the zero-knowledge property of $\mathcal{NIZK}$ and from the knowledge soundness of Π. In fact, one can consider a mental experiment where the verifier generates a simulated proof π instead of a real one. This proof does not carry any information about the randomness but it is indistinguishable from a real one. A successful prover in the real world is still successful in this mental experiment and, therefore, we reduced to the knowledge soundness of Π. The zero-knowledge of Π' follows from the fact that PAoK are honest-verifier zero-knowledge, and from the knowledge soundness of $\mathcal{NIZK}$. In particular, given a maliciously generated challenge (c^*, π^*), the simulator can use the knowledge extractor of $\mathcal{NIZK}$ on π^*, extract a valid witness r^*, and then produce a valid answer.

5.2 Compiler in the NPRO Model

We start by recalling the definition of zero-knowledge in the NPRO model, for interactive protocols. Recall that a NPRO is weaker than a programmable random oracle. Intuitively, in the NPRO model the simulator can observe the verifier's queries to the hash function, but is not allowed to program the behaviour of the hash function. The definition below is adapted from Wee [41].

Definition 4 (Zero-knowledge protocol in the NPRO model). *Let* $(\mathcal{P}, \mathcal{V})$ *be an interactive protocol for an NP relation R. We say that* $(\mathcal{P}, \mathcal{V})$ *satisfies the* zero-knowledge *property in the NPRO model if for every PPT malicious verifier* $\mathcal{V}^*$ *there exists a PPT simulator* $\mathcal{Z}$ *and a negligible function* $\nu : \mathbb{N} \to [0,1]$ *such that for all PPT distinguishers* $\mathcal{D}$, *all* $(x, w) \in R$, *and all auxiliary inputs* $z \in \{0,1\}^*$, *the following holds:*

$$\Delta(\Pi, \mathcal{Z}, \mathcal{V}^*) := \max_{\mathcal{D}, z} \Big| \Pr\left[\mathcal{D}^H(x, \tau, z) = 1 : \; \tau \leftarrow (\mathcal{P}^H(x, w) \leftrightarrows \mathcal{V}^{*H}(x, z))\right]$$

$$- \Pr\left[\mathcal{D}^H(x, \tau, z) = 1 : \; \tau \leftarrow \mathcal{Z}^H(x, z)\right]\Big| \leqslant \nu(|x|).$$

The Compiler. Let $\Pi = (\mathsf{Chall}, \mathsf{Resp})$ be a PAoK for a relation R with ℓ-bit prover's answer, and assume that Chall uses at most $\rho(|x|, \kappa)$ random bits for a polynomial ρ. Let H be a random oracle with output length $\rho(\kappa)$. Consider the following derived one-round PAoK $\Pi' = (\mathsf{Chall}', \mathsf{Resp}')$.

- Algorithm Chall' takes as input $(1^\kappa, x)$ and proceeds as follows:
  1. Sample a random tag $t_1 \leftarrow\!\!{}_{\$} \{0,1\}^\rho$ and compute $r := H(t_1)$.
  2. Run $(c, b) := \mathsf{Chall}(1^\kappa, x; r)$.
  3. Define $t_2 := H(b)$, and set the challenge to $c' := (c, t)$ where $t := t_1 \oplus t_2$.
- Algorithm Resp' takes as input (x, w, c) and proceeds as follows:
  1. Parse $c' := (c, t)$ and run $a \leftarrow\!\!{}_{\$} \mathsf{Resp}(1^\kappa, x, w, c)$.
  2. Define $t_1 := t \oplus H(a)$, and check whether $(c, a) = \mathsf{Chall}(1^\kappa, x; H(t_1))$. If this is the case, output a and otherwise output $\bot$.

The main idea behind the above construction is to force the malicious verifier to follow the underlying protocol Π; in order to do so we generate the challenge feeding the algorithm Chall with the uniformly random string $H(t_1)$. What we need now is to both make able the prover to check that the verifier followed the algorithm Chall and to maintain soundness. Unfortunately, since PAoK are private-coin protocols, we can't simply make the verifier output t_1; what we do instead is to one-time pad the value with the value t_2 which is computable only knowing the answer. We show the following result:

Theorem 6. *If Π is a PAoK with ℓ-bit prover's answer for the relation R, and $\ell = \omega(\log \kappa)$, then the protocol Π' is a ZK-PAoK in the NPRO model.*

To prove soundness we show that $t = t_1 \oplus t_2$ is essentially uniformly random if the prover does not know b: this explains why we need $\ell = \omega(\log \kappa)$, otherwise a malicious prover could just brute force the right value of b and check for consistency. Note that here we are leveraging the power of the random oracle model, that allows us to produce polynomially-long pseudorandomness from unpredictability. To prove zero-knowledge we note that a simulator can look into the random-oracle calls made by the malicious verifier while running it. Given the output (c^*, t^*) produced by the malicious verifier two cases can happen:

- The simulator finds an oracle call t' that "explains" the challenge c^*, namely $(c^*, b) = \mathsf{Chall}(1^\kappa, x; H(t'))$; in this case the simulator just outputs b. We argue that the simulator produces an indistinguishable view because the protocol Π has overwhelming completeness.
- The simulator does not find any t' that explains the challenge. Then it outputs $\perp$. Let b' be the answer that the real prover would compute using the algorithm Resp. We argue that the malicious verifier can find a challenge (c^*, t^*) that passes the check, namely $(c^*, b') = \mathsf{Chall}(1^\kappa, x; H(H(b') \oplus t^*))$ only with negligible probability. Therefore the real prover would output $\perp$ as well, and so the views are indistinguishable.

Proof (of Theorem 6). Completeness follows readily from the completeness of the underlying PAoK.

We proceed to prove knowledge soundness of Π'. Given a prover $\mathcal{P}'^*$ for Π' that makes the verifier accept with probability $p(\kappa)$, we define a prover $\mathcal{P}^*$ for Π that is successful with probability $p(\kappa)/Q(\kappa)$ where Q is a polynomial that upper bounds the number of oracle calls made by $\mathcal{P}'^*$ to the NPRO H. Prover $\mathcal{P}^*$ proceeds as follow:

1. Upon input $(1^\kappa, c, z)$, set $c' := (c, t)$ for uniformly random $t \leftarrow_\$ \{0, 1\}^\rho$ and run $\mathcal{P}^*(1^\kappa, c', z)$. Initialize counter j to $j := 1$, $\mathcal{Q} := \emptyset$, and pick a uniformly random index $i^* \leftarrow_\$ [Q(\kappa)]$.
2. Upon input a random oracle query x from $\mathcal{P}'^*$, pick $y \leftarrow_\$ \{0, 1\}^\rho$ and add the tuple (x, y, j) to H. If $j = i^*$, then output x and stop. Otherwise set $j \leftarrow j+1$ and forward y to $\mathcal{P}'^*$.
3. In case $\mathcal{P}^*$ aborts or terminates, output $\perp$ and stop.

Without loss of generality we can assume that the prover $\mathcal{P}'^*$ does not repeat random oracle queries, and that before outputting an answer a^*, it checks that $(c, a^*) := \mathsf{Chall}(1^\kappa, x; H(t \oplus H(a^*)))$. We now analyse the winning probability of $\mathcal{P}^*$. Let a be the correct answer corresponding to the challenge c. Observe that the view produced by $\mathcal{P}^*$ is exactly the same as the real view (i.e., the view that $\mathcal{P}'^*$, with access to the random oracle, expects from an execution with the verifier $\mathcal{V}'$ from Π'), until $\mathcal{P}'^*$ queries H with the value a. In this case, in fact, $\mathcal{P}'^*$ expects to receive a tag t_2 such that $(c, a) := \mathsf{Chall}(1^\kappa, x; H(t \oplus t_2))$. We can write,

$\Pr\left[\mathcal{P}^*(1^\kappa, c, z) \text{ returns } a\right]$

$= \Pr\left[(a, *, i^*) \in \mathcal{Q}\right]$

$= \Pr\left[a \text{ is the } i^*\text{-th query to } H \wedge a = \mathcal{P}'^*(1^\kappa, c', z)\right]$

$= \Pr\left[a \text{ is the } i^*\text{-th query to } H \mid a = \mathcal{P}^*(1^\kappa, c', z)\right] \Pr\left[a = \mathcal{P}^*(1^\kappa, c', z)\right]$

$\geqslant 1/Q(\kappa) \cdot p(\kappa). \hspace{5cm} (2)$

Notice that in Eq.(2) the two probabilities are taken over two different probability spaces, namely the view provided by $\mathcal{P}'^*$ to the prover $\mathcal{P}^*$ together with i^* on the left hand side and the view that $\mathcal{P}'^*$ would expect in an execution with a honest prover together with the index i^* in the right hand side. Knowledge soundness of Π' follows.

We now prove the zero-knowledge property. Upon input $(1^\kappa, x, z)$ the simulator $\mathcal{Z}$ proceeds as follows:

1. Execute algorithm $\mathcal{V}^*(1^\kappa, x, z)$ and forward all queries to H; let $\mathcal{Q}$ be the set of queries made by $\mathcal{V}^*$.
2. Eventually $\mathcal{V}^*$ outputs a challenge $c^* = (c'^*, t^*)$. Check if there exist $(a^*, t_1^*) \in \mathcal{Q}$ such that $(c'^*, a^*) = \mathsf{Chall}(1^\kappa, x; H(t_1^*))$ and $t^* = t_1^* \oplus H(a^*)$. Output the transcript $\tau := (c^*, a^*)$. If no such pair is found, output $(c^*, \perp)$.

Let r' be the randomness used by the prover. For any challenge c, instance x and witness w, we say that r is *good* for c w.r.t. x, w, r' if $(c, a) = \mathsf{Chall}(1^\kappa, x; r) \wedge a = \mathsf{Resp}(1^\kappa, x, w, c; r')$. By completeness, the probability that r is not good, for $r \leftarrow_\$ \{0, 1\}^\rho$, is negligible. Therefore by letting *Good* be the event that $\mathcal{V}^*$ queries H only on inputs that output good randomness for some c, by taking a union bound over all queries we obtain

$$\Pr[\mathit{Good}] \geqslant 1 - Q(\kappa) \cdot \nu'(\kappa) \geqslant 1 - \nu(\kappa), \hspace{3cm} (3)$$

for negligible functions $\nu, \nu' : \mathbb{N} \to [0, 1]$.

From now on we assume that the event *Good* holds; notice that this only modifies by a negligible factor the distinguishing probability of the distinguisher $\mathcal{D}$.

We proceed with a case analysis on the possible outputs of the simulator and the prover:

- The second output of $\mathcal{Z}$ is $a \neq \perp$, whereas the second output of $\mathcal{P}$ is $\perp$. Conditioning on $\mathcal{Z}$'s second output being $a \neq \perp$, we get that the challenge c is *well formed*, namely, c is in the set of all possible challenges for the instance x and security parameter 1^κ. On the other hand, the fact that $\mathcal{P}$ outputs $\perp$ means that either algorithm Resp aborted or the check in step 2 of the description of Π' failed. However, neither of the two cases can happen unless event *Good* does not happen. Namely, if Resp outputs $\perp$ the randomness $H(t^* \oplus H(a))$ is not good for c (w.r.t. x, w, r'), and therefore Resp must have output a which, together with t^*, would pass the test in step 2 by definition of $\mathcal{Z}$. It follows that this case happens only with negligible probability.

- The second output returned by $\mathcal{Z}$ is $\perp$, whereas $\mathcal{P}$'s second output is $a \neq \perp$. Conditioning on $\mathcal{Z}$'s second output being $\perp$, we get that $\mathcal{V}^*$ made no queries (a^*, t_1^*) such that $(c, a^*) = \mathsf{Chall}(1^\kappa, x; t_1^*)$ and $t_1^* = H(t^* \oplus H(a^*))$. In such a case, there exists a negligible function $\nu : \mathbb{N} \to [0, 1]$ such that:

$$\Pr[(c, a) = \mathsf{Chall}(1^\kappa, x; H(t^* \oplus H(a^*)))]$$
$$\leqslant \Pr\left[t_1^* := (H(a) \oplus t) \in \mathcal{Q} \vee \mathsf{Chall}(1^\kappa, x; H(t_1^*)) = (c, a)\right]$$
$$\leqslant Q \cdot 2^{-\rho} + 2^{-\gamma} + \epsilon \leqslant \nu(\kappa), \tag{4}$$

where 2^γ is the size of the challenge space. Notice that by overwhelming completeness and $\ell = \omega(\log \kappa)$, it follows that $\gamma = \omega(\log \kappa)$.
- Both $\mathcal{Z}$'s and $\mathcal{P}$'s second output are not $\perp$, but they are different. This event cannot happen, since we are conditioning on *Good*.

Combining Eqs. (3) and (4) we obtain that $\Delta(\Pi, \mathcal{Z}, \mathcal{V}^*)$ is negligible, as desired.

On RO-Dependent Auxiliary Input. Notice that Definition 4 does not allow the auxiliary input to depend on the random oracle. Wee [41] showed that this is necessary for one-round protocols, namely zero-knowledge w.r.t. RO-dependent auxiliary input is possible only for trivial languages. This is because the result of [29] relativizes.

In a similar fashion, for the case of multi-round protocols, one can show that also the proof of [29, Theorem 4.5] relativizes. It follows that the assumption of disallowing RO-dependent auxiliary input is necessary also in our case.

6   Predictable ZAPs

We recall the concept of ZAP introduced by Dwork and Naor [17]. ZAPs are two-message (i.e., one-round) protocols in which:

(i) The first message, going from the verifier to the prover, can be fixed "once and for all," and is independent of the instance being proven;
(ii) The verifier's message consists of public coins.

Typically a ZAP satisfies two properties. First, it is witness indistinguishable meaning that it is computationally hard to tell apart transcripts of the protocols generated using different witnesses (for a given statement). Second, the protocol remains sound even if the statement to be proven is chosen after the first message is fixed.

In this section we consider the notion of Predictable ZAP (PZAP). With the terminology "ZAP" we want to stress the particular structure of the argument system we are interested in, namely a one-round protocol in which the first message can be fixed "once and for all." However, there are a few important differences between the notion of ZAPs and PZAPs. First off, PZAPs cannot be public coin, because the predictability requirement requires that the verifier uses private coins. Second, we relax the privacy requirement and allow PZAPs not to be witness indistinguishable; notice that, in contrast to PZAPs, ZAPs become uninteresting in this case as the prover could simply forward the witness to the verifier. Third, ZAPs are typically only computationally sound, whereas we insist on knowledge soundness.

More formally, a PZAP is fully specified by a tuple of PPT algorithms $\Pi = (\mathsf{Chall}, \mathsf{Resp}, \mathsf{Predict})$ as described below:

1. $\mathcal{V}$ samples $(c, \vartheta) \leftarrow_{\$} \mathsf{Chall}(1^\kappa)$ and sends c to $\mathcal{P}$.
2. $\mathcal{P}$ samples $a \leftarrow_{\$} \mathsf{Resp}(1^\kappa, x, w, c)$ and sends a to $\mathcal{V}$.
3. $\mathcal{V}$ computes $b := \mathsf{Predict}(1^\kappa, \vartheta, x)$ and outputs acc iff $a = b$.

Notice that, in contrast to the syntax of PAoK, now the verifier runs two algorithms $\mathsf{Chall}, \mathsf{Predict}$, where Chall is independent of the instance x being proven, and $\mathsf{Predict}$ uses the trapdoor ϑ and the instance x in order to predict the prover's answer.

Care needs to be taken while defining (knowledge) soundness for PZAPs. In fact, observe that while the verification algorithm needs private coins, in many practical circumstances the adversary might be able to infer the outcome of the verifier, and thus learn one bit of information about the verifier's private coins. For this reason, as we aim to constructing argument systems where the first message can be re-used, we enhance the adversary with oracle access to the verifier in the definition of soundness.

Definition 5 (Predictable ZAP). *Let $\Pi = (\mathsf{Chall}, \mathsf{Resp}, \mathsf{Predict})$ be as specified above, and let R be an NP relation. Consider the properties below.*

Completeness: *There exists a negligible function $\nu : \mathbb{N} \to [0, 1]$ such that for all $(x, w) \in R$:*

$$\Pr_{c, \vartheta}\left[\mathsf{Predict}(1^\kappa, \vartheta, x) \neq \mathsf{Resp}(1^\kappa, x, w, c) : (c, \vartheta) \leftarrow \mathsf{Chall}(1^\kappa)\right] \leq \nu(\kappa).$$

(Adaptive) Knowledge soundness with error ϵ: *For all PPT provers $\mathcal{P}^*$ making polynomially many queries to its oracle, there exists a PPT extractor $\mathcal{K}$ such that for any auxiliary input $z \in \{0, 1\}^*$ the following holds. Whenever*

$$p_z(\kappa) := \Pr\left[a = b \; : \; \begin{array}{l} (c, \vartheta) \leftarrow_{\$} \mathsf{Chall}(1^\kappa), \\ (x, a) \leftarrow_{\$} \mathcal{P}^{*\mathcal{V}(1^\kappa, \vartheta, \cdot, \cdot)}(c, z) \text{ where } |x| = \kappa, \\ b := \mathsf{Predict}(1^\kappa, \vartheta, x). \end{array}\right] > \epsilon(\kappa),$$

we have

$$\Pr\left[(x, w) \in R \; : \; \begin{array}{l} (c, \vartheta) \leftarrow_{\$} \mathsf{Chall}(1^\kappa), \\ (x, a) \leftarrow_{\$} \mathcal{P}^{*\mathcal{V}(1^\kappa, \vartheta, \cdot, \cdot)}(c, z) \text{ where } |x| = \kappa, \\ w \leftarrow_{\$} \mathcal{K}(1^\kappa, x, z, \mathcal{Q}). \end{array}\right] \geq p_z(\kappa) - \epsilon(\kappa).$$

In the above equations, we denote by $\mathcal{V}(1^\kappa, \vartheta, \cdot, \cdot)$ the oracle machine that upon input a query (x, a) computes $b := \mathsf{Predict}(1^\kappa, \vartheta, x)$ and outputs 1 iff $a = b$; we also write $\mathcal{Q}$ for the list $\{((x_i, a_i), d_i)\}$ of oracle queries (and answers to these queries) made by $\mathcal{P}^*$.

Let ℓ be the size of the prover's answer, we call Π a predictable ZAP (PZAP) for R if Π satisfies completeness and adaptive knowledge soundness with error ϵ, and moreover $\epsilon - 2^{-\ell}$ is negligible. In case knowledge soundness holds provided that no verification queries are allowed, we call Π a weak PZAP.

The definition of *laconic* PZAPs is obtained as a special case of the above defn by setting $\ell = 1$. Note, however, that in this case we additionally need to require that the value x returned by $\mathcal{P}^*$ is not contained in $\mathcal{Q}$.[13]

In the full version of the paper [21] we show a construction of PZAP based on any extractable witness pseudo-random function (Ext-WPRF), a primitive recently introduced in [43].

6.1   On Weak PZAP Versus PZAP

We investigate the relation between the notions of weak PZAP and PZAP. On the positive side, we show that weak PZAP for *NP* can be generically leveraged to PZAP for *NP* in a generic (non-black-box) manner. On the negative side, we show an impossibility result ruling out a broad class of black-box reductions from weak PZAP to PZAP. Both results assume the existence of one-way functions.

From Weak PZAP to PZAP. We show the following result:

Theorem 7. *Under the assumption that non-interactive zero-knowledge proof of knowledge systems for NP and non-interactive computationally-hiding commitment schemes exist, weak PZAP for NP imply PZAP for NP.*

Before coming to the proof, let us introduce some useful notation. Given a set $I \subseteq \{0,1\}^\kappa$, we will say that I is *bit-fixing* if there exists a string in $x \in \{0,1,\star\}^\kappa$ such that $I_x = I$ where $I_x := \{y \in \{0,1\}^\kappa : \forall i \in [\kappa], (x_i = y_i \lor x_i = \star)\}$ is the set of all κ-bit strings matching x in the positions where x is equal to 0/1. The symbol $\star$ takes the role of a special "don't care" symbol. Notice that there is a bijection between the set $\{0,1,\star\}^\kappa$ and the family of all bit-fixing sets contained in $\{0,1\}^\kappa$; in particular, for any $I \subseteq \{0,1\}^\kappa$ there exists a unique $x \in \{0,1,\star\}$ such that $I = I_x$ (and viceversa). Therefore, in what follows, we use x and I_x interchangeably. We also enforce the empty set to be part of the family of all bit-fixing sets, by letting $I_\perp = \emptyset$ (corresponding to $x = \perp$).

We now give some intuition for the proof of Theorem 7. The proof is divided in two main steps. In the first step, we define three algorithms (Gen, Sign, Verify). Roughly speaking, such a tuple constitutes a special type of signature scheme where the key generation algorithm Gen additionally takes as input a bit-fixing set I and returns a secret key that allows to sign messages $m \notin I$. There are two main properties we need from such a signature scheme: (i) The verification key and any set of polynomially many (adaptively chosen) signature queries do not

---

[13] This is necessary, as otherwise a malicious prover could query both $(x,0)$ and $(x,1)$, for $x \notin L$, and succeed with probability 1.

reveal any information on the set I; (ii) It should be hard to forge signatures on messages $m \in I$, even when given the set I and the secret key corresponding to I. A variation of such a primitive, with a few crucial differences, already appeared in the literature under the name of functional signatures [11].[14] Fix now some NP-relation R. In the second step of the proof, we consider an augmented NP-relation where the witness of an instance (x, VK) is either a witness w for $(x, w) \in R$, or a valid signature of x under VK. We then construct a PZAP based on a weak PZAP and on a NIZK-PoK for the above augmented NP-relation.

The reduction from weak PZAP to PZAP uses a partitioning technique, similar to the one used to prove unforgeability of several signature schemes (see, e.g., [10,12,20,34,35]). Intuitively, we can set the reduction in such a way that by sampling a random bit-fixing set I all the verification queries made by a succeeding prover for the PZAP will not be in I with good probability (and therefore such queries can be dealt with using knowledge of the signature key corresponding to I); this holds because the prover has no information on the set I, as ensured by property (i) defined above. On the other hand, the challenge x^* output by the prover will be contained in the set I, which will allow the reduction to break the weak PZAP. Here, is where we rely on property (ii) described above, so that the reduction is not able to forge a signature for x^*, and thus the extracted witness w^* must be a valid witness for $(x^*, w^*) \in R$.

Proof (of Theorem 7). Let Com be a computationally hiding commitment scheme with message space $\{0, 1, \star\}^\kappa \cup \{\bot\}$. Consider the following relation:

$$R_{\mathsf{com}} := \left\{ (m, com), (x, r) : \; com = \mathsf{Com}(x; r) \; \wedge \; m \notin I_x \right\}.$$

Let $\mathcal{NIZK} = (\ell, \mathsf{Prove}, \mathsf{Ver})$ be a NIZK-PoK for the relation R_{com}. We define the following tuple of algorithms $(\mathsf{Gen}, \mathsf{Sign}, \mathsf{Verify})$.

- Algorithm Gen takes as input the security parameter and a string $x \in \{0, 1, \star\}^\kappa \cup \{\bot\}$, samples $\omega \leftarrow_\$ \{0, 1\}^{\ell(\kappa)}$, and defines $com := \mathsf{Com}(x; r)$ for some random tape r. It then outputs $VK := (\omega, com)$ and $SK := (\omega, x, r)$.
- Algorithm Sign takes as input a secret key SK and a message m, and outputs $\sigma := \pi \leftarrow_\$ \mathsf{Prove}(\omega, (m, com), (x, r))$.
- Algorithm Verify takes as input a verification key VK and a pair (m, σ), parses $VK := (\omega, com)$, and outputs the same as $\mathsf{Ver}(\omega, (m, com), \sigma)$.

The lemmas below show two main properties of the above signature scheme.

Lemma 2. *For any PPT distinguisher $\mathcal{D}$, and any bit-fixing set $I \subseteq \{0, 1\}^\kappa$, there exists a negligible function $\nu : \mathbb{N} \to [0, 1]$ such that:*

$$\big| \Pr[\mathcal{D}^{\mathsf{Sign}(SK_I, \cdot)}(VK, I) : \; (VK, SK_I) \leftarrow_\$ \mathsf{Gen}(1^\kappa, I)]$$
$$- \Pr[\mathcal{D}^{\mathsf{Sign}(SK, \cdot)}(VK, I) : \; (VK, SK) \leftarrow_\$ \mathsf{Gen}(1^\kappa, \bot)] \big| \leqslant \nu(\kappa),$$

where $\mathcal{D}$ is not allowed to query its oracle on messages $m \in I$.

---

[14] On a high level, the difference is that functional signatures allow to generate punctured signature keys, whereas our signature scheme allows to puncture the message space.

Proof. We consider a series of hybrid experiments, where each hybrid is indexed by a bit-fixing set I and outputs the view of a distinghuisher $\mathcal{D}$ taking as input a verification key and the set I, while given oracle access to a signing oracle.

Hybrid $\mathcal{H}_1^I$: The first hybrid samples $(VK, SK) \leftarrow\!\!{}_\$ \; \mathsf{Gen}(1^\kappa, I)$ and runs the distinghuisher $\mathcal{D}$ upon input (VK, I) and with oracle access to $\mathsf{Sign}(SK, \cdot)$.

Hybrid $\mathcal{H}_2^I$: Let $\mathcal{Z}$ be the simulator of the underlying NIZK-PoK. The second hybrid samples $(\tilde{\omega}, \vartheta) \leftarrow\!\!{}_\$ \; \mathcal{Z}_0(1^\kappa)$ and defines $com := \mathsf{Com}(x; r)$ (for random tape r) and $\tilde{VK} = (\tilde{\omega}, com)$. It then runs the distinghuisher $\mathcal{D}$ upon input $(\tilde{VK}, I)$, and answers its oracle queries m by returning $\tilde{\sigma} \leftarrow\!\!{}_\$ \; \mathcal{Z}_1(\vartheta, (m, com))$.

The two claims below imply the statement of Lemma 2.

Claim. For all bit-fixing sets I, we have $\{\mathcal{H}_1^I\}_{\kappa\in\mathbb{N}} \stackrel{c}{\approx} \{\mathcal{H}_2^I\}_{\kappa\in\mathbb{N}}$.

Proof (of Claim). The only difference between the two experiments is in the way the verification key is computed and in how the signature queries are answered. In particular, the second experiment replaces the CRS with a simulated CRS and answers signature queries by running the ZK simulator of the NIZK. Note that the commitment com has the same distribution in both experiments.

Clearly, given any distinguisher that tells apart the two hybrids for some set I we can derive a distinguisher contradicting the unbounded zero-knowledge property of the NIZK. This concludes the proof.

Claim. Let $I_\perp := \emptyset$. For all bit-fixing sets I, we have $\{\mathcal{H}_2^I\}_{\kappa\in\mathbb{N}} \stackrel{c}{\approx} \{\mathcal{H}_2^{I_\perp}\}_{\kappa\in\mathbb{N}}$.

Proof (of Claim). Given a PPT distinguisher $\mathcal{D}$ telling apart $\mathcal{H}_2^I$ and $\mathcal{H}_2^{I_\perp}$, we construct a PPT distinguisher $\mathcal{D}$ that breaks computational hiding of the commitment scheme. Distinguisher $\mathcal{D}'$ is given as input a value com' which is either a commitment to I or a commitment to $I_\perp$. Thus, $\mathcal{D}'$ simply emulates the view for $\mathcal{D}$ but uses com' instead of com.

The claim follows by observing that in case com' is a commitment to I the view generated by $\mathcal{D}'$ is identical to that in hybrid $\mathcal{H}_2^I$, whereas in case com' is a commitment to $I_\perp$ the view generated by $\mathcal{D}'$ is identical to that in hybrid $\mathcal{H}_2^{I_\perp}$. Hence, $\mathcal{D}'$ retains the same advantage as $\mathcal{D}$, a contradiction.

Lemma 3. *For any PPT forger $\mathcal{F}$, and for any bit-fixing set I, there exists a negligible function $\nu : \mathbb{N} \to [0, 1]$ such that the following holds:*

$$\Pr\left[m^* \in I \wedge \mathsf{Verify}(VK, m^*, \sigma^*) = 1 : \begin{array}{l} (m^*, \sigma^*) \leftarrow\!\!{}_\$ \; \mathcal{F}(I, r), \\ (VK, SK_I) := \mathsf{Gen}(1^\kappa, I; r) \end{array} \right] \leqslant \nu(\kappa).$$

Proof. We rely on the knowledge soundness property of the NIZK-PoK and on the binding property of the commitment scheme. By contradiction, assume that there exists a PPT forger $\mathcal{F}$, a bit-fixing set I_x, and some polynomial $p(\cdot)$, such that for infinitely many values of $\kappa \in \mathbb{N}$

$$\Pr\left[m^* \in I_x \wedge \mathsf{Ver}(\omega, (m^*, com), \sigma^*) = 1 : \begin{array}{l} r \leftarrow\!\!{}_\$ \; \{0,1\}^*, \omega \leftarrow\!\!{}_\$ \; \{0,1\}^\ell \\ com \leftarrow\!\!{}_\$ \; \mathsf{Com}(x; r) \\ (m^*, \sigma^*) \leftarrow\!\!{}_\$ \; \mathcal{F}(\omega, r, I_x) \end{array} \right] \geq 1/p(\kappa).$$

Consider the following adversary $\mathcal{B}$ attacking the binding property of the commitment scheme:

(i) Upon input 1^κ, run $(\tilde{\omega}, \vartheta) \leftarrow_\$ \mathcal{K}_0(1^\kappa)$;
(ii) Obtain $(m^*, \sigma^*) \leftarrow_\$ \mathcal{F}(\tilde{\omega}, r, I_x)$ for some $x \in \{0, 1, \star\}^\kappa$ and $r \leftarrow_\$ \{0, 1\}^*$;
(iii) Extract $(x', r') \leftarrow_\$ \mathcal{K}_1(\tilde{\omega}, \vartheta, (m^*, com), \sigma^*)$, where $com = \mathsf{Com}(x; r)$;
(iv) Output $(x, r), (x', r')$ and m (as an auxiliary output).

By relying on the knowledge soundness property of the NIZK-PoK, and using the fact that the forger outputs an accepting proof with non-negligible probability, we obtain:

$$
\begin{aligned}
&\Pr[\mathcal{B} \text{ wins}] \\
&= \Pr\left[com = \mathsf{Com}(x'; r') \wedge (x, r) \neq (x', r') :\ ((x, r), (x', r')), m) \leftarrow_\$ \mathcal{B}(1^\kappa)\right] \\
&\geq \Pr\left[\begin{array}{l} com = \mathsf{Com}(x'; r'), \\ m \notin I_{x'}, \\ m \in I_x \end{array} :\ ((x, r), (x', r')), m) \leftarrow_\$ \mathcal{B}(1^\kappa)\right] - \nu(\kappa) \\
&\geq \Pr\left[\begin{array}{c} m^* \in I_x, \\ \mathsf{Ver}(\omega, (m^*, com), \sigma^*) = 1 \end{array} :\ \begin{array}{c} r \leftarrow_\$ \{0, 1\}^*, \omega \leftarrow_\$ \{0, 1\}^\ell \\ com \leftarrow_\$ \mathsf{Com}(x; r) \\ (m^*, \sigma^*) \leftarrow_\$ \mathcal{F}(\omega, r, I_x) \end{array}\right] \\
&\geq 1/p(\kappa) - \nu(\kappa),
\end{aligned}
$$

for some negligible function $\nu(\cdot)$. The first inequality uses the fact that the condition $(m \notin I_{x'}) \wedge (m \in I_x)$ implies $I_x \neq I_{x'}$ (and thus $x \neq x'$), and thus is sufficient for violating the binding property. This concludes the proof.

We can now explain how to transform a weak PZAP for NP into a PZAP for NP. Let R be an NP-relation. Consider the following derived relation:

$$R' = \{((x, VK), w) :\ (x, w) \in R \ \vee \ \mathsf{Verify}(VK, x, w) = 1)\}.$$

Clearly, R' is in NP, so let $\Pi = (\mathsf{Chall}, \mathsf{Resp}, \mathsf{Predict})$ be a weak PZAP for R'. Define the following PZAP $\Pi' = (\mathsf{Chall}', \mathsf{Resp}', \mathsf{Predict}')$ for the relation R.

- Algorithm Chall' takes as input $(1^\kappa, x)$ and proceeds as follows:
  • Run $(c, \vartheta) \leftarrow_\$ \mathsf{Chall}(1^\kappa)$.
  • Sample $(VK, SK) \leftarrow_\$ \mathsf{Gen}(1^\kappa, \bot)$, and let the challenge be $c' := (c, VK)$ and the trapdoor be $\vartheta' = (\vartheta, VK)$.
- Algorithm Resp' takes as input $(1^\kappa, x, w, c')$, parses $c' := (c, VK)$, and outputs $a := \mathsf{Resp}(1^\kappa, (x, VK), w, c)$.
- Algorithm $\mathsf{Predict}'$ takes as input $1^\kappa, \vartheta', x$, parses $\vartheta' := (\vartheta, VK)$, and outputs $b := \mathsf{Predict}(\vartheta, (x, VK))$.

The lemma below concludes the proof of Theorem 7.

Lemma 4. *Let Π and Π' be as above. If Π is a weak PZAP for R', then Π' is a PZAP for R.*

Proof. Given a prover $\mathcal{P}^*$ for Π', we construct a prover $\mathcal{P}_\alpha$ for Π' for a parameter $\alpha \in [\kappa]$ to be determined later. The description of $\mathcal{P}_\alpha$ follows.

- Upon input challenge c, choose $s \in \{0, 1, \star\}^\kappa$ in such a way that $\alpha := |\{i \in [\kappa] : s_i = \star\}|$. Sample $(VK, SK_I) \leftarrow\!\!\text{\tiny\$}\ \mathsf{Gen}(1^\kappa, I)$ for $I := I_s$, and forward the challenge $c' := (c, VK)$ to $\mathcal{P}^*$.
- Upon input a verification query (x_i, a_i) from $\mathcal{P}^*$ behave as follows:
  - In case $x_i \in I$, stop simulating $\mathcal{P}^*$, pick a random $x^* \leftarrow\!\!\text{\tiny\$}\ \{0,1\}^\kappa \backslash I$, and return the instance (x^*, VK) and answer $a^* := \mathsf{Resp}(1^\kappa, c, (x^*, VK), \mathsf{Sign}(SK_I, x^*))$.
  - In case $x_i \notin I$, compute $\sigma \leftarrow\!\!\text{\tiny\$}\ \mathsf{Sign}(SK_I, x_i)$ and answer the verification query with 1 iff $a = \mathsf{Resp}(1^\kappa, c, (x, VK), \sigma)$.
- Whenever $\mathcal{P}^*$ outputs (x^*, a^*), if $x^* \in I$ output $((x^*, VK), a^*)$. Else pick a random $x^* \leftarrow\!\!\text{\tiny\$}\ \{0,1\}^\kappa \backslash I$ and return the instance (x^*, VK) and answer $a^* := \mathsf{Resp}(1^\kappa, c, (x^*, VK), \mathsf{Sign}(SK_I, x^*))$.

We define the extractor for Π' (w.r.t. the relation R) to be the same as the extractor $\mathcal{K}$ for Π (w.r.t. the relation R'). It remains to bound the probability that $\mathcal{K}$ output a valid witness for the relation R.

Let *Good* be the event that $x^* \in I$ and all the x_i's corresponding to $\mathcal{P}^*$'s verification queries are such that $x_i \notin I$. Moreover, let Ext_R (resp. $Ext_{R'}$) be the event that $(x, w) \in R$ (resp. $((x, VK), w) \in R'$) where w comes from running the extractor $\mathcal{K}$ in the definition of PZAP. We can write:

$$\Pr[Ext_R] \geqslant \Pr[Ext_R \wedge Good] \tag{5}$$
$$\geqslant \Pr[Ext_{R'} \wedge Good] - \nu(\kappa)$$
$$\geqslant \Pr[Ext_{R'}] - \Pr[\neg Good] - \nu(\kappa)$$
$$\geqslant \left(\Pr[\mathcal{P}' \text{ succeeds}] - \nu'(\kappa) \right) - \Pr[\neg Good] - \nu(\kappa), \tag{6}$$

for negligible functions $\nu(\cdot), \nu'(\cdot)$. Here, Eq. (5) holds because of Lemma 3, whereas Eq. (6) follows by knowledge soundness of Π.

Observe that, by definition of $\mathcal{P}_\alpha$, the success probability when we condition on the event *Good* not happening is overwhelming (this is because in that case $\mathcal{P}_\alpha$ just computes a valid signature, and thus it succeeds with overwhelming probability by completeness of Π), therefore:

$$\Pr[\mathcal{P}_\alpha \text{ succeeds}] \geqslant \Pr[\mathcal{P}_\alpha \text{ succeeds}| Good] \cdot \Pr[Good] + (1 - \nu''(\kappa)) \Pr[\neg Good],$$

for some negligible function $\nu''(\cdot)$. Combining the last two equations, we obtain that there exists a negligible function $\nu'''(\cdot)$ such that:

$$\Pr[Ext_R] \geqslant \Pr[\mathcal{P}_\alpha \text{ succeeds}| Good] \cdot \Pr[Good] - \nu'''(\kappa).$$

We analyse the probability that $\mathcal{P}_\alpha$ succeeds conditioning on *Good* and the probability of event *Good* separately. We claim that the first term is negligibly close to the success probability of $\mathcal{P}^*$. In fact, when the event *Good* happens, by Lemma 2, the view generated by $\mathcal{P}_\alpha$ is indistinguishable from the view in the knowledge soundness definition of PZAP.

As for the second term, again by Lemma 2, it is not hard to see that it is negligibly close to $(1 - 2^{-\kappa+\alpha})^Q \cdot 2^{-\kappa+\alpha}$, where Q is an upper bound for the number of verification queries made by the prover. Since when $2^{-\kappa+\alpha} := 1 - Q/(Q+1)$, then $(1 - 2^{-\kappa+\alpha})^Q \cdot 2^{-\kappa+\alpha} \geqslant 1/e$, it suffices to set $\alpha := \kappa + \log(1 - Q/(Q+1))$ to enforce that the probability of *Good* is noticeable. This concludes the proof.

Ruling-Out Challenge-Passing Reductions We show an impossibility result ruling out a broad class of black-box reductions from weak laconic PZAP to laconic PZAP. This negative result holds for so-called "challenge-passing" black-box reductions, which simply forward their input to the inner prover of the PZAP protocol.

Theorem 8. *Assume that pseudo-random generators exist, and let Π be laconic weak PZAP for NP. There is no challenge-passing black-box reduction from weak knowledge soundness to knowledge soundness of Π.*

The impossibility exploits the fact that oracle access to the verifier $\mathcal{V}^*$ in the adaptive-knowledge soundness of laconic PZAP is equivalent to oracle access to a succeeding prover for the same relation. Consider the relation of pseudo-random string produced by a PRG G. The adversary can query the reduction with either a valid instance, namely a value x such that $x = G(s)$ for $s \leftarrow_{\$} \{0,1\}^\kappa$, or an invalid instance $x \leftarrow_{\$} \{0,1\}^{\kappa+1}$. Notice that, since the reduction is black-box the two instances are indistinguishable, therefore a good reduction must be able to answer correctly both kind of instances. This allows us to use the reduction itself as a succeeding prover. We refer the reader to the full version of the paper [21] for the formal proof.

7   Conclusion and Open Problems

We initiated the study of Predictable Arguments of Knowledge (PAoK) systems for *NP*. Our work encompasses a full characterization of PAoK (showing in particular that they can without loss of generality assumed to be extremely laconic), provides several constructions of PAoK (highlighting that PAoK are intimately connected to witness encryption and program obfuscation), and studies PAoK with additional properties (such as zero-knowledge and Predictable ZAP).

Although, the notions of PAoK and Ext-WE are equivalent, we think that they give two different points of view on the same object. Ultimately, this can only give more insights.

There are several interesting questions left open by our work. First, one could try to see whether there are other ways (beyond the ones we explored in the paper) how to circumvent the implausibility result of [23]. For instance it remains open if full-fledged PAoK for *NP* exist in the random oracle model.

Second, while it is impossible to have PAoK that additionally satisfy the zero-knowledge property in the plain model—in fact, we were able to achieve zero-knowledge in the CRS model and in the non-programmable random oracle model)—such a negative result does not apply to witness indistinguishability. Hence, it would be interesting to construct PAoK that are additionally witness indistinguishable in the plain model. An analogous question holds for PZAP.

Third, we believe the relationship between the notions of weak PZAP (where the prover is not allowed any verification query) and PZAP deserves further study. Our impossibility result for basing PZAP on weak PZAP in a black-box way, in fact, only rules out very basic types of reductions (black-box, and challenge-passing), and additionally only works for laconic PZAP. It remains open whether the impossibility proof can be extended to rule-out larger classes of reductions for non-laconic PZAP, or if the impossibility can somehow be circumvented using non-black-box techniques.

Acknowledgement. The first author and the second author acknowledge support by European Research Council Starting Grant 279447. The first author and the second author acknowledge support from the Danish National Research Foundation and The National Science Foundation of China (under the grant 61361136003) for the Sino-Danish Center for the Theory of Interactive Computation.

References

1. Abusalah, H., Fuchsbauer, G., Pietrzak, K.: Offline witness encryption. IACR Cryptology ePrint Archive, 2015:838 (2015)
2. Ananth, P., Boneh, D., Garg, S., Sahai, A., Zhandry, M.: Differing-inputs obfuscation and applications. IACR Cryptology ePrint Archive, 2013:689 (2013)
3. Angluin, D., Lichtenstein, D.: Provable security of cryptosystems: a survey. Technical report TR-288, Yale University, October 1983
4. Barak, B., Goldreich, O., Impagliazzo, R., Rudich, S., Sahai, A., Vadhan, S.P., Yang, K.: On the (im)possibility of obfuscating programs. J. ACM **59**(2), 6 (2012)
5. Bellare, M., Impagliazzo, R., Naor, M.: Does parallel repetition lower the error in computationally sound protocols? In: FOCS, pp. 374–383 (1997)
6. Bellare, M., Stepanovs, I., Tessaro, S.: Poly-many hardcore bits for any one-way function and a framework for differing-inputs obfuscation. In: Sarkar, P., Iwata, T. (eds.) ASIACRYPT 2014. LNCS, vol. 8874, pp. 102–121. Springer, Heidelberg (2014). doi:10.1007/978-3-662-45608-8_6
7. Bellare, M., Stepanovs, I., Waters, B.: New negative results on differing-inputs obfuscation. In: Fischlin, M., Coron, J.-S. (eds.) EUROCRYPT 2016. LNCS, vol. 9666, pp. 792–821. Springer, Heidelberg (2016). doi:10.1007/978-3-662-49896-5_28
8. Benhamouda, F., Blazy, O., Chevalier, C., Pointcheval, D., Vergnaud, D.: New techniques for SPHFs and efficient one-round PAKE protocols. In: Canetti, R., Garay, J.A. (eds.) CRYPTO 2013. LNCS, vol. 8042, pp. 449–475. Springer, Heidelberg (2013). doi:10.1007/978-3-642-40041-4_25
9. Bitansky, N., Canetti, R., Halevi, S.: Leakage-tolerant interactive protocols. In: Cramer, R. (ed.) TCC 2012. LNCS, vol. 7194, pp. 266–284. Springer, Heidelberg (2012). doi:10.1007/978-3-642-28914-9_15

10. Boneh, D., Boyen, X.: Secure identity based encryption without random oracles. In: Franklin, M. (ed.) CRYPTO 2004. LNCS, vol. 3152, pp. 443–459. Springer, Heidelberg (2004). doi:10.1007/978-3-540-28628-8_27

11. Boyle, E., Goldwasser, S., Ivan, I.: Functional signatures and pseudorandom functions. In: Krawczyk, H. (ed.) PKC 2014. LNCS, vol. 8383, pp. 501–519. Springer, Heidelberg (2014). doi:10.1007/978-3-642-54631-0_29

12. Boyle, E., Segev, G., Wichs, D.: Fully leakage-resilient signatures. J. Cryptol. **26**(3), 513–558 (2013)

13. Canetti, R., Halevi, S., Steiner, M.: Hardness amplification of weakly verifiable puzzles. In: Kilian, J. (ed.) TCC 2005. LNCS, vol. 3378, pp. 17–33. Springer, Heidelberg (2005). doi:10.1007/978-3-540-30576-7_2

14. Chung, K.-M., Liu, F.-H.: Parallel repetition theorems for interactive arguments. In: Micciancio, D. (ed.) TCC 2010. LNCS, vol. 5978, pp. 19–36. Springer, Heidelberg (2010). doi:10.1007/978-3-642-11799-2_2

15. Chung, K.-M., Pass, R.: Tight parallel repetition theorems for public-coin arguments using KL-divergence. In: Dodis, Y., Nielsen, J.B. (eds.) TCC 2015. LNCS, vol. 9015, pp. 229–246. Springer, Heidelberg (2015). doi:10.1007/978-3-662-46497-7_9

16. Derler, D., Slamanig, D.: Practical witness encryption for algebraic languages and how to reply an unknown whistleblower. IACR Cryptology ePrint Archive, 2015:1073 (2015)

17. Dwork, C., Naor, M.: ZAPs and their applications. SIAM J. Comput. **36**(6), 1513–1543 (2007)

18. Dziembowski, S., Pietrzak, K., Wichs, D.: Non-malleable codes, pp. 434–452. In: Innovations in Computer Science (2010)

19. Faonio, A., Nielsen, J.B.: Fully leakage-resilient codes. IACR Cryptology ePrint Archive, 2015:1151 (2015)

20. Faonio, A., Nielsen, J.B., Venturi, D. Mind your coins: fully leakage-resilient signatures with graceful degradation. In: ICALP, pp. 456–468 (2015)

21. Faonio, A., Nielsen, J.B., Venturi, D.: Predictable arguments of knowledge. Cryptology ePrint Archive, Report 2015/740 (2015). http://eprint.iacr.org/2015/740

22. Faust, S., Mukherjee, P., Nielsen, J.B., Venturi, D.: A tamper and leakage resilient von Neumann architecture. In: Katz, J. (ed.) PKC 2015. LNCS, vol. 9020, pp. 579–603. Springer, Heidelberg (2015). doi:10.1007/978-3-662-46447-2_26

23. Garg, S., Gentry, C., Halevi, S., Wichs, D.: On the implausibility of differing-inputs obfuscation and extractable witness encryption with auxiliary input. In: Garay, J.A., Gennaro, R. (eds.) CRYPTO 2014. LNCS, vol. 8616, pp. 518–535. Springer, Heidelberg (2014). doi:10.1007/978-3-662-44371-2_29

24. Garg, S., Gentry, C., Sahai, A., Waters, B.: Witness encryption and its applications. In: STOC, pp. 467–476 (2013)

25. Garg, S., Ostrovsky, R., Visconti, I., Wadia, A.: Resettable statistical zero knowledge. In: Cramer, R. (ed.) TCC 2012. LNCS, vol. 7194, pp. 494–511. Springer, Heidelberg (2012). doi:10.1007/978-3-642-28914-9_28

26. Goldreich, O.: The Foundations of Cryptography, Basic Techniques, vol. 1. Cambridge University Press, Cambridge (2001)

27. Goldreich, O., Håstad, J.: On the complexity of interactive proofs with bounded communication. Inf. Process. Lett. **67**(4), 205–214 (1998)

28. Goldreich, O., Levin, L.A.: A hard-core predicate for all one-way functions. In: STOC, pp. 25–32 (1989)

29. Goldreich, O., Oren, Y.: Definitions and properties of zero-knowledge proof systems. J. Cryptol. **7**(1), 1–32 (1994)

30. Goldreich, O., Vadhan, S.P., Wigderson, A.: On interactive proofs with a laconic prover. Comput. Complex. **11**(1–2), 1–53 (2002)
31. Goldwasser, S., Kalai, Y.T., Popa, R.A., Vaikuntanathan, V., Zeldovich, N.: How to run turing machines on encrypted data. In: Canetti, R., Garay, J.A. (eds.) CRYPTO 2013. LNCS, vol. 8043, pp. 536–553. Springer, Heidelberg (2013). doi:10.1007/978-3-642-40084-1_30
32. Haitner, I.: A parallel repetition theorem for any interactive argument. SIAM J. Comput. **42**(6), 2487–2501 (2013)
33. Håstad, J., Pass, R., Wikström, D., Pietrzak, K.: An efficient parallel repetition theorem. In: Micciancio, D. (ed.) TCC 2010. LNCS, vol. 5978, pp. 1–18. Springer, Heidelberg (2010). doi:10.1007/978-3-642-11799-2_1
34. Hofheinz, D., Kiltz, E.: Programmable hash functions and their applications. In: Wagner, D. (ed.) CRYPTO 2008. LNCS, vol. 5157, pp. 21–38. Springer, Heidelberg (2008). doi:10.1007/978-3-540-85174-5_2
35. Malkin, T., Teranishi, I., Vahlis, Y., Yung, M.: Signatures resilient to continual leakage on memory and computation. In: Ishai, Y. (ed.) TCC 2011. LNCS, vol. 6597, pp. 89–106. Springer, Heidelberg (2011). doi:10.1007/978-3-642-19571-6_7
36. Nielsen, J.B., Venturi, D., Zottarel, A.: On the connection between leakage tolerance and adaptive security. In: Kurosawa, K., Hanaoka, G. (eds.) PKC 2013. LNCS, vol. 7778, pp. 497–515. Springer, Heidelberg (2013). doi:10.1007/978-3-642-36362-7_30
37. Okamoto, T., Ohta, K.: Divertible zero knowledge interactive proofs and commutative random self-reducibility. In: Quisquater, J.-J., Vandewalle, J. (eds.) EUROCRYPT 1989. LNCS, vol. 434, pp. 134–149. Springer, Heidelberg (1990). doi:10.1007/3-540-46885-4_16
38. Pass, R., Venkitasubramaniam, M.: An efficient parallel repetition theorem for Arthur-Merlin games. In: STOC, pp. 420–429 (2007)
39. Pietrzak, K., Wikström, D.: Parallel repetition of computationally sound protocols revisited. J. Cryptol. **25**(1), 116–135 (2012)
40. Tompa, M., Woll, H.: Random self-reducibility and zero knowledge interactive proofs of possession of information. In: FOCS, pp. 472–482 (1987)
41. Wee, H.: Zero knowledge in the random oracle model, revisited. In: Matsui, M. (ed.) ASIACRYPT 2009. LNCS, vol. 5912, pp. 417–434. Springer, Heidelberg (2009). doi:10.1007/978-3-642-10366-7_25
42. Wee, H.: Efficient chosen-ciphertext security via extractable hash proofs. In: Rabin, T. (ed.) CRYPTO 2010. LNCS, vol. 6223, pp. 314–332. Springer, Heidelberg (2010). doi:10.1007/978-3-642-14623-7_17
43. Zhandry, M.: How to avoid obfuscation using witness PRFs. In: Kushilevitz, E., Malkin, T. (eds.) TCC 2016. LNCS, vol. 9563, pp. 421–448. Springer, Heidelberg (2016). doi:10.1007/978-3-662-49099-0_16

Removing Erasures with Explainable Hash Proof Systems

Michel Abdalla[1], Fabrice Benhamouda[2(✉)], and David Pointcheval[1]

[1] ENS, CNRS, INRIA, and PSL Research University, Paris, France
{michel.abdalla,david.pointcheval}@ens.fr
[2] IBM Research, Yorktown Heights, NY, USA
fabrice.benhamouda@normalesup.org
http://www.di.ens.fr/~abdalla
http://www.normalesup.org/~fbenhamo
http://www.di.ens.fr/~pointche

Abstract. An important problem in secure multi-party computation is the design of protocols that can tolerate adversaries that are capable of corrupting parties dynamically and learning their internal states. In this paper, we make significant progress in this area in the context of password-authenticated key exchange (PAKE) and oblivious transfer (OT) protocols. More precisely, we first revisit the notion of projective hash proofs and introduce a new feature that allows us to *explain* any message sent by the simulator in case of corruption, hence the notion of *Explainable Projective Hashing*. Next, we demonstrate that this new tool generically leads to efficient PAKE and OT protocols that are secure against semi-adaptive adversaries without erasures in the Universal Composability (UC) framework. We then show how to make these protocols secure even against adaptive adversaries, using *non-committing encryption*, in a much more efficient way than generic conversions from semi-adaptive to adaptive security. Finally, we provide concrete instantiations of explainable projective hash functions that lead to the most efficient PAKE and OT protocols known so far, with UC-security against adaptive adversaries, without assuming reliable erasures, in the single global CRS setting.

As an important side contribution, we also propose a new commitment scheme based on DDH, which leads to the construction of the first one-round PAKE adaptively secure under plain DDH without pairing, assuming reliable erasures, and also improves previous constructions of OT and two- or three-round PAKE schemes.

Keywords: Oblivious transfer · Password authenticated key exchange · Erasures · Universal composability · Adaptive adversaries

1 Introduction

1.1 Motivation

One of the most difficult problems in secure multi-party computation is the design of protocols that can tolerate adaptive adversaries. These are adversaries

© International Association for Cryptologic Research 2017
S. Fehr (Ed.): PKC 2017, Part I, LNCS 10174, pp. 151–174, 2017.
DOI: 10.1007/978-3-662-54365-8_7

which can corrupt parties dynamically and learn their internal states. As stated in the seminal work of Canetti *et al.* [12], this problem is even more difficult when uncorrupted parties may deviate from the protocol by keeping record of past configurations, instead of erasing them, or just because erasures are not reliable. To deal with this problem, they introduced the concept of non-committing encryption (NCE) and showed how to use it to build general multi-party computation protocols that remained secure even in the presence of such adversaries. Unfortunately, the gain in security came at the cost of a significant loss in efficiency. Though these results were later improved (e.g., [6,17,21,27]), NCE still requires a large amount of communication and achieving efficient constructions with adaptive security without assuming reliable erasures remains a difficult task.

To address the efficiency issue with previous solutions, Garay, Wichs, and Zhou [24] (GWZ) introduced two new notions. The first one was the notion of semi-adaptive security in which an adversary is not allowed to corrupt a party if all the parties are honest at the beginning of the protocol. The main advantage of the new notion is that it is only slightly more difficult to achieve than static security but significantly easier than fully-adaptive security. The second new notion was the concept *somewhat non-committing encryption*. Unlike standard NCE schemes, somewhat non-committing encryption only allows the sender of a ciphertext to open it in a limited number of ways, according to an equivocality parameter ℓ.

In addition to being able to build very efficient somewhat non-committing encryption schemes for small values of ℓ, Garay *et al.* [24] also showed how to build a generic compiler with the help of such schemes that converts any semi-adaptively secure cryptographic scheme into a fully-adaptively secure one. Since the equivocality parameter ℓ needed by their compiler is proportional to the input and output domains of the functionality being achieved, they were able to obtain very efficient constructions for functionalities with small domains, such as 1-out-of-2 oblivious transfers (OT). In particular, their results do not require reliable erasures and hold in the universal composability (UC) framework [8,9].

Building on the results of Garay *et al.* [24], Canetti *et al.* [10] showed how to use 1-out-of-2 OT protocols to build reasonably efficient password-based authenticated key exchange (PAKE) protocols in the UC framework against adaptive corruptions without erasures. The number of OT instances used in their protocol is proportional to the number of bits of the password.

Even though both works provide efficient constructions of UC-secure OT and PAKE schemes with adaptive security without erasures, the efficiency gap between these protocols and those which assume reliable erasures (e.g., [1,18]) remains significant. In this work, we aim to reduce this gap.

1.2   Our Approach

In order to build more efficient OT and PAKE schemes with adaptive security without erasures, we start from the constructions of Abdalla *et al.* [1], which were the most efficient OT and PAKE constructions in the UC model with adaptive corruptions, with a single global common reference string (CRS)[1], and assuming reliable erasures. We then improve them to make them secure against *semi-adaptive* adversaries, without erasures. Finally, we show how to enhance these protocols with *non-committing encryption* (NCE) in order to achieve adaptive security without erasures and without impacting too much their efficiency. All our constructions assume the existence of a single global CRS (notice that even with static corruptions, OT and PAKE in the UC model do not exist in the plain model without CRS [14]).

Hash Proof Systems. At the heart of the OT and PAKE constructions in [1] is the following idea: one party commits to his index (for OT) or his password (for PAKE), and the other party derives from this commitment some hash value which the first party can compute if his commitment was valid and contained some given value (a valid password or a given index), or appears random otherwise. This hash value is then used to mask the values to be transferred in the OT case or is used to derive the session key in the PAKE case.

More precisely, this hash value is computed through a hash proof system or smooth projective hash functions (SPHF) [20]. An SPHF is defined for a language $\mathcal{L} \subseteq \mathcal{X}$. In our case, this language is the language of valid commitments of some value. The first property of an SPHF is that, for a word C in $\mathcal{L}$, the hash value can be computed using either a *secret* hashing key hk (generated by the first party) or a *public* projected key hp (derived from hk and given to the second party) together with a witness w to the fact that C is indeed in $\mathcal{L}$. However, for a word C not in $\mathcal{L}$, the hash value computed with hk is perfectly random, even knowing hp. The latter is known as the *smoothness* property.

Explainable Hash Proof Systems. To make the protocol secure against semi-adaptive adversaries, we face two main problems. The first is the fact the commitment scheme has at the very least to be UC-secure against semi-adaptive adversaries, without relying on erasures. While this is not the case for the original commitment scheme in [1], we show that it is true for a slight variant of it.

The second problem is the main challenge: in case of corruption of an honest player, after this player sent some projection key hp, we need to exhibit a hashing key hk that is compatible with the view of the adversary. In particular, this view may contain a hash value of some commitment under hk. For that purpose, we introduce the notion of explainable hash proof systems (EPHFs) which basically are SPHFs with a trapdoor enabling to generate a projection key hp, and later exhibit a hashing key hk for any hash value.

We propose two constructions of EPHFs. The first one works with any SPHF, as long as there exists a trapdoor which enables to generate, for any hashing key hk, a random hashing key hk′ associated to the same projection key as hp. This property is achieved by most known SPHFs. Then to generate a hashing key hk′ corresponding to a given projection key hp (associated to some known hk) and a given hash value H, we can draw hk′ as above until it corresponds to the hash

---

[1] Here, global CRS just means multiple parties can share the same CRS, as in [18]. Our notion of global CRS is different from that in [11].

value H. Unfortunately, this can only be done if the set of possible hash values is small. One way to ensure this fact is to truncate the hash value to only ν bits instead of keeping the entire hash value. In this case, the reduction requires $O(2^\nu)$ drawing of hk'.

This reduction gap means that ν has to be logarithmic in the security parameter. If we look carefully at current SPHF constructions over cyclic groups, we remark that hashing keys are usually vectors of scalars, while hash values are typically group elements. Therefore, intuitively, it does not seem possible to recover a hashing key from a hash value, without performing some kind of discrete logarithm computation on the hash value.[2] As a result, it appears that the best we can hope for in this case is to drop the cost from $O(2^\nu)$ down to $O(2^{\nu/2})$, through the use of a baby-step giant-step algorithm, or the Pollard's kangaroo method [30]. A straightforward application of this idea to an SPHF, however, would require computing the discrete logarithm of the hash value, which is impractical. Our second construction consists largely in making this idea work.

From Semi-adaptive to Adaptive Adversaries. Once we obtain OT and PAKE protocols secure against semi-adaptive adversaries using EPHFs, we still need to transform them into protocols secure against adaptive adversaries.

First, for PAKE, the GWZ transformation cannot directly be used because channels are not authenticated, and some ideas of Canetti *et al.* in [4] need to be combined to deal with this issue. Even then, the GWZ improvement of using somewhat NCE cannot be applied directly because PAKE outputs are session keys, and therefore there is an exponential number of them, which means the equivocality parameter and the communication complexity of the resulting protocol would be exponential in the security parameter. Hence, to transform a semi-adaptively secure PAKE protocol into an adaptively secure one, each bit of each flow of the original protocol needs to be sent through an NCE channel. While the resulting protocol would only be 3-round, its communication complexity would be impractical: even with the most efficient NCE schemes known so far [17], this would multiply the communication complexity of the original protocol by about 320.[3] This is why we propose a new transformation from semi-adaptively secure to adaptively-secure PAKE, in which only $\mathfrak{K} + 8\nu_m$ bits are sent via NCE channels (where $\mathfrak{K}$ is the security parameter and ν_m is the password length).

Second, for OT, while the GWZ transformation is very practical for bit OT (i.e., OT for one-bit messages), it cannot be used for long messages nor for

---

[2] We could alternatively use group elements for the hashing key, but that would require bilinear maps, and the hash value would be in the target group $\mathbb{G}_T$ of the pairing $e : \mathbb{G} \times \mathbb{G} \to \mathbb{G}_T$. So we would still need to be able to convert a group element from the target group $\mathbb{G}_T$ to the original group $\mathbb{G}$. In any case, the whole comment just highlights our intuition. There might be other ways of avoiding any discrete logarithm computation, using some novel ideas we have not thought about.

[3] We are interested in minimizing the total communication complexiy of the NCE scheme. With regards to this measure of efficiency, the NCE scheme of Hemenway, Ostrovsky, and Rosen in [27] is less efficient than the scheme of Choi *et al.* [17].

1-out-of-k OT for large k (e.g., polynomial in the security parameter) for similar reasons as in the PAKE case. Garay *et al.* [24] proposed a solution for long messages consisting in running ν_m-bit string OT together with zero-knowledge proofs to make sure the same index is used in all protocols. Here, we show how to directly construct ν_m-bit string OT from our specific semi-adaptive protocol at a much lower cost, by avoiding zero-knowledge proofs and reducing the number of bits sent via NCE channels. Contrary to a solution obtained by the GWZ transformation, the communication complexity of this new protocol is polynomial in k (instead of being exponential in k).

Relying only on DDH. As an important side contribution, we propose a new SPHF-friendly commitment scheme based on the plain Decisional Diffie-Hellman assumption (DDH). In addition to being more efficient than the one of Abdalla *et al.* [1], the new commitment scheme also does not require pairings. As a result, the new scheme can be used to significantly improve previous OT and PAKE schemes in the UC model with adaptive adversaries, assuming reliable erasures. Moreover, it also yields to the *first one-round PAKE scheme under plain DDH*, using [1]. All the previously known one-round PAKE schemes (even only secure against statistical corruptions) use pairings, including the recent extremely efficient scheme of Jutla and Roy in [28], where each user only sends four group elements.

For our protocols to be secure, the underlying commitment scheme has to possess strong properties, which makes its design quite challenging. First, we need to be able to extract the inputs of the parties and, in particular, the commitments produced by the adversary. Second, we also need to be able to simulate a party without knowing its input and, in particular, his commitments; but we still need to be able to later open these commitments to the correct input, in case of corruption. In other words, the commitment has to be both equivocable and extractable. Third, to be compatible with SPHF, an additional twist is required: the language $\mathcal{L}$ of commitments of a given value need to be non-trivial. More precisely, it should not be possible for a (polynomial-time) adversary to generate a commitment which may be opened in multiple ways (even if a polynomial-time adversary may not be able to find it), or in other words, a commitment generated by a polynomial-time adversary has to be perfectly binding. This last property is called robustness. Roughly speaking, a commitment satisfying all these three properties is said to be SPHF-friendly.

Efficient constructions of equivocable and extractable commitments fall in two categories: the one following the ideas of Canetti and Fischlin [13] (including [1,3]), and the ones using non-interactive zero-knowledge proofs as decommitment information as the Fischlin-Libert-Manulis schemes [23]. The latter ones are not robust and cannot be used for our purpose. The first basically consists, when the committed value is just one bit b, to commit in an equivocable way to b, and provide two ciphertexts C_0 and C_1, where C_b contains the decommitment information for b and C_{1-b} is random. Extracting such a commitment can be done by decrypting C_0 and C_1 and finding which of them contains a valid decommitment information, while simulating such a commitment just consists of encryptions of valid decommitment information in C_0 and C_1 (for 0 and 1, respectively).

The difficulty is to find an equivocable commitment and an encryption scheme compatible with an SPHF, which essentially means that they have to be structure-preserving. In [3], the Pedersen [31] commitment scheme is used. But then the decommitment information has to be done bit by bit as it is a scalar, which is very inefficient[4]. To solve this issue, in [1], one of the Haralambiev structure-preserving commitment schemes [26] is used, at the expense of relying on SXDH and pairings. Unfortunately, there does not seem to exist structure-preserving commitment schemes under plain DDH. This is why we developed a new way of constructing SPHF-friendly commitment schemes.

1.3   Organization of the Paper

Due to space restrictions, we focus on OT in the core of the paper. PAKE constructions are detailed in the full version [2].

After recalling some definitions in Sect. 2, we introduce our new notion of explainable hash proof systems (EPHFs) in Sect. 3 and present our two constructions. This is our first main contribution. Then, we show how to use EPHFs and SPHF-friendly commitments to construct OT UC-secure against semi-adaptive adversaries, in Sect. 4. Next, we introduce our new SPHF-friendly commitment scheme under plain DDH, which is our second main contribution. Using the latter, we also provide substantial improvements for OT and PAKE schemes in the UC model, assuming reliable erasures. Finally, in Sect. 6, we show how to efficiently enhance our OT semi-adaptive protocols with *non-committing encryption* (NCE) in order to achieve adaptive security. In particular, we propose several adaptive versions of our semi-adaptive OT protocols, yielding different trade-offs in terms of communication complexity and number of rounds. In each case, at least one of our new protocols outperforms existing ones. A detailed related work coverage can be found in the full version [2].

To better focus on the core ideas, standard definitions and notations are recalled in the full version [2]. Additional details and proofs for EPHFs, all the proofs of our semi-adaptively and adaptively secure protocols, and proofs and some technical parts of our new SPHF-friendly commitment are in the full version [2].

2   Definitions

Notations. As usual, all the players and algorithms will be possibly probabilistic and stateful. Namely, adversaries can keep a state st during the different phases, and we denote $\xleftarrow{\$}$ the outcome of a probabilistic algorithm or the sampling from a uniform distribution. For example, $\mathcal{A}(x; r)$ will denote the execution of $\mathcal{A}$ with

---

[4] In addition, the SPHF we can build is a weak form of SPHF, and cannot be used in one-round PAKE protocol for example.

input x and random tape r. For the sake of clarity, sometimes, the latter random tape will be dropped, with the notation $\mathcal{A}(x)$.

Smooth Projective Hash Functions. Projective hashing was first introduced by Cramer and Shoup [20]. Here we use the formalization of SPHF from [7].

Let $(\mathcal{X}_{crs})_{crs}$ be a family of domains for the hash functions indexed by crs, and let $(\mathcal{L}_{crs,par})_{crs,par}$ be a family of languages, i.e., $\mathcal{L}_{crs,par}$ is a subset of $\mathcal{X}_{crs}$. For the sake of simplicity, we write crs-par $=$ (crs, par). In this paper, we focus on languages of commitments, whose corresponding plaintexts satisfy some relations, and even more specifically here equal to some value par. The value crs will be the common reference string for these commitments. The value par is a parameter which is not necessarily public. In case of PAKE for example, it is the expected password.

A key property of an SPHF is that, for a word C in $\mathcal{L}_{crs\text{-}par}$, the hash value can be computed by using either a *secret* hashing key hk or a *public* projection key hp but with a witness w of the fact that C is indeed in $\mathcal{L}$. More precisely, an SPHF is defined by four algorithms:

- HashKG(crs) generates a hashing key hk for crs;
- ProjKG(hk, crs, C) derives the projection key hp;
- Hash(hk, crs-par, C) outputs the hash value (in a set Π, called the *range* of the SPHF) from the hashing key hk, for any word $C \in \mathcal{X}$;
- ProjHash(hp, crs-par, C, w) outputs the hash value from the projection key hp, and the witness w, for a word $C \in \mathcal{L}$.

On the one hand, the *correctness* of the SPHF assures that if $C \in \mathcal{L}_{crs\text{-}par}$ with w a witness of this fact, then Hash(hk, crs-par, C) $=$ ProjHash(hp, crs-par, C, w). On the other hand, the security is defined through the *smoothness*, which guarantees that, if $C \notin \mathcal{L}_{crs\text{-}par}$, Hash(hk, crs-par, C) is *statistically* indistinguishable from a random element, even knowing hp. More formally, an SPHF is smooth if, for any crs, any par, and any $C \notin \mathcal{L}_{crs\text{-}par}$, the following two distributions are statistically indistinguishable:

$$\{(hp, H) \,|\, hk \xleftarrow{\$} HashKG(crs); hp \leftarrow ProjKG(hk, crs, C); H \leftarrow Hash(hk, crs\text{-}par, C)\}$$
$$\{(hp, H) \,|\, hk \xleftarrow{\$} HashKG(crs); hp \leftarrow ProjKG(hk, crs, C); H \xleftarrow{\$} \Pi\}.$$

We chose to restrict HashKG and ProjKG not to use the parameter par, but just crs (instead of crs-par), as for some applications, such as PAKE, hk and hp have to be independent of par, since par is a secret (the password in case of PAKE). We know that this is a stronger restriction than required for our purpose, since one can use par without leaking any information about it; and some of our applications such as OT do not require par to be private at all. But, this is not an issue, since none of our SPHFs uses par.

If ProjKG does not depend on C and satisfies a slightly stronger smoothness property (called adaptive smoothness, which holds even if C is chosen after hp), we say the SPHF is a KV-SPHF, as such an SPHF was introduced by Katz and Vaikuntanathan in [29]. Otherwise, it is said to be a GL-SPHF, as such an

SPHF was introduced by Gennaro and Lindell in [25]. More formally, a KV-SPHF is said to be smooth if for any crs, any par, and any function f from the set of projection keys to $\mathcal{X}_{\text{crs-par}} \setminus \mathcal{L}_{\text{crs-par}}$, the following two distributions are statistically indistinguishable:

$$\{(\mathsf{hp}, H) \mid \mathsf{hk} \xleftarrow{\$} \mathsf{HashKG}(\mathsf{crs}); \mathsf{hp} \leftarrow \mathsf{ProjKG}(\mathsf{hk}, \mathsf{crs}); H \leftarrow \mathsf{Hash}(\mathsf{hk}, \mathsf{crs\text{-}par}, f(\mathsf{hp}))\}$$

$$\{(\mathsf{hp}, H) \mid \mathsf{hk} \xleftarrow{\$} \mathsf{HashKG}(\mathsf{crs}); \mathsf{hp} \leftarrow \mathsf{ProjKG}(\mathsf{hk}, \mathsf{crs}); H \xleftarrow{\$} \Pi\}.$$

See [7] for details on GL-SPHF and KV-SPHF and language definitions.

We would like to remark that one can easily extend the range of an existing SPHF by concatenating several hash values with independent hashing keys on the same word. In this case, the global projection key would be the concatenation of the respective projection keys. It is straightforward to see that the smoothness property of the global SPHF follows directly from a classic hybrid argument over the smoothness property of the underlying SPHF.

SPHF-Friendly Commitment Schemes. In this section, we briefly sketch the definition of SPHF-friendly commitment schemes we will use in this paper (more details are given in the full version [2]). This is a slightly stronger variant of the one in [1], since it requires an additional polynomial-time algorithm C.IsBinding. But the construction in [1] still satisfies it. This is a commitment scheme that is both equivocable and extractable. It is defined by the following algorithms: $\mathsf{C.Setup}(1^{\mathfrak{K}})$ generates the global parameters, passed through the global CRS crs to all other algorithms, while $\mathsf{C.SetupT}(1^{\mathfrak{K}})$ is an alternative that additionally outputs a trapdoor τ; $\mathsf{C.Com}^{\ell}(M)$ outputs a pair (C, δ), where C is the commitment of the message M for the label ℓ, and δ is the corresponding opening data, used by $\mathsf{C.Ver}^{\ell}(C, M, \delta)$ to check the correct opening for C, M and ℓ. It always outputs 0 (false) on $M = \bot$. The trapdoor τ can be used by $\mathsf{C.Sim}^{\ell}(\tau)$ to output a pair (C, eqk), where C is a commitment and eqk an equivocation key that is later used by $\mathsf{C.Open}^{\ell}(\mathsf{eqk}, C, M)$ to open C on any message M with an appropriate opening data δ. The trapdoor τ can also be used by $\mathsf{C.Ext}^{\ell}(\tau, C)$ to output the committed message M in C, or $\bot$ if the commitment is invalid. Eventually, the trapdoor τ also allows $\mathsf{C.IsBinding}^{\ell}(\tau, C, M)$ to check whether the commitment C is binding to the message M or not: if there exists $M' \neq M$ and δ', such that $\mathsf{C.Ver}^{\ell}(C, M', \delta') = 1$, then it outputs 0.

All these algorithms should satisfy some correctness properties: all honestly generated commitments open and verify correctly, can be extracted and are binding to the committed value, while the simulated commitments can be opened on any message.

Then, some security guarantees should be satisfied as well, when one denotes the generation of fake commitments $(C, \delta) \xleftarrow{\$} \mathsf{C.SCom}^{\ell}(\tau, M)$, computed as $(C, \mathsf{eqk}) \xleftarrow{\$} \mathsf{C.Sim}^{\ell}(\tau)$ and then $\delta \leftarrow \mathsf{C.Open}^{\ell}(\mathsf{eqk}, C, M)$:

– *Setup Indistinguishability*: one cannot distinguish the CRS generated by C.Setup from the one generated by C.SetupT;

– *Strong Simulation Indistinguishability*: one cannot distinguish a real commitment (which is generated by C.Com) from a fake commitment (generated by C.SCom), even with oracle access to the extraction oracle (C.Ext), the binding test oracle (C.IsBinding), and to fake commitments (using C.SCom);
– *Robustness*: one cannot produce a commitment and a label that extracts to M (possibly $M = \bot$) such that C.IsBinding$^\ell(\tau, C, M) = 0$, even with oracle access to the extraction oracle (C.Ext), the binding test oracle (C.IsBinding), and to fake commitments (using C.SCom).

Note that, for excluding trivial attacks, on fake commitments, the extraction oracle outputs the C.SCom-input message and the binding test oracle accepts for the C.SCom-input message too. Finally, an SPHF-friendly commitment scheme has to admit an SPHF for the following language:

$$\mathcal{L}_{\text{crs-par}} = \{(\ell, C) \mid \exists \delta, \ \text{C.Ver}^\ell(C, M, \delta) = 1\},$$

where crs-par $=$ (crs, par) and $M = $ par.

Basically, compared to the original definition in [1], the main difference is that it is possible to check in polynomial time (using C.IsBinding) whether a commitment is perfectly binding or not, i.e., does not belong to any $\mathcal{L}_{(\text{crs},M')}$ for $M' \neq M$, where M is the value extracted from the commitment via C.Ext. In addition, in the games for the strong simulation indistinguishability and the robustness, the adversary has access to this oracle C.IsBinding.

Finally, for our PAKE protocols, as in [1], we need another property called strong pseudo-randomness. This property is a strong version of the pseudo-randomness property. However, while the latter is automatically satisfied by any SPHF-friendly commitment scheme, the former may not, because of an additional information provided to the adversary. But, it is satisfied by the SPHF-friendly commitment scheme in [1] and by our new commitment scheme introduced in Sect. 5, which is the most efficient known so far, based on the plain DDH.

SPHF-Friendly Commitment Schemes without Erasures. We will say that an SPHF-friendly commitment scheme is *without erasures* if this is an SPHF-friendly commitment scheme where δ (and thus the witness) just consists of the random coins used by the algorithm C.Com. Then, an SPHF-friendly commitment scheme without erasures yields directly a commitment scheme that achieves UC-security without erasures.

We remark that slight variants of the constructions in [1,3] are actually *without erasures*, as long as it is possible to sample obliviously an element from a cyclic group. To make these schemes without erasures, it is indeed sufficient to change the commitment algorithm C.Com to generate random ciphertexts (with elements obliviously sampled from the corresponding cyclic groups) instead of ciphertexts of 0, for the unused ciphertexts (i.e., the ciphertexts $b_{i,\overline{M_i}}$, for [1], using the notations in that paper). This does not change anything else, since these ciphertexts are not used in the verification algorithm C.Ver.

In the sequel, all SPHF-friendly commitment schemes are assumed to be *without erasures*. Variants of [1,3] are possible instantiations, but also our quite efficient constructions presented in Sect. 5 and the full version [2].

3 Explainable Projective Hashing

In this section, we define the notion of explainable projective hash function (EPHF) and then give two generic constructions of EPHF from SPHF. Both constructions work with any SPHF built using the generic framework of [7], basically as long as there is a way to generate the CRS so that the discrete logarithms of all elements are known. This encompasses most SPHFs over cyclic groups. The second construction is more efficient, but only enable building GL-EPHF, while the first construction enables building both GL-EPHF and KV-EPHF and is slightly more generic (it may work with SPHFs which are not built using the generic framework).

3.1 Definition

Let us first suppose there exists an algorithm Setup which takes as input the security parameter $\mathfrak{K}$ and outputs a CRS crs together with a trapdoor τ. In our case Setup will be C.SetupT, and the trapdoor τ will be the commitment trapdoor, which may need to be slightly modified, as we will see in our constructions. This modification generally roughly consists in adding the discrete logarithms of all used elements in the trapdoor C.SetupT and is possible with most concrete commitment schemes.

An *explainable projective hashing* (EPH) is an SPHF with the following additional property: it is possible to generate a random-looking projection key hp, and then receive some hash value H, some value par and some word $C \notin \mathcal{L}_{\text{crs-par}}$, and eventually generate a valid hashing key hk which corresponds to hp and H, as long as we know τ. In other words, it is possible to generate hp and then "explain" any hash H for a word outside the language $\mathcal{L}_{\text{crs-par}}$, by giving the appropriate hk.

While dual projective hashing [33] implies a weak version of smoothness, our notion of EPH implies the usual notion of smoothness, and is thus stronger than SPHF. Then, an EPHF can be either a GL-EPHF or a KV-EPHF, depending on whether the word C is known when hp is generated.

GL-EPHF. Formally, a GL-EPHF is defined by the following algorithms:

- Setup($1^{\mathfrak{K}}$) takes as input the security parameter $\mathfrak{K}$ and outputs the global parameters, passed through the global CRS crs or crs-par to all the other algorithms, plus a trapdoor τ;
- HashKG, ProjKG, Hash, and ProjHash behave as for a classical SPHF;
- SimKG(crs, τ, C) outputs a projection key hp together with an explainability key expk (C is not given as input for KV-EPHF);
- Explain(hp, crs-par, C, H, expk) outputs an hashing key hk corresponding to hp, crs-par, C, and H.

It must satisfy the same properties as an SPHF together with the following properties, for any (crs, τ) $\overset{\$}{\leftarrow}$ Setup($1^{\mathfrak{K}}$):

- *Explainability Correctness.* For any par, any $C \notin \mathcal{L}_{\text{crs-par}}$ and any hash value H, if $(\text{hp}, \text{expk}) \xleftarrow{\$} \text{SimKG}(\text{crs}, \tau, C)$ and $\text{hk} \xleftarrow{\$} \text{Explain}(\text{hp}, \text{crs-par}, C, H, \text{expk})$, then $\text{hp} = \text{ProjKG}(\text{hk}, \text{crs}, C)$ and $H = \text{Hash}(\text{hk}, \text{crs-par}, C)$, with overwhelming probability (over the random tape of Explain);
- *Indistinguishability.* As for smoothness, we consider two types of indistinguishability: a GL-EPHF is indistinguishable, if for any par and any $C \notin \mathcal{L}_{\text{crs-par}}$, the two following distributions are statistically indistinguishable:

$$\left\{ (\text{hk}, \text{hp}) \left| \begin{array}{l} H \xleftarrow{\$} \Pi; (\text{hp}, \text{expk}) \xleftarrow{\$} \text{SimKG}(\text{crs}, \tau, C); \\ \text{hk} \xleftarrow{\$} \text{Explain}(\text{hp}, \text{crs-par}, C, H, \text{expk}) \end{array} \right. \right\}$$

$$\left\{ (\text{hk}, \text{hp}) | \text{hk} \xleftarrow{\$} \text{HashKG}(\text{crs}); \text{hp} \leftarrow \text{ProjKG}(\text{hk}, \text{crs}, C) \right\}.$$

KV-EPHF. A KV-EPHF is a GL-EPHF, for which ProjKG and SimKG does not take as input the word C, and which satisfies the same smoothness as a KV-SPHF, and a stronger indistinguishability property. A KV-EPHF is ε-indistinguishable, if for any par and any function f from the set of projection keys to $\mathcal{X} \backslash \mathcal{L}_{\text{crs-par}}$, the two following distributions are statistically indistinguishable:

$$\left\{ (\text{hk}, \text{hp}) \left| \begin{array}{l} H \xleftarrow{\$} \Pi; (\text{hp}, \text{expk}) \xleftarrow{\$} \text{SimKG}(\text{crs}, \tau, \perp); \\ \text{hk} \xleftarrow{\$} \text{Explain}(\text{hp}, \text{crs-par}, f(\text{hp}), H, \text{expk}) \end{array} \right. \right\}$$

$$\left\{ (\text{hk}, \text{hp}) | \text{hk} \xleftarrow{\$} \text{HashKG}(\text{crs}); \text{hp} \leftarrow \text{ProjKG}(\text{hk}, \text{crs}, \perp) \right\}.$$

3.2   First Construction

This first construction enables to transform any GL-SPHF (or KV-SPHF) satisfying some properties of re-randomization of the hashing key into a GL-EPHF (respectively, a KV-SPHF). These properties are satisfied by any GL-SPHF (or KV-SPHF) built from the generic framework [7], when τ contains the discrete logarithms of all elements defining the language, as shown in the full version [2]. We first present the construction for GL-EPHF.

GL-EPHF. Here are the properties we require:

(a) For any hashing key hk and associated projection key hp, it is possible to draw a random hk' corresponding to hp, such that hk' looks like a fresh hashing key (conditioned on the fact that its projection key is hp). More precisely, we suppose there exists a randomized algorithm InvProjKG, which takes as input τ, a hashing key hk, crs-par, and a word $C \notin \mathcal{L}_{\text{crs-par}}$, and outputs a random hashing key hk', satisfying $\text{ProjKG}(\text{hk}', \text{crs}, C) = \text{hp}$. For any crs-par, for any $C \notin \mathcal{L}_{\text{crs-par}}$, for any hashing key $\text{hk} \xleftarrow{\$} \text{HashKG}(\text{crs})$, the two following distributions are supposed to be statistically indistinguishable:

$\{\text{hk}' \mid \text{hk}' \xleftarrow{\$} \text{HashKG}(\text{crs}) \text{ such that } \text{ProjKG}(\text{hk}, \text{crs}, C) = \text{ProjKG}(\text{hk}', \text{crs}, C)\}$

$\{\text{hk}' \mid \text{hk}' \xleftarrow{\$} \text{InvProjKG}(\tau, \text{hk}, \text{crs}, C)\}.$

For GL-SPHFs built from the generic framework [7], if we look at the discrete logarithms of all the group elements defining the language and all the ones in the projection key, hashing keys corresponding to a given projection key hp essentially are the solutions of a linear system (the right-hand side of the system corresponds to hp, while coefficients of the system depend on the language). InvProjKG can then output a uniform solution of this linear system.

(b) A stronger property than smoothness, called strong smoothness, is required. Informally, it ensures that smoothness holds even when the hashing key is conditioned on any projection key. Formally, a GL-SPHF is strongly smooth if for any crs-par, for any $C \notin \mathcal{L}_{\text{crs-par}}$, for any projection key hp (generated by hk $\xleftarrow{\$}$ HashKG(crs) and hp $\leftarrow$ ProjKG(hk, crs, C)), the two following distributions are statistically indistinguishable:

$$\left\{ \text{Hash}(\text{hk}', \text{crs-par}, C) \,\middle|\, \begin{array}{l} \text{hk}' \xleftarrow{\$} \text{HashKG(crs) such that} \\ \text{ProjKG}(\text{hk}', \text{crs}, C) = \text{hp} \end{array} \right\}$$

$$\left\{ H \,\middle|\, H \xleftarrow{\$} \Pi \right\};$$

(c) There exists a parameter ν linear in $\log \mathfrak{K}$ and a randomness extractor Extract with range $\{0, 1\}^\nu$, such that the two following distributions are statistically indistinguishable:

$$\{\text{Extract}(H) \mid H \xleftarrow{\$} \Pi\} \qquad \{H \mid H \xleftarrow{\$} \{0, 1\}^\nu\}.$$

Details on the randomness extractor can be found in the full version [2]. But we can use either a deterministic extractor exists for Π, which is possible for many cyclic groups [16], or a probabilistic extractor with an independent random string in the CRS.

Then, if the hash values H computed by Hash or ProjHash are replaced by Extract(H), the resulting SPHF is a GL-EPHF. Indeed, if SimKG(crs, τ, C) just generates hk $\xleftarrow{\$}$ HashKG(crs) and hp $\leftarrow$ ProjKG(hk, crs, C), and outputs hp and expk $= (\tau, \text{hk})$. Then, Explain(hp, crs-par, C, H, expk) just runs hk' $\xleftarrow{\$}$ InvProjKG(τ, hk, crs, C) many times until it finds hk' such that Hash(hk', crs-par, C) $= H$. It aborts if does not find a valid hk' after $2^\nu \mathfrak{K}$ times. Thanks to the smoothness and the above properties, its abort probability is negligible in the security parameter $\mathfrak{K}$.[5] Since ν is linear in $\log \mathfrak{K}$, the resulting algorithm Explain runs in polynomial time in $\mathfrak{K}$. A formal proof can be found in the full version [2].

We observe that ν impacts on the running time of SimKG which will only be used in the proofs of our PAKE and OT protocols (and not in their constructions), so that ν only impacts on the tightness of the proofs of the resulting protocols. In all comparisons in this article, we will use $\nu = 1$, which hinders performances of our scheme; but our schemes are still very efficient. In practice, to gain constant

---

[5] Notice that the strong smoothness is necessary to prove that as, otherwise, it would have been possible that for some projection key hp, no such hk' exist, and Explain would not run in expected polynomial time. See details in the full version [2].

factors, it would be advisable to use a greater ν, and thus larger blocks. Finally, the range of the EPHF can be easily extended just by using multiple copies of the EPHF: for a range of ν', hk becomes a tuple of $\lceil \nu'/\nu \rceil$ original hashing keys, the same for hp and H.

KV-EPHF. In the first generic construction for GL-SPHF, we get a KV-EPHF, if Property (a) and Property (b) hold even if C can depend on hp. In other words, instead of quantifying on any $C \notin \mathcal{L}_{\text{crs-par}}$, we quantify on any function f from the set of projection keys to $\mathcal{X} \backslash \mathcal{L}_{\text{crs-par}}$, and replace C by $f(\text{hp})$ in the definition (similarly to what is done for the smoothness of KV-SPHF or the indistinguishability of KV-EPHF).

As for GL-EPHF, any KV-SPHF built using the generic framework satisfies these properties and so can be transformed into KV-EPHF, as long as discrete logarithms of all elements in the matrix Γ can be known from τ.

3.3 Second Construction

We show a more efficient construction for GL-EPHF from any GL-SPHF built using the generic framework in the full version [2]. The idea is to use the algebraic properties of this framework to replace the costly search for hk' in Explain (which requires $O(2^\nu)$ guesses) by the computation of a small (less than 2^ν) discrete logarithm in ProjHash. This can be done in $O(2^{\nu/2})$ group operations by ProjHash, using Pollard's kangaroo method in [30]. The parameter ν can therefore be twice larger in our second construction, which makes it approximately twice more efficient.

4 Semi-adaptive OT Without Erasures

In this section, we propose a new OT protocol that is UC-secure against semi-adaptive adversaries, without requiring reliable erasures. The new protocol is very similar to the UC-secure OT construction in [1], except that the underlying SPHF-friendly commitment scheme has to be *without erasures* and the underlying SPHF has to be *explainable*. The security proof, which can be found in the full version [2], is however more complex.

4.1 Semi Adaptivity

The semi-adaptive setting has been introduced in [24], for two-party protocols when channels are authenticated: the adversary is not allowed to corrupt any player if the two players were honest at the beginning of the protocol. When channels are not authenticated, as for PAKE, we restrict the adversary not to corrupt a player P_i if an honest flow has been sent on its behalf, and it has been received by P_j, without being altered.

In addition to those restrictions on the adversary, there are also some restrictions on the simulator and the protocol. First, the simulator has to be *setup-preserving*, which means, in our case, that it first has to generate the CRS, before simulating the protocol execution. Second, the simulator has to be *input-preserving*, which means that if the adversary corrupts some user and honestly runs the protocol for some input x, the simulator submits the same input to the functionality. Third, the protocol has to be *well-formed*, which means that the number of flows and the size of each flow is independent of the input and the random tapes of the users. All these restrictions are clearly satisfied by our simulators and protocols. Formal definitions can be found in [24].

4.2   Oblivious Transfer

The ideal functionality of an Oblivious Transfer (OT) protocol is depicted in Fig. 1. It is inspired from [18]. In Fig. 2, we describe a 2-round 1-out-of-k OT for ν_m-bit messages, that is UC-secure against semi-adaptive adversaries. It can be built from any SPHF-friendly commitment scheme, admitting a GL-EPHF, with range $\Pi = \{0,1\}^{\nu_m}$, for the language: $\mathcal{L}_{\mathsf{crs\text{-}par}} = \{(\ell, C) \mid \exists \delta, \mathsf{C.Ver}^\ell(C, M, \delta) = 1\}$, where crs-par $= (\mathsf{crs}, \mathsf{par})$ and $M = \mathsf{par}$.

The functionality $\mathcal{F}_{(1,k)\text{-}\mathsf{OT}}$ is parameterized by a security parameter $\mathfrak{K}$. It interacts with an adversary $\mathcal{S}$ and a set of parties $P_1, \ldots, P_n$ via the following queries:

- **Upon receiving an input** (Send, sid, ssid, $P_i, P_j, (m_1, \ldots, m_k)$) **from party** P_i, with $m_i \in \{0,1\}^{\mathfrak{K}}$: record the tuple (sid, ssid, $P_i, P_j, (m_1, \ldots, m_k)$) and reveal (Send, sid, ssid, P_i, P_j) to the adversary $\mathcal{S}$. Ignore further Send-message with the same ssid from P_i.
- **Upon receiving an input** (Receive, sid, ssid, P_i, P_j, s) **from party** P_j, with $s \in \{1, \ldots, k\}$: record the tuple (sid, ssid, P_i, P_j, s), and reveal (Receive, sid, ssid, P_i, P_j) to the adversary $\mathcal{S}$. Ignore further Receive-message with the same ssid from P_j.
- **Upon receiving a message** (Sent, sid, ssid, P_i, P_j) **from the adversary** $\mathcal{S}$: ignore the message if (sid, ssid, $P_i, P_j, (m_1, \ldots, m_k)$) or (sid, ssid, P_i, P_j, s) is not recorded; otherwise send (Sent, sid, ssid, P_i, P_j) to P_i and ignore further Sent-message with the same ssid from the adversary.
- **Upon receiving a message** (Received, sid, ssid, P_i, P_j) **from the adversary** $\mathcal{S}$: ignore the message if (sid, ssid, $P_i, P_j, (m_1, \ldots, m_k)$) or (sid, ssid, P_i, P_j, s) is not recorded; otherwise send (Received, sid, ssid, P_i, P_j, m_s) to P_j and ignore further Received-message with the same ssid from the adversary.

Fig. 1. Ideal functionality for 1-out-of-k oblivious transfer $\mathcal{F}_{(1,k)\text{-}\mathsf{OT}}$

In case of corruption of the database (sender) after it has sent its flow, since we are in the semi-adaptive setting, the receiver was already corrupted and thus the index s was known to the simulator. The latter can thus generate "explainable" hp_t for all $t \neq s$, so that when the simulator later learns the messages m_t, it can explain hp_t with appropriate hk_t. Erasures are no longer required, contrarily to [1].

CRS: crs $\xleftarrow{\$}$ C.Setup($1^{\Re}$).

Index query on s:

1. P_j computes $(C, \delta) \xleftarrow{\$}$ C.Com$^\ell(s)$ with $\ell = (\text{sid}, \text{ssid}, P_i, P_j)$
2. P_j sends C to P_i

Database input $(m_1, \ldots, m_k)$:

1. P_i computes hk$_t \xleftarrow{\$}$ HashKG(crs), hp$_t \leftarrow$ ProjKG(hk$_t$, crs, (ℓ, C)),
   $K_t \leftarrow$ Hash(hk$_t$, (crs, t), (ℓ, C)), and $M_t \leftarrow K_t$ xor m_t, for $t = 1, \ldots, k$
2. P_i sends (hp$_t$, M_t)$_{t=1,\ldots,k}$

Data recovery:
Upon receiving (hp$_t$, M_t)$_{t=1,\ldots,k}$, P_j computes $K_s \leftarrow$ ProjHash(hp$_s$, (crs, s), (ℓ, C), δ) and gets $m_s \leftarrow K_s$ xor M_s.

Fig. 2. UC-secure 1-out-of-k OT from an SPHF-friendly commitment for semi-adaptive adversaries

The restriction that Π has to be of the form $\{0, 1\}^{\nu_m}$ is implicit in [1]. Any SPHF can be transformed to an SPHF with range Π of the form $\{0, 1\}^{\nu_m}$, using a randomness extractor, as long as the initial range is large enough. However, this is not necessarily the case for EPHF, since the extractor might not be efficiently invertible. That is why we prefer to make this assumption on Π explicit.[6]

5 A New SPHF-Friendly Commitment Scheme

In this section, we present our new efficient SPHF-friendly commitment scheme under the plain DDH. Due to lack of space, we only give an overview of the scheme and a comparison with previous SPHF-friendly commitment schemes. Details are left to the full version [2].

5.1 Scheme

High-Level Intuition. The basic idea of our scheme is a generalization of the schemes in [1,3,13,15]. In these schemes, the commitment of a bit b consists of an equivocable commitment[7] (also known as trapdoor commitment [22]) a of b

---

[6] As pointed out by an anonymous reviewer, if ν_m is linear in log $\Re$, this assumption is not necessary, as any extractor can be inversed by evaluating it on $2^{\nu_m}\Re$ randomly chosen inputs, similarly to what Explain does in the construction of Sect. 3.2.

[7] For the resulting commitment scheme to not require erasures, we suppose that it is not only possible to generate the opening data of a simulated commitment for any message, but also the corresponding random coins used by C.Com. Please note that we do not require the opening data to be the random coins, to provide more efficient construction, as the one in [1] using the Haralambiev commitment scheme TC4 [26] (see details in the sequel).

together with two ciphertexts C_0 and C_1 (with an IND-CCA encryption scheme), such that C_b contains a valid opening d_b of the commitment a for b, while C_{1-b} is sampled obliviously.

To extract some commitment C, it is sufficient to know the decryption key of the underlying IND-CCA encryption scheme and check whether C_0 or C_1 contains a valid opening d_0 or d_1 of a for 0 or 1. To simulate a commitment C, it is sufficient to know a trapdoor enabling to construct a commitment a and two valid openings d_0 and d_1 for both 0 and 1.

The robustness property basically comes from the fact the adversary cannot generate a commitment a and two valid openings d_0 and d_1, without breaking the binding property of the commitment a. Therefore, any commitment C generated by a polynomial-time adversary is perfectly binding.

However, for the resulting commitment to be compatible with SPHF, the underlying primitives (equivocable commitment and IND-CCA encryption scheme) have to be algebraic. In [3], Abdalla et al. propose to use the Pedersen commitment [31], as the equivocable commitment, together with the Cramer-Shoup [19] encryption scheme. Unfortunately, as the openings of the Pedersen commitments are scalars, they have to be encrypted bit-by-bit for the resulting commitment to be SPHF-friendly. This makes the commitment size of one bit to be quadratic in the security parameter (or the commitment to contain a linear number of group elements). This issue was solved in [1] by replacing the Pedersen commitment, by the Haralambiev commitment TC4 [26], for which the opening is a group element. However, this was at the expense on relying on bilinear groups (and SXDH) instead of plain DDH.

More precisely, the Haralambiev commitment of a bit b consists in a group element $a = g^{r_b}T^b$, with r_b a random scalar, and g, T two public generators of a cyclic group $\mathbb{G}$ of prime order p. The opening of a is $d_b = \hat{h}^{r_b}$ with $\hat{h}$ another generator of $\mathbb{G}$. This can be check using a pairing as follows: $e(a/T^b, \hat{h}) \stackrel{?}{=} e(g, d_b)$.

Pairings are only used to check the validity of an opening, and are only required in the security proof, as the committer needs to reveal r_b anyway (as it is part of his random tape), and r_b is sufficient to check the validity of the opening information d_b of a without pairing.

In our new scheme, we replace the need of a pairing by adding a 2-universal hash [20]. A 2-universal hash proof system can be seen as a designated-verifier one-time-simulation-sound zero-knowledge proof, which basically means that (i) it can only be checked by the simulator which generated the CRS, (ii) the simulator can generate fake or simulated proof for false statement, (ii) and the adversary cannot generate proof for false statement even if it sees one fake proof. Finally, the Cramer-Shoup (IND-CCA) encryption scheme can be replaced by the ElGamal encryption scheme, as the 2-universal hash provides a form of non-malleability which is sufficient for our purpose[8]. As the construction is no longer black-box, new ideas are required in the proof of security of the scheme.

---

[8] Actually, a Cramer-Shoup ciphertext basically consists in an ElGamal ciphertext plus a Diffie-Hellman element and a proof that everything is well-formed.

Our New Scheme. Our new scheme is formally described and proven in the full version [2].

Basically, the setup $\mathsf{C.SetupT}(1^\mathfrak{K})$ generates a cyclic group $\mathbb{G}$ of order p, together with four generators g, $h = g^x$, $\hat{h} = g^{\hat{x}}$, $T = g^t$, a tuple $(\alpha, \beta, \gamma, \alpha', \beta', \gamma') \leftarrow \mathbb{Z}_p^6$, and H is a random collision-resistant hash function from some family $\mathcal{H}$. It then computes the tuple $(c = g^\alpha \hat{h}^\gamma, d = g^\beta h^\gamma, c' = g^{\alpha'} \hat{h}^{\gamma'}, d' = g^{\beta'} h^{\gamma'})$. The CRS crs is set as $(g, h, \hat{h}, H, c, d, c', d', T)$ and the trapdoor τ is the tuple $(\alpha, \alpha', \beta, \beta', \gamma, \gamma')$ (a.k.a., extraction trapdoor) together with t (a.k.a., equivocation trapdoor) and $(x, \hat{x})$ (only used in the EPHF).

To commit a vector of bits $\boldsymbol{M} = (M_i)_i \in \{0,1\}^m$ under a label ℓ, for $i = 1, \ldots, m$, we choose two random scalars $r_{i,M_i}, s_{i,M_i} \overset{\$}{\leftarrow} \mathbb{Z}_p$ and set

$$u_{i,M_i} = g^{s_{i,M_i}} \qquad v_{i,M_i} = h^{s_{i,M_i}} \hat{h}^{r_{i,M_i}} \qquad w_{i,M_i} = (c^{r_{i,M_i}} \cdot d^{s_{i,M_i}}) \cdot (c'^{r_{i,M_i}} d'^{s_{i,M_i}})^\xi$$

$$u_{i,\overline{M_i}} \overset{\$}{\leftarrow} \mathbb{G} \qquad v_{i,\overline{M_i}} \overset{\$}{\leftarrow} \mathbb{G} \qquad w_{i,\overline{M_i}} \overset{\$}{\leftarrow} \mathbb{G},$$

together with $a_i \leftarrow g^{r_{i,M_i}} T^{M_i}$, where $\xi = H(\ell, (a_i, (u_{i,b}, v_{i,b})_b)_i)$. The commitment is then $C = (a_i, (u_{i,b}, v_{i,b}, w_{i,b})_b)_i \in \mathbb{G}^{8m}$, while the opening information is the $2m$-tuple $\delta = (r_{i,M_i}, s_{i,M_i})_i \in \mathbb{Z}_p^{2m}$.

The pair (u_{i,M_i}, v_{i,M_i}) is the ElGamal encryption of the opening $d_{i,M_i} = \hat{h}^{r_{i,M_i}}$ of the equivocable commitment a_i, while w_{i,M_i} is the 2-universal hash proving that $\log_g a_i / T^{M_i}$, the discrete logarithm in base g of a_i (i.e., r_{i,M_i} when generated honestly), is equal to the discrete logarithm in base $\hat{h}$ of the plaintext d_{i,M_i}.

The equivocation trapdoor t enables to open a_i to both 0 and 1, and so enables simulating commitments, while the equivocation trapdoor $(\alpha, \alpha', \beta, \beta', \gamma, \gamma')$ is the hashing key for the 2-universal hash proof system, i.e., enables to check the validity of the proof w_{i,M_i} as follows: $w_{i,b} \overset{?}{=} (a_i / T^b)^{\alpha + \xi \alpha'} \cdot u_{i,b}^{\beta + \xi \beta'} \cdot v_{i,b}^{\gamma + \xi \gamma'}$.

5.2   Complexity and Comparison

Table 1 compares our new schemes with existing non-interactive UC-secure commitments with a single global CRS. Since in most cryptographic schemes relying on SPHF-friendly commitments, such as the OT and PAKE schemes in [1], the most important metrics tend to be the size of the commitments and the size of the projection keys, Table 1 focuses on these parameters. In this context, as Table 1 shows, our new construction is the most efficient SPHF-friendly commitment scheme (even for KV-SPHF, since group elements in $\mathbb{G}_2$ are larger than elements in $\mathbb{G}_1$) resulting in the most efficient OT and PAKE schemes so far (adaptively secure, assuming reliable erasures, under any assumption, with a single global CRS). In addition, since the new commitment scheme is secure under plain DDH, it allows for the construction of the first one-round PAKE (adaptively secure, assuming reliable erasures) under plain DDH, since the scheme of Abdalla, Chevalier, and Pointcheval [3] does not support KV-SPHF (which is required for one-round PAKE construction [1]).

Table 1. Comparison with existing non-interactive UC-secure commitments with a single global CRS

	SPHF-friendly	W/o erasure	Assumption	C size	δ size	KV/GL SPHF hp size
[13]		✓ᵃ	DDH	$9m \times \mathbb{G}$	$2m \times \mathbb{Z}_p$	—
[3]ᵇ	✓	✓ᵃ	DDH	$(m + 16m\mathfrak{K}) \times \mathbb{G}$	$2m\mathfrak{K} \times \mathbb{Z}_p$	$-/(3m+2) \times \mathbb{G} + (\mathbb{Z}_p)^{\mathrm{a}}$
[23]ᶜ, 1			DLin	$5 \times \mathbb{G}$	$16 \times \mathbb{G}$	—
[23]ᶜ, 2			DLin	$37 \times \mathbb{G}$	$3 \times \mathbb{G}$	—
[1]	✓	✓ᵃ	SXDH	$8m \times \mathbb{G}_1 + m \times \mathbb{G}_2$	$m \times \mathbb{Z}_p$	$2m \times \mathbb{G}_1/\mathbb{G}_1 + (\mathbb{Z}_p)^{\mathrm{a}}$
Section 5.1	✓	✓	DDH	$7m \times \mathbb{G}$	$2m \times \mathbb{Z}_p$	$4m \times \mathbb{G}/2 \times \mathbb{G} + (\mathbb{Z}_p)^{\mathrm{d}}$

$m =$ bit-length of the committed value, $\mathfrak{K} =$ security parameter; we suppose there exists a family of efficient collision-resistant hash functions (for efficiency reason, since DDH implies the existence of such families).
ᵃ commitments in [1,3,13] were not described as without erasures, but slight variants of them are, as explained in Sect. 2.
ᵇ we consider a slight variant without one-time signature but using labels and multi-Cramer-Shoup ciphertexts, as in the scheme in [1] (which makes the scheme more efficient). The size of the projection key is computed using the most efficient methods in [1];
ᶜ we use a Pedersen commitment as a chameleon hash and multi-Cramer-Shoup ciphertexts to commit to multiple bits in a non-malleable way (see [1] for a description of the multi-Cramer-Shoup encryption scheme). We do not know a SPHF on such commitment, since the opening information of a Pedersen commitment is a scalar;
ᵈ this $\mathbb{Z}_p$ element may only be $\mathfrak{K}$-bit long and is useless when $m = 1$.

6   Adaptive OT Without Erasures

As explained in [24], one can transform any semi-adaptive protocols into adaptive ones by sending all the flows through secure channels. Such secure channels can be constructed using non-committing encryption (NCE) [5,12,17,21]. However, even the most efficient instantiation of NCE [17] requires $8\nu_{\mathsf{NCE}}\mathfrak{K}$ group elements to send ν_{NCE} bits securely, with ElGamal encryption scheme as (trapdoor) simulatable encryption scheme. If ν_{NCE} is $\Omega(\mathfrak{K})$, this can be reduced to about $320\nu_{\mathsf{NCE}}$ group elements.

In this section, we propose several adaptive versions of our semi-adaptive OT and PAKE protocols. Some are optimized for the number of rounds, while others are optimized for the communication complexity. In each case, at least one of our new protocols performs better than existing protocols. Only the high-level intuition is given in this section. Details are given in the full version [2].

First Scheme. A first efficient way to construct a bit (i.e., $\nu_m = 1$) 1-out-of-2 OT secure against adaptive adversary consists in applying the generic transformation of Garay *et al.* [24] to our semi-adaptive OT.

This transformation uses the notion of ℓ-somewhat non-committing encryption scheme. This scheme enables to send securely long messages, but which restricts the non-committing property to the following: it is only possible to produce random coins corresponding to ℓ different messages. Then, to get an adaptive OT from a semi-adaptive OT, it is sufficient to execute the protocol in a 8-somewhat non-committing channel. Indeed, the simulator can send via this channel 8 versions of the transcript of the protocol: depending on which user gets corrupted first and on which were their inputs and outputs. There are two choices of inputs for the sender (the two index queries) and two outputs (the message m_s), hence four choices in total; and there are four choices of inputs for the receiver (the two messages m_0 and m_1). Hence the need for 8 versions.

In [24], the authors also show how to extend their bit OT based on the DDH version of the static OT of Peikert *et al.* [32] to string OT by repeating the protocol in parallel and adding an equivocable commitment to the index and a zero-knowledge proof to ensure that the sender always uses the same index s. Actually, for both of our instantiations and for the one in [24], we can do better, just by using the same commitment C to s (in our case) or the same CRS (the one obtained by coin tossing) and the same public key of the dual encryption system (in their case). This enables us to get rid off the additional zero-knowledge proof and can also be applied to the QR instantiation in [24]. In addition, the commitment C to s (in our case) or the CRS and the public key (in their case) only needs to be sent in the first somewhat non-committing channel.

Furthermore, if the original semi-adaptive OT is a 1-out-of-k OT (with $k = 2^{\nu_k}$), then we just need to use a 2^{k+1}-somewhat NCE instead of a 8-somewhat NCE encrypt (because there are 2^k possible inputs for the sender, and k possible inputs and 2 possible outputs for the receiver, so $2^k + 2k \leq 2^{k+1}$ possible versions for the transcript).

Finally, the combination of all the above remarks yields a ν_m-bit string 1-out-of-k OT scheme requiring only ν_m 2^{k+1}-somewhat NCE channels, and so only $\nu_m(k + 1)$ bits sent through NCE.

Second Scheme. Our second scheme can be significantly more efficient than our first one, for several parameter choices. Essentially, it consists in using NCE channels to send $k\nu_m$ random bits to mask the messages (in case the sender is corrupted first) and $2\nu_k$ random bits to enable the simulator to make the commitment binding to the index s (in case the receiver gets corrupted first). Methods used for this second part are specific to our new SPHF-friendly commitment scheme, but can also be applied to the commitment scheme in [1].

The scheme is depicted in Fig. 3. Our 1-out-of-k OT protocol uses a NCE channel of $\nu_{\mathsf{NCE}} = 2\nu_k + k\nu_m$ bits, where $k = 2^{\nu_k}$, for ν_m-bit strings. This channel is used to send a random value R. The last $k\nu_m$ bits of R are k ν_m-bit values $R_1, \ldots, R_k$. These values are used to mask the messages $m_1, \ldots, m_k$ sent by the sender, to be able to reveal the correct messages, in case of corruption of the sender (when both the sender and the receiver were honest at the beginning, and so when $m_1, \ldots, m_k$ were completely unknown to the simulator).

CRS: crs $\xleftarrow{\$}$ C.Setup($1^\Re$) and NCE.param $\xleftarrow{\$}$ NCE.Setup($1^\Re$).

Pre-flow:

1. P_i generates (ek, dk) $\xleftarrow{\$}$ NCE.KG(NCE.param)
2. P_i sends ek to P_j

Index query on s:

1. P_j chooses a random $R \xleftarrow{\$} \{0,1\}^{\nu_{\text{NCE}}}$ and computes $\chi \xleftarrow{\$}$ NCE.Enc(ek, R)
2. P_j computes $(C = ((e_{I,b}, u_{I,b}, v_{I,b}, w_{I,b})_{I,b}), \delta) \xleftarrow{\$}$ C.Com$^\ell(s)$ with $\ell =$ (sid, ssid, P_i, P_j)
3. P_j sets $w'_{I,b} = w_{I,b}$ if $R_{2I+b-1} = 0$ and $w'_{I,b} = 1/w_{I,b}$ otherwise, for $I = 1, \ldots, \nu_k$ and $b = 0, 1$;
   and sets $C' = ((e_{I,b}, u_{I,b}, v_{I,b}, w'_{I,b})_{I,b})$
4. P_j sends χ and C' to P_i

Database input $(m_1, \ldots, m_k)$:

1. P_i computes $R \xleftarrow{\$}$ NCE.Dec(dk, χ)
2. P_i sets $w_{I,b} = w'_{I,b}$ if $R_{2I+b-1} = 0$ and $w_{I,b} = 1/w'_{I,b}$ otherwise, for $I = 1, \ldots, \nu_k$ and $b = 0, 1$;
   and sets $C = ((e_{I,b}, u_{I,b}, v_{I,b}, w_{I,b})_{I,b})$
3. P_i sets $(R_t)_t$ to the last $k\nu_m$ bits of R (R_t being a ν_m-bit variable)
4. P_i computes hk$_t \xleftarrow{\$}$ HashKG(crs), hp$_t \leftarrow$ ProjKG(hk$_t$, crs, (ℓ, C)),
   $K_t \leftarrow$ Hash(hk$_t$, (crs, t), (ℓ, C)), and $M_t \leftarrow R_t$ xor K_t xor m_t, for $t = 1, \ldots, k$
5. P_i sends (hp$_t$, M_t)$_{t=1,\ldots,k}$

Data recovery:
Upon receiving (hp$_t$, M_t)$_{t=1,\ldots,k}$, P_j computes $K_s \leftarrow$ ProjHash(hp$_s$, (crs, s), $(\ell, C), \delta$)
and gets $m_s \leftarrow R_s$ xor K_s xor M_s, with $(R_t)_t$ the last $k\nu_m$ bits of R.

Fig. 3. UC-secure 1-out-of-k OT from our SPHF-friendly commitment for adaptive adversaries

The first $2\nu_k$ bits of R are used to make the commitment C (which is normally simulated when the receiver is honest) perfectly binding to the revealed index s, in case of corruption of the receiver (when both the sender and the receiver were honest at the beginning, and so when s was completely unknown to the simulator). More precisely, they are used to partially hide the last component of commitments: the $w_{i,b}$; the bit R_{2i+b-1} indicates whether $w_{i,b}$ has to be inverted or not before use. The full security proof is given in the full version [2].

Remark 1. Though the new protocol uses our new commitment scheme, it could alternatively use the commitment scheme in [1], by just replacing $w_{i,b}$ by the last part of the Cramer-Shoup ciphertexts in these schemes. The proof would be very similar. This replacement may yield a more efficient scheme (under SXDH however) when ν_m is large, since the projection key in [1] is shorter than for our scheme and multiple projection keys need to be sent due to the generic transformation of SPHF to EPH.

Comparison. In Table 2, we give a detailed comparison of our OT schemes with the DDH-based OT in [24]. The QR-based one in less efficient anyway. We see that, for every parameters ν_m and k, at least one of our two schemes (if not both) is the most efficient scheme regarding both the number of rounds and the communication complexity.

The exact communication complexity cost depends on the exact instantiation of NCE. But in all cases, at least one of our schemes outperforms existing schemes both in terms of number of bits sent via a NCE channel, and in terms of auxiliary elements (elements which are not directly used by the NCE scheme). In addition, our second scheme always uses the smallest number of auxiliary elements; and it requires $k\nu_m + 2\nu_k$ bits to be sent via a NCE channel, which is not worse than the $(k+1)\nu_m$ bits required by our first scheme, as long as $\nu_m \geq 2\nu_k$.

Table 2. Comparison of 1-out-of-k OT UC-secure against adaptive adversaries, without erasures, with $k = 2^{\nu_k}$

	Rnd[a]	Communication complexity
[24]	≥ 8	$(k+1) \cdot \nu_m \times \mathsf{NCE} + 3 \cdot (2^k + 2k) \cdot \nu_m \times \mathbb{G}$ $+(2^k + 2k) \cdot \left(\mathsf{com}(4 \times \mathbb{G}) + 2\nu_k \times \mathbb{G} + \nu_k \times \mathsf{ZK} + 4\nu_m\nu_k \times \mathbb{G}\right)$
1st	4	$(k+1) \cdot \nu_m \times \mathsf{NCE} + 3 \cdot (2^k + 2k) \cdot \nu_m \times \mathbb{G}$ $+(2^k + 2k) \cdot \left(7\nu_k \times \mathbb{G} + \nu_m \cdot (2 \times \mathbb{G} + (\mathbb{Z}_p)^{\mathrm{b}} + 2)\right)$
2nd	3	$(k\nu_m + 2\nu_k) \times \mathsf{NCE} + 7\nu_k \times \mathbb{G} + \nu_m \cdot \left(2 \times \mathbb{G} + (\mathbb{Z}_p)^{\mathrm{b}} + 2\right)$

[a] number of rounds
[b] this element in $\mathbb{Z}_p$ is not required when $\nu_m = \nu_k = 1$
Legend:
– ZK: zero-knowledge proof used in [24].
– $\mathsf{com}(x)$: communication complexity of a UC-commitment scheme for x bits. This is used to generate the CRS for the scheme in [32]. If this commitment is interactive, this increases the number of required rounds.
– $x \times \mathsf{NCE}$: x bits sent by non-committing encryption scheme.

Here are some details on the comparison. We suppose we use the NCE scheme proposed in [17] (which is 2-round) and the ElGamal encryption as simulation encryption scheme for the NCE scheme and the somewhat NCE construction (which also requires a simulation encryption scheme). So all our schemes are secure under DDH (plus existence of collision resistant hash functions and symmetric key encryption, but only for efficiency, since DDH implies that also).

In the comparison, we extend the schemes in [24] to 1-out-of-k schemes using the method explained in Sect. 6 and the 1-out-of-k version of the schemes of Peikert *et al.* [32], which consists in doing ν_k schemes in parallel and secret sharing the messages (where $k = 2^{\nu_k}$).

To understand the costs in the table, recall that a 2^l-somewhat non-committing encryption scheme works as follows: one player sends a l-bit value I using a full NCE scheme (2 rounds) together with 2^l public keys all samples obviously except the Ith one, and then the other player sends 2^l ciphertexts samples obliviously except the Ith one which contains a symmetric key K. Then to send any message through this 2^l-somewhat NCE channel, a player just sends 8 messages all random except the Ith one which is an encryption of the actual message under K. This means that if the original semi-adaptive protocol is x-round, then the protocol resulting from the transformation of Garay et al., is $(x+2)$-round; and this costs a total of $3 \cdot 2^l$ group elements, in addition of the group elements for the l-bit non-committing encryption.

Acknowledgments. This work was partially done while the second author was student at ENS, CNRS, INRIA, and PSL Research University, Paris, France. The first author and the third author were supported by the European Research Council under the European Community's Seventh Framework Programme (FP7/2007–2013 Grant Agreement no. 339563 – CryptoCloud). The second author was supported in part by the CFM Foundation and by the Defense Advanced Research Projects Agency (DARPA) and Army Research Office (ARO) under Contract No. W911NF-15-C-0236.

References

1. Abdalla, M., Benhamouda, F., Blazy, O., Chevalier, C., Pointcheval, D.: SPHF-friendly non-interactive commitments. In: Sako, K., Sarkar, P. (eds.) ASIACRYPT 2013. LNCS, vol. 8269, pp. 214–234. Springer, Heidelberg (2013). doi:10.1007/978-3-642-42033-7_12

2. Abdalla, M., Benhamouda, F., Pointcheval, D.: Removing erasures with explainable hash proof systems. Cryptology ePrint Archive, Report 2014/125 (2014). http://eprint.iacr.org/2014/125

3. Abdalla, M., Chevalier, C., Pointcheval, D.: Smooth projective hashing for conditionally extractable commitments. In: Halevi, S. (ed.) CRYPTO 2009. LNCS, vol. 5677, pp. 671–689. Springer, Heidelberg (2009). doi:10.1007/978-3-642-03356-8_39

4. Barak, B., Canetti, R., Lindell, Y., Pass, R., Rabin, T.: Secure computation without authentication. In: Shoup, V. (ed.) CRYPTO 2005. LNCS, vol. 3621, pp. 361–377. Springer, Heidelberg (2005). doi:10.1007/11535218_22

5. Beaver, D.: Commodity-based cryptography (extended abstract). In: 29th ACM STOC, pp. 446–455. ACM Press, May 1997

6. Beaver, D.: Plug and play encryption. In: Kaliski, B.S. (ed.) CRYPTO 1997. LNCS, vol. 1294, pp. 75–89. Springer, Heidelberg (1997). doi:10.1007/BFb0052228

7. Benhamouda, F., Blazy, O., Chevalier, C., Pointcheval, D., Vergnaud, D.: New techniques for SPHFs and efficient one-round PAKE protocols. In: Canetti, R., Garay, J.A. (eds.) CRYPTO 2013. LNCS, vol. 8042, pp. 449–475. Springer, Heidelberg (2013). doi:10.1007/978-3-642-40041-4_25

8. Canetti, R.: Universally composable security: a new paradigm for cryptographic protocols. Cryptology ePrint Archive, Report 2000/067 (2000). http://eprint.iacr.org/2000/067

9. Canetti, R.: Universally composable security: a new paradigm for cryptographic protocols. In: 42nd FOCS, pp. 136–145. IEEE Computer Society Press, October 2001

10. Canetti, R., Dachman-Soled, D., Vaikuntanathan, V., Wee, H.: Efficient password authenticated key exchange via oblivious transfer. In: Fischlin, M., Buchmann, J., Manulis, M. (eds.) PKC 2012. LNCS, vol. 7293, pp. 449–466. Springer, Heidelberg (2012). doi:10.1007/978-3-642-30057-8_27

11. Canetti, R., Dodis, Y., Pass, R., Walfish, S.: Universally composable security with global setup. In: Vadhan, S.P. (ed.) TCC 2007. LNCS, vol. 4392, pp. 61–85. Springer, Heidelberg (2007). doi:10.1007/978-3-540-70936-7_4

12. Canetti, R., Feige, U., Goldreich, O., Naor, M.: Adaptively secure multi-party computation. In: 28th ACM STOC, pp. 639–648. ACM Press, May 1996

13. Canetti, R., Fischlin, M.: Universally composable commitments. In: Kilian, J. (ed.) CRYPTO 2001. LNCS, vol. 2139, pp. 19–40. Springer, Heidelberg (2001). doi:10.1007/3-540-44647-8_2

14. Canetti, R., Halevi, S., Katz, J., Lindell, Y., MacKenzie, P.: Universally composable password-based key exchange. In: Cramer, R. (ed.) EUROCRYPT 2005. LNCS, vol. 3494, pp. 404–421. Springer, Heidelberg (2005). doi:10.1007/11426639_24

15. Canetti, R., Lindell, Y., Ostrovsky, R., Sahai, A.: Universally composable two-party and multi-party secure computation. In: 34th ACM STOC, pp. 494–503. ACM Press, May 2002

16. Chevalier, C., Fouque, P.-A., Pointcheval, D., Zimmer, S.: Optimal random-ness extraction from a Diffie-Hellman element. In: Joux, A. (ed.) EUROCRYPT 2009. LNCS, vol. 5479, pp. 572–589. Springer, Heidelberg (2009). doi:10.1007/978-3-642-01001-9_33

17. Choi, S.G., Dachman-Soled, D., Malkin, T., Wee, H.: Improved non-committing encryption with applications to adaptively secure protocols. In: Matsui, M. (ed.) ASIACRYPT 2009. LNCS, vol. 5912, pp. 287–302. Springer, Heidelberg (2009). doi:10.1007/978-3-642-10366-7_17

18. Choi, S.G., Katz, J., Wee, H., Zhou, H.-S.: Efficient, adaptively secure, and com-posable oblivious transfer with a single, global CRS. In: Kurosawa, K., Hanaoka, G. (eds.) PKC 2013. LNCS, vol. 7778, pp. 73–88. Springer, Heidelberg (2013). doi:10.1007/978-3-642-36362-7_6

19. Cramer, R., Shoup, V.: A practical public key cryptosystem provably secure against adaptive chosen ciphertext attack. In: Krawczyk, H. (ed.) CRYPTO 1998. LNCS, vol. 1462, pp. 13–25. Springer, Heidelberg (1998). doi:10.1007/BFb0055717

20. Cramer, R., Shoup, V.: Universal hash proofs and a paradigm for adaptive cho-sen ciphertext secure public-key encryption. In: Knudsen, L.R. (ed.) EURO-CRYPT 2002. LNCS, vol. 2332, pp. 45–64. Springer, Heidelberg (2002). doi:10.1007/3-540-46035-7_4

21. Damgård, I., Nielsen, J.B.: Improved non-committing encryption schemes based on a general complexity assumption. In: Bellare, M. (ed.) CRYPTO 2000. LNCS, vol. 1880, pp. 432–450. Springer, Heidelberg (2000). doi:10.1007/3-540-44598-6_27

22. Feige, U., Shamir, A.: Witness indistinguishable and witness hiding protocols. In: 22nd ACM STOC. pp. 416–426. ACM Press (May 1990)

23. Fischlin, M., Libert, B., Manulis, M.: Non-interactive and re-usable universally composable string commitments with adaptive security. In: Lee, D.H., Wang, X. (eds.) ASIACRYPT 2011. LNCS, vol. 7073, pp. 468–485. Springer, Heidelberg (2011). doi:10.1007/978-3-642-25385-0_25

24. Garay, J.A., Wichs, D., Zhou, H.-S.: Somewhat non-committing encryption and efficient adaptively secure oblivious transfer. In: Halevi, S. (ed.) CRYPTO 2009. LNCS, vol. 5677, pp. 505–523. Springer, Heidelberg (2009). doi:10.1007/978-3-642-03356-8_30

25. Gennaro, R., Lindell, Y.: A framework for password-based authenticated key exchange. ACM Trans. Inf. Syst. Secur. 9(2), 181–234 (2006)

26. Haralambiev, K.: Efficient cryptographic primitives for non-interactive zero-knowledge proofs and applications. Ph.D. thesis, New York University (2011)

27. Hemenway, B., Ostrovsky, R., Rosen, A.: Non-committing encryption from Φ-hiding. In: Dodis, Y., Nielsen, J.B. (eds.) TCC 2015. LNCS, vol. 9014, pp. 591–608. Springer, Heidelberg (2015). doi:10.1007/978-3-662-46494-6_24

28. Jutla, C.S., Roy, A.: Dual-system simulation-soundness with applications to UC-PAKE and more. In: Iwata, T., Cheon, J.H. (eds.) ASIACRYPT 2015. LNCS, vol. 9452, pp. 630–655. Springer, Heidelberg (2015). doi:10.1007/978-3-662-48797-6_26

29. Katz, J., Vaikuntanathan, V.: Round-optimal password-based authenticated key exchange. In: Ishai, Y. (ed.) TCC 2011. LNCS, vol. 6597, pp. 293–310. Springer, Heidelberg (2011). doi:10.1007/978-3-642-19571-6_18

30. Montenegro, R., Tetali, P.: How long does it take to catch a wild kangaroo? In: Mitzenmacher, M. (ed.) 41st ACM STOC, pp. 553–560. ACM Press, May–June 2009

31. Pedersen, T.P.: Non-interactive and information-theoretic secure verifiable secret sharing. In: Feigenbaum, J. (ed.) CRYPTO 1991. LNCS, vol. 576, pp. 129–140. Springer, Heidelberg (1992). doi:10.1007/3-540-46766-1_9

32. Peikert, C., Vaikuntanathan, V., Waters, B.: A framework for efficient and composable oblivious transfer. In: Wagner, D. (ed.) CRYPTO 2008. LNCS, vol. 5157, pp. 554–571. Springer, Heidelberg (2008). doi:10.1007/978-3-540-85174-5_31

33. Wee, H.: Dual projective hashing and its applications—lossy trapdoor functions and more. In: Pointcheval, D., Johansson, T. (eds.) EUROCRYPT 2012. LNCS, vol. 7237, pp. 246–262. Springer, Heidelberg (2012). doi:10.1007/978-3-642-29011-4_16

Scalable Multi-party Private Set-Intersection

Carmit Hazay[1](✉) and Muthuramakrishnan Venkitasubramaniam[2]

[1] Bar-Ilan University, Ramat-Gan, Israel
carmit.hazay@biu.ac.il
[2] University of Rochester, Rochester, NY 14611, USA
muthuv@cs.rochester.edu

Abstract. In this work we study the problem of private set-intersection in the multi-party setting and design two protocols with the following improvements compared to prior work. First, our protocols are designed in the so-called star network topology, where a designated party communicates with everyone else, and take a new approach of leveraging the 2PC protocol of [FNP04]. This approach minimizes the usage of a broadcast channel, where our semi-honest protocol does not make any use of such a channel and all communication is via point-to-point channels. In addition, the communication complexity of our protocols scales with the number of parties.

More concretely, (1) our first semi-honest secure protocol implies communication complexity that is linear in the input sizes, namely $O((\sum_{i=1}^{n} m_i) \cdot \kappa)$ bits of communication where κ is the security parameter and m_i is the size of P_i's input set, whereas overall computational overhead is quadratic in the input sizes only for a designated party, and linear for the rest. We further reduce this overhead by employing two types of hashing schemes. (2) Our second protocol is proven secure in the malicious setting. This protocol induces communication complexity $O((n^2 + nm_{\mathrm{MAX}} + nm_{\mathrm{MIN}} \log m_{\mathrm{MAX}})\kappa)$ bits of communication where m_{MIN} (resp. m_{MAX}) is the minimum (resp. maximum) over all input sets sizes and n is the number of parties.

Keywords: Scalable multi-party computation · Private set-intersection

1 Introduction

Background on Secure Multi-party Computation. Secure multi-party computation enables a set of parties to mutually run a protocol that computes some

---

C. Hazay—Supported by the European Research Council under the ERC consolidators grant agreement n. 615172 (HIPS) and by the BIU Center for Research in Applied Cryptography and Cyber Security in conjunction with the Israel National Cyber Bureau in the Prime Ministers Office, and by a grant from the Israel Ministry of Science and Technology (grant No. 3-10883).

M. Venkitasubramaniam—Supported by Google Faculty Research Grant and NSF Award CNS-1526377.

© International Association for Cryptologic Research 2017
S. Fehr (Ed.): PKC 2017, Part I, LNCS 10174, pp. 175–203, 2017.
DOI: 10.1007/978-3-662-54365-8_8

function f on their private inputs, while preserving a number of security properties. Two of the most important properties are privacy and correctness. The former implies data confidentiality, namely, nothing leaks by the protocol execution but the computed output. The latter requirement implies that the protocol enforces the integrity of the computations made by the parties, namely, honest parties learn the correct output. Feasibility results are well established [Yao86, GMW87, MR91, Bea91], proving that any efficient functionality can be securely computed under full simulation-based definitions (following the ideal/real paradigm). Security is typically proven with respect to two adversarial models: the semi-honest model (where the adversary follows the instructions of the protocol but tries to learn more than it should from the protocol transcript), and the malicious model (where the adversary follows an arbitrary polynomial-time strategy), and feasibility holds in the presence of both types of attacks.

Following these works, many constructions focused on improving the *efficiency* of the computational and communication costs. Conceptually, this line of works can be split into two sub-lines: (**1**) Improved generic protocols that compute any boolean or arithmetic circuit; see [IPS08, LOP11, BDOZ11, DPSZ12, LPSY15] for just a few examples. (**2**) Protocols for concrete functionalities. In the latter approach attention is given to constructing efficient protocols for specific functions while exploiting their internal structure. While this approach has been proven useful for many different two-party functions in both the semi-honest and malicious settings such as calculating the kth ranked element [AMP04], pattern matching and related search problems [HT10, Ver11], set-intersection [JL09, HN12], greedy optimizations [SV15] and oblivious pseudorandom function (PRF) evaluation [FIPR05], only minor progress has been achieved for concrete multi-party functions.

2PC Private Set-Intersection. The set-intersection problem is a fundamental functionality in secure computation and has been widely studied in the past decade. In this problem a set of parties $P_1, \ldots, P_n$, holding input sets $X_1, \ldots, X_n$ of sizes $m_1, \ldots, m_n$, respectively, wish to compute $X_1 \cap X_2 \cap \ldots \cap X_n$. In the two-party setting this problem has been intensively studied by researchers in the last few years mainly due to its potential applications for dating services, datamining, recommendation systems, law enforcement and more, culminating with highly efficient protocols with practically linear overhead in the set sizes; see for instance [FNP04, DSMRY09, JL09, HL10, HN12, Haz15]. For example, consider two security agencies that wish to compare their lists of suspects without revealing their contents, or an airline company that would like to check its list of passengers against the list of people that are not allowed to go abroad.

Two common approaches are known to concretely solve this problem securely in the plain model for two parties: (**1**) oblivious polynomial evaluation (OPE) and (**2**) committed oblivious PRF evaluation.

In the first approach based on OPE, one party, say P_1, computes a polynomial $Q(\cdot)$ such that $Q(x) = 0$ for all $x \in X_1$. The set of coefficients of $Q(\cdot)$ are then encrypted using a homomorphic encryption scheme and sent to the other party P_2, who then computes the encryption of $r_{x'} \cdot Q(x') + x'$ for all $x' \in X_2$

using fresh randomness $r_{x'}$ via homomorphic evaluation. Finally, P_1 decrypts these computed ciphertexts and outputs the intersection of its input set X_1 and these plaintexts. This is the approach (and variants thereof) taken by the works [FNP04, DSMRY09, HN12].

The second approach uses a secure implementation of oblivious PRF evaluation. More precisely, in this approach, party P_1 chooses a PRF key K and computes the set $\mathsf{PRF}_{X_1} = \{\mathsf{PRF}_K(x)\}_{x \in X_1}$. The parties then execute an oblivious PRF protocol where P_1 inputs the key K and P_2 inputs its private set X_2. At the end of this protocol P_2 learns the set $\mathsf{PRF}_{X_2} = \{\mathsf{PRF}_K(x')\}_{x' \in X_2}$. Finally, P_1 sends the set PRF_{X_1} to P_2, and P_2 computes $S = \mathsf{PRF}_{X_1} \cap \mathsf{PRF}_{X_2}$ and outputs the corresponding elements $x' \in X_2$ whose PRF values are in S as the actual intersection. This idea was introduced in [FIPR05] and further used in [HL10, JL09, JL10]. Other solutions in the random oracle model such as [CT10, CKT10, ACT11] take a different approach by applying the random oracle on (one of) the sets members, or apply oblivious transfer extension [DCW13] to implement a garbled Bloom filter.

By now, major progress had already been achieved for general two-party protocols [KSS12, FJN+13, GLNP15, Lin16]. Moreover, it has been surprisingly demonstrated that general protocols can be more efficient than the concrete "custom-made" protocols for set-intersection [HEK12].

MPC Private Set-Intersection. While much progress has been made towards achieving practical protocols in the two-party setting to realize set-intersection, only few works have considered so far the multi-party setting. Moreover, most of the previous approaches fail to leverage the highly efficient techniques that were developed for the two-party case with scalable efficiency. Specifically, while several recent works improve the efficiency of generic multi-party protocols [LPSY15, LSS16, KOS16], they still remain inefficient for concrete applications on big data.

The first concrete protocols that securely implemented the set-intersection functionality were designed by Kissner and Song [KS05]. The core technique underlying these protocols is based on OPE and extends the [FNP04] approach, relying on expensive generic zero-knowledge proofs to achieve correctness. Following that, Sang and Shen introduced a new protocol with quadratic overhead in the size of the input sets [SS07], which was followed by another protocol in the honest majority setting based on Bilinear groups [SS08]. Cheon et al. improved the communication complexity of these works by reducing the dependency on the input sets from quadratic to quasi linear [CJS12]. Nevertheless, each party still needs to broadcast $O(m_i)$ elements, where m_i is the size of its input set, implying that the overall communication complexity and group multiplications per player grow quadratically with the number of parties. In [DMRY11], the authors considered a new approach based on multivariate polynomials achieving broadcast communication complexity of $O(n \cdot m_{\mathrm{MAX}} + m_{\mathrm{MAX}} \cdot \log^2 m_{\mathrm{MAX}})$ and computational complexity $O(n \cdot m_{\mathrm{MAX}}^2)$, where m_{MAX} is the maximum over all input sets sizes and n is the number of parties. Finally, in a recent work [MN15], Miyaji and Nishida introduced a semi-honest secure protocol based on Bloom filters that achieves communication complexity $O(n \cdot m_{\mathrm{MAX}})$ and computational complexity $O(n \cdot m_{\mathrm{MAX}})$ for the designated party.

One can also consider using standard secure computation to securely realize set-intersection. One popular approach for efficient protocols is [DPSZ12] protocol, dubbed SPDZ, that describes a flavour of [GMW87] protocol for arithmetic circuits. This protocol consists of a preprocessing phase that uses somewhat homomorphic encryption scheme to generate correlated randomness, that is later used in an information theoretic online phase. The total overhead of this approach is $O(n \cdot s + n^3)$ where s is the size of the computed circuit. An alternative approach to compute the offline phase, avoiding these costly primitives, was recently introduced in [KOS16]. This protocol achieves a significant improvement, and is only six times less efficient than a semi-honest version of the protocol (where their experiments were shown for up to five parties), yet its cost still approaches $O(n^2)$ overhead per multiplication triple. Finally, we note that the round complexity of this approach is proportional to the circuit's multiplication depth.

A different approach was taken in [BMR90], extending the celebrated garbled circuits technique of [Yao86] to the multi-party setting. This constant-round protocol, developed by Beaver, Micali and Rogaway, has proven secure in the presence of semi-honest adversaries (and malicious adversaries in the honest majority setting). It is comprised of an offline phase for which the garbled circuit is created, and an online phase for which the garbled circuit is evaluated. Recently, Lindell et al. [LPSY15] extended the [BMR90] protocol to the malicious honest majority setting. For the offline phase the authors presented an instantiation based on [DPSZ12]. In a more recent work, Lindell et al. [LSS16] introduced a concretely efficient MPC protocol with malicious security, focusing on reducing the round complexity into 9 rounds. The efficiency of this approach is dominated by the efficiency of the protocol that realizes the offline phase.

Our main motivation in this paper is to develop a new approach for securely realizing set-intersection in the multi-party setting. Concretely, we study whether the multi-party variant of set-intersection can be reduced to the two-party case. Meaning, can we securely realize private multi-party set-intersection using two-party set-intersection protocols. Generally speaking, the paradigm of constructing multi-party protocols from two-party protocols has several important advantages. First, it may require using a broadcast channel fewer times than in the classic approach (where every party typically communicates with everyone else all the time). Moreover, it enables to leverage the extensive knowledge and experience gained while studying the two-party variant in order to achieve efficient multi-party protocols. Finally, the mere idea of working on smaller pieces of the inputs/problems also implies that we can achieve better running times and implementations. Our new approach has not been considered yet in the past, specifically because it is quite challenging to use two-party protocols for intermediate computations without violating the privacy of the multi-party construction, and required pursuing a new approach.

In light of this overview we pose the following questions,

Can we securely realize the set-intersection functionality with linear communication complexity (and sub-quadratic computational complexity) in the input sets sizes?

In particular, to what extent can multi-party set-intersection be reduced to its two-party variant. Considering the set-intersection functionality, at first sight, it seems that the answer to this question is negative as any 2PC protocol that operates only on two input sets leaks information about the these intersections, which is more than what should be leaked about the outputs by the protocol. One potential solution would be to split the parties into pairs that repetitively compute their pairwise intersection. While it is not clear how to prevent any leakage within iterations, we further note that the round complexity induced by such an approach is $O(\log n)$ where n is the number of parties, and that the number of 2PC invocations is quadratic. It is worth noting that [CKMZ14] also considered an approach of designing a three parties protocol by emulating a two-party protocol, yet their techniques are quite different.

1.1 Our Results

In this paper we devise new protocols that securely compute the set-intersection functionality in the multiparty setting while exploiting known techniques from the two-party setting. In particular, we are able to save on quadratic overhead in pairwise communication that is incurred in typical multiparty protocols and obtain efficient protocols. More specifically, we consider a different network topology than point-to-point fully connected network for which a single designated party communicates with every party (i.e. star topology). An added benefit of this topology is that not all parties must be online at the same time. This topology has been recently considered in [HLP11] in a different context. In this work we consider both the semi-honest and malicious settings.

The Semi-honest Setting. The main building block in our design is a threshold additively homomorphic public-key encryption scheme (PKE). Our main observation is that one can employ the 2-round semi-honest variant of the [FNP04] protocol, where a designated party P_1 first interacts individually with every other party via a variant of this protocol and learns the (encrypted) cross intersection with every other party. Then in a second stage, P_1 combines these results and computes the outcome. More specifically, we leverage the following core insight, where any element in P_1's input that appears in all other input sets is part of the set-intersection. On the other hand, if some element from P_1's set does not appear in one of the other sets then surely this element is not part of the set-intersection. Therefore, it is sufficient to only examine P_1's set against the other sets rather than examine all pairwise sets, which is the common approach in prior works. Note that our protocol is the first multi-party protocol for realizing private set-intersection that does not need to employ any broadcast channel at any phase during its execution, since all the communication is conducted directly between P_1 and each other party at a point-to-point level. More formally,

Theorem 11 (Informal). *Assume the existence of a threshold additively homomorphic encryption scheme. Then, there exists a protocol that securely realizes the private set-intersection functionality in the presence of semi-honest adversaries with no use of a broadcast channel and for $n \geq 2$ parties.*

Moreover, the communication complexity of our protocol is linear in the input sets sizes, namely, $O((\sum_{i=1}^{n} m_i) \cdot \kappa)$ bits of communication where κ is the security parameter, whereas the computational overhead is quadratic in the input sizes only the designated party P_1, namely $O(m_1^2)$ exponentiations (where the overhead of the rest of the parties is a linear number of exponentiations in their input sets). Consequently, the designated party can be set as the party with the *smallest input set*. Finally, by employing hash functions techniques, as in [FNP04], we can further reduce P_1's overhead by splitting the input elements into bins. We consider two hash schemes: simple hashing and balanced allocation hashing. For simple hashing, this approach induces $O((n-1) \cdot m_{\mathrm{MIN}} \cdot \log m_{\mathrm{MAX}})$ overhead where m_{MIN} (resp. m_{MAX}) is the minimum (resp. maximum) over all input sets sizes and n is the number of parties. Whereas for balanced allocation hash functions this approach induces $O((n-1) \cdot m_{\mathrm{MIN}} \cdot \log \log m_{\mathrm{MAX}})$ overhead. In both cases the communication complexity is $O(\mathcal{B} \cdot M \cdot (n-1))$ where $\mathcal{B}$ is the number of bins and M is the maximum bin size.

We note that the first variant based on simple hashing induces a simpler protocol and the modification compared to the original protocol are minor. On the other hand, the protocol based on balanced allocation hashing is slightly more complicated as this hashing, that uses two hash functions, implies two oblivious polynomial evaluations per elements from P_1's input. Consequently, P_1 must somehow learn which of the evaluations (if any) has evaluated to zero. We solve this issue in two ways: either the parties communicate and compute the product of the two evaluations, or the underlying additively homomorphic encryption scheme supports single multiplication as well (e.g., [BGN05]). Finally, we note that our approach is the first to employ these techniques due to its internal design that heavily relies on a 2PC approach.

The Malicious Setting. Next, we extend our semi-honest approach for the malicious setting. In this setting we need to work harder in order to ensure correctness since a corrupted P_1 can easily cheat, by using different input sets in the 2PC executions against different parties. It is therefore crucial that P_1 first broadcasts its committed input to the rest of the parties. Where later, each 2PC protocol is carried out with respect to these commitments. It turns out that even by adding this broadcast phase it is not enough to boost the security of our semi-honest protocol since P_1 may still abuse the security of the [FNP04] protocol. Specifically, the main challenge is to prevent P_1 from learning additional information about the intersection with individual parties as a corrupted P_1 may use ill formed ciphertexts or ciphertexts for which it does not know their corresponding plaintexts, exploiting the honest parties as a decryption oracle.

We recall that the [FNP04] follows by having the parties send encryptions of polynomials defined by their input sets (as explained above). Then, towards achieving malicious security, we design a polynomial check that verifies that P_1 indeed assembled the encrypted polynomials correctly. This check follows by asking the parties to sample a random element u which they later evaluate their encrypted polynomials on and then compare these outcomes against the evaluation of the combined protocol (which is publicly known). To avoid malleability issues, we enforce correctness using a non-malleable proof of knowledge that is provided by each party relative to its computation. This crucial phase allows the simulator to extract the parties' inputs by rewinding them on distinct random values. Interestingly, this proof is only invoked once and thus induces an overhead that is independent of the set sizes. We prove the following theorem.

Theorem 12 (Informal). *Assume the existence of a threshold additively homomorphic encryption scheme and simulation sound zero-knowledge proof of knowledge. Then, there exists a protocol that securely realizes the private set-intersection functionality in the presence of malicious adversaries and for $n \geq 2$ parties.*

The communication complexity of the maliciously secure protocol is bounded by $O((n^2 + nm_{\text{MAX}} + nm_{\text{MIN}} \cdot \log m_{\text{MAX}})\kappa)$ bits of communication where m_{MIN} (resp. m_{MAX}) is the minimum (resp. maximum) over all input sets sizes and n is the number of parties. The significant term in this complexity is $O(n \cdot m_{\text{MAX}} \cdot \kappa)$ and this is linearly dependent on both the number of parties and the database size. In contrast, previous works required higher complexity [DMRY11, CJS12]. In terms of of computational overhead, except for party P_1, the computational complexity of each party P_i is $O(m_{\text{MAX}})$ exponentiations plus $O(m_{\text{MIN}} \cdot m_{\text{MAX}})$ groups multiplications, whereas party P_1 needs to perform $O(m_1 \cdot m_{\text{MAX}})$ exponentiations.

Finally, we note that our building blocks can be instantiated based on the El Gamal [Gam85] or Piallier [Pai99] public key encryptions schemes for the semi-honest protocol. In the malicious setting, we either consider the El Gamal scheme together with a Σ-protocol zero-knowledge proof of knowledge, that can be made non-interactive using the Fiat-Shamir heuristic [FS86] which is analyzed in the Random Oracle Model of Bellare and Rogaway [BR93]. The analysis in this model implies the simulation soundness property we need for non-malleability. A second instantiation can be shown based on the [BBS04] public key encryption scheme and the simulation-sound non-interactive zero-knowledge (NIZK) by Groth [Gro06].

2   Preliminaries

2.1   Basic Notations

We denote the security parameter by κ. We say that a function $\mu : \mathbb{N} \to \mathbb{N}$ is *negligible* if for every positive polynomial $p(\cdot)$ and all sufficiently large κ it holds that $\mu(\kappa) < \frac{1}{p(\kappa)}$. We use the abbreviation PPT to denote probabilistic polynomial-time. We further denote by $a \leftarrow A$ the random sampling of a from a distribution A, by $[d]$ the set of elements $(1, \ldots, d)$ and by $[0, d]$ the set of elements $(0, \ldots, d)$.

We now specify the definition of computationally indistinguishable.

Definition 21. *Let* $X = \{X(a, \kappa)\}_{a \in \{0,1\}^*, \kappa \in \mathbb{N}}$ *and* $Y = \{Y(a, \kappa)\}_{a \in \{0,1\}^*, \kappa \in \mathbb{N}}$ *be two distribution ensembles. We say that* X *and* Y *are* computationally indistinguishable, *denoted* $X \overset{c}{\approx} Y$, *if for every PPT machine* D, *every* $a \in \{0,1\}^*$, *every positive polynomial* $p(\cdot)$ *and all sufficiently large* κ:

$$\left| \Pr\left[D(X(a, \kappa), 1^\kappa) = 1\right] - \Pr\left[D(Y(a, \kappa), 1^\kappa) = 1\right] \right| < \frac{1}{p(\kappa)}.$$

We define a d-degree polynomial $Q(\cdot)$ by its set of coefficients $(q_0, \ldots, q_d)$, or simply write $Q(x) = q_0 + q_1 x + \ldots q_d x^d$. Typically, these coefficients will be picked from $\mathbb{Z}_p$ for a prime p. We further write $g^{Q(\cdot)}$ to denote the coefficients of $Q(\cdot)$ in the exponent of a generator g of a multiplicative group $\mathbb{G}$ of prime order p.

2.2   Hardness Assumptions

Let $\mathcal{G}$ be a group generation algorithm, which outputs $(p, \mathbb{G}, \mathbb{G}_1, e, g)$ given 1^κ, where $\mathbb{G}, \mathbb{G}_1$ is the description of groups of prime order p, e is a bilinear mapping (see below) and g is a generator of $\mathbb{G}$.

Definition 22 (DLIN). *We say that the* decisional linear *problem is hard relative to* $\mathcal{G}$, *if for any PPT distinguisher* D *there exists a negligible function* negl *such that*

$$(p, \mathbb{G}, \mathbb{G}_1, e, g, g^x, g^y, g^{xr}, g^{ys}, g^{r+s}) \approx_c (p, \mathbb{G}, \mathbb{G}_1, e, g, g^x, g^y, g^{xr}, g^{ys}, g^d)$$

where $(p, \mathbb{G}, \mathbb{G}_1, e, g) \leftarrow \mathcal{G}(1^\kappa)$ *and* $x, y, r, s, d \leftarrow \mathbb{Z}_p$.

Definition 23 (DDH). *We say that* the decisional Diffie-Hellman (DDH) problem *is hard relative to* $\mathcal{G}$, *if for any PPT distinguisher* D *there exists a negligible function* negl *such that*

$$\left| \Pr\left[D(\mathbb{G}, p, g, g^x, g^y, g^z) = 1\right] - \Pr\left[D(\mathbb{G}, p, g, g^x, g^y, g^{xy}) = 1\right] \right| \leq \mathsf{negl}(\kappa),$$

where $(\mathbb{G}, p, g) \leftarrow \mathcal{G}(1^\kappa)$ *and the probabilities are taken over the choices of* $x, y, z \leftarrow_R \mathbb{Z}_p$.

Definition 24 (Bilinear pairing). *Let* $\mathbb{G}$, $\mathbb{G}_T$ *be multiplicative cyclic groups of prime order* p *and let* g *be a generator of* $\mathbb{G}$. *A map* $e \colon \mathbb{G} \times \mathbb{G} \to \mathbb{G}_T$ *is a bilinear map for* $\mathbb{G}$ *if it has the following properties:*

1. *Bi-linearity:* $\forall u, v \in \mathbb{G}$, $\forall a, b \in \mathbb{Z}_p$, $e(u^a, v^b) = e(u, v)^{ab}$.
2. *Non-degeneracy:* $e(g, g)$ *generates* $\mathbb{G}_T$.
3. e *is efficiently computable.*

We assume that the D-linear assumption holds in $\mathbb{G}$.

2.3   Public Key Encryption Schemes (PKE)

We specify first the definitions of public key encryption and IND-CPA.

Definition 25 (PKE). *We say that Π = (Gen, Enc, Dec) is a public key encryption scheme if Gen, Enc, Dec are polynomial-time algorithms specified as follows:*

- Gen, *given a security parameter 1^{κ}, outputs keys* (PK, SK), *where* PK *is a public key and* SK *is a secret key. We denote this by* (PK, SK) $\leftarrow$ Gen(1^{κ}).
- Enc, *given the public key* PK *and a plaintext message m, outputs a ciphertext c encrypting m. We denote this by $c \leftarrow$ Enc$_{PK}(m)$; and when emphasizing the randomness r used for encryption, we denote this by $c \leftarrow$ Enc$_{PK}(m; r)$.*
- Dec, *given the public key* PK, *secret key* SK *and a ciphertext c, outputs a plaintext message m s.t. there exists randomness r for which $c =$ Enc$_{PK}(m; r)$ (or $\perp$ if no such message exists). We denote this by $m \leftarrow$ Dec$_{PK,SK}(c)$.*

For a public key encryption scheme Π = (Gen, Enc, Dec) and a non-uniform adversary $\mathcal{A} = (\mathcal{A}_1, \mathcal{A}_2)$, we consider the following *IND-CPA game*:

$$(PK, SK) \leftarrow \text{Gen}(1^{\kappa}).$$
$$(m_0, m_1, history) \leftarrow \mathcal{A}_1(PK), \text{ s.t. } |m_0| = |m_1|.$$
$$c \leftarrow \text{Enc}_{PK}(m_b), \text{ where } b \leftarrow \{0, 1\}.$$
$$b' \leftarrow \mathcal{A}_2(c, history).$$
$$\mathcal{A} \text{ wins if } b' = b.$$

Denote by $\text{ADV}_{\Pi, \mathcal{A}}(\kappa)$ the probability that $\mathcal{A}$ wins the IND-CPA game.

Definition 26 (IND-CPA). *A public key encryption scheme Π = (Gen, Enc, Dec) has* indistinguishable encryptions under chosen plaintext attacks *(IND-CPA), if for every non-uniform adversary $\mathcal{A} = (\mathcal{A}_1, \mathcal{A}_2)$ there exists a negligible function* negl *such that $\text{ADV}_{\Pi, \mathcal{A}}(\kappa) \leq \frac{1}{2} + \text{negl}(\kappa)$.*

Additively Homomorphic PKE. A public key encryption scheme is additively homomorphic if given two ciphertexts $c_1 = \text{Enc}_{PK}(m_1; r_1)$ and $c_2 = \text{Enc}_{PK}(m_2; r_2)$ it is possible to efficiently compute $\text{Enc}_{PK}(m_1 + m_2; r)$ with independent r, and without the knowledge of the secret key. Clearly, this assumes that the plaintext message space is a group; we actually assume that both the plaintext and ciphertext spaces are groups (with respective group operations $+$ or $\cdot$). We abuse notation and use $\text{Enc}_{PK}(m)$ to denote the random variable induced by $\text{Enc}_{PK}(m; r)$ where r is chosen uniformly at random. We have the following formal definition,

Definition 27 (Homomorphic PKE). *We say that a public key encryption scheme* (Gen, Enc, Dec) *is homomorphic if for all k and all* (PK, SK) *output by* Gen(1^{κ}), *it is possible to define groups $\mathcal{M}, \mathcal{C}$ such that:*

- *The plaintext space is $\mathcal{M}$, and all ciphertexts output by $\mathsf{Enc_{PK}}(\cdot)$ are elements of $\mathcal{C}$.[1]*
- *For every $m_1, m_2 \in \mathcal{M}$ it holds that*

$$\{PK, c_1 = \mathsf{Enc_{PK}}(m_1), c_1 \cdot \mathsf{Enc_{PK}}(m_2)\} \equiv \{PK, \mathsf{Enc_{PK}}(m_1), \mathsf{Enc_{PK}}(m_1 + m_2)\}$$

where the group operations are carried out in $\mathcal{C}$ and $\mathcal{M}$, respectively, and the randomness for the distinct ciphertexts are independent.

Note that any such a scheme supports a multiplication of a plaintext by a scalar. We implicitly assume that each homomorphic operation on a set of ciphertexts is concluded with a refresh operation, where the party multiplies the result ciphertext with an independently generated ciphertext that encrypts zero. This is required in order to ensure that the randomness of the outcome ciphertext is not related to the randomness of the original set of ciphertexts.

Threshold PKE. In a distributed scheme, the parties hold shares of the secret key so that the combined key remains a secret. In order to decrypt, each party uses its share to generate an intermediate computation which are eventually combined into the decrypted plaintext. To formalize this notion, we consider two multi-party functionalities: One for securely generating a secret key while keeping it a secret from all parties, whereas the second functionality jointly decrypts a given ciphertext. We denote the key generation functionality by $\mathcal{F}_{\mathrm{GEN}}$, which is defined as follows,

$$(1^\kappa, \ldots, 1^\kappa) \mapsto \Big((PK, SK_1), \ldots, (PK, SK_n)\Big)$$

where $(PK, SK) \leftarrow \mathsf{Gen}(1^\kappa)$, and SK_1 through SK_n are random shares of SK. In the simulation, the simulator obtains a public key $\widetilde{PK}$, either from the trusted party or from the reduction, and enforces that outcome. Namely, that $PK = \widetilde{PK}$. Moreover, the decryption functionality $\mathcal{F}_{\mathrm{DEC}}$ is defined by,

$$(c, PK, \ldots, PK) \mapsto \Big((m : c = \mathsf{Enc_{PK}}(m)), -, \ldots, -\Big).$$

In the simulation, the simulator sends ciphertexts on behalf of the honest parties which do not necessarily match the distribution of ciphertexts in the real execution (as it computes these ciphertexts based on arbitrary inputs). Moreover, in the reduction the simulator is given a ciphertext (or more) from an external source and must be able to decrypt it, jointly with the rest of the corrupted parties, without knowing the secret key. We therefore require that in the simulation, the simulator cheats in the decryption by biasing the decrypted value into some predefined plaintext m_S. It is required that the corrupted parties' view is computationally indistinguishable in both real and simulated decryption protocols. One can view the pair of simulators $(\mathcal{S}_{\mathrm{GEN}}, \mathcal{S}_{\mathrm{DEC}})$ as a stateful algorithm where

---

[1] The plaintext and ciphertext spaces may depend on PK; we leave this implicit.

$\mathcal{S}_{\text{DEC}}$ obtains a state returned by $\mathcal{S}_{\text{GEN}}$ which includes the public key enforced by $\mathcal{S}_{\text{GEN}}$ as well as the corrupted parties' shares. For simplicity we leave this state implicit. Finally, we consider a variation of $\mathcal{F}_{\text{DEC}}$, denoted by $\mathcal{F}_{\text{DecZero}}$, that allows the parties to learn whether a ciphertext encrypts zero or not, but nothing more. Similarly to $\mathcal{S}_{\text{DEC}}$ we can define a simulator $\mathcal{S}_{\text{DecZero}}$ that receives as output, either zero or a random group element and enforces that value as the outcome plaintext. These functionalities can be securely realized relative to the El Gamal and [BBS04], and Paillier and [BGN05], PKEs as specified next. We denote the corresponding protocols that respectively realize $\mathcal{F}_{\text{GEN}}$ and $\mathcal{F}_{\text{DEC}}$ in the semi-honest setting by $\pi_{\text{GEN}}^{\text{SH}}$ and $\pi_{\text{DEC}}^{\text{SH}}$, and by $\pi_{\text{GEN}}^{\text{ML}}$ and $\pi_{\text{DEC}}^{\text{ML}}$ their malicious variants.

The El Gamal PKE. A useful implementation of homomorphic PKE is the El Gamal [Gam85] scheme that has two variations of additive and multiplicative definitions (where the former is only useful for small domains plaintexts). In this paper we exploit the additive variation. Let $\mathbb{G}$ be a group of prime order p in which DDH is hard. Then the public key is a tuple $\text{PK} = \langle \mathbb{G}, p, g, h \rangle$ and the corresponding secret key is $\text{SK} = s$, s.t. $g^s = h$. Encryption is performed by choosing $r \leftarrow \mathbb{Z}_p$ and computing $\text{Enc}_{\text{PK}}(m; r) = \langle g^r, h^r \cdot g^m \rangle$. Decryption of a ciphertext $c = \langle \alpha, \beta \rangle$ is performed by computing $g^m = \beta \cdot \alpha^{-s}$ and then finding m by running an exhaustive search. Consequently, this variant is only applicable for small plaintext domains, which is the case in our work.

Threshold El Gamal. In El Gamal the parties first agree on a group $\mathbb{G}$ of order p and a generator g. Then, each party P_i picks $s_i \leftarrow \mathbb{Z}_p$ and sends $h_i = g^{s_i}$ to the others. Finally, the parties compute $h = \prod_{i=1}^{n} h_i$ and set $\text{PK} = \langle \mathbb{G}, p, g, h \rangle$. Clearly, the secret key $s = \sum_{i=1}^{n} s_n$ associated with this public key is correctly shared amongst the parties. In order to ensure correct behavior, the parties must prove knowledge of their s_i by running on (g, h_i) the zero-knowledge proof π_{DL}, specified in Sect. 2.6. To ensure simulation based security, each party must commit to its share first and decommit this commitment only after the commit phase is completed. Note that the simulator can enforce the public key outcome by rewinding the corrupted parties after seeing their decommitment information.

Moreover, decryption of a ciphertext $c = \langle c_1, c_2 \rangle$ follows by computing the product $c_2 \cdot (\prod_{i=1}^{n} c_1^{s_i})^{-1}$, where each party sends c_1 to the power of its share together with a corresponding proof for proving a Diffie-Hellman relation. Here the simulator can cheat in the proof and return a share of the form $c_2/(m_{\mathcal{S}} \cdot (\prod_{i \in \mathcal{I}} c_1^{s_i}))$ where $\mathcal{I}$ is the set of corrupted parties and $m_{\mathcal{S}}$ is the message to be biased. Note that the simulated share may not distribute as the real share (this happens in case $m_{\mathcal{S}}$ is different than the actual plaintext within c). Indistinguishability can be shown by a reduction to the DDH hardness assumption.

The variation of $\mathcal{F}_{\text{DEC}}$ allows the parties to learn whether a ciphertext $c = \langle \alpha, \beta \rangle$ encrypts zero or not, but nothing more. This can be carried out as follows. Each party first raises c to a random non-zero power and rerandomizes the result (proving correctness using a zero-knowledge proof). The parties then decrypt the final ciphertext and conclude that $m = 0$ if and only if the masked plaintext was 0.

2.4   The Paillier PKE

The Paillier encryption scheme [Pai99] is another example of a public-key encryption scheme that meets Definition 27. We focus our attention on the following, widely used, variant of Paillier due to Damgård and Jurik [DJ01]. Specifically, the key generation algorithm chooses two equal length primes p and q and computes $N = pq$. It further picks an element $g \in \mathbb{Z}^*_{N^{s+1}}$ such that $g = (1+N)^j r^N \bmod N^{s+1}$ for a known j relatively prime to N and r^N. Let λ be the least common multiple of $p-1$ and $q-1$, then the algorithm chooses d such that $d \bmod N \in \mathbb{Z}^*_N$ and $d = 0 \bmod \lambda$. The public key is N, g and the secret key is d. Next, encryption of a plaintext $m \in \mathbb{Z}_{N^s}$ is computed by $g^m r^{N^s} \bmod N^{s+1}$. Finally, decryption of a ciphertext c follows by first computing $c^d \bmod N^{s+1}$ which yields $(1 + N)^{jmd \bmod N^s}$, and then computing the discrete logarithm of the result relative to $(1 + N)$ which is an easy task.

In this work we consider a concrete case where $s = 1$. Thereby, encryption of a plaintext m with randomness $r \leftarrow_R \mathbb{Z}^*_N$ ($\mathbb{Z}_N$ in practice) is computed by,

$$\mathsf{Enc}_N(m, r) = (N + 1)^m \cdot r^N \bmod N^2.$$

Finally, decryption is performed by,

$$\mathsf{Dec}_{sk}(c) = \frac{[c^{\phi(N)} \bmod N^2] - 1}{N} \cdot \phi(N)^{-1} \bmod N.$$

The security of Paillier is implied by the Decisional Composite Residuosity (DCR) hardness assumption.

Threshold Paillier. The threshold variant of Paillier PKE in the semi-honest setting can be found in [Gil99], where the parties mutually generate an RSA composite N. A malicious variant realizing this functionality can be found in [HMRT12]. These protocols are fully simulatable in the two-party setting, but can be naturally extended to the multi-party setting (in fact, Hazay et al. also shows a variant that applies for any number of parties). In addition to a key generation protocol, Hazay et al. also designed a threshold decryption protocol which allows to bias the plaintext as required above.

The [BBS04] PKE. To setup the keys we choose at random $x, y \leftarrow \mathbb{Z}^*_p$. The public key is (f, h) where $f = g^x, h = g^y$, and the secret key is (x, y). To encrypt a message $m \in \mathbb{G}$ we choose $r, s \leftarrow \mathbb{Z}_p$ and let the ciphertext be $(u, v, w) = (f^r, h^s, g^{r+s} \cdot m)$. To decrypt a ciphertext $(u, v, w) \in \mathbb{G}^3$ we compute $m = \mathsf{Dec}(u, v, w) = w/u^x v^y$. This homomorphic scheme is IND-CPA secure assuming the hardness of the DLIN assumption and can be viewed as an extension of the El Gamal PKE. Specifically, the protocols we discussed above with respect to El Gamal can be directly extended for this PKE as well.

The [BGN05] PKE. The public key is PK $= (N, \mathbb{G}, \mathbb{G}_1, e, g, h)$ where $N = q_1 q_2$, $h = u^{q_2}$, g, u are random generators of $\mathbb{G}$, and the secret key is SK $= q_1$. To encrypt a message $m \in \mathbb{Z}_{q_2}$ we pick a random $r \leftarrow [N-1]$ and compute $g^m h^r$. To decrypt a ciphertext c we observe that $c^{q_1} = (g^m h^r)^{q_1} = (g^{q_1})^m$. Security follows assuming the subgroup decision problem. In a threshold variant, the parties first mutually generate a product of two primes N, so that the factorization of N is shared amongst the parties. To decrypt, each party raises the ciphertext to the power of its share. This scheme supports multiplication in the exponent via the pairing operation, see Definition 24. Furthermore, the scheme is additively homomorphic in both groups.

2.5 The Pedersen Commitment Scheme

The Pedersen commitment scheme [Ped91] is defined as follows. A key generation algorithm $(p, g, h, \mathbb{G}) \leftarrow \mathcal{G}(1^\kappa)$ for which the commitment key is $|ck = (\mathbb{G}, p, g, h)$. To commit to a message $m \in \mathbb{Z}_p$ the committer picks randomness $r \leftarrow \mathbb{Z}_p$ and computes $\mathsf{Com}_{\mathrm{CK}}(m; r) = g^m h^r$. The Pedersen commitment scheme is computationally binding under the discrete logarithm assumption, i.e., any two different openings of the same commitment are reduced to computing $\log_g h$. Finally, it is perfectly hiding since a commitment is uniformly distributed in $\mathbb{G}$. Another appealing property of this scheme is its additively homomorphism.

2.6 Zero-Knowledge Proofs

To prevent malicious behavior, the parties must demonstrate that they are well-behaved. To achieve this, our protocols utilize zero-knowledge (ZK) proofs of knowledge. The following proof π_{DL} is required for proving consistency in our maliciously secure threshold decryption protocol. Namely, π_{DL} is employed for demonstrating the knowledge of a solution x to a discrete logarithm problem [Sch89]. Formally stating,

$$\mathcal{R}_{\mathrm{DL}} = \{((\mathbb{G}, g, h), x) \mid h = g^x\}.$$

2.7 Hash Functions

The main computational overhead of our basic semi-honest protocol is carried out by P_1, which essentially has to do $m_1 \cdot m_i$ comparisons for each $i \in [2, n]$ in order to compare each of its inputs to each of the other parties' inputs. This overhead can be reduced using hashing, if both parties use the same hash scheme to map their respective items into different $\mathcal{B}$ bins. In that case, the items mapped by some party to a certain bin must only be compared to those mapped by P_1 to the same bin. Thus the number of comparisons can be reduced to be in the order of the number of P_1's inputs times the maximum number of items mapped to a bin. (Of course, care must be taken to ensure that the result of the hashing does not reveal information about the inputs.) In this work we consider two hash schemes: simple hashing and balanced allocations hashing; see [FHNP16] for a thorough discussion.

Simple Hashing. Let h be a randomly chosen hash function mapping elements into bins numbered $1, \ldots, \mathcal{B}$. It is well known that if the hash function h maps m items to random bins, then, if $m \geq \mathcal{B} \log \mathcal{B}$, each bin contains with high probability at most $M = \frac{m}{\mathcal{B}} + \sqrt{\frac{m \log \mathcal{B}}{\mathcal{B}}}$ (see, e.g., [RS98, Wie07]). Setting $\mathcal{B} = m / \log m$ and applying the Chernoff bound shows that $M = O(\log m)$ except with probability $(m)^{-s}$, where s is a constant that depends on the exact value of M.[2]

Balanced Allocation. A different hash construction with better parameters is the balanced allocation scheme of [ABKU99] where elements are inserted into $\mathcal{B}$ bins as follows. Let $h_0, h_1 : \{0,1\}^{p(n)} \to [\mathcal{B}]$ be two randomly chosen hash functions mapping elements from $\{0,1\}^{p(n)}$ into bins $1, \ldots, \mathcal{B}$. An element $x \in \{0,1\}^{p(n)}$ is inserted into the less occupied bin from $\{h_0(x), h_1(x)\}$, where ties are broken arbitrarily. If m elements are inserted, then except with negligible probability over the choice of the hash functions h_0, h_1, the maximum number of elements allocated to any single bin is at most $M = O(m/\mathcal{B} + \log \log \mathcal{B})$. Setting $\mathcal{B} = \frac{m}{\log \log m}$ implies that $M = O(\log \log m)$.[3]

3   The Semi-honest Construction

We begin with a description of a private MPC protocol that securely realizes the following functionality in the presence of semi-honest adversaries. Specifically, the private set-intersection functionality $\mathcal{F}_{\mathrm{PSI}}$ for n parties is defined by $(X_1, \ldots, X_n) \mapsto (X_1 \cap \ldots, \cap X_n, \lambda, \ldots, \lambda)$ where λ is the empty string. For simplicity we consider a functionality where only the first party receives an output. Our protocol takes a new approach where party P_1 interacts with every party using a 2PC protocol that implements $\mathcal{F}_{\mathrm{PSI}}$ for two parties. At the end, P_1 combines the results of all these protocols and learns the intersection.

To be concrete, assume that P_1 learns for each element $x_1^j \in X_1$ whether it is in X_i or not, for all $j \in [m_1]$ and $i \in [2, n]$. Then, P_1 can conclude the overall intersection. This is because an element from X_1 that intersects with all other sets must be in the overall intersection. On the other hand, any element that is joint for all sets must be in X_1 as well. Thus, we conclude that it is sufficient to individually compare X_1 with all other sets. This protocol, of course, is insecure as it leaks the pairwise intersections (which is much more information than P_1

---

[2] As stated in [FHNP16], by setting $\mathcal{B} = m \log \log m / \log m$ we can make the error probability negligible in m. However, any actual implementation will have to examine the exact value of $\mathcal{B}$ which results in a sufficiently small error probability for the input sizes that are expected. As for theoretical analysis, the subsequent construction, based on balanced allocation hashing, presents a negligible error probability.

[3] A constant factor improvement is achieved using the *Always Go Left* scheme in [Vöc03] where $h_0 : \{0,1\}^{p(n)} \to [1, \ldots, \frac{\mathcal{B}}{2}], h_1 : \{0,1\}^{p(n)} \to [\frac{b}{2} + 1, \ldots, \mathcal{B}]$. An element x is inserted into the less occupied bin from $\{h_0(x), h_1(x)\}$; in case of a tie x is inserted into $h_0(x)$.

should learn from a secure realization of $\mathcal{F}_{\mathrm{PSI}}$). In order to hide this leakage we suggest to use a subprotocol for which P_1 learns an encryption of zero in case the corresponding element is in the intersection, and an encryption of a random element otherwise. If the encryption is additively homomorphic then P_1 can combine all the results with respect to each element $x_1^j \in X_1$, so that x_1^j is in the overall intersection if and only if the combined ciphertext encrypts the zero string. We implement this subprotocol using a variant of the [FNP04] protocol; see below for a complete description.

The [FNP04] *protocol (the semi-honest variant).* More concretely, the [FNP04] protocol is based on oblivious polynomial evaluation. The basic two-round semi-honest protocol, executed between parties $\widetilde{P}_1$ and $\widetilde{P}_2$ on the respective inputs X_1 and X_2 of sizes m_1 and m_2, works as follows:

1. Party $\widetilde{P}_2$ chooses encryption/decryption keys $(\mathrm{PK}, \mathrm{SK}) \leftarrow \mathsf{Gen}(1^\kappa)$ for an additively homomorphic encryption scheme $(\mathsf{Gen}, \mathsf{Enc}, \mathsf{Dec})$.
   $\widetilde{P}_2$ further computes the coefficients of a polynomial $Q(\cdot)$ of degree m_2, with roots set to the m_2 elements of X_2, and sends the encrypted coefficients, as well as PK, to $\widetilde{P}_1$.
2. For each element $x_1^j \in X_1$ (in random order), party $\widetilde{P}_1$ chooses a random value r_j (taken from an appropriate set depending on the encryption scheme), and uses the homomorphic properties of the encryption scheme to compute an encryption of $r_j \cdot Q(x_1^j) + x_1^j$. $\widetilde{P}_1$ sends the encrypted values to $\widetilde{P}_2$.
3. Upon receiving these ciphertexts, $\widetilde{P}_2$ extracts $X_1 \cap X_2$ by decrypting each value and then checking if the result is in X_2. Note that if $z \in X_1 \cap X_2$ then by the construction of the polynomial $Q(\cdot)$ we get that $r \cdot Q(z) + z = r \cdot 0 + z = z$ for any r. Otherwise, $r \cdot Q(z) + z$ is a random value that reveals no information about z and (with high probability) is not in X_2.

Towards realizing $\mathcal{F}_{\mathrm{PSI}}$ we slightly modify the [FNP04] protocol as follows. The role of $\widetilde{P}_2$ remains almost the same and played by all parties P_i for $i \in [2, n]$, except that these parties do not generate a pair of keys but rather use a public key that was previously generated by the whole set of parties in a key generation phase. Whereas for each element $x_1^j \in X_1$ (picked in random order), $\widetilde{P}_1$ computes the encryption of $r_j \cdot Q(x_1^j)$ and keeps it for itself. This role is computed by party P_1 that aggregates the polynomial evaluations and concludes the intersection as explained in the beginning of this section. We denote $\widetilde{P}_\tau$'s message sent within this modified protocol by π_{FNP}^τ for $\tau \in \{1, 2\}$.

Our Complete Protocol. Let $(\mathsf{Gen}, \mathsf{Enc}, \mathsf{Dec})$ denote a threshold additively homomorphic cryptosystem with a public key generation and decryption protocols $\pi_{\mathrm{GEN}}^{\mathrm{SH}}$ and $\pi_{\mathrm{DEC}}^{\mathrm{SH}}$, respectively (in fact, we will be using protocol $\pi_{\mathrm{DecZero}}^{\mathrm{SH}}$; see Sect. 2.3). Then our protocol can be described using three phases. In the first phase the parties run protocol $\pi_{\mathrm{GEN}}^{\mathrm{SH}}$ in order to agree on a public key without disclosing its corresponding secret key to anyone. In the second 2PC phase P_1 individually interacts with each party in order to generate the set of ciphertexts as specified above (via the [FNP04] modified protocol). Finally, in the last phase, the parties carry out protocol $\pi_{\text{DecZero}}^{\text{SH}}$ for which P_1 concludes the overall intersection. More formally,

Protocol 1 (Protocol π_{PSI} with semi-honest security).

- **Input:** *Party P_i is given a set X_i of size m_i for all $i \in [n]$. All parties are given a security parameter 1^κ and a description of a group $\mathbb{G}$.*
- **The protocol:**
  - **Key Generation.** *The parties mutually generate a public key PK and the corresponding secret key shares $(\text{SK}_1, \ldots, \text{SK}_n)$ by running a semi-honestly secure protocol $\pi_{\text{GEN}}^{\text{SH}}$ that realizes $\mathcal{F}_{\text{GEN}}$.*
  - **The 2PC phase.** *Party P_1 engages in an execution of protocol $(\pi_{\text{FNP}}^1, \pi_{\text{FNP}}^2)$ specified above with each party P_i, for every $i \in [2, n]$. Let $(c_1^i, \ldots, c_{m_1}^i)$ denote the outcome of party P_1 from the $(i-1)$th execution of 2PC protocol. (Recall that P_1 has m_1 elements in its set.)*
  - **Concluding the intersection.**
    1. *The parties mutually decrypt for P_1 the set of ciphertexts*

    $$\prod_{i=2}^{n} c_1^i, \ldots, \prod_{i=2}^{n} c_{m_1}^i$$

    by engaging in a semi-honestly secure protocol $\pi_{\text{DecZero}}^{\text{SH}}$ that realizes $\mathcal{F}_{\text{DecZero}}$.
    2. *P_1 outputs x_j only if the decryption of $\prod_{i=2}^n c_j^i$ equals zero.*

We continue with the proof of the following theorem,

Theorem 31. *Assume that $(\text{Gen}, \text{Enc}, \text{Dec})$ is IND-CPA secure threshold additively homomorphic encryption scheme. Then, Protocol 1 securely realizes $\mathcal{F}_{\text{PSI}}$ in the presence of semi-honest adversaries in the $\{\mathcal{F}_{\text{GEN}}, \mathcal{F}_{\text{DecZero}}\}$-hybrid for $n \geq 2$ parties.*

Proof: We already argued for correctness, we thus directly continue with the privacy proof. We consider two classes of adversaries. The first class involves adversaries that corrupt a subset of parties that includes party P_1, whereas the second class does not involve the corruption of P_1. We provide a separate simulation for each class.

Consider an adversary $\mathcal{A}$ that corrupts a strict subset $\mathcal{I}$ of parties from the set $\{P_1, \ldots, P_n\}$, including P_1. We define a simulator $\mathcal{S}$ as follows.

1. Given $\{X_i\}_{i \in \mathcal{I}}$ and $Z = \cap_{i=1}^n X_i$, the simulator invokes the corrupted parties on their corresponding inputs and randomness.
2. $\mathcal{S}$ generates $(\text{PK}, \text{SK}) \leftarrow \text{Gen}(1^\kappa)$ and invokes the simulator $\mathcal{S}_{\text{GEN}}(\text{PK})$ for $\pi_{\text{GEN}}^{\text{SH}}$ in the key generation phase.
3. Next, $\mathcal{S}$ plays the role of the honest parties against P_1 on arbitrary sets of inputs. Namely, $\mathcal{S}$ sends ciphertexts encrypting the polynomials induced by these inputs.

4. Finally, at the concluding phase the simulator completes the decryption protocol as follows. For each $x_1^j \in Z$, $\mathcal{S}$ invokes $\mathcal{S}_{\text{DecZero}}(0)$, forcing the decryption outcome to be zero. Whereas for each $x_1^j \notin Z$, the simulator invokes $\mathcal{S}_{\text{DecZero}}(r)$ for a uniformly distributed $r \leftarrow \mathbb{G}$.

Note that the difference between the two views is with respect to the encrypted polynomials sent by the simulator as opposed to the real parties. Then indistinguishability follows from the privacy of π_{DecZero} which boils down to the privacy of the threshold homomorphic encryption scheme. This can be shown via a reduction to the indistinguishability of ciphertexts of the encryption scheme. More formally, assume by construction the existence of an adversary $\mathcal{A}$ and a distinguisher D that distinguishes the real and simulated executions with non-negligible probability. We construct an adversary $\mathcal{A}_\Pi$ that distinguishes two sets of ciphertexts. Concretely, upon receiving a public key PK, $\mathcal{A}_\Pi$ invokes the simulator $\mathcal{S}_{\text{GEN}}(\text{PK})$ as would the simulator $\mathcal{S}$ do. Next, it outputs two sets of vectors. One corresponds to the set of polynomials computed from the honest parties' inputs. Whereas the other set is arbitrarily fixed as generated in the simulation. Upon receiving the vector of ciphertexts $\tilde{c}$ from its oracle, $\mathcal{A}_\Pi$ sends $\tilde{c}$ to the corrupted P_1 and completes the reduction as in the simulation.

Note that if $\tilde{c}$ corresponds to encryptions of the honest parties' inputs, then the adversary's view is distributed as in the real execution. In particular, $\mathcal{A}_\Pi$ always knows the correct plaintext to be decrypted (which is either zero or a random value where this randomness is also known in the semi-honest model). Therefore, the shares handed by $\mathcal{A}_\Pi$ are as in the real execution. On the other hand, in case $\tilde{c}$ corresponds to the set of arbitrary inputs, then the adversary's view is distributed as in the simulation since the decrypted plaintext is not correlated with the actual plaintext. This concludes the proof.

Next, we consider an adversary which does not corrupt P_1. In this case the simulator $\mathcal{S}$ is defined as follows.

1. Given $\{X_i\}_{i \in \mathcal{I}}$ and $Z = \cap_{i=1}^n X_i$, the simulator invokes the corrupted parties on their corresponding inputs and randomness.
2. $\mathcal{S}$ generates $(\text{PK}, \text{SK}) \leftarrow \text{Gen}(1^\kappa)$ and invokes the simulator $\mathcal{S}_{\text{GEN}}(\text{PK})$ for π_{GEN} in the key generation phase.
3. Next, $\mathcal{S}$ plays the role of P_1 against the corrupted parties on an arbitrary set of inputs and concludes the simulation by playing the role of P_1 on these arbitrary inputs. (Note that this corruption case is even simpler as only P_1 learns the output. In case all parties should learn the output then we apply the same simulation technique as in the previous corruption case.)

Note that the difference is with respect to the polynomial evaluations made by the simulated P_1 which uses an arbitrary input. Then the indistinguishability argument follows similarly as above via a reduction to the privacy of the encryption scheme as only P_1 receives an output. ■

3.1 Communication and Computation Complexities

Note that the complexity of the protocol is dominated by the overhead of the threshold cryptosystem as well as the underlying 2PC protocol for implementing $\mathcal{F}_{\mathrm{PSI}}^{\mathrm{2PC}}$. We instantiate the latter using the [FNP04] and either the El Gamal PKE [Gam85] or the Paillier PKE [Pai99] for the former. Note that the communication complexity of the [FNP04] variant we consider here is linear in m_2, as m_2+1 encrypted values are sent from $\tilde{P}_2$ to $\tilde{P}_1$ (these are the encrypted coefficients of $Q(\cdot)$). However, the work performed by $\tilde{P}_1$ is high, as each of the m_1 oblivious polynomial evaluations includes performing $O(m_2)$ exponentiations, totaling in $O(m_1 \cdot m_2)$ exponentiations. To save on computational work, Freedman et al. introduced hash functions into their schemes. Below we consider two instantiations of simple hashing (cf. Sect. 2.7) and balanced allocation hash function (cf. Sect. 2.7).

Furthermore, the underlying threshold additively homomorphic encryption scheme can be instantiated using either the additive variant of the El Gamal PKE, for which the public key can be generated using the Diffie-Hellman approach [DH76], or the Paillier PKE for which the public key can be generated using [Gil99]. Finally, we note that our protocol is constant round and does not need to use any broadcast channel.

Improved Computation Using Simple Hashing. In our protocol, the hash function h will be picked by one of the parties (say $\tilde{P}_2$) and known to both. Moreover, $\tilde{P}_2$ defines a polynomial of degree M for each bin by fixing its mapped elements to be the set of roots. As some of the bins contain less than M elements, $\tilde{P}_2$ pads each polynomial with zero coefficients up to degree M, so that the total degree of the polynomial is M (since P_2 must hide the actual number of elements allocated to each bin). This results in $\mathcal{B}$ polynomials, all of degree M, with exactly m_2 non-zero roots. The rest of the protocol remains unchanged. Now, $\tilde{P}_1$ needs to first map each element x_1^j in its set and then obliviously evaluate the polynomial that corresponds to that bin. Neglecting small constant factors, the communication complexity is not affected as $\tilde{P}_i$ now sends $\mathcal{B} \cdot M_i = O(m_i)$ encrypted values. There is, however, a dramatic reduction in the work performed by $\tilde{P}_1$ as each of the oblivious polynomial evaluations amounts now to performing just $O(M_i)$ exponentiations, and hence $\tilde{P}_1$ performs $O(m_1 \cdot \sum_i M_i)$ exponentiations overall, where M_i is a bin size for allocating P_i's input.

Improved Computation Using Balanced Allocation Hashing. Loosely speaking, they used the balanced allocation scheme of [ABKU99] with $\mathcal{B} = \frac{m_2}{\log\log m_2}$ bins, each of size $M = O(m_2/\mathcal{B} + \log\log\mathcal{B}) = O(\log\log m_2)$. Party $\tilde{P}_2$ now uses the balanced allocation scheme to hash every $x \in X$ into one of the $\mathcal{B}$ bins resulting (with high probability) with each bin's load being at most M. Instead of a single polynomial of degree m_2 party $\tilde{P}_2$ now constructs a degree-M polynomial for each of the $\mathcal{B}$ bins, i.e., polynomials $Q_1(\cdot), \ldots, Q_{\mathcal{B}}(\cdot)$ such that the roots of $Q_i(\cdot)$ are the elements put in the ith bin. Upon receiving the encrypted polynomials, party

$\widetilde{P}_1$ obliviously evaluates the encryption of $r_0^j \cdot Q_{h_0(x_j^1)}(x_j^1)$ and $r_1^j \cdot Q_{h_1(x_j^1)}(x_j^1)$ for each of the two bins $h_0(x_j^1), h_1(x_j^1)$ in which x_j^1 can be allocated, enabling $\widetilde{P}_1$ to extract $X \cap Y$ as above.

The communication and computational overheads are as above. Nevertheless, a subtlety emerges in our semi-honest protocol that employs this tool, as P_1 cannot tell which of the two bins contains the particular element. Consequently, it cannot tell which of the two associated polynomials is evaluated to zero, where this information is crucial in order to conclude the intersection. We suggest two solutions in order to overcome this issue. Our first solution supports the El Gamal and Paillier PKEs but requires more communication. Namely, the parties run a protocol to compute the encryption of the product of plaintexts. This is easily done by having $\widetilde{P}_1$ additively mask the two evaluations and then have $\widetilde{P}_2$ multiply the decrypted results and send the encrypted product back to $\widetilde{P}_1$. At the end, $\widetilde{P}_1$ unmasks this ciphehrtext and continues with the protocol execution. Note that all the products can be computed in parallel.

Our second solution uses an encryption scheme that is additively homomorphic and multiplicative with respect to a single plaintexts multiplication. In this case, it is possible to multiply the two results of the polynomials evaluations, which will result zero if one of the evaluations is zero. An additively homomorphic encryption scheme that supports such a property is due to Boneh et al. [BGN05] (cf. Sect. 2.4).

4   The Malicious Construction

Towards designing a protocol with stronger security we need to handle new challenges that emerge due to the fact that party P_1 may behave maliciously. The main challenge is to prevent P_1 from learning additional information about the intersection with individual parties. To be concrete, we recall that our semi-honest protocol follows by having P_1 individually interacting with each party via 2PC protocol, where this stage is followed by decrypting the combined ciphertexts generated in these executions. Then upon corrupting a subset of parties which includes P_1, a malicious adversary may use ill formed ciphertexts or ciphertexts for which it does not know their corresponding plaintext, exploiting the honest parties as a decryption oracle. Towards dealing with malicious attacks we modify Protocol 1 as follows (for simplicity we concretely consider the El Gamal PKE and adapt our ZK proofs for this encryption scheme).

1. First, P_1 broadcasts commitments to its input X_1 together with a zero-knowledge proof. This phase is required in order to ensure that P_1 uses the *same input* against every underlying 2PC evaluation with every other party. One particular instantiation for this commitment scheme can be based in Pedersen's scheme (cf. Sect. 2.5). This scheme is consistent with El Gamal PKE (cf. 2.3) and the BBS PKE (cf. 2.4). An alternative scheme, e.g. [DN02], can be considered when using the Paillier or the BGN PKEs (cf. Sect. 2.4); see below for more details.

2. To prevent P_1 from cheating when assembling the encrypted polynomial, each party chooses a random element $\lambda_i \leftarrow \mathbb{G}$ and encrypts the product of each coefficient of $Q_i(\cdot)$ with λ_i. More specifically, P_i sends an encryption of polynomial $\lambda_i \cdot Q_i(\cdot)$, where the underlying set of roots remains unchanged. This later allows the other parties to verify the correctness of P_1's computation, which will allow to claim that P_1 can only learn a random group element upon deviating.

3. Next, the parties pick a random group element $u \leftarrow \mathbb{G}$ and compare the evaluation of P_1's combined polynomial against the evaluations of their own individual polynomials. Namely, each party broadcasts the value $\sum_j (c_j^i)^{u^j}$ together with a zero-knowledge proof of knowledge. If concluded correctly, this phase is followed by the parties verifying the equality of the following equation

$$\sum_{j=1}^{m_{\mathrm{MAX}}} (c_j)^{x^j} = \sum_{i=2}^{n} \tilde{\lambda}_i$$

where m_{MAX} is the maximum over all input sets sizes and n is the number of parties. Note that equality is performed over the ciphertexts. For this reason we can only work with additively homomorphic PKEs for which the homomorphic operation does not add noise to the ciphertext. Our crucial observation here is that the simulator can run the extractor of the proof of knowledge and obtain the polynomials evaluations. Now, if the adversary convinces the honest parties with a non-negligible probability that it indeed knows the plaintext, then the simulator can rewind it sufficiently many times in order to extract enough evaluation points for which it can fully recover the corrupted parties' polynomials, and hence their inputs.

4. Finally, P_1 must prove that it correctly evaluated the combined polynomial on its committed input X_1 from Item 1. This phase is backed up with a ZK proof due to Bayer and Groth [BG13], denoted by π_{EVAL}, and formally stated in Sect. 2.6.

Building blocks. Our protocol uses the following sub-protocols.

1. A coin tossing protocol π_{COIN} employed in order to sample a random group element $u \leftarrow \mathbb{G}$. Our protocol employs π_{COIN} only once, where u is locally substituted by the parties in their private polynomials. These values are then used by the parties to verify the behaviour of P_1. The overhead of π_{COIN} is $O(n^2)$ where n is the number of parties.

2. A ZK proof of knowledge π_{EXP} for demonstrating the knowledge of the message with respect to an additively homomorphic commitment scheme. We employ this proof in two distinct places in our protocol, and for two different purposes. First, when P_1 broadcasts its polynomial in Step 2 and proves the knowledge of these coefficients and second, in Step 4c when each party sends its polynomial evaluation. As we demonstrate below, for both instantiations we can use the same proof for the two purposes. Importantly, since we are in the multi-party setting, where each party uses a homomorphic encryption to

encrypt its polynomial, we must avoid the case for which an adversary may "reuse" one of the encrypted polynomials as the polynomial of one of the corrupted parties. We will require the proof to be simulation-extractable. We will ensure this by showing that our proofs are non-malleable and straight-line extractable.

3. A ZK proof of knowledge π_{EVAL} for demonstrating the correctness of a polynomial evaluation for a secret committed value [BG13]. This proof is an argument of knowledge such that given a polynomial $P(\cdot) = (p_0, \ldots, p_d)$ and two commitments $,,,'$, proves the knowledge of a pair v, u such that $P(v) = u$ where $, = \mathsf{Com}(u)$, $,' = \mathsf{Com}(v)$ and $\mathsf{Com}(\cdot)$ denotes an homomorphic commitment scheme (as noted in [BG13] any homomorphic commitment can be used). Moreover, the polynomial can be committed as well. Formally stating,

$$
\mathcal{R}_{\mathrm{EVAL}} = \left\{ (P(\cdot) = (p_0, \ldots, p_d),,,,'),(r,r',u,v) \ \middle| \ \begin{array}{c} , = \mathsf{Com}(u;r) \\ \wedge \ ,' = \mathsf{Com}(v;r') \\ \wedge \ P(u) = v \end{array} \right\}.
$$

Importantly, the communication complexity of this proof is logarithmic in the degree of the polynomial, whereas the computational overhead by the verifier is $O(d)$ multiplications.

We next formally describe our protocol.

Protocol 2 (Protocol π_{ML} (with malicious security).

- **Input:** *Party P_i is given a set $X_i = \{x_i^1, \ldots, x_i^{m_i}\}$ of size m_i for all $i \in [n]$. All parties are given a security parameter 1^κ and a description of a group $\mathbb{G}$.*
- **The protocol:**
    1. **Key Generation.** *The parties mutually generate a public key PK and the corresponding secret key shares $(\mathrm{SK}_1, \ldots, \mathrm{SK}_n)$ by running a maliciously secure protocol $\pi_{\mathrm{GEN}}^{\mathrm{ML}}$ that realizes $\mathcal{F}_{\mathrm{GEN}}$.*
    2. **The commitment phase.** *P_1 creates commitments to its inputs $\{,1, \ldots, ,m_1\}$ and broadcasts them to all parties and proves the knowledge of their decommitments using threshold π_{EXP}.*
    3. **The 2PC phase.** *For all $i \in [2, n]$, party P_i computes the coefficients of a polynomial $Q_i(\cdot) = (q_0^i, \ldots, q_{m_i}^i)$ of degree m_i, with roots set to the m_i elements of X_i. In addition, P_i chooses a random element $\lambda_i \leftarrow \mathbb{G}$ and computes the product $\lambda_i \cdot q_j^i$ for every coefficient within Q_i. Finally, P_i sends P_1 the sets of ciphertexts $(c_1^i, \ldots, c_{m_i}^i)$, encrypting the coefficients of $\lambda_i \cdot Q_i(\cdot)$.*
    4. **Concluding the intersection.**
        (a) *Upon receiving the ciphertexts from all parties, party P_1 combines the following ciphertexts*

$$
c_1 = \prod_{i=2}^{n} c_1^i, \ldots, c_{m_{\mathrm{MAX}}} = \prod_{i=2}^{n} c_{m_{\mathrm{MAX}}}^i
$$

where $m_{\mathrm{MAX}} = \max(m_2, \ldots, m_n)$. Note that P_1 calculates the ciphertexts encrypting the coefficients of the combined polynomial $\lambda_2 \cdot Q_2(\cdot) + \cdots + \lambda_n \cdot Q_n(\cdot)$. P_1 then broadcasts ciphertexts $(c_1, \ldots, c_{m_{\mathrm{MAX}}})$ to all parties.

(b) Next, the parties verify the correctness of these ciphertexts. Specifically, the parties first agree on a random element u from the appropriate plaintext domain using the coin tossing protocol π_{COIN}.

(c) Then, each party broadcasts the ciphertext computed by $\sum_j (c_j^i)^{u^j}$, denoted by $\tilde{\lambda}_i$, together with a ZK proof of knowledge π_{EXP} for proving the knowledge of the plaintext.
If all the proofs are verified correctly, then the parties check that $\sum_{j=1}^{m_{\text{MAX}}} (c_j)^{x^j} = \sum_{i=2}^{n} \tilde{\lambda}_i$ using the homomorphic property of the encryption scheme.

(d) If the verification phase is completed correctly, for every $x_1^j \in X_1$, P_1 evaluates the polynomial that is induced by the coefficients encrypted within ciphertexts $(c_1, \ldots, c_{m_{\text{MAX}}})$ on x_1^j and proves consistency with the commitments from Step 2 using the ZK proof π_{EVAL}.

(e) Upon completing the evaluation, the parties decrypt the evaluation outcomes for P_1 using protocol $\pi_{\text{DecZero}}^{\text{ML}}$, who concludes the intersection.

We continue with the proof for this theorem,

Theorem 41. *Assume that* $(\text{Gen}, \text{Enc}, \text{Dec})$ *is IND-CPA secure threshold additively homomorphic encryption scheme, and that* $\pi_{\text{COIN}}, \pi_{\text{EXP}}, \pi_{\text{EVAL}}, \pi_{\text{GEN}}$ *and* π_{DecZero} *are as above. Then, Protocol 2 securely realizes* $\mathcal{F}_{\text{PSI}}$ *in the presence of malicious adversaries for* $n \geq 2$ *parties.*

Proof: Intuitively, correctness follows easily due to a similar argument as in the semi-honest case, where each element in P_1's set must zero all the other polynomials if it belongs to the intersection. Next, we consider two classes of adversaries. The first class involves adversaries that corrupt a subset of parties that includes party P_1, whereas the second class does not involve the corruption of P_1. We provide a separate simulation for each class.

Consider an adversary $\mathcal{A}$ that corrupts a strict subset $\mathcal{I}$ of parties from the set $\{P_1, \ldots, P_n\}$, including P_1. We define a simulator $\mathcal{S}$ as follows.

1. Given $\{X_i\}_{i \in \mathcal{I}}$ the simulator invokes the corrupted parties on their corresponding inputs and randomness.
2. $\mathcal{S}$ generates $(\text{PK}, \text{SK}) \leftarrow \text{Gen}(1^\kappa)$ and invokes the simulator $\mathcal{S}_{\text{GEN}}(\text{PK})$ for $\pi_{\text{GEN}}^{\text{ML}}$ in the key generation phase.
3. Next, $\mathcal{S}$ extracts the input X_1' of P_1 by invoking the extractor of the proof of knowledge π_{EXP}.
4. $\mathcal{S}$ plays the role of the honest parties against P_1 on arbitrary sets of inputs.
5. Finally, at the concluding phase the simulator completes the execution of the protocol as follows. $\mathcal{S}$ completes the verification phase as the honest parties would do. If the verification phase fails $\mathcal{S}$ aborts, sending $\perp$ to the trusted party.
6. Otherwise, $\mathcal{S}$ extracts the corrupted parties' inputs (excluding party P_1 for which its input has already been extracted). More concretely, the simulator repetitively rewinds the adversary to the beginning of Step 4b, where for every iteration the parties evaluate their polynomial at a randomly chosen point u and the simulator extracts the individual evaluations by running the

extractor of the proof of knowledge π_{EXP} and records these values only if they pass the verification phase.

Upon recording $d+1$ values for each corrupted party, the simulator reconstructs their polynomials and calculates the set of roots X_i of each polynomial $\lambda_i \cdot Q_i(\cdot)$ for $i \in \mathcal{I}$. In case $\mathcal{S}$ fails to record this many values, it outputs $\perp$.

7. $\mathcal{S}$ sends $\{X_i\}_{i\in\mathcal{I}}$ to the trusted party, receiving Z. $\mathcal{S}$ further verifies the π_{EVAL} proofs and aborts in case the verification fails.

8. Finally, for every $x_1^j \in Z$, $\mathcal{S}$ biases the decryption of the combined polynomials to be zero. Whereas for each $x_1^j \notin Z$, the simulator biases the decryption into a random group element by running the simulator $\mathcal{S}_{\mathrm{DecZero}}^{\mathrm{ML}}$ on the appropriate plaintext.

We briefly discuss the running time of the simulator. Observe that its running time is dominated by Step 6, when it repeatedly rewinds the adversary. Nevertheless, using a standard analysis, the expected number of rewindings can be shown to be polynomial. We next prove that the real and simulated executions are computationally indistinguishable. Note that the difference between the executions boils down to the privacy of the encryption scheme. Namely, the simulator sends encryptions of polynomials that were computed based on arbitrary inputs, as opposed to the honest parties' real inputs. Our proof follows via a sequence of hybrid games. We will begin with a scenario where P_1 is in the set of corrupted parties $\mathcal{I}$. When P_1 is honest, the proof is simpler and we discuss this at the end.

Hybrid$_0$: The first game is the real execution.

Hybrid$_1$: This hybrid is identical to the real world with the exception that the simulator $\mathcal{S}_1$ in this experiment extracts the corrupted parties inputs as in the simulation. More precisely, it extracts the inputs of all corrupted parties from π_{EXP} and π_{EVAL}, and aborts if it fails to extract. Since the probability that the simulator fails to extract is negligible, it follows that this hybrid is statistically close to the real world execution. Specifically, consider two cases. If the adversary passes the verification check in Step 4b with non-negligible probability, then using a standard argument the simulator will be able to extract enough evaluation points. On the other hand, if the probability that the simulator reaches the rewinding phase is negligible then indistinguishability will follow from the aborting views output by the simulator.

Hybrid$_2$: In this hybrid, the simulator extracts just as in **Hybrid$_1$** with the following modifications. First, it invokes simulator $\mathcal{S}_{\mathrm{GEN}}$ for protocol π_{GEN} in Step 1. In addition, if the simulator does not abort when executing Step 4b, it computes the set-intersection result Z based on the extracted inputs and the honest parties' inputs (which it knows in this hybrid). Next, it invokes simulator $\mathcal{S}_{\mathrm{DecZero}}$ of the decryption protocols that is invoked in Step 4e. Note that $\mathcal{S}_{\mathrm{DecZero}}$ is handed as plaintexts result of the set-intersection and needs to bias the outcome towards these set of plaintexts. That is, for each element $z \in X_1$ substituted in the combined polynomial in Step 4d, the simulator enforces the decryption to be zero, and a random element otherwise. Note that indistinguishability follows from the properties of the threshold decryption. In particular, the adversary's view in the previous hybrid includes the real execution of protocols π_{GEN} and π_{DEC}, whereas in the current hybrid the adversary's view includes the simulated protocols executions. We further claim that the adversary's set-intersection result is identical in both executions condition on the even that extraction follows successfully. This is due to the correctness enforced by the decryption protocol.

Hybrid$_3$: In this hybrid, the simulator changes all the proofs given by the honest parties in Step 4b to simulated ones. Moreover, recall that the simulator continues to extract the inputs of the corrupted parties. Now, since the zero-knowledge proof we employ in this step is simulation extractable, it follows that **Hybrid$_2$** and **Hybrid$_3$** are computationally indistinguishable. Namely, as we require this proof to be non-malleable and straight-line extractable, indistinguishability follows by simply posting either the real or the simulated proofs.

Hybrid$_4$: In this hybrid, the simulator changes the inputs of the honest parties in the 2PC phase to random inputs. Namely, the simulator sends the encryptions of a random polynomial on behalf of each honest party in Step 3. Then indistinguishability of **Hybrid$_3$** and **Hybrid$_4$** follows from the IND-CPA security of the underlying encryption scheme. Specifically, the simulator never needs to know the secret key of the encryption scheme, so that the ciphertexts obtained from the encryption oracle in the IND-CPA reduction can be directly plugged into the protocol. More concretely, a simple reduction can follow by providing an adversary $\mathcal{A}'$, who wishes to break the IND-CPA security of the underlying PKE, a public-key PK and a sequence of ciphertexts that either encrypt the real honest parties' polynomials or a set of random polynomials. $\mathcal{A}'$ emulates the simulator for this hybrid, with the exception that it plugs-in these ciphertexts on behalf of the honest parties in Step 3. Note that the adversary's view is either distributed according to the current or the prior hybrid execution, where the no information about the polynomials is revealed in Step 4c due to the random λ masks that yield random polynomials evaluations.

As **Hybrid$_4$** is identical to the real simulator, the proof of indistinguishabiliy follows via a standard hybrid argument.

Next, in the case that P_1 is not corrupted, the simulator further plays the role of this party in the simulation. In this case the proof follows almost as above with the difference that now the simulator uses a fake input for P_1 when emulating Step 4d. This requires two extra hybrid games in the proof for which the simulator switches to P_1's real input, reducing security to the privacy of the underlying encryption scheme and the zero-knowledge property of π_{EVAL}. ∎

4.1   An Instantiation of π_{EXP} Based on DDH and the Random Oracle

Our first instantiation uses the following building blocks. First, we use the El Gamal PKE as the threshold additively homomorphic encryption scheme;

we elaborate in Sect. 2.3 regarding this scheme. We further consider Pedersen's commitment scheme [Ped91] for the commitment scheme made by P_1 in Step 2 (see Sect. 2.5 for the details of this commitment scheme). Finally we realize π_{EXP} using a standard Σ-protocol for the following relation

$$\mathcal{R}_{\mathrm{EXP}} = \{((\mathbb{G}, g, h, h'), (m, r)) \mid h' = g^m h^r\}.$$

We invoke this proof in two places in our protocol. First, P_1 proves the knowledge of its committed input in Step 2. Next, the parties prove the knowledge of their evaluated polynomial in Step 4b (where for any El Gamal type ciphertext $\langle c_1, c_2 \rangle = \langle g^r, h^r \cdot g^m \rangle$ it is sufficient to prove the knowledge with respect to the second group element c_2, which can be viewed as a Pedersen's commitment). Importantly, as the latter proof must meet the non-malleability property, we consider its non-interactive variant using the Fiat-Shamir heuristic [FS86] which is analyzed in the Random Oracle Model of Bellare and Rogaway [BR93]. Finally, we note that the overhead of this proof is constant. As mentioned before, we need the proofs to satisfy the stronger simulation-extractability property. If we assume the stronger programmability property of random oracles, we can show that these proofs are non-malleable and straight-line extractable. For more details, see [FKMV12].

4.2 An Instantiation of π_{EXP} Based on the DLIN Hardness Assumption

Our second instantiation is based on the [BBS04] PKE that is based on the DLIN hardness assumption and the simulation-sound NIZK by Groth [Gro06]. In this work, Groth demonstrates NIZK proofs of knowledge for Pedersen's commitment scheme, which can be used by P_1 in Step 2 as in the previous instantiation, and for a plaintext knowledge relative to [BBS04] which can be used by the parties in Step 4b. To achieve non-malleability we will require that an independent common reference string is sampled between every pair of parties.

4.3 Communication and Computation Complexities

Denoting by m_{MIN} (resp. m_{MAX}) the minimum (resp. maximum) over all input sets sizes and n is the number of parties, we set $m_1 = m_{\mathrm{MIN}}$. Next, note that the communication complexity of Protocol 2 is dominated by the following factors: (1) First, $O(n^2)$ groups elements in the threshold key generation phase in Step 1, in the coin tossing generation phase in Step 4b and in Step 4c where the parties broadcast their polynomial evaluation. (2) Second, the 2PC step for which each party P_i computes its own polynomial boils down to $O(\sum_i m_i)$ and finally, (3) the broadcast of the combined protocol and the overhead of the zero-knowledge proof π_{EVAL} yield $O(n \cdot m_{\mathrm{MAX}} + n \cdot m_{\mathrm{MIN}} \cdot \log m_{\mathrm{MAX}})$. All together this implies $O((n^2 + n \cdot m_{\mathrm{MAX}} + n \cdot m_{\mathrm{MIN}} \cdot \log m_{\mathrm{MAX}})\kappa)$ bits of communication.

In addition to the above, except for party P_1, the computational complexity of each party P_i is $O(m_{\mathrm{MAX}})$ exponentiations plus $O(m_{\mathrm{MIN}} \cdot m_{\mathrm{MAX}})$ groups multiplications, whereas party P_1 needs to perform $O(m_1 \cdot m_{\mathrm{MAX}})$ exponentiations.

References

[ABKU99] Azar, Y., Broder, A.Z., Karlin, A.R., Upfal, E.: Balanced allocations. SIAM J. Comput. **29**(1), 180–200 (1999)

[ACT11] Ateniese, G., De Cristofaro, E., Tsudik, G.: (If) size matters: size-hiding private set intersection. In: Catalano, D., Fazio, N., Gennaro, R., Nicolosi, A. (eds.) PKC 2011. LNCS, vol. 6571, pp. 156–173. Springer, Heidelberg (2011). doi:10.1007/978-3-642-19379-8_10

[AMP04] Aggarwal, G., Mishra, N., Pinkas, B.: Secure computation of the kth-ranked element. In: Cachin, C., Camenisch, J.L. (eds.) EUROCRYPT 2004. LNCS, vol. 3027, pp. 40–55. Springer, Heidelberg (2004). doi:10.1007/978-3-540-24676-3_3

[BBS04] Boneh, D., Boyen, X., Shacham, H.: Short group signatures. In: Franklin, M. (ed.) CRYPTO 2004. LNCS, vol. 3152, pp. 41–55. Springer, Heidelberg (2004). doi:10.1007/978-3-540-28628-8_3

[BDOZ11] Bendlin, R., Damgård, I., Orlandi, C., Zakarias, S.: Semi-homomorphic encryption and multiparty computation. In: Paterson, K.G. (ed.) EURO-CRYPT 2011. LNCS, vol. 6632, pp. 169–188. Springer, Heidelberg (2011). doi:10.1007/978-3-642-20465-4_11

[Bea91] Beaver, D.: Foundations of secure interactive computing. In: Feigenbaum, J. (ed.) CRYPTO 1991. LNCS, vol. 576, pp. 377–391. Springer, Heidelberg (1992). doi:10.1007/3-540-46766-1_31

[BG13] Bayer, S., Groth, J.: Zero-knowledge argument for polynomial evaluation with application to blacklists. In: Johansson, T., Nguyen, P.Q. (eds.) EUROCRYPT 2013. LNCS, vol. 7881, pp. 646–663. Springer, Heidelberg (2013). doi:10.1007/978-3-642-38348-9_38

[BGN05] Boneh, D., Goh, E.-J., Nissim, K.: Evaluating 2-DNF formulas on cipher-texts. In: Kilian, J. (ed.) TCC 2005. LNCS, vol. 3378, pp. 325–341. Springer, Heidelberg (2005). doi:10.1007/978-3-540-30576-7_18

[BMR90] Beaver, D., Micali, S., Rogaway, P.: The round complexity of secure pro-tocols. In: STOC 1990, pp. 503–513 (1990)

[BR93] Bellare, M., Rogaway, P.: Random oracles are practical: a paradigm for designing efficient protocols. In: CCS, pp. 62–73 (1993)

[CJS12] Cheon, J.H., Jarecki, S., Seo, J.H.: Multi-party privacy-preserving set intersection with quasi-linear complexity. IEICE Trans. **95–A**(8), 1366–1378 (2012)

[CKMZ14] Choi, S.G., Katz, J., Malozemoff, A.J., Zikas, V.: Efficient three-party computation from cut-and-choose. In: Garay, J.A., Gennaro, R. (eds.) CRYPTO 2014. LNCS, vol. 8617, pp. 513–530. Springer, Heidelberg (2014). doi:10.1007/978-3-662-44381-1_29

[CKT10] De Cristofaro, E., Kim, J., Tsudik, G.: Linear-complexity private set intersection protocols secure in malicious model. In: Abe, M. (ed.) ASI-ACRYPT 2010. LNCS, vol. 6477, pp. 213–231. Springer, Heidelberg (2010). doi:10.1007/978-3-642-17373-8_13

[CT10] De Cristofaro, E., Tsudik, G.: Practical private set intersection protocols with linear complexity. In: Sion, R. (ed.) FC 2010. LNCS, vol. 6052, pp. 143–159. Springer, Heidelberg (2010). doi:10.1007/978-3-642-14577-3_13

[DCW13] Dong, C., Chen, L., Wen, Z.: When private set intersection meets big data: an efficient and scalable protocol. In: CCS, pp. 789–800 (2013)

[DH76] Diffie, W., Hellman, M.E.: New directions in cryptography. IEEE Trans. Inf. Theor. **22**(6), 644–654 (1976)

[DJ01] Damgård, I., Jurik, M.: A generalisation, a simplification and some applications of paillier's probabilistic public-key system. In: Kim, K. (ed.) PKC 2001. LNCS, vol. 1992, pp. 119–136. Springer, Heidelberg (2001). doi:10.1007/3-540-44586-2_9

[DMRY11] Dachman-Soled, D., Malkin, T., Raykova, M., Yung, M.: Secure efficient multiparty computing of multivariate polynomials and applications. In: Lopez, J., Tsudik, G. (eds.) ACNS 2011. LNCS, vol. 6715, pp. 130–146. Springer, Heidelberg (2011). doi:10.1007/978-3-642-21554-4_8

[DN02] Damgård, I., Nielsen, J.B.: Perfect hiding and perfect binding universally composable commitment schemes with constant expansion factor. In: Yung, M. (ed.) CRYPTO 2002. LNCS, vol. 2442, pp. 581–596. Springer, Heidelberg (2002). doi:10.1007/3-540-45708-9_37

[DPSZ12] Damgård, I., Pastro, V., Smart, N.P., Zakarias, S.: Multiparty computation from somewhat homomorphic encryption. In: Safavi-Naini, R., Canetti, R. (eds.) CRYPTO 2012. LNCS, vol. 7417, pp. 643–662. Springer, Heidelberg (2012). doi:10.1007/978-3-642-32009-5_38

[DSMRY09] Dachman-Soled, D., Malkin, T., Raykova, M., Yung, M.: Efficient robust private set intersection. In: Abdalla, M., Pointcheval, D., Fouque, P.-A., Vergnaud, D. (eds.) ACNS 2009. LNCS, vol. 5536, pp. 125–142. Springer, Heidelberg (2009). doi:10.1007/978-3-642-01957-9_8

[FHNP16] Freedman, M.J., Hazay, C., Nissim, K., Pinkas, B.: Efficient set intersection with simulation-based security. J. Cryptol. **29**(1), 115–155 (2016)

[FIPR05] Freedman, M.J., Ishai, Y., Pinkas, B., Reingold, O.: Keyword search and oblivious pseudorandom functions. In: Kilian, J. (ed.) TCC 2005. LNCS, vol. 3378, pp. 303–324. Springer, Heidelberg (2005). doi:10.1007/978-3-540-30576-7_17

[FJN+13] Frederiksen, T.K., Jakobsen, T.P., Nielsen, J.B., Nordholt, P.S., Orlandi, C.: MiniLEGO: efficient secure two-party computation from general assumptions. In: Johansson, T., Nguyen, P.Q. (eds.) EUROCRYPT 2013. LNCS, vol. 7881, pp. 537–556. Springer, Heidelberg (2013). doi:10.1007/978-3-642-38348-9_32

[FKMV12] Faust, S., Kohlweiss, M., Marson, G.A., Venturi, D.: On the non-malleability of the fiat-shamir transform. In: Galbraith, S., Nandi, M. (eds.) INDOCRYPT 2012. LNCS, vol. 7668, pp. 60–79. Springer, Heidelberg (2012). doi:10.1007/978-3-642-34931-7_5

[FNP04] Freedman, M.J., Nissim, K., Pinkas, B.: Efficient private matching and set intersection. In: Cachin, C., Camenisch, J.L. (eds.) EUROCRYPT 2004. LNCS, vol. 3027, pp. 1–19. Springer, Heidelberg (2004). doi:10.1007/978-3-540-24676-3_1

[FS86] Fiat, A., Shamir, A.: How to prove yourself: practical solutions to identification and signature problems. In: Odlyzko, A.M. (ed.) CRYPTO 1986. LNCS, vol. 263, pp. 186–194. Springer, Heidelberg (1987). doi:10.1007/3-540-47721-7_12

[Gam85] El Gamal, T.: A public key cryptosystem and a signature scheme based on discrete logarithms. IEEE Trans. Inf. Theor. **31**(4), 469–472 (1985)

[Gil99] Gilboa, N.: Two party RSA key generation. In: Wiener, M. (ed.) CRYPTO 1999. LNCS, vol. 1666, pp. 116–129. Springer, Heidelberg (1999). doi:10.1007/3-540-48405-1_8

[GLNP15] Gueron, S., Lindell, Y., Nof, A., Pinkas, B.: Fast garbling of circuits under standard assumptions. In: CCS, pp. 567–578 (2015)

[GMW87] Goldreich, O., Micali, S., Wigderson, A.: How to play any mental game or a completeness theorem for protocols with honest majority. In: STOC, pp. 218–229 (1987)

[Gro06] Groth, J.: Simulation-sound NIZK proofs for a practical language and constant size group signatures. In: Lai, X., Chen, K. (eds.) ASIACRYPT 2006. LNCS, vol. 4284, pp. 444–459. Springer, Heidelberg (2006). doi:10. 1007/11935230_29

[Haz15] Hazay, C.: Oblivious polynomial evaluation and secure set-intersection from algebraic PRFs. In: Dodis, Y., Nielsen, J.B. (eds.) TCC 2015. LNCS, vol. 9015, pp. 90–120. Springer, Heidelberg (2015). doi:10.1007/ 978-3-662-46497-7_4

[HEK12] Huang, Y., Evans, D., Katz, J.: Private set intersection: are garbled circuits better than custom protocols? In: NDSS (2012)

[HL10] Hazay, C., Lindell, Y.: Efficient protocols for set intersection and pattern matching with security against malicious and covert adversaries. J. Cryptol. **23**(3), 422–456 (2010)

[HLP11] Halevi, S., Lindell, Y., Pinkas, B.: Secure computation on the web: computing without simultaneous interaction. In: Rogaway, P. (ed.) CRYPTO 2011. LNCS, vol. 6841, pp. 132–150. Springer, Heidelberg (2011). doi:10. 1007/978-3-642-22792-9_8

[HMRT12] Hazay, C., Mikkelsen, G.L., Rabin, T., Toft, T.: Efficient RSA key generation and threshold paillier in the two-party setting. In: Dunkelman, O. (ed.) CT-RSA 2012. LNCS, vol. 7178, pp. 313–331. Springer, Heidelberg (2012). doi:10.1007/978-3-642-27954-6_20

[HN12] Hazay, C., Nissim, K.: Efficient set operations in the presence of malicious adversaries. J. Cryptol. **25**(3), 383–433 (2012)

[HT10] Hazay, C., Toft, T.: Computationally secure pattern matching in the presence of malicious adversaries. In: Abe, M. (ed.) ASIACRYPT 2010. LNCS, vol. 6477, pp. 195–212. Springer, Heidelberg (2010). doi:10.1007/ 978-3-642-17373-8_12

[IPS08] Ishai, Y., Prabhakaran, M., Sahai, A.: Founding cryptography on oblivious transfer – efficiently. In: Wagner, D. (ed.) CRYPTO 2008. LNCS, vol. 5157, pp. 572–591. Springer, Heidelberg (2008). doi:10.1007/ 978-3-540-85174-5_32

[JL09] Jarecki, S., Liu, X.: Efficient oblivious pseudorandom function with applications to adaptive OT and secure computation of set intersection. In: Reingold, O. (ed.) TCC 2009. LNCS, vol. 5444, pp. 577–594. Springer, Heidelberg (2009). doi:10.1007/978-3-642-00457-5_34

[JL10] Jarecki, S., Liu, X.: Fast secure computation of set intersection. In: Garay, J.A., Prisco, R. (eds.) SCN 2010. LNCS, vol. 6280, pp. 418–435. Springer, Heidelberg (2010). doi:10.1007/978-3-642-15317-4_26

[KOS16] Keller, M., Orsini, E., Scholl, P.: MASCOT: faster malicious arithmetic secure computation with oblivious transfer. IACR Cryptology ePrint Archive 2016:505 (2016)

[KS05] Kissner, L., Song, D.X.: Privacy-preserving set operations. In: Shoup, V. (ed.) CRYPTO 2005. LNCS, vol. 3621, pp. 241–257. Springer, Heidelberg (2005). doi:10.1007/11535218_15

[KSS12] Kreuter, B., Shelat, A., Shen, C.-H.: Billion-gate secure computation with malicious adversaries. In: USENIX, pp. 285–300 (2012)

[Lin16] Lindell, Y.: Fast cut-and-choose-based protocols for malicious and covert adversaries. J. Cryptol. **29**(2), 456–490 (2016)

[LOP11] Lindell, Y., Oxman, E., Pinkas, B.: The IPS compiler: optimizations, variants and concrete efficiency. In: Rogaway, P. (ed.) CRYPTO 2011. LNCS, vol. 6841, pp. 259–276. Springer, Heidelberg (2011). doi:10.1007/978-3-642-22792-9_15

[LPSY15] Lindell, Y., Pinkas, B., Smart, N.P., Yanai, A.: Efficient constant round multi-party computation combining BMR and SPDZ. In: Gennaro, R., Robshaw, M. (eds.) CRYPTO 2015. LNCS, vol. 9216, pp. 319–338. Springer, Heidelberg (2015). doi:10.1007/978-3-662-48000-7_16

[LSS16] Lindell, Y., Smart, N.P., Soria-Vazquez, E.: More efficient constant-round multi-party computation from BMR and SHE. In: Hirt, M., Smith, A. (eds.) TCC 2016. LNCS, vol. 9985, pp. 554–581. Springer, Heidelberg (2016). doi:10.1007/978-3-662-53641-4_21

[MN15] Miyaji, A., Nishida, S.: A scalable multiparty private set intersection. In: Qiu, M., Xu, S., Yung, M., Zhang, H. (eds.) NSS 2015. LNCS, vol. 9408, pp. 376–385. Springer, Cham (2015). doi:10.1007/978-3-319-25645-0_26

[MR91] Micali, S., Rogaway, P.: Secure computation. In: Feigenbaum, J. (ed.) CRYPTO 1991. LNCS, vol. 576, pp. 392–404. Springer, Heidelberg (1992). doi:10.1007/3-540-46766-1_32

[Pai99] Paillier, P.: Public-key cryptosystems based on composite degree residuosity classes. In: Stern, J. (ed.) EUROCRYPT 1999. LNCS, vol. 1592, pp. 223–238. Springer, Heidelberg (1999). doi:10.1007/3-540-48910-X_16

[Ped91] Pedersen, T.P.: Non-interactive and information-theoretic secure verifiable secret sharing. In: Feigenbaum, J. (ed.) CRYPTO 1991. LNCS, vol. 576, pp. 129–140. Springer, Heidelberg (1992). doi:10.1007/3-540-46766-1_9

[RS98] Raab, M., Steger, A.: "Balls into Bins" — a simple and tight analysis. In: Luby, M., Rolim, J.D.P., Serna, M. (eds.) RANDOM 1998. LNCS, vol. 1518, pp. 159–170. Springer, Heidelberg (1998). doi:10.1007/3-540-49543-6_13

[Sch89] Schnorr, C.P.: Efficient identification and signatures for smart cards. In: Brassard, G. (ed.) CRYPTO 1989. LNCS, vol. 435, pp. 239–252. Springer, New York (1990). doi:10.1007/0-387-34805-0_22

[SS07] Sang, Y., Shen, H.: Privacy preserving set intersection protocol secure against malicious behaviors. In: PDCAT, pp. 461–468 (2007)

[SS08] Sang, Y., Shen, H.: Privacy preserving set intersection based on bilinear groups. In: ACSC, pp. 47–54 (2008)

[SV15] Shelat, A., Venkitasubramaniam, M.: Secure computation from millionaire. In: Iwata, T., Cheon, J.H. (eds.) ASIACRYPT 2015. LNCS, vol. 9452, pp. 736–757. Springer, Heidelberg (2015). doi:10.1007/978-3-662-48797-6_30

[Ver11] Vergnaud, D.: Efficient and secure generalized pattern matching via fast fourier transform. In: Nitaj, A., Pointcheval, D. (eds.) AFRICACRYPT 2011. LNCS, vol. 6737, pp. 41–58. Springer, Heidelberg (2011). doi:10.1007/978-3-642-21969-6_3

[Vöc03] Vöcking, B.: How asymmetry helps load balancing. J. ACM **50**(4), 568–589 (2003)

[Wie07] Wieder, U.: Balanced allocations with heterogenous bins. In: SPAA, pp. 188–193 (2007)

[Yao86] Yao, A.C.-C.: How to generate and exchange secrets (extended abstract). In: FOCS, pp. 162–167 (1986)

Encryption Schemes

Tightly Secure IBE Under Constant-Size Master Public Key

Jie Chen[1,2](✉), Junqing Gong[3,4](✉), and Jian Weng[5](✉)

[1] East China Normal University, Shanghai, China
S080001@e.ntu.edu.sg
[2] State Key Laboratory of Information Security,
Institute of Information Engineering, Chinese Academy of Sciences, Beijing, China
[3] Shanghai Jiao Tong University, Shanghai, China
gongjunqing@126.com
[4] Laboratoire LIP, École Normale Supérieure de Lyon, Lyon, France
[5] Jinan University, Guangzhou, China
cryptjweng@gmail.com

Abstract. Chen and Wee [CRYPTO, 2013] proposed the first almost tightly and adaptively secure IBE in the standard model and left two open problems which called for a tightly secure IBE with (1) constant-size master public key and/or (2) constant security loss. In this paper, we propose an IBE scheme with *constant-size* master public key and *tighter* security reduction. This (partially) solves Chen and Wee's first open problem and makes progress on the second one. Technically, our IBE scheme is built based on Wee's petit IBE scheme [TCC, 2016] in the composite-order bilinear group whose order is product of four primes. The sizes of master public key, ciphertexts, and secret keys are not only constant but also nearly optimal as Wee's petit IBE. We can prove its adaptive security in the *multi-instance, multi-ciphertext* setting [PKC, 2015] based on the decisional subgroup assumption and a subgroup variant of DBDH assumption. The security loss is $\mathcal{O}(\log q)$ where q is the upper bound of the total number of secret keys and challenge ciphertexts per instance. It's much smaller than those for all known adaptively secure IBE schemes in a concrete sense.

1 Introduction

In 1984, Shamir introduced the notion of *identity based encryptions* [Sha84] (IBE). The entire system is maintained by an authority called *Key Generation*

J. Chen—Supported by the National Natural Science Foundation of China (Nos. 61472142, 61632012) and the Science and Technology Commission of Shanghai Municipality (No. 14YF1404200). Part of this work was done while at École Normale Supérieure de Lyon in France. http://www.jchen.top

J. Gong—Supported by the French ANR ALAMBIC project (ANR-16-CE39-0006).

J. Weng—Supported by the National Natural Science Foundation of China (Nos. 61272413, 61472165, 61133014).

© International Association for Cryptologic Research 2017
S. Fehr (Ed.): PKC 2017, Part I, LNCS 10174, pp. 207–231, 2017.
DOI: 10.1007/978-3-662-54365-8_9

Center (KGC) who publishes a master public key MPK and keeps the master secret key MSK. Each user receives his/her secret key SK for decryption from KGC which is produced using MSK. To encrypt a message to a user in the system, one only needs MPK and user's identity ID, which can be a descriptive tag such as email address.

Boneh and Franklin, in their seminal work [BF01] in 2001, formulated the security notion of IBE and proposed a pairing-based IBE in the random oracle model. Their security model has been accepted as standard model for IBE which ensures that a ciphertext for target identity ID* reveals nothing of the plaintext even when adversary $\mathcal{A}$ holding MPK can obtain secret keys for any identity other than ID*. We call it *adaptive security* in the paper. After that, a series of work were devoted to constructing IBE schemes in the standard model (i.e., without random oracle) including Boneh and Boyen's IBE [BB04a] in the selective model[1], Boneh and Boyen's IBE [BB04b] with huge security loss, Waters' IBE [Wat05] with large MPK, and Gentry's IBE [Gen06] based on q-type assumption. The *dual system methodology* was proposed in 2009 by Waters [Wat09]. With this novel and powerful proof technique, Waters proposed an IBE scheme with constant-size MPK in the standard model. The adaptive security is proven based on standard and static complexity assumptions, and the security loss is proportional to the amount of secret keys held by the adversary. This is the first IBE scheme achieving all these features simultaneously.

Since Waters deals with only one secret key at a time in the proof, a security loss of such an order of magnitude seems to be inherent. Fortunately, Chen and Wee [CW13] combined the proof idea underlying Naor-Reingold PRF [NR04] and the dual system methodology and showed an *almost-tightly* secure IBE scheme. Here *almost tight* means the security loss can be bounded by a polynomial in security parameter λ instead of the number of revealed secret keys. Soon afterwards, Blazy *et al.* [BKP14] described a generic transformation from affine MAC to IBE and constructed an affine MAC with almost-tight reduction. Their method essentially follows Chen and Wee's [CW13] but leads to a more efficient IBE. Recently, the study of almost-tightly secure IBE has extended to the *multi-instance, multi-ciphertext setting* [HKS15, GCD+16, AHY15, GDCC16]. However the following two problems left by Chen and Wee [CW13] still remain open.

Question 1. Can we achieve master public key of constant size?
Question 2. Can we achieve constantly tight reduction?

It's worth noting that Attrapadung *et al.* [AHY15] provided a technique achieving a trade-off between the size of master public key and sizes of secret keys and ciphertexts. As a special case, they can indeed reach constant-size master public key but at the cost of larger secret keys and ciphertexts (and vice

---

[1] In the selective model, the adversary has to choose the target identity ID* before seeing MPK. This is weaker than Boneh and Franklin's adaptive security model.

versa). Here we do not consider this as a satisfactory solution to Chen and Wee's first open problem. One must preserve advantages of Chen and Wee's IBE such as constant-size secret keys and ciphertexts.

1.1 Our Contribution

In this paper, we present an IBE scheme in the composite-order bilinear group [BGN05] with constant-size master public key, ciphertexts, and secret keys. The adaptive security in the multi-instance, multi-ciphertext setting relies on several concrete decisional subgroup assumptions [BWY11] and a subgroup variant of decisional bilinear Diffie-Hellman (DBDH) assumption. The security reduction arises a probability loss of $\mathcal{O}(\log q)$ in which q is the upper bound of the total number of secret keys and challenge ciphertexts per instance.

We make a comparison in Table 1. On one hand, our IBE has the shortest master public key, ciphertexts, secret keys and fastest decryption algorithm Dec. In fact the performance is nearly optimal as Wee's petit IBE [Wee16]. On the other hand, we achieve a tighter reduction in a concrete sense[2]. Under typical setting where $q = 2^{30}$ and $n = 128$, the security loss of our IBE scheme is just a quarter of those for all previous ones [CW13, HKS15, AHY15]. Therefore our result (partially) answers Chen and Wee's first open problem and makes a significant progress on the second one. We emphasize that the multi-instance, multi-ciphertext setting [HKS15] is more realistic and complex than Boneh and Franklin's standard security notion [BF01]. This means that we are actually working on Chen and Wee's open problems in a more complex setting.

Our Strategy. Chen and Wee [CW13] have pointed out that solving these two open problems may require some kinds of progresses in the underlying PRF, which is another long-standing problem. As our high-level strategy, we reverse the problem in order to circumvent the technical difficulty. In particular, instead of reducing the size of master public key of a tightly secure IBE to constant, we try to *improve the tightness of an IBE scheme already with constant-size master public key*. Technically, we propose a variant of Wee's petit IBE [Wee16] which is tightly secure and inherits all advantages from Wee's petit IBE. Our work is inspired by Chen and Wee's tight reduction technique from a very high level and brings Chase and Meiklejohn's idea [CM14] back to Wee's petit IBE [Wee16] in order to fulfil the intuition.

Our Method. Assume composite-order bilinear group $(N = p_1 p_2 p_3, \mathbb{G}, \mathbb{G}_T, e)$. Let's review Wee's petit IBE [Wee16]. From a high level, Wee followed the dual system methodology [Wat09] and employed Déjà Q technique [CM14] with an

---

[2] Let λ be the security parameter. In the common case that $n = \text{poly}(\lambda)$ and $q = \text{poly}(\lambda)$, we can see that $\mathcal{O}(n)$ and $\mathcal{O}(\log q)$ are equivalent to $\mathcal{O}(\lambda)$ and $\mathcal{O}(\log \lambda)$, respectively. Superficially, our reduction is also tighter in an asymptotical sense. However $\mathcal{O}(\log \lambda)$ here contains an adversarially-dependent constant while $\mathcal{O}(\lambda)$ is totally independent of adversary.

Table 1. Comparing existing tightly secure IBE in the composite-order bilinear group.

Scheme	$|\text{MPK}|$	$|\text{SK}|$	$|\text{CT}| + |\text{KEY}|$	Dec	Tightness	$\# p_i$	Mimc
[CW13]	$\mathcal{O}(n)|\mathbb{G}| + |\mathbb{G}_T|$	$2|\mathbb{G}|$	$2|\mathbb{G}| + |\mathbb{G}_T|$	2$\mathbb{P}$	$\mathcal{O}(n)$	3	No
[HKS15]	$\mathcal{O}(n)|\mathbb{G}| + |\mathbb{G}_T|$	$2|\mathbb{G}|$	$2|\mathbb{G}| + |\mathbb{G}_T|$	2$\mathbb{P}$	$\mathcal{O}(n)$	4	Yes
[AHY15]	$\mathcal{O}(n)|\mathbb{G}| + |\mathbb{G}_T|$	$2|\mathbb{G}|$	$2|\mathbb{G}| + |\mathbb{G}_T|$	2$\mathbb{P}$	$\mathcal{O}(n)$	4	Yes
	$8|\mathbb{G}| + |\mathbb{G}_T|$	$\mathcal{O}(n)|\mathbb{G}|$	$\mathcal{O}(n)|\mathbb{G}| + |\mathbb{G}_T|$	$\mathcal{O}(n)\mathbb{P}$	$\mathcal{O}(n)$	4	Yes
Ours	$2|\mathbb{G}| + |\mathbb{G}_T|$	$|\mathbb{G}|$	$|\mathbb{G}| + |\mathbb{G}_T|$	1$\mathbb{P}$	$\mathcal{O}(\log q)$	4	Yes

- In the table, n is the binary length of identities, q is the upper bound of total number of secret keys and challenge ciphertexts revealed to adversary in each instance.
- Column "$\# p_i$" shows the number of prime factors of group order N.
- Column "mimc" indicates whether the scheme can be proved in the multi-instance, multi-ciphertext setting.
- The two sub-rows of row "[AHY15]" are for scheme $\Phi_{\text{cc}}^{\text{comp}}$ and $\Phi_{\text{slp}}^{\text{comp}}$, respectively. Note that $\Phi_{\text{slp}}^{\text{comp}}$ employs the trade-off technique we have mentioned, and we just show the parameter of an instantiation with constant MPK in the table.

extension. The IBE scheme is quite elegant as we described below.

$$\text{MPK} : g_1, \; g_1^\alpha, \; e(g_1, u), \; \mathsf{H}$$

$$\text{SK}_{\text{ID}} : u^{\frac{1}{\alpha+\text{ID}}} \cdot R_3$$

$$\text{CT}_{\text{ID}} : g_1^{(\alpha+\text{ID})s}, \; \mathsf{H}(e(g_1, u)^s) \cdot \text{M}$$

where $g_1, u \leftarrow \mathbb{G}_{p_1}$, $\alpha, s \leftarrow \mathbb{Z}_N$, $R_3 \leftarrow \mathbb{G}_{p_3}$, H is selected from a pairwise independent hash family. Here we consider $\mathbb{G}_{p_1}$ as normal space and $\mathbb{G}_{p_2}$ as semi-functional space. Subgroup $\mathbb{G}_{p_3}$ is used to randomize secret keys.

To prove the adaptive security, he first transformed the challenge ciphertext into the form

$$\text{CT}_{\text{ID}^*} : S, \; \mathsf{H}(e(S, \text{SK}_{\text{ID}^*})) \cdot \text{M}$$

where $S \leftarrow \mathbb{G}_{p_1}\mathbb{G}_{p_2}$ and SK_{ID^*} is a secret key for target identity ID^*. The core step is to inject enough entropy into the semi-functional space of SK_{ID} for all ID "touched" by adversary (including the target identity ID^*). More formally, define

$$f_i(x) = \sum_{j=1}^{i} \frac{r_j}{\alpha_j + x} \in \mathbb{Z}_{p_2}$$

where $r_1, \ldots, r_i, \alpha_1, \ldots, \alpha_i \leftarrow \mathbb{Z}_{p_2}$. It has been proved that f_q behaves like a truly random function given only q input-output pairs [Wee16, CM14] where q depends on the total number of identities involved (in secret keys revealed to adversary and the challenge ciphertext). The remaining task is to transform all involved secret keys (including that used in CT_{ID^*})

$$\text{from} \quad u^{\frac{1}{\alpha+\text{ID}}} \cdot \boxed{g_2^{f_0(\text{ID})}} \cdot R_3 \quad \text{into} \quad u^{\frac{1}{\alpha+\text{ID}}} \cdot \boxed{g_2^{f_q(\text{ID})}} \cdot R_3$$

where $f_0(\text{ID}) = 0$ for all ID. Wee reached f_q in q steps following the roadmap

$$f_0 \to f_1 \to f_2 \to \cdots \to f_q.$$

In the kth step, he extracted one unit of entropy r_k and α_k from the normal space (i.e., from u and α) and injected them into the semi-functional space (i.e., into f_{k-1}). We illustrate the process in the graph below.

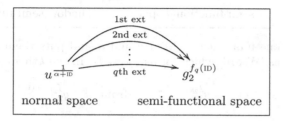

Chen and Wee's success [CW13] teaches us that one must reach f_q much more quickly in order to obtain tighter reduction. In other word, we should try to extract and inject more entropy each time. Our idea is to extract entropy from f_k ($1 \le k \le q$) itself rather than from u and α, and then inject them back into f_k. A key observation is that f_k already has k units of entropy (i.e., $\alpha_1, r_1, \ldots, \alpha_k, r_k$) and the structure of f_k allows us to reach f_{2k} directly which will include $2k$ units of entropy. This significantly accelerates the process towards f_q. In particular, the roadmap now becomes

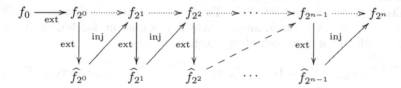

where $\widehat{f_k}$ indicates the entropy extracted from f_k, both of which have the same structure but $\widehat{f_k}$ are defined by independent randomness over $\mathbb{Z}_{p_3}$. It's not hard to see that we only need $n = \lceil \log q \rceil + 1$ steps to reach f_q.

To fulfill the above intuition, we introduce another semi-functional space, which we call *shadow semi-functional space*, to temporarily store the entropy extracted from f_k (i.e., $\widehat{f_k}$ in the above graph) since we obviously can not put them into the normal space. Furthermore the new semi-functional space should allow us to flip all entropy back to the old semi-functional space as Chase and Meiklejohn [CM14] did. We sketch our method in the following graph where the IBE is now put into a bilinear group of order $N = p_1 p_2 p_3 p_4$. Subgroup $\mathbb{G}_{p_3}$ acts as the shadow semi-functional space and $\mathbb{G}_{p_4}$ is used to randomize secret key.

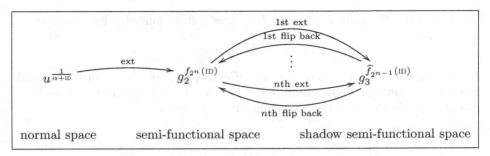

We first extract one unit entropy from u and α and puts them into the semi-functional space as [Wee16] which forms $f_{2^0} = f_1$. In the kth step, we first

$$\text{extract} \quad g_3^{\widehat{f}_{2^{k-1}}(\text{ID})} \quad \text{from} \quad g_2^{f_{2^{k-1}}(\text{ID})}$$

and then

$$\text{flip} \quad g_3^{\widehat{f}_{2^{k-1}}(\text{ID})} \quad \text{back as} \quad g_2^{\widehat{f}_{2^{k-1}}(\text{ID})}$$

which forms $g_2^{f_{2^k}(\text{ID})}$ together with $g_2^{f_{2^{k-1}}(\text{ID})}$. All these technical steps can be realized under several concrete instantiations of decisional subgroup assumption.

On the Multi-ciphertext Setting. We find that Wee's proof idea [Wee16] and our extension (see above) can be directly extended to the (single-instance) multi-ciphertext setting but with the restriction that only one challenge ciphertext is allowed for each target identity. This is the *weak* version of adaptive security in the multi-ciphertext setting [HKS15]. The first observation is that each challenge ciphertext has its own randomness s which is sufficient for hiding α on the ciphertext side. That is we can always argue

$$\{g_1^{(\alpha+\text{ID})s}, \ e(g_1, u)^s\} = \{g_1^{(\alpha+\text{ID})s}, \ e(g_1^{(\alpha+\text{ID})s}, u^{\frac{1}{\alpha+\text{ID}}})\} = \{g_1^s, \ e(g_1^s, u^{\frac{1}{\alpha+\text{ID}}})\}$$

even when there are more than one challenge ciphertexts; the second observation is that it's adequate to cope with more than one target identity by setting $n = \lceil \log q_\sigma \rceil$ where q_σ is the total number of reveal keys and challenge ciphertexts. The restriction is set here so as to avoid the following situation: After reaching f_{2^n}, all l challenge ciphertexts for target identity ID^* will be in the form

$$S_1, \ \mathsf{H}(e(S_1, u^{\frac{1}{\alpha+\text{ID}^*}}) \cdot \boxed{e(S_1, g_2^{f_{2^n}(\text{ID}^*)})}) \cdot \mathsf{M}_1, \quad S_1 \leftarrow \mathbb{G}_{p_1}\mathbb{G}_{p_2};$$

$$S_2, \ \mathsf{H}(e(S_2, u^{\frac{1}{\alpha+\text{ID}^*}}) \cdot \boxed{e(S_2, g_2^{f_{2^n}(\text{ID}^*)})}) \cdot \mathsf{M}_2, \quad S_2 \leftarrow \mathbb{G}_{p_1}\mathbb{G}_{p_2};$$

$$\vdots$$

$$S_l, \ \mathsf{H}(e(S_l, u^{\frac{1}{\alpha+\text{ID}^*}}) \cdot \boxed{e(S_l, g_2^{f_{2^n}(\text{ID}^*)})}) \cdot \mathsf{M}_l, \quad S_l \leftarrow \mathbb{G}_{p_1}\mathbb{G}_{p_2}$$

where boxed terms have their own randomness $S_1, \ldots, S_l$, but share the same $f_{2^n}(\text{ID}^*)$.

To remove this restriction and achieve the *full* adaptive security [HKS15], we employ a subgroup variant of decisional bilinear Diffie-Hellman (DBDH) assumption (in subgroup $\mathbb{G}_{p_2}$). This allows us to utilize randomness $S_1, \ldots, S_l$ and argues that the joint distribution of all boxed terms sharing $f_{2^n}(\text{ID}^*)$ are pseudorandom. Our proof idea is almost the same as [HKS15] but our assumption is slightly simpler.

On the Multi-instance Setting. Hofheinz *et al.* [HKS15] also investigated the so-called *multi-instance* setting where adversary $\mathcal{A}$ is allowed to attack multiple IBE instances at the same time. Fortunately, our technique and result in the single-instance setting (see above) can be extended to the multi-instance setting with a tiny adjustment. The high-level idea is to apply our proof technique (for the single-instance setting) to each instance in an *independent* but *concurrent* manner.

Assume there are τ instances. For the ι-th ($1 \leq \iota \leq \tau$) instance, we define a series of functions $f_{2^0}^{(\iota)}, \ldots, f_{2^n}^{(\iota)}$ as in the single-instance setting, which are independent of those for other instances. Here we let $n = \lceil \log \hat{q}_\sigma \rceil$ in which $\hat{q}_\sigma$ is the upper bound of the total number of revealed secret keys and challenge ciphertexts per instance. We depict the process in the graph below. In the ith step, we create τ functions $f_{2^i}^{(1)}, \ldots, f_{2^i}^{(\tau)}$ at a time using the random self-reducibility of decisional subgroup assumption.

$$
\begin{array}{lccccc}
\text{1st instance:} & f_{2^0}^{(1)} & f_{2^1}^{(1)} & f_{2^2}^{(1)} & & f_{2^n}^{(1)} \\
\text{2nd instance:} & f_{2^0}^{(2)} \longrightarrow & f_{2^1}^{(2)} \longrightarrow & f_{2^2}^{(2)} & \longrightarrow \cdots \longrightarrow & f_{2^n}^{(2)} \\
\vdots & & & & & \\
\tau\text{th instance:} & f_{2^0}^{(\tau)} & f_{2^1}^{(\tau)} & f_{2^2}^{(\tau)} & & f_{2^n}^{(\tau)} \\
& & \text{1st step} & \text{2nd step} & & n\text{th step}
\end{array}
$$

Then, utilizing the random self-reducibility of the subgroup variant of DBDH assumption, we can prove the full adaptive security in the multi-instance setting.

1.2   Related Work

The dual system methodology has been applied to broader area of functional encryptions [OT10,LOS+10]. In 2014, Wee [Wee14] and Attrapadung [Att14] independently gave generic constructions of a large class of functional encryptions with adaptive security including attribute based encryption, inner-product encryption, and even functional encryption for regular language. They introduced the notion of predicate/pair encoding and employed the dual system methodology in the composite-order bilinear group. Their work have been extended to the prime-order setting in [AC16, Att16, CGW15] recently.

Tight reduction under short public parameter has been studied in the field of digital signature. Very recently, Hofheinz developed algebraic partitioning technique [Hof16b] and adaptive partitioning technique [Hof16a] based on Chen and Wee's result [CW13], which leaded to tightly secure signatures with constant verification key and public key encryption against chosen ciphertext attack with similar features. However it's not quite direct to apply their technique to IBE.

Déjà Q technique was proposed by Chase and Meiklejohn [CM14]. They showed that one can avoid the use of (a class of) q-type assumptions with the help of a composite-order bilinear group equipped with decisional subgroup assumption using the dual system methodology. Recently, Wee gave a petit IBE scheme and broadcast encryption scheme [Wee16] with a extended Déjà Q technique. Their results have been used to build non-zero inner-product encryptions [CLR16] and functional commitments for linear functions [LRY16] (which implies many other important primitives such as accumulators.)

A recent work by Boyen and Li [BL16] established a generic framework from PRF to signatures and IBE utilizing the powerful tools in the lattice world. The reduction is constantly tight and the security loss of resulting scheme solely depends on that of underlying PRF. We remark that all tightly secure IBE schemes they showed still require non-constant-size master public key.

Independent Work. An independent work by Chase, Maller and Meiklejohn [CMM16] developed the basic Déjà Q technique [CM14] in a similar way to us. We focus on solving or making progress on two open problems left by Chen and Wee [CW13] in a specific area (i.e., tightly secure IBE) while Chase *et al.* focus on a more general goal, i.e., tightly translating a broader class of q-type assumptions into static one. Although they described four functional encryptions including an IBE scheme, its master public key consists of $\mathcal{O}(n)$ group elements with identity space $\{0,1\}^n$. As a matter of fact, neither Wee's IBE nor ours can be derived from an IBE under q-type assumption using Chase *et al.*'s new framework [CMM16]. Therefore we believe it's still necessary to propose and analyze the IBE directly.

Open Problem. Our proposed IBE scheme works in the composite-order bilinear group which can be a drawback. We leave it as an open problem to find a prime-order IBE with tight(er) reduction, constant-size master public key, secret keys and ciphertexts.

Organization. The paper will be organized as follows. Section 2 reviews several basic notions, the decisional subgroup assumption and a core lemma given by Wee [Wee16]. Section 3 describes our IBE scheme and proves the *weak* adaptive security in the single-instance, multi-ciphertext setting. We then extend the basic result to *full* adaptive security and *multi-instance* setting in Sects. 4 and 5, respectively.

2   Preliminaries

Notation. Let S be a finite set. The notation $s \leftarrow S$ means that we pick s from S at random. "p.p.t." is the abbreviation of "probabilistic polynomial time".

2.1 Composite-Order Bilinear Groups

Our IBE scheme is constructed in composite-order bilinear groups [BGN05]. We assume a group generator GrpGen which takes as input the security parameter 1^λ and outputs group description $\mathcal{G} = (N, \mathbb{G}, \mathbb{G}_T, e)$, where order N is product of 4 distinct $\Theta(\lambda)$-bit primes, group $\mathbb{G}$ and $\mathbb{G}_T$ are all finite cyclic groups of order N and e is an efficient, non-degenerated bilinear map from $\mathbb{G} \times \mathbb{G}$ to $\mathbb{G}_T$. With $N = p_1 p_2 p_3 p_4$ for primes p_1, p_2, p_3, p_4, we let $\mathbb{G}_{p_i}$ be the subgroup of order p_i in $\mathbb{G}$ and use $\mathbb{G}_{p_i}^*$ to refer to the set of all generators in $\mathbb{G}_{p_i}$, i.e., $\mathbb{G}_{p_i} \backslash \{1\}$.

We review several concrete instantiations of decisional subgroup assumption [BWY11]. Since we can uniquely decompose $\mathbb{G} = \mathbb{G}_{p_1} \times \mathbb{G}_{p_2} \times \mathbb{G}_{p_3} \times \mathbb{G}_{p_4}$, we employ a special notation for sampling random elements from a composite-order subgroup of $\mathbb{G}$. For any two prime factors p_i, p_j of N with $1 \leq i < j \leq 4$, we use $X_i X_j \leftarrow \mathbb{G}_{p_i} \mathbb{G}_{p_j}$ to indicate that we uniformly sample an element from the subgroup of order $p_i p_j$, whose respective components in $\mathbb{G}_{p_i}$, $\mathbb{G}_{p_j}$ are X_i, X_j. The notation can also be applied to more general cases.

Assumption 1 (SD1). *For any p.p.t. adversary $\mathcal{A}$ the following advantage function is negligible in λ.*

$$\mathsf{Adv}_{\mathcal{A}}^{\mathrm{SD1}}(\lambda) = |\Pr[\mathcal{A}(\mathcal{G}, g_1, g_4, T_0) = 1] - \Pr[\mathcal{A}(\mathcal{G}, g_1, g_4, T_1)]|,$$

where $\mathcal{G} \leftarrow \mathsf{GrpGen}(1^\lambda)$, $g_1 \leftarrow \mathbb{G}_{p_1}^*$, $g_4 \leftarrow \mathbb{G}_{p_4}^*$,

$$T_0 \leftarrow \mathbb{G}_{p_1} \quad and \quad T_1 \leftarrow \mathbb{G}_{p_1} \mathbb{G}_{p_2} \mathbb{G}_{p_3}.$$

Assumption 2 (SD2). *For any p.p.t. adversary $\mathcal{A}$ the following advantage function is negligible in λ.*

$$\mathsf{Adv}_{\mathcal{A}}^{\mathrm{SD2}}(\lambda) = |\Pr[\mathcal{A}(\mathcal{G}, g_1, g_4, X_1 X_2 X_3, T_0) = 1] - \Pr[\mathcal{A}(\mathcal{G}, g_1, g_4, X_1 X_2 X_3, T_1)]|,$$

where $\mathcal{G} \leftarrow \mathsf{GrpGen}(1^\lambda)$, $g_1 \leftarrow \mathbb{G}_{p_1}^*$, $g_4 \leftarrow \mathbb{G}_{p_4}^*$, $X_1 X_2 X_3 \leftarrow \mathbb{G}_{p_1} \mathbb{G}_{p_2} \mathbb{G}_{p_3}$,

$$T_0 \leftarrow \mathbb{G}_{p_1} \quad and \quad T_1 \leftarrow \mathbb{G}_{p_1} \mathbb{G}_{p_2}.$$

Assumption 3 (SD3). *For any p.p.t. adversary $\mathcal{A}$ the following advantage function is negligible in λ.*

$$\mathsf{Adv}_{\mathcal{A}}^{\mathrm{SD3}}(\lambda) = |\Pr[\mathcal{A}(\mathcal{G}, g_1, g_4, X_1 X_2 X_3, T_0) = 1] - \Pr[\mathcal{A}(\mathcal{G}, g_1, g_4, X_1 X_2 X_3, T_1)]|,$$

where $\mathcal{G} \leftarrow \mathsf{GrpGen}(1^\lambda)$, $g_1 \leftarrow \mathbb{G}_{p_1}^*$, $g_4 \leftarrow \mathbb{G}_{p_4}^*$, $X_1 X_2 X_3 \leftarrow \mathbb{G}_{p_1} \mathbb{G}_{p_2} \mathbb{G}_{p_3}$,

$$T_0 \leftarrow \mathbb{G}_{p_2} \quad and \quad T_1 \leftarrow \mathbb{G}_{p_2} \mathbb{G}_{p_3}.$$

Assumption 4 (SD4). *For any p.p.t. adversary $\mathcal{A}$ the following advantage function is negligible in λ.*

$$\mathsf{Adv}_{\mathcal{A}}^{\mathrm{SD4}}(\lambda) = |\Pr[\mathcal{A}(\mathcal{G}, g_1, g_4, X_1 X_2 X_3, Y_2 Y_4, T_0) = 1]$$
$$- \Pr[\mathcal{A}(\mathcal{G}, g_1, g_4, X_1 X_2 X_3, Y_2 Y_4, T_1)]|,$$

where $\mathcal{G} \leftarrow \mathsf{GrpGen}(1^\lambda)$, $g_1 \leftarrow \mathbb{G}_{p_1}^*$, $g_4 \leftarrow \mathbb{G}_{p_4}^*$, $X_1 X_2 X_3 \leftarrow \mathbb{G}_{p_1} \mathbb{G}_{p_2} \mathbb{G}_{p_3}$, $Y_2 Y_4 \leftarrow \mathbb{G}_{p_2} \mathbb{G}_{p_4}$,

$$T_0 \leftarrow \mathbb{G}_{p_2} \mathbb{G}_{p_4} \quad and \quad T_1 \leftarrow \mathbb{G}_{p_3} \mathbb{G}_{p_4}.$$

2.2   Identity Based Encryptions

In the paper we define the notion of identity based encryption (IBE) in the framework of key encapsulation mechanism (KEM).

Algorithms. An IBE (in the single-instance setting) is composed of the following four p.p.t. algorithms:

- Setup(1^λ) → (MPK, MSK). The *setup algorithm* Setup takes as input the security parameter 1^λ and outputs master public/secret key pair (MPK, MSK). We assume that MPK includes ciphertext space $\mathcal{C}$ and key space $\mathcal{K}$.
- KeyGen(MPK, MSK, ID) → SK. The *key generation algorithm* KeyGen takes as input the master public key MPK, the master secret key MSK and an identity ID and outputs its secret key SK.
- Enc(MPK, ID) → (CT, KEY). The *encryption algorithm* Enc takes as input the master public key MPK and an identity ID and outputs a ciphertext CT ∈ $\mathcal{C}$ along with key KEY ∈ $\mathcal{K}$.
- Dec(MPK, CT, SK) → KEY. The *decryption algorithm* Dec takes as input the master public key MPK, a ciphertext CT and a secret key SK and outputs key KEY or ⊥.

Correctness. For any $\lambda \in \mathbb{N}$, (MPK, MSK) $\in [\mathsf{Setup}(1^\lambda)]$, identity ID, we require

$$\Pr\left[\mathsf{Dec}(\text{MPK}, \text{CT}, \text{SK}) = \text{KEY} \,\middle|\, \begin{array}{l} \text{SK} \leftarrow \mathsf{KeyGen}(\text{MPK}, \text{MSK}, \text{ID}) \\ (\text{CT}, \text{KEY}) \leftarrow \mathsf{Enc}(\text{MPK}, \text{ID}) \end{array}\right] \geq 1 - 2^{-\Omega(\lambda)}.$$

The probability space is defined by random coins of KeyGen and Enc.

Security notion. For any adversary $\mathcal{A}$, we define the advantage function as

$$\mathsf{Adv}_{\mathcal{A}}^{\mathrm{IBE}}(\lambda) = \left| \Pr\left[\beta = \beta' \,\middle|\, \begin{array}{l} (\text{MPK}, \text{MSK}) \leftarrow \mathsf{Setup}(1^\lambda), \ \beta \leftarrow \{0, 1\} \\ \beta' \leftarrow \mathcal{A}^{\mathsf{O}^{\mathsf{KeyGen}}(\cdot), \mathsf{O}_\beta^{\mathsf{Enc}}(\cdot)}(1^\lambda, \text{MPK}) \end{array}\right] - \frac{1}{2} \right|$$

where oracles are defined as

- $\mathsf{O}^{\mathsf{KeyGen}}$: On input (ID), the oracle returns KeyGen(MPK, MSK, ID) and sets $Q_K = Q_K \cup \{\text{ID}\}$.
- $\mathsf{O}_\beta^{\mathsf{Enc}}$: On input (ID*), the oracle samples $(\text{CT}_1^*, \text{KEY}_1^*) \leftarrow \mathsf{Enc}(\text{MPK}, \text{ID}^*)$, $(\text{CT}_0^*, \text{KEY}_0^*) \leftarrow \mathcal{C} \times \mathcal{K}$ and returns $(\text{CT}_\beta^*, \text{KEY}_\beta^*)$. It then sets $Q_C = Q_C \cup \{\text{ID}^*\}$.

The probability is defined over random coins used by Setup, oracle $\mathsf{O}^{\mathsf{KeyGen}}$ and $\mathsf{O}_\beta^{\mathsf{Enc}}$, and adversary $\mathcal{A}$ as well as random bit β. We say an IBE is *adaptively secure and anonymous* if and only if the above advantage function is negligible in λ for any p.p.t. adversary such that $Q_C \cap Q_K = \emptyset$.

2.3   A Core Lemma

We review the lemma by Wee [Wee16] as follows.

Lemma 1. *Fix a prime p. For any adversary $\mathcal{A}$ making at most q queries, we have*

$$\left| \Pr\left[\mathcal{A}^{O^f(\cdot)}(1^q) = 1 \right] - \Pr\left[\mathcal{A}^{O^{RF}(\cdot)}(1^q) = 1 \right] \right| \leq \frac{q^2}{p}$$

where oracles are defined as

- O^f: *The oracle is initialized by picking $r_1, \ldots, r_q, \alpha_1, \ldots, \alpha_q \leftarrow \mathbb{Z}_p$. On input $x \in \mathbb{Z}_p$, it outputs*

$$\sum_{i=1}^{q} \frac{r_i}{\alpha_i + x} \in \mathbb{Z}_p.$$

  Every queries are answered using the same $r_1, \ldots, r_q, \alpha_1, \ldots, \alpha_q$ we picked at the very beginning.
- O^{RF}: *This oracle behaves as a truly random function $RF : \mathbb{Z}_p \to \mathbb{Z}_p$. On input $x \in \mathbb{Z}_p$, it returns $RF(x)$ if it has been defined, otherwise it returns $y \leftarrow \mathbb{Z}_p$ and defines $RF(x) = y$.*

3 Our IBE Scheme

This section describes our IBE scheme. At current stage, we prove its *weak* adaptive security and anonymity in the *single-instance*, multi-challenge setting, i.e., adversary can access only one IBE instance and only one challenge ciphertext is allowed for *each* target identity.

3.1 Construction

Our IBE scheme is described as follows.

- Setup(1^λ). Run $\mathcal{G} = (N, \mathbb{G}, \mathbb{G}_T, e) \leftarrow \mathsf{GrpGen}(1^\lambda)$. Sample

$$\alpha \leftarrow \mathbb{Z}_N, \quad g_1 \leftarrow \mathbb{G}_{p_1}^*, \quad u \leftarrow \mathbb{G}_{p_1}, \quad g_4 \leftarrow \mathbb{G}_{p_4}^*.$$

  Pick $H : \mathbb{G}_T \to \{0,1\}^\lambda$ from a pairwise independent hash family. Output

$$\mathrm{MPK} = (g_1, \ g_1^\alpha, \ e(g_1, u), \ H) \quad \text{and} \quad \mathrm{MSK} = (\alpha, u, g_4).$$

- KeyGen(MPK, MSK, ID). Sample $R_4 \leftarrow \mathbb{G}_{p_4}$ and output

$$\mathrm{SK} = u^{\frac{1}{\alpha + \mathrm{ID}}} \cdot R_4.$$

- Enc(MPK, ID). Sample $s \leftarrow \mathbb{Z}_N$ and output

$$\mathrm{CT} = g_1^{(\alpha + \mathrm{ID})s} \quad \text{and} \quad \mathrm{KEY} = H(e(g_1, u)^s).$$

- Dec(MPK, CT, SK). Return

$$\mathrm{KEY} = H(e(\mathrm{CT}, \mathrm{SK})).$$

Correctness. We have

$$e(\mathrm{CT}, \mathrm{SK}) = e(g_1^{(\alpha + \mathrm{ID})s}, u^{\frac{1}{\alpha + \mathrm{ID}}} \cdot R_4) = e(g_1, u)^{(\alpha + \mathrm{ID})s \cdot \frac{1}{\alpha + \mathrm{ID}}} = e(g_1, u)^s.$$

This immediately proves the correctness.

3.2 Security Analysis: An Overview

We prove the following theorem.

Theorem 1. *For any p.p.t. adversary $\mathcal{A}$ sending at most q_σ queries to $\mathsf{O}^{\mathsf{KeyGen}}$ and $\mathsf{O}^{\mathsf{Enc}}_\beta$, there exist $\mathcal{B}_1$, $\mathcal{B}_2$, $\mathcal{B}_3$, $\mathcal{B}_4$ such that*

$$\mathsf{Adv}^{\mathrm{IBE}}_{\mathcal{A}}(\lambda) \leq \frac{5}{2} \cdot \mathsf{Adv}^{\mathrm{SD1}}_{\mathcal{B}_1}(\lambda) + 2 \cdot \mathsf{Adv}^{\mathrm{SD2}}_{\mathcal{B}_2}(\lambda) + 2 \cdot \lceil \log q_\sigma \rceil \cdot \mathsf{Adv}^{\mathrm{SD3}}_{\mathcal{B}_3}(\lambda)$$

$$+ \left(2 \cdot \lceil \log q_\sigma \rceil + \frac{1}{2}\right) \cdot \mathsf{Adv}^{\mathrm{SD4}}_{\mathcal{B}_4}(\lambda) + 2^{-\Omega(\lambda)}$$

and $\max\{\mathsf{T}(\mathcal{B}_1), \mathsf{T}(\mathcal{B}_2), \mathsf{T}(\mathcal{B}_3), \mathsf{T}(\mathcal{B}_4)\} \approx \mathsf{T}(\mathcal{A}) + q_\sigma^2 \cdot \mathsf{poly}(\lambda)$.

We prove the theorem using hybrid argument. We define the advantage function of any p.p.t. adversary $\mathcal{A}$ in Game_{xxx} as

$$\mathsf{Adv}^{\mathsf{Game}_{xxx}}_{\mathcal{A}}(\lambda) = |\Pr[\beta = \beta'] - 1/2|$$

Let $n = \lceil \log q_\sigma \rceil$. Our proof employs the following game sequence.

$\boxed{\mathsf{Game}_{\mathsf{real}}}$ is the real game.

$\boxed{\mathsf{Game}_0}$ is the real game with the following assumptions:

- $\mathcal{A}$ can not find $\mathrm{ID}, \mathrm{ID}' \in \mathbb{Z}_N$ such that $\mathrm{ID} \neq \mathrm{ID}'$ but $\mathrm{ID} = \mathrm{ID}' \mod p_2$;
- $\mathcal{A}$ can not find $\mathrm{ID} \in \mathbb{Z}_N$ such that $\alpha + \mathrm{ID} = 0 \mod p_1$ even given α.

One may notice that $\mathcal{A}$ can efficiently factorize the order N and break the general decisional subgroup assumption when it violates one of the above two assumptions. Technically, Game_0 aborts immediately when $\mathcal{A}$ submits $\mathrm{ID} \in \mathbb{Z}_N$ (through $\mathsf{O}^{\mathsf{KeyGen}}$ or $\mathsf{O}^{\mathsf{Enc}}_\beta$) such that

- $\gcd(\mathrm{ID} - \mathrm{ID}', N) \notin \{1, N\}$ for some previous identity $\mathrm{ID}' \in \mathbb{Z}_N$;
- $\gcd(\alpha + \mathrm{ID}, N) \notin \{1, N\}$.

Note that both $N \in \mathbb{Z}$ and $\alpha \in \mathbb{Z}_N$ are always available throughout our proof. We prove the following lemma.

Lemma 2 (from $\mathsf{Game}_{\mathsf{real}}$ to Game_0). *For any p.p.t. adversary $\mathcal{A}$ sending at most q_σ queries to $\mathsf{O}^{\mathsf{KeyGen}}$ and $\mathsf{O}^{\mathsf{Enc}}_\beta$, there exist $\mathcal{B}_1$, $\mathcal{B}_2$ such that $\max\{\mathsf{T}(\mathcal{B}_1), \mathsf{T}(\mathcal{B}_2)\} \approx \mathsf{T}(\mathcal{A}) + q_\sigma \cdot \mathsf{poly}(\lambda)$ and*

$$|\mathsf{Adv}^{\mathsf{Game}_0}_{\mathcal{A}}(\lambda) - \mathsf{Adv}^{\mathsf{Game}_{\mathsf{real}}}_{\mathcal{A}}(\lambda)| \leq \frac{1}{2} \cdot \mathsf{Adv}^{\mathrm{SD1}}_{\mathcal{B}_1}(\lambda) + \frac{1}{2} \cdot \mathsf{Adv}^{\mathrm{SD4}}_{\mathcal{B}_2}(\lambda) + 2^{-\Omega(\lambda)}.$$

$\boxed{\mathsf{Game}'_0}$ is identical to Game_0 except that, for each query (ID^*) to $\mathsf{O}^{\mathsf{Enc}}_\beta$, we compute KEY^*_1 as

$$\mathrm{KEY}^*_1 = \mathsf{H}(e(\mathrm{CT}^*_1, \mathrm{SK}_{\mathrm{ID}^*}))$$

where CT^*_1 is produced as before and $\mathrm{SK}_{\mathrm{ID}^*}$ is obtained via a $\mathsf{O}^{\mathsf{KeyGen}}$ query (ID^*). From the correctness, we have that

$$\mathsf{Adv}^{\mathsf{Game}'_0}_{\mathcal{A}}(\lambda) = \mathsf{Adv}^{\mathsf{Game}_0}_{\mathcal{A}}(\lambda)$$

for any p.p.t. adversary $\mathcal{A}$.

Game_0'' is identical to Game_0' except that, for each query (ID^*) to $\mathsf{O}_\beta^{\mathsf{Enc}}$, we compute CT_1^* as

$$g_1^s \qquad \text{instead of} \qquad g_1^{(\alpha+\text{ID}^*)s}$$

where $s \leftarrow \mathbb{Z}_N$. We have

$$\mathsf{Adv}_{\mathcal{A}}^{\mathsf{Game}_0''}(\lambda) = \mathsf{Adv}_{\mathcal{A}}^{\mathsf{Game}_0'}(\lambda)$$

for any p.p.t. adversary $\mathcal{A}$ since the two games are exactly the same unless $\alpha + \text{ID}^* = 0 \bmod p_1$ for some query (ID^*). We emphasize that it holds even for the multiple challenge setting since s is freshly picked for each query. Game_1 is identical to Game_0'' except that, for each query (ID^*) to $\mathsf{O}_\beta^{\mathsf{Enc}}$, we compute CT_1^* as

$$(g_1 g_2 g_3)^s \qquad \text{instead of} \qquad g_1^s$$

where $s \leftarrow \mathbb{Z}_N$, $g_2 \leftarrow \mathbb{G}_{p_2}^*$ and $g_3 \leftarrow \mathbb{G}_{p_3}^*$. We prove the lemma.

Lemma 3 (from Game_0'' to Game_1). *For any p.p.t. adversary $\mathcal{A}$ sending at most q_σ queries to $\mathsf{O}^{\mathsf{KeyGen}}$ and $\mathsf{O}_\beta^{\mathsf{Enc}}$, there exists $\mathcal{B}$ with $\mathsf{T}(\mathcal{B}) \approx \mathsf{T}(\mathcal{A}) + q_\sigma \cdot \mathsf{poly}(\lambda)$ and*

$$|\mathsf{Adv}_{\mathcal{A}}^{\mathsf{Game}_1}(\lambda) - \mathsf{Adv}_{\mathcal{A}}^{\mathsf{Game}_0''}(\lambda)| \leq \mathsf{Adv}_{\mathcal{B}}^{\mathsf{SD1}}(\lambda) + 2^{-\Omega(\lambda)}.$$

$\mathsf{Game}_{2.i}$ $(0 \leq i \leq n, n = \lceil \log q_\sigma \rceil)$ is identical to Game_1 except that, for each query (ID) to $\mathsf{O}^{\mathsf{KeyGen}}$ (including those involved in $\mathsf{O}_\beta^{\mathsf{Enc}}$), we return

$$u^{\frac{1}{\alpha+\text{ID}}} \cdot \boxed{g_2^{\sum_{j=1}^{2^i} \frac{r_j}{\alpha_j+\text{ID}}}} \cdot R_4$$

where $g_2 \leftarrow \mathbb{G}_{p_2}^*$ and $\alpha_j, r_j \leftarrow \mathbb{Z}_N$ for all $j \in [2^i]$. We must prove the following lemma first.

Lemma 4 (from Game_1 to $\mathsf{Game}_{2.0}$). *For any p.p.t. adversary $\mathcal{A}$ sending at most q_σ queries to $\mathsf{O}^{\mathsf{KeyGen}}$ and $\mathsf{O}_\beta^{\mathsf{Enc}}$, there exists $\mathcal{B}$ with $\mathsf{T}(\mathcal{B}) \approx \mathsf{T}(\mathcal{A}) + q_\sigma \cdot \mathsf{poly}(\lambda)$ and*

$$|\mathsf{Adv}_{\mathcal{A}}^{\mathsf{Game}_{2.0}}(\lambda) - \mathsf{Adv}_{\mathcal{A}}^{\mathsf{Game}_1}(\lambda)| \leq \mathsf{Adv}_{\mathcal{B}}^{\mathsf{SD2}}(\lambda) + 2^{-\Omega(\lambda)}.$$

To move from $\mathsf{Game}_{2.i}$ to $\mathsf{Game}_{2.(i+1)}$, we need two additional games:

- $\mathsf{Game}_{2.i.1}$ is identical to $\mathsf{Game}_{2.i}$ except that, for each query (ID) to $\mathsf{O}^{\mathsf{KeyGen}}$, we return

$$u^{\frac{1}{\alpha+\text{ID}}} \cdot g_2^{\sum_{j=1}^{2^i} \frac{r_j}{\alpha_j+\text{ID}}} \cdot \boxed{g_3^{\sum_{j=1}^{2^i} \frac{\widehat{r}_j}{\widehat{\alpha}_j+\text{ID}}}} \cdot R_4$$

where $g_3 \leftarrow \mathbb{G}_{p_3}^*$ and $\alpha_j, r_j, \widehat{\alpha}_j, \widehat{r}_j \leftarrow \mathbb{Z}_N$ for all $j \in [2^i]$.
- $\mathsf{Game}_{2.i.2}$ is identical to $\mathsf{Game}_{2.i}$ except that, for each query (ID) to $\mathsf{O}^{\mathsf{KeyGen}}$, we return

$$u^{\frac{1}{\alpha+\text{ID}}} \cdot g_2^{\sum_{j=1}^{2^i} \frac{r_j}{\alpha_j+\text{ID}} + \boxed{\sum_{j=1}^{2^i} \frac{\widehat{r}_j}{\widehat{\alpha}_j+\text{ID}}}} \cdot R_4$$

where $\alpha_j, r_j, \widehat{\alpha}_j, \widehat{r}_j \leftarrow \mathbb{Z}_N$ for all $j \in [2^i]$.

We prove the following two lemmas.

Lemma 5 (from $\mathsf{Game}_{2.i}$ to $\mathsf{Game}_{2.i.1}$). *For any p.p.t. adversary $\mathcal{A}$ sending at most q_σ queries to $\mathsf{O}^{\mathsf{KeyGen}}$ and $\mathsf{O}^{\mathsf{Enc}}_\beta$, there exists $\mathcal{B}$ with $\mathsf{T}(\mathcal{B}) \approx \mathsf{T}(\mathcal{A}) + q_\sigma^2 \cdot \mathsf{poly}(\lambda)$ and*

$$|\mathsf{Adv}_{\mathcal{A}}^{\mathsf{Game}2.i.1}(\lambda) - \mathsf{Adv}_{\mathcal{A}}^{\mathsf{Game}2.i}(\lambda)| \leq \mathsf{Adv}_{\mathcal{B}}^{\mathsf{SD3}}(\lambda) + 2^{-\Omega(\lambda)}.$$

Lemma 6 (from $\mathsf{Game}_{2.i.1}$ to $\mathsf{Game}_{2.i.2}$). *For any p.p.t. adversary $\mathcal{A}$ sending at most q_σ queries to $\mathsf{O}^{\mathsf{KeyGen}}$ and $\mathsf{O}^{\mathsf{Enc}}_\beta$, there exists $\mathcal{B}$ with $\mathsf{T}(\mathcal{B}) \approx \mathsf{T}(\mathcal{A}) + q_\sigma^2 \cdot \mathsf{poly}(\lambda)$ and*

$$|\mathsf{Adv}_{\mathcal{A}}^{\mathsf{Game}2.i.2}(\lambda) - \mathsf{Adv}_{\mathcal{A}}^{\mathsf{Game}2.i.1}(\lambda)| \leq \mathsf{Adv}_{\mathcal{B}}^{\mathsf{SD4}}(\lambda) + 2^{-\Omega(\lambda)}.$$

Observe that all r_j and all $\widehat{r}_j$ are i.i.d. variables in $\mathsf{Game}_{2.i.2}$. By setting $\alpha_{2^i+k} = \widehat{\alpha}_k$ and $r_{2^i+k} = \widehat{r}_k$ for all $k \in [2^i]$, one can claim that

$$\mathsf{Adv}_{\mathcal{A}}^{\mathsf{Game}2.i.2}(\lambda) = \mathsf{Adv}_{\mathcal{A}}^{\mathsf{Game}2.(i+1)}(\lambda)$$

for any adversary $\mathcal{A}$.

Game_3 is identical to $\mathsf{Game}_{2.n}$ except that, for each query (ID) to $\mathsf{O}^{\mathsf{KeyGen}}$, we return

$$u^{\frac{1}{\alpha+\mathrm{ID}}} \cdot g_2^{\mathsf{RF}(\mathrm{ID})} \cdot R_4$$

where $g_2 \leftarrow \mathbb{G}^*_{p_2}$ and RF is a truly random function. By the core lemma shown in Sect. 2.3, we have

$$|\mathsf{Adv}_{\mathcal{A}}^{\mathsf{Game}2.n}(\lambda) - \mathsf{Adv}_{\mathcal{A}}^{\mathsf{Game}3}(\lambda)| \leq 2^{-\Omega(\lambda)}$$

for any adversary $\mathcal{A}$.

Game_4 is identical to Game_3 except that, for each query (ID^*) to $\mathsf{O}^{\mathsf{Enc}}_\beta$, we directly sample $\mathrm{KEY}_1^* \leftarrow \{0,1\}^\lambda$. In Game_3, we compute a challenge for ID^* as follows:

$$\mathrm{CT}_1^* = (g_1 g_2 g_3)^s \quad \text{and} \quad \mathrm{KEY}_1^* = \mathsf{H}(e(g_1^s, u^{\frac{1}{\mathrm{ID}^*}}) \cdot \boxed{e(g_2, g_2)^{s \cdot \mathsf{RF}(\mathrm{ID}^*)}}).$$

Due to the restrictions in the security game, $\mathsf{RF}(\mathrm{ID}^*)$ will be evaluated only in this place and the boxed term has entropy of $p_2 = \Theta(\lambda)$ which means we can sample $\mathrm{KEY}_1^* \leftarrow \{0,1\}^\lambda$ instead but with small error. This comes from the leftover hash lemma and the fact that the pairwise independent hash family is a stronger extractor. Formally we have

$$|\mathsf{Adv}_{\mathcal{A}}^{\mathsf{Game}4}(\lambda) - \mathsf{Adv}_{\mathcal{A}}^{\mathsf{Game}3}(\lambda)| \leq 2^{-\Omega(\lambda)}$$

for any adversary $\mathcal{A}$.

Utilizing, in a reversed manner, a game sequence which is identical to the above except that we always sample $\mathrm{KEY}_1^* \leftarrow \{0,1\}^\lambda$ when answering queries to $\mathsf{O}^{\mathsf{Enc}}_\beta$, we may reach a game where we create

$$\boxed{\mathrm{CT}_1^* \leftarrow \mathbb{G}_{p_1}} \quad \text{and} \quad \mathrm{KEY}_1^* \leftarrow \{0,1\}^\lambda \quad \text{for all } \mathrm{ID}^*.$$

This means we can answer all queries to $\mathsf{O}^{\mathsf{Enc}}_\beta$ without β and this readily proves the main theorem.

3.3 Security Analysis: Proving All Lemmas

This subsection provides all omitted proofs.

Proof of Lemma 2.

Proof (a sketch). Let $\mathsf{Abort}_{\mathcal{A}}$ be the event that Game_0 aborts with adversary $\mathcal{A}$. We have

$$|\mathsf{Adv}_{\mathcal{A}}^{\mathsf{Game}_0}(\lambda) - \mathsf{Adv}_{\mathcal{A}}^{\mathsf{Game}_{\mathsf{real}}}(\lambda)| \leq \Pr[\mathsf{Abort}_{\mathcal{A}}].$$

As we have discussed, when $\mathsf{Abort}_{\mathcal{A}}$ occurs, one can reach a non-trivial factorization of N. That is we can efficiently compute $N_1, N_2 \in \mathbb{Z}$ such that $N = N_1 N_2$ and $1 < N_1, N_2 < N$. Let us consider the following three cases:

1. If $p_4|N_1$ and $p_2 \nmid N_1$, given $(\mathcal{G}, g_1, g_4, X_1 X_2 X_3, Y_2 Y_4, T)$ where either $T \leftarrow \mathbb{G}_{p_2}\mathbb{G}_{p_4}$ or $T \leftarrow \mathbb{G}_{p_3}\mathbb{G}_{p_4}$, we observe that $(Y_2 Y_4)^{N_1} \in \mathbb{G}_{p_2}$. This allows us to break SD4 assumption by checking whether $e((Y_2 Y_4)^{N_1}, T) = 1$.
2. If $p_2 p_4|N_1$ and $p_3 \nmid N_1$, given $(\mathcal{G}, g_1, g_4, X_1 X_2 X_3, Y_2 Y_4, T)$ where either $T \leftarrow \mathbb{G}_{p_2}\mathbb{G}_{p_4}$ or $T \leftarrow \mathbb{G}_{p_3}\mathbb{G}_{p_4}$, we can break SD4 assumption by checking whether $T^{N_1} = 1$.
3. If $p_2 p_3 p_4|N_1$, it must be the case that $N_2 = p_1$. Given $(\mathcal{G}, g_1, g_4, T)$ where either $T \leftarrow \mathbb{G}_{p_1}$ or $T \leftarrow \mathbb{G}_{p_1}\mathbb{G}_{p_2}\mathbb{G}_{p_3}$, we can break SD1 assumption by checking whether $T^{N_2} = 1$.

In all three cases, we have access to $(\mathcal{G}, g_1, g_4)$ which is sufficient for simulating Game_0 for $\mathcal{A}$. Therefore we can claim that there exist $\mathcal{B}_1$, $\mathcal{B}_2$ such that $\max\{\mathsf{T}(\mathcal{B}_1), \mathsf{T}(\mathcal{B}_2)\} \approx \mathsf{T}(\mathcal{A}) + q_\sigma \cdot \mathsf{poly}(\lambda)$ and

$$\Pr[\mathsf{Abort}_{\mathcal{A}}] \leq \frac{1}{2} \cdot \mathsf{Adv}_{\mathcal{B}_1}^{\mathsf{SD1}}(\lambda) + \frac{1}{2} \cdot \mathsf{Adv}_{\mathcal{B}_2}^{\mathsf{SD4}}(\lambda) + 2^{-\Omega(\lambda)}.$$

This proves the lemma. $\square$

Proof of Lemma 3.

Proof. Given $(\mathcal{G}, g_1, g_4, T)$ where either $T \leftarrow \mathbb{G}_{p_1}$ or $T \leftarrow \mathbb{G}_{p_1}\mathbb{G}_{p_2}\mathbb{G}_{p_3}$, algorithm $\mathcal{B}$ works as follows:

Initialization. Pick $\alpha \leftarrow \mathbb{Z}_N$ and $u \leftarrow \mathbb{G}_{p_1}$. Select hash function H. Output

$$\mathrm{MPK} = (g_1, \; g_1^\alpha, \; e(g_1, u), \; \mathsf{H})$$

and store $\mathrm{MSK} = (\alpha, \; u, \; g_4)$.

Answering $\mathsf{O}^{\mathsf{KeyGen}}$. On input (ID), return $\mathsf{KeyGen}(\mathrm{MPK}, \mathrm{MSK}, \mathrm{ID})$ directly.

Answering $\mathsf{O}_\beta^{\mathsf{Enc}}$. On input (ID^*), obtain $\mathrm{SK}_{\mathrm{ID}^*}$ via a query (ID^*) to $\mathsf{O}^{\mathsf{KeyGen}}$. Sample $s' \leftarrow \mathbb{Z}_N$ and compute

$$\mathrm{CT}_1^* = T^{s'} \quad \text{and} \quad \mathrm{KEY}_1^* = \mathsf{H}(e(T^{s'}, \mathrm{SK}_{\mathrm{ID}^*})).$$

$\mathcal{B}$ then picks $(\mathrm{CT}_0^*, \mathrm{KEY}_0^*) \leftarrow \mathbb{G}_{p_1} \times \{0,1\}^\lambda$ and returns $(\mathrm{CT}_\beta^*, \mathrm{KEY}_\beta^*)$.

Finalize. $\mathcal{B}$ returns 1 if $\beta = \beta'$ and returns 0 in the other case.

When $T \leftarrow \mathbb{G}_{p_1}$, the simulation is identical to Game_0''; when $T \leftarrow \mathbb{G}_{p_1}\mathbb{G}_{p_2}\mathbb{G}_{p_3}$, the simulation is identical to Game_1. The additive probability error $2^{-\Omega(\lambda)}$ is caused by trivial subgroup components in T. Because we actually take T as a generator, our simulation will deviate from both or one of the games if there exists any trivial subgroup component in it. $\square$

Proof of Lemma 4.

Proof. Given $(\mathcal{G}, g_1, g_4, X_1 X_2 X_3, T)$ where either $T = u \leftarrow \mathbb{G}_{p_1}$ or $T = u g_2^r \leftarrow \mathbb{G}_{p_1}\mathbb{G}_{p_2}$ for $g_2 \leftarrow \mathbb{G}_{p_2}^*$ and $r \leftarrow \mathbb{Z}_N$, algorithm $\mathcal{B}$ works as follows:

Initialization. Pick $\alpha \leftarrow \mathbb{Z}_N$ and select hash function H. Output

$$\mathrm{MPK} = (g_1, \ g_1^\alpha, \ e(g_1, T), \ \mathsf{H}).$$

Observe that $e(g_1, T) = e(g_1, u)$ in both cases.

Answering $\mathsf{O}^{\mathsf{KeyGen}}$. On input (ID), sample $R_4 \leftarrow \mathbb{G}_{p_4}$ and return

$$T^{\frac{1}{\alpha + \mathrm{ID}}} \cdot R_4.$$

Answering $\mathsf{O}_\beta^{\mathsf{Enc}}$. On input (ID^*), sample $s' \leftarrow \mathbb{Z}_N$ and compute

$$\mathrm{CT}_1^* = (X_1 X_2 X_3)^{s'} \quad \text{and} \quad \mathrm{KEY}_1^* = \mathsf{H}(e((X_1 X_2 X_3)^{s'}, \mathrm{SK}_{\mathrm{ID}^*}))$$

where $\mathrm{SK}_{\mathrm{ID}^*}$ is obtained via oracle $\mathsf{O}^{\mathsf{KeyGen}}$. $\mathcal{B}$ then picks $(\mathrm{CT}_0^*, \mathrm{KEY}_0^*) \leftarrow \mathbb{G}_{p_1} \times \{0,1\}^\lambda$ and returns $(\mathrm{CT}_\beta^*, \mathrm{KEY}_\beta^*)$.

Finalize. $\mathcal{B}$ returns 1 if $\beta = \beta'$ and returns 0 in the other case.

When $T = u$, the simulation is identical to Game_1; when $T = u g_2^r$, the simulation is identical to $\mathsf{Game}_{2.0}$ where $\alpha_1 = \alpha \bmod p_2$ and $r_1 = r \bmod p_2$. The additive probability error $2^{-\Omega(\lambda)}$ is caused by trivial subgroup components in $X_1 X_2 X_3$. $\square$

Proof of Lemma 5.

Proof. Given $(\mathcal{G}, g_1, g_4, X_1 X_2 X_3, T)$ where either $T = g_2 \leftarrow \mathbb{G}_{p_2}$ or $T = g_2 g_3 \leftarrow \mathbb{G}_{p_2}\mathbb{G}_{p_3}$, algorithm $\mathcal{B}$ works as follows:

Initialization. Pick $\alpha \leftarrow \mathbb{Z}_N$ and $u \leftarrow \mathbb{G}_{p_1}$. Select hash function H. Output

$$\mathrm{MPK} = (g_1, \ g_1^\alpha, \ e(g_1, u), \ \mathsf{H}).$$

Sample $\alpha_1', \ldots, \alpha_{2^i}', r_1', \ldots, r_{2^i}' \leftarrow \mathbb{Z}_N$.

Answering $\mathsf{O}^{\mathsf{KeyGen}}$. On input (ID), sample $R_4 \leftarrow \mathbb{G}_{p_4}$ and return

$$u^{\frac{1}{\alpha + \mathrm{ID}}} \cdot T^{\sum_{j=1}^{2^i} \frac{r_j'}{\alpha_j' + \mathrm{ID}}} \cdot R_4.$$

Answering $\mathsf{O}_\beta^{\mathsf{Enc}}$. On input (ID^*), sample $s' \leftarrow \mathbb{Z}_N$ and compute

$$\mathrm{CT}_1^* = (X_1 X_2 X_3)^{s'} \quad \text{and} \quad \mathrm{KEY}_1^* = \mathsf{H}(e((X_1 X_2 X_3)^{s'}, \mathrm{SK}_{\mathrm{ID}^*}))$$

where $\mathrm{SK}_{\mathrm{ID}^*}$ is obtained via oracle $\mathsf{O}^{\mathsf{KeyGen}}$. $\mathcal{B}$ then picks $(\mathrm{CT}_0^*, \mathrm{KEY}_0^*) \leftarrow \mathbb{G}_{p_1} \times \{0,1\}^\lambda$ and returns $(\mathrm{CT}_\beta^*, \mathrm{KEY}_\beta^*)$.

Finalize. $\mathcal{B}$ returns 1 if $\beta = \beta'$ and returns 0 in the other case.

When $T = g_2$, the simulation is identical to $\mathsf{Game}_{2.i}$; when $T = g_2g_3$, the simulation is identical to $\mathsf{Game}_{2.i.1}$. We set

$$\alpha_j = \alpha'_j \bmod p_2, \quad r_j = r'_j \bmod p_2, \quad \text{for all } j \in [2^i]$$

for both cases and set

$$\widehat{\alpha}_j = \alpha'_j \bmod p_3, \quad \widehat{r}_j = r'_j \bmod p_3, \quad \text{for all } j \in [2^i]$$

in the case of $T = g_2g_3$. The additive probability error $2^{-\Omega(\lambda)}$ is caused by trivial subgroup components in $X_1X_2X_3$ and T. $\qquad\qquad\square$

Proof of Lemma 6.

Proof. Given $(\mathcal{G}, g_1, g_4, X_1X_2X_3, Y_2Y_4, T)$ where either $T = g_2R_4 \leftarrow \mathbb{G}_{p_2}\mathbb{G}_{p_4}$ or $T = g_3R_4 \leftarrow \mathbb{G}_{p_3}\mathbb{G}_{p_4}$, algorithm $\mathcal{B}$ works as follows:

Initialization. Pick $\alpha \leftarrow \mathbb{Z}_N$ and $u \leftarrow \mathbb{G}_{p_1}$. Select hash function H. Output

$$\mathrm{MPK} = (g_1, \ g_1^{\alpha}, \ e(g_1, u), \ \mathsf{H}).$$

Sample $\alpha'_1, \ldots, \alpha'_{2^i}, r'_1, \ldots, r'_{2^i}, \widehat{\alpha}_1, \ldots, \widehat{\alpha}_{2^i}, \widehat{r}_1, \ldots, \widehat{r}_{2^i} \leftarrow \mathbb{Z}_N$.
Answering $\mathsf{O}^{\mathsf{KeyGen}}$. On input (ID), sample $R'_4 \leftarrow \mathbb{G}_{p_4}$ and return

$$u^{\frac{1}{\alpha+\mathrm{ID}}} \cdot (Y_2Y_4)^{\sum_{j=1}^{2^i} \frac{r'_j}{\alpha'_j+\mathrm{ID}}} \cdot T^{\sum_{j=1}^{2^i} \frac{\widehat{r}_j}{\widehat{\alpha}_j+\mathrm{ID}}} \cdot R'_4.$$

Answering $\mathsf{O}^{\mathsf{Enc}}_{\beta}$. On input (ID^*), sample $s' \leftarrow \mathbb{Z}_N$ and compute

$$\mathrm{CT}^*_1 = (X_1X_2X_3)^{s'} \quad \text{and} \quad \mathrm{KEY}^*_1 = \mathsf{H}(e((X_1X_2X_3)^{s'}, \mathrm{SK}_{\mathrm{ID}^*}))$$

where $\mathrm{SK}_{\mathrm{ID}^*}$ is obtained via oracle $\mathsf{O}^{\mathsf{KeyGen}}$. $\mathcal{B}$ then picks $(\mathrm{CT}^*_0, \mathrm{KEY}^*_0) \leftarrow \mathbb{G}_{p_1} \times \{0,1\}^{\lambda}$ and returns $(\mathrm{CT}^*_{\beta}, \mathrm{KEY}^*_{\beta})$.
Finalize. $\mathcal{B}$ returns 1 if $\beta = \beta'$ and returns 0 in the other case.

Let $Y_2Y_4 = g_2^{y_2} g_4^{y_4}$, we implicitly set

$$\alpha_j = \alpha'_j \bmod p_2 \quad \text{and} \quad r_j = r'_j \cdot y_2 \bmod p_2 \quad \text{for all } j \in [2^i].$$

When $T = g_3R_4$, the simulation is identical to $\mathsf{Game}_{2.i.1}$; when $T = g_2R_4$, the simulation is identical to $\mathsf{Game}_{2.i.2}$. The additive probability error $2^{-\Omega(\lambda)}$ is caused by trivial subgroup components in $X_1X_2X_3$, Y_2Y_4 and T. $\qquad\square$

4   Towards *Full* Adaptive Security

To prove the full adaptive security of our IBE scheme (in the single-instance setting), we still employ the game sequence described in the previous section. In fact, *nearly* all lemmas and results we have established still hold in the *full* adaptive security model where each target identity may have more than one challenge ciphertexts. The only exception is that we can not prove the indistinguishability between Game$_3$ and Game$_4$ just from the property of random function as before.

Following the work by Hofheinz *et al.* [HKS15], we find that we can prove the indistinguishability between them under a subgroup variant of DBDH assumption (see Assumption 5). This assumption is motivated by *Dual System Bilinear DDH assumption* from [HKS15] but is simpler.

Assumption 5 (DBDH in $\mathbb{G}_{p_2}$). *For any p.p.t. adversary $\mathcal{A}$ the following advantage function is negligible in λ.*

$$\mathsf{Adv}_{\mathcal{A}}^{\mathrm{DBDH}}(\lambda) = |\Pr[\mathcal{A}(\mathcal{G}, D, T_0) = 1] - \Pr[\mathcal{A}(\mathcal{G}, D, T_1)]|,$$

where $\mathcal{G} \leftarrow \mathsf{GrpGen}(1^\lambda)$, $g_1 \leftarrow \mathbb{G}_{p_1}^*$, $g_2 \leftarrow \mathbb{G}_{p_2}^*$, $g_3 \leftarrow \mathbb{G}_{p_3}^*$, $g_4 \leftarrow \mathbb{G}_{p_4}^*$, $a, b, c,$ $r \leftarrow \mathbb{Z}_N$,

$$D = (\mathcal{G}, g_1, g_3, g_4, g_2, g_2^a, g_2^b, g_2^c);$$
$$T_0 = e(g_2, g_2)^{abc} \quad and \quad T_1 \leftarrow e(g_2, g_2)^r.$$

We can define two efficient algorithms to re-randomize DBDH problem instances as Hofheinz *et al.* [HKS15]. Given a DBDH instance, algorithm ReRand produces an entirely fresh instance while algorithm ReRand$_a$ creates a fresh instance sharing b and c with its input. Their formal definitions are given below.

– ReRand$_a(g_2, g_2^a, g_2^b, g_2^c, T) \rightarrow (g_2^{a'}, T')$ where $a' \leftarrow \mathbb{Z}_N$ and

$$T' = \begin{cases} e(g_2, g_2)^{a'bc} & \text{when } T = e(g_2, g_2)^{abc} \\ e(g_2, g_2)^{r'} \text{ for } r' \leftarrow \mathbb{Z}_N & \text{when } T = e(g_2, g_2)^r \end{cases}$$

– ReRand$(g_2, g_2^a, g_2^b, g_2^c, T) \rightarrow (g_2^{a'}, g_2^{b'}, g_2^{c'}, T')$ where $a', b', c' \leftarrow \mathbb{Z}_N$ and

$$T' = \begin{cases} e(g_2, g_2)^{a'b'c'} & \text{when } T = e(g_2, g_2)^{abc} \\ e(g_2, g_2)^{r'} \text{ for } r' \leftarrow \mathbb{Z}_N & \text{when } T = e(g_2, g_2)^r \end{cases}$$

We now prove that Game$_3$ and Game$_4$ are *computationally* indistinguishable in the *full* adaptive security model. This will immediately derive the full adaptive security of our IBE scheme in the single-instance setting.

Lemma 7 (from Game$_3$ to Game$_4$). *For any p.p.t. adversary $\mathcal{A}$ sending at most q_σ queries to $\mathsf{O}^{\mathsf{KeyGen}}$ and $\mathsf{O}_\beta^{\mathsf{Enc}}$, there exists $\mathcal{B}$ with $\mathsf{T}(\mathcal{B}) \approx \mathsf{T}(\mathcal{A}) + q_\sigma \cdot \mathsf{poly}(\lambda)$ and*

$$|\mathsf{Adv}_{\mathcal{A}}^{\mathsf{Game}_3}(\lambda) - \mathsf{Adv}_{\mathcal{A}}^{\mathsf{Game}_4}(\lambda)| \leq \mathsf{Adv}_{\mathcal{B}}^{\mathrm{DBDH}}(\lambda) + 2^{-\Omega(\lambda)}.$$

Proof. Given $(\mathcal{G}, g_1, g_3, g_4, g_2, g_2^a, g_2^b, g_2^c, T)$ where either $T = e(g_2, g_2)^{abc}$ or $T = e(g_2, g_2)^r$ for some $r \leftarrow \mathbb{Z}_N$, algorithm $\mathcal{B}$ works as follows:

Initialization. Pick $\alpha \leftarrow \mathbb{Z}_N$ and $u \leftarrow \mathbb{G}_{p_1}$. Select hash function H. Output

$$\text{MPK} = (g_1, \; g_1^\alpha, \; e(g_1, u), \; \text{H}).$$

Answering O^{KeyGen}. On input (ID), return

$$u^{\frac{1}{\alpha + \text{ID}}} \cdot g_2^{\text{RF}(\text{ID})} \cdot R_4$$

where $R_4 \leftarrow \mathbb{G}_{p_4}$ and RF is a truly random function.

Answering O_β^{Enc}. $\mathcal{B}$ maintains a list $\mathcal{L}$. On input (ID*), sample $s' \leftarrow \mathbb{Z}_N$. If one can find a entry $(\text{ID}^*, g_2^{a'}, g_2^{b'}, g_2^{c'}, T') \in \mathcal{L}$, get

$$(g_2^{a^*}, T^*) \leftarrow \mathsf{ReRand}_a(g_2^{a'}, g_2^{b'}, g_2^{c'}, T');$$

otherwise get

$$(g_2^{a^*}, g_2^{b^*}, g_2^{c^*}, T^*) \leftarrow \mathsf{ReRand}(g_2^a, g_2^b, g_2^c, T)$$

and update the list as $\mathcal{L} = \mathcal{L} \cup \{(\text{ID}^*, g_2^{a^*}, g_2^{b^*}, g_2^{c^*}, T^*)\}$. $\mathcal{B}$ then computes

$$\text{CT}_1^* = (g_1 g_3)^{s'} \cdot g_2^{a^*} \quad \text{and} \quad \text{KEY}_1^* = \text{H}(e(g_1^{s'}, u^{\frac{1}{\alpha + \text{ID}^*}}) \cdot T^*).$$

Finally $\mathcal{B}$ picks $(\text{CT}_0^*, \text{KEY}_0^*) \leftarrow \mathbb{G}_{p_1} \times \{0, 1\}^\lambda$ and returns $(\text{CT}_\beta^*, \text{KEY}_\beta^*)$.

Finalize. $\mathcal{B}$ returns 1 if $\beta = \beta'$ and returns 0 in the other case.

We implicitly define RF as

$$\text{RF}(\text{ID}^*) = b^* c^* \quad \text{for all } (\text{ID}^*, g_2^{a^*}, g_2^{b^*}, g_2^{c^*}, T^*) \in \mathcal{L} \; (\text{or } \text{ID}^* \in Q_C).$$

For all $(\text{ID}^*, \star, \star, \star, \star) \in \mathcal{L}$ (or $\text{ID}^* \in Q_C$), we have $\text{ID}^* \notin Q_K$. Therefore our simulation of RF is consistent. When $T = e(g_2, g_2)^{abc}$, the simulation is identical to Game_3 where

$$T^* = e(g_2^{a^*}, g_2^{\text{RF}(\text{ID}^*)});$$

when $T = e(g_2, g_2)^r$ for some $r \leftarrow \mathbb{Z}_N$, the simulation is identical to Game_4 since all inputs of H have min-entropy $\Theta(\lambda)$ and thus distributions of all KEY_1^* are statistically close to the uniform distribution over $\{0, 1\}^\lambda$. $\qquad \square$

5   Towards *Multi-instance* Setting

Having obtained full adaptive security of our IBE scheme in the basic single-instance setting, we now extend the result to the *multi-instance setting* [HKS15]. Typically, all instances in question will share some parameters. Formally, we define two additional algorithms following [HKS15]:

- Param$(1^\lambda) \to$ GP. The *parameter generation algorithm* Param takes as input the security parameter 1^λ and outputs global parameter GP.
- Setup$_m$(GP) $\to$ (MPK, MSK). The *setup algorithm* Setup$_m$ takes as input the global parameter GP and outputs master public/secret key pair (MPK, MSK).

Each instance is established by running algorithm Setup$_m$ with the global parameter GP (shared among all instances) and a fresh random coin. For simplicity, we assume that all instances have common ciphertext space $\mathcal{C}$ and key space $\mathcal{K}$. With master public/secret key pair (MPK, MSK) generated by algorithm Setup$_m$, one can invoke algorithms KeyGen, Enc, Dec as in the single-instance setting. Therefore the correctness can be defined in a natural way.

The full adaptive security and anonymity in the multi-instance setting can be formulated by defining the advantage function as

$$\mathsf{Adv}_{\mathcal{A}}^{\mathrm{mIBE}}(\lambda) = \left| \Pr\left[\beta = \beta' \middle| \begin{array}{c} \mathrm{GP} \leftarrow \mathsf{Param}(1^\lambda), \ \beta \leftarrow \{0,1\} \\ (\mathrm{MPK}^{(\iota)}, \mathrm{MSK}^{(\iota)}) \leftarrow \mathsf{Setup}_m(\mathrm{GP}), \quad \forall \iota \in [\tau] \\ \beta' \leftarrow \mathcal{A}^{\mathsf{O}^{\mathsf{KeyGen}}(\cdot,\cdot), \mathsf{O}_\beta^{\mathsf{Enc}}(\cdot,\cdot)}(1^\lambda, \mathrm{MPK}^{(1)}, \ldots, \mathrm{MPK}^{(\tau)}) \end{array} \right] - \frac{1}{2} \right|$$

where τ is the number of instances and oracles work as follows

- $\mathsf{O}^{\mathsf{KeyGen}}$: On input (ι, ID), the oracle returns KeyGen(MPK$^{(\iota)}$, MSK$^{(\iota)}$, ID) and sets $Q_K = Q_K \cup \{(\iota, \mathrm{ID})\}$.
- $\mathsf{O}_\beta^{\mathsf{Enc}}$: On input (ι^*, ID^*), the oracle samples (CT$_1^*$, KEY$_1^*$) $\leftarrow$ Enc(MPK$^{(\iota^*)}$, ID*), (CT$_0^*$, KEY$_0^*$) $\leftarrow \mathcal{C} \times \mathcal{K}$ and returns (CT$_\beta^*$, KEY$_\beta^*$). Set $Q_C = Q_C \cup \{(\iota^*, \mathrm{ID}^*)\}$.

5.1 Construction

We describe a multi-instance variant of our basic IBE scheme (shown in Sect. 3.1) as follows.

- Param(1^λ). Run $\mathcal{G} = (N, \mathbb{G}, \mathbb{G}_T, e) \leftarrow$ GrpGen(1^λ). Sample

$$g_1 \leftarrow \mathbb{G}_{p_1}^*, \quad g_4 \leftarrow \mathbb{G}_{p_4}^*.$$

Pick H : $\mathbb{G}_T \to \{0,1\}^\lambda$ from a pairwise independent hash family. Output

$$\mathrm{GP} = (\mathcal{G}, \ g_1, \ g_4, \ \mathsf{H}).$$

- Setup$_m$(GP). Sample $\alpha \leftarrow \mathbb{Z}_N$ and $u \leftarrow \mathbb{G}_{p_1}$. Output

$$\mathrm{MPK} = (g_1, \ g_1^\alpha, \ e(g_1, u), \ \mathsf{H}) \quad \text{and} \quad \mathrm{MSK} = (\alpha, u, g_4).$$

The remaining algorithms KeyGen, Enc, Dec are defined as in Sect. 3.1.

5.2 Security

We prove the following theorem.

Theorem 2. *For any p.p.t. adversary $\mathcal{A}$ sending at most $\hat{q}_\sigma$ queries to O^{KeyGen} and O_β^{Enc} for each of τ instances, there exist $\mathcal{B}_1$, $\mathcal{B}_2$, $\mathcal{B}_3$, $\mathcal{B}_4$ such that*

$$\mathsf{Adv}_{\mathcal{A}}^{\mathrm{mIBE}}(\lambda) \leq \frac{5}{2} \cdot \mathsf{Adv}_{\mathcal{B}_1}^{\mathrm{SD1}}(\lambda) + 2 \cdot \mathsf{Adv}_{\mathcal{B}_2}^{\mathrm{SD2}}(\lambda) + 2 \cdot \lceil \log \hat{q}_\sigma \rceil \cdot \mathsf{Adv}_{\mathcal{B}_3}^{\mathrm{SD3}}(\lambda)$$

$$+ \left(2 \cdot \lceil \log \hat{q}_\sigma \rceil + \frac{1}{2} \right) \cdot \mathsf{Adv}_{\mathcal{B}_4}^{\mathrm{SD4}}(\lambda) + 2^{-\Omega(\lambda)}$$

and $\max\{\mathsf{T}(\mathcal{B}_1), \mathsf{T}(\mathcal{B}_2), \mathsf{T}(\mathcal{B}_3), \mathsf{T}(\mathcal{B}_4)\} \approx \mathsf{T}(\mathcal{A}) + \tau^2 \cdot q_\sigma^2 \cdot \mathrm{poly}(\lambda)$.

One may find that the above theorem is almost the same as Theorem 1. As a matter of fact, it can be proved in a similar way. As we have discussed, our main idea in this setting is to build an *independent* random function for *each* instance in a *concurrent* manner. The remaining of this subsection is devoted to showing how to upgrade the proof of Theorem 1 (c.f. Sect. 3.2 for game sequence and Sect. 3.3 for proof details) to prove Theorem 2.

Game Sequence. It's quite straightforward to extend $\mathsf{Game}_{\mathsf{real}}$, Game_0, Game_0', Game_0'', Game_1 and Game_4 to the multi-instance setting. The remaining $\mathsf{Game}_{2.i}$, $\mathsf{Game}_{2.i.1}$, $\mathsf{Game}_{2.i.2}$, Game_3 can be described as follows: Let $\mathcal{G} = (N, \mathbb{G}, \mathbb{G}_T, e) \leftarrow \mathsf{GrpGen}(1^\lambda)$. In all these games, master public keys given to adversary $\mathcal{A}$ are

$$\mathrm{MPK}^{(1)} = (g_1, g_1^{\alpha^{(1)}}, e(g_1, u^{(1)}), \mathsf{H}), \ \ldots \ , \ \mathrm{MPK}^{(\tau)} = (g_1, g_1^{\alpha^{(\tau)}}, e(g_1, u^{(\tau)}), \mathsf{H})$$

where $g_1 \leftarrow \mathbb{G}_{p_1}^*$, $\alpha^{(1)}, \ldots, \alpha^{(\tau)} \leftarrow \mathbb{Z}_N$, $u^{(1)}, \ldots, u^{(\tau)} \leftarrow \mathbb{G}_{p_1}$ and H is picked from a family of pairwise-independent hash family; oracle O_β^{Enc} works as follows:

– On input (ι^*, ID^*), sample $\mathrm{CT}_1^* \leftarrow \mathbb{G}_{p_1} \mathbb{G}_{p_2} \mathbb{G}_{p_3}$ and compute

$$\mathrm{KEY}_1^* = \mathsf{H}(e(\mathrm{CT}_1^*, \mathrm{SK}_{\mathrm{ID}^*}^{(\iota^*)}))$$

where $\mathrm{SK}_{\mathrm{ID}^*}^{(\iota^*)}$ is obtained via a O^{KeyGen} query (ι^*, ID^*). Sample $(\mathrm{CT}_0^*, \mathrm{KEY}_0^*) \leftarrow \mathbb{G}_{p_1} \times \{0,1\}^\lambda$ and return $(\mathrm{CT}_\beta^*, \mathrm{KEY}_\beta^*)$.

However, on input (ι, ID), oracle O^{KeyGen} behaves differently in those games:

– In $\mathsf{Game}_{2.i}$, it returns

$$(u^{(\iota)})^{\frac{1}{\alpha^{(\iota)} + \mathrm{ID}}} \cdot \boxed{g_2^{\sum_{j=1}^{2^i} \frac{r_j^{(\iota)}}{\alpha_j^{(\iota)} + \mathrm{ID}}}} \cdot R_4$$

where $g_2 \leftarrow \mathbb{G}_{p_2}^*$ and $\alpha_j^{(1)}, r_j^{(1)}, \ldots, \alpha_j^{(\tau)}, r_j^{(\tau)} \leftarrow \mathbb{Z}_N$ for all $j \in [2^i]$.
– In $\mathsf{Game}_{2.i.1}$, it returns

$$(u^{(\iota)})^{\frac{1}{\alpha^{(\iota)} + \mathrm{ID}}} \cdot g_2^{\sum_{j=1}^{2^i} \frac{r_j^{(\iota)}}{\alpha_j^{(\iota)} + \mathrm{ID}}} \cdot \boxed{g_3^{\sum_{j=1}^{2^i} \frac{\widehat{r}_j^{(\iota)}}{\widehat{\alpha}_j^{(\iota)} + \mathrm{ID}}}} \cdot R_4,$$

where $g_3 \leftarrow \mathbb{G}_{p_3}^*$ and $\alpha_j^{(1)}, r_j^{(1)}, \widehat{\alpha}_j^{(1)}, \widehat{r}_j^{(1)}, \ldots, \alpha_j^{(\tau)}, r_j^{(\tau)}, \widehat{\alpha}_j^{(\tau)}, \widehat{r}_j^{(\tau)} \leftarrow \mathbb{Z}_N$ for all $j \in [2^i]$.

– In $\mathsf{Game}_{2.i.2}$, it returns

$$(u^{(\iota)})^{\frac{1}{\alpha^{(\iota)}+\mathrm{ID}}} \cdot g_2^{\sum_{j=1}^{2^i} \frac{r_j^{(\iota)}}{\alpha_j^{(\iota)}+\mathrm{ID}} + \boxed{\sum_{j=1}^{2^i} \frac{\widehat{r}_j^{(\iota)}}{\widehat{\alpha}_j^{(\iota)}+\mathrm{ID}}}} \cdot R_4,$$

where $g_2 \leftarrow \mathbb{G}_{p_2}^*$ and $\alpha_j^{(1)}, r_j^{(1)}, \widehat{\alpha}_j^{(1)}, \widehat{r}_j^{(1)}, \ldots, \alpha_j^{(\tau)}, r_j^{(\tau)}, \widehat{\alpha}_j^{(\tau)}, \widehat{r}_j^{(\tau)} \leftarrow \mathbb{Z}_N$ for all $j \in [2^i]$.

– In Game_3, it returns

$$(u^{(\iota)})^{\frac{1}{\alpha^{(\iota)}+\mathrm{ID}}} \cdot g_2^{\mathsf{RF}^{(\iota)}(\mathrm{ID})} \cdot R_4$$

where $g_2 \leftarrow \mathbb{G}_{p_2}^*$ and $\mathsf{RF}^{(1)}, \ldots, \mathsf{RF}^{(\tau)}$ are τ independent random functions.

Lemmas and Proofs. Most lemmas and proofs (including arguments) in Sects. 3.3, 3.2 and 4 can be extended directly to cope with multiple instances. In particular, in order to prove $\mathsf{Game}_{2.i} \approx \mathsf{Game}_{2.i.1}$, $\mathsf{Game}_{2.i.1} \approx \mathsf{Game}_{2.i.2}$, and $\mathsf{Game}_3 \approx \mathsf{Game}_4$ (where "$\mathsf{Game}_{xxx} \approx \mathsf{Game}_{yyy}$" means two games are computationally indistinguishable) in the multi-instance setting, one can just invoke simulators described in the proofs of Lemmas 5, 6, and 7 for *each* instance using *independent* random coins. It remains to give the following lemma showing $\mathsf{Game}_1 \approx \mathsf{Game}_{2.0}$ with proof.

Lemma 8. (from Game_1 to $\mathsf{Game}_{2.0}$, multi-instance case). *For any p.p.t. adversary $\mathcal{A}$ sending at most $\hat{q}_\sigma$ queries to $\mathsf{O}^{\mathsf{KeyGen}}$ and $\mathsf{O}_\beta^{\mathsf{Enc}}$ for each of τ instances, there exists $\mathcal{B}$ with $\mathsf{T}(\mathcal{B}) \approx \mathsf{T}(\mathcal{A}) + \tau \cdot \hat{q}_\sigma \cdot \mathsf{poly}(\lambda)$ and*

$$|\mathsf{Adv}_{\mathcal{A}}^{\mathsf{Game}_{2.0}}(\lambda) - \mathsf{Adv}_{\mathcal{A}}^{\mathsf{Game}_1}(\lambda)| \leq \mathsf{Adv}_{\mathcal{B}}^{\mathsf{SD2}}(\lambda) + 2^{-\Omega(\lambda)}.$$

Proof. Given $(\mathcal{G}, g_1, g_4, X_1 X_2 X_3, T)$ where either $T = g_1^\mu \leftarrow \mathbb{G}_{p_1}$ or $T = g_1^\mu g_2^r \leftarrow \mathbb{G}_{p_1} \mathbb{G}_{p_2}$ for $g_2 \leftarrow \mathbb{G}_{p_2}^*$ and $\mu, r \leftarrow \mathbb{Z}_N$, algorithm $\mathcal{B}$ works as follows:

Initialization. Pick $\alpha^{(1)}, \ldots, \alpha^{(\tau)}, \mu^{(1)}, \ldots, \mu^{(\tau)} \leftarrow \mathbb{Z}_N$ and select hash function H. Compute

$$T^{(1)} = T^{\mu^{(1)}}, \ \ldots, \ T^{(\tau)} = T^{\mu^{(\tau)}}$$

and output

$$\mathsf{MPK}^{(1)} = (g_1, \ g_1^{\alpha^{(1)}}, \ e(g_1, T^{(1)}), \ \mathsf{H}), \ \ldots, \ \mathsf{MPK}^{(\tau)} = (g_1, \ g_1^{\alpha^{(\tau)}}, \ e(g_1, T^{(\tau)}), \ \mathsf{H}).$$

Here we implicitly set

$$u^{(1)} = g_1^{\mu\mu^{(1)}}, \ \ldots, \ u^{(\tau)} = g_1^{\mu\mu^{(\tau)}}.$$

Answering $\mathsf{O}^{\mathsf{KeyGen}}$. On input (ι, ID), sample $R_4 \leftarrow \mathbb{G}_{p_4}$ and return

$$(T^{(\iota)})^{\frac{1}{\alpha^{(\iota)}+\mathrm{ID}}} \cdot R_4.$$

Answering O_β^{Enc}. On input (ι^*, ID^*), sample $s' \leftarrow \mathbb{Z}_N$ and compute

$$\mathrm{CT}_1^* = (X_1 X_2 X_3)^{s'} \quad \text{and} \quad \mathrm{KEY}_1^* = \mathsf{H}(e((X_1 X_2 X_3)^{s'}, \mathrm{SK}_{\mathrm{ID}^*}))$$

where $\mathrm{SK}_{\mathrm{ID}^*}$ is obtained via a O^{KeyGen} query. $\mathcal{B}$ then picks $(\mathrm{CT}_0^*, \mathrm{KEY}_0^*) \leftarrow \mathbb{G}_{p_1} \times \{0,1\}^\lambda$ and returns $(\mathrm{CT}_\beta^*, \mathrm{KEY}_\beta^*)$.

Finalize. $\mathcal{B}$ returns 1 if $\beta = \beta'$ and returns 0 in the other case.

When $T = g_1^\mu$, the simulation is identical to Game_1; when $T = g_1^\mu g_2^r$, the simulation is identical to $\mathsf{Game}_{2.0}$ where we implicitly set

$$\begin{aligned} \alpha_1^{(1)} &= \alpha^{(1)} \bmod p_2 \qquad \alpha_1^{(\tau)} = \alpha^{(\tau)} \bmod p_2 \\ r_1^{(1)} &= r\mu^{(1)} \bmod p_2 \, , \cdots , \; r_1^{(\tau)} = r\mu^{(\tau)} \bmod p_2 \end{aligned}.$$

This proves the lemma. $\qquad\qquad\qquad\qquad\qquad\qquad\qquad\qquad\qquad\qquad\square$

Acknowledgement. We thank Benoît Libert, Somindu Ramanna and Kai Zhang for their advices. We also greatly thank all anonymous reviewers of PKC 2017. Their constructive comments motivated us to extend our basic result to the multi-instance setting and helped us to clarify some technical subtlety.

References

[AC16] Agrawal, S., Chase, M.: A study of pair encodings: predicate encryption in prime order groups. In: Kushilevitz, E., Malkin, T. (eds.) TCC 2016. LNCS, vol. 9563, pp. 259–288. Springer, Heidelberg (2016). doi:10.1007/978-3-662-49099-0_10

[AHY15] Attrapadung, N., Hanaoka, G., Yamada, S.: A framework for identity-based encryption with almost tight security. In: Iwata, T., Cheon, J.H. (eds.) ASIACRYPT 2015. LNCS, vol. 9452, pp. 521–549. Springer, Heidelberg (2015). doi:10.1007/978-3-662-48797-6_22

[Att14] Attrapadung, N.: Dual system encryption via doubly selective security: framework, fully secure functional encryption for regular languages, and more. In: Nguyen, P.Q., Oswald, E. (eds.) EUROCRYPT 2014. LNCS, vol. 8441, pp. 557–577. Springer, Heidelberg (2014). doi:10.1007/978-3-642-55220-5_31

[Att16] Attrapadung, N.: Dual system encryption framework in prime-order groups via computational pair encodings. In: Cheon, J.H., Takagi, T. (eds.) ASIACRYPT 2016. LNCS, vol. 10032, pp. 591–623. Springer, Heidelberg (2016). doi:10.1007/978-3-662-53890-6_20

[BB04a] Boneh, D., Boyen, X.: Efficient selective-ID secure identity-based encryption without random oracles. In: Cachin, C., Camenisch, J.L. (eds.) EUROCRYPT 2004. LNCS, vol. 3027, pp. 223–238. Springer, Heidelberg (2004). doi:10.1007/978-3-540-24676-3_14

[BB04b] Boneh, D., Boyen, X.: Secure identity based encryption without random oracles. In: Franklin, M. (ed.) CRYPTO 2004. LNCS, vol. 3152, pp. 443–459. Springer, Heidelberg (2004). doi:10.1007/978-3-540-28628-8_27

[BF01]   Boneh, D., Franklin, M.: Identity-based encryption from the Weil pairing. In: Kilian, J. (ed.) CRYPTO 2001. LNCS, vol. 2139, pp. 213–229. Springer, Heidelberg (2001). doi:10.1007/3-540-44647-8_13

[BGN05] Boneh, D., Goh, E.-J., Nissim, K.: Evaluating 2-DNF formulas on ciphertexts. In: Kilian, J. (ed.) TCC 2005. LNCS, vol. 3378, pp. 325–341. Springer, Heidelberg (2005). doi:10.1007/978-3-540-30576-7_18

[BKP14] Blazy, O., Kiltz, E., Pan, J.: (Hierarchical) identity-based encryption from affine message authentication. In: Garay, J.A., Gennaro, R. (eds.) CRYPTO 2014. LNCS, vol. 8616, pp. 408–425. Springer, Heidelberg (2014). doi:10.1007/978-3-662-44371-2_23

[BL16]   Boyen, X., Li, Q.: Towards tightly secure lattice short signature and ID-based encryption. In: Cheon, J.H., Takagi, T. (eds.) ASIACRYPT 2016. LNCS, vol. 10032, pp. 404–434. Springer, Heidelberg (2016). doi:10.1007/978-3-662-53890-6_14

[BWY11] Bellare, M., Waters, B., Yilek, S.: Identity-based encryption secure against selective opening attack. In: Ishai, Y. (ed.) TCC 2011. LNCS, vol. 6597, pp. 235–252. Springer, Heidelberg (2011). doi:10.1007/978-3-642-19571-6_15

[CGW15] Chen, J., Gay, R., Wee, H.: Improved dual system ABE in prime-order groups via predicate encodings. In: Oswald, E., Fischlin, M. (eds.) EUROCRYPT 2015. LNCS, vol. 9057, pp. 595–624. Springer, Heidelberg (2015). doi:10.1007/978-3-662-46803-6_20

[CLR16] Chen, J., Libert, B., Ramanna, S.C.: Non-zero inner product encryption with short ciphertexts and private keys. In: Zikas, V., Prisco, R. (eds.) SCN 2016. LNCS, vol. 9841, pp. 23–41. Springer, Heidelberg (2016). doi:10.1007/978-3-319-44618-9_2

[CM14]   Chase, M., Meiklejohn, S.: Déjà Q: using dual systems to revisit q-type assumptions. In: Nguyen, P.Q., Oswald, E. (eds.) EUROCRYPT 2014. LNCS, vol. 8441, pp. 622–639. Springer, Heidelberg (2014). doi:10.1007/978-3-642-55220-5_34

[CMM16] Chase, M., Maller, M., Meiklejohn, S.: Déjà Q all over again: tighter and broader reductions of q-type assumptions. In: Cheon, J.H., Takagi, T. (eds.) ASIACRYPT 2016. LNCS, vol. 10032, pp. 655–681. Springer, Heidelberg (2016). doi:10.1007/978-3-662-53890-6_22

[CW13]   Chen, J., Wee, H.: Fully, (Almost) tightly secure IBE and dual system groups. In: Canetti, R., Garay, J.A. (eds.) CRYPTO 2013. LNCS, vol. 8043, pp. 435–460. Springer, Heidelberg (2013). doi:10.1007/978-3-642-40084-1_25

[GCD+16] Gong, J., Chen, J., Dong, X., Cao, Z., Tang, S.: Extended nested dual system groups, revisited. In: Cheng, C.-M., Chung, K.-M., Persiano, G., Yang, B.-Y. (eds.) PKC 2016. LNCS, vol. 9614, pp. 133–163. Springer, Heidelberg (2016). doi:10.1007/978-3-662-49384-7_6

[GDCC16] Gong, J., Dong, X., Chen, J., Cao, Z.: Efficient IBE with tight reduction to standard assumption in the multi-challenge setting. In: Cheon, J.H., Takagi, T. (eds.) ASIACRYPT 2016. LNCS, vol. 10032, pp. 624–654. Springer, Heidelberg (2016). doi:10.1007/978-3-662-53890-6_21

[Gen06] Gentry, C.: Practical identity-based encryption without random oracles. In: Vaudenay, S. (ed.) EUROCRYPT 2006. LNCS, vol. 4004, pp. 445–464. Springer, Heidelberg (2006). doi:10.1007/11761679_27

[HKS15] Hofheinz, D., Koch, J., Striecks, C.: Identity-based encryption with (Almost) tight security in the multi-instance, multi-ciphertext setting. In: Katz, J. (ed.) PKC 2015. LNCS, vol. 9020, pp. 799–822. Springer, Heidelberg (2015). doi:10.1007/978-3-662-46447-2_36

[Hof16a] Hofheinz, D.: Adaptive partitioning. IACR Cryptology ePrint Archive 2016:373 (2016)

[Hof16b] Hofheinz, D.: Algebraic partitioning: fully compact and (almost) tightly secure cryptography. In: Kushilevitz, E., Malkin, T. (eds.) TCC 2016. LNCS, vol. 9562, pp. 251–281. Springer, Heidelberg (2016). doi:10.1007/978-3-662-49096-9_11

[LOS+10] Lewko, A., Okamoto, T., Sahai, A., Takashima, K., Waters, B.: Fully secure functional encryption: attribute-based encryption and (hierarchical) inner product encryption. In: Gilbert, H. (ed.) EUROCRYPT 2010. LNCS, vol. 6110, pp. 62–91. Springer, Heidelberg (2010). doi:10.1007/978-3-642-13190-5_4

[LRY16] Libert, B., Ramanna, S.C., Yung, M.: Functional commitment schemes: from polynomial commitments to pairing-based accumulators from simple assumptions. In: ICALP 2016 (2016)

[NR04] Naor, M., Reingold, O.: Number-theoretic constructions of efficient pseudo-random functions. J. ACM $51(2)$, 231–262 (2004)

[OT10] Okamoto, T., Takashima, K.: Fully secure functional encryption with general relations from the decisional linear assumption. In: Rabin, T. (ed.) CRYPTO 2010. LNCS, vol. 6223, pp. 191–208. Springer, Heidelberg (2010). doi:10.1007/978-3-642-14623-7_11

[Sha84] Shamir, A.: Identity-based cryptosystems and signature schemes. In: Blakley, G.R., Chaum, D. (eds.) CRYPTO 1984. LNCS, vol. 196, pp. 47–53. Springer, Heidelberg (1985). doi:10.1007/3-540-39568-7_5

[Wat05] Waters, B.: Efficient identity-based encryption without random oracles. In: Cramer, R. (ed.) EUROCRYPT 2005. LNCS, vol. 3494, pp. 114–127. Springer, Heidelberg (2005). doi:10.1007/11426639_7

[Wat09] Waters, B.: Dual system encryption: realizing fully secure IBE and HIBE under simple assumptions. In: Halevi, S. (ed.) CRYPTO 2009. LNCS, vol. 5677, pp. 619–636. Springer, Heidelberg (2009). doi:10.1007/978-3-642-03356-8_36

[Wee14] Wee, H.: Dual system encryption via predicate encodings. In: Lindell, Y. (ed.) TCC 2014. LNCS, vol. 8349, pp. 616–637. Springer, Heidelberg (2014). doi:10.1007/978-3-642-54242-8_26

[Wee16] Wee, H.: Déjà Q: Encore! un petit IBE. In: Kushilevitz, E., Malkin, T. (eds.) TCC 2016. LNCS, vol. 9563, pp. 237–258. Springer, Heidelberg (2016). doi:10.1007/978-3-662-49099-0_9

Separating IND-CPA and Circular Security for Unbounded Length Key Cycles

Rishab Goyal[(✉)], Venkata Koppula, and Brent Waters

University of Texas at Austin, Austin, USA
{rgoyal,kvenkata,bwaters}@cs.utexas.edu

Abstract. A public key encryption scheme is said to be n-circular secure if no PPT adversary can distinguish between encryptions of an n length key cycle and n encryptions of zero.

One interesting question is whether circular security comes for free from IND-CPA security. Recent works have addressed this question, showing that for all integers n, there exists an IND-CPA scheme that is not n-circular secure. However, this leaves open the possibility that for every IND-CPA cryptosystem, there exists a cycle length l, dependent on the cryptosystem (and the security parameter) such that the scheme is l-circular secure. If this is true, then this would directly lead to many applications, in particular, it would give us a fully homomorphic encryption scheme via Gentry's bootstrapping.

In this work, we show that is not true. Assuming indistinguishability obfuscation and leveled homomorphic encryption, we construct an IND-CPA scheme such that for all cycle lengths l, the scheme is not l-circular secure.

1 Introduction

Key dependent message security [9] extends the basic notion of semantic security [22] by allowing the adversary to query for encryptions of function evaluations on the hidden secret key. One of the most prominent examples of key dependent message security is that of circular security, which addresses the following question: "What can the adversary learn when given an encryption of the secret key, or more generally, an encryption of a key cycle?". An n length key cycle consists of n ciphertexts, where the ith ciphertext is an encryption of the $(i+1)^{th}$ secret key using the ith public key.[1] The notion of circular security is captured formally via a security game in which the adversary must distinguish between an n length key cycle and n encryptions of zero (under the n different public keys). An encryption scheme is said to be n-circular secure if no polynomial time adversary can perform this task with non-negligible advantage.

B. Waters—Supported by NSF CNS-1228599 and CNS-1414082, DARPA SafeWare, Microsoft Faculty Fellowship, and Packard Foundation Fellowship.

[1] The nth ciphertext is an encryption of the first secret key using the nth public key.

© International Association for Cryptologic Research 2017
S. Fehr (Ed.): PKC 2017, Part I, LNCS 10174, pp. 232–246, 2017.
DOI: 10.1007/978-3-662-54365-8_10

The problem of circular security has received a considerable amount of attention recently because it is a natural question giving rise to different applications [2,14,26]. Most notably, it gives us a path to achieve fully homomorphic encryption from leveled homomorphic encryption via Gentry's bootstrapping approach [20].

In the past several years, there have been many interesting works [4–7,10–13,23,27] that have addressed the question of circular security (or more generally, key dependent message security), leading to circular secure encryption schemes under fairly standard assumptions such as bilinear decisional Diffie Hellman assumption (BDDH) and the Learning with Errors assumption (LWE)[29].

However, an important related question is whether *any* IND-CPA scheme is also circular secure. If so, circular security would come for free and no additional construction mechanisms would need to be designed (beyond what we already needed for IND-CPA security). Unfortunately, this is not true. For $n = 1$, there exists a trivial counterexample — an IND-CPA scheme where the encryption of the secret key is the secret key itself. The question for $n > 1$ was open for some time, and was resolved by Acar et al. [1]. They showed, under the SXDH assumption, an IND-CPA secure encryption scheme that was not 2-circular secure. A similar counterexample with additional features was proposed by Cash, Green and Hohenberger [16], also under the SXDH assumption. In a recent work, Bishop, Hohenberger and Waters [8] expanded the state-of-the-art for $n = 2$ by showing counterexamples under the k-linear assumption and the LWE assumption. For arbitrary n, the first counterexamples were proposed by Koppula, Ramchen and Waters [24], and Marcedone and Orlandi [28]. Given any fixed integer n, Koppula, Ramchen and Waters showed how to construct an IND-CPA scheme that is not n-circular secure using indistinguishability obfuscation (iO). Marcedone and Orlandi concurrently achieved a similar result under the stronger notion of virtual black-box obfuscation (VBB). Recently, Alamati and Peikert [3], and Koppula and Waters [25] proved similar results using LWE assumption.

At first sight, these results might seem to shut the door on the prospect of getting circular security automatically from IND-CPA security. However, they miss an important distinction in the order of quantifiers. All prior works [3,24, 25,28] show that for every integer n, there exists an IND-CPA scheme which is not n-circular secure. In particular, the parameters of their schemes (i.e. the size of public parameters, secret keys and ciphertexts) depend on n. However, this leaves open the possibility that for every cryptosystem, there exists some polynomial function $\alpha(\cdot)$, particular to that cryptosystem, such that the scheme is $\alpha(\cdot)$-circular secure. More formally, we are interested in the following question:

Is it possible that for every IND-CPA secure public key encryption scheme, there exists an integer α such that the scheme is also α-circular secure?[2]

If this were true, then this would provide an automatic path to Gentry's bootstrapping, and potentially other applications. For instance, suppose we

---

[2] In comparison, the previous works addressed the following question: "Is it possible that there exists an integer n such that every IND-CPA secure public key encryption scheme is also n-circular secure?".

have a bootstrappable homomorphic encryption scheme (that is, a homomorphic encryption scheme for circuit class $\mathcal{C}$ where the decryption circuit is also in $\mathcal{C}$), and let us assume the scheme is α-circular secure. Then, in order to get a homomorphic encryption scheme for all circuits, one simply needs to include an α length key cycle as part of the public key. This key cycle can be used to reduce the amount of noise in homomorphically evaluated ciphertexts, thereby allowing us to perform arbitrary homomorphic evaluations.

With this motivation, we study the aforementioned question. Unfortunately, the answer is in the negative, and we show this by constructing a class of public key encryption schemes for which there does not exist any α such that they are α-circular secure. Our construction uses indistinguishability obfuscator (iO) for polynomial sized circuits, coupled with a leveled homomorphic encryption (LHE) scheme that is capable of homomorphically evaluating its own decryption circuit[3]. Such LHE schemes [13,21] are realizable from the LWE assumption. Current iO candidates [19,32], on the other hand, rely on strong assumptions like multilinear maps [17,18] and therefore, the reader might question the underlying security of current construction. However, we would like to emphasize that our result is a counterexample and it would hold as long as some iO scheme exists, thus the concern over reliability of current candidates is somewhat mitigated.

Our Approach. Below, we sketch an outline of our construction, which has the feature of being very intuitive. In our system, each public key consists of an LHE public key $\mathsf{PK_{HE}}$ and an auxiliary program Prog (to be described momentarily), whose purpose is to aid the circular security adversary. The secret key consists of the corresponding LHE secret key $\mathsf{SK_{HE}}$. The encryption and decryption procedures are simply the LHE encryption and decryption algorithms. The program Prog is the obfuscation of a program that on input an LHE ciphertext, under public key $\mathsf{PK_{HE}}$, decrypts it using (hardwired) secret key $\mathsf{SK_{HE}}$ and outputs 1 iff the plaintext is $\mathsf{SK_{HE}}$ itself. In other words, Prog acts as a publicly available self-cycle (1-cycle) tester.

Our idea for testing secret key cycles of any (unbounded) length is to iteratively reduce size of the cycle by homomorphically decrypting last ciphertext in the chain using the second-last ciphertext to generate a fresh ciphertext that will act as a new end of the chain. More formally, consider a key cycle of length n in which the last two ciphertexts ct_{n-1} and ct_n are encryptions of sk_n and sk_1 under public keys pk_{n-1} and pk_n (respectively), and let $C_{\mathsf{Dec},n}$ be a circuit that takes an input x and uses it to decrypt ct_n. Our cycle tester will homomorphically evaluate circuit $C_{\mathsf{Dec},n}$ on input ct_{n-1}. Since ct_{n-1} is an encryption of sk_n, the homomorphic evaluation will output a new ciphertext ct'_{n-1} which would be an encryption of sk_1 under public key pk_{n-1}. Thus, this successfully reduces the length of key cycle from n to $n-1$, and iteratively applying this procedure would eventually reduce the cycle size to 1. At this point, we could use the program

---

[3] Recently, [15] provided constructions for LHE from sub-exponentially hard indistinguishability obfuscation, one-way functions, and re-randomizable encryption schemes.

Prog_1 which is part of first public key pk_1 to test for a self-cycle. The crucial idea in our cycle tester is that we start slicing the cycle from the end, thus existence of a leveled homomorphic encryption scheme suffices, and we do not require a fully homomorphic scheme for testing unbounded length key cycles.

Now let us move on to the IND-CPA security proof. Ideally we would like to directly leverage the IND-CPA security of LHE scheme to prove IND-CPA security of our construction because intuitively, the obfuscated program Prog should not reveal the hardwired LHE secret key. However, indistinguishability obfuscation is a relatively weak notion of program obfuscation, therefore using it directly is a bit tricky so we need to tweak our scheme slightly as in [24]. In our modified scheme, our secret key also contains a random string s, and the program Prog has both $\mathsf{SK_{HE}}$ and t hardwired, where $t = \mathrm{PRG}(s)$. On any input ciphertext ct, it first decrypts using $\mathsf{SK_{HE}}$ to recover (a, b) and then checks if $a = \mathsf{SK_{HE}}$ and $t = \mathrm{PRG}(b)$.

In order to use the IND-CPA security of the LHE scheme, we first need to modify program Prog such that it does not contain $\mathsf{SK_{HE}}$ anymore. To remove $\mathsf{SK_{HE}}$ from Prog, we make a hybrid jump in which we choose t randomly instead of setting it as $t = \mathrm{PRG}(s)$. This hybrid jump is indistinguishable due to the security of the pseudorandom generator. Note that if t is chosen uniformly at random, then with high probability, this program outputs $\bot$ on all inputs. As a result, by the security of $i\mathcal{O}$, this program is indistinguishable from one that always outputs $\bot$. In this manner, we can remove the secret key $\mathsf{SK_{HE}}$ from Prog. Once this is done, we can directly reduce a successful attack on our construction to a successful attack on IND-CPA security of LHE scheme. Our construction is described in detail in Sect. 4.

Organization. In Sect. 2, we describe the required notations and preliminaries. The definition of circular security can be found in Sect. 3. In Sect. 4, we describe our counterexample scheme. The circular security attack is included in Sect. 4.1 and the corresponding IND-CPA security proof in Sect. 4.2. Finally, in Sect. 5, we discuss (informally) how our construction can be modified to achieve a stronger negative result.

2   Preliminaries

Notation. Let $\mathcal{R}$ be a ring, and let $\mathcal{C}_{\mathcal{R},\lambda,k}$ denote the set of circuits of size at most $\mathsf{poly}(\lambda)$ and depth at most k, with domain and co-domain being $\mathcal{R}$. For simplicity of notation, we will skip the dependence of $\mathcal{C}_{\mathcal{R},\lambda,\ell}$ on $\mathcal{R}$, λ when it is clear from the context.

2.1   Public Key Encryption

A public key encryption scheme $\mathcal{PKE}$ with message space $\mathcal{M}$ consists of three algorithms Setup, Enc and Dec with the following syntax:

- Setup(1^λ) → (pk, sk) The setup algorithm takes as input the security parameter 1^λ and outputs a public key pk and secret key sk.
- Enc(pk, $m \in \mathcal{M}$) → ct The encryption algorithm takes as input a public key pk and a message $m \in \mathcal{M}$ and outputs a ciphertext ct.
- Dec(sk, ct) → $x \in \mathcal{M} \cup \{\bot\}$ The decryption algorithm takes as input a secret key sk, ciphertext ct and outputs $x \in \mathcal{M} \cup \{\bot\}$.

Correctness: For correctness, we require that for all security parameters λ, (pk, sk) ← Setup(1^λ) and messages $m \in \mathcal{M}$, Dec(sk, Enc(pk, m)) = m.

Definition 1 (IND-CPA Security). *A public key encryption scheme* $\mathcal{PKE} =$ (Setup, Enc, Dec) *is said to be* IND-CPA *secure if for all security parameters* λ, *stateful PPT adversaries* $\mathcal{A}$, $\mathrm{Adv}^{\mathsf{ind\text{-}cpa}}_{\mathcal{A}, \mathcal{PKE}}(\lambda)$ *is negligible in* λ, *where advantage of* $\mathcal{A}$ *is defined as* $\mathrm{Adv}^{\mathsf{ind\text{-}cpa}}_{\mathcal{A}, \mathcal{PKE}}(\lambda) = |\Pr[\mathsf{Exp\text{-}IND\text{-}CPA}(\mathcal{PKE}, \mathcal{A}, \lambda) = 1] - 1/2|$, *and* Exp-IND-CPA *is defined in Fig. 1.*

$$
\begin{array}{l}
\underline{\mathsf{Exp\text{-}IND\text{-}CPA}(\mathcal{PKE}, \mathcal{A}, \lambda)} \\
\quad b \leftarrow \{0, 1\} \\
\quad (\mathsf{pk}, \mathsf{sk}) \leftarrow \mathsf{Setup}(1^\lambda) \\
\quad (m_0, m_1) \leftarrow \mathcal{A}(\mathsf{pk}) \\
\quad y \leftarrow \mathsf{Enc}(\mathsf{pk}, m_b) \\
\quad \hat{b} \leftarrow \mathcal{A}(y) \\
\quad \text{Output } (\hat{b} \overset{?}{=} b)
\end{array}
$$

Fig. 1. IND-CPA security game

2.2   Homomorphic Encryption

Homomorphic encryption [20,30] is a powerful extension of public key encryption that allows one to evaluate functions on ciphertexts. In this work, we will be using leveled homomorphic encryption schemes. Let $\mathcal{R}$ be a ring. A leveled homomorphic encryption scheme $\mathcal{HE}$ with message space $\mathcal{R}$ consists of four algorithms Setup, Enc, Dec, Eval with the following syntax:

1. Setup($1^\lambda, 1^\ell$) → (pk, sk) The setup algorithm takes as input the security parameter λ, bound on circuit depth ℓ and outputs a public key pk and secret key sk.
2. Enc(pk, $m \in \mathcal{R}$) → ct The encryption algorithm takes as input a public key pk, message $m \in \mathcal{R}$ and outputs a ciphertext ct.
3. Eval($C \in \mathcal{C}_\ell$, ct) → ct' The evaluation algorithm takes as input a circuit $C \in \mathcal{C}_\ell$, a ciphertext ct and outputs a ciphertext ct'.
4. Dec(sk, ct) → x The decryption algorithm takes as input a secret key sk and ciphertext ct and outputs $x \in \mathcal{R} \cup \{\bot\}$.

We will now define some properties of leveled homomorphic encryption schemes. Let $\mathcal{HE}$ be any homomorphic encryption scheme with message space $\mathcal{R}$. First, we have the correctness property, which states that the decryption of a homomorphic evaluation on a ciphertext must be equal to the evaluation on the underlying message.

Definition 2 (Correctness). *The scheme* $\mathcal{HE}$ *is said to be perfectly correct if for all security parameter* λ*, circuit-depth bound* ℓ*,* $(\mathsf{pk}, \mathsf{sk}) \leftarrow \mathsf{Setup}(1^\lambda, 1^\ell)$*, circuit* $C \in \mathcal{C}_\ell$ *and message* $m \in \mathcal{R}$*,* $\mathsf{Dec}(\mathsf{sk}, \mathsf{Eval}(C, \mathsf{Enc}(\mathsf{pk}, m))) = C(m)$*.*

Next, we have the compactness property which requires that the size of the output of an evaluation on a ciphertext must not depend upon the evaluation circuit. In particular, we require that there exists one decryption circuit such that this circuit can decrypt any bounded-depth evaluations on ciphertexts.

Definition 3 (Compactness). *The scheme* $\mathcal{HE}$ *is said to be compact if for all* λ*,* ℓ *there is a decryption circuit* $C_{\lambda,\ell}^{\mathsf{Dec}}$ *such that for all* $(\mathsf{pk}, \mathsf{sk}) \leftarrow \mathsf{Setup}(1^\lambda, 1^\ell)$*,* $m \in \mathcal{R}$*,* $C \in \mathcal{C}_\ell$*,* $C_{\lambda,\ell}^{\mathsf{Dec}}(\mathsf{sk}, \mathsf{Eval}(C, \mathsf{Enc}(\mathsf{pk}, m))) = C(m)$*.*

Finally, we define the notion of *bootstrappability*. Gentry [20] showed that if the decryption circuit is of low depth, then a homomorphic encryption scheme for low depth circuits can be bootstrapped to a homomorphic encryption scheme for polynomial depth circuits where the polynomial is apriori defined. We will use this property for constructing our unbounded circular security counterexample. We would like to emphasize that the following notion of bootstrappability does not directly imply fully homomorphic encryption since an FHE scheme must successfully evaluate a ciphertext on all polynomial depth circuits, and not just on apriori defined polynomials.

Definition 4. *A compact homomorphic encryption scheme* $\mathcal{HE}$ *is said to be bootstrappable if for all security parameters* λ*, there exists a depth bound* $D = D(\lambda)$ *such that for all* $\ell \geq D$*,* $\mathsf{depth}(C_{\lambda,\ell}^{\mathsf{Dec}}) \leq \ell$*.*

Security: For security, we require that the underlying scheme is IND-CPA secure.

Definition 5. *The scheme* $\mathcal{HE}$ *is secure if* $\Gamma = (\mathsf{Setup}, \mathsf{Enc}, \mathsf{Dec})$ *is* IND-CPA *secure (as per Definition 1).*

2.3 Indistinguishability Obfuscation

Next, we recall the definition of indistinguishability obfuscation from [31].

Definition 6 *(Indistinguishability Obfuscation). A uniform PPT machine* $i\mathcal{O}$ *is called an indistinguishability obfuscator for a circuit class* $\{\mathcal{C}_\lambda\}_\lambda$ *if it satisfies the following conditions:*

– *(Preserving Functionality) For all security parameters* $\lambda \in \mathbb{N}$*, for all* $C \in \mathcal{C}_\lambda$*, for all inputs* x*, we have that* $C'(x) = C(x)$ *where* $C' \leftarrow i\mathcal{O}(C)$*.*

- *(Indistinguishability of Obfuscation) For any (not necessarily uniform) PPT distinguisher $(Samp, D)$, there exists a negligible function $negl(\cdot)$ such that the following holds: if for all security parameters $\lambda \in \mathbb{N}, \Pr[\forall x, C_0(x) = C_1(x) : (C_0; C_1; \sigma) \leftarrow Samp(1^\lambda)] > 1 - negl(\lambda)$, then*

$$| \Pr[D(\sigma, i\mathcal{O}(C_0)) = 1 : (C_0; C_1; \sigma) \leftarrow Samp(1^\lambda)] -$$
$$\Pr[D(\sigma, i\mathcal{O}(C_1)) = 1 : (C_0; C_1; \sigma) \leftarrow Samp(1^\lambda)]| \leq negl(\lambda)$$

[19] showed a candidate indistinguishability obfuscator for the circuit class $P/poly$.

3   Circular Security

In this section, we define the notion of n-circular security. At a high level, n-circular security deals with the following question: "What additional information can a PPT adversary learn given an n-length encryption cycle (that is, a sequence of n ciphertexts where the ith ciphertext is an encryption of the $(i+1)^{th}$ secret key using the ith public key)?". In this work, we consider the following notion of circular security, where the adversary must distinguish between an n-encryption cycle and n encryptions of **0** (where the ith encryption is computed using the ith public key).

Definition 7. *A public key cryptosystem $\mathcal{PKE}$ is said to n-circular secure if for all security parameters λ, PPT adversaries $\mathcal{A}$, $\mathsf{Adv}^{circ}_{\mathcal{A}, \mathcal{PKE}}(\lambda, n)$ is negligible in λ, where advantage of $\mathcal{A}$ is defined as $\mathsf{Adv}^{circ}_{\mathcal{A}, \mathcal{PKE}}(\lambda, n) = | \Pr[\mathsf{Exp\text{-}circ}(n, \mathcal{PKE}, \mathcal{A}, \lambda) = 1] - 1/2|$, and $\mathsf{Exp\text{-}circ}$ is defined in Fig. 2.*

$\mathsf{Exp\text{-}circ}(n, \mathcal{PKE}, \mathcal{A}, \lambda)$
$b \leftarrow \{0, 1\}$
$(\mathsf{pk}_i, \mathsf{sk}_i) \leftarrow \mathsf{Setup}(1^\lambda)$ for $i \leq n$
$\mathsf{ct}_i^{(0)} \leftarrow \mathsf{Enc}(\mathsf{pk}_i, \mathsf{sk}_{(i \bmod n)+1})$
$\mathsf{ct}_i^{(1)} \leftarrow \mathsf{Enc}(\mathsf{pk}_i, \mathbf{0})$
$\hat{b} \leftarrow \mathcal{A}\left(\{(\mathsf{pk}_i, \mathsf{ct}_i^{(b)})\}_i\right)$
Output $(\hat{b} \stackrel{?}{=} b)$

Fig. 2. Security game for n-circular security

3.1   Separating IND-CPA and Circular Security

First, let us recall the theorem statement from [24].

Theorem 1 ([24]). *If there exists a secure indistinguishability obfuscator for polynomial size circuits (Defintion 6) and a secure pseudorandom generator, then for every positive integer n, there exists a public key encryption scheme $\mathcal{PKE}$ such that*

- For all PPT adversaries $\mathcal{A}$, there exists a negligible function $negl_1(\cdot)$ and λ_0 such that for all security parameters $\lambda > \lambda_0$, $\mathsf{Adv}^{\mathsf{ind\text{-}cpa}}_{\mathcal{A},\mathcal{PKE}}(\lambda) \leq negl_1(\lambda)$, and
- There exists a PPT algorithm Test and a negligible function $negl_2(\cdot)$ such that for all security parameters λ, $\mathsf{Adv}^{\mathsf{circ}}_{\mathsf{Test},\mathcal{PKE}}(\lambda, n) \geq 1/2 - negl_2(\lambda)$.

We observe that the counterexample provided by Koppula, Ramchen, and Waters could be trivially extended to prove the following (slightly stronger) statement.

Theorem 2. *If there exists a secure indistinguishability obfuscator for polynomial size circuits (Defintion 6) and a secure pseudorandom generator, then there exists a public key encryption scheme $\mathcal{PKE}$ such that*

- For all PPT adversaries $\mathcal{A}$, there exists a negligible function $negl_1(\cdot)$ and λ_0 such that for all security parameters $\lambda > \lambda_0$, $\mathsf{Adv}^{\mathsf{ind\text{-}cpa}}_{\mathcal{A},\mathcal{PKE}}(\lambda) \leq negl_1(\lambda)$, and
- There exists a PPT algorithm Test, polynomial $p(\cdot)$ and a negligible function $negl_2(\cdot)$ such that for all security parameters λ and $n \leq p(\lambda)$, $\mathsf{Adv}^{\mathsf{circ}}_{\mathsf{Test},\mathcal{PKE}}(\lambda, n) \geq 1/2 - negl_2(\lambda)$.

The KRW counterexample could be extended as follows — For security parameter λ and polynomial $p(\cdot)$, instantiate $p(\lambda)$ copies of KRW scheme where each scheme is designed to be insecure for a certain length key cycle.

Our result proves a stronger statement which is not implied by the KRW counterexample. It is formally stated below.

Theorem 3. *If there exists a secure indistinguishability obfuscator for polynomial size circuits (Defintion 6), secure bootstrappable homomorphic encryption scheme (Definitions 4 and 5), and a secure pseudorandom generator, then there exists a public key encryption scheme $\mathcal{PKE}$ such that*

- For all PPT adversaries $\mathcal{A}$, there exists a negligible function $negl_1(\cdot)$ and λ_0 such that for all security parameters $\lambda > \lambda_0$, $\mathsf{Adv}^{\mathsf{ind\text{-}cpa}}_{\mathcal{A},\mathcal{PKE}}(\lambda) \leq negl_1(\lambda)$, and
- There exists a PPT algorithm Test, a negligible function $negl_2(\cdot)$ such that for all security parameters λ and positive integers α, $\mathsf{Adv}^{\mathsf{circ}}_{\mathsf{Test},\mathcal{PKE}}(\lambda, \alpha) \geq 1/2 - negl_2(\lambda)$.

4 Unbounded Circular Insecure Public Key Encryption Scheme

In this section, we prove Theorem 3 by constructing a public key encryption scheme $\mathcal{PKE} = (\mathsf{Setup}_{\mathrm{PKE}}, \mathsf{Enc}_{\mathrm{PKE}}, \mathsf{Dec}_{\mathrm{PKE}})$ that breaks circular security with unbounded length key cycles. Let $\mathcal{HE} = (\mathsf{Setup}_{\mathrm{HE}}, \mathsf{Enc}_{\mathrm{HE}}, \mathsf{Eval}_{\mathrm{HE}}, \mathsf{Dec}_{\mathrm{HE}})$ be a secure bootstrappable homomorphic encryption scheme, $i\mathcal{O}$ be a secure indistinguishability obfuscator and PRG be a secure pseudorandom generator that maps ℓ bit inputs to 2ℓ bit outputs. The construction is described as follows:

SelfCycleTest

Constants: Secret key $\mathsf{SK_{HE}}$, Value t.
Inputs: Ciphertext ct.

1. Decrypt ct as $(\mathsf{sk}, s) = \mathsf{Dec_{PKE}}(\mathsf{SK_{HE}}, \mathsf{ct})$.
2. If $\mathsf{sk} = \mathsf{SK_{HE}}$ and $\mathsf{PRG}(s) = t$ output 1, otherwise output 0.

Fig. 3. SelfCycleTest

- $\mathsf{Setup_{PKE}}(1^\lambda)$: It runs HE setup algorithm to obtain a public and secret key pair as $(\mathsf{PK_{HE}}, \mathsf{SK_{HE}}) \leftarrow \mathsf{Setup_{HE}}(1^\lambda, 1^D)$, where D is a depth such that $\mathsf{depth}(C_{\lambda,D}^{\mathsf{Dec_{HE}}}) \leq D$.[4] It uniformly samples $s \leftarrow \{0,1\}^\ell$, sets $t = \mathsf{PRG}(s)$, and computes the obfuscation of program SelfCycleTest (described in Fig. 3) as $\mathsf{Prog} \leftarrow i\mathcal{O}(\mathsf{SelfCycleTest})$. It sets the public key and secret key as $\mathsf{PK_{PKE}} = (\mathsf{PK_{HE}}, \mathsf{Prog}), \mathsf{SK_{PKE}} = (\mathsf{SK_{HE}}, s)$.
- $\mathsf{Enc_{PKE}}(\mathsf{PK_{PKE}}, m; r)$: It computes ciphertext as $\mathsf{ct} = \mathsf{Enc_{HE}}(\mathsf{PK_{HE}}, m; r)$, where $\mathsf{PK_{PKE}} = (\mathsf{PK_{HE}}, \mathsf{Prog})$.
- $\mathsf{Dec_{PKE}}(\mathsf{SK_{PKE}}, \mathsf{ct})$: It outputs $\mathsf{Dec_{HE}}(\mathsf{SK_{HE}}, \mathsf{ct})$, where $\mathsf{SK_{PKE}} = (\mathsf{SK_{HE}}, s)$.

The proof of Theorem 3 is described in two parts. First, we show a poly-time attack on circular security of $\mathcal{PKE}$ in Sect. 4.1. Next, we prove it to be IND-CPA secure in Sect. 4.2.

4.1 Attack on Unbounded Circular Security

We construct a PPT adversary $\mathcal{A}$ which breaks unbounded circular security of above construction as follows:

1. Challenger generates n public and secret key pairs as $\{(\mathsf{pk}_i, \mathsf{sk}_i)\}_{i=1}^n$ by independently running the setup algorithm n times $((\mathsf{pk}_i, \mathsf{sk}_i) \leftarrow \mathsf{Setup_{PKE}}(1^\lambda)$ for $i \leq n$). It uniformly chooses a bit $b \leftarrow \{0,1\}$, and computes ciphertexts $\mathsf{ct}_i \leftarrow \mathsf{Enc_{PKE}}(\mathsf{pk}_i, m_{i,b})$ for $i \leq n$, where $m_{i,0} = \mathsf{sk}_{(i \bmod n)+1}$ and $m_{i,1} = 0^{|m_{i,0}|}$. Finally, it sends $\{(\mathsf{pk}_i, \mathsf{ct}_i)\}_{i=1}^n$ to $\mathcal{A}$.
2. $\mathcal{A}$ receives n public key and ciphertext pairs $\{(\mathsf{pk}_i, \mathsf{ct}_i)\}_{i=1}^n$, and proceeds as follows:
   - It sets $\mathsf{ct}_n' = \mathsf{ct}_n$.
   - For $i = n-1$ to $i = 1$:
     - Compute $\mathsf{ct}_i' = \mathsf{Eval_{HE}}(C_i, \mathsf{ct}_i)$, where C_i is the HE decryption circuit $C^{\mathsf{Dec_{HE}}}$ with ct_{i+1}' hardwired as the its second input, i.e. $C_i(x) = C^{\mathsf{Dec_{HE}}}(x, \mathsf{ct}_{i+1}')$.[5]

---

[4] Note that such a depth D exists since our HE scheme is bootstrappable (Definition 4).

[5] Actually, the circuits C_i are not standard HE decryption circuits because ciphertexts ct_i are encryptions of $(i+1)^{th}$ secret key and an extra element, therefore the circuit must ignore the second element during homomorphic decryption.

- $\mathcal{A}$ runs program Prog_1 on input ct'_1, and outputs $b' = \mathsf{Prog}_1(\mathsf{ct}'_1)$ as its guess, where $\mathsf{pk}_1 = (\mathsf{pk}'_1, \mathsf{Prog}_1)$.
3. $\mathcal{A}$ wins if its guess is correct $(b' = b)$.

Lemma 1. *If* PRG *is a secure pseudorandom generator, then there exists a negligible function* $\mathsf{negl}(\cdot)$ *such that for all security parameters* λ *and positive integers* n, $\mathsf{Adv}^{\mathsf{circ}}_{\mathcal{A},\mathcal{PKE}}(\lambda, n) \geq 1/2 - \mathsf{negl}(\lambda)$.

Proof. We prove this lemma in two parts. First, we consider a length n key cycle and show that adversary $\mathcal{A}$ always correctly guesses challenger's bit b as 1. Next, we show that, with all but negligible probability, $\mathcal{A}$ correctly guesses b as 0.

As we described earlier, the basic idea is to slice the ring structure of n ciphertexts by iteratively reducing an n-circular attack to an $(n-1)$-circular attack and finally, reducing it to a 1-circular attack. For slicing the ring of ciphertexts, we use bootstrappability of the underlying scheme. The correctness of the above reduction is proven by induction over cycle length n. The base case $n = 1$ follows directly from the correctness of program Prog_1. For the induction step, assume that $\mathcal{A}$ correctly identifies a length k key cycle. To prove that $\mathcal{A}$ also identifies length $k + 1$ key cycle, we only need to show that $\mathcal{A}$ correctly reduces a $(k + 1)$-circular instance to a k-circular instance. Note that given $k + 1$ public key, ciphertext pairs $(\{(\mathsf{pk}_i, \mathsf{ct}_i)\}^{k+1}_{i=1})$. $\mathcal{A}$ computes ct'_k as $\mathsf{ct}'_k = \mathsf{Eval}_{\mathrm{HE}}(C_k, \mathsf{ct}_k)$. If ct_{k+1} is an encryption of sk_1 under pk_{k+1}, and ct_k is an encryption of sk_{k+1} under pk_k, then ct'_k will be an encryption of sk_1 under pk_k as the scheme $\mathcal{HE}$ is bootstrappable satisfying Definition 4. Therefore, using inductive hypothesis, we can conclude that $\mathcal{A}$ correctly identifies length $k + 1$ key cycle. Thus, the above reduction correctly reduces circular instances with unbounded length key cycles to 1-circular instances, and therefore $\mathcal{A}$ guesses the bit b as 1 with probability 1.

To conclude our proof we just need to show that if the cycle is encryption of all zeros, then $\mathcal{A}$ outputs 0 with all but negligible probability. This follows from the fact that PRG is a secure pseudorandom generator. Consider a hybrid experiment in which the value t_1 is sampled uniformly at random instead of being computed as $t_1 = \mathrm{PRG}(s_1)$. Since PRG is a length doubling pseudorandom generator, we can claim that in the hybrid experiment (with all but negligible probability) Prog_1 outputs 0 because there does not exist any pre-image s for t_1. Therefore, if PRG is a secure pseudorandom generator, $\mathcal{A}$ will always output 0 with all but negligible probability. Thus, $\mathcal{A}$ wins the n-circular security game with all but negligible probability.

4.2   IND-CPA Security

Lemma 2. *If* $i\mathcal{O}$ *is a secure indistinguishability obfuscator for polynomial size circuits (Definition 6),* $\mathcal{HE}$ *is a secure bootstrappable homomorphic encryption scheme (Definitions 4 and 5), and* PRG *is a secure pseudorandom generator, then public key encryption scheme* $\mathcal{PKE}$ *is IND-CPA secure (Definition 1).*

Proof. We prove above lemma by contradiction. Let $\mathcal{A}$ be any PPT adversary that wins the IND-CPA security game against $\mathcal{PKE}$ with non-negligible advantage. We argue that such an adversary must break security of at least one underlying primitive. To formally prove security, we construct a series of hybrid games as follows.

Game 1: This game is the original IND-CPA security game described in Definition 1.

1. Challenger runs HE setup algorithm to obtain a public and secret key pair as $(\mathsf{PK_{HE}, SK_{HE}}) \leftarrow \mathsf{Setup_{HE}}(1^\lambda)$. It uniformly samples $s \leftarrow \{0,1\}^\ell$, sets $t = \mathrm{PRG}(s)$, and computes the obfuscation of program SelfCycleTest (described in Fig. 3) as $\mathsf{Prog} \leftarrow i\mathcal{O}(\mathrm{SelfCycleTest})$. It sets the public key and secret key as $\mathsf{PK_{PKE}} = (\mathsf{PK_{HE}, Prog}), \mathsf{SK_{PKE}} = (\mathsf{SK_{HE}}, s)$. Finally, it sends $\mathsf{PK_{PKE}}$ to $\mathcal{A}$.
2. $\mathcal{A}$ receives $\mathsf{PK_{PKE}}$ from challenger, and computes messages m_0, m_1. It sends (m_0, m_1) to the challenger.
3. Challenger chooses bit $b \leftarrow \{0,1\}$, computes $\mathsf{ct}^* \leftarrow \mathsf{Enc_{PKE}}(\mathsf{PK_{PKE}}, m_b)$, and sends ct^* to $\mathcal{A}$.
4. $\mathcal{A}$ receives challenge ciphertext ct^* from challenger, and outputs its guess b'.
5. $\mathcal{A}$ wins if it guesses correctly, that is if $b = b'$.

Game 2: Game 2 is same as Game 1, except challenger uniformly samples t from $\{0,1\}^{2\ell}$ instead of computing it as $t = \mathrm{PRG}(s)$.

1. Challenger runs HE setup algorithm to obtain a public and secret key pair as $(\mathsf{PK_{HE}, SK_{HE}}) \leftarrow \mathsf{Setup_{HE}}(1^\lambda)$. It uniformly samples $s \leftarrow \{0,1\}^\ell$, $\underline{t \leftarrow \{0,1\}^{2\ell}}$, and computes the obfuscation of program SelfCycleTest (described in Fig. 3) as $\mathsf{Prog} \leftarrow i\mathcal{O}(\mathrm{SelfCycleTest})$. It sets the public key and secret key as $\mathsf{PK_{PKE}} = (\mathsf{PK_{HE}, Prog}), \mathsf{SK_{PKE}} = (\mathsf{SK_{HE}}, s)$. Finally, it sends $\mathsf{PK_{PKE}}$ to $\mathcal{A}$.

2–5. Same as before.

Game 3: Game 3 is same as Game 2, except challenger computes Prog as obfuscation of program Zero.

1. Challenger runs HE setup algorithm to obtain a public and secret key pair as $(\mathsf{PK_{HE}, SK_{HE}}) \leftarrow \mathsf{Setup_{HE}}(1^\lambda)$. It uniformly samples $s \leftarrow \{0,1\}^\ell, t \leftarrow \{0,1\}^{2\ell}$, and $\underline{\text{computes the obfuscation of program Zero (described in Fig. 4) as } \mathsf{Prog}} \leftarrow i\mathcal{O}(\mathrm{Zero})^6$. It sets the public key and secret key as $\mathsf{PK_{PKE}} = (\mathsf{PK_{HE}, Prog})$, $\overline{\mathsf{SK_{PKE}} = (\mathsf{SK_{HE}}, s)}$. Finally, it sends $\mathsf{PK_{PKE}}$ to $\mathcal{A}$.

2–5. Same as before.

We now establish via a sequence of claims that the adversary's advantage between each adjacent game is negligible. Let $\mathsf{Adv}_i = |\Pr[b' = b] - 1/2|$ denote the advantage of adversary $\mathcal{A}$ in Game i of guessing the bit b.

---

[6] Note that program Zero must be padded such that it is of same size as program SelfCycleTest.

```
                                   Zero

    Inputs: Ciphertext ct.

    1. Output 0.
```

Fig. 4. Zero

Claim 1. *If* PRG *is a secure pseudorandom generator, then for all PPT* $\mathcal{A}$, $|\mathsf{Adv}_1 - \mathsf{Adv}_2| \leq negl(\lambda)$ *for some negligible function* $negl(\cdot)$.

Proof. We describe and analyze a PPT reduction algorithm $\mathcal{B}$ that plays the pseudorandom generator security game. $\mathcal{B}$ first receives a PRG challenge $T \in \{0,1\}^{2\ell}$. It then plays the security game with $\mathcal{A}$ as described in Game 1 with the exception that in step 1 it lets $t = T$. If $\mathcal{A}$ wins (i.e. $b' = b$), then $\mathcal{B}$ guesses '1' to indicate that T was chosen in the image space of PRG$(\cdot)$; otherwise, it outputs '0' to that T was chosen randomly.

We observe that when T is generated as $T = \text{PRG}(r)$, then $\mathcal{B}$ gives exactly the view of Game 1 to $\mathcal{A}$. Otherwise if T is chosen randomly the view is of Game 2. Therefore if $|\mathsf{Adv}_1 - \mathsf{Adv}_2|$ is non-negligble, $\mathcal{B}$ must also have non-negligible advantage against the pseudorandom generator.

Claim 2. *If* $i\mathcal{O}$ *is a secure indistinguishability obfuscator, then for all PPT* $\mathcal{A}$, $|\mathsf{Adv}_2 - \mathsf{Adv}_3| \leq negl(\lambda)$ *for some negligible function* $negl(\cdot)$.

Proof. We describe and analyze a PPT reduction algorithm $\mathcal{B}$ that plays the indistinguishability obfuscation security game with $\mathcal{A}$. $\mathcal{B}$ runs steps 1 as in Game 2, except it creates two programs as $C_0 = \text{SelfCycleTest}$ and $C_1 = \text{Zero}$. It submits both of these to the IO challenger and receives back a program P. It sets $\text{Prog} = P$ and finishes step 1. It executes steps 2–5 as in Game 2. If the attacker wins (i.e. $b' = b$), then $\mathcal{B}$ guesses '0' to indicate that P was and obfuscation of C_0; otherwise, it guesses '1' to indicate it was an obfuscation of C_1.

We observe that when P is generated as an obfuscation of C_0, then $\mathcal{B}$ gives exactly the view of Game 2 to $\mathcal{A}$. Otherwise if P is chosen as an obfuscation of C_1 the view is of Game 2. In addition, the programs are functionally equivalent with all but negligible probability. The reason is that t is outside the image of the pseudorandom generator with probability at least $1 - 2^\ell$. Therefore if $|\mathsf{Adv}_2 - \mathsf{Adv}_3|$ is non-negligble, $\mathcal{B}$ must also have non-negligible advantage against the indisguishability obfuscation game.

Claim 3. *If* $\mathcal{HE}$ *is a secure bootstrappable homomorphic encryption scheme, then for all PPT* $\mathcal{A}$, $\mathsf{Adv}_3 \leq negl(\lambda)$ *for some negligible function* $negl(\cdot)$.

Proof. We describe and analyze a PPT reduction algorithm $\mathcal{B}$ that plays the IND-CPA security game with $\mathcal{HE}$ challenger. $\mathcal{B}$ receives public key PK_{HE} from $\mathcal{HE}$ challenger. It runs step 1 as described in Game 3 with the exception that it uses PK_{HE} generated by $\mathcal{HE}$ challenger instead of running the setup algorithm.

$\mathcal{B}$ forwards the challenge messages (m_0, m_1) it receives from $\mathcal{A}$ to $\mathcal{HE}$ challenger as its challenge, and receives ct^* as the challenge ciphertext, which it then forwards to $\mathcal{A}$. Finally, $\mathcal{B}$ outputs the same bit as $\mathcal{A}$.

We observe that if $\mathcal{A}$ wins (i.e. $b' = b$), then $\mathcal{B}$ also wins because it exactly simulates the view of Game 3 for $\mathcal{A}$. Therefore if Adv_3 is non-negligble, $\mathcal{B}$ must also have non-negligible advantage against $\mathcal{HE}$ challenger.

5   Unbounded Counterexamples with Mixed Cryptosystems

We conclude by making the following observation pertaining to our counterexample. In our construction, we started slicing the key cycle from the end, and after every cycle length reduction iteration, the new (homomorphically) evaluated ciphertext is encrypted under a different public key. Concretely, if we consider an n-length key cycle, then after i^{th} cycle reduction iteration, the ciphertext ct'_{n-i} generated is encrypted under public key pk_{n-i}. Therefore, the cycle testing algorithm works in the presence of a LHE scheme. We observe that if we instantiate our idea with an unbounded fully homomorphic encryption (FHE) scheme as opposed to a leveled one, then the cycle testing algorithm could be alternatively evaluated by slicing the key cycle from the start. More formally, in the first iteration, our new cycle tester would homomorphically evaluate circuit $C_{\mathsf{Dec},2}$ on ct_1, where $C_{\mathsf{Dec},2}$ is a circuit that takes an input x and uses it to decrypt ct_2. Since ct_1 and ct_2 are encryptions of sk_2 and sk_3 under public keys pk_1 and pk_2 (respectively), the homomorphic evaluation would generate a new ciphertext ct'_2 that would be an encryption of sk_3 under public key pk_1. Note that this also reduces the key cycle length by one, but in the forward direction and it requires the encryption scheme to be fully homomorphic. Therefore, iteratively applying this procedure would finally generate a ciphertext ct'_1 which encrypts secret key sk_1 under public key pk_1, and as before, the self-cycle could be tested using Prog_1.

The crucial observation in the alternative cycle testing procedure is that we require only one encryption scheme to be homomorphic encryption scheme. This opens up the possibility of creating a counterexample for circular security under *mixed* public key encryption (PKE) framework, where the cycle could comprise of distinct and variegated PKE schemes with a universal message and key space. In particular, this shows that just one "bad" key could poison the circular security for any arbitrary length cycle.

References

1. Acar, T., Belenkiy, M., Bellare, M., Cash, D.: Cryptographic agility and its relation to circular encryption. In: Gilbert, H. (ed.) EUROCRYPT 2010. LNCS, vol. 6110, pp. 403–422. Springer, Heidelberg (2010). doi:10.1007/978-3-642-13190-5_21
2. Adão, P., Bana, G., Herzog, J., Scedrov, A.: Soundness and completeness of formal encryption: the cases of key cycles and partial information leakage. J. Comput. Secur. **17**(5), 737–797 (2009)

3. Alamati, N., Peikert, C.: Three's compromised too: circular insecurity for any cycle length from (ring-)LWE. Cryptology ePrint Archive, Report 2016/110 (2016)
4. Alperin-Sheriff, J., Peikert, C.: Circular and KDM security for identity-based encryption. In: Fischlin, M., Buchmann, J., Manulis, M. (eds.) PKC 2012. LNCS, vol. 7293, pp. 334–352. Springer, Heidelberg (2012). doi:10.1007/978-3-642-30057-8_20
5. Applebaum, B.: Key-dependent message security: generic amplification and completeness. In: Paterson, K.G. (ed.) EUROCRYPT 2011. LNCS, vol. 6632, pp. 527–546. Springer, Heidelberg (2011). doi:10.1007/978-3-642-20465-4_29
6. Applebaum, B., Cash, D., Peikert, C., Sahai, A.: Fast cryptographic primitives and circular-secure encryption based on hard learning problems. In: Halevi, S. (ed.) CRYPTO 2009. LNCS, vol. 5677, pp. 595–618. Springer, Heidelberg (2009). doi:10.1007/978-3-642-03356-8_35
7. Barak, B., Haitner, I., Hofheinz, D., Ishai, Y.: Bounded key-dependent message security. In: Gilbert, H. (ed.) EUROCRYPT 2010. LNCS, vol. 6110, pp. 423–444. Springer, Heidelberg (2010). doi:10.1007/978-3-642-13190-5_22
8. Bishop, A., Hohenberger, S., Waters, B.: New circular security counterexamples from decision linear and learning with errors. In: Iwata, T., Cheon, J.H. (eds.) ASIACRYPT 2015. LNCS, vol. 9453, pp. 776–800. Springer, Heidelberg (2015). doi:10.1007/978-3-662-48800-3_32
9. Black, J., Rogaway, P., Shrimpton, T.: Encryption-scheme security in the presence of key-dependent messages. In: Nyberg, K., Heys, H. (eds.) SAC 2002. LNCS, vol. 2595, pp. 62–75. Springer, Heidelberg (2003). doi:10.1007/3-540-36492-7_6
10. Boneh, D., Halevi, S., Hamburg, M., Ostrovsky, R.: Circular-secure encryption from decision diffie-hellman. In: Wagner, D. (ed.) CRYPTO 2008. LNCS, vol. 5157, pp. 108–125. Springer, Heidelberg (2008). doi:10.1007/978-3-540-85174-5_7
11. Brakerski, Z., Goldwasser, S.: Circular and leakage resilient public-key encryption under subgroup indistinguishability (or: Quadratic residuosity strikes back). IACR Cryptology ePrint Archive 2010/226 (2010)
12. Brakerski, Z., Goldwasser, S., Kalai, Y.T.: Black-box circular-secure encryption beyond affine functions. In: Ishai, Y. (ed.) TCC 2011. LNCS, vol. 6597, pp. 201–218. Springer, Heidelberg (2011). doi:10.1007/978-3-642-19571-6_13
13. Brakerski, Z., Vaikuntanathan, V.: Efficient fully homomorphic encryption from (standard) LWE. In: IEEE 52nd Annual Symposium on Foundations of Computer Science, FOCS 2011, Palm Springs, CA, USA, 22–25 October, 2011, pp. 97–106 (2011)
14. Camenisch, J., Lysyanskaya, A.: An efficient system for non-transferable anonymous credentials with optional anonymity revocation. IACR Cryptology ePrint Archive 2001/19 (2001)
15. Canetti, R., Lin, H., Tessaro, S., Vaikuntanathan, V.: Obfuscation of probabilistic circuits and applications. In: Dodis, Y., Nielsen, J.B. (eds.) TCC 2015. LNCS, vol. 9015, pp. 468–497. Springer, Heidelberg (2015). doi:10.1007/978-3-662-46497-7_19
16. Cash, D., Green, M., Hohenberger, S.: New definitions and separations for circular security. In: Fischlin, M., Buchmann, J., Manulis, M. (eds.) PKC 2012. LNCS, vol. 7293, pp. 540–557. Springer, Heidelberg (2012). doi:10.1007/978-3-642-30057-8_32
17. Coron, J.-S., Lepoint, T., Tibouchi, M.: Practical multilinear maps over the integers. In: Canetti, R., Garay, J.A. (eds.) CRYPTO 2013. LNCS, vol. 8042, pp. 476–493. Springer, Heidelberg (2013). doi:10.1007/978-3-642-40041-4_26
18. Garg, S., Gentry, C., Halevi, S.: Candidate multilinear maps from ideal lattices. In: Johansson, T., Nguyen, P.Q. (eds.) EUROCRYPT 2013. LNCS, vol. 7881, pp. 1–17. Springer, Heidelberg (2013). doi:10.1007/978-3-642-38348-9_1

19. Garg, S., Gentry, C., Halevi, S., Raykova, M., Sahai, A., Waters, B.: Candidate indstinguishability obfuscation and functional encryption for all circuits. In: FOCS (2013)

20. Gentry, C.: Fully homomorphic encryption using ideal lattices. In: Proceedings of the 41st Annual ACM Symposium on Theory of Computing, STOC 2009, Bethesda, MD, USA, 31 May–2 June, 2009, pp. 169–178 (2009)

21. Gentry, C., Sahai, A., Waters, B.: Homomorphic encryption from learning with errors: conceptually-simpler, asymptotically-faster, attribute-based. In: Canetti, R., Garay, J.A. (eds.) CRYPTO 2013. LNCS, vol. 8042, pp. 75–92. Springer, Heidelberg (2013). doi:10.1007/978-3-642-40041-4_5

22. Goldwasser, S., Micali, S.: Probabilistic encryption. J. Comput. Syst. Sci. **28**(2), 270–299 (1984)

23. Haitner, I., Holenstein, T.: On the (im)possibility of key dependent encryption. In: Reingold, O. (ed.) TCC 2009. LNCS, vol. 5444, pp. 202–219. Springer, Heidelberg (2009). doi:10.1007/978-3-642-00457-5_13

24. Koppula, V., Ramchen, K., Waters, B.: Separations in circular security for arbitrary length key cycles. In: Dodis, Y., Nielsen, J.B. (eds.) TCC 2015. LNCS, vol. 9015, pp. 378–400. Springer, Heidelberg (2015). doi:10.1007/978-3-662-46497-7_15

25. Koppula, V., Waters, B.: Circular security separations for arbitrary length cycles from lWE. Cryptology ePrint Archive, Report 2016/117 (2016)

26. Laud, P.: Encryption cycles and two views of cryptography. In: NORDSEC 2002 - Proceedings of the 7th Nordic Workshop on Secure IT Systems (Karlstad University Studies 2002:31, pp. 85–100 (2002)

27. Malkin, T., Teranishi, I., Yung, M.: Efficient circuit-size independent public key encryption with KDM security. In: Paterson, K.G. (ed.) EUROCRYPT 2011. LNCS, vol. 6632, pp. 507–526. Springer, Heidelberg (2011). doi:10.1007/978-3-642-20465-4_28

28. Marcedone, A., Orlandi, C.: Obfuscation $\Rightarrow$ (IND-CPA Security $\nRightarrow$ Circular Security). In: Abdalla, M., Prisco, R. (eds.) SCN 2014. LNCS, vol. 8642, pp. 77–90. Springer, Cham (2014). doi:10.1007/978-3-319-10879-7_5

29. Regev, O.: On lattices, learning with errors, random linear codes, and cryptography. In: Proceedings of the 37th Annual ACM Symposium on Theory of Computing, Baltimore, MD, USA, 22–24 May, 2005, pp. 84–93 (2005)

30. Rivest, R.L., Adleman, L., Dertouzos, M.L.: On data banks and privacy homomorphisms. In: Foundations of Secure Computation, pp. 169–179. Academia Press (1978)

31. Sahai, A., Waters, B.: How to use indistinguishability obfuscation: deniable encryption, and more. In: Symposium on Theory of Computing, STOC 2014, New York, NY, USA, 31 May–03 June, 2014, pp. 475–484 (2014)

32. Zimmerman, J.: How to obfuscate programs directly. In: Oswald, E., Fischlin, M. (eds.) EUROCRYPT 2015. LNCS, vol. 9057, pp. 439–467. Springer, Heidelberg (2015). doi:10.1007/978-3-662-46803-6_15

Structure-Preserving Chosen-Ciphertext Security with Shorter Verifiable Ciphertexts

Benoît Libert[1], Thomas Peters[2([envelope])], and Chen Qian[3]

[1] CNRS, Laboratoire LIP (CNRS, ENSL, U. Lyon, Inria, UCBL),
ENS de Lyon, Lyon, France
[2] FNRS & UCLouvain, ICTEAM, Louvain-la-Neuve, Belgium
thomas.peters@uclouvain.be
[3] IRISA, Rennes, France

Abstract. Structure-preserving cryptography is a world where messages, signatures, ciphertexts and public keys are entirely made of elements of a group over which a bilinear map is efficiently computable. While structure-preserving signatures have received much attention the last 6 years, structure-preserving encryption schemes have undergone slower development. In particular, the best known structure-preserving cryptosystems with chosen-ciphertext (IND-CCA2) security either rely on symmetric pairings or require long ciphertexts comprised of hundreds of group elements or do not provide publicly verifiable ciphertexts. We provide a publicly verifiable construction based on the SXDH assumption in asymmetric bilinear groups $e : \mathbb{G} \times \hat{\mathbb{G}} \to \mathbb{G}_T$, which features relatively short ciphertexts. For typical parameters, our ciphertext size amounts to less than 40 elements of $\mathbb{G}$. As a second contribution, we provide a structure-preserving encryption scheme with perfectly randomizable ciphertexts and replayable chosen-ciphertext security. Our new RCCA-secure system significantly improves upon the best known system featuring similar properties in terms of ciphertext size.

Keywords: Structure-preserving encryption · Chosen-ciphertext security · RCCA security · Public ciphertext verifiability

1 Introduction

Structure-preserving cryptography is a paradigm where handled objects all live in discrete-log-hard abelian groups over which a bilinear map is efficiently computable. The structure-preserving property allows for a smooth interaction of the considered primitives with Groth-Sahai (GS) proof systems [36], making them very powerful tools for the modular design of privacy-preserving cryptographic protocols [3, 8, 16, 17, 19, 27, 32, 37, 44, 51].

In structure-preserving signatures (SPS) [6, 8], messages, signatures, public keys all live in the source groups $(\mathbb{G}, \hat{\mathbb{G}})$ of a bilinear map $e : \mathbb{G} \times \hat{\mathbb{G}} \to \mathbb{G}_T$. The roots of SPS schemes can be traced back to the work of Groth [34], which initiated a line of work seeking to obtain short signatures [4–6, 23, 40, 45], security

© International Association for Cryptologic Research 2017
S. Fehr (Ed.): PKC 2017, Part I, LNCS 10174, pp. 247–276, 2017.
DOI: 10.1007/978-3-662-54365-8_11

under standard assumptions [4,18,24,37,40,45], tight security proofs [5,37] or lower bounds [1,7]. Beyond signatures, structure-preserving cryptography was also developed in the context of commitment schemes [6,9,10,35,42], public-key [5,16] and identity-based encryption [41,52] as well as in deterministic primitives [2].

STRUCTURE-PRESERVING ENCRYPTION. Camenisch *et al.* [16] came up with the first chosen-ciphertext-secure (IND-CCA2) structure-preserving public-key encryption scheme. Structure-preserving CCA2 security is motivated by applications in the realization of oblivious third parties protocols [20] or proofs of knowledge of leakage-resilient signatures [28]. Among the use cases of structure-preserving CCA-secure encryption, [16] mentions various settings where a user, who has a ciphertext and a Groth-Sahai proof of its well-formedness, wants to convince a third party that it is in possession of such a ciphertext without revealing it. Structure-preserving encryption also allows two users to jointly compute an encryption (of a function) of two plaintexts such that neither player learns the plaintext of the other player and only one of them obtains the ciphertext.

As pointed out in [16], structure-preserving encryption should make it possible to efficiently and non-interactively prove possession of a valid ciphertext, which rules out the use of standard techniques – like hash functions [26] or ordinary (i.e., non-structure-preserving) one-time signatures [21,29,50] – that are typically used to achieve chosen-ciphertext security [49] in the standard model. In particular, the original Cramer-Shoup cryptosystem [26] does not provide the sought-after structure-preserving property and neither do direct applications of the Canetti-Halevi-Katz paradigm [21]: for example, merely combining Kiltz's tag-based encryption [39] with a one-time SPS does not work as the security proof of [39] requires (hashed) verification keys to be encoded as exponents. Nevertheless, Camenisch *et al.* [16] managed to twist the design principle of Cramer-Shoup [26] so as to obtain a variant of the scheme that only resorts to algebraic operations when it comes to tying all ciphertexts components altogether in a non-malleable manner.

While efficient and based on the standard Decision Linear assumption [14], the initial construction of [16] still suffers from certain disadvantages. In the first variant of their scheme, for example, one of the ciphertext components lives in the target group $\mathbb{G}_T$ of a bilinear map $e : \mathbb{G} \times \hat{\mathbb{G}} \to \mathbb{G}_T$ which complicates its use in applications requiring to prove knowledge of a ciphertext: recall that Groth-Sahai proofs require witnesses to live in the *source* group of a bilinear (i.e., they need *strictly* structure-preserving components in the sense of [9]). While Camenisch *et al.* [16] suggested a technique of moving all ciphertext components to the source groups in their scheme, this is only known to be possible using symmetric bilinear groups (where $\mathbb{G} = \hat{\mathbb{G}}$) as it relies on the one-sided pairing randomization technique of [8]. Another limitation of [16] is that, analogously to the original Cramer-Shoup system [26], valid ciphertexts (i.e., which lie in the range of the legitimate encryption algorithm) are not publicly recognizable. As a result, only the sender of a ciphertext (who knows the random encryption coins) can generate a proof that this particular ciphertext is indeed a valid ciphertext without revealing it. Ideally, any ciphertext observer should be able to commit to that ciphertext and prove statements about it without any interaction with the sender, which would be possible with publicly verifiable ciphertexts.

Abe *et al.* [5] provided several constructions of structure-preserving CCA2-secure encryption with publicly verifiable ciphertexts. On the downside, their solutions incur substantially longer ciphertexts than [16]: under the Decision Linear assumption, the most efficient solution of [5] entails 321 group elements per ciphertext. Moreover, it was only described in terms of symmetric pairings.

In addition, symmetric pairings have become significantly less efficient (see, e.g., [31]) as the use of small-characteristic fields is now considered insecure [11]. This motivates the search for efficient structure-preserving CCA2-secure systems which provide shorter ciphertexts and can operate in asymmetric pairings.

OUR CONTRIBUTIONS. We provide a new CCA2-secure structure-preserving encryption scheme wherein the validity of ciphertexts is publicly verifiable and ciphertexts only consist of 16 elements of $\mathbb{G}$ and 11 elements of $\hat{\mathbb{G}}$. By "public verifiability", we mean that ciphertexts which are rejected by the decryption algorithm should be recognizable given the public key. While stronger definitions of verifiability could be used[1], this notions suffices to ensure confidentiality in settings – like threshold decryption [13,46,54] – where potentially harmful decryption queries should be publicly detectable. In particular, our first scheme readily implies a CCA2-secure structure-preserving cryptosystem that enables threshold decryption in the adaptive corruption setting.

In our first scheme, the ciphertext size amounts to 38 elements of $\mathbb{G}$ assuming that each element of $\hat{\mathbb{G}}$ has a representation which is twice as large as the representation of $\mathbb{G}$ elements. The security is proved under the standard symmetric eXternal Diffie-Hellman (SXDH) assumption [53] in asymmetric bilinear maps.

As a second contribution, we provide a different structure-preserving cryptosystem which features perfectly re-randomizable ciphertexts and replayable chosen-ciphertext (RCCA) security. As defined by Canetti, Krawczyk and Nielsen [22], RCCA security is a meaningful relaxation of CCA2 security that tolerates a "benign" form of malleability: namely, anyone should be able to randomize a given ciphertext into another encryption of the same plaintext. Under the SXDH assumption, our construction features statistically randomizable ciphertexts which only consist of 34 elements of $\mathbb{G}$ and 18 elements of $\hat{\mathbb{G}}$. Under the same[2] assumption, the best known RCCA-secure realization thus far was the scheme of Chase *et al.* [25] which costs 49 elements of $\mathbb{G}$ and 20 elements of $\hat{\mathbb{G}}$.

OUR TECHNIQUES. Our structure-preserving CCA2 secure cryptosystem builds on a public-key encryption scheme suggested by Libert and Yung [46], which is

---

[1] For example, we could additionally require that all ciphertexts outside the range of the decryption algorithm are rejected by the decryption procedure.

[2] The authors of [25] only described a construction from the DLIN assumption with 93 elements per ciphertext. Their approach extends to the SXDH assumption and happens to provide structure-preserving schemes.

not structure-preserving in its original form. Our starting observation is that, unlike Kiltz's tag-based encryption scheme [39], the security proof of [46] does not require to interpret one-time signature verification keys as exponents. The construction of [46] is obtained by tweaking the Cramer-Shoup paradigm [26] and replacing the designated verifier NIZK proofs of ciphertext validity by a universally verifiable Groth-Sahai proof. In order to obtain publicly verifiable proofs with the desired security property called *simulation-soundness* [50], the authors of [46] used Groth-Sahai common reference strings (CRSes) which depend on the verification key of a one-time signature. In the security proof, the key idea was to enable the simulation of fake NIZK proofs of ciphertext validity while making it impossible for the adversary to create such a fake proof himself. In Groth-Sahai proofs, this can be achieved by programming the Groth-Sahai CRSes in such a way that they form a linear subspace of dimension 1 in the challenge ciphertext whereas adversarially-generated ciphertexts involve CRSes of dimension 2 (which are perfectly sound CRSes).

We build on the observation that the approach of [46] still works if one-time verification keys consist of group elements instead of exponents. One difficulty is that we need one-time signature verification keys comprised of a single group element while the best known one-time SPS [6] have longer verification keys. Our solution is to "hash" the one-time verification keys of [6] in a structure-preserving manner. For this purpose, we apply a strictly structure-preserving commitment scheme proposed by Abe *et al.* [10] as if it was a chameleon hash function: namely, we replace the hash value by a commitment to the one-time verification key while the corresponding de-commitment information is included in the ciphertext. One caveat is that [10] considers a relaxed security notion for strictly structure-preserving commitments, called *chosen-message target collision-resistance*, which appears insufficient for our purposes. We actually need a stronger notion, called *enhanced chosen-message target collision-resistance* (ECM-TCR), where the adversary should also be able to come up with a different opening to the same message for a given commitment. Fortunately, we can prove that the strictly structure-preserving commitment of [10] *does* provide ECM-TCR security under the SXDH assumption.

The security proof of our construction addresses another technical hurdle which arises from the fact that ciphertexts contain elements from both sources groups $\mathbb{G}$ and $\hat{\mathbb{G}}$. Directly adapting the security proof of [46] would require to sign all elements of $\mathbb{G}$ and $\hat{\mathbb{G}}$ that are contained in the ciphertext, which would require a one-time SPS where messages contain elements of both groups $(\mathbb{G}, \hat{\mathbb{G}})$. While such schemes exist [4], they are less efficient than one-time SPS schemes for unilateral messages. Our solution to this problem is to modify the security proof of Libert and Yung [46] in such a way that not all ciphertexts components have to be signed using the one-time signature. In short, we leverage the fact that only Groth-Sahai commitments have to live in the group $\hat{\mathbb{G}}$: proof elements and other components of the ciphertext can indeed dwell in $\mathbb{G}$. In GS commitments for linear multi-exponentiation equations, we notice that Groth-Sahai commitments are uniquely determined by the proof elements and the statement.

For this reason, even if the adversary tampers with the GS commitments of the challenge ciphertext, it will be unable to create another ciphertext that will be accepted by the decryption oracle. This saves us from having to one-time-sign the Groth-Sahai commitments in the encryption algorithm, which is the reason why we only need such a system for unilateral messages.

Our construction of RCCA-secure encryption extends the ideas of Chase *et al.* [25]. In a nutshell, the RCCA-secure scheme of [25] combines a semantically secure encryption scheme and a randomizable witness indistinguishable proof of a statement of the form "Either I know the plaintext OR a signature of a ciphertext that this ciphertext is a randomization of". Our construction proceeds in an analogous way by demonstrating a statement of the form "Either I know the plaintext OR this ciphertext is a randomization of the challenge ciphertext".

In a high level, for the two branches of the statement we rely on proofs which nicely share a common structure to optimize our OR-proof. On the one hand, for the knowledge of the plaintext we use a quasi-adaptive NIZK (QA-NIZK) proof, which are NIZK proofs introduced by [38] where the CRS may depend on the specific language for which proofs have to be generated. Our QA-NIZK is built from the one-time structure-preserving linearly homomorphic signature (LHSPS) of Libert, Peters, Joye and Yung [42]. On the other hand, for the one-time signature we use the strongly unforgeable one-time SPS of Abe et al. [5] that we make re-randomizable thanks to LHSPS. These tools allows to combine some of the verification equations for which Groth-Sahai proofs of satisfiability are included in ciphertexts.

RELATED WORK. Several different approaches [15,30,47,48] were taken to reconcile chosen-ciphertext-security and homomorphism. Relaxed flavors of chosen-ciphertext security [22] opened the way to perfectly randomizable encryption schemes offering stronger guarantees than just semantic security. Groth described [33] a weakly RCCA secure variant of Cramer-Shoup which only encrypts messages in a bit-by-bit manner. Prabhakaran and Rosulek [47] showed how to more efficiently encrypt many bits at once in a RCCA-secure realization from the DDH assumption. While their solution features shorter ciphertexts than our RCCA-secure scheme, it is not structure-preserving as it cannot be readily instantiated in groups with a bilinear maps. On the other hand, unlike our scheme and the one of [25], it allows re-randomizing ciphertexts without knowing under which public key they were encrypted.

Prabhakaran and Rosulek subsequently generalized the RCCA security notion [22] into a model [48] of homomorphic encryption that only supports a limited form of malleability. Boneh, Segev and Waters [15] took a different approach aiming for restricted malleability properties. Chase *et al.* [25] considered a modular design of HCCA-secure encryption [48] based on malleable proof systems. Their proposals turn out to be the only known HCCA/RCCA-secure structure-preserving candidates thus far.

2 Background and Definitions

2.1 Hardness Assumptions

We consider groups $(\mathbb{G}, \hat{\mathbb{G}}, \mathbb{G}_T)$ of prime-order p endowed with a bilinear map $e : \mathbb{G} \times \hat{\mathbb{G}} \to \mathbb{G}_T$.

Definition 1. *The **Diffie-Hellman problem** (DDH) in $\mathbb{G}$, is to distinguish the distributions (g, g^a, g^b, g^{ab}) and (g, g^a, g^b, g^c) with $a, b, c \xleftarrow{R} \mathbb{Z}_p$. The Diffie-Hellman assumption asserts the intractability of DDH for any PPT distinguisher.*

In the asymmetric setting $(\mathbb{G}, \hat{\mathbb{G}}, \mathbb{G}_T)$, we consider the SXDH assumption, which posits that the DDH assumption holds in both $\mathbb{G}$ and $\hat{\mathbb{G}}$.

Definition 2. *The **Double Pairing problem** (DP) in $(\mathbb{G}, \hat{\mathbb{G}}, \mathbb{G}_T)$ is, given a pair of group elements $(\hat{g}_z, \hat{g}_r) \in \hat{\mathbb{G}}^2$, to find a non-trivial triple $(z, r) \in \mathbb{G}^2 \backslash \{(1_{\mathbb{G}}, 1_{\mathbb{G}})\}$ such that $e(z, \hat{g}_z) \cdot e(r, \hat{g}_r) = 1_{\mathbb{G}_T}$.*

It is known [8] that the DP assumption is implied by the DDH assumption in $\mathbb{G}$. By exchanging the roles of $\mathbb{G}$ and $\hat{\mathbb{G}}$ in the definition of DP, we obtain a variant of the assumption which implies the hardness of DDH in $\hat{\mathbb{G}}$.

2.2 One-Time Structure-Preserving Signatures

Structure-preserving signatures (SPS) [6,8] are signature schemes where messages and public keys all consist of elements of a group over which a bilinear map $e : \mathbb{G} \times \hat{\mathbb{G}} \to \mathbb{G}_T$ is efficiently computable. Constructions based on simple assumptions were put forth in [4,5].

In the forthcoming sections, we will rely on one-time SPS schemes.

Definition 3. *A one-time signature scheme is a tuple of efficient algorithms $\mathcal{OTS} = (\mathsf{Setup}, \mathsf{KeyGen}, \mathsf{Sign}, \mathsf{Verify})$ where:*

Setup(λ): *This algorithm takes as input a security parameter λ and generates the public parameters PP for the scheme.*

KeyGen (PP): *This algorithm takes as input PP and generates a one-time secret key osk and a one-time verification key ovk.*

Sign(PP, osk, M): *Given as input $(\mathsf{PP}, \mathsf{osk})$ and a message M, this algorithm produces a signature σ for M.*

Verify(PP, ovk, M, σ): *The verification algorithm takes $(\mathsf{PP}, \mathsf{ovk}, M, \sigma)$ and returns 1 or 0.*

Correctness mandates that, for any $\lambda \in \mathbb{N}$, any $\mathsf{PP} \leftarrow \mathsf{Setup}(\lambda)$, any pair $(\mathsf{osk}, \mathsf{ovk}) \leftarrow \mathsf{KeyGen}(\mathsf{PP})$, we have $\mathsf{Verify}(\mathsf{PP}, \mathsf{ovk}, M, \mathsf{Sign}(\mathsf{PP}, \mathsf{osk}, M)) = 1$ for any message M.

In addition, a one-time signature is said *structure-preserving* if the components of ovk, M and σ all live in the source groups $(\mathbb{G}, \hat{\mathbb{G}})$ of a configuration $(\mathbb{G}, \hat{\mathbb{G}}, \mathbb{G}_T)$ of bilinear groups.

Definition 4. *A one-time signature scheme* $\mathcal{OTS}$ = (Setup, KeyGen, Sign, Verify) *is strongly unforgeable against chosen message attack* $(SUF\text{-}CMA)$ *if*

$$\mathbf{Adv}_{OTS,\mathcal{A}}^{SUF\text{-}CMA} = \Pr\left[\begin{array}{l|l} (m^\star, \sigma^\star) \notin Q_{\mathsf{Sign}^{OT}} \wedge & \mathsf{PP} \leftarrow \mathsf{Setup}(1^\lambda) \\ \mathsf{Verify}(\mathsf{ovk}, m^\star, \sigma^\star) = 1 & (\mathsf{ovk}, \mathsf{osk}) \leftarrow \mathsf{KeyGen}(\mathsf{PP}) \\ & (m^\star, \sigma^\star) \leftarrow \mathcal{A}^{\mathsf{Sign}_{\mathsf{osk}}^{OT}(\cdot)}(\mathsf{ovk}) \end{array} \right]$$

is negligible against any PPT adversary $\mathcal{A}$*. Here,* $\mathsf{Sign}_{\mathsf{osk}}^{OT}(\cdot)$ *is a signing oracle which allows the adversary to obtain a signature* σ_m *of only one message* m *for which* (m, σ_m) *is stored in* $Q_{\mathsf{Sign}^{OT}}$*.*

We recall a construction of the one-time Structure-Preserving Signature scheme which was proposed in [5].

Setup(λ)**:** Choose asymmetric bilinear groups $(\mathbb{G}, \hat{\mathbb{G}}, \mathbb{G}_T)$ of prime order $p > 2^\lambda$ and output $\mathsf{PP} = (\mathbb{G}, \hat{\mathbb{G}}, \mathbb{G}_T)$.

KeyGen(PP)**:** Generates the signing key osk and the verification key ovk using the security parameter λ and the number n of messages to be signed.
1. Choose $\hat{g}_z, \hat{g}_r, g \xleftarrow{R} \hat{\mathbb{G}}$.
2. For $i = 1$ to n, pick $(\chi_i, \gamma_i) \xleftarrow{R} \mathbb{Z}_p^2$ and compute $\hat{g}_i = \hat{g}_z^{\chi_i} \hat{g}_r^{\gamma_i}$.
3. Pick $(\zeta, \rho) \xleftarrow{R} \mathbb{Z}_p^2$ and compute $\hat{A} = g_z^\zeta \cdot g_r^\rho$.
4. Set $\mathsf{osk} = (\{(\chi_i, \gamma_i)\}_{i=1}^n, \zeta, \rho) \in \mathbb{G}^{2n+2}$ and

$$\mathsf{ovk} = (\hat{g}_z, \hat{g}_r, \{\hat{g}_i\}_{i=1}^n, \hat{A}) \in \hat{\mathbb{G}}^{n+3}.$$

Sign(osk, $M = (M_1, \ldots, M_n)$)**:** In order to sign $M = (M_1, \ldots, M_n) \in \mathbb{G}^n$, compute $z = g^\zeta \prod_{i=1}^n M_i^{\chi_i}$ and $r = g^\rho \prod_{i=1}^n M_i^{\gamma_i}$. Output $\sigma = (z, r)$.

Verify(ovk, $M = (M_1, \ldots, M_n), \sigma = (z, r)$)**:** Return 1 if and only if the following equations are satisfied: $e(z, \hat{g}_z) \cdot e(r, \hat{g}_r) = e(g, \hat{A}) \cdot \prod_{i=1}^n e(M_i, \hat{g}_i)$.

2.3 Partial One-Time Signature

A special case of the one-time signature presented in Sect. 2.2 is called Partial One-Time Signature (POTS) [12]. In a such scheme, part of the verification key can be re-used in multiple signatures and the remaining part must be refreshed at every signature generation.

Definition 5. *A partial one-time signature (POTS) scheme is a tuple of algorithms* $POTS$ = (Setup, KeyGen, OKeyGen, Sign, Verify).

Setup(λ)**:** *The setup algorithm takes as input a security parameter* λ *and generates the public parameters* PP *for the scheme.*

KeyGen(PP)**:** *The key generation algorithm takes as input the public parameters* PP *and generates the long-term signing key* sk *and long-term verification key* vk*.*

OKeyGen(PP)**:** *The key generation algorithm takes* PP *and generates the one-time signing key* osk *and the one-time verification key* ovk*.*

Sign(PP, sk, osk, M): *The signature algorithm uses the* (PP, osk) *to produce a valid signature σ for the message vector M.*

Verify(PP, vk, ovk, M, σ): *The verification algorithm takes* (PP, vk, ovk, M, σ) *and returns* 1 *or* 0.

Correctness requires that, for any PP $\leftarrow$ Setup(λ), (sk, vk) $\leftarrow$ KeyGen(PP) and (osk, ovk) $\leftarrow$ OKeyGen(PP), the partial one-time signature scheme is correct if and only if Verify(PP, vk, ovk, M, Sign(PP, sk, osk, M)) = 1.

We focus on the strong unforgeability against one-time chosen-message attack of our POTS.

Definition 6. *A POTS scheme POTS* = (Setup, KeyGen, OKeyGen, Sign, Verify) *is strongly unforgeable against one-time chosen-message attack (or OT-CMA secure) if:*

$$\mathbf{Adv}^{OT\text{-}SU\text{-}CMA}_{POTS,\mathcal{A}}(\lambda)$$

$$= \Pr \left[\begin{array}{l} \exists \, (m', \sigma') \text{ s.t. } (\mathsf{ovk}^\star, \sigma', m') \in Q \\ \wedge \, (\mathsf{ovk}^\star, \sigma^\star, m^\star) \notin Q \\ \wedge \, \mathsf{Verify}(\mathsf{vk}, \mathsf{ovk}^\star, m^\star, \sigma^\star) = 1 \end{array} \middle| \begin{array}{l} \mathsf{PP} \leftarrow \mathsf{Setup}(1^\lambda) \\ (\mathsf{vk}, \mathsf{sk}) \leftarrow \mathsf{KeyGen}(\mathsf{PP}) \\ (\mathsf{ovk}^\star, \sigma^\star, m^\star) \leftarrow \mathcal{A}^{\mathcal{O}_{\mathsf{sk}}}(\mathsf{PP}, \mathsf{vk}) \end{array} \right]$$

is negligible for any PPT adversary $\mathcal{A}$. Here, the signing oracle takes as input a message m, generates (ovk, osk) $\leftarrow$ OKeyGen(PP), $\sigma \leftarrow$ Sign(sk, osk, m). *Then, it records* (ovk, m) *to Q and returns* (σ, ovk).

Here, we recall an instantiation of the POTS scheme [4], which is strongly unforgeable against the one-time chosen-message attack (SU-OTCMA) under the DP assumption.

Setup(λ, ℓ): On input of a security parameter λ and an integer $\ell \in poly(\lambda)$, the setup algorithm chooses a large prime $p > 2^\lambda$, asymmetric groups $(\mathbb{G}, \hat{\mathbb{G}}, \mathbb{G}_T)$ of prime order p, with a bilinear map $e : \mathbb{G} \times \hat{\mathbb{G}} \to \mathbb{G}_T$ and the corresponding generators $(g, \hat{g}) \in \mathbb{G} \times \hat{\mathbb{G}}$. The algorithm outputs

$$\mathsf{PP} = (p, \mathbb{G}, \hat{\mathbb{G}}, \mathbb{G}_T, e, g, \hat{g}, \ell).$$

KeyGen(PP): Parse PP as $(p, \mathbb{G}, \hat{\mathbb{G}}, \mathbb{G}_T, e, g, \hat{g}, \ell)$. Choose $w_z \xleftarrow{R} \mathbb{Z}_p^*$ and compute $g_z \leftarrow g^{w_z}$. For $i \in \{1, \dots, \ell\}$, choose $\chi_i \xleftarrow{R} \mathbb{Z}_p$ and compute $g_i \leftarrow g^{\chi_i}$. Return

$$\mathsf{vk} = (g_z, g_1, \dots, g_\ell) \in \mathbb{G}^{\ell+1} \qquad \mathsf{sk} = (w_z, \chi_1, \dots, \chi_\ell) \in \mathbb{Z}_p^{\ell+1}$$

OKeyGen(PP): Parse PP, choose $a \leftarrow \mathbb{Z}_p$, compute $A \leftarrow g^a$ and output

$$\mathsf{ovk} = A \qquad \mathsf{osk} = a$$

Sign(sk, osk, $\hat{M}$): Parse $\hat{M}$ as $(\hat{M}_1, \dots, \hat{M}_\ell) \in \hat{\mathbb{G}}^\ell$. Parse sk and osk, choose $\zeta \xleftarrow{R} \mathbb{Z}_p^*$, then compute and output

$$\hat{Z} = \hat{g}^\zeta \qquad \hat{R} = \hat{g}^{a - \zeta w_z} \prod_{i=1}^\ell \hat{M}_i^{-\chi_i}.$$

Verify(vk, ovk, $\hat{M}, \sigma$): Parse σ as $(\hat{Z}, \hat{R}) \in \hat{\mathbb{G}}^2$, $\hat{M}$ as $(\hat{M}_1, \ldots, \hat{M}_\ell) \in \hat{\mathbb{G}}^\ell$ and ovk as $A \in \mathbb{G}$. The algorithm returns 1 if the following equation holds:

$$e(A, \hat{g}) = e(g_z, \hat{Z}) \cdot e(g, \hat{R}) \cdot \prod_{i=1}^{\ell} e(g_i, \hat{M}_i)$$

otherwise the algorithm returns 0.

2.4 One-Time Linearly Homomorphic Structure-Preserving Signatures

Libert et al. [42] considered structure-preserving with linear homomorphic properties (see the full version of the paper for formal definitions). This section recalls the one-time linearly homomorphic structure-preserving signature (LHSPS) of [42].

Keygen(λ, n): Given a security parameter λ and the dimension $n \in \mathbb{N}$ of the subspace to be signed, choose bilinear group $(\mathbb{G}, \hat{\mathbb{G}}, \mathbb{G}_T)$ of prime order p. Then, choose $\hat{g}_z, \hat{g}_r \xleftarrow{R} \hat{\mathbb{G}}$. For $i = 1$ to n, pick $\chi_i, \gamma_i \xleftarrow{R} \mathbb{Z}_p$ and compute $\hat{g}_i = \hat{g}_z^{\chi_i} \hat{g}_r^{\gamma_i}$. The private key is defined to be $\mathsf{sk} = \{(\chi_i, \gamma_i)\}_{i=1}^n$ while the public key is $\mathsf{pk} = (\hat{g}_z, \hat{g}_r, \{\hat{g}_i\}_{i=1}^n) \in \hat{\mathbb{G}}^{n+2}$.

Sign(sk, $(M_1, \ldots, M_n)$): To sign a $(M_1, \ldots, M_n) \in \mathbb{G}^n$ using $\mathsf{sk} = \{(\chi_i, \gamma_i)\}_{i=1}^n$, output $\sigma = (z, r) \in \mathbb{G}^2$, where $z = \prod_{i=1}^n M_i^{\chi_i}$, $r = \prod_{i=1}^n M_i^{\gamma_i}$.

SignDerive(pk, $\{(\omega_i, \sigma^{(i)})\}_{i=1}^\ell$): given pk as well as ℓ tuples $(\omega_i, \sigma^{(i)})$, parse $\sigma^{(i)}$ as $\sigma^{(i)} = (z_i, r_i)$ for $i = 1$ to ℓ. Compute and return $\sigma = (z, r)$, where $z = \prod_{i=1}^\ell z_i^{\omega_i}$, $r = \prod_{i=1}^\ell r_i^{\omega_i}$.

Verify(pk, σ, $(M_1, \ldots, M_n)$): Given a signature $\sigma = (z, r) \in \mathbb{G}^2$ and a vector $(M_1, \ldots, M_n)$, return 1 iff $(M_1, \ldots, M_n) \neq (1_{\mathbb{G}}, \ldots, 1_{\mathbb{G}})$ and (z, r) satisfy

$$e(z, \hat{g}_z) \cdot e(r, \hat{g}_r) = \prod_{i=1}^n e(M_i, \hat{g}_i).$$

The one-time security of the scheme (of which the definition is recalled in the full version of the paper) was proved [42] under the DP assumption. In short, the security notion implies the infeasibility of deriving a signature on a vector outside the subspace spanned by the vectors authenticated by the signer. Here, "one-time" security means that a given public key allows signing only one subspace.

We remark that the one-time structure-preserving signature of Sect. 2.2 can be seen as a special case of the above LHSPS scheme, in which we fix the first element of the vector to be signed. The one-time security of this signature scheme can be directly deduced from the security of the LHSPS scheme.

2.5 Strictly Structure-Preserving (Trapdoor) Commitments

In this section, we recall the notion of Chosen-Message Target Collision Trapdoor Commitment as it was defined by Abe *et al.* [10].

Definition 7. *A non-interactive commitment scheme is a tuple of polynomial-time algorithms* {Setup, KeyGen, Commit, Verify} *that:*

Setup(λ): *The parameter generation algorithm takes the security parameter* λ *and outputs a public parameter* PP.

KeyGen(PP): *The key generation algorithm takes* PP *and outputs the commitment key* ck.

Com(PP, ck, m): *The commitment algorithm takes* (PP, ck) *and a message* m, *then it outputs a commitment* com *and an opening information* open.

Verify(PP, com, m, open): *The verification algorithm takes* (PP, com, m, open) *and outputs 1 or 0.*

In trapdoor commitment schemes, the Setup algorithm additionally outputs a trapdoor tk which, on input of a message m and random coins r such that $c = \mathsf{Com}(\mathsf{PP}, \mathsf{ck}, m; r)$, allows opening the commitment c to any message m'. In our construction, we need a length-reducing commitment scheme which satisfies a stronger notion of Chosen-Message Target Collision Resistance (CM-TCR) than the one considered in [10, Definition 10].

Definition 8. *A Commitment Scheme provides* **enhanced chosen-message target collision-resistance** *(ECM-TCR) if the advantage*

$$\mathbf{Adv}_{\mathcal{A}}^{ECM\text{-}TCR}(\lambda)$$

$$= \Pr \left[\begin{array}{l} \exists (m^{\dagger}, \mathsf{open}^{\dagger}) \text{ s.t. } (\mathsf{com}^{\star}, m^{\dagger}, \mathsf{open}^{\dagger}) \in Q \\ \wedge \ (\mathsf{com}^{\star}, m^{\star}, \mathsf{open}^{\star}) \notin Q \\ \wedge \ \mathsf{Verify}(\mathsf{ck}, \mathsf{com}^{\star}, m^{\star}, \mathsf{open}^{\star}) = 1 \end{array} \ \middle| \ \begin{array}{l} \mathsf{PP} \leftarrow \mathsf{Setup}(1^{\lambda}) \\ \mathsf{ck} \leftarrow \mathsf{KeyGen}(\mathsf{PP}) \\ (\mathsf{com}^{\star}, m^{\star}, \mathsf{open}^{\star}) \leftarrow \mathcal{A}^{\mathcal{O}_{\mathsf{ck}}}(\mathsf{ck}) \end{array} \right]$$

is negligible for any PPT adversary $\mathcal{A}$. Here, $\mathcal{O}_{\mathsf{ck}}$ is an oracle that, given a message m, executes (com, open) $\leftarrow$ Com(PP, ck, m), *records* (com, m, open) *in Q and returns* (com, open).

We note that Definition 8 captures a stronger requirement than the original definition [10, Definition 10] in that the latter only requires that the adversary be unable to open a target commitment com* to a different message than the one queried to the oracle $\mathcal{O}_{\mathsf{ck}}$. Here, the adversary is also considered successful if it provides a different opening open$^{\star} \neq$ open$'$ of com* to the same message $m^{\star} = m^{\dagger}$ as the one queried to $\mathcal{O}_{\mathsf{ck}}$.

We now recall the Strictly Structure-Preserving Trapdoor Commitment of Abe *et al.* [10] and show that it actually satisfies our stronger notion of ECM-TCR security.

TC.Setup(λ, ℓ): On input of a security parameter λ and an integer $\ell \in \mathsf{poly}(\lambda)$, the public parameters are generated by choosing a large prime $p > 2^\lambda$, asymmetric groups $(\mathbb{G}, \hat{\mathbb{G}}, \mathbb{G}_T)$ of prime order p, with a bilinear map $e : \mathbb{G} \times \hat{\mathbb{G}} \to \mathbb{G}_T$ and group generators $(g, \hat{g}) \in \mathbb{G} \times \hat{\mathbb{G}}$. The algorithm outputs

$$\mathsf{PP} = (p, \mathbb{G}, \hat{\mathbb{G}}, \mathbb{G}_T, e, g, \hat{g}, \ell).$$

TC.KeyGen(PP): For $i = 1, \ldots, \ell + 2$, choose $\rho_i \xleftarrow{R} \mathbb{Z}_p^*$ and compute

$$\hat{X}_i \leftarrow \hat{g}^{\rho_i} \qquad \forall i \in \{1, \ldots, \ell + 2\}.$$

Output the commitment key $\mathsf{ck} := \{\hat{X}_i\}_{i=1}^{\ell+2}$. Optionally, the algorithm may output the trapdoor $tk := \{\rho_i\}_i^{\ell+2}$.

TC.Commit(PP, ck, M): To commit to $\hat{M} = (\hat{M}_1, \ldots, \hat{M}_\ell) \in \hat{\mathbb{G}}^\ell$, conduct the following step.

1. Generate a key pair $(\mathsf{vk}_{pots}, \mathsf{sk}_{pots})$ for the partial one-time signature of Sect. 2.3. Namely, choose $\mathsf{sk}_{pots} \xleftarrow{R} (w_z, \chi_1, \ldots, \chi_\ell) \in \mathbb{Z}_p^{\ell+1}$ and set

$$\mathsf{vk}_{pots} = (g_z, g_1, \ldots, g_\ell) = (g^{w_z}, g^{\chi_1}, \ldots, g^{\chi_\ell}) \in \mathbb{G}^{\ell+1}.$$

2. Choose $a \xleftarrow{R} \mathbb{Z}_p$ and compute $\mathsf{ovk}_{pots} = A = g^a$ and $\mathsf{osk}_{pots} = a$.
3. Using sk_{pots}, generate a partial one-time signature on the message $\hat{M}$ w.r.t. to the one-time secret key osk_{pots}. To this end,
   a. Pick $\zeta_1 \in \mathbb{Z}_p$.
   b. Compute $(\hat{Z}, \hat{R}) \in \hat{\mathbb{G}}^2$ as a partial one-time signature of $\hat{M}$ as

$$\hat{Z} = \hat{g}^{\zeta_1} \qquad\qquad \hat{R} = \hat{g}^{a - \zeta_1 w_z} \prod_{i=1}^{\ell} \hat{M}_i^{\chi_i}$$

4. Generate a commitment to the message.
   a. Set $(m_1, \ldots, m_{\ell+2}) \leftarrow (\chi_1, \ldots, \chi_\ell, w_z, a)$
   b. Parse ck as $(\hat{X}_1, \ldots, \hat{X}_{\ell+2})$.
   c. Choose a random value $\zeta_2 \leftarrow \mathbb{Z}_p^*$ and compute:

$$\hat{C} = \hat{g}^{\zeta_2} \cdot \prod_{i=1}^{\ell+2} \hat{X}_i^{m_i} \qquad\qquad D = g^{\zeta_2}$$

5. Output the commitment $\hat{\mathsf{com}} = \hat{C}$ as well as the opening information

$$\mathsf{open} = \left(D, g_z, g_1, \ldots, g_\ell, A = g^a, \hat{Z}, \hat{R}\right) \in \mathbb{G}^{\ell+3} \times \hat{\mathbb{G}}^2. \qquad (1)$$

TC.Verify(ck, $\hat{\mathsf{com}}$, $\hat{M}$, open): Given $\hat{\mathsf{com}} = \hat{C} \in \hat{\mathbb{G}}$, parse $\hat{M}$ as $(\hat{M}_1, \ldots, \hat{M}_\ell)$ and open as in (1).
   1. Set $N = (N_1, \ldots, N_{\ell+2}) = (g_1, \ldots, g_\ell, g_z, A)$

2. Using $\mathsf{ovk}_{pots} = A \in \mathbb{G}$, return 1 if the following equalities hold:

$$e(g, \hat{C}) = e(D, \hat{g}) \cdot \prod_{i=1}^{\ell+2} e(N_i, \hat{X}_i) \tag{2}$$

$$e(A, \hat{g}) = e(g_z, \hat{Z}) \cdot e(g, \hat{R}) \cdot \prod_{i=1}^{\ell} e(g_i, \hat{M}_i).$$

Otherwise, return 0.

Using $tk := \{\rho_i\}_i^{\ell+2}$, it is possible to trapdoor-open a commitment $\hat{\mathsf{com}} = \hat{C}$ in the same way as a Pedersen commitment since $\hat{C}$ is nothing but a Pedersen commitment to $(\mathsf{sk}_{pots}, \mathsf{osk}_{pots})$.

We now prove that the above commitment does not only provide CM-TCR security as defined in [10], but also ECM-TCR security. The proof builds on the same ideas as that of [10] but also takes advantage of the strong unforgeability[3] of the underlying partial one-time signature.

Theorem 1. *The scheme provides ECM-CTR security under the SXDH assumption.*

Proof. For the sake of contradiction, let us assume that a PPT adversary $\mathcal{A}$ can win the game of Definition 8 with noticeable probability. We observe that the adversary can only win in two mutually exclusive cases.

I. $\mathcal{A}$ outputs a commitment $\hat{C}^\star \in \hat{\mathbb{G}}$ for which it provides an opening

$$\boldsymbol{M}^\star = (M_1^\star, \ldots, M_n^\star)$$
$$\mathsf{open}^\star = (D^\star, g_z^\star, g_1^\star, \ldots, g_\ell^\star, A^\star, \hat{Z}^\star, \hat{R}^\star),$$

where $(D^\star, g_z^\star, g_1^\star, \ldots, g_\ell^\star, A^\star)$ differs from the tuple $(D^\dagger, g_z^\dagger, g_1^\dagger, \ldots, g_\ell^\dagger, A^\dagger)$ returned by $\mathcal{O}_{\mathsf{ck}}$ as part of the opening

$$\mathsf{open}^\dagger = (D^\dagger, g_z^\dagger, g_1^\dagger, \ldots, g_\ell^\dagger, A^\dagger, \hat{Z}^\dagger, \hat{R}^\dagger),$$

of $\hat{C}^\star$ when $\mathcal{A}$ queried $\mathcal{O}_{\mathsf{ck}}$ to obtain a commitment to $\hat{\boldsymbol{M}}^\dagger = (\hat{M}_1^\dagger, \ldots, \hat{M}_\ell^\dagger)$.

II. $\mathcal{A}$ outputs a commitment $\hat{C}^\star \in \hat{\mathbb{G}}$ which it opens by revealing a pair

$$\boldsymbol{M}^\star = (M_1^\star, \ldots, M_n^\star)$$
$$\mathsf{open}^\star = (D^\star, g_z^\star, g_1^\star, \ldots, g_\ell^\star, A^\star, \hat{Z}^\star, \hat{R}^\star),$$

such that $(D^\dagger, g_z^\dagger, g_1^\dagger, \ldots, g_\ell^\dagger, A^\dagger) = (D^\star, g_z^\star, g_1^\star, \ldots, g_\ell^\star, A^\star)$. In this case, we must have either $\boldsymbol{M}^\star \neq \boldsymbol{M}^\dagger$ or $(\hat{Z}^\star, \hat{R}^\star) \neq (\hat{Z}^\dagger, \hat{R}^\dagger)$.

---

[3] Note that, while [4] only considered the standard notion of unforgeability, it is straightforward that their scheme also provides strong unforgeability.

Let us first assume that situation I occurs with noticeable probability. We show that $\mathcal{A}$ can be turned into an algorithm $\mathcal{B}_I$ that breaks the DDH assumption in $\hat{G}$ by finding a pair (Z, R) such that $e(Z, \hat{g}) \cdot e(R, \hat{h}) = 1_{\mathbb{G}_T}$ for a given pair $(\hat{g}, \hat{h}) \in \hat{\mathbb{G}}^2$. This algorithm $\mathcal{B}_I$ proceeds in the same way as in [10]. Namely, it creates the commitment key ck by choosing $\rho_i, \theta_i \xleftarrow{R} \mathbb{Z}_p$ and setting $\hat{X}_i = \hat{g}^{\rho_i} \cdot \hat{h}^{\theta_i}$ for each $i \in \{1, \ldots, \ell + 2\}$. It faithfully answers all queries made by $\mathcal{A}$ to $\mathcal{O}_{\text{ck}}$. By hypothesis, $\mathcal{A}$ outputs a commitment $\hat{C}^\star \in \hat{G}$ as well as an opening $(M^\star, \text{open}^\star)$ which satisfy the conditions of situation I. In particular, open$^\star = \left(D^\star, g_z^\star, g_1^\star, \ldots, g_\ell^\star, A^\star, \hat{Z}^\star, \hat{R}^\star\right)$ satisfies

$$e(g, \hat{C}^\star) = e(D^\star, \hat{g}) \cdot \prod_{i=1}^{\ell} e(g_i^\star, \hat{X}_i) \cdot e(g_z^\star, \hat{X}_{\ell+1}) \cdot e(A^\star, \hat{X}_{\ell+2}) \qquad (3)$$

and the set Q must contain $\text{open}^\dagger = \left(D^\dagger, g_z^\dagger, g_1^\dagger, \ldots, g_\ell^\dagger, A^\dagger, \hat{Z}^\dagger, \hat{R}^\dagger\right)$ such that

$$e(g, \hat{C}^\star) = e(D^\dagger, \hat{g}) \cdot \prod_{i=1}^{\ell} e(g_i^\dagger, \hat{X}_i) \cdot e(g_z^\dagger, \hat{X}_{\ell+1}) \cdot e(A^\dagger, \hat{X}_{\ell+2}). \qquad (4)$$

Dividing (4) out of (3), we find that the pair

$$Z = \left(\frac{D^\star}{D^\dagger}\right) \cdot \left(\frac{g_z^\star}{g_z^\dagger}\right)^{\rho_{\ell+1}} \cdot \left(\frac{A^\star}{A^\dagger}\right)^{\rho_{\ell+2}} \cdot \prod_{i=1}^{\ell} \left(\frac{g_i^\star}{g_i^\dagger}\right)^{\rho_i}$$

$$R = \left(\frac{D^\star}{D^\dagger}\right) \cdot \left(\frac{g_z^\star}{g_z^\dagger}\right)^{\theta_{\ell+1}} \cdot \left(\frac{A^\star}{A^\dagger}\right)^{\theta_{\ell+2}} \cdot \prod_{i=1}^{\ell} \left(\frac{g_i^\star}{g_i^\dagger}\right)^{\theta_i}$$

satisfies $e(Z, \hat{g}) \cdot e(R, \hat{h}) = 1_{\mathbb{G}_T}$. Moreover, we have $Z \neq 1_{\mathbb{G}}$ with all but negligible probability since $\{\rho_i\}_{i=1}^{\ell}$ are completely independent of $\mathcal{A}$'s view.

We now turn to situation II and show that it implies an algorithm $\mathcal{B}_{II}$ that defeats the strong unforgeability of the partial one-time signature scheme. Algorithm $\mathcal{B}_{II}$ takes as input a POTS verification key $\text{vk}_{pots} = (g_z^\dagger, g_1^\dagger, \ldots, g_\ell^\dagger)$ supplied by its own challenger in the POTS security game. It generates $\text{ck} = \{\hat{X}_i\}_{i=1}^{\ell+2}$ by picking $\rho_i \xleftarrow{R} \mathbb{Z}_p$ and defining $\hat{X}_i = \hat{g}^{\rho_i}$ for each $i \in \{1, \ldots, \ell + 2\}$. Letting $Q_c \in \text{poly}(\lambda)$ denote the number of queries made by $\mathcal{A}$ to $\mathcal{O}_{\text{ck}}$, $\mathcal{B}_{II}$ draws a random index $k^\star \xleftarrow{R} \{1, \ldots, Q_c\}$ as a guess that $\mathcal{A}$ will choose to equivocate the commitment $\hat{C}^\dagger$ returned as the output of the $k^\star$-th query. It answers all queries to $\mathcal{O}_{\text{ck}}$ as follows. For each $k \in \{1, \ldots, Q_c\} \backslash \{k^\star\}$, the k-th query is answered by faithfully running the commitment algorithm. When the $k^\star$-th query occurs, $\mathcal{B}_{II}$ embeds $\text{vk}_{pots} = (g_z^\dagger, g_1^\dagger, \ldots, g_\ell^\dagger)$ into the opening of the $k^\star$-th commitment. To this end, it chooses $\zeta \xleftarrow{R} \mathbb{Z}_p^\star$ and computes $\hat{C}^\dagger = \hat{g}^\zeta$.

Next, $\mathcal{B}_{II}$ queries its own POTS challenger to obtain a signature $(A^\dagger, (\hat{Z}, \hat{R}))$ on the message $\hat{M} = (\hat{M}_1, \ldots, \hat{M}_\ell) \in \hat{\mathbb{G}}^\ell$ queried by $\mathcal{A}$ at this $k^\star$-th query. Upon receiving a partial one-time signature $(A^\dagger, (\hat{Z}^\dagger, \hat{R}^\dagger))$ from its POTS challenger, $\mathcal{B}_{II}$ defines $(N_1, \ldots, N_\ell, N_{\ell+1}, N_{\ell+2}) = (g_1^\dagger, \ldots, g_\ell^\dagger, g_z^\dagger, A^\dagger)$ and computes

$$D^\dagger = g^\zeta \cdot \prod_{i=1}^{\ell+2} N_i^{-\rho_i} \in \mathbb{G},$$

which satisfies $e(g, \hat{C}^\dagger) = e(D^\dagger, \hat{g}) \cdot \prod_{i=1}^{\ell+2} e(N_i, \hat{X}_i)$. Given that $(A^\dagger, (\hat{Z}^\dagger, \hat{R}^\dagger))$ satisfies the second verification equation of (2) by construction, we observe that

$$\mathsf{open}^\dagger = \left(D^\dagger, g_z^\dagger, g_1^\dagger, \ldots, g_\ell^\dagger, A^\dagger, \hat{Z}^\dagger, \hat{R}^\dagger \right)$$

forms a valid opening of $\hat{C}^\dagger$. When $\mathcal{A}$ halts, we know that, with probability $1/Q_c$, it chooses to output a pair $(M^\star, \mathsf{open}^\star)$ which opens $\hat{C}^\star = \hat{C}^\dagger$. Given that $(D^\star, g_z^\star, g_1^\star, \ldots, g_\ell^\star, A^\star) = (D^\dagger, g_z^\dagger, g_1^\dagger, \ldots, g_\ell^\dagger, A^\dagger)$ and since we must have $(M^\star, \mathsf{open}^\star) \neq (M^\dagger, \mathsf{open}^\dagger)$ by the definition of ECM-TCR security, we know that $(M^\star, (\hat{Z}^\star, \hat{R}^\star)) \neq (M^\dagger, (\hat{Z}^\dagger, \hat{R}^\dagger))$. This means that $\mathcal{B}_{II}$ can win the game against its POTS challenger by outputting $(M^\star, (A^\star, \hat{Z}^\star, \hat{R}^\star))$. In turn, the result of [4] implies that $\mathcal{B}_{II}$ would contradict the DDH assumption in $\mathbb{G}$.   □

3 A Structure-Preserving CCA2-Secure Public-Key Cryptosystem with Shorter Publicly Verifiable Ciphertexts

In this section, we use the all-but-one hash proof systems of [46] and combine them with the structure-preserving commitment scheme of Sect. 2.5 and a strongly unforgeable signature scheme. We show that the ECMTCR property of the commitment scheme suffices to construct the sought-after CCA2-secure structure preserving encryption scheme with publicly verifiable ciphertexts.

In the notations hereafter, for any vector $\hat{\boldsymbol{h}} = (\hat{h}_1, \hat{h}_2) \in \hat{\mathbb{G}}^2$ and any $g \in \mathbb{G}$, we denote by $E(g, \hat{\boldsymbol{h}})$ the vector $(e(g, \hat{h}_1), e(g, \hat{h}_2))$. For any vectors $\hat{\boldsymbol{u}}_1, \hat{\boldsymbol{u}}_2 \in \hat{\mathbb{G}}^2$, the product $\hat{\boldsymbol{u}}_1 \cdot \hat{\boldsymbol{u}}_2 \in \hat{\mathbb{G}}^2$ refers to the component-wise multiplication in $\hat{\mathbb{G}}$.

KeyGen(λ):
1. Run the setup algorithm of the commitment scheme in Sect. 2.5 to obtain $\mathsf{PP} = (p, \mathbb{G}, \hat{\mathbb{G}}, \mathbb{G}_T, e, g, \hat{g}, \ell = 6) \leftarrow TC.\mathsf{Setup}(\lambda, 6)$, which will be used to commit to messages in $\hat{\mathbb{G}}^6$.
2. Generate $(\mathsf{ck}, \mathsf{tk}) \leftarrow TC.\mathsf{KeyGen}(\mathsf{PP})$, where $\mathsf{ck} \in \hat{\mathbb{G}}^8$ is the commitment key and $\mathsf{tk} \in \mathbb{Z}_p^8$ is the trapdoor key which can be erased.
3. Choose also group generators $g_1, g_2 \xleftarrow{R} \mathbb{G}$ and random values $x_1, x_2 \xleftarrow{R} \mathbb{Z}_p$ and set $X = g_1^{x_1} g_2^{x_2}$.
4. Choose $\rho_u \xleftarrow{R} \mathbb{Z}_p$ and $\hat{h} \xleftarrow{R} \hat{\mathbb{G}}^2$ at random.
5. Define $(\hat{\boldsymbol{u}}_1, \hat{\boldsymbol{u}}_2)$ with $\hat{\boldsymbol{u}}_1 = (\hat{g}, \hat{h}) \in \hat{\mathbb{G}}^2$ and $\hat{\boldsymbol{u}}_2 = (\hat{g}^{\rho_u}, \hat{h}^{\rho_u}) \in \hat{\mathbb{G}}^2$. Note that $\hat{\boldsymbol{u}}_1$ and $\hat{\boldsymbol{u}}_2$ are linearly dependent.

6. Define $\mathsf{SK} = (x_1, x_2)$ and

$$\mathsf{PK} = (g_1, g_2, \hat{u}_1, \hat{u}_2, X, \mathsf{PP}, \mathsf{ck}).$$

Encrypt(M, PK): To encrypt $M \in \mathbb{G}$, conduct the following steps.

1. Generate a key pair $(\mathsf{SSK}, \mathsf{SVK}) \leftarrow OT1.\mathsf{KeyGen}(\mathsf{PP}, 5)$ for the one-time SPS of Sect. 2.2 so as to sign messages in $\mathbb{G}^5$. Let the resulting key pair consist of $\mathsf{SSK} = (\{\chi_i, \gamma_i\}_{i=1}^5, \zeta, \rho) \in \mathbb{Z}_p^{14}$ and $\mathsf{SVK} = (\{\hat{g}_i\}_{i=1}^5, \hat{A}) \in \hat{\mathbb{G}}^6$, where $\hat{g}_i = \hat{g}_z^{\chi_i} \cdot \hat{g}_r^{\delta_i}$ and $\hat{A} = \hat{g}_z^\zeta \cdot \hat{g}_r^\rho$.
2. Choose $\theta \xleftarrow{R} \mathbb{Z}_p$ and compute

$$C_0 = M \cdot X^\theta, \qquad C_1 = g_1^\theta, \qquad C_2 = g_2^\theta.$$

3. Generate a commitment to $\mathsf{SVK} = (\{\hat{g}_i\}_{i=1}^5, \hat{A})$ and let

$$(\hat{\mathsf{com}}, \mathsf{open}) \leftarrow TC.\mathsf{Commit}(\mathsf{PP}, ck, \mathsf{SVK}) \in \hat{\mathbb{G}} \times (\mathbb{G}^9 \times \hat{\mathbb{G}}^2)$$

be the resulting commitment/opening pair.
4. Define vector $\hat{u}_{\hat{\mathsf{com}}} = \hat{u}_2 \cdot (1, \hat{\mathsf{com}}) \in \hat{\mathbb{G}}^2$ as well as the Groth-Sahai CRS $\hat{u}_{\hat{\mathsf{com}}} = (\hat{u}_{\hat{\mathsf{com}}}, \hat{u}_1) \in \hat{\mathbb{G}}^2$.
5. Pick $r \xleftarrow{R} \mathbb{Z}_p$. Compute $\hat{C}_\theta = \hat{u}_{\hat{\mathsf{com}}}^\theta \cdot \hat{u}_1^r$.
6. Using the randomness of the commitment C_θ, generate proof elements $\pi = (\pi_1, \pi_2) = (g_1^r, g_2^r) \in \mathbb{G}^2$ showing that the committed $\theta \in \mathbb{Z}_p$ satisfies the multi-exponentiation equations

$$C_1 = g_1^\theta \qquad\qquad C_2 = g_2^\theta$$

7. Output the ciphertext

$$C = (\mathsf{SVK}, \hat{\mathsf{com}}, \mathsf{open}, C_0, C_1, C_2, \hat{C}_\theta, \pi, \sigma) \in \mathbb{G}^{16} \times \hat{\mathbb{G}}^{11} \qquad (5)$$

where $\sigma \leftarrow OT1.\mathsf{Sign}(\mathsf{SSK}, (C_0, C_1, C_2, \pi_1, \pi_2)) \in \mathbb{G}^2$.

Decrypt$(\mathsf{PK}, C, \mathsf{SK})$: Parse the ciphertext C as in (5). Then, conduct the following steps.

1. Parse PK as $(g_1, g_2, X, \mathsf{PP}, ck)$ and SK as (x_1, x_2).
2. Return $\perp$ if $OT1.\mathsf{Verify}(\mathsf{SVK}, (C_0, C_1, C_2, \pi_1, \pi_2), \sigma) = 0$.
3. Return $\perp$ if $\hat{\mathsf{com}} = 1_{\hat{\mathbb{G}}}$ or $TC.\mathsf{Verify}(ck, \hat{\mathsf{com}}, \mathsf{SVK}, \mathsf{open}) = 0$.
4. Verify that $\pi = (\pi_1, \pi_2)$ is a valid Groth-Sahai proof w.r.t. $(C_1, C_2, C_\theta, \hat{\mathsf{com}})$. Namely, it should satisfy

$$E(g_1, \hat{C}_\theta) = E(C_1, \hat{u}_{\hat{\mathsf{com}}}) \cdot E(\pi_1, \hat{u}_1) \qquad (6)$$
$$E(g_2, \hat{C}_\theta) = E(C_2, \hat{u}_{\hat{\mathsf{com}}}) \cdot E(\pi_2, \hat{u}_1)$$

5. If the above verifications all succeed, output $M = C_0/(C_1^{x_1} \cdot C_2^{x_2})$.

Note that, in step 3 of the decryption algorithm, the condition $\text{côm} \neq 1_{\hat{\mathbb{G}}}$ ensures that vectors $(\hat{\boldsymbol{u}}_{\text{côm}}, \hat{\boldsymbol{u}}_1)$ form a perfectly sound Groth-Sahai CRS, so that ciphertexts such that $\log_{g_1}(C_1) \neq \log_{g_2}(C_2)$ are always rejected.

The proof of the following theorem follows the strategy of [46] with additional arguments showing that omitting to sign the Groth-Sahai commitments does not affect the security of the scheme.

Theorem 2. *The scheme provides IND-CCA2 security under the SXDH assumption. More precisely,* $\mathbf{Adv}^{\mathsf{CCA}}(\lambda) \leq 5 \times \mathbf{Adv}^{\mathsf{SXDH}}(\lambda) + q_d \times 2^{-\lambda}$.

Proof. The proof proceeds with a sequence of games that begins with the real game and ends with a game where no advantage is left to the adversary whatsoever. In each game, we call W_i the event that the experiment outputs 1. The security parameter λ is implicitly given in all the games. Let q_d denote the number of decryption queries made by the adversary.

Game 0: This is the real game. The adversary is given the public key PK which contains vectors $(\hat{\boldsymbol{u}}_1, \hat{\boldsymbol{u}}_2)$ such that

$$\hat{\boldsymbol{u}}_1 = (\hat{g}, \hat{h}) \in \hat{\mathbb{G}}^2 \qquad\qquad \hat{\boldsymbol{u}}_2 = (\hat{g}^{\rho_u}, \hat{h}^{\rho_u}) \in \hat{\mathbb{G}}^2, \qquad (7)$$

where $\hat{g}, \hat{h} \xleftarrow{R} \hat{\mathbb{G}}$, $\rho_u \xleftarrow{R} \mathbb{Z}_p$. In the challenge phase, it chooses two messages $M_0, M_1 \in \mathbb{G}$ and obtains a challenge ciphertext

$$\boldsymbol{C}^{\star} = (\mathsf{SVK}^{\star}, \text{côm}^{\star}, \text{open}^{\star}, C_0^{\star}, C_1^{\star}, C_2^{\star}, \hat{\boldsymbol{C}}_{\theta}^{\star}, \boldsymbol{\pi}^{\star}, \boldsymbol{\sigma}^{\star})$$

where, for some random bit $\beta \xleftarrow{R} \{0, 1\}$,

$$C_0^{\star} = M_{\beta} \cdot X^{\theta^{\star}}, \qquad\qquad C_1^{\star} = g_1^{\theta^{\star}}, \qquad\qquad C_2^{\star} = g_2^{\theta^{\star}},$$

as well as $(\text{côm}, \text{open}) \leftarrow TC.\mathsf{Commit}(\mathsf{PP}_{TC}, ck, \mathsf{SVK})$, $\hat{\boldsymbol{C}}_{\theta}^{\star} = \hat{\boldsymbol{u}}_{\text{côm}^{\star}}^{\theta^{\star}} \cdot \hat{\boldsymbol{u}}_1^{r^{\star}}$ and $\boldsymbol{\pi}^{\star} = (\pi_1^{\star}, \pi_2^{\star}) = (g_1^{r^{\star}}, g_2^{r^{\star}})$, where $\hat{\boldsymbol{u}}_{\text{côm}^{\star}} = \hat{\boldsymbol{u}}_2 \cdot (1, \text{côm}^{\star})$. We assume w.l.o.g. that $\mathsf{SVK}^{\star}$ and $\text{côm}^{\star} = \hat{C}^{\star}$ are generated at the outset of the game.

The adversary's decryption queries are always faithfully answered by the challenger. When the adversary halts, it outputs $\beta' \in \{0, 1\}$ and wins if $\beta' = \beta$. In this case, the experiment outputs 1. Otherwise, it outputs 0. The adversary's advantage is thus $|\Pr[W_0] - 1/2|$.

Game 1: This game is like Game 0 except that, if the adversary makes a pre-challenge decryption query $\boldsymbol{C} = (\mathsf{SVK}, \text{côm}, \text{open}, C_0, C_1, C_2, \hat{C}_{\theta}, \boldsymbol{\pi}, \boldsymbol{\sigma})$ such that $\text{côm} = \text{côm}^{\star}$, the experiment halts and outputs a random bit. Since Game 1 is identical to Game 0 until this event F_1 occurs, we have the inequality $|\Pr[W_1] - \Pr[W_0]| \leq \Pr[F_1]$. Moreover, since $\text{côm}^{\star}$ was chosen uniformly in $\hat{\mathbb{G}}$ and remains independent of $\mathcal{A}$'s view until the challenge phase, we have $|\Pr[W_1] - \Pr[W_0]| \leq \Pr[F_1] \leq q_d/p$.

Game 2: In this game, we modify the generation of the public key and define

$$\hat{\boldsymbol{u}}_1 = (\hat{g}, \hat{h}) \in \hat{\mathbb{G}}^2 \qquad\qquad\qquad (8)$$
$$\hat{\boldsymbol{u}}_2 = (\hat{g}^{\rho_u}, \hat{h}^{\rho_u}) \cdot (1, \text{côm}^{\star})^{-1} \in \hat{\mathbb{G}}^2,$$

for a random $\rho_u \xleftarrow{R} \mathbb{Z}_p$, instead of computing $(\hat{u}_1, \hat{u}_2)$ as in (7). Note that $(\hat{u}_1, \hat{u}_2)$ are now linearly independent and côm* is no longer statistically hidden before the challenge phase. However, a straightforward argument based on the semantic security of ElGamal (and thus the DDH assumption in $\hat{\mathbb{G}}$) shows that this modification does not affect the adversary's view. We have $|\Pr[W_2] - \Pr[W_1]| \le 2 \times \mathbf{Adv}_{\hat{\mathbb{G}}, \mathcal{B}}^{\mathrm{DDH}}(\lambda)$.

Game 3: This game is like Game 2 but we modify the decryption oracle. Namely, if the adversary makes a post-challenge decryption query for a valid ciphertext $C = (\mathsf{SVK}, \hat{\mathsf{com}}, \mathsf{open}, C_0, C_1, C_2, \hat{C}_\theta, \boldsymbol{\pi}, \boldsymbol{\sigma})$ such that côm $=$ côm* but $(\mathsf{SVK}, \mathsf{open}) \neq (\mathsf{SVK}^*, \mathsf{open}^*)$, the experiment halts and outputs a random bit. If we call F_3 the latter event, we have $|\Pr[W_3] - \Pr[W_2]| \le \Pr[F_3]$. As shown by Lemma 1, event F_3 implies an adversary $\mathcal{B}_3$ against the ECM-TCR property (as formalized by Definition 8) of the trapdoor commitment in Sect. 2.5, which contradicts the SXDH assumption. We thus have $|\Pr[W_3] - \Pr[W_2]| \le \mathbf{Adv}_{TC, \mathcal{B}_3}^{\mathrm{ECM\text{-}TCR}}(\lambda) \le \mathbf{Adv}_{\mathcal{B}_3}^{\mathrm{SXDH}}(\lambda)$.

Game 4: We modify again the decryption oracle in post-challenge decryption queries. After the challenge phase, if the adversary $\mathcal{A}$ queries the decryption of a ciphertext $C = (\mathsf{SVK}, \hat{\mathsf{com}}, \mathsf{open}, C_0, C_1, C_2, \hat{C}_\theta, \boldsymbol{\pi}, \boldsymbol{\sigma})$ such that we have $(\hat{\mathsf{com}}, \mathsf{open}) = (\hat{\mathsf{com}}^*, \mathsf{open}^*)$ but $(C_0, C_1, C_2, \pi_1, \pi_2) \neq (C_0^\star, C_1^\star, C_2^\star, \pi_1^\star, \pi_2^\star)$, the experiment halts and outputs a random bit. If we call F_4 this event, we have the inequality $|\Pr[W_4] - \Pr[W_3]| \le \Pr[F_4]$ since Game 4 is identical to Game 3 until F_4 occurs. Moreover, F_4 would contradict the strong unforgeability of the one-time structure-preserving signature and thus the DP assumption. This implies $|\Pr[W_4] - \Pr[W_3]| \le \mathbf{Adv}_{\mathcal{B}}^{\mathrm{SUF\text{-}OTS}}(\lambda) \le \mathbf{Adv}_{\mathcal{B}}^{\mathrm{DP}}(\lambda)$.

Game 5: We introduce another modification in the decryption oracle. We reject all ciphertexts $C = (\mathsf{SVK}, \hat{\mathsf{com}}, \mathsf{open}, C_0, C_1, C_2, \hat{C}_\theta, \boldsymbol{\pi}, \boldsymbol{\sigma})$ such that

$$(\hat{\mathsf{com}}, \mathsf{open}) = (\hat{\mathsf{com}}^*, \mathsf{open}^*) \quad \wedge$$
$$(C_0, C_1, C_2, \pi_1, \pi_2) = (C_0^\star, C_1^\star, C_2^\star, \pi_1^\star, \pi_2^\star) \quad \wedge \quad \hat{C}_\theta \neq \hat{C}_\theta^\star. \qquad (9)$$

Let F_5 be the event that the decryption oracle rejects a ciphertext that would not have been rejected in Game 4. We argue that $\Pr[W_5] = \Pr[W_4]$ since Game 5 is identical to Game 4 until event F_5 occurs and we have $\Pr[F_5] = 0$. Indeed, for a given $(C_1^\star, C_2^\star, \pi_1^\star, \pi_2^\star) \in \mathbb{G}^4$, there exists only one commitment $\hat{C}_\theta^\star \in \hat{\mathbb{G}}^2$ that satisfies the equalities (6). This follows from the fact that, since $(C_1^\star, C_2^\star, \pi_1^\star, \pi_2^\star) = (g_1^{\theta^*}, g_2^{\theta^*}, g_1^{r^*}, g_2^{r^*})$, relations (6) can be written

$$E(g_1, \hat{C}_\theta^\star) = E(g_1^{\theta^*}, \hat{u}_{\hat{\mathsf{com}}}) \cdot E(g_1^{r^*}, \hat{u}_1) = E(g_1, \hat{u}_{\hat{\mathsf{com}}}^{\theta^*}) \cdot E(g_1, \hat{u}_1^{r^*})$$
$$E(g_2, \hat{C}_\theta^\star) = E(g_2^{\theta^*}, \hat{u}_{\hat{\mathsf{com}}}) \cdot E(g_2^{r^*}, \hat{u}_1) = E(g_2, \hat{u}_{\hat{\mathsf{com}}}^{\theta^*}) \cdot E(g_2, \hat{u}_1^{r^*})$$

which uniquely determines the only commitment $\hat{C}_\theta^\star = \hat{u}_{\hat{\mathsf{com}}}^{\theta^*} \cdot \hat{u}_1^{r^*} \in \hat{\mathbb{G}}^2$ that satisfies (6). This shows that $\Pr[F_5] = 0$, as claimed.

Game 6: In this game, we modify the distribution of the public key. Namely, instead of generating the vectors $(\hat{u}_1, \hat{u}_2)$ as in (8), we set

$$\hat{u}_1 = (\hat{g}, \hat{h}) \in \hat{\mathbb{G}}^2 \qquad \hat{u}_2 = (\hat{g}^{\rho_u}, \hat{h}^{\rho_u}) \cdot (1, \hat{C}^{\star-1}) \in \hat{\mathbb{G}}^2. \qquad (10)$$

Said otherwise, $\hat{u}_2$ is now the product of two terms, the first one of which lives in the one-dimensional subspace spanned by $\hat{u}_1$. Under the DDH assumption in $\hat{\mathbb{G}}$, this modified distribution of PK should have not noticeable impact on the adversary's behavior. A straightforward reduction shows that $|\Pr[W_6] - \Pr[W_5]| \leq \mathbf{Adv}_B^{\mathrm{DDH}}(\lambda)$. Note that, although the vectors $(\hat{u}_{\mathsf{com}^\star}, \hat{u}_1) \in \hat{\mathbb{G}}^2$ are no longer linearly independent, $\hat{C}_\theta^\star = \hat{u}_1^{\rho_u \cdot \theta^\star + r^\star}$ remains the only commitment that satisfies the verification equations for a given tuple $(C_1^\star, C_2^\star, \pi_1^\star, \pi_2^\star)$.

Game 7: In this game, we modify the challenge ciphertext and replace the NIZK proof $\boldsymbol{\pi}^\star = (\pi_1^\star, \pi_2^\star) \in \mathbb{G}^2$ by a simulated proof which is produced using $\rho_u \in \mathbb{Z}_p$ as a simulation trapdoor. Namely, $(\hat{C}_\theta^\star, \boldsymbol{\pi}^\star)$ is obtained by picking $r \xleftarrow{R} \mathbb{Z}_p$ and computing

$$\hat{C}_\theta^\star = u_1^r, \qquad\qquad \pi_1^\star = g_1^r \cdot C_1^{\star -\rho_u}, \qquad\qquad \pi_2^\star = g_2^r \cdot C_2^{\star -\rho_u}$$

Observe that, although $(\hat{C}_\theta^\star, \pi_1^\star, \pi_2^\star)$ are generated without using the witness $\theta^\star = \log_{g_1}(C_1^\star) = \log_{g_2}(C_2^\star)$, the NIZK property of GS proofs ensures that their distribution remains exactly as in Game 6: indeed, if we define $\tilde{r} = r - \rho_u \cdot \theta^\star$, we have

$$\hat{C}_\theta^\star = \hat{u}_{\mathsf{com}^\star}^{\theta^\star} \cdot \hat{u}_1^{\tilde{r}}, \qquad\qquad \pi_1^\star = g_1^{\tilde{r}}, \qquad\qquad \pi_2^\star = g_2^{\tilde{r}},$$

which implies $\Pr[W_7] = \Pr[W_6]$.

Game 8: We modify the generation of the challenge ciphertext, which is generated using the private key $\mathsf{SK} = (x_1, x_2)$ instead of the public key: Namely, the challenger computes

$$C_1^\star = g_1^{\theta^\star}, \qquad\qquad C_2^\star = g_2^{\theta^\star}, \qquad\qquad C_0^\star = M_\beta \cdot C_1^{\star x_1} \cdot C_2^{\star x_2},$$

while $(\hat{C}_\theta^\star, \pi_1^\star, \pi_2^\star)$ are computed using the NIZK simulation trapdoor $\rho_u \in \mathbb{Z}_p$ as in Game 7. This change does not affect the adversary's view since the ciphertext retains the same distribution. We have $\Pr[W_8] = \Pr[W_7]$.

Game 9: We modify again the distribution of the challenge ciphertext which is obtained as

$$C_1^\star = g_1^{\theta_1^\star}, \qquad\qquad C_2^\star = g_2^{\theta_2^\star}, \qquad\qquad C_0^\star = M_\beta \cdot C_1^{\star x_1} \cdot C_2^{\star x_2},$$

for random and independent $\theta_1^\star, \theta_2^\star \xleftarrow{R} \mathbb{Z}_p$, while the NIZK proof $(\hat{C}_\theta^\star, \pi_1^\star, \pi_2^\star)$ is simulated using $\rho_u \in \mathbb{Z}_p$ as in Game 8. Since the witness $\theta^\star \in \mathbb{Z}_p$ was not used anymore in Game 8, a straightforward reduction shows that any noticeable change in $\mathcal{A}$'s output distribution implies a DDH distinguisher in $\mathbb{G}$. We have $|\Pr[W_9] - \Pr[W_8]| \leq \mathbf{Adv}_{B,\mathbb{G}}^{\mathrm{DDH}}(\lambda)$.

In the final game, it is easy to see that $\Pr[W_9] = 1/2$ since the challenge ciphertext does not carry any information about $\beta \in \{0, 1\}$. Indeed, we have

$$C_1^\star = g_1^{\theta_1^\star}, \qquad\qquad C_2^\star = g_2^{\theta_1^\star + \theta_1'}, \qquad\qquad C_0^\star = M_\beta \cdot X^{\theta_1^\star} \cdot g_2^{\theta_1' \cdot x_2},$$

for some random $\theta_1' \in_R \mathbb{Z}_p$, which implies that the term $g_2^{\theta_1' \cdot x_2}$ perfectly hides M_β in the expression of $C_0^\star$. This follows from the fact that $x_2 \in \mathbb{Z}_p$ is perfectly independent of the adversary's view. Indeed, the public key leaves $x_2 \in \mathbb{Z}_p$ completely undetermined as it only reveals $X = g_1^{x_1} g_2^{x_2}$. During the game, decryption queries are guaranteed not to reveal anything about x_2 since all NIZK proofs $(\hat{C}_\theta, \pi_1, \pi_2)$ take place on Groth-Sahai CRSes $(\hat{u}_{\mathsf{côm}}, \hat{u}_1)$ which are perfectly sound (as they span the entire vector space $\hat{\mathbb{G}}^2$) whenever $\mathsf{côm} \neq \mathsf{côm}^\star$. This implies that, although the adversary can see a simulated NIZK proof $(\hat{C}_\theta^\star, \pi_1^\star, \pi_2^\star)$ for a false statement in the challenge phase, it remains unable to trick the decryption oracle into accepting a ciphertext $C = (\mathsf{SVK}, \mathsf{côm}, \mathsf{open}, C_0, C_1, C_2, \hat{C}_\theta, \boldsymbol{\pi}, \boldsymbol{\sigma})$ such that $\log_{g_1}(C_1) \neq \log_{g_2}(C_2)$. As a consequence, the adversary does not learn anything about x_2 from responses of the decryption oracle. $\qquad\qquad\square$

Lemma 1. *In Game 3, there exists an ECM-TCR adversary with advantage $\epsilon \geq \Pr[F_3]$ against the trapdoor commitment scheme of Sect. 2.5 and which runs in about the same time as $\mathcal{A}$.*

Proof. Let $\mathcal{A}$ be an adversary against the SP-CCA encryption scheme as in the proof of Theorem 2 and let the event F_3 be defined as in Game 3. Then, we build an adversary $\mathcal{B}_3$ against the ECM-CTR security of the structure-preserving trapdoor commitment defined in Sect. 2.5 which efficiently runs $\mathcal{A}$.

The challenger $\mathcal{B}_3$ is given the public parameter PP_{TC} and a commitment key ck generated as in the trapdoor commitment scheme as well as an access to a commit-open oracle $\mathcal{O}_{\mathsf{ck}}$ as defined in Definition 8. Then, $\mathcal{B}_3$ runs step 3 to step 6 of the key generation algorithm of the encryption scheme to get PK and $\mathsf{SK} = (x_1, x_2)$ as specified in Game 2 and Game 3.

The adversary $\mathcal{A}$ is given PK and $\mathcal{B}_3$ is easily able to answer to $\mathcal{A}$'s decryption queries as described in Game 2 and Game 3 thanks to SK. In order to compute the challenge ciphertext given $\{m_0, m_1\}$, $\mathcal{B}_3$ picks $\beta \xleftarrow{R} \{0, 1\}$, runs all the steps of the encryption algorithm with m_β except for step 3 for which $\mathcal{B}_3$ queries $\mathcal{O}_{\mathsf{ck}}$ on $\mathsf{SVK}^\star$ to get $(\mathsf{côm}^\star, \mathsf{open}^\star)$. The computed ciphertext $C^\star$ is then given to $\mathcal{A}$.

Assuming that F_3 occurs, which means that $\mathcal{A}$ makes a post-challenge decryption query for a valid ciphertext $C = (\mathsf{SVK}, \mathsf{côm}, \mathsf{open}, C_0, C_1, C_2, \hat{C}_\theta, \boldsymbol{\pi}, \boldsymbol{\sigma})$ such that $\mathsf{côm} = \mathsf{côm}^\star$ but $(\mathsf{SVK}, \mathsf{open}) \neq (\mathsf{SVK}^\star, \mathsf{open}^\star)$, the challenger simply outputs $(\mathsf{côm}^\star, \mathsf{SVK}, \mathsf{open})$.

Obviously, we have $TC.\mathsf{Verify}(\mathsf{ck}, \mathsf{côm}^\star, \mathsf{SVK}, \mathsf{open}) = 1$ since C is valid. However, during the ECM-TR experiment $\mathcal{B}_3$ only chose a single message $\mathsf{SVK}^\star$ so that there is only one target in $Q = \{(\mathsf{côm}^\star, \mathsf{SVK}^\star, \mathsf{open}^\star)\}$. Moreover, since we also have $(\mathsf{côm}^\star, \mathsf{SVK}, \mathsf{open}) \notin Q$, we find $\Pr[F_3] = \mathbf{Adv}_{TC, \mathcal{B}_3}^{ECM\text{-}TCR}(\lambda)$. $\qquad\square$

While we do not explicit provide a threshold decryption mechanism in the paper, this can be easily achieved in the same way as in the SXDH-based threshold cryptosystem described in [46]. As a result, we readily obtain a robust and non-interactive structure-preserving threshold cryptosystem with CCA2-security in the adaptive corruption setting.

It would be interesting to improve the efficiency of the scheme using quasi-adaptive NIZK arguments [38] in the same way as in [43]. Unfortunately, we did not manage to obtain the required simulation-soundness property while keeping the QA-NIZK arguments structure-preserving.

4   A Randomizable RCCA-Secure Construction

Given a message M over $\mathbb{G}$, the encryption algorithm computes an ElGamal-like encryption of the form $(c_0, c_1, c_2) = (f^\theta, g^\theta, M \cdot h^\theta)$. In order to have an alternative decryption in the reduction as well as publicly verifiable ciphertexts, the algorithm then derives an LHSP signature (Sect. 2.4) on the vector $\boldsymbol{v} = (c_0^b, c_1^b, g^{1-b}, c_1^{1-b}, c_2^{1-b})$, where $b = 1$ is a hidden bit. This is made possible by giving an LHSP signature on $\boldsymbol{v}_1 = (f, g, 1, 1, 1)$ and $\boldsymbol{v}_2 = (1, 1, 1, g, h)$ in the public key since $\boldsymbol{v} = \boldsymbol{v}_1^\theta$. Note that, if $b = 0$, the encryption algorithm cannot derive a signature on $\boldsymbol{v}$ since $(1, 1, g, c_1, c_2)$ is outside the linear span of $\boldsymbol{v}_1$ and $\boldsymbol{v}_2$. The goal of the security reduction is to compute the challenge ciphertext with $b = 0$ (using the signing key) and force the adversary to keep this $b = 0$ in any re-randomization of the challenge. This allows detecting when the adversary attempts to obtain the decryption of a *replayed* ciphertext.

In order to make freshly generated ciphertexts indistinguishable from (re-randomizations of) the challenge ciphertext, we use Groth-Sahai commitments and NIWI proofs to hide b. The encryption algorithm computes a commitment to g^b and $\boldsymbol{v}$ and proves that $b \in \{0, 1\}$ and that $\boldsymbol{v}$ is well-formed with respect to (c_0, c_1, c_2). Then, it proves that the LHSP signature on $\boldsymbol{v}$ is valid.

This proof can be seen as a quasi-adaptive NIZK proof [38] that either (c_0, c_1, c_2) is well-formed or that I know a one-time signature on (c_1, c_2) (of Sect. 2.2) which corresponds to an LHSP signature on (g, c_1, c_2), where g is the fixed element of the verification-key.

In order to statistically re-randomize ciphertext, the OR-proof should be efficiently and publicly adaptable and at the same time it should not support any other kind of malleability. Even though in the NIWI setting the Groth-Sahai proofs are perfectly re-randomizable the constants of the proofs are modified when we compute $(c_0', c_1', c_2') = (c_0, c_1, c_2) \cdot (f, g, h)^{\theta'}$ as well as the variables $\boldsymbol{v}' = \boldsymbol{v} \cdot (\boldsymbol{v}_1^b \cdot \boldsymbol{v}_2^{1-b})^{\theta'}$. Since proving that $\boldsymbol{v}'$ has the correct form requires the same random coins as those used in the commitment of g^b, the encryption algorithm simply adds in the ciphertext a commitment to $\boldsymbol{v}_1^b \cdot \boldsymbol{v}_2^{1-b}$, a proof of well-formedness and a Groth-Sahai NIWI proof of an LHSP signature that can be derived from the public key.

At a first glance, ciphertexts may appear not to prevent malleability of the encrypted message M since nothing seems to "freeze" c_2 in the ciphertext when $c_2^{1-b} = 1$ in honest execution. However, the ciphertext actually binds c_2 in the proof elements which depend on the random coins of the commitments.

Keygen(λ): Choose bilinear groups $(\mathbb{G}, \hat{\mathbb{G}}, \mathbb{G}_T)$ of prime order $p > 2^\lambda$ with generators $f, g \xleftarrow{R} \mathbb{G}$, $\hat{g}, \hat{h} \xleftarrow{R} \hat{\mathbb{G}}$ and do the following.

1. Choose a random exponent $\alpha \xleftarrow{R} \mathbb{Z}_p$ and set $h = g^\alpha$.
2. Choose random $\boldsymbol{u}_1, \boldsymbol{u}_2 \xleftarrow{R} \mathbb{G}^2$ and $\hat{\boldsymbol{u}}_1, \hat{\boldsymbol{u}}_2 \xleftarrow{R} \hat{\mathbb{G}}^2$.
3. Define $\boldsymbol{v}_1 = (f, g, 1, 1, 1)$ and $\boldsymbol{v}_2 = (1, 1, 1, g, h)$, then generate a crs for a QA-NIZK proof system for the language of vectors in $\mathsf{span}\langle \boldsymbol{v}_1, \boldsymbol{v}_2 \rangle$: pick $\mathsf{tk} = (\chi_j, \gamma_j)_{j=1}^5 \xleftarrow{R} \mathbb{Z}_p^{2 \times 5}$ and compute $\hat{g}_j = \hat{g}^{\chi_j} \hat{h}^{\gamma_j}$, for each $1 \leq j \leq 5$, as well as the language dependent parameters $(z_1, r_1) = (f^{\chi_1} g^{\chi_2}, f^{\gamma_1} g^{\gamma_2})$ and $(z_2, r_2) = (g^{\chi_4} h^{\chi_5}, g^{\gamma_4} h^{\gamma_5})$. Then, we have

$$e(z_1, \hat{g}) \cdot e(r_1, \hat{h}) = (f, \hat{g}_1) \cdot (g, \hat{g}_2),$$
$$e(z_2, \hat{g}) \cdot e(r_2, \hat{h}) = (g, \hat{g}_4) \cdot (h, \hat{g}_5).$$

4. Define the private key as $\mathsf{SK} = \alpha \in \mathbb{Z}_p$ and erase tk. The public key $\mathsf{PK} \in \mathbb{G}^{11} \times \hat{\mathbb{G}}^{16}$ is defined to be

$$\mathsf{PK} = \left(f,\ g,\ h,\ \boldsymbol{u}_1,\ \boldsymbol{u}_2,\ z_1,\ r_1,\ r_2,\ z_2,\ \hat{g},\ \hat{h},\ \hat{\boldsymbol{u}}_1,\ \hat{\boldsymbol{u}}_2,\ \{\hat{g}_j\}_{j=1}^5 \right).$$

Encrypt(PK, M): To encrypt $M \in \mathbb{G}$, conduct the following steps:
1. Pick $\theta \xleftarrow{R} \mathbb{Z}_p$ and compute $(c_0, c_1, c_2) = (f^\theta, g^\theta, M \cdot h^\theta)$.
2. Define the bit $b = 1$ and set $G = g^b \in \mathbb{G}$ and $\hat{g}^b \in \hat{\mathbb{G}}$. Prove that

$$e(\boxed{G}, \hat{g}) = e(g, \boxed{\hat{g}^b}) \qquad\qquad e(\boxed{G}, \hat{g}/\boxed{\hat{g}^b}) = 1_{\mathbb{G}_T}. \tag{11}$$

Namely, compute commitments to $G = g^b$ (resp. $\hat{g}^b$), which are obtained as $C_G = (1, G) \cdot \boldsymbol{u}_1^{r_g} \cdot \boldsymbol{u}_2^{s_g}$ (resp. $\hat{C}_b = (1, \hat{g}^b) \cdot \hat{\boldsymbol{u}}_1^{r_b} \cdot \hat{\boldsymbol{u}}_2^{s_b}$), for random $r_g, s_g, r_b, s_b \xleftarrow{R} \mathbb{Z}_p$. Let $\pi_G \in \mathbb{G}^2 \times \hat{\mathbb{G}}^2$ and $\pi_{bit} \in \mathbb{G}^4 \times \hat{\mathbb{G}}^4$ be the proof elements for relations (11).
3. Define $(\Theta_0, \Theta_1, \Theta_2) = (c_0^b, c_1^b, c_2^b)$ and prove that[4]

$$e(\boxed{\Theta_1}, \hat{g}) = e(c_1, \boxed{\hat{g}^b}) \qquad\qquad e(\boxed{\Theta_2}, \hat{g}) = e(c_2, \boxed{\hat{g}^b}). \tag{12}$$

More precisely, compute commitments to Θ_i as $C_i = (1, \Theta_i) \cdot \boldsymbol{u}_1^{\bar{r}_i} \cdot \boldsymbol{u}_2^{\bar{s}_i}$, for each $i \in \{0, 1, 2\}$, and for random $\bar{r}_i, \bar{s}_i \xleftarrow{R} \mathbb{Z}_p$. The corresponding proof elements π_1, π_2 both live in $\mathbb{G}^2 \times \hat{\mathbb{G}}^2$.
4. Derive a QA-NIZK proof $(z, r) = (z_1^\theta, r_1^\theta)$ that $\boldsymbol{v} := \boldsymbol{v}_1^\theta \in \mathbb{G}^5$ belongs to $\mathsf{span}\langle \boldsymbol{v}_1, \boldsymbol{v}_2 \rangle$. Since $b = 1$, we have

$$\boldsymbol{v} = (\boldsymbol{v}_1^\theta)^b \cdot (\boldsymbol{v}_2^\theta)^{1-b} = (c_0^b, c_1^b, 1, 1, 1) = (c_0^b, c_1^b, g^{1-b}, c_1^{1-b}, c_2^{1-b}),$$

which allows generating a NIWI proof $\pi_{enc} \in \hat{\mathbb{G}}^2$ that $(z, r, \Theta_0, \Theta_1, \Theta_2, g^b)$ satisfy

$$e(\boxed{z}, \hat{g}) \cdot e(\boxed{r}, \hat{h}) = e(\boxed{\Theta_0}, \hat{g}_1) \cdot e(\boxed{\Theta_1}, \hat{g}_2) \cdot e(g/\boxed{g^b}, \hat{g}_3)$$
$$\cdot e(c_1/\boxed{\Theta_1}, \hat{g}_4) \cdot e(c_2/\boxed{\Theta_2}, \hat{g}_5). \tag{13}$$

together with the Groth-Sahai commitments $C_z, C_r \in \mathbb{G}^2$ of $z, r \in \mathbb{G}$.

---

[4] Note that we intentionally omit to prove the validity of Θ_0 as the unforgeability of the LHSP signature is sufficient for this purpose. As a consequence, c_0 does not have to be in the ciphertext.

5. To enable re-randomization, define $H = h^b$ and $F = f^b$ and compute Groth-Sahai commitments to H and F as $C_H = (1, h^b) \cdot \boldsymbol{u_1}^{r_h} \cdot \boldsymbol{u_2}^{s_h} \in \mathbb{G}^2$ and $C_F = (1, f^b) \cdot \boldsymbol{u_1}^{r_f} \cdot \boldsymbol{u_2}^{s_f} \in \mathbb{G}^2$ for random $r_h, r_f, s_h, s_f \xleftarrow{R} \mathbb{Z}_p$. Then, generate a NIWI proof $\pi_H \in \mathbb{G}^2 \times \hat{\mathbb{G}}^2$ that

$$e(\boxed{H}, \hat{g}) = e(h, \boxed{\hat{g}^b}).$$

6. Derive a QA-NIZK argument $(z_{rand}, r_{rand}) = (z_1^b \cdot z_2^{1-b}, r_1^b \cdot r_2^{1-b})$ that $\boldsymbol{w} := v_1^b \cdot v_2^{1-b}$ belongs to $\mathsf{span}\langle \boldsymbol{v_1}, \boldsymbol{v_2}\rangle$. Since $\boldsymbol{w} = (f^b, g^b, 1, g^{1-b}, h^{1-b})$, generate a proof $\pi_{rand} \in \hat{\mathbb{G}}^2$ that

$$e(\boxed{z_{rand}}, \hat{g}) \cdot e(\boxed{r_{rand}}, \hat{h})$$
$$= e(\boxed{F}, \hat{g}_1) \cdot e(\boxed{G}, \hat{g}_2) \cdot e(g/\boxed{G}, \hat{g}_4) \cdot e(h/\boxed{H}, \hat{g}_5),$$

together with the commitments $C_{z_{rand}}, C_{r_{rand}} \in \mathbb{G}^2$.
Return the ciphertext $\boldsymbol{c} = (c_1, c_2, \pi_{\mathsf{Enc}}, \pi_{\mathsf{Rand}})$ of $\mathbb{G}^{34} \times \hat{\mathbb{G}}^{18}$ where,

$$\pi_{\mathsf{Enc}} = (C_G, \hat{C}_b, \pi_G, \pi_{bit}, C_0, C_1, C_2, \pi_1, \pi_2, C_z, C_r, \pi_{enc}),$$
$$\pi_{\mathsf{Rand}} = (C_H, \pi_H, C_F, C_{z_{rand}}, C_{r_{rand}}, \pi_{rand}).$$

ReRand(PK, c): Parse $\boldsymbol{c} = (c_1, c_2, \pi_{\mathsf{Enc}}, \pi_{\mathsf{Rand}})$ as above and do the following:
1. Pick $\theta' \xleftarrow{R} \mathbb{Z}_p$ and compute $(c_1', c_2') = (c_1 \cdot g^{\theta'}, c_2 \cdot h^{\theta'})$.
2. Update[5] the commitments C_0, C_1, C_2 and the proofs π_1, π_2 of relations (12) according to the update of the constants c_1, c_2 into c_1', c_2'. Namely, compute $(C_0', C_1', C_2') = (C_0 \cdot C_F^{\theta'}, C_1 \cdot C_G^{\theta'}, C_2 \cdot C_H^{\theta'})$ as well as $\pi_1' = \pi_1 \cdot \pi_G^{\theta'}$ and $\pi_2' = \pi_2 \cdot \pi_H^{\theta'}$.
2. Update[6] C_z, C_r and the NIWI proof π_{enc} for relation (13). Namely, compute $C_z' = C_z \cdot C_{z_{rand}}^{\theta'}$ and $C_r' = C_r \cdot C_{r_{rand}}^{\theta'}$ as well as $\pi_{enc}' = \pi_{enc} \cdot \pi_{rand}^{\theta'}$. We should have

$$\Theta_0' = f^{b \cdot (\theta + \theta')}, \qquad \Theta_1' = g^{b \cdot (\theta + \theta')}, \qquad \Theta_2' = M^b \cdot h^{b \cdot (\theta + \theta')},$$

while C_z^i and C_r' are now commitments to

$$z' = z \cdot z_{rand}^{\theta'} = (z_1^b \cdot z_2^{1-b})^{\theta + \theta'}$$
$$r' = r \cdot r_{rand}^{\theta'} = (r_1^b \cdot r_2^{1-b})^{\theta + \theta'}.$$

3. Re-randomize $C_G, \hat{C}_b, C_0', C_1', C_2', C_z', C_r', C_H, C_F, C_{z_{rand}}, C_{r_{rand}}$ and the proofs $\pi_G, \pi_{bit}, \pi_1', \pi_2', \pi_{enc}', \pi_H, \pi_{rand}$ so as to get $C_G'', \hat{C}_b'', C_0'', C_1'', C_2'', C_z'', C_r'', C_H'', C_F'', C_{z_{rand}}'', C_{r_{rand}}''$ and $\pi_G'', \pi_{bit}'', \pi_1'', \pi_2'', \pi_{enc}'', \pi_H'', \pi_{rand}''$.

---

[5] This is can be done efficiently because $\boldsymbol{c}$ contains the commitments and the proofs $C_G, \pi_G \in \pi_{\mathsf{Enc}}$ and $C_H, \pi_H, C_F \in \pi_{\mathsf{Rand}}$ for which π_G, π_H should not only be associated to the bit b but should also contain the same random coins of $\hat{C}_b$ used in π_1, π_2.

[6] At this point, $\{C_i'\}_{i=0,1,2}$ are no longer commitments to $\{\Theta_i\}_{i=0,1,2}$ since the variables have changed into $\Theta_0' = \Theta_0 \cdot F^{\theta'}$, $\Theta_1' = \Theta_1 \cdot G^{\theta'}$ and $\Theta_2' = \Theta_2 \cdot H^{\theta'}$.

Return the ciphertext $c' = (c'_1, c'_2, \pi'_{\text{Enc}}, \pi'_{\text{Rand}})$ where,

$$\pi'_{\text{Enc}} = (C''_G, \hat{C}''_b, \pi''_G, \pi''_{bit}, C''_0, C''_1, C''_2, \pi''_1, \pi''_2, C''_z, C''_r, \pi''_{enc}),$$
$$\pi'_{\text{Rand}} = (C''_H, \pi''_H, C''_F, C''_{z_{rand}}, C''_{r_{rand}}, \pi''_{rand}).$$

Decrypt(SK, c): Parse $c = (c_1, c_2, \pi_{\text{Enc}}, \pi_{\text{Rand}})$ as above and check whether all the proofs are valid. If not, output $\perp$, and otherwise return $M = c_1/c_2^{\alpha}$.

As far as efficiency goes, ciphertexts consist of 34 elements of $\mathbb{G}$ and 18 elements of $\hat{\mathbb{G}}$. Correctness follows from the correctness of the Groth-Sahai proofs and the correctness of the underlying LHSP signatures.

We show that the above scheme, denoted by $\mathcal{E}$, is statistically re-randomizable even for adversarially chosen ciphertexts, as defined in [47] (with the difference that the randomization algorithm uses the public key).

Theorem 3. *The above scheme $\mathcal{E}$ provides statistical unlinkability.*

Proof. We only consider valid adversarially-generated ciphertext c since the validity of ciphertext is efficiently recognizable. Given $c \leftarrow \mathcal{A}(\text{PK})$, we define two distributions on ciphertexts as in the definition of unlikability. The first distribution generates $c' \leftarrow \text{Encrypt}(\text{PK}, \text{Decrypt}(\text{SK}, c))$ while the second distribution generates $c' \leftarrow \text{ReRand}(\text{PK}, c)$. Clearly if we write $c' = (c'_1, c'_2, \pi'_{\text{Enc}}, \pi'_{\text{Rand}})$, the first distribution generates (c_1, c_2) as a fresh ElGamal ciphertext and the perfectly NIWI proofs $(\pi'_{\text{Enc}}, \pi'_{\text{Rand}})$ are completely random subject to the verification of all the pairing product equations detailed in the encryption algorithm of $\mathcal{E}$. Indeed, the key generation algorithm sets the CRSes $(\boldsymbol{u}_1, \boldsymbol{u}_2)$ and $(\hat{\boldsymbol{u}}_1, \hat{\boldsymbol{u}}_2)$ as random elements as in the perfect NIWI setting of the Groth-Sahai proof system [36]. For the same reason, ReRand transforms c into a perfectly re-randomized ciphertext c'. Indeed, step 1 leads to a perfectly re-randomized ElGamal ciphertext $(c'_1, c'_2) = (c_1, c_2) \cdot (g, h)^{\theta'}$. Steps 2 and 3 adapt the Groth-Sahai commitments and proofs with respect to the constant (c'_1, c'_2) to keep the validity of the ciphertext. Finally, step 4 completely re-randomizes these commitments and proofs and the NIWI setting ensures that the resulting $(\pi'_{\text{Enc}}, \pi'_{\text{Rand}})$ are uniformly re-distributed among all the valid proofs satisfying the same pairing product equations with the constant (c'_1, c'_2). Consequently, c' is distributed as a fresh ciphertext of $\text{Decrypt}(\text{SK}, c)$ even if the adversary tried to put some subliminal information in c. $\square$

Next, we show that $\mathcal{E}$ is secure against a Replayable Chosen-Ciphertext Attack (RCCA) in the sense of [22].

Theorem 4. *The above scheme $\mathcal{E}$ provides RCCA security under the SXDH assumption. More precisely, we have* $\mathbf{Adv}_{\mathcal{A}, \mathcal{E}}^{\text{RCCA}}(\lambda) \leq 4 \times \mathbf{Adv}^{\text{SXDH}}(\lambda) + q_d \times 2^{-\lambda}$.

Proof. The proof uses a sequence of games starting with the real game and ending with a game where even an unbounded adversary has no advantage. For each i, S_i is the event that the challenger outputs 1 in Game i meaning that the adversary rightly guesses which message is encrypted in the challenge ciphertext. We assume that security parameter λ is given in each game.

Game 1: This is the real attack game where the adversary chooses M_0 and M_1 and obtains a challenge ciphertext $c^\star$ as a real encryption of M_β, for some $\beta \xleftarrow{R} \{0, 1\}$ chosen by the challenger, in the challenge phase. We recall that the adversary may query the decryption of any ciphertext. In the post-challenge phase, when the challenger uses SK to faithfully reply to the decryption queries it runs the decryption algorithm and returns $\perp$ if the (public) verification fails. If the decryption returns M, the challenger sends back M except if $M \in \{M_0, M_1\}$, in which case *"replay"* is returned. We denote by S_1 the event that the adversary outputs $\beta' = \beta$, which causes the challenger to output 1.

Game 2: This game is like Game 1 except that, in the challenge phase, the challenge ciphertext $c^\star = (c_1^\star, c_2^\star, \pi_{\mathsf{Enc}}^\star, \pi_{\mathsf{Rand}}^\star)$, the proofs

$$\pi_{\mathsf{Enc}}^\star = (C_G^\star, \hat{C}_b^\star, \pi_G^\star, \pi_{bit}^\star, C_0^\star, C_1^\star, C_2^\star, \pi_1^\star, \pi_2^\star, C_z^\star, C_r^\star, \pi_{enc}^\star),$$
$$\pi_{\mathsf{Rand}}^\star = (C_H^\star, \pi_H^\star, C_F^\star, C_{z_{rand}}^\star, C_{r_{rand}}^\star, \pi_{rand}^\star).$$

are obtained by computing $\pi_{\mathsf{Enc}}^\star, \pi_{\mathsf{Rand}}^\star$ as simulated proofs using the trapdoor $\mathsf{tk} = \{(\chi_i, \gamma_i)\}_{i=1}^5$. This is achieved by computing $(\tilde{z}, \tilde{r}) \in \mathbb{G}^2$ as a linearly homomoprhic signature on the vector $v^\star = (1_\mathbb{G}, 1_\mathbb{G}, g, c_1^\star, c_2^\star)$. In step 2 of the encryption algorithm, the challenger thus sets $b = 0$, and conducts the remaining steps of the encryption algorithm except for $(\tilde{z}, \tilde{r})$ at step 4. Thanks to the perfect witness indistinguishability of Groth-Sahai proofs (recall that (u_1, u_2) and $(\hat{u}_1, \hat{u}_2)$ form CRSes for the perfect NIWI setting in the real game), the NIWI proofs $\pi_{\mathsf{Enc}}^\star, \pi_{\mathsf{Rand}}^\star$ have exactly the same distribution as in Game 1 and $\mathcal{A}$'s view remains unchanged. We have $\Pr[S_2] = \Pr[S_1]$. Note that tk is also used to generate the LHSP signatures on the vectors v_1, v_2 of the public key.

Game 3: In this game, we modify the distribution of the public key. In step 2 of the key generation algorithm, we choose $u_2 = u_1^\xi$ and $\hat{u}_2 = \hat{u}_1^\zeta$, with $\xi, \zeta \xleftarrow{R} \mathbb{Z}_p$, instead of choosing $u_2 \xleftarrow{R} \mathbb{G}^2$ and $\hat{u}_2 \xleftarrow{R} \mathbb{G}^2$ uniformly. Under the SXDH assumption, this change should not significantly affect $\mathcal{A}$'s behavior and we have $|\Pr[S_3] - \Pr[S_2]| \leq 2 \times \mathbf{Adv}^{\mathrm{SXDH}}(\lambda)$. Note that (u_1, u_2) and $(\hat{u}_1, \hat{u}_2)$ now form perfectly sound CRSes.

Game 4: We modify the decryption oracle. When the adversary $\mathcal{A}$ queries the decryption of $c = (c_1, c_2, \pi_{\mathsf{Enc}}, \pi_{\mathsf{Rand}})$, the challenger parses the proofs as

$$\pi_{\mathsf{Enc}} = (C_G, \hat{C}_b, \pi_G, \pi_{bit}, C_0, C_1, C_2, \pi_1, \pi_2, C_z, C_r, \pi_{enc}),$$
$$\pi_{\mathsf{Rand}} = (C_H, \pi_H, C_F, C_{z_{rand}}, C_{r_{rand}}, \pi_{rand})$$

and rejects c if the proofs do not properly verify. Otherwise, instead of merely using the private key $\mathsf{SK} = \alpha$ to compute $M = c_1/c_2^\alpha$ as in the real decryption algorithm, the challenger $\mathcal{B}$ uses the extraction trapdoor $\beta = \log_{u_{1,1}}(u_{1,2})$ of the Groth-Sahai CRS (u_1, u_2), where $u_1 = (u_{1,1}, u_{1,2})$, to extract the witnesses g^b, (z, r) and $v = (\Theta_0, \Theta_1, g/g^b, c_1/\Theta_1, c_2/\Theta_2)$ from their commitments C_G, C_z, C_r and $\{C_i\}_{i=0}^2$ which are contained in π_{Enc}. Then, the challenger uses

$\mathsf{tk} = \{(\chi_i, \gamma_i)\}_{i=1}^5$ to compute an LHSP signatures on $v = (v_1, v_2, v_3, v_4, v_5)$

$$z^\dagger = \textstyle\prod_{i=1}^5 v_i^{\chi_i}, \qquad\qquad r^\dagger = \textstyle\prod_{i=1}^5 v_i^{\gamma_i},$$

and rejects the ciphertext in the event that $z^\dagger \neq z$. If c is not rejected, $\mathcal{B}$ computes $M = c_1/c_2^\alpha$. If $M \in \{M_0, M_1\}$ in the post-challenge phase, $\mathcal{B}$ returns *"replay"* as in the actual RCCA game. Otherwise, it returns M to $\mathcal{A}$. It is easy to see that, if $\mathcal{B}$ rejects a ciphertext that would not have been rejected in Game 3, then $\mathcal{B}$ is able to solve the DP problem. This is because (u_1, u_2) and $(\hat{u}_1, \hat{u}_2)$ are perfectly sound Groth-Sahai CRSes and the validity of the proof π_{enc} implies that (z, r) would be another valid homomorphic signature on $v \in \mathbb{G}^5$ than the one that $\mathcal{B}$ can compute. Therefore, this would provide $\mathcal{B}$ with two distinct linearly homomorphic signatures on the same vector and allow $\mathcal{B}$ to solve an instance of the DP problem as done in the proof of [42, Theorem 1]. We thus have $|\Pr[S_4] - \Pr[S_3]| \leq \mathbf{Adv}_{\mathcal{B}}^{\mathrm{DP}}(\lambda)$.

Game 5: We modify the decryption oracle in all pre-challenge and post-challenge decryption queries $c = (c_1, c_2, \pi_{\mathsf{Enc}}, \pi_{\mathsf{Rand}})$ to avoid the use of the secret key $\mathsf{SK} = \alpha = \log_g h$. This change allows modifying the generation of the public element $h = g^x f^y$ with uniformly sampled $x, y \xleftarrow{R} \mathbb{Z}_p$.

In the case of pre-challenge queries, if the commitment C_G contained in π_{Enc} opens to $g^b = 1$ (meaning that $b = 0$), $\mathcal{B}$ rejects the ciphertext. In the case of post-challenge queries c, if $g^b = 1$ (i.e., $b = 0$) and the ciphertext is not rejected by the rules of Game 4, the challenger $\mathcal{B}$ returns "replay" without extracting the encrypted message. Additionally, in all decryption queries, if $g^b = g$ (namely, $b = 1$), $\mathcal{B}$ computes $M := c_2 \cdot c_1^{-x} \cdot \Theta_0^{-y}$. Before the challenge phase, it always outputs M. In the case of post-challenge queries, $\mathcal{B}$ returns "replay" if $M \in \{M_0, M_1\}$ and M otherwise. We now analyze the adversary's view in this game under the light of the unforgeability of LHSP signatures:

Before the challenge: It is easy to see that the probability to reject a ciphertext that would not have been rejected in Game 4 is statistically negligible. This follows from the fact that, from the public key, $\mathcal{A}$ has only obtained linearly homomorphic signatures on (v_1, v_2), the span of which clearly does not contain $v = (\Theta_0, \Theta_1, g/g^b, C_1/\Theta_1, C_2/\Theta_2)$ when $g/g^b \neq 1_{\mathbb{G}}$. Therefore, pre-challenge decryption queries for which $g^b = 1$ are rejected in Game 4 except in the event that $z^\dagger = z$. This event only occurs with probability at most $1/p$ at each such query since $z^\dagger$ (as computed from v using tk) is completely unpredictable from the public key. This follows from the fact that honestly-generated LHSP signatures are deterministic functions of tk while there exist exponentially many valid signatures on each vector of messages. The signing key tk retains sufficient entropy to make it statistically impossible to predict the honestly-generated signature on a vector outside the span of (v_1, v_2), which are given in PK.

After the challenge: First, the perfect soundness of the Groth-Sahai proofs $\{\pi_i\}_{i=1}^2$ for relation (12) allows extracting witnesses that satisfy $\Theta_i = c_i^b$, for each $i \in \{1,2\}$, and then $\boldsymbol{v} = (\Theta_0, c_1^b, g^{1-b}, c_1^{1-b}, c_2^{1-b})$. The difference with pre-challenge queries is that the adversary is also given information on the signature on $\boldsymbol{v}^\star$ from the challenge ciphertext $\boldsymbol{c}^\star$. Hence, in post-challenge queries, LHSP signatures must be in $\mathsf{span}\langle \boldsymbol{v}_1, \boldsymbol{v}_2, \boldsymbol{v}^\star \rangle$. Secondly, we consider the two cases $b \in \{0,1\}$:

- If $g^b = 1_{\mathbb{G}}$ (i.e., $b = 0$), we have $\boldsymbol{v} = (\Theta_0, 1_{\mathbb{G}}, g, c_1, c_2)$. Since $\boldsymbol{c}$ was not rejected, the vector $\boldsymbol{v}$ must be in $\mathsf{span}\langle \boldsymbol{v}_2, (1_{\mathbb{G}}, 1_{\mathbb{G}}, g, c_1^\star, c_2^\star) \rangle$ (i.e. without $\boldsymbol{v}_1$ because the second component of $\boldsymbol{v}$ is $1_{\mathbb{G}}$) except with probability $1/p$. Indeed, otherwise, the same argument as in Game 4 shows that $\boldsymbol{c}$ can only avoid rejection if it contains a commitment C_z to $z^\dagger = z$ and we argued that it is statistically independent of $\mathcal{A}$'s view for vectors outside $\mathsf{span}\langle \boldsymbol{v}_1, \boldsymbol{v}_2, (1_{\mathbb{G}}, 1_{\mathbb{G}}, g, c_1^\star, c_2^\star) \rangle$. This means that $\boldsymbol{v} = \boldsymbol{v}_0 \cdot \boldsymbol{v}_2^\theta$, for some θ, where $\boldsymbol{v}_0 := (1_{\mathbb{G}}, 1_{\mathbb{G}}, g, 1_{\mathbb{G}}, M_\beta)$. Said otherwise, the queried ciphertext is a randomization of the challenge ciphertext, so that $\mathcal{B}$ can rightfully return "*replay*" without changing the view of $\mathcal{A}$.

- If $g^b = g$ (i.e., $b = 1$), we have $\boldsymbol{v} = (\Theta_0, c_1, 1_{\mathbb{G}}, 1_{\mathbb{G}}, 1_{\mathbb{G}})$. Since $\boldsymbol{c}$ was not rejected, $\boldsymbol{v}$ must be in the span of $\boldsymbol{v}_1$ except with probability $1/p$ (via the same argument on the event $z^\dagger = z$ as above). With overwhelming probability $(p-1)/p$, we thus have $\Theta_0 = f^{\log_g c_1}$, which implies that

$$c_1^x \cdot \Theta_0^y = h^{\log_g c_1} = c_1^\alpha$$

if $\mathsf{SK} := \alpha = x + \log_g(f) \cdot y$ is the secret key that underlies $h = g^x f^y$. It follows that $\mathcal{A}$ obtains the same response as in Game 4.

At each decryption query, $\mathcal{B}$'s response deviates from its response in Game 4 with probability at most $1/p$. A union bound over all decryption queries leads to $|\Pr[S_5] - \Pr[S_4]| \le q_d/p$ if q_d is the number of decryption queries.

Game 6: We modify the distribution of the challenge ciphertext. Namely, we choose $(c_0^\star, c_1^\star, c_2^\star)$ as a completely random triple $(c_0^\star, c_1^\star, c_2^\star) \xleftarrow{R} \mathbb{G}^3$ instead of a well-formed tuple $(1_{\mathbb{G}}, 1_{\mathbb{G}}, M_\beta) \cdot (f, g, h)^{\theta^\star}$, for a random $\theta^\star \xleftarrow{R} \mathbb{Z}_p$. Under the SXDH assumption, this modification has no noticeable impact on $\mathcal{A}$'s output distribution since, given a DDH_1 instance (g, f, g^a, f^{a+c}) (where either $c = 0$ or $c \in_R \mathbb{Z}_p$), it is sufficient to define $h = g^x \cdot f^y$, as previously, and set $c_0^\star = f^{a+c}$, $c_1^\star = g^a$ and $c_2^\star = M_\beta \cdot (g^a)^x \cdot (f^{a+c})^y$ during the challenge phase. At this point, $(g^a)^x \cdot (f^{a+c})^y = h^a \cdot f^{cy}$ and we obtain the inequality $|\Pr[S_6] - \Pr[S_5]| \le \mathbf{Adv}^{\mathrm{SXDH}}(\lambda)$.

In Game 6, no information about $\beta \in \{0,1\}$ is leaked anywhere, so that we get $\Pr[S_6] = 1/2$. Since the SXDH assumption implies the DP assumption, we thus find the following advantage

$$|\Pr[S_1] - 1/2| \le 4 \times \mathbf{Adv}^{\mathrm{SXDH}}(\lambda) + q_d \times 2^{-\lambda},$$

which concludes the proof. $\qquad\qquad\square$

Acknowledgements. The first author was supported in part by the "Programme Avenir Lyon Saint-Etienne de l'Université de Lyon" in the framework of the programme "Investissements d'Avenir" (ANR-11-IDEX-0007) and in part by the French ANR ALAMBIC project (ANR-16-CE39-0006). The second author is supported by the F.R.S-FNRS as a postdoctoral researcher.

References

1. Abe, M., Groth, J., Haralambiev, K., Ohkubo, M.: Optimal structure-preserving signatures in asymmetric bilinear groups. In: Rogaway, P. (ed.) CRYPTO 2011. LNCS, vol. 6841, pp. 649–666. Springer, Heidelberg (2011). doi:10.1007/978-3-642-22792-9_37

2. Abe, M., Camenisch, J., Dowsley, R., Dubovitskaya, M.: On the impossibility of structure-preserving deterministic primitives. In: Lindell, Y. (ed.) TCC 2014. LNCS, vol. 8349, pp. 713–738. Springer, Heidelberg (2014). doi:10.1007/978-3-642-54242-8_30

3. Abe, M., Camenisch, J., Dubovitskaya, M., Nishimaki, R.: Universally composable adaptive oblivious transfer (with access control) from standard assumptions. In: Digital Identity Management 2013, pp. 1–12. ACM Press (2013)

4. Abe, M., Chase, M., David, B., Kohlweiss, M., Nishimaki, R., Ohkubo, M.: Constant-size structure-preserving signatures: generic constructions and simple assumptions. In: Wang, X., Sako, K. (eds.) ASIACRYPT 2012. LNCS, vol. 7658, pp. 4–24. Springer, Heidelberg (2012). doi:10.1007/978-3-642-34961-4_3

5. Abe, M., David, B., Kohlweiss, M., Nishimaki, R., Ohkubo, M.: Tagged one-time signatures: tight security and optimal tag size. In: Kurosawa, K., Hanaoka, G. (eds.) PKC 2013. LNCS, vol. 7778, pp. 312–331. Springer, Heidelberg (2013). doi:10.1007/978-3-642-36362-7_20

6. Abe, M., Fuchsbauer, G., Groth, J., Haralambiev, K., Ohkubo, M.: Structure-preserving signatures and commitments to group elements. In: Rabin, T. (ed.) CRYPTO 2010. LNCS, vol. 6223, pp. 209–236. Springer, Heidelberg (2010). doi:10.1007/978-3-642-14623-7_12

7. Abe, M., Groth, J., Ohkubo, M.: Separating short structure-preserving signatures from non-interactive assumptions. In: Lee, D.H., Wang, X. (eds.) ASIACRYPT 2011. LNCS, vol. 7073, pp. 628–646. Springer, Heidelberg (2011). doi:10.1007/978-3-642-25385-0_34

8. Abe, M., Haralambiev, K., Ohkubo, M.: Signing on elements in bilinear groups for modular protocol design. IACR Cryptology ePrint Archive 2010/133 (2010)

9. Abe, M., Haralambiev, K., Ohkubo, M.: Group to group commitments do not shrink. In: Pointcheval, D., Johansson, T. (eds.) EUROCRYPT 2012. LNCS, vol. 7237, pp. 301–317. Springer, Heidelberg (2012). doi:10.1007/978-3-642-29011-4_19

10. Abe, M., Kohlweiss, M., Ohkubo, M., Tibouchi, M.: Fully structure-preserving signatures and shrinking commitments. In: Oswald, E., Fischlin, M. (eds.) EUROCRYPT 2015. LNCS, vol. 9057, pp. 35–65. Springer, Heidelberg (2015). doi:10.1007/978-3-662-46803-6_2

11. Barbulescu, R., Gaudry, P., Joux, A., Thomé, E.: A heuristic quasi-polynomial algorithm for discrete logarithm in finite fields of small characteristic. In: Nguyen, P.Q., Oswald, E. (eds.) EUROCRYPT 2014. LNCS, vol. 8441, pp. 1–16. Springer, Heidelberg (2014). doi:10.1007/978-3-642-55220-5_1

12. Bellare, M., Shoup, S.: Two-tier signatures, strongly unforgeable signatures, and fiat-shamir without random oracles. In: Okamoto, T., Wang, X. (eds.) PKC 2007. LNCS, vol. 4450, pp. 201–216. Springer, Heidelberg (2007). doi:10.1007/978-3-540-71677-8_14

13. Boneh, D., Boyen, X., Halevi, S.: Chosen ciphertext secure public key threshold encryption without random oracles. In: Pointcheval, D. (ed.) CT-RSA 2006. LNCS, vol. 3860, pp. 226–243. Springer, Heidelberg (2006). doi:10.1007/11605805_15

14. Boneh, D., Boyen, X., Shacham, H.: Short group signatures. In: Franklin, M. (ed.) CRYPTO 2004. LNCS, vol. 3152, pp. 41–55. Springer, Heidelberg (2004). doi:10.1007/978-3-540-28628-8_3

15. Boneh, D., Segev, G., Waters, B.: Targeted malleability: homomorphic encryption for restricted computations. In: Innovations in Theoretical Computer Science (ITCS 2012), pp. 350–366 (2012)

16. Camenisch, J., Chandran, N., Shoup, V.: A public key encryption scheme secure against key dependent chosen plaintext and adaptive chosen ciphertext attacks. In: Joux, A. (ed.) EUROCRYPT 2009. LNCS, vol. 5479, pp. 351–368. Springer, Heidelberg (2009). doi:10.1007/978-3-642-01001-9_20

17. Camenisch, J., Dubovitskaya, M., Enderlein, R.R., Neven, G.: Oblivious transfer with hidden access control from attribute-based encryption. In: Visconti, I., Prisco, R. (eds.) SCN 2012. LNCS, vol. 7485, pp. 559–579. Springer, Heidelberg (2012). doi:10.1007/978-3-642-32928-9_31

18. Camenisch, J., Dubovitskaya, M., Haralambiev, K.: Efficient structure-preserving signature scheme from standard assumptions. In: Visconti, I., Prisco, R. (eds.) SCN 2012. LNCS, vol. 7485, pp. 76–94. Springer, Heidelberg (2012). doi:10.1007/978-3-642-32928-9_5

19. Camenisch, J., Dubovitskaya, M., Haralambiev, K., Kohlweiss, M.: Composable and modular anonymous credentials: definitions and practical constructions. In: Iwata, T., Cheon, J.H. (eds.) ASIACRYPT 2015. LNCS, vol. 9453, pp. 262–288. Springer, Heidelberg (2015). doi:10.1007/978-3-662-48800-3_11

20. Camenisch, J., Gross, T., Heydt-Benjamin, T.: Rethinking accountable privacy supporting services. In: 2008 Digital Identity Management, pp. 1–8. ACM Press (2008)

21. Canetti, R., Halevi, S., Katz, J.: Chosen-ciphertext security from identity-based encryption. In: Cachin, C., Camenisch, J.L. (eds.) EUROCRYPT 2004. LNCS, vol. 3027, pp. 207–222. Springer, Heidelberg (2004). doi:10.1007/978-3-540-24676-3_13

22. Canetti, R., Krawczyk, H., Nielsen, J.B.: Relaxing chosen-ciphertext security. In: Boneh, D. (ed.) CRYPTO 2003. LNCS, vol. 2729, pp. 565–582. Springer, Heidelberg (2003). doi:10.1007/978-3-540-45146-4_33

23. Cathalo, J., Libert, B., Yung, M.: Group encryption: non-interactive realization in the standard model. In: Matsui, M. (ed.) ASIACRYPT 2009. LNCS, vol. 5912, pp. 179–196. Springer, Heidelberg (2009). doi:10.1007/978-3-642-10366-7_11

24. Chase, M., Kohlweiss, M.: A new hash-and-sign approach and structure-preserving signatures from DLIN. In: Visconti, I., Prisco, R. (eds.) SCN 2012. LNCS, vol. 7485, pp. 131–148. Springer, Heidelberg (2012). doi:10.1007/978-3-642-32928-9_8

25. Chase, M., Kohlweiss, M., Lysyanskaya, A., Meiklejohn, S.: Malleable proof systems and applications. In: Pointcheval, D., Johansson, T. (eds.) EUROCRYPT 2012. LNCS, vol. 7237, pp. 281–300. Springer, Heidelberg (2012). doi:10.1007/978-3-642-29011-4_18

26. Cramer, R., Shoup, V.: A practical public key cryptosystem provably secure against adaptive chosen ciphertext attack. In: Krawczyk, H. (ed.) CRYPTO 1998. LNCS, vol. 1462, pp. 13–25. Springer, Heidelberg (1998). doi:10.1007/BFb0055717

27. David, B.M., Nishimaki, R., Ranellucci, S., Tapp, A.: Generalizing efficient multiparty computation. In: Lehmann, A., Wolf, S. (eds.) ICITS 2015. LNCS, vol. 9063, pp. 15–32. Springer, Heidelberg (2015). doi:10.1007/978-3-319-17470-9_2
28. Dodis, Y., Haralambiev, K., López-Alt, A., Wichs, D.: Efficient public-key cryptography in the presence of key leakage. In: Abe, M. (ed.) ASIACRYPT 2010. LNCS, vol. 6477, pp. 613–631. Springer, Heidelberg (2010). doi:10.1007/978-3-642-17373-8_35
29. Dolev, D., Dwork, C., Naor, M.: Non-malleable cryptography. In: STOC 1991, pp. 542–552. ACM Press, New York (1991)
30. Emura, K., Hanaoka, G., Ohtake, G., Matsuda, T., Yamada, S.: Chosen ciphertext secure keyed-homomorphic public-key encryption. In: Kurosawa, K., Hanaoka, G. (eds.) PKC 2013. LNCS, vol. 7778, pp. 32–50. Springer, Heidelberg (2013). doi:10.1007/978-3-642-36362-7_3
31. Granger, R., Kleinjung, T., Zumbrägel, J.: Breaking '128-bit secure' supersingular binary curves. In: Garay, J.A., Gennaro, R. (eds.) CRYPTO 2014. LNCS, vol. 8617, pp. 126–145. Springer, Heidelberg (2014). doi:10.1007/978-3-662-44381-1_8
32. Green, M., Hohenberger, S.: Universally composable adaptive oblivious transfer. In: Pieprzyk, J. (ed.) ASIACRYPT 2008. LNCS, vol. 5350, pp. 179–197. Springer, Heidelberg (2008). doi:10.1007/978-3-540-89255-7_12
33. Groth, J.: Rerandomizable and replayable adaptive chosen ciphertext attack secure cryptosystems. In: Naor, M. (ed.) TCC 2004. LNCS, vol. 2951, pp. 152–170. Springer, Heidelberg (2004). doi:10.1007/978-3-540-24638-1_9
34. Groth, J.: Simulation-sound NIZK proofs for a practical language and constant size group signatures. In: Lai, X., Chen, K. (eds.) ASIACRYPT 2006. LNCS, vol. 4284, pp. 444–459. Springer, Heidelberg (2006). doi:10.1007/11935230_29
35. Groth, J.: Homomorphic trapdoor commitments to group elements. In: Cryptology ePrint Archive: Report 2009/007 (2009)
36. Groth, J., Sahai, A.: Efficient non-interactive proof systems for bilinear groups. In: Smart, N. (ed.) EUROCRYPT 2008. LNCS, vol. 4965, pp. 415–432. Springer, Heidelberg (2008). doi:10.1007/978-3-540-78967-3_24
37. Hofheinz, D., Jager, T.: Tightly secure signatures and public-key encryption. In: Safavi-Naini, R., Canetti, R. (eds.) CRYPTO 2012. LNCS, vol. 7417, pp. 590–607. Springer, Heidelberg (2012). doi:10.1007/978-3-642-32009-5_35
38. Jutla, C.S., Roy, A.: Shorter quasi-adaptive NIZK proofs for linear subspaces. In: Sako, K., Sarkar, P. (eds.) ASIACRYPT 2013. LNCS, vol. 8269, pp. 1–20. Springer, Heidelberg (2013). doi:10.1007/978-3-642-42033-7_1
39. Kiltz, E.: Chosen-ciphertext security from tag-based encryption. In: Halevi, S., Rabin, T. (eds.) TCC 2006. LNCS, vol. 3876, pp. 581–600. Springer, Heidelberg (2006). doi:10.1007/11681878_30
40. Kiltz, E., Pan, J., Wee, H.: Structure-preserving signatures from standard assumptions, revisited. In: Gennaro, R., Robshaw, M. (eds.) CRYPTO 2015. LNCS, vol. 9216, pp. 275–295. Springer, Heidelberg (2015). doi:10.1007/978-3-662-48000-7_14
41. Libert, B., Joye, M.: Group signatures with message-dependent opening in the standard model. In: Benaloh, J. (ed.) CT-RSA 2014. LNCS, vol. 8366, pp. 286–306. Springer, Heidelberg (2014). doi:10.1007/978-3-319-04852-9_15
42. Libert, B., Peters, T., Joye, M., Yung, M.: Linearly homomorphic structure-preserving signatures and their applications. In: Canetti, R., Garay, J.A. (eds.) CRYPTO 2013. LNCS, vol. 8043, pp. 289–307. Springer, Heidelberg (2013). doi:10.1007/978-3-642-40084-1_17

43. Libert, B., Peters, T., Joye, M., Yung, M.: Non-malleability from malleability: simulation-sound quasi-adaptive NIZK proofs and CCA2-secure encryption from homomorphic signatures. In: Nguyen, P.Q., Oswald, E. (eds.) EUROCRYPT 2014. LNCS, vol. 8441, pp. 514–532. Springer, Heidelberg (2014). doi:10.1007/978-3-642-55220-5_29

44. Libert, B., Peters, T., Yung, M.: Group signatures with almost-for-free revocation. In: Safavi-Naini, R., Canetti, R. (eds.) CRYPTO 2012. LNCS, vol. 7417, pp. 571–589. Springer, Heidelberg (2012). doi:10.1007/978-3-642-32009-5_34

45. Libert, B., Peters, T., Yung, M.: Short group signatures via structure-preserving signatures: standard model security from simple assumptions. In: Gennaro, R., Robshaw, M. (eds.) CRYPTO 2015. LNCS, vol. 9216, pp. 296–316. Springer, Heidelberg (2015). doi:10.1007/978-3-662-48000-7_15

46. Libert, B., Yung, M.: Non-interactive CCA-secure threshold cryptosystems with adaptive security: new framework and constructions. In: Cramer, R. (ed.) TCC 2012. LNCS, vol. 7194, pp. 75–93. Springer, Heidelberg (2012). doi:10.1007/978-3-642-28914-9_5

47. Prabhakaran, M., Rosulek, M.: Rerandomizable RCCA encryption. In: Menezes, A. (ed.) CRYPTO 2007. LNCS, vol. 4622, pp. 517–534. Springer, Heidelberg (2007). doi:10.1007/978-3-540-74143-5_29

48. Prabhakaran, M., Rosulek, M.: Homomorphic encryption with CCA security. In: Aceto, L., Damgård, I., Goldberg, L.A., Halldórsson, M.M., Ingólfsdóttir, A., Walukiewicz, I. (eds.) ICALP 2008. LNCS, vol. 5126, pp. 667–678. Springer, Heidelberg (2008). doi:10.1007/978-3-540-70583-3_54

49. Rackoff, C., Simon, D.R.: Non-interactive zero-knowledge proof of knowledge and chosen ciphertext attack. In: Feigenbaum, J. (ed.) CRYPTO 1991. LNCS, vol. 576, pp. 433–444. Springer, Heidelberg (1992). doi:10.1007/3-540-46766-1_35

50. Sahai, A.: Non-malleable non-interactive zero knowledge and adaptive chosen-ciphertext security. In: 1999 40th Annual Symposium on Foundations of Computer Science, FOCS, 17–18, 1999, New York, NY, USA, pp. 543–553. IEEE Computer Society, October 1999

51. Sakai, Y., Attrapadung, N., Hanaoka, G.: Attribute-based signatures for circuits from bilinear map. In: Cheng, C.-M., Chung, K.-M., Persiano, G., Yang, B.-Y. (eds.) PKC 2016. LNCS, vol. 9614, pp. 283–300. Springer, Heidelberg (2016). doi:10.1007/978-3-662-49384-7_11

52. Sakai, Y., Emura, K., Hanaoka, G., Kawai, Y., Matsuda, T., Omote, K.: Group signatures with message-dependent opening. In: Abdalla, M., Lange, T. (eds.) Pairing 2012. LNCS, vol. 7708, pp. 270–294. Springer, Heidelberg (2013). doi:10.1007/978-3-642-36334-4_18

53. Scott, M.: Authenticated id-based key exchange and remote log-in with simple token and pin number. Cryptology ePrint Archive: Report 2002/164 (2002)

54. Shoup, V., Gennaro, R.: Securing threshold cryptosystems against chosen ciphertext attack. In: Nyberg, K. (ed.) EUROCRYPT 1998. LNCS, vol. 1403, pp. 1–16. Springer, Heidelberg (1998). doi:10.1007/BFb0054113

Leakage-Resilient and Non-Malleable Codes

Non-malleable Codes with Split-State Refresh

Antonio Faonio and Jesper Buus Nielsen[✉]

Aarhus University, Aarhus, Denmark
jbn@cs.au.dk

Abstract. Non-Malleable Codes for the split state model allow to encode a message into two parts such that arbitrary independent tampering on the parts either destroys completely the content or maintains the message untouched. If the code is also leakage resilient it allows limited independent leakage from the two parts. We propose a model where the two parts can be refreshed independently. We give an abstract framework for building codes for this model, instantiate the construction under the external Diffie-Hellman assumption and give applications of such split-state refreshing. An advantage of our new model is that it allows arbitrarily many tamper attacks and arbitrarily large leakage over the life-time of the systems as long as occasionally each part of the code is refreshed. Our model also tolerates that the refreshing occasionally is leaky or tampered with.

1 Introduction

Non-malleable codes (NMCs) are a natural relaxation of the notions of error correcting codes and error detecting codes, which tolerates more attacks by relaxing the security guarantees. An error correcting code guarantees that the encoded message is always correctly decoded. The price for this guarantee is that the code can tolerate only limited attacks, e.g., that some small constant fraction of the codeword is tampered with. An error detecting code decodes either the correct message or returns some special symbol $\perp$ signalling an error. They can tolerate more general attacks, e.g., that some larger constant fraction of the codeword is tampered with. A NMC only guarantees that either the encoded message is correctly decoded or the decoder outputs a message which is unrelated to the encoded message. This weak guarantee allows much more general tampering. It is for instance possible to tolerate tampering that modifies the entire codeword.

Despite the weaker security guarantee, NMCs can be used to protect against physical attacks. Consider a physical device D with an embedded secret key K. For instance a signature card which on input m outputs $\sigma = \mathsf{Sign}_K(m)$. Assume the device might fall into the hands of an adversary that can apply a physical attack on the device to tamper with K, producing a different but related key K'. Now, on input m the device outputs $\sigma = \mathsf{Sign}_{K'}(m)$. We would like to ensure that the adversary cannot learn any information about K from seeing $\mathsf{Sign}_{K'}(m)$. Let Encode and Decode denote the encoding and decoding algorithms of a NMC. Consider now a device $\tilde{D}$ on which we store an encoded key $X \leftarrow \mathsf{Encode}(K)$. On

© International Association for Cryptologic Research 2017
S. Fehr (Ed.): PKC 2017, Part I, LNCS 10174, pp. 279–309, 2017.
DOI: 10.1007/978-3-662-54365-8_12

input m the device outputs $\sigma = \mathsf{Sign}_{\mathsf{Decode}(X)}(m)$. We call $\tilde{D}$ the strengthened device. In face of a tampering with the key the strengthened device outputs $\sigma = \mathsf{Sign}_{\mathsf{Decode}(X')}(m)$. The value of $\mathsf{Decode}(X')$ will either be K or an unrelated key K'. NMC security guarantees that when K' is an unrelated key, then the adversary could in fact have computed K' itself without any access to K. It follows that the adversary either learns a correct signature $\sigma = \mathsf{Sign}_K(m)$ or a value $\sigma = \mathsf{Sign}_{K'}(m)$ it could have computed itself without access to the device. This ensures that tampering does not result in information leaking from the device.

Formally security is defined as a tampering game between an adversary and a simulator S. The adversary submits to the tampering game a message m and the game computes a random encoding $X \leftarrow \mathsf{Encode}(m)$. The adversary then submits a tampering function T. Now the game either computes $m' = \mathsf{Decode}(T(X))$ and gives m' to the adversary. Or, it computes $m' = \mathsf{S}(T)$ and gives m' to the adversary. The code is called secure if for all adversaries there exists an efficient simulator such that the adversary cannot guess which of the two cases occurred except with negligible advantage. A small but crucial modification of the game is needed. Notice that the adversary might for instance submit T equal to the identity function. In that case $m' = m$ in the first case, so the simulator would be required to compute m too, which is impossible as it is not given m as input and m might be a random value. The game is therefore modified to allow S to give a special output $*$ in which case the game sets $m' = m$ before giving m' to the adversary. Security therefore demonstrates that the adversary when submitting a tampering function T could itself efficiently have computed whether the tampering will have no effect (when $\mathsf{S}(T) = *$) and in case there is an effect, which message $m' = \mathsf{S}(T)$ would be the result of the tampering.

It is clear that we need to put some restriction on the tampering function. If the adversary submits the function $T(X) = \mathsf{Encode}(\mathsf{Decode}(X)+1)$ the simulator would have to output $m+1$ without knowing m. The most popular way to restrict the tampering functions is to assume the split-state model (STM), which was first used to get leakage-resilient cryptography (see Dziembowski et al. [21]). In this model we assume that the encoding X consists of two parts $X = (X^0, X^1)$ stored on two separate storage devices or separate parts of a chip. The assumption is that the adversary can only tamper independently with the two parts, i.e., in the model it submits tampering functions $T = (T^0, T^1)$ and the result of tampering is $(X'^0, X'^1) = (T^0(X^0), T^1(X^1))$. This is also the model we consider in this paper. In the split state model it is possible to construct codes which tolerates arbitrary tampering, except that the two parts must be tampered independently.

Unfortunately NMC security is not sufficient for device strengthening if the adversary can repeatedly tamper with the device. To see this assume for simplicity that the encoding has the property that if a single bit is flipped in an encoding X, then $\mathsf{Decode}(X') = \bot$. Consider then the tampering function O_i which overwrites the i'th bit in X by 0. Each O_i is allowed in the split-state model. Now, $\mathsf{Decode}(O_i(X)) = \bot$ if and only if the i'th bit of X is 1. Hence by applying $O_1, \ldots, O_{|X|}$ an adversary can learn X and then compute $m = \mathsf{Decode}(X)$. This means that if the code is secure then by definition the simulator can also compute m, which it cannot. Let us call the above attack the fail-or-not attack.

Two different ways to circumvent the fail-or-not attack has been proposed in the literature. In [34] Liu and Lysyanskaya propose that the strengthened device whenever it reconstructed the key $K = \mathsf{Decode}(X)$ resamples a new encoding $X' \leftarrow \mathsf{Encode}(K)$ and overrides X by X' on the storage medium. This way the adversary gets to tamper with each fresh encoding only once and the NMC assumption is sufficient. In [25] Faust et al. propose a model where the encoding X remains the same in all tamperings. Instead the authors assume that the strengthened device self destructs when it detects that $\mathsf{Decode}(X) = \bot$. In the fail-or-not attack the adversary is using failure or not to leak information on the encoding X. If the device self destructs on failure this can however only be exploited to leak logarithmic many bits, namely in which round of tampering the self destruction happened. The authors in [25] then use a code which can tolerate limited leakage on the two halves of the encoding and constructs the code such that computing in which round the device would have self-destructed can be done using only limited independent leakage from the two halves, reducing tampering to leakage, an idea we use in our new code too.

Both [25,34] consider codes which are additionally leakage resilient in the split state model. In [25] this is needed anyway to protect against tampering and in [34] it is argued to be a natural requirement as we assume the device to be in the hands of an adversary which might learn leakage on the two parts X^0 and X^1 by measuring the device during operation. In both [25,34] it is assumed that the circuitry doing the encoding (and refreshing) cannot be tampered with and that it is leakage free, i.e., only the storage devices are subject to tampering and leakage. Below we will partially relax this assumption by allowing occasional leakage and tampering of the refresh procedure.

Our Contributions We propose a new model in line with [34]. In particular we do not assume the device can self destruct and we use refreshing to protect against the fail-or-not attack. We propose two extra requirements on the refreshing which we motivate below. First, we want the refreshing to be split-state, i.e., the refreshing algorithm should be of the form $\mathsf{Refresh}(X) = (\mathsf{Refresh}_0(X^0), \mathsf{Refresh}_1(X^1))$. Second, the code should tolerate multiple tampering attacks in between refreshes.

To motivate the model, imagine the following application for strengthening a device. The parts X^0 and X^1 are placed in separate storages. When the key is needed the device computes $K = \mathsf{Decode}(X)$ and outputs $\mathsf{Sign}_K(m)$. In addition to this, occasionally the device will read up a part X^i and write back $X'^i = \mathsf{Refresh}(X^i)$. The refreshing of the parts might also be done by separate processes sitting in the storage device of the part, as opposed to the circuitry doing the decoding. The practical motivation is as follows. In all existing codes the encoding process is considerably more complex than the decoding process. For instance encoding necessarily needs cryptographic strength randomness, whereas decoding can be deterministic. It could therefore be much harder to create a leakage and tamper free implementation of Encode. Also, refreshing by decoding and re-encoding is unnecessarily risky as (real-world) leakage from this process could be leakage on the decoded key K.

Notice on the other hand that if a partial refreshing $X'^i = \mathsf{Refresh}(X^i)$ is tampered with, then it can simply be considered just another tampering attack on X^i in the split state model. In the same way, if a partial refreshing $X'_i = \mathsf{Refresh}(X_i)$ is leaky, then it can simply be considered just another leakage attack on X_i in the split state model. For this to be true it is important that the refreshing is split state, motivating our first extra requirement. As a consequence, if only occasionally the refreshing succeeds in being tamper and leakage free, all the failed attempts can be recast as tamper and leakage attacks. This means the code remains secure if it can tolerate several tamper and leakage attacks in between refreshes, motivating our second extra requirement. Notice that for this to be true, the security of the code should not depend on the two parts being refreshed at the same time. We can only assume that each part occasionally gets refreshed.

Our model works as follows. The adversary submits to the game a message m and the game samples $(X^0, X^1) \leftarrow \mathsf{Encode}(m)$. The adversary can then repeatedly submit leakage or tamper queries. In a leakage query the adversary submits (i, L) and is given $R = L(X^i)$. In a tampering query the adversary submits (T^0, T^1) and is given $m' = \mathsf{Decode}(T^0(X^0), T^1(X^1))$.[1] The adversary can also make a refresh query by submitting an index j to the game. Then the game refreshes the corresponding part: $E^j \leftarrow \mathsf{Refresh}_j(E^j)$. We give a simulation-based security definition. The simulator is not given m. To simulate a leakage query the simulator is given (j, L) and must return some value R to the adversary. To simulate a tampering query the simulator is given (T^0, T^1) and must return some value m', where $m' = *$ is replaced with $m' = m$ before m' is returned to the adversary. To simulate a refresh query the simulator is given j and has to return nothing. The adversary must not be able to tell whether it is interacting with the real world or the simulator. The only restriction on the adversary is that the length of the leakage and the number of tampering attacks in between refreshes must be limited. For any polynomials $p(\kappa), q(\kappa)$ we construct a code that can tolerate $p(\kappa)$ bits of leakage and $q(\kappa)$ many tampering attacks in between successful refreshes.

Our definition is *not strong* according to the notions of Non-Malleable Codes given in the original paper [20]. In the security experiment of the strong NMCs the adversary receives either the entire tampered codeword (as opposed to receive the decoded message of the tampered codeword) or $*$ in case that the tampering function keeps the codeword unaltered. The goal of the adversary is to distinguish the codewords of two different message given the result of the tampering function. However, such definition cannot be met in presence of a split-state refresh algorithm. In fact the adversary could forward, as tampering function,

---

[1] Notice that tampering does not overwrite the codeword. This is called non-persistent tampering and is stronger than persistent tampering in the split state model as the set of tampering functions is closed under composition—subsequent tamperings can just first reapply all previous tampering functions (cf. Jafargholi and Wichs [32]).

the refreshing function itself and receives a valid codeword (since it won't be the same codeword). Given the codeword, it can easily distinguish by decoding.

Our techniques borrow ideas from both [25, 34]. In X^1 we will keep a secret key sk for a public-key encryption scheme. In X^0 we will keep the corresponding public key $pk = \mathsf{PK}(sk)$, an encryption $c = \mathsf{Enc}(pk, m)$ of the encoded message and a simulation-sound NIZK proof of knowledge π of some sk such that $pk = \mathsf{PK}(sk)$ using c as a label. Decoding will check the proof and if it is correct and sk matches pk. If so, it outputs $\mathsf{Dec}(sk', c)$. To tolerate leakage and to allow refreshing we use a leakage resilient encryption scheme which allows to refresh sk and c independently. The public key pk in X^1 will never be refreshed, which is secure as pk might in fact be public. To allow the proof of knowledge to be refreshed we use a non-malleable proof with some controlled malleability. We give a concrete instantiation of this framework based on the Continual Leakage-Resilient scheme of Dodis et al. [18] and the Controlled-Malleable NIZK system of Chase et al. [10] instantiated with Groth-Sahai proofs [30].

The structure of the encoding scheme is very similar to the one proposed by [34], however there are few substantial differences: 1. We substitute the PKE and the NIZK scheme with cryptographic primitives that allow efficient refresh mechanisms; 2. The NP relationship of the NIZK is different. (In fact, it is inspired by the scheme of [25].)

The main proof technique is to reduce tampering to legal leakage queries on the encryption scheme. In the reduction we are given separate leakage oracles of sk and c. To simulate leakage from X^1, leak from sk. To simulate leakage from X^0, once and for all produce a simulated proof π with label c and simulate each leakage query from X^0 by leaking from (pk, c, π). As for tampering queries, assume that the parts have been tampered into $X'^1 = sk'$ and $X'^0 = (pk', c', \pi')$. First we use leakage to check whether the decoding would fail. Leak from X'^1 the value $pk'' = \mathsf{PK}(sk')$. Then leak from X'^0 a single bit telling whether $pk' = pk''$ and whether π' is a valid proof. This is exactly enough to determine whether the decoding would fail or not. If the decoding would fail, output $\bot$. Otherwise, if the proof π' still has c as label (which implies that $X'^0 = (pk'', c, \pi')$ when the proof is valid), then output $*$ indicating that the decoding would output the original encoded message. If the label of π' is not c, then use the extraction trapdoor of the proof to extract the secret key sk' matching pk''. Then output $\mathsf{Dec}(sk', c')$. This allows to simulate each tampering attack with limited leakage on X^0 and X^1. Therefore the scheme remains secure as long as refreshing happens often enough for the leakage needed to simulate tampering to not grow about the leakage tolerance of the encryption scheme.

In [18], it was shown that Continually Leakage-Resilient Codes with Split-State Refresh are impossible to construct without computational assumptions. The result holds even when the leakage between each updates is 1 bit. It is easy to see that the same result holds for Non-Malleable Codes with Split-State Refresh. (This is because a tampering attack corresponds at least to 1 bit of leakage.)

More Related Work. Non-Malleable Codes were introduced to achieve tamper-proof security of arbitrary cryptographic primitives. Since their introduction many works have constructed NMCs in different models both under cryptographic assumptions or information theoretically (see [1–3, 12, 15, 19, 26, 32, 38]).

A related line of work on tamper resilience (see [14, 27, 31, 33]) aims at constructing secure compilers protecting against tampering attacks targeting the computation carried out by a cryptographic device (typically in the form of boolean and arithmetic circuits).

A third line of work on tamper resilience instead aims at constructing ad hoc solutions for different contexts like for example symmetric encryption [6, 28, 36], public-key encryption [5, 7, 16, 17, 24, 35, 39], hash functions [29] and more [8, 13, 38].

Roadmap. In the following we will first introduce some known notation and abstract definitions of the properties we need from the primitives in the abstract framework. Then we describe and prove the abstract framework, followed by an instantiation based on External Diffie-Hellman assumption [4, 9]. At the end we will present the application to continual-tamper-and-leakage resilient cryptography in more details.

2 Preliminaries

2.1 Notation and Probability Preliminaries

We let $\mathbb{N}$ denote the naturals and $\mathbb{R}$ denote the reals. For $a, b \in \mathbb{R}$, we let $[a, b] = \{x \in \mathbb{R} : a \leq x \leq b\}$; for $a \in \mathbb{N}$ we let $[a] = \{0, 1, \ldots, a\}$. If x is a bit-string, we denote its length by $|x|$ and for any $i \leq |x|$ we denote with $x_{(i)}$ the i-th bit of x; If $\mathcal{X}$ is a set, $|\mathcal{X}|$ represents the number of elements in $\mathcal{X}$. When x is chosen randomly in $\mathcal{X}$, we write $x \leftarrow_\$ \mathcal{X}$. When A is an algorithm, we write $y \leftarrow \mathsf{A}(x)$ to denote a run of A on input x and output y; if A is randomized, then y is a random variable and $\mathsf{A}(x; r)$ denotes a run of A on input x and randomness r. An algorithm A is *probabilistic polynomial-time* (PPT) if A is allowed to use random choices and the computation of $\mathsf{A}(x; r)$ terminates in at most $poly(|x|)$ steps for any input $x \in \{0, 1\}^*$ and randomness $r \in \{0, 1\}^*$.

Let κ be a security parameter. A function *negl* is called *negligible* in κ (or simply negligible) if it vanishes faster than the inverse of any polynomial in κ. For a relation $\mathcal{R} \subseteq \{0, 1\}^* \times \{0, 1\}^*$, the language associated with $\mathcal{R}$ is $L_\mathcal{R} = \{x : \exists w \text{ s.t. } (x, w) \in \mathcal{R}\}$.

For two ensembles $\mathcal{X} = \{X_\kappa\}_{\kappa \in \mathbb{N}}$, $\mathcal{Y} = \{Y_\kappa\}_{\kappa \in \mathbb{N}}$, we write $\mathcal{X} \overset{c}{\approx}_\epsilon \mathcal{Y}$, meaning that every probabilistic polynomial-time distinguisher D has $\epsilon(\kappa)$ advantage in distinguishing $\mathcal{X}$ and $\mathcal{Y}$, i.e., $\frac{1}{2}|\mathbb{P}[D(\mathcal{X}_\kappa) = 1] - \mathbb{P}[D(\mathcal{Y}_\kappa) = 1]| \leq \epsilon(\kappa)$ for all sufficiently large values of κ.

We simply write $\mathcal{X} \overset{c}{\approx} \mathcal{Y}$ when there exists a negligible function ϵ such that $\mathcal{X} \overset{c}{\approx}_\epsilon \mathcal{Y}$. Similarly, we write $\mathcal{X} \approx_\epsilon \mathcal{Y}$ (statistical indistinguishability), meaning that every unbounded distinguisher has $\epsilon(\kappa)$ advantage in distinguishing $\mathcal{X}$ and $\mathcal{Y}$.

Given a string $X = (X^1, X^2) \in (\{0,1\}^*)^2$ and a value $\ell \in \mathbb{N}$ let $\mathcal{O}_\ell(X)$ be *the split-state leakage oracle*. $\mathcal{O}_\ell(X)$ accepts as input tuple of the form (i, f) where the first element i is an index in $\{0,1\}$ and the the second element f is a function defined as a circuit. If the total amount of leakage is below ℓ, $\mathcal{O}_\ell(X)$ outputs $f_1(X^{i_1})$ otherwise it outputs the special symbol $\perp$. More formally, the oracle $\mathcal{O}_\ell(X)$ is a state machine that maintains state variables $\mathcal{O}_\ell(X).l^0$ and $\mathcal{O}_\ell(X).l_1$ and upon input (i, f) where f is an efficiently computable function with co-domain $\{0,1\}^o$ for a value $o \in \mathbb{N}$ outputs $f(X^i)$ if $(l^i + o) \leq \ell$ and then updates the value l^i to $l^i + o$, otherwise it outputs the value $\perp$.

Given two PPT interactive algorithms A and B we write $(y, k) \leftarrow \mathsf{A}(x) \leftrightarrows \mathsf{B}(z)$ to denote the joint execution of the algorithm A with input x and the algorithm B with input z. The string y (resp. z) is the output of A (resp. B) after the interaction. In particular we write $\mathsf{A} \leftrightarrows \mathcal{O}_\ell(X)$ to denote A having oracle access to the leakage oracle with input X. Moreover, we write $\mathsf{A} \leftrightarrows \mathcal{B}, \mathcal{C}$ to denote A interacting in an interleaved fashion both with $\mathcal{B}$ and with $\mathcal{C}$.

2.2 Cryptographic Primitives

NIZK Proof of Knowledge. We first introduce the necessary notation for *label-malleable* NIZK (lM-NIZK for short) argument system. A label-malleable NIZK is intuitively a non-malleable NIZK except that from a proof under a given label one can generate a new proof for the same statement under a different label without using the witness. A lM-NIZK $\mathcal{NIZK} := (\mathsf{I}, \mathsf{P}, \mathsf{V}, \mathsf{RandProof}, \mathsf{LEval})$ with label space $\mathcal{L}$ is a tuple of PPT algorithms where: (1) The algorithm I upon input the security parameter 1^κ, creates a common reference string (CRS) ω; (2) The prover algorithm P upon input ω, a label $L \in \mathcal{L}$ and a valid instance x together with a witness w produces a proof π. We write $\mathsf{P}^L(\omega, x, w)$; (3) The verifier algorithm V upon input ω, a label L an instance x together with a proof π outputs a verdict in $\{0,1\}$. We write $\mathsf{V}^L(\omega, x, \pi)$; (4) The label-derivation algorithm LEval upon input ω, a transformation ϕ, a label L an instance x and a proof π outputs a new proof π'.

Definition 1 (Adaptive multi-theorem zero-knowledge). *Let $\mathcal{NIZK}$ be a non-interactive argument system for a relation $\mathcal{R}$. We say that $\mathcal{NIZK}$ satisfies adaptive multi-theorem zero-knowledge if the following holds:*

(i) There exists a PPT algorithm S_0 that outputs a CRS ω and a trapdoor τ_{sim}.

(ii) There exist a PPT simulator S_1 and a negligible function ν such that, for all PPT adversaries A, we have that

$$\left| \mathbb{P}\left[\mathsf{A}(\omega) \leftrightarrows \mathsf{P}(\omega, \cdot) = 1 \mid \omega \leftarrow \mathsf{I}(1^\kappa)\right] \right.$$

$$\left. - \mathbb{P}\left[\mathsf{A}(\omega) \leftrightarrows \mathcal{SIM}(\tau_{sim}, \cdot) = 1 \mid (\omega, \tau_{sim}) \leftarrow \mathsf{S}_0(1^\kappa)\right] \right| \leq \nu(\kappa).$$

The simulation oracle $\mathcal{SIM}(\tau_{sim}, \cdot)$ takes as input a tuple (L, x, w) and checks if $(x, w) \in \mathcal{R}$, and, if true, ignores w and outputs a simulated argument $\mathsf{S}_1(\tau_{sim}, L, x)$, and otherwise outputs $\perp$.

Experiment $\mathbf{Exp}_{\text{Ext},S,A}^{\mathcal{T}-\text{lmSE}}(\kappa)$:

$(\omega, \tau_{sim}, \tau_{ext}) \leftarrow S_0(1^{\kappa}); \mathcal{Q} \leftarrow \emptyset;$
$(x^*, L^*, \pi^*) \leftarrow A(\omega) \leftrightarrows \mathcal{SIM}^*(\tau_{sim});$
$(w, \phi, L) \leftarrow \text{Ext}_1(\tau_{ext}, L^*, x^*, \pi);$
Return $(w, \phi, L), \mathcal{Q}.$

Oracle $\mathcal{SIM}^*(\tau_{sim}, \mathcal{Q})$:

Upon message $(L, x) \in \mathcal{L} \times L_{\mathcal{R}};$
$\mathcal{Q} \leftarrow \mathcal{Q} \cup \{(L, x)\};$
Return $S_1(\tau_{sim}, L, x).$

Experiment $\mathbf{Exp}_{\mathcal{NIZK}}^{\mathcal{T}-\text{IDP}}(\kappa)$:

$\omega \leftarrow I(1^{\kappa}); b \leftarrow^\$ \{0, 1\};$
$(\phi, L, x, w, \pi), st \leftarrow A(\omega);$
if $(x, w) \notin \mathcal{R} \vee (V^L(\omega, x, \pi) = 0)$
    then Return 0;
if $(b = 0)$ then $\pi' \leftarrow P(\omega, \phi(L), x, w);$
else $\pi' \leftarrow \text{LEval}(\omega, \phi, (x, L, \pi));$
$b' \leftarrow A(st, \pi');$
Return $(b = b').$

Fig. 1. Experiments defining $\mathcal{T}$-ml-SE and label derivation privacy of $\mathcal{NIZK}$.

Given $\mathcal{NIZK}$ that supports the set of labels $\mathcal{L}$, we say that a set $\mathcal{T}$ is a set of label transformations for $\mathcal{NIZK}$ iff for any $\phi \in \mathcal{T}$ the co-domain of ϕ is a subset of $\mathcal{L}$.

Definition 2 ($\mathcal{T}$-Malleable Label Simulation Extractability). *Let $\mathcal{T}$ be a set of label transformations for $\mathcal{NIZK}$. Let $\mathcal{NIZK}$ be a non-interactive argument system for a relation $\mathcal{R}$. We say that $\mathcal{NIZK}$ is $\mathcal{T}$-malleable label simulation extractable ($\mathcal{T}$-ml-SE) if the following holds:*

(i) *There exists an algorithm S_0 that outputs a CRS ω, a simulation trapdoor τ_{sim}, and an extraction trapdoor τ_{ext}.*

(ii) *There exists a PPT algorithm Ext such that, for all PPT adversaries A, the probability, taken over the experiment $\mathbf{Exp}_{\text{Ext},S,A}^{\mathcal{T}-\text{lmSE}}$ (as defined in Fig. 1), of the conjunction of the following events is negligible in the security parameter κ:*

(a) *$(L^*, x^*) \notin \mathcal{Q}$ and $V(\omega, L^*, x^*, \pi^*) = 1;$*
(b) *$(x^*, w) \notin \mathcal{R};$*
(c) *Either $\phi \notin \mathcal{T}$ or for any (L, x) either $(L, x) \notin \mathcal{Q}$ or $\phi(L) \neq L^*$.*
Moreover, we say that A wins the $\mathcal{T}$-lm SE Experiment when all the above events happen.

Definition 3 (Label Derivation Privacy). *Let $\mathcal{NIZK}$ a lM-NIZK, and let $\mathcal{T}$ be a set of label transformations. We say that $\mathcal{NIZK}$ has label derivation privacy if for all PPT A, there exists a negligible function negl such that $(P \left[\mathbf{Exp}_{\mathcal{NIZK}}^{\mathcal{T}-\text{IDP}}(\kappa) = 1 \right] - \frac{1}{2}) \leq negl(\kappa)$ (where the experiment is defined in Fig. 1).*

Public-Key Encryption. A public-key encryption (PKE) scheme is a tuple of algorithms $E = (\text{Setup}, \text{Gen}, \text{Enc}, \text{Dec})$ defined as follows. (1) Algorithm Setup takes as input the security parameter and outputs public parameters $pub \in \{0, 1\}^*$. all algorithms are implicitly given pub as input. (2) Algorithm Gen takes as input the security parameter and outputs a public/secret key pair (pk, sk); the set of all secret keys is denoted by $\mathcal{SK}$ and the set of all public keys by $\mathcal{PK}$. Additionally, we require the existence of a PPT function PK which upon an input $sk \in \mathcal{SK}$ produces a valid public key pk. (3) The randomized algorithm Enc takes as input the public key pk, a message $m \in \mathcal{M}$, and randomness $r \in \mathcal{R}$, and outputs a ciphertext $c = \mathsf{Enc}(pk, m; r)$; the set of all ciphertexts is denoted by $\mathcal{C}$. (4) The deterministic algorithm Dec takes as input the secret key sk and a ciphertext c, and outputs $m = \mathsf{Dec}(sk, c)$ which is either equal to some message $m \in \mathcal{M}$ or to an error symbol $\bot$. Additionally, we also consider two PPT algorithms: 1. Algorithm UpdateC takes as input a public key pk a ciphertext c and outputs a new ciphertext c. 2. Algorithm UpdateS takes as input a secret key sk and outputs a new secret key sk'.

Correctness (with Updates). We say that E satisfies *correctness* if for all $pub \leftarrow \mathsf{Setup}(1^\kappa)$ and $(pk, sk) \leftarrow \mathsf{Gen}(pub)$ we have that:

$$\mathbb{P}\left[\mathsf{Dec}(\mathsf{UpdateS}(sk), \mathsf{UpdateC}(pk, \mathsf{Enc}(pk, m))) = m\right] = 1,$$

where the randomness is taken over the internal coin tosses of algorithms Enc, UpdateS and UpdateC. Additionally, we require that for any $pk, sk \leftarrow \mathsf{Gen}(pub)$: (A) any sk' such that $\mathsf{PK}(sk') = pk$ and any $c \in \mathcal{C}$ we have that $\mathsf{Dec}(sk, c) = \mathsf{Dec}(sk', c)$; (B) any $sk' \leftarrow \mathsf{UpdateS}(sk)$ we have that $\mathsf{PK}(sk) = \mathsf{PK}(sk')$.

CLRS Friendly PKE Security. We now turn to define Continual-Leakage Resilient Storage Friendly public key encryption.

Definition 4. *For $\kappa \in \mathbb{N}$, let $\ell = \ell(\kappa)$ be the leakage parameter. We say that $E = (\mathsf{Setup}, \mathsf{Gen}, \mathsf{Enc}, \mathsf{Dec}, \mathsf{UpdateC}, \mathsf{UpdateS})$ is ℓ-CLRS Friendly if for all PPT adversaries A there exists a negligible function $\nu : \mathbb{N} \to [0, 1]$ such that $\left|\mathbb{P}\left[\mathbf{Exp}^{\mathrm{clrs}}_{E,A}(\kappa, \ell) = 1\right] - \frac{1}{2}\right| \leq \nu(\kappa)$, (where the experiment is defined in Fig. 2).*

We observe that Definition 4 is weaker than the definition of Dodis *et al.* [18], in fact we do not consider leakage from the update process. We introduce an extra property on the UpdateC algorithm of a CLRS Friendly PKE.

Experiment $\mathbf{Exp}^{\mathrm{clrs}}_{E,A}(\kappa, \ell)$:

$pub \leftarrow \mathsf{Setup}(1^\kappa)$
$(pk, sk) \leftarrow \mathsf{Gen}(pub)$
$b \leftarrow^\$ \{0, 1\}; j \leftarrow 1$
$l_0 := 0; l_1 := 0$
$(m_0, m_1) \leftarrow \mathsf{A}(pub, pk)$
if $|m_0| \neq |m_1|$ set $m_0 \leftarrow m_1$
$c \leftarrow \mathsf{Enc}(pk, m_b)$
$\mathsf{state}^0 := sk, \mathsf{state}^1 := c;$
$st \leftarrow \mathsf{A}(pk) \leftrightharpoons \mathsf{Update}, \mathcal{O}_\ell(\mathsf{state})$
$b' \leftarrow \mathsf{A}(pk, c)$
Return $(b' = b)$

Oracle Update(i):

$\mathcal{O}_\ell(\mathsf{state}).l^i := 0$
$r' \leftarrow^\$ \{0, 1\}^{p(\kappa)}$
if $(i = 0)$
$\quad c = \mathsf{state}^0$
$\quad c' \leftarrow \mathsf{UpdateC}(pk, c)$
$\quad \mathsf{state}^0 := c'$
if $(i = 1)$
$\quad sk = \mathsf{state}^1$
$\quad sk' \leftarrow \mathsf{UpdateS}(sk)$
$\quad \mathsf{state}^1 := sk'$

Fig. 2. Experiment defining CLRS security of E.

Definition 5. *We say that E is* perfectly ciphertext-update private *if for any* $\kappa \in \mathbb{N}$, $pub \leftarrow \mathsf{Setup}(1^\kappa)$, $(pk, sk) \leftarrow \mathsf{Gen}(pub)$ *and any* $m \in \mathcal{M}$ *the distributions* $\{\mathsf{Encode}(pk, m)\}$ *and* $\{\mathsf{UpdateC}(pk, \mathsf{Enc}(pk, m))\}$ *are equivalent.*

If E is a CLRS Friendly PKE then the weaker version of the property above where the two distributions are computationally indistinguishable already holds. The construction in Sect. 4 can be proved secure using the computational ciphertext-update privacy property. However, we prefer to include the perfectly ciphertext-update privacy property because it simplifies the exposition.

3   Definition

In this section we consider three definitions of Non-Malleable Codes with Refresh (NMC-R). The syntax given allows the scheme to depends on a common reference string following [34].

A coding scheme in the CRS model is a tuple $\Sigma = (\mathsf{Init}, \mathsf{Encode}, \mathsf{Decode})$ of PPT algorithms with the following syntax: (1) Init on input 1^κ outputs a common reference string crs. (2) Encode on inputs crs and a message $m \in \mathcal{M}_\kappa$ outputs $X \in \mathcal{C}_\kappa$; (3) Decode is a deterministic algorithm that on inputs crs and a codeword $X \in \mathcal{C}_\kappa$ decodes to $m' \in \mathcal{M}_\kappa$. A coding scheme is correct if for any κ and any $m \in \mathcal{M}_\kappa$ we have $\mathbb{P}_{crs, r_e}[\mathsf{Decode}(crs, \mathsf{Encode}(crs, m; r_e)) = m] = 1$.

We consider coding schemes with an efficient refreshing algorithm. Specifically, for a coding scheme Σ there exists an algorithm Rfrsh that upon inputs crs and a codeword $X \in \mathcal{C}_\kappa$ outputs a codeword $X \in \mathcal{C}_\kappa$. For correctness we require that $\mathbb{P}[\mathsf{Decode}(crs, \mathsf{Rfrsh}(crs, X)) = \mathsf{Decode}(crs, X)] = 1$, where the probability is over the randomness used by the algorithms and the generation of the CRS.

We are interested in coding schemes in the split-state model where the two parts can be refreshed independently and without the need of any interactions. Given a codeword $X := (X^0, X^1)$, we consider the procedure $\mathsf{Rfrsh}(crs, (i, X^i))$ for $i \in \{0, 1\}$ that takes the i-th piece of the codeword and outputs a new piece X'^i. Abusing of notation, given a codeword $X := (X^0, X^1)$ when we write $\mathsf{Rfrsh}(crs, X)$ we implicitly mean the execution of both $\mathsf{Rfrsh}(crs, (i, X^0))$ and $\mathsf{Rfrsh}(crs, (i, X^1))$. Similarly, given a split-state function $T = (T^0, T^1)$ we equivalently write $T(X)$ meaning the application of both $T^0(X^0)$ and $T^1(X^1)$.

We require that for any codeword $X := (X^0, X^1)$ and for any $i \in \{0, 1\}$, let $\bar{X}$ such that $\bar{X}^i \leftarrow \mathsf{Rfrsh}(crs, (i, X^i))$ and $\bar{X}^{i-1} = X^i$ then $\mathbb{P}[\mathsf{Decode}(crs, \bar{X}) = \mathsf{Decode}(crs, X)] = 1$.

NMC with Refresh in the STM. We now give the security definition for Non-Malleable Codes with Refresh. Although the definition would be meaningful for a more general setting, for the sake of concreteness, we specialize it for the split-state model. Let I_m be a function from $\mathcal{M} \cup \{*\}$ to $\mathcal{M}$ which substitutes the symbol $*$ in input with the message m and acts as the identity function otherwise. Let **Tamper** and **SimTamper** be the experiments described in Fig. 3.

Experiment **Tamper**$_{A,\Sigma}(\kappa, \ell, \rho, \tau)$:

Variables i, t^0, t^1 set to 0;

$crs \leftarrow \mathsf{Init}(1^\kappa)$;

$(m, z) \leftarrow A_0(crs)$; $(m_0, st_0) := (m, z)$;

$X_0 := (X_0^0, X_0^1) \leftarrow \mathsf{Encode}(crs, m_0)$;

forall $i < \rho(\kappa)$:

  $(T_{i+1}, st_{i+1}, j) \leftarrow A_1(m_i, st_i) \leftrightarrows \mathcal{O}^\ell(X_i)$,

  where T_{i+1} is a split-state function;

  $\tilde{X}_{i+1} := T_{i+1}(X_i)$;

  $m_{i+1} := \mathsf{Decode}(crs, \tilde{X}_{i+1})$;

  $X_{i+1} := X_i$;

  For $j' \in \{0, 1\}$ if $(t^{j'} > \tau)$ or $(j' = j)$

    $X_{i+1}^{j'} \leftarrow \mathsf{Rfrsh}(crs, (j', X_i^{j'}))$

    Set $\mathcal{O}_\ell(X_i).l^{j'}$ and $t^{j'}$ to 0;

  Increment t^0, t^1 and i;

Return $A_2(st_p)$.

Experiment **SimTamper**$_{A,S}(\kappa, \ell, \rho, \tau)$:

Variable i set to 0;

$(crs, aux) \leftarrow S_0(1^\kappa)$;

$(m, z) \leftarrow A(crs)$; $(m_0, st_0) := (m, z)$;

forall $i < \rho(\kappa)$:

  $(T_{i+1}, st_{i+1}, j) \leftarrow A_1(m_i, st_i) \leftrightarrows S_2(z)$;

  $\bar{m}_{i+1} \leftarrow S_1(T_{i+1}, z)$;

  $m_{i+1} := I_{m_0}(\bar{m}_{i+1})$;

  $S_3(j, z)$

  $i := i + 1$;

Return $A_2(st_p)$.

Fig. 3. Experiments defining the security of NMC with Refresh Σ. Notice that t^j for $j \in \{0, 1\}$ counts the number of rounds since the last refresh of X^j. If $t^j > \tau$ or if the adversary triggers it then a refresh of X^j is executed.

Definition 6 (Non-Malleable Codes with Refresh). *For $\kappa \in \mathbb{N}$, let $\ell = \ell(\kappa), \rho = \rho(\kappa), \tau = \tau(\kappa)$ be parameters. We say that the coding scheme Σ is a (ℓ, ρ, τ)-Non-Malleable Code with Refresh (NMC-R) in the split state model if for any adversary $A = (A_0, A_1, A_2)$ where A_0 and A_2 are a PPT algorithm and A_1 is deterministic polynomial time, there exists a PPT simulator $S = (S_0, S_1, S_2, S_3)$ and a negligible function ν such that*

$$\left| \mathbb{P}\left[\mathbf{Tamper}_{A,\Sigma}(\kappa, \ell, \rho, \tau) = 1 \right] - \mathbb{P}\left[\mathbf{SimTamper}_{A,S}(\kappa, \ell, \rho, \tau) = 1 \right] \right| \leq \nu(\kappa).$$

We give some remarks regarding the definition above. The simulator S is composed of four different parts S_0, S_1, S_2, S_3. The algorithm S_0 upon input 1^κ produces a CRS together with some trapdoor information aux, the CRS produced and the output of Init are computationally indistinguishable.

For simplicity, we assume that the state information aux is stored in a common read-and-write memory that the simulators S_0, S_1, S_2, S_3 have access to. We will sometime referee to S_1 as the *tampering simulator*, to S_2 as the *leakage simulator* and to S_3 as the *refresh simulator*.

The adversary A is composed by a PPT algorithm A_0, a deterministic algorithm A_1 and PPT distinguishing algorithm A_2. The adversary A_0 can sample a message m (as function of the CRS) and some state information z. The latter may encode some side information z about the message m and other information that A_0 wants to pass to A_1. Notice that we can assume without loss of any generality A_1 to be deterministic, in fact, z may also contain random coins. The tampering simulator, the leakage simulator and the refresh simulator take as input the state information z. In addition, in each round, the tampering simulator S_1 receives a split-state tampering function T_{i+1} and it outputs a message $\bar{m}_{i+1}$. First, we notice that, in general, the tampering T_{i+1} can be produced as a function of the initial message m, therefore the simulator (which does not know m) cannot compute the tampering function by its own, even given z. Secondly, the adversary can efficiently produce a tampering function that keeps the same encoded message but modifies the codeword (for example, by submitting the refreshing algorithm Rfrsh as tampering function). The task of the tampering simulator is to detect this (outputting the special symbol $*$), in this case the function I_m forwards to A the initial message m. (We stress that the simulator does not know the message m, so it cannot forward m directly to A but it needs to pass by I_m.)

The tamper experiment takes four parameters: the security parameter κ, the leakage parameter ℓ, the round parameter ρ and the tampering parameter τ. The tampering parameter τ counts how many times the adversary can tamper with the codeword before a refresh of the codeword is needed.

4 Construction

Let $E = (\mathsf{Setup}, \mathsf{Gen}, \mathsf{Enc}, \mathsf{Dec}, \mathsf{UpdateC}, \mathsf{UpdateS})$ be a CLRS friendly PKE with ciphertext space $\mathcal{C}_E$. Let $\mathcal{R}$ be the *NP* relation defined below:

$$\mathcal{R} := \{(pk, sk) \; : \; pk = \mathsf{PK}(sk), sk \in \mathcal{SK}\}.$$

Let $\mathcal{T}$ be a set of label transformations defined below:

$$\mathcal{T} := \{\phi \; : \; \exists pk, sk : \forall m, r : \mathsf{Dec}(sk, \phi(\mathsf{Enc}(pk, m; r))) = m, pk = \mathsf{PK}(sk)\}.$$

Notice that both $\mathcal{R}$ and $\mathcal{T}$ are implicitly parametrized by the public parameters *pub* of the PKE scheme. Let $\mathcal{U}$ be the following set of label transformations:

$$\mathcal{U} := \{\mathsf{UpdateC}(pk, \cdot \; ; r_u) : \; r_u \in \{0, 1\}^\kappa, pk \in \mathcal{PK}\}.$$

It is easy to check that $\mathcal{U} \subseteq \mathcal{T}$. In fact, by the correctness of PKE, there exists sk such that $\mathbb{P}[\mathsf{Dec}(sk, \mathsf{UpdateC}(pk, \mathsf{Enc}(pk, m))) = m] = 1$ and $pk = \mathsf{PK}(sk)$.

Let $\mathcal{NIZK} := (\mathsf{I}, \mathsf{P}, \mathsf{V}, \mathsf{LEval})$ be a lM-NIZK argument system for the relation $\mathcal{R}$ with label space $\mathcal{C}_E$ and set of transformation $\mathcal{T}$. Let Σ be the following coding scheme with refresh in the CRS model:

- $\mathsf{Init}(1^\kappa)$: Sample $\omega \leftarrow \mathsf{I}(1^\kappa)$ and $pub \leftarrow \mathsf{Setup}(1^\kappa)$. Return $crs = (\omega, pub)$.
- $\underline{\mathsf{Encode}(crs, m)}$: Parse $crs = (\omega, pub)$, sample $(sk, pk) \leftarrow \mathsf{Gen}(pub)$, compute $c \leftarrow \mathsf{Enc}(pk, m)$ and $\pi \leftarrow \mathsf{P}^c(\omega, pk, sk)$. Set $X^0 := (pk, c, \pi)$ and $X^1 := sk$ and return $X := (X^0, X^1)$.
- $\underline{\mathsf{Decode}(crs, X)}$: Parse $crs = (\omega, pub)$ and $X = (X^0, X^1)$ where $X^1 = sk$ and $X^0 = (pk, c, \pi)$. Check: (A) $pk = \mathsf{PK}(sk)$ and (B) $\mathsf{V}^c(\omega, pk, \pi) = 1$.

  If both checks (A) and (B) hold then return $\mathsf{Dec}(sk, c)$, otherwise return $\bot$.
- $\mathsf{Rfrsh}(crs, (j, X^j))$:
  - $j = 0$, parse $X^0 = (c, pk, \pi)$, $r \leftarrow_\$ \{0, 1\}^\kappa$, compute $c' := \mathsf{UpdateC}(pk, c; r)$ and $\pi' \leftarrow \mathsf{LEval}(\omega, \mathsf{UpdateC}(pk, \cdot; r), (pk, c, \pi))$, return $X^0 := (pk, c', \pi')$.

– $j = 1$, parse $X^1 = sk$ and compute $sk' \leftarrow \mathsf{UpdateS}(sk)$, return $X^1 :=$ (sk').

Theorem 1. *For any polynomial $\tau(\kappa)$, if E is an ℓ'-CLRS-Friendly PKE scheme (Definition 4) with public key space $\mathcal{PK}$ and message space $\mathcal{M}$ and where $\ell'(\kappa) := \ell(\kappa) + \tau(\kappa) \cdot (\max(\kappa + 1, \log(|\mathcal{M}| + 2) + 1, \log|\mathcal{PK}|))$ and if $\mathcal{NIZK}$ is an adaptive multi-theorem zero-knowledge (Definition 1) label-malleable non-interactive argument of knowledge system with malleable label simulation extractability (Definition 2) and label derivation privacy (Definition 3) then the scheme above is a (ℓ, ρ, τ)-Non-Malleable Code with Refresh for any polynomial $\rho(\kappa)$.*

The leakage rate of the encoding scheme depends on the relation between the size of the proofs of the NIZK system and the parameters of the CLRS Friendly PKE. Roughly, setting τ be a constant, assuming the size of the secret key and the size of the ciphertext of the PKE be approximately the same and let $r = |sk|/\ell$ be the leakage ratio of the CLRS-Friendly PKE then the leakage ratio of the coding scheme is strictly less than $r/(2 + 1/poly(\kappa))$. This comes from the extractability property[2] of the NIZK system and the $O(\kappa)$-bits of leakage needed to support tampering attacks.

Proof. The correctness follows immediately from the correctness of the E and $\mathcal{NIZK}$ and $\mathcal{U} \subseteq \mathcal{T}$. The proof of security is divided in two parts. We first define a simulator, then we define a sequence of mental experiments starting with the initial **Tamper** experiment and proceeding toward the **SimTamper** experiment and we prove that the experiments are computationally indistinguishable.

The Simulator. Let $\widetilde{\mathsf{S}}$ be the simulator of the $\mathcal{NIZK}$ as postulated by Definition 1. Given an adversary $\mathsf{A} = (\mathsf{A}_0, \mathsf{A}_1, \mathsf{A}_2)$ consider the following simulator $\mathsf{S} = (\mathsf{S}_0, \mathsf{S}_1, \mathsf{S}_2, \mathsf{S}_3)$ for the **SimTamper** experiment:

Simulator $\mathsf{S}_0(1^\kappa)$:

– Set the variables t^0, t^1, l^0, l^1 to 0.
– Run the $\mathcal{NIZK}$ simulator $(\omega, \tau_{sim}, \tau_{ext}) \leftarrow \widetilde{\mathsf{S}}_0(1^\kappa)$.
– Sample $(pk, sk) \leftarrow \mathsf{Gen}(pub)$, $c \leftarrow \mathsf{Enc}(pk, 0^\kappa)$ and $\pi \leftarrow \widetilde{\mathsf{S}}_1(\omega, c, pk)$.
– Set the joint state aux to $(\tau_{sim}, \tau_{ext}, X^0, X^1, t^0, t^1)$ where $(X^0, X^1) = ((pk, c, \pi), (sk))$.

Simulator $\mathsf{S}_1(T, z)$:

– Parse $T = (T^0, T^1)$ and aux as $(\tau_{sim}, \tau_{ext}, X^0, X^1, t^0, t^1)$ where $(X^0, X^1) = ((pk, c, \pi), (sk))$.
– Compute $\tilde{X}^i = T^i(X^i)$ for $i \in \{0, 1\}$.
– Check $\tilde{pk} = \mathsf{PK}(\tilde{sk})$ and $\mathsf{V}^{\tilde{c}}(\omega, \tilde{pk}, \tilde{\pi}) = 1$ (check (A) and (B) of Decode), if at least one of the checks fails then return $\bot$.

---

[2] We also are assuming that the NIZK system is not succinct.

- Compute $(sk', \phi, c') \leftarrow \mathsf{Ext}(\tau_{ext}, \tilde{c}, \tilde{pk}, \tilde{\pi})$:
  - (I) If $\tilde{pk} = \mathsf{PK}(sk')$ then output $\tilde{m} = \mathsf{Dec}(sk', \tilde{c})$;
  - (II) If $\phi(c') = \tilde{c}$, $c' = c$ and $T \in \mathcal{T}$ return $*$;
  - (III) Else abort.

Simulator $\mathsf{S}_2(z)$:

- Parse aux as $(\tau_{sim}, \tau_{ext}, X^0, X^1, t^0, t^1, l^0, l^1)$ where $(X^0, X^1) = ((pk, c, \pi), (sk))$.
- Upon message (i, L) where $i \in \{0, 1\}$, compute $y \leftarrow L(X^i)$. If $l^i + |y| \leq \lambda$ then update $l^i := l^i + |y|$ and output y else output $\perp$.

Simulator $\mathsf{S}_3(j, z)$:

- Parse aux as $(\tau_{sim}, \tau_{ext}, X^0, X^1, t^0, t^1, l^0, l^1)$ where $(X^0, X^1) = ((pk, c, \pi), (sk))$; If $j \notin \{0, 1\}$ and $t^0, t^1 \leq \tau$ set $X_{i+1} := X_i$; Else:
  - If $j = 0$ or $(t^0 > \tau)$ then compute $c' \leftarrow \mathsf{UpdateC}(pk, c)$ and $\pi' \leftarrow \tilde{\mathsf{S}}_1(\tau_{sim}, c', pk)$ and reset l^0, t^0 to 0;
  - If $j = 1$ or $(t^1 > \tau)$ then compute $sk' \leftarrow \mathsf{UpdateS}(sk)$ and reset l^1, t^1 to 0.
- Set aux as $(\tau_{sim}, \tau_{ext}, X'^0, X'^1, t^0, t^1, l^0, l^1)$ where $(X'^0, X'^1) = ((pk, c', \pi'), (sk'))$.

The Hybrids. We consider a sequence of mental experiments, starting with the initial **Tamper** experiment which for simplicity we denote by $\mathbf{G}_0$. We summarize the sequence of mental experiments in Fig. 4.

Game $\mathbf{G}_0$. This is exactly the game defined by the experiment **Tamper**, where Σ is the coding scheme described above. In particular, the Init algorithm of Σ samples a CRS $\omega \leftarrow \mathsf{I}(1^\kappa)$ for $\mathcal{NIZK}$, a pair $(pk, sk_0) \leftarrow \mathsf{Gen}(pub)$, encrypts $c_0 \leftarrow \mathsf{Enc}(pk, m)$ and computes $\pi_0 \leftarrow \mathsf{P}^c(\omega, pk, sk)$. The Rfrsh^* algorithm if Σ upon input $j = 0$ samples randomness $r_u \leftarrow_\$ \{0, 1\}^\kappa$, defines the transformation $\phi_u(\cdot) := \mathsf{UpdateC}(pk, \cdot; r_u)$ and computes $c_{i+i} := \phi_u(c_i)$ and $\pi_{i+1} := \mathsf{LEval}(\omega, \phi_u, (pk, c_i, \pi_i))$.

Game $\mathbf{G}_1$. We change the way the proofs π_{i+1} are refreshed. For each iteration $i \in [\rho(\kappa)]$, the refresh procedure Rfrsh^* upon input $j = 0$ parses X_i^0 as (pk, c_i, π_i), samples randomness $r_u \leftarrow_\$ \{0, 1\}^\kappa$, defines the transformation $\phi_u(\cdot) := \mathsf{UpdateC}(pk, \cdot; r_u)$, computes $c_{i+1} \leftarrow \phi_u(c_i)$ and a *fresh* proof:

$$\pi_{i+1} \leftarrow \mathsf{P}^{c_{i+1}}(\omega, pk, sk_i).$$

Finally, it sets $X_{i+1}^0 := (pk, c_{i+1}, \pi_{i+1})$.

Game $\mathbf{G}_2$. We change the way the CRS for the $\mathcal{NIZK}$ and the proofs π_i are computed. Let $\omega, \tau_{sim}, \tau_{ext} \leftarrow \tilde{\mathsf{S}}_0(1^\kappa)$ and for $i \in [\rho(\kappa)]$ if Rfrsh^* is called at the i-th iteration with input $j = 0$ then the proof π_{i+1} is computed as:

$$\pi_{i+1} \leftarrow \tilde{\mathsf{S}}_1(\tau_{sim}, c_{i+1}, pk).$$

Also the proof π_0 is computed in the same way.

$\mathbf{G_0}$, $\boxed{\mathbf{G_1}}$, $\boxed{\mathbf{G_2}}$, $\mathbf{G_3}$, $\mathbf{G_4}$, $\mathbf{G_5}$, $\dashbox{\mathbf{G_6}}$, $\mathbf{G_7}$, $\boxed{\mathbf{G_8}}$,

Variables i, l^0, l^1, t^0, t^1 set to 0;

$\omega \leftarrow \mathsf{I}(1^\kappa)$; $\quad \omega, \tau_{sim}, \tau_{ext} \leftarrow \widetilde{\mathsf{S}}_0(1^\kappa)$;

$pub \leftarrow E.\mathsf{Setup}(1^\kappa)$;

$crs := (\omega, pub)$;

$(m, z) \leftarrow \mathsf{A}_0(crs)$; $(m_0, st_0) := (m, z)$;

$pk, sk \leftarrow \mathsf{KGen}(pub)$;

$\boxed{c_0 \leftarrow \mathsf{Encode}(pk, m);}$ $\quad c_0 \leftarrow \mathsf{Encode}(pk, 0^\kappa)$;

$\pi_0 \leftarrow \mathsf{P}^c(\omega, pk, sk)$; $\quad \pi_0 \leftarrow \widetilde{\mathsf{S}}_1(\tau_{sim}, c_0, pk)$;

$X_0^0 := (pk, c_0, \pi_0)$;

$X_0^1 := sk_0$; $X_0 := (X_0^0, X_0^1)$;

forall $i < \rho(\kappa)$:

$\quad (T_{i+1}, st_{i+1}, j) \leftarrow \mathsf{A}_1(m_i, st_i) \leftrightarrows \mathcal{O}^\ell(X_i)$;

$\quad \tilde{X}_{i+1} := T_{i+1}(X_i)$;

$\quad (\tilde{pk}, \tilde{c}, \tilde{\pi}), (\tilde{sk}) = \tilde{X}_{i+1}$;

$\quad$ if $(\mathsf{V}^{\tilde{c}}(\omega, \tilde{pk}, \tilde{\pi}) = 1$ and $\mathsf{PK}(\tilde{sk}) = \tilde{pk})$ then

$\quad \dashbox{m_{i+1} := \mathsf{Dec}(\tilde{sk}, \tilde{c});}$

$\quad \boxed{C := \{c_0, \ldots, c_i\};}$ $\quad C := \{c_i\}$;

$\quad sk', \phi, c' \leftarrow \mathsf{Ext}(\tau_{ext}, \tilde{\pi})$;

$\quad$ if $(\tilde{pk} \neq \mathsf{PK}(sk'))$ and

$\qquad (\phi(c) \neq c'$ or $c' \notin C$ or $\phi \notin \mathcal{T})$;

$\quad$ then $\mathbf{Abort}$

$\quad$ if $\tilde{pk} = \mathsf{PK}(sk')$

$\qquad$ then $m_{i+1} := I_m(\mathsf{Dec}(sk', \tilde{c}))$;

$\quad$ if $(\phi(c') = \tilde{c}, c' \in C, \phi \in \mathcal{T})$

$\qquad$ then $m_{i+1} := I_m(*)$;

$\quad$ else $m_{i+1} := \bot$;

$\quad X_{i+1} := X_i$;

$\quad$ For $j' \in \{0, 1\}$ if $(t^{j'} > \tau)$ or $(j' = j)$

$\quad X_{i+1}^{j'} \leftarrow \mathsf{Rfrsh}(crs, (j', X_i^{j'}))$

$\quad$ Set $\mathcal{O}_\ell(X_i).l^{j'}, t^{j'}$ to 0;

$\quad$ Increment t^0, t^1 and i;

Return $\mathsf{A}_2(st_\rho)$.

Procedure $\mathsf{Rfrsh}(crs, (j, X_i^j))$:

if $j = 0$ then:

$\quad (pk, c_i, \pi_i) = X_i^0$;

$\quad r_u \leftarrow_\$ \{0, 1\}^\kappa$;

$\quad \phi_u(\cdot) := \mathsf{UpdateC}(pk, \cdot \, ; r_u)$;

$\quad c_{i+1} := \phi_u(c_i)$;

$\quad \pi_{i+1} \leftarrow \mathsf{LEval}(\omega, \phi_u, X_i^0)$;

$\quad \boxed{\pi_{i+1} \leftarrow \mathsf{P}^{c_{i+1}}(\omega, pk, sk);}$

$\quad \boxed{\pi_{i+1} \leftarrow \widetilde{\mathsf{S}}_1(\tau_{sim}, c_{i+1}, pk);}$

$\quad X_{i+1}^0 := (pk, c_{i+1}, \pi_{i+1})$;

if $j = 1$ then;

$\quad sk_i = X_i^1$;

$\quad sk_{i+1} \leftarrow \mathsf{UpdateS}(sk_i)$;

$\quad X_{i+1}^1 := (sk_{i+1})$;

Fig. 4. Games in the proof of Theorem 1. Game $\mathbf{G_0}$ does not execute any of the colored actions, whereas each colored game executes all actions from the previous game plus the ones of the corresponding color. $\mathbf{G_6}$ executes all actions from the previous game but it does not execute the dash-boxed instructions. Additionally, $\mathbf{G_8}$ does not execute any of the boxed instructions.

Game G_3. We extract the witness from the proof $\tilde{\pi}$ and abort if the extraction procedure fails. The game is the same as G_2 but, for each iteration i, let $\tilde{X}_{i+1}$ be the tampered codeword where $\tilde{X}_{i+1} = (\tilde{pk}, \tilde{c}, \tilde{\pi}), (\tilde{sk})$. The game first checks if $V^{\tilde{c}}(\omega, \tilde{pk}, \tilde{\pi}) = 1$ and if so then it runs:

$$sk', \phi, c' \leftarrow \mathsf{Ext}(\tau_{ext}, \tilde{\pi}).$$

Let C be the set of ciphertexts produced by the game until the i-th iteration. Namely $C := \{c_0, \ldots, c_i\}$. If both the conditions: (i) $\tilde{pk} = \mathsf{PK}(sk')$ and (ii) $\phi(c') = \tilde{c}$, $c' \in C$ and $\phi \in \mathcal{T}$ do not hold then the game outputs a special symbol **Abort**.

Game G_4. We change the output of Decode to match point (I) of the simulator S_1. The game is the same as G_3 but, for each iteration $i \in [\rho(\kappa)]$, after the extraction, if the condition $\tilde{pk} = \mathsf{PK}(sk')$ holds, it sets the message $m_{i+1} := I_m(\mathsf{Dec}(sk', \tilde{c}))$.

Game G_5. We change the output of Decode. The game is the same as G_4 but, for each iteration $i \in [\rho(\kappa)]$, after the i-th extraction, if the conditions $\phi(c') = \tilde{c}$, $c' \in C$, where $C = \{c_0, \ldots, c_i\}$ and $\phi \in \mathcal{T}$ hold, it sets the message $m_{i+1} := I_m(*)$ (the original message).

Game G_6. We do not decode explicitly anymore. The game is the same as G_5 but, for each iteration $i \in [\rho(\kappa)]$, in the execution of the decoding algorithm Decode, we do not execute the instruction $m_{i+1} := \mathsf{Dec}(\tilde{sk}, \tilde{c})$.

Game G_7. We change the output of Decode to match point (II) of the simulator S_1. The game is the same as G_6 but, for each iteration $i \in [\rho(\kappa)]$, after the i-th extraction, let the set C be redefined as the singleton containing the ciphertext produced after the last refresh, namely $C := \{c_i\}$, the game checks that the conditions $\phi(c') = \tilde{c}$, $c' \in C$ (instead of $c' \in \{c_0, \ldots, c_i\}$) and $\phi \in \mathcal{T}$ hold then it sets the message $m_{i+1} := I_m(*)$ (the original message).

Game G_8. We replace the ciphertext c with a dummy ciphertext. The game is the same as G_7 but it sets $c \leftarrow \mathsf{Enc}(pk, 0^\kappa)$ (instead of $c \leftarrow \mathsf{Enc}(pk, m)$).

It is easy to check that G_8 is equivalent to the **SimTamper**$_{A,S}$.

Lemma 1. *For all PPT adversaries A there exists a negligible function $\nu_{0,1}$: $\mathbb{N} \to [0,1]$ such that $|\mathbb{P}[G_0(\kappa) = 1] - \mathbb{P}[G_1(\kappa) = 1]| \le \nu_{0,1}(\kappa)$.*

Proof. We reduce to label derivation privacy of $\mathcal{NIZK}$ via an hybrid argument. For any $l \in [\rho(\kappa)+1]$, let **Hyb**$_l$ be the hybrid experiment that executes the same code of G_1 until the l-th iteration (the proofs are *new*) and then executes the same code of G_1 (the proofs are *re-labeled*). In particular, for any l, in the hybrid **Hyb**$_l$, for any $0 \le i < l$ the proof π_i is computed as $P^{c_{i+1}}(\sigma, pk, sk)$ while for $i \ge l$ the proof π_i is computed as $\mathsf{LEval}(\omega, \phi_u, (pk, c_i, \pi_i))$. Moreover, **Hyb**$_{\rho+1}$ is equivalent to G_1 while **Hyb**$_1$ is equivalent to G_0.

Suppose there exist a PPT adversary A, an index $l \in [\rho(\kappa)]$ and a polynomial $p(\cdot)$ such that, for infinitely many values of $\kappa \in \mathbb{N}$, the adversary A distinguishes between **Hyb**$_l$ and **Hyb**$_{l+1}$ with probability at least $1/p(\kappa)$.

We can construct an adversary B that breaks label derivation privacy. The adversary B with input $\omega \leftarrow \mathsf{I}(1^\kappa)$ runs the code of hybrid $\mathbf{Hyb}_l$ on A until the l-th iteration. At this point B forwards to its own challenger the tuple $(\phi_u, c_{l-1}, pk, sk, \pi_{l-1})$ where $\phi_u(\cdot) := \mathsf{UpdateC}(pk, \cdot \,; r_u)$ with $r_u \leftarrow_\$ \{0,1\}^\kappa$, and receives back the proof π'. Notice that $c_l := \phi_u(c_{l-1})$.

If the challenge bit is $b = 0$ then $\pi' \leftarrow \mathsf{P}^{c_l}(\omega, pk, sk)$, and therefore B perfectly simulates $\mathbf{Hyb}_{l+1}$ otherwise if $b = 1$ then $\pi' \leftarrow \mathsf{LEval}(\omega, \phi_u, (pk, c_{l-1}, \pi_{l-1}))$, therefore B perfectly simulates $\mathbf{Hyb}_l$. Therefore B can break label derivation privacy of $\mathcal{NIZK}$ with advantage $1/p(\kappa)$.

Lemma 2. *For all PPT adversaries A there exists a negligible function $\nu_{1,2}$: $\mathbb{N} \to [0,1]$ such that $|\mathbb{P}[\mathbf{G}_1(\kappa) = 1] - \mathbb{P}[\mathbf{G}_2(\kappa) = 1]| \leq \nu_{1,2}(\kappa)$.*

Proof. We reduce to adaptive multi-theorem zero-knowledge of $\mathcal{NIZK}$.

Suppose there exist a PPT adversary A and a polynomial p such that, for infinitely many values of $\kappa \in \mathbb{N}$, $|\mathbb{P}[\mathbf{G}_1(\kappa) = 1] - \mathbb{P}[\mathbf{G}_2(\kappa) = 1]| \geq 1/p(\kappa)$. Let B be a PPT adversary for the multi-theorem zero-knowledge game that runs the same code of $\mathbf{G}_2$ but for any i, instead of computing the proof π_i, forwards to its oracle the query (c_i, pk, sk).

The view provided by B to A is equivalent to $\mathbf{G}_2$ if B's oracle is P and equivalent to $\mathbf{G}_3$ if B's oracle is $\mathcal{SIM}(\tau_{sim}, \cdot)$. Therefore B can break multi-theorem zero-knowledge of $\mathcal{NIZK}$ with advantage $1/p(\kappa)$.

Lemma 3. *For all PPT adversaries A there exists a negligible function $\nu_{2,3}$: $\mathbb{N} \to [0,1]$ such that $|\mathbb{P}[\mathbf{G}_2(\kappa) = 1] - \mathbb{P}[\mathbf{G}_3(\kappa) = 1]| \leq \nu_{2,3}(\kappa)$.*

Proof. We reduce to the $\mathcal{T}$-Malleable label simulation extractability of $\mathcal{NIZK}$. Let Abort be the event that the game $\mathbf{G}_3$ aborts with message **Abort**. Notice that the two games proceed exactly the same until the event Abort happens. Therefore, we have

$$|\mathbb{P}[\mathbf{G}_2(\kappa) = 1] - \mathbb{P}[\mathbf{G}_3(\kappa) = 1]| \leq \mathbb{P}[\mathsf{Abort}].$$

Suppose there exist a PPT adversary A and a polynomial p such that, for infinitely many values of $\kappa \in \mathbb{N}$, $\mathbb{P}[\mathsf{Abort}] \geq 1/p(\kappa)$, where the probability is over the game $\mathbf{G}_3$ with adversary A.

Let B be a PPT adversary for the malleable label simulation extractability that runs the same code of $\mathbf{G}_3$ but for any i, instead of computing the proof π_i, forwards to its oracle the query (c_i, pk) and, if the event during the i-th iteration the message **Abort** is raised, outputs the value $\tilde{X}^0_{i+1} = (\tilde{pk}, \tilde{c}, \tilde{\pi})$. Notice, that the message **Abort** is raised only if the winning condition of the malleable label simulation extractability experiment are met. Therefore the winning probability of B is the probability of the event Abort in $\mathbf{G}_3$.

Lemma 4. $\mathbb{P}[\mathbf{G}_3(\kappa) = 1] = \mathbb{P}[\mathbf{G}_4(\kappa) = 1].$

Proof. Notice that the two games proceed the same until $\mathsf{PK}(\tilde{sk}) = \mathsf{PK}(sk')$ but $\mathsf{Dec}(\tilde{sk}, \tilde{c}) \neq \mathsf{Dec}(sk', \tilde{c})$. Let WrongDec be such event. Then we have

$$|\mathbb{P}[\mathbf{G}_3(\kappa) = 1] - \mathbb{P}[\mathbf{G}_4(\kappa) = 1]| \leq \mathbb{P}[\mathsf{WrongDec}].$$

By the correctness of E we have that the event WrongDec has probability 0.

Lemma 5. $\mathbb{P}[\mathbf{G}_4(\kappa) = 1] = \mathbb{P}[\mathbf{G}_5(\kappa) = 1]$.

Proof. Notice that two games proceed the same until $\phi(c_i) = \tilde{c}$ and $\phi \in \mathcal{T}$ but $\mathsf{Dec}(sk', \tilde{c}) \neq m$ (the original message). Let NotSame be such event. Therefore, we have

$$|\mathbb{P}[\mathbf{G}_3(\kappa) = 1] - \mathbb{P}[\mathbf{G}_4(\kappa) = 1]| \leq \mathbb{P}[\mathsf{NotSame}].$$

The definition of the set $\mathcal{T}$ and $\phi \in \mathcal{T}$ together with the fact that c_i is an encryption of m under pk and $\phi(c_i) = \tilde{c}$ imply that $\mathsf{Dec}(sk', \tilde{c}) = m$. In fact $\phi \in \mathcal{T}$ implies that $\mathsf{Dec}(sk, \phi(c))$ decrypts correctly if c is a valid ciphertext under pk and $pk = \mathsf{PK}(sk)$. Therefore, we have that the event NotSame has probability 0.

Lemma 6. $\mathbb{P}[\mathbf{G}_5(\kappa) = 1] = \mathbb{P}[\mathbf{G}_6(\kappa) = 1]$.

Proof. $\mathbf{G}_6$ does not execute the instruction $m_{i+1} := \mathsf{Dec}(\tilde{sk}, \tilde{c})$, however notice that already in game $\mathbf{G}_5$ either the value m_{i+1} is overwritten or the game outputs **Abort**. So the two game are semantically the same.

Lemma 7. *For all PPT adversaries* A *there exists a negligible function* $\nu_{6,7} :$ $\mathbb{N} \to [0,1]$ *such that* $|\mathbb{P}[\mathbf{G}_6(\kappa) = 1] - \mathbb{P}[\mathbf{G}_7(\kappa) = 1]| \leq \nu_{6,7}(\kappa)$.

Proof. We reduce to the CLRS security of E via an hybrid argument. For $l \in [\rho(\kappa)]$ let $\mathbf{Hyb}_l$ be an hybrid experiment that executes the code of $\mathbf{G}_6$ until the $(l-1)$-th iteration and, after that, executes the code of $\mathbf{G}_7$. Specifically, for every $i < l$ the hybrid $\mathbf{Hyb}_l$, at the i-th iteration, runs the extractor and checks if the conditions $T'(c) = \tilde{c}$, $c' \in \{c_0, \ldots, c_i\}$ and $T \in \mathcal{T}$ hold, and, if yes, it sets $m_{i+1} := m$. For every $i \geq l$ the hybrid $\mathbf{Hyb}_l$, at the i-th iteration, runs the extractor and checks if the conditions $T'(c) = \tilde{c}$, $c' = c_i$ and $T \in \mathcal{T}$ hold, and, if yes, it sets $m_{i+1} := m$. In particular, $\mathbf{Hyb}_0$ is equivalent to $\mathbf{G}_7$ while $\mathbf{Hyb}_\rho$ is equivalent to $\mathbf{G}_8$.

Given an adversary A and an index $k \in [l-1]$ define the event OldCT_k over the random experiment $\mathbf{Hyb}_l$ to hold if A at the l-th iteration outputs a tampering function T_l such that $T_l(X_l^0) = (\tilde{pk}, \tilde{c}, \tilde{\pi})$ and, let $(\bot, T', c') \leftarrow \mathsf{Ext}(\tau_{ext}, \tilde{c}, \tilde{\pi})$, then $c' = c_k$.

Let OldCT be the event $\{\exists k \in [l-1] : \mathsf{OldCT}_k\}$. It is easy to check that

$$|\mathbb{P}[\mathbf{Hyb}_l = 1] - \mathbb{P}[\mathbf{Hyb}_{l+1} = 1]| \leq \mathbb{P}[\mathsf{OldCT}].$$

In fact, if the event OldCT does not happen in $\mathbf{Hyb}_l$ then the condition $c' = c_l$ holds, therefore the two hybrids behave exactly the same.

Suppose there exist an adversary A and a polynomial $p(\cdot)$ such that, for infinitely many values of $\kappa \in \mathbb{N}$, the adversary A distinguishes between game $\mathbf{G}_6$ and $\mathbf{G}_7$ with probability at least $1/p(\kappa)$. Then $\mathbb{P}[\mathsf{OldCT}] \geq 1/p(\kappa)$.

We build a PPT adversary B that breaks CLRS Friendly PKE Security of E. Let $\mathcal{H}$ a family of 2-wise independent hash functions with domain $\mathcal{C}_E$ and co-domain $\{0,1\}^\kappa$. We introduce some useful notation in Fig. 5. A formal description of B follows:

Adversary B:

1. Receive pub, pk from the challenger of the CLRS security experiment and get oracle access to $\mathcal{O}_\ell(,)$.
2. Set variables i, t^0, t^1 to 0 (as in the **Tamper** experiment).
3. Run $\omega, \tau_{sim}, \tau_{ext} \leftarrow \widetilde{S}_0(1^\kappa)$, set $crs := (pub, \omega)$ and send crs to A_0.
4. Let m, z be the output from A_0, let m' be a valid plaintext for E such that the first bit of m' differs from the first bit of m and $|m'| = |m|$. Send the tuple m, m' to the challenger. Set $st_0 := z$.
5. For $i = 0$ to $(l-1)$ execute the following loop:
   (a) Sample $r_i \leftarrow\!\!\!{}^{\$} \{0,1\}^\kappa$ and run the adversary $A_1(m_i, st_i)$, upon query (j, L) from A_1, if $j = 1$ forward the same query to the leakage oracle, if $j = 0$ forward the query $(0, \mathbf{L}_{L,r_i,pk})$ to the leakage oracle.
   (b) Eventually, the adversary A_1 outputs (T_{i+1}, st_{i+1}, j).
   (c) Forward the query $(1, \mathsf{PK}(T^1_{i+1}(\cdot)))$ to the leakage oracle and let pk' be the answer. Forward the query $(0, \mathbf{V}_{T^0_{i+1}, r_i, pk, pk'})$ to the leakage oracle and let a be the answer, if $a = 0$ then set $m_{i+1} := \bot$ and continue to the next cycle.
   (d) Otherwise, forward the query $(0, \mathbf{M}_{T_{i+1}, r_i, pk})$ and let m' be the answer, if m' is **Abort*** then abort, otherwise set $m_{i+1} := m'$. Execute the refresh algorithm $\mathsf{Rfrsh}^*(j)$ as defined by $\mathbf{G}_6$. (In particular, use the trapdoor τ_{sim} to sample $\pi_{i+1} \leftarrow \widetilde{S}_1(\tau_{sim}, c_{i+1}, pk)$.)
6. Sample $H \leftarrow\!\!\!{}^{\$} \mathcal{H}$ and $r_l \leftarrow\!\!\!{}^{\$} \{0,1\}^\kappa$ and run the adversary A_1 on input (m_{l-1}, st_{l-1}) and reply to the leakage oracle queries as in step (5a). Eventually, the adversary A_1 outputs (T_l, st_l, j) forward the leakage query $(0, \mathbf{H}_{T_l, r_l, pk, H})$, let h be the answer of the leakage oracle.
7. Set x to be the empty string. For $i := 1$ to η, where $\eta := 2p^2(\kappa) + 2p(\kappa)|c|$, execute the following:
   (a) Sample $r_{l+i} \leftarrow\!\!\!{}^{\$} \{0,1\}^\kappa$ and run the adversary A_1 on input (m_{l-1}, st_{l-1}) and reply to the leakage oracle queries as in step (5a).
   (b) Eventually the adversary A_1 outputs (T_l, st_l, j), forward the query $(0, \mathbf{H}_{T_l, r, pk, x})$ to the leakage oracle, let a the answer, if $a \neq \bot$ set $x := x \| a$.
   (c) Call the oracle $\mathsf{Update}(0)$ and increase the counter i.
8. If $|x| < |c|$ then sample $b' \leftarrow\!\!\!{}^{\$} \{0,1\}$ and output b'. Otherwise, query the leakage oracle with $(1, (\mathsf{Dec}(\cdot, x))_{(0)})$ and let a be the answer. If $a = m_{(0)}$ output 0 else output 1.

We compute the amount of leakage performed by B. For any executions of the loop in step (5) the adversary B forwards all the leakage queries made by A and, additionally:

- In step (5c) leaks $\log |\mathcal{PK}|$ bits from the secret key and 1 bit from the ciphertext;

- $\underline{\mathbf{L}_{L,r,pk}(c)}$:

  Return $L(pk, c, \mathsf{S}_1(\tau_{sim}, c, pk; r))$.

- $\underline{\mathbf{V}_{T,r,pk,pk'}(c)}$:

  $(\tilde{pk}, \tilde{c}, \tilde{\pi}) := T(pk, c, \mathsf{S}_1(\tau_{sim}, c, pk; r))$;
  Output $(\mathsf{V}^{\tilde{c}}(\omega, \tilde{pk}, \tilde{\pi}) = 1 \ \wedge \ \tilde{pk} = pk')$.

- $\underline{\mathbf{M}_{T,r,pk}(c)}$:

  $(\tilde{pk}, \tilde{c}, \tilde{\pi}) := T(pk, c, \mathsf{S}_1(\tau_{sim}, c, pk; r))$;
  $sk', T', c' \leftarrow \mathsf{Ext}(\tau_{ext}, \tilde{\pi})$;
  if $\tilde{pk} = \mathsf{PK}(sk')$ output $\mathsf{Dec}(sk', \tilde{c})$;
  if $(T'(c) = c', c' \in C, T' \in \mathcal{T})$ output $*$;
  Output **Abort***.

- $\underline{\mathbf{H}_{T,r,pk,H}(c)}$:

  $(\tilde{pk}, \tilde{c}, \tilde{\pi}) := T(pk, c, \mathsf{S}_1(\tau_{sim}, c, pk; r))$;
  $sk', T', c' \leftarrow \mathsf{Ext}(\tau_{ext}, \tilde{\pi})$;
  If $(c' \notin \{c, \bot\})$ output $H(c)$.
  else output $\bot$.

- $\underline{\mathbf{C}_{T,r,pk,H,x,h}(c)}$:

  $(\tilde{pk}, \tilde{c}, \tilde{\pi}) := T(pk, c, \mathsf{S}_1(\tau_{sim}, c, pk; r))$;
  $sk', T', c' \leftarrow \mathsf{Ext}(\tau_{ext}, \tilde{\pi})$;
  if $(T'(c) \neq c'$ or $T' \notin \mathcal{T})$ then output $\bot$;
  if $h = H(c)$ then
     if $|x| < |c|$ then output $(c_{(|x|+1)})$,
     else output the empty string.

Fig. 5. Leakage functions on the ciphertext of E.

- In step (5d) leaks $\log(|\mathcal{M}| + 2)$ bits from the ciphertext (the output is either a message or $*$ or **Abort**);

Notice that τ many of the leakage queries described above are allowed before an invocation of Update is forced. Moreover, in step (6) the adversary B leaks κ bit from the ciphertext and for any executions of the loop in step (7) leaks 1 bit from the ciphertext and then it calls the Update algorithm.

Let ℓ_A the maximum amount of leakage between each invocation of the Rfrsh* algorithm done by A, then the amount of leakage done by B is:

$$\ell' = \ell_A + \tau \cdot (\max(\kappa + 1, \log(|\mathcal{M}| + 2) + 1, \log|\mathcal{PK}|))$$

We compute the winning probability of B. Let $c_0, \ldots, c_{l+\eta}$ be the set of ciphertexts produced (either by Enc, in the case of c_0, or by the UpdateC procedure otherwise) during the CLRS Security Experiment with B. Consider the following events and random variables:

- Let Collision be the event $\{\exists i, j \leq [l + \eta] : i \neq j \wedge H(c_i) = H(c_j)\}$;
- Let Hit be the event that $\{\exists k < l : h = H(c_k)\}$, where h is the output of the leakage query $(0, \mathbf{H}_{T_l,r_l,pk,H})$ (see step 6).
- Let Hit$_i$ be the random variable equal to 1 if the condition $(h = H(c))$ in the i-th execution of the leakage query $(0, \mathbf{H}_{T_l,r_{l+i},pk,x})$ (see step 7) holds, 0 otherwise.
- Let Complete be the event $|x| = |c|$.

It is easy to check that if $(\neg\mathsf{Collision} \wedge \mathsf{Hit} \wedge \mathsf{Complete})$ holds then, at step (8), there exist a positive index $k < l$ such that $(x = c_k)$ holds. Therefore conditioned on the conjunction of the events the adversary B wins[3] with probability 1.

---

[3] Notice we assume perfect correctness of E.

Claim. $\mathbb{P}\left[\mathsf{Collision}\right] \leq (\eta + l)^2 \cdot 2^{-\kappa}$.

Proof. Recall that H is 2-wise independent, therefore for any fixed $x, y \in \mathcal{C}_E$ such that $x \neq y$, $\mathbb{P}\left[H(x) = H(y)\right] = 2^{-\kappa}$, where the probability is taken over the sampling of H. Moreover, the ciphertexts c_i for $i \in [l+\eta]$ are sampled independently of the choice of H, therefore given two indices i, j where $i \neq j$, by averaging over all the possible assignment of c_i, c_j we have that $\mathbb{P}\left[H(c_i) = H(c_j)\right] = 2^{-\kappa}$. By union bound we get the claim.

Claim. $\mathbb{P}\left[\mathsf{Hit} \mid b = 0\right] = \mathbb{P}\left[\mathsf{OldCT}\right]$.

Proof. In fact, the adversary B (on challenge the ciphertext $\mathsf{Enc}(pk, m)$) follows the code of $\mathbf{Hyb}_l$ until step 6. In particular, B has only oracle access to the ciphertext and the secret key (as prescribed by the CLRS Security experiment), while the hybrid $\mathbf{Hyb}_l$ has full access to them. However, the adversary B can perform the same operations via its own leakage oracle access. Therefore, in the execution of the leakage query $(0, \mathbf{H}_{T_l, r_l, pk, H})$ at step (6), the event $c' = c_k$ where $sk', T', c' \leftarrow \mathsf{Ext}(\tau_{ext}, \tilde{pk})$ holds with the same probability of the event OldCT in the hybrid $\mathbf{Hyb}_l$.

Claim. $\mathbb{P}\left[\mathsf{Complete}\right] \leq 2^{-2\kappa+1}$.

Proof. Let φ be the variable that denotes all the randomness used (including the challenger randomness) in the CLRS experiment between the challenger and the adversary B just before the execution of the step 7. Let Good the event that $\{\mathbb{P}\left[\mathsf{Hit}\right] \geq 1/2p(\kappa)\}$. By a Markov argument the probability $\mathbb{P}\left[\varphi \in \mathsf{Good}\right]$ is at least $1/2$. We can condition on the event Good.

We analyze the random variables $\{\mathsf{Hit}_i\}_{i \in [\eta]}$. Fixing the choice of the randomness φ, for any i, the random variable Hit_i depends only on r_{l+i} and on the output of $\mathsf{UpdateC}$ at the $(l + i)$-th invocation. Notice that the adversary B at each iteration of step 7 samples a fresh r_{l+i}, moreover by the perfectly ciphertext-update privacy (see Definition 5) of E, for any $j \neq i$ the ciphertext c_i and c_j are independent (in fact, for any k the distribution of c_{k+1} does not depend on the value of c_k). Therefore, the random variables $\{\mathsf{Hit}_i\}_{i \in [\eta]}$ for any assignment of φ are independent. Let $Z := \sum_{j \in [\eta]} \mathsf{Hit}_j$, we have that $\mathbb{E}\left[Z \mid \mathsf{Good}\right] \geq \eta/2p(\kappa)$.

$$\mathbb{P}\left[\neg\mathsf{Complete} \mid \mathsf{Good}\right]$$
$$= \mathbb{P}\left[Z < |c| \mid \mathsf{Good}\right] = \mathbb{P}\left[Z < \mathbb{E}\left[Z \mid \mathsf{Good}\right] - (\mathbb{E}\left[Z \mid \mathsf{Good}\right] - |c|) \mid \mathsf{Good}\right]$$
$$= \mathbb{P}\left[Z < \mathbb{E}\left[Z \mid \mathsf{Good}\right] - p(\kappa) \cdot \kappa \mid \mathsf{Good}\right] \leq 2^{-2\kappa}$$

Where, in the last step of the above disequations, we used the Chernoff bound.

Let $\mathsf{Guess} := (\neg\mathsf{Hit} \vee \neg\mathsf{Complete})$, namely the event that triggers B to guess the challenge bit at random. Obviously, for any $a \in \{0, 1\}$, $\mathbb{P}\left[b' = b \mid \mathsf{Guess}, b = a\right] = \frac{1}{2}$. For any $a \in \{0, 1\}$ and infinitely many κ:

$$\mathbb{P}[b' = b]$$
$$\geq \tfrac{1}{2}\mathbb{P}\left[\mathsf{Guess}\right] + \mathbb{P}\left[b' = b \wedge \mathsf{Hit} \wedge \mathsf{Complete}\right]$$
$$\geq \tfrac{1}{2}\mathbb{P}\left[\mathsf{Guess}\right] + \mathbb{P}\left[\neg\mathsf{Collision} \wedge \mathsf{Hit} \wedge \mathsf{Complete}\right] \tag{1}$$
$$\geq \tfrac{1}{2}\mathbb{P}\left[\mathsf{Guess}\right] + (\mathbb{P}\left[\mathsf{Hit}\right] - \mathbb{P}\left[\neg\mathsf{Complete}\right] - \mathbb{P}\left[\mathsf{Collision}\right])$$
$$\geq \tfrac{1}{2}\mathbb{P}\left[\mathsf{Guess}\right] + \mathbb{P}\left[\mathsf{Hit}\right] - 2^{-2\kappa+1} - (\eta + l)^2 \cdot 2^{-\kappa}$$
$$\geq \left(\tfrac{1}{2} - \tfrac{1}{2}\mathbb{P}\left[\mathsf{Hit}\right]\right) + \mathbb{P}\left[\mathsf{Hit}\right] - 2^{-2\kappa+1} - (\eta + l)^2 \cdot 2^{-\kappa} \tag{2}$$
$$\geq \tfrac{1}{2} + \tfrac{1}{4} \cdot (\mathbb{P}\left[\mathsf{OldCT}\right] + \mathbb{P}\left[\mathsf{Hit} \mid b = 1\right]) - ((\eta + l)^2 + 1) \cdot 2^{-\kappa}.$$

Where Eq. (1) follows because $\mathbb{P}\left[b' = b \mid \neg\mathsf{Collision} \wedge \mathsf{Hit} \wedge \mathsf{Complete}\right] = 1$ and Eq. (2) follows because $\mathbb{P}\left[\mathsf{Guess}\right] \geq 1 - \mathbb{P}\left[\mathsf{Hit}\right]$.

Lemma 8. *For all PPT adversaries* A *there exists a negligible function* $\nu_{7,8}$: $\mathbb{N} \to [0,1]$ *such that* $|\mathbb{P}\left[\mathbf{G}_7(\kappa) = 1\right] - \mathbb{P}\left[\mathbf{G}_8(\kappa) = 1\right]| \leq \nu_{7,8}(\kappa)$.

Proof. We reduce to the CLRS Friendly PKE Security of E.

By contradiction, assume that there exists a PPT an adversary and a polynomial $p(\cdot)$ such that for infinitely many values of $\kappa \in \mathbb{N}$, we have that A distinguishes between game $\mathbf{G}_7$ and game $\mathbf{G}_8$ with probability at least $1/p(\kappa)$. We build a PPT adversary B that breaks CLRS Friendly PKE Security of E. The adversary B follows the points (1) to (5) of the adversary defined in Lemma 7 with the following modifications: (i) The adversary B runs internally D; (ii) The messages for the challenge are m and 0^κ; (iii) The cycle in step (5) runs for $i = 0$ to $\rho(\kappa)$; (iv) The adversary B eventually outputs the same output bit as A. Let ℓ_A the maximum amount of leakage between each invocation of the Rfrsh* algorithm done by A, then the amount of leakage done by B is:

$$\ell' = \ell_A + \tau \cdot (\max(\log(|\mathcal{M}| + 2) + 1, \log|\mathcal{PK}|))$$

A formal description of B follows.

Adversary B:
1. Receive pub, pk from the challenger of the CLRS security experiment and get oracle access to $\mathcal{O}_\ell()$.
2. Set variables $i, \mathsf{flg}, l^0, l^1, t^0, t^1$ to 0 (as in the **Tamper** experiment).
3. Run $\omega, \tau_{sim}, \tau_{ext} \leftarrow \tilde{\mathsf{S}}_0(1^\kappa)$, set $crs := (pub, \omega)$ and send crs to A_0.
4. Let m, z be the output from A_0. Send $(m, 0^\kappa)$ to the challenger and set $st_0 := z$.
5. For $i = 0$ to $\rho(\kappa)$ execute the following loop:
   (a) Sample $r_i \leftarrow_\$ \{0,1\}^\kappa$ and run the adversary $\mathsf{A}_1(m_i, st_i)$, upon query (j, L) from A_1, if $j = 1$ forward the same query to the leakage oracle, if $j = 0$ forward the query $(0, \mathbf{L}_{L,r_i,pk})$ to the leakage oracle.
   (b) Eventually, the adversary A_1 outputs (T_{i+1}, st_{i+1}, j).
   (c) Forward the query $(1, \mathsf{PK}(T^1_{i+1}(\cdot)))$ to the leakage oracle and let pk^i be the answer. Forward the query $(0, \mathbf{V}_{T^0_{i+1}, r_i, pk, pk'})$ to the leakage oracle and let a be the answer, if $a = 0$ then set $m_{i+1} := \bot$ and continue to the next cycle.

(d) Otherwise, forward the query $(0, \mathbf{M}_{T_i, r_i, pk})$ and let m' be the answer, if m' is **Abort*** then abort, otherwise set $m_{i+1} := m'$.

(e) Execute the refresh algorithm $\mathsf{Rfrsh}^*(j)$ as defined by $\mathbf{G}_6$. (In particular, use the trapdoor τ_{sim} to sample $\pi_{i+1} \leftarrow \widetilde{\mathsf{S}}_1(\tau_{sim}, c_{i+1}, pk)$.)

6. Output $\mathsf{A}_2(st_\rho)$.

The view provided by B to A is equivalent to $\mathbf{G}_7$ if the challenge bit b of the PKE Friendly Security experiment is 0. (This because the encrypted message is m.) Otherwise the view is equivalent to $\mathbf{G}_8$.

Wrapping up all together we have that:

$$\left| \mathbb{P}\left[\mathbf{G}_0 = 1\right] - \mathbb{P}\left[\mathbf{G}_8 = 1\right] \right|$$
$$\leq \sum_{i \in [7]} \left| \mathbb{P}\left[\mathbf{G}_i = 1\right] - \mathbb{P}\left[\mathbf{G}_{i+1} = 1\right] \right| \leq \sum_{i \in [7]} \nu_{i,i+1} \leq negl(\kappa).$$

5 Concrete Instantiations

For a group $\mathbb{G}$ of prime order q and a generator g of $\mathbb{G}$, we denote by $[a]_g := g^a \in \mathbb{G}$ the *implicit representation* of an element $a \in \mathbb{Z}_q$. Let $\mathcal{G}$ be a PPT pairing generation algorithm that upon input the security parameter 1^κ outputs a tuple $gd = (\mathbb{G}_1, \mathbb{G}_2, \mathbb{G}_T, q, g, h, e)$ where the first three elements are the description of groups of prime order $q > 2^\kappa$, g (resp. h) is a generator for the group $\mathbb{G}_1$ (resp. $\mathbb{G}_2$) and e is an efficiently computable non-degenerate pairing function from $\mathbb{G}_1 \times \mathbb{G}_2 \to \mathbb{G}_T$. In what follow, we indicate vectors with bold chars and matrices with capital bold chars, all vectors are row vectors, given a group $\mathbb{G}$, two matrices $\mathbf{X} \in \mathbb{G}^{n \times m}$, $\mathbf{Y} \in \mathbb{G}^{m \times t}$ for $n, m, t \geq 1$ and an element $a \in \mathbb{G}$ we denote with $\mathbf{X} \cdot \mathbf{Y}$ the matrix product of $\mathbf{X}$ and $\mathbf{Y}$ and with $a \cdot \mathbf{X}$ the scalar multiplication of $\mathbf{X}$ by a. Given two elements $[a]_g \in \mathbb{G}_1$ and $[b]_h \in \mathbb{G}_2$ we denote with $[a]_g \bullet [b]_h = [a \cdot b]_{e(g,h)}$ the value $e([a]_g, [b]_h)$, the notation is extended to vectors and matrices in the natural way. Given a field $\mathbb{F}$ and natural numbers $n, m, j \in \mathbb{N}$ where $j \leq \min(n, m)$ we define $\mathsf{Rk}_j(\mathbb{F}^{n \times m})$ to be the set of matrices in $\mathbb{F}^{n \times m}$ with rows rank j; given a matrix $\mathbf{B}$ we let $\mathsf{Rank}(\mathbf{B})$ be the rank of $\mathbf{B}$.

Definition 7. *The k-rank hiding assumption for a pairing generation algorithm $pub := (\mathbb{G}_1, \mathbb{G}_2, \mathbb{G}_T, q, g_1, g_2, e) \leftarrow_{\$} \mathcal{G}(1^\kappa)$ states that for any $i \in \{1, 2\}$ and for any $k \leq j, j' \leq \min(n, m)$ the tuple $(g_i, [\mathbf{B}]_{g_i})$ and the tuple $(g_i, [\mathbf{B}']_{g_i})$ for random $\mathbf{B} \leftarrow_{\$} \mathsf{Rk}_j$ and $\mathbf{B}' \leftarrow_{\$} \mathsf{Rk}_{j'}$ are computational indistinguishable.*

The k-rank hiding assumption was introduced by Naor and Segev in [37] where the authors showed to be implied by the more common k-linear (DLIN) assumption. The assumption gets weaker as k increases. In fact for $k = 1$ this assumption is equivalent to DDH assumption. Unfortunately, it is known that DDH cannot hold in symmetric pairings where $\mathbb{G}_1 = \mathbb{G}_2$. However, it is reasonable to assume that DDH holds in asymmetric pairings. This assumption is often called *external Diffie-Hellman* assumption (SXDH) (see [4, 9]).

5.1   The Encryption Scheme

We consider a slight variation of the CLRS Friendly PKE scheme of [18]. Consider the following PKE scheme $E = (\mathsf{Setup}, \mathsf{Gen}, \mathsf{Enc}, \mathsf{Dec}, \mathsf{UpdateC}, \mathsf{UpdateS})$ with message space $\mathcal{M} := \{0, 1\}$ and parameters $n, m, d \in \mathbb{N}$.

- $\mathsf{Setup}(1^\kappa)$: Sample $gd \leftarrow \mathcal{G}(1^\kappa)$ and vectors $\boldsymbol{p}, \boldsymbol{w} \leftarrow_\$ \mathbb{Z}_q^m$ such that $\boldsymbol{p} \cdot \boldsymbol{w}^T = 0$ mod q. Return $pub := (gd, [\boldsymbol{p}]_g, [\boldsymbol{w}]_h)$. (Recall that all algorithms implicitly take pub as input.)

- $\mathsf{Gen}(pub)$: Sample $\boldsymbol{t} \leftarrow_\$ \mathbb{Z}_q^m$, $\boldsymbol{r} \leftarrow_\$ \mathbb{Z}_q^n$ and compute $sk := [\boldsymbol{r}^T \cdot \boldsymbol{w} + \boldsymbol{1}_n^T \cdot \boldsymbol{t}]_h$, set $\alpha := \boldsymbol{p} \cdot \boldsymbol{t}^T$ and compute $pk := [\alpha]_g$. The latter can be computed given only $[\boldsymbol{p}]_g \in \mathbb{G}_1^m$ and $\boldsymbol{t} \in \mathbb{Z}_q^m$. Return (pk, sk).

- $\mathsf{Enc}(pk, b)$: Sample $\boldsymbol{u} \leftarrow_\$ \mathbb{Z}_q^n$ and compute $c_1 := [\boldsymbol{u}^T \cdot \boldsymbol{p}]_g$ and $c_2 := [\alpha \boldsymbol{u} + b \boldsymbol{1}_n]_g$. Return $C := (c_1, c_2)$.

- $\mathsf{Dec}(sk, C)$: Let $f = e(g, h)$, parse $sk = [\boldsymbol{S}]_h \in \mathbb{G}_2^{n \times m}$, let $\boldsymbol{S}_1$ be the first row of $\boldsymbol{S}$ and parse $C = ([\boldsymbol{C}]_g, [\boldsymbol{c}]_g) \in (\mathbb{G}_1^{n \times m} \times \mathbb{G}_1^n)$. Compute $\boldsymbol{b} := [\boldsymbol{c} - \boldsymbol{C} \cdot \boldsymbol{S}_1^T]_f$ and output 1 if and only if $\boldsymbol{b} = [\boldsymbol{1}_n]_f$. In particular, $[\boldsymbol{b}]_f$ can be computed by first computing $[\boldsymbol{c}]_f := e([\boldsymbol{c}]_g, h)$ and then $[\boldsymbol{C} \cdot \boldsymbol{S}_1^T]_f := \prod_i e(\boldsymbol{C}[i], \boldsymbol{S}[i])$.

- $\mathsf{UpdateC}(pk, C)$: Parse $C = ([\boldsymbol{C}]_g, [\boldsymbol{c}]_g) \in (\mathbb{G}_1^{n \times m} \times \mathbb{G}_1^n)$. Sample $\boldsymbol{B} \leftarrow_\$ \mathbb{Z}_q^{n \times n}$ such that $\boldsymbol{B} \cdot \boldsymbol{1}_n^T = \boldsymbol{1}_n$ and the rank of $\boldsymbol{B}$ is d. Return $([\boldsymbol{B} \cdot \boldsymbol{C}], [\boldsymbol{B} \cdot \boldsymbol{c}^T])$.

- $\mathsf{UpdateS}(sk)$: Parse $sk = [\boldsymbol{S}]_h \in \mathbb{G}_2^{n \times m}$. Sample $\boldsymbol{A} \leftarrow_\$ \mathbb{Z}_q^{n \times n}$ such that $\boldsymbol{A} \cdot \boldsymbol{1}_n^T = \boldsymbol{1}_n$ and the rank of $\boldsymbol{A}$ is d. Return $[\boldsymbol{A} \cdot \boldsymbol{S}]_h$.

Some remarks are in order. First, the main difference between the scheme above and the PKE of [18] is in the public-keys and in the ciphertexts spaces. Let E_{DLWW} be the scheme proposed by [18]. A public key for E_{DLWW} is the target group element $[\boldsymbol{p} \cdot \boldsymbol{t}^T]_f$, while in the scheme above, a public key belongs to the group $\mathbb{G}_1$. Similarly, a ciphertext for E_{DLWW} is a tuple (c_1, c_2) where $c_2 \in \mathbb{G}_T^n$. The message space of E_{DLWW} is $\mathbb{G}_T$, while the message space of the scheme above is $\{0, 1\}$. This is a big disadvantage, however, thanks to this modification, the public keys, secret keys and ciphertexts belong either to $\mathbb{G}_1$ or $\mathbb{G}_2$. As we will see, this modification is necessary to use lM-NIZK based on Groth-Sahai proof systems [30].

Second, we cannot directly derive from the secret key the public key. However, we can define the function PK' that upon input $sk = [\boldsymbol{S}]_h$ produces $pk' = [\boldsymbol{p}]_g \bullet [\boldsymbol{S}_1]_h$, where $\boldsymbol{S}_1$ is the first row of $\boldsymbol{S}$. Notice that the NMC Σ and the simulator S_1 of Theorem 1 need to check if the public key stored in one side is *valid* for the secret key stored in the other side. We can fix[4] this issue by checking the condition $e(pk, h) = \mathsf{PK}'(sk)$ instead.

Theorem 2. *For any $m \geq 6, n \geq 3m - 6, d := n - m + 3$ the above scheme is an ℓ-CLRS-friendly encryption scheme under the External Diffie-Hellman Assumption on $\mathcal{G}$ for $\ell = \min\{m/6 - 1, n - 3m + 6\} \cdot \log(q) - \omega(\log \kappa)$.*

---

[4] In particular, the reduction in Lemma 7 in steps 5c can leak $(1, \mathsf{PK}'(T_{i+1}(\cdot)))$ and then, in step 5d, we need to modify the function $\mathbf{V}_{T_{i+1}^0, r_i, pk, pk'}$ to check if $e(pk, h) = pk'$ and the function $\mathbf{M}_{T_{i+1}, r_i, pk}$ to check if $e(\tilde{pk}, h) = \mathsf{PK}'(sk')$.

The proof of security follows the same line of [18]. The PKE scheme E is perfectly ciphertext-update private. See the full version [23] of the paper for more details.

Unfortunately, the message space of the PKE is $\{0, 1\}$ which limits the number of applications of NMC-R. We propose two different way to overcome this weakness:

- For any $k \in \mathbb{N}$ let $E^{\times k}$ the direct product encryption scheme that given a message in $\{0, 1\}^\kappa$ encrypts it bit by bit. In the full version of the paper we show that if E is a ℓ-CLRS-Friendly secure PKE then $E^{\times k}$ is a ℓ-CLRS-Friendly secure PKE. Unfortunately, the leakage-rate of the encoding scheme gets much worse. In fact, the size of the chipertexts increase κ times but the leakage parameter stays the same.
- We define CLRS-Friendly Key Encapsulation Mechanisms and the Non-Malleable Key-Encoding schemes with Refresh. The latter notion is strictly weaker than Non-Malleable Codes, however, it still allows useful applications in the setting of tamper resilience cryptography. We defer all the details to the full version of the paper.

5.2 The Label-Malleable NIZK

We can cast a lM-NIZK as a special case of the Controlled-Malleable NIZK (cM-NIZK) argument of knowledge systems [10]. Roughly speaking, cM-NIZK systems allow malleability (from a specific set of allowable transformation) both on the instance and on the NIZK proof. Similarly to lM-NIZK AoK systems, cM-NIZK systems have a form of simulation sound extractability called Controlled-Malleable Simulation Sound Extractability (cM-SSE). Informally, the extractor will either extract a valid witness or will *track back* to a tuple formed by an instance queried to the simulation oracle and the associated simulated proof.

The elegant framework of [10] (full version [11]) builds on the malleability of Groth-Sahai proof systems [30] and provides a set of sufficient conditions to have efficient cM-NIZK systems. Here we translate the conditions to the setting of lM-NIZK systems.

Definition 8. *For a relation $\mathcal{R}$ and a set of transformations $\mathcal{T}$ on the set of labels $\mathcal{L}$, we say $(\mathcal{R}, \mathcal{T})$ is* LM-friendly *if the following five properties hold:*

1. **Representable statements and labels:** *any instance and witness of $\mathcal{R}$ can be represented as a set of group elements; i.e., there are efficiently computable bijections $F_s : L_\mathcal{R} \to \mathbb{G}_{i_s}^{d_s}$ for some d_s and i_s, $F_w : W_\mathcal{R} \to \mathbb{G}_{i_d}^{d_w}$ for some d_w and i_w where $L_\mathcal{R} := \{x | \exists w : (x, w) \in \mathcal{R}\}$ and $L_\mathcal{R} := \{w | \exists x : (x, w) \in \mathcal{R}\}$ and $F_l : \mathcal{L} \to \mathbb{G}_{i_l}^{d_l}$ for some d_l and $i_l = i_s$.*
2. **Representable transformations:** *any transformation in $\mathcal{T}$ can be represented as a set of group elements; i.e., there is an efficiently computable bijection $F_t : \mathcal{T} \to \mathbb{G}_{i_t}^{d_t}$ for some d_t and some i_t.*
3. **Provable statements:** *we can prove the statement $(x, w) \in \mathcal{R}$ (using the above representation for x and w) using pairing product equations; i.e., there is a pairing product statement that is satisfied by $F_s(x)$ and $F_w(w)$ iff $(x, w) \in \mathcal{R}$.*

4. **Provable transformations:** *we can prove the statement "$\phi(L') = L \wedge \phi \in \mathcal{T}$" (using the above representations for labels L, L' and transformation ϕ) using a pairing product equation, i.e. there is a pairing product statement that is satisfied by $F_t(\phi), F_l(L), F_l(L')$ iff $T \in \mathcal{T} \wedge \phi(L') = L$.*

5. **Transformable transformations:** *for any $\phi, \phi' \in \mathcal{T}$ there is a valid transformation $t(\phi)$ that takes the statement "$\phi(L') = L \wedge \phi \in \mathcal{T}$" (phrased using pairing products as above) for the statement "$(\phi' \circ \phi)(L') = \phi(L) \wedge (\phi' \circ \phi) \in \mathcal{T}$" and that preserves[5] the label L'.*

The definition above is almost verbatim from [11], the only differences are that the point (1) is extended to support labels and that the original definition has a condition on the malleability of the tuple statement/witness (which trivially holds for lM-NIZK). We adapt a theorem of [11] to the case of Label Malleability:

Theorem 3. *If the DLIN assumption holds then we can construct a lM-NIZK that satisfies derivation privacy for any LM-friendly relation and transformation set $(\mathcal{R}, \mathcal{T})$.*

With this powerful tool in our hand, we are now ready to show that there exists a lM-NIZK for the relation and transformation set $(\mathcal{R}_{pub}, \mathcal{T}_{pub})$ defined above:

$$\mathcal{R}_{pub} = \{([\alpha]_g, [\boldsymbol{S}]_h) : [\alpha]_g = [\boldsymbol{p} \cdot \boldsymbol{S}_1^T]_g\},$$

$$\mathcal{T}_{pub} = \left\{\phi_{\boldsymbol{B}}(\boldsymbol{C}, \boldsymbol{c}) := \left([\boldsymbol{B} \cdot \boldsymbol{C}^T]_g, [\boldsymbol{B} \cdot \boldsymbol{c}^T]_g\right) \ : \ \boldsymbol{1} = \boldsymbol{B} \cdot \boldsymbol{1}^T\right\}.$$

where $pub = (gd, [\boldsymbol{p}]_g, [\boldsymbol{w}]_h) \leftarrow \mathsf{Setup}(1^\kappa)$. Notice that the set of all the possible updates of a ciphertext,

$$\left\{\phi \ : \phi(\cdot) = \mathsf{UpdateC}(pub, pk, \cdot \ ; \boldsymbol{B}), \boldsymbol{B} \in \mathbb{Z}_q^{n \times n}, \boldsymbol{1}_n = \boldsymbol{B} \cdot \boldsymbol{1}_n^T, \mathsf{rank}(\boldsymbol{B}) = d\right\},$$

is a subset of $\mathcal{T}_{pub}$. Therefore, we can apply the generic transformation of Sect. 4 given a lM-NIZK for the relation $\mathcal{R}_{pub}$ and the set of transformations $\mathcal{T}_{pub}$ and the CLRS-Friendly PKE defined above. We show that the tuple $(\mathcal{R}_{pub}, \mathcal{T}_{pub})$ is LM-Friendly.

Representable statements and labels: Notice that $L_{\mathcal{R}_{pub}} \subseteq \mathbb{G}_1$, while the set of valid label is the set $\mathbb{G}_1^{n \times m} \times \mathbb{G}_1^n$.

Representable transformations: We can describe a transformation $\phi_{\boldsymbol{B}} \in \mathcal{T}_{pub}$ as a matrix of elements $[\boldsymbol{B}]_h \in \mathbb{G}_2^{n \times n}$.

Provable statements: The relation $\mathcal{R}_{pub}$ can be represented by the pairing product statement $[\alpha]_g \bullet [\boldsymbol{1}]_h = [\boldsymbol{p}] \bullet [\boldsymbol{S}_1^T]_h$.

Provable transformations: Given a transformation $\phi_{\boldsymbol{B}} \in \mathcal{T}_{pub}$ and labels $c = ([\boldsymbol{C}]_g, [\boldsymbol{c}]_g), c' = ([\boldsymbol{C}']_g, [\boldsymbol{c}']_g)$, the statement "$\phi_{\boldsymbol{B}}(c') = c \wedge \phi_{\boldsymbol{B}} \in \mathcal{T}$" is transformed as the system of pairing product statements:

$$\begin{cases} [\boldsymbol{B}]_h \bullet [\boldsymbol{C}'^T]_g = [\boldsymbol{C}]_g \bullet [\boldsymbol{1}]_h \\ [\boldsymbol{B}]_h \bullet [\boldsymbol{c}'^T]_g = [\boldsymbol{c}]_g \bullet [\boldsymbol{1}]_h \\ [\boldsymbol{B}]_h \bullet [\boldsymbol{1}^T]_g = [\boldsymbol{1}]_f \end{cases} \tag{3}$$

---

[5] See full version for the formal definition.

Transformable transformations: Let ϕ_B, c, c' be as before and let $\phi_{B'} \in \mathcal{T}_{pub}$. We show that we can transform the system in Eq. (3) to be a valid system of pairing product statement for the statement $(\phi_{B'} \circ \phi_B)(c') = \phi_{B'}(c) \wedge (\phi_{B'} \circ \phi_B) \in \mathcal{T}$. Given the system of pairing product equations in Eq. (3) and $B' \in \mathbb{Z}_q^{n \times n}$ we can perform operations at the exponent and derive:

$$
\begin{cases}
[B' \cdot B]_h \bullet [C'^T]_g = [B' \cdot C^T]_g \bullet [1]_h \\
[B' \cdot B]_h \bullet [c'^T]_g = [B' \cdot c^T]_g \bullet [1]_h \\
[B' \cdot B]_h \bullet [1^T]_g = [1]_f
\end{cases}
$$

The Set $\mathcal{T}_{pub}^{\times k}$ of Transformations for $E^{\times k}$. For any $k \in \mathbb{N}$, let the PKE scheme $E^{\times k}$ be defined as in Sect. 5.1, let $\mathcal{C}_{E^{\times k}} = (\mathcal{C}_E)^k$ be the ciphertexts space of $E^{\times k}$ and let $\mathcal{T}_{pub}^{\times k} = (\mathcal{T}_{pub})^k$. Explicitly, the set of transformations is defined as:

$$
\mathcal{T}_{pub}^{\times k} = \left\{ \phi_{\bar{B}} : \begin{array}{l} \phi_{\bar{B}}(\bar{c}) = \left([B^i \cdot C^{iT}]_g, [B^i \cdot c^{iT}]_g : i \in [k] \right), \\ \bar{c} = (C^1, c^1), \ldots, (C^k, c^k), \\ \bar{B} = B^1, \ldots, B^k, \ \forall i \in [k] : 1 = B^i \cdot 1^T \end{array} \right\}
$$

For any positive polynomial $k(\kappa)$, the tuple $(\mathcal{R}_{pub}, \mathcal{T}_{pub}^{\times k})$ is LM-Friendly. The result follows straight forward from the framework presented in Sect. B.3 of [11] where it is shown that the for any pair of transformations on statements over pairing product equations we can derive a new transformation for the conjunction of the statements.

6 Applications

Following the same approach of [22,34] we show a compiler that maps any functionality $G(s, \cdot)$ to a Continually-Leakage-and-Tamper Resilient functionality $G'(s', \cdot)$ equipped with refresh procedure Rfrsh. Consider the experiments in Fig. 6.

Definition 9. *A compiler* $\Phi = (\mathsf{Setup}, \mathsf{FCompile}, \mathsf{MCompile}, \mathsf{Rfrsh})$ *is a Split-State* (ℓ, ρ, τ)-*Continually-Leakage-and-Tamper (for short* (ℓ, ρ, τ)-*CLT) Compiler in the CRS model if for every PPT adversary* A *there exists a simulator* S *such that for every efficient functionality* $G : \{0,1\}^\kappa \times \{0,1\}^i \to \{0,1\}^o$ *for* $\kappa, i, o \in \mathbb{N}$ *and any secret state* $s \in \{0,1\}^\kappa$, *the output of the real experiment* $\mathbf{TamperFunc}_{\mathsf{A}, \Phi}^{(G,s)}(\kappa, \ell, \rho, \tau)$ *and the output of the simulated experiment* $\mathbf{IdealFunc}(\kappa)$ *are indistinghuishable.*

Given a NMC-R Σ, consider the following compiler $\Pi = (\mathsf{Setup}, \mathsf{MCompile}, \mathsf{Enc}, \mathsf{FCompile}, \mathsf{Rfrsh})$:

- $\underline{\mathsf{Setup}(1^\kappa)}$: Output $crs \leftarrow_{\$} \Sigma.\mathsf{Init}(1^\kappa)$;
- $\underline{\mathsf{MCompile}(crs, s)}$: Output $s' \leftarrow_{\$} \Sigma.\mathsf{Enc}(crs, s)$;
- $\underline{\mathsf{FCompile}(crs, G)}$: Output $G'(s', x) := G(\Sigma.\mathsf{Dec}(crs, s'))$;

Experiment $\mathbf{IdealFunc}_S^{(G,s)}(\kappa)$:

Variables $\bar{\mathcal{Q}}$ set to $\emptyset$;

$(crs, \mathcal{Q}', st) \leftarrow\!\!\text{\$}\ \mathsf{S}(1^\kappa, G) \leftrightarrows \bar{\mathcal{E}}(G, s)$;

Return $(crs, \bar{\mathcal{Q}} \cup \mathcal{Q}', st)$.

Experiment $\mathbf{TamperFunc}_{A,\Phi}^{(G,s)}(\kappa, \ell, \rho, \tau)$:

Variables i, k, t^0, t^1, st_0 set to 0 and $\mathcal{Q} := \emptyset$;

Variables $s'_{j'} := \bot$ for $j' \in [\tau \cdot \rho]$;

$crs \leftarrow\!\!\text{\$}\ \mathsf{Setup}(1^\kappa)$;

$s'_0 \leftarrow\!\!\text{\$}\ \mathsf{MCompile}(crs, s)$;

$G' \leftarrow\!\!\text{\$}\ \mathsf{FCompile}(crs, G)$;

forall $i < \rho(\kappa)$:

$\quad (st_{i+1}, T, j) \leftarrow \mathsf{A}(crs, st_i) \leftrightarrows \mathcal{O}_\ell(s'_i), \mathcal{E}(G')$;

$\quad s'_{k+1} := T(s'_0)$;

$\quad$ If $j \in \{0,1\}$ then $\mathsf{Rfrsh}^*(j)$,

$\quad$ else $s'_{i+1} := s'_i$;

$\quad$ For $j' \in \{0,1\}$ if $(t^{j'} > \tau)$

$\quad\quad$ then $\mathsf{Rfrsh}^*(j')$;

$\quad$ Increment k, t^0, t^1 and i;

Return $(crs, \mathcal{Q}, st_\rho)$.

Oracle $\bar{\mathcal{E}}(G, s)$:

Upon message x;

Compute $y \leftarrow G(s, x)$;

$\bar{\mathcal{Q}} := \bar{\mathcal{Q}} \cup \{(x, y)\}$;

Return y.

Oracle $\mathcal{E}(G')$:

Upon message (t, x);

If $t \notin [\rho \cdot \tau]$ Return $\bot$

Else $y \leftarrow G'(s'_t, x)$;

$\quad \mathcal{Q} := \mathcal{Q} \cup \{(x, y)\}$;

$\quad$ Return y.

Procedure $\mathsf{Rfrsh}^*(j)$:

Set $\mathcal{O}_\ell(X_i).l^j, t^j$ to 0;

Increment t^{1-j};

$s'^{1-j}_{i+1} := s'^{1-j}_i$;

$s'^j_{i+1} \leftarrow\!\!\text{\$}\ \mathsf{Rfrsh}(crs, (j, s'^j_i))$

Fig. 6. Experiment defining the security of CLT Resilient Compiler.

- $\underline{\mathsf{Rfrsh}(crs, s')}$: Output $\Sigma.\mathsf{Rfrsh}(crs, s')$.

Theorem 4. *Let Σ be a (ℓ, ρ, τ)-Non-Malleable Code with Refresh then Π as defined above is a Split-State (ℓ, ρ, τ)-CTL Compiler in the CRS model.*

Acknowledgement. The authors acknowledge support by European Research Council Starting Grant 279447. The authors acknowledge support from the Danish National Research Foundation and The National Science Foundation of China (under the grant 61361136003) for the Sino-Danish Center for the Theory of Interactive Computation.

References

1. Aggarwal, D., Dodis, Y., Lovett, S.: Non-malleable codes from additive combinatorics. In: Proceedings of the STOC, pp. 774–783 (2014)
2. Agrawal, S., Gupta, D., Maji, H.K., Pandey, O., Prabhakaran, M.: A rate-optimizing compiler for non-malleable codes against bit-wise tampering and permutations. In: Dodis, Y., Nielsen, J.B. (eds.) TCC 2015. LNCS, vol. 9014, pp. 375–397. Springer, Heidelberg (2015). doi:10.1007/978-3-662-46494-6_16
3. Ball, M., Dachman-Soled, D., Kulkarni, M., Malkin, T.: Non-malleable codes for bounded depth, bounded fan-in circuits. In: Fischlin, M., Coron, J.-S. (eds.) EUROCRYPT 2016. LNCS, vol. 9666, pp. 881–908. Springer, Heidelberg (2016). doi:10.1007/978-3-662-49896-5_31
4. Ballard, L., Green, M., de Medeiros, B., Monrose, F.: Correlation-resistant storage via keyword-searchable encryption. Cryptology ePrint Archive, Report 2005/417 (2005). http://ia.cr/2005/417

5. Bellare, M., Cash, D., Miller, R.: Cryptography secure against related-key attacks and tampering. In: Lee, D.H., Wang, X. (eds.) ASIACRYPT 2011. LNCS, vol. 7073, pp. 486–503. Springer, Heidelberg (2011). doi:10.1007/978-3-642-25385-0_26

6. Bellare, M., Kohno, T.: A theoretical treatment of related-key attacks: RKA-PRPs, RKA-PRFs, and applications. In: Biham, E. (ed.) EUROCRYPT 2003. LNCS, vol. 2656, pp. 491–506. Springer, Heidelberg (2003). doi:10.1007/3-540-39200-9_31

7. Bellare, M., Paterson, K.G., Thomson, S.: RKA security beyond the linear barrier: IBE, encryption and signatures. In: Wang, X., Sako, K. (eds.) ASIACRYPT 2012. LNCS, vol. 7658, pp. 331–348. Springer, Heidelberg (2012). doi:10.1007/978-3-642-34961-4_21

8. Boldyreva, A., Cash, D., Fischlin, M., Warinschi, B.: Foundations of non-malleable hash and one-way functions. In: Matsui, M. (ed.) ASIACRYPT 2009. LNCS, vol. 5912, pp. 524–541. Springer, Heidelberg (2009). doi:10.1007/978-3-642-10366-7_31

9. Boneh, D., Boyen, X., Shacham, H.: Short group signatures. In: Franklin, M. (ed.) CRYPTO 2004. LNCS, vol. 3152, pp. 41–55. Springer, Heidelberg (2004). doi:10.1007/978-3-540-28628-8_3

10. Chase, M., Kohlweiss, M., Lysyanskaya, A., Meiklejohn, S.: Malleable proof systems and applications. In: Pointcheval, D., Johansson, T. (eds.) EUROCRYPT 2012. LNCS, vol. 7237, pp. 281–300. Springer, Heidelberg (2012). doi:10.1007/978-3-642-29011-4_18

11. Chase, M., Kohlweiss, M., Lysyanskaya, A., Meiklejohn, S.: Malleable proof systems and applications. IACR Cryptology ePrint Archive, 2012:12 (2012)

12. Chattopadhyay, E., Zuckerman, D.: Non-malleable codes against constant split-state tampering. In: Proceedings of the FOCS, pp. 306–315 (2014)

13. Chen, Y., Qin, B., Zhang, J., Deng, Y., Chow, S.S.M.: Non-malleable functions and their applications. In: Cheng, C.-M., Chung, K.-M., Persiano, G., Yang, B.-Y. (eds.) PKC 2016. LNCS, vol. 9615, pp. 386–416. Springer, Heidelberg (2016). doi:10.1007/978-3-662-49387-8_15

14. Dachman-Soled, D., Kalai, Y.T.: Securing circuits and protocols against 1/poly(k) tampering rate. In: Lindell, Y. (ed.) TCC 2014. LNCS, vol. 8349, pp. 540–565. Springer, Heidelberg (2014). doi:10.1007/978-3-642-54242-8_23

15. Dachman-Soled, D., Liu, F.-H., Shi, E., Zhou, H.-S.: Locally decodable and updatable non-malleable codes and their applications. In: Dodis, Y., Nielsen, J.B. (eds.) TCC 2015. LNCS, vol. 9014, pp. 427–450. Springer, Heidelberg (2015). doi:10.1007/978-3-662-46494-6_18

16. Damgård, I., Faust, S., Mukherjee, P., Venturi, D.: Bounded tamper resilience: how to go beyond the algebraic barrier. In: Sako, K., Sarkar, P. (eds.) ASIACRYPT 2013. LNCS, vol. 8270, pp. 140–160. Springer, Heidelberg (2013). doi:10.1007/978-3-642-42045-0_8

17. Damgård, I., Faust, S., Mukherjee, P., Venturi, D.: The chaining lemma and its application. In: Lehmann, A., Wolf, S. (eds.) ICITS 2015. LNCS, vol. 9063, pp. 181–196. Springer, Heidelberg (2015). doi:10.1007/978-3-319-17470-9_11

18. Dodis, Y., Lewko, A.B., Waters, B., Wichs, D.: Storing secrets on continually leaky devices. In: Proceedings of the FOCS, pp. 688–697 (2011)

19. Dziembowski, S., Kazana, T., Obremski, M.: Non-malleable codes from two-source extractors. In: Canetti, R., Garay, J.A. (eds.) CRYPTO 2013. LNCS, vol. 8043, pp. 239–257. Springer, Heidelberg (2013). doi:10.1007/978-3-642-40084-1_14

20. Dziembowski, S., Kazana, T., Wichs, D.: One-time computable self-erasing functions. In: Ishai, Y. (ed.) TCC 2011. LNCS, vol. 6597, pp. 125–143. Springer, Heidelberg (2011). doi:10.1007/978-3-642-19571-6_9

21. Dziembowski, S., Pietrzak, K.: Leakage-resilient cryptography. In: Proceedings of the FOCS, pp. 293–302 (2008)
22. Dziembowski, S., Pietrzak, K., Wichs, D.: Non-malleable codes. In: Innovations in Computer Science, pp. 434–452 (2010)
23. Faonio, A., Nielsen, J.B.: Non-malleable codes with split-state refresh. Cryptology ePrint Archive, Report 2016/1192 (2016). http://eprint.iacr.org/2016/1192
24. Faonio, A., Venturi, D.: Efficient public-key cryptography with bounded leakage and tamper resilience. In: Cheon, J.H., Takagi, T. (eds.) ASIACRYPT 2016. LNCS, vol. 10031, pp. 877–907. Springer, Heidelberg (2016). doi:10.1007/978-3-662-53887-6_32
25. Faust, S., Mukherjee, P., Nielsen, J.B., Venturi, D.: Continuous non-malleable codes. In: Lindell, Y. (ed.) TCC 2014. LNCS, vol. 8349, pp. 465–488. Springer, Heidelberg (2014). doi:10.1007/978-3-642-54242-8_20
26. Faust, S., Mukherjee, P., Venturi, D., Wichs, D.: Efficient non-malleable codes and key-derivation for poly-size tampering circuits. In: Nguyen, P.Q., Oswald, E. (eds.) EUROCRYPT 2014. LNCS, vol. 8441, pp. 111–128. Springer, Heidelberg (2014). doi:10.1007/978-3-642-55220-5_7
27. Faust, S., Pietrzak, K., Venturi, D.: Tamper-proof circuits: how to trade leakage for tamper-resilience. In: Aceto, L., Henzinger, M., Sgall, J. (eds.) ICALP 2011. LNCS, vol. 6755, pp. 391–402. Springer, Heidelberg (2011). doi:10.1007/978-3-642-22006-7_33
28. Goldenberg, D., Liskov, M.: On related-secret pseudorandomness. In: Micciancio, D. (ed.) TCC 2010. LNCS, vol. 5978, pp. 255–272. Springer, Heidelberg (2010). doi:10.1007/978-3-642-11799-2_16
29. Goyal, V., O'Neill, A., Rao, V.: Correlated-input secure hash functions. In: Ishai, Y. (ed.) TCC 2011. LNCS, vol. 6597, pp. 182–200. Springer, Heidelberg (2011). doi:10.1007/978-3-642-19571-6_12
30. Groth, J., Sahai, A.: Efficient noninteractive proof systems for bilinear groups. SIAM J. Comput. 41(5), 1193–1232 (2012)
31. Ishai, Y., Prabhakaran, M., Sahai, A., Wagner, D.: Private circuits II: keeping secrets in tamperable circuits. In: Vaudenay, S. (ed.) EUROCRYPT 2006. LNCS, vol. 4004, pp. 308–327. Springer, Heidelberg (2006). doi:10.1007/11761679_19
32. Jafargholi, Z., Wichs, D.: Tamper detection and continuous non-malleable codes. In: Dodis, Y., Nielsen, J.B. (eds.) TCC 2015, Part I. LNCS, vol. 9014, pp. 451–480. Springer, Heidelberg (2015). doi:10.1007/978-3-662-46494-6_19
33. Kiayias, A., Tselekounis, Y.: Tamper resilient circuits: the adversary at the gates. In: Sako, K., Sarkar, P. (eds.) ASIACRYPT 2013. LNCS, vol. 8270, pp. 161–180. Springer, Heidelberg (2013). doi:10.1007/978-3-642-42045-0_9
34. Liu, F.-H., Lysyanskaya, A.: Tamper and leakage resilience in the split-state model. In: Safavi-Naini, R., Canetti, R. (eds.) CRYPTO 2012. LNCS, vol. 7417, pp. 517–532. Springer, Heidelberg (2012). doi:10.1007/978-3-642-32009-5_30
35. Lu, X., Li, B., Jia, D.: Related-key security for hybrid encryption. In: Chow, S.S.M., Camenisch, J., Hui, L.C.K., Yiu, S.M. (eds.) ISC 2014. LNCS, vol. 8783, pp. 19–32. Springer, Cham (2014). doi:10.1007/978-3-319-13257-0_2
36. Lucks, S.: Ciphers secure against related-key attacks. In: Roy, B., Meier, W. (eds.) FSE 2004. LNCS, vol. 3017, pp. 359–370. Springer, Heidelberg (2004). doi:10.1007/978-3-540-25937-4_23
37. Naor, M., Segev, G.: Public-key cryptosystems resilient to key leakage. In: Halevi, S. (ed.) CRYPTO 2009. LNCS, vol. 5677, pp. 18–35. Springer, Heidelberg (2009). doi:10.1007/978-3-642-03356-8_2

38. Qin, B., Liu, S., Yuen, T.H., Deng, R.H., Chen, K.: Continuous non-malleable key derivation and its application to related-key security. In: Katz, J. (ed.) PKC 2015. LNCS, vol. 9020, pp. 557–578. Springer, Heidelberg (2015). doi:10.1007/978-3-662-46447-2_25

39. Wee, H.: Public key encryption against related key attacks. In: Fischlin, M., Buchmann, J., Manulis, M. (eds.) PKC 2012. LNCS, vol. 7293, pp. 262–279. Springer, Heidelberg (2012). doi:10.1007/978-3-642-30057-8_16

Tight Upper and Lower Bounds
for Leakage-Resilient, Locally Decodable
and Updatable Non-malleable Codes

Dana Dachman-Soled, Mukul Kulkarni, and Aria Shahverdi[(⊠)]

University of Maryland, College Park, USA
danadach@ece.umd.edu, {mukul,ariash}@terpmail.umd.edu

Abstract. In a recent result, Dachman-Soled et al. (TCC 2015) proposed a new notion called locally decodable and updatable non-malleable codes, which informally, provides the security guarantees of a non-malleable code while also allowing for efficient random access. They also considered locally decodable and updatable non-malleable codes that are *leakage-resilient*, allowing for adversaries who continually leak information in addition to tampering. Unfortunately, the locality of their construction in the continual setting was $\Omega(\log n)$, meaning that if the original message size was n blocks, then $\Omega(\log n)$ blocks of the codeword had to be accessed upon each decode and update instruction.

In this work, we ask whether super-constant locality is inherent in this setting. We answer the question affirmatively by showing tight upper and lower bounds. Specifically, in any threat model which allows for a rewind attack—wherein the attacker leaks a small amount of data, waits for the data to be overwritten and then writes the original data back—we show that a locally decodable and updatable non-malleable code with block size $\mathcal{X} \in \text{poly}(\lambda)$ number of bits requires locality $\delta(n) \in \omega(1)$, where $n = \text{poly}(\lambda)$ is message length and λ is security parameter. On the other hand, we re-visit the threat model of Dachman-Soled et al. (TCC 2015)—which indeed allows the adversary to launch a rewind attack—and present a construction of a locally decodable and updatable non-malleable code with block size $\mathcal{X} \in \Omega(\lambda^{1/\mu})$ number of bits (for constant $0 < \mu < 1$) with locality $\delta(n)$, for any $\delta(n) \in \omega(1)$, and $n = \text{poly}(\lambda)$.

1 Introduction

Non-malleable codes were introduced by Dziembowski, Pietrzak and Wichs [22] as a relaxation of error-correcting codes, and are useful in settings where privacy—but not necessarily correctness–is desired. Informally, a coding scheme is **non-malleable** against a tampering function if by tampering with the codeword, the function can either keep the underlying message unchanged or change it to an unrelated message. The main application of non-malleable codes proposed in the literature is for achieving security against leakage and tampering

D. Dachman-Soled—This work is supported in part by an NSF CAREER Award #CNS-1453045 and by a Ralph E. Powe Junior Faculty Enhancement Award.

© International Association for Cryptologic Research 2017
S. Fehr (Ed.): PKC 2017, Part I, LNCS 10174, pp. 310–332, 2017.
DOI: 10.1007/978-3-662-54365-8_13

attacks on memory (so-called *physical attacks* or *hardware attacks*), although non-malleable codes have also found applications in other areas of cryptography [16, 17, 29] and theoretical computer science [12].

Standard non-malleable codes are useful for protecting small amounts of secret data stored on a device (such as a cryptographic secret key) but unfortunately are not suitable in settings where, say, an entire database must be protected. This is due to the fact that non-malleable codes do not allow for random access: Once the database is encoded via a non-malleable code, in order to access just a single location, the entire database must first be decoded, requiring a linear scan over the database. Similarly, in order to update a single location, the entire database must be decoded, updated and re-encoded. In a recent result, [18] proposed a new notion called locally decodable and updatable non-malleable codes, which informally speaking, provides the security guarantees of a non-malleable code while also allowing for efficient random access. In more detail, we consider a message $m = m_1, \ldots, m_n$ consisting of n blocks, and an encoding algorithm $\text{ENC}(m)$ that outputs a codeword $\hat{C} = \hat{c}_1, \ldots, \hat{c}_{\hat{n}}$ consisting of $\hat{n}$ blocks. As introduced by Katz and Trevisan [35], local decodability means that in order to retrieve a single block of the underlying message, one does not need to read through the whole codeword but rather, one can access just a few blocks of the codeword. Similarly, local updatability means that in order to update a single block of the underlying messages, one only needs to update a few blocks of the codeword.

As observed by [18], achieving these locality properties requires a modification of the previous definition of non-malleability: Suppose a tampering function f only modifies one block of the codeword, then it is likely that the output of the decoding algorithm, DEC, remains unchanged in most locations. (Recall DEC gets as input an index $i \in [n]$ and will only access a few blocks of the codeword to recover the i-th block of the message, so it may not detect the modification.) In this case, the (overall) decoding of the tampered codeword $f(\hat{C})$ (i.e. $(\text{DEC}^{f(\hat{C})}(1), \ldots, \text{DEC}^{f(\hat{C})}(n))$) can be highly related to the original message, which intuitively means it is highly malleable.

To handle this issue, [18] consider a more fine-grained experiment. Informally, they require that for any tampering function f (within some class), there exists a simulator that, after every update instruction, computes a vector of decoded messages $\boldsymbol{m}^*$, and a set of indices $\mathcal{I} \subseteq [n]$. Here $\mathcal{I}$ denotes the coordinates of the underlying messages that have been tampered with. If $\mathcal{I} = [n]$, then the simulator thinks that the decoded messages are $\boldsymbol{m}^*$, which should be unrelated to the most recent messages placed in each position by the updater. On the other hand, if $\mathcal{I} \subsetneq [n]$, the simulator thinks that all the messages not in $\mathcal{I}$ remain unchanged (equivalent to the *most recent values* placed there by the simulator or the original message, if no update has occurred in that position), while those in $\mathcal{I}$ become $\bot$. This intuitively means the tampering function can do only one of the following cases:

1. It destroys a block (or blocks) of the underlying messages while keeping the other blocks unchanged, OR

2. If it modifies a block of the underlying message to a valid encoding, then it must have modified *all* blocks to encodings of unrelated messages, thus destroying the original message.

It turns out, as shown by [18], that the above is sufficient for achieving tamper-resilience for RAM computations. Specifically, the above (together with an ORAM scheme) yields a compiler for any RAM program with the guarantee that any adversary who gets input/output access to the compiled RAM program Π running on compiled database D who can additionally apply tampering functions $f \in \mathcal{F}$ to the database D adaptively throughout the computation, learns no more than what can be learned given only input/output access to Π running on database D. Dachman-Soled et al. in [18] considered locally decodable and updatable non-malleable codes that are also *leakage-resilient*, thus allowing for adversaries who continually leak information about D in addition to tampering. The locality achieved by the construction of [18] is $\Theta(\log(n))$, meaning that when encoding messages of length n number of blocks, the decode and update procedures each require access to $\Theta(\log(n))$ number of blocks of the encoding. Thus, when using the encoding scheme of [18] to compile a RAM program into its secure version, the overhead is at least $\Omega(\log(n))$ memory accesses for each read/write access in the underlying program. In practice, such an overhead is often prohibitive.[1] In this work, we ask whether it is possible to construct leakage-resilient, locally decodable and updatable non-malleable codes that achieve significantly better locality.

Rewind attacks. When considering both leakage and tampering attacks (even just a single leakage query followed in a later round by a single tampering query) so-called *rewind attacks* become possible. In a rewind attack, the attacker does the following (1) **leak** information on only a "few" blocks of memory in rounds $1, \ldots, i$; (2) **wait** during rounds $i + 1, \ldots, j$ until these memory locations are (with high probability) modified by the "updater" (the entity that models the honest computation on the data); (3) **re-write** the old information into these memory locations in round $j + 1$, with the goal of causing the state of the computation to be *rewound*. Rewind attacks can be thwarted by ensuring that when the old information is written back, it becomes *inconsistent* with other positions of the codeword and an error is detected. On the other hand, a bad outcome of a rewind attack occurs if when decoding certain blocks of memory, with non-negligible probability, the old values from round i are recovered and no error is detected. This is a problem since such an outcome cannot be simulated by a simulator as required in the security definition: The decoding of these blocks depends on the original message and yet is no longer equal to "same" (since the values decoded are not the most recent values placed in those positions by the updater).

---

[1] Although the ORAM scheme used in the compiler also has $\omega(\log(n))$ overhead, in many applications of interest, properties of the specific RAM program can be leveraged so that the overhead of ORAM can be reduced such that it becomes practically feasible. On the other hand, the $\Theta(\log(n))$ overhead of the encoding scheme of [18] is entirely agnostic to the RAM program being run on top and thus, the high overhead would be incurred in all applications.

1.1   Our Results

Our results show that any construction of locally decodable and updatable non-malleable codes in a threat model which allows for a rewind attack as above will require "high locality." Specifically, we show tight upper and lower bounds: (1) Every such construction will require super-constant locality, moreover; (2) Super-constant locality is sufficient for achieving constructions in the same threat model as [18] (which, as discussed, allows for rewind attacks). Throughout the paper, we assume that the decode and update procedures are *non-adaptive* in the sense that once an encoding scheme $\Pi = (\text{ENC}, \text{DEC})$ is specified, then for each $n \in \mathbb{N}$, the sets of codeword blocks $S_i := S_i^{\text{DEC}} \cup S_i^{\text{UP}}$ accessed in order to decode/update the i-th message block, $i \in [n]$, are fixed (and do not depend on the codeword $\hat{C}$). This is a natural requirement, which holds true for the encoding scheme of [18].

Specifically, we show the following:

Theorem 1 (Informal). *Let λ be security parameter and let $\Pi = (\text{ENC}, \text{DEC})$ be a locally decodable and updatable non-malleable code with non-adaptive decode and update which takes messages over alphabet Σ and outputs codewords over alphabet $\hat{\Sigma}$, where $|\Sigma|, |\hat{\Sigma}| \in \text{poly}(\lambda)$, in a threat model which allows for a rewind attack. Then, for $n = \text{poly}(\lambda)$, Π has locality $\delta(n) \in \omega(1)$.*

Moreover, for every $\delta(n) \in \omega(1)$, there exists a $\Pi = (\text{ENC}, \text{DEC})$ with non-adaptive decode and update in a threat model which allows for a rewind attack, which takes messages over alphabet Σ and outputs codewords over alphabet $\hat{\Sigma}$, where $|\Sigma| \in \text{poly}(\lambda)$ and $|\hat{\Sigma}| \in \Omega(\lambda^{1/\mu})$ for constant $0 < \mu < 1$, such that for $n = \text{poly}(\lambda)$, Π has locality $\delta(n)$.

Specifically, for the positive result, the construction of leakage resilient locally decodable updatable codes is secure against the same classes of tampering and leakage functions, $\mathcal{F}, \mathcal{G}$, as the construction of [18], but improves the locality from $O(\log n)$ to $\delta(n)$, for any $\delta(n) \in \omega(1)$.

We emphasize that, for the lower bound, our attack works even in a threat model which allows only a *single* bit of leakage in each round. We leave as an open question extending our lower bound to the setting where decode and update may be adaptive (i.e. the next position accessed by decode and/or update depends on the values read in the previous positions) or randomized.

1.2   Our Techniques

Lower Bound. We assume that there exists a locally decodable and updatable non-malleable code with non-adaptive decode and update and constant locality, c, for all message lengths $n = \text{poly}(\lambda)$ (where n is the number of blocks in the message). We then arrive at contradiction by showing that for every constant c, there exists a constant $c' > c$, such that the security guarantee cannot hold when encoding messages of length $\mathcal{X}^{c'}$ number of blocks, where $\mathcal{X} \in \text{poly}(\lambda)$ is the bit length of the codeword blocks. Specifically, for messages of length $n := \mathcal{X}^{c'} \in \text{poly}(\lambda)$ number of blocks, we will present an explicit attacker and an explicit updater for which there cannot exist a simulator as required by the definition of locally decodable and updatable non-malleable codes.

The attack we present is a *rewind* attack, as discussed before. Intuitively, the main difficulty of designing the attack is to determine *which* positions of the codeword are to be leaked and subsequently re-wound to their original values so that with high probability in the real game, the corresponding message block will decode (with no error detected) to the original value in that position, as opposed to the most recently updated value. For purposes of our attack, we assume that the original message is either equal to 0 in all n blocks or equal to 1 in all n blocks.

Sunflower Lemma. For $i \in [n]$, let the sets $S_i \subseteq [\hat{n}]$ correspond to the blocks (where each block has size $\mathcal{X} \in \text{poly}(\lambda)$ bits) of the codeword accessed in order to decode/update the i-th block of the message. Note that by the locality assumption, the size of each set S_i is $|S_i| = c$. We use the Sunflower Lemma of Erdős and Rado [24] to choose constant c' large enough such that when the message is of length $n := \mathcal{X}^{c'}$ number of blocks, we are guaranteed to have a Sunflower $\mathsf{SF} := \{S_{i_0}, S_{i_1}, \ldots, S_{i_k}\}$, where $i_0, \ldots, i_k \in [n]$, of size $k + 1$, where $k \gg \mathcal{X} \cdot c$. A sunflower is a collection of sets such that the intersection of any pair is equal to the core core, i.e. $S_{i_j} \cap S_{i_\ell} = \mathsf{core}$ for all $j \neq \ell$. There exists k petals, $S_{i_j} \setminus \mathsf{core}$, and it is required that none of them are empty. See Sects. 3.1 and 3.2 for more details.

The Compression Function. Given a *fixed* initial codeword $\hat{C}$ and sunflower SF (as defined above) we define a (randomized) compression function $F_{\hat{C}} : \{0, 1, \mathsf{same}\}^k \rightarrow \{0, 1\}^{\mathcal{X} \cdot c}$ which takes as input values $x_1, \ldots, x_k \in \{0, 1, \mathsf{same}\}$ indicating how to update (or not) the corresponding message block i_j, $j \in [k]$, where S_{i_j} is in the sunflower. Specifically, for $j = 1$ to k: If $x_j = \mathsf{same}$, message block i_j does not get updated. Otherwise $\text{UPDATE}^{\hat{C}}(i_j, x_j)$ is executed. The output of the function $F_{\hat{C}}$ is the contents of the sunflower core, core, after all the updates have been completed. Note that core can consist of at most c codeword blocks since $\mathsf{core} \subseteq S_{i_j}$ for all $j \in [k]$. Therefore, the output length of $F_{\hat{C}}$ is at most $\mathcal{X} \cdot c$ bits. Note that this means that $F_{\hat{C}}$ is a compression function, since we chose $k \gg \mathcal{X} \cdot c$. Now this, in turn, means that the output of $F_{\hat{C}}$ cannot contain all of the information in its input. Indeed, it can be shown (cf. [20]) that with high probability over the choice of $j^* \in [k]$, the two distributions $F_{\hat{C}}(X_1, \ldots, X_{j^*-1}, \mathsf{same}, X_{j^*+1}, \ldots, X_k)$ and $F_{\hat{C}}(X_1, \ldots, X_{j^*-1}, X_{j^*}, X_{j^*+1}, \ldots, X_k)$ are statistically close when each X_j, $j \in [k]$ is chosen uniformly at random from $\{0, 1, \mathsf{same}\}$. See Sects. 3.1, 3.3 and 3.4 for more details.

The Attacker and the Updater. The *attacker* first finds the sunflower $\mathsf{SF} := \{S_{i_0}, S_{i_1}, \ldots, S_{i_k}\}$ in polynomial time and then chooses $j^* \in [k]$ at random. In the first round (or multiple rounds if the attacker is allowed only a single bit of leakage) the attacker leaks the contents of the positions in $\hat{C}$ corresponding to decoding of i_{j^*} ($S_{i_{j^*}}$), minus the contents of the blocks in the core of the sunflower. We denote the entire leaked information by y_{j^*}. The attacker then writes those same values, y_{j^*}, back in the $k + 1$-st round. The *updater* chooses values $x_1, \ldots, x_k \in \{0, 1, \mathsf{same}\}$ and in each round from 1 to k, requests the corresponding update (i.e. update message block i_j to 0, if $x_j = 0$, update to 1 if $x_j = 1$ and do not update this block at all, if $x_j = \mathsf{same}$). See Sect. 3.5 for more details.

Putting it All Together. Note that the input to the decoding algorithm when decoding position i_{j^*} is exactly: $(y_{j^*}, F_{\hat{C}_0}(X_1, \ldots, X_{j^*-1}, X_{j^*}, X_{j^*+1}, \ldots, X_k))$ (the contents of the positions in $\hat{C}$ corresponding to decoding of i_{j^*}, minus the contents of the blocks in the core of the sunflower, and the core itself). Additionally, note that since $\{S_{i_0}, S_{i_1}, \ldots, S_{i_k}\}$ form a sunflower, if $x_{j^*} = \mathsf{same}$, then the rewind attack has *no effect* (since the blocks in $S_{i_{j^*}} \backslash \mathsf{core}$ were not accessed during any update request) and so decode on input $(y_{j^*}, F_{\hat{C}_0}(X_1, \ldots, X_{j^*-1},$ $\mathsf{same}, X_{j^*+1}, \ldots, X_k))$ must correctly output 1 if the original encoding was 1 and 0 if the original encoding was 0 (without outputting $\bot$). Since $F_{\hat{C}}$ is a compression function, it means that with high probability decode on input $(y_{j^*}, F_{\hat{C}}(X_1, \ldots, X_{j^*-1}, X_{j^*}, X_{j^*+1}, \ldots, X_k))$ will output 1 if the original encoding was 1 and 0 if the original encoding was 0, regardless of the value of X_{j^*}. Intuitively, since the output of decode now depends on the *original* message block in the i_{j^*}-th position, as opposed to the *most recently updated* value, the simulator must fail in at least one of the two cases (either when the original message was 0 or 1) and so the encoding scheme cannot satisfy the non-malleability definition. See Sect. 3.6 for more details.

Upper Bound. Here we take advantage of the fact that codeword blocks are large—$\mathcal{X} \in \Omega(\lambda^{1/\mu})$ number of bits, for constant $0 < \mu < 1$–to replace the Merkle Tree used in the original construction of [18] with an alternative data structure we call a t-slice Merkle Tree. Note that the $\Omega(\log \lambda)$ locality of the construction of [18] came from the fact that an entire path (and siblings) of the binary Merkle tree from root to leaf of length $\log(n)$ had to be traversed for each decode and update instruction. Our new data structure is a $t := \mathcal{X}^{1-\mu}$-ary tree for constant $0 < \lambda < 1$ and uses as a building block a collision resistant hash function $h : \{0,1\}^{\mathcal{X}} \to \{0,1\}^{\mathcal{X}^{\mu}}$ (note h has output length $\mathcal{X}^{\mu} \in \Omega(\lambda)$) and so, for messages of length $n = \mathrm{poly}(\lambda)$ blocks, an entire path of the tree from root to leaf will always have length less than $\delta(n)$, for any $\delta(n) \in \omega(1)$. Moreover, the root of the tree can be updated and verified without reading any of the siblings along the path from root to leaf, due to the use of a carefully constructed hash function with a specific structure. This allows us to achieve a locally decodable and updatable code with locality $\delta(n)$, for any $\delta(n) \in \omega(1)$. See Sect. 4 for more details.

1.3   Related Work

Non-Malleable Codes. The concept of non-malleability was introduced by Dolev, Dwork and Naor [19] and has been applied widely in cryptography since. It has since been studied in both the computational as well as the information-theoretic setting. Error-correcting codes and early works on tamper resilience [28, 32] gave rise to the study of non-malleable codes. The notion of non-malleable codes was formalized in the seminal work of Dziembowski, Pietrzak and Wichs [22]. Split state classes of tampering functions introduced by Liu and Lysyanskaya [37], have subsequently received a lot of attention with a sequence of improvements achieving reduced number of states, improved rate, or adding desirable features to the scheme [1–3, 6, 11, 21]. Recently [5, 7] gave efficient constructions of non-malleable codes for "non-compartmentalized" tampering function classes. Other works on non-malleable codes include [2, 4, 8, 10, 15, 25, 33]. We guide the interested reader to [34, 37] for illustrative discussion of various models for tamper and leakage resilience. There are also several inefficient, existential or randomized constructions for much more general classes of functions (sometimes presented as efficient constructions in a random-oracle model) in addition to those above [14, 22, 27].

Locally Decodable Codes. The idea of *locally decodable* codes was introduced by Katz and Trevisan in [35], when they considered the possibility of recovering the message by looking at a limited number of bits from a (possibly) corrupted encoding obtained from an error correcting code. They also showed the impossibility of achieving the same for schemes with linear encoding length. This work was followed by [13, 23, 38] who achieved constant locality with super-polynomial code length, while on the other hand locally decodable codes with constant rate and sub-linear locality have been constructed by [30, 31, 36]. We refer the interested reader to [39], a survey on locally decodable codes by Yekhanin.

Locally Updatable and Locally Decodable Codes. The notion of *locally updatable and locally decodable codes* was introduced by Chandran et al. in [9] where the constraint of *locality*, i.e. restricting the number of bits accessed, is also applied to updating any codeword obtained from encoding of another message. They gave information theoretic construction with amortized update locality of $\mathcal{O}(\log^2 k)$ and read locality of (super-linear) polynomial in k, where k is the length of input message. Another variant called *locally updatable and locally decodable-detectable codes* was also introduced in the same work which ensures that decoding never outputs an incorrect message. Chandran et al. in [9] gave the construction of such codes in computational setting with poly-logarithmic locality.

Locally Decodable and Updatable Non-Malleable Codes. Dachman-Soled et al. in [18] introduced the notion of *locally decodable and updatable non-malleable codes* and presented a construction in the computational setting. The construction of [18] also achieves leakage resilience in addition to the tamper resilience. Dachman-Soled et al. in [18] then used this notion to construct compilers that transform any RAM machine into a RAM machine secure against leakage and tampering. This application was also studied by Faust et al. [26], who presented a different approach which does not use locally decodable and updatable non-malleable codes. Recently, Chandran et al. [10] gave a construction of locally decodable and updatable non-malleable codes in the information-theoretic setting. However, they addressed only the one-time leakage and tampering case, and to achieve continual leakage and tampering, require a periodic refresh of the entire memory. The locality of their construction is super-constant, thus affirming our results.

Bounds on Non-Malleable Codes. Cheragachi and Guruswami [14] studied the "capacity" of non-malleable codes in order to understand the optimal bounds on the efficiency of non-malleable codes. This work has been instrumental in asserting the claims of efficient constructions for non-malleable codes since then (cf. [1,5,6]). We note that our work is the first study establishing similar tight bounds for the locality of the *locally decodable and updatable non-malleable codes.*

2 Definitions

Definition 1 (Locally Decodable and Updatable Code). *Let $\Sigma, \hat{\Sigma}$ be sets of strings, and $n, \hat{n}, p, q$ be some parameters. An $(n, \hat{n}, p, q)$ locally decodable and updatable coding scheme consists of three algorithms* (ENC, DEC, UPDATE) *with the following syntax:*

- *The encoding algorithm* ENC *(perhaps randomized) takes input an n-block (in Σ) message and outputs an $\hat{n}$-block (in $\hat{\Sigma}$) codeword.*
- *The (local) decoding algorithm* DEC *takes input an index in $[n]$, reads at most p blocks of the codeword, and outputs a block of message in Σ. The overall decoding algorithm simply outputs* (DEC(1), DEC(2), . . . , DEC(n)).
- *The (local) updating algorithm* UPDATE *(perhaps randomized) takes inputs an index in $[n]$ and a string in $\Sigma \cup \{\epsilon\}$, and reads/writes at most q blocks of the codeword. Here the string ϵ denotes the procedure of refreshing without changing anything.*

Let $\hat{C} \in \hat{\Sigma}^{\hat{n}}$ be a codeword. For convenience, we denote DEC$^{\hat{C}}$, UPDATE$^{\hat{C}}$ *as the processes of reading/writing individual block of the codeword, i.e. the codeword oracle returns or modifies individual block upon a query. Here we view $\hat{C}$ as a random access memory where the algorithms can read/write to the memory $\hat{C}$ at individual different locations. In binary settings, we often set $\Sigma = \{0,1\}^\kappa$ and $\hat{\Sigma} = \{0,1\}^{\hat{\kappa}}$.*

Definition 2 (Correctness). *An $(n, \hat{n}, p, q)$ locally decodable and updatable coding scheme (with respect to $\Sigma, \hat{\Sigma}$) satisfies the following properties. For any message $M = (m_1, m_2, \ldots, m_n) \in \Sigma^n$, let $\hat{C} = (\hat{c}_1, \hat{c}_2, \ldots, \hat{c}_{\hat{n}}) \leftarrow$ ENC(M) be a codeword output by the encoding algorithm. Then we have:*

- *for any index $i \in [n]$, $\Pr[\text{DEC}^{\hat{C}}(i) = m_i] = 1$, where the probability is over the randomness of the encoding algorithm.*

- *for any update procedure with input $(j, m') \in [n] \times \Sigma \cup \{\epsilon\}$, let $\hat{C}'$ be the resulting codeword by running* UPDATE$^{\hat{C}}(j, m')$. *Then we have* $\Pr[\text{DEC}^{\hat{C}'}(j) = m'] = 1$, *where the probability is over the encoding and update procedures. Moreover, the decodings of the other positions remain unchanged.*

Remark 1. The correctness definition can be directly extended to handle any sequence of updates.

Definition 3 (Continual Tampering and Leakage Experiment). *Let k be the security parameter, $\mathcal{F}, \mathcal{G}$ be some families of functions. Let* (ENC, DEC, UPDATE) *be an $(n, \hat{n}, p, q)$-locally decodable and updatable coding scheme with respect to $\Sigma, \hat{\Sigma}$. Let $\mathcal{U}$ be an updater that takes input a message $M \in \Sigma^n$ and outputs an index $i \in [n]$ and $m \in \Sigma$. Then for any blocks of messages $M = (m_1, m_2, \ldots, m_n) \in \Sigma^n$, and any (non-uniform) adversary $\mathcal{A}$, any updater $\mathcal{U}$, define the following continual experiment* **CTamperLeak**$_{\mathcal{A}, \mathcal{U}, M}$:

- *The challenger first computes an initial encoding $\hat{C}^{(1)} \leftarrow$ ENC(M).*
- *Then the following procedure repeats, at each round j, let $\hat{C}^{(j)}$ be the current codeword and $M^{(j)}$ be the underlying message:*
    - *$\mathcal{A}$ sends either a tampering function $f \in \mathcal{F}$ and/or a leakage function $g \in \mathcal{G}$ to the challenger.*
    - *The challenger replaces the codeword with $f(\hat{C}^{(j)})$, or sends back a leakage $\ell^{(j)} = g(\hat{C}^{(j)})$.*
    - *We define $\boldsymbol{m}^{(j)} \stackrel{\text{def}}{=} \left(\text{DEC}^{f(\hat{C}^{(j)})}(1), \ldots, \text{DEC}^{f(\hat{C}^{(j)})}(n) \right)$.*
    - *Then the updater computes $(i^{(j)}, m) \leftarrow \mathcal{U}(\boldsymbol{m}^{(j)})$ for the challenger.*
    - *Then the challenger runs* UPDATE$^{f(\hat{C}^{(j)})}(i^{(j)}, m)$ *and sends the index $i^{(j)}$ to $\mathcal{A}$.*
    - *$\mathcal{A}$ may terminate the procedure at any point.*
- *Let t be the total number of rounds above. At the end, the experiment outputs*

$$\left(\ell^{(1)}, \ell^{(2)}, \ldots, \ell^{(t)}, \boldsymbol{m}^{(1)}, \ldots, \boldsymbol{m}^{(t)}, i^{(1)}, \ldots, i^{(t)} \right).$$

Definition 4 (Non-malleability and Leakage Resilience against Continual Attacks). *An $(n, \hat{n}, p, q)$-locally decodable and updatable coding scheme with respect to $\Sigma, \hat{\Sigma}$ is continual non-malleable against $\mathcal{F}$ and leakage resilient against $\mathcal{G}$ if for all* PPT *(non-uniform) adversaries $\mathcal{A}$, and* PPT *updaters $\mathcal{U}$, there exists some* PPT *(non-uniform) simulator $\mathcal{S}$ such that for any $M = (m_1, \ldots, m_n) \in \Sigma^n$,* **CTamperLeak**$_{\mathcal{A}, \mathcal{U}, M}$ *is (computationally) indistinguishable to the following ideal experiment* **Ideal**$_{\mathcal{S}, \mathcal{U}, M}$:

- *The experiment proceeds in rounds. Let $M^{(1)} = M$ be the initial message.*
- *At each round j, the experiment runs the following procedure:*
    - *At the beginning of each round, $\mathcal{S}$ outputs $(\ell^{(j)}, \mathcal{I}^{(j)}, \boldsymbol{w}^{(j)})$, where $\mathcal{I}^{(j)} \subseteq [n]$.*

– *Define*

$$\boldsymbol{m}^{(j)} = \begin{cases} \boldsymbol{w}^{(j)} & if \mathcal{I}^{(j)} = [n] \\ \boldsymbol{m}^{(j)}|_{\mathcal{I}^{(j)}} := \bot, \boldsymbol{m}^{(j)}|_{\bar{\mathcal{I}}^{(j)}} := M^{(j)}|_{\bar{\mathcal{I}}^{(j)}} & otherwise, \end{cases}$$

where $\boldsymbol{x}|_{\mathcal{I}}$ denotes the coordinates $\boldsymbol{x}[v]$ where $v \in \mathcal{I}$, and the bar denotes the complement of a set.

– *The updater runs $(i^{(j)}, m) \leftarrow \mathcal{U}(\boldsymbol{m}^{(j)})$ and sends the index $i^{(j)}$ to the simulator. Then the experiment updates $M^{(j+1)}$ as follows: set $M^{(j+1)} := M^{(j)}$ for all coordinates except $i^{(j)}$, and set $M^{(j+1)}[i^{(j)}] := m$.*

– *Let t be the total number of rounds above. At the end, the experiment outputs*

$$\left(\ell^{(1)}, \ell^{(2)}, \ldots, \ell^{(t)}, \boldsymbol{m}^{(1)}, \ldots, \boldsymbol{m}^{(t)}, i^{(1)}, \ldots, i^{(t)} \right).$$

3   Lower Bound

In this section we prove the following theorem:

Theorem 2. *Let λ be security parameter and let $\Pi = (\text{ENC}, \text{DEC})$ be a locally decodable and updatable non-malleable code with non-adaptive decode and update which takes messages over alphabet Σ and outputs codewords over alphabet $\widehat{\Sigma}$, where $\log|\Sigma|, \log|\widehat{\Sigma}| \in \text{poly}(\lambda)$, in a threat model which allows for a rewind attack. Then, for $n := n(\lambda) \in \text{poly}(\lambda)$, Π has locality $\delta(n) \in \omega(1)$.*

We denote by $\mathcal{X} := \log|\widehat{\Sigma}| \in \text{poly}(\lambda)$ the number of bits in each block of the codeword. For purposes of the lower bound, we can take $\mathcal{X}$ to be any polynomial in λ (or smaller).

In the following, we assume that $\Pi = (\text{ENC}, \text{DEC})$ is a locally decodable and updatable non-malleable code with non-adaptive decode and update and with *constant* locality. We then present an efficient rewind attacker along with an updater that break the security of Π, thus proving the theorem.

3.1   Attack Preliminaries

Definition 5 (Sunflower). *A sunflower (or Δ-system) is a collection of sets S_i for $1 \leq i \leq k$ such that the intersection of any two set is core Y, i.e. $S_i \cap S_j = \text{core}$ for all $i \neq j$. There exists k petals $S_i \backslash \text{core}$ and it's required that none of them are empty. A family of pairwise disjoint sets form a sunflower with an empty core.*

The following famous lemma is due to Erdős and Rado.

Lemma 1 (Sunflower Lemma [24]). *Let $\mathcal{F}$ be family of sets each of cardinality s. If $|\mathcal{F}| > s!(k-1)^s$ then $\mathcal{F}$ contains a sunflower with k petals.*

Definition 6 (Statistical Distance). *Let $\mathcal{D}_1$ and $\mathcal{D}_2$ be two distribution over a shared universe of outcomes. let $supp(\mathcal{D})$ be the set of values assumed by $\mathcal{D}$ with nonzero probability, and let $\mathcal{D}(u) := \Pr[\mathcal{D} = u]$. The statistical distance of $\mathcal{D}_1$ and $\mathcal{D}_2$ is defined as*

$$||\mathcal{D}_1 - \mathcal{D}_2||_{stat} := \frac{1}{2} \sum_{u \in supp(\mathcal{D}_1) \cup supp(\mathcal{D}_2)} |\mathcal{D}_1(u) - \mathcal{D}_2(u)|.$$

Definition 7 (Distributional Stability [20]). *Let $\mathcal{U}$ be a finite universe and $t, n \geq 1$ be integers. Let $\mathcal{D}_i$ for $1 \leq i \leq t$ be a collection of t mutually independent distributions over $\{0, 1\}^n$ and F be a possibly-randomized mapping $F(x^1, \ldots, x^t) : \{0, 1\}^{n \times t} \to \mathcal{U}$, for $j \in [t]$ let*

$$\gamma_j := \underset{y \sim \mathcal{D}_j}{\mathbb{E}} [||F(\mathcal{D}_1, \ldots, \mathcal{D}_{j-1}, y, \mathcal{D}_{j+1}, \ldots, \mathcal{D}_t) - F(\mathcal{D}_1, \ldots, \mathcal{D}_t)||_{stat}].$$

F is δ-distributionally stable for $\delta \in [0, 1]$ with respect to $\mathcal{D}_1, \ldots, \mathcal{D}_t$ if

$$\frac{1}{t} \sum_{j=1}^{t} \gamma_j \leq \delta.$$

Lemma 2 (Compression Functions are Distributionally Stable [20]). *Let $R(x^1, \ldots, x^t) : \{0, 1\}^{n \times t} \to \{0, 1\}^{\leq t'}$ be any possibly-randomized mapping, for any $n, t, t' \in \mathbb{N}^+$. R is δ-distributionally stable with respect to any independent input distributions $\mathcal{D}_1, \ldots, \mathcal{D}_t$, where it may take either of the following two bounds:*

1. $\delta := \sqrt{\frac{\ln 2}{2} \cdot \frac{t'+1}{t}}$

2. $\delta := 1 - 2^{-\frac{t'}{t} - 3}$.

3.2 Applying the Sunflower Lemma

For $i \in [n]$, the sets $S_i \subseteq [\hat{n}]$ correspond to the blocks (each of size $\mathcal{X}$) of the codeword accessed in order to update/decode m_i (i.e. the set $S_i := S_i^{\text{DEC}} \cup S_i^{\text{UP}}$, where S_i^{DEC}, S_i^{UP} are the sets of blocks accessed by the decode and update procedures, respectively). By hypothesis, we have that for $i \in [n]$, $|S_i| = c$, for constant c. Choose $n = \mathcal{X}^{c'} \in \text{poly}(\lambda)$, where c' is a constant such that

$$\mathcal{X}^{c'} > c! \cdot (22,500 \cdot c \cdot \mathcal{X})^c$$

Then by the Sunflower Lemma, $\{S_1, \ldots, S_n\}$ contains a sunflower with $k + 1 := 22,500 \cdot c \cdot \mathcal{X} + 1$ petals. Let $\mathsf{SF} := \{S_{i_0}, S_{i_1}, \ldots, S_{i_k}\}$, where $i_0, \ldots, i_k \in [n]$. For codeword $\hat{C}$, Let $\mathsf{core}(\hat{C})$ denote the content of the set of blocks that make up the core of the sunflower. For set S_ℓ, $\ell \in [n]$, let $\mathsf{set}_\ell(\hat{C})$ denote the content of the blocks in set S_ℓ.

3.3   The Compression Functions

Given a *fixed* initial codeword $\hat{C}$, sunflower $\mathsf{SF} := \{S_{i_0}, \ldots, S_{i_k}\}$, where $i_0, \ldots, i_k \in [n]$ (as defined above) with $k + 1 := 22{,}500 \cdot c \cdot \mathcal{X} + 1$ petals, define the following (randomized) function $F_{\hat{C}} : \{0, 1, \mathsf{same}\}^k \to \{0, 1\}^{\mathcal{X} \cdot c}$ as follows:

- On input $x_1, \ldots, x_k \in \{0, 1, \mathsf{same}\}$
- For $j = 1$ to k:
  - If $x_j = \mathsf{same}$, run $\text{UPDATE}^{\hat{C}}(i_0, 0)$.
  - Otherwise run $\text{UPDATE}^{\hat{C}}(i_j, x_j)$.
  where $\hat{C}$ denotes the current codeword at any point in time.
- Run $\text{UPDATE}^{\hat{C}}(i_0, 0)$.
- Output the contents of $\mathsf{core}(\hat{C})$.

3.4   Closeness of Distributions

For $\ell \in [k]$, let X_ℓ be a random variable distributed as X, where X is distributed as $U_{\{0,1,\mathsf{same}\}}$, i.e. its value is chosen uniformly from the set $\{0, 1, \mathsf{same}\}$. Let $\hat{C}_0 \leftarrow \text{ENC}(0 \ldots 0)$ and $\hat{C}_1 \leftarrow \text{ENC}(1 \ldots 1)$. Let $y_j^0 := \mathsf{set}_{i_j}(\hat{C}_0) \backslash \mathsf{core}(\hat{C}_0)$ denote the contents of the positions in $\hat{C}_0$ corresponding to decoding of i_j, minus the contents of the blocks in the core of the sunflower. Similarly, let $y_j^1 := \mathsf{set}_{i_j}(\hat{C}_1) \backslash \mathsf{core}(\hat{C}_1)$ denote the contents of the positions in $\hat{C}_1$ corresponding to decoding of i_j, minus the contents of the blocks in the core of the sunflower. We prove the following claim, which will be useful in the subsequent analysis.

Claim 3.1. For every $\hat{C}_0 \leftarrow \text{ENC}(0 \ldots 0)$ and $\hat{C}_1 \leftarrow \text{ENC}(1 \ldots 1)$, we have that:

- With probability at least 0.8 over $j \sim [k]$, the statistical distance between $(y_j^0, F_{\hat{C}_0}(X_1, \ldots, X_{j-1}, \mathsf{same}, X_{j+1}, \ldots, X_k))$ and $(y_j^0, F_{\hat{C}_0}(X_1, \ldots, X_k))$ is at most 0.1.
- With probability at least 0.8 over $j \sim [k]$, the statistical distance between $(y_j^1, F_{\hat{C}_1}(X_1, \ldots, X_{j-1}, \mathsf{same}, X_{j+1}, \ldots, X_k))$ and $(y_j^1, F_{\hat{C}_1}(X_1, \ldots, X_k))$ is at most 0.1.

Proof. First, by Lemma 2 and the fact that $F_{\hat{C}}$ is a compression function, we have that for every codeword $\hat{C}$:

$$\frac{1}{k} \sum_{j=1}^{k} \mathop{\mathbb{E}}_{x \sim X} [\|F_{\hat{C}}(X_1, \ldots, X_{j-1}, x, X_{j+1}, \ldots, X_k) - F_{\hat{C}}(X_1, \ldots, X_k)\|_{stat}] < \sqrt{\frac{c \cdot \mathcal{X}}{k}}.$$

By linearity of expectation, we have

$$\mathop{\mathbb{E}}_{x \sim X} \left[\frac{1}{k} \sum_{j=1}^{k} (\|F_{\hat{C}}(X_1, \ldots, X_{j-1}, x, X_{j+1}, \ldots, X_k) - F_{\hat{C}}(X_1, \ldots, X_k)\|_{stat}) \right] < \sqrt{\frac{c \cdot \mathcal{X}}{k}}.$$

Now, by Markov's inequality, we have that

$$\frac{1}{k}\sum_{j=1}^{k}(\|F_{\hat{C}}(X_1,\ldots,X_{j-1},\mathsf{same},X_{j+1},\ldots,X_k) - F_{\hat{C}}(X_1,\ldots,X_k)\|_{stat}) < 3\sqrt{\frac{c\cdot\mathcal{X}}{k}}.$$

Applying Markov's inequality again, we have that with probability at least 0.8 over choice of $j \sim [k]$,

$$\|F_{\hat{C}}(X_1,\ldots,X_{j-1},\mathsf{same},X_{j+1},\ldots,X_k) - F_{\hat{C}}(X_1,\ldots,X_k)\|_{stat} < 15\cdot\sqrt{\frac{c\cdot\mathcal{X}}{k}} = 0.1,$$

where the final equality holds since we take $k + 1 := 22,500\cdot c\cdot\mathcal{X}+1$. Finally, since the above holds for every $\hat{C}$, we have that for every $\hat{C}_0 \leftarrow \mathrm{ENC}(0\ldots0)$, and $\hat{C}_1 \leftarrow \mathrm{ENC}(1\ldots1)$:

- With probability at least 0.8 over $j \sim [k]$, the statistical distance between $F_{\hat{C}_0}(X_1,\ldots,X_{j-1},\mathsf{same},X_{j+1},\ldots,X_k)$ and $F_{\hat{C}_0}(X_1,\ldots,X_k)$ is at most 0.1.
- With probability at least 0.8 over $j \sim [k]$, the statistical distance between $F_{\hat{C}_1}(X_1,\ldots,X_{j-1},\mathsf{same},X_{j+1},\ldots,X_k)$ and $F_{\hat{C}_1}(X_1,\ldots,X_k)$ is at most 0.1.

The above implies that for every $\hat{C}_0 \leftarrow \mathrm{ENC}(0\ldots0)$ and $\hat{C}_1 \leftarrow \mathrm{ENC}(1\ldots1)$, we have that with probability at least 0.8 over $j \sim [k]$, the statistical distance between $(y_j^0, F_{\hat{C}_0}(X_1,\ldots,X_{j-1},\mathsf{same},X_{j+1},\ldots,X_k))$ and $(y_j^0, F_{\hat{C}_0}(X_1,\ldots,X_k))$ is at most 0.1, and with probability at least 0.8 over $j \sim [k]$, the statistical distance between $(y_j^1, F_{\hat{C}_1}(X_1,\ldots,X_{j-1},\mathsf{same},X_{j+1},\ldots,X_k))$ and $(y_j^1, F_{\hat{C}_1}(X_1,\ldots,X_k))$ is at most 0.1, since y_j^0, y_j^1 can be deduced from $\hat{C}_0$, $\hat{C}_1$, respectively, and $\hat{C}_0$, $\hat{C}_1$ are part of the description of the functions. This concludes the proof of the claim.

3.5   The Attack

In this section we describe the polynomial-time attacker and updater:
   Description of attacker:

- Find the Sunflower $\mathsf{SF} := \{S_{i_0},\ldots,S_{i_k}\}$, where $i_0,\ldots,i_k \in [n]$ and $k + 1 := 22,500\cdot c\cdot\mathcal{X}+1$, contained in $\{S_1,\ldots,S_n\}$ in $O(n^2)$ time.[2]
- Choose $j^* \sim [k]$
- In the first round, submit leakage function $\ell(\hat{C})$ defined as $\ell(\hat{C}) := \mathsf{set}_{i_{j^*}}(\hat{C})\backslash\mathsf{core}(\hat{C})$ which returns Leaked, i.e. the contents of the positions in $\hat{C}$ corresponding to decoding of i_{j^*}, minus the contents of the blocks in the core of the sunflower.[3]

---

[2] This can be done by finding the pairwise intersection $S_i \cap S_j$ for all $i,j \in [n]$, yielding sets $\mathsf{core}_1,\ldots,\mathsf{core}_{n^2}$ and the sorting these sets lexicographically. The core of the sunflower $\mathsf{core} := \mathsf{core}_i$, where core_i is the most frequently appearing core. The petals are the corresponding sets that share that pairwise intersection.

[3] If the attacker may leak only a single bit per round, we instead add here $r < \mathcal{X}\cdot c$ number of rounds where in each round the attacker leaks a single bit from $\mathsf{set}_{i_{j^*}}(\hat{C})\backslash\mathsf{core}(\hat{C})$. During each of these rounds, the updater requests a "dummy" update, $\mathrm{UPDATE}^{\hat{C}^{(j)}}(i_0,0)$.

– Wait until the $k+1$-st round. In the $k+1$-st round, choose tampering function f which replaces the contents of $\text{set}_{i_{j_*}}(\hat{C}^{(k)}) \backslash \text{core}(\hat{C}^{(k)})$, i.e. the positions in $\hat{C}^{(k)}$ corresponding to decoding of i_{j_*}, minus the contents of the blocks in the core of the sunflower, with the values, Leaked, that were leaked via ℓ.

Description of Updater:

– Choose $x_1, \ldots, x_k \sim \{0, 1, \text{same}\}^k$.
– For $j = 1$ to k:
  - If $x_j = \text{same}$, request $\text{UPDATE}^{\hat{C}^{(j)}}(i_0, 0)$
  - Otherwise request $\text{UPDATE}^{\hat{C}^{(j)}}(i_j, x_j)$
  where $\hat{C}^{(j)}$ denotes the current codeword in round j.
– In round $j > k$, request $\text{UPDATE}^{\hat{C}^{(j)}}(i_0, 0)$.

3.6 Attack Analysis

Let J^* be the random variable corresponding to choice of j^* in the attack described above. For $j \in [k]$, let UP_{i_j} be the event that location i_j gets updated and let $\overline{\text{UP}_{i_j}}$ be the event that location i_j does not get updated. Recall that for $j \in [k]$, m_{i_j} denotes the original message in block i_j. We have the following properties, which can be verified by inspection:

Fact 1.(a) For $j \in [k]$, $\Pr[\text{UP}_{i_j} \mid m_{i_j} = 0] = \Pr[\text{UP}_{i_j} \mid m_{i_j} = 1] = 0.67$; $\Pr[\overline{\text{UP}_{i_j}} \mid m_{i_j} = 0] = \Pr[\overline{\text{UP}_{i_j}} \mid m_{i_j} = 1] = 0.33$.
(b) For $j \in [k]$, if the i_j-th block of original message was a $m_{i_j} = 0$, then conditioned on an update occurring on block i_j, $m_{i_j}^{(k)} = 0$ with probability 0.5 and $m_{i_j}^{(k)} = 1$ with probability 0.5. Conditioned on no update occurring on block i_j, $m_{i_j}^{(k)} = 0$ with probability 1.
(c) For $j \in [k]$, if the i_j-th block of original message was a $m_{i_j} = 1$, then conditioned on an update occurring on block i_j, $m_{i_j}^{(k)} = 1$ with probability 0.5 and $m_{i_j}^{(k)} = 0$ with probability 0.5. Conditioned on no update occurring on block i_j, $m_i^{(k)} = 1$ with probability 1.

We next present the main technical claim of this section:

Claim 3.2. For the attack and updater specified in Sect. 3.5:

Case 1: If the original message was $\boldsymbol{m} = \boldsymbol{0}$, then with probability at least 0.7, $m_{i_{J^*}}^{(k+1)} = 0$.
Case 2: If the original message was $\boldsymbol{m} = \boldsymbol{1}$, then with probability at least 0.7, $m_{i_{J^*}}^{(k+1)} = 1$.

We first show how to use Claim 3.2 to complete the proof of Theorem 2 and then present the proof of Claim 3.2.

Proof (of Theorem 2). We show that the above claim implies that the candidate scheme is not secure under Definitions 3 and 4. Definition 4 requires the existence of a simulator $\mathcal{S}$ which (for the above attack and updater) outputs one of $\{\mathsf{same}, \bot\} \cup \{0,1\}^\kappa$ for the decoding of position i in round $k+1$. Recall that if $\mathcal{S}$ outputs same, then the output of the experiment in the corresponding position, denoted $m_{i_{J^*},\mathcal{S}}^{(k+1)}$, is set to $m_{i_{J^*},\mathcal{S}}^{(k+1)} := m_{i_{J^*}}^{(k)}$. We begin by defining the following notation for each $j \in [k]$:

$$p_{up,j}^0 := \Pr[\mathcal{S} \text{ outputs same} \mid m_{i_j} = 0 \wedge \mathrm{UP}_{i_j}]$$

$$p_{up,j}^1 := \Pr[\mathcal{S} \text{ outputs same} \mid m_{i_j} = 1 \wedge \mathrm{UP}_{i_j}]$$

$$p_{\overline{up},j}^0 := \Pr[\mathcal{S} \text{ outputs same} \mid m_{i_j} = 0 \wedge \overline{\mathrm{UP}_{i_j}}]$$

$$p_{0,j}^0 := \Pr[\mathcal{S} \text{ outputs } 0 \mid m_{i_j} = 0]$$

$$p_{0,j}^1 := \Pr[\mathcal{S} \text{ outputs } 0 \mid m_{i_j} = 1]$$

Note that since $\mathcal{S}$ does not see the original message, we have that for each $j \in [k]$:

$$(a)\, p_{up,j}^0 = p_{up,j}^1 \qquad (b)\, p_{0,j}^0 = p_{0,j}^1. \tag{1}$$

Additionally we have, for each $j \in [k]$::

$$\Pr[\mathcal{S} \text{ outputs same} \wedge m_{i_j}^{(k)} = 0 \wedge \mathrm{UP}_{i_j} \mid m_{i_j} = 0]$$
$$= \Pr[\mathrm{UP}_{i_j} \mid m_{i_j} = 0] \cdot \Pr[\mathcal{S} \text{ outputs same} \mid m_{i_j} = 0 \wedge \mathrm{UP}_{i_j}]$$
$$\cdot \Pr[m_{i_j}^{(k)} = 0 \mid m_{i_j} = 0 \wedge \mathrm{UP}_{i_j}]$$
$$= 0.67 \cdot p_{up,j}^0 \cdot 0.5, \tag{2}$$

where the first equality follows since $(\mathcal{S} \text{ outputs same} \mid m_{i_j} = 0 \wedge \mathrm{UP}_{i_j})$ and $(m_{i_j}^{(k)} = 0 \mid m_{i_j} = 0 \wedge \mathrm{UP}_{i_j})$ are independent events and the last line follows from Fact 1, items (a) and (b). Similarly, for each $j \in [k]$:

$$\Pr[\mathcal{S} \text{ outputs same} \wedge m_{i_j}^{(k)} = 0 \wedge \mathrm{UP}_{i_j} \mid m_{i_j} = 1]$$
$$= \Pr[\mathrm{UP}_{i_j} \mid m_{i_j} = 1] \cdot \Pr[\mathcal{S} \text{ outputs same} \mid m_{i_j} = 1 \wedge \mathrm{UP}_{i_j}]$$
$$\cdot \Pr[m_{i_j}^{(k)} = 0 \mid m_{i_j} = 1 \wedge \mathrm{UP}_{i_j}]$$
$$= 0.67 \cdot p_{up,j}^1 \cdot 0.5$$
$$= 0.67 \cdot p_{up,j}^0 \cdot 0.5, \tag{3}$$

where the second to last line follows from Fact 1, items (a) and (c), and the last line follows due to (1a). Moreover, we have for each $j \in [k]$:

$$\Pr[\mathcal{S} \text{ outputs same} \wedge m_{i_j}^{(k)} = 0 \wedge \overline{\mathrm{UP}_{i_j}} \mid m_{i_j} = 0]$$
$$= \Pr[\overline{\mathrm{UP}_{i_j}} \mid m_{i_j} = 0] \cdot \Pr[\mathcal{S} \text{ outputs same} \mid m_{i_j} = 0 \wedge \overline{\mathrm{UP}_{i_j}}]$$
$$= 0.33 \cdot p_{\overline{up},j}^0, \tag{4}$$

where the last line follows from Fact 1, item (a). Finally, for each $j \in [k]$:

$$\Pr[\mathcal{S} \text{ outputs same} \wedge m_{i_j}^{(k)} = 0 \wedge \overline{\text{UP}_{i_j}} \mid m_{i_j} = 1] = 0. \tag{5}$$

Given Claim 3.2, in order for $\mathcal{S}$ to succeed, if the original message was $\boldsymbol{m} = \boldsymbol{0}$, then $m_{i_{J^*},\mathcal{S}}^{(k+1)}$ must be equal to 0 with probability (nearly) 0.7, whereas if the original message was $\boldsymbol{m} = \boldsymbol{1}$, then $m_{i_{J^*},\mathcal{S}}^{(k+1)}$ must be equal to 1 with probability (nearly) 0.7. Thus we have that:

$$\begin{aligned}
0.7 = &\sum_{j \in [k]} \Pr[J^* = j] \cdot \Pr[m_{i_j,\mathcal{S}}^{(k+1)} = 0 \mid m_{i_j} = 0] \\
= &\sum_{j \in [k]} \frac{1}{k} \cdot (\Pr[\mathcal{S} \text{ outputs same} \wedge m_{i_j}^{(k)} = 0 \wedge \text{UP}_{i_j} \mid m_{i_j} = 0] \\
& + \Pr[\mathcal{S} \text{ outputs same} \wedge m_{i_j}^{(k)} = 0 \wedge \overline{\text{UP}_{i_j}} \mid m_{i_j} = 0] \\
& + \Pr[\mathcal{S} \text{ outputs } 0 \mid m_{i_j} = 0]) \\
= &\sum_{j \in [k]} \frac{1}{k} \cdot (0.67 \cdot p_{up,j}^0 \cdot 0.5 + 0.33 \cdot p_{\overline{up},j}^0 + p_{0,j}^0), \tag{6}
\end{aligned}$$

where the last line follows due to (2) and (4). On the other hand we have:

$$\begin{aligned}
0.3 \geq &\sum_{j \in [k]} \Pr[J^* = j] \cdot \Pr[m_{i_j,\mathcal{S}}^{(k+1)} = 0 \mid m_{i_j} = 1] \\
= &\sum_{j \in [k]} \frac{1}{k} \cdot (\Pr[\mathcal{S} \text{ outputs same} \wedge m_{i_j}^{(k)} = 0 \wedge \text{UP}_{i_j} \mid m_{i_j} = 1] \\
& + \Pr[\mathcal{S} \text{ outputs same} \wedge m_{i_j}^{(k)} = 0 \wedge \overline{\text{UP}_{i_j}} \mid m_{i_j} = 1] \\
& + \Pr[\mathcal{S} \text{ outputs } 0 \mid m_{i_j} = 1]) \\
= &\sum_{j \in [k]} \frac{1}{k} \cdot (0.67 \cdot p_{up,j}^0 \cdot 0.5 + p_{0,j}^1) \\
= &\sum_{j \in [k]} \frac{1}{k} \cdot (0.67 \cdot p_{up,j}^0 \cdot 0.5 + p_{0,j}^0). \tag{7}
\end{aligned}$$

where the second to last line follows due to (3) and (5) and the last line follows due to (1b). But subtracting (7) from (6), this implies that $0.33 \cdot \sum_{j \in [k]} \frac{1}{k} \cdot p_{\overline{up},j}^0 \geq 0.4$, which is impossible since for each $j \in [k]$, $p_{\overline{up},j} \leq 1$. Thus we have reached contradiction and so the theorem is proved.

We conclude by proving the Claim.

Proof (of Claim 3.2). The proof of the claim relies on the fact that decode takes as input $\text{DEC}(y_{j^*}^0, F_{\hat{C}_0}(X_1, \ldots, X_k))$ in Case 1 and $\text{DEC}(y_{j^*}^1, F_{\hat{C}_1}(X_1, \ldots, X_k))$ in Case 2, where $y_j^0 := \text{set}_{i_j}(\hat{C}_0) \backslash \text{core}(\hat{C}_0)$ denotes the contents of the positions in

$\hat{C}_0$ corresponding to decoding of i_j, minus the contents of the blocks in the core of the sunflower, and similarly, $y_j^1 := \mathsf{set}_{i_j}(\hat{C}_1)\backslash\mathsf{core}(\hat{C}_1)$ denotes the contents of the positions in $\hat{C}_1$ corresponding to decoding of i_j, minus the contents of the blocks in the core of the sunflower.

But note that, due to the structure of the Sunflower, updates to positions $i_0, \ldots, i_{j^*-1}, i_{j^*+1}, \ldots, i_k$ do not modify the contents of $\mathsf{set}_{i_{j^*}}(\hat{C}_0)\backslash\mathsf{core}(\hat{C}_0)$ (and $\mathsf{set}_{i_{j^*}}(\hat{C}_1)\backslash\mathsf{core}(\hat{C}_1)$) and so $\mathsf{DEC}(y_{j^*}^0, F_{\hat{C}_0}(X_1, \ldots, X_{j^*-1}, \mathsf{same}, X_{j^*+1}, \ldots, X_k)) = 0$ with overwhelming probability and $\mathsf{DEC}(y_{j^*}^1, F_{\hat{C}_1}(X_1, \ldots, X_{j^*-1}, \mathsf{same}, X_{j^*+1}, \ldots, X_k)) = 1$ with overwhelming probability, since when $X_j = \mathsf{same}$, the rewind attack has no effect and decode outputs the original message.

Moreover, we have shown in Claim 3.1 that for every $\hat{C}_0 \leftarrow \mathrm{ENC}(0\ldots0)$ and $\hat{C}_1 \leftarrow \mathrm{ENC}(1\ldots1)$, we have that:

1. With probability at least 0.8 over $j^* \sim [k]$, the statistical distance between $(y_j^0, F_{\hat{C}_0}(X_1, \ldots, X_{j-1}, \mathsf{same}, X_{j+1}, \ldots, X_k))$ and $(y_j^0, F_{\hat{C}_0}(X_1, \ldots, X_k))$ is at most 0.1.
2. With probability at least 0.8 over $j^* \sim [k]$, the statistical distance between $(y_j^1, F_{\hat{C}_1}(X_1, \ldots, X_{j-1}, \mathsf{same}, X_{j+1}, \ldots, X_k))$ and $(y_j^1, F_{\hat{C}_1}(X_1, \ldots, X_k))$ is at most 0.1.

Hence with each will not be satisfied with probability at most 0.2. Now, conditioned on each being satisfied, it can be concluded from (1) that the probability of $\mathsf{DEC}(y_j^0, F_{\hat{C}_0}(X_1, \ldots, X_k)) = 1$ is at most 0.1. Similarly from (2), $\mathsf{DEC}(y_j^1, F_{\hat{C}_1}(X_1, \ldots, X_k)) = 0$ with probability at most 0.1. Taking a union bound, we have that in each case, DEC procedure will fail to output the original message with probability at most 0.3. This means that with probability at least 0.7 over all coins, $\mathsf{DEC}(y_{j^*}^0, F_{\hat{C}_0}(X_1, \ldots, X_k)) = 0$, whereas with probability at least 0.7 over all coins $\mathsf{DEC}(y_{j^*}^1, F_{\hat{C}_1}(X_1, \ldots, X_k)) = 1$, completing the proof of the claim.

4 Matching Upper Bound

In this section we show how to construct a locally updatable and decodable non-malleable code with super-constant locality. This is achieved by replacing the Merkle Tree in the construction presented in [18] by a new data structure, *t-slice Merkle Tree* which we defined below (see Definition 8). Intuitively, the locality of updating/decoding in the construction given by Dachman-Soled et al. [18] is lower-bounded by the depth of the Merkle Tree, since, in order to detect tampering, each update/decode instruction must check the consistency of a leaf by traversing the path from leaf to root. Our initial idea is to replace the binary Merkle Tree of depth $\log(n)$ with a t-ary Merkle tree (where t is a super-constant function of n defined below) of constant depth. Unfortunately, this simple solution does not quite work. Recall that in order to verify consistency of a leaf in a standard Merkle tree, one needs to access not only the path from leaf to root, but also the *siblings* of each node on the path. This would mean that in the t-ary tree, we would need to access at least $\Omega(t)$ sibling nodes, where t is super-constant, thus still requiring super-constant locality. Our solution, therefore, is to construct t-ary Merkle trees of a particular form, where verifying consistency of a leaf can be done by traversing only the path from leaf to root, *without* accessing any sibling nodes. We call such trees t-slice Merkle trees. Details of the construction follow in Definitions 8, 9, 10 and 11. Finally, in Theorem 3 we show that the t-slice Merkle Tree is collision resistant, which allows us to retain security while replacing the Merkle tree in the construction of [18] with our t-slice Merkle Tree. This then leads to our matching upper bound in Theorem 4.

Definition 8 (t-slice Merkle Tree). *Let $\mathcal{X}$ and $h : \{0,1\}^{\mathcal{X}} \to \{0,1\}^{\mathcal{X}/t}$ be a hash function that maps a block of size $\mathcal{X}$ to block of size $\mathcal{X}/t$. Let a block of data at level j with index i denoted by α_i^j and $M = (m_1, m_2, \ldots, m_n)$ being the input data and set $\alpha_i^0 := m_{i+1}$ for $0 \leq i \leq n-1$. A t-slice Merkle Tree $\mathsf{Tree}_h^t(M)$ is defined recursively in the following way:*

- *Bottom layer of the tree contains n blocks of data each of size $\mathcal{X}$, i.e., $(\alpha_0^0, \alpha_1^0, \ldots, \alpha_{n-1}^0)$.*
- *To compute the content of non-leaf node at level j with index i set $\alpha_i^j := h(\alpha_{i \cdot t}^{j-1}) || \ldots || h(\alpha_{((i+1) \cdot t)-1}^{j-1})$.*
- *Once a single block α_i^j remains, set the root of Merkle Tree $\mathsf{Root}_h^t(M) := h(\alpha_i^j)$ and the height of tree $\mathcal{H} := j+1$ and terminate.*

For $k \in [0, \ldots, t-1]$, we denote the k-th slice of α_i^j by $\alpha_i^j[k]$ The internal blocks of Merkle Tree (including the root) are denoted as $\mathsf{Tree}_h^t(M)$.

Definition 9 (Path). *Given a Merkle Tree $\mathsf{Tree}_h^t(M)$ with n leaves of height $\mathcal{H}$ and its root $\mathsf{Root}_h^t(M)$, a path $p_i := p_i^0, \ldots, p_i^{\mathcal{H}-1}$, for $i \in [0, \ldots n-1]$ is a sequence of $\mathcal{H}$ blocks from leaf to root defined as follows: For $j \in [0, \ldots, \mathcal{H}-1]$, $p_i^j := \alpha_\ell^j$, where $\ell := \sum_{k=j}^{\mathcal{H}-1} \beta_k \cdot t^{k-j}$ and $\beta_{\mathcal{H}-1}, \ldots, \beta_0$ is the base t representation of i, where $\beta_{\mathcal{H}-1}$ is the most significant digit and β_0 is the least significant digit.*

Definition 10 (Consistency). *Let $\beta_{\mathcal{H}-1}, \ldots, \beta_0$ be the base t representation of i, where $\beta_{\mathcal{H}-1}$ is the most significant digit and β_0 is the least significant digit. Path $p_i := p_i^0, \ldots, p_i^{\mathcal{H}-1}$ is consistent with $\mathsf{Root}_h^t(M)$ if the following hold:*

- $p_i^{\mathcal{H}-1} = \mathsf{Root}_h^t(M)$.
- *For $j \in [\mathcal{H}-2]$, $h(p_i^j) = p_i^{j+1}[\ell \mod t]$, where $\ell := \sum_{k=j}^{\mathcal{H}-1} \beta_k \cdot t^{k-j}$ (i.e. the hash of the j-th element on the path is equal to the $(\ell \mod t)$-th slice of the $j+1$-st element on the path).*

Definition 11 (Update). *Given a path $p_i := p_i^0, \ldots, p_i^{\mathcal{H}-1}$ in Merkle Tree $\mathsf{Tree}_h^t(M)$ and new message block α'^0_i, Let $\beta_{\mathcal{H}-1}, \ldots, \beta_0$ be the base t representation of i, where $\beta_{\mathcal{H}-1}$ is the most significant digit and β_0 is the least significant digit. The update procedure computes a modified path $p_i' := p'^0_i, \ldots, p'^{\mathcal{H}-1}_i$ as follows (the rest of the tree remains the same):*

- $p'^0_i := \alpha'^0_i$.
- For $j \in [1, \ldots, \mathcal{H} - 1]$, $p'^{j+1}_i[\ell \mod t] := h(p'^j_i)$, where $\ell := \sum_{k=j}^{\mathcal{H}-1} \beta_k \cdot t^{k-j}$ (i.e. the $(\ell \mod t)$-th slice of the $j + 1$-st element on the path is equal to the hash of the j-th element on the path).
- For $j \in [\mathcal{H} - 1]$, $\gamma \in [0, \ldots, t] \backslash \{\ell \mod t\}$, where $\ell := \sum_{k=j}^{\mathcal{H}-1} \beta_k \cdot t^{k-j}$, $p'^{j+1}_i[\gamma] := p^{j+1}_i[\gamma]$ (i.e. all other slices of the $j + 1$-st element on the path stay the same as in the original path p_i).

Lemma 3. Let $\mathcal{X} \in \Omega(\lambda^{1/\mu})$, $h : \{0, 1\}^{\mathcal{X}} \to \{0, 1\}^{\mathcal{X}^\mu}$, and $t := \mathcal{X}^{1-\mu}$, for constant $0 < \mu < 1$. Assuming $n = \text{poly}(\lambda) := \mathcal{X}^c$ for constant c, the height of the t-slice Merkle Tree will be constant $\mathcal{H} = \frac{c-1}{1-\mu}$.

Proof. In the beginning the message blocks $M = (m_1, m_2, \ldots, m_n)$ are at the leaves of the tree and size of each block is $\mathcal{X}$, i.e. $|m_i| = \mathcal{X}$. After applying a hash function to each of the blocks separately, their size becomes $\mathcal{X}^\mu$ and by concatenating $\mathcal{X}^{1-\mu}$ number of hashes a single block of size $\mathcal{X}$ will be formed. In this level there will therefore be $\frac{\mathcal{X}^c}{\mathcal{X}^{1-\mu}} = \mathcal{X}^{c+\mu-1}$ block of size $\mathcal{X}$. Applying hash function to each of them will form new blocks of size $\mathcal{X}^\mu$ and there will be $\mathcal{X}^{c+2\mu-2}$ blocks of size $\mathcal{X}$. In general in level i-th there will be $\mathcal{X}^{c+i\mu-i}$ blocks of size $\mathcal{X}$. The root of the t-slice Merkle Tree is of size $\mathcal{X}$, so the height of the tree is for the case where $\mathcal{X}^{c+i\mu-i} = \mathcal{X}$ resulting the i and hence the height of tree is $\frac{c-1}{1-\mu}$. $\square$

Theorem 3. Let $\mathcal{X} \in \Omega(\lambda^{1/\mu})$, $h : \{0, 1\}^{\mathcal{X}} \to \{0, 1\}^{\mathcal{X}^\mu}$, and $t := \mathcal{X}^{1-\mu}$, for constant $0 < \mu < 1$. Assuming h is a collision resistant hash function, consider the resulting t-slice Merkle Tree. Then for any message $M = (m_1, m_2, \ldots, m_n)$ with $m_i \in \{0, 1\}^{\mathcal{X}}$, any polynomial time adversary $\mathcal{A}$,

$$\Pr\left[(m'_i, p_i) \leftarrow \mathcal{A}(M, h) : m'_i \neq m_i, p_i \text{ is a consistent path with } \mathsf{Root}^t_h(M)\right] \leq \mathsf{negl}(k).$$

Moreover, given a path p_i passing the leaf m_i, and a new value m'_i, the update algorithm computes $\mathsf{Root}^t_h(M')$ in constant time $\mathcal{H} := \frac{c-1}{1-\mu}$, where $M' = (m_1, \ldots, m_{i-1}, m'_i, m_{i+1}, \ldots, m_n)$.

Proof. The second part of Theorem 3 is immediate by inspection of Definition 11.

For the first part of the theorem, we assume towards contradiction that for some message $M = (m_1, m_2, \ldots, m_n)$ with $m_i \in \{0, 1\}^{\mathcal{X}}$, there is an efficient adversary $\mathcal{A}$ such that

$$\Pr\left[(m'_i, p'_i) \leftarrow \mathcal{A}(M, h) : m'_i \neq m_i, p'_i \text{ is a consistent path with } \mathsf{Root}^t_h(M)\right] = 1/\text{poly}(\lambda).$$

We construct adversary $\mathcal{A}'$ which finds a collision in hash function h. The procedure is as follows:

- On input h, adversary $\mathcal{A}'$ instantiates $\mathcal{A}$ on input (M, h).
- Adversary $\mathcal{A}$ returns (m'_i, p'_i), where $p'_i := p'^0_i, \ldots, p'^{\mathcal{H}-1}_i$.
- $\mathcal{A}'$ checks that $p'^{\mathcal{H}-1}_i = \mathsf{Root}^t_h(M)$.

– For $j \in [\mathcal{H} - 2]$, if $p'^{j+1}_i = p^{j+1}_i$, $p'^j_i \neq p^j_i$ and $h(p'^j_i) = p'^{j+1}_i[\ell \mod t]$, where $\ell := \sum_{k=j}^{\mathcal{H}-1} \beta_k \cdot t^{k-j}$, then $\mathcal{A}'$ returns collision (p'^j_i, p^j_i).

Note that if $m'_i \neq m_i$, then $p'_i \neq p_i$ and so at some point the "if statement" above must hold. Moreover, if p'_i is a consistent path, then it must be the case that $p'^{\mathcal{H}-1}_i = \mathsf{Root}^t_h(M)$ and for $j \in [\mathcal{H} - 2]$, $h(p'^j_i) = p'^{j+1}_i[\ell \mod t]$, where $\ell := \sum_{k=j}^{\mathcal{H}-1} \beta_k \cdot t^{k-j}$, by definition of consistency. Thus, the above adversary $\mathcal{A}'$ will succeeds with same probability as the adversary $\mathcal{A}$ and breaks collision resistance of h with probability $1/\text{poly}(\lambda)$. Thus, we arrive at contradiction and so the theorem is proved.

Theorem 4. *Assume there exists a semantically secure symmetric encryption scheme, and a non-malleable code against the tampering function class $\mathcal{F}$, and leakage resilient against the function class $\mathcal{G}$. Then there exists a leakage resilient, locally decodable and updatable coding scheme that is non-malleable against continual attacks of the tampering class*

$$\bar{\mathcal{F}} \stackrel{\text{def}}{=} \left\{ \begin{array}{l} f : \hat{\Sigma}^{2n+1} \to \hat{\Sigma}^{2n+1} \text{ and } |f| \leq \text{poly}(k), \text{ such that} : \\ f = (f_1, f_2), \; f_1 : \hat{\Sigma}^{2n+1} \to \hat{\Sigma}, \; f_2 : \hat{\Sigma}^{2n} \to \hat{\Sigma}^{2n}, \\ \forall (x_2, \ldots, x_{2n+1}) \in \hat{\Sigma}^{2n}, f_1(\; \cdot \;, x_2, \ldots, x_{2n+1}) \in \mathcal{F}, \\ f(x_1, x_2, \ldots, x_{2n+1}) = (f_1(x_1, x_2, \ldots, x_{2n+1}), f_2(x_2, \ldots, x_{2n+1})). \end{array} \right\},$$

and is leakage resilient against the class

$$\bar{\mathcal{G}} \stackrel{\text{def}}{=} \left\{ \begin{array}{l} g : \hat{\Sigma}^{2n+1} \to \mathcal{Y} \text{ and } |g| \leq \text{poly}(k), \text{ such that} : \\ g = (g_1, g_2), \; g_1 : \hat{\Sigma}^{2n+1} \to \mathcal{Y}', \; g_2 : \hat{\Sigma}^{2n} \to \hat{\Sigma}^{2n}, \\ \forall \; (x_2, \ldots, x_{2n+1}) \in \hat{\Sigma}^{2n}, g_1(\; \cdot \;, x_2, \ldots, x_{2n+1}) \in \mathcal{G}. \end{array} \right\}.$$

Moreover, for $n := \mathcal{X}^c \in \text{poly}(\lambda)$, the coding scheme has locality $\delta(n)$, for any $\delta(n) \in \omega(1)$.

Our construction is exactly the same as that of Dachman-Soled et al. [18], except we replace their (standard) Merkle tree with our t-slice Merkle tree with the parameters described above. We note that the only property of the Merkle hash used in the security proof of [18] is the "collision resistance" property, analogous to our Theorem 3 above for the t-slice Merkle tree. Thus, our security proof follows exactly as theirs does and we therefore omit the full proof. On the other hand, as described in Definitions 10 and 11, updates and consistency checks require time and number of accesses to memory proportional to the height of the tree, $\mathcal{H}$, which is $\frac{c-1}{1-\mu}$ for our choice of parameters, as shown in Lemma 3 above. Since $n = \mathcal{X}^c \in \text{poly}(\lambda)$, it means that the height of the tree will always be less than $\delta(n)$, for any $\delta(n) \in \omega(1)$. On the other hand, [18] used a standard (binary) Merkle tree with height $\Theta(\log n)$. Therefore, while [18] requires locality $\Theta(\log n)$, we achieve locality $\delta(n)$, for any $\delta(n) \in \omega(1)$.

Finally, we give a concrete example of the resulting leakage and tampering classes we can tolerate via Theorem 4 when instantiating the underlying non-malleable code with a concrete construction. Specifically, we consider instantiating the underlying non-malleable code with the construction of

Liu and Lysyanskaya [37], which achieves both leakage and tamper resilience for split-state functions. Combining the constructions of [18,37] yields codewords consisting of $2n + 1$ blocks. We next describe the leakage and tampering classes $\bar{\mathcal{G}}, \bar{\mathcal{F}}$ that can be tolerated on the $2n + 1$-block codeword. $\bar{\mathcal{G}}$ consists of leakage functions g such that g restricted to the first block (i.e. g_1) is any (poly-sized) length-bounded split-state function; g_2 on the other hand, can leak all other parts. $\bar{\mathcal{F}}$ consists of tampering functions f such that f restricted to the first block (i.e. f_1) is any (poly-sized) split-state function. On the other hand f restricted to the rest (i.e. f_2) is any poly-sized function. We also remark that the function f_2 itself can depend on the split-state leakage on the first part.

References

1. Aggarwal, D., Agrawal, S., Gupta, D., Maji, H.K., Pandey, O., Prabhakaran, M.: Optimal computational split-state non-malleable codes. In: Kushilevitz, E., Malkin, T. (eds.) TCC 2016. LNCS, vol. 9563, pp. 393–417. Springer, Heidelberg (2016). doi:10.1007/978-3-662-49099-0_15

2. Aggarwal, D., Dodis, Y., Kazana, T., Obremski, M.: Non-malleable reductions and applications. In: Servedio, R.A., Rubinfeld, R. (eds.) 47th ACM STOC, pp. 459–468. ACM Press, June 2015

3. Aggarwal, D., Dodis, Y., Lovett, S.: Non-malleable codes from additive combinatorics. In: Shmoys, D.B. (ed.) 46th ACM STOC, pp. 774–783. ACM Press, May/June 2014

4. Aggarwal, D., Dziembowski, S., Kazana, T., Obremski, M.: Leakage-resilient non-malleable codes. In: Dodis, Y., Nielsen, J.B. (eds.) TCC 2015. LNCS, vol. 9014, pp. 398–426. Springer, Heidelberg (2015). doi:10.1007/978-3-662-46494-6_17

5. Agrawal, S., Gupta, D., Maji, H.K., Pandey, O., Prabhakaran, M.: Explicit non-malleable codes against bit-wise tampering and permutations. In: Gennaro, R., Robshaw, M. (eds.) CRYPTO 2015. LNCS, vol. 9215, pp. 538–557. Springer, Heidelberg (2015). doi:10.1007/978-3-662-47989-6_26

6. Agrawal, S., Gupta, D., Maji, H.K., Pandey, O., Prabhakaran, M.: A rate-optimizing compiler for non-malleable codes against bit-wise tampering and permutations. In: Dodis, Y., Nielsen, J.B. (eds.) TCC 2015. LNCS, vol. 9014, pp. 375–397. Springer, Heidelberg (2015). doi:10.1007/978-3-662-46494-6_16

7. Ball, M., Dachman-Soled, D., Kulkarni, M., Malkin, T.: Non-malleable codes for bounded depth, bounded fan-in circuits. In: Fischlin, M., Coron, J.-S. (eds.) EURO-CRYPT 2016. LNCS, vol. 9666, pp. 881–908. Springer, Heidelberg (2016). doi:10.1007/978-3-662-49896-5_31

8. Chandran, N., Goyal, V., Mukherjee, P., Pandey, O., Upadhyay, J.: Block-wise non-malleable codes. Cryptology ePrint Archive, Report 2015/129 (2015). http://eprint.iacr.org/2015/129

9. Chandran, N., Kanukurthi, B., Ostrovsky, R.: Locally updatable and locally decodable codes. In: Lindell, Y. (ed.) TCC 2014. LNCS, vol. 8349, pp. 489–514. Springer, Heidelberg (2014). doi:10.1007/978-3-642-54242-8_21

10. Chandran, N., Kanukurthi, B., Raghuraman, S.: Information-theoretic local non-malleable codes and their applications. In: Kushilevitz, E., Malkin, T. (eds.) TCC 2016. LNCS, vol. 9563, pp. 367–392. Springer, Heidelberg (2016). doi:10.1007/978-3-662-49099-0_14

11. Chattopadhyay, E., Zuckerman, D.: Non-malleable codes against constant split-state tampering. In: 55th FOCS, pp. 306–315. IEEE Computer Society Press, October 2014

12. Chattopadhyay, E., Zuckerman, D.: Explicit two-source extractors and resilient functions. In: Wichs, D., Mansour, Y. (eds.) 48th ACM STOC, pp. 670–683. ACM Press, June 2016

13. Chee, Y.M., Feng, T., Ling, S., Wang, H., Zhang, L.F.: Query-efficient locally decodable codes of subexponential length. Comput. Complex. **22**(1), 159–189 (2013). http://dx.doi.org/10.1007/s00037-011-0017-1

14. Cheraghchi, M., Guruswami, V.: Capacity of non-malleable codes. In: Naor, M. (ed.) ITCS 2014, pp. 155–168. ACM, January 2014

15. Cheraghchi, M., Guruswami, V.: Non-malleable coding against bit-wise and split-state tampering. In: Lindell, Y. (ed.) TCC 2014. LNCS, vol. 8349, pp. 440–464. Springer, Heidelberg (2014). doi:10.1007/978-3-642-54242-8_19

16. Coretti, S., Dodis, Y., Tackmann, B., Venturi, D.: Non-malleable encryption: simpler, shorter, stronger. In: Kushilevitz, E., Malkin, T. (eds.) TCC 2016. LNCS, vol. 9562, pp. 306–335. Springer, Heidelberg (2016). doi:10.1007/978-3-662-49096-9_13

17. Coretti, S., Maurer, U., Tackmann, B., Venturi, D.: From single-bit to multi-bit public-key encryption via non-malleable codes. In: Dodis, Y., Nielsen, J.B. (eds.) TCC 2015. LNCS, vol. 9014, pp. 532–560. Springer, Heidelberg (2015). doi:10.1007/978-3-662-46494-6_22

18. Dachman-Soled, D., Liu, F.-H., Shi, E., Zhou, H.-S.: Locally decodable and updatable non-malleable codes and their applications. In: Dodis, Y., Nielsen, J.B. (eds.) TCC 2015. LNCS, vol. 9014, pp. 427–450. Springer, Heidelberg (2015). doi:10.1007/978-3-662-46494-6_18

19. Dolev, D., Dwork, C., Naor, M.: Nonmalleable cryptography. SIAM J. Comput. **30**(2), 391–437 (2000)

20. Drucker, A.: New limits to classical and quantum instance compression. SIAM J. Comput. **44**(5), 1443–1479 (2015)

21. Dziembowski, S., Kazana, T., Obremski, M.: Non-malleable codes from two-source extractors. In: Canetti, R., Garay, J.A. (eds.) CRYPTO 2013. LNCS, vol. 8043, pp. 239–257. Springer, Heidelberg (2013). doi:10.1007/978-3-642-40084-1_14

22. Dziembowski, S., Pietrzak, K., Wichs, D.: Non-malleable codes. In: Yao, A.C.C. (ed.) ICS 2010, pp. 434–452. Tsinghua University Press, January 2010

23. Efremenko, K.: 3-query locally decodable codes of subexponential length. In: Mitzenmacher, M. (ed.) 41st ACM STOC, pp. 39–44. ACM Press, May/June 2009

24. Erdős, P., Rado, R.: Intersection theorems for systems of sets. J. Lond. Math. Soc. **35**(1), 85–90 (1960)

25. Faust, S., Mukherjee, P., Nielsen, J.B., Venturi, D.: Continuous non-malleable codes. In: Lindell, Y. (ed.) TCC 2014. LNCS, vol. 8349, pp. 465–488. Springer, Heidelberg (2014). doi:10.1007/978-3-642-54242-8_20

26. Faust, S., Mukherjee, P., Nielsen, J.B., Venturi, D.: A tamper and leakage resilient von neumann architecture. In: Katz, J. (ed.) PKC 2015. LNCS, vol. 9020, pp. 579–603. Springer, Heidelberg (2015). doi:10.1007/978-3-662-46447-2_26

27. Faust, S., Mukherjee, P., Venturi, D., Wichs, D.: Efficient non-malleable codes and key-derivation for poly-size tampering circuits. In: Nguyen, P.Q., Oswald, E. (eds.) EUROCRYPT 2014. LNCS, vol. 8441, pp. 111–128. Springer, Heidelberg (2014). doi:10.1007/978-3-642-55220-5_7

28. Gennaro, R., Lysyanskaya, A., Malkin, T., Micali, S., Rabin, T.: Algorithmic Tamper-Proof (ATP) security: theoretical foundations for security against hardware tampering. In: Naor, M. (ed.) TCC 2004. LNCS, vol. 2951, pp. 258–277. Springer, Heidelberg (2004). doi:10.1007/978-3-540-24638-1_15

29. Goyal, V., Pandey, O., Richelson, S.: Textbook non-malleable commitments. In: Wichs, D., Mansour, Y. (eds.) 48th ACM STOC, pp. 1128–1141. ACM Press, June 2016

30. Guo, A., Kopparty, S., Sudan, M.: New affine-invariant codes from lifting. In: Kleinberg, R.D. (ed.) ITCS 2013, pp. 529–540. ACM, January 2013

31. Hemenway, B., Ostrovsky, R., Wootters, M.: Local correctability of expander codes. In: Fomin, F.V., Freivalds, R., Kwiatkowska, M., Peleg, D. (eds.) ICALP 2013. LNCS, vol. 7965, pp. 540–551. Springer, Heidelberg (2013). doi:10.1007/978-3-642-39206-1_46

32. Ishai, Y., Prabhakaran, M., Sahai, A., Wagner, D.: Private circuits II: keeping secrets in tamperable circuits. In: Vaudenay, S. (ed.) EUROCRYPT 2006. LNCS, vol. 4004, pp. 308–327. Springer, Heidelberg (2006). doi:10.1007/11761679_19

33. Jafargholi, Z., Wichs, D.: Tamper detection and continuous non-malleable codes. In: Dodis, Y., Nielsen, J.B. (eds.) TCC 2015. LNCS, vol. 9014, pp. 451–480. Springer, Heidelberg (2015). doi:10.1007/978-3-662-46494-6_19

34. Kalai, Y.T., Kanukurthi, B., Sahai, A.: Cryptography with tamperable and leaky memory. In: Rogaway, P. (ed.) CRYPTO 2011. LNCS, vol. 6841, pp. 373–390. Springer, Heidelberg (2011). doi:10.1007/978-3-642-22792-9_21

35. Katz, J., Trevisan, L.: On the efficiency of local decoding procedures for error-correcting codes. In: 32nd ACM STOC, pp. 80–86. ACM Press, May 2000

36. Kopparty, S., Saraf, S., Yekhanin, S.: High-rate codes with sublinear-time decoding. In: Fortnow, L., Vadhan, S.P. (eds.) 43rd ACM STOC, pp. 167–176. ACM Press, June 2011

37. Liu, F.-H., Lysyanskaya, A.: Tamper and leakage resilience in the split-state model. In: Safavi-Naini, R., Canetti, R. (eds.) CRYPTO 2012. LNCS, vol. 7417, pp. 517–532. Springer, Heidelberg (2012). doi:10.1007/978-3-642-32009-5_30

38. Yekhanin, S.: Towards 3-query locally decodable codes of subexponential length. J. ACM 55(1), 1:1–1:16. http://doi.acm.org/10.1145/1326554.1326555

39. Yekhanin, S.: Locally decodable codes: a brief survey. In: Chee, Y.M., Guo, Z., Ling, S., Shao, F., Tang, Y., Wang, H., Xing, C. (eds.) IWCC 2011. LNCS, vol. 6639, pp. 273–282. Springer, Heidelberg (2011). doi:10.1007/978-3-642-20901-7_18

Fully Leakage-Resilient Codes

Antonio Faonio$^{(\boxtimes)}$ and Jesper Buus Nielsen

Aarhus University, Aarhus, Denmark
afaonio@gmail.com

Abstract. Leakage resilient codes (LRCs) are probabilistic encoding schemes that guarantee message hiding even under some bounded leakage on the codeword. We introduce the notion of *fully* leakage resilient codes (FLRCs), where the adversary can leak λ_0 bits from the encoding process, namely, the message and the randomness involved during the encoding process. In addition the adversary can as usual leak from the codeword. We give a simulation-based definition requiring that the adversary's leakage from the encoding process and the codeword can be simulated given just λ_0 bits of leakage from the message. We give a fairly general impossibility result for FLRCs in the popular split-state model, where the codeword is broken into independent parts and where the leakage occurs independently on the parts. We then give two feasibility results for weaker models. First, we show that for NC^0-bounded leakage from the randomness and arbitrary poly-time leakage from the parts of the codeword the inner-product construction proposed by Daví *et al.* (SCN'10) and successively improved by Dziembowski and Faust (ASIACRYPT'11) is a FLRC for the split-state model. Second, we provide a compiler from any LRC to a FLRC in the *common reference string model* where the leakage on the encoding comes from a fixed leakage family of small cardinality. In particular, this compiler applies to the split-state model but also to other models.

Keywords: Leakage-resilient cryptography · Impossibility · Fully-leakage resilience · Simulation-based definition · Feasibility results

1 Introduction

Leakage-resilient codes (LRCs) (also known as leakage-resilient storages) allow to store safely a secret information in a physical memory that may leak some side-channel information. Since their introduction (see Daví *et al.* [12]) they have found many applications either by their own or as building blocks for other leakage and tamper resilient primitives. To mention some, Dziembowski and Faust [15] proposed an efficient and continuous leakage-resilient identification scheme and a continuous leakage-resilient CCA2 cryptosystem, while Andrychowicz *et al.* [5] proposed a practical leakage-resilient LPN-based version of the Lapin protocol (see Heyse *et al.* [28]) both relying on LRCs based on the inner-product extractor. LRC found many applications also in the context

© International Association for Cryptologic Research 2017
S. Fehr (Ed.): PKC 2017, Part I, LNCS 10174, pp. 333–358, 2017.
DOI: 10.1007/978-3-662-54365-8_14

of non-malleable codes (see Dziembowski *et al.* [17]), which, roughly speaking, can be seen as their tamper-resilience counterpart. Faust *et al.* [23] showed a non-malleable code based on LRC, Aggarwal *et al.* [1] proposed a construction of leakage and tamper resilient code and Faust *et al.* [21] showed continuous non-malleable codes based on LRC [21] (see also Jafargholi and Wichs [29]).

The security requirement of LRC states that given two encoded messages, arbitrarily but bounded length leakage on the codeword is indistinguishable. Ideally, a good LRC should be resilient to a leakage that can be much longer than the size of the message protected, however, to get such strong guarantee some restriction on the class of leakage allowed must be set. Intuitively, any scheme where the adversary can even partially compute the decoding function as leakage cannot be secure. A way to fix this problem is to consider randomly chosen LRCs. As showed in [12], and successively improved in [23,29], for any fixed set of leakage functions, there exists a family of efficiently computable codes such that with high probability a code from this family is leakage resilient. From a cryptographic perspective, the results known in this direction can be interpreted as being the "common reference string" model, where the leakage class is set and, then, the LRC is sampled.

Another way, more relevant for our paper, is to consider the split-state model [16,27] where the message is encoded in two (or more) codewords and the leakage happens adaptively but independently from each codeword, thus the decoding function cannot automatically be part of the allowed leakage, which opens the possibility of constructing a LRC.

It is easy to see that the encoding algorithm must be randomized, otherwise two fixed messages can be easily distinguished. However, the security of LRC does not give any guarantee when there is leakage from the randomness used in the encoding process. In other words, while the encoded message can be stored in a leaky device the encoding process must be executed in a completely leak-free environment. A stronger flavour of security where we allow leakage from the encoding process is usually called *fully* leakage resilient.

Our Contributions. We generalize the notion of LRC to the setting of fully leakage resilience. Roughly speaking, a fully leakage-resilient code (FLRC) hides information about the secret message even when the adversary leaked information during the encoding process. Our contributions are summarized as follow:

1. We provide a simulation-based definition of fully leakage-resilient codes. The definition postulates that for any adversary leaking λ_0 bits from the encoding process and λ_1 bits from the codewords there exists a simulator which provides a view that is indistinguishable. Our definition is, in some sense, the minimal one suitable for the fully leakage resilience setting. As a sanity check, we show that our new notion is implied by the indistinguishability-based definition of [12] for $\lambda_0 = 0$.
2. We show that there does not exist an efficient coding scheme in the split-state model that is a fully leakage resilient code if the leakage function is allowed to be any poly-time function. Our result holds for coding schemes

where the length of the messages is at least linear in the security parameter and under the sole assumption that collision-resistant hash functions exist. We can generalize the impossibility result to the case of constant-length messages under the much stronger assumption that differing-input obfuscation (diO) exists (see [3, 9]).

3. We provide two feasibility results for weaker models. We show that, if the leakage from the randomness is computable by bounded-depth constant fan-in circuits (i.e. NC^0-computable leakage), the inner-product extractor LRC of [12] is fully leakage resilient. We show a compiler from any LRC to a fully leakage resilient code in the common reference string model for any fixed leakage-from-the-encoding-process family of small cardinality.

Simulation-Based Security. Consider the naive fully leakage-resilient extension of the indistinguishability-based security definition of LRC. Roughly speaking, the adversary plays against a challenger and it can leak $\lambda_0 > 0$ bits from a random string $\omega \leftarrow_\$ \{0,1\}^*$, in a second phase, the adversary sends to the challenger two messages m_0, m_1, the challenger chooses a random bit b and encodes the message m_b using the randomness ω. After this, the adversary gets access to leakage from the codewords. We show an easy attack on this definition. The attacker can compute, via one leakage function on the randomness, the encoding of both m_0 and m_1 and find a coordinate in which the two codewords differ, successively, by leaking from the codeword only one bit, it can check whether m_0 or m_1 has been encoded.

The problem with the indistinguishability-based security definition sketched above is that it concentrates on preserving, in the presence of leakage on the randomness, the same security guarantees as the (standard) leakage resilient definition. However, the ability of leaking before and after the challenge generation, as shown for many other cryptographic primitives, gives to the adversary too much power.

Following the *leakage-tolerant* paradigm introduced by Bitansky et al. [7], we instead consider a simulation-based notion of security. The definition postulates that for any adversary leaking λ_0 bits from the encoding process and λ_1 bits from the codeword there exists a simulator which provide a view that is indistinguishable. In particular, the adversary chooses one input message and forwards it to the challenger of the security game. After that, the adversary can leak first from the encoding process and then from the codeword. The job of the simulator is to produce an indistinguishable view of the leakage oracles to the adversary given only leakage oracle access to the message. It is not hard to see that, without the help of leakage oracle on the message, the task would be impossible. In fact, the adversary can leak bits of the input message, if the input message is randomly chosen the simulator cannot provide an indistinguishable view. Therefore, the simulator can leak up to $\lambda_0(1+\gamma)$ bits from the message for a "slack parameter" $\gamma \geqslant 0$. The idea is that some information about the message can unavoidably leak from the encoding process, however the amount of information about the message that the adversary gathers by jointly leaking from the encoding process and from the codeword should not exceed by too much the the bound given by the leakage on the encoding process. The slack parameter is often considered as a reasonable weakening of the model in the context of fully leakage resilience (see for example [19,26,27,39]), we include it in our model to make the impossibility results stronger. For the feasibility results we will instead ignore it.

The Impossibility Results. We give an impossibility result for FLRCs in the split-state model. Recall that, in the split state model, the codeword is divided in two parts which are stored in two independent leaky devices. Each leakage query can be any poly-time function of the data stored in one of the parts.

Here we give the intuition behind the attacker. For simplicity let us set the slack parameter γ equal to 0. In our attack we leak from the encoding process a hash of each of the two parts of the codeword. The leakage function takes the message and the randomness, runs the encoding algorithm to compute the two parts L and R (the left part and the right part) and leaks two hash values $h_l = h(L)$ and $h_r = h(R)$. Then we use a succinct argument of knowledge system to leak an argument of knowledge of pre-images L and R of h_l and h_r for which it holds that (L, R) decodes to m. Let λ_0 be equal to the length of the two hashed values and the transcript of the succinct argument. After this the message can be encoded. The adversary uses its oracle access to L to leak, in sequence, several succinct arguments of knowledge of L such that $h_l = h(L)$. Similarly, the adversary uses its oracle access to R to leak, in sequence, several succinct arguments of knowledge of R such that $h_r = h(R)$. By setting $\lambda_1 \gg \lambda_0$ we can within the leakage bound λ_1 on L and R leak $17\lambda_0$ succinct arguments of knowledge of L and R. Suppose that the code is secure, then there exists a simulator which can simulate the leakage of h_l and h_r and all the arguments given at most λ_0 bits of leakage on m. Since the arguments are accepting in the real world and the simulator is assumed to be good it follows that the simulated arguments are accepting with probability close to 1. Since the simulator has access to only λ_0 bits of leakage on m it follows that for one of the $17\lambda_0$ simulated arguments produced by the simulator it uses the leakage oracle on m with probability at most $\frac{1}{4}$. This means that with probability $\frac{3}{4}$ the simulator is not even using the leakage oracle to simulate this argument, so if we remove the access to leakage from m the argument will still be acceptable with probability close to $\frac{3}{4}$. Hence if the argument systems has knowledge error just $\frac{1}{2}$ we can extract L from this argument with probability close to $\frac{1}{4}$. Similarly we can extract from one of the arguments of knowledge of R the value R with probability close to $\frac{1}{4}$. By collision resistance and soundness of the first argument leaked from the encoding process it follows that (L, R) decodes to m. This means that we can extract from the simulator the message m with probability negligibly close to $\frac{1}{16}$ while using only λ_0 bits of leakage on m. If m is uniformly random and just $\lambda_0 + 6$ bits long, this is a contradiction. In fact, the amount of min-entropy of m after have leaked λ_0 bits is $\lambda_0 + 6 - \lambda_0 = 6$, therefore m cannot be guessed with probability better than 2^{-6}.

Similar proof techniques have been used already by Nielsen *et al.* [38] to prove a connection between leakage resilience and adaptive security and recently by Ostrovsky *et al.* [40] to prove an impossibility result for certain flavors of leakage-resilient zero-knowledge proof systems. The way we apply this type of argument here is novel. It is in particular a new idea to use many arguments of knowledge in sequence to sufficient restrict the simulators ability to leak from its leakage oracle in one of the proofs.

The definition of FLR makes sense only when the leakage parameter λ_0 is strictly smaller than the size of the message. The proposed attack needs to leak at least a collision resistant hash function of the codeword, therefore the length of the message needs to be super-logarithmic in the security parameter. Thus the technique cannot be used to give an impossibility result for FLRC with message space of constant length. We can overcome this problem relying on the concept of Predictable ZAP (PZAP) recently proposed by Faonio et al. [20]. A PZAP is an extremely succinct 2-message argument of knowledge where the prover can first see the challenge from the verifier and then decide the instance. This allows the attacker to implement the first check by just leaking a constant-length argument that the hashed values of the two parts of the codeword are well formed (without actually leaking the hashed values) and then, successively, leak the hashed values from the codeword and check the validity of the argument. PZAP are shown to imply extractable witness encryption (see Boyle et al. [9]) and therefore the "implausibility" result of Garg et al. [25] applies. We interpret our second impossibility result as an evidence that constant-length FLRC are hard to construct as such a code would not only make extractable witness encryption implausible, but it would prove it *impossible* under the only assumption that collision-resistant hash functions exists. We provide more details in the full version of the paper [18].

The Feasibility Results. The ability to leak a collision resistant hash function of the randomness is necessary for the impossibility result. Therefore, the natural question is: If we restrict the leakage class so that collision resistant hash functions cannot be computed as leakage on the randomness, can we find a coding scheme that is fully leakage resilient? We answer this question affirmatively.

We consider the class NC^0 of constant-depth constant fan-in circuits and we show that the LRC based on the inner-product extractor (and more general LRCs where there is an NC^0 function that maps the randomness to the codeword) are fully leakage resilient. The intuition is that NC^0 leakage is not powerful enough to break all the "independence" between the two parts of the codeword. Technically, we are able to cast every leakage query on the randomness into two slightly bigger and independent leakage queries on the two parts of the codeword. Notice that collision resistant hash functions cannot be computed by NC^0 circuits. This is necessary. In fact, proving a similar result for a bigger complexity class automatically implies a lower bound on the complexity of computing either collision resistant hash functions or arguments of knowledge. Intuitively, this provides a strong evidence that is hard to construct FLRC even for bounded classes of leakage.

Another important property that we exploit in the impossibility result is that, given access to the leakage oracle on the randomness, we can compute the codeword. A second path to avoid the impossibility results is to consider weaker models of security where this is not permitted. We point out that the schemes proposed by [12,23,29] in the common reference string model can be easily proved to be fully leakage resilient. Inspired by the above results we provide a compiler that maps any LRC to FLRC for any fixed leakage-from-the-encoding family $\mathcal{F}$ of small cardinality. Notice that the bound is on the cardinality of the leakage class and not on its complexity (in principle, the leakage class could contain collision resistant hash functions).

We remark that the definition of FLRC already assumes a CRS (this to include in our model the result of Liu and Lysyanskaya [34]). The key point is that, by fixing $\mathcal{F}$ ahead (namely, before the common reference string is sampled) and because of the small cardinality, the adversary cannot make the leakage on the encoding "depends" from the common reference string, disabling therefore the computation of the encoded word as leakage on the encoding process.

Technically, we use a result of Trevisan and Vadhan [43] which proves that for any fixed leakage class $\mathcal{F}$ a t-wise independent hash function (the parameter t depends on the cardinality of $\mathcal{F}$) is a deterministic extractor with high probability. The proof mostly follows the template given in [23].

Related Work. Cryptographic schemes are designed under the assumption that the adversary cannot learn any information about the secret key. However, side-channel attacks (see [32,33,42]) have showed that this assumption does not always hold. These attacks have motivated the design of leakage-resilient cryptosystems which remain secure even against adversaries that may obtain partial information about the secret state. Starting from the groundbreaking result of Micali and Reyzin [36], successively either gradually stronger or different models have been considered (see for example [2,16,24,37]). Fully leakage resilient schemes are known for signatures [11,19,35], zero-knowledge proof system [4,26,41] and multi-party computation protocols [8,10]. Similar concepts of leakage resilient codes have been considered, Liu and Lysyanskaya [34] and successively Aggarwal et al. [1] constructed leakage and tamper resilient codes while Dodis et al. [13] constructed continual leakage resilient storage. Simulation-based definitions in the context of leakage-resilient cryptography were also adopted in the case of zero-knowledge proof (see [4,26,41]), public-key encryption (see [27]) and signature schemes (see [39]). As mentioned already, our proof technique for the impossibility result is inspired by the works of Nielsen et al. [38] and Ostrovsky et al. [40], however, part of the analysis diverges, and instead resembles an information theoretic argument already known in leakage-resilient cryptography (see for example [2,19,30]).

In [22] the authors present a RAM model of computation where a CPU is connected to some constant number of memories, paralleling the split-state model that we use here. The memories and buses are assumed to be leaky, but the CPU is assumed to be leakage free. Besides leakage, the paper also shows how to handle tampering, like moving around codewords in the memories. They show how to use a leakage-resilient and tamper-resilient code to securely compute on this platform. In each step the CPU will read from the disks a number of codewords, decode these, do a computation on the plaintext, re-encode the results and write the codewords back in the memories. One should wonder if it is possible to get a similar result for the more realistic model where there is a little leakage from the CPU? It is clear that if the CPU can leak, then it can also leak from the plaintexts it is working on. This can be handled by having the computation that is done on the plaintexts being leakage resilient in itself. The challenging part is then to show that the leakage from the CPU during re-encoding of the results to be stored in the memories can be simulated given just a little leakage on the results themeselves. This would in particular require that the code is fully leakage-resilient in the sense we define in this paper. Our negative results therefore do not bode well for this proof strategy. On the other hand, our positive results open up the possibility of tolerating some simple leakage from the CPU or getting a result for weaker models, like the random oracle model. Note, however, that the code would have to be tamper-resilient in addition to being fully leakage resilient, so there still seem to be significant obstacles towards proving such a result.

Roadmap. In Sect. 2 we introduce the necessary notation for probability and cryptographic tools. In Sect. 3 we provide the simulation-based definition for Fully Leakage-Resilient Codes. In Sect. 4 we state and prove the main impossibility result for linear-size message spaces. In Sect. 5 we provide the two feasibility results, specifically, in Sect. 5.1 we give a FLR code for the class NC^0 and in Sect. 5.2 we give a compiler from Leakage-Resilient Codes to Fully Leakage-Resilient Codes for any fixed class of small cardinality.

2   Preliminaries

We let $\mathbb{N}$ denote the naturals and $\mathbb{R}$ denote the reals. For $a, b \in \mathbb{R}$, we let $[a, b] = \{x \in \mathbb{R} \ : \ a \leq x \leq b\}$; for $a \in \mathbb{N}$ we let $[a] = \{1, 2, \ldots, a\}$. If x is a string, we denote its length by $|x|$; if $\mathcal{X}$ is a set, $|\mathcal{X}|$ represents the number of elements in $\mathcal{X}$. When x is chosen randomly in $\mathcal{X}$, we write $x \leftarrow_\$ \mathcal{X}$. When $\mathcal{A}$ is an algorithm, we write $y \leftarrow \mathcal{A}(x)$ to denote a run of $\mathcal{A}$ on input x and output y; if $\mathcal{A}$ is randomized, then y is a random variable and $\mathcal{A}(x; r)$ denotes a run of $\mathcal{A}$ on input x and randomness r. An algorithm $\mathcal{A}$ is *probabilistic polynomial-time* (ppt) if $\mathcal{A}$ is allowed to use random choices and for any input $x \in \{0, 1\}^*$ and randomness $r \in \{0, 1\}^*$ the computation of $\mathcal{A}(x; r)$ terminates in at most $\mathsf{poly}(|x|)$ steps.

Let κ be a security parameter. A function negl is called *negligible* in κ (or simply negligible) if it vanishes faster than the inverse of any polynomial in κ. For a relation $\mathcal{R} \subseteq \{0, 1\}^* \times \{0, 1\}^*$, the language associated with $\mathcal{R}$ is $\mathcal{L}_\mathcal{R} = \{x : \exists w \text{ s.t. } (x, w) \in \mathcal{R}\}$.

For two ensembles $\mathcal{X} = \{X_\kappa\}_{\kappa \in \mathbb{N}}$, $\mathcal{Y} = \{Y_\kappa\}_{\kappa \in \mathbb{N}}$, we write $\mathcal{X} \overset{c}{\approx}_\epsilon \mathcal{Y}$, meaning that every probabilistic polynomial-time distinguisher D has $\epsilon(\kappa)$ advantage in distinguishing $\mathcal{X}$ and $\mathcal{Y}$, i.e., $\frac{1}{2}|\Pr[D(\mathcal{X}_\kappa) = 1] - \Pr[D(\mathcal{Y}_\kappa) = 1]| \leq \epsilon(\kappa)$ for all sufficiently large values of κ.

We simply write $\mathcal{X} \stackrel{c}{\approx} \mathcal{Y}$ when there exists a negligible function ϵ such that $\mathcal{X} \stackrel{c}{\approx}_\epsilon \mathcal{Y}$. Similarly, we write $\mathcal{X} \approx_\epsilon \mathcal{Y}$ (statistical indistinguishability), meaning that every unbounded distinguisher has $\epsilon(\kappa)$ advantage in distinguishing $\mathcal{X}$ and $\mathcal{Y}$. Given two ensembles $\mathcal{X}$ and $\mathcal{Y}$ such that $\mathcal{X} \approx_\epsilon \mathcal{Y}$ the following holds:

$$\frac{1}{2} \sum_z |\Pr[X_\kappa = z] - \Pr[Y_\kappa = z]| \leqslant \epsilon(\kappa).$$

We recall the notion of (average) conditional min-entropy. We adopt the definition given in [2], where the authors generalize the notion of conditional min-entropy to *interactive* predictors that participate in some randomized experiment **E**. The conditional min-entropy of random variable X given any randomized experiment **E** is defined as $\widetilde{\mathbb{H}}_\infty (X \mid \mathbf{E}) = \max_{\mathcal{B}} \left(-\log \Pr[\mathcal{B}()^{\mathbf{E}} = X] \right)$, where the maximum is taken over all predictors without any requirement on efficiency. Note that w.l.o.g. the predictor $\mathcal{B}$ is deterministic, in fact, we can de-randomize $\mathcal{B}$ by hardwiring the random coins that maximize its outcome. Sometimes we write $\widetilde{\mathbb{H}}_\infty(X|Y)$ for a random variable Y, in this case we mean the average conditional min-entropy of X given the random experiment that gives Y as input to the predictor. Given a string $X \in \{0,1\}^*$ and a value $\lambda \in \mathbb{N}$ let the oracle $\mathcal{O}_\lambda^X(\cdot)$ be *the leakage oracle* that accepts as input functions $f_1, f_2, \ldots$ defined as circuits and outputs $f_1(X), f_2(X), \ldots$ under the restriction that $\sum_i |f_i(X)| \leqslant \lambda$.

We recall here a lemma of Alwen *et al.* [2] and a lemma from Bellare and Rompel [6] that we make us of.

Lemma 1. *For any random variable X and for any experiment* **E** *with oracle access to $\mathcal{O}_\lambda^X(\cdot)$, consider the experiment* **E'** *which is the same as* **E** *except that the predictor does not have oracle access to $\mathcal{O}_\lambda^X(\cdot)$. Then $\widetilde{\mathbb{H}}_\infty (X \mid \mathbf{E}) \geqslant \widetilde{\mathbb{H}}_\infty (X \mid \mathbf{E'}) - \lambda$.*

Lemma 2. *Let $t \geqslant 4$ be an even integer. Suppose $X_1, \ldots, X_n$ are t-wise independent random variables taking values in $[0,1]$. Let $X := \sum_i X_i$ and define $\mu := \mathbb{E}[X]$ to be the expectation of the sum. Then, for any $A > 0$, $\Pr[|X - \mu| \geqslant A] \leqslant 8 \left(\frac{t\mu + t^2}{A^2} \right)^{t/2}$.*

2.1 Cryptographic Primitives

Arguments of Knowledge. Our results are based on the existence of round-efficient interactive argument systems. We follow some of the notation of Wee [44]. The knowledge soundness definition is taken from [40]. A public-coin argument system $(P(w), V)(x)$ with round complexity $\rho(\kappa)$ is fully described by the tuple of ppt algorithms (Prove, Judge) where:

- V on input x samples uniformly random strings $y_1, \ldots, y_{\rho(\kappa)} \leftarrow_\$ \{0,1\}^\kappa$, P on inputs x, w samples uniformly random string $r_P \leftarrow_\$ \{0,1\}^\kappa$.
- For any $i \in [\rho(\kappa)]$, V sends the message y_i and P replies with the message $x_i := \mathsf{Prove}(x, w, y_1, \ldots, y_i; r_P)$.

– The verifier V executes $j := \mathsf{Judge}\big(x, y_1, \ldots, y_{\rho(\kappa)}, x_1, \ldots, x_{\rho(\kappa)}\big)$ and accepts if $j = 1$.

Definition 1 (Argument of knowledge). *An interactive protocol (P, V) is an argument of knowledge for a language $\mathcal{L}$ if there is a relation $\mathcal{R}$ such that $\mathcal{L} = \mathcal{L}_{\mathcal{R}} := \{x | \exists w : (x, w) \in \mathcal{R}\}$, and functions $\nu, s : \mathbb{N} \to [0, 1]$ such that $1 - \nu(\kappa) > s(\kappa) + 1/\mathsf{poly}(\kappa)$ and the following conditions hold.*

– *(Efficiency): The length of all the exchanged messages is polynomially bounded, and both P and V are computable in probabilistic polynomial time;*
– *(Completeness): If $(x, w) \in \mathcal{R}$, then V accepts in $(P(w), V)(x)$ with probability at least $1 - \nu(|x|)$.*
– *(Knowledge Soundness): For every* ppt *prover strategy P^*, there exists an expected polynomial-time algorithm* K *(called the* knowledge extractor*) such that for every $x, z, r \in \{0, 1\}^*$ if we denote by $p^*(x, z, r)$ the probability that V accepts in $(P(z; r), V)(x)$, then $p^*(x, z, r) > s(|x|)$ implies that*

$$\Pr[\mathsf{K}(P^*, x, z, r) \in \mathcal{R}(x)] \geqslant p^*(x, z, r) - s(|x|).$$

The value $\nu(\cdot)$ is called the *completeness error* and the value $s(\cdot)$ is called the *knowledge error*. We say (P, V) has perfect completeness if $\nu = 0$. The communication complexity of the argument system is the total length of all messages exchanged during an execution; the round complexity is the total number of exchanged messages. We write $\mathsf{AoK}_{\nu,s}(\rho(\kappa), \lambda(\kappa))$ to denote interactive argument on knowledge systems with completeness error ν, knowledge error s, round-complexity $\rho(\kappa)$ and communication complexity $\lambda(\kappa)$. Sometimes we also write $\lambda(\kappa) = \lambda_P(\kappa) + \lambda_V(\kappa)$ to differentiate between the communication complexity of the prover and of the verifier. We say (P, V) is *succinct* if $\lambda(\kappa)$ is poly-logarithmic in the length of the witness and the statement being proven.

We remark that for our results interactive arguments are sufficient; in particular our theorems can be based on the assumption that collision-resistant function ensembles exist [31].

Collision Resistant Hash Functions. Let $(\mathsf{Gen}^{\mathrm{CRH}}, \mathsf{Eval}^{\mathrm{CRH}})$ be a tuple of ppt algorithms such that upon input 1^κ the algorithm Gen outputs an evaluation key h and upon inputs h and a string $x \in \{0, 1\}^*$ the deterministic algorithm $\mathsf{Eval}^{\mathrm{CRH}}$ outputs a string $y \in \{0, 1\}^{\ell_{\mathrm{CRH}}(\kappa)}$. We shorten the notation by writing $h(x)$ for $\mathsf{Eval}^{\mathrm{CRH}}(h, x)$.

Definition 2. *A tuple $(\mathsf{Eval}^{\mathrm{CRH}}, \mathsf{Gen}^{\mathrm{CRH}})$ is a collision-resistant hash function (family) with output length $\ell_{\mathrm{CRH}}(\kappa)$ if for all non-uniform polynomial time adversary $\mathcal{B}_{coll}$ there exists a negligible function* negl *such that the following holds:*

$$\Pr_{h \,\leftarrow\$\, \mathsf{Gen}^{\mathrm{CRH}}(1^\kappa)} \big[h(x_0) = h(x_1) \wedge x_0 \neq x_1 \,|\, (x_0, x_1) := \mathcal{B}_{coll}(h)\big] < \mathsf{negl}(\kappa).$$

For simplicity we consider the model of non-uniform polynomial time adversaries. Note, however, that our results hold also if we consider the model ppt adversaries.

3 Definition

In this section we give the definition of Fully Leakage Resilient Codes. The definition given is specialized for the 2-split-state model, we adopt this definition instead of a more general one for simplicity. The results given in Sect. 4 can be adapted to hold for the more general k-split model (see Remark 1). LRCs of [12,21,29] in the common reference string model can be proved fully-leakage resilience (see Sect. 5). Therefore the syntax given allows the scheme to depends on a common reference string to include the scheme of [34].

An (α, β)-split-coding scheme is a tuple $\Sigma = (\mathsf{Gen}, \mathsf{Enc}, \mathsf{Dec})$ of ppt algorithms with the following syntax:

- Gen on input 1^κ outputs a common reference string crs;
- Enc on inputs crs and a message $m \in \mathcal{M}_\kappa$ outputs a tuple $(L, R) \in \mathcal{C}_\kappa \times \mathcal{C}_\kappa$;
- Dec is a deterministic algorithm that on inputs crs and a codeword $(L, R) \in \mathcal{C}_\kappa \times \mathcal{C}_\kappa$ decodes to $m' \in \mathcal{M}_\kappa$.

Here $\mathcal{M}_\kappa = \{0,1\}^{\alpha(\kappa)}$, $\mathcal{C}_\kappa = \{0,1\}^{\beta(\kappa)}$ and the randomness space of Enc is $\mathcal{R}_k = \{0,1\}^{p(\kappa)}$ for a fixed polynomial p.

A split-coding scheme is correct if for any κ and any $m \in \mathcal{M}_\kappa$ we have $\Pr_{\mathsf{crs},r_e}[\mathsf{Dec}(\mathsf{crs}, \mathsf{Enc}(\mathsf{crs}, m; r_e)) = m] = 1$. In what follows, whenever it is clear from the context, we will omit the security parameter κ so we will write α, β instead of $\alpha(\kappa), \beta(\kappa)$, etc.

Given an (α, β)-split-coding scheme Σ, for any $\mathcal{A} = (\mathcal{A}_0, \mathcal{A}_1)$ and any function λ_0, λ_1 let $\mathsf{Real}_{\mathcal{A},\Sigma}^{\lambda_0,\lambda_1}(\kappa)$ be the following experiment:

Sampling Phase. The experiment runs the adversary $\mathcal{A}_0$ on input $\mathsf{crs} \leftarrow_\$ \mathsf{Gen}(1^\kappa)$ and randomness $r_A \leftarrow_\$ \{0,1\}^{p(\kappa)}$ for a polynomial p that bounds the running time of $\mathcal{A}_0$. The adversary outputs a message $m \in \mathcal{M}_\kappa$ and a state value st. The experiment samples $\omega \leftarrow_\$ \mathcal{R}_\kappa$ and instantiates a leakage oracle $\mathcal{O}_{\lambda_0}^{\omega\|m}$.

Encoding Phase. The experiment runs the adversary $\mathcal{A}_1$ on input st and crs. Moreover, the experiment sets an index $i := 0$.

- Upon query $(\mathbf{rand}, f)$ from the adversary where f is the description of a function with domain $\mathcal{R}_\kappa \times \mathcal{M}_\kappa$, the experiment sets $i := i + 1$, computes $\mathsf{lk}_\omega^i := \mathcal{O}_{\lambda_0}^{\omega\|m}(f)$ and returns the value to the adversary.
- Eventually, the adversary notifies the experiment by sending the message **encode**.

The message is encoded, namely the experiment defines $(L, R) := \mathsf{Enc}(\mathsf{crs}, m; \omega)$ and instantiates the oracles $\mathcal{O}_{\lambda_1}^L, \mathcal{O}_{\lambda_1}^R$. Moreover, the experiment sets two indexes $l := 0$ and $r := 0$.

- Upon query (L, f) from the adversary where f is the description of a function with domain $\mathcal{C}_\kappa$, the experiment sets $l := l + 1$, computes $\mathsf{lk}_L^l := \mathcal{O}_{\lambda_1}^L(f)$ and returns the value to the adversary.

- Upon query (R, f) from the adversary where f is the description of a function with domain $\mathcal{C}_\kappa$, the experiment sets $r := r + 1$, computes $\mathsf{lk}_R^r := \mathcal{O}_{\lambda_1}^R(f)$ and returns the value to the adversary.

By overloading the notation, we let $\mathsf{Real}_{\mathcal{A},\Sigma}^{\lambda_0,\lambda_1}$ be also the tuple of random variables that describes the view of $\mathcal{A}$ in the experiment:

$$\mathsf{Real}_{\mathcal{A},\Sigma}^{\lambda_0,\lambda_1} := \begin{pmatrix} r_A, \mathsf{crs}, \\ \mathsf{lk}_\omega := (\mathsf{lk}_\omega^1, \mathsf{lk}_\omega^2, \dots, \mathsf{lk}_\omega^i), \\ \mathsf{lk}_L := (\mathsf{lk}_L^1, \mathsf{lk}_L^2, \dots, \mathsf{lk}_L^l), \\ \mathsf{lk}_R := (\mathsf{lk}_R^1, \mathsf{lk}_R^2, \dots, \mathsf{lk}_R^r) \end{pmatrix},$$

Given an adversary $\mathcal{A} = (\mathcal{A}_0, \mathcal{A}_1)$, a simulator $\mathcal{S}$ and a slack parameter $\gamma(\kappa)$ such that $0 \leqslant \gamma(\kappa) < \frac{\alpha(\kappa)}{\lambda_0(\kappa)} - 1$ let $\mathsf{Ideal}_{\mathcal{A},\mathcal{S},\gamma}^{\lambda_0,\lambda_1}(\kappa)$ be the following experiment:

Sampling Phase. The experiment runs the adversary $\mathcal{A}_0$ on input $\mathsf{crs} \leftarrow\!\!{}_\$ \mathsf{Gen}(1^\kappa)$ and randomness $r_A \leftarrow\!\!{}_\$ \{0,1\}^{p(\kappa)}$ for a polynomial p that bounds the running time of $\mathcal{A}_0$. The adversary outputs a message $m \in \mathcal{M}_\kappa$ and a state value st. The experiment instantiates an oracle $\mathcal{O}_{\lambda_0 \cdot (1+\gamma)}^m$.

Encoding Phase. The experiment runs the adversary $\mathcal{A}_1$ on input st and crs, and the simulator $\mathcal{S}$ on input crs.

- Upon query (X, f) from the adversary where $X \in \{\mathtt{rand}, \mathtt{L}, \mathtt{R}\}$ the experiment forwards the query to the simulator $\mathcal{S}$ which returns an answer to the adversary.
- Upon query $(\mathtt{msg}, f)$ from the simulator the experiment computes $\mathsf{lk}_m := \mathcal{O}_{\lambda_0 \cdot (1+\gamma)}^m(f)$ and returns an answer to the simulator.

As we did with $\mathsf{Real}_{\mathcal{A},\Sigma}^{\lambda_0,\lambda_1}$ we denote with $\mathsf{Ideal}_{\mathcal{A},\mathcal{S},\gamma}^{\lambda_0,\lambda_1}$ also the tuple of random variables that describe the view of $\mathcal{A}$ in the experiment. To mark the distinction between the real experiment and ideal experiment we upper script the "simulated" components of the ideal experiment with a tilde, namely:

$$\mathsf{Ideal}_{\mathcal{A},\mathcal{S},\gamma}^{\lambda_0,\lambda_1} = \left(r_A, \mathsf{crs}, \widetilde{\mathsf{lk}}_\omega, \widetilde{\mathsf{lk}}_L, \widetilde{\mathsf{lk}}_R \right)$$

Given a class of leakage functions Λ we say that an adversary is Λ-bounded if it submits only queries $(\mathtt{rand}, f)$ where the function $f \in \Lambda$.

Definition 3 (Simulation-based Λ-fully leakage resilient code). *An (α, β)-split-coding scheme is said to be $(\Lambda, \lambda_0, \lambda_1, \epsilon)$-FLR-sim-secure with slack parameter $0 \leqslant \gamma < \alpha/\lambda_0 - 1$ if for any ppt adversary $\mathcal{A}$ that is Λ-bounded there exists a ppt simulator $\mathcal{S}$ such that $\left\{ \mathsf{Real}_{\mathcal{A},\Sigma}^{\lambda_0,\lambda_1}(\kappa) \right\}_{\kappa\in\mathbb{N}} \overset{c}{\approx}_\epsilon \left\{ \mathsf{Ideal}_{\mathcal{A},\mathcal{S},\gamma}^{\lambda_0,\lambda_1}(\kappa) \right\}_{\kappa\in\mathbb{N}}.$*

Let $\mathsf{P}_{/\mathsf{poly}}$ be the set of all polynomial-sized circuits.

Definition 4 (Simulation-based fully leakage resilient code). *An (α, β)-split-coding scheme is said to be $(\lambda_0, \lambda_1, \epsilon)$-FLR-sim-secure with slack parameter γ if it is $(\mathsf{P}_{/\mathsf{poly}}, \lambda_0, \lambda_1, \epsilon)$-FLR-sim-secure with slack parameter γ. We simply say that a split-coding scheme is (λ_0, λ_1)-FLR-sim-secure if there exists a negligible function negl and a constant $\gamma < \alpha/\lambda_0 - 1$ such that the scheme is $(\lambda_0, \lambda_1, \mathsf{negl})$-FLR-sim-secure with slack parameter γ.*

In the full version of the paper [18] we prove that the game-based definition of [12] implies FLR-sim-security for $\lambda_0 = 0$.

4   Impossibility Results

In this section we show the main result of this paper. Throughout the section we let the class of leakage functions be $\Lambda = P_{/\text{poly}}$. We prove that (α, β)-split-coding schemes that are (λ_0, λ_1)-FLR-sim-secure don't exist for many interesting parameters of α, β, λ_0 and λ_1. We start with the case $\alpha(\kappa) = \Omega(\kappa)$, the impossibility results holds under the only assumption that collision resistant hash functions exist. For the case $\alpha(\kappa) = O(1)$, the impossibility results holds under the stronger assumption that adaptive-secure PAoK exists.

Theorem 1. *If public-coin* $\text{AoK}_{\text{negl}(\kappa), 1/2}(O(1), \ell_{\text{AoK}}(\kappa))$ *for* NP *and collision-resistant hash functions with output length* $\ell_{\text{CRH}}(\kappa)$ *exist then for any* $\lambda_0 \geq \ell_{\text{AoK}}(\kappa) + 2 \cdot \ell_{\text{CRH}}(\kappa)$ *for any* $\gamma \geq 0$ *and for any* (α, β)-*split-coding scheme* Σ *with* $\alpha(\kappa) \geq \lambda_0(\kappa) \cdot (1 + \gamma) + \ell_{\text{CRH}}(\kappa) + 7$ *and if* $\lambda_1(\kappa) \geq 17\lambda_0(\kappa) \cdot (1 + \gamma) \cdot \ell_{\text{AoK}}(\kappa)$ *then* Σ *is not* (λ_0, λ_1)-*FLR-sim-secure.*

Proof. We first set some necessary notation. Given a random variable x we use the notation $\bar{x}$ to refer to a possible assignment of the random variable. Let $(\text{Gen}^{\text{CRH}}, \text{Eval}^{\text{CRH}})$ be a collision resistant hash function with output length $\ell_{\text{CRH}}(\kappa)$.

Leakage-Aided Prover. Let $\Pi = (\text{Prove}, \text{Judge})$ be in $\text{AoK}_{1/2, \text{negl}(\kappa)}(O(1), \ell_{\text{AoK}}(\kappa))$ and a public-coin argument system for NP. For concreteness let ρ be the round complexity of the Π. We say that an attacker leaks an argument of knowledge for $x \in \mathcal{L}_{\mathcal{R}}$ from $X \in \{\text{rand}, L, R\}$ if the attacker proceeds with the following sequence of instructions and leakage-oracle queries:

- Let r_p be a random string long enough to specify all random choices done by the prover of Π. For $j \in [\rho]$ do the following:
  1. Sample a random string $y_j \leftarrow_\$ \{0, 1\}^\kappa$;
  2. Send the query $\big(X, \text{Prove}(x, \cdot, y_1, \ldots, y_j; r_p)\big)$ and let z_j be the answer to such query.
- Let $\pi := y_1, \ldots, y_\rho, z_1, \ldots, z_\rho$ be the leaked transcript, compute the value $j := \text{Judge}(x, \pi))$, if $j = 1$ we say that the leaked argument of knowledge is accepting.

Consider the adversary $\mathcal{A}' = (\mathcal{A}'_0, \mathcal{A}'_1)$ that does the following:

1. Pick a collision resistant hash function $h \leftarrow \text{Gen}^{\text{CRH}}(1^\kappa)$;
2. Pick $m \leftarrow_\$ \mathcal{M}_\kappa$ and send it to the challenger;
3. Compute $h(m)$.

This ends the code of $\mathcal{A}'_0$, formally, $\mathcal{A}'_0(1^\kappa)$ outputs m that is forwarded to the experiment which instantiates a leakage oracle $\mathcal{O}^m_{\lambda_0 \cdot (1+\gamma)}$, also $\mathcal{A}'_0(1^\kappa)$ outputs the state $st := (h, h(m))$. Here starts the code of $\mathcal{A}'_1(h, h(m))$:

4. **Leak Hashed Values.** Define the following function:

$$f_0(\omega\|m) := (h(L), h(R) \text{ where } L, R = \mathsf{Enc}(\mathsf{crs}, m; \omega));$$

Send the query $(\mathbf{rand}, f_0)$. Let (h_l, h_r) be the answer to the query.

5. **Leak Argument of Knowledge of Consistency.** Consider the following relation:

$$\mathcal{R}^{\mathsf{st}} := \left\{ (x_{crs}, x_l, x_r, x_m), (w_l, w_r) : \begin{array}{c} h(w_l) = x_l \\ h(w_r) = x_r \\ h(\mathsf{Dec}(x_{crs}, w_l, w_r)) = x_m \end{array} \right\}$$

Leak an argument of knowledge for $(\mathsf{crs}, h_l, h_r, h(m)) \in \mathcal{L}_{\mathcal{R}^{\mathsf{st}}}$ from $\mathbf{rand}$. Notice that a witness for the instance can be defined as function of $(\omega\|m)$. If the leaked argument is not accepting then abort. Let π_0 be the leaked transcript.

6. Send the message encode.

7. **Leak Arguments of Knowledge of the Left part.** Consider the following relation:

$$\mathcal{R}^{\mathsf{hash}} := \{(y, x) : h(x) = y\}$$

Let $\tau := 17\lambda_0 \cdot (1 + \gamma)$, for all $i \in [\tau]$ leak an argument of knowledge for $h_l \in \mathcal{L}_{\mathcal{R}^{\mathsf{hash}}}$ from $\mathbf{L}$. If the leaked argument is not accepting then abort. Let π_i^L be the leaked transcript.

8. **Leak Arguments of Knowledge of the Right part.** For all $i \in [\tau]$ leak an argument of knowledge for $h_r \in \mathcal{L}_{\mathcal{R}^{\mathsf{hash}}}$ from $\mathbf{R}$. If the leaked argument is not accepting then abort. Let π_i^R be the leaked transcript.

Consider the following randomized experiment $\mathbf{E}$:

– Pick uniformly random $m \leftarrow_\$ \mathcal{M}_\kappa$ and $h \leftarrow_\$ \mathsf{Gen}^{\mathsf{CRH}}(1^\kappa)$ and set $st = (h, h(m))$ and forward to the predictor the state st.
– Instantiate an oracle $\mathcal{O}^m_{\lambda_0 \cdot (1+\gamma)}$ and give the predictor access to it.

Lemma 3. $\widetilde{\mathbb{H}}_\infty(m \mid \mathbf{E}) \geqslant \alpha - \ell_{\mathsf{CRH}} - \lambda_0 \cdot (1 + \gamma)$.

Proof. Consider the experiment $\mathbf{E}'$ which is the same as $\mathbf{E}$ except that the predictor's input is h (instead of $(h, h(m))$). We apply Lemma 1:

$$\widetilde{\mathbb{H}}_\infty(m \mid \mathbf{E}) \geqslant \widetilde{\mathbb{H}}_\infty(m \mid \mathbf{E}') - \ell_{\mathsf{CRH}}.$$

Consider the experiment $\mathbf{E}''$ which is the same as $\mathbf{E}'$ except that the predictor's oracle access to $\mathcal{O}^m_{\lambda_0 \cdot (1+\gamma)}$ is removed. We apply Lemma 1:

$$\widetilde{\mathbb{H}}_\infty(m \mid \mathbf{E}') \geqslant \widetilde{\mathbb{H}}_\infty(m \mid \mathbf{E}'') - \lambda_0 \cdot (1 + \gamma).$$

In the last experiment $\mathbf{E}''$ the predictor has no information about m and moreover h is independently chosen with respect to m, therefore:

$$\widetilde{\mathbb{H}}_\infty(m \mid \mathbf{E}'') = \log|\mathcal{M}| = \alpha.$$

$\square$

Lemma 4. *If Σ is (λ_0, λ_1)-FLR-sim-secure then $\widetilde{\mathbb{H}}_\infty(m|\mathbf{E}) \leqslant 6$.*

Proof. Assume that Σ is an $(\lambda_0, \lambda_1, \epsilon)$-FLR-sim-secure split-coding scheme for a negligible function ϵ and a slack parameter γ. Since $\mathcal{A}'$ is ppt there exists a ppt simulator $\mathcal{S}'$ such that:

$$\{\mathsf{Real}_{\mathcal{A}',\Sigma}^{\lambda_0,\lambda_1}(\kappa)\}_\kappa \overset{c}{\approx}_{\epsilon(\kappa)} \{\mathsf{Ideal}_{\mathcal{A}',\mathcal{S}',\gamma}^{\lambda_0,\lambda_1}(\kappa)\}_\kappa. \tag{1}$$

For the sake of the proof we first build a predictor which tries to guess m. We then use this predictor to prove the lemma. Let K be the extractor given by the knowledge soundness property of the argument of knowledge for the relation $\mathcal{R}^{\mathsf{hash}}$. Consider the following predictor $\mathcal{B}$ that takes as input $(h, h(m))$ and has oracle access to $\mathcal{O}_{\lambda_0 \cdot (1+\gamma)}^m$:

1. Pick two random tapes r_a, r_s for the adversary $\mathcal{A}'_1$ and the simulator $\mathcal{S}'$ and run both of them (with the respective randomness r_a, r_s) forwarding all the queries from $\mathcal{A}'_1$ to $\mathcal{S}'$ and from $\mathcal{S}'$ to $\mathcal{O}_{\lambda_0 \cdot (1+\gamma)}^m$. (The adversary $\mathcal{A}'_1$ starts by leaking the values h_l, h_r and an argument of knowledge for $(h_l, h_r) \in \mathcal{L}_{\mathcal{R}^{\mathsf{st}}}$. Eventually the adversary sends the message encode.)

2.L. **Extract $(h_l, L') \in \mathcal{R}^{\mathsf{hash}}$ using the knowledge extractor K.** For any $i \in [\tau]$, let $\bar{st}_i^L$ be the actual internal state of $\mathcal{S}'$ during the above run of $\mathcal{S}'$ and $\mathcal{A}'_1$ just before the i-th iteration of step 7 of $\mathcal{A}'_1$.

   Let $\mathcal{P}_{\mathsf{leak}}$ be a prover of Π for $\mathcal{R}^{\mathsf{hash}}$ that upon input the instance h_l, randomness r_p and auxiliary input $\bar{st}_i^L$ does the following:

   - Run a new instance $\mathcal{S}'_i$ of $\mathcal{S}'$ with the internal state set to $\bar{st}_i^L$.
   - Upon message y_j with $j \in [\rho]$ from the verifier, send to $\mathcal{S}'_i$ the message $(\mathsf{L}, \mathsf{Prove}(h_l, \cdot, y_1, \ldots, y_j; r_p))$.
   - Upon message (msg, f') from the simulator $\mathcal{S}'_i$ reply $\bot$ to $\mathcal{S}'_i$.

   Notice that $\mathcal{P}_{\mathsf{leak}}$ makes no leakage oracle queries.

   (i) If the value L' is unset, run the knowledge extractor K on the prover $\mathcal{P}_{\mathsf{leak}}$ on input h_l and auxiliary input st_i^L and proper randomness[1]. The knowledge extractor K outputs a value L' or aborts. If $h_l = h(L')$ then set L' otherwise we say that the i-th extraction aborts.
   (ii) Keep on running $\mathcal{A}'_1$ and $\mathcal{S}'$ as in the simulated experiment until reaching the next iteration.
   If all the extractions abort, the predictor aborts.

2.R. **Extract $(h_r, R') \in \mathcal{R}^{\mathsf{hash}}$ using the knowledge extractor K.** The procedure is the same as step 2.L of the predictor, for notational completeness let us denote with st_i^R the internal state of $\mathcal{S}'$ just before the i-th iteration of step 8.

3. The predictor outputs $m' := \mathsf{Dec}(L', R')$ as its own guess.

We compute the probability that $\mathcal{B}$ predicts m correctly. We set up some useful notation:

---

[1] The randomness for $\mathcal{P}_{\mathsf{leak}}$ is implicitly defined in the random string r_a.

- Let Ext_L (resp. Ext_R) be the event that K successfully extracts a value L' (resp. R').
- Let CohSt be the event $\{h(\mathsf{Dec}(L', R')) = h(m)\}$.
- Let Coll be the event $\{h(\mathsf{Dec}(L', R')) = h(m) \wedge \mathsf{Dec}(L', R') \neq m\}$.

Recall that $m' := \mathsf{Dec}(L', R')$ is the guess of $\mathcal{B}$. We can easily derive that:

$$\Pr\left[m' = m\right] = \Pr\left[\mathsf{Ext}_L \wedge \mathsf{Ext}_R \wedge \mathsf{CohSt} \wedge \neg\mathsf{Coll}\right] \tag{2}$$

In fact, Ext_L and Ext_R imply that L' and R' are well defined and the event $(\mathsf{CohSt} \wedge \neg\mathsf{Coll})$ implies that $\mathsf{Dec}(L', R') = m$.

Claim 1. $\Pr[\mathsf{Ext}_L] \geqslant \frac{1}{4} - \mathsf{negl}(\kappa)$.

Proof. Consider the execution of step 7 between the adversary and the simulator. Let $\bar{\mathbf{st}} = \bar{st}_1^L, \ldots, \bar{st}_\tau^L \in \{0, 1\}^*$ be a fixed observed value of the states of $\mathcal{S}'$ in the different rounds, i.e., $\bar{st}_i^L$ is the observed state of $\mathcal{S}'$ just before the i-th iteration in step 7.

We define a probability $\mathsf{Free}_L(\bar{st}_i^L)$ of the simulator not asking a leakage query in round i, i.e., the probability that the simulator queries its leakage oracle if run with fresh randomness starting in round i. We can assume without loss of generality that the randomness r_s of the simulator is part of $\bar{st}_i^L$. Therefore the probability is taken over just the randomness r_a of the adversary, m, h and the challenges used in the proof in round i. Notice that even though it might be fixed in $\bar{\mathbf{st}} = \bar{st}_1^L, \ldots, \bar{st}_\tau^L$ whether or not the simulator leaked in round i (this information might be contained in the final state $\bar{st}_\tau^L$), the probability $\mathsf{Free}_L(\bar{st}_i^L)$ might not be 0 or 1, as it is the probability that the simulator leaked in round i if we would rerun round i with fresh randomness of the adversary consistent with $\bar{st}_i^L$.

Recall that $\bar{\mathbf{st}} = \bar{st}_1^L, \ldots, \bar{st}_\tau^L \in \{0, 1\}^*$ is a fixed observed value of the states of $\mathcal{S}'$ in the different rounds. Let $\mathsf{Good}(\bar{\mathbf{st}})$ be a function which is 1 if

$$\exists i \in [\tau] : \mathsf{Free}_L(\bar{st}_i^L) \geqslant \frac{3}{4}$$

and which is 0 otherwise.[2] After having defined $\mathsf{Good}(\bar{\mathbf{st}})$ relative to a fixed observed sequence of states, we apply it to the random variable $\mathbf{st}$ describing the states of $\mathcal{S}'$ in a random run. When applied to $\mathbf{st}$, we simply write Good.

We use the law of total probability to condition to the event $\{\mathsf{Good} = 1\}$:

$$\Pr[\mathsf{Ext}_L] \geqslant \Pr[\mathsf{Ext}_L \mid \mathsf{Good} = 1] \cdot \Pr[\mathsf{Good} = 1] . \tag{3}$$

We will now focus on bounding $\Pr[\mathsf{Ext}_L \mid \mathsf{Good} = 1] \cdot \Pr[\mathsf{Good} = 1]$. We first bound $\Pr[\mathsf{Good} = 1]$ and then bound $\Pr[\mathsf{Ext}_L \mid \mathsf{Good} = 1]$. We first prove that

$$\Pr[\mathsf{Good} = 1] = 1 - \mathsf{negl}(\kappa) .$$

---

[2] Intuitively, Good is an indicator for a good event, that, as we will show, has overwhelming probability.

To see this notice that the simulator by the rules of the experiment never queries its leakage oracle in more than $\lambda_0 \cdot (1+\gamma)$ rounds: it is not allowed to leak more than $\lambda_0 \cdot (1+\gamma)$ bits and each leakage query counts as at least one bit. Therefore there are at least $\tau - \lambda_0 \cdot (1+\gamma)$ rounds in which the simulator did not query its oracle. If $\mathsf{Good} = 0$, then in each of these rounds the probability of leaking, before the round was executed, was at least $\frac{1}{4}$ and hence the probability of not leaking was at most $\frac{3}{4}$. Set $\lambda' := \lambda \cdot (1+\gamma)$, we can use a union bound to bound the probability of observing this event

$$\Pr[\mathsf{Good} = 0] \leq \binom{\tau}{\tau - \lambda'} \left(\frac{3}{4}\right)^{\tau - \lambda'} \leq \binom{\tau}{\lambda'} 2^{\log_2(3/4)(\tau - \lambda')} . \tag{4}$$

We now use that $\tau = 17\lambda_0 \cdot (1+\gamma) = 17\lambda'$ and that it holds for any constant $c \in (0,1)$ that $\lim_{n \to \infty} \binom{n}{cn} = 2^{H_2(c) \cdot n}$, where H_2 is the binary entropy function. We get that

$$\Pr[\mathsf{Good} = 0] \leq 2^{H_2(1/17)17\lambda'} 2^{\log_2(3/4)16\lambda'} = (2^{H_2(1/17)17 + \log_2(3/4)16})^{\lambda'} < 2^{-\lambda_0} .$$

We now bound $\Pr[\mathsf{Ext}_L | \mathsf{Good} = 1]$. Let $\mathsf{Ext}_L(i)$ be the event that K successfully extracts the value L' at the i-th iteration of the step 7 of the adversary $\mathcal{A}$. Let $\mathsf{Accept}_L(i)$ be the event that $\mathcal{P}_{\mathsf{leak}}$ on input h_l and auxiliary input st_i^L gives an accepting proof. It follows from knowledge soundness of Π that

$$\Pr\left[\mathsf{Ext}_L(i) | \mathsf{Good} = 1\right] \geqslant \Pr\left[\mathsf{Accept}_L(i) | \mathsf{Good} = 1\right] - \frac{1}{2} .$$

Let $\mathsf{Leak}_L(i)$ be the event that the simulator queries its leakage oracle in round i. It holds for all i that

$$\Pr\left[\mathsf{Accept}_L(i) | \mathsf{Good} = 1\right] \geq 1 - \Pr\left[\mathsf{Leak}_L(i) | \mathsf{Good} = 1\right] - \mathsf{negl}(\kappa) .$$

To see this assume that $\mathcal{P}_{\mathsf{leak}}$ upon message $(\mathtt{msg}, f')$ from $\mathcal{S}_i'$ would send to the simulator $f'(\omega \| m)$ instead of $\bot$. In that case it gives an acceptable proof with probability $1 - \mathsf{negl}(\kappa)$ as the adversary leaks an acceptable proof in the real world and the simulator simulates the real world up to negligible difference. Furthermore, sending $\bot$ when the simulator queries its oracle can only make a difference when it actually sends a query, which happens with probability $\Pr[\mathsf{Leak}_L(i)]$. Combining the above inequalities we get that

$$\Pr\left[\mathsf{Ext}_L(i) | \mathsf{Good} = 1\right] \geqslant 1 - \Pr\left[\mathsf{Leak}_L(i) | \mathsf{Good} = 1\right] - \mathsf{negl}(\kappa) - \frac{1}{2} .$$

When $\mathsf{Good} = 1$ there exists some round i^* such that $\mathsf{Free}_L(\bar{st}_{i^*}^L) \geqslant \frac{3}{4}$, which implies that $\Pr\left[\mathsf{Ext}_L(i^*) | \mathsf{Good} = 1\right] \geqslant \frac{3}{4} - \mathsf{negl}(\kappa) - \frac{1}{2}$. Clearly $\mathsf{Ext}_L(i^*)$ implies Ext_L, so we conclude that $\Pr\left[\mathsf{Ext}_L | \mathsf{Good} = 1\right] \geqslant \frac{1}{4} - \mathsf{negl}(\kappa)$.

Claim 2. $\Pr[\mathsf{Ext}_R | \mathsf{Ext}_L] \geqslant \frac{1}{4} - \mathsf{negl}(\kappa)$.

The proof proceeds similar to the proof of Claim 1, therefore it is omitted. The reason why the condition Ext_L does not matter is that the proof exploits only the knowledge soundness of the proof system. Whether the extraction of the left part succeeded or not does not remove the knowledge soundness of the proofs for the right part, as they are done *after* the proofs for the left part.

Claim 3. $\Pr[\mathsf{CohSt} \,|\mathsf{Ext}_L \wedge \mathsf{Ext}_R] \geqslant \frac{1}{2} - \mathsf{negl}(\kappa)$.

Proof. We reduce to the collision resistance property of h and the knowledge soundness of the argument system Π. Suppose that

$$\Pr[h(\mathsf{Dec}(L', R')) \neq h(m) \,|\mathsf{Ext}_L \wedge \mathsf{Ext}_R] \geqslant 1/\mathsf{poly}(\kappa)$$

Consider the following collision finder adversary $\mathcal{B}_{coll}(h)$:

1. Sample uniformly random $m \leftarrow_{\!\!\$} \mathcal{M}$ and random $h \leftarrow_{\!\!\$} \mathsf{Gen}^{\mathsf{CRH}}(1^\kappa)$;
2. Run an instance of the predictor $\mathcal{B}^{\mathcal{O}^m_{\lambda_0 \cdot (1+\gamma)}}(h, h(m))$. The predictor needs oracle access to $\mathcal{O}^m_{\lambda_0 \cdot (1+\gamma)}$ which can be simulated by $\mathcal{B}_{coll}(h)$.
3. Let L', R' be defined as by the execution of the predictor $\mathcal{B}$ and let r_a, r_s be the same randomness used by $\mathcal{B}$ in its step 1. Simulate an execution of $\mathcal{A}_1(h, h(m); r_a)$ and $\mathcal{S}'(1^\kappa; r_s)$ and break them just before the adversary leaks an argument of knowledge for $\mathcal{R}^{\mathsf{st}}$. Let st' be the internal state of $\mathcal{S}(1^\kappa; r_s)$. Let $\mathcal{P}'_{\mathsf{leak}}$ be a prover for Π for the relation $\mathcal{R}^{\mathsf{st}}$ that upon input the instance $(\mathsf{crs}, h(L'), h(R'), h(m))$ and auxiliary input $z := (st', m)$ does the following:
   - Run an $\mathcal{S}'$ with the internal state set to st'. Sample a random string r_p long enough to specify all random choices done by the prover of Π.
   - Upon message y_j with $j \in [\rho]$ from the verifier, send to $\mathcal{S}'$ the message $(\mathsf{rand}, \mathsf{Prove}((\mathsf{crs}, h(L'), h(R'), h(m)), \mathsf{Enc}(\mathsf{crs}, \cdot \;; \cdot), y_1, \ldots, y_j; r_p))$. (The next-message function of the prover of Π that uses as input the witness $\mathsf{Enc}(\mathsf{crs}, m; \omega)$ and the internal randomness set to r_p.)
   - Upon message (msg, f') from the simulator $\mathcal{S}'$ reply forwarding $f'(m)$.
4. Run K_{st} on the prover $\mathcal{P}'_{\mathsf{leak}}$ on input $(\mathsf{crs}, h(L'), h(R'), h(m))$ and auxiliary input z. Let L'', R'' be the witness output by the extractor.
5. If $L' \neq L''$ output (L', L'') else (R', R'').

It is easy to check that $\mathcal{B}_{coll}$ simulates perfectly the randomized experiment **E**. Therefore:

$$\Pr[h(\mathsf{Dec}(L', R')) \neq h(m)] \geqslant \tag{5}$$
$$\geqslant \Pr[h(\mathsf{Dec}(L', R')) \neq h(m) \,|\mathsf{Ext}_L \wedge \mathsf{Ext}_R] \Pr[\mathsf{Ext}_L \wedge \mathsf{Ext}_R]$$
$$\geqslant 1/\mathsf{poly}(\kappa) \cdot (\tfrac{1}{16} - \mathsf{negl}(\kappa))$$

On the other hand, the extractor K_{st} succeeds with probability at least $1 - \mathsf{negl}(\kappa) - \frac{1}{2}$. Therefore, L'' and R'' are such that $h(L'') = h(L')$, $h(R'') = h(R')$ and $h(\mathsf{Dec}(L'', R'')) = h(m)$.

Combining the latter and the statement of the event in Eq. (5), we have $h(\mathsf{Dec}(L', R')) \neq h(m) = h(\mathsf{Dec}(L'', R''))$ which implies that either $L'' \neq L'$ or $R'' \neq R'$. Lastly, notice that $\mathcal{B}_{coll}$ is an expected polynomial time algorithm. However we can make it polynomial time by aborting if the number of step exceeds some fixed polynomial. By setting the polynomial big enough the probability of $\mathcal{B}_{coll}$ finding a collision is still noticeable.

Claim 4. $\Pr\left[\mathsf{Coll} \mid \mathsf{CohSt} \wedge \mathsf{Ext}_L \wedge \mathsf{Ext}_R\right] \leqslant \mathsf{negl}(\kappa)$.

Recall that Coll is the event that $h(m) = h(m')$ but $m \neq m'$. It can be easily verified that under collision resistance of h the claim holds, therefore the proof is omitted. Summarizing, we have:

$$\Pr[m' = m] = \Pr\left[\mathsf{Ext}_L \wedge \mathsf{Ext}_R \wedge \mathsf{CohSt} \wedge \neg\mathsf{Coll}\right]$$
$$\geqslant \left(\tfrac{1}{16} - \mathsf{negl}(\kappa)\right) \cdot \left(\tfrac{1}{2} - \mathsf{negl}(\kappa)\right) \cdot \left(1 - \mathsf{negl}(\kappa)\right) \geqslant \tfrac{1}{64}.$$

which implies the statement of the lemma.

We conclude the proof of the theorem noticing that, if Σ is (λ_0, λ_1)-FLR-sim-secure split-coding scheme by the parameter given in the statement of the theorem we have that Lemmas 3 and 4 are in contraction. $\qquad\square$

Remark 1. The result can be generalized for a weaker version of the split-state model where the codeword is split in many parts. The probability that the predictor in Lemma 4 guesses the message m degrades exponentially in the number of splits (the adversary needs to leak one hash for each split and then executes step 7 for any split). Therefore, the impossibility holds when the number of splits is $o((\alpha - \lambda_0(1 + \gamma))/\ell_{\mathsf{CRH}})$. We present the theorem, as stated here, for sake of simplicity.

The Case of Constant-Size Message. For space reason we defer the impossibility result for the case of constant-size message fully leakage resilient codes the full version of the paper [18].

5   Feasibility Results

In this section we give two feasibility results for weaker models of security.

5.1   The Inner-Product Extractor is a NC^0-Fully LR Code

We start by giving a well-known characterization of the class NC^0.

Lemma 5. *Let* $f \in \mathsf{NC}^0$ *where* $f := \left(f^n : \{0,1\}^n \to \{0,1\}^{m(n)}\right)_{n \in \mathbb{N}}$ *for a function* m. *For any* n *there exists a value* $c = O(m)$, *a set* $\{i_1, \ldots, i_c\} \subseteq [n]$ *of indexes and a function* g *such that for any* $x \in \{0,1\}^n$, $f(x) = g(x_{i_1}, x_{i_2}, \ldots, x_{i_c})$.

The lemma above shows that any function in NC^0 with output length m such that $m(n)/n = o(1)$ cannot be collision resistant, because an adversary can guess an index $i \notin \{i_1, \ldots, i_c\}$ and output $0^n, (0^{i-1}\|1\|0^{n-i})$ as collision.

Let $\mathbb{F}$ be a finite field and let $\Phi_{\mathbb{F}}^n = (\mathsf{Enc}, \mathsf{Dec})$ be as follows:

- Enc on input $m \in \mathbb{F}$ picks uniformly random $\boldsymbol{L}, \boldsymbol{R} \leftarrow_{\$} \mathbb{F}^n$ under the condition that $\langle \boldsymbol{L}, \boldsymbol{R} \rangle = m$.

– Dec on input L, R outputs $\langle L, R \rangle$.

Theorem 2 (from [15]). *The encoding scheme $\Phi_{\mathbb{F}}^n$ as defined above for $|\mathbb{F}| = \Omega(\kappa)$ is a $(0, 0.3 \cdot n \log |\mathbb{F}||)$-FLR-SIM-secure for $n > 20$.*

We will show now that the scheme is also fully leakage resilient for NC^0-bounded adversaries.

Theorem 3. *For any $n \in \mathbb{N}$ and $n > 20$ there exists a positive constant $\delta \in \mathbb{R}$ such that, for any λ_0, λ_1 such that $\delta \cdot \lambda_0 + \lambda_1 < 0.3 \cdot |\mathbb{F}^n|$ the encoding scheme $\Phi_{\mathbb{F}}^n$ is $(NC^0, \lambda_0, \lambda_1)$-FLR-SIM-secure.*

We reduce an adversary $\mathcal{A}$ for the $(NC^0, \lambda_0, \lambda_1)$-FLR-SIM game (with $\lambda_0 > 0$) to an adversary for the $(0, \delta \cdot \lambda_0 + \lambda_1)$-FLR-SIM game. Given Lemma 5 and the structure of $\Phi_{\mathbb{F}}^n$, the task is very easy. In fact, the randomness ω picked by Enc can be parsed as $(L_0, \ldots, L_{n-1}, R_0, \ldots, R_{n-2})$. Whenever the adversary $\mathcal{A}$ queries the oracle $\mathcal{O}_{\lambda_0}^\omega$ the reduction splits the leakage function in two pieces and leak from $\mathcal{O}^L$ and $\mathcal{O}^R$ the relative piece of information necessary to compute the leakage function. Because of Lemma 5 we know that for each function the amount of leakage done on the two states is bounded by a constant δ.

Proof. Given a vector $X \in \mathbb{F}^n$ let $\mathsf{bit}(X)_i$ be the i-th bit of a canonical bit-representation of X. Given $\mathcal{A} = (\mathcal{A}_0, \mathcal{A}_1)$ we define a new adversary $\mathcal{A}'$ that works as follows:

0. Instantiate an execution of $(m, st) \leftarrow_{\$} \mathcal{A}_0(1^\kappa)$;
1. Execute $\mathcal{A}_1(st)$ and reply to the leakage oracle queries it makes as follow:
   – Upon message (rand, f) from $\mathcal{A}_1$, let I be the set of indexes such that f depends on I only. Define $I_L := I \cap [qn]$ and $I_R := I \cap [qn + 1, 2qn]$. Define the functions:

   $$f_L(L) := (\mathsf{bit}(L)_i \text{ for } i \in I_L) \text{ and } f_R(R) := (\mathsf{bit}(R)_i \text{ for } i \in I_R).$$

   Send the queries (L, f_L) and (R, f_R) and let lk_L and lk_R be the answers to the queries. Hardwire such values and evaluate the function f on input m. Namely, compute $\mathsf{lk}_f := f(f_L(L), f_R(R), m)$ and send it back to $\mathcal{A}_1(st)$.
   – Upon message (X, f) where $\mathsf{X} \in \{\mathsf{L}, \mathsf{R}\}$ from $\mathcal{A}_1$ forward the message.

W.l.o.g. assume that every leakage query to $\mathcal{O}_{\lambda_0}^{\omega \| m}$ has output length 1 and that the adversary makes exactly λ_0 queries. By Lemma 5 there exists a constant $\delta \in \mathbb{N}$ such that for the i-th leakage query made by $\mathcal{A}_1$ to $\mathcal{O}_{\lambda_0}^{\omega \| m}$ the adversary $\mathcal{A}'$ leaks δ bits from $\mathcal{O}_{\lambda_1}^L, \mathcal{O}_{\lambda_1}^R$. By construction:

$$\{\mathsf{Real}_{\mathcal{A}, \Phi_{\mathbb{F}}^n}^{\lambda_0, \lambda_1}(\kappa)\}_{\kappa \in \mathbb{N}} \equiv \{\mathsf{Real}_{\mathcal{A}', \Phi_{\mathbb{F}}^n}^{0, \lambda_1 + \delta \cdot \lambda_0}(\kappa)\}_{\kappa \in \mathbb{N}}.$$

Let $\mathcal{S}'$ be the simulator for the adversary $\mathcal{A}'$ as provided by Theorem 2, thus:

$$\{\mathsf{Real}_{\mathcal{A}', \Phi_{\mathbb{F}}^n}^{0, \lambda_1 + \delta \cdot \lambda_0}(\kappa)\}_{\kappa \in \mathbb{N}} \approx_{\mathsf{negl}(\kappa)} \{\mathsf{Ideal}_{\mathcal{A}', \mathcal{S}'}^{0, \lambda_1 + \delta \cdot \lambda_0}(\kappa)\}_{\kappa \in \mathbb{N}}.$$

Let $\mathcal{S}$ be defined as the machine that runs the adversary $\mathcal{A}'$ interacting with the simulator $\mathcal{S}'$. Notice that:

$$\{\mathsf{Ideal}_{\mathcal{A}',\mathcal{S}'}^{0,\lambda_1+\delta\cdot\lambda_0}(\kappa)\}_{\kappa\in\mathbb{N}} \equiv \{\mathsf{Ideal}_{\mathcal{A},\mathcal{S}}^{\lambda_0,\lambda_1}(\kappa)\}_{\kappa\in\mathbb{N}}.$$

This conclude the proof of the theorem.   □

The proof exploits only marginally the structure of $\Phi_{\mathbb{F}}^n$. It is not hard to see that the theorem can be generalized for any coding scheme (Gen, Enc, Dec) where for any message $m \in \mathcal{M}$ and any crs the function $\mathsf{Enc}(\mathsf{crs}, m; \cdot)$ is invertible in NC^0. We present the theorem, as stated here, only for sake of concreteness. Moreover, the The construction is secure under the slightly stronger definition where the adversary does not lose access to $\mathcal{O}_{\lambda_0}^{\omega\|m}$ after having sent the message encode.

5.2 A Compiler from LRC to FLRC

Given a (α, β)-split-coding scheme $\Sigma = (\mathsf{Gen}, \mathsf{Enc}, \mathsf{Dec})$ with randomness space $\mathcal{R}$, let $\mathcal{H}_{r,t}$ denote a family of efficiently computable t-wise independent hash function with domain $\{0,1\}^r$ and co-domain $\mathcal{R}$. We define $\Sigma' = (\mathsf{Gen}', \mathsf{Enc}', \mathsf{Dec}' := \mathsf{Dec})$:

- Gen$'$ on input 1^κ executes crs $\leftarrow$ $\mathsf{Gen}(1^\kappa)$ and samples a function $h \leftarrow$ $\mathcal{H}_{r,t}$. It outputs crs$' = (h, \mathsf{crs})$.
- Enc$'$ on input a message $m \in \mathcal{M}$ and (h, crs) picks a random string $\omega \leftarrow$ $\{0,1\}^r$ and returns as output $\mathsf{Enc}(\mathsf{crs}, m; h(\omega))$.

Theorem 4. *For any encoding scheme Σ and any leakage class $\mathcal{F}$, if Σ is $(0, \lambda_1, \epsilon)$-FLR-SIM-secure then Σ' is $(\mathcal{F}, \lambda_0, \lambda_1, 3\epsilon)$-FLR-SIM-secure for any $0 \leqslant \lambda_0 < \alpha$ whenever:*

$$r \geqslant \lambda_0 + \lambda_1 + 2\log(1/\epsilon) + \log(t) + 3,$$

$$t \geqslant \lambda_0 \cdot \log|\mathcal{F}| + \alpha + \lambda_0 + \lambda_1 + 2\log(1/\epsilon).$$

We leverage on the fact that with overwhelming probability a t-wise independent hash function (where t is set as in the statement of the theorem) is a deterministic strong randomness extractor for the class of of sources defined by adaptively leaking from the randomness using functions from $\mathcal{F}$. We can, therefore, reduce an adversary for the $(\mathcal{F}, \lambda_0, \lambda_1)$-FLR-SIM game to an adversary for the $(0, \lambda_1)$-FLR-SIM game. The reduction samples a uniformly random string $\omega' \leftarrow$ $\{0,1\}^r$ and replies all the leakage oracle queries on the randomness by applying the the leakage function on ω'. By the property of the randomness extractor, this leakage is indistinguishable from to the leakage on the real randomness. It is not hard to see that the above result can be generalized to every class of leakage that allows an efficient average-case strong randomness extractor [14]. We present the result, as stated here, only for sake of concreteness.

Proof. Given an adversary $\mathcal{A}'$ against Σ', we define a ppt adversary $\mathcal{A} = (\mathcal{A}_0, \mathcal{A}_1)$ against Σ as follow:

- **Adversary $\mathcal{A}_0$:** On input crs, it picks at random $h \leftarrow_\$ \mathcal{H}_{r,t}$, a random string $\omega \leftarrow_\$ \{0,1\}^r$ and a random string $r \leftarrow_\$ \{0,1\}^{p(\kappa)}$ for a polynomial p that bounds the running time of $\mathcal{A}'$ and runs $\mathcal{A}'_0(1^\kappa; r)$. Upon leakage oracle query f to $\mathcal{O}^\omega_{\lambda_0}$ from $\mathcal{A}'_0$, it replies $f(\omega)$. Eventually, the adversary $\mathcal{A}'_0$ outputs a a message $m \in \mathcal{M}$ and a state value st, $\mathcal{A}_0$ outputs m and $st' = (st, h)$.
- **Adversary $\mathcal{A}_1$:** On inputs $st' = (st, h)$ and crs, it runs $\mathcal{A}'_1(st, (h, \mathrm{crs}))$ and forwards all the queries made by $\mathcal{A}'_1$.

W.l.o.g. the adversary $\mathcal{A}_0$ makes the sequence $(\mathbf{rand}, f_1), (\mathbf{rand}, f_2), \ldots,$ $(\mathbf{rand}, f_{\lambda_0})$ of queries. Let $\boldsymbol{f} := (f_1, \ldots, f_{\lambda_0}) \in \mathcal{F}^{\lambda_0}$, therefore view of $\mathcal{A}'$ in the real experiment is:

$$\mathsf{Real}^{\lambda_0, \lambda_1}_{\mathcal{A}', \Sigma'}(\kappa) = \left(r, (h, \mathrm{crs}), \boldsymbol{f}(\omega), \mathsf{lk}_L, \mathsf{lk}_R\right)$$

On the other hand, by definition of the adversary $\mathcal{A}$, the view provided to $\mathcal{A}'$ is:

$$\mathsf{Hyb}(\kappa) = \left(r, \boldsymbol{f}(\omega), (h, \mathrm{crs}), \mathsf{lk}_{L'}, \mathsf{lk}_{R'}\right),$$

where $L', R' = \mathsf{Enc}(\mathrm{crs}, m; \omega')$ and $\omega \leftarrow_\$ \{0,1\}^r$ and $\omega' \leftarrow_\$ \mathcal{R}$.

Claim 5 $\left\{\mathsf{Real}^{\lambda_0, \lambda_1}_{\mathcal{A}', \Sigma'}(\kappa)\right\}_{\kappa \in \mathbb{N}} \approx_{2\epsilon(\kappa)} \left\{\mathsf{Hyb}(\kappa)\right\}_{\kappa \in \mathbb{N}}.$

Before proceeding with the proof of the claim we show how the theorem follows. Let $\mathcal{S}$ be the simulator for the adversary $\mathcal{A}$ as given by the hypothesis of the theorem:

$$\{\mathsf{Real}^{0, \lambda_1}_{\mathcal{A}, \Sigma}(\kappa)\}_{\kappa \in \mathbb{N}} \overset{c}{\approx}_{\epsilon(\kappa)} \{\mathsf{Ideal}^{0, \lambda_1}_{\mathcal{A}, \mathcal{S}}(\kappa)\}_{\kappa \in \mathbb{N}}. \tag{6}$$

Let $\mathcal{S}'$ be defined as the adversary $\mathcal{A}$ interacting with the simulator $\mathcal{S}$. Therefore, if we consider $\mathsf{Ideal}^{0, \lambda_1}_{\mathcal{A}, \mathcal{S}}(\kappa) = \left((r, h, \omega), \mathrm{crs}, \widetilde{\mathsf{lk}}_L, \widetilde{\mathsf{lk}}_R\right)$, it holds that:

$$\mathsf{Ideal}^{\lambda_0, \lambda_1}_{\mathcal{A}', \mathcal{S}'}(\kappa) = \left(r, (h, \mathrm{crs}), \boldsymbol{f}(\omega), \widetilde{\mathsf{lk}}_L, \widetilde{\mathsf{lk}}_R\right).$$

It follows from a simple reduction to Eq. (6) that:

$$\left\{\mathsf{Hyb}(\kappa)\right\}_{\kappa \in \mathbb{N}} \overset{c}{\approx}_{\epsilon(\kappa)} \{\mathsf{Ideal}^{\lambda_0, \lambda_1}_{\mathcal{A}', \mathcal{S}'}(\kappa)\}_{\kappa \in \mathbb{N}}.$$

We conclude by applying Claim 5 to equation above. $\qquad \square$

Proof (of the claim). Since we are proving statistical closeness we can de-randomize the adversary $\mathcal{A}'$ by setting the random string that maximize the distinguishability of the two random variables. Similarly we can de-randomize the common reference string generation algorithm Gen. Therefore, w.l.o.g., we can consider them fixed in the views.

Recall that the adversary $\mathcal{A}$ defines for $\mathcal{A}'$ a hybrid environment where the leakage on the randomness is on $\omega \leftarrow_\$ \{0,1\}^r$ but the codeword is instantiated using fresh randomness $\omega' \leftarrow_\$ \mathcal{R}$. We prove the stronger statement that the two views are statistical close with high probability over the choice of the t-wise hash function h. For convenience, we define two tuples of random variables:

$$\mathsf{Real}_h := \left(\boldsymbol{f}(\omega), \mathsf{lk}_L, \mathsf{lk}_R \,\middle|\, (L, R) = \mathsf{Enc}(\mathrm{crs}, m;\, h(\omega))\right)$$
$$\mathsf{Hyb}_h := \left(\boldsymbol{f}(\omega), \mathsf{lk}_{L'}, \mathsf{lk}_{R'} \,\middle|\, (L', R') = \mathsf{Enc}(\mathrm{crs}, m;\, \omega')\right)$$

Notice that in both distributions above the function $\boldsymbol{f}$ are random variable. For any fixed sequence of functions $\boldsymbol{f} = f_0, \ldots, f_{\lambda_0}$, let $\mathsf{Real}_{h,\boldsymbol{f}}$ (resp. $\mathsf{Hyb}_{h,\boldsymbol{f}}$) be the distribution Real_h (resp. Hyb_h) where the leakage functions are set. We prove that

$$\Pr[\mathsf{Hyb}_h \approx_\epsilon \mathsf{Real}_h] \geqslant 1 - \epsilon \,,$$

where the probability is over the choice of $h \leftarrow^{\$} \mathcal{H}_{r,t}$. Let Bad be the event $\{\mathsf{Hyb}_h \not\approx_\epsilon \mathsf{Real}_h\}$.

$$\Pr[\mathsf{Bad}] \leq \Pr_{h \leftarrow^{\$} \mathcal{H}_{r,t}} \left[\exists f_1, \ldots, f_{\lambda_0} \in \mathcal{F}, m \in \mathcal{M} : \mathsf{Real}_{h,\boldsymbol{f}} \not\approx_\epsilon \mathsf{Hyb}_{h,\boldsymbol{f}} \right]$$

$$\leqslant \sum_{\boldsymbol{f} \in \mathcal{F}^{\lambda_0}} \sum_{m \in \mathcal{M}} \Pr_{h \leftarrow^{\$} \mathcal{H}_{r,t}} \left[\sum_v \left| \Pr_\omega[\mathsf{Real}_{h,\boldsymbol{f}} = v] - \Pr_{\omega,\omega'}[\mathsf{Hyb}_{h,\boldsymbol{f}} = v] \right| > 2\epsilon \right]$$

Let $\lambda := \lambda_0 + \lambda_1$ and let $p_v := \Pr_{\omega,\omega'}[\mathsf{Hyb}_{h,\boldsymbol{f}} = v]$. Define $\tilde{p}_v := \max\{p_v, 2^{-\lambda}\}$. Note that:

$$\sum_{v \in \{0,1\}^\lambda} \tilde{p}_v \leqslant \sum_v p_v + \sum_v 2^{-\lambda} \leqslant 2$$

Define the indicator random variable $Y_{\bar{\omega},v}$ for the event $\{\mathsf{Real}_{h,\boldsymbol{f}} = v \mid \omega = \bar{\omega}\}$, where the randomness is over the choice of $h \leftarrow^{\$} \mathcal{H}_{r,t}$.

For any view v, the random variables $\{Y_{\bar{\omega},v}\}_{\bar{\omega} \in \{0,1\}^r}$ are t-wise independent. Moreover, $\mathbb{E}[\sum_{\bar{\omega} \in \{0,1\}^r} Y_{\bar{\omega},v}] = 2^r p_v$. In fact, for any $\bar{h} \in \mathcal{H}$, any $\bar{\omega} \in \{0,1\}^r$ and any $v \in \{0,1\}^\lambda$ it holds that $\Pr_h[\mathsf{Real}_{h,\boldsymbol{f}} = v \mid \omega = \bar{\omega}] = \Pr_{\omega'}[\mathsf{Hyb}_{h,\boldsymbol{f}} = v \mid \omega = \bar{\omega}, h = \bar{h}]$. It follows that

$$\Pr_{h \leftarrow^{\$} \mathcal{H}_{r,t}} \left[\sum_v \left| \Pr_\omega[\mathsf{Real}_{h,\boldsymbol{f}} = v] - p_v \right| > 2\epsilon \right]$$

$$\leqslant \Pr_{h \leftarrow^{\$} \mathcal{H}_{r,t}} \left[\exists v : \left| \Pr_\omega[\mathsf{Real}_{h,\boldsymbol{f}} = v] - p_v \right| > \epsilon \cdot \tilde{p}_v \right]$$

$$\leqslant \sum_{v \in \{0,1\}^\lambda} \Pr_{h \leftarrow^{\$} \mathcal{H}_{r,t}} \left[\left| \Pr_\omega[\mathsf{Real}_{h,\boldsymbol{f}} = v] - p_v \right| > \epsilon \cdot \tilde{p}_v \right]$$

$$\leqslant \sum_{v \in \{0,1\}^\lambda} \Pr_{h \leftarrow^{\$} \mathcal{H}_{r,t}} \left[\left| \sum_{\bar{\omega}} Y_{\bar{\omega},v} - 2^r p_v \right| > 2^r \epsilon \cdot \tilde{p}_v \right]$$

$$\leqslant \sum_{v \in \{0,1\}^\lambda} 8 \left(\frac{t \cdot 2^r p_v + t^2}{(2^r \epsilon \cdot \tilde{p}_v)^2} \right)^{t/2} \tag{7}$$

$$\leqslant \sum_{v \in \{0,1\}^\lambda} 8 \left(\frac{2t \cdot 2^r \tilde{p}_v}{(2^r \epsilon \cdot \tilde{p}_v)^2} \right)^{t/2} \tag{8}$$

$$\leqslant 2^\lambda \cdot 8 \left(\frac{2t}{2^{r-\lambda} \cdot \epsilon^2} \right)^{t/2} \tag{9}$$

where Eq. (7) follows by Lemma 2 and Eqs. (8) and (9) follow because $2^r \cdot \tilde{p}_v \geqslant 2^{r-\lambda} \geqslant t$. Combining all together we have:

$$\Pr[\mathsf{Bad}] \leqslant |\mathcal{F}|^{\lambda_0} \cdot |\mathcal{M}| \cdot 2^{\lambda_0 + \lambda_1} \cdot 8 \left(\frac{2t}{2^{r-\lambda_0-\lambda_1} \cdot \epsilon^2} \right)^{t/2}.$$

To make the above negligible we can set:

$$r \geqslant \lambda_0 + \lambda_1 + 2\log(1/\epsilon) + \log(t) + 3,$$

$$t \geqslant \lambda_0 \cdot \log|\mathcal{F}| + \alpha + \lambda_0 + \lambda_1 + 2\log 1/\epsilon.$$

6   Conclusion and Open Problems

We defined the notion of Fully Leakage Resilient Codes. Although natural, our definition is too strong to be met in the popular split-state model. Fortunately, by restricting the class of leakage from the randomness we were able to achieve two different feasibility results.

There is still a gap between our impossibility result and the possibility results. As we showed, in the plain model the problem of finding a FLR Code in the split-state model is strictly connected to the complexity of computing the next-message function of a prover of a succinct argument of knowledge and to the complexity of computing an collision resistant hash function. A construction of FLR code for, let say, the class NC provides, therefore, a complexity lower bound for at least one of the two mentioned tasks and it would be a very surprising result. An interesting open problem is to show FLR codes for AC^0.

Our definition restricts the simulator to be efficient, this seems a natural restriction and it is necessary for our impossibility result. It would be interesting to show either a FLR code with unbounded-time simulator or to generalize our impossibility result in this setting.

Acknowledgement. The authors acknowledge support by European Research Council Starting Grant 279447. The authors acknowledge support from the Danish National Research Foundation and The National Science Foundation of China (under the grant 61361136003) for the Sino-Danish Center for the Theory of Interactive Computation.

References

1. Aggarwal, D., Dziembowski, S., Kazana, T., Obremski, M.: Leakage-resilient non-malleable codes. In: Dodis, Y., Nielsen, J.B. (eds.) TCC 2015. LNCS, vol. 9014, pp. 398–426. Springer, Heidelberg (2015). doi:10.1007/978-3-662-46494-6_17
2. Alwen, J., Dodis, Y., Wichs, D.: Leakage-resilient public-key cryptography in the bounded-retrieval model. In: Halevi, S. (ed.) CRYPTO 2009. LNCS, vol. 5677, pp. 36–54. Springer, Heidelberg (2009). doi:10.1007/978-3-642-03356-8_3
3. Ananth, P., Boneh, D., Garg, S., Sahai, A., Zhandry, M.: Differing-inputs obfuscation and applications. Cryptology ePrint Archive, Report 2013/689 (2013). http://ia.cr/2013/689
4. Ananth, P., Goyal, V., Pandey, O.: Interactive proofs under continual memory leakage. In: Garay, J.A., Gennaro, R. (eds.) CRYPTO 2014. LNCS, vol. 8617, pp. 164–182. Springer, Heidelberg (2014). doi:10.1007/978-3-662-44381-1_10

5. Andrychowicz, M., Masny, D., Persichetti, E.: Leakage-resilient cryptography over large finite fields: theory and practice. In: Malkin, T., Kolesnikov, V., Lewko, A.B., Polychronakis, M. (eds.) ACNS 2015. LNCS, vol. 9092, pp. 655–674. Springer, Heidelberg (2015). doi:10.1007/978-3-319-28166-7_32

6. Bellare, M., Rompel, J.: Randomness-efficient oblivious sampling. In: FOCS, pp. 276–287 (1994)

7. Bitansky, N., Canetti, R., Halevi, S.: Leakage-tolerant interactive protocols. In: Cramer, R. (ed.) TCC 2012. LNCS, vol. 7194, pp. 266–284. Springer, Heidelberg (2012). doi:10.1007/978-3-642-28914-9_15

8. Bitansky, N., Dachman-Soled, D., Lin, H.: Leakage-tolerant computation with input-independent preprocessing. In: Garay, J.A., Gennaro, R. (eds.) CRYPTO 2014. LNCS, vol. 8617, pp. 146–163. Springer, Heidelberg (2014). doi:10.1007/978-3-662-44381-1_9

9. Boyle, E., Chung, K.-M., Pass, R.: On extractability obfuscation. In: Lindell, Y. (ed.) TCC 2014. LNCS, vol. 8349, pp. 52–73. Springer, Heidelberg (2014). doi:10.1007/978-3-642-54242-8_3

10. Boyle, E., Goldwasser, S., Kalai, Y.T.: Leakage-resilient coin tossing. Distrib. Comput. 27(3), 147–164 (2014)

11. Boyle, E., Segev, G., Wichs, D.: Fully leakage-resilient signatures. J. Cryptol. 26(3), 513–558 (2013)

12. Davì, F., Dziembowski, S., Venturi, D.: Leakage-resilient storage. In: Garay, J.A., Prisco, R. (eds.) SCN 2010. LNCS, vol. 6280, pp. 121–137. Springer, Heidelberg (2010). doi:10.1007/978-3-642-15317-4_9

13. Dodis, Y., Lewko, A.B., Waters, B., Wichs, D.: Storing secrets on continually leaky devices. In: FOCS, pp. 688–697 (2011)

14. Dodis, Y., Ostrovsky, R., Reyzin, L., Smith, A.D.: Fuzzy extractors: how to generate strong keys from biometrics and other noisy data. SIAM J. Comput. 38(1), 97–139 (2008)

15. Dziembowski, S., Faust, S.: Leakage-resilient cryptography from the inner-product extractor. In: Lee, D.H., Wang, X. (eds.) ASIACRYPT 2011. LNCS, vol. 7073, pp. 702–721. Springer, Heidelberg (2011). doi:10.1007/978-3-642-25385-0_38

16. Dziembowski, S., Pietrzak, K.: Leakage-resilient cryptography. In: FOCS, pp. 293–302 (2008)

17. Dziembowski, S., Pietrzak, K., Wichs, D.: Non-malleable codes. In: ICS, pp. 434–452 (2010)

18. Faonio, A., Nielsen, J.B.: Fully leakage-resilient codes. IACR Cryptology ePrint Archive 2015:1151 (2015)

19. Faonio, A., Nielsen, J.B., Venturi, D.: Mind your coins: fully leakage-resilient signatures with graceful degradation. IACR Cryptology ePrint Archive 2014:913 (2014)

20. Faonio, A., Nielsen, J.B., Venturi, D.: Predictable arguments of knowledge (2015). http://ia.cr/2015/740

21. Faust, S., Mukherjee, P., Nielsen, J.B., Venturi, D.: Continuous non-malleable codes. In: Lindell, Y. (ed.) TCC 2014. LNCS, vol. 8349, pp. 465–488. Springer, Heidelberg (2014). doi:10.1007/978-3-642-54242-8_20

22. Faust, S., Mukherjee, P., Nielsen, J.B., Venturi, D.: A tamper and leakage resilient von neumann architecture. In: Katz, J. (ed.) PKC 2015. LNCS, vol. 9020, pp. 579–603. Springer, Heidelberg (2015). doi:10.1007/978-3-662-46447-2_26

23. Faust, S., Mukherjee, P., Venturi, D., Wichs, D.: Efficient non-malleable codes and key-derivation for poly-size tampering circuits. In: Nguyen, P.Q., Oswald, E. (eds.) EUROCRYPT 2014. LNCS, vol. 8441, pp. 111–128. Springer, Heidelberg (2014). doi:10.1007/978-3-642-55220-5_7

24. Faust, S., Rabin, T., Reyzin, L., Tromer, E., Vaikuntanathan, V.: Protecting circuits from leakage: the computationally-bounded and noisy cases. In: Gilbert, H. (ed.) EUROCRYPT 2010. LNCS, vol. 6110, pp. 135–156. Springer, Heidelberg (2010). doi:10.1007/978-3-642-13190-5_7

25. Garg, S., Gentry, C., Halevi, S., Wichs, D.: On the implausibility of differing-inputs obfuscation and extractable witness encryption with auxiliary input. In: Garay, J.A., Gennaro, R. (eds.) CRYPTO 2014. LNCS, vol. 8616, pp. 518–535. Springer, Heidelberg (2014). doi:10.1007/978-3-662-44371-2_29

26. Garg, S., Jain, A., Sahai, A.: Leakage-resilient zero knowledge. In: Rogaway, P. (ed.) CRYPTO 2011. LNCS, vol. 6841, pp. 297–315. Springer, Heidelberg (2011). doi:10.1007/978-3-642-22792-9_17

27. Halevi, S., Lin, H.: After-the-fact leakage in public-key encryption. In: Ishai, Y. (ed.) TCC 2011. LNCS, vol. 6597, pp. 107–124. Springer, Heidelberg (2011). doi:10.1007/978-3-642-19571-6_8

28. Heyse, S., Kiltz, E., Lyubashevsky, V., Paar, C., Pietrzak, K.: Lapin: an efficient authentication protocol based on ring-lpn. In: Canteaut, A. (ed.) FSE 2012. LNCS, vol. 7549, pp. 346–365. Springer, Heidelberg (2012). doi:10.1007/978-3-642-34047-5_20

29. Jafargholi, Z., Wichs, D.: Tamper detection and continuous non-malleable codes. In: Dodis, Y., Nielsen, J.B. (eds.) TCC 2015. LNCS, vol. 9014, pp. 451–480. Springer, Heidelberg (2015). doi:10.1007/978-3-662-46494-6_19

30. Katz, J., Vaikuntanathan, V.: Signature schemes with bounded leakage resilience. In: Matsui, M. (ed.) ASIACRYPT 2009. LNCS, vol. 5912, pp. 703–720. Springer, Heidelberg (2009). doi:10.1007/978-3-642-10366-7_41

31. Kilian, J.: A note on efficient zero-knowledge proofs and arguments (extended abstract). In: STOC, pp. 723–732 (1992)

32. Kocher, P.C.: Timing attacks on implementations of Diffie-Hellman, RSA, DSS, and other systems. In: Koblitz, N. (ed.) CRYPTO 1996. LNCS, vol. 1109, pp. 104–113. Springer, Heidelberg (1996). doi:10.1007/3-540-68697-5_9

33. Kocher, P., Jaffe, J., Jun, B.: Differential power analysis. In: Wiener, M. (ed.) CRYPTO 1999. LNCS, vol. 1666, pp. 388–397. Springer, Heidelberg (1999). doi:10.1007/3-540-48405-1_25

34. Liu, F.-H., Lysyanskaya, A.: Tamper and leakage resilience in the split-state model. In: Safavi-Naini, R., Canetti, R. (eds.) CRYPTO 2012. LNCS, vol. 7417, pp. 517–532. Springer, Heidelberg (2012). doi:10.1007/978-3-642-32009-5_30

35. Malkin, T., Teranishi, I., Vahlis, Y., Yung, M.: Signatures resilient to continual leakage on memory and computation. In: Ishai, Y. (ed.) TCC 2011. LNCS, vol. 6597, pp. 89–106. Springer, Heidelberg (2011). doi:10.1007/978-3-642-19571-6_7

36. Micali, S., Reyzin, L.: Physically observable cryptography. In: Naor, M. (ed.) TCC 2004. LNCS, vol. 2951, pp. 278–296. Springer, Heidelberg (2004). doi:10.1007/978-3-540-24638-1_16

37. Naor, M., Segev, G.: Public-key cryptosystems resilient to key leakage. IACR Cryptology ePrint Archive 2009:105 (2009)

38. Nielsen, J.B., Venturi, D., Zottarel, A.: On the connection between leakage tolerance and adaptive security. In: Kurosawa, K., Hanaoka, G. (eds.) PKC 2013. LNCS, vol. 7778, pp. 497–515. Springer, Heidelberg (2013). doi:10.1007/978-3-642-36362-7_30

39. Nielsen, J.B., Venturi, D., Zottarel, A.: Leakage-resilient signatures with graceful degradation. In: Public Key Cryptography, pp. 362–379 (2014)

40. Ostrovsky, R., Persiano, G., Visconti, I.: Impossibility of black-box simulation against leakage attacks. In: Gennaro, R., Robshaw, M. (eds.) CRYPTO 2015. LNCS, vol. 9216, pp. 130–149. Springer, Heidelberg (2015). doi:10.1007/978-3-662-48000-7_7
41. Pandey, O.: Achieving constant round leakage-resilient zero-knowledge. In: Lindell, Y. (ed.) TCC 2014. LNCS, vol. 8349, pp. 146–166. Springer, Heidelberg (2014). doi:10.1007/978-3-642-54242-8_7
42. Quisquater, J.-J., Samyde, D.: Electromagnetic analysis (EMA): measures and counter-measures for smart cards. In: E-smart, pp. 200–210 (2001)
43. Trevisan, L., Vadhan, S.P.: Extracting randomness from samplable distributions. In: FOCS, pp. 32–42 (2000)
44. Wee, H.: On round-efficient argument systems. In: Caires, L., Italiano, G.F., Monteiro, L., Palamidessi, C., Yung, M. (eds.) ICALP 2005. LNCS, vol. 3580, pp. 140–152. Springer, Heidelberg (2005). doi:10.1007/11523468_12

Number Theory and Diffie-Hellman

On the Bit Security of Elliptic Curve Diffie–Hellman

Barak Shani[✉]

Department of Mathematics, University of Auckland, Auckland,
New Zealand
barak.shani@auckland.ac.nz

Abstract. This paper gives the first bit security result for the elliptic curve Diffie–Hellman key exchange protocol for elliptic curves defined over prime fields. About 5/6 of the most significant bits of the x-coordinate of the Diffie–Hellman key are as hard to compute as the entire key. A similar result can be derived for the 5/6 lower bits. The paper improves the result for elliptic curves over extension fields, that shows that computing one component (in the ground field) of the Diffie–Hellman key is as hard to compute as the entire key.

Keywords: Hidden number problem · Bit security · Elliptic curve Diffie–Hellman

1 Introduction

The notion of *hardcore functions* goes back almost to the invention of public key cryptography. Loosely speaking, for a one-way function f, a function b is a *hardcore function for* f if given $f(x)$ it is hard to compute $b(x)$ (while given x, computing $b(x)$ is easy).

The main interest is in functions b that output some bits of x, which gives this research field the name *bit security*. That is, while computing x from $f(x)$ is computationally hard by definition, one tries to assess the hardness of computing partial information about x. This can be done by providing an (efficient) algorithm that computes $b(x)$, or more commonly by reducing the problem of computing x to computing $b(x)$. That is, one provides an (efficient) algorithm that inverts f given an algorithm that computes b on f.

For popular candidates for one-way functions, such as the RSA function ($RSA_{N,e}(x) = x^e \bmod N$) and discrete exponentiation in a subgroup of prime order ($EXP_g(x) = g^x$; g has prime order), all single-bit functions are known to be hardcore. This result, which is standard these days, took more than 15 years to achieve, where year after year small improvements were made. An important aspect to consider is the success in computing $b(x)$. The mentioned result applies to every algorithm that computes $b(x)$ with a non-negligible success over a trivial guess. See [11] for a survey on hardcore functions which presents the developments over the years.

© International Association for Cryptologic Research 2017
S. Fehr (Ed.): PKC 2017, Part I, LNCS 10174, pp. 361–387, 2017.
DOI: 10.1007/978-3-662-54365-8_15

The notion of a hardcore function can be generalized to suit the Diffie–Hellman key exchange protocol. Let $(G, \cdot)$ be a group and let $g \in G$. For a function b, given g^u and g^v, we consider the hardness of computing $b(s)$ for (the Diffie–Hellman key) $s = g^{uv}$. Proving bit security for Diffie–Hellman key exchange has known less success than the aforementioned results. For $G = \mathbb{Z}_p^*$, the multiplicative group of integers modulo a prime p, the $\sqrt{\log p} + \log \log p$ most (and least) significant bits of s are hard to compute as s itself [9] (see also [13]; a similar result holds for twice as many consecutive inner bits, as a consequence of [19, Sect. 5.1]). For $G = \mathbb{F}_{p^m}^*$, the multiplicative group of a finite extension field, represented as a vector space over $\mathbb{F}_p$, computing a single component of s is as hard to compute as s itself [25], which follows from the fact that a single component of a product st is linear in all of the components of s. Moreover, using this linearity, a result in a similar fashion to the case of $G = \mathbb{Z}_p^*$ can be obtained from [22] for a single component (see also [16]). These results need – essentially – a perfect success in computing the partial information.

The case of the elliptic curve Diffie–Hellman key exchange protocol has known even fewer results, mainly because of the inherent nonlinearity of the problem. For elliptic curves over prime fields there are no known (non-trivial) results. For the group of elliptic curve points over an extension field of degree 2, computing a single component of the x-coordinate of s is as hard to compute as s itself [14, Remark 3.1]. This result requires perfect success in computing the component. We mention that for the case of elliptic curves over prime fields it is claimed in [7] that computing the top $(1 - \epsilon)$ fraction of bits of the x-coordinate of s, for $\epsilon \approx 0.02$, is as hard as computing all of them, but a proof is not provided, probably since it is a weak result, as the authors mentioned. Obtaining bit security results for elliptic curve Diffie–Hellman keys has been an open problem for almost 20 years [6, Sect. 5] (see also [11, Sect. 5]).

Some results on hardness of bits, related to the elliptic curve Diffie–Hellman protocol, were given by Boneh and Shparlinski [8] and by Jetchev and Venkatesan [15] (building on [8] and assuming the generalized Riemann hypothesis). These results differ from ours in two aspects. They do not provide hardness of bits for the elliptic curve Diffie–Hellman protocol for a single fixed curve. Furthermore, the techniques used to achieve these results are very different from ours, as they reduce the problem to an easier linear problem, while we keep working with the non-linear addition law.

In this paper we study the bit security of the elliptic curve Diffie–Hellman key exchange protocol. Our main result is Theorem 2, where we show that about $5/6$ of the most significant bits of the x-coordinate of the Diffie–Hellman key are as hard to compute as the entire key. As above, this result holds if one assumes a perfect success in computing these bits. This result directly follows from the solution to the *elliptic curve hidden number problem* given in Theorem 1. This solution is based on the ideas behind the solution to the *modular inversion hidden number problem* given in [7] and follows the formal proof given by Ling, Shparlinski, Steinfeld and Wang [17] (earlier ideas already appear in [2,3]).

Additional results are given in Sect. 6. In Sect. 6.1 we show how to derive the same result for the least significant bits. Section 6.2 addresses the case of elliptic curves over extension fields. This problem was first studied by Jao, Jetchev and Venkatesan [14]. We improve the known result to hold for both coordinates of the Diffie–Hellman key and to any constant extension degree. More details on these results appear in the full version of this paper [21].

As the literature on the elliptic curve hidden number problem is very minimal and incomplete, short discussions – some of which are quite trivial – appear throughout the paper in order to give a complete and comprehensive study of the problem. We hope that this work will initiate the study of bit security of elliptic curve Diffie–Hellman key exchange that will lead to improvements either in the number of hardcore bits or in the required success probability for computing them.

2   Mathematical Background

Throughout the paper $p > 3$ is an m-bit prime number and $\mathbb{F}_p$ is the field with p elements represented by $\{-\frac{p-1}{2}, \ldots, \frac{p-1}{2}\}$. For $k > 0$ and $x \in \mathbb{F}_p$, we denote by $\mathrm{MSB}_k(x)$ any $h \in \mathbb{F}_p$ such that $|x - h| \leq \frac{p}{2^{k+1}}$.[1] We have $h = \mathrm{MSB}_k(x) = x - e$ for $|e| \leq \frac{p}{2^{k+1}}$, which we loosely call *noise*.

2.1   Elliptic Curves

Throughout the paper E is an elliptic curve over $\mathbb{F}_p$, given in a short Weierstrass form

$$y^2 = x^3 + ax + b, \quad a, b \in \mathbb{F}_p \quad \text{and} \quad 4a^3 + 27b^2 \neq 0.$$

A point $P = (x, y) \in \mathbb{F}_p^2$ that satisfies this equation is a point on the curve E. We denote the x-coordinate (resp. y-coordinate) of a given point P by x_P or P_x (resp. y_P or P_y). The set of points on E, together with the *point at infinity* O, is known to be an abelian group. Hasse's theorem states that the number of points $\#E$ on the curve $E(\mathbb{F}_p)$ satisfies

$$|\#E - p - 1| \leq 2\sqrt{p}.$$

The (additive) inverse of a point $Q = (x_Q, y_Q)$ is $-Q = (x_Q, -y_Q)$. For an integer n we denote by $[n]P$ the successive n-time addition of a point P; $[-n]P = [n](-P)$. Addition of points $P = (x_P, y_P)$ and $Q = (x_Q, y_Q)$, where $P \neq \pm Q$, is given by the following formula. Let $s = s_{P+Q} = \frac{y_P - y_Q}{x_P - x_Q}$, then

$$(P + Q)_x = s^2 - x_P - x_Q \quad \text{and} \quad (P + Q)_y = -(y_P + s((P + Q)_x - x_P)).$$

---

[1] The function MSB_k is standard and thought of as providing the k most significant bits of x. It differs from the classical definition of most-significant-bits functions by (at most) 1 bit. For broad discussions see [4, Sect. 5], [5, Sect. 3] and [19, Sect. 5.1].

2.2 Lattices

Let $B = \{b_1, \ldots, b_r\}$ a set of linearly independent vectors in the Euclidean space $\mathbb{R}^s$, for some integers $r \leq s$. The set $L = \{\sum_{i=1}^{r} n_i b_i \mid n_i \in \mathbb{Z}\}$ is called an r-*dimensional lattice* and B is a *basis for L*. The (Euclidean) norm of a vector $v \in \mathbb{R}^s$ is denoted by $\|v\|$.

For a lattice L in $\mathbb{R}^s$ and a real number $\gamma \geq 1$, the γ-*shortest vector problem* (γ-SVP) is to find a non-zero lattice vector $v \in L$ with norm not larger than γ times the norm of the shortest non-zero vector in L. In other words, $\|v\| \leq \gamma \min\{\|u\| \mid 0 \neq u \in L\}$.

This problem is a fundamental problem in lattice cryptography. References to surveys and state-of-the-art algorithms for γ-SVP are given in Sect. 1.2 in the work of Ling, Shparlinski, Steinfeld and Wang [17], and like their work our result uses the γ-SVP algorithms of Schnorr [20] and Micciancio–Voulgaris [18].

3 Hidden Number Problems

The *hidden number problem* was introduced by Boneh and Venkatesan [9] in order to study bit security of the Diffie–Hellman key exchange protocol in the multiplicative group of integers modulo a prime p. This problem is formulated as follows.

> HNP: Fix a prime p, an element $g \in \mathbb{Z}_p^*$ and a positive number k. Let $\alpha \in \mathbb{Z}_p^*$ be a hidden number and let $\mathcal{O}_{\alpha,g}$ be an oracle that on input x computes the k most significant bits of $\alpha g^x \bmod p$. That is, $\mathcal{O}_{\alpha,g}(x) = \mathrm{MSB}_k(\alpha \cdot g^x \bmod p)$. The goal is to recover the hidden number α, given query access to the oracle $\mathcal{O}_{\alpha,g}$.

Various natural variants of this problem can be considered, such as changing the group the elements are taken from and the function the oracle is simulating. Moreover, one can consider oracles with different probability of producing the correct answer. The survey [24] covers many of these generalizations as well as different applications.

The elliptic curve equivalent, known as the *elliptic curve hidden number problem*, is formulated as follows for $\psi \in \{x, y\}$.

> EC-HNP$_\psi$: Fix a prime p, an elliptic curve E over $\mathbb{F}_p$, a point $R \in E$ and a positive number k. Let $P \in E$ be a hidden point and let $\mathcal{O}_{P,R}$ be an oracle that on input t computes the k most significant bits of the ψ-coordinate of $P+[t]R$. That is, $\mathcal{O}_{P,R}(t) = \mathrm{MSB}_k((P+[t]R)_\psi)$. The goal is to recover the hidden point P, given query access to the oracle $\mathcal{O}_{P,R}$.

The elliptic curve hidden number problem, to the best of our knowledge, was first considered (more generally, and only for the x-coordinate) by Boneh, Halevi and Howgrave-Graham [7], and besides being mentioned in the surveys

[23, 24] there is no other literature about it.[2] We remark that there are no known solutions to this problem, even for large k's (except, of course, of trivial cases, i.e., $k \geq \log p - O(\log \log p)$).

A related[3] non-linear problem is the *modular inversion hidden number problem*, which was introduced by Boneh, Halevi and Howgrave-Graham [7]. It is formulated as follows.

> MIHNP: Fix a prime p and positive numbers k, d. Let $\alpha \in \mathbb{Z}_p$ be a hidden number and let $t_1, \ldots, t_d \in \mathbb{Z}_p \backslash \{-\alpha\}$ chosen independently and uniformly at random. The goal is to find the secret number α given the d pairs $\left(t_i, \mathrm{MSB}_k \left(\frac{1}{\alpha + t_i} \right) \right)$.

We now explain the relation between the elliptic curve hidden number problem and bit security of the elliptic curve Diffie–Hellman key exchange protocol.

Remark 1. Given an elliptic curve E over a field $\mathbb{F}_q$, a point $Q \in E$ and the values $[a]Q$ and $[b]Q$, the Diffie–Hellman key P is the value $P = ECDH_Q([a]Q, [b]Q) = [ab]Q$. Suppose one has an oracle that on input $[u]Q$ and $[v]Q$ outputs some partial information on $[uv]Q$. Then, one can choose an integer t and calculate $[t]Q$, and by adding $[t]Q$ and $[a]Q$, one gets $[a]Q + [t]Q = [a + t]Q$. Querying the oracle on $[b]Q$ and $[a + t]Q$, one gets partial information on $[(a + t)b]Q = [ab]Q + [tb]Q = P + [t]([b]Q) = P + [t]R$, for $R = [b]Q$. Repeating for several t's, if it is possible to solve the elliptic curve hidden number problem, one can find the Diffie–Hellman key $P = [ab]Q$.

In the proof below we use the fact that one can get $\mathrm{MSB}_k(x_P)$ for the secret point P. This can be easily justified by taking $t = 0$ in EC-HNP, or equivalently querying the oracle from Remark 1 on $[a]Q$ and $[b]Q$. Moreover,

Remark 2. Similar to HNP [9, Sect. 4.1] and MIHNP [7, Sect. 2.1], EC-HNP can be self-randomized. Indeed, given $\{(Q_i, \mathcal{O}((P + Q_i)_\psi))\}_{1 \leq i \leq n}$, for an oracle $\mathcal{O}$, choose $1 \leq i_0 \leq n$, and define a new secret $P' := P + Q_{i_0}$. Let $Q'_i := Q_i - Q_{i_0}$, then we have $P + Q_i = P' + Q'_i$, and so $\mathcal{O}((P' + Q'_i)_\psi) = \mathcal{O}((P + Q_i)_\psi)$. If one can find P', recovering $P = P' - Q_{i_0}$ is easy. This shows that given $\{(Q_i, \mathcal{O}((P + Q_i)_\psi))\}_i$, one can randomize the secret P as well as the 'multipliers' Q_i. Alternatively, if access to the oracle is still provided, one can query on $t_{i_0} + t_i$ to receive $\mathcal{O}((P' + Q_i)_\psi)$, as well as taking the approach of [9, Sect. 4.1]. This self-randomization allows us to assume without loss of generality that R in EC-HNP is a generator for $\langle Q \rangle$.

---

[2] In [14] (a variant of) this problem is studied for elliptic curves over extension fields.

[3] We show below that the technique used to solve this problem also applies to EC-HNP. In addition, [23] reveals that obtaining bit security results for the elliptic curve Diffie–Hellman scheme has been a primary motivation for studying this problem.

4   Main Results

The main result is Theorem 2, which gives the first bit security result for prime-field elliptic curve Diffie–Hellman key exchange. This result follows from the following theorem, which shows how to recover the secret point in EC-HNP$_x$ given a γ-SVP algorithm.

Theorem 1. *Let E be an elliptic curve over a prime field $\mathbb{F}_p$, let n be an integer and k a real number. Let an unknown $P = (x_P, y_P) \in E\backslash\{O\}$ and a known generator $R \in E\backslash\{O\}$ be points on the curve. Let $\mathcal{O}$ be a function such that $\mathcal{O}(t) = MSB_k((P + [t]R)_x)$, and denote $Q_i := [t_i]R$. Then, given a γ-SVP algorithm, there exists a deterministic polynomial-time algorithm that recovers the unknown x_P with $2n + 1$ calls to $\mathcal{O}$ and a single call to the γ-SVP algorithm on a $(3n + 3)$-dimensional lattice with polynomially bounded basis, except with probability*

$$\mathcal{P}_1 \leq \frac{8^n(6\eta\Delta + 1)^{6n+3}}{(p - 2\sqrt{p} - 2)^n} + \frac{16(6\eta\Delta + 1)^6}{p - 2\sqrt{p} - 2} + \frac{2n + 3}{p - 2\sqrt{p}}$$

over the choices of $x_{Q_1}, \ldots, x_{Q_n}$, when it returns no answer or a wrong answer, where $\eta = 2\gamma\sqrt{3n + 1}$ and $\Delta = \lceil \frac{p}{2^{k+1}} \rceil$.[4] If the correct x-coordinate x_P has been recovered, the algorithm determines which of the two candidates $\pm y_P$ is the correct y-coordinate, except with probability

$$\mathcal{P}_2 \leq \frac{(16\Delta)^n}{(p - 2\sqrt{p} - 2)^n}$$

over the choices of $x_{Q_1}, \ldots, x_{Q_n}$.

Remark 3. In the theorem, as in the corollary below, R is taken to be a generator of E in order to give precise bounds on the probabilities. Both results hold even if R is not a generator of E, as long as it generates a "large enough" subgroup. The size of the subgroup appears in the denominator of the probabilities bounds (see footnote 7), and so the results also hold if the subgroup's order is greater than $p/poly(\log(p))$, for example. For substantially smaller subgroups, one would need to adjust the value for k.

The following corollary shows that one can solve EC-HNP$_x$ given an oracle for $k > (\frac{5}{6} + \epsilon)m$ most significant bits (where m is the bit length of p, and for any constant ϵ). Similar to Ling et al. [17], we consider two different SVP approximation algorithms to show the influence of ϵ on the running time and the minimum allowed value for p.

Corollary 1. *Fix $0 < \delta \leq 3\epsilon < 1/2$. Let $n_0 = \lceil \frac{1}{6\epsilon} \rceil$, p be an m-bit prime, E be an elliptic curve over $\mathbb{F}_p$ and $k > (5/6 + \epsilon)m$. There exist deterministic*

---

[4] As the matter of exact precision is not important, we set Δ to be an integer.

algorithms A_i, for $i = 1, 2$, that solve EC-HNP$_x$ (with MSB$_k$ and a generator R) for $m \geq m_i$, with probability at least $1 - p^{-\delta}$ over the choices of $x_{Q_1}, \ldots, x_{Q_{n_0}}$ where

$$m_1 = \lceil c_1 \epsilon^{-1} \log \epsilon^{-1} \rceil \quad and \quad m_2 = \lceil c_2 \epsilon^{-2} \frac{(\log \log \epsilon^{-1})^2}{\log \epsilon^{-1}} \rceil,$$

for some absolute effectively computable constants c_1, c_2, and their running time is T_i where

$$T_1 = (2^{\epsilon^{-1}} m)^{O(1)} \quad and \quad T_2 = (\epsilon^{-1} m)^{O(1)}.$$

As a consequence, following Remark 1, we get a hardcore function for the elliptic curve Diffie–Hellman problem and the following bit security result for elliptic curve Diffie–Hellman key exchange.

Theorem 2. *Fix $0 < \delta \leq 3\epsilon < 1/2$. Let p be an m-bit prime, E be an elliptic curve over $\mathbb{F}_p$, a point $P \in E \backslash \{O\}$ of order at least $p/poly(\log(p))$ and $k > (5/6 + \epsilon)m$. Given an efficient algorithm to compute MSB$_k$ $(([ab]P)_x)$ from $[a]P$ and $[b]P$, there exists a deterministic polynomial-time algorithm that computes $[ab]P$ with probability at least $1 - p^{\delta}$.*

In a nutshell, the approach of solving non-linear problems like MIHNP and EC-HNP is to form some polynomials with desired small roots, and use a lattice basis reduction algorithm to find some of these roots. The polynomials' degree, the number of their monomials, and subsequently the dimension of the lattice, play a main role in the quality of the result one can obtain.

4.1 Our Approach

The first obstacle in approaching EC-HNP is the nonlinearity (over the ground field) of the addition rule. This can be easily overcome by the "linearization" approach of Boneh et al. [7], which we adopt, but at the cost of not being able to use Babai's algorithm for closest lattice point [1]. This prevents non-linear problems, like MIHNP and EC-HNP, of achieving results as good as the result for the linear HNP.

The second obstacle in approaching EC-HNP$_x$ (and similarly EC-HNP$_y$) is that while one only gets partial information of x_P, the formula for $(P + Q)_x$ also involves (the unbounded unknown) y_P. Similar to the approach of [7], one can isolate this unknown in one equation, and substitute to all of the other equations, hence 'losing' one equation. Doing so will impose an extra bounded unknown in each equation, as well as many additional monomials, coming from the noise term of the equation we use to eliminate y_P.[5] This will therefore result in a significantly large dimension of the lattice one constructs.[6] Instead, we show

---

[5] Alternatively, once y_P is isolated, one can square both sides of the equation to eliminate y_P using the elliptic curve equation. While this allows us to keep all initial equations, doing so will result in polynomials of a larger degree with many more monomials.

[6] We speculate that this is the reason why [7] can only rigorously solve EC-HNP$_x$ given $(1 - \epsilon)$ fraction of the bits, for $\epsilon \approx 0.02$.

how one can combine two correlated equations to eliminate y_P. This helps us to define one bounded unknown (twice as large) while keeping the number of monomials relatively small. Taking this approach we form new equations from pairs of initial equations, causing a 'loss' of about half of the equations.

Formally, we proceed as follows.

Eliminating y_P. For some integer t consider the pair $Q = [t]R$, $-Q = [-t]R \in E$, and suppose $P \neq \pm Q$. Let $P = (x_P, y_P)$ and $Q = (x_Q, y_Q)$, therefore $-Q = (x_Q, -y_Q)$, and write $s_{P+Q} = \frac{y_P - y_Q}{x_P - x_Q}$ and $s_{P-Q} = \frac{y_P - y_{-Q}}{x_P - x_{-Q}} = \frac{y_P + y_Q}{x_P - x_Q}$. The following operations take place in $\mathbb{F}_p$.

$$
\begin{aligned}
(P+Q)_x - (P-Q)_x &= s_{P+Q}^2 - x_P - x_Q + s_{P-Q}^2 - x_P - x_Q \\
&= \left(\frac{y_P - y_Q}{x_P - x_Q} \right)^2 + \left(\frac{y_P + y_Q}{x_P - x_Q} \right)^2 - 2x_P - 2x_Q \\
&= 2 \left(\frac{y_P^2 + y_Q^2}{(x_P - x_Q)^2} - x_P - x_Q \right) \\
&= 2 \left(\frac{x_Q x_P^2 + (a + x_Q^2)x_P + ax_Q + 2b}{(x_P - x_Q)^2} \right).
\end{aligned}
\tag{1}
$$

Constructing Polynomials with Small Roots. Write $h_0 = \mathrm{MSB}_k(x_P) = x_P - e_0$, $h = \mathrm{MSB}_k((P+Q)_x) = (P+Q)_x - e$ and $h' = \mathrm{MSB}_k((P-Q)_x) = (P-Q)_x - e'$. Letting $\tilde{h} = h + h'$ and $\tilde{e} = e + e'$ and plugging $x_P = h_0 + e_0$ in (1) we get

$$
\begin{aligned}
\tilde{h} + \tilde{e} &= (P+Q)_x + (P-Q)_x \\
&= 2 \left(\frac{x_Q(h_0 + e_0)^2 + (a + x_Q^2)(h_0 + e_0) + ax_Q + 2b}{(h_0 + e_0 - x_Q)^2} \right).
\end{aligned}
$$

Multiplying by $(h_0 + e_0 - x_Q)^2$ and rearranging we get that the following bivariate polynomial

$$
\begin{aligned}
F(X, Y) = \ & X^2 Y + (\tilde{h} - 2x_Q)X^2 + 2(h_0 - x_Q)XY \\
& + 2[\tilde{h}(h_0 - x_Q) - 2h_0 x_Q - a - x_Q^2]X + (h_0 - x_Q)^2 Y \\
& + [\tilde{h}(h_0 - x_Q)^2 - 2h_0^2 x_Q - 2(a + x_Q^2)h_0 - 2ax_Q - 4b]
\end{aligned}
$$

satisfies $F(e_0, \tilde{e}) \equiv 0 \mod p$.

Repeating with n different Q_i leads to n polynomials of the form

$$
F_i(X, Y) = X^2 Y + A_i X^2 + A_{0,i} XY + B_i X + B_{0,i} Y + C_i,
\tag{2}
$$

that satisfy $F_i(e_0, \tilde{e}_i) \equiv 0 \mod p$. Our aim is to find "small" roots for F_i; if one of these roots satisfies $X = e_0$, we can substitute in h_0 and recover x_P.

We start with a simple argument that shows that indeed we expect to solve EC-HNP$_x$ with more than the top 5/6 fraction of the bits. The argument is identical to the argument given in [7, Sect. 3.1].

4.2   A Simple Heuristic Argument

The solutions to the system of the n polynomials in (2) can be represented by a lattice of dimension $4n + 3$, as follows. The lattice is spanned by the rows of a matrix M of the following structure

$$M = \begin{pmatrix} E & R \\ 0 & P \end{pmatrix}$$

where E and P are diagonal square matrices of dimensions $3n+3$ and n, respectively, and R is a $(3n + 3) \times n$ matrix. Each of the first $3n + 3$ rows of M is associated with one of the terms in (2), and each of the last n columns is associated with one of these equations. For example, for $n = 2$ we get the matrix (m is the bit size of p and k the number of bits we get)

$$M = \begin{pmatrix}
1 & 0 & 0 & 0 & 0 & 0 & 0 & 0 & 0 & C_1 & C_2 \\
0 & 2^{k-m} & 0 & 0 & 0 & 0 & 0 & 0 & 0 & B_{0,1} & 0 \\
0 & 0 & 2^{k-m} & 0 & 0 & 0 & 0 & 0 & 0 & 0 & B_{0,2} \\
0 & 0 & 0 & 2^{k-m} & 0 & 0 & 0 & 0 & 0 & B_1 & B_2 \\
0 & 0 & 0 & 0 & 2^{2(k-m)} & 0 & 0 & 0 & 0 & A_{0,1} & 0 \\
0 & 0 & 0 & 0 & 0 & 2^{2(k-m)} & 0 & 0 & 0 & 0 & A_{0,2} \\
0 & 0 & 0 & 0 & 0 & 0 & 2^{2(k-m)} & 0 & 0 & A_1 & A_2 \\
0 & 0 & 0 & 0 & 0 & 0 & 0 & 2^{3(k-m)} & 0 & 1 & 0 \\
0 & 0 & 0 & 0 & 0 & 0 & 0 & 0 & 2^{3(k-m)} & 0 & 1 \\
0 & 0 & 0 & 0 & 0 & 0 & 0 & 0 & 0 & p & 0 \\
0 & 0 & 0 & 0 & 0 & 0 & 0 & 0 & 0 & 0 & p
\end{pmatrix}.$$

For $e_0, \tilde{e}_i$, the last n columns give us equations over the integers:

$$e_0^2 \tilde{e}_i + A_i e_0^2 + A_{0,i} e_0 \tilde{e}_i + B_i e_0 + B_{0,i} \tilde{e}_i + C_i - k_i p = 0.$$

For the corresponding solution vector

$$\mathbf{v} := \langle 1, \tilde{e}_1, \ldots, \tilde{e}_n, e_0, e_0 \tilde{e}_1, \ldots, e_0 \tilde{e}_n, e_0^2, e_0^2 \tilde{e}_1, \ldots, e_0^2 \tilde{e}_n, k_1, \ldots, k_n \rangle,$$

we get that $\mathbf{v}M =$

$$\langle 1, \frac{\tilde{e}_1}{2^{m-k}}, \ldots, \frac{\tilde{e}_n}{2^{m-k}}, \frac{e_0}{2^{m-k}}, \frac{e_0 \tilde{e}_1}{2^{2(m-k)}}, \ldots, \frac{e_0 \tilde{e}_n}{2^{2(m-k)}}, \frac{e_0^2}{2^{2(m-k)}}, \frac{e_0^2 \tilde{e}_1}{2^{3(m-k)}}, \ldots, \frac{e_0^2 \tilde{e}_n}{2^{3(m-k)}}, 0, \ldots, 0 \rangle.$$

Therefore, $\mathbf{v}M$ is a lattice point with $3n + 3$ non-zero entries, all of which are smaller than 1, so its Euclidean norm is smaller than $\sqrt{3n + 3}$.

The determinant of the lattice is $\frac{p^n}{2^{(m-k)(6n+3)}}$. We apply the heuristic for short lattice vectors and expect that $\mathbf{v}M$ is the shortest vector if $\sqrt{3n + 3} \ll \sqrt{4n + 3} \left(2^{(k-m)(6n+3)} p^n \right)^{1/(4n+3)}$. Substituting $p = 2^{m+O(1)}$ and ignoring lower terms we get $2^k \gg 2^{5/6m}$, and so we expect that $\mathbf{v}M$ is the shortest lattice vector when we get more than $\frac{5}{6}m$ bits. Therefore, this becomes a problem of recovering the shortest lattice vector.

Boneh et al. [7] suggest using Coppersmith's method [10] and construct a lattice that leads to a smaller bound on the number of bits one needs in order to recover the secret element in this kind of non-linear problems. This approach has to assume linear independence of the equations involved, and therefore does not provide a proof, but only a heuristic. Since the aim of this paper is to prove bit security, we do not follow this path.

We now turn to a complete formal proof of Theorem 1. It follows the same arguments as in the proof of Theorem 1 in [17], where necessary adaptations have been made.

5   Proofs

The proof of Theorem 1 is very technical. The algorithm of recovering x_P appears in Algorithm 1, but we first lay the groundwork, so that the probability analysis that appears after the algorithm could be understood. We first give an overview of the key points of the proof.

Overview

In the algorithmic part:

- Using $\mathcal{O}$, we construct the polynomial relations (as in (2) above)

$$F_i(X, Y) = X^2 Y + A_i X^2 + A_{0,i} XY + B_i X + B_{0,i} Y + C_i$$

for which $F_i(e_0, \widetilde{e}_i) \equiv 0 \mod p$.
- Using these relations, we construct a lattice (see (4)), such that the vector

$$\mathbf{e} := (\Delta^3, \Delta^2 e_0, \Delta^2 \widetilde{e}_1, \ldots, \Delta^2 \widetilde{e}_n, \Delta e_0^2, \Delta e_0 \widetilde{e}_1, \ldots, \Delta e_0 \widetilde{e}_n, e_0^2 \widetilde{e}_1, \ldots, e_0^2 \widetilde{e}_n)$$

is a short lattice vector.
- We run a γ-SVP algorithm on the lattice to receive a short lattice vector

$$\mathbf{f} := (\Delta^3 f_0', \Delta^2 f_0, \Delta^2 f_1 \ldots, \Delta^2 f_n, \Delta f_{0,0}, \Delta f_{0,1}, \ldots, \Delta f_{0,n}, f_{00,1}, \ldots, f_{00,n}).$$

As $\mathbf{e}$ and $\mathbf{f}$ are two short lattice vectors, we expect them to be a (scalar) multiple of each other.
- Supposing this is the case, the scalar f_0' is found by observing the first coordinate of $\mathbf{e}$ and $\mathbf{f}$. We then compute $e_0 = f_0/f_0'$ provided $f_0' \neq 0$.
- From the relation $h_0 = x_P - e_0$ we derive $x_P = h_0 + e_0$.

The second part of the proof analyzes the success probability of the algorithm, as follows:

- If $e_0 \neq f_0/f_0'$ or $f_0' = 0$ the algorithm fails.

- To derive the probability of these events we form a certain family of low-degree polynomials (see (12)), for which we are interested in their set of zeros. The number of polynomials in the family is a function of $\Delta = \lceil \frac{p}{2^{k+1}} \rceil$, and so a function of k.
- Claim 5.1 shows that if $y_P \neq 0$, then the polynomials are not identically zero.
- We show that these events occur if the points x_{Q_i} are roots of some of these polynomials. Thus, we derive an exact expression of the probability of these events to hold.

The last part of the proof shows how one can determine the correct value for y_P using a consistency check with all of the given values.

5.1 Proof of Theorem 1

Assume without loss of generality $3\eta\Delta \leq 3\eta\Delta^3 < p$, as otherwise the bound on the probability makes the claim trivial, and that the unknown P is chosen uniformly at random (see Remark 2). Throughout, unless stated otherwise, i, j are indices such that $1 \leq i \leq n$ and $0 \leq j \leq n$. Set $t_0 = 0$, choose $t_i \in [1, \#E - 1]$ independently and uniformly at random, and query the oracle $\mathcal{O}$ on $\pm t_j$ to get the $2n + 1$ values $\mathcal{O}(\pm t_j)$ denoted by $h_0 = \mathrm{MSB}_k(P_x) = x_P - e_0$, $h_i = \mathrm{MSB}_k((P+Q_i)_x) = (P+Q_i)_x - e_i$ and $h_{i'} = \mathrm{MSB}_k((P-Q_i)_x) = (P-Q_i)_x - e_{i'}$, for some integers $-\Delta \leq e_j, e_{i'} \leq \Delta$. Denote $\widetilde{h}_i = h_i + h_{i'}$ and $\widetilde{e}_i = e_i + e_{i'}$, and suppose $P \neq \pm Q_i$.

The following has been shown in Sect. 4.1. For every $1 \leq i \leq n$, one has

$$\widetilde{h}_i + \widetilde{e}_i = h_i + e_i + h_{i'} + e_{i'} = (P+Q_i)_x + (P-Q_i)_x$$
$$\equiv 2\left(\frac{x_{Q_i}(h_0+e_0)^2 + (a + x_{Q_i}^2)(h_0+e_0) + ax_{Q_i} + 2b}{(h_0 + e_0 - x_{Q_i})^2}\right) \pmod{p}.$$

Consider the polynomials

$$F_i(X, Y) := X^2Y + A_iX^2 + A_{0,i}XY + B_iX + B_{0,i}Y + C_i,$$

where (all congruences hold mod p)

$$A_i \equiv \widetilde{h}_i - 2x_{Q_i}, \qquad\qquad\qquad A_{0,i} \equiv 2(h_0 - x_{Q_i}),$$
$$B_i \equiv 2[\widetilde{h}_i(h_0 - x_{Q_i}) - 2h_0x_{Q_i} - a - x_{Q_i}^2], \qquad B_{0,i} \equiv (h_0 - x_{Q_i})^2, \text{ and}$$
$$C_i \equiv \widetilde{h}_i(h_0 - x_{Q_i})^2 - 2((h_0^2 + a)x_{Q_i} + (a + x_{Q_i}^2)h_0 + 2b).$$

It holds that $F(e_0, \widetilde{e}_i) \equiv 0 \pmod{p}$ for every $1 \leq i \leq n$. As $e_0, \widetilde{e}_i$ are relatively small, one hopes that finding a *small solution* to one of these polynomials would allow to recover e_0 and subsequently P. To achieve this goal, we use these relations to construct a lattice and apply the γ-SVP algorithm.

Formally, we start by 'balancing' the coefficients (as lattice basis reduction algorithms work better where all the coefficients are of similar size). For every $1 \leq i \leq n$, set

$$a_i \equiv \Delta^{-1}A_i \pmod{p}, \quad a_{0,i} \equiv \Delta^{-1}A_{0,i} \pmod{p},$$
$$b_i \equiv \Delta^{-2}B_i \pmod{p}, \quad b_{0,i} \equiv \Delta^{-2}B_{0,i} \pmod{p}, \text{ and} \tag{3}$$
$$c_i \equiv \Delta^{-3}C_i \pmod{p}.$$

The vector

$$\mathbf{e} = (\Delta^3, \Delta^2 e_0, \Delta^2 \widetilde{e}_1, \ldots, \Delta^2 \widetilde{e}_n, \Delta e_0^2, \Delta e_0 \widetilde{e}_1, \ldots, \Delta e_0 \widetilde{e}_n, e_0^2 \widetilde{e}_1, \ldots, e_0^2 \widetilde{e}_n)$$

belongs to the lattice L consisting of solutions

$$\mathbf{x} = (x_0', x_0, x_1, \ldots, x_n, x_{0,0}, x_{0,1}, \ldots, x_{0,n}, x_{00,1}, \ldots, x_{00,n}) \in \mathbb{Z}^{3n+3}$$

of the congruences

$$c_i x_0' + b_i x_0 + b_{0,i} x_i + a_i x_{0,0} + a_{0,i} x_{0,i} + x_{00,i} \equiv 0 \pmod{p}, \ 1 \le i \le n,$$
$$x_0' \equiv 0 \pmod{\Delta^3},$$
$$x_j \equiv 0 \pmod{\Delta^2} \ \ 0 \le j \le n, \text{ and}$$
$$x_{0,j} \equiv 0 \pmod{\Delta} \ \ 0 \le j \le n.$$

The lattice L is generated by the rows of a $(3n+3) \times (3n+3)$ matrix M of the following structure:

$$M = \begin{pmatrix} \mathbf{\Delta^2} & 0 & M_1 \\ 0 & \mathbf{\Delta} & M_2 \\ 0 & 0 & P \end{pmatrix} \tag{4}$$

where $\mathbf{\Delta^2}$, $\mathbf{\Delta}$ and P are diagonal square matrices of dimensions $n+2$, $n+1$ and n, respectively, such that the diagonal of P consists of the prime p, the matrix $\mathbf{\Delta}$ consists of Δ and the matrix $\mathbf{\Delta^2}$ of Δ^2, except of the first diagonal entry which is Δ^3; and the matrices M_1 and M_2 are of dimensions $(n+2) \times n$ and $(n+1) \times n$ respectively, given by

$$M_1 = \begin{pmatrix} -C_1 & -C_2 & \cdots & -C_n \\ -B_1 & -B_2 & & -B_n \\ -B_{0,1} & 0 & & 0 \\ 0 & -B_{0,2} & & \\ \vdots & 0 & \ddots & \\ & \vdots & & \\ 0 & 0 & & -B_{0,n} \end{pmatrix}, \quad M_2 = \begin{pmatrix} -A_1 & -A_2 & \cdots & -A_n \\ -A_{0,1} & 0 & & 0 \\ 0 & -A_{0,2} & & \vdots \\ \vdots & 0 & \ddots & \\ & \vdots & & \\ 0 & 0 & & -A_{0,n} \end{pmatrix}.$$

As $|\widetilde{e}_i| = |e_i + e_{i'}| \le 2\Delta$ for every $1 \le i \le n$, we have

$$\|\mathbf{e}\| \le \sqrt{3\Delta^6 + 12n\Delta^6} = \sqrt{3 + 12n}\,\Delta^3 \le 2\Delta^3\sqrt{3n+1}.$$

Run the γ-SVP algorithm and denote the vector it outputs by

$$\mathbf{f} = (\Delta^3 f_0', \Delta^2 f_0, \Delta^2 f_1 \ldots, \Delta^2 f_n, \Delta f_{0,0}, \Delta f_{0,1}, \ldots, \Delta f_{0,n}, f_{00,1}, \ldots, f_{00,n}), \tag{5}$$

where $f'_0, f_j, f_{0,j}, f_{00,i} \in \mathbb{Z}$. Notice that

$$\|\mathbf{f}\| \leq \gamma\|\mathbf{e}\| \leq 2\gamma\Delta^3\sqrt{3n+1} = \eta\Delta^3 \text{ for } \eta = 2\gamma\sqrt{3n+1},$$

and also that

$$|f'_0| \leq \|\mathbf{f}\|\Delta^{-3} \leq \eta,$$
$$|f_j| \leq \|\mathbf{f}\|\Delta^{-2} \leq \eta\Delta,$$
$$|f_{0,j}| \leq \|\mathbf{f}\|\Delta^{-1} \leq \eta\Delta^2, \text{ and}$$
$$|f_{00,i}| \leq \|\mathbf{f}\| \leq \eta\Delta^3.$$

As $\mathbf{e}, \mathbf{f}$ are both short lattice vectors, we expect them to be scalar multiples of each other. Therefore, let

$$\mathbf{d} = f'_0\mathbf{e} - \mathbf{f} = (0, \Delta^2 d_0, \Delta^2 d_1, \ldots, \Delta^2 d_n, \Delta d_{0,0}, \Delta d_{0,1}, \ldots, \Delta d_{0,n}, d_{00,1}, \ldots, d_{00,n}),$$

where

$$
\begin{aligned}
d_0 &= f'_0 e_0 - f_0, & |d_0| &= |f'_0 e_0 - f_0| \leq \eta|e_0| + |f_0| \leq \eta\Delta + \eta\Delta = 2\eta\Delta, \\
d_i &= f'_0 \widetilde{e}_i - f_i, & |d_i| &= |f'_0 \widetilde{e}_i - f_i| \leq \eta|\widetilde{e}_i| + |f_i| \leq \eta 2\Delta + \eta\Delta = 3\eta\Delta, \\
d_{0,0} &= f'_0 e_0^2 - f_{0,0}, & |d_{0,0}| &= |f'_0 e_0^2 - f_{0,0}| \leq \eta|e_0|^2 + |f_{0,0}| \\
& & &\qquad\qquad \leq \eta\Delta^2 + \eta\Delta^2 = 2\eta\Delta^2, \quad (6) \\
d_{0,i} &= f'_0 e_0 \widetilde{e}_i - f_{0,i}, & |d_{0,i}| &= |f'_0 e_0 \widetilde{e}_i - f_{0,i}| \leq \eta|e_0 \widetilde{e}_i| + |f_{0,i}| \\
& & &\qquad\qquad \leq \eta 2\Delta^2 + \eta\Delta^2 = 3\eta\Delta^2, \text{ and} \\
d_{00,i} &= f'_0 e_0^2 \widetilde{e}_i - f_{00,i}, & |d_{00,i}| &= |f'_0 e_0^2 \widetilde{e}_i - f_{00,i}| \leq \eta|e_0^2 \widetilde{e}_i| + |f_{00,i}| \\
& & &\qquad\qquad \leq \eta 2\Delta^3 + \eta\Delta^3 = 3\eta\Delta^3.
\end{aligned}
$$

Notice that if $f'_0 \neq 0$ and also one of the coordinates of $\mathbf{d}$ (except of the first one) is zero, we can recover some previously unknown information. More precisely, suppose $f'_0 \neq 0$, then

$$\text{If } d_0 = 0, \text{ then } e_0 = f_0/f'_0; \qquad\qquad\qquad\qquad (7)$$
$$\text{If } d_i = 0, \text{ then } \widetilde{e}_i = f_i/f'_0, \quad 1 \leq i \leq n; \qquad\qquad (8)$$
$$\text{If } d_{0,0} = 0, \text{ then } e_0^2 = f_{0,0}/f'_0; \qquad\qquad\qquad\quad (9)$$
$$\text{If } d_{0,i} = 0, \text{ then } e_0\widetilde{e}_i = f_{0,i}/f'_0, \quad 1 \leq i \leq n; \qquad (10)$$
$$\text{If } d_{00,i} = 0, \text{ then } e_0^2\widetilde{e}_i = f_{00,i}/f'_0, \quad 1 \leq i \leq n. \qquad (11)$$

As $\widetilde{e}_i = e_i + e_{i'}$ it is unclear how to use these values in general to recover the secret x_P. We therefore focus on e_0, from which we derive x_P. Although there are several ways to recover e_0 from these equations, for the sake of the proof we only focus on (7), thus in case $f'_0 \neq 0$ we take $h_0 + f_0/f'_0$ as the candidate for x_P, and if $f'_0 = 0$, we fail. We remark that a more involved approach can be taken (to determine e_0 and in the case $f'_0 = 0$), using the consistency check in Appendix A.

A pseudocode for the algorithm that recovers x_P is the following.

Algorithm 1. Find x_P

1: Construct a lattice, generated by the rows of the matrix M as in (4).
2: Run the γ-SVP algorithm on the lattice to get the vector $\mathbf{f}$ as in (5).
3: **if** $f_0' \neq 0$ **then**
    return $h_0 + f_0/f_0'$
    else
    Fail

Probability of Failure

We now define the following events:

(E-1) $y_P = 0$;
(E-2) $d_0 \neq 0$ and (E-1) does not hold;
(E-3) $f_0' = 0$ and (E-1) and (E-2) do not hold.

It is clear that if none of the events hold, one can recover x_P. The requirement $y_P \neq 0$ will be made clear in Claim 5.1 below.

As there are at most 3 values for $x_P \in \mathbb{F}_p$ that satisfy the equation $x_P^3 + ax_P + b \equiv 0 \pmod{p}$, and since P is assumed to be chosen uniformly at random, the probability that (E-1) holds satisfies

$$\Pr[(\text{E-1})] \leq \frac{3}{\#E - 1} \leq \frac{3}{p - 2\sqrt{p}} .$$

In order to derive a bound on the probability of the other events we form some useful equations. As

$$c_i \Delta^3 + b_i \Delta^2 e_0 + b_{0,i} \Delta^2 \widetilde{e}_i + a_i \Delta e_0^2 + a_{0,i} \Delta e_0 \widetilde{e}_i + e_0^2 \widetilde{e}_i \equiv 0 \pmod{p}, \ 1 \leq i \leq n,$$

and

$$c_i \Delta^3 f_0' + b_i \Delta^2 f_0 + b_{0,i} \Delta^2 f_i + a_i \Delta f_{0,0} + a_{0,i} \Delta f_{0,i} + f_{00,i} \equiv 0 \pmod{p}, \ 1 \leq i \leq n,$$

we get (by the definition of $\mathbf{d}$)

$$b_i \Delta^2 d_0 + b_{0,i} \Delta^2 d_i + a_i \Delta d_{0,0} + a_{0,i} \Delta d_{0,i} + d_{00,i} \equiv 0 \pmod{p}, \ 1 \leq i \leq n,$$

and therefore (using (3) above)

$$B_i d_0 + B_{0,i} d_i + A_i d_{0,0} + A_{0,i} d_{0,i} + d_{00,i} \equiv 0 \pmod{p}, \ 1 \leq i \leq n.$$

Multiplying by $(x_P - x_{Q_i})^2$ and using the definitions for $A_i, A_{0,i}, B_i$ and $B_{0,i}$ we get for every $1 \leq i \leq n$

$$(x_P - x_{Q_i})^2 \Big(2[\widetilde{h}_i(h_0 - x_{Q_i}) - 2h_0 x_{Q_i} - a - x_{Q_i}^2]d_0 + (h_0^2 - 2h_0 x_{Q_i} + x_{Q_i}^2)d_i$$
$$+ (\widetilde{h}_i - 2x_{Q_i})d_{0,0} + 2(h_0 - x_{Q_i})d_{0,i} + d_{00,i} \Big) \equiv 0 \pmod{p},$$

which simplifies, as a polynomial in x_{Q_i}, to

$$U_i x_{Q_i}^4 - V_i x_{Q_i}^3 + W_i x_{Q_i}^2 + Y_i x_{Q_i} + Z_i \equiv 0 \pmod{p}, \ 1 \le i \le n, \qquad (12)$$

where (all congruences hold mod p)

$$U_i \equiv d_i - 2d_0,$$
$$V_i \equiv 2(2x_P - 2e_0 - \tilde{e}_i)d_0 + (4x_P - 2e_0)d_i + 2d_{0,0} + 2d_{0,i},$$
$$W_i \equiv 2(3x_P^3 - 6e_0 x_P - 3\tilde{e}_i x_P + e_0 \tilde{e}_i - 3a)d_0 + (6x_P^2 - 6e_0 x_P + e_0^2)d_i$$
$$\quad + (6x_P - \tilde{e}_i)d_{0,0} + (6x_P - 2e_0)d_{0,i} + d_{00,i},$$
$$Y_i \equiv 2(3\tilde{e}_i x_P^2 - 2e_0 \tilde{e}_i x_P + 2ax_P - 2ae_0 - 4b)d_0 - 2(2x_P^3 - 3e_0 x_P^2 + e_0^2 x_P)d_i$$
$$\quad + (2\tilde{e}_i x_P + 2a)d_{0,0} - (6x_P^2 - 4e_0 x_P)d_{0,i} - 2x_P d_{00,i}, \ \text{and} \qquad (13)$$
$$Z_i \equiv 2(-\tilde{e}_i x_P^3 + e_0 \tilde{e}_i x_P^2 + ax_P^2 - 2ae_0 x_P + 4bx_P - 4be_0)d_0$$
$$\quad + (x_P^4 - 2e_0 x_P^3 + e_0^2 x_P^2)d_i + (-\tilde{e}_i x_P^2 + 2ax_P + 4b)d_{0,0}$$
$$\quad + (2x_P^3 - 2e_0 x_P^2)d_{0,i} + x_P^2 d_{00,i}.$$

We now show that if for some $1 \le i \le n$ the left hand side of (12) is the constant zero polynomial, then $d_0 = 0 = d_{0,0}$. We conclude that if $d_0 \ne 0$ or $d_{0,0} \ne 0$, then the left hand side of (12) is a non-constant polynomial in x_{Q_i} (of degree at most 4) for every $1 \le i \le n$.

Claim. Let $1 \le i \le n$, and assume $y_P \ne 0$. The left hand side of (12) is constant if and only if $d_0 = d_{0,0} = d_i = d_{0,i} = d_{00,i} = 0$.

Proof. The first implication is clear from (13). Suppose that the left hand side of (12) is constant for some $1 \le i \le n$. Then $U_i \equiv V_i \equiv W_i \equiv Y_i \equiv Z_i \equiv 0$ (mod p). One can express the latter as a system of 5 equations in the 5 variables $d_0, d_i, d_{0,0}, d_{0,i}$ and $d_{00,i}$. A non-zero solution exists if and only if the system is singular. We show that the system is nonsingular if and only if $y_P \ne 0$, which completes the proof.

We use the first 4 equations to eliminate $d_i, d_{0,i}, d_{00,i}$ and remain with the "global" variables $d_0, d_{0,0}$. One then has

$$-2(2x_P^3 + 3e_0 x_P^2 + 2ax_P + ae_0 + 2b)d_0 + (3x_P^2 + a)d_{0,0} \equiv 0 \pmod{p},$$

which simplifies to

$$-4y_P d_0 - 2e_0(3x_P^2 + a)d_0 + (3x_P^2 + a)d_{0,0} \equiv 0 \pmod{p}.$$

If $3x_P^2 + a \equiv 0$ (mod p), then $y_P d_0 \equiv 0$ (mod p). Otherwise, one can express $d_{0,0}$ in terms of d_0. Plugging this value, with the other recovered variables, to the last equation, one gets

$$(x_P^6 + 2ax_P^4 + 2bx_P^3 + a^2 x_P^2 + 2abx_P + b^2)d_0 \equiv y_P^4 d_0 \equiv 0 \pmod{p}.$$

In both cases, since $y_P \ne 0$, we have $d_0 \equiv d_{0,0} \equiv d_i \equiv d_{0,i} \equiv d_{00,i} \equiv 0$ (mod p), and since all of these values are of size smaller than p (as we suppose $3\eta\Delta < 3\eta\Delta^3 < p$), the claim follows. ∎

We use this claim to bound the probabilities of (E-2) and (E-3), which will prove the first claim in the theorem. The probability of events (E-2) and (E-3) is taken over the choice of the points Q_i for $1 \leq i \leq n$. That is, we consider the number of n-tuples

$$(x_{Q_1}, \ldots, x_{Q_n}) \in (E_x \backslash \{x_P\})^n$$

such that (E-2) holds or (E-3) holds, where $E_x := \{z \in \mathbb{F}_p \mid \exists Q \in E, Q_x = z\}$.[7] Note that $\#E - 1 \leq 2|E_x| \leq \#E + 2$.

Probability of Event (E-2). Assume (E-2) holds, that is $d_0 \neq 0$ and $y_P \neq 0$, and fix some values of $d_j, d_{0,j}$ for $0 \leq j \leq n$ and $d_{00,i}$ for $1 \leq i \leq n$. Let us consider the number of n-tuples

$$(x_{Q_1}, \ldots, x_{Q_n}) \in (E_x \backslash \{x_P\})^n$$

satisfying (12).

Since $d_0 \neq 0$ Claim 5.1 shows that the left hand side of (12) is nonconstant for all $1 \leq i \leq n$. Thus, as all the relations in (12) are satisfied, there are at most 4 values x_{Q_i} that satisfy each relation, and so there are at most 4^n n-tuples that satisfy these n non-constant polynomials.

From (6) above we get: as $d_0 \neq 0$ it can take at most $4\eta\Delta$ values, each d_i can take at most $6\eta\Delta + 1$ values, $d_{0,0}$ can take at most $4\eta\Delta^2 + 1$ values, each $d_{0,i}$ can take at most $6\eta\Delta^2 + 1$ values, and each $d_{00,i}$ can take at most $6\eta\Delta^3 + 1$ values. Therefore, there are at most

$$4^n 4\eta\Delta(6\eta\Delta + 1)^n(4\eta\Delta^2 + 1)(6\eta\Delta^2 + 1)^n(6\eta\Delta^3 + 1)^n <$$
$$4^n 4\eta\Delta(6\eta\Delta + 1)^n(4\eta\Delta + 1)^2(6\eta\Delta + 1)^{2n}(6\eta\Delta + 1)^{3n} < 4^n(6\eta\Delta + 1)^{6n+3}$$

n-tuples $(x_{Q_1}, \ldots, x_{Q_n})$ for which event (E-2) happens. Denote them by $\mathcal{Q}$. The probability that $d_0 \neq 0$ (given $y_P \neq 0$) satisfies

$$\Pr[(\text{E-2})] \leq \frac{|\mathcal{Q}|}{|E_x \backslash \{x_P\}|^n} < \frac{4^n(6\eta\Delta + 1)^{6n+3}}{\left(\frac{1}{2}(\#E - 1) - 1\right)^n} \leq \frac{8^n(6\eta\Delta + 1)^{6n+3}}{(p - 2\sqrt{p} - 2)^n}.$$

Probability of Event (E-3). Assume (E-3) holds, that is $f_0' = 0, d_0 = 0$ and $y_P \neq 0$. We may suppose that for all the n-tuples in $\mathcal{Q}$ event (E-3) holds, and thus consider the remaining n-tuples which are not in $\mathcal{Q}$. We first notice that $d_{0,0} = 0$. Indeed, if $d_{0,0} \neq 0$, then by Claim 5.1 the left hand side of (12) is nonconstant for all $1 \leq i \leq n$. In that case, the only n-tuples that satisfy (12) are in $\mathcal{Q}$. We therefore have $f_0 = f_0' e_0 - d_0 = 0 = f_0' e_0^2 - d_{0,0} = f_{0,0}$.

Consider the set $S = \{i \in \{1, \ldots, n\} \mid d_i = d_{0,i} = d_{00,i} = 0\}$. Let $l = |S|$, and notice that if $l = n$ then $f_0 = f_i = f_{0,0} = f_{0,i} = f_{00,i} = 0$, and since $f_0' = 0$ by assumption then $\mathbf{f} = 0$. As $\mathbf{f}$ is a non-zero vector by construction, $l < n$.

---

[7] In the case that R is not a generator of E, one would define $E_x := \{z \in \mathbb{F}_p \mid \exists Q \in \langle R \rangle, Q_x = z\}$. Proving the theorem for *any* R boils down to proving that the roots of (12) are not restricted to E_x.

Fix some values of $d_i, d_{0,i}, d_{00,i}$ for $1 \leq i \leq n$. We now consider the number of n-tuples

$$(x_{Q_1}, \ldots, x_{Q_n}) \notin \mathcal{Q}$$

satisfying (12). If $i \in S$ then the left hand side of (12) is the constant zero, and so there are $|E_x| - 1$ possible values for x_{Q_i} satisfying (12). If $i \notin S$ then either $d_i \neq 0$ or $d_{0,i} \neq 0$ or $d_{00,i} \neq 0$ and by Claim 5.1 the left hand side of (12) is nonconstant, so there are at most 4 solutions x_{Q_i} to the corresponding equation in (12).

Overall, there are at most $4^{n-l}(|E_x| - 1)^l$ n-tuples $(x_{Q_1}, \ldots, x_{Q_n}) \notin \mathcal{Q}$ that satisfy (12). The possible values for each $d_i, d_{0,i}, d_{00,i}$ for each $i \notin S$ are given above. So overall there are at most

$$4^{n-l}(|E_x| - 1)^l (6\eta\Delta + 1)^{n-l} (6\eta\Delta^2 + 1)^{n-l} (6\eta\Delta^3 + 1)^{n-l}$$
$$< 4^{n-l}(|E_x| - 1)^l (6\eta\Delta + 1)^{n-l} (6\eta\Delta + 1)^{2(n-l)} (6\eta\Delta + 1)^{3(n-l)}$$
$$= 4^{n-l}(|E_x| - 1)^l (6\eta\Delta + 1)^{6(n-l)}$$

n-tuples $(x_{Q_1}, \ldots, x_{Q_n}) \notin \mathcal{Q}$ for which event (E-3) happens. Denote them by $\mathcal{Q}'$. Over these tuples (not in Q), the probability that $f_0' = 0$ (given $d_0 = 0$ and $y_P \neq 0$) is bounded by

$$\frac{|\mathcal{Q}'|}{|E_x \setminus \{x_P\}|^n} \leq \sum_{l=0}^{n-1} \left(\frac{4(6\eta\Delta + 1)^6}{|E_x| - 1} \right)^{n-l} \leq \sum_{l=1}^{n} \left(\frac{4(6\eta\Delta + 1)^6}{\frac{1}{2}(\#E - 1) - 1} \right)^l$$
$$= \sum_{l=1}^{n} \left(\frac{1}{2} \frac{16(6\eta\Delta + 1)^6}{\#E - 3} \right)^l \leq \sum_{l=1}^{n} \left(\frac{1}{2} \right)^l \left(\frac{16(6\eta\Delta + 1)^6}{p - 2\sqrt{p} - 2} \right)^l.$$

If $\frac{16(6\eta\Delta+1)^6}{p-2\sqrt{p}-2} < 1$, then the latter is smaller than $\frac{16(6\eta\Delta+1)^6}{p-2\sqrt{p}-2}$. In any case we get that this probability is bounded by

$$\frac{16(6\eta\Delta + 1)^6}{p - 2\sqrt{p} - 2}.$$

We finally get that the probability that event (E-3) happens satisfies

$$\Pr[(\text{E-3})] \leq \frac{|\mathcal{Q}|}{|E_x \setminus \{x_P\}|^n} + \frac{|\mathcal{Q}'|}{|E_x \setminus \{x_P\}|^n} < \frac{8^n (6\eta\Delta + 1)^{6n+3}}{(p - 2\sqrt{p} - 2)^n} + \frac{16(6\eta\Delta + 1)^6}{p - 2\sqrt{p} - 2}.$$

Notice that the probability that $Q_i = \pm P$ for some $1 \leq i \leq n$ is

$$\frac{2}{\#E - 1} \leq \frac{2}{p - 2\sqrt{p}}.$$

Thus, the probability that $Q_i = \pm P$ for any $1 \leq i \leq n$ is bounded by

$$\frac{2n}{p - 2\sqrt{p}}.$$

This concludes the first claim in the theorem.

Now suppose x_P has been recovered. To determine which of the two values $\pm\sqrt{x_P^3 + ax_P + b}$ is the correct y-coordinate of P, we run the consistency check, which is presented in Appendix A, on both candidates. It is clear that the correct candidate will pass the test. If both candidates pass the consistency check then we cannot determine the point P. We analyze the probability of the event in which the incorrect candidate $-P = (x_P, -y_P)$ passes the test.

We consider how many Q_i lead the system to be consistent with both $\pm y_P$. Recall that

$$h_i + e_i = \left(\frac{y_{Q_i} - y_P}{x_{Q_i} - x_P}\right)^2 - x_P - x_{Q_i} = \frac{x_P x_{Q_i}^2 + (a + x_P^2)x_{Q_i} + ax_P + 2b - 2y_{Q_i}y_P}{(x_{Q_i} - x_P)^2}.$$

If $-P$ passes the test, then there exist $\bar{e}_i$ with $|\bar{e}_i| \le \Delta$ such that $h_i = (P - Q_i)_x - \bar{e}_i$, for all $1 \le i \le n$. We therefore have

$$h_i + \bar{e}_i = \left(\frac{y_{Q_i} - y_P}{x_{Q_i} - x_P}\right)^2 - x_P - x_{Q_i} = \frac{x_P x_{Q_i}^2 + (a + x_P^2)x_{Q_i} + ax_P + 2b + 2y_{Q_i}y_P}{(x_{Q_i} - x_P)^2}.$$

Subtracting one from the other and multiplying by $(x_P - x_{Q_i})^2$ we get

$$(e_i - \bar{e}_i)(x_P - x_{Q_i})^2 = -4y_P y_{Q_i}.$$

Squaring both sides and rearranging results in

$$(e_i - \bar{e}_i)^2(x_P - x_{Q_i})^4 - 16y_P^2(x_{Q_i}^3 + ax_{Q_i} + b) \equiv 0 \pmod{p}.$$

This is a non-constant polynomial in x_{Q_i} of degree 4 and therefore for every $\bar{e}_i$ there are at most 4 values for x_{Q_i} that satisfy this equation. Since there are at most 2Δ possible values for each $\bar{e}_i$, and since we can form n such equations,[8] we conclude that the probability that the point $(x_P, -y_P)$ passes the consistency check is bounded by

$$\frac{4^n(2\Delta)^n}{(|E_x| - 1)^n} \le \frac{(16\Delta)^n}{(p - 2\sqrt{p} - 2)^n}.$$

This concludes the proof.

5.2   Proof of Corollary 1

Consider the bounds on $\mathcal{P}_1$ and $\mathcal{P}_2$ in Theorem 1. One needs $1 - \mathcal{P}_1 - \mathcal{P}_2 \ge 1 - p^{-\delta}$, therefore $\mathcal{P}_1 + \mathcal{P}_2 \le p^{-\delta}$, for the claim to hold. As $\mathcal{P}_2$ is smaller than the first bound on $\mathcal{P}_1$ in Theorem 1 we get that $\mathcal{P}_1 + \mathcal{P}_2$ is bounded by

$$2\frac{8^n(6\eta\Delta + 1)^{6n+3}}{(p - 2\sqrt{p} - 2)^n} + \frac{16(6\eta\Delta + 1)^6}{p - 2\sqrt{p} - 2} + \frac{2n + 3}{p - 2\sqrt{p}}. \tag{14}$$

---

[8] Notice that we can also form n equations from the values $h_{i'}$. For each i each solution x_{Q_i} should satisfy an additional equation $(e_{i'} - \bar{e}_{i'})(x_P - x_{Q_i})^2 = 4y_P y_{Q_i}$. However, adding the two equations results in the condition $e_i + e_{i'} - \bar{e}_i - \bar{e}_{i'} = 0$. While this condition can be always satisfied (e.g. $\bar{e}_{i'} = e_i, \bar{e}_i = e_{i'}$), the probability it holds depends on the model for the oracle, i.e. how the noise terms $e_i, e_{i'}$ are generated.

It is sufficient to bound the latter by $p^{-\delta}$.

Consider the third term in (14). For the claim to hold, one needs

$$\frac{2n_0 + 3}{p - 2\sqrt{p}} < \frac{1}{p^\delta},$$

from which it is easy to derive the minimal p (thus the minimal bit size m of p) for the condition to hold. We therefore let δ' such that $p^{-\delta'} = p^{-\delta} - \frac{2n_0+3}{p-2\sqrt{p}}$ (assuming the later is positive) and bound each of the other terms in (14) by $\frac{p^{-\delta'}}{2}$. Notice that $\delta' > \delta$.

Plugging $p = 2^{m+O(1)}$ and $\Delta = 2^{m-k+O(1)}$ in the first term (14), and since $k > (5/6 + \epsilon)m$, we have

$$\frac{2 \cdot 8^n (6\eta\Delta + 1)^{6n+3}}{(p - 2\sqrt{p} - 2)^n} = \frac{2^{3n+1}(2^{O(1)}\eta 2^{m-k+O(1)} + 1)^{6n+3}}{(2^{m+O(1)} - 2^{m/2+O(1)} - 2)^n}$$

$$= \eta^{6n+3} 2^{(6n+3)(m-k+O(1))-(m+O(1))n}$$

$$\leq \eta^{6n+3} 2^{(6n+3)(m/6-m\epsilon+O(1))-(m+O(1))n}$$

$$= 2^{(6n+3)(\log \eta - m\epsilon)+m/2+O(n)}.$$

The latter is smaller than $\frac{p^{-\delta'}}{2} = 2^{-\delta'(m-1+O(1))}$ if $(6n+3)(\log \eta - \epsilon m) + m/2 + O(n) \leq -\delta'(m + O(1))$, which simplifies to (for some sufficiently large absolute constant C_0)

$$(6n + 3)(\epsilon - m^{-1}(\log \eta + C_0)) \geq \delta' + \frac{1}{2} > \delta + \frac{1}{2}. \tag{15}$$

Using $3\epsilon \geq \delta$ and $n \geq n_0$, it is easy to verify that (for a sufficiently large absolute constant C_1)

$$m > \epsilon^{-1}(2 \log \eta + C_1) \tag{16}$$

implies (15).

Similarly, to show that the second term in (14) is bounded by $\frac{p^{-\delta'}}{2}$ one gets the condition (for some sufficiently large absolute constant C_2)

$$6(\epsilon - m^{-1}(\log \eta + C_3)) \geq \delta' > \delta,$$

which can be shown to hold when (for a sufficiently large absolute constant C_3)

$$m > (6 \log \eta + C_3)(6\epsilon - \delta)^{-1}.$$

The latter is implied by (15), therefore by (16), provided C_0 is large enough.

For A_1 we apply the 1-SVP algorithm (with running time $\tilde{O}(2^{2d})$) of Micciancio and Voulgaris [18] to a lattice of dimension $d = 3n_0 + 3$, which gives $\eta = 2\sqrt{3n_0 + 1}$. For A_2, we use the $2^{O(d(\log \log d)^2/\log d)}$-SVP algorithm (with running time $\tilde{O}(d)$) of Schnorr [20] for the dimension $d = 3n_0 + 3$, which gives $\eta = 2^{n_0+2}\sqrt{3n_0 + 1}$. Using $n_0 = \lceil \frac{1}{6\epsilon} \rceil$, the bounds m_i follow.

6   Additional Results

The techniques presented in the previous sections can be used to show some additional results, which we briefly sketch here. Considering EC-HNP with the LSB_k function, similar results can be derived for the least significant $5/6$ bits of the x-coordinate as we show in Sect. 6.1. In Sect. 6.2 we address the bit security of the Diffie–Hellman key exchange protocol in elliptic curves over extension fields $\mathbb{F}_q$. We refer to the full version of this paper [21] for more details.

6.1   EC-HNP with Least Significant Bits

As we allow k to take any (positive) real value, we define LSB_k by $\mathrm{LSB}_k(x) := x$ (mod $\lceil 2^k \rceil$). In other words, $\mathrm{LSB}_k(x)$ gives x mod l for $2 \le l = \lceil 2^k \rceil \le p$, not necessarily a power of 2.

Let $h = \mathrm{LSB}_k((P+Q)_x) = (P+Q)_x \mod l = (s_{P+Q}^2 - x_P - x_Q - qp) - le$ for some q and $|e| < \frac{p}{2l} \le \frac{p}{2^{k+1}}$. For $u = l^{-1} \in \mathbb{Z}_p^*$ we have (where the operations are in $\mathbb{F}_p$)

$$
\overline{h} := hu = \left(\left(\frac{y_P - y_Q}{x_P - x_Q} \right)^2 - x_P - x_Q - qp - le \right) u
$$

$$
= u \left(\left(\frac{y_P - y_Q}{x_P - x_Q} \right)^2 - x_P - x_Q \right) - q'p - e \equiv u \left(\left(\frac{y_P - y_Q}{x_P - x_Q} \right)^2 - x_P - x_Q \right) - e .
$$

Now let $h_0 = \mathrm{LSB}_k(x_P) = x_P - le_0$ and $h' = \mathrm{LSB}_k((P-Q)_x) = (P-Q)_x$ mod $l = (s_{P-Q}^2 - x_P - x_Q - rp) - le'$ for some r and $|e_0|, |e'| < \frac{p}{2l} \le \frac{p}{2^{k+1}}$. Then

$$
\overline{h}' := h'u \equiv u \left(\left(\frac{y_P + y_Q}{x_P - x_Q} \right)^2 - x_P - x_Q \right) - e' \quad (\mathrm{mod}\ p) .
$$

Letting $\widetilde{h} = \overline{h} + \overline{h}'$ and $\widetilde{e} = e + e'$ and plugging $x_P = h_0 + le_0$ in (1) above we get

$$
\widetilde{h} + \widetilde{e} = u \left((P+Q)_x + (P-Q)_x \right)
$$

$$
\equiv 2u \left(\frac{x_Q(h_0 + le_0)^2 + (a + x_Q^2)(h_0 + le_0) + a x_Q + 2b}{(h_0 + le_0 - x_Q)^2} \right) \quad (\mathrm{mod}\ p) .
$$

Multiplying by $(h_0 + le_0 - x_Q)^2$ results in a bivariate polynomial in $e_0, \widetilde{e}$ of degree 3, similar to (2) above. We expect to get a similar result to the one presented above.

6.2   Bit Security of Elliptic Curve Diffie–Hellman over Extension Fields

The field $\mathbb{F}_q = \mathbb{F}_{p^d}$ is a d-dimensional vector space over $\mathbb{F}_p$. We fix a basis $\{\mathbf{b}_1, \ldots, \mathbf{b}_d\}$ for $\mathbb{F}_q$, and represent points $\mathbf{x} \in \mathbb{F}_q$ with respect to that basis:

for $\mathbf{x} = \sum_{i=1}^{d} x^i \mathbf{b_i}$ we write $\mathbf{x} = (x^1, \ldots, x^d)$. We consider $E(\mathbb{F}_q)$, the group of elliptic curve points over $\mathbb{F}_q$.

For the elliptic curve hidden number problem in this setting, a natural question is whether the ability to recover one component allows to recover the entire secret point. This problem, in the elliptic curve context, was studied by Jao, Jetchev and Venkatesan (JJV) [14]. They consider the following hidden number problem for elliptic curves, which they call *multiplier elliptic curve hidden number problem*: Given an oracle $\mathcal{O}$ that computes a single component of the x-coordinate of the map $r \to [r]P$, that is $\mathcal{O}(r) = ([r]P)_x^i$, recover the point P.

The algorithm given by JJV to this problem is polynomial in $\log(p)$ but not in d, and therefore suits problems where one fixes the degree d and let $\log p$ grow. That is, for extension fields $\mathbb{F}_{p^d}$ of a constant degree. However, there is a drawback in JJV's approach: they can only work with small multipliers r. As a consequence, it is not clear that by considering only small multipliers, this hidden number problem has a unique solution, or a small set of solutions.[9]

This leads them to give precise statements only for degrees 2 and 3 (Propositions 3.1 and 3.2), but to leave the constant degree case (Sect. 3.3) with a description of a general approach, and so a proof of bit security cannot be derived in this case. Moreover, we show that the solution for $d = 3$ is incomplete. The approach presented here overcomes this drawback, and therefore gives a complete solution to any constant extension degree. Moreover, the solution holds for the y-coordinate as well. Our solution is based on (a generalization of) the algorithm given by JJV.

In a nutshell, the essence of the solution is to construct a system of (small degree) polynomials for which $\mathbf{x_P} = (x_P^1, \ldots, x_P^d)$ is a simultaneous solution, which will result in some small number of candidates for P.

Improved Results. Our approach overcomes the drawback in the previous work, as the 'multipliers' Q are not restricted to any (short) interval. As already mentioned in [14], in the case of random multipliers, it is easy to argue for uniqueness.[10]

Proposition 1. *Let E be an elliptic curve over an extension field $\mathbb{F}_{p^d}$. There exists an algorithm, polynomial in $\log p$, that solves EC-HNP given an oracle that outputs a complete component of either the x or y coordinates.*

Proof (sketch). Consider the x-coordinate case. Similar to the solution of EC-HNP over a prime field, one queries the oracle $\mathcal{O}$ on $\pm t$ to get one component of $(P + [t]R)_x$ and $(P - [t]R)_x$. Denote $Q := [t]R$, and let $\{\mathbf{b_1}, \ldots, \mathbf{b_d}\}$ be a basis for $\mathbb{F}_p^d$. It holds that

---

[9] For comparison, it is easy to show that restricting to small multipliers in HNP in $\mathbb{F}_p^*$ yields exponentially many solutions.

[10] We note that the multipliers here and in [14] have different context, as the elliptic curve hidden number problem is defined differently. However, the arguments for uniqueness stay the same.

$$(P+Q)_x+(P-Q)_x=2\left(\frac{\mathbf{x}_Q\mathbf{x}_P^2+(\mathbf{a}+\mathbf{x}_Q^2)\mathbf{x}_P+\mathbf{ax}_Q+2\mathbf{b}}{(\mathbf{x}_P-\mathbf{x}_Q)^2}\right)=\frac{R_1(x_P^1,\ldots,x_P^d)}{R_2(x_P^1,\ldots,x_P^d)},$$

where R_1,R_2 are polynomials (depending on x_Q) of degree 2 in $\mathbb{F}_p^d[x^1,\ldots,x^d]$. Rewrite

$$\frac{R_1(x^1,\ldots,x^d)}{R_2(x^1,\ldots,x^d)}=\frac{R_1^1\mathbf{b}_1+\ldots+R_1^d\mathbf{b}_d}{R_2^1\mathbf{b}_1+\ldots+R_2^d\mathbf{b}_d},$$

where for $1\leq j\leq d$ each polynomial $R_1^j(x^1,\ldots,x^d),R_2^j(x^1,\ldots,x^d)$ has coefficients in $\mathbb{F}_p$. We "rationalize" the denominator to express

$$\frac{R_1(x^1,\ldots,x^d)}{R_2(x^1,\ldots,x^d)}=r^1(x^1,\ldots,x^d)\mathbf{b}_1+\ldots+r^d(x^1,\ldots,x^d)\mathbf{b}_d,$$

where r^j are rational functions with coefficients in $\mathbb{F}_p$, of degree at most $2d$.

We suppose to have access to component i, that is, we know $(P+Q)_x^i$ and $(P-Q)_x^i$. We have

$$\mathcal{O}(t)+\mathcal{O}(-t)=(P+Q)_x^i+(P-Q)_x^i=r^i(x_P^1,\ldots,x_P^d)=\frac{r_{Q,1}^i(x_P^1,\ldots,x_P^d)}{r_{Q,2}^i(x_P^1,\ldots,x_P^d)}.$$

Multiplying by $r_{Q,2}^i(x^1,\ldots,x^d)$ and rearranging we get the following polynomial

$$g_Q(x^1,\ldots,x^d):=r_{Q,1}^i(x^1,\ldots,x^d)-r_{Q,2}^i(x^1,\ldots,x^d)\left((P+Q)_x^i+(P-Q)_x^i\right),$$

where $g_Q(\mathbf{x}_P)=g_Q(x_P^1,\ldots,x_P^d)=0$, and g_Q is of degree at most $2d$.

We repeat with different points Q and look for a simultaneous solution to the system $\{g_Q=0\}$. When choosing the Q's uniformly and independently, standard arguments (like the root counting above) can be used to show that a sufficiently large system $\{g_Q\}$ is expected to have a unique (simultaneous) root.

The case of the y-coordinate is a simple adaptation of the method, where one takes the third-degree polynomial

$$(P+Q)_y-(P-Q)_y=2\mathbf{y}_Q\left(\frac{\mathbf{x}_P^3+3\mathbf{x}_Q\mathbf{x}_P^2+3\mathbf{ax}_P+\mathbf{ax}_Q+4\mathbf{b}}{(\mathbf{x}_P-\mathbf{x}_Q)^3}\right).$$

∎

Corollary 2. *For an elliptic curve defined over a constant-degree extension field, computing a single component of the Diffie–Hellman key (for either the x or y coordinates) is as hard as computing the entire key.*

We refer to the full version of this paper [21] for a general method and a comparison between JJV's approach and our approach. We finish with a correction to JJV's work.

Correction. We finish with a couple of remarks regarding the solution for $d = 3$ in [14, Sect. 3.2]. In this case JJV take the resultant of two bivariate polynomials of degree $10, 25$ in each variable. First, as we show in Appendix B, this resultant is a univariate polynomial of degree at most 500, not 250 as written there. More importantly, while the resultant's degree is bounded by a constant value, in general it can also be identically zero, which will then not yield a constant-sized set of possible solutions (as the zero polynomial is satisfied by every point). This point is important, especially because the authors identify a problem with showing uniqueness of the solution, or the existence of a small set of solutions. However, the paper [14] does not treat this point.

7 Comments

It is desirable to get bit security results also in the case of an imperfect oracle. The main obstacle in achieving such a result is that the lattice constructed by the algorithm has to be of an exact shape, which will not be achieved in general if some equations are not of the right form. It should be noted that like other problems (see for example [9, Sect. 4.1] for HNP) one can consider an imperfect oracle which is very likely to answer all the queries correctly, when its inputs are random. In addition, one can consider the approach suggested in [12] for imperfect oracles.

A natural question is whether a similar strong bit security result can be shown for the y-coordinate of the elliptic curve Diffie–Hellman key. Unfortunately, the trick presented in this paper, using 2 correlated equations to eliminate one variable, seems out of reach when one works with the y-coordinate. We remark that one can still get some results using the approaches described in Sect. 4.1, but they ought to be weak results.

Moreover, while Weierstrass equations are normally used to represent elliptic curves, Edwards curves are also of interest. The y-coordinate in Edwards curves is considered analogous to the x-coordinate in Weierstrass curves. One therefore expects to have analogous equations for $(P + Q)_y + (P - Q)_y$ and for the y-coordinate of point multiplication, i.e. $([r]P)_y$. It is of interest to get solutions for the elliptic curve hidden number problem using Edwards curves as well.

Acknowledgements. Many thanks to my supervisor Steven Galbraith for his help and guidance.

A   Consistency Check – Filtering Impossible Secrets

We introduce a test that takes a candidate P' for the secret point P, and determines whether P' is not the secret. That is, after running the test, P' is either guaranteed not to be P or it is potentially the secret point P. We give a bound on the probability that the outcome of the test is inconclusive, for $P' \neq P$ (it is clear that if $P' = P$ the test is inconclusive). Specifically, given the candidate for

x_P from Theorem 1, one can test which value (if any) is the correct y-coordinate y_P. Moreover, one can test whether $y_P \neq 0$ or $P \neq \pm Q_i$.

Given a candidate $P' = (x_{P'}, y_{P'})$, the consistency check goes over the pairs $(Q, h = \mathrm{MSB}_k((P+Q)_x))$ and checks if these values are consistent with the problem's settings. That is, we use h to derive a candidate $\bar{e}$ for the noise e, and check if $|\bar{e}| \leq \Delta$. Formally, using $h_0 = x_P - e_0$ we compute

$$\bar{e}_0 := x_{P'} - h_0 \mod p,$$

and check if $|\bar{e}_0| \leq \Delta$. If so then for every $1 \leq i \leq n$ using $h_i = \mathrm{MSB}_k((P+Q_i)_x)$ we compute

$$\bar{e}_i := \left(\frac{y_{P'} - y_Q}{x_{P'} - x_Q}\right)^2 - x_{P'} - x_Q - h_i \mod p,$$

and check if $|\bar{e}_i| \leq \Delta$. We do the same process with $h_{i'}$. If at any point this inequality does not hold, we can stop the test and determine that $P' \neq P$. Otherwise, P' passes the consistency check and is potentially the secret point P.

For completeness, we analyze the probability (over the samples Q_i) of the event in which a candidate $P' \neq P$ passes the consistency check. Hence, suppose that $P' = (x_{P'}, y_{P'})$ passed the consistency check.

Probability of $x_{P'} \neq x_P$. Given $h_i, h_{i'}$, from Sect. 4.1 above we have

$$h_i + h_{i'} = 2\left(\frac{x_P x_{Q_i}^2 + (a + x_P^2)x_{Q_i} + ax_P + 2b}{(x_P - x_{Q_i})^2}\right) - e_i - e_{i'}.$$

Since P' passed the consistency check there exist $|\bar{e}_i|, |\bar{e}_{i'}| \leq \Delta$ such that

$$h_i + h_{i'} = 2\left(\frac{x_{P'} x_{Q_i}^2 + (a + x_{P'}^2)x_{Q_i} + ax_{P'} + 2b}{(x_{P'} - x_{Q_i})^2}\right) - \bar{e}_i - \bar{e}_{i'}.$$

Subtracting these two equations and multiplying by $(x_P - x_{Q_i})^2 (x_{P'} - x_{Q_i})^2$ we get

$$(e_i + e_{i'} - \bar{e}_i - \bar{e}_{i'})(x_P - x_{Q_i})^2(x_{P'} - x_{Q_i})^2 =$$
$$2\left((x_P x_{Q_i}^2 + (a + x_P^2)x_{Q_i} + ax_P + 2b)(x_{P'} - x_{Q_i})^2\right.$$
$$\left. - (x_{P'} x_{Q_i}^2 + (a + x_{P'}^2)x_{Q_i} + ax_{P'} + 2b)(x_P - x_{Q_i})^2\right).$$

By rearranging we get a polynomial in x_{Q_i} of degree 4. By simple algebra one can check that this polynomial is identically zero if and only if $x_{P'} = x_P$ (thus $e_i + e_{i'} - \bar{e}_i - \bar{e}_{i'} = 0$). We assume $x_{P'} \neq x_P$. Therefore for every $\bar{e}_i, \bar{e}_{i'}$ there are at most 4 values for x_{Q_i} that satisfy this equation. Since there are $2\Delta + 1$ possible values for each $\bar{e}_i, \bar{e}_{i'}$ we conclude that the probability that $x_{P'} \neq x_P$ is bounded by

$$\frac{4^n(2\Delta + 1)^{2n}}{(|E_x| - 1)^n} \leq \frac{2^n(4\Delta + 2)^{2n}}{(p - 2\sqrt{p} - 2)^n}.$$

Probability of $x_{P'} = x_P$ and $y_{P'} \neq y_P$. The probability that $P' = (x_P, -y_P)$ passes the consistency check, is analyzed at the end of the proof of Theorem 1, and shown to be bounded by

$$\frac{4^n (2\Delta)^n}{(|E_x| - 1)^n} \leq \frac{(16\Delta)^n}{(p - 2\sqrt{p} - 2)^n}.$$

Remark 4. Although the aim of this paper is to give a bit security result and not a practical algorithm, for completeness purposes we consider a matter of practice. In the case in which the value $d_0 \neq 0$, the recovered value $e := f_0/f_0' \neq e_0$, and therefore $x_{P'} := h + e \neq x_P$. Running the consistency check on P' might reveal that indeed $P' \neq P$. One can derive from Eqs. (8)–(11) other candidates for e_0 and subsequently candidates for x_P, and apply the consistency check on them. If none of these candidates pass the consistency check, then one can test P' where $y_{P'} = 0$ and $P' = \pm Q_i$. We analyze the probability that there exists $P' \neq P$ that is consistent with all $2n + 1$ samples.

We use the analysis above which shows that the probability that a candidate P' with $x_{P'} \neq x_P$ passes the test with the $2n$ equations is bounded by

$$\frac{(4\Delta + 2)^{2n}}{(|E_x| - 1)^n} \leq \frac{2^n (4\Delta + 2)^{2n}}{(p - 2\sqrt{p} - 2)^n}.$$

We also have $x_{P'} - \bar{e}_0 = h_0 = x_P - e_0$, so $x_{P'} = x_P - e_0 + \bar{e}_0$ can take 2Δ values. Thus, the probability that any P' with $x_{P'} \neq x_P$ passes the consistency check is bounded by

$$\frac{2^{n+1} \Delta (4\Delta + 2)^{2n}}{(p - 2\sqrt{p} - 2)^n}.$$

With the above bound for $y_{P'} \neq -y_P$ we get that the probability that there exists $P' \neq P$ that passes the consistency check is bounded by

$$\frac{2^{n+1} \Delta (4\Delta + 2)^{2n}}{(p - 2\sqrt{p} - 2)^n} + \frac{(16\Delta)^n}{(p - 2\sqrt{p} - 2)^n}.$$

B Resultant's Degree

Claim. Let $p, q \in k[x, y]$ be two polynomials with

$$\deg_x p = n_x, \ \deg_y p = n_y,$$

$$\deg_x q = m_x, \ \deg_y q = m_y.$$

Then the degree (in x) of the resultant of p and q in variable y is at most $m_y n_x + n_y m_x$.

Proof. The Sylvester matrix of p and q with respect to y is a $(m_y + n_y) \times (m_y + n_y)$ matrix. The first m_y rows, coming from the coefficients of p, contain polynomials in x of degree at most n_x. Similarly, the last n_y rows contain polynomials in x of degree at most m_x. The resultant of p and q in variable y is given by the determinant of this matrix, which is formed by summing products of an entry from each row. The first m_y rows contribute at most $m_y n_x$ to the degree of x, and the last n_y rows contribute at most $n_y m_x$. ∎

References

1. Babai, L.: On Lovász' lattice reduction and the nearest lattice point problem. Combinatorica **6**(1), 1–13 (1986)
2. Blackburn, S.R., Gomez-Perez, D., Gutierrez, J., Shparlinski, I.E.: Predicting the inversive generator. In: Paterson, K.G. (ed.) Cryptography and Coding 2003. LNCS, vol. 2898, pp. 264–275. Springer, Heidelberg (2003). doi:10.1007/978-3-540-40974-8_21
3. Blackburn, S.R., Gomez-Perez, D., Gutierrez, J., Shparlinski, I.E.: Predicting nonlinear pseudorandom number generators. Math. Comput. **74**(251), 1471–1494 (2005)
4. Blake, I.F., Garefalakis, T.: On the complexity of the discrete logarithm and Diffie-Hellman problems. J. Complex. **20**(2–3), 148–170 (2004)
5. Blake, I.F., Garefalakis, T., Shparlinski, I.E.: On the bit security of the Diffie-Hellman key. Appl. Algebra Eng. Commun. Comput. **16**(6), 397–404 (2006)
6. Boneh, D.: The decision Diffie-Hellman problem. In: Buhler, J.P. (ed.) ANTS 1998. LNCS, vol. 1423, pp. 48–63. Springer, Heidelberg (1998). doi:10.1007/BFb0054851
7. Boneh, D., Halevi, S., Howgrave-Graham, N.: The modular inversion hidden number problem. In: Boyd, C. (ed.) ASIACRYPT 2001. LNCS, vol. 2248, pp. 36–51. Springer, Heidelberg (2001). doi:10.1007/3-540-45682-1_3
8. Boneh, D., Shparlinski, I.E.: On the unpredictability of bits of the elliptic curve Diffie-Hellman scheme. In: Kilian, J. (ed.) CRYPTO 2001. LNCS, vol. 2139, pp. 201–212. Springer, Heidelberg (2001). doi:10.1007/3-540-44647-8_12
9. Boneh, D., Venkatesan, R.: Hardness of computing the most significant bits of secret keys in Diffie-Hellman and related schemes. In: Koblitz, N. (ed.) CRYPTO 1996. LNCS, vol. 1109, pp. 129–142. Springer, Heidelberg (1996). doi:10.1007/3-540-68697-5_11
10. Coppersmith, D.: Small solutions to polynomial equations, and low exponent RSA vulnerabilities. J. Cryptol. **10**(4), 233–260 (1997)
11. González Vasco, M.I., Näslund, M.: A survey of hard core functions. In: Lam, K.-Y., Shparlinski, I., Wang, H., Xing, C. (eds.) Proceedings of Workshop on Cryptography and Computational Number Theory 1999. Progress in Computer Science and Applied Logic, pp. 227–255. Birkhäuser, Basel (2001)
12. González Vasco, M.I., Näslund, M., Shparlinski, I.E.: New results on the hardness of Diffie-Hellman bits. In: Bao, F., Deng, R., Zhou, J. (eds.) PKC 2004. LNCS, vol. 2947, pp. 159–172. Springer, Heidelberg (2004). doi:10.1007/978-3-540-24632-9_12
13. González Vasco, M.I., Shparlinski, I.E.: On the security of Diffie-Hellman bits. In: Lam, K.-Y., Shparlinski, I., Wang, H., Xing, C. (eds.) Proceedings of Workshop on Cryptography and Computational Number Theory 1999. Progress in Computer Science and Applied Logic, pp. 257–268. Birkhäuser, Basel (2001)
14. Jao, D., Jetchev, D., Venkatesan, R.: On the bits of elliptic curve Diffie-Hellman keys. In: Srinathan, K., Rangan, C.P., Yung, M. (eds.) INDOCRYPT 2007. LNCS, vol. 4859, pp. 33–47. Springer, Heidelberg (2007). doi:10.1007/978-3-540-77026-8_4
15. Jetchev, D., Venkatesan, R.: Bits security of the elliptic curve Diffie–Hellman secret keys. In: Wagner, D. (ed.) CRYPTO 2008. LNCS, vol. 5157, pp. 75–92. Springer, Heidelberg (2008). doi:10.1007/978-3-540-85174-5_5
16. Li, W.-C.W., Näslund, M., Shparlinski, I.E.: Hidden number problem with the trace and bit security of XTR and LUC. In: Yung, M. (ed.) CRYPTO 2002. LNCS, vol. 2442, pp. 433–448. Springer, Heidelberg (2002). doi:10.1007/3-540-45708-9_28

17. Ling, S., Shparlinski, I.E., Steinfeld, R., Wang, H.: On the modular inversion hidden number problem. J. Symbolic Comput. **47**(4), 358–367 (2012)
18. Micciancio, D., Voulgaris, P.: A deterministic single exponential time algorithm for most lattice problems based on Voronoi cell computations. SIAM J. Comput. **42**(3), 1364–1391 (2013)
19. Nguyen, P.Q., Shparlinski, I.E.: The insecurity of the digital signature algorithm with partially known nonces. J. Cryptol. **15**(3), 151–176 (2002)
20. Schnorr, C.P.: A hierarchy of polynomial time lattice basis reduction algorithms. Theoret. Comput. Sci. **53**(2–3), 201–224 (1987)
21. Shani, B.: On the bit security of elliptic curve Diffie-Hellman. In: Cryptology ePrint Archive, Report 2016/1189 (2016). http://eprint.iacr.org/2016/1189
22. Shparlinski, I.E.: Sparse polynomial approximation in finite fields. In: Proceedings of 33rd ACM Symposium on Theory of Computing - STOC 2001, pp. 209–215. ACM, New York (2001)
23. Shparlinski, I.E.: Playing "Hide-and-Seek" in finite fields: hidden number problem and its applications. In: Proceedings of 7th Spanish Meeting on Cryptology and Information Security, pp. 49–72 (2002)
24. Shparlinski, I.E.: Playing "Hide-and-Seek" with numbers: the hidden number problem, lattices and exponential sums. In: Garrett, P., Lieman, D. (eds.) Public-Key Cryptography; Proceedings of Symposia in Applied Mathematics, vol. 62, pp. 153–177. AMS (2005)
25. Verheul, E.R.: Certificates of recoverability with scalable recovery agent security. In: Imai, H., Zheng, Y. (eds.) PKC 2000. LNCS, vol. 1751, pp. 258–275. Springer, Heidelberg (2000). doi:10.1007/978-3-540-46588-1_18

Extended Tower Number Field Sieve with Application to Finite Fields of Arbitrary Composite Extension Degree

Taechan Kim[1(✉)] and Jinhyuck Jeong[2]

[1] NTT Secure Platform Laboratories, Tokyo, Japan
taechan.kim@lab.ntt.co.jp
[2] Seoul National University, Seoul, Korea
wlsyrlekd@snu.ac.kr

Abstract. We propose a generalization of exTNFS algorithm recently introduced by Kim and Barbulescu (CRYPTO 2016). The algorithm, exTNFS, is a state-of-the-art algorithm for discrete logarithm in $\mathbb{F}_{p^n}$ in the medium prime case, but it only applies when $n = \eta\kappa$ is a composite with nontrivial factors η and κ such that $\gcd(\eta, \kappa) = 1$. Our generalization, however, shows that exTNFS algorithm can be also adapted to the setting with an arbitrary composite n maintaining its best asymptotic complexity. We show that one can compute a discrete logarithm in medium case in the running time of $L_{p^n}(1/3, \sqrt[3]{48/9})$ (resp. $L_{p^n}(1/3, 1.71)$ if multiple number fields are used), where n is an *arbitrary composite*. This should be compared with a recent variant by Sarkar and Singh (Asiacrypt 2016) that has the fastest running time of $L_{p^n}(1/3, \sqrt[3]{64/9})$ (resp. $L_{p^n}(1/3, 1.88)$) when n is a power of prime 2. When p is of special form, the complexity is further reduced to $L_{p^n}(1/3, \sqrt[3]{32/9})$. On the practical side, we emphasize that the key-size of pairing-based cryptosystems should be updated following to our algorithm if the embedding degree n remains composite.

Keywords: Discrete logarithm problem · Number field sieve · Finite fields · Cryptanalysis

1   Introduction

Discrete logarithm problem (DLP) over a multiplicative subgroup of finite fields $\mathbb{F}_Q$, $Q = p^n$, gathers its particular interest due to its prime importance in pairing-based cryptography. Over a generic group, the best known algorithm of the DLP takes exponential running time in the bitsize of the group order. However, in the case for the multiplicative group of finite fields one can exploit a special algebraic structure of the group to design better algorithms, where the DLP can be solved much more efficiently than in exponential time. For example, when the characteristic p is small compared to the extension degree n, the best known algorithms have quasi-polynomial time complexity [3,11].

© International Association for Cryptologic Research 2017
S. Fehr (Ed.): PKC 2017, Part I, LNCS 10174, pp. 388–408, 2017.
DOI: 10.1007/978-3-662-54365-8_16

Recall the usual L_Q-notation,

$$L_Q(\ell, c) = \exp\left((c + o(1))(\log Q)^\ell (\log\log Q)^{1-\ell}\right),$$

for some constants $0 \le \ell \le 1$ and $c > 0$. We call the characteristic $p = L_Q(\ell_p, c_p)$ medium when $1/3 < \ell_p < 2/3$ and large when $2/3 < \ell_p \le 1$. We say that a field $\mathbb{F}_{p^n}$ is in the boundary case when $\ell_p = 2/3$.

For medium and large characteristic, all the best known attacks are variants of the number field sieve (NFS) algorithm. Initially used for factoring, NFS was rapidly introduced in DLP to target prime fields [10, 23]. It was about a decade later by Schirokauer [24] that NFS was adapted to target non-prime fields $\mathbb{F}_{p^n}$ with $n > 1$. This is known today as tower number field sieve (TNFS) [4]. On the other hand, an approach by Joux et al. [14], which we denote by JLSV, was on a main stream of recent improvements on DLP over medium and large characteristic case. JLSV's idea is similar to the variant used to target prime fields, except the step called polynomial selection. This polynomial selection method was later supplemented with generalized Joux-Lercier (GJL) method [2, 18], Conjugation (Conj) method [2], and Sarkar-Singh (SS) method [22] leading improvements on the complexity of the NFS algorithm. However, in all these algorithms the complexity for the medium prime case is slightly larger than that of large prime case. Moreover there was an anomaly that the best complexity was obtained in the boundary case, $\ell_p = 2/3$.

Finally, in a recent breakthrough by Kim and Barbulescu [17], they obtained an algorithm, called exTNFS, of better complexity for the medium prime case than in the large prime case. Although this approach only applies to fields of extension degree n where $n = \eta\kappa$ has factors $\eta, \kappa > 1$ such that $\gcd(\eta, \kappa) = 1$, it was enough to frighten pairing-based community since a number of popular pairing-friendly curves, such as Barreto-Naehrig curve [7], are in the category that exTNFS applies.

Then one might ask a question whether transitioning into pairing-friendly curves with embedding degree n, a prime power, would be immune to this recent attack by Kim and Barbulescu. In practice, pairings with embedding degree of a prime power, such as Kachisa-Schafer-Scott curve with embedding degree 16 [16] or Barreto-Lynn-Scott curve with embedding degree 27 [6], were considered to be suitable for protocols in which products of pairings play a major part [25]. Unfortunately, our answer is also negative to use such pairings: we show that our algorithm has the same complexity as exTNFS algorithm for any composite n, so the keysize of the pairing-based cryptosystems should be also updated according to our algorithm whenever the embedding degree is composite.

Related Works. When the extension degree n, which is composite, cannot be factored into relatively prime factors (for example, n is a prime power), the best known attacks for the medium prime case still had the complexity $L_Q(1/3, \sqrt[3]{96/9})$ until Sarkar and Singh proposed an algorithm [20] of the best complexity $L_Q(1/3, \sqrt[3]{64/9})$. Note that, however, this is still slightly larger than the best complexity of Kim-Barbulescu's exTNFS. Recently, soon after a preprint

Table 1. The complexity of each algorithm. Each cell in the second indicates c if the complexity is $L_Q(1/3, (c/9)^{\frac{1}{3}})$ when $p = L_Q(\ell_p)$, $1/3 < \ell_p < 2/3$.

Method	Complexity in the medium case	Conditions on n
NFS-(Conj and GJL) [2]	96	n: any integers
exTNFS-$\mathcal{C}$ [20]	$\geq 64^{a}$	$n = 2^i$ for some $i > 1$
exTNFS-KimBar [17]	$\geq 48^{a}$	$n = \eta\kappa$ $(\eta, \kappa \neq 1)$, $\gcd(\eta, \kappa) = 1$
exTNFS-$\mathcal{D}$ [21]	$\geq 48^{a}$	n: any composite
exTNFS-new (this article)	$\geq 48^{a}$	n: any composite
	≤ 54.28	$n = 2^i$ for some $i > 1$

[a]The best complexity is obtained when n has a factor of the appropriate size (refer to each paper for details).

Table 2. The complexity of each algorithm using multiple number fields. Each cell in the second column indicates an approximation of c if the complexity is $L_Q(1/3, (c/9)^{\frac{1}{3}})$ when $p = L_Q(\ell_p)$, $1/3 < \ell_p < 2/3$.

Method	Complexity in the medium case	Conditions on n
MNFS-(Conj and GJL) [19]	89.45	n: any integers
MexTNFS-$\mathcal{C}$ [20]	$\geq 61.29^{a}$	$n = 2^i$ for some $i > 1$
MexTNFS-KimBar [17]	$\geq 45.00^{a}$	$n = \eta\kappa$ $(\eta, \kappa \neq 1)$, $\gcd(\eta, \kappa) = 1$
MexTNFS-$\mathcal{D}$ [21]	$\geq 45.00^{a}$	n: any composite
MexTNFS-new (this article)	$\geq 45.00^{a}$	n: any composite
	≤ 59.80	$n = 2^i 3^j$ for some $i + j > 1$
	≤ 50.76	$n = 2^i$ for some $i > 1$

[a]The best complexity is obtained when n has a factor of the appropriate size (refer to each paper for details).

of our paper [13] has been published, Sarkar and Singh proposed an algorithm called exTNFS-$\mathcal{D}$ [21]. Their algorithm has the best complexity as same as our new algorithm, but it provides a wider range of finite fields for which the algorithm achieves a lower complexity than the previous algorithms. One can see Table 1 for a comparison of these previous algorithms on the asymptotic complexity.

All currently known variants of NFS admit variants with multiple number fields (MNFS) which have a slightly better asymptotic complexity. The complexity of these variants is shown in Table 2.

When the characteristic p has a special form, as it is the case for fields in pairing-based cryptosystems, one can further accelerate NFS algorithms using variants called special number field sieve (SNFS). In Table 3 we list asymptotic complexity of each algorithm. When n is a prime power, the algorithm suggested by Joux and Pierrot had been the best algorithm before our algorithm.

Table 3. The complexity of each algorithm used when the characteristic has a special form (SNFS). Each cell indicates an approximation of c if the complexity is $L_Q(1/3, (c/9)^{\frac{1}{3}})$ when $p = L_Q(\ell_p)$, $1/3 < \ell_p < 2/3$.

Method	Complexity in the medium case	Conditions on n
SNFS-JP [15]	64	n: any integers
SexTNFS-KimBar [17]	32	$n = \eta\kappa$ $(\eta, \kappa \neq 1)$, $\gcd(\eta, \kappa) = 1$
SexTNFS-new (this article)	32	n: any composite

Recently, Guillevic, Morain, and Thomé [12] observed that Kim-Barbulescu's technique can be adapted to target the fields of extension degree 4. However, they did not pursue the idea to analyze further its complexity.

Our Contributions. We propose an algorithm that is a state-of-the-art algorithm for the DLP over finite fields of composite extension degrees in the medium prime case as far as we aware. We remark that our algorithm applies to target fields of arbitrary composite extension degree n. If n can be written as $n = \eta\kappa$ for some η and κ with $\gcd(\eta, \kappa) = 1$, our algorithm has the same complexity as Kim-Barbulescu's exTNFS [17]. However, our algorithm allows to choose factors η and κ freely from the co-primality condition, so we have more choices for the pair (η, κ). This helps us to find a better (η, κ) that practically yields a better performance, although the asymptotic complexity is unchanged.

If n is a prime power, the complexity of our algorithm is less than that of Sarkar-Singh's variant [20], a currently best-known algorithm for this case.

When n is a b-smooth integer for an integer $b \leq 4$, we obtain an upper bound for the asymptotic complexity of our algorithm. For example, when n is a power of 2, our algorithm always has the asymptotic complexity less than $L_Q(1/3, 1.82)$. If multiple NFS variants are used, the complexity can always be lowered to $L_Q(1/3, c)$, $c \leq 1.88$, when n is a 4-smooth composite integer, and $L_Q(1/3, c)$, $c \leq 1.78$, when n is a power of 2.

When p is of special form, pairings with embedding degree such as $n = 4, 9, 16$ was not affected by Kim-Barbulescu's algorithm, however, due to our variant of SNFS, the keysize of such pairings should be also updated following to our new complexity.

Our Main Idea. Our main idea comes from a simple modification during the polynomial selection in exTNFS algorithm. In exTNFS algorithm, for a field of a composite extension degree, one represents it as $\mathbb{F}_{p^n} = \mathbb{F}_{(p^\eta)^\kappa}$, where $\mathbb{F}_{p^\eta} = R/pR$ and $R = \mathbb{Z}[t]/h(t)$ for an irreducible polynomial h of degree η, and selects polynomials f and g such that they have a common irreducible factor k of degree κ modulo p, where $\mathbb{F}_{(p^\eta)^\kappa} = \mathbb{F}_{p^\eta}[x]/k(x)$.

In Kim-Barbulescu's exTNFS, f and g are chosen so that they have coefficients in $\mathbb{Z}$, therefore k has its coefficients in $\mathbb{F}_p$. Since any irreducible polynomial of degree κ over $\mathbb{F}_p$ is still irreducible over $\mathbb{F}_{p^\eta}$ if and only if η and κ are relatively prime, Kim-Barbulescu's algorithm only works under the prescribed condition. Although they mentioned that drawing f and g from $R[x]$ instead of $\mathbb{Z}[x]$ can get rid of this condition, all known NFS algorithms only discuss the polynomial selections with integer coefficients and the possibility of using polynomials in $R[x]$ in NFS algorirhtms has remained rather unclear.

In this work, we observe that the idea described above is actually well adapted to the setting of exTNFS algorithm. Indeed, we simply modify most of known polynomial selection methods described in [17] so that the coefficients of polynomials are chosen from R and they can be used in exTNFS algorithm. Furthermore, we show that the formula of the size of norms in number fields constructed by those polynomials, which plays important role in the complexity analysis, has the same bound as in Kim-Barbulescu's exTNFS. Consequently, this leads us to get an algorithm with the same complexity as Kim-Barbulescu's algorithm while our algorithm applies to fields of any composite extension degrees. Recently, Sarkar-Singh's algorithm [20] exploited a similar idea, but their polynomial selection methods are slightly different from ours and it has slightly larger complexity than ours.

Organization. We briefly recall exTNFS algorithm and introduce our algorithm in Sect. 2. The complexity analysis is given in Sect. 3. The variants such as multiple number field sieve and special number field sieve are discussed in Sect. 4. In Sect. 5, we make a precise comparison to the state-of-the-art algorithms at cryptographic sizes. We conclude with cryptographic implications of our result in Sect. 6.

2   Extended TNFS

2.1   Setting

Throughout this paper, we target fields $\mathbb{F}_Q$ with $Q = p^n$ where $n = \eta\kappa$ such that $\eta, \kappa \neq 1$ and the characteristic p is medium or large, i.e. $\ell_p > 1/3$.

We briefly review exTNFS algorithm and then explain our algorithm. Recall the commutative diagram that is familiar in the context of NFS algorithm (Fig. 1). First we select an irreducible polynomial $h(t) \in \mathbb{Z}[t]$ of degree η which is also irreducible modulo p. We put $R := \mathbb{Z}[t]/h(t) = \mathbb{Z}(\iota)$ then $R/pR \simeq \mathbb{F}_{p^\eta}$. We select two polynomials f and g with coefficients in R so that they have a common factor $k(x)$ of degree κ modulo p. We further require k to be irreducible over $\mathbb{F}_{p^\eta}$. Note that the only difference of our algorithm from Kim-Barbulescu's exTNFS is that the coefficients of f and g are chosen from R instead of $\mathbb{Z}$.

The conditions on f, g and h yield two ring homomorphisms from $R[x]$ to $(R/pR)/k(x) = \mathbb{F}_{p^{\eta\kappa}}$ through $R[x]/f(x)$ (or $R[x]/g(x)$). Thus one has the commutative diagram in Fig. 1 which is a generalization of the classical diagram of NFS.

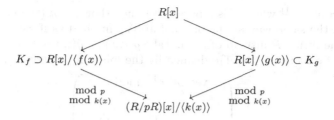

Fig. 1. Commutative diagram of exTNFS. We can choose f and g to be irreducible polynomials over R such that $k = \gcd(f, g) \mod p$ is irreducible over $R/pR = \mathbb{F}_{p^\eta}$.

After the polynomial selection, the exTNFS algorithm proceeds as all other variants of NFS, following the same steps: relations collection, linear algebra and individual logarithm. We skip the description on it and refer to [17] for further details.

2.2 Detailed Descriptions

Polynomial Selection

Choice of h. We have to select a polynomial $h(t) \in \mathbb{Z}[t]$ of degree η which is irreducible modulo p and whose coefficients are as small as possible. As in TNFS [4] we try random polynomials h with small coefficients and factor them in $\mathbb{F}_p[t]$ to test irreducibility. The ratio of irreducible polynomials over all monic polynomials of degree η over $\mathbb{F}_p$ is close to $1/\eta$, thus one succeeds after η trials and since $\eta \leq 3^\eta$ we expect to find h such that $\|h\|_\infty = 1$.

Choice of f and g. Next we select f and g in $R[x]$ which have a common factor $k(x)$ modulo p of degree κ which remains irreducible over $\mathbb{F}_{p^\eta} = R/pR$. We can adapt all the polynomial selection methods discussed in the previous NFS algorithms, such as JLSV's method [14], GJL and Conj [2] method, and so on [5,15,19,22], except that one chooses the coefficients of f and g from R instead of $\mathbb{Z}$. To fix ideas, we describe polynomial selection methods based on $JLSV_2$ method and Conjugation method. A similar idea also applies with GJL method, but we skip the details.

Generalized $JLSV_2$ Method. We describe a generalized method of polynomial selection based on $JLSV_2$ method [14]. To emphasize that the coefficients of polynomial are taken from a ring $R = \mathbb{Z}[\iota]$ instead of a smaller ring $\mathbb{Z}$, we call it as *generalized $JLSV_2$ method* (g$JLSV_2$ method).

First, we select a bivariate polynomial $\widetilde{g}(t, x) \in \mathbb{Z}[t, x]$ such that

$$\widetilde{g}(t, x) = g_0(t) + g_1(t)x + \cdots + g_{\kappa-1}(t)x^{\kappa-1} + x^\kappa,$$

where $g_i(t) \in \mathbb{Z}[t]$'s are polynomials of degree less than η with small integer coefficients. We also require $\widetilde{g} \mod (p, h(t))$ to be irreducible in $\mathbb{F}_{p^\eta}[x]$. Set an integer $W \approx p^{1/(d+1)}$ where d is a parameter such that $d \geq \kappa$ (the parameter W is chosen in the same way as the original JLSV$_2$ method as if we are targeting $\mathbb{F}_{P^\kappa}$ for some prime P instead of $\mathbb{F}_{p^n}$). Take $g(t, x) := \widetilde{g}(t, x + W)$ and consider the lattice of dimension $(d+1)\eta$ defined by the following matrix M:

$$M := \begin{pmatrix} \boxed{\text{vec}(pt^0 x^0 \mod h)} \\ \vdots \\ \boxed{\text{vec}(pt^i x^j \mod h)} \\ \vdots \\ \boxed{\text{vec}(pt^{\eta-1} x^{\kappa-1} \mod h)} \\ \boxed{\text{vec}(g \mod h)} \\ \vdots \\ \boxed{\text{vec}(t^i x^j g \mod h)} \\ \vdots \\ \boxed{\text{vec}(t^{\eta-1} x^{d-\kappa} g \mod h)} \end{pmatrix} \tag{1}$$

where, for all bivariate polynomial $w(t, x) = \sum_{i=0}^{d} w_j(t) x^j$ with $w_j(t) = \sum_{i=0}^{\eta-1} w_{j,i} t^i$, $\text{vec}(w) = (w_{0,0}, \ldots, w_{0,\eta-1}, \ldots, w_{d,0}, \ldots, w_{d,\eta-1})$ of dimension $(d+1)\eta$. For instance, $\text{vec}(pt^i x^j) = (0, \ldots, 0, p, 0, \ldots, 0)$ where only $(j\eta + i + 1)$-th entry is nonzero and $\text{vec}(g) = (g_{0,0}, \ldots, g_{0,\eta-1}, \ldots, g_{\kappa-1,0}, \ldots, g_{\kappa-1,\eta-1}, 1, 0, \ldots, 0)$ for a monic polynomial g of degree κ with respect to x. Note that the determinant of M is $|\det(M)| = p^{\kappa\eta}$.

Finally, take the coefficients of $f(t, x) = \sum_{j=0}^{d} f_j(t) x^j$ with $f_j(t) = \sum_{i=0}^{\eta-1} f_{j,i} t^i$ as the shortest vector of an LLL-reduced basis of the lattice L and set $k = g \mod p$. Then by construction we have

- $\deg_x(f) = d \geq \kappa$ and $\|f\|_\infty := \max\{f_{i,j}\} = O(p^{\frac{\kappa\eta}{(d+1)\eta}}) = O(p^{\frac{\kappa}{d+1}})$;
- $\deg_x(g) = \kappa$ and $\|g\|_\infty = \max\{g_{i,j}\} = O(p^{\frac{\kappa}{d+1}})$.

Example 1. We target a field $\mathbb{F}_{p^4}$ for $p \equiv 7 \mod 8$ prime. For example, we take $p = 1000010903$. Set $\eta = \kappa = 2$ and $d = 2 \geq \kappa$. Choose $h(t) = t^2 + 1$ so that $h \mod p$ is irreducible over $\mathbb{F}_p$. Consider $R = \mathbb{Z}(\iota) = \mathbb{Z}[t]/h(t)$ and $\mathbb{F}_{p^2} = \mathbb{F}_p(\iota) = \mathbb{F}_p[t]/h(t)$. Choose $\widetilde{g} = x^2 + (t+1)x + 1$ and $W = 1001 \geq p^{1/(d+1)}$. Then we set

$$g = (\widetilde{g}(t, x + W) \mod h) = x^2 + (\iota + 2003)x + 1001\iota + 1003003.$$

Construct a lattice of dimension 6 defined by the following matrix (blank entries are filled with zeros)

$$\begin{pmatrix} p & & & & & \\ & p & & & & \\ & & p & & & \\ & & & p & & \\ 1003003 & 1001 & 2003 & 1 & 1 & 0 \\ -1001 & 1003003 & -1 & 2003 & 0 & 1 \end{pmatrix}.$$

Run the LLL algorithm with this lattice and we obtain

$$f = (499\iota - 499505)x^2 + (499992\iota - 498111)x + 493992\iota - 50611.$$

One can check that $f, g, k = g \mod p$ and h are suitable for exTNFS algorithm. Note that $\|f\|_\infty$ and $\|g\|_\infty$ are of order $p^{2/3}$.

Algorithm   1.   Polynomial   selection   with   the   generalized   JLSV$_2$ method (gJLSV)

Input: p prime, $n = \eta\kappa$ integer such that $\eta, \kappa > 1$ and $d \geq \kappa$ integer
Output: f, g, k, h with $h \in \mathbb{Z}[t]$ irreducible of degree η, and $f, g \in R[x]$ irreducible over $R = \mathbb{Z}[t]/h\mathbb{Z}[t]$, and $k = \gcd(f \mod p, g \mod p)$ in $\mathbb{F}_{p^\eta} = \mathbb{F}_p[t]/h(t)$ irreducible of degree κ
1: Choose $h \in \mathbb{Z}[t]$ with small coefficients, irreducible of degree η such that p is inert in $\mathbb{Q}[t]/h(t)$;
2: Choose a bivariate polynomial $\tilde{g}(t, x) = x^\kappa + \sum_{i=0}^{\kappa-1} g_j(t)x^j$ with small coefficients;
3: Choose an integer $W \approx p^{1/(d+1)}$ and set $g = \tilde{g}(t, x + W) \mod h$;
4: Reduce the rows of the matrix L as defined in (1) using LLL, to get

$$\text{LLL}(M) = \begin{pmatrix} f_{0,0} \ f_{0,1} \ \cdots \ f_{d,\eta-1} \\ * \end{pmatrix}$$

5: **return** $(f = \sum_{0 \leq i \leq d, 0 \leq j < \eta} f_{i,j}t^j x^i, g, k = g \mod p, h)$

Generalized Conjugation Method. We describe a polynomial selection method based on Conjugation method [2,17]. Again, we call it as *the generalized Conjugation method* (gConj method).

First, one chooses two bivariate polynomials $g^{(1)}(t, x)$ and $g^{(0)}(t, x)$ in $\mathbb{Z}[t, x]$ of form

$$g^{(1)}(t, x) = g_0^{(1)}(t) + g_1^{(1)}(t)x + \cdots + g_{\kappa-1}^{(1)}(t)x^{\kappa-1}$$

and

$$g^{(0)}(t, x) = g_0^{(0)}(t) + g_1^{(0)}(t)x + \cdots + g_\kappa^{(0)}(t)x^\kappa,$$

where $g_i^{(s)}(t) \in \mathbb{Z}[t]$ are polynomials with small coefficients in $\mathbb{Z}$ and of degree less than or equal to $\eta - 1$. Then $g^{(s)} \mod (p, h(t))$ is a polynomial of degree $\leq \kappa$ over $\mathbb{F}_{p^\eta} = \mathbb{F}_p(\iota)$ for each $s = 0, 1$.

Next one chooses a quadratic, monic, irreducible polynomial $\mu(x) \in \mathbb{Z}[x]$ with small coefficients. If $\mu(x)$ has a root δ modulo p and $g^{(0)} + \delta g^{(1)} \mod (p, h)$ is irreducible over $\mathbb{F}_{p^\eta}$, then set $k(x) = g^{(0)} + \delta g^{(1)} \mod (p, h)$. Otherwise, one repeats the above steps until such $g^{(1)}, g^{(0)},$ and δ are found. Once it has been done, find u and v such that $\delta \equiv u/v \pmod{p}$ and $u, v \leq O(\sqrt{p})$ using rational reconstruction. Finally, we set $f = \text{Res}_Y(\mu(Y), g^{(0)} + Yg^{(1)})$ and $g = vg^{(0)} + ug^{(1)}$. By construction we have

- $\deg_x(f) = 2\kappa$ and $\|f\|_\infty = \max\{f_{i,j}\} = O(1)$;
- $\deg_x(g) = \kappa$ and $\|g\|_\infty = \max\{g_{i,j}\} = O(\sqrt{p}) = O(Q^{\frac{1}{2\eta\kappa}})$.

The bound on $\|f\|_\infty$ depends on the number of polynomials $g^{(0)} + \delta g^{(1)}$ tested before we find one which is irreducible over $\mathbb{F}_{p^\eta}$. Heuristically this happens on average after κ trials. Since there are $3^{2\eta\kappa} > \kappa$ choices of $g^{(0)}$ and $g^{(1)}$ of norm 1 we have $\|f\|_\infty = O(1)$. We give some examples in the followings.

Example 2. We target a field $\mathbb{F}_{p^4}$ for $p \equiv 7 \mod 8$ prime. For example, we take $p = 1000010903$. If we choose $h(t) = t^2 + 1$ then $h \mod p$ is irreducible over $\mathbb{F}_p$. Consider $R = \mathbb{Z}(\iota) = \mathbb{Z}[t]/h(t)$ and $\mathbb{F}_{p^2} = \mathbb{F}_p(\iota) = \mathbb{F}_p[t]/h(t)$. Choose an irreducible polynomial $\mu(x) = x^2 - 2 \in \mathbb{Z}[x]$ with small coefficients. It has a root $\sqrt{2} = 219983819 \in \mathbb{F}_p$ modulo p. We take $k(x) = (x^2 + \iota) + \sqrt{2}x \in \mathbb{F}_{p^2}[x]$ and $f(x) = (x^2 + \iota + \sqrt{2}x)(x^2 + \iota - \sqrt{2}x) = x^4 + (2\iota - 2)x^2 + 1 \in R[x]$. Then we find $u, v \in \mathbb{Z}$ such that $u/v \equiv \sqrt{2} \mod p$ where their orders are of $\sqrt{p}$. Now we take $g(x) = v(x^2 + \iota) + ux = 25834(x^2 + \iota) + 18297x \in R[x]$. One easily checks that f and g are irreducible over R and k is irreducible over $\mathbb{F}_{p^2}$ so that they are suitable for exTNFS algorithm.

Example 3. Now we target a field $\mathbb{F}_{p^9}$. Again, we take $p = 1000010903$ for example. Choose $h(t) = t^3 + t + 1 \in \mathbb{Z}[t]$ which remains irreducible modulo p. Let $R = \mathbb{Z}(\iota) = \mathbb{Z}[t]/h(t)$ and $\mathbb{F}_{p^3} = \mathbb{F}_p(\iota) = \mathbb{F}_p[t]/h(t)$. We set $\mu(x) = x^2 - 3$. Compute u and v such that $u/v \equiv \sqrt{3} \mod p$. Then the polynomials $k(x) = (x^3 + \iota) + \sqrt{3}x \in \mathbb{F}_{p^3}[x]$, $f(x) = (x^3 + \iota)^2 - 3x^2 \in R[x]$ and $g(x) = v(x^3 + \iota) + ux \in R[x]$ satisfy the conditions of polynomial selection for exTNFS algorithm.

Relation Collection. Recall the elements of $R = \mathbb{Z}[t]/h(t)$ can be represented uniquely as polynomials of $\mathbb{Z}[t]$ of degree less than $\deg h = \eta$. In the setting of exTNFS, we sieve all the pairs $(a, b) \in \mathbb{Z}[t]^2$ of degree $\leq \eta - 1$ such that $\|a\|_\infty$, $\|b\|_\infty \leq A$ (a parameter A to be determined later) until we obtain a relation satisfying

$$N_f(a, b) := \mathrm{Res}_t(\mathrm{Res}_x(a(t) - b(t)x, f(x)), h(t)) \text{ and}$$
$$N_g(a, b) := \mathrm{Res}_t(\mathrm{Res}_x(a(t) - b(t)x, g(x)), h(t))$$

are B-smooth for a parameter B to be determined (an integer is B-smooth if all its prime factors are less than B). It is equivalent to say that the norm of $a(\iota) - b(\iota)\alpha_f$ and $a(\iota) - b(\iota)\alpha_g$ are simultaneously B-smooth in $K_f = \mathbb{Q}(\iota, \alpha_f)$ and $K_g = \mathbb{Q}(\iota, \alpha_g)$, respectively.

For each pair (a, b) one obtains a linear equation where the unknowns are logarithms of elements of the factor base as in the classical variant of NFS for discrete logarithms where the factor base is chosen as in [17]. Other than the polynomial selection step, our algorithm follows basically the same as the description of the exTNFS algorithm. For full description of the algorithm, refer to [17].

Algorithm 2. Polynomial selection with the generalized Conjugation method (gConj)

Input: p prime and $n = \eta\kappa$ integer such that $\eta, \kappa > 1$
Output: f, g, k, h with $h \in \mathbb{Z}[t]$ irreducible of degree η, and $f, g \in R[x]$ irreducible over $R = \mathbb{Z}[t]/h\mathbb{Z}[t]$, and $k = \gcd(f \mod p, g \mod p)$ in $\mathbb{F}_{p^\eta} = \mathbb{F}_p[t]/h(t)$ irreducible of degree κ

1: Choose $h \in \mathbb{Z}[t]$, irreducible of degree η such that p is inert in $\mathbb{Q}[t]/h(t)$
2: **repeat**
3:   Select $g_0^{(0)}(t), \ldots, g_{\kappa-1}^{(0)}(t)$, polynomials of degree $\leq \eta - 1$ with small integer coefficients;
4:   Select $g_0^{(1)}(t), \ldots, g_{\kappa'-1}^{(1)}(t)$, polynomials of degree $\leq \eta - 1$, and $g_{\kappa'}^{(1)}(t)$, a constant polynomial with small integer coefficients, for an integer $\kappa' < \kappa$;
5:   Set $g^{(0)}(t, x) = x^\kappa + \sum_{i=0}^{\kappa-1} g_i^{(0)}(t)x^i$ and $g^{(1)}(t, x) = \sum_{i=0}^{\kappa'} g_i^{(1)}(t)x^i$;
6:   Select $\mu(x)$ a quadratic, monic, irreducible polynomial over $\mathbb{Z}$ with small coefficients;
7: **until** $\mu(x)$ has a root δ modulo p and $k = g^{(0)} + \delta g^{(1)} \mod (p, h)$ is irreducible over $\mathbb{F}_{p^\eta}$;
8: $(u, v) \leftarrow$ a rational reconstruction of δ;
9: $f \leftarrow \mathrm{Res}_Y(\mu(Y), g_0 + Y g_1 \mod h)$;
10: $g \leftarrow v g_0 + u g_1 \mod h$;
11: **return** (f, g, k, h)

---

3   Complexity

From now on, we often abuse the notation for a bivariate polynomial $f(t, x)$ in $\mathbb{Z}[t, x]$ and a polynomial $f(x) = f(t, x) \mod h = f(\iota, x)$ in $R[x]$. Unless stated, $\deg(f)$ denotes both the degree of $f(x) \in R[x]$ and the degree of $f(t, x) \in \mathbb{Z}[t, x]$ with respect to x. The norm of $f(x) \in R[x]$, denoted by $\|f\|_\infty$, is defined by the maximum of the absolute value of the integer coefficients of $f(t, x)$.

The complexity analysis of our algorithm basically follows that of all the other NFS variants. Recall that in the algorithm we test the smoothness of the norm of an element from the number field K_f and K_g. As a reminder to readers, we quote the formula for the complexity of exTNFS algorithm [17]: For a smoothness parameter B, the factor base has $(2 + o(1))B/\log B$ elements, so the cost of linear algebra is $B^{2+o(1)}$. Thus the complexity of exTNFS algorithm is given by (up to an exponent $1 + o(1)$)

$$\text{complexity(exTNFS)} = \frac{B}{\mathrm{Prob}(N_f, B)\mathrm{Prob}(N_g, B)} + B^2, \qquad (2)$$

where N_f denotes the norm of an element from K_f over $\mathbb{Q}$, B is a smoothness parameter, and $\mathrm{Prob}(x, y)$ denotes the probability that an integer less than x is y-smooth.

It leads us to consider the estimation of the norm sizes. We need the following lemma that can be found in [17, Lemma 2].

Lemma 1 ([17], **Lemma 2**). *Let $h \in \mathbb{Z}[t]$ be an irreducible polynomial of degree η and f be an irreducible polynomial over $R = \mathbb{Z}[t]/h(t)$ of degree $\deg(f)$. Let ι (resp. α) be a root of h (resp. f) in its number field and set $K_f := \mathbb{Q}(\iota, \alpha)$. Let $A > 0$ be a real number and T an integer such that $2 \leq T \leq \deg(f)$. For each $i = 0, \ldots, \deg(f) - 1$, let $a_i(t) \in \mathbb{Z}[t]$ be polynomials of degree $\leq \eta - 1$ with $\|a_i\|_\infty \leq A$.*

1. We have

$$\left| N_{K_f/\mathbb{Q}}\left(\sum_{i=0}^{T-1} a_i(\iota)\alpha^i \right) \right| < A^{\eta \deg(f)} \|f\|_\infty^{(T-1)\eta} \|h\|_\infty^{(T+\deg(f)-1)(\eta-1)} D(\eta, \deg(f)),$$

where $D(\eta, \kappa) = \left((2\kappa - 1)(\eta - 1) + 1\right)^{\eta/2}(\eta + 1)^{(2\kappa-1)(\eta-1)/2}\left((2\kappa - 1)!\eta^{2\kappa}\right)^\eta$.

2. Assume in addition that $\|h\|_\infty$ is bounded by an absolute constant H and that $p = L_Q(\ell_p, c)$ for some $\ell_p > 1/3$ and $c > 0$. Then

$$N_f(a, b) \leq E^{\deg(f)} \|f\|_\infty^\eta L_Q(2/3, o(1)), \tag{3}$$

where $E = A^\eta$

The above formula remains the same when we restrict the coefficients of f to be integers.

Proof. The proof can be found in [17]. □

We summarize our results in the following theorem. The results are similar to Theorem 1 in [17], however, we underline that in our algorithm n is any composite. We also add the results on the upper bound of the complexity when n is a b-smooth number for $b \leq 4$.

Theorem 1 *(under the classical NFS heuristics). If $Q = p^n$ is a prime power such that $p = L_Q(\ell_p, c_p)$ with $1/3 < \ell_p$ and $n = \eta\kappa$ is a composite such that $\eta, \kappa \neq 1$, then the discrete logarithm over $\mathbb{F}_Q$ can be solved in $L_Q(1/3, (C/9)^{1/3})$ where C and the additional conditions are listed in Table 4.*

For each polynomial selection, the degree and the norm of the polynomials have the same formula as in [17]. Although in our case the polynomials f and g have coefficients in R, the formula for the upper bound of the norm $N_f(a, b)$ remains the same as Kim-Barbulescu's algorithm by Lemma 1. Finally, the analysis is simply rephrasing of the previous results, so we simply omit the proof. In the next subsection, we briefly explain how to obtain the upper bound of the complexity when n has prime factors 2 or 3. The case is interesting since most pairings use such fields to utilize tower extension field arithmetic for efficiency.

3.1   exTNFS When $n = 2^i$

Recall that our algorithm with Conjugation method has the same expression for the norms as in [2] replacing p with $P = p^\eta$. Write $P = L_Q(2/3, c_P)$ and denote

Table 4. Complexity of exTNFS variants.

Algorithm	C	Conditions
exTNFS-gJLSV$_2$	64	$\kappa = o\left(\left(\frac{\log Q}{\log\log Q}\right)^{\frac{1}{3}}\right)$
exTNFS-gGJL	64	$\kappa \leq \left(\frac{8}{3}\right)^{-\frac{1}{3}}\left(\frac{\log Q}{\log\log Q}\right)^{\frac{1}{3}}$
exTNFS-gConj	48	$\kappa = 12^{-\frac{1}{3}}\left(\frac{\log Q}{\log\log Q}\right)^{\frac{1}{3}}$
	≤ 54.28	$n = 2^i\ (i > 1)$
MexTNFS-gJLSV$_2$	$\frac{92+26\sqrt{13}}{3}$	$\kappa = o\left(\left(\frac{\log Q}{\log\log Q}\right)^{\frac{1}{3}}\right)$
MexTNFS-gGJL	$\frac{92+26\sqrt{13}}{3}$	$\kappa \leq \left(\frac{7+2\sqrt{13}}{6}\right)^{-1/3}\left(\frac{\log Q}{\log\log Q}\right)^{\frac{1}{3}}$
MexTNFS-gConj	$\frac{(3+\sqrt{33+12\sqrt{6}})^3}{14+6\sqrt{6}}$	$\kappa = \left(\frac{56+24\sqrt{6}}{12}\right)^{-1/3}\left(\frac{\log Q}{\log\log Q}\right)^{\frac{1}{3}}$
	≤ 59.80	$n = 2^i3^j\ (i+j > 1)$
	≤ 50.76	$n = 2^i\ (i > 1)$
SexTNFS-new	32	$\kappa = o\left(\left(\frac{\log Q}{\log\log Q}\right)^{\frac{1}{3}}\right)$
		p is d-SNFS with $d = \frac{(2/3)^{\frac{1}{3}}+o(1)}{\kappa}\left(\frac{\log Q}{\log\log Q}\right)^{\frac{1}{3}}$

$\tau - 1$ by the degree of sieving polynomials. Then the complexity of exTNFS-gConj is $L_Q(1/3, C_{\mathrm{NFS}}(\tau, c_P))$ where

$$C_{\mathrm{NFS}}(\tau, c_P) = \frac{2}{c_P\tau} + \sqrt{\frac{4}{(c_P\tau)^2} + \frac{2}{3}c_P(\tau - 1)}. \qquad (4)$$

Let $k_0 = \left(\frac{\log Q}{\log\log Q}\right)^{1/3}$. When $n = 2^i$ for some $i > 1$, we can always find a factor κ of n in the interval $\left[\frac{k_0}{3.31}, \frac{k_0}{1.64}\right]$ so that c_P lies in the interval $[1.64, 3.31]$ (observe that the ratio $(k_0/1.64)/(k_0/3.31)$ is larger than 2). Since $C(\tau, c_P)$ is less than 1.82 when $\tau = 2$ and $1.64 \leq c_P \leq 3.31$, the complexity of exTNFS is always less than $L_Q(1/3, 1.82)$ in this case.

This result shows that the DLP over $\mathbb{F}_{p^n}$ can always be solved in the running time less than $L_Q(1/3, 1.82)$ when n is a power of 2. Compare that exTNFS-$\mathcal{C}$ [20] has a larger asymptotic complexity of $L_Q(1/3, 1.92)$ and they even require the specified condition on a factor of n.

4 Variants

4.1 The Case When p Has a Special Form (SexTNFS)

A generalized polynomial selection method also admits a variant when the characteristic has a special form. It includes the case for the fields used in pairing-based cryptosystems. The previous SexTNFS by Kim and Barbulescu cannot be applied to pairing-friendly fields with prime power embedding degree, such as Kachisa-Schaefer-Scott curve [16] $p = (u^{10} + 2u^9 + 5u^8 + 48u^6 + 152u^5 + 240u^4 + 625u^2 + 2398u + 3125)/980$ of embedding degree 16.

For a given integer d, an integer p is d-SNFS if there exists an integer u and a polynomial $\Pi(x)$ with small integer coefficients (up to a small denominator) so that

$$p = \Pi(u),$$

$\deg \Pi = d$ and $\|\Pi\|_\infty$ is bounded by an absolute constant not depending on p.

We consider the case when $n = \eta\kappa$ $(\eta, \kappa \neq 1)$ with $\kappa = o\left(\left(\frac{\log Q}{\log \log Q}\right)^{1/3}\right)$ and p is d-SNFS. In this case our exTNFS selects h, f and g so that

- h is a polynomial over $\mathbb{Z}$ and irreducible modulo p, $\deg h = \eta$ and $\|h\|_\infty = O(1)$;
- f and g are two polynomials with coefficients from $R = \mathbb{Z}[\iota]$, have a common factor $k(x)$ modulo p which is irreducible over $R/pR = \mathbb{F}_{p^\eta} = \mathbb{F}(\iota)$ of degree κ.

We choose such polynomials using the method of Joux and Pierrot [15]. Find a bivariate polynomial S of degree $\kappa - 1$ with respect to x such that

$$S(t, x) = S_0(t) + S_1(t)x + \cdots + S_{\kappa-1}(t)x^{\kappa-1} \in \mathbb{Z}[t, x],$$

where $S_i(t)$'s have their coefficients in $\{-1, 0, 1\}$ and are of degree $\leq \eta - 1$. We further require that $k = x^\kappa + S(t, x) - u \mod (p, h)$ is irreducible over $\mathbb{F}_{p^\eta}$. Since the proportion of irreducible polynomials in $\mathbb{F}_q$ (q: a prime power) of degree κ is $1/\kappa$ and there are $3^{\eta\kappa}$ choices we expect this step to succeed. Then we set

$$\begin{cases} g = x^\kappa + S(t, x) - u \mod h \\ f = \Pi(x^\kappa + S(t, x)) \mod h. \end{cases}$$

If f is not irreducible over $R[x]$, which happens with low probability, start over. Note that g is irreducible modulo p and that f is a multiple of g modulo p. More precisely, as in [15], we choose $S(t, x)$ so that the number of its terms is approximately $O(\log n)$. Since $3^{\log n} > \kappa$, this allows us enough chance to get an irreducible polynomial g. The size of the largest integer coefficient of f comes from the part $S(t, x)^d$ and it is bounded by $\sigma^d = O\left((\log n)^d\right)$, where σ denotes the number of the terms in $S(t, x)$. By construction we have:

- $\deg(g) = \kappa$ and $\|g\|_\infty = u = O(p^{1/d})$;
- $\deg(f) = \kappa d$ and $\|f\|_\infty = O((\log n)^d)$.

We inject these values in Eq. (1) and obtain the same formula as in Kim-Barbulescu's SexTNFS variant. Thus we obtain the same complexity as in their paper. Again, we note that our polynomial selection applies to fields of arbitrary composite extension degree n.

4.2   The Multiple Polynomial Variants (MexTNFS-gConj)

One can also accelerate the complexity of exTNFS with the generalized Conjugation method using multiple polynomial variants. The description is similar to the previous multiple variant of NFS: choose an irreducible quadratic polynomial

$\mu(x) \in \mathbb{Z}[x]$ such that it has small coefficients, and has a root δ modulo p. As before, choose $k = g_0 + \delta g_1 \in \mathbb{F}_{p^\eta}[x]$ and set $f = Res_Y(\mu(Y), g_0 + Yg_1) \in R[x]$, where g_0 and g_1 are polynomials in $R[x]$. We find two pairs of integers (u, v) and (u', v') using rational reconstruction such that

$$\delta \equiv u/v \equiv u'/v' \mod p,$$

where we require (u, v) and (u', v') are linearly independent over $\mathbb{Q}$ and the integers u, v, u', v' are all of the size of $\sqrt{p}$.

Next we set $f_1 = f$, $f_2 = vg_0 + ug_1$ and $f_3 = v'g_0 + u'g_1$ and select other $V - 3$ irreducible polynomials $f_i := \mu_i f_2 + \nu_i f_3$ where $\mu_i = \sum_{j=0}^{\eta-1} \mu_{i,j} \iota^j$ and $\nu_i = \sum_{j=0}^{\eta-1} \nu_{i,j} \iota^j$ are elements of R such that $\|\mu_i\|_\infty, \|\nu_i\|_\infty \le V^{\frac{1}{2\eta}}$ where $V = L_Q(1/3, c_v)$ is a parameter which will be selected later. Denote α_i a root of f_i for $i = 1, 2, \ldots, V$.

By construction, we have:

- $\deg(f_1) = 2\kappa$ and $\|f_1\|_\infty = O(1)$;
- $\deg(f_i) = \kappa$ and $\|f_i\|_\infty = V^{\frac{1}{2\eta}}(p^{\eta\kappa})^{1/(2\kappa)}$ for $2 \le i \le V$.

As before, evaluating these values into Eq. (1), we obtain:

$$|N_{f_1}(a, b)| < E^{2\kappa} L_Q(2/3, o(1))$$
$$|N_{f_i}(a, b)| < E^\kappa (p^{\kappa\eta})^{\frac{1}{2\kappa}} L_Q(2/3, o(1)) \text{ for } 2 \le i \le V.$$

We emphasize that $\left(V^{1/(2\eta)}\right)^\eta = V^{1/2} = L_Q(2/3, o(1))$.

Then, one can proceed the computation identical to [19]. When $P = p^\eta = L_Q(2/3, c_P)$ such that $c_P > \left(\frac{7+2\sqrt{13}}{6}\right)^{1/3}$ and $\tau - 1$ is the degree of the enumerated polynomials r, then the complexity obtained is $L_Q(1/3, C_{\mathrm{MNFS}}(\tau, c_P))$ where

$$C_{\mathrm{MNFS}}(\tau, c_P) = \frac{2}{c_P \tau} + \sqrt{\frac{20}{9(c_P \tau)^2} + \frac{2}{3} c_P(\tau - 1)}. \tag{5}$$

The best case occurs when $c_P = \left(\frac{56+24\sqrt{6}}{12}\right)^{1/3}$ and $\tau = 2$ (linear polynomials):

$$\text{complexity(best case of MexTNFS-gConj)} = L_Q\left(1/3, \frac{3 + \sqrt{3(11 + 4\sqrt{6})}}{(18(7 + 3\sqrt{6}))^{1/3}}\right).$$

MexTNFS when n $=2^i 2^j$. We separate this case into following two cases.

Case 1: $n = 2^i 3^j$ *for* $i + j > 1$. In this case, we can always find a factor κ of n in the interval $\left[\frac{k_0}{3.89}, \frac{k_0}{1.27}\right]$ where $k_0 = \left(\frac{\log Q}{\log\log Q}\right)^{1/3}$ so that c_P, where $p^\eta = L_Q(1/3, c_P)$, is in the interval $[1.27, 3.89]$. Observe that the ratio $(k_0/1.27)/(k_0/3.89)$ is larger than 3. Since $C_{\mathrm{MNFS}}(\tau, c_P)$ in Eq. (5) is less than 1.88 when $\tau = 2$ and $1.27 \le c_P \le 3.89$, we have a result that the complexity of MexTNFS is always less than $L_Q(1/3, 1.88)$.

Case 2: $n = 2^i$ *for some* $i > 1$. If n is a power of 2 we get a better result than Case 1. In this case we can always find a factor κ of n in the interval $\left[\frac{k_0}{3.09}, \frac{k_0}{1.52}\right]$ where k_0 is the same as Case 1. Again we check that the ratio $(k_0/1.52)/(k_0/3.09)$ is larger than 2. Since $C_{\text{MNFS}}(\tau, c_P) \leq 1.78$ for $\tau = 2$ and $1.52 \leq c_P \leq 3.09$, the complexity of MexTNFS is always less than $L_Q(1/3, 1.78)$ in this case.

This result shows that, if multiple variants are used, the DLP over $\mathbb{F}_{p^n}$ can always be solved in the running time less than $L_Q(1/3, 1.88)$ when n is 4-smooth or less than $L_Q(1/3, 1.78)$ when n is a power of 2 using MexTNFS algorithm. Recall that MexTNFS-$\mathcal{C}$ [20] has the best asymptotic complexity $L_Q(1/3, 1.88)$ only when n is a power of 2 and has a factor of the specified size.

5   Comparison and Examples

In the context of NFS algorithm including its variants such as TNFS, exTNFS, we compute a large number of integers that are usually given by the norms of elements in number fields, and factor these numbers to test if they are B-smooth for a parameter B. These B-smooth numbers are used to produce a linear relation of the discrete logarithm of the factor base elements, and we solve a linear system from those relations. Thus if we reduce the size of the norms computed in the algorithm we reduce the work of finding B-smooth numbers, further it allows us to improve the total complexity.

The term, the norm size, in this section is used for the bitsize of the product of the norms $|N_f(r \mod f)N_g(r \mod g)|$, where $r \in R[x]$ is a polynomial over R of degree less than τ and f and g are polynomials selected by each polynomial selection method. Each coefficient of r is considered as a polynomial in $\mathbb{Z}[x]$ of degree less than η whose coefficients are bounded by a parameter $A = E^{1/\eta}$.

As recent results [17, 20] show, the exTNFS variants have a smaller size of the norms than that in classical NFS. Thus, in this section, we mainly compare the norm size with exTNFS variants.

5.1   A Precise Comparison When p Is Arbitrary

We present the norm sizes in Table 5 depending on each variant of polynomial selection from exTNFS variants. Note that in our algorithm the extension degree n can be any composite integer.

We remark that a recent variant by Sarkar and Singh, exTNFS-$\mathcal{C}$ [20], is only interested in the case of $\lambda = \eta$ where $\lambda \leq \eta$ denotes a parameter if $k = k_0 + k_1 x + \cdots + k_\kappa x^\kappa \in \mathbb{F}_{p^n}[x]$ such that $k_i \in \mathbb{F}_{p^n}$'s are represented as polynomials over $\mathbb{F}_p$ of degree $\lambda - 1$. When $\lambda = 1$, all the coefficients of k are in $\mathbb{F}_p$. Then $\kappa = \deg(k)$ and η should be relatively prime so that k is irreducible over $\mathbb{F}_{p^n}$. Thus this case is not interesting since the case is already covered by Kim-Barbulescu's exTNFS. We do not consider the case when $1 < \lambda < \eta$ as mentioned in [20].

We extrapolate the parameter E using the formula $E = cL_Q(1/3, (8/9)^{1/3})$ such that $\log_2 E = 30$ when $\log_2 Q = 600$ (chosen from the record by Bouvier et al. [8]).

Table 5. Comparison of norm sizes, where $\tau=\deg r(x)$, $d=\deg(f)$ and K,λ are integer parameters subject to the conditions in the last column.

Method	Norms product	Conditions and parameters
exTNFS-JLSV$_2$ [17]	$E^{\frac{2(\kappa+d)}{\tau}} Q^{\frac{\tau-1}{d+1}}$	$n=\eta\kappa, \gcd(\eta,\kappa)=1, d:=\deg(f)\geq\kappa$
exTNFS-GJL [17]	$E^{\frac{2(2d+1)}{\tau}} Q^{\frac{\tau-1}{d+1}}$	$n=\eta\kappa, \gcd(\eta,\kappa)=1, d\geq\kappa$
exTNFS-Conj [17]	$E^{\frac{6\kappa}{\tau}} Q^{\frac{(\tau-1)}{2\kappa}}$	$n=\eta\kappa, \gcd(\eta,\kappa)=1$
exTNFS-$\mathcal{C}$ [20]	$E^{\frac{2\kappa_0(2K+1)}{\tau}} Q^{\frac{(\tau-1)(K(\lambda-1)+\kappa_1)}{\kappa(K\lambda+1)}}$	$n=\eta\kappa=\eta\kappa_0\kappa_1, K\geq\kappa_1, \lambda=\eta^a$
exTNFS-gJLSV$_2$ (this)	$E^{\frac{2(\kappa+d)}{\tau}} Q^{\frac{\tau-1}{d+1}}$	$n=\eta\kappa, d:=\deg(f)\geq\kappa$
exTNFS-gGJL (this)	$E^{\frac{2(2d+1)}{\tau}} Q^{\frac{\tau-1}{d+1}}$	$n=\eta\kappa, d\geq\kappa$
exTNFS-gConj (this)	$E^{\frac{6\kappa}{\tau}} Q^{\frac{(\tau-1)}{2\kappa}}$	$n=\eta\kappa$

[a] If $\lambda=1$, exTNFS-$\mathcal{C}$ is only applicable when $\gcd(\eta,\kappa)=1$.

The Case of Fields $\mathbb{F}_{p^9}$. One of the interesting cases is when the extension degree n is a prime power, e.g. $n=4,9,16,32$ and so on. In this section, we particularly focus on the case $n=9$ although one can also carry out a similar analysis for other cases.

In this case the previous best polynomial selection method is exTNFS-$\mathcal{C}$ [20], so we compare our method with exTNFS-$\mathcal{C}$. We apply the algorithms with $\eta=3$ and $\kappa=3$. In particular, we have the following choices:

- exTNFS-$\mathcal{C}$ with $\kappa_0=3$, $K=\kappa_1=1$ and $\lambda=3$ has the optimal norm size of $E^9 Q^{1/4}$ when $\tau=2$.
- exTNFS-$\mathcal{C}$ with $\kappa_0=1$, $K=\kappa_1=3$ and $\lambda=3$ has the optimal norm size of $E^7 Q^{3/10}$ when $\tau=2$.
- exTNFS-gJLSV$_2$ has the optimal size of the norms $E^6 Q^{1/4}$ when $\tau=2$.
- exTNFS-gGJL has the optimal size of the norms $E^7 Q^{1/4}$ when $\tau=2$.
- exTNFS-gConj has the optimal size of the norms $E^9 Q^{1/6}$ when $\tau=2$.

We plot the values of the norms in Fig. 2. Note that exTNFS-gJLSV seems to be the best choice when the bitsize of target fields is between 300 and 1800 bits, otherwise exTNFS-gConj seems to be the best choice as the size of fields grows.

The Case of Fields $\mathbb{F}_{p^{12}}$. When n is a composite that is not a prime power, such as $n=6,12,18$, and so on, one can always find factors η and κ such that $n=\eta\kappa$ and $\gcd(\eta,\kappa)=1$. Thus it is possible to apply the polynomial selection as in Kim-Barbulescu's exTNFS that is already the best choice in the sense of asymptotic complexity. However, from a practical perspective, one might have better choice by allowing to choose η and κ that are not necessarily relatively prime. We plot the case of $n=12$ as an example. Note that exTNFS-gConj with $\kappa=2$ seems to be the best choice when the size of fields is small (say, less than 500 bits) and exTNFS-gJLSV with $\kappa=2$ seems to be the best choice as the size of fields grows as shown in Fig. 3. Remark that $\kappa=2$ seems to be the best choice in both cases. Note that this choice is not applicable with Kim-Barbulescu's method since $\eta=6$ and $\kappa=2$ are not relatively prime.

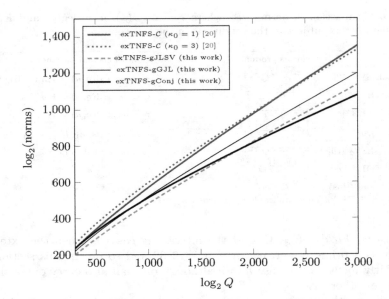

Fig. 2. Plot of the norms bitsize for several variants of NFS targeting $\mathbb{F}_Q = \mathbb{F}_{p^9}$ with $\eta = \kappa = 3$. Horizontal axis indicates the bitsize of p^n while the vertical axis the bitsize of the norms product.

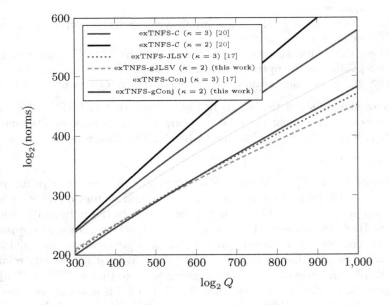

Fig. 3. Plot of the norms bitsize for several variants of NFS targeting $\mathbb{F}_Q = \mathbb{F}_{p^{12}}$ with various choices for κ. Horizontal axis indicates the bitsize of p^n while the vertical axis the bitsize of the norms product.

5.2   Precise Comparison When p Is a Special Prime

In Table 6, we provide precise norm sizes when p is a d-SNFS prime. Note that our SexTNFS can be applied with arbitrary composite n maintaining the same formula for the norm sizes as in [17].

To compare the precise norm sizes, we choose the parameter E using the formula $E = cL_Q(1/3, (4/9)^{1/3})$ and the pair $\log_2 Q = 1039, \log_2 E = 30.38$ (due to the records by Aoki et al. [1]).

We plot the norm sizes for each method in Figs. 4 and 5. In our range of interest, each of the norm sizes has the minimum value when $\tau = 2$, i.e. sieving only linear polynomials, so we only consider the case when $\tau = 2$.

The Case of $n = 12$ and p is a $4 - SNFS$ Prime. This case is interesting due to Barreto-Naehrig pairing construction [7]. We plot the norm size in Fig. 4

Table 6. Comparison of norm sizes when p is d-SNFS prime.

Method	Norms product	Conditions
STNFS [4]	$E^{\frac{2(d+1)}{\tau}} Q^{\frac{\tau-1}{d}}$	
SNFS-JP [15]	$E^{\frac{2n(d+1)}{\tau}} Q^{\frac{\tau-1}{nd}}$	
SexTNFS-KimBar [17]	$E^{\frac{2\kappa(d+1)}{\tau}} Q^{\frac{\tau-1}{\kappa d}}$	$n = \eta\kappa, \gcd(\kappa, \eta) = 1 \; 2 \le \eta < n$
SexTNFS-new (this work)	$E^{\frac{2\kappa(d+1)}{\tau}} Q^{\frac{\tau-1}{\kappa d}}$	$n = \eta\kappa, 2 \le \eta < n$

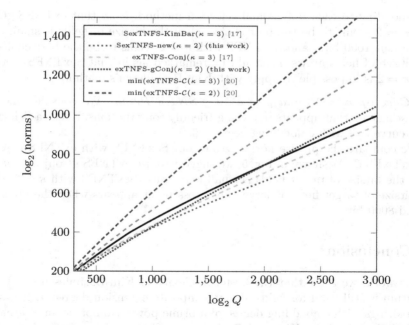

Fig. 4. Comparison when $n = 12$ and p is a 4-SNFS for $300 \le \log_2 Q \le 3000$. Horizontal axis indicates the bitsize of $Q = p^n$ while the vertical axis the bitsize of the norms product.

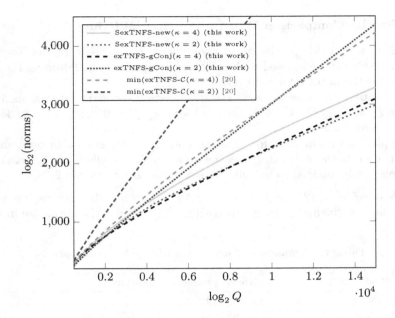

Fig. 5. Comparison when $n = 16$ and p is a $d = 10$-SNFS prime. Horizontal axis indicates the bitsize of p^n while the vertical axis the bitsize of the norms product.

corresponding to each polynomial selection method. Note that exTNFS-gConj with $\kappa = 2$ seems to be the best choice when the bitsize of fields is small (less than about 1000 bits) and SexTNFS with $\kappa = 2$ seems to be the best choice as the bitsize of fields grows. It should be remarked again that SexTNFS method with $\kappa = 2$ is impossible to apply with Kim-Barbulescu's method.

The Case of $n = 16$ and p is a $10 - SNFS$ Prime. We consider another interesting case that appears in pairing-friendly constructions, Kachisa-Schaefer-Scott curve [16] with embedding degree 16.

We compare the precise norm sizes of our SexTNFS with exTNFS-(g)Conj and exTNFS-$\mathcal{C}$. As shown in Fig. 5, we suggest to use exTNFS-gConj with $\kappa = 4$ when the bitsize of target fields is small and to use SexTNFS with $\kappa = 2$ when the bitsize of target fields is large. The cross point appears when the bitsize is around 8000 bits.

6   Conclusion

In this work, we show that the best complexity of Kim-Barbulescu's exTNFS algorithm is still valid for fields of any composite extension degree n. It asserts that pairings with embedding degree of a prime power cannot be an alternative to avoid the attack by Kim and Barbulescu and the keysize for such pairings also needs to be updated following to our attack.

It is also interesting to remark that fields with extension degree of form $n = 2^i 3^j$ tend to be vulnerable to our attack compared to fields of any other extension degree. It is because when n is a smooth number it is more likely to find a factor of n so that its size is close to the desired size to obtain the best asymptotic complexity. Note that a large number of pairings have embedding degree only divisible by 2 or 3 for an efficient field arithmetic.

From a practical point of view, our algorithm also performs better than Kim-Barbulescu's algorithm although the asymptotic complexity remains the same. For example, when $n = 12$, the choice of $(\eta, \kappa) = (6, 2)$ is better than $(\eta, \kappa) = (4, 3)$ in terms of the norm sizes where the former case can only be covered by our algorithm.

Precise evaluation of the keysize for pairing-based cryptosystems should be further studied. It would be also an interesting question to find efficient alternatives for Barreto-Naehrig curve that are not affected by our attack. Such curves potentially have a large embedding degree or a prime embedding degree. Pairings of embedding degree one might be also alternatives as considered in [9]. Nevertheless, such pairings might be very slow and still need to be further improved for cryptographers to use them.

Acknowledgement. The authors would like to thank Razvan Barbulescu for his fruitful comments on an early draft of this paper.

References

1. Aoki, K., Franke, J., Kleinjung, T., Lenstra, A.K., Osvik, D.A.: A kilobit special number field sieve factorization. In: Kurosawa, K. (ed.) ASIACRYPT 2007. LNCS, vol. 4833, pp. 1–12. Springer, Heidelberg (2007). doi:10.1007/978-3-540-76900-2_1
2. Barbulescu, R., Gaudry, P., Guillevic, A., Morain, F.: Improving NFS for the discrete logarithm problem in non-prime finite fields. In: Oswald, E., Fischlin, M. (eds.) EUROCRYPT 2015. LNCS, vol. 9056, pp. 129–155. Springer, Heidelberg (2015). doi:10.1007/978-3-662-46800-5_6
3. Barbulescu, R., Gaudry, P., Joux, A., Thomé, E.: A heuristic quasi-polynomial algorithm for discrete logarithm in finite fields of small characteristic. In: Nguyen, P.Q., Oswald, E. (eds.) EUROCRYPT 2014. LNCS, vol. 8441, pp. 1–16. Springer, Heidelberg (2014). doi:10.1007/978-3-642-55220-5_1
4. Barbulescu, R., Gaudry, P., Kleinjung, T.: The tower number field sieve. In: Iwata, T., Cheon, J.H. (eds.) ASIACRYPT 2015. LNCS, vol. 9453, pp. 31–55. Springer, Heidelberg (2015). doi:10.1007/978-3-662-48800-3_2
5. Barbulescu, R., Pierrot, C.: The multiple number field sieve for medium and high characteristic finite fields. LMS J. Comput. Math. **17**, 230–246 (2014). The published version contains an error which is corrected in version 2 available at https://hal.inria.fr/hal-00952610
6. Barreto, P.S.L.M., Lynn, B., Scott, M.: Constructing elliptic curves with prescribed embedding degrees. In: Cimato, S., Persiano, G., Galdi, C. (eds.) SCN 2002. LNCS, vol. 2576, pp. 257–267. Springer, Heidelberg (2003). doi:10.1007/3-540-36413-7_19
7. Barreto, P.S.L.M., Naehrig, M.: Pairing-friendly elliptic curves of prime order. In: Preneel, B., Tavares, S. (eds.) SAC 2005. LNCS, vol. 3897, pp. 319–331. Springer, Heidelberg (2006). doi:10.1007/11693383_22

8. Bouvier, C., Gaudry, P., Imbert, L., Jeljeli, H., Thom, E.: Discrete logarithms in GF(p) - 180 digits. Announcement available at the NMBRTHRY archives, item 004703 (2014)
9. Chatterjee, S., Menezes, A., Rodriguez-Henriquez, F.: On implementing pairing-based protocols with elliptic curves of embedding degree one. Cryptology ePrint Archive, Report 2016/403 (2016). http://eprint.iacr.org/2016/403
10. Gordon, D.M.: Discrete logarithms in $GF(p)$ using the number field sieve. SIAM J. Discret. Math. 6(1), 124–138 (1993)
11. Granger, R., Kleinjung, T., Zumbrägel, J.: On the powers of 2. Cryptology ePrint Archive, Report 2014/300 (2014). http://eprint.iacr.org/
12. Guillevic, A., Morain, F., Thomé, E.: Solving discrete logarithms on a 170-bit MNT curve by pairing reduction. In: Selected Areas in Cryptography - SAC 2016 (2016)
13. Jeong, J., Kim, T.: Extended tower number field sieve with application to finite fields of arbitrary composite extension degree. IACR Cryptology ePrint Archive 2016/526 (2016)
14. Joux, A., Lercier, R., Smart, N., Vercauteren, F.: The number field sieve in the medium prime case. In: Dwork, C. (ed.) CRYPTO 2006. LNCS, vol. 4117, pp. 326–344. Springer, Heidelberg (2006). doi:10.1007/11818175_19
15. Joux, A., Pierrot, C.: The special number field sieve in $\mathbb{F}_{p^n}$. In: Cao, Z., Zhang, F. (eds.) Pairing 2013. LNCS, vol. 8365, pp. 45–61. Springer, Cham (2014). doi:10.1007/978-3-319-04873-4_3
16. Kachisa, E.J., Schaefer, E.F., Scott, M.: Constructing brezing-weng pairing-friendly elliptic curves using elements in the cyclotomic field. In: Galbraith, S.D., Paterson, K.G. (eds.) Pairing 2008. LNCS, vol. 5209, pp. 126–135. Springer, Heidelberg (2008). doi:10.1007/978-3-540-85538-5_9
17. Kim, T., Barbulescu, R.: Extended tower number field sieve: a new complexity for the medium prime case. In: Robshaw, M., Katz, J. (eds.) CRYPTO 2016. LNCS, vol. 9814, pp. 543–571. Springer, Heidelberg (2016). doi:10.1007/978-3-662-53018-4_20
18. Matyukhin, D.V.: Effective version of the number field sieve for discrete logarithm in a field $GF(p^k)$. Trudy po Diskretnoi Matematike 9, 121–151 (2006)
19. Pierrot, C.: The multiple number field sieve with conjugation and generalized joux-lercier methods. In: Oswald, E., Fischlin, M. (eds.) EUROCRYPT 2015. LNCS, vol. 9056, pp. 156–170. Springer, Heidelberg (2015). doi:10.1007/978-3-662-46800-5_7
20. Sarkar, P., Singh, S.: A general polynomial selection method and new asymptotic complexities for the tower number field sieve algorithm. IACR Cryptology ePrint Archive 2016/485 (2016)
21. Sarkar, P., Singh, S.: A generalisation of the conjugation method for polynomial selection for the extended tower number field sieve algorithm. IACR Cryptology ePrint Archive 2016/537 (2016)
22. Sarkar, P., Singh, S.: New complexity trade-offs for the (multiple) number field sieve algorithm in non-prime fields. In: Fischlin, M., Coron, J.-S. (eds.) EUROCRYPT 2016. LNCS, vol. 9665, pp. 429–458. Springer, Heidelberg (2016). doi:10.1007/978-3-662-49890-3_17
23. Schirokauer, O.: Discrete logarithms and local units. Philos. Trans. R. Soc. Lond. A: Math. Phys. Eng. Sci. 345(1676), 409–423 (1993)
24. Schirokauer, O.: Using number fields to compute logarithms in finite fields. Math. Comput. 69(231), 1267–1283 (2000)
25. Zhang, X., Lin, D.: Analysis of optimum pairing products at high security levels. In: Galbraith, S., Nandi, M. (eds.) INDOCRYPT 2012. LNCS, vol. 7668, pp. 412–430. Springer, Heidelberg (2012). doi:10.1007/978-3-642-34931-7_24

Provably Secure **NTRU** Instances over Prime Cyclotomic Rings

Yang Yu[1], Guangwu Xu[2], and Xiaoyun Wang[3]($\boxtimes$)

[1] Department of Computer Science and Technology,
Tsinghua University, Beijing 100084, China
`y-y13@mails.tsinghua.edu.cn`
[2] Department of EE and CS, University of Wisconsin-Milwaukee,
Milwaukee 53201, WI, USA
`gxu4uwm@uwm.edu`
[3] Institute for Advanced Study, Tsinghua University, Beijing 100084, China
`xiaoyunwang@mail.tsinghua.edu.cn`

Abstract. Due to its remarkable performance and potential resistance to quantum attacks, NTRUEncrypt has drawn much attention recently; it also has been standardized by IEEE. However, classical NTRUEncrypt lacks a strong security guarantee and its security still relies on heuristic arguments. At Eurocrypt 2011, Stehlé and Steinfeld first proposed a variant of NTRUEncrypt with a security reduction from standard problems on ideal lattices. This variant is restricted to the family of rings $\mathbb{Z}[X]/(X^n + 1)$ with n a power of 2 and its private keys are sampled by rejection from certain discrete Gaussian so that the public key is shown to be almost uniform. Despite the fact that partial operations, especially for RLWE, over $\mathbb{Z}[X]/(X^n + 1)$ are simple and efficient, these rings are quite scarce and different from the classical NTRU setting. In this work, we consider a variant of NTRUEncrypt over prime cyclotomic rings, *i.e.* $\mathbb{Z}[X]/(X^{n-1} + \cdots + X + 1)$ with n an odd prime, and obtain IND-CPA secure results in the standard model assuming the hardness of worst-case problems on ideal lattices. In our setting, the choice of the rings is much more flexible and the scheme is closer to the original NTRU, as $\mathbb{Z}[X]/(X^{n-1} + \cdots + X + 1)$ is a large subring of the NTRU ring $\mathbb{Z}[X]/(X^n - 1)$. Some tools for prime cyclotomic rings are also developed.

Keywords: Lattice-based cryptography · NTRU · Learning with errors · Provable security

1 Introduction

The well-known public key system NTRU was created and refined by Hoffstein, Pipher and Silverman in [17,18]. The NTRU encryption scheme, NTRUEncrypt,

© IACR 2017. This article is the final version submitted by the authors to the IACR and to Springer-Verlag on January 7, 2017. The version published by Springer-Verlag is available at doi:10.1007/978-3-662-54365-8_17.

© International Association for Cryptologic Research 2017
S. Fehr (Ed.): PKC 2017, Part I, LNCS 10174, pp. 409–434, 2017.
DOI: 10.1007/978-3-662-54365-8_17

is one of the fastest known lattice-based cryptosystems and regarded as an alternative to RSA and ECC due to its potential of countering attacks by quantum computers. The underlying problem of NTRUEncrypt has been used to design various cryptographic primitives including digital signatures [16], identity-based encryption [8] and multi-linear maps [11,23]. In the course of assessing the security of NTRU, Coppersmith and Shamir first claimed in [5] that one can convert breaking NTRU to solving hard problems on the so-called NTRU lattice. Then an army of cryptanalyses [1,2,4,9,10,12,15,19,21,22,29,34] have brought security estimations on NTRU and its variants, and NTRU is still considered secure in practice.

The *Learning With Errors* problem (LWE), introduced by Regev in 2005 [32], is shown to be as hard as certain lattice problems in the worst case. The *Ring Learning With Errors* problem (RLWE) is an algebraic variant of LWE, proposed by Lyubashevsky, Peikert and Regev [25], whose hardness is guaranteed by some hard problems over ideal lattices. Due to its better compactness and efficiency over LWE, RLWE has been used as the foundation of new cryptographic applications. In a celebrated paper [33], Stehlé and Steinfeld first modified NTRUEncrypt by incorporating RLWE and proved that the security of NTRU follows by a reduction from RLWE provided that a right set of parameters are used, which is the first sound theoretical base for the security of NTRU in the asymptotic sense. It is worth noting that several novel ideas and powerful techniques have been developed in [33]. One remarkable contribution is to show that, for n being a power of 2, and private keys f, g sampled according suitable conditions and parameters from the ring $\mathbb{Z}[X]/(X^n + 1)$, the public key $h = \frac{f}{g}$ is close to that uniformly sampled under the statistical distance. Based on the provably secure NTRU scheme, more interesting cryptographic primitives are achieved, such as fully homomorphic encryption [3,24], proxy re-encryption [30].

In most known ring-based cryptosystems, the rings of the form $\mathbb{Z}[X]/(X^{2^m} + 1)$ are preferred choices. This family of rings has some nice algebraic features and various results on it have been already established. However, as these rings are very scarce, it has a limitation on the choice of the rings. It is noted that another family of rings, the prime cyclotomic rings of the form $\mathcal{R} = \mathbb{Z}[X]/(X^{n-1} + \cdots + X + 1)$ with n being a prime, is also of particular interest in many aspects, especially in the context of RLWE and NTRU. As a large subring, this ring is much closer to the original NTRU ring. It is also remarked that a class of subfield attacks [1] is proposed recently and affects the asymptotic security of NTRU for large moduli q. Note that the subfield attack is not applicable to the setting of [33], but it is still meaningful to consider NTRU over the fields with no subfields of desired relative degree. In this sense, prime cyclotomic ring seems a good choice of the potential to counter the subfield attack. Establishing IND-CPA (*indistinguishability under chosen-plaintext attack*) secure results with respect to this class of rings will be an important topic. Indeed, as stated in [33], the results for $\mathbb{Z}[X]/(X^{2^m} + 1)$ are likely to hold for more general cases including that for prime cyclotomic rings. However, to the best of our knowledge, there were no actual discussions on this issue found in literature.

Our Contribution. The main purpose of this paper is to study the problem of provable security of NTRU in a modified setting with respect to prime cyclotomic rings. We show results similar to that of [33] still hold over prime cyclotomic rings. Consequently, to instantiate a provably secure NTRU, the density of usable cyclotomic polynomial degree $n < N$ is increased from $\Theta\left(\frac{\log N}{N}\right)$ to $\Theta\left(\frac{1}{\log N}\right)$. Even though some main ideas of [33] are applicable in our discussion, many technical differences also need to be taken care of. Furthermore, some new results on prime cyclotomic rings developed here might be of general interest. We believe that these results could be used to design more applications based on prime cyclotomic rings.

Organization. We start in Sect. 2 with some notations and basic facts that will be useful to our discussion. We shall develop and prove a series of relevant results over prime cyclotomic rings in Sect. 3. Section 4 describes a modified NTRUEncrypt over prime cyclotomic rings and a reduction to its IND-CPA security from RLWE which has been proven hard under worst-case assumptions on ideal lattices. We conclude in Sect. 5. We have a couple of results whose proofs are similar to that in [33], these proofs are included in Appendices A, B and C for completeness.

2   Preliminaries

Lattice. A lattice $\mathcal{L}$ is a discrete subgroup of $\mathbb{R}^m$ and represented by a basis, *i.e.* there is a set of linearly independent vectors $\mathbf{b}_1, \cdots, \mathbf{b}_n \in \mathbb{R}^m$ such that $\mathcal{L} = \{\sum_i x_i \mathbf{b}_i | x_i \in \mathbb{Z}\}$. The integer m is the dimension and the integer n is the rank of $\mathcal{L}$. A lattice is full-rank if its rank equals its dimension. The first minimum $\lambda_1(\mathcal{L})$ (resp. $\lambda_1^\infty(\mathcal{L})$) is the minimum of Euclidean (resp. ℓ_∞) norm of all non-zero vectors of the lattice $\mathcal{L}$. More generally, the k-th minimum $\lambda_k(\mathcal{L})$ for $k \leq n$ is the smallest r such that there are at least k linearly independent vectors of $\mathcal{L}$ whose norms are not greater than r. Given a basis $\mathbf{B} = (\mathbf{b}_1, \cdots, \mathbf{b}_n)$ of a full-rank lattice $\mathcal{L}$, the set $\mathcal{P}(\mathbf{B}) = \{\sum_i c_i \mathbf{b}_i | c_i \in [0,1)\}$ is the fundamental parallelepiped of $\mathbf{B}$ whose volume $|\det(\mathbf{B})|$ is an invariant of $\mathcal{L}$, called the volume of $\mathcal{L}$ and denoted by $\det(\mathcal{L})$. The dual lattice of $\mathcal{L}$ is the lattice $\widehat{\mathcal{L}} = \{\mathbf{c} \in \mathbb{R}^m | \forall i, \langle \mathbf{c}, \mathbf{b}_i \rangle \in \mathbb{Z}\}$ of the same dimension and rank with $\mathcal{L}$.

Given a ring $\mathcal{R}$ with an additive isomorphism θ mapping $\mathcal{R}$ to the lattice $\theta(\mathcal{R})$ in an inner product space and an ideal I of $\mathcal{R}$, we call the sublattice $\theta(I)$ an *ideal lattice*. Due to their smaller space requirement and faster operation speed, ideal lattices have been a popular choice for most lattice-based cryptosystems. More importantly, the hardness of classical lattice problems, SVP (*Shortest Vector Problem*) and γ-SVP (*Approximate Shortest Vector Problem with approximation factor γ*), does not seem to substantially decrease (except maybe very large approximate factors [6]). Thus, it is believed that the worst-case hardness of γ-SVPover ideal lattices, denoted by γ-Ideal-SVP, is against subexponential quantum attacks, for any $\gamma \leq \text{poly}(n)$.

Probability and Statistics. Let D be a distribution over a discrete domain E. We write $z \hookleftarrow D$ to represent the random variable z that is sampled from the distribution D and denote by $D(x)$ the probability of z evaluates to $x \in E$. We denote by $U(E)$ the uniform distribution over a finite domain E. For two distributions D_1, D_2 over a same discrete domain E, their statistical distance is $\Delta(D_1; D_2) = \frac{1}{2} \sum_{x \in E} |D_1(x) - D_2(x)|$. Two distributions D_1, D_2 are said to be statistically close with respect to n if their statistical distance $\Delta(D_1; D_2) = o(n^{-c})$ for any constant $c > 0$.

Gaussian Measures. We denote by $\rho_{r,\mathbf{c}}(\mathbf{x})$ the n-dimensional Gaussian function with center $\mathbf{c} \in \mathbb{R}^n$ and width r, *i.e.* $\rho_{r,\mathbf{c}}(\mathbf{x}) = \exp\left(-\frac{\pi \|\mathbf{x}-\mathbf{c}\|^2}{r^2}\right)$. When the center is $\mathbf{0}$, the Gaussian function is simply written as $\rho_r(\mathbf{x})$. Let S be a subset of $\mathbb{R}^n$, we denote by $\rho_{r,\mathbf{c}}(S)$ (resp. $\rho_r(S)$) the sum $\sum_{\mathbf{x} \in S} \rho_{r,\mathbf{c}}(\mathbf{x})$ (resp. $\sum_{\mathbf{x} \in S} \rho_r(\mathbf{x})$). Let $D_{\mathcal{L},r,\mathbf{c}}$ be the *discrete Gaussian distribution* over a lattice $\mathcal{L}$ with center $\mathbf{c}$ and width r, the probability of a vector $\mathbf{x} \in \mathcal{L}$ under this distribution is $D_{\mathcal{L},r,\mathbf{c}}(\mathbf{x}) = \frac{\rho_{r,\mathbf{c}}(\mathbf{x})}{\rho_{r,\mathbf{c}}(\mathcal{L})}$. For $\delta > 0$, the *smoothing parameter* $\eta_\delta(\mathcal{L})$ is the smallest $r > 0$ such that $\rho_{1/r}(\widehat{\mathcal{L}}) \leq 1 + \delta$. The smoothing parameter is bounded in terms of some lattice quantities. The following lemmata will be useful in our discussion.

Lemma 1 ([28], Lemma 3.3). *Let $\mathcal{L} \subseteq \mathbb{R}^n$ be a full-rank lattice and $\delta \in (0, 1)$. Then $\eta_\delta(\mathcal{L}) \leq \sqrt{\frac{\ln(2n(1+1/\delta))}{\pi}} \cdot \lambda_n(\mathcal{L})$.*

Lemma 2 ([31], Lemma 3.5). *Let $\mathcal{L} \subseteq \mathbb{R}^n$ be a full-rank lattice and $\delta \in (0, 1)$. Then $\eta_\delta(\mathcal{L}) \leq \frac{\sqrt{\ln(2n(1+1/\delta))/\pi}}{\lambda_1^\infty(\widehat{\mathcal{L}})}$.*

Lemma 3 ([28], Lemma 4.4). *Let $\mathcal{L} \subseteq \mathbb{R}^n$ be a full-rank lattice and $\delta \in (0, 1)$. For $\mathbf{c} \in \mathbb{R}^n$ and $r \geq \eta_\delta(\mathcal{L})$, we have $\Pr_{\mathbf{b} \hookleftarrow D_{\mathcal{L},r,\mathbf{c}}}(\|\mathbf{b} - \mathbf{c}\| \geq r\sqrt{n}) \leq \frac{1+\delta}{1-\delta} 2^{-n}$.*

Lemma 4 ([14], Corollary 2.8). *Let $\mathcal{L}' \subseteq \mathcal{L} \subseteq \mathbb{R}^n$ be full-rank lattices and $\delta \in (0, \frac{1}{2})$. For $\mathbf{c} \in \mathbb{R}^n$ and $r \geq \eta_\delta(\mathcal{L}')$, we have $\Delta(D_{\mathcal{L},r,\mathbf{c}} \bmod \mathcal{L}'; U(\mathcal{L}/\mathcal{L}')) \leq 2\delta$.*

Lemma 5 ([14], Theorem 4.1). *There exists a polynomial-time algorithm that, given a basis $(\mathbf{b}_1, \cdots, \mathbf{b}_n)$ of a lattice $\mathcal{L} \subseteq \mathbb{Z}^n$, a parameter $r = \omega(\sqrt{\log n}) \max \|\mathbf{b}_i\|$ and $\mathbf{c} \in \mathbb{R}^n$, outputs samples from a distribution statistically close to $D_{\mathcal{L},r,\mathbf{c}}$ with respect to n.*

Furthermore, we denote by ψ_r the Gaussian distribution with mean 0 and width r over $\mathbb{R}$ and by ψ_r^n the *spherical Gaussian distribution* over $\mathbb{R}^n$ of the vector $(v_1, \cdots, v_n)$ in which each v_i is drawn from ψ_r independently. In this paper, we shall restrict ψ_r over $\mathbb{Q}$ rather than $\mathbb{R}$. As explained in [7], this will only lead to a negligible impact on our results.

Cyclotomic Ring. Let ξ_n be a primitive n-th complex root of unity and $\Phi_n(X)$ the n-th cyclotomic polynomial. It is known that $\Phi_n(X) \in \mathbb{Z}[X]$ and is of degree $\varphi(n)$, the totient of n. All roots of $\Phi_n(X)$ form the set $\{\xi_n^i | i \in \mathbb{Z}_n^*\}$. In this paper, we will be working with a cyclotomic ring of the form $\mathcal{R} = \mathbb{Z}[X]/\Phi_n(X)$. For any prime n, if a prime q satisfies $q = 1 \bmod n$, then $\Phi_n(X)$ splits into $n-1$ distinct linear factors modulo q. Given n, the existence of infinite such primes is guaranteed by Dirichlet's theorem on arithmetic progressions. Furthermore, by Linnik's theorem, the smallest such q can be bounded by $\mathrm{poly}(n)$ (a more precise bound $O(n^{5.2})$ has been proven in [36]). Another important class of rings involved in our discussion is the family of rings of the form $\mathcal{R}_q = \mathcal{R}/q\mathcal{R}$. As indicated earlier, our main focus will be *prime cyclotomic rings*, *i.e.* those rings associate with polynomials $\Phi_n(X) = X^{n-1} + X^{n-2} + \cdots + 1$ with n a prime.

Given a positive integer n, we define the polynomial $\Theta_n(X)$ to be $X^n - 1$ if n is odd, and $X^{\frac{n}{2}} + 1$ if n is even. It is easy to see that there is a natural ring extension $\mathcal{R}' = \mathbb{Z}[X]/\Theta_n(X)$ of the cyclotomic ring $\mathcal{R} = \mathbb{Z}[X]/\Phi_n(X)$. In particular, when $n > 1$ is a power of 2, $\mathcal{R} = \mathcal{R}'$; when n is a prime, the relation $\Theta_n(X) = \Phi_n(X) \cdot (X-1)$ implies a ring isomorphism $\mathcal{R}' \simeq \mathcal{R} \times \mathbb{Z}$ by the Chinese Remainder Theorem.

Hardness of RLWE. The "pure" Ring Learning With Errors problem (RLWE) introduced in [25] involves the dual of the ring. For the ring $\mathbb{Z}[X]/(X^{2^m}+1)$, its dual is just a scaling of itself. Therefore, many RLWE instances are established over such rings to avoid dual. In [7], Ducas and Durmus proposed an "easy-to-use" RLWE setting and instantiated RLWE over prime cyclotomic rings. In this paper, we follow the setting of [7].

Definition 1 (RLWE error distribution in [7]). *Let* $\mathcal{R} = \mathbb{Z}[X]/\Phi_n(X)$. *Given* ψ *a distribution over* $\mathbb{Q}[X]/\Theta_n(X)$, *we define* $\overline{\psi}$ *as the distribution over* $\mathcal{R}$ *obtained by* $e = \lfloor e' \bmod \Phi_n(X) \rceil \in \mathcal{R}$ *with* $e' \hookleftarrow \psi$. *Here we denote by* $\lfloor f \rceil$ *the polynomial whose coefficients are derived by rounding coefficients of f to the nearest integers.*

Definition 2 (RLWE distribution in [7]). *Let* $\mathcal{R} = \mathbb{Z}[X]/\Phi_n(X)$ *and* $\mathcal{R}_q = \mathcal{R}/q\mathcal{R}$. *For* $s \in \mathcal{R}_q$ *and* ψ *a distribution over* $\mathbb{Q}[X]/\Theta_n(X)$, *we define* $A_{s,\psi}$ *as the distribution over* $\mathcal{R}_q \times \mathcal{R}_q$ *obtained by sampling the pair* $(a, as + e)$ *where* $a \hookleftarrow U(\mathcal{R}_q)$ *and* $e \hookleftarrow \overline{\psi}$.

Definition 3 (RLWE$_{q,\psi,k}$). *Let* $\mathcal{R} = \mathbb{Z}[X]/\Phi_n(X)$ *and* $\mathcal{R}_q = \mathcal{R}/q\mathcal{R}$. *The problem* RLWE$_{q,\psi,k}$ *in the ring* $\mathcal{R}$ *is defined as follows. Given* k *samples drawn from* $A_{s,\psi}$ *where* $s \hookleftarrow U(\mathcal{R}_q)$ *and* k *samples from* $U(\mathcal{R}_q \times \mathcal{R}_q)$, *distinguish them with an advantage* $1/\mathrm{poly}(n)$.

The following theorem indicates that RLWE under the above settings is hard based on the worst-case hardness of γ-Ideal-SVP. The ideal lattices we discuss here are with respect to the so-called *canonical embedding*, *i.e.* $\theta(f) = (f(\xi_n^i))_{i \in \mathbb{Z}_n^*}$.

Theorem 1 ([7], Theorem 2). *Let n be an odd prime, and let $\mathcal{R}_q$ be the ring $\mathbb{Z}_q[X]/\Phi_n(X)$ where q is a prime congruent to 1 modulo $2n$. Also, let $\alpha \in (0,1)$ be a real number such that $\alpha q > \omega(\sqrt{\log n})$. There exists a randomized quantum* *reduction from γ-Ideal-SVP on ideal lattices in $\mathbb{Z}[X]/\Phi_n(X)$ to* $\mathsf{RLWE}_{q,\psi_t^n,k}$ *for*

$t = \sqrt{n}\alpha q \left(\frac{(n-1)k}{\log((n-1)k)}\right)^{1/4}$ *(with $\gamma = \tilde{O}\left(\frac{\sqrt{n}}{\alpha}\right)$) that runs in time $O(q \cdot \mathrm{poly}(n))$.*

Let $\mathcal{R}_q^\times$ be the set of all invertible elements of $\mathcal{R}_q$. By restricting $A_{s,\psi}$ to $\mathcal{R}_q^\times \times \mathcal{R}_q$, we obtain a modified RLWE distribution and denote it by $A_{s,\psi}^\times$. Replacing $A_{s,\psi}$ and $U(\mathcal{R}_q \times \mathcal{R}_q)$ by $A_{s,\psi}^\times$ and $U(\mathcal{R}_q^\times \times \mathcal{R}_q)$ respectively, we get a variant of RLWE which is denoted by $\mathsf{RLWE}^\times$. When $q = \Omega(n)$, the invertible elements account for a non-negligible fraction in the $\mathcal{R}_q$. Thus $\mathsf{RLWE}^\times$ remains hard. Furthermore, as explained in [33], the nonce s in $A_{s,\psi}^\times$ can be sampled from ψ without incurring security loss. We denote by $\mathsf{RLWE}_{HNF}^\times$ this variant of $\mathsf{RLWE}^\times$.

3   New Results on Prime Cyclotomic Rings

In this section, we will report on a series of results on prime cyclotomic rings. Some of the results are adapted from corresponding conclusions in [33], but the modifications are not trivial considering the differences between the cyclotomic rings of prime and a power of 2 orders. Firstly, we present several notations and basic properties aiming at prime cyclotomic rings.

3.1   Notations and Properties

Let n be a prime and $\mathcal{R}$ be the ring $\mathbb{Z}[X]/\Phi_n(X) = \mathbb{Z}[X]/(X^{n-1} + \cdots + 1)$. For any $f \in \mathcal{R}$, we call a vector $(f_0, \cdots, f_{n-2}) \in \mathbb{Z}^{n-1}$ the coefficient vector of f if $f = \sum_{i=0}^{n-2} f_i X^i$. For any $\mathbf{s} = (s_1, \cdots, s_m) \in \mathcal{R}^m$, we view $\mathbf{s}$ as a $m(n-1)$-dimensional vector in $\mathbb{Z}^{m(n-1)}$ by coefficient embedding. Given $\mathbf{s}, \mathbf{t} \in \mathcal{R}^m$, their Euclidean inner product is denoted by $\langle \mathbf{s}, \mathbf{t} \rangle$. To get a clean expression of $\langle \mathbf{s}, \mathbf{t} \rangle$ as a coefficient of a polynomial related to $\mathbf{s}$ and $\mathbf{t}$, we introduce two operations on $f \in \mathcal{R}$ as follows.

Let $f \in \mathcal{R}$ of coefficient vector $(f_0, \cdots, f_{n-2})$, we define $f^\smile$ to be the polynomial $\sum_{i=0}^{n-2}(\sum_{j=i}^{n-2} f_j)X^i$ and $f^\frown$ the polynomial $\sum_{i=0}^{n-3}(f_i - f_{i+1})X^i + f_{n-2}X^{n-2}$, respectively. One important consequence is that, regarding $\smile$ and $\frown$ as two functions over $\mathcal{R}$, these operations are inverse to each other, namely

Proposition 1. *Let n be a prime and $\mathcal{R} = \mathbb{Z}[X]/\Phi_n(X)$, then*

$$\forall f \in \mathcal{R}, (f^\smile)^\frown = (f^\frown)^\smile = f.$$

Proof. Let $(g_0, \cdots, g_{n-2})$ and $(h_0, \cdots, h_{n-2})$ be the coefficient vectors of the polynomials $f^\smile$ and $f^\frown$ respectively. According to the definitions of these two operations, we have

$$g_i = \sum_{j=i}^{n-2} f_j \text{ for } i \in \{0, \cdots, n-2\}$$

and
$$h_i = f_i - f_{i+1} \text{ for } i < n - 2 \quad \text{and} \quad h_{n-2} = f_{n-2}.$$
Then, a straightforward computation leads to that
$$g_i - g_{i+1} = f_i \text{ for } i < n - 2 \quad \text{and} \quad g_{n-2} = f_{n-2}$$
and
$$\sum_{j=i}^{n-2} h_j = f_i \text{ for } i \in \{0, \cdots, n - 2\}.$$
Thus we conclude that $g^\wedge = h^\vee = f$, i.e. $(f^\vee)^\wedge = (f^\wedge)^\vee = f$. $\square$

The following lemma manifests an expression of the Euclidean inner product of two elements in $\mathcal{R}$.

Lemma 6. *Let n be a prime and $\mathcal{R} = \mathbb{Z}[X]/\Phi_n(X)$. Denote by X^{-1} the inverse of X. Let $f \in \mathcal{R}$ of coefficient vector $(f_0, \cdots, f_{n-2})$ and $g \in \mathcal{R}$ of coefficient vector $(g_0, \cdots, g_{n-2})$. Then*

$$\sum_{i=0}^{n-2} f_i g_i = \text{the constant coefficient of the polynomial } f(X)g^\vee(X^{-1}).$$

Proof. Let $(g'_0, \cdots, g'_{n-2})$ be the coefficient vector of the polynomial $g^\vee$. Notice that the term X^n is equivalent to the identity element of $\mathcal{R}$. Hence X^{-1} is equivalent to X^{n-1} when it comes to the algebraic computations over $\mathcal{R}$. Then we have

$$f(X)g^\vee(X^{-1}) = f(X)g^\vee(X^{n-1}) = \sum_{i,j \in \{0, \cdots, n-2\}} f_i g'_j X^{i+(n-1)j}.$$

The constant coefficient of $f(X)g^\vee(X^{-1})$ is only contributed by the term $X^{i+(n-1)j}$ with $i + (n-1)j = 0, n - 1 \bmod n$, i.e. $i = j$ or $j - 1$. Note that $X^{n-1} = -(X^{n-2} + \cdots + 1)$, thus the constant coefficient of $f(X)g^\vee(X^{-1})$ equals $\sum_{i=0}^{n-2} f_i g'_i - \sum_{i=0}^{n-3} f_i g'_{i+1} = \sum_{i=0}^{n-3} f_i(g'_i - g'_{i+1}) + f_{n-2}g'_{n-2}$. The terms $\{g'_i - g'_{i+1}\}_{i=0}^{n-3}$ and g'_{n-2} are the coefficients of the polynomial $(g^\vee)^\wedge = g$. Consequently, the constant coefficient of $f(X)g^\vee(X^{-1})$ equals $\sum_{i=0}^{n-2} f_i g_i$. $\square$

Corollary 1. *Let n be a prime and $\mathcal{R} = \mathbb{Z}[X]/\Phi_n(X)$. For any $\mathbf{s} = (s_1, \cdots, s_m) \in \mathcal{R}^m$ and $\mathbf{t} = (t_1, \cdots, t_m) \in \mathcal{R}^m$, then*

$$\langle \mathbf{s}, \mathbf{t} \rangle = \text{the constant coefficient of the polynomial } \sum_{i=1}^{m} s_i(X)t_i^\vee(X^{-1}).$$

Remark. For the ring $\mathbb{Z}[X]/(X^n + 1)$, the Euclidean inner product of any two elements f and g equals the constant coefficient of the polynomial $f(X)g(X^{-1})$, which is simpler than the case in our discussion. The rather involved expression of Euclidean inner product contributes to a sequence of technical differences compared to that in [33].

Now we introduce several norms and demonstrate some relations among them. For any $t \in \mathcal{R}$, we define its T_2-*norm* by $T_2(t)^2 = \sum_{i=1}^{n-1} |t(\xi_n^i)|^2$ and its *algebraic norm* by $N(t) = \prod_{i=1}^{n-1} |t(\xi_n^i)|$. Also we define the *polynomial norm* $\|t\|$ by the Euclidean norm of the coefficient vector of t.

Lemma 7. *Let n be a prime and $\mathcal{R} = \mathbb{Z}[X]/\Phi_n(X)$. For any $t \in \mathcal{R}$, we have*

$$N(t)^{\frac{2}{n-1}} \leq \frac{1}{n-1} T_2(t)^2 \quad and \quad \|t\|^2 = \frac{T_2(t)^2 + t(1)^2}{n} \geq \frac{T_2(t)^2}{n}.$$

Proof. The first inequality can be proven directly by arithmetic-geometric inequality. Since $\|t\|^2 = \frac{\sum_{i=0}^{n-1} |t(\xi_n^i)|^2}{n} = \frac{T_2(t)^2 + t(1)^2}{n}$ is the Parseval's identity [35], the second one follows immediately, as $t(1)^2 \geq 0$.   □

Moreover, we present the following result to illustrate that the product of two polynomials in $\mathcal{R}$ is of well-bounded norm.

Lemma 8. *Let n be a prime and $\mathcal{R} = \mathbb{Z}[X]/\Phi_n(X)$. For any $f, g \in \mathcal{R}$, we have*

$$\|fg\|_\infty \leq 2\|f\|\|g\| \quad and \quad \|fg\| \leq 2\sqrt{n-1}\|f\|\|g\|.$$

Proof. Let $\mathcal{R}' = \mathbb{Z}[X]/(X^n - 1)$ and $f', g' \in \mathcal{R}'$ be the polynomials with the same coefficients as f, g respectively, *i.e.* the coefficients of X^{n-1} are 0. Let $h' = \sum_{i=0}^{n-1} h_i' X^i$ be the product of f' and g' in $\mathcal{R}'$ where $h_i' \in \mathbb{Z}$ for $i \in \{0, \cdots, n-1\}$. Let $h = f \cdot g \in \mathcal{R}$. Notice that $\Phi_n(X)$ is a factor of $X^n - 1$, hence we know that $h' \mod \Phi_n(X) = h \in \mathcal{R}$, *i.e.* $h = h' \mod \Phi_n(X) = \sum_{i=0}^{n-2} (h_i' - h_{n-1}') X^i$.

Let $(f_0, \cdots, f_{n-2})$ and $(g_0, \cdots, g_{n-2})$ be the coefficient vectors of f and g. We also set $f_{n-1} = g_{n-1} = 0$. For any $i \in \{0, \cdots, n-1\}$, we have $h_i' = \sum_{j=0}^{n-1} f_j g_{(i-j) \mod n}$. By Cauchy-Schwarz inequality, we know that $|h_i'| \leq \|f\|\|g\|$. Therefore

$$\|h\|_\infty = \max_{0 \leq i \leq n-2} |h_i' - h_{n-1}'| \leq \max_{0 \leq i \leq n-2} (|h_i'| + |h_{n-1}'|) \leq 2\|f\|\|g\|.$$

By equivalence of norms, we conclude that $\|h\| \leq \sqrt{n-1}\|h\|_\infty \leq 2\sqrt{n-1}\|f\|\|g\|$.   □

Remark. The second inequality indicates that an upper bound of the multiplicative expansion factor of $\mathcal{R}$, which is $\gamma_\times(\mathcal{R}) = \max_{f,g \in \mathcal{R}} \frac{\|fg\|}{\|f\|\|g\|}$, is $2\sqrt{n-1}$. This is comparable to that of power-of-2 cyclotomic rings in the asymptotic sense, as the expansion factor of the ring $\mathbb{Z}[X]/(X^n + 1)$ is exactly $\sqrt{n}$ (see [13]).

3.2   Duality Results for Module Lattices

In [33], Stehlé and Steinfeld reveals a nice duality between two module lattices for the n-th cyclotomic ring with n a power of 2. However, that duality cannot be simply generalized to the case of prime cyclotomic rings. Next, we will propose a new duality relationship between two module lattices for a prime cyclotomic ring.

To begin with, we introduce a few families of $\mathcal{R}$-modules. Let q be a prime such that $\Phi_n(X)$ splits into $n-1$ distinct linear factors modulo q and $\mathcal{R}_q = \mathcal{R}/q\mathcal{R}$. We denote by $\{\phi_i\}_{i=1,\cdots,n-1}$ all roots of $\Phi_n(X)$ modulo q. Note that if ϕ is a root of $\Phi_n(X)$ modulo q, then so is $\phi^{-1} \bmod q$. By the Chinese Remainder Theorem, we see that

$$\mathcal{R}_q \simeq \mathbb{Z}_q[X]/(X - \phi_1) \times \cdots \times \mathbb{Z}_q[X]/(X - \phi_{n-1}) \simeq (\mathbb{Z}_q)^{n-1}.$$

From this, we see that each ideal of $\mathcal{R}_q$ is of the form $\prod_{i \in S}(X - \phi_i) \cdot \mathcal{R}_q$ with $S \subseteq \{1, \cdots, n-1\}$, and we denote it by I_S. Let $\mathcal{R}_q^\times$ be the set of all invertible elements of $\mathcal{R}_q$. Given $\mathbf{a} \in \mathcal{R}_q^m$, we define two $\mathcal{R}$-modules $\mathbf{a}^\perp(I_S)$ and $\mathcal{L}(\mathbf{a}, I_S)$ in exactly the same manner as in [33]:

$$\mathbf{a}^\perp(I_S) := \left\{ (t_1, \cdots, t_m) \in \mathcal{R}^m \mid \forall i, (t_i \bmod q) \in I_S \text{ and } \sum_{i=1}^m t_i a_i = 0 \bmod q \right\},$$

$$\mathcal{L}(\mathbf{a}, I_S) := \{(t_1, \cdots, t_m) \in \mathcal{R}^m \mid \exists s \in \mathcal{R}_q, \forall i, (t_i \bmod q) = a_i \cdot s \bmod I_S\}.$$

Then we can define a new $\mathcal{R}$-module $\mathcal{L}^\frown(\mathbf{a}, I_S)$ to be

$$\mathcal{L}^\frown(\mathbf{a}, I_S) := \left\{ (t_1, \cdots, t_m) \in \mathcal{R}^m \mid (t_1^\smile, \cdots, t_m^\smile) \in \mathcal{L}(\mathbf{a}, I_S) \right\}.$$

Module lattices $\mathbf{a}^\perp(I_S)$ and $\mathcal{L}^\frown(\mathbf{a}, I_S)$ can be related by duality argument. More precisely,

Lemma 9. *Let n be a prime and $\mathcal{R} = \mathbb{Z}[X]/\Phi_n(X)$. Let q be a prime such that $\Phi_n(X)$ splits into $n-1$ distinct linear factors modulo q and $\mathcal{R}_q = \mathcal{R}/q\mathcal{R}$. Given $S \subseteq \{1, \cdots, n-1\}$ and $\mathbf{a} \in \mathcal{R}_q^m$, let $\mathbf{a}^\times \in \mathcal{R}_q^m$ be defined by $a_i^\times = a_i(X^{-1})$ and $I_{\bar{S}}^\times$ be the ideal $\prod_{i \in \bar{S}}(X - \phi_i^{-1}) \cdot \mathcal{R}_q$ where $\bar{S}$ is the complement of S. Then (considering both sets as $m(n-1)$-dimensional lattices by identifying $\mathcal{R}$ with $\mathbb{Z}^{n-1}$)*

$$\widehat{\mathbf{a}^\perp(I_S)} = \frac{1}{q}\mathcal{L}^\frown(\mathbf{a}^\times, I_{\bar{S}}^\times).$$

Proof. Firstly, we prove that $\frac{1}{q}\mathcal{L}^\frown(\mathbf{a}^\times, I_{\bar{S}}^\times) \subseteq \widehat{\mathbf{a}^\perp(I_S)}$. For any $\mathbf{t} = (t_1, \cdots, t_m) \in \mathbf{a}^\perp(I_S)$ and $\mathbf{t}' = (t_1', \cdots, t_m') \in \mathcal{L}^\frown(\mathbf{a}^\times, I_{\bar{S}}^\times)$, Corollary 1 says that their inner product $\langle \mathbf{t}, \mathbf{t}' \rangle$ equals the constant coefficient of the polynomial $\sum_{i=1}^m t_i(X)t_i'^\smile(X^{-1})$. According to the definition of $\mathcal{L}^\frown(\mathbf{a}^\times, I_{\bar{S}}^\times)$ and Proposition 1, there exists $s \in \mathcal{R}_q$ such that $(t_i'^\smile \bmod q) = a_i^\times \cdot s + b_i'$ for some $b_i' \in I_{\bar{S}}^\times$. Then we get

$$\sum_{i=1}^m t_i(X)t_i'^\smile(X^{-1}) = s(X^{-1}) \cdot \sum_{i=1}^m t_i(X)a_i(X) + \sum_{i=1}^m t_i(X)b_i'(X^{-1}) \bmod q$$

Both two sums in the right hand side evaluate to 0 in $\mathcal{R}_q$, which means that $\langle \mathbf{t}, \mathbf{t}' \rangle = 0 \bmod q$. Therefore, we finish the proof of this part.

Secondly, it suffices to prove that $\mathcal{L}^\frown(\widehat{\mathbf{a}^\times, I_{\bar{S}}^\times}) \subseteq \frac{1}{q}\mathbf{a}^\perp(I_S)$. For any $\mathbf{t} \in \mathcal{L}^\frown(\mathbf{a}^\times, I_{\bar{S}}^\times)$ and $\mathbf{t}' \in \mathcal{L}^\frown(\widehat{\mathbf{a}^\times, I_{\bar{S}}^\times})$, the constant coefficient of $\sum_{i=1}^m t_i'(X) t_i^\vee(X^{-1}) = \langle \mathbf{t}', \mathbf{t} \rangle$ is an integer due to duality. Notice that if $(t_1, \cdots, t_m) \in \mathcal{L}^\frown(\mathbf{a}^\times, I_{\bar{S}}^\times)$, then $\left((t_1^\vee \cdot X^k)^\frown, \cdots, (t_m^\vee \cdot X^k)^\frown \right) \in \mathcal{L}^\frown(\mathbf{a}^\times, I_{\bar{S}}^\times)$. Thus, for $k \in \{1, \cdots, n-2\}$, the constant coefficient of $\sum_{i=1}^m t_i'(X) t_i^\vee(X^{-1}) X^{-k}$ is also an integer, which implies that all coefficients of $\sum_{i=1}^m t_i'(X) t_i^\vee(X^{-1})$ are integers. For any $(t_1, \cdots, t_m) \in \mathcal{L}^\frown(\widehat{\mathbf{a}^\times, I_{\bar{S}}^\times})$, we deduce from the fact $(q^\frown, 0, \cdots, 0) \in \mathcal{L}^\frown(\mathbf{a}^\times, I_{\bar{S}}^\times)$ that $q t_1 \in \mathbb{Z}^{n-1}$. Let $\nu_{I_{\bar{S}}^\times}$ be the polynomial $\prod_{i \in \bar{S}}(X - \phi_i^{-1})$. Since $\left(\nu_{I_{\bar{S}}^\times}^\frown, 0, \cdots, 0 \right) \in \mathcal{L}^\frown(\mathbf{a}^\times, I_{\bar{S}}^\times)$, we obtain $q t_1(X) \cdot \nu_{I_{\bar{S}}^\times}(X^{-1}) = 0 \bmod \mathcal{R}_q$, that means $(q t_1 \bmod q) \in I_S$. For the same reason, we have $(q t_i \bmod q) \in I_S$ for any $i \in \{1, \cdots, m\}$. If we set $s = 1$, then $(a_1^{\times\frown}, \cdots, a_m^{\times\frown}) \in \mathcal{L}^\frown(\mathbf{a}^\times, I_{\bar{S}}^\times)$. It shows that the polynomial $\sum_{i=1}^m (q t_i(X) a_i(X)) = q \sum_{i=1}^m (t_i(X) a_i^\times(X^{-1})) = 0 \bmod q$. Combining the fact that $(q t_i \bmod q) \in I_S$, we conclude that $q(t_1, \cdots, t_m) \in \mathbf{a}^\perp(I_S)$. The proof is completed.   □

Remark. The above result on the duality is different from that proven in [33], because the inner product has a more involved form. The original ideas of [33] have been exploited here, but we also add more details to treat technical differences.

3.3   On the Absence of Unusually Short Vector in $\mathcal{L}^\frown(\mathbf{a}, I_S)$

We now show that for $\mathbf{a} \hookleftarrow \mathbf{U}((\mathcal{R}_q^\times)^m)$, the first minimum of $\mathcal{L}^\frown(\mathbf{a}, I_S)$ for the ℓ_∞ norm is overwhelming unlikely unusually small. First we observe that the lattice $\mathcal{L}^\frown(\mathbf{a}, I_S)$ is transformed from the lattice $\mathcal{L}(\mathbf{a}, I_S)$. To describe the transformation, we define a matrix $\mathbf{H} \in \mathbb{Z}^{m(n-1) \times m(n-1)}$ as

$$\mathbf{H} = \begin{pmatrix} 1 & & & \\ -1 & 1 & & \\ & -1 & \ddots & \\ & & \ddots & 1 \\ & & & -1 & 1 \end{pmatrix} \otimes \mathbf{Id}_m,$$

where $\mathbf{Id}_m$ is an m-dimensional identity matrix. Let $\mathbf{B} \in \mathbb{Z}^{m(n-1) \times m(n-1)}$ be a basis of $\mathcal{L}(\mathbf{a}, I_S)$ whose rows correspond to the basis vectors, then $\mathbf{B}' = \mathbf{B} \cdot \mathbf{H}$ is a basis of $\mathcal{L}^\frown(\mathbf{a}, I_S)$. It is thus easy to see that $\mathcal{L}^\frown(\mathbf{a}, I_S)$ and $\mathcal{L}(\mathbf{a}, I_S)$ are of the same volume, *i.e.* $\det\left(\mathcal{L}^\frown(\mathbf{a}, I_S) \right) = \det\left(\mathcal{L}(\mathbf{a}, I_S) \right) = q^{(m-1)|S|}$. This is because there are $q^{m(n-1-|S|)+|S|}$ points of $\mathcal{L}(\mathbf{a}, I_S)$ in the cube $[0, q-1]^{m(n-1)}$. Also, the first minimums of these two lattices may not have a significant difference. Hence we first present a result on $\mathcal{L}(\mathbf{a}, I_S)$ which is a variant on prime cyclotomic rings of Lemma 8 in [33].

Lemma 10. *Let $n \geq 7$ be a prime and $\mathcal{R} = \mathbb{Z}[X]/\Phi_n(X)$. Let q be a prime such that $\Phi_n(X)$ splits into $n - 1$ distinct linear factors modulo q and $\mathcal{R}_q = \mathcal{R}/q\mathcal{R}$. For any $S \subseteq \{1, \cdots, n-1\}$, $m \geq 2$ and $\epsilon > 0$, set*

$$\beta := 1 - \frac{1}{m} + \frac{1 - \sqrt{1 + 4m(m-1)\left(1 - \frac{|S|}{n-1}\right) + 4m\epsilon}}{2m} \geq 1 - \frac{1}{m} - \epsilon - (m-1)\left(1 - \frac{|S|}{n-1}\right),$$

then we have $\lambda_1^\infty(\mathcal{L}(\mathbf{a}, I_S)) \geq \frac{1}{\sqrt{n}} q^\beta$ with probability $\geq 1 - \frac{2^{n-1}}{(q-1)^{\epsilon(n-1)}}$ over the uniformly random choice of $\mathbf{a}$ in $(\mathcal{R}_q^\times)^m$.

Remark. The above lemma can be shown by following the original idea but with some slight modifications on the inequalities for different norms in prime cyclotomic rings. For completeness, we give a proof in Appendix A. It is also noted that our statement of the lemma is essentially the same as that in Lemma 8 of [33], this is primarily because there is a simple relation for the Euclidean and algebraic norms in both prime and power-of-2 cyclotomic rings.

Next, we shall show that the first minimum $\lambda_1^\infty(\mathcal{L}(\mathbf{a}, I_S))$ is at most $\frac{n}{2}$ times that of $\mathcal{L}^\frown(\mathbf{a}, I_S)$.

Lemma 11. *Let $n \geq 7$ be a prime and $\mathcal{R} = \mathbb{Z}[X]/\Phi_n(X)$. Let q be a prime such that $\Phi_n(X)$ splits into $n - 1$ distinct linear factors modulo q and $\mathcal{R}_q = \mathcal{R}/q\mathcal{R}$. Then, for any $\mathbf{a} \in (\mathcal{R}_q^\times)^m$ and $S \subseteq \{1, \cdots, n-1\}$, we have*

$$\lambda_1^\infty(\mathcal{L}(\mathbf{a}, I_S)) \leq \frac{n-1}{2} \lambda_1^\infty(\mathcal{L}^\frown(\mathbf{a}, I_S)).$$

Proof. We first show that $\|X^{\frac{n-1}{2}} t^\vee\|_\infty \leq \frac{n-1}{2}\|t\|_\infty$ for any $t \in \mathcal{R}$. Let $(t_0, \cdots, t_{n-2})$ be the coefficient vector of t. We denote by $(t_0^\vee, \cdots, t_{n-2}^\vee)$ and $(t'_0, \cdots, t'_{n-2})$ the coefficient vectors of the polynomials $t^\vee$ and $X^{\frac{n-1}{2}} t^\vee$, then:

$$t'_i = \begin{cases} t_{\frac{n+1}{2}+i}^\vee - t_{\frac{n-1}{2}}^\vee, & i < \frac{n-3}{2} \\ -t_{\frac{n-1}{2}}^\vee, & i = \frac{n-3}{2} \\ t_{i-\frac{n-1}{2}}^\vee - t_{\frac{n-1}{2}}^\vee, & i > \frac{n-3}{2} \end{cases}.$$

From $t_i^\vee = \sum_{j=i}^{n-2} t_j$, we get

$$t'_i = \begin{cases} -\sum_{j=\frac{n-1}{2}}^{\frac{n-1}{2}+i} t_j, & i < \frac{n-3}{2} \\ -\sum_{j=\frac{n-1}{2}}^{n-2} t_j, & i = \frac{n-3}{2} \\ \sum_{j=i-\frac{n-1}{2}}^{\frac{n-3}{2}} t_j, & i > \frac{n-3}{2} \end{cases}.$$

Notice that each t_i' is a sum of consecutive t_j's of length at most $\frac{n-1}{2}$, thus $\|X^{\frac{n-1}{2}}t^{\smile}\|_\infty = \max_i |t_i'| \le \frac{n-1}{2}\max_i |t_i| = \frac{n-1}{2}\|t\|_\infty$ holds.

For any $\mathbf{s} = (s_1, \cdots, s_m) \in \mathcal{L}^{\frown}(\mathbf{a}, I_S)$, the vector $\mathbf{s}^{\smile} = (s_1^{\smile}, \cdots, s_m^{\smile})$ belongs to $\mathcal{L}(\mathbf{a}, I_S)$ and thus the vector $\mathbf{s}' = \left(X^{\frac{n-1}{2}}s_1^{\smile}, \cdots, X^{\frac{n-1}{2}}s_m^{\smile}\right)$ is also in $\mathcal{L}(\mathbf{a}, I_S)$. Then

$$\|\mathbf{s}'\|_\infty = \max_i \|X^{\frac{n-1}{2}}s_i^{\smile}\|_\infty \le \frac{n-1}{2}\max_i \|s_i\|_\infty = \frac{n-1}{2}\|\mathbf{s}\|_\infty.$$

Since there exists a unique $\mathbf{s} \in \mathcal{L}(\mathbf{a}, I_S)$ such that $\mathbf{r} = \mathbf{s}^{\frown}$ for any $\mathbf{r} \in \mathcal{L}^{\frown}(\mathbf{a}, I_S)$, we conclude that $\lambda_1^\infty(\mathcal{L}(\mathbf{a}, I_S)) \le \frac{n-1}{2}\lambda_1^\infty(\mathcal{L}^{\frown}(\mathbf{a}, I_S))$. □

Lemmata 10 and 11 lead to the following result on $\mathcal{L}^{\frown}(\mathbf{a}, I_S)$ immediately.

Lemma 12. *Let $n \ge 7$ be a prime and $\mathcal{R} = \mathbb{Z}[X]/\Phi_n(X)$. Let q be a prime such that $\Phi_n(X)$ splits into $n-1$ distinct linear factors modulo q and $\mathcal{R}_q = \mathcal{R}/q\mathcal{R}$. For any $S \subseteq \{1, \cdots, n-1\}$, $m \ge 2$ and $\epsilon > 0$, set*

$$\beta := 1 - \frac{1}{m} + \frac{1 - \sqrt{1 + 4m(m-1)\left(1 - \frac{|S|}{n-1}\right) + 4m\epsilon}}{2m} \ge 1 - \frac{1}{m} - \epsilon - (m-1)\left(1 - \frac{|S|}{n-1}\right),$$

then we have $\lambda_1^\infty(\mathcal{L}^{\frown}(\mathbf{a}, I_S)) \ge \frac{2}{(n-1)\sqrt{n}}q^\beta$ with probability $\ge 1 - \frac{2^{n-1}}{(q-1)^{\epsilon(n-1)}}$ over the uniformly random choice of $\mathbf{a}$ in $(\mathcal{R}_q^\times)^m$.

3.4 Results on Regularity

Let $\mathbb{D}_\chi$ be the distribution of the tuple $(a_1, \cdots, a_m, \sum_{i=1}^m t_i a_i) \in (\mathcal{R}_q^\times)^m \times \mathcal{R}_q$ with a_i's being independent and uniformly random in $\mathcal{R}_q^\times$ and t_i's being sampled from the distribution χ over $\mathcal{R}_q$. We call the statistical distance between $\mathbb{D}_\chi$ and the uniform distribution over $(\mathcal{R}_q^\times)^m \times \mathcal{R}_q$ the *regularity* of the generalized knapsack function $(t_1, \cdots, t_m) \mapsto \sum_{i=1}^m t_i a_i$. In [27], Micciancio gave some results on regularity for general finite rings and constructed a class of one-way functions. In [33], an improved result was claimed for the ring $\mathbb{Z}[X]/(X^n + 1)$ with n a power of 2 and a Gaussian distribution χ.

We can derive the result of the regularity for prime cyclotomic rings. It provides a foundation of security for more cryptographic primitives based on prime cyclotomic rings. In the later part, we will concentrate on NTRU applications corresponding to the case $m = 2$.

Lemma 13. *Let $n \ge 7$ be a prime and $\mathcal{R} = \mathbb{Z}[X]/\Phi_n(X)$. Let q be a prime such that $\Phi_n(X)$ splits into $n-1$ distinct linear factors modulo q and $\mathcal{R}_q = \mathcal{R}/q\mathcal{R}$. Let $S \subseteq \{1, \cdots, n-1\}$, $m \ge 2, \epsilon > 0, \delta \in (0, \frac{1}{2})$, $\mathbf{c} \in \mathbb{R}^{m(n-1)}$ and $\mathbf{t} \hookleftarrow D_{\mathbb{Z}^{m(n-1)}, r, \mathbf{c}}$, with $r \ge \frac{n-1}{2}\sqrt{\frac{n\ln(2m(n-1)(1+1/\delta))}{\pi}} \cdot q^{\frac{1}{m}+(m-1)\frac{|S|}{n-1}+\epsilon}$. Then for all except a fraction $\le \frac{2^{n-1}}{(q-1)^{\epsilon(n-1)}}$ of $\mathbf{a} \in (\mathcal{R}_q^\times)^m$, we have*

$$\Delta\left(\mathbf{t} \bmod \mathbf{a}^\perp(I_S); U(\mathbb{Z}^{m(n-1)}/\mathbf{a}^\perp(I_S))\right) \le 2\delta.$$

In particular, for all except a fraction $\leq 2^{n-1}(q-1)^{-\epsilon(n-1)}$ of $\mathbf{a} \in (\mathcal{R}_q^{\times})^m$, *we have*

$$\left| D_{\mathbb{Z}^{m(n-1)}, r, \mathbf{c}}(\mathbf{a}^{\perp}(I_S)) - q^{-(n-1)-(m-1)|S|} \right| \leq 2\delta.$$

Proof. By combining Lemmata 2, 4, 9 and 12, the first part follows. For $\mathbf{a} \in (\mathcal{R}_q^{\times})^m$, the lattice $\mathbf{a}^{\perp}(I_S)$ is of the volume $\det(\mathbf{a}^{\perp}(I_S)) = \det\left(\frac{1}{q}\mathcal{L}^{\frown}(\mathbf{a}^{\times}, I_{\bar{S}}^{\times})\right)^{-1} = q^{m(n-1)}/q^{(m-1)(n-1-|S|)} = q^{n-1+(m-1)|S|}$. Notice that $|\mathbb{Z}^{m(n-1)}/\mathbf{a}^{\perp}(I_S)| = \det(\mathbf{a}^{\perp}(I_S))$, thus we complete the proof of the second part. □

Remark. Our regularity result is under the coefficient embedding. We have also considered the canonical embedding and generalized some results of [26]. In the latter case, for $\delta = q^{-\epsilon n}$ with $\epsilon \in (0,1)$, the polynomial factor of the lower bound of required width gets reduced to $O(n^{1.5})$ from $O(n^2)$ in Lemma 13 and the power exponent can also be slightly smaller. However, our key result, which is Theorem 2 in next section, requires the parameter δ in Lemma 13 to be very small. Under the canonical embedding and with $\delta = q^{-n-\epsilon n}$, a desired result similar to the lemma is not currently available. Thus we only work with the coefficient embedding in this paper and leave the relevant results for our next work.

3.5   Bounded Gap of Ideal Lattices

Let I be an ideal of the n-th cyclotomic ring and $\mathcal{L}_I$ be the ideal lattice corresponding to I (under the coefficient embedding). For the case that n is a power of 2, one has $\lambda_{\varphi(n)}(\mathcal{L}_I) = \lambda_1(\mathcal{L}_I)$. For n being a prime, however, we do not know whether this nice property hold or not, but we are able to show that the gap between $\lambda_{n-1}(\mathcal{L}_I)$ and $\lambda_1(\mathcal{L}_I)$ is bounded by $\sqrt{n}$.

Lemma 14. *Let n be a prime and $\mathcal{R} = \mathbb{Z}[X]/\Phi_n(X)$. For any non-zero ideal I of $\mathcal{R}$, we have:*

$$\lambda_{n-1}(\mathcal{L}_I) \leq \sqrt{n} \cdot \lambda_1(\mathcal{L}_I).$$

Proof. Let $\mathbf{a} = (a_0, \cdots, a_{n-2})$ be a non-zero shortest vector of $\mathcal{L}_I$ and $a \in \mathcal{R}$ be the polynomial of coefficient vector $\mathbf{a}$. Then the polynomial $X^k \cdot a$ also induces a vector of $\mathcal{L}_I$ denoted by $\mathbf{a}^{(k)} = \left(a_0^{(k)}, \cdots, a_{n-2}^{(k)}\right)$. For any $k \in \{1, \cdots, n-2\}$, the coordinates of $\mathbf{a}^{(k)}$ can be represented by the a_i's as follows:

$$a_i^{(k)} = \begin{cases} a_{n-k+i} - a_{n-1-k}, & i < k-1 \\ -a_{n-1-k}, & i = k-1 \\ a_{i-k} - a_{n-1-k}, & i > k-1 \end{cases}$$

Then, we have

$$
\begin{aligned}
\|\mathbf{a}^{(k)}\| &= \sqrt{\sum_{i=0}^{n-2} a_i^2 - 2a_{n-1-k}\Big(\sum_{i \neq n-1-k} a_i\Big) + (n-2)a_{n-1-k}^2} \\
&\leq \sqrt{\sum_{i=0}^{n-2} a_i^2 + (n-1)a_{n-1-k}^2 + \Big(\sum_{i \neq n-1-k} a_i\Big)^2} \\
&\leq \sqrt{\sum_{i=0}^{n-2} a_i^2 + (n-1)a_{n-1-k}^2 + (n-2)\Big(\sum_{i \neq n-1-k} a_i^2\Big)} \\
&\leq \sqrt{n} \cdot \|\mathbf{a}\|.
\end{aligned}
$$

All these $\mathbf{a}^{(k)}$'s and $\mathbf{a}$ are linearly independent so that we conclude that $\lambda_{n-1}(\mathcal{L}_{I_S}) \leq \sqrt{n} \cdot \lambda_1(\mathcal{L}_{I_S})$. ☐

Back to the ring $\mathcal{R}_q$, combining Minkowski's theorem, we obtain the following corollary.

Corollary 2. *Let $n \geq 7$ be a prime and $\mathcal{R} = \mathbb{Z}[X]/\Phi_n(X)$. Let q be a prime such that $\Phi_n(X)$ splits into $n-1$ distinct linear factors modulo q and $\mathcal{R}_q = \mathcal{R}/q\mathcal{R}$. Let $S \subseteq \{1, \cdots, n-1\}$ and denote by $\mathcal{L}_{I_S}$ the lattice generated by the ideal $\langle q, \prod_{i \in S}(X - \phi_i)\rangle$. Then*

$$
\lambda_{n-1}(\mathcal{L}_{I_S}) \leq \sqrt{n} \cdot \lambda_1(\mathcal{L}_{I_S}) \leq n \cdot q^{\frac{|S|}{n-1}}.
$$

4   Revised **NTRUEncrypt** over Prime Cyclotomic Rings

In this section, we will describe a variant of NTRUEncrypt over prime cyclotomic rings with provable security under the worst-case hardness assumption. The revised NTRUEncrypt is determined by parameters n, q, p, r, α, k and denoted by NTRUEncrypt(n, q, p, r, α, k). First, we choose a prime $n \geq 7$ and let $\mathcal{R}$ be the ring $\mathbb{Z}[X]/\Phi_n(X)$. Then we pick a prime $q = 1 \bmod n$ so that $\Phi_n(X) = \prod_{i=1}^{n-1}(X - \phi_i) \bmod q$ with distinct ϕ_i's, and let $\mathcal{R}_q = \mathcal{R}/q\mathcal{R}$. The parameter $p \in \mathcal{R}_q^\times$ is chosen to be of small norm, such as $p = 2, 3$ or $p = x+2$. The parameter r is the width of discrete Gaussian distribution used for key generation. The parameters α and k are used for RLWE error generation. We list below three main components of NTRUEncrypt(n, q, p, r, α, k):

- **Key Generation.** Sample f' from $D_{\mathbb{Z}^{n-1}, r}$; if $f = pf' + 1 \bmod q \notin \mathcal{R}_q^\times$, resample. Sample g from $D_{\mathbb{Z}^{n-1}, r}$; if $g \bmod q \notin \mathcal{R}_q^\times$, resample. Then return private key $sk = f \in \mathcal{R}_q^\times$ with $f = 1 \bmod p$ and public key $pk = h = pg/f \in \mathcal{R}_q^\times$.

- **Encryption.** Given message $M \in \mathcal{R}/p\mathcal{R}$, let $t = \sqrt{n}\alpha q \left(\frac{(n-1)k}{\log((n-1)k)}\right)^{1/4}$, set $s, e \hookleftarrow \overline{\psi_t^n}$ and return ciphertext $C = hs + pe + M \in \mathcal{R}_q$.

– **Decryption.** Given ciphertext C and private key f, compute $C' = f \cdot C \bmod q$ and return $C' \bmod p$.

Next we explain when and why the scheme works and how to assess its security.

4.1 Key Generation

In the above key generation algorithm, we generate the polynomials f and g by using a discrete Gaussian sampler. Lemma 5 provides a sampler outputting a distribution within exponentially small statistical distance to a certain discrete Gaussian. Actually, the conditions in our results are more demanding than that in Lemma 5. Ignoring the negligible impact, we assume we already have a polynomial-time perfect discrete Gaussian sampler.

To ensure both f and g are invertible modulo q, we may need to resample quite a few times. The following result indicates that the key generation algorithm terminates in expected polynomial time for some selective parameters.

Lemma 15. *Let $n \geq 7$ be a prime and $\mathcal{R} = \mathbb{Z}[X]/\Phi_n(X)$. Let q be a prime such that $\Phi_n(X)$ splits into $n - 1$ distinct linear factors modulo q and $\mathcal{R}_q = \mathcal{R}/q\mathcal{R}$. For any $\delta \in (0, 1/2)$, let $r \geq n\sqrt{\frac{\ln(2(n-1)(1+1/\delta))}{\pi}} \cdot q^{1/(n-1)}$. Then*

$$\Pr_{f' \hookleftarrow D_{\mathbb{Z}^{n-1}, r}} \left((p \cdot f' + a \bmod q) \notin \mathcal{R}_q^\times \right) \leq (n-1)\left(\frac{1}{q} + 2\delta\right)$$

holds for $a \in \mathcal{R}$ and $p \in \mathcal{R}_q^\times$.

Proof. It suffices to bound the probability that $p \cdot f' + a$ belongs to $I := \langle q, X - \phi_k \rangle$ by $(1/q + 2\delta)$ for any $k \leq n - 1$. First we have $\lambda_{n-1}(\mathcal{L}_I) \leq nq^{\frac{1}{n-1}}$ by Corollary 2 since the ideal I corresponds to $I_{\{k\}}$. This, together with Lemma 1, implies that $r \geq \eta_\delta(\mathcal{L}_I)$. Applying Lemma 4, we have that the probability of $p \cdot f' + a = 0 \bmod I$ does not exceed $1/q + 2\delta$. □

Next, we claim that the norms of f and g are small with overwhelming probability.

Lemma 16. *Let $n \geq 7$ be a prime and $\mathcal{R} = \mathbb{Z}[X]/\Phi_n(X)$. Suppose $q > 8n$ is a prime such that $\Phi_n(X)$ splits into $n - 1$ distinct linear factors modulo q and $\mathcal{R}_q = \mathcal{R}/q\mathcal{R}$. Let $r \geq n\sqrt{\frac{2\ln(6(n-1))}{\pi}} \cdot q^{1/(n-1)}$. The secret key polynomials f, g satisfy, with probability $\geq 1 - 2^{-n+4}$,*

$$\|f\| \leq 2n\|p\|r \quad and \quad \|g\| \leq \sqrt{n-1}r.$$

If $\deg p = 0$, then $\|f\| \leq 2\sqrt{n-1} \cdot \|p\|r$ with probability $\geq 1 - 2^{-n+4}$.

Proof. Setting $\delta = \frac{1}{10(n-1)-1}$, then we get $r \geq \sqrt{\frac{\ln(2(n-1)(1+1/\delta))}{\pi}}$ from the assumption. Applying Lemma 1 to $\mathbb{Z}^{n-1}$, we know that $r \geq \eta_\delta(\mathbb{Z}^{n-1})$. Therefore, we can use Lemma 3 to get,

$$\Pr_{g \hookleftarrow D_{\mathbb{Z}^{n-1},r}} \left(\|g\| \geq r\sqrt{n-1} \right) \leq \frac{1+\delta}{1-\delta} 2^{1-n}.$$

Since $r \geq n\sqrt{\frac{\ln(2(n-1)(1+1/\delta))}{\pi}} \cdot q^{1/(n-1)}$, Lemma 15 yields

$$\Pr_{g \hookleftarrow D_{\mathbb{Z}^{n-1},r}} \left(\|g\| \geq r\sqrt{n-1} \mid g \in \mathcal{R}_q^\times \right) \leq \frac{\Pr_{g \hookleftarrow D_{\mathbb{Z}^{n-1},r}} \left(\|g\| \geq r\sqrt{n-1} \right)}{\Pr_{g \hookleftarrow D_{\mathbb{Z}^{n-1},r}} \left(g \in \mathcal{R}_q^\times \right)}$$

$$\leq \frac{1+\delta}{1-\delta} 2^{1-n} \cdot \frac{1}{1 - (n-1)(1/q+2\delta)} \leq 2^{4-n}.$$

This means that the norm of the key polynomial g is less than $r\sqrt{n-1}$ with probability $\geq 1 - 2^{4-n}$. The same argument holds true for the polynomial f' such that $f = p \cdot f' + 1$.

If $\deg p = 0$, we have $\|f\| \leq 1 + \|p\|\|f'\| \leq 2\|p\| r\sqrt{n-1}$ with probability $\geq 1 - 2^{4-n}$. For general cases, applying Lemma 8, we know that $\|f\| \leq 1 + \|p\|\|f'\| \leq 1 + 2(n-1)\|p\|r \leq 2n \cdot \|p\|r$ with probability $\geq 1 - 2^{4-n}$. □

We are also able to prove that the public key h, the ratio of pg and $f = pf'+1$, enjoys a favorable uniformity for some well-chosen r's, just like that shown in [33]. We denote by $D_{r,z}^\times$ the discrete Gaussian $D_{\mathbb{Z}^{n-1},r}$ restricted to $\mathcal{R}_q^\times + z$.

Theorem 2. *Let $n \geq 7$ be a prime and $\mathcal{R} = \mathbb{Z}[X]/\Phi_n(X)$. Suppose $q > 8n$ is a prime such that $\Phi_n(X)$ splits into $n - 1$ distinct linear factors modulo q and $\mathcal{R}_q = \mathcal{R}/q\mathcal{R}$. Let $0 < \epsilon < \frac{1}{2}$ and $r \geq (n-1)^2 \sqrt{\ln(8nq)} \cdot q^{\frac{1}{2}+2\epsilon}$. Then*

$$\Delta \left(\frac{y_1 + p \cdot D_{r,z_1}^\times}{y_2 + p \cdot D_{r,z_2}^\times} \bmod q; U(\mathcal{R}_q^\times) \right) \leq \frac{2^{3(n-1)}}{q^{\lfloor \epsilon(n-1) \rfloor}}$$

for $p \in \mathcal{R}_q^\times$, $y_i \in \mathcal{R}_q$ and $z_i = -y_i p^{-1} \bmod q$ for $i \in \{1,2\}$.

Remark. Our proof follows essentially the same approach as in [33]. For completeness, we include it in Appendix B. This result provides a new instance of Decisional Small Polynomial Ratio (DSPR) assumption introduced in [24].

4.2   Decryption

Just like in the classical NTRUEncrypt, the correctness of decryption is based on the fact that a polynomial of ℓ_∞ norm $< q/2$ is invariant under modulo q reduction. In our decryption procedure, we have $C' = f \cdot C = pgs + pfe + fM \bmod q$. When $\|pgs + pfe + fM\|_\infty < \frac{q}{2}$, C' is in fact $pgs + pfe + fM$ and hence $C' \bmod p = fM \bmod p = M$ due to $f = 1 \bmod p$, *i.e.* the decryption succeeds. Now we are to confirm that, given a set of proper parameters, the ℓ_∞ norms of pgs, pfe and fM will be small enough (e.g., less than $\frac{q}{6}$) with high probability. This ensures a successful decryption.

We first show that the polynomial drawn from RLWE error distribution has a relatively small norm with a high probability.

Lemma 17. *Let $n \geq 7$ be a prime and $\mathcal{R} = \mathbb{Z}[X]/\Phi_n(X)$. For $t > 1$ and $u > 0$, we have*

$$\Pr_{\mathbf{b} \hookleftarrow \psi_t^n}\left(\|\mathbf{b}\| \geq \left(\sqrt{2n}(\sqrt{u}+2)\right)t\right) \leq \exp(-u).$$

Proof. We will need the following inequality in our proof:

$$\lfloor x \rceil^2 \leq \frac{1}{4\epsilon} + \frac{1}{1-\epsilon}x^2.$$

In fact, for $x \in \mathbb{R}$, we have $(\lfloor x \rceil - x)^2 \leq \frac{1}{4}$. For any $\epsilon \in (0,1)$, we have $\lfloor x \rceil^2 \leq \frac{1}{4} - x^2 + 2\lfloor x \rceil x \leq \frac{1}{4} - x^2 + \frac{1}{1-\epsilon}x^2 + (1-\epsilon)\lfloor x \rceil^2 = \frac{1}{4} + \frac{\epsilon}{1-\epsilon}x^2 + (1-\epsilon)\lfloor x \rceil^2$. A routine computation leads to the result.

Let $\mathbf{b} = \lfloor \mathbf{b}' \bmod \Phi_n(X) \rceil \in \mathcal{R}$ with $\mathbf{b}' \hookleftarrow \psi_t^n$. Let vector $\mathbf{v} = \frac{1}{t}(b_0, \cdots, b_{n-1})$ where $(b_0, \cdots, b_{n-1})$ is the coefficient vector of $\mathbf{b}'$. Then we obtain

$$\|\mathbf{b}\|^2 \leq \frac{1}{1-\epsilon}\sum_{i=0}^{n-2}(b_i - b_{n-1})^2 + \frac{n-1}{4\epsilon} = \frac{t^2}{1-\epsilon}\|\mathbf{Mv}\|^2 + \frac{n-1}{4\epsilon},$$

where

$$\mathbf{M} = \begin{pmatrix} 1 & & & -1 \\ & 1 & & -1 \\ & & \ddots & \vdots \\ & & 1 & -1 \\ & & & 0 \end{pmatrix} \in \mathbb{R}^{n \times n}.$$

Let $\Sigma = \mathbf{M}^\top \mathbf{M}$, we have

$$\Sigma = \begin{pmatrix} 1 & & & -1 \\ & 1 & & -1 \\ & & \ddots & \vdots \\ & & 1 & -1 \\ -1 & -1 & \cdots & -1 & (n-1) \end{pmatrix} \in \mathbb{R}^{n \times n}.$$

In our estimation, we need traces $\mathbf{tr}(\Sigma)$, $\mathbf{tr}(\Sigma^2)$ and the operator norm $\|\Sigma\|$. It is easy to check that $\mathbf{tr}(\Sigma) = 2(n-1)$, $\mathbf{tr}(\Sigma^2) = (n-1)(n+2)$. It can be calculated that the characteristic polynomial of Σ is $\lambda(\lambda-1)^{n-2}(\lambda-n)$, so n is the largest eigenvalue of Σ and hence $\|\Sigma\| = n$.

All coordinates of $\mathbf{b}'$ follow the distribution ψ_t independently, so the coordinates of $\mathbf{v}$ follow standard Gaussian independently. As shown in [20], an tail bound for $\|\mathbf{Mv}\|^2$ holds

$$\Pr\left(\|\mathbf{Mv}\|^2 > 2(n-1) + 2\sqrt{(n-1)(n+2)u} + 2nu\right)$$
$$= \Pr\left(\|\mathbf{Mv}\|^2 > \mathbf{tr}\,(\Sigma) + 2\sqrt{\mathbf{tr}\,(\Sigma^2)\,u} + 2\|\Sigma\|u\right) \le \exp(-u).$$

Let

$$\epsilon = \left(1 + \sqrt{\frac{4t^2\left(2(n-1) + 2\sqrt{(n-1)(n+2)u} + 2nu\right)}{n-1}}\right)^{-1} \in (0,1)$$

and

$$A = \sqrt{\frac{2(n-1) + 2\sqrt{(n-1)(n+2)u} + 2nu}{1-\epsilon} + \frac{n-1}{4t^2\epsilon}}.$$

Then it can be verified that

$$A = \sqrt{2(n-1) + 2\sqrt{(n-1)(n+2)u} + 2nu + \sqrt{\frac{n-1}{4t^2}}} < \sqrt{2n}(\sqrt{u}+2),$$

thus we have

$$\Pr_{\mathbf{b}\hookleftarrow\psi_t^n}\left(\|\mathbf{b}\| \ge \left(\sqrt{2n}(\sqrt{u}+2)\right)t\right)$$
$$\le \Pr_{\mathbf{b}\hookleftarrow\psi_t^n}\left(\|\mathbf{b}\| > At\right)$$
$$\le \Pr_{\mathbf{v}\hookleftarrow\psi_1^n}\left(\frac{1}{1-\epsilon}\|\mathbf{Mv}\|^2 + \frac{n-1}{4t^2\epsilon} > A^2\right)$$
$$= \Pr\left(\|\mathbf{Mv}\|^2 > 2(n-1) + 2\sqrt{(n-1)(n+2)u} + 2nu\right)$$
$$\le \exp(-u). \qquad \square$$

Setting u in Lemma 17 to $\Theta(\log^{1+\kappa} n)$ and applying Lemmata 8 and 16, we are able to get the following:

Lemma 18. *In* $\mathsf{NTRUEncrypt}(n,q,p,r,\alpha,k)$, *let* $t = \sqrt{n}\alpha q\left(\frac{(n-1)k}{\log((n-1)k)}\right)^{1/4} > 1$. *Then for* $\kappa > 0$, *we have*

$$\|pgs\|_\infty, \|pfe\|_\infty \le 8\sqrt{2}n^2\Theta\left(\log^{\frac{1+\kappa}{2}} n\right)\|p\|^2 rt$$

with probability at least $1 - n^{-\Theta(\log^\kappa n)}$.

Furthermore, if $\deg p = 0$, *then*

$$\|pgs\|_\infty, \|pfe\|_\infty \le 4\sqrt{2}n\Theta\left(\log^{\frac{1+\kappa}{2}} n\right)\|p\|^2 rt$$

with probability at least $1 - n^{-\Theta(\log^\kappa n)}$.

It is also hoped that fM has smaller norm. Indeed, we can prove

Lemma 19. *In* NTRUEncrypt(n, q, p, r, α, k), *we have*

1. $\|M\| \leq (n-1)\|p\|$.
2. $\|fM\|_\infty \leq 4n^2\|p\|^2 r$ *with probability at least* $1 - 2^{-n+4}$.

Furthermore, if $\deg p = 0$, *we have* $\|M\| \leq \frac{\sqrt{n-1}}{2}\|p\|$ *holds, and with probability at least* $1 - 2^{-n+4}$, $\|fM\|_\infty \leq 2n\|p\|^2 r$ *holds.*

Proof. By reducing modulo the pX^i's, we can write M into $\sum_{i=0}^{n-2} \epsilon_i p X^i$ with $-1/2 < \epsilon_i \leq 1/2$. Using Lemma 8, we have

$$\|M\| \leq 2\sqrt{n-1}\|\sum_{i=0}^{n-2} \epsilon_i X^i\|\|p\| \leq (n-1)\|p\|.$$

For the case $\deg p = 0$, we have $\|M\| = \|p\| \cdot \|\sum_{i=0}^{n-2} \epsilon_i X^i\| \leq \frac{\sqrt{n-1}}{2}\|p\|$. Then, combining Lemmata 8 and 16 with the above result, the proof is completed. $\square$

Overall, we give a set of parameters such that NTRUEncrypt decrypts correctly with high probability.

Theorem 3. *If* $\omega\left(n^2 \log^{0.5} n\right)\|p\|^2 rt/q < 1$ *(resp.* $\omega\left(n \log^{0.5} n\right)\|p\|^2 rt/q < 1$ *if* $\deg p = 0$*) and* $t = \sqrt{n}\alpha q\left(\frac{(n-1)k}{\log((n-1)k)}\right)^{1/4} > 1$, *then the decryption algorithm of* NTRUEncrypt *recovers M with probability* $1 - n^{-\omega(1)}$ *over the choice of* s, e, f, g.

4.3 Security Reduction and Parameters

In a manner similar to [33], we are able to establish a security reduction of NTRUEncrypt from the decisional RLWE$^\times_{HNF}$. One technical idea is that one can produce a legal pair of public key and ciphertext pair $(h = pa, C = pb + M = hs + pe + M)$ by using the pair $(a, b = as + e)$ sampled from RLWE distribution. The proof of Lemma 20 is shown in Appendix C.

Lemma 20. *Let* $n \geq 8$ *be a prime and* $\mathcal{R} = \mathbb{Z}[X]/\Phi_n(X)$. *Suppose* $q > 8n$ *is a prime such that* $\Phi_n(X)$ *splits into* $n - 1$ *distinct linear factors modulo* q *and* $\mathcal{R}_q = \mathcal{R}/q\mathcal{R}$. *Let* $\epsilon, \delta > 0$, $p \in \mathcal{R}_q^\times$, $t = \sqrt{n}\alpha q\left(\frac{(n-1)k}{\log((n-1)k)}\right)^{1/4}$, *and* $r \geq (n-1)^2\sqrt{\ln(8nq)} \cdot q^{\frac{1}{2}+\epsilon}$. *If there exists an* IND-CPA *attack against the variant of* NTRUEncrypt *that runs in time T and has success probability* $1/2 + \delta$, *then there exists an algorithm solving* RLWE$_{q,\psi,k}$ *with* $\psi = \overline{\psi_t^n}$ *that runs in time* $T' = T + O(kn)$ *and has success probability* $\frac{1}{2} + \delta'$ *where* $\delta' = \frac{\delta}{2} - q^{-\Omega(n)}$.

Now we integrate all above results and discuss the parameter requirements. To ensure the uniformity of public keys, the parameters r, n and q should satisfy the condition claimed in Theorem 2, i.e. $r \geq (n-1)^2\sqrt{\ln(8nq)} \cdot q^{\frac{1}{2}+2\epsilon}$ for $0 < \epsilon < \frac{1}{2}$. To ensure a high probability of success decryption, we need that $t = \sqrt{n}\alpha q \left(\frac{(n-1)k}{\log((n-1)k)}\right)^{1/4} > 1$ and $\omega\left(n^2 \log^{0.5} n\right) \|p\|^2 rt/q < 1$ (resp. $\omega\left(n \log^{0.5} n\right) \|p\|^2 rt/q < 1$ if $\deg p = 0$) as stated in Theorem 3. To satisfy the condition of RLWE (Theorem 1), it requires that $\alpha q > \omega(\sqrt{\log n})$. From these requirements, to obtain a variant of NTRUEncrypt with provable security against IND-CPA attack, we may set main parameters as follows.

- $q = \text{poly}(n)$, $\epsilon \in \left(0, \frac{1}{2}\right)$, and $q^{\frac{1}{2}-\epsilon} = \omega\left(n^{4.75} \log^{1.5} n \|p\|^2\right)$,
- $r = n^2 \sqrt{\ln(8nq)} \cdot q^{\frac{1}{2}+\epsilon}$,
- $k = O(1)$, $\alpha q = \Omega(\log^{0.75} n)$ and $t = \sqrt{n}\alpha q \left(\frac{(n-1)k}{\log((n-1)k)}\right)^{1/4} = \Omega(n^{0.75} \log^{0.5} n)$.

If p is set to be an integer (*i.e.* $\deg p = 0$) which is a most routine case used in NTRUEncrypt scheme, the parameters may be relaxed:

- $q = \text{poly}(n)$, $\epsilon \in \left(0, \frac{1}{2}\right)$, and $q^{\frac{1}{2}-\epsilon} = \omega\left(n^{3.75} \log^{1.5} n \|p\|^2\right)$,
- $r = n^2 \sqrt{\ln(8nq)} \cdot q^{\frac{1}{2}+\epsilon}$,
- $k = O(1)$, $\alpha q = \Omega(\log^{0.75} n)$ and $t = \sqrt{n}\alpha q \left(\frac{(n-1)k}{\log((n-1)k)}\right)^{1/4} = \Omega(n^{0.75} \log^{0.5} n)$.

Combining with Theorem 1, we have obtained our main result.

Theorem 4. *Let $n \geq 8$ be a prime and $\mathcal{R} = \mathbb{Z}[X]/\Phi_n(X)$. Suppose $q = \text{poly}(n)$ is a prime such that $\Phi_n(X)$ splits into $n - 1$ distinct linear factors modulo q and $q^{\frac{1}{2}-\epsilon} = \omega\left(n^{4.75} \log^{1.5} n \|p\|^2\right)$ (resp. $q^{\frac{1}{2}-\epsilon} = \omega\left(n^{3.75} \log^{1.5} n \|p\|^2\right)$, if $\deg p = 0$), for arbitrary $\epsilon \in \left(0, \frac{1}{2}\right)$ and $p \in \mathcal{R}_q^{\times}$. Let $r = n^2 \sqrt{\ln(8nq)} \cdot q^{\frac{1}{2}+\epsilon}$ and $t = \sqrt{n}\alpha q \left(\frac{(n-1)k}{\log((n-1)k)}\right)^{1/4}$ where $k = O(1)$ and $\alpha q = \Omega(\log^{0.75} n)$. If there exists an IND-CPA attack against the variant of NTRUEncrypt(n, q, p, r, α, k) that runs in time $\text{poly}(n)$ and has success probability $\frac{1}{2} + \frac{1}{\text{poly}(n)}$, then there exists a $\text{poly}(n)$-time algorithm solving γ-Ideal-SVP on ideal lattices in $\mathbb{Z}[X]/\Phi_n(X)$ with $\gamma = O\left(\sqrt{n}q/\log^{0.75} n\right)$. Moreover, the decryption success probability exceeds $1 - n^{-\omega(1)}$ over the choice of the encryption randomness.*

In the modified NTRUEncrypt, the parameter r is $\tilde{\Omega}(n^2 \cdot q^{\frac{1}{2}+\epsilon})$ and that in [33] is $\tilde{\Omega}(n \cdot q^{\frac{1}{2}+\epsilon})$. Note that the term $q^{\frac{1}{2}+\epsilon}$ is much greater than its polynomial coefficient n^2 or n, thus, in this sense, our result is close to that for power-of-2 cyclotomic rings. By setting $\epsilon = o(1)$ and p to be of degree 0, the smallest modulus q and approximate factor γ reach $\tilde{\Omega}(n^{7.5})$ and $\tilde{\Omega}(n^8)$ respectively. These compare to $\tilde{\Omega}(n^5)$ and $\tilde{\Omega}(n^{5.5})$ for NTRUEncrypt over power-of-2 cyclotomic rings.

5   Conclusion and Future Work

In this paper, we extended the provable security of an NTRU variant, originally proposed by Stehlé and Steinfeld for power-of-2 cyclotomic rings, to the family of prime cyclotomic rings. As this class of rings is closer to the original NTRU rings, the results here may bring a new security estimation for the original NTRU settings. We also developed a series of tools for prime cyclotomic rings that provide a foundation to generalize more cryptosystems to this class of rings. These tools might be of some independent interest.

We present a theoretical construction with suggested parameters in the asymptotic sense. There are a batch of cryptanalyses work aiming at NTRU, such as hybrid attack [19], subfield attack [1] and straightforward attack [22]. Detailed analyses of our NTRU variant against these attacks should be well-considered. Furthermore, the operations over the rings $\mathbb{Z}[X]/(X^n \pm 1)$ are still more efficient than that over prime cyclotomic rings. The further investigation of the relation between the prime cyclotomic ring and NTRU ring may improve the efficiency of related cryptosystems. We leave them to the future work.

As shown in [25,26], canonical embedding provides a neat description of the geometry of cyclotomic rings, which may lead to more compact and general results. To get similar conclusions with respect to the canonical embedding, we need to develop more powerful tools and that is left as a future investigation.

The ideal lattices (under the coefficient embedding) over prime cyclotomic rings are not (anti-)circulant, thus to study the gap between their minimums could be useful in cryptanalysis. Another interesting problem is a finer estimation of Euclidean norm of elements in an ideal of the prime cyclotomic ring, as it is useful in reducing some complexity estimations.

Acknowledgements. We thank Léo Ducas, Dianyan Xiao and the anonymous PKC'17 reviewers for their helpful comments. This work is supported in part by China's 973 Program (No. 2013CB834205), the Strategic Priority Research Program of the Chinese Academy of Sciences (No. XDB01010600) and NSF of China (No. 61502269).

A Proof of Lemma 10

Let p be the probability over the randomness of $\mathbf{a}$ that $\lambda_1^\infty(\mathcal{L}(\mathbf{a}, I_S)) < B$, where $B = \frac{1}{\sqrt{n}} q^\beta$. For a non-zero vector $\mathbf{t}$ of ℓ_∞ norm $< B$ and $s \in \mathcal{R}_q/I_S$, let $p(\mathbf{t}, s) = \Pr_{\mathbf{a}}(\forall i, t_i = a_i s \bmod I_S)$ and $p_i(t_i, s) = \Pr_{a_i}(t_i = a_i s \bmod I_S)$, then we have $p(\mathbf{t}, s) = \prod_{i=1}^m p_i(t_i, s)$.

Let ν_{I_S} be the polynomial $\prod_{i \in S}(X - \phi_i)$. We only need to consider such $(\mathbf{t}, s)$ pairs that $\gcd(t_i, \nu_{I_S}) = \gcd(s, \nu_{I_S})$ for all $i \in \{1, \cdots, m\}$: if not so, we can prove $p(\mathbf{t}, s) = 0$ due to the invertibility of a_i. For each such pair, we denote by d the degree of $\gcd(s, \nu_{I_S})$. Notice that there are $(q-1)^{d+n-1-|S|}$ distinct a_i's in $\mathcal{R}_q^\times$ such that $t_i = a_i s \bmod I_S$, i.e. $p_i(t_i, s) = (q-1)^{d-|S|}$, then we have $p(\mathbf{t}, s) = \prod_{i=1}^m p_i(t_i, s) = (q-1)^{m(d-|S|)}$.

The probability p is bounded by

$$p \leq \sum_{s \in \mathcal{R}_q/I_S} \sum_{0 < \|\mathbf{t}\|_\infty < B} p(\mathbf{t}, s)$$

$$\leq \sum_{\substack{0 \leq d \leq |S| \\ h = \prod_{i \in S'}(X - \phi_i)}} \sum_{S' \subseteq S, |S'| = d} \sum_{\substack{s \in \mathcal{R}_q/I_S \\ h | s}} \sum_{\substack{t \in \mathcal{R}_q^m \\ \forall i, 0 < \|t_i\|_\infty < B \\ h | t_i}} (q-1)^{m(d-|S|)}.$$

For $h = \prod_{i \in S'}(X - \phi_i)$ of degree d, let $N(B,d)$ be the number of $t \in \mathcal{R}_q$ such that $\|t\|_\infty \in (0, B)$ and $t = ht'$ for $t' \in \mathcal{R}_q$ of degree $< n-1-d$. We now show two bounds for $N(B,d)$ depending on d.

Suppose that $d \geq \beta(n-1)$, then $N(B,d) = 0$. Indeed, for any $t = ht'$ with $t' \in \mathcal{R}_q$, the ideal $\langle t \rangle$ is a full-rank sub-ideal of the ideal $\langle h, q \rangle$. Thus, we have $N(t) = N(\langle t \rangle) \geq N(\langle h, q \rangle) = q^d$. Combined with Lemma 7 and equivalence of norms, we conclude that $\|t\|_\infty \geq \frac{\|t\|}{\sqrt{n-1}} \geq \frac{T_2(t)}{\sqrt{n(n-1)}} \geq \frac{N(t)^{1/(n-1)}}{\sqrt{n}} \geq \frac{q^\beta}{\sqrt{n}}$, which implies $N(B,d) = 0$ when $d \geq \beta(n-1)$.

Suppose that $d < \beta(n-1)$, then $N(B,d) \leq (2B)^{n-1-d}$. Let $t = \sum_{i=0}^{n-2} t_i X^i$, $h = \sum_{i=0}^{d} h_i X^i$ and $t' = \sum_{i=0}^{n-2-d} t_i' X^i$. From $t = ht'$, we have

$$(t_0, \cdots, t_{n-2-d}) = (t_0', \cdots, t_{n-2-d}') \begin{pmatrix} h_0 & h_1 & \cdots & & h_{n-2-d} \\ & h_0 & h_1 & & \vdots \\ & & h_0 & \ddots & \\ & & & \ddots & h_1 \\ & & & & h_0 \end{pmatrix}$$

The constant coefficient of h_0 is non-zero modulo prime q, so the polynomial t' will be determined once the $(n-1-d)$ low-order coefficients of t are determined, and vice versa. Thus each possible t is uniquely decided by its $(n-1-d)$ low-order coefficients and this leads to $N(B,d) \leq (2B)^{n-1-d}$.

Notice that the number of subsets of S is $2^{|S|}$ and the number of $s \in \mathcal{R}_q/I_S$ divisible by $h = \prod_{i \in S'}(X - \phi_i)$ of degree d is $q^{|S|-d}$. Thus the probability p can be bounded as follows:

$$p \leq 2^{|S|} \max_{d < \beta(n-1)} \frac{(2B)^{m(n-1-d)}}{(q-1)^{m(|S|-d)}} \cdot q^{|S|-d} \leq 2^{n-1} \max_{d < \beta(n-1)} \frac{(2B)^{m(n-1-d)}(\frac{q}{q-1})^{n-1-d}}{(q-1)^{(m-1)(|S|-d)}}.$$

Since $n \geq 7$, $q = 1 \bmod n$ and $\beta \leq 1 - \frac{1}{m}$, we have $(2B)^m(\frac{q}{q-1}) < (q-1)^{\beta m}$ and then

$$\max_{d < \beta(n-1)} \frac{(2B)^{m(n-1-d)}(\frac{q}{q-1})^{n-1-d}}{(q-1)^{(m-1)(|S|-d)}} < (q-1)^{\beta m(n-1) - (m-1)|S| + \beta(n-1)(m-1-\beta m)} = (q-1)^{-\epsilon(n-1)}.$$

We now complete the proof.

B   Proof of Theorem 2

For $a \in \mathcal{R}_q^\times$, we define $Pr_a = Pr_{f_1, f_2}((y_1 + pf_1)/(y_2 + pf_2) = a)$, where $f_i \hookleftarrow \mathbf{D}_{r, z_i}^\times$. It suffices to prove that $|Pr_a - (q-1)^{-(n-1)}| \leq \frac{2^{2(n-1)+5}}{q^{\lfloor \epsilon(n-1) \rfloor}} \cdot (q-1)^{-(n-1)} =: \epsilon'$ for all except a fraction $\leq \frac{2^{2(n-1)}}{(q-1)^{\epsilon(n-1)}}$ of $a \in \mathcal{R}_q^\times$.

To translate Pr_a into a more straightforward form, we introduce another probability $Pr_\mathbf{a} = Pr_{f_1, f_2}[a_1 f_1 + a_2 f_2 = a_1 z_1 + a_2 z_2]$ for $\mathbf{a} = (a_1, a_2) \in (\mathcal{R}_q^\times)^2$, and then obtain $Pr_\mathbf{a} = Pr_{-a_2 \cdot a_1^{-1}}$ after a simple computation. For $(a_1, a_2) \in (\mathcal{R}_q^\times)^2$, we consider the equation $a_1 f_1 + a_2 f_2 = a_1 z_1 + a_2 z_2$ of the pair (f_1, f_2). All its solutions form the set $\mathbf{z} + \mathbf{a}^{\perp \times}$, where $\mathbf{z} = (z_1, z_2)$ and $\mathbf{a}^{\perp \times} = \mathbf{a}^\perp \bigcap (\mathcal{R}_q^\times + q\mathbb{Z}^{n-1})^2$. Then, we have

$$Pr_\mathbf{a} = \frac{\mathbf{D}_{\mathbb{Z}^{2(n-1)}, r}(\mathbf{z} + \mathbf{a}^{\perp \times})}{\mathbf{D}_{\mathbb{Z}^{n-1}, r}(z_1 + \mathcal{R}_q^\times + q\mathbb{Z}^{n-1}) \cdot \mathbf{D}_{\mathbb{Z}^{n-1}, r}(z_2 + \mathcal{R}_q^\times + q\mathbb{Z}^{n-1})}.$$

Thanks to $\mathbf{a} \in (\mathcal{R}_q^\times)^2$, for any $(x_1, x_2) \in \mathbf{a}^\perp$, the elements x_1 and x_2 lie in the same ideal I_S of $\mathcal{R}_q$. To circumvent the restriction on invertibility, we exploit the inclusion-exclusion principle and change the three above sums into the following forms.

$$\mathbf{D}_{\mathbb{Z}^{2(n-1)}, r}(\mathbf{z} + \mathbf{a}^{\perp \times}) = \sum_{S \subseteq \{1, \cdots, n-1\}} (-1)^{|S|} \cdot \mathbf{D}_{\mathbb{Z}^{2(n-1)}, r}(\mathbf{z} + \mathbf{a}^\perp(I_S)), \quad (1)$$

$$\mathbf{D}_{\mathbb{Z}^{n-1}, r}(z_i + \mathcal{R}_q^\times + q\mathbb{Z}^{n-1}) = \sum_{S \subseteq \{1, \cdots, n-1\}} (-1)^{|S|} \cdot \mathbf{D}_{\mathbb{Z}^{2(n-1)}, r}(z_i + I_S + q\mathbb{Z}^{n-1}), \text{ for } i \in \{1, 2\}. \quad (2)$$

First, let's prove the Eq. 1. For $\mathbf{D}_{\mathbb{Z}^{2(n-1)}, r}(\mathbf{z} + \mathbf{a}^\perp(I_S))$ with $|S| \leq \epsilon(n-1)$, let $\delta = q^{-(n-1)-\lfloor \epsilon(n-1) \rfloor}$ and $m = 2$, then Lemma 13 implies that, for all except a fraction $\leq \frac{2^{n-1}}{(q-1)^{\epsilon(n-1)}}$ of $\mathbf{a} \in (\mathcal{R}_q^\times)^2$,

$$\left| \mathbf{D}_{\mathbb{Z}^{2(n-1)}, r}(\mathbf{z} + \mathbf{a}^\perp(I_S)) - q^{-(n-1)-|S|} \right| = \left| \mathbf{D}_{\mathbb{Z}^{2(n-1)}, r, -\mathbf{z}}(\mathbf{a}^\perp(I_S)) - q^{-(n-1)-|S|} \right| \leq 2\delta.$$

For the case $|S| > \epsilon(n-1)$, we can find $S' \subseteq S$ with $|S'| = \lfloor \epsilon(n-1) \rfloor$. Because $\mathbf{a}^\perp(I_S) \subseteq \mathbf{a}^\perp(I_{S'})$, we have $\mathbf{D}_{\mathbb{Z}^{2(n-1)}, r, -\mathbf{z}}(\mathbf{a}^\perp(I_S)) \leq \mathbf{D}_{\mathbb{Z}^{2(n-1)}, r, -\mathbf{z}}(\mathbf{a}^\perp(I_{S'}))$. Using the result proven before, we conclude that $\mathbf{D}_{\mathbb{Z}^{2(n-1)}, r, -\mathbf{z}}(\mathbf{a}^\perp(I_S)) \leq 2\delta + q^{-(n-1)-\lfloor \epsilon(n-1) \rfloor}$. Therefore, the following inequality holds

$$\left| \mathbf{D}_{\mathbb{Z}^{2(n-1)}, r}(\mathbf{z} + \mathbf{a}^{\perp \times}) - \frac{(q-1)^{n-1}}{q^{2(n-1)}} \right|$$

$$= \left| \sum_{S \subseteq \{1, \cdots, n-1\}} (-1)^{|S|} \left(\mathbf{D}_{\mathbb{Z}^{2(n-1)}, r}(\mathbf{z} + \mathbf{a}^\perp(I_S)) - q^{-(n-1)-|S|} \right) \right|$$

$$\leq 2^n \delta + 2 \sum_{k=\lceil \epsilon(n-1) \rceil}^{n-1} \binom{n-1}{k} q^{-(n-1)-\lfloor \epsilon(n-1) \rfloor} \leq 2^{n+1} q^{-(n-1)-\lfloor \epsilon(n-1) \rfloor},$$

for all except a fraction $\leq \frac{2^{2(n-1)}}{(q-1)^{\epsilon(n-1)}}$ of $\mathbf{a} \in (\mathcal{R}_q^\times)^2$.

Next, we are to prove the Eq. 2. Let $\delta = q^{-(n-1)/2}$. Lemma 2 shows that $\lambda_{n-1}(\mathcal{L}_{I_S}) \leq n \cdot q^{|S|/(n-1)}$. For S of cardinality $\leq (n-1)/2$, by Lemma 1, we get that $r \geq \eta_\delta(I_S + q\mathbb{Z}^{n-1})$. Using Lemma 4, we know $|\mathbf{D}_{\mathbb{Z}^{n-1}, r, -z_i}(I_S + q\mathbb{Z}^{n-1}) - q^{-|S|}| \leq 2\delta$. For the case $|S| > (n-1)/2$, using the same argument, we have $\mathbf{D}_{\mathbb{Z}^{n-1}, r, -z_i}(I_S + q\mathbb{Z}^{n-1}) \leq 2\delta + q^{-(n-1)/2}$. Therefore,

$$\left| \mathbf{D}_{\mathbb{Z}^{n-1}, r}(z_i + \mathcal{R}_q^\times + q\mathbb{Z}^{n-1}) - \frac{(q-1)^{n-1}}{q^{n-1}} \right|$$

$$= \left| \sum_{S \subseteq \{1, \cdots, n-1\}} (-1)^{|S|} \left(\mathbf{D}_{\mathbb{Z}^{2(n-1)}, r}(z_i + I_S + q\mathbb{Z}^{n-1}) - q^{-|S|} \right) \right|$$

$$\leq 2^n (\delta + q^{-(n-1)/2}) = 2^{n+1} q^{-(n-1)/2}.$$

Overall, we prove that, except for a fraction $\leq \frac{2^{2(n-1)}}{(q-1)^{\epsilon(n-1)}}$ of $\mathbf{a} \in (\mathbb{R}_q^\times)^2$,

$$\mathbf{D}_{\mathbb{Z}^{2(n-1)}, r}(\mathbf{z} + \mathbf{a}^{\perp \times}) = (1 + \delta_0) \cdot \frac{(q-1)^{n-1}}{q^{2(n-1)}},$$

$$\mathbf{D}_{\mathbb{Z}^{n-1}, r}(z_i + \mathcal{R}_q^\times + q\mathbb{Z}^{n-1}) = (1 + \delta_i) \cdot \frac{(q-1)^{n-1}}{q^{n-1}}, \text{ for } i \in \{1, 2\}.$$

where $|\delta_i| \leq 2^{2n} q^{-\lfloor \epsilon(n-1) \rfloor}$ for $i \in \{0, 1, 2\}$, which implies that $|Pr_a - (q - 1)^{-(n-1)}| \leq \epsilon'$.

C   Proof of Lemma 20

Let $\mathcal{A}$ be the given IND-CPA attack algorithm. Given oracle $\mathcal{O}$ that outputs k samples drawn from either $U(\mathcal{R}_q^\times \times \mathcal{R}_q)$ or $A_{s,\psi}^\times$ for previously chosen $s \hookleftarrow \psi$. We construct an algorithm $\mathcal{B}$ to solve $\text{RLWE}_{HNF}^\times$. Algorithm $\mathcal{B}$ first calls $\mathcal{O}$ to get k samples $(h_1', C_1'), \cdots, (h_k', C_k')$. Then algorithm $\mathcal{B}$ picks $i \hookleftarrow U(\{1, \cdots, k\})$ and calculates the public key $h_i = p \cdot h_i'$. When $\mathcal{A}$ outputs a challenge message pair (M_0, M_1), $\mathcal{B}$ picks $b \hookleftarrow U(\{0, 1\})$, computes the challenge ciphertext $C_i = p \cdot C_i' + M_b$ and sends it to $\mathcal{A}$. Finally, $\mathcal{A}$ outputs its guess b', and then $\mathcal{B}$ outputs 1 if $b' = b$ and 0 otherwise.

All h_i''s are uniformly random in $\mathcal{R}_q^\times$, and thus so are the public keys h_i's due to $p \in \mathcal{R}_q^\times$. Theorem 2 shows that the statistical distance between the distribution of the public key given to $\mathcal{A}$ and that in the genuine attack is $q^{-\Omega(n)}$. Furthermore, if $\mathcal{O}$ outputs samples from $A_{s,\psi}^\times$, the pair (h_i, C_i) is of the form $(h_i, h_i s + pe + M_b)$ which corresponds to actual "public key and ciphertext" pair in the IND-CPA attack. Therefore $\mathcal{A}$ succeeds and $\mathcal{B}$ outputs 1 with probability $\geq \frac{1}{2} + \delta - q^{-\Omega(n)}$.

If $\mathcal{O}$ outputs samples from $U(\mathcal{R}_q^\times \times \mathcal{R}_q)$, then C_i is uniformly random in $\mathcal{R}_q$ and independent of b. Algorithm $\mathcal{B}$ outputs 1 with probability $1/2$ in this case. Thus the advantage of $\mathcal{B}$ in distinguishing $U(\mathcal{R}_q^\times \times \mathcal{R}_q)$ and $A_{s,\psi}^\times$ is greater than $\delta/2 - q^{-\Omega(n)}$.

References

1. Albrecht, M., Bai, S., Ducas, L.: A subfield lattice attack on overstretched NTRU assumptions. In: Robshaw, M., Katz, J. (eds.) CRYPTO 2016. LNCS, vol. 9814, pp. 153–178. Springer, Heidelberg (2016). doi:10.1007/978-3-662-53018-4_6

2. Bi, J., Cheng, Q.: Lower bounds of shortest vector lengths in random NTRU lattices. In: Agrawal, M., Cooper, S.B., Li, A. (eds.) TAMC 2012. LNCS, vol. 7287, pp. 143–155. Springer, Heidelberg (2012). doi:10.1007/978-3-642-29952-0_18

3. Bos, J.W., Lauter, K., Loftus, J., Naehrig, M.: Improved security for a ring-based fully homomorphic encryption scheme. In: Stam, M. (ed.) IMACC 2013. LNCS, vol. 8308, pp. 45–64. Springer, Heidelberg (2013). doi:10.1007/978-3-642-45239-0_4

4. Cheon, J.H., Jeong, J., Lee, C.: An algorithm for NTRU problems and cryptanalysis of the GGH multilinear map without an encoding of zero. Cryptology ePrint Archive, Report 2016/139 (2016). http://eprint.iacr.org/2016/139

5. Coppersmith, D., Shamir, A.: Lattice attacks on NTRU. In: Fumy, W. (ed.) EUROCRYPT 1997. LNCS, vol. 1233, pp. 52–61. Springer, Heidelberg (1997). doi:10.1007/3-540-69053-0_5

6. Cramer, R., Ducas, L., Wesolowski, B.: Short stickelberger class relations and application to Ideal-SVP. Cryptology ePrint Archive, Report 2016/885 (2016). http://eprint.iacr.org/2016/885

7. Ducas, L., Durmus, A.: Ring-LWE in polynomial rings. In: Fischlin, M., Buchmann, J., Manulis, M. (eds.) PKC 2012. LNCS, vol. 7293, pp. 34–51. Springer, Heidelberg (2012). doi:10.1007/978-3-642-30057-8_3

8. Ducas, L., Lyubashevsky, V., Prest, T.: Efficient identity-based encryption over NTRU lattices. In: Sarkar, P., Iwata, T. (eds.) ASIACRYPT 2014. LNCS, vol. 8874, pp. 22–41. Springer, Heidelberg (2014). doi:10.1007/978-3-662-45608-8_2

9. Ducas, L., Nguyen, P.Q.: Learning a zonotope and more: cryptanalysis of NTRUSign countermeasures. In: Wang, X., Sako, K. (eds.) ASIACRYPT 2012. LNCS, vol. 7658, pp. 433–450. Springer, Heidelberg (2012). doi:10.1007/978-3-642-34961-4_27

10. Gama, N., Nguyen, P.Q.: New chosen-ciphertext attacks on NTRU. In: Okamoto, T., Wang, X. (eds.) PKC 2007. LNCS, vol. 4450, pp. 89–106. Springer, Heidelberg (2007). doi:10.1007/978-3-540-71677-8_7

11. Garg, S., Gentry, C., Halevi, S.: Candidate multilinear maps from ideal lattices. In: Johansson, T., Nguyen, P.Q. (eds.) EUROCRYPT 2013. LNCS, vol. 7881, pp. 1–17. Springer, Heidelberg (2013). doi:10.1007/978-3-642-38348-9_1

12. Gentry, C.: Key recovery and message attacks on NTRU-composite. In: Pfitzmann, B. (ed.) EUROCRYPT 2001. LNCS, vol. 2045, pp. 182–194. Springer, Heidelberg (2001). doi:10.1007/3-540-44987-6_12

13. Gentry, C.: Fully homomorphic encryption using ideal lattices. In: STOC 2009, pp. 169–178 (2009)

14. Gentry, C., Peikert, C., Vaikuntanathan, V.: Trapdoors for hard lattices and new cryptographic constructions. In: STOC 2008, pp. 197–206 (2008)

15. Gentry, C., Szydlo, M.: Cryptanalysis of the revised NTRU signature scheme. In: Knudsen, L.R. (ed.) EUROCRYPT 2002. LNCS, vol. 2332, pp. 299–320. Springer, Heidelberg (2002). doi:10.1007/3-540-46035-7_20

16. Hoffstein, J., Howgrave-Graham, N., Pipher, J., Silverman, J.H., Whyte, W.: NTRUSign: digital signatures using the NTRU lattice. In: Joye, M. (ed.) CT-RSA 2003. LNCS, vol. 2612, pp. 122–140. Springer, Heidelberg (2003). doi:10.1007/3-540-36563-X_9

17. Hoffstein, J., Pipher, J., Silverman, J.H.: NTRU: a new high speed public key cryptosystem. Presented at the Rump Session of Crypto 1996 (1996)
18. Hoffstein, J., Pipher, J., Silverman, J.H.: NTRU: a ring-based public key cryptosystem. In: Buhler, J.P. (ed.) ANTS 1998. LNCS, vol. 1423, pp. 267–288. Springer, Heidelberg (1998). doi:10.1007/BFb0054868
19. Howgrave-Graham, N.: A hybrid lattice-reduction and meet-in-the-middle attack against NTRU. In: Menezes, A. (ed.) CRYPTO 2007. LNCS, vol. 4622, pp. 150–169. Springer, Heidelberg (2007). doi:10.1007/978-3-540-74143-5_9
20. Hsu, D., Kakade, S.M., Zhang, T.: A tail inequality for quadratic forms of subgaussian random vectors. Electron. Commun. Probab. **17**(25), 1–6 (2011)
21. Jaulmes, É., Joux, A.: A chosen-ciphertext attack against NTRU. In: Bellare, M. (ed.) CRYPTO 2000. LNCS, vol. 1880, pp. 20–35. Springer, Heidelberg (2000). doi:10.1007/3-540-44598-6_2
22. Kirchner, P., Fouque, P.A.: Comparison between subfield and straightforward attacks on NTRU. Cryptology ePrint Archive, Report 2016/717 (2016). http://eprint.iacr.org/2016/717
23. Langlois, A., Stehlé, D., Steinfeld, R.: GGHLite: more efficient multilinear maps from ideal lattices. In: Nguyen, P.Q., Oswald, E. (eds.) EUROCRYPT 2014. LNCS, vol. 8441, pp. 239–256. Springer, Heidelberg (2014). doi:10.1007/978-3-642-55220-5_14
24. López-Alt, A., Tromer, E., Vaikuntanathan, V.: On-the-fly multiparty computation on the cloud via multikey fully homomorphic encryption. In: STOC 2012, pp. 1219–1234 (2012)
25. Lyubashevsky, V., Peikert, C., Regev, O.: On ideal lattices and learning with errors over rings. In: Gilbert, H. (ed.) EUROCRYPT 2010. LNCS, vol. 6110, pp. 1–23. Springer, Heidelberg (2010). doi:10.1007/978-3-642-13190-5_1
26. Lyubashevsky, V., Peikert, C., Regev, O.: A toolkit for Ring-LWE cryptography. Cryptology ePrint Archive, Report 2013/293 (2013). http://eprint.iacr.org/2013/293
27. Micciancio, D.: Generalized compact knapsacks, cyclic lattices, and efficient one-way functions. Comput. Complex. **16**(4), 365–411 (2007)
28. Micciancio, D., Regev, O.: Worst-case to average-case reductions based on gaussian measures. SIAM J. Comput. **37**(1), 267–302 (2007)
29. Nguyen, P.Q., Regev, O.: Learning a parallelepiped: cryptanalysis of GGH and NTRU signatures. In: Vaudenay, S. (ed.) EUROCRYPT 2006. LNCS, vol. 4004, pp. 271–288. Springer, Heidelberg (2006). doi:10.1007/11761679_17
30. Nuñez, D., Agudo, I., Lopez, J.: NTRUReEncrypt: An efficient proxy re-encryption scheme based on NTRU. In: ASIACCS 2015, pp. 179–189 (2015)
31. Peikert, C.: Limits on the hardness of lattice problems in ℓ_p norms. Comput. Complex. **17**(2), 300–351 (2008)
32. Regev, O.: On lattices, learning with errors, random linear codes, and cryptography. In: STOC 2005, pp. 84–93 (2005)
33. Stehlé, D., Steinfeld, R.: Making NTRU as secure as worst-case problems over ideal lattices. In: Paterson, K.G. (ed.) EUROCRYPT 2011. LNCS, vol. 6632, pp. 27–47. Springer, Heidelberg (2011). doi:10.1007/978-3-642-20465-4_4
34. Szydlo, M.: Hypercubic lattice reduction and analysis of GGH and NTRU signatures. In: Biham, E. (ed.) EUROCRYPT 2003. LNCS, vol. 2656, pp. 433–448. Springer, Heidelberg (2003). doi:10.1007/3-540-39200-9_27
35. Terras, A.: Fourier Analysis on Finite Groups and Applications. Cambridge University Press, Cambridge (1999)
36. Xylouris, T.: On Linnik's constant (2009). http://arxiv.org/abs/0906.2749

Equivalences and Black-Box Separations of Matrix Diffie-Hellman Problems

Universitat Politècnica de Catalunya, Barcelona, Spain
jorge.villar@upc.edu

Abstract. In this paper we provide new algebraic tools to study the relationship between different Matrix Diffie-Hellman (MDDH) Problems, which are recently introduced as a natural generalization of the so-called Linear Problem. Namely, we provide an algebraic criterion to decide whether there exists a generic black-box reduction, and in many cases, when the answer is positive we also build an explicit reduction with the following properties: it only makes a single oracle call, it is tight and it makes use only of operations in the base group.

It is well known that two MDDH problems described by matrices with a different number of rows are separated by an oracle computing certain multilinear map. Thus, we put the focus on MDDH problems of the same size. Then, we show that MDDH problems described with a different number of parameters are also separated (meaning that a successful reduction cannot decrease the amount of randomness used in the problem instance description).

When comparing MDDH problems of the same size and number of parameters, we show that they are either equivalent or incomparable. This suggests that a complete classification into equivalence classes could be done in the future. In this paper we give some positive and negative partial results about equivalence, in particular solving the open problem of whether the Linear and the Cascade MDDH problems are reducible to each other.

The results given in the paper are limited by some technical restrictions in the shape of the matrices and in the degree of the polynomials defining them. However, these restrictions are also present in most of the work dealing with MDDH Problems. Therefore, our results apply to all known instances of practical interest.

Keywords: Matrix Diffie-Hellman problems · Black-box reductions · Decisional linear assumption · Black-box separations

1 Introduction

Matrix Decisional Diffie-Hellman (MDDH) Problems were recently introduced in [9] as a natural generalization of the Linear Problem, and they have found

J.L. Villar—This work has been supported by the Spanish research project MTM2013-41426-R.

© International Association for Cryptologic Research 2017
S. Fehr (Ed.): PKC 2017, Part I, LNCS 10174, pp. 435–464, 2017.
DOI: 10.1007/978-3-662-54365-8_18

many applications (see, for instance [1–9]) and they are further generalized to computational problems in [13,15]. A MDDH problem is defined as a set of matrices $\mathbf{A} \in \mathbb{Z}_q^{\ell \times k}$, for $\ell > k$, sampled from a probability distribution $\mathcal{D}_{\ell,k}$. Informally, the $\mathcal{D}_{\ell,k}$-MDDH problem is telling apart the two probability distributions $([\mathbf{A}], [\mathbf{A}\boldsymbol{w}])$ and $([\mathbf{A}], [\boldsymbol{z}])$, where $\mathbf{A} \leftarrow \mathcal{D}_{\ell,k}$, $\boldsymbol{w} \leftarrow \mathbb{Z}_q^k$ and $\boldsymbol{z} \leftarrow \mathbb{Z}_q^\ell$. The bracket notation (also called 'implicit' notation) means giving the vectors and matrices "in the exponent" (see Sect. 2). Most interesting examples correspond to the case $\ell = k + 1$, and usually $\mathcal{D}_{\ell,k}$ is defined by evaluating a degree-one polynomial map $\mathbf{A}(\boldsymbol{t})$ on a random point $\boldsymbol{t} \in \mathbb{Z}_q^d$ (we denote this problem as $\mathcal{D}_k^{\mathbf{A}}$-MDDH).[1]

The broadly used DDH and k-Lin problems are indeed instances of MDDH problems (namely, $\mathcal{L}_1$-MDDH and $\mathcal{L}_k$-MDDH problems). Other useful instances were introduced in [9,15], like the Cascade ($\mathcal{C}_k$-MDDH) and the Symmetric Cascade ($\mathcal{SC}_k$-MDDH) problems (see Sect. 2.3 for more details on these examples). This wide range of decisional problems is typically organized into families of increasing hardness, allowing us to trade compactness for hardness. In particular, $\mathcal{C}_k$-MDDH and $\mathcal{L}_k$-MDDH both depend on k parameters, and they offer the same security guarantees (generically), while $\mathcal{SC}_k$-MDDH has optimal representation size (only one parameter) but it is supposed to be easier than $\mathcal{C}_k$-MDDH. The applications of the MDDH problems that appeared in the papers listed above suggest that, in most scenarios, the k-Lin problem can be successfully replaced by any other hard MDDH problem.

Using tools from algebraic geometry, in [9] a general criterion for the hardness of $\mathcal{D}_k^{\mathbf{A}}$-MDDH in the (symmetric) k-linear generic group model is given, based on the properties of the so-called determinant polynomial $\partial_{\mathbf{A}}$ associated to the MDDH problem. This criterion is one of the few known general theorems that transforms the problem of proving the generic hardness of a computational problem, chosen from a wide family, into a simple algebraic problem. This can be done thanks to a purely algebraic reformulation of the generic group model formalized by Maurer in [14], including also the multilinear map functionality. A clear and detailed reference for this algebraic reformulation, applied to a very general generic group model supporting several groups and homomorphisms among them, can be found in [4].

Although proving the hardness of a problem in a generic model does not give all the guarantees about the security of the protocols based on it, at least, it constitutes a proof that the protocol is well-designed. Indeed, the meaning of a

---

[1] MDDH problems beyond these technical limitations are hard to use because, firstly, there are no known efficient algebraic tools to show the generic hardness of unbounded families of $\mathcal{D}_{\ell,k}$-MDDH problems with $\ell > k + 1$, meaning that the hardness must be proven individually for every instance in the family. Secondly, dealing with MDDH problems defined by non-linear polynomial maps produces the same effect in the generic hardness analysis, and in addition, it limits the practical applicability of the MDDH problem instances. Indeed, in the linear case, $[\mathbf{A}]$ (typically required to be publicly known) can be easily recovered by evaluating the polynomial map in the exponent, given only the parameters $[\boldsymbol{t}]$. This compression of the public information is partially lost when using polynomial maps of higher degree.

problem being hard on a generic group is that the only possible successful algorithms solving it are specific to a particular choice of the base group. Moreover, even when a specific attack against a protocol based on such problem is found, there is still the possibility to avoid it by properly changing the base group. For instance, the subexponential algorithms solving the Discrete Logarithm problem in certain groups have no known equivalent in the realm of random elliptic curves. On the other hand, even if we know that two problems are generically hard, it still makes sense looking for reductions (or separations) between them, because they have implications about the impact of solving one of the problems implemented on a specific group family.

Indeed, in the current candidates for multilinear maps (or the richer structure called graded encodings) considered in the literature, most decisional problems inspired on DDH (including the MDDH problems) are easy. However, these attacks are specific to the platforms considered in the constructions, and they do not rule out the existence of other constructions in the future. Therefore, the research on general results about the hardness and relationship of decisional problems related to DDH remains to be of great theoretical interest.

Finding reductions between decisional problems is a rather difficult task: A decisional problem typically specifies two probability distributions that are hard to tell apart, and then the reduction has to transform the two specific probability distributions defining one of the problems into the two distributions defining the other, tolerating only a negligible error probability. One can find many subtleties when trying to build such reductions, or to rule out their existence, as shown for example in [16]. Most known reductions fall in the class of black-box reductions, and they typically use the base groups in a generic way. This suggests the possibility of finding an algebraic formulation that captures the notion of generic black-box reducibility for a wide family of decisional problems, assuming that their description is uniform enough. A natural candidate is the family of MDDH problems. However, known results about equivalence or separation of MDDH problems essentially reduce to:

- [9]. $\mathcal{D}_{\ell,k}$-MDDH and $\mathcal{D}_{\ell',k'}$-MDDH problems with $k < k'$ are separated by an oracle that computes a $(k + 1)$-linear map.[2] Namely, $\mathcal{D}_{\ell,k}$-MDDH is easily solved by means of the oracle, while $\mathcal{D}_{\ell',k'}$-MDDH could remain hard (e.g., it can still be hard in the generic k'-linear group model).
- [10]. All hard $\mathcal{D}_{\ell,k}^{\mathbf{A}}$-MDDH problems with $\ell = k + 1$, described by a univariate degree-one polynomial map $\mathbf{A}(t)$ are equivalent.
- [10]. By using randomization and "algebraic reductions" one can obtain reductions between some known families of MDDH problems. For instance, $\mathcal{SC}_k$-MDDH is reduced to $\mathcal{C}_k$-MDDH, and all $\mathcal{D}_{\ell,k}$-MDDH problems reduce to $\mathcal{U}_{\ell,k}$-MDDH problems (based on the uniform matrix distribution).

---

[2] This is actually valid in the general case provided that k is constant (i.e., independent of the security parameter). However, for some compact matrix distributions, including $\mathcal{L}_k$, $\mathcal{C}_k$ and $\mathcal{SC}_k$), a $(k + 1)$-linear map can efficiently solve the $\mathcal{D}_{\ell,k}$-MDDH problem even when k grows linearly in the complexity parameter.

Many other questions remain unanswered. For instance, it is an open problem whether a reduction between $\mathcal{C}_k$-MDDH and $\mathcal{L}_k$-MDDH exists, in either way.

In this paper we focus on the general problem of finding a simple algebraic criterion for the existence of reductions between two MDDH problems with the same size k. When the answer is positive, we also try to build a simple reduction. The results we provide here are a first step of the big project of classifying all MDDH assumptions (or at least a wide family of them) into equivalence classes.

1.1 Our Results

The main theorem in [9,10] gives sufficient conditions for the hardness, in the generic k-linear group model, of a wide family of MDDH problems defined by polynomial matrix distributions $\mathcal{D}_k^{\mathbf{A}}$, based on some properties (degree and irreducibility) of the determinant polynomial $\mathfrak{d}_{\mathbf{A}}$ (i.e., the determinant of $\mathbf{A}(t)\|z$ as a polynomial in (t, z), see Definition 8). In the particular case of one-parameter polynomial matrix distributions, the converse theorem is also proved in [10]. We prove that a similar converse also holds for matrix distributions with many parameters in Theorem 3, by using different techniques. We also give additional technical properties that any $\mathfrak{d}_{\mathbf{A}}$ must fulfil when $\mathcal{D}_k^{\mathbf{A}}$ is hard (i.e., the $\mathcal{D}_k^{\mathbf{A}}$-MDDH problem is hard in the generic k-linear group model), and they are based on the geometric notion called elusiveness, recently introduced in [15].

Our main contribution is giving positive and negative results about the existence of black-box reductions between the two generically hard problems $\mathcal{D}_k^{\mathbf{A}}$-MDDH and $\mathcal{D}_k^{\mathbf{B}}$-MDDH defined by degree-one polynomial matrix distributions with d and e parameters, respectively. The first result shows how to extract from any successful generic black-box reduction with polynomially-many oracle calls a polynomial map f of degree one fulfilling the simple polynomial equation

$$\lambda \mathfrak{d}_{\mathbf{A}} = \mathfrak{d}_{\mathbf{B}} \circ f \tag{1}$$

(Informal) Theorem 4. *If there exists a generic black-box reduction from the* $\mathcal{D}_k^{\mathbf{A}}$-MDDH *problem to the* $\mathcal{D}_k^{\mathbf{B}}$-MDDH *problem, then Eq. 1 is satisfied by some polynomial map* f, *for some nonzero constant* λ.

This polynomial map is also shown to be injective, which means that necessarily $e \geq d$, that is, a successful generic black-box reduction cannot decrease the number of parameters, or equivalently, it cannot derandomize the instance of $\mathcal{D}_k^{\mathbf{A}}$-MDDH to build an instance of $\mathcal{D}_k^{\mathbf{B}}$-MDDH. This result itself is enough to show a black-box separation between MDDH problems defined from the distributions $\mathcal{SC}_k$ and $\mathcal{C}_k$, and also $\mathcal{L}_k$ and $\mathcal{U}_k$, for the same size k. At this point, we know many black-box separations between MDDH problems. Informally, bigger problems do not reduce to smaller problems, and problems with many parameters do not reduce to problems with fewer parameters.

To gain a deeper understanding of the reducibility of MDDH problems, we show that Eq. 1 captures it by proving the converse of Theorem 4.

(Informal) Theorem 5. *If there exists a solution to Eq. 1, then*

1. *there exists a black-box deterministic reduction from $\mathcal{D}_k^{\mathbf{A}}$-MDDH to $\mathcal{D}_k^{\mathbf{B}}$-MDDH, using a single oracle call, that succeeds with overwhelming probability if the oracle is perfect.*
2. *if in addition f is surjective, then the reduction is actually a tight black-box reduction, and it works for any imperfect oracle.*
3. *otherwise, if $\mathcal{D}_k^{\mathbf{B}}$ is random self-reducible, then there also exists a (probabilistic) tight black-box reduction with the same properties.*

The last item requires a stronger notion of random self-reducibility, compared to the one used in [9,10], in which not only the vector $\mathbf{z}$, but also the matrix $\mathbf{A}$ is randomized. We prove in this paper that the usual matrix distributions $\mathcal{C}_k$, $\mathcal{SC}_k$, $\mathcal{L}_k$, $\mathcal{RL}_k$ and the uniform one are random self-reducible in this stronger way. These results directly show that, among other relations, $\mathcal{SC}_k$-MDDH reduces to $\mathcal{C}_k$-MDDH, and $\mathcal{L}_k$-MDDH reduces to $\mathcal{RL}_k$-MDDH, as one can expect.

The previous theorem is extremely powerful when $e = d$, since then any possible solution f to Eq. 1 must be a bijective map. Thus, using the inverse map we also show in Theorem 6 that $\mathcal{D}_k^{\mathbf{A}}$-MDDH and $\mathcal{D}_k^{\mathbf{B}}$-MDDH are either equivalent (by simple tight reductions involving only operations in the base group), or they are incomparable by generic black-box reductions. This fact opens the possibility to build an entire classification of all degree-one polynomial MDDH problems into equivalence classes. Although we leave the general problem open, we also provide some partial results and tools to carry out the classification. Recall that all MDDH problems in an equivalence class must have the same size and number of parameters.

In the positive way, we give two easy-to-check sufficient conditions for equivalence: the first one directly uses the determinant polynomial, while the second is related to a polynomial vector space $X_{\mathbf{A}}$ associated to any polynomial matrix distribution (in the way defined in [12]),

(Informal) Corollary 2. *If $\mathfrak{d}_{\mathbf{A}} = \mathfrak{d}_{\mathbf{B}}$, then $\mathcal{D}_k^{\mathbf{A}}$-MDDH $\Leftrightarrow \mathcal{D}_k^{\mathbf{B}}$-MDDH.*

(Informal) Corollary 3. *If $X_{\mathbf{A}} = X_{\mathbf{B}}$, then $\mathcal{D}_k^{\mathbf{A}}$-MDDH $\Leftrightarrow \mathcal{D}_k^{\mathbf{B}}$-MDDH.*

Actually, the second result implies the first, since the polynomial vector space $X_{\mathbf{A}}$ is determined by $\mathfrak{d}_{\mathbf{A}}$. However, the equality of determinant polynomials can be checked trivially, while the equality of two vector spaces (given by generating sets) involves some linear algebra computations.

Although most natural algebraic reductions of matrix problems keep $X_{\mathbf{A}}$ invariant, there are other less natural reductions that do not, and therefore the equality of polynomial vector spaces does not solve the equivalence problem completely. Nevertheless, the special case of the one-parameter family of degree-one polynomial matrix distributions is completely solved since there is only one possible choice for the vector space $X_{\mathbf{A}}$, and then all hard one-parameter MDDH problems are equivalent. This result has proved in [10] in a rather different way.

Next, we address the problem of showing separations between $\mathcal{D}_k^{\mathbf{A}}$-MDDH and $\mathcal{D}_k^{\mathbf{B}}$-MDDH with $e = d \geq 1$, like for instance $\mathcal{C}_k$-MDDH and $\mathcal{L}_k$-MDDH. Although one can try to show directly that Eq. 1 has no solutions, it is a cumbersome task when k and d grow. This kind of problem is often solved by looking for invariant objects. Namely, we look for easy-to compute objects associated to matrix distributions, such that they are constant within an equivalence class, while they typically change between different equivalence classes. In this paper, we propose two invariant objects: the singular locus and the automorphism group. Roughly speaking, for every matrix distribution $\mathcal{D}_k^{\mathbf{A}}$ we can define the algebraic variety $V_{\mathbf{A}}$ containing all the zeros of the determinant polynomial, and also the automorphism group $\mathrm{Aut_A}$ containing all bijective polynomial maps that leave $V_{\mathbf{A}}$ invariant. Then,

(Informal) Lemma 6. *If $\mathcal{D}_k^{\mathbf{A}}$-MDDH $\Leftrightarrow \mathcal{D}_k^{\mathbf{B}}$-MDDH, then $V_{\mathbf{A}}$ and $V_{\mathbf{B}}$ have the same number of (rational) singular points.*

(Informal) Lemma 7. *If $\mathcal{D}_k^{\mathbf{A}}$-MDDH $\Leftrightarrow \mathcal{D}_k^{\mathbf{B}}$-MDDH, then $\mathrm{Aut_A} \cong \mathrm{Aut_B}$.*

The singular locus turns to be quite easy to compute for matrix distributions. Indeed we use it to solve the open problem of the black-box separation between $\mathcal{L}_k$-MDDH and $\mathcal{C}_k$-MDDH. Namely, we show that the variety associated to $\mathcal{L}_k$ has singular points, while the one corresponding to $\mathcal{C}_k$ has not. This suggests that $\mathcal{C}_k$ is "cleaner" than $\mathcal{L}_k$, so the former would be a preferable choice (as singular points are associated to easy problem instances).

However, the singular locus is a too coarse invariant, meaning that many non-equivalent matrix distributions have no singular points, and then they cannot be separated using this technique. We propose a second invariant which is presumably finer that the singular locus, the group of black-box self-reductions, or the group of automorphisms of the matrix distribution. Although computing the whole group is a hard task, we could compute only some property of the group, like the number of elements of order two. However, we could not give any concrete example such that this technique is simpler than directly showing the nonexistence of solutions to Eq. 1.

1.2   Roadmap

In Sect. 2 we describe the basics about MDDH problems, the known generic hardness results, and a new more general "converse" theorem is given in Sect. 3. The main contributions are in Sects. 4 and 5. In the former we show the importance of Eq. 1 for the reducibility of MDDH problems, while the latter deals with the classification of MDDH problems with the same number of parameters. In particular, we give the separation result between of the most used MDDH problems: the $\mathcal{C}_k$-MDDH and the $\mathcal{L}_k$-MDDH problems.

2   Preliminaries

2.1   Additive Notation for Group Elements

In this paper we adopt the additive notation for group operations, as it is now a *de facto* standard for papers dealing with matrix problems. Let $\mathbb{G}$ be a cyclic group of prime-order q and g a generator of $\mathbb{G}$. We will denote every group element $h \in \mathbb{G}$ by its (possibly unknown) discrete logarithm with respect to the generator g. More precisely, we will write $h = [x]$, where $x \in \mathbb{Z}_q$ such that $h = g^x$. We naturally extend this notation to vectors and matrices. Thus, for a matrix $\mathbf{A} = (a_{ij}) \in \mathbb{Z}_q^{n \times m}$, we will write $[\mathbf{A}] = (g^{a_{ij}}) \in \mathbb{G}^{n \times m}$.

Notice that computing $x \in \mathbb{Z}_q$ from $[x] \in \mathbb{G}$ is hard, since it means solving the Discrete Logarithm Problem in $\mathbb{G}$. Similarly, given $[x], [y] \in \mathbb{G}$ and $z \in \mathbb{Z}_q$, one can efficiently compute $[x + y], [xz], [yz] \in \mathbb{G}$ but not $[xy] \in \mathbb{G}$, since the latter would mean solving the Computational Diffie-Hellman Problem in $\mathbb{G}$.

For a non-degenerated bilinear symmetric pairing $e : \mathbb{G} \times \mathbb{G} \to \mathbb{G}_T$ we use a similar notation. For $[x], [y] \in \mathbb{G}$ we will write $[z]_T = [xy]_T = e([x], [y])$, where, as one would expect, $[z]_T = g_T^z \in \mathbb{G}_T$ and $[1]_T = g_T = e(g, g)$ is a generator of $\mathbb{G}_T$. Similarly, for a k-linear map $e : \mathbb{G}^k \to \mathbb{G}_T$ we will write $[z]_T = [x_1 \cdots x_k]_T = e([x_1], \ldots, [x_k])$.

2.2 A Generic Model for Groups with a Multilinear Map

In this section we sketch the random-encodings based and the purely-algebraic generic models for groups with a multilinear map, used in the paper. The latter is similar to the model used in [4,9,11], and it is a purely algebraic version of Maurer's generic group model [14] including the k-linear map functionality.

As we are dealing with decisional problems entirely described by group elements, we can notably simplify the exposition. Consider first Maurer's model, in which an algorithm $\mathcal{A}$ does not deal with proper group elements in $\mathbb{G}$ or $\mathbb{G}_T$, but only with labels, and it has access to an additional oracle internally performing the group operations. Namely, on start $\mathcal{A}$ receives the labels $(X_1, 1), \ldots, (X_n, 1)$, corresponding to some group elements $[x_1], \ldots, [x_n] \in \mathbb{G}$ (along with some additional labels $(0, 1), (1, 1), (0, T), (1, T)$ corresponding to $[0], [1], [0]_T, [1]_T$, which we assume are implicitly given to $\mathcal{A}$). Then $\mathcal{A}$ can adaptively make the following queries to the generic group oracle:

- GroupOp$((Y_1, i), (Y_2, i))$, $i \in \{1, T\}$: group operation in $\mathbb{G}$ or $\mathbb{G}_T$ for two previously issued labels, resulting in a new label (Y_3, i).
- GroupInv$((Y_1, i))$, $i \in \{1, T\}$: group inversion in $\mathbb{G}$ or $\mathbb{G}_T$, resulting in a new label (Y_2, i).
- GroupML$((Y_1, 1), \ldots, (Y_k, 1))$: k-linear map of k previously issued labels in $\mathbb{G}$, resulting in a new label (Y_{k+1}, T).
- GroupEqTest$((Y_1, i), (Y_2, i))$, $i \in \{1, T\}$: test two previously issued labels in $\mathbb{G}$ or $\mathbb{G}_T$ for equality of the corresponding group elements, resulting in a bit (1 indicates equality). Here, the oracle stores the actual input group elements and the results of the operations corresponding to the oracle calls.

Every badly formed query (for instance, containing an unknown label) is answered with a special rejection symbol $\perp$. Similarly, the output of $\mathcal{A}$ consists of some labels $(Z_1, 1), \ldots, (Z_a, 1), (Z_{a+1}, T), \ldots, (Z_{a+b}, T)$ representing group elements in either $\mathbb{G}$ or $\mathbb{G}_T$, and perhaps some non-group elements $\tilde{z}$.

In a generic group model based on random encodings, every group element handled by the algorithm is replaced by a random label (just a string selected from a large enough set, in order to prevent guessing a valid label from scratch). The generic oracle keeps the real group elements (or elements in an isomorphic copy of the group) associated to the labels, and carries out all group operations queried by the algorithm. The label mapping is injective, meaning that equal group elements (perhaps resulting from different computations) are assigned to the same label. Therefore, only the first three oracle queries (GroupOp, GroupInv and GroupML) are necessary in this generic group model. The GroupEqTest query is now trivial due to the mentioned injectivity.

On the other hand, in the purely algebraic generic model, the labels are indeed polynomials in $\boldsymbol{X} = (X_1, \ldots, X_n)$. More precisely the labels are (Y, i) for $Y \in \mathbb{Z}_q[\boldsymbol{X}]$ and $i \in \{1, T\}$. The oracle no longer performs group operations but only polynomial operations in the labels. As a consequence, the labels received by $\mathcal{A}$ are completely predictable to it, that is, $\mathcal{A}$ knows the coefficients of every label Y as a polynomial in $\boldsymbol{X}$, for every intermediate group element handled during the computations, including the group elements in the output. Observe that due to the limitation in the oracle syntax, the elements in $\mathbb{G}$ correspond to polynomials of degree at most 1, while the elements in $\mathbb{G}_T$ correspond to polynomials of degree at most k. And these are the only polynomials that can appear in the labels.

To model the possible constraints in the inputs $[x_1], \ldots, [x_n]$, we assume that $\boldsymbol{x} = (x_1, \ldots, x_n)$ is sampled by evaluating a polynomial map $\mathfrak{h}$ at a a uniformly distributed random point $\boldsymbol{s} \in \mathbb{Z}_q^d$. Thus, the generic group oracle formally assigns polynomials $X_1, \ldots, X_n \in \mathbb{Z}_q[\boldsymbol{S}]$ to the input labels. Then, the oracle call GroupEqTest is modified and it just compares the labels as polynomials in $\boldsymbol{S}$. This modification in the oracle only amounts into a negligible difference between the models. Indeed, as a usual step in generic model proofs, detecting the model difference means finding a (bounded degree) polynomial that vanishes at a random point $\boldsymbol{s}$, and this probability is shown to be negligible by using Schwartz-Zippel Lemma and the union bound.

All the information $\mathcal{A}$ can obtain from the purely algebraic generic group oracle is via the equality test queries, since for any intermediate group element $\mathcal{A}$ knows the corresponding polynomial in $\boldsymbol{X}$, but not necessarily the associated polynomial in $\boldsymbol{S}$. When dealing with a decisional problem, there are two different sampling polynomial maps $\mathfrak{h}_0, \mathfrak{h}_1$, and $\mathcal{A}$'s goal is guessing which one is used by the generic group oracle. In this setting, $\mathcal{A}$ wins if it finds two different "computable" polynomials (i.e., of degree at most k) in $\boldsymbol{X}$ such that they are equal when composed to $\mathfrak{h}_0$, but they are different when composed to $\mathfrak{h}_1$, or vice versa. Proving that the decisional problem is generically hard exactly means proving that such polynomials do not exist.

When dealing with algorithms in the generic group model with access to extra oracles (e.g. reductions), the transition between a generic group model based on random encodings to its purely algebraic counterpart is a bit more subtle. This is mainly due to the interaction of the generic model with the extra oracle, which can leak some information about the group elements themselves. For the reducibility results given in Sect. 4, we will use in the proofs both the random encodings based generic model and the purely algebraic one.

2.3 The Matrix DDH Problem Family

We recall some definitions from [9,10,15].

Definition 1 (Matrix Distribution). *Let $\ell, k \in \mathbb{N}$ with $\ell > k$.[3] We call $\mathcal{D}_{\ell,k}$ a matrix distribution if it is a probabilistic algorithm that, given any large enough prime q [4], it outputs matrices in $\mathbb{Z}_q^{\ell \times k}$, in time polynomial in $\log q$, that have full rank k with overwhelming probability. We actually identify $\mathcal{D}_{\ell,k}$ to the probability distribution of its output. For simplicity, we write $\mathcal{D}_k = \mathcal{D}_{k+1,k}$.*

Definition 2 (Polynomial Matrix Distribution). *We call $\mathcal{D}_{\ell,k}$ a polynomial matrix distribution with d parameters if there exists a polynomial map $\mathbf{A} : \mathbb{Z}_q^d \to \mathbb{Z}_q^{\ell \times k}$ of constant degree (i.e., not depending on q) such that for a uniformly sampled $t \in \mathbb{Z}_q^d$, the matrix $\mathbf{A}(t)$ follows the distribution $\mathcal{D}_{\ell,k}$. We will write $\mathcal{D}_{\ell,k}^{\mathbf{A}}$ to emphasize that the matrix distribution is defined via a polynomial map. We call the degree of $\mathcal{D}_{\ell,k}^{\mathbf{A}}$ to the minimum possible degree of a polynomial map $\mathbf{A}$ producing the distribution $\mathcal{D}_{\ell,k}$.*

We define the $\mathcal{D}_{\ell,k}$-matrix decision problem as to distinguish the two distributions $([\mathbf{A}], [\mathbf{A}w])$ and $([\mathbf{A}], [z])$, where $\mathbf{A} \leftarrow \mathcal{D}_{\ell,k}$, $w \leftarrow \mathbb{Z}_q^k$ and $z \leftarrow \mathbb{Z}_q^\ell$.

Definition 3 ($\mathcal{D}_{\ell,k}$-MDDH Problem). *Let $\mathcal{D}_{\ell,k}$ be a matrix distribution and IG an instance generator algorithm. The $\mathcal{D}_{\ell,k}$-Matrix Decision Diffie-Hellman ($\mathcal{D}_{\ell,k}$-MDDH) Problem, defined with respect to IG, is telling apart the two probability distributions*

$$D_{real} = (q, \mathbb{G}, g, [\mathbf{A}], [\mathbf{A}w]), \qquad D_{random} = (q, \mathbb{G}, g, [\mathbf{A}], [z]),$$

where $(q, \mathbb{G}, g) \leftarrow \mathsf{IG}(1^\lambda)$, $\mathbf{A} \leftarrow \mathcal{D}_{\ell,k}$, $w \leftarrow \mathbb{Z}_q^k$ and $z \leftarrow \mathbb{Z}_q^\ell$.

The $\mathcal{D}_{\ell,k}$-MDDH Assumption for an instance generator IG says that for all probabilistic polynomial time distinguishers A,

$$|\Pr[\mathsf{A}(D_{\text{real}}) = 1] - \Pr[\mathsf{A}(D_{\text{random}}) = 1]| \in negl.$$

Definition 4 (Hard Matrix Distribution). *We say that a matrix distribution $\mathcal{D}_{\ell,k}$ is hard if the $\mathcal{D}_{\ell,k}$-MDDH Problem is hard in the generic k-linear group model.[5]*

---

[3] We assume that k and ℓ are constant (*i.e.*, independent of the security parameter).

[4] From now on we assume that q is implicitly given as input to $\mathcal{D}_{\ell,k}$.

[5] This is the maximum level of generic security achievable, since a $(k+1)$-linear map solves all $\mathcal{D}_{\ell,k}$-MDDH problem instances.

Some particular families of matrix distributions were presented in [9,15]. Namely,

$$
\mathcal{L}_k : \begin{pmatrix} a_1 & & 0 \\ & \ddots & \\ 0 & & a_k \\ 1 & \cdots & 1 \end{pmatrix}, \qquad
\mathcal{C}_k : \begin{pmatrix} a_1 & & 0 \\ 1 & \ddots & \\ & \ddots & a_k \\ 0 & & 1 \end{pmatrix}, \qquad
\mathcal{RL}_k : \begin{pmatrix} a_1 & & 0 \\ & \ddots & \\ 0 & & a_k \\ b_1 & \cdots & b_k \end{pmatrix},
$$

where $a_i, b_i \leftarrow \mathbb{Z}_q$. $\mathcal{L}_k$, $\mathcal{C}_k$ and $\mathcal{RL}_k$ are respectively called the Linear, the Cascade and the Randomized Linear matrix distributions. The Symmetric Cascade distribution, $\mathcal{SC}_k$, is defined from $\mathcal{C}_k$ by taking $a_1 = \cdots = a_k = a$, and similarly the Incremental Linear distribution, $\mathcal{IL}_k$, is defined from $\mathcal{L}_k$ by taking $a_i = a + i - 1$. The Uniform matrix distribution $\mathcal{U}_{\ell,k}$ is simply taking uniformly distributed matrices in $\mathbb{Z}_q^{\ell \times k}$. Also from the same source, the Circulant matrix distribution is defined as follows

$$
\mathcal{CI}_{k,d} : \begin{pmatrix}
a_1 & & & 0 \\
\vdots & a_1 & & \\
a_d & \vdots & \ddots & \\
1 & a_d & & a_1 \\
& 1 & \ddots & \vdots \\
& & \ddots & a_d \\
0 & & & 1
\end{pmatrix} \in \mathbb{Z}_q^{(k+d) \times k}, \qquad \text{where } a_i \leftarrow \mathbb{Z}_q.
$$

2.4   Algebraic Reductions and Random Self-Reducibility

The algebraic nature of matrix distributions makes it easy to find some natural generic reductions among the corresponding problems. The following set of transformations were introduced in [10].

Definition 5 (Algebraic Reductions[6]). *We say that a matrix distribution $\mathcal{D}_{\ell,k}^1$ is algebraically reducible to another one $\mathcal{D}_{\ell,k}^2$ if there exists an efficiently samplable distribution $\mathcal{T}$ that, on the input of a large prime q, it outputs a pair of matrices $(\mathbf{L}, \mathbf{R})$, $\mathbf{L} \in \mathbb{Z}_q^{\ell \times \ell}$ and $\mathbf{R} \in \mathbb{Z}_q^{k \times k}$, with the following property: Given $\mathbf{A} \leftarrow \mathcal{D}_{\ell,k}^1$ the distribution of $\mathbf{LAR}$ is statistically close to $\mathcal{D}_{\ell,k}^2$. In this case we write $\mathcal{D}_{\ell,k}^1 \stackrel{alg}{\Rightarrow} \mathcal{D}_{\ell,k}^2$, or simply $\mathcal{D}_{\ell,k}^2 = \mathcal{T}^*(\mathcal{D}_{\ell,k}^1)$.*

As shown in [10] and later in [15], algebraic reductions between matrix distributions also imply generic reductions between the MDDH problems.

Lemma 1 (from [15]). $\mathcal{D}_{\ell,k}^1 \stackrel{alg}{\Rightarrow} \mathcal{D}_{\ell,k}^2$ *implies* $\mathcal{D}_{\ell,k}^1$-MDDH $\Rightarrow \mathcal{D}_{\ell,k}^2$-MDDH.

---

[6] This definition can be extended to deal with matrix distributions of different sizes, by adding some restrictions to the shapes of $\mathbf{R}$ and $\mathbf{L}$. However, here we are mainly focusing on self-reductions.

By taking $\mathcal{T}$ to produce independent uniformly distributed invertible matrices, it is easy to see that for any matrix distribution $\mathcal{D}_{\ell,k}$, $\mathcal{D}_{\ell,k} \overset{alg}{\Rightarrow} \mathcal{U}_{\ell,k}$, which implies that $\mathcal{U}_{\ell,k}$-MDDH is the hardest of the MDDH problems of size $\ell \times k$. It is also easy to prove that $\mathcal{L}_k \overset{alg}{\Rightarrow} \mathcal{RL}_k$ and $\mathcal{SC}_k \overset{alg}{\Rightarrow} \mathcal{C}_k$.

As mentioned in [9], MDDH problems show some random self-reducibility properties. In particular, all variants of the $\mathcal{D}_k$-MDDH problems (that is, with $\ell = k + 1$) with a nonuniform distribution of the vector z (either in the real or the random instances) can be reduced to the corresponding proper $\mathcal{D}_k$-MDDH problem (i.e., with z distributed as in Definition 3). Indeed, it suffices to apply the map $(\mathbf{A}, z) \mapsto (\mathbf{A}, \lambda z + \mathbf{A}w)$ for random $w \leftarrow \mathbb{Z}_q^k$ and $\lambda \leftarrow \mathbb{Z}_q^\times$, which works fine for both real and random instances.

Stronger self-reducibility properties of the $\mathcal{D}_k$-MDDH problems (i.e., including also the distribution of the matrix $\mathbf{A}$) are known for specific matrix distributions, like $\mathcal{C}_k$, $\mathcal{SC}_k$, $\mathcal{RL}_k$, $\mathcal{RL}_k$ or the uniform distribution. To this end, we can use the algebraic reductions, given in Definition 5, to explicitly build random self-reductions (according to Lemma 1) transforming any probability distribution of the parameters $t \in \mathbb{Z}_q^d$ into some probability distribution statistically close to the uniformly one. In particular, for $\mathcal{C}_k$ we can choose an algebraic reduction $\mathcal{T}$ producing diagonal matrices

$$\mathbf{L}(\boldsymbol{\lambda}) = \begin{pmatrix} 1 & & & 0 \\ & \lambda_1^{-1} & & \\ & & \ddots & \\ 0 & & & \lambda_k^{-1} \end{pmatrix} \qquad \mathbf{R}(\boldsymbol{\lambda}) = \begin{pmatrix} \lambda_1 & & 0 \\ & \ddots & \\ 0 & & \lambda_k \end{pmatrix}$$

where $\lambda_1, \ldots, \lambda_k \leftarrow \mathbb{Z}_q^\times$ are taken at random. Observe that $\mathcal{T}$ can be seen as the transformation in the parameter space $(a_1, \ldots, a_k) \mapsto (\lambda_1 a_1, \ldots, \lambda_k a_k)$. Using now $\lambda_1 = \cdots = \lambda_k$, we can show the strong random self-reducibility of $\mathcal{SC}_k$-MDDH. Similarly, for $\mathcal{RL}_k$ we can take

$$\mathbf{L}(\boldsymbol{\lambda}) = \begin{pmatrix} \lambda_1 & & 0 \\ & \ddots & \\ & & \lambda_k \\ 0 & & 1 \end{pmatrix} \qquad \mathbf{R}(\boldsymbol{\mu}) = \begin{pmatrix} \mu_1 & & 0 \\ & \ddots & \\ 0 & & \mu_k \end{pmatrix}$$

for random $\lambda_1, \ldots, \lambda_k, \mu_1, \ldots, \mu_k \leftarrow \mathbb{Z}_q^\times$, corresponding to the map $(a_1, \ldots, a_k, b_1, \ldots, b_k) \mapsto (\lambda_1\mu_1 a_1, \ldots, \lambda_k\mu_k a_k, \mu_1 b_1, \ldots, \mu_k b_k)$. Finally, for $\mathcal{L}_k$ we just set $\mu_1 = \cdots = \mu_k = 1$.[7] We formally define this stronger notion of self-reducibility.

Definition 6 (Random Self-reducibility). *A matrix distribution $\mathcal{D}_k$ (or the $\mathcal{D}_k$-MDDH problem) is defined to be random self-reducible if there exists a probabilistic polynomial-time transformation $\mathcal{R}$ such that on the input of any possible*

---

[7] Actually, these transformations do not randomize some 'badly selected' parameters, that is, when some $a_i = 0$ or $b_i = 0$. In practice, we can discard these values in the sampling algorithm, incurring only in a negligible difference, but here we are forced to include them due to the algebraic framework.

instance[8] $(q, \mathbb{G}, g, [\mathbf{A}], [\mathbf{z}])$ of the $\mathcal{D}_k$-MDDH problem, it outputs $([\widetilde{\mathbf{A}}], [\widetilde{\mathbf{z}}])$ with the following properties

1. if there exists $\mathbf{w} \in \mathbb{Z}_q^k$ such that $\mathbf{z} = \mathbf{A}\mathbf{w}$, then the probability distribution of $(q, \mathbb{G}, g, [\widetilde{\mathbf{A}}], [\widetilde{\mathbf{z}}])$ is statistically close to D_{real}.
2. otherwise, the probability distribution is statistically close to D_{random}.

where D_{real} and D_{random} are given in Definition 3.

Definition 7 (Quasi Random Self-reducibility). We say that $\mathcal{D}_k$ is quasi random self-reducible if there exists a transformation $\mathcal{R}$ fulfiling the properties required in Definition 6 only when the matrix $\mathbf{A}$ in the input instance of $\mathcal{R}$ belongs to a subset $\mathcal{X} \subset \mathbb{Z}_q^{(k+1) \times k}$ such that $\Pr[\mathbf{A} \notin \mathcal{X}; \mathbf{A} \leftarrow \mathcal{D}_k] \in negl$.

Clearly, for the above families, the composition of $\mathcal{T}$ and the map $(\mathbf{A}, \mathbf{z}) \mapsto (\mathbf{A}, \lambda\mathbf{z} + \mathbf{A}\mathbf{w})$, for random $\mathbf{w} \leftarrow \mathbb{Z}_q^k$ and $\lambda \leftarrow \mathbb{Z}_q^\times$, behaves as the transformation $\mathcal{R}$ in the previous definitions. This proves the following result.

Theorem 1. The matrix distributions $\mathcal{C}_k$, $\mathcal{SC}_k$, $\mathcal{L}_k$, $\mathcal{RL}_k$ and the uniform distribution are quasi random self-reducible[9] in the sense of Definition 7.

2.5   Generic Hardness of the MDDH Problems

Here we will focus on the case $\ell = k + 1$, as presented in [9]. However, in [11] more general results for the case $\ell > k + 1$ are given, and they are applied to the particular family $\mathcal{CI}_{k,d}$ in [15].

Given a polynomial matrix distribution $\mathcal{D}_k^{\mathbf{A}}$, the hardness of the $\mathcal{D}_k^{\mathbf{A}}$-MDDH problem in the k-linear generic group model (i.e., the hardness of $\mathcal{D}_k^{\mathbf{A}}$) is tightly related to the properties of the so-called *determinant polynomial* corresponding to $\mathcal{D}_k^{\mathbf{A}}$.

Definition 8 (Determinant Polynomial). Given a polynomial matrix distribution $\mathcal{D}_k^{\mathbf{A}}$, described by the polynomial map $\mathbf{A} : \mathbb{Z}_q^d \to \mathbb{Z}_q^{(k+1) \times k}$, the associated determinant polynomial $\mathfrak{d}_{\mathbf{A}} \in \mathbb{Z}_q[t_1, \ldots, t_d, z_1, \ldots, z_{k+1}]$ is defined as the determinant $\mathfrak{d}_{\mathbf{A}}(\mathbf{t}, \mathbf{z}) = \det(\mathbf{A}(\mathbf{t}) \| \mathbf{z})$.

Observe that developing the determinant by its last column, we can write

$$\mathfrak{d}_{\mathbf{A}}(\mathbf{t}, \mathbf{z}) = \sum_{i=1}^{k+1} \mathfrak{d}_{\mathbf{A},i}(\mathbf{t}) z_i \tag{2}$$

which means that $\mathfrak{d}_{\mathbf{A}}(\mathbf{t}, \mathbf{z})$ is linear (i.e., homogeneous of degree one) in $\mathbf{z}$.

---

[8] That is, $\mathcal{R}$ transforms every particular real instance into a randomly distributed real one, and the same for random instances. Therefore, $([\widetilde{\mathbf{A}}], [\widetilde{\mathbf{z}}])$ is independent of $([\mathbf{A}], [\mathbf{z}])$ for real and random instances.

[9] Indeed, $\mathcal{SC}_k$ can be shown to be random self-reducible by using a more sophisticated transformation leading to $a \mapsto a + \lambda$ for $\lambda \in \mathbb{Z}_q$.

Once we associate a polynomial $\mathfrak{d}_\mathbf{A}$ to the polynomial matrix distribution $\mathcal{D}_k^\mathbf{A}$, other mathematical objects are automatically defined, like the principal ideal $\mathfrak{I}_\mathbf{A} = (\mathfrak{d}_\mathbf{A}) \subset \mathbb{Z}_q[t, z]$ or the associated algebraic variety $V_\mathbf{A} = V(\mathfrak{I}_\mathbf{A}) = \{(t, z) \in \mathbb{Z}_q^d \times \mathbb{Z}_q^{k+1} \mid \mathfrak{d}_\mathbf{A}(t, z) = 0\}$[10]. It is precisely using these objects how the following hardness criterion is derived.

Theorem 2 (Determinant Hardness Criterion (from [9])). *Let $\mathcal{D}_k^\mathbf{A}$ be a polynomial matrix distribution, which outputs matrices $\mathbf{A}(t)$ for uniform $t \in \mathbb{Z}_q^d$. Let $\mathfrak{d}_\mathbf{A}$ be the associated determinant polynomial.*

1. *If all matrices $\mathbf{A}(t)$ have full rank even for t_i in the algebraic closure $\overline{\mathbb{Z}}_q$, then the determinant polynomial $\mathfrak{d}_\mathbf{A}$ is irreducible over $\overline{\mathbb{Z}}_q$.*
2. *If $\mathbf{A}(t)$ has degree one, $\mathfrak{d}_\mathbf{A}$ is irreducible over $\overline{\mathbb{Z}}_q$, and the total degree of $\mathfrak{d}_\mathbf{A}$ is $k + 1$, then $\mathcal{D}_k^\mathbf{A}$ is a hard matrix distribution (i.e., $\mathcal{D}_k^\mathbf{A}$-MDDH problem is hard in the generic k-linear group model). In particular, for any polynomial $\mathfrak{h} \in \mathbb{Z}_q[t, z]$, if $\mathfrak{h}((t, \mathbf{A}(t)w)) = 0$ for all $t \in \mathbb{Z}_q^d$ and $w \in \mathbb{Z}_q^k$, then $\mathfrak{h} \in \mathfrak{I}_\mathbf{A}$ (i.e., $\mathfrak{h}$ is a multiple of $\mathfrak{d}_\mathbf{A}$).*

The intuition behind this result is that in the generic k-linear group model[11], any successful strategy to solve the $\mathcal{D}_k^\mathbf{A}$-MDDH problem amounts to evaluate a known nonzero polynomial $\mathfrak{h}$ of degree at most k that vanishes at all points $(t, \mathbf{A}(t)w)$, for $t \in \mathbb{Z}_q^d$ and $w \in \mathbb{Z}_q^k$. The irreducibility of $\mathfrak{d}_\mathbf{A}$ is used to show that $\mathfrak{h}$ must belong to the principal ideal $\mathfrak{I}_\mathbf{A}$. Finally, the degree requirement for $\mathfrak{d}_\mathbf{A}$ just shows that no such polynomial $\mathfrak{h}$ exists.

This powerful result allows to directly prove at once the generic hardness of a whole family of MDDH problems, by just analyzing the properties of a particular polynomial, or a family of polynomials. For instance, in [9] the criterion is applied to the $\mathcal{SC}$, $\mathcal{C}$ and $\mathcal{L}$ families (actually, the hardness of $\mathcal{C}_k$ is implied by the hardness of $\mathcal{SC}_k$, and similarly with $\mathcal{RL}_k$ and $\mathcal{L}_k$, from the results on algebraic reductions given above).

3   A Partial Converse of Theorem 2

From now on, we restrict the study to the particular case of polynomial matrix distributions $\mathcal{D}_{\ell,k}^\mathbf{A}$ of degree one with $\ell = k + 1$, as considered also in Theorem 2. Namely, $\mathcal{D}_{\ell,k}^\mathbf{A}$ can be sampled by the map $\mathbf{A}(t) = \mathbf{A}_0 + \mathbf{A}_1 t_1 + \ldots + \mathbf{A}_d t_d$ for uniformly distributed $t = (t_1, \ldots, t_d) \in \mathbb{Z}_q^d$, and fixed matrices $\mathbf{A}_0, \ldots, \mathbf{A}_d \in \mathbb{Z}_q^{(k+1) \times k}$. This family covers the most useful instances among the matrix distributions, including $\mathcal{C}_k$, $\mathcal{L}_k$, $\mathcal{SC}_k$, $\mathcal{RL}_k$ and the uniform one. We also assume that the parameters $t_1, \ldots, t_d$ are all meaningful, that is, the map $\mathbf{A} : \mathbb{Z}_q^d \to \mathbb{Z}_q^{(k+1) \times k}$ is injective, or equivalently, $\mathbf{A}_1, \ldots, \mathbf{A}_d$ are linearly independent matrices. This in particular implies that the parameters $t_1, \ldots, t_d$ can be expressed as linear

---

[10] To properly define the variety we need to consider the algebraic closure of the field. But here we only consider the subset of rational points, *i.e.*, with coordinates in $\mathbb{Z}_q$.
[11] See Sect. 2.2 for details.

combinations of the entries of the matrix $\mathbf{A}(t)$. Therefore, there exist efficient (generic) algorithms computing $[t]$ from $[\mathbf{A}(t)]$, and vice versa. We call these polynomial matrix distributions *compact degree-one*.

Recall that the determinant polynomial $\mathfrak{d}_{\mathbf{A}}$ is defined as the determinant of $(\mathbf{A}(t)\|z)$ as a polynomial in $\mathbb{Z}_q[t,z]$, $\mathfrak{I}_{\mathbf{A}}$ is the ideal generated by $\mathfrak{d}_{\mathbf{A}}$, and $V_{\mathbf{A}}$ is the set of (rational) zeros of $\mathfrak{d}_{\mathbf{A}}$. For notational convenience, we also define the set $V_{\mathbf{A}}^{\mathrm{def}} = \{t \in \mathbb{Z}_q^d \mid \mathrm{rank}\, \mathbf{A}(t) < k\}$ (which is also the set of rational points in an algebraic variety).

We start the exposition with a few technical lemmas stating additional properties of the compact degree-one matrix distributions.

Lemma 2. *Define* $r = \max_{t\in\mathbb{Z}_q^d} \mathrm{rank}\, \mathbf{A}(t)$. *Then* $\mathrm{rank}\, \mathbf{A}(t) = r$ *with overwhelming probability, and there exists a nonzero polynomial* $\mathfrak{h} \in \mathbb{Z}_q[t,z]$ *of total degree at most* $r + 1$ *such that* $\mathfrak{h}(t, \mathbf{A}(t)w) = 0$ *for all* $t \in \mathbb{Z}_q^d$ *and* $w \in \mathbb{Z}_q^k$.

Proof. Clearly, there exists a r-minor of $\mathbf{A}(t)$ that is nonzero, as a polynomial in $\mathbb{Z}_q[t]$. By Schwartz-Zippel Lemma [17] this polynomial, whose degree cannot exceed $r < k$, can only vanish at a negligible fraction of $\mathbb{Z}_q^d$ (a fraction $\frac{r}{q}$), which proves that $\mathrm{rank}\, \mathbf{A}(t) = r$ with overwhelming probability. Let $\widehat{\mathbf{A}}(t)$ be any $(r + 1) \times r$ submatrix of $\mathbf{A}(t)$ containing the previous r-minor, and let $(\widehat{\mathbf{A}}(t)\|\widehat{z})$ be the same matrix but adding as an extra column the part of z corresponding to the rows of $\widehat{\mathbf{A}}(t)$. As before, $\mathrm{rank}\, \widehat{\mathbf{A}}(t) = r$ with overwhelming probability. In addition, $\mathrm{rank}(\widehat{\mathbf{A}}(t)\|\widehat{z}) = r + 1$ with overwhelming probability if $z \leftarrow \mathbb{Z}_q^\ell$, while $\mathrm{rank}(\widehat{\mathbf{A}}(t)\|\widehat{z}) \leq \mathrm{rank}(\mathbf{A}(t)\|z) \leq r$ when $z = \mathbf{A}(t)w$. Therefore $\mathfrak{h} = \det(\widehat{\mathbf{A}}(t)\|\widehat{z})$ fulfils the required properties: $\mathfrak{h}$ is a nonzero polynomial of total degree at most $r + 1$, and $\mathfrak{h}(t, \mathbf{A}(t)w) = 0$ for all $t \in \mathbb{Z}_q^d$ and $w \in \mathbb{Z}_q^k$. $\square$

Another interesting property of a hard matrix distribution $\mathcal{D}_{\ell,k}$ is the so-called k-elusiveness, introduced in [15].

Definition 9 (m-Elusiveness (from [15])). *A matrix distribution* $\mathcal{D}_{\ell,k}$ *is called m-elusive for some $m < \ell$ if for all m-dimensional subspaces $F \subset \mathbb{Z}_q^\ell$,* $\Pr(F \cap \ker \mathbf{A}^\top \neq \{\mathbf{0}\}) \in \mathrm{negl}$, *where the probability is computed with respect to* $\mathbf{A} \leftarrow \mathcal{D}_{\ell,k}$.

Lemma 3 (proved in [15]). *All hard matrix distributions* $\mathcal{D}_{\ell,k}$ *are k-elusive.*

We will need another technical lemma about the determinant polynomial of a hard compact degree-one matrix distribution, which essentially states that $\mathfrak{d}_{\mathbf{A}}$ cannot be constant along any line in the space $\mathbb{Z}_q^d \times \mathbb{Z}_q^{k+1}$.

Lemma 4. *Let* $\mathcal{D}_k^{\mathbf{A}}$ *be a hard compact degree-one matrix distribution with d parameters. If there exist vectors* $\boldsymbol{\tau} \in \mathbb{Z}_q^d$ *and* $\boldsymbol{\zeta} \in \mathbb{Z}_q^{k+1}$ *such that* $\mathfrak{d}_{\mathbf{A}}(t + \boldsymbol{\tau}, z + \boldsymbol{\zeta}) = \mathfrak{d}_{\mathbf{A}}(t, z)$, *for all* $t \in \mathbb{Z}_q^d$ *and* $z \in \mathbb{Z}_q^{k+1}$, *then necessarily* $(\boldsymbol{\tau}, \boldsymbol{\zeta}) = (\mathbf{0}, \mathbf{0})$.

Proof. Recall the linearity property of the determinant polynomial $\mathfrak{d}_{\mathbf{A}}(t, z_1 + z_2) = \mathfrak{d}_{\mathbf{A}}(t, z_1) + \mathfrak{d}_{\mathbf{A}}(t, z_2)$. In particular, $\mathfrak{d}_{\mathbf{A}}(t, z + \mathbf{A}(t)w) = \mathfrak{d}_{\mathbf{A}}(t, z)$ for any $w \in \mathbb{Z}_q^k$, since clearly $\mathfrak{d}_{\mathbf{A}}(t, \mathbf{A}(t)w) = 0$.

Using now that $\mathbf{A}(t + \tau) = \mathbf{A}(t) + \mathbf{B}$, where $\mathbf{B} = \sum_{i=1}^{d} \tau_i \mathbf{A}_i$, and $\mathfrak{d}_{\mathbf{A}}(t + \tau, z + \zeta) = \mathfrak{d}_{\mathbf{A}}(t, z)$ for any $z \in \mathbb{Z}_q^{k+1}$, we have for any $w \in \mathbb{Z}_q^k$,

$$\mathfrak{d}_{\mathbf{A}}(t+\tau, \mathbf{A}(t+\tau)w+\zeta) = \mathfrak{d}_{\mathbf{A}}(t, \mathbf{A}(t+\tau)w) = \mathfrak{d}_{\mathbf{A}}(t, \mathbf{A}(t)w+\mathbf{B}w) = \mathfrak{d}_{\mathbf{A}}(t, \mathbf{B}w)$$

and, on the other hand, by the linearity property

$$\mathfrak{d}_{\mathbf{A}}(t + \tau, \mathbf{A}(t + \tau)w + \zeta) = \mathfrak{d}_{\mathbf{A}}(t + \tau, \zeta) = \mathfrak{d}_{\mathbf{A}}(t, 0) = 0$$

Thus, $\mathfrak{d}_{\mathbf{A}}(t, \mathbf{B}w) = 0$ which implies that $\mathbf{B}w \in \operatorname{Im} \mathbf{A}(t)$ for all $w \in \mathbb{Z}_q^k$ and $t \in \mathbb{Z}_q^d \setminus V_{\mathbf{A}}^{\text{def}}$. Therefore, for all such t we have $\operatorname{Im} \mathbf{B} \subseteq \operatorname{Im} \mathbf{A}(t)$ or equivalently $\ker \mathbf{A}(t)^\top \subseteq \ker \mathbf{B}^\top$.

By the k-elusiveness property, this is only possible if $\dim \ker \mathbf{B}^\top > k$, that is, $\mathbf{B} = \mathbf{0}$. In addition, by the compactness property, necessarily $\tau = \mathbf{0}$. But now, for all $t \in \mathbb{Z}_q^d$, $\mathfrak{d}_{\mathbf{A}}(t, \zeta) = \mathfrak{d}_{\mathbf{A}}(t, 0) = 0$ which implies $\zeta \in \operatorname{Im} \mathbf{A}(t)$ for all $t \in \mathbb{Z}_q^d \setminus V_{\mathbf{A}}^{\text{def}}$. Then, $\ker \mathbf{A}(t)^\top$ is included in the orthogonal subspace $\{\zeta\}^\perp$, which contradicts again the k-elusiveness property, unless $\dim\{\zeta\}^\perp > k$ or equivalently $\zeta = \mathbf{0}$. □

Now we state and prove a partial converse of Theorem 2.[12]

Theorem 3. *Let $\mathcal{D}_k^{\mathbf{A}}$ be a hard compact degree-one matrix distribution, producing matrices $\mathbf{A}(t) = \mathbf{A}_0 + \mathbf{A}_1 t_1 + \ldots + \mathbf{A}_d t_d$. Then, the set $V_{\mathbf{A}}^{def}$ is a negligible fraction of $\mathbb{Z}_q^d$, and the determinant polynomial $\mathfrak{d}_{\mathbf{A}}$ has the following properties:*

1. *$\mathfrak{d}_{\mathbf{A}}$ is irreducible in $\overline{\mathbb{Z}}_q[t, z]$ with total degree $k + 1$.*
2. *$\mathfrak{d}_{\mathbf{A}}$ cannot be constant along any direction in the space $\mathbb{Z}_q^d \times \mathbb{Z}_q^{k+1}$, i.e., $\mathfrak{d}_{\mathbf{A}}(t + \tau, z + \zeta) = \mathfrak{d}_{\mathbf{A}}(t, z)$ for all $t \in \mathbb{Z}_q^d$ and all $z \in \mathbb{Z}_q^{k+1}$ only if $(\tau, \zeta) = (\mathbf{0}, \mathbf{0})$.*
3. *The polynomials $\mathfrak{d}_{\mathbf{A},1}, \ldots, \mathfrak{d}_{\mathbf{A},k+1}$ in Eq. 2 are linearly independent[13].*

Proof. If $\mathcal{D}_k^{\mathbf{A}}$ is hard then no nonzero polynomial $\mathfrak{h} \in \mathbb{Z}_q[t, z]$ of degree at most k fulfils $\mathfrak{h}(t, \mathbf{A}(t)w) = 0$ for all $t \in \mathbb{Z}_q^d$ and $w \in \mathbb{Z}_q^k$. Otherwise, a distinguisher only needs to check whether $\mathfrak{h}(t, z) = 0$ (using the k-linear map) to tell apart 'real' and 'random' instances of the $\mathcal{D}_k^{\mathbf{A}}$-MDDH problem.

Consider the maximal rank $r = \max_{t \in \mathbb{Z}_q^d} \operatorname{rank} \mathbf{A}(t)$. If $r < k$ then, according to Lemma 2, the $\mathcal{D}_k^{\mathbf{A}}$-MDDH problem is easy in a k-linear group (as shown also in [9]). Thus, it must be $r = k$, and the same lemma states in addition that $\operatorname{rank} \mathbf{A}(t) = k$ with overwhelming probability, or equivalently, $V_{\mathbf{A}}^{\text{def}}$ only holds a negligible fraction of the parameter space $\mathbb{Z}_q^d$. Actually, all instances (t, z) of the $\mathcal{D}_k^{\mathbf{A}}$-MDDH problem with $t \in V_{\mathbf{A}}^{\text{def}}$ are easy.

---

[12] A more limited converse of the same theorem appeared in [10], but for the special case of $d = 1$. It is worth mentioning that for $d = 1$, $V_{\mathbf{A}}^{\text{def}}$ is not only a negligible fraction of $\mathbb{Z}_q^d$, but it is the empty set.

[13] In [12] this property is named irredundancy of the matrix distribution.

Moreover, the total degree of the determinant polynomial $\mathfrak{d}_{\mathbf{A}}$ must be $k+1$ (it cannot be larger because the degree of $\mathbf{A}$ is one). Otherwise, we could let $\mathfrak{h} = \mathfrak{d}_{\mathbf{A}}$ and solve the $\mathcal{D}_k^{\mathbf{A}}$-MDDH problem, as explained in the first paragraph of the proof. Notice that $\mathfrak{d}_{\mathbf{A}}$ cannot be the zero polynomial because it would contradict the fact that rank $\mathbf{A}(t) = k$ with overwhelming probability.

Consider now the irreducibility of the determinant polynomial. If $\mathfrak{d}_{\mathbf{A}}$ were reducible in $\overline{\mathbb{Z}}_q[t, z]$, it follows that $\mathfrak{d}_{\mathbf{A}}$ can be split as $\mathfrak{d}_{\mathbf{A}} = \mathfrak{c}\mathfrak{d}_0$, where $\mathfrak{c} \in \overline{\mathbb{Z}}_q[t]$ and $\mathfrak{d}_0 \in \overline{\mathbb{Z}}_q[t, z]$ are nonconstant. Indeed, the degree of $\mathfrak{d}_{\mathbf{A}}$ in z is one. Thus, only one of the irreducible factors of $\mathfrak{d}_{\mathbf{A}}$ can depend explicitly on z, and its coefficients must be elements in the base field $\mathbb{Z}_q$ (as there is no other conjugate irreducible factor)[14]. Clearly, for any t such that $\mathfrak{c}(t) \neq 0$, we know that $\mathfrak{d}_0(t, \mathbf{A}(t)w) = 0$ for all $w \in \mathbb{Z}_q^k$. Hence, by Schwartz-Zippel lemma, as a polynomial in $\mathbb{Z}_q[t, w]$, $\mathfrak{d}_0(t, \mathbf{A}(t)w)$ is the zero polynomial. Again, we could use $\mathfrak{h} = \mathfrak{d}_0$ to solve the $\mathcal{D}_k^{\mathbf{A}}$-MDDH problem, since $\deg \mathfrak{d}_0 < \deg \mathfrak{d}_{\mathbf{A}} = k+1$.

On the other hand, under the conditions of the theorem Lemma 4 ensures that $\mathfrak{d}_{\mathbf{A}}$ cannot be constant along any direction in the space $\mathbb{Z}_q^d \times \mathbb{Z}_q^{k+1}$.

We now proceed in a similar way with the last item in the theorem statement. According to Eq. 2, any nontrivial linear dependency relation of the polynomials $\mathfrak{d}_{\mathbf{A},1}, \ldots, \mathfrak{d}_{\mathbf{A},k+1}$ can be written as

$$\mathfrak{d}_{\mathbf{A}}(t, \zeta) = \sum_{i=1}^{k+1} \mathfrak{d}_{\mathbf{A},i}(t)\zeta_i = 0$$

for a fixed nonzero $\zeta \in \mathbb{Z}_q^{k+1}$ and for all $t \in \mathbb{Z}_q^d$. Again, Lemma 4 implies that such nonzero vector ζ does not exist. $\square$

Notice that the last item in the theorem statement allow us to associate every hard polynomial matrix distribution of degree one $\mathcal{D}_k^{\mathbf{A}}$ with a polynomial vector space $X_{\mathbf{A}} \subset \mathbb{Z}_q[t]$ of dimension $k+1$, generated by $\mathfrak{d}_{\mathbf{A},1}, \ldots, \mathfrak{d}_{\mathbf{A},k+1}$. This association is actually at the heart of the polynomial view of MDDH problems, introduced in [12]. Moreover, since the total degree of $\mathfrak{d}_{\mathbf{A}}$ is $k+1$ then the maximum of the degrees of $\mathfrak{d}_{\mathbf{A},1}, \ldots, \mathfrak{d}_{\mathbf{A},k+1}$ is exactly k. Clearly, for $d=1$ the only possible choice is $X_{\mathbf{A}} = \mathbb{Z}_q[t]_{\leq k}$, the vector space of all polynomials of degree at most k. We will show later that this actually means that there is essentially a unique hard polynomial matrix distribution of degree one with only one parameter, and this matrix distribution is the symmetric cascade distribution $\mathcal{SC}_k$. This was proved for the first time in [10] by means of completely different algebraic tools, more related to matrix Jordan normal forms. This uniqueness does not directly extend to the case $d \geq 2$, because the number of possible choices for the vector space $X_{\mathbf{A}}$ increases fast with d.

4   MDDH Problems of the Same Size

The goal of this section is to obtain some criteria to analyze in a compact way the possible black-box reductions between MDDH problems, in terms of

---

[14] All these facts are indeed used in [9] to prove Theorem 2.

the determinant polynomials or other mathematical objects associated to the matrix distributions. The idea is then to avoid the classical case-by-case approach to show reductions or separation results between computational problems, and deal instead with large families of problems at once. As explained in the previous section, we restrict ourselves to the study of compact degree-one matrix distributions, but we also restrict to the case of reductions between $\mathcal{D}_k$-MDDH problems, that is with the same size and with $\ell = k + 1$.

In a more general approach we would take into consideration the possible reductions between two $\mathcal{D}_{k_1}$-MDDH and $\mathcal{D}_{k_2}$-MDDH problems with $k_1 < k_2$. However, since any $\mathcal{D}_k$-MDDH problem is easy in a m-linear group with $m > k$, then $\mathcal{D}_{k_1}$-MDDH and $\mathcal{D}_{k_2}$-MDDH are separated by an oracle computing a (k_1+1)-linear map, meaning that the large problem could remain hard while the small one is clearly easy. Therefore, we focus only on the case $k_2 = k_1$, in which there is no a priori hardness implication.

Recall that the determinant polynomial $\mathfrak{d}_\mathbf{A}$ is defined as the determinant of $(\mathbf{A}(t)\|z)$ as a polynomial in $\mathbb{Z}_q[t, z]$, $\mathfrak{I}_\mathbf{A}$ is the ideal generated by $\mathfrak{d}_\mathbf{A}$, $V_\mathbf{A}$ is the set of (rational) zeros of $\mathfrak{d}_\mathbf{A}$, and $V_\mathbf{A}^{\text{def}} = \{t \in \mathbb{Z}_q^d \mid \text{rank}\,\mathbf{A}(t) < k\}$.

Once the properties of the determinant polynomials of hard polynomial matrix distributions of degree one are understood, we can find a purely algebraic criterion for the existence of generic reductions among them. Indeed, as usually in the generic algebraic models, the criterion either gives an explicit reduction or completely rules out its existence.

Theorem 4. *Let $\mathcal{D}_k^\mathbf{A}$ and $\mathcal{D}_k^\mathbf{B}$ be hard compact degree-one matrix distributions, producing matrices $\mathbf{A}(t) = \mathbf{A}_0 + \mathbf{A}_1 t_1 + \ldots + \mathbf{A}_d t_d$ and $\mathbf{B}(s) = \mathbf{B}_0 + \mathbf{B}_1 s_1 + \ldots + \mathbf{B}_e s_e$, and let $\mathfrak{d}_\mathbf{A}$ and $\mathfrak{d}_\mathbf{B}$ be the corresponding determinant polynomials. If there exists a generic black-box reduction from the $\mathcal{D}_k^\mathbf{A}$-MDDH problem to the $\mathcal{D}_k^\mathbf{B}$-MDDH problem, then there exists a polynomial map $f : \mathbb{Z}_q^{d+k+1} \to \mathbb{Z}_q^{e+k+1}$ of degree one such that $\lambda \mathfrak{d}_\mathbf{A} = \mathfrak{d}_\mathbf{B} \circ f$ for some nonzero constant $\lambda \in \mathbb{Z}_q$.*

Proof. Because of the compactness of the two matrix distributions we know that the matrices $\mathbf{A}_1, \ldots, \mathbf{A}_d$ are linearly independent, and so are $\mathbf{B}_1, \ldots, \mathbf{B}_e$. Then there are efficient linear maps computing $[t]$ from $[\mathbf{A}(t)]$, and $[s]$ from $[\mathbf{B}(s)]$. Thus, we can consider the instances of the two $\mathcal{D}_k^\mathbf{A}$-MDDH and $\mathcal{D}_k^\mathbf{B}$-MDDH problems respectively defined by $([t], [z])$ and $([s], [u])$.

Let $\mathcal{R}$ be a black-box reduction in the generic k-linear group model from the $\mathcal{D}_k^\mathbf{A}$-MDDH problem to the $\mathcal{D}_k^\mathbf{B}$-MDDH problem, and assume that $\mathcal{D}_k^\mathbf{A}$ is a hard matrix distribution, and there is no polynomial map $f : \mathbb{Z}_q^{d+k+1} \to \mathbb{Z}_q^{e+k+1}$ of degree one such that $\lambda \mathfrak{d}_\mathbf{A} = \mathfrak{d}_\mathbf{B} \circ f$ for some nonzero constant $\lambda \in \mathbb{Z}_q$. We use a sequence of games in order to prove that $\mathcal{R}$ can only have a negligible advantage even when it has access to an oracle solving the $\mathcal{D}_k^\mathbf{B}$-MDDH problem with overwhelming probability. Each game in the sequence, Game G_i, is played by the reduction $\mathcal{R}$ and a (possibly inefficient) challenger $\mathcal{C}_i$, specific for that game, that simulates all the environment for $\mathcal{R}$. Namely it provides the input for $\mathcal{R}$, and simulates the oracle $\mathcal{O}$ solving the $\mathcal{D}_k^\mathbf{B}$-MDDH problem with overwhelming probability and the generic group oracle.

Notice that in the generic k-linear group model $\mathcal{R}$'s input is an encoding of an instance of $\mathcal{D}_k^A$-MDDH, $([t], [z])$, consisting only of elements in $\mathbb{G}$. These group elements are generated by evaluating a polynomial map $\mathfrak{h}$ at a random point. Namely, for a 'real' instance $\mathfrak{h}_1(t, w) = (t, \mathbf{A}(t)w) = (t, z)$, and for a 'random' instance, $\mathfrak{h}_0$ is the identity map. Observe that both polynomials $\mathfrak{h}_0$, $\mathfrak{h}_1$ have degree 1. For notational convenience, we will denote 'real' instances by $b = 1$ and 'random' instances by $b = 0$, where b is a variable defined by the challenger. Thus, in the generic k-linear group model every group element $[y] \in \mathbb{G}$ or $[y]_T \in \mathbb{G}_T$ handled by $\mathcal{R}$ can be seen as a polynomial in the formal variables (T, W) or (T, Z), depending on the type of input instance given to $\mathcal{R}$. To give more notational uniformity to the proof we will consider that the polynomial Y associated to a group element $[y]$ or $[y]_T$ depends on the variables (T, Z), formally representing the entries of (t, z). Thus, $Y \in \mathbb{Z}_q[T, Z]$ but then composing Y with the sampling polynomial, $\mathfrak{h} = Y \circ \mathfrak{h}_b$ is either in $\mathbb{Z}_q[T, W]$ if $b = 1$, or it is in $\mathbb{Z}_q[T, Z]$ if $b = 0$.[15]

The combination of the generic k-linear group model with algorithms with additional oracle access is not a trivial task, since depending of the oracle definition, some essential information about the representation of the group elements can be leaked to the algorithm, thus breaking the usual arguments in the generic model proofs. For this reason we give a more detailed proof that analyzes step-by-step the transition between a generic k-linear group model based on random encodings to its purely algebraic counterpart. It is worth noticing that the methodology used here is specific for the MDDH problem structure, and therefore it cannot be directly applied to other scenarios.

In the proof we will consider two different simulation strategies for both the generic group oracle and the oracle $\mathcal{O}$. We describe them before detailing the sequence of games.

Real (value-based) simulation of the generic group oracle. This is the usual strategy for the simulation. The challenger maintains two tables $\mathcal{T}_1$, $\mathcal{T}_k$ with entries $(y, Y, \mathfrak{h}, L_y)$, where $y \in \mathbb{Z}_q$, $Y \in \mathbb{Z}_q[T, Z]$ is a polynomial representing y, $\mathfrak{h} = Y \circ \mathfrak{h}_b$ ($\mathfrak{h}_b$ is the sampling polynomial defined above), and L_y is a string called 'label', randomly drawn from a large enough set (making hard for $\mathcal{R}$ to guess a valid label).[16] The tuple $(y, Y, \mathfrak{h}, L_y)$ represents either the group element $[y]$ or $[y]_T$, depending on the table it belongs to. The tables are initialized with $(0, 0, 0, L_0)$ and $(1, 1, 1, L_1)$ and $(0, 0, 0, L_{0,k})$ and $(1, 1, 1, L_{1,k})$, for the neutral element and generator of $\mathbb{G}$ and $\mathbb{G}_T$. Group elements in the input of $\mathcal{R}$, $([t], [z])$, are replaced by freshly generated labels, which are stored in the table $\mathcal{T}_1$ along with their discrete logarithms (t, z) and the corresponding formal variables T, Z and their composition with $\mathfrak{h}_b$.

All operations queried by $\mathcal{R}$ to the generic group oracle are performed on the discrete logarithms stored in the tables and on the associated polynomials. For

---

[15] Indeed, the polynomial Y models what $\mathcal{R}$ knows about $[y]$ in the generic k-linear group model, while the challenger also knows $\mathfrak{h}$, or even the discrete logarithm y.

[16] It suffices, for instance, taking a set of size greater than q^5.

instance, for a query $\mathsf{GroupOp}(L_1, L_2)$, two tuples $(y_1, Y_1, \mathfrak{y}_1, L_1)$, $(y_2, Y_2, \mathfrak{y}_2, L_2)$ are located at either one of the tables $\mathcal{T}_1$ or $\mathcal{T}_k$. If a tuple $(y_1 + y_2, Y_3, \mathfrak{y}_3, L_3)$ already exists in the same table then L_3 is answered to $\mathcal{R}$. Otherwise, a fresh random label L_3 is generated, the tuple $(y_1 + y_2, Y_1 + Y_2, \mathfrak{y}_1 + \mathfrak{y}_2, L_3)$ is added to the table and L_3 is answered to $\mathcal{R}$. The other oracle queries $\mathsf{GroupInv}(L_1)$ and $\mathsf{GroupML}(L_1, \ldots, L_k)$ work similarly, except that in the last case labels $L_1, \ldots, L_k$ are looked only at table $\mathcal{T}_1$ and the resulting tuple is added to table $\mathcal{T}_k$. Any improper query (e.g., containing an unknown or invalid label) made by $\mathcal{R}$ is rejected by the oracle.

Observe that the polynomials stored in the tables are unused in this simulation. But always in any tuple $(y, Y, \mathfrak{y}, L_y)$, y is the result of evaluating Y at the point $(\boldsymbol{t}, \boldsymbol{z})$ sampled by the challenger (or evaluating $\mathfrak{y}$ at either $(\boldsymbol{t}, \boldsymbol{w})$ if $b = 1$ or $(\boldsymbol{t}, \boldsymbol{z})$ if $b = 0$).

Algebraic (polynomial-based) simulation of the generic group oracle. In this simulation the discrete logarithms stored in the tables are no longer used, and the polynomial components are used instead. Namely, in a query $\mathsf{GroupOp}(L_1, L_2)$, instead of looking for a tuple $(y_1 + y_2, Y_3, \mathfrak{y}_3, L_3)$, it looks for $(y_3, Y_3, \mathfrak{y}_1 + \mathfrak{y}_2, L_3)$. Notice that now a label is not associated to a true group element, but to an algebraic relation with the parameters used in the sampling procedure. Therefore, the two simulations will differ when after some query to the real generic group oracle there exist two different tuples $(y_1, Y_1, \mathfrak{y}_1, L_1)$, $(y_2, Y_2, \mathfrak{y}_2, L_2)$ in the same table such that $y_1 = y_2$ while $\mathfrak{y}_1 \neq \mathfrak{y}_2$. This implies that the non-zero polynomial $\mathfrak{y}_2 - \mathfrak{y}_1$ vanishes at the random point $((\boldsymbol{t}, \boldsymbol{w})$ if $b = 1$ or $(\boldsymbol{t}, \boldsymbol{z})$ if $b = 0)$ used in the sampling procedure.

In a standard proof in the generic k-linear group model we can easily upper bound the probability that such a difference occurs between the two simulation strategies, by just considering the degree of the polynomials and applying Schwartz-Zippel lemma. However, things are not so simple when $\mathcal{R}$ has access to extra oracles, that could leak some information about the group elements outside of the generic k-linear group model. We then consider also an algebraic simulation of the additional oracle $\mathcal{O}$.

For technical reasons, we need to ensure that only 'good' instances of $\mathcal{D}_k^A$-MDDH and $\mathcal{D}_k^B$-MDDH are handled by $\mathcal{R}$, i.e., instances with $\mathrm{rank}\,\mathbf{A}(\boldsymbol{t}) = \mathrm{rank}\,\mathbf{B}(\boldsymbol{s}) = k$. This is not an issue since for any black-box reduction $\mathcal{R}$ there exists another one $\mathcal{R}'$ with at least the same advantage solving $\mathcal{D}_k^A$-MDDH, and running essentially within the same time, fulfilling the previous requirement. The only differences between both reductions are that $\mathcal{R}'$ directly solves any instance $([\boldsymbol{t}], [\boldsymbol{z}])$ of $\mathcal{D}_k^A$-MDDH with $\mathrm{rank}\,\mathbf{A}(\boldsymbol{t}) < k$ via the k-linear map (as already described in the proof of Theorem 3), and all queries $([\boldsymbol{s}], [\boldsymbol{u}])$ to the oracle $\mathcal{O}$ made by $\mathcal{R}$ with $\mathrm{rank}\,\mathbf{B}(\boldsymbol{s}) < k$ are directly solved by $\mathcal{R}'$ itself, also with the k-linear map. From now on, we will assume that $\mathcal{R} = \mathcal{R}'$.

Real (value-based) simulation of the oracle $\mathcal{O}$. We will simulate an oracle $\mathcal{O}$ that solves the $\mathcal{D}_k^B$-MDDH problem with overwhelming probability. Since we are considering $\mathcal{R} = \mathcal{R}'$, we only deal with instances $([\boldsymbol{s}], [\boldsymbol{u}])$ such that $\mathrm{rank}\,\mathbf{B}(\boldsymbol{s}) = k$.

With this restriction, $\boldsymbol{u} \in \operatorname{Im} \mathbf{B}(\boldsymbol{s})$ if and only if $\det(\mathbf{B}(\boldsymbol{s})\|\boldsymbol{u}) = 0$, or equivalently, $\mathfrak{d}_\mathbf{B}(\boldsymbol{s}, \boldsymbol{u}) = 0$. Thus, we define $\mathcal{O}$ to output 1 if and only if $\mathfrak{d}_\mathbf{B}(\boldsymbol{s}, \boldsymbol{u}) = 0$. Notice that 'real' instances are correctly solved with probability one, while 'random' instances are solved correctly only with probability $1 - 1/q$, because the latter instances include the former ones.[17] In this simulation, in order to compute $\mathfrak{d}_\mathbf{B}(\boldsymbol{s}, \boldsymbol{u})$ the challenger needs the real values of $([\boldsymbol{s}], [\boldsymbol{u}])$. But in the generic k-linear group model (either value-based or polynomial-based one) the simulator can recover the discrete logarithms $(\boldsymbol{s}, \boldsymbol{u})$ from the labels queried by $\mathcal{R}$ and the table $\mathcal{T}_1$, maintained by the generic group oracle. As before, any improper query (e.g., containing an unknown or invalid label) made by $\mathcal{R}$ is rejected by the oracle. Once $(\boldsymbol{s}, \boldsymbol{u})$ are known, the challenger directly evaluates $\mathfrak{d}_\mathbf{B}(\boldsymbol{s}, \boldsymbol{u})$ and obtains the oracle answer.

Algebraic (polynomial-based) simulation of the oracle $\mathcal{O}$. Similarly as happens to the generic group oracle, in the algebraic version the challenger retrieves from the table $\mathcal{T}_1$ the polynomials $(\boldsymbol{S}, \boldsymbol{U})$ corresponding to the labels queried by $\mathcal{R}$, and not the discrete logarithms. This means that the simulator obtains a polynomial map f of degree one,[18] expressing the variables $(\boldsymbol{S}, \boldsymbol{U})$ as polynomials in $(\boldsymbol{T}, \boldsymbol{Z})$. Now the challenger computes the composition $\mathfrak{g} = \mathfrak{d}_\mathbf{B} \circ f \circ \mathfrak{h}_b$, which is also a polynomial. If $\mathfrak{g} = 0$ (as a polynomial) then the oracle answer is set to 1, otherwise the answer is 0. Again, both simulations can differ only when $\mathfrak{g}$ is a non-zero polynomial but it vanishes at the random point $((\boldsymbol{t}, \boldsymbol{w})$ or $(\boldsymbol{t}, \boldsymbol{z}))$ used in the sampling procedure.

Essentially, switching from the value-based simulation to the polynomial-based one means delaying the sampling of the parameters, which could cause some inconsistencies in the simulation. We introduce a sequence of games such that the oracles switch gradually from one model to the other, and we bound the error probability in each step in the sequence. Let Q be the number of calls to $\mathcal{O}$ made by $\mathcal{R}$, let n_i for $i = 1, \ldots, Q$ be the number of calls to the generic group oracle made by $\mathcal{R}$ before the i-th oracle call to $\mathcal{O}$, and let n_∞ be the total number of calls to the generic group oracle made by $\mathcal{R}$.

Game $G_{real,b}$, $b \in \{0,1\}$: This game perfectly simulates the environment for $\mathcal{R}$ as a distinguisher for the $\mathcal{D}_k^\mathrm{A}$-MDDH problem (fed with a 'real' instance if $b = 1$, and a 'random' instance if $b = 0$), with oracle access to a solver for the $\mathcal{D}_k^\mathrm{B}$-MDDH problem, that answers correctly with an overwhelming probability. In this game, the challenger $\mathcal{C}_{real,b}$ initializes the tables $\mathcal{T}_1$ and $\mathcal{T}_k$ and computes the input labels for $\mathcal{R}$, as explained in the previous paragraph "Real (value-based) simulation of the generic group oracle". Then $\mathcal{C}_{real,b}$ uses the real simulation of both the generic group oracle and the oracle $\mathcal{O}$. Finally, $\mathcal{C}_{real,b}$ just forwards $\mathcal{R}$'s output bit.

---

[17] This problem could be overcome by redefining the MDDH problems as telling apart 'real' from non-'real' instances.

[18] Observe that all the group elements considered here are in $\mathbb{G}$, and the group operation in $\mathbb{G}$ corresponds to linear combinations of the associated polynomials.

Game $G_{i,b}$, $i = 1, \ldots, Q$, $b \in \{0, 1\}$: The challenger performs the same initialization as $\mathcal{C}_{\text{real},b}$, but it uses instead the algebraic simulation of both the generic group oracle and the oracle $\mathcal{O}$, until $\mathcal{R}$ makes the i-th query to $\mathcal{O}$. Then, $\mathcal{C}_{i,b}$ switches to the real simulation to answer this query and all subsequent queries to the two oracles. Finally, $\mathcal{C}_{i,b}$ just forwards $\mathcal{R}$'s output bit.

Game $G'_{i,b}$, $i = 1, \ldots, Q$, $b \in \{0, 1\}$: The challenger $\mathcal{C}'_{i,b}$ only differs from $\mathcal{C}_{i,b}$ in that it uses the algebraic simulation also to answer the i-th query to $\mathcal{O}$ (thus, the switching point is moved to just after answering that query).

Game $G_{\text{alg},b}$, $b \in \{0, 1\}$: The challenger performs the same initialization as $\mathcal{C}_{\text{real},b}$, but it uses instead the algebraic simulation of both the generic group oracle and the oracle $\mathcal{O}$ all the time. Finally, $\mathcal{C}_{i,b}$ just forwards $\mathcal{R}$'s output bit.

Now we analyze the differences between the games. It should be mentioned that during the simulation, $\mathcal{R}$ itself can partially maintain the tables $\mathcal{T}_1$ and $\mathcal{T}_k$. Namely, it can associate each label L_y to the corresponding polynomial Y.

Step $G_{real,b} \to G_{1,b}$, $b \in \{0, 1\}$: The only possible difference between games can occur if in some query to the generic group oracle before the first query to $\mathcal{O}$ it happens that there exist two different tuples $(y_1, Y_1, \mathfrak{y}_1, L_1)$, $(y_2, Y_2, \mathfrak{y}_2, L_2)$ in the same table ($\mathcal{T}_1$ or $\mathcal{T}_k$) such that $y_1 = y_2$ while $\mathfrak{y}_1 \neq \mathfrak{y}_2$, which implies that the non-zero polynomial $\mathfrak{y}_2 - \mathfrak{y}_1$ vanishes at the random point $((t, w)$ if $b = 1$ or (t, z) if $b = 0)$ used in the sampling procedure. Lets call this event $F_{1,b}$. Then, by Schwartz-Zippel lemma,

$$\Pr[F_{1,b}] \leq \binom{n_1}{2} \frac{k}{q}$$

since there are at most $\binom{n_1}{2}$ different pairs of polynomials $(\mathfrak{y}_1, \mathfrak{y}_2)$ in the tables. Indeed, the degree of the polynomial $\mathfrak{y}_2 - \mathfrak{y}_1$ is upper bounded by k, since the sampling polynomial $\mathfrak{h}_b$ has degree 1.

Step $G_{i,b} \to G'_{i,b}$, $b \in \{0, 1\}$, $1 \leq i \leq Q$: The games are identical until the i-th query to $\mathcal{O}$ is made. Moreover, at this point, conditioned to b, the view of $\mathcal{R}$ is independent of the true values (t, z) if $b = 0$, or (t, w) if $b = 1$. The only difference between the two games can occur because of the simulation of $\mathcal{O}$ in this query. Namely, there exists a nonzero polynomial $\mathfrak{g} = \partial_{\mathbf{B}} \circ f \circ \mathfrak{h}_b$, of degree at most $\deg \partial_{\mathbf{B}} = k + 1$ that vanishes at the random point $((t, w)$ or $(t, z))$ used in the sampling procedure. Lets call this event $F'_{i,b}$. Again, by Schwartz-Zippel lemma,

$$\Pr[F'_{i,b}] \leq \frac{k + 1}{q}.$$

Step $G'_{i,b} \to G_{i+1,b}$, $b \in \{0, 1\}$, $1 \leq i \leq Q - 1$: The games proceed identically until the i-th query to $\mathcal{O}$ is answered. Again, at this point, conditioned to b, the view of $\mathcal{R}$ is independent of the true values (t, z) if $b = 0$, or (t, w) if $b = 1$. As in the step $G_{real,b} \to G_{1,b}$, the only difference between games is due to the simulation of the generic group oracle. Lets call $F_{i+1,b}$ to the event that between the i-th and the $(i + 1)$-th calls to $\mathcal{O}$, as a consequence of a query to the generic group oracle, there exist two different tuples $(y_1, Y_1, \mathfrak{y}_1, L_1)$, $(y_2, Y_2, \mathfrak{y}_2, L_2)$ in the same table ($\mathcal{T}_1$ or $\mathcal{T}_k$) such that $y_1 = y_2$ while $\mathfrak{y}_1 \neq \mathfrak{y}_2$, but at least one of them is generated within this period. By Schwartz-Zippel lemma,

$$\Pr[F_{i+1,b}] \leq \left(\binom{n_{i+1}}{2} - \binom{n_i}{2} \right) \frac{k}{q}.$$

Step $G'_{Q,b} \to G_{alg,b}$, $b \in \{0,1\}$: This step follows exactly the same argument as any other $G'_{i,b} \to G_{i+1,b}$ with $i < Q$. Therefore, we define $F_{alg,b}$ accordingly, and

$$\Pr[F_{alg,b}] \leq \left(\binom{n_\infty}{2} - \binom{n_Q}{2} \right) \frac{k}{q}.$$

Step $G_{alg,0} \to G_{alg,1}$: As a final step, we argue that the two games must be identical. Otherwise, either $\mathcal{D}_k^{\mathbf{A}}$ is not a hard matrix distribution, or there exists a polynomial map $f : \mathbb{Z}_q^{d+k+1} \to \mathbb{Z}_q^{e+k+1}$ of degree one such that $\lambda \mathfrak{d}_{\mathbf{A}} = \mathfrak{d}_{\mathbf{B}} \circ f$ for some nonzero constant $\lambda \in \mathbb{Z}_q$. Firstly let us assume that the first difference in the oracle answers given to $\mathcal{R}$ occurs in a query to the generic group oracle. Then there exists two different tuples $(y_1, Y_1, \mathfrak{y}_1, L_1)$, $(y_2, Y_2, \mathfrak{y}_2, L_2)$ in the same table ($\mathcal{T}_1$ or $\mathcal{T}_k$) such that $\mathfrak{y}_1 = \mathfrak{y}_2$ in one game while $\mathfrak{y}_1 \neq \mathfrak{y}_2$ in the other. But this can only happen if $Y_1 \neq Y_2$ and $Y_1 \circ \mathfrak{y}_1 = Y_2 \circ \mathfrak{y}_1$, because $\mathfrak{h}_0$ is the identity map. Therefore, by Theorem 2 the existence of the polynomial $Y_2 - Y_1$, which has degree at most k, contradicts the fact that $\mathcal{D}_k^{\mathbf{A}}$ is a hard matrix distribution.

Suppose now that the first difference between games occur in a query to $\mathcal{O}$. This implies that there exists a polynomial map f of degree one such that the composition $\mathfrak{g} = \mathfrak{d}_{\mathbf{B}} \circ f \circ \mathfrak{h}_b$ is the zero polynomial only in one of the games. Again, using that $\mathfrak{h}_0$ is the identity, it must happen that $\mathfrak{d}_{\mathbf{B}} \circ f \neq 0$ and $\mathfrak{d}_{\mathbf{B}} \circ f \circ \mathfrak{h}_1 = 0$. But then, Theorem 2 applied to the hard matrix distribution $\mathcal{D}_k^{\mathbf{A}}$ implies that $\mathfrak{d}_{\mathbf{B}} \circ f$ is a multiple of $\mathfrak{d}_{\mathbf{A}}$. Finally, $k+1 = \deg \mathfrak{d}_{\mathbf{A}} \leq \deg(\mathfrak{d}_{\mathbf{B}} \circ f) \leq \deg \mathfrak{d}_{\mathbf{B}} = k+1$ and then $\mathfrak{d}_{\mathbf{B}} \circ f$ can only be a nonzero scalar multiple of $\mathfrak{d}_{\mathbf{A}}$, which contradicts the assumption about the nonexistence of such map f.

Summing up, using the triangle inequality, the advantage of $\mathcal{R}$ solving the $\mathcal{D}_k^{\mathbf{A}}$-MDDH problem is

$$|\Pr[G_{real,1}[\mathcal{R}] = 1] - \Pr[G_{real,0}[\mathcal{R}] = 1]| \leq$$
$$\leq \Pr[F_{alg,1}] + \Pr[F_{alg,0}] + \sum_{i=1}^{Q} \left(\Pr[F'_{i,1}] + \Pr[F_{i,1}] + \Pr[F_{i,0}] + \Pr[F'_{i,0}] \right) \leq$$
$$\leq \frac{n_\infty^2 k}{q} + \frac{2Q(k+1)}{q} \in negl \qquad \qquad \square$$

Not all polynomial maps of degree one can actually fulfil the equation $\lambda \mathfrak{d}_{\mathbf{A}} = \mathfrak{d}_{\mathbf{B}} \circ f$. In particular, any such f must be injective.

Lemma 5. *Let $\mathcal{D}_k^{\mathbf{A}}$ and $\mathcal{D}_k^{\mathbf{B}}$ be as in Theorem 4. Any polynomial map of degree one such that $\lambda \mathfrak{d}_{\mathbf{A}} = \mathfrak{d}_{\mathbf{B}} \circ f$ for a nonzero $\lambda \in \mathbb{Z}_q$ is injective.*

Proof. For any non-injective map f there exists $(\tau, \zeta) \in \mathbb{Z}_q^d \times \mathbb{Z}_q^{k+1} \setminus \{(0,0)\}$ such that $f(\tau, \zeta) = f(0,0)$. Indeed, since f is a polynomial map of degree one, we can write $f(t, z) = f(0,0) + g(t, z)$ where the map g is linear. Then, for all $t, \tau \in \mathbb{Z}_q^d$ and all $z, \zeta \in \mathbb{Z}_q^{k+1}$,

$$f(t+\tau, z+\zeta) - f(t, z) = g(t+\tau, z+\zeta) - g(t, z) = g(\tau, \zeta) = f(\tau, \zeta) - f(0,0)$$

Then, any collision $f(t_1, z_1) = f(t_2, z_2)$ implies $f(\tau, \zeta) = f(0,0)$ for $\tau = t_1 - t_2$ and $\zeta = z_1 - z_2$. Conversely, $f(\tau, \zeta) = f(0,0)$ implies $f(t+\tau, z+\zeta) = f(t, z)$ for all $t \in \mathbb{Z}_q^d$ and $z \in \mathbb{Z}_q^{k+1}$. Now, from the equation $\lambda \eth_{\mathbf{A}} = \eth_{\mathbf{B}} \circ f$ we know that $\eth_{\mathbf{A}}(t+\tau, z+\zeta) = \lambda \eth_{\mathbf{B}}(f(t+\tau, z+\zeta)) = \lambda \eth_{\mathbf{B}}(f(t, z)) = \eth_{\mathbf{A}}(t, z)$ for all $t \in \mathbb{Z}_q^d$ and $z \in \mathbb{Z}_q^{k+1}$, which contradicts Lemma 4 unless $(\tau, \zeta) = (0,0)$. This finally proves the injectivity of f. □

The necessary injectivity of the map f gives us the following result, that essentially claims that a successful generic black-box reduction between MDDH problems cannot reduce the amount of randomness in the problem instance.

Corollary 1. *Let $\mathcal{D}_k^{\mathbf{A}}$ and $\mathcal{D}_k^{\mathbf{B}}$ be as in Theorem 4. If there exists a generic black-box reduction from the $\mathcal{D}_k^{\mathbf{A}}$-MDDH problem to the $\mathcal{D}_k^{\mathbf{B}}$-MDDH problem, then $e \geq d$.*

We now address the natural question about whether the converse of Theorem 4 is also true. We easily show that the converse actually holds, but for reductions using a perfect oracle (*i.e.*, that correctly solves all instances of the problem). Building a more general reduction from the map f, working with imperfect oracles, is a bit more involved. Indeed, it requires some extra properties of f, or some random self-reducibility properties of the MDDH problems.

Theorem 5. *Let $\mathcal{D}_k^{\mathbf{A}}$ and $\mathcal{D}_k^{\mathbf{B}}$ be as in Theorem 4. If there exists a degree one polynomial map $f : \mathbb{Z}_q^{d+k+1} \to \mathbb{Z}_q^{e+k+1}$ such that $\lambda \eth_{\mathbf{A}} = \eth_{\mathbf{B}} \circ f$ for some nonzero constant $\lambda \in \mathbb{Z}_q$, then*

1. *there exists a black-box deterministic reduction from the $\mathcal{D}_k^{\mathbf{A}}$-MDDH problem to the $\mathcal{D}_k^{\mathbf{B}}$-MDDH problem, using a single oracle call, that succeeds with overwhelming probability if the oracle is perfect.*
2. *if in addition f is surjective, then the above reduction is actually a tight black-box reduction using a single oracle call, for any imperfect oracle.*
3. *otherwise, if $\mathcal{D}_k^{\mathbf{B}}$ is random self-reducible (see Definition 6)[19], then there also exists a (probabilistic) tight black-box reduction with the same properties.*

Proof. To prove the theorem, we just show a reduction $\mathcal{R}$ making a single oracle call, based on the map f. Namely, on the input of an instance $([t], [z])$ of $\mathcal{D}_k^{\mathbf{A}}$-MDDH, $\mathcal{R}$ computes $([s], [u])$ by applying f to it. Observe that these computations only involve group operations in $\mathbb{G}$, since $\deg f = 1$. Then $\mathcal{R}$ queries the oracle on $([s], [u])$ and just forwards its answer.

---

[19] If it is only quasi random self-reducible, then one have to additionally check whether the image of f intersects properly with the set $\mathcal{X}$ of randomizable instances (see again Definition 7 for more details).

For convenience, we classify the problem instances $([t], [z])$ of $\mathcal{D}_k^A$-MDDH (we omit here $(q, \mathbb{G}, g)$ for simplicity) into four types: 'good real', 'bad real', 'good non-real', 'bad non-real'. Here 'real' refers to instances such that $z \in \text{Im}\,\mathbf{A}(t)$, while 'bad' corresponds to $t \in V_A^{\text{def}}$. Let $\mathcal{Y}_A$ and $\mathcal{N}_A$ respectively denote the sets of good real and good non-real instances, and $U_{\mathcal{Y}_A}$ and $U_{\mathcal{N}_A}$ the corresponding uniform probability distributions. Notice that $\mathfrak{d}_A(t, z) \neq 0$ if and only if $(t, z) \in \mathcal{N}_A$. On the other hand, the probability distribution D_{real}^A given in Definition 3 produces both good and bad real instances, while D_{random}^A produces the four types. Theorem 3 ensures that V_A^{def} is a negligible fraction of the set $\mathbb{Z}_q^d$, that is, there exists a negligible function ε_A such that $\left|V_A^{\text{def}}\right| = \varepsilon_A q^d$ (where $|\mathcal{X}|$ denotes the cardinality of a set $\mathcal{X}$). Thus D_{random}^A produces elements in $\mathcal{N}_A$ with overwhelming probability, while D_{real}^A produces elements in $\mathcal{Y}_A$ with overwhelming probability. Therefore, we can replace the distributions D_{real}^A and D_{random}^A by $U_{\mathcal{Y}_A}$ and $U_{\mathcal{N}_A}$ without any noticeable change in Definition 3. We also apply the same considerations to the $\mathcal{D}_k^B$-MDDH problem.

The map f transforms $\mathcal{N}_A$ into $\mathcal{N}_B$, since $\lambda \mathfrak{d}_A = \mathfrak{d}_B \circ f$ and then $\mathfrak{d}_A(t, z) \neq 0$ if and only if $\mathfrak{d}_B(s, u) \neq 0$. The case of good real instances is not so easy, as f can map the elements in $\mathcal{Y}_A$ into either of the three types: good real, bad real and bad non-real. However, we can show that f maps uniformly distributed elements in $\mathcal{Y}_A$ into $\mathcal{Y}_B$ with overwhelming probability. Namely, consider a generic distinguisher A solving the $\mathcal{D}_k^A$-MDDH problem in the following way: First, A computes $([s], [u])$ from $([t], [z])$ using f. Then, A checks whether $s \in V_B^{\text{def}}$, that is, $\text{rank}\,\mathbf{B}(s) < k$ using the k-linear map. If so, A decides that $([t], [z]) \in \mathcal{Y}_A$. Otherwise, it decides $([t], [z]) \in \mathcal{N}_A$. It is easy to see that the advantage of A is $\Pr[f(t, z) \notin \mathcal{Y}_B; (t, z) \leftarrow \mathcal{Y}_A]$, since bad $\mathcal{D}_k^B$-MDDH instances never come from $\mathcal{N}_A$. Then A breaks the generic hardness of $\mathcal{D}_k^A$-MDDH unless f maps uniformly distributed elements in $\mathcal{Y}_A$ into $\mathcal{Y}_B$ with overwhelming probability.

With these ideas in mind we consider now the three cases in the theorem separately. Since f preserves good real and good non-real instances with overwhelming probability, the reduction $\mathcal{R}$ succeeds with overwhelming probability for a perfect oracle solving the $\mathcal{D}_k^B$-MDDH problem. However, the general case of an imperfect oracle is harder, because we need to show that $f(U_{\mathcal{Y}_A}) \approx U_{\mathcal{Y}_B}$ and $f(U_{\mathcal{N}_A}) \approx U_{\mathcal{N}_B}$, where $\approx$ denotes that two distributions are statistically close.

Let us assume that f is surjective (*i.e.*, the second case in the theorem). According to Lemma 5, f is injective, so it is a bijection and then $e = d$. Therefore, $f(U_{\mathcal{N}_A}) = U_{\mathcal{N}_B}$.[20] Similarly, consider the subset $\mathcal{Y}_A' = \mathcal{Y}_A \cap f^{-1}(\mathcal{Y}_B)$, containing all good real instances of $\mathcal{D}_k^A$-MDDH transformed by f into good real instances of $\mathcal{D}_k^B$-MDDH. Because of the above discussion, $U_{\mathcal{Y}_A'} \approx U_{\mathcal{Y}_A}$. In particular, there exists a negligible function ε such that $|\mathcal{Y}_A'| = (1 - \varepsilon)|\mathcal{Y}_A|$. We also claim that $f(U_{\mathcal{Y}_A'}) \approx U_{\mathcal{Y}_B}$. Indeed, $|\mathcal{Y}_A| = (1 - \varepsilon_A)q^d q^k$, since every good real instance can be uniquely written as $(t, \mathbf{A}(t)w)$ for $t \in \mathbb{Z}_q^d \setminus V_A^{\text{def}}$ and $w \in \mathbb{Z}_q^k$, and similarly $|\mathcal{Y}_B| = (1 - \varepsilon_B)q^d q^k$ for some negligible function ε_B. Moreover, by definition, $f(\mathcal{Y}_A') \subset \mathcal{Y}_B$, and by the injectivity of f,

---

[20] An injective map f always transforms the uniform probability distribution on a subset $\mathcal{X}$ into the uniform distribution on the image subset $\mathcal{Y} = f(\mathcal{X})$.

$|f(\mathcal{Y}'_\mathbf{A})| = |\mathcal{Y}'_\mathbf{A}| = (1 - \varepsilon)|\mathcal{Y}_\mathbf{A}| = (1 - \varepsilon)(1 - \varepsilon_\mathbf{A})q^d q^k$, that differs from $|\mathcal{Y}_\mathbf{B}|$ only in a negligible fraction. Finally, we have that $\mathsf{U}_{\mathcal{Y}_\mathbf{A}} \approx \mathsf{U}_{\mathcal{Y}'_\mathbf{A}}$ implies $f(\mathsf{U}_{\mathcal{Y}_\mathbf{A}}) \approx f(\mathsf{U}_{\mathcal{Y}'_\mathbf{A}})$, and along with $f(\mathsf{U}_{\mathcal{Y}'_\mathbf{A}}) \approx \mathsf{U}_{\mathcal{Y}_\mathbf{B}}$ imply that $f(\mathsf{U}_{\mathcal{Y}_\mathbf{A}}) \approx \mathsf{U}_{\mathcal{Y}_\mathbf{B}}$. This proves that $\mathcal{R}$ has the same advantage as the oracle, up to a negligible function.

Concerning the third part of the theorem, if f is not surjective then we would need to randomize it. This is actually possible when $\mathcal{D}_k^\mathbf{B}$ is random self-reducible (according to Definition 6). Indeed, we have seen that except for a negligible error probability f maps real instances into real instances, and also non-real instances into non-real instances. Therefore, the composition of the reduction in Definition 6 and the map f produces the right distributions (except for a negligible statistical distance) for real and random instances, even when f is not surjective. Therefore, a tight reduction from the $\mathcal{D}_k^\mathbf{A}$-MDDH problem to the $\mathcal{D}_k^\mathbf{B}$-MDDH problem is obtained also in this case.   □

It is easy to see that when $\mathcal{D}_k^\mathbf{B}$ is only quasi random self-reducible, if the images $(\boldsymbol{s}, \boldsymbol{u}) = f(\boldsymbol{t}, \boldsymbol{z})$ both for $(\boldsymbol{t}, \boldsymbol{z}) \leftarrow D_{\mathrm{real}}^\mathbf{A}$ and $(\boldsymbol{t}, \boldsymbol{z}) \leftarrow D_{\mathrm{random}}^\mathbf{A}$ fulfil $\boldsymbol{s} \in \mathcal{X}$ with overwhelming probability, where $\mathcal{X}$ is the set of rerandomizable matrices in Definition 7, then we can also prove the existence of the reduction.

It is noticeable that, as a byproduct of the last two theorems, whenever a generic black-box reduction from $\mathcal{D}_k^\mathbf{A}$-MDDH to $\mathcal{D}_k^\mathbf{B}$-MDDH exists, and either $d = e$ or $\mathcal{D}_k^\mathbf{B}$-MDDH is random self-reducible, then there also exists a simple reduction with the following properties: (1) The reduction only makes a single oracle query. (2) It never uses the multilinear map, and then it only performs some group operations in the base group $\mathbb{G}$. (3) It is probabilistic only when the random self-reducibility property is needed. Intuitively, this means that there is little hope in that making many oracle calls or trying to use the multilinear map helps finding a reduction between two reasonable MDDH problems.

Some examples of reductions from MDDH families can be easily obtained by combining the previous theorem and the quasi random self-reducibility of $\mathcal{C}_k$, $\mathcal{L}_k$ and $\mathcal{RL}_k$. In particular, using the trivial inclusions as the map f, one obtains $\mathcal{IL}_k \Rightarrow \mathcal{L}_k \Rightarrow \mathcal{RL}_k$ and $\mathcal{SC}_k \Rightarrow \mathcal{C}_k$. It is also known that $\mathcal{IL}_k$ and $\mathcal{SC}_k$ are equivalent. Thus, $\mathcal{SC}_k \Rightarrow \mathcal{L}_k$.

5   MDDH Problems of the Same Size and Randomness

We now focus on the case $e = d$, that is, the two MDDH problems have the same (minimal) number of parameters. From Corollary 1 this is the only case in which two MDDH problems can be equivalent by generic black-box reductions. Notice that $e = d$ implies that any injective polynomial map $f : \mathbb{Z}_q^{d+k+1} \to \mathbb{Z}_q^{d+k+1}$ of degree one is indeed a bijection, and its inverse map g is also a polynomial map of degree one. Therefore, if there exists a generic black-box reduction from the $\mathcal{D}_k^\mathbf{A}$-MDDH problem to the $\mathcal{D}_k^\mathbf{B}$-MDDH problem then there exists a bijective polynomial map $f : \mathbb{Z}_q^{d+k+1} \to \mathbb{Z}_q^{d+k+1}$ (of degree one) such that $\lambda \partial_\mathbf{A} = \partial_\mathbf{B} \circ f$ for $\lambda \in \mathbb{Z}_q^\times$, which also implies $\lambda^{-1} \partial_\mathbf{B} = \partial_\mathbf{A} \circ g$, where g is the inverse of f.

As a consequence of the previous results, this shows the existence of a generic black-box reduction in the opposite way (observe that we are in the case g is bijective). In summary, we conclude that either the two problems are equivalent or they are incomparable via generic black-box reductions.

Theorem 6. *Let $\mathcal{D}_k^{\mathbf{A}}$ and $\mathcal{D}_k^{\mathbf{B}}$ be hard polynomial degree one matrix distributions, both with d parameters. Then either $\mathcal{D}_k^{\mathbf{A}}$-MDDH and $\mathcal{D}_k^{\mathbf{B}}$-MDDH are equivalent or they are incomparable, by generic black-box reductions.*

This result suggests the possibility of classifying all MDDH problems of the same size and number of parameters into equivalence classes. In particular, we can consider the following positive consequences of the previous theorems.

Corollary 2. *Let $\mathcal{D}_k^{\mathbf{A}}$ and $\mathcal{D}_k^{\mathbf{B}}$ be hard polynomial matrix distributions of degree one. If $\eth_{\mathbf{A}} = \eth_{\mathbf{B}}$ then $\mathcal{D}_k^{\mathbf{A}}$-MDDH and $\mathcal{D}_k^{\mathbf{B}}$-MDDH are equivalent.*

Proof. The identity map is a particular bijective degree one polynomial map f, and we just need to apply Theorem 5.   □

This means that the determinant polynomials hold enough information about the MDDH problems to decide their equivalence. However, $\eth_{\mathbf{A}} \neq \eth_{\mathbf{B}}$ does not mean the separation of the MDDH problems. The following result using the polynomial vector spaces is more complete, since $\eth_{\mathbf{A}} = \eth_{\mathbf{B}}$ implies $X_{\mathbf{A}} = X_{\mathbf{B}}$, but the converse is not true in general.

Corollary 3. *Let $\mathcal{D}_k^{\mathbf{A}}$ and $\mathcal{D}_k^{\mathbf{B}}$ be hard polynomial matrix distributions of degree one. If the polynomial vector spaces $X_{\mathbf{A}}$ and $X_{\mathbf{B}}$ are equal, then $\mathcal{D}_k^{\mathbf{A}}$-MDDH and $\mathcal{D}_k^{\mathbf{B}}$-MDDH are equivalent.*

Proof. The equality of the two vector spaces implies the existence of an invertible matrix $M \in \mathbb{Z}_q^{d \times d}$ such that $\eth_{\mathbf{A},i} = \sum_{j=1}^{d} m_{i,j} \eth_{\mathbf{B},j}$. Then

$$\eth_{\mathbf{A}}(t, z) = \sum_{i=1}^{d} \eth_{\mathbf{A},i}(t) z_i = \sum_{i=1}^{d} \sum_{j=1}^{d} \eth_{\mathbf{B},j}(t) z_i m_{i,j} =$$

$$= \sum_{j=1}^{d} \eth_{\mathbf{B},j}(t) \sum_{i=1}^{d} z_i m_{i,j} = \eth_{\mathbf{B}}(t, M^{\top} z)$$

and finally $\eth_{\mathbf{A}} = \eth_{\mathbf{B}} \circ f$ for $f(t, z) = (t, M^{\top} z)$, which is a bijective polynomial map of degree one.   □

As pointed out in previous section, for $d = 1$ there is a unique choice for the vector space $X_{\mathbf{A}}$. Thus, there exists a unique hard one-parameter polynomial matrix distribution of degree one, up to equivalence of the corresponding MDDH problems, which is the symmetric cascade distribution $\mathcal{SC}_k$.

The story does not end here, as still equivalent MDDH problems could have different vector spaces, $X_{\mathbf{A}} \neq X_{\mathbf{B}}$. We failed to provide a simple and efficient way to show the equivalence of two MDDH problems in the general case. Although we managed to notably simplify the set of possible reductions between MDDH problems, it is still hard taking into account all possible bijective polynomial maps f fulfilling the equation $\lambda \partial_{\mathbf{A}} = \partial_{\mathbf{B}} \circ f$, specially for large k and d, or for large problem subfamilies. Observe that some maps f transform only the z_i (as in the last corollary), or only the t_i, or they can mix both types of variables, as in the following toy example. Consider the self-reduction of C_2-MDDH induced by the map $f(a_1, a_2, z_1, z_2, z_3) = (a_1, z_3, z_1, z_2, a_2)$, that exchanges the second parameter a_2 and z_3. It solves the equation $\lambda \partial_{\mathbf{A}} = \partial_{\mathbf{A}} \circ f$ for $\lambda = 1$, due to the symmetry of $\partial_{\mathbf{A}}$. Namely, $\partial_{\mathbf{A}}(a_1, a_2, z_1, z_2, z_3) = a_1 a_2 z_3 - a_1 z_2 + z_1$, and a_2 and z_3 only appear in one of the monomials. A similar construction could be used to show a reduction between two more complex but differently looking MDDH problems. At this point, we can consider the complementary approach of proving separations between (families of) MDDH problems.

5.1   Invariants, Singularities and Separations

When the goal is obtaining a separation between two MDDH problems, one has to rule out the existence of any map f satisfying the equation $\lambda \partial_{\mathbf{A}} = \partial_{\mathbf{B}} \circ f$. Trying to show the nonexistence of solutions directly form the equation is not an impossible task for well-structured determinant polynomials, but it takes a lot of computations and one have to deal with many unknowns (in principle, the description of f requires $(k + 1 + d)(k + 2 + d)$ unknowns).

However, we can consider the following simple example with $k = 3$ and $d = 2$, for two variants of C_3, one $\mathbf{A}$ with parameters (a_1, a_2, a_2) and the other $\mathbf{B}$ with parameters (b_1, b_1, b_2),

$$\mathbf{A}(a_1, a_2) = \begin{pmatrix} a_1 & 0 & 0 \\ 1 & a_1 & 0 \\ 0 & 1 & a_2 \\ 0 & 0 & 1 \end{pmatrix} \qquad \mathbf{B}(b_1, b_2) = \begin{pmatrix} b_1 & 0 & 0 \\ 1 & b_2 & 0 \\ 0 & 1 & b_2 \\ 0 & 0 & 1 \end{pmatrix}$$

where $\partial_{\mathbf{A}}(\boldsymbol{a}, \boldsymbol{z}) = a_1^2 a_2 z_4 - a_1^2 z_3 + a_1 z_2 - z_1$ and $\partial_{\mathbf{B}}(\boldsymbol{b}, \boldsymbol{u}) = b_1 b_2^2 u_4 - b_1 b_2 u_3 + b_1 u_2 - u_1$. Here, $\partial_{\mathbf{A}}$ has only one monomial of total degree 4. Therefore if the equation $\lambda \partial_{\mathbf{A}} = \partial_{\mathbf{B}} \circ f$ holds for a degree one polynomial map f, then necessarily $\lambda a_1^2 a_2 z_4$ comes from the terms of degree 4 of $b_1 b_2^2 u_4$. Since we are in a unique factorization domain, this means that b_1 can only depend on one of a_1, a_2 or z_4, and the same happens to b_2 and u_4. Actually, because of the square, b_2 can only depend on a_1 (i.e., $b_2 = \beta_{20} + \beta_{21} a_1$, for some constants β_{20}, β_{21}), while we can still choose whether b_1 depends only on a_2 and u_4 depends only on z_4, or vice versa. But now, moving to the degree 3 terms, $b_1 b_2^2 u_4$ does not depend on z_3 and the monomial $a_1^2 z_3$ can only come from $b_1 b_2 u_3$, and u_3 must depend (among other variables) on z_3. But then the degree of $b_1 b_2$ in a_1 must be at least 2, which contradicts what happened with the degree 4 terms. Therefore, we conclude that no such f exists, and the two MDDH problems are incomparable. This approach can be applied to obtain more general separation results, but the computations scale badly with the size and the number of parameters of the matrix distribution, and also depends heavily on the configuration of the matrix itself. Thus, we look for a different strategy.

Another natural way separate two MDDH problems is looking for some easy to compute invariants associated to the determinant polynomial (or to other mathematical objects related to it), where 'invariant' means here a quantity that is preserved by all bijective polynomial maps f of degree one. If the invariant takes different values for two MDDH problems, then no such map f can exist, and both problems are incomparable. One possible candidate for invariant is the singular locus, *i.e.*, the set of points $(t, z) \in \mathbb{Z}_q^d \times \mathbb{Z}_q^{k+1}$ such that both $\mathfrak{d}_\mathbf{A}$ and its gradient $\nabla \mathfrak{d}_\mathbf{A}$ are zero.

Lemma 6. *Given two hard polynomial matrix distributions $\mathcal{D}_k^\mathbf{A}$ and $\mathcal{D}_k^\mathbf{B}$ of degree 1 such that there exists a bijective polynomial map f and $\lambda \neq 0$ such that $\lambda \mathfrak{d}_\mathbf{A} = \mathfrak{d}_\mathbf{B} \circ f$, then $V_\mathbf{A}$ and $V_\mathbf{B}$ have the same number of rational singular points.*

Proof. It is easy to see that any bijective polynomial f satisfying $\lambda \mathfrak{d}_\mathbf{A} = \mathfrak{d}_\mathbf{B} \circ f$ maps singular points to singular points. Indeed, the map f can be written as $(s, u) = f(t, z) = f(0, 0) + M(t \| z)$ for an invertible matrix M. Thus, $\nabla \mathfrak{d}_\mathbf{A}(t, z) = \lambda^{-1} \nabla \mathfrak{d}_\mathbf{B}(s, u) \cdot M$ and $\nabla \mathfrak{d}_\mathbf{A}(t, z) = 0$ if and only if $\nabla \mathfrak{d}_\mathbf{B}(s, u) = 0$. Therefore, the number of singular points of $V_\mathbf{A}$ and $V_\mathbf{B}$ must be the same. $\square$

If (t, z) is a singular point of $\mathcal{D}_k^\mathbf{A}$, so is $(t, 0)$, and the singular points of $\mathcal{D}_k^\mathbf{A}$ with $z = 0$ are precisely the points $(t, 0)$ such that $\operatorname{rank} \mathbf{A}(t) < k$, (or simply $t \in V_\mathbf{A}^{\text{def}}$. Indeed, using Eq. 2 the gradient of $\mathfrak{d}_\mathbf{A}$ is

$$\left(\frac{\partial \mathfrak{d}_\mathbf{A}}{\partial t_1}, \dots, \frac{\partial \mathfrak{d}_\mathbf{A}}{\partial t_d}, \mathfrak{d}_{\mathbf{A},1}, \dots, \mathfrak{d}_{\mathbf{A},k+1} \right) \qquad \text{where} \qquad \frac{\partial \mathfrak{d}_\mathbf{A}}{\partial t_j}(t, z) = \sum_{i=1}^{k+1} \frac{\partial \mathfrak{d}_{\mathbf{A},i}}{\partial t_j}(t) z_i$$

Then, the first d components of the gradient at a point $(t, 0)$ are necessarily zero, and $(t, 0)$ is singular if and only if $\mathfrak{d}_{\mathbf{A},i}(t) = 0$ for $i = 1, \dots, k+1$, since this implies that $\nabla \mathfrak{d}_\mathbf{A} = \mathbf{0}$ and it always holds that $\mathfrak{d}_\mathbf{A}(t, 0) = 0$. This also shows that if (t, z) is singular, then so is $(t, 0)$. Moreover, the polynomials $\mathfrak{d}_{\mathbf{A},i}$ are by construction the k-minors of $\mathbf{A}$, and then the above means that $(t, 0)$ is singular if and only if $\operatorname{rank} \mathbf{A}(t) < k$, or equivalently $t \in V_\mathbf{A}^{\text{def}}$. This allows us to prove the separation between the cascade and the linear MDDH problems.

Theorem 7. *There is no generic black-box reduction between the $\mathcal{C}_k$-MDDH and $\mathcal{L}_k$-MDDH problems (in either way), for any $k \geq 2$.*

Proof. According to Lemma 6, to prove the theorem it is enough showing that $V_{\mathcal{C}_k}$ has no singular points, while $V_{\mathcal{L}_k}$ has. Indeed, $V_{\mathcal{C}_k}^{\text{def}} = \emptyset$, since $\operatorname{rank} \mathbf{A}(t) = k$ for all $t \in \mathbb{Z}_q^k$. Thus, $V_{\mathcal{C}_k}$ has no singular points. However, for $\mathcal{L}_k$, $\operatorname{rank} \mathbf{A}(t) < k$ whenever two or more t_i are zero, which happens for all $k \geq 2$. $\square$

The singular locus is a too coarse invariant, as there are many non-equivalent polynomial matrix distributions without singular points. Another interesting invariant is the group of "automorphisms" of the matrix distribution, that is the group $\mathrm{Aut}_\mathbf{A}$ of the bijective polynomial maps f such that $\lambda \partial_\mathbf{A} = \partial_\mathbf{A} \circ f$ for some nonzero constant λ. These maps actually correspond to the black-box generic self-reductions of the $\mathcal{D}_k^\mathbf{A}$-MDDH problem.

Lemma 7. *Given two hard polynomial matrix distributions $\mathcal{D}_k^\mathbf{A}$ and $\mathcal{D}_k^\mathbf{B}$ of degree 1 such that there exists a bijective polynomial map f and a nonzero constant λ such that $\lambda \partial_\mathbf{A} = \partial_\mathbf{B} \circ f$, then the groups $\mathrm{Aut}_\mathbf{A}$ and $\mathrm{Aut}_\mathbf{B}$ are isomorphic.*

Proof. As usually for this type of statement, we show that for any map $g_\mathbf{A} \in \mathrm{Aut}_\mathbf{A}$, the conjugate $g_\mathbf{B} = f \circ g_\mathbf{A} \circ f^{-1}$ is in $\mathrm{Aut}_\mathbf{B}$. Firstly, it is clear that $g_\mathbf{B}$ is a bijective polynomial map, because f and $g_\mathbf{A}$ are. In addition, using now $\mu \partial_\mathbf{A} = \partial_\mathbf{A} \circ g_\mathbf{A}$ for certain nonzero constant μ, $\partial_\mathbf{B} \circ g_\mathbf{B} = \partial_\mathbf{B} \circ f \circ g_\mathbf{A} \circ f^{-1} = \lambda \partial_\mathbf{A} \circ g_\mathbf{A} \circ f^{-1} = \mu \lambda \partial_\mathbf{A} \circ f^{-1} = \mu \partial_\mathbf{B} \circ f \circ f^{-1} = \mu \partial_\mathbf{B}$ Similarly, f^{-1} transforms $g_\mathbf{B} \in \mathrm{Aut}_\mathbf{B}$ into $g_\mathbf{A} = f^{-1} \circ g_\mathbf{B} \circ f \in \mathrm{Aut}_\mathbf{A}$. $\square$

Now we can use this invariant to separate MDDH problems with no singular points. Computing the whole group $\mathrm{Aut}_\mathbf{A}$ is in general a complex task, but for our purposes we only need to find a difference between $\mathrm{Aut}_\mathbf{A}$ and $\mathrm{Aut}_\mathbf{B}$ that prevents the isomorphism. For instance, two isomorphic groups have the same number of elements of order two, or they have to be either both abelian or both nonabelian, etcetera. Unfortunately, we could not find examples of matrix distributions such that showing that the automorphism groups are non isomorphic is easier than proving that the equation $\lambda \partial_\mathbf{A} = \partial_\mathbf{B} \circ f$ has no solutions.

Acknowledgments. The author is very thankful to Carla Ràfols, Gottfried Herold and Eike Kiltz, for the insightful discussions about the subject. In fact, the core of this paper were developed during a fruiful stage at HGI Bochum. He is also thankful to some of the anonymous referees for their valuable remarks.

References

1. Abdalla, M., Benhamouda, F., Pointcheval, D.: Disjunctions for hash proof systems: new constructions and applications. In: Oswald, E., Fischlin, M. (eds.) EUROCRYPT 2015. LNCS, vol. 9057, pp. 69–100. Springer, Heidelberg (2015). doi:10.1007/978-3-662-46803-6_3
2. Attrapadung, N.: Dual system encryption framework in prime-order groups via computational pair encodings. In: Cheon, J.H., Takagi, T. (eds.) ASIACRYPT 2016. LNCS, vol. 10032, pp. 591–623. Springer, Heidelberg (2016). doi:10.1007/978-3-662-53890-6_20
3. Bader, C., Hofheinz, D., Jager, T., Kiltz, E., Li, Y.: Tightly-secure authenticated key exchange. In: Dodis, Y., Nielsen, J.B. (eds.) TCC 2015. LNCS, vol. 9014, pp. 629–658. Springer, Heidelberg (2015). doi:10.1007/978-3-662-46494-6_26
4. Barthe, G., Fagerholm, E., Fiore, D., Mitchell, J., Scedrov, A., Schmidt, B.: Automated analysis of cryptographic assumptions in generic group models. In: Garay, J.A., Gennaro, R. (eds.) CRYPTO 2014. LNCS, vol. 8616, pp. 95–112. Springer, Heidelberg (2014). doi:10.1007/978-3-662-44371-2_6

5. Benhamouda, F., Couteau, G., Pointcheval, D., Wee, H.: Implicit zero-knowledge arguments and applications to the malicious setting. In: Gennaro, R., Robshaw, M. (eds.) CRYPTO 2015. LNCS, vol. 9216, pp. 107–129. Springer, Heidelberg (2015). doi:10.1007/978-3-662-48000-7_6

6. Blazy, O., Kakvi, S.A., Kiltz, E., Pan, J.: Tightly-secure signatures from chameleon hash functions. In: Katz, J. (ed.) PKC 2015. LNCS, vol. 9020, pp. 256–279. Springer, Heidelberg (2015). doi:10.1007/978-3-662-46447-2_12

7. Blazy, O., Kiltz, E., Pan, J.: (Hierarchical) identity-based encryption from affine message authentication. In: Garay, J.A., Gennaro, R. (eds.) CRYPTO 2014. LNCS, vol. 8616, pp. 408–425. Springer, Heidelberg (2014). doi:10.1007/978-3-662-44371-2_23

8. Chen, J., Gay, R., Wee, H.: Improved dual system ABE in prime-order groups via predicate encodings. In: Oswald, E., Fischlin, M. (eds.) EUROCRYPT 2015. LNCS, vol. 9057, pp. 595–624. Springer, Heidelberg (2015). doi:10.1007/978-3-662-46803-6_20

9. Escala, A., Herold, G., Kiltz, E., Ràfols, C., Villar, J.: An algebraic framework for diffie-hellman assumptions. In: Canetti, R., Garay, J.A. (eds.) CRYPTO 2013. LNCS, vol. 8043, pp. 129–147. Springer, Heidelberg (2013). doi:10.1007/978-3-642-40084-1_8

10. Escala, A., Herold, G., Kiltz, E., Ràfols, C., Villar, J.: An algebraic framework for Diffie-Hellman assumptions. Cryptology ePrint Archive, Report 2013/377 (2013). http://eprint.iacr.org/2013/377 (full version of [9])

11. Herold, G.: Applications of classical algebraic geometry to cryptography. Ph.D. thesis, Ruhr-Universität Bochum (2014)

12. Herold, G., Hesse, J., Hofheinz, D., Ràfols, C., Rupp, A.: Polynomial spaces: a new framework for composite-to-prime-order transformations. In: Garay, J.A., Gennaro, R. (eds.) CRYPTO 2014. LNCS, vol. 8616, pp. 261–279. Springer, Heidelberg (2014). doi:10.1007/978-3-662-44371-2_15

13. Kiltz, E., Wee, H.: Quasi-adaptive NIZK for linear subspaces revisited. In: Oswald, E., Fischlin, M. (eds.) EUROCRYPT 2015. LNCS, vol. 9057, pp. 101–128. Springer, Heidelberg (2015). doi:10.1007/978-3-662-46803-6_4

14. Maurer, U.: Abstract models of computation in cryptography. In: Smart, N.P. (ed.) Cryptography and Coding 2005. LNCS, vol. 3796, pp. 1–12. Springer, Heidelberg (2005). doi:10.1007/11586821_1

15. Morillo, P., Ràfols, C., Villar, J.L.: Matrix computational assumptions in multilinear groups. Cryptology ePrint Archive, Report 2015/353 (2015). http://eprint.iacr.org/2015/353

16. Sadeghi, A.-R., Steiner, M.: Assumptions related to discrete logarithms: why subtleties make a real difference. In: Pfitzmann, B. (ed.) EUROCRYPT 2001. LNCS, vol. 2045, pp. 244–261. Springer, Heidelberg (2001). doi:10.1007/3-540-44987-6_16

17. Schwartz, J.T.: Fast probabilistic algorithms for verification of polynomial identities. J. ACM **27**(4), 701–717 (1980)

Author Index